T0180318

Lecture Notes in Computer Science 12510

More information about this subseries at http://www.springer.com/series/7412

George Bebis · Zhaozheng Yin ·
Edward Kim · Jan Bender ·
Kartic Subr · Bum Chul Kwon ·
Jian Zhao · Denis Kalkofen ·
George Baciu (Eds.)

Advances in
Visual Computing

15th International Symposium, ISVC 2020
San Diego, CA, USA, October 5–7, 2020
Proceedings, Part II

Springer

Editors
George Bebis
University of Nevada Reno
Reno, NV, USA

Edward Kim
Drexel University
Philadelphia, PA, USA

Kartic Subr
University of Edinburgh
Edinburgh, UK

Jian Zhao
University of Waterloo
Waterloo, ON, Canada

George Baciu
The Hong Kong Polytechnic University
Hong Kong, Hong Kong

Zhaozheng Yin
Stony Brook University
Stony Brook, NY, USA

Jan Bender
RWTH Aachen University
Aachen, Germany

Bum Chul Kwon
IBM Research – Cambridge
Cambridge, MA, USA

Denis Kalkofen
Graz University of Technology
Graz, Austria

ISSN 0302-9743 ISSN 1611-3349 (electronic)
Lecture Notes in Computer Science
ISBN 978-3-030-64558-8 ISBN 978-3-030-64559-5 (eBook)
https://doi.org/10.1007/978-3-030-64559-5

LNCS Sublibrary: SL6 – Image Processing, Computer Vision, Pattern Recognition, and Graphics

This Springer imprint is published by the registered company Springer Nature Switzerland AG
The registered company address is: Gewerbestrasse 11, 6330 Cham, Switzerland

Preface

It is with great pleasure that we welcome you to the proceedings of the 15th International Symposium on Visual Computing (ISVC 2020), which was held virtually during October 5–7, 2020. ISVC provides a common umbrella for the four main areas of visual computing including vision, graphics, visualization, and virtual reality. The goal is to provide a forum for researchers, scientists, engineers, and practitioners throughout the world to present their latest research findings, ideas, developments, and applications in the broader area of visual computing.

This year, the program consisted of 6 keynote presentations, 16 oral sessions, 2 poster sessions, 2 special tracks, and 1 tutorial. We received 175 submissions for the main symposium from which we accepted 65 papers for oral presentation and 41 papers for poster presentation. Special track papers were solicited separately through the Organizing and Program Committees of each track. A total of 12 papers were accepted for oral presentation from 18 submissions.

All papers were reviewed with an emphasis on the potential to contribute to the state of the art in the field. Selection criteria included accuracy and originality of ideas, clarity and significance of results, and presentation quality. The review process was quite rigorous, involving three independent blind reviews followed by several days of discussion. During the discussion period we tried to correct anomalies and errors that might have existed in the initial reviews. Despite our efforts, we recognize that some papers worthy of inclusion may not have been included in the program. We offer our sincere apologies to authors whose contributions might have been overlooked.

We wish to thank everybody who submitted their work to ISVC 2020 for review. It was because of their contributions that we succeeded in having a technical program of high scientific quality. In particular, we would like to thank the keynote speakers, the program chairs, the Steering Committee, the International Program Committee, the special track organizers, the tutorial organizers, the reviewers, the sponsors, and especially the authors who contributed their work to the symposium. In particular, we would like to express our appreciation to Springer for sponsoring the Best Paper Award this year.

Despite all the difficulties due to the pandemic, we sincerely hope that ISVC 2020 offered participants opportunities for professional growth.

October 2020

George Bebis
Zhaozheng Yin
Edward Kim
Jan Bender
Kartic Subr
Bum Chul Kwon
Jian Zhao
Denis Kalkofen
George Baciu

Organization

Steering Committee

George Bebis   University of Nevada, Reno, USA
Sabine Coquillart   Inria, France
James Klosowski   AT&T Labs Research, USA
Yoshinori Kuno   Saitama University, Japan
Steve Lin   Microsoft, USA
Peter Lindstrom   Lawrence Livermore National Laboratory, USA
Kenneth Moreland   Sandia National Laboratories, USA
Ara Nefian   NASA Ames Research Center, USA
Ahmad P. Tafti   Mayo Clinic, USA

Computer Vision Chairs

Zhaozheng Yin   Stony Brook University, USA
Edward Kim   Drexel University, USA

Computer Graphics Chairs

Jan Bender   RWTH Aachen University, Germany
Kartic Subr   The University of Edinburgh, UK

Virtual Reality Chairs

Denis Kalkofen   Graz University of Technology, Austria
George Baciu   The Hong Kong Polytechnic University, Hong Kong

Visualization Chairs

Jian Zhao   University of Waterloo, Canada
Bum Chul Kwon   IBM Research, USA

Publicity

Ali Erol   Eksperta Software, Turkey

Tutorials and Special Tracks

Emily Hand   University of Nevada, Reno, USA
Alireza Tavakkoli   University of Nevada, Reno, USA

Awards

Zehang Sun   Apple, USA
Gholamreza Amayeh   Aurora, USA

Web Master

Isayas Berhe Adhanom   University of Nevada, Reno, USA

Program Committee

Nabil Adam	Rutgers University, USA
Emmanuel Agu	Worcester Polytechnic Institute, USA
Touqeer Ahmad	University of Colorado Colorado Springs, USA
Alfonso Alba	Universidad Autónoma de San Luis Potosí, Mexico
Kostas Alexis	University of Nevada, Reno, USA
Usman Alim	University of Calgary, Canada
Amol Ambardekar	Microsoft, USA
Mehdi Ammi	University Paris 8, France
Mark Apperley	University of Waikato, New Zealand
Antonis Argyros	Foundation for Research and Technology - Hellas, Greece
Vijayan K. Asari	University of Dayton, USA
Aishwarya Asesh	Adobe, USA
Vassilis Athitsos	The University of Texas at Arlington, USA
Melinos Averkiou	University of Cyprus, Cyprus
George Baciu	The Hong Kong Polytechnic University, Hong Kong
Chris Holmberg Bahnsen	Aalborg University, Denmark
Abdul Bais	University of Regina, Canada
Abhishek Bajpayee	Massachusetts Institute of Technology, USA
Peter Balazs	University of Szeged, Hungary
Selim Balcisoy	Sabanci University, Turkey
Reneta Barneva	State University of New York at Fredonia, USA
Ronen Barzel	Independent
Fereshteh S Bashiri	University of Wisconsin-Madison, USA
Aryabrata Basu	Emory University, USA
Anil Ufuk Batmaz	Simon Fraser University, Canada
George Bebis	University of Nevada, Reno, USA
Jan Bender	RWTH Aachen University, Germany
Ayush Bhargava	Key Lime Interactive, USA
Harsh Bhatia	Lawrence Livermore National Laboratory, USA
Sanjiv Bhatia	University of Missouri-St. Louis, USA
Mark Billinghurst	University of Canterbury, New Zealand
Ankur Bist	G. B. Pant University of Agriculture and Technology, India
Ayan Biswas	Los Alamos National Laboratory, USA

Dibio Borges	Universidade de Brasília, Brazil
David Borland	RENCI, The University of North Carolina at Chapel Hill, USA
Nizar Bouguila	Concordia University, Canada
Alexandra Branzan Albu	University of Victoria, Canada
Jose Braz Pereira	EST Setúbal, IPS, Portugal
Wolfgang Broll	Ilmenau University of Technology, Germany
Gerd Bruder	University of Central Florida, USA
Tolga Capin	TED University, Turkey
Bruno Carvalho	Federal University of Rio Grande do Norte, Brazil
Sek Chai	SRI International, USA
Jian Chang	Bournemouth University, UK
Sotirios Chatzis	Cyprus University of Technology, Cyprus
Rama Chellappa	University of Maryland, USA
Cunjian Chen	Michigan State University, USA
Yang Chen	HRL Laboratories, LLC, USA
Zhonggui Chen	Xiamen University, China
Yi-Jen Chiang	New York University, USA
Isaac Cho	North Carolina A&T State University, USA
Amit Chourasia	University of California, San Diego, USA
Kichung Chung	Oracle Corporation, USA
Sabine Coquillart	Inria, France
Andrew Cunningham	University of South Australia, Australia
Tommy Dang	Texas Tech University, USA
Aritra Dasgupta	New York University, USA
Jeremie Dequidt	University of Lille, France
Sotirios Diamantas	Tarleton State University, USA
Alexandra Diehl	University of Konstanz, Germany
John Dingliana	Trinity College Dublin, Ireland
Cosimo Distante	CNR, Italy
Ralf Doerner	RheinMain University of Applied Sciences, Germany
Anastasios Doulamis	Technical University of Crete, Greece
Shengzhi Du	Tshwane University of Technology, South Africa
Ye Duan	University of Missouri, USA
Soumya Dutta	Los Alamos National Laboratory, USA
Achim Ebert	University of Kaiserslautern, Germany
Christian Eckhardt	California Polytechnic State University, USA
Mohamed El Ansari	Ibn Zohr University, Morocco
El-Sayed M. El-Alfy	King Fahd University of Petroleum and Minerals, Saudi Arabia
Barrett Ens	Monash University, Australia
Alireza Entezari	University of Florida, USA
Ali Erol	Sigun Information Technologies, UK
Thomas Ertl	University of Stuttgart, Germany
Mohammad Eslami	Technical University of Munich, Germany
Guoliang Fan	Oklahoma State University, USA

Stefan Jeschke	NVIDIA, USA
Ming Jiang	Lawrence Livermore National Laboratory, USA
Sungchul Jung	HIT Lab NZ, New Zealand
Stefan Jänicke	Leipzig University, Germany
Denis Kalkofen	Graz University of Technology, Austria
Ho Chuen Kam	The Chinese University of Hong Kong, Hong Kong
George Kamberov	University of Alaska Anchorage, USA
Gerda Kamberova	Hofstra University, USA
Martin Kampel	Vienna University of Technology, Austria
Takashi Kanai	The University of Tokyo, Japan
Kenichi Kanatani	Okayama University, Japan
David Kao	NASA Ames Research Center, USA
Hirokatsu Kataoka	National Institute of Advanced Industrial Science and Technology (AIST), Japan
Rajiv Khadka	Idaho National Laboratory, USA
Waqar Khan	Wellington Institute of Technology, New Zealand
Deepak Khosla	HRL Laboratories, USA
Edward Kim	Drexel University, USA
Hyungseok Kim	Konkuk University, South Korea
Kangsoo Kim	University of Central Florida, USA
Min H. Kim	Korea Advanced Institute of Science and Technology, South Korea
James Klosowski	AT&T Labs Research, USA
Steffen Koch	University of Stuttgart, Germany
Stefanos Kollias	National Technical University of Athens, Greece
Takashi Komuro	Saitama University, Japan
Dimitris Kosmopoulos	University of Patras, Greece
Jens Krueger	COVIDAG, SCI Institute, USA
Arjan Kuijper	TU Darmstadt, Germany
Yoshinori Kuno	Saitama University, Japan
Tsz Ho Kwok	Concordia University, Canada
Bum Chul Kwon	IBM Research, USA
Hung La	University of Nevada, Reno, USA
Robert Laganière	University of Ottawa, Canada
Yu-Kun Lai	Cardiff University, UK
Robert S Laramee	Swansea University, UK
Manfred Lau	City University of Hong Kong, Hong Kong
D. J. Lee	Brigham Young University, UK
Gun Lee	University of South Australia, Australia
Robert R. Lewis	Washington State University, USA
Frederick Li	Durham University, UK
Xin Li	Louisiana State University, USA
Kuo-Chin Lien	XMotors.ai, USA
Chun-Cheng Lin	National Chiao Tung University, Taiwan
Stephen Lin	Microsoft, China

Scott Nykl   Air Force Institute of Technology, USA
Yoshihiro Okada   Kyushu University, Japan
Gustavo Olague   CICESE, Mexico
Francisco Ortega   Florida International University, USA
Francisco Ortega   Colorado State University, USA
Masaki Oshita   Kyushu Institute of Technology, Japan
Volker Paelke   Hochschule Bremen, Germany
Kalman Palagyi   University of Szeged, Hungary
Alex Pang   University of California, Santa Cruz, USA
George Papagiannakis   University of Crete, Greece
George Papakostas   EMT Institute of Technology, Greece
Michael Papka   Argonne National Laboratory and Northern Illinois
                                University, USA
Giuseppe Patanè   CNR-IMATI, Italy
Maurizio Patrignani   Roma Tre University, Italy
Shahram Payandeh   Simon Fraser University, Canada
Helio Pedrini   University of Campinas, Brazil
Jaako Peltonen   Tampere University, Finland
Euripides Petrakis   Technical University of Crete, Greece
Bill Pike   Pacific Northwest National Laboratory, USA
Claudio Pinhanez   IBM Research, Brazil
Giuseppe Placidi   University of L'Aquila, Italy
Vijayakumar Ponnusamy   SRM Institute of Science and Technology, India
Kevin Ponto   University of Wisconsin-Madison, USA
Jiju Poovvancheri   University of Victoria, Canada
Nicolas Pronost   Université Claude Bernard Lyon 1, France
Helen Purchase   The University of Glasgow, UK
Hong Qin   Stony Brook University, USA
Christopher Rasmussen   University of Delaware, USA
Emma Regentova   University of Nevada, Las Vegas, USA
Guido Reina   University of Stuttgart, Germany
Erik Reinhard   InterDigital, USA
Banafsheh Rekabdar   Southern Illinois University Carbondale, USA
Paolo Remagnino   Kingston University, UK
Hongliang Ren   National University of Singapore, Singapore
Benjamin Renoust   Osaka University, Japan
Theresa-Marie Rhyne   Consultant
Eraldo Ribeiro   Florida Institute of Technology, USA
Peter Rodgers   University of Kent, UK
Paul Rosen   University of South Florida, USA
Isaac Rudomin   BSC, Spain
Amela Sadagic   Naval Postgraduate School, USA
Filip Sadlo   Heidelberg University, Germany
Punam Saha   University of Iowa, USA
Naohisa Sakamoto   Kobe University, Japan
Kristian Sandberg   Computational Solutions, Inc., USA

Alberto Santamaria Pang	General Electric Research, USA
Nickolas S. Sapidis	University of Western Macedonia, Greece
Muhammad Sarfraz	Kuwait University, Kuwait
Andreas Savakis	Rochester Institute of Technology, USA
Fabien Scalzo	University of California, Los Angeles, USA
Jacob Scharcanski	UFRGS, Brazil
Thomas Schultz	University of Bonn, Germany
Jurgen Schulze	University of California, San Diego, USA
Muhammad Shahzad	National University of Sciences and Technology, Pakistan
Puneet Sharma	Uit The Arctic University of Norway, Norway
Mohamed Shehata	Memorial University, USA
Hubert P. H. Shum	Durham University, UK
Adalberto Simeone	KU Leuven, Belgium
Gurjot Singh	Fairleigh Dickinson University, USA
Robert Sisneros	University of Illinois at Urbana-Champaign, USA
Alexei Skurikhin	Los Alamos National Laboratory, USA
Pavel Slavik	Czech Technical University in Prague, Czech Republic
Jack Snoeyink	The University of North Carolina at Chapel Hill, USA
Fabio Solari	University of Genoa, DIBRIS, Italy
Paolo Spagnolo	CNR, Italy
Jaya Sreevalsan-Nair	IIIT Bangalore, India
Diane Staheli	Massachusetts Institute of Technology, USA
Chung-Yen Su	National Taiwan Normal University, Taiwan
Kartic Subr	The University of Edinburgh, UK
Changming Sun	CSIRO, Australia
Zehang Sun	Apple, USA
Tanveer Syeda-Mahmood	IBM Almaden Research Center, USA
Carlo H. Séquin	University of California, Berkeley, USA
Ahmad Tafti	Mayo Clinic, USA
Tieniu Tan	Institute of Automation, CAS, China
Jules-Raymond Tapamo	University of KwaZulu-Natal, South Africa
Alireza Tavakkoli	University of Nevada, Reno, USA
João Manuel R. S. Tavares	FEUP, INEGI, Portugal
Daniel Thalmann	Ecole Polytechnique Fédérale de Lausanne, Switzerland
Holger Theisel	Otto-von-Guericke University, Germany
Yuan Tian	InnoPeak Technology, USA
Yan Tong	University of South Carolina, USA
Thomas Torsney-Weir	Swansea University, UK
Mehmet Engin Tozal	University of Louisiana at Lafayette, USA
Gavriil Tsechpenakis	Indiana University and Purdue University, USA

Stefano Tubaro	Politecnico di Milano, Italy
Georg Umlauf	HTWG Konstanz, Germany
Georg Umlauf	University of Applied Science Constance, Germany
Daniela Ushizima	Lawrence Berkeley National Laboratory, USA
Dimitar Valkov	University of Münster, Germany
Krishna Venkatasubramanian	University of Rhode Island, USA
Jonathan Ventura	California Polytechnic State University San Luis Obispo, USA
Athanasios Voulodimos	University of West Attica, Greece
Chaoli Wang	University of Notre Dame, USA
Cuilan Wang	Georgia Gwinnett College, USA
Benjamin Weyers	University of Trier, Germany
Thomas Wischgoll	Wright State University, USA
Kin Hong Wong	The Chinese University of Hong Kong, Hong Kong
Panpan Xu	Bosch Research North America, USA
Wei Xu	Brookhaven National Lab, USA
Yasuyuki Yanagida	Meijo University, Japan
Fumeng Yang	Brown University, USA
Xiaosong Yang	Bournemouth University, UK
Hsu-Chun Yen	National Taiwan University, Taiwan
Lijun Yin	State University of New York at Binghamton, USA
Zhaozheng Yin	Stony Brook University, USA
Zeyun Yu	University of Wisconsin-Milwaukee, USA
Chunrong Yuan	Technische Hochschule Köln, Germany
Xiaoru Yuan	Peking University, China
Xenophon Zabulis	FORTH-ICS, Greece
Jiri Zara	Czech Technical University in Prague, Czech Republic
Wei Zeng	Florida International University, USA
Zhao Zhang	Hefei University of Technology, China
Jian Zhao	University of Waterloo, Canada
Ye Zhao	Kent State University, USA
Ying Zhu	Georgia State University, USA
Changqing Zou	University of Maryland, USA
Ignacio Zuleta	University of California, San Francisco, USA

Special Tracks

Computational Bioimaging

Organizers

| Tavares João Manuel R. S. | Universidade do Porto, Portugal |
| Jorge Renato Natal | Universidade do Porto, Portugal |

Computer Vision Advances in Geo-Spatial Applications and Remote Sensing

Organizers

Nefian Ara	NASA Ames Research Center, USA
Nestares Oscar	Intel Research, USA
Edwards Laurence	NASA Ames Research Center, USA
Zuleta Ignacio	Planet Labs, USA
Coltin Brian	NASA Ames Research Center, USA
Fong Terry	NASA Ames Research Center, USA

Tutorial

Evolutionary Computer Vision

Organizers

Olague Gustavo	CICESE Research Center, Mexico

Contents – Part II

Posters

Contents – Part I

Deep Learning

Segmentation

Visualization

Video Analysis and Event Recognition

ST: Computational Bioimaging

Applications

Biometrics

Motion and Tracking

Computer Graphics

Virtual Reality

ST: Computer Vision Advances in Geo-Spatial Applications and Remote Sensing

Object Recognition/Detection/Categorization

Few-Shot Image Recognition
with Manifolds

Debasmit Das$^{(\boxtimes)}$, J. H. Moon, and C. S. George Lee

School of Electrical and Computer Engineering, Purdue University,
West Lafayette, IN, USA
{das35,moon92,csglee}@purdue.edu

Abstract. In this paper, we extend the traditional few-shot learning
(FSL) problem to the situation when the source-domain data is not accessible but only high-level information in the form of class prototypes is
available. This limited information setup for the FSL problem deserves
much attention due to its implication of privacy-preserving inaccessibil-
ity to the source-domain data but it has rarely been addressed before.
Because of limited training data, we propose a non-parametric approach
to this FSL problem by assuming that all the class prototypes are structurally arranged on a manifold. Accordingly, we estimate the novel-class
prototype locations by projecting the few-shot samples onto the average
of the subspaces on which the surrounding classes lie. During classification, we again exploit the structural arrangement of the categories
by inducing a Markov chain on the graph constructed with the class
prototypes. This manifold distance obtained using the Markov chain is
expected to produce better results compared to a traditional nearest-
neighbor-based Euclidean distance. To evaluate our proposed framework,
we have tested it on two image datasets – the large-scale ImageNet and
the small-scale but fine-grained CUB-200. We have also studied parameter sensitivity to better understand our framework.

1 Introduction

Deep learning has produced breakthrough in many areas like computer vision [7,
9], speech recognition [1], natural language processing [4] etc., mainly due to the
availability of lots of labeled data, complex neural network architectures and efficient training procedures. Even though these deep learning models are trained on
large labeled datasets, they still fail to generalize to new classes or environments.
Humans, on the other hand, can quickly recognize new objects from very few
samples. They do that by using their previously obtained *knowledge* and apply
it to new situations. This difference in the way machines and humans learn provides motivation to carry out research on few-shot learning (FSL). Accordingly,
most few-shot learning methods strive for a transfer-learning approach where
they extract useful transferable knowledge from data-abundant base classes and
use it to recognize data-starved novel classes.

Most previous methods in FSL assumed that abundant labeled data is available across the base categories from which a robust and generalizable knowledge

© Springer Nature Switzerland AG 2020
G. Bebis et al. (Eds.): ISVC 2020, LNCS 12510, pp. 3–14, 2020.
https://doi.org/10.1007/978-3-030-64559-5_1

representation can be learned. However, in certain situations, it is difficult to have access to all the labeled data of these base categories due to privacy restrictions and/or inefficiency in maintaining such a large database. Hence, alternatively class exemplars or prototypes can be retained. These prototypes summarize the class information by averaging over the data samples without revealing sensitive information about the data. For example, the prototype of the dog category can be the arithmetic mean of all the dog sample features. Previous work on *hypothesis transfer learning* (HTL) [8,10,15] assumed access to base class models, where recognition performance would depend on the choice of these models. As a result, this HTL-based setting does not allow for fair comparison. On the other hand, our proposed setting involving base-class prototypes allow for fair comparison where performance depends only on the data and the proposed transfer learning approach. This proposed FSL setting is depicted in Fig. 1.

Previous FSL methods cannot be applied to this proposed restrictive setting. This is because they assume that lots of labeled data are available from the source domain. Consequently, they use neural-network-based parametric approaches. The neural-network-based approaches can be categorized depending on the type of transferable knowledge extracted from the base categories and encoded in the neural network architecture: (a) *Metric-learning* methods [13,14,16] learn a metric space; (b) *Meta-learning* methods [2,5,12] learn the learning procedure; (c) *Generative* methods [6,11,17] generate data for the novel classes. However, the neural-network-based parametric models might

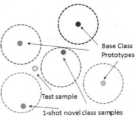

Fig. 1. In this FSL setting, the base-class prototypes are known but not the novel-class prototypes. The spread of the classes (dashed boundaries) are also unknown.

severely overfit if we only have limited data in the form of class prototypes available from the source domain. Hence, in order to solve this restrictive FSL problem, it is natural to seek a non-parametric approach.

In this paper, we address this restricted FSL setting by formulating it as a case of *ill-sampling*. As depicted in Fig. 1, the correct locations of the base category prototypes are known but that of the novel categories are unknown. This is because the few-shot data from a novel category might be sampled from the periphery of the class distribution. These non-representative samples when used for classification will result in poor recognition performance. Therefore, a non-parametric-based prior is used to produce a biased estimate of the novel-class prototype location.

For the non-parametric-based prior, we find inspiration from the idea [3] that data samples from one class lie on a low-dimensional subspace. Therefore, we can consider all the classes as a collection of piece-wise linear subspaces. This set of subspaces can be considered as an approximation of a non-linear manifold close to which the class-prototypes lie. This manifold serves as a prior to estimate the location of the novel-class prototype. The subspace near the novel-class prototype is found by calculating the mean of the subspaces on which the nearby base classes lie. The subspace on which the nearby base classes lie is again found using their nearest neighbors as shown in Fig. 2. Finally, the novel-class sample can be projected onto the mean subspace to obtain the novel-class prototype.

Once the novel-class prototypes are estimated, one can use the nearest-neighbor (NN) approach to assign a test sample to a class based on the Euclidean distance to all the prototypes. However, the estimation procedure for the novel-class prototype might still be error prone. Hence, there is a need to exploit the structural arrangement of the manifold containing all the classes to assign a class to a test sample. The neighboring class locations can provide better estimate of class-prototype distances. This can be achieved by constructing a graph using all the class prototypes and then using equilibrium probability of an induced absorbing Markov-chain process to output the most probable class. Finally, to validate the proposed approach, we perform experiments and analyses on this framework to set a benchmark for future research.

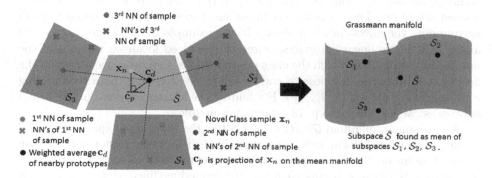

Fig. 2. The surrounding subspaces $\mathcal{S}_1$, $\mathcal{S}_2$ and $\mathcal{S}_3$ for a novel-class sample $\mathbf{x}_n$ are found by using its Nearest Neighbors (NN) and the NNs of its NNs. Their mean can be calculated to obtain the subspace $\bar{\mathcal{S}}$ on which the novel-class sample $\mathbf{x}_n$ is projected to obtain $\mathbf{c}_p$. The weighted average $\mathbf{c}_d$ of the nearby prototypes are also used to obtain the novel-class prototype.

2 Proposed Approach

In this section, we describe the proposed framework, which consists of two steps - estimating novel-class prototypes using the manifold approach and classification using the Markov chain method.

2.1 Estimating Novel-Class Prototypes

Consider that we have access to the base-category prototypes collected in the form of a matrix $\mathbf{C} \in \mathbb{R}^{n_b \times d}$, where n_b is the number of base prototypes and d

is the dimensionality of the feature space. Let the one-shot sample from a novel class be $\mathbf{x}_n \in \mathbb{R}^d$. Our goal is to estimate the prototype location $\mathbf{c}_n \in \mathbb{R}^d$ of the novel class. Our assumption is that all the base and novel-class prototypes, i.e., all rows of $\mathbf{C}$ and $\mathbf{c}_n$ lie close to a non-linear manifold. Since the mathematical expression of the manifold is unknown, we express it as a collection of piecewise linear subspaces. First, we find the surrounding classes of the novel class by finding r nearest-neighboring prototypes of the novel-class sample $\mathbf{x}_n$. Let these nearest-neighboring prototypes be denoted as $\mathbf{c}_{ni} \in \mathbb{R}^d$ for $i \in \{1, 2, ..., r\}$. For each of the r neighboring prototypes, we find q neighboring prototypes. These new prototypes can be expressed as $\mathbf{c}_{nij} \in \mathbb{R}^d$ for $j \in \{1, 2, ..., q\}$ and $i \in \{1, 2, ..., r\}$. Hence, $\mathbf{c}_{nij}$ represents the jth nearest neighbor of the ith nearest neighbor of the novel-class sample $\mathbf{x}_n$. To represent the non-linear manifold, we form r linear subspaces using the r nearest neighbors of the novel sample as well as the q nearest neighbors of each of the r prototypes. The linear subspace $\mathcal{S}_i$ corresponding to the ith nearest neighbor of $\mathbf{x}_n$ is represented as a column space such that $\mathcal{S}_i \equiv [\mathbf{c}_{ni} \vdots \mathbf{c}_{ni1} \vdots \mathbf{c}_{ni2} \vdots ... \vdots \mathbf{c}_{niq}]$. The linear subspace can be orthonormalized to obtain $\mathcal{S}_i^\perp$ and the operation can be repeated for all the r nearest neighbors. The net result is r linear subspaces with dimensionality $(q+1)$ surrounding the novel-class sample $\mathbf{x}_n$. In the example in Fig. 2, we chose $r = 3$ and $q = 3$. These linear subspaces represent linearized localized versions of the non-linear manifold on which the class prototypes lie. The subspace on which the novel-class prototype lies close to can be found by averaging these surrounding r subspaces $\mathcal{S}_i^\perp$ for $i \in \{1, 2, ..., r\}$. For finding the average of these orthonormal subspaces, we use the concept of Grassmann manifold.

A Grassmann manifold $\mathcal{G}(n, l)$ for $n, l > 0$ is the topological space composed of all l-dimensional linear subspaces embedded in an n-dimensional Euclidean space. A point on the Grassmann manifold is represented as an $n \times l$ orthonormal matrix $\mathbf{S}$ whose columns span the corresponding linear subspace $\mathcal{S}$. It is represented as: $\mathcal{G}(n, l) = \{\text{span}(\mathbf{S}): \mathbf{S} \in \mathbb{R}^{n \times l}, \mathbf{S}^T\mathbf{S} = \mathbf{I}_l\}$, where $\mathbf{I}_l$ is a $l \times l$-dimensional identity matrix and superscript T indicates matrix transpose.

Following the definition, the r orthonormal subspaces $\mathcal{S}_i^\perp$ for $i \in \{1, 2, ..., r\}$ are points lying on a $\mathcal{G}(d, q + 1)$ Grassmann manifold. The average of these points on the Grassmann manifold will represent the linear subspace to which the novel-class prototype lies close to. The average of these points is found using the *extrinsic mean*. For a set of points on the Grassmann manifold $\mathcal{G}(d, q+1)$, the extrinsic mean is the point that minimizes the Frobenius-norm-squared difference of the projections of the points onto the space of $(q + 1)$ ranked $d \times d$ matrices. Therefore, the optimization problem for finding the extrinsic mean $\bar{\mathbf{S}}$ is

$$\underset{\mathbf{S}^T\mathbf{S}=\mathbf{I}}{\text{argmin}} \sum_{i=1}^{r} d(\mathbf{S}_i, \mathbf{S})^2, \quad \text{where} \quad d(\mathbf{S}_i, \mathbf{S}) = \frac{||\mathbf{SS}^T - \mathbf{S}_i\mathbf{S}_i^T||_{\mathcal{F}}}{\sqrt{2}}. \tag{1}$$

Here $|| \cdot ||_{\mathcal{F}}$ is the Frobenius norm. Let $\mathbf{S}^*$ be the solution to the optimization problem (1), which can be found using eigenvalue decomposition. $\mathbf{S}^*$ is the spanning matrix of the extrinsic mean of the surrounding subspaces $\mathcal{S}_i^\perp$'s. Setting the extrinsic mean $\bar{\mathbf{S}} = \mathbf{S}^*$, we project the novel-class sample $\mathbf{x}_n$ onto the subspace spanned by the matrix $\bar{\mathbf{S}}$. The projected point $\mathbf{c}_p$ can be obtained as $\mathbf{c}_p = \bar{\mathbf{S}}\bar{\mathbf{S}}^+\mathbf{x}_n$, where $\bar{\mathbf{S}}^+ = (\bar{\mathbf{S}}^T\bar{\mathbf{S}})^{-1}\bar{\mathbf{S}}^T$. Superscripts -1 and $+$ indicate matrix inverse and matrix pseudo-inverse, respectively.

We also consider the direct contribution of the surrounding class prototypes into estimating the novel-class prototype. If $\mathbf{C}_r \in \mathbb{R}^{r \times d}$ consists of the r nearest neighbors of the novel-class sample $\mathbf{x}_n$, then their contribution $\mathbf{c}_d$ to the novel-class prototype location can be found using the equation $\mathbf{c}_d = \mathbf{C}_r^T\mathbf{p}_d$, where $\mathbf{p}_d \in \mathbb{R}^r$ is the probability vector formed by carrying out the exponential mapping of the Euclidean distances of the class prototypes to $\mathbf{x}_n$, followed by normalization. Hence, the contributions $\mathbf{x}_n$, $\mathbf{c}_p$ and $\mathbf{c}_d$ can be used to estimate the novel-class prototype location $\mathbf{c}_n$ as

$$\mathbf{c}_n = \alpha_2[\alpha_1\mathbf{x}_n + (1 - \alpha_1)\mathbf{c}_p] + (1 - \alpha_2)\mathbf{c}_d, \tag{2}$$

where $\alpha_1, \alpha_2 \in [0, 1]$ are scalar weights that are manually set. In case $\mathbf{x}_n$ is very close to the novel-class prototype, $\alpha_1 = \alpha_2 \approx 1$ will produce optimal classification performance.

2.2 Classification Using Absorbing Markov Chain

Once the class prototype locations of the novel classes are known, the structural arrangement of the prototypes of both the base and novel classes are again used to recognize a test sample to obtain a more informed decision about the classification. The structural arrangement of the classes is represented using a k'-nearest-neighbor (k'-NN) graph, where each node represents a class prototype. The k'-NN graph formulation allows nodes to only be connected to its k'-NN nodes. The weights between the nodes are defined using the exponential of the negative Euclidean distances. Upon defining this

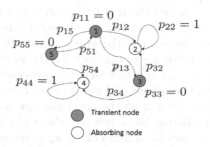

Fig. 3. Possible transitions are shown with directed arrows. The transition probability from a state i to a state j is p_{ij}. The transient state and the absorbing state have self-transition probabilities p_{ii} as 0 and 1, respectively.

graph, an absorbing Markov-chain process is induced on it. Each state of the Markov chain corresponds to a node in the graph and therefore a category. The transition probability from a state i to a state j is found as $p_{ij} = w_{ij}/\sum_l w_{il}$, where w_{il} is the weight connecting nodes i and l. In the absorbing Markov chain process, there are two kinds of states - *transient* and *absorbing*. The transient state and the absorbing state have self-transition probabilities p_{ii} as 0 and 1, respectively. This suggests that a random walker on a graph cannot stay on the transient node for the next step but for the absorbing node it will stay there forever. An example of an absorbing Markov chain is given in Fig. 3, where the arrows represent the possible transitions from one node to another. Overall, the Markov chain is represented using the transition matrix $\mathbf{P}$, which models the dynamics of the process. Using $\mathbf{P}$, the Markov-chain equations are described as follows:

$$\mathbf{u}^{t+1} = \mathbf{u}^t\mathbf{P}, \quad \text{where} \quad \mathbf{P} = \begin{bmatrix} \mathbf{T}_{n_t \times n_t} & \mathbf{A}_{n_t \times n_a} \\ \mathbf{0}_{n_a \times n_t} & \mathbf{I}_{n_a \times n_a} \end{bmatrix}, \mathbf{P}^\infty = \begin{bmatrix} \mathbf{0}_{n_t \times n_t} & (\mathbf{I} - \mathbf{T})^{-1}\mathbf{A} \\ \mathbf{0}_{n_a \times n_t} & \mathbf{I}_{n_a \times n_a} \end{bmatrix}.$$

$$(3)$$

$\mathbf{u}^t$ and $\mathbf{u}^{t+1}$ are the states of the process at instants t and $t + 1$, respectively, and they are represented as a probability vector over all the states. $\mathbf{T}$ describes the transition probabilities from one transient state to another. $\mathbf{A}$ describes the transition probabilities from transient states to absorbing states. n_t and n_a are the number of transient and absorbing states, respectively, and the zero and identity matrices $\mathbf{0}_{n_a \times n_t}$ and $\mathbf{I}_{n_a \times n_a}$ imply that the process cannot leave the absorbing state. Our goal is to find the equilibrium state $\mathbf{u}^t$ as $t \to \infty$ for a given initial state $\mathbf{u}^0$. Accordingly, $\mathbf{u}^\infty = \mathbf{u}^0\mathbf{P}^m$ as $m \to \infty$. The closed-form solution of $\mathbf{P}^m$ as $m \to \infty$ is treated as $\mathbf{P}^\infty$. Using this formulation, the equilibrium state probabilities can only be distributed among the absorbing states with zero probabilities on the transient states.

The initial state $\mathbf{u}^0$ is calculated using the Euclidean distances of the test sample to all the base- and novel-class prototypes and normalizing it to obtain a probability vector. Using the absorbing Markov-chain formulation in Eq. (3), we choose the novel categories and base categories as transient and absorbing states, respectively, to obtain the most probable base category from $\mathbf{u}^\infty$. Then, we interchange the order of absorbing and transient states to obtain the most probable novel category. In the final step, we apply one nearest neighbor approach on the test sample to choose the most probable class among the most probable base and novel categories obtained in the previous steps. The overall procedure from the novel-class prototype estimation to the Markov-chain-based prediction for a test sample is given in Algorithm 1. In case we have multiple samples for a novel class, $\mathbf{x}_n$ is set as the mean of these samples.

3   Experiments and Discussions

3.1   Dataset Description

To evaluate our proposed approach, we used two image recognition datasets – ImageNet and CUB-200. Originally, the ImageNet dataset consists of 21K categories of which we used 1000 for our experiments. These 1000 categories are accordingly split into base and novel classes. The CUB-200 is a fine-grained dataset that consists of 200 categories of different bird species. Of these 200 classes, we used a total of 150 of which 100 are base and 50 are novel classes. For both datasets, the image features used were the 2048-dimensional ResNet-101 [7].

3.2   Effects of Varying the Number of Classes and Samples

In this section, we study how recognition performance is affected by the number of categories and the number of samples per category in the base and novel

---

Algorithm 1: Proposed two-step FSL procedure using manifolds.

Given: Base category prototypes $\mathbf{C} \in \mathbb{R}^{n_b \times d}$, Novel class one-shot samples $\mathbf{x}_n, n \in \{1, 2, ..., n_{nov}\}$, Test sample $\mathbf{x}_{te}$.

Parameters: $r, q, k', \alpha_1, \alpha_2$

Goal: Classify $\mathbf{x}_{te}$ into one of the $n_b + n_{nov}$ categories

Step 1 *Estimate class prototype for each novel class*

for each novel class $n \in \{1, 2, ..., n_{nov}\}$

    Obtain r nearest base prototypes for $\mathbf{x}_n$ to form $\mathbf{C}_r \in \mathbb{R}^{r \times d}$

    Obtain q nearest base prototypes for each of the r base prototypes

    Obtain orthonormal subspaces $\mathcal{S}_i^{\perp}$ for $i \in \{1, 2, ..., r\}$ using the q neighbors

    $\bar{\mathcal{S}} \leftarrow \mathtt{ExtrinsicManifoldMean}(\mathcal{S}_1^{\perp}, \mathcal{S}_2^{\perp}, ..., \mathcal{S}_r^{\perp})$

    Project $\mathbf{x}_n$ onto $\bar{\mathcal{S}}$ to obtain $\mathbf{c}_p$ followed by $\mathbf{c}_d$

    Obtain novel-class prototypes as $\mathbf{c}_n \leftarrow \alpha_2(\alpha_1\mathbf{x}_n + (1 - \alpha_1)\mathbf{c}_p) + (1 - \alpha_2)\mathbf{c}_d$

end for

Step 2 *Predict class of test sample $\mathbf{x}_{te}$*

Construct k'-nearest-neighbor graph with n_b base prototypes and n_{nov} novel prototypes as nodes.

Find initial probability vector $\mathbf{u}_0$ using distance of $\mathbf{x}_{te}$ to all the prototypes.

Construct Markov chain and obtain most probable base class.

Construct Markov chain and obtain most probable novel class.

Use nearest neighbor to obtain the most probable class among the two.

---

datasets. For training purposes, we used the prototypes of the base categories and the few-shot samples from the novel categories. For evaluation purposes, test samples from both base and novel categories were used. Recognition performance is reported as class-wise averaged accuracy. This ensures that major classes do not dominate the performance and minor classes containing less number of samples are not ignored. It is noted that performing cross-validation is impossible since we do not have access to enough data to be held out as a validation set and therefore results were reported by fixing the hyper-parameters. For evaluation, we used the following models: (NA) The No-adaptation baseline which consists of just using nearest neighbor on the few-shot sample mean; (M1) It uses nearest neighbor on the estimated novel-class prototypes; (M2) It uses the Markov-chain-based manifold distance on the few-shot sample mean; (Oracle) It assumes access to novel-class prototypes and uses nearest neighbor for prediction; (M1+M2) involves computing the manifold distance on the estimated class prototypes.

For the first set of experiments, we used the ImageNet dataset with 800 base and 200 novel categories and studied the effect of changing the number of shots per novel category. The results were taken over 10 trials and reported in Table 1. From the results, it is seen that M1 improves the recognition performance over the no-adaptation baseline but the difference diminishes as the number of shots increases. This is because for the novel categories, the few-shot mean becomes closer to the prototype location as the number of shots increases. Also, the contribution of M2 over the baseline or over M1 is incremental. This can be attributed to the fact that the ResNet-101 features are not trained using the manifold-based distance and there is a mis-match between the training and testing evaluation measures. The standard error reduces with the increasing number of shots because of reduced variance in the few-shot mean and eventually the estimated prototype over the trials. We repeated the same experiment for the CUB-200 dataset, the results of which are reported in Table 2. In this case, we have 100 base and 50 novel categories, all of which are fine-grained. As a result, the recognition performance is poorer compared to ImageNet, even though CUB-200 has lesser number of categories. Still, the observed recognition performance has a pattern similar to that of the ImageNet dataset. However, there is no reduction in the standard error with increasing shots. This can be attributed to larger overlap between the fine-grained classes of CUB-200. For the

Table 1. Average accuracy results over 10 trials of the ImageNet dataset with 800 base and 200 novel categories as the number of shots per novel category is changed. Standard error is shown in the parentheses. The hyper-parameter setting is $r = 20, q = 20, k' = 3, \alpha_1 = 0.9, \alpha_2 = 0.7$.

	1 shot	2 shot	5 shot	10 shot	20 shot
NA	64.31 (0.05)	67.60 (0.05)	71.09 (0.03)	72.24 (0.02)	72.89 (0.01)
M1	66.58 (0.05)	69.67 (0.05)	71.62 (0.03)	72.31 (0.02)	72.91 (0.01)
M1+M2	66.91 (0.05)	69.88 (0.05)	72.05 (0.03)	72.72 (0.02)	72.97 (0.02)
M2	65.21 (0.05)	67.98 (0.05)	71.33 (0.02)	72.07 (0.02)	72.60 (0.01)
Oracle	73.3	73.3	73.3	73.3	73.3

Table 2. Accuracy results over 10 trials of the CUB-200 dataset with 100 base and 50 novel categories as the number of shots per novel category is changed. The hyper-parameter setting is $r = 20, q = 20, k' = 5, \alpha_1 = 0.5, \alpha_2 = 0.5$.

	1 shot	2 shot	5 shot	10 shot	20 shot
NA	43.40 (0.12)	45.28 (0.13)	51.19 (0.18)	55.70 (0.20)	58.16 (0.16)
M1	45.91 (0.23)	48.80 (0.20)	51.90 (0.16)	55.94 (0.18)	57.63 (0.14)
M1+ M2	46.13 (0.28)	49.01 (0.22)	52.13 (0.11)	55.57 (0.17)	58.67 (0.12)
M2	43.81 (0.11)	45.86 (0.15)	51.45 (0.15)	55.91 (0.18)	58.31 (0.14)
Oracle	60.51	60.51	60.51	60.51	60.51

next set of experiments, we considered the performance change on the ImageNet dataset for the 1-shot setting as the numbers of base and novel categories are varied. We considered two such scenarios. In the first case, the total number of categories was fixed at 1000 while the proportion of base categories was changed.

Table 3. Accuracy results over 10 trials of the ImageNet dataset for the 1-shot setting as the ratio of number of base categories to the total number of categories is changed. (x-b, y-n) implies x base and y novel categories.

	0.1 (100-b, 900-n)	0.2 (200-b,800-n)	0.4 (400-b, 600-n)	0.6 (600-b, 400-n)
NA	38.29 (0.30)	39.59 (0.29)	46.50 (0.18)	55.28 (0.11)
M1	47.70 (0.28)	49.65 (0.30)	54.65 (0.23)	60.71 (0.12)
M1+M2	47.89 (0.28)	50.33 (0.29)	55.13 (0.23)	61.34 (0.11)
M2	38.36 (0.30)	39.68 (0.29)	46.57 (0.19)	55.31 (0.11)
Oracle	73.3	73.3	73.3	73.3

This setting considers less number of base categories compared to novel categories and it has rarely been studied in previous work. The results of this setting are reported in Table 3. From the table, it can be seen that M1 improves over NA by a large margin (9 points) especially when the number of base categories is very less (ratio of 0.1). This is alluded to our assumption that all the class prototypes have a structural arrangement on a manifold. Therefore, the use of this structure is especially beneficial in the few-class regime. However, the difference between M1 and NA decreases mainly due to more base categories and lesser difficult novel categories. After that, we considered the experimental setting where the total number of categories was varied but the proportion of base and novel categories was kept the same at 4:1, the results of which are reported in Table 4. The results show that the upper bound of the recognition performance, i.e., the oracle performance, decreases with an increase in the number of categories. This is because classification becomes more difficult as the number of categories increases. As expected, M1 performs better compared to NA and the contribution of M2 is incremental.

Our proposed few-shot learning setting is new and therefore we do not have previous work to compare and benchmark against. However, we can study whether our approach can improve existing relevant work. Prototypical networks [13] consider the mean of the few-shot samples to represent class prototypes. Therefore, there is a possibility of obtaining the class prototypes using our manifold-based approach and further improving the performance. Accordingly, we tested the contribution of M1 and M2 over prototypical networks on *miniImageNet*, which is a subset of the ImageNet dataset. The results are shown in Table 5. In the table, K-way N-shot implies that K novel categories are sampled per testing episode with N samples per category. From the results, it is clear that M1 improves the performance, however M2 declines it. This is mainly because of the discrepancy between the Euclidean distance metric used during training ProtoNets and the manifold-based distance metric used during testing.

3.3 Parameter Sensitivity Studies

In this section, we study the effect of hyper-parameters on the recognition performance. We only report results of sensitivity with respect to r, α_1 and α_2 in

Table 4. Accuracy results over 10 trials of the ImageNet dataset for the 1-shot setting as the total number of categories is changed but keeping the ratio of base categories to novel categories as 4:1.

	50 (40-b, 10-n)	100 (80-b, 20-n)	200 (160-b, 40-n)	500 (400-b, 100-n)
NA	81.76 (0.54)	75.98 (0.34)	70.25 (0.16)	67.43 (0.10)
M1	86.10 (0.45)	79.92 (0.36)	73.50 (0.16)	69.59 (0.08)
M1+M2	86.43 (0.47)	80.61 (0.51)	74.09 (0.34)	70.41 (0.08)
M2	82.52 (0.53)	75.48 (0.39)	70.88 (0.23)	67.44 (0.10)
Oracle	92.20	86.76	80.85	76.87

Table 5. Few-shot classification accuracies on the miniImageNet dataset averaged over 600 test episodes for different ways and shots. 95% confidence intervals are shown in the parentheses.

	5-way 1-shot	5-way 5-shot	20-way 1-shot	20-way 5-shot
ProtoNet	47.21 (0.69)	63.62 (0.61)	20.51 (0.46)	35.20 (0.59)
ProtoNet+M1	48.79 (0.51)	65.67 (0.56)	21.93 (0.62)	35.66 (0.53)
ProtoNet+M2	41.36 (0.47)	57.48 (0.43)	16.94 (0.57)	31.52 (0.64)

Fig. 4. We found our recognition performance to be negligibly sensitive to q and k'. This suggests that the location of the novel-class prototype estimate only depends on the number of subspaces (r) rather than its dimensionality ($q + 1$). Similarly, the Markov-chain-based prediction does not depend on the number of nearest neighbors k' used for connecting the graph. In Fig. 4(a), the number of subspaces (r) is varied, keeping rest of the hyper-parameters the same. This is done for both the ImageNet (denoted as (I)) and the CUB-200 dataset (denoted as (C)). From the plot, it is seen that the performance increases as the number of subspaces increases but then decreases after reaching a peak. Initially, more linear subspaces in the neighborhood are required for estimating the local structure of the non-linear manifold but becomes irrelevant after more supbspaces.

Next, we studied the effects of α_1 and α_2 on the recognition performance for the 1- and 5-shot settings of the ImageNet and the CUB-200 datasets as reported in Figs. 4(b) and 4(c), respectively. Accordingly, we obtained an optimal performance when α_1 or α_2 is between 0 and 1. From Eq. (2), it suggests that the location of the novel-class prototype is within the space bounded by the few-shot sample mean ($\mathbf{x}_n$), the subspace projection ($\mathbf{c}_p$) and the weighted mean of the nearby class prototypes ($\mathbf{c}_d$). For higher number of shots, the maxima seems to move towards the right; that is, closer to α_1, α_2 values of 1. This implies more contribution from the few-shot class mean as visible from Eq. (2). This is intuitive because as the number of shots increases, we expect the few-shot sample mean to converge to the class prototype. In fact, for shots of 10 and higher, we obtained the maxima at $\alpha_1 = \alpha_2 = 0.9$ on both datasets. For low values of α_1, α_2 (less contribution of the few-shot sample mean), we observed a dip in

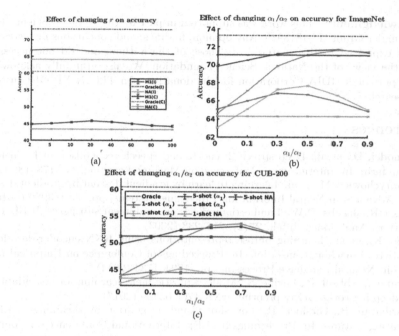

Fig. 4. (a) Effect of the number of subspaces r on recognition performance for both ImageNet (I) and CUB-200 (C). Effect of α_1 and α_2 on 1-shot and 5-shot recognition performance for (b) ImageNet and (c) CUB-200. Legends of (c) hold for (b) as well. α_1 in parenthesis suggests that α_1 is varied while $\alpha_2 = 1$ and vice versa. All results are over 10 trials.

performance, even sometimes worse than the NA baseline. This suggests that the contribution of the few-shot mean is important in estimating the novel-class prototype. From the plot, we see that the setting $\alpha_1 = 0$, $\alpha_2 = 1$ produces much better performance as compared to $\alpha_1 = 1$, $\alpha_2 = 0$. According to Eq. (2), it means that the contribution of the projection (c_p) is more important compared to contribution of nearby prototypes (c_d).

4   Conclusions

In this paper, we have introduced a new setting in few-shot learning that assumes access to only the base-class prototypes. To address this problem, we used the structural arrangement of the class prototypes on a manifold, firstly to estimate the novel-class prototypes and secondly to induce an absorbing Markov-chain for test-time prediction. From the experiments, it is evident that our proposed method improved over the no-adaptation baseline but there is still a lot of room for improvement to reach the oracle-level performance. Therefore, our results serve as a benchmark for future researchers to work upon.

Acknowledgments. This work was supported in part by the National Science Foundation under Grant IIS-1813935. Any opinion, findings, and conclusions or recommendations expressed in this material are those of the authors and do not necessarily reflect the views of the National Science Foundation. We also gratefully acknowledge the support of NVIDIA Corporation for the donation of a TITAN XP GPU used for this research.

References

1. Amodei, D., et al.: Deep speech 2: end-to-end speech recognition in English and Mandarin. In: International Conference on Machine Learning, pp. 173–182 (2016)
2. Andrychowicz, M., et al.: Learning to learn by gradient descent by gradient descent. In: Advances in Neural Information Processing Systems, pp. 3981–3989 (2016)
3. Basri, R., Jacobs, D.W.: Lambertian reflectance and linear subspaces. IEEE Trans. Pattern Anal. Mach. Intell. **25**(2), 218–233 (2003)
4. Cho, K., et al.: Learning phrase representations using RNN encoder-decoder for statistical machine translation. In: Proceedings of Conference on Empirical Methods in Natural Language Processing, pp. 1724–1734 (2014)
5. Finn, C., Abbeel, P., Levine, S.: Model-agnostic meta-learning for fast adaptation of deep networks. arXiv preprint arXiv:1703.03400 (2017)
6. Hariharan, B., Girshick, R.: Low-shot visual recognition by shrinking and hallucinating features. In: Proceedings of IEEE International Conference on Computer Vision (ICCV), Venice, Italy (2017)
7. He, K., Zhang, X., Ren, S., Sun, J.: Deep residual learning for image recognition. In: Proceedings of the IEEE Conference on Computer Vision and Pattern Recognition (CVPR), pp. 770–778 (2016)
8. Jie, L., Tommasi, T., Caputo, B.: Multiclass transfer learning from unconstrained priors. In: Proceedings of IEEE International Conference on Computer Vision, pp. 1863–1870 (2011)
9. Krizhevsky, A., Sutskever, I., Hinton, G.E.: ImageNet classification with deep convolutional neural networks. In: Advances in Neural Information Processing Systems, pp. 1097–1105 (2012)
10. Kuzborskij, I., Orabona, F., Caputo, B.: Scalable greedy algorithms for transfer learning. Comput. Vis. Image Under. **156**, 174–185 (2017)
11. Mehrotra, A., Dukkipati, A.: Generative adversarial residual pairwise networks for one shot learning. arXiv preprint arXiv:1703.08033 (2017)
12. Ravi, S., Larochelle, H.: Optimization as a model for few-shot learning. In: International Conference on Learning Representations (2017)
13. Snell, J., Swersky, K., Zemel, R.: Prototypical networks for few-shot learning. In: Advances in Neural Information Processing Systems, pp. 4080–4090 (2017)
14. Sung, F., Yang, Y., Zhang, L., Xiang, T., Torr, P.H., Hospedales, T.M.: Learning to compare: relation network for few-shot learning. In: Proceedings of the IEEE Conference on Computer Vision and Pattern Recognition (2018)
15. Tommasi, T., Orabona, F., Caputo, B.: Learning categories from few examples with multi model knowledge transfer. IEEE Trans. Pattern Anal. Mach. Intell. **36**(5), 928–941 (2014)
16. Vinyals, O., Blundell, C., Lillicrap, T., Kavukcuoglu, K., Wierstra, D.: Matching networks for one shot learning. In: Advances in Neural Information Processing Systems, pp. 3630–3638 (2016)
17. Wang, Y.X., Girshick, R., Herbert, M., Hariharan, B.: Low-shot learning from imaginary data. In: Computer Vision and Pattern Recognition (CVPR) (2018)

A Scale-Aware YOLO Model
for Pedestrian Detection

Xingyi Yang[1]([✉]), Yong Wang[3], and Robert Laganière[2]

[1] Department of Electrical and Computer Engineering, UC San Diego,
San Diego, USA
x3yang@ucsd.edu
[2] School of Electrical Engineering and Computer Science, University of Ottawa,
Ottawa, Canada
laganier@eecs.uottawa.ca
[3] School of Aeronautics and Astronautics, Sun Yat-Sen University,
Guangzhou, China
wangyong5@mail.sysu.edu.cn

Abstract. Pedestrian detection is considered one of the most challenging problems in computer vision, as it involves the combination of classification and localization within a scene. Recently, convolutional neural networks (CNNs) have been demonstrated to achieve superior detection results compared to traditional approaches. Although YOLOv3 (an improved You Only Look Once model) is proposed as one of state-of-the-art methods in CNN-based object detection, it remains very challenging to leverage this method for real-time pedestrian detection. In this paper, we propose a new framework called SA YOLOv3, a scale-aware You Only Look Once framework which improves YOLOv3 in improving pedestrian detection of small scale pedestrian instances in a real-time manner. Our network introduces two sub-networks which detect pedestrians of different scales. Outputs from the sub-networks are then combined to generate robust detection results. Experimental results show that the proposed SA YOLOv3 framework outperforms the results of YOLOv3 on public datasets and run at an average of 11 fps on a GPU.

Keywords: Pedestrian detection · YOLO · CNN

1 Introduction

Pedestrian detection is one of the most challenging problems in the field of computer vision. The goal of pedestrian detection is to localize different pedestrians in a scene and assign bounding boxes. It has been the object of many studies in the computer vision community as an important component in many applications including intelligent vehicles, person re-identification and robotics, to name a few.

Traditional methods [1,2] use a sliding window approach and a classifier is employed to determine the presence of a pedestrian. However, this type of approach has a high detection error rate. Recently, convolutional neural networks

© Springer Nature Switzerland AG 2020
G. Bebis et al. (Eds.): ISVC 2020, LNCS 12510, pp. 15–26, 2020.
https://doi.org/10.1007/978-3-030-64559-5_2

(CNNs) have shown significant performance in a range of different applications, with pedestrian detection being one of the key areas where CNNs clearly outperforms traditional approaches [3–7]. For example, in [6], an end-to-end CNN architecture is employed to generate pedestrian bounding boxes via multiple layers in an image, and a classifier performs classification on bounding boxes. Although these two-stage methods are able to produce high accuracy, the whole procedure is computationally expensive.

To speed up detection procedure, a framework called You Only Look Once (YOLO) [8] is proposed which formulate the detection problem as a single regression problem, where bounding box position and class probabilities are solved at the same time. YOLO has demonstrated its ability to provide appealing speed advantages compared to two-stage methods, but it has significantly higher location error than these methods. Recently, YOLOv3 [9] was proposed with the objective of further reducing detection errors. A feature pyramid to improve small object detection is used.

Small pedestrian detection is one of the fundamental problem in pedestrian detection. Existing approaches handle the scale-variance problem mainly from two aspects. First, a multi-scale scheme is employed on pedestrians of various sizes [10,11]. Second, data augmentation is utilized to improve scale-invariance [12,13]. However, it is difficult to integrate object features of different scale within a single model as the intra-class variance of large-size and small-size objects is large. In [14], a scale-aware architecture network is proposed to exploit the different characteristics of pedestrians at various scales. However, this is a two stage approach that needs ACF [15] to provide candidate bounding boxes first, which reduces its detection efficiency and accuracy.

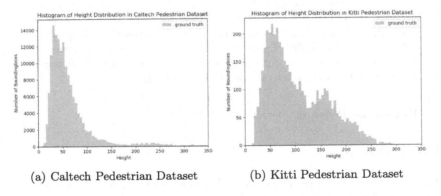

(a) Caltech Pedestrian Dataset   (b) Kitti Pedestrian Dataset

Fig. 1. Histogram of object height (in pixel) distribution for two pedestrian detection dataset

To address this problem, we further investigate some statistics properties of pedestrian detection. First, small objects dominate pedestrian datasets. Figure 1 shows the histograms of object height on two pedestrian detection dataset. Half of bounding boxes in Caltech dataset [31] and one third from the Kitti dataset [3] have a height less than 50 pixels. Second, small pedestrians tend to appear at the center of the images. Figure 2 visualizes the location heatmap for small pedestrian (height less than 50). Most bounding boxes center around the middle line of the whole images. Findings above give us two valuable inspirations: 1. We need to design a separated component for small object detection due to its large quantity. 2. We need to specially focus on central image to detect tiny pedestrians.

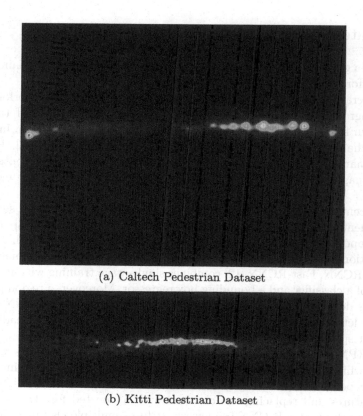

(a) Caltech Pedestrian Dataset

(b) Kitti Pedestrian Dataset

Fig. 2. Pedestrian location heatmap with height less than 50 pixels for two pedestrian detection dataset. Brighter colors indicate more objects gathered abound that location. (Color figure online)

Motivated by the above observations, we develop a novel scale-aware YOLOv3 framework which is built on the YOLOv3 [9]. Different from [14], this framework is an end-to-end architecture and one-stage detector. The proposed scale-aware YOLOv3 integrates a large-size sub-network and a small-size sub-network. Different scales pedestrians are trained with different sub-networks.

The contribution of our work is as follows. First, we propose a novel scale-aware YOLOv3 model for pedestrian detection by integrating a large-size sub-network and a small-size sub-network into a unified architecture. Second, different training strategies are implemented on the two sub-networks. Third, extensive experiments on challenging pedestrian datasets demonstrate that our method achieve state-of-the-art performance.

The paper is organized as follows. Section 2 reviews the related works. In Sect. 3, the methodology of our method is described in details. In Sect. 4, experimental results demonstrating the efficacy of our method are presented. Conclusions are drawn in Sect. 5.

2   Related Works

There are a great number of literatures on pedestrian detection. We mainly focus here on efforts that are closely related to our method.

Hand-crafted features have played a key role in obtaining good performance. The histogram of oriented gradient (HOG) descriptor [1] is one of the most well-known features constructed for pedestrian detection. It has been improved through the introduction of integral channel features (ICF) in [17]. Features such as Haar features, histograms, and local sums are efficiently computed using integral images. This work has been further extended in several ways, e.g., ACF [15].

In recent years, CNN-based approaches [18–21] have made significant improvements in pedestrian detection. The RCNN developed in [13] combines object proposals with CNN features. This leads to SPPnet [22] which enhances the detection speed of RCNN by computing CNN features once per image. Built on top of RCNN, Fast-RCNN [12] combines single-stage training with multi-task learning of a classifier and a bounding box regressor. Moreover, a region proposal network is developed in Faster-RCNN [23]. It shares entire image CNN features with the detection network to effectively predict object position, leading to a significant speedup for detection.

The RPN+BF model [7] demonstrated that the RPN performs well as a detector while the classifier degrades in performance due to collapsing bins of small-size pedestrians. This problem can be alleviated by using higher resolution features and replacing the classifier with a boosted forest. F-DNN [24] also adopts the Faster R-CNN framework. It fuses multiple classifiers including ResNet [25] and GoogLeNet [26] by using soft-reject and incorporates multiple training datasets.

A convolutional sparse coding based method is employed in [27] to pre-train CNN for pedestrian detection. In [21] pedestrian detection is jointly optimized with other semantic tasks including scene attributes. Complexity-aware cascaded detectors are introduced in [18] by leveraging both CNN and hand-crafted features for trade-off between speed and accuracy.

Multi-layer methods have also been proposed for detecting objects across various sizes. Up-sampling inputs training and testing are used in [6,22] to improve the scale-invariance of Faster RCNN [23]. SA-FastRCNN [14] proposes two subnetworks based on Fast-RCNN to adaptively detect pedestrians across different scales. Similarly, multiple layers are utilized in MSCNN [6] to match objects of different sizes.

Complementary detectors can be integrated to create a strong multi-scale detector. A single classifier is trained at a fixed resolution [13,22]. Then the input image is resized to several different scales and the associated features are computed independently.

Various one-stage detector methods have been proposed to better balance the detection accuracy and speed [8,9,28,29]. SSD [28] discretizes the output space of bounding boxes into a set of template boxes over varying aspect ratios and scales. An improved YOLO is proposed in [29] (named YOLOv2) where anchor boxes are employed to predict bounding boxes. In addition, there is no fully-connected layer in YOLOv2. To improve the training model accuracy, k-means clustering is adopted on the training set to automatically select good priors. The Darknet-19 model was developed to make YOLOv2 faster.

This motivates us to consider a simpler grouping of pedestrians into two sizes, large size and small size, which corresponds to near vs. far instances in dataset. The focus of this paper is to achieve a more balanced detection performance for both large and small-size pedestrian images.

3   Our Detection Algorithm

3.1   Overview of Our Framework

As shown in Fig. 3, given an input image, the SA YOLOv3 first divides the image into two parts. The whole image is for large scale pedestrian detection. And the center part is for small scale pedestrian detection. These two parts are first passed through the shared convolutional layers to extract corresponding feature maps. Then they are separately sent to two sub-networks. Different confidence scores and bounding boxes are assigned which are then combined to generate the final detection results using NMS.

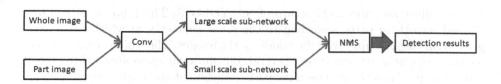

Fig. 3. Illustration of our SA YOLOv3. A large-scale and a small-scale sub-network are learned specifically to detect pedestrians with different scales. The final result is obtained by fusing the outputs of the two sub-networks.

3.2   YOLOv3

YOLOv3 improves YOLO by proposing several extensions. The first is class prediction. Binary cross-entropy loss is utilized during training. The second is the introduction of a new network, Darknet-53, as illustrated in Fig. 4. This network is an improved version of Darknet-19 and more efficient than ResNet-101 and ResNet-152. The third is multiple scale prediction. Three layers are employed to predict bounding boxes using a feature pyramid similar to [30]. These multiple features can provide more meaningful semantic information from the deeper layers and finer grained information from the earlier feature maps.

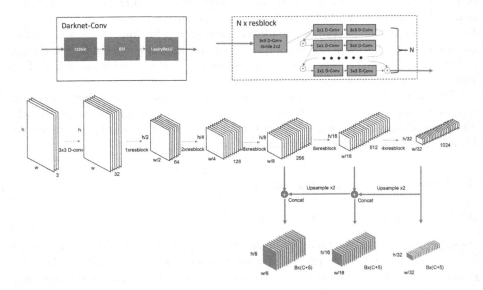

Fig. 4. The Darknet-53 model.

3.3   Architecture of SA YOLOv3

Figure 5 illustrates the architecture of SA YOLOv3. The input image is first divided into three parts according to the scene geometry in which small scale pedestrians usually appear in the middle of the images. The whole image and center part are sent into the network. Several convolutional layers are used to extract feature maps. Then the proposed network branches into two sub-networks, which are learned specifically to detect large-scale and small-scale pedestrians respectively.

Each sub-network takes as input the feature maps generated from the previous convolutional layers. These feature maps are further extracted through a sequence of convolutional layers to generate feature specialized for a specific scale. Feature maps are pooled into a fixed-length feature vector which is fed into a sequence of fully connected layers.

Each sub-network follows two output layers which produce two output vectors per instance proposal. Specifically, one layer outputs classification scores, the other one regresses the bounding box coordinate. Finally, the outputs from the two sub-networks are fused via NMS.

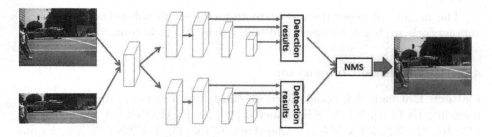

Fig. 5. The architecture of our SA YOLOv3. The features of the entire input image are first extracted by a set of convolutional layers, and then fed into two sub-networks. A sequence of convolutional layers is utilized to further extract scale-specific features in each sub-network. Next, the produced feature maps are pooled into a fixed-length feature vector via a RoI pooling layer. Then several fully connected layers generate scale-specific detection results: one outputs classification scores and the other outputs refined bounding box coordinate for each pedestrian. Finally, the outputs of the two sub-networks are fused by applying NMS.

4 Experiment

We evaluate our method on the popular Caltech dataset [31]. Comprehensive analysis and ablation experiments are carried out using the Caltech dataset. In addition, to test generalization of our model, pedestrian detection is also carried out on the KITTI dataset [3].

4.1 Implementation Details

The Caltech dataset [31] consists of 350K pedestrian bounding box annotations across 10 h of urban driving. The log average miss rate against a false positive per image (FPPI) range of [10 2; 10 0] is utilized for evaluating performance. A minimum intersection over union (IoU) threshold of 0.5 is required for a detected box to match with a ground truth box. For training, we sample every 5 frames from the standard training set, which contains 10734 training images. We evaluate on the standard 4024 images in the testing set. In our experiments, six subsets are considered to demonstrate the performance on occlusion and small size issues: reasonable, all-scale, far-scale, large, medium-scale, heavy occluded. In the reasonable subset, pedestrians are over 50 pixels. In the all-scale subset, pedestrians are over 20 pixels. In the far-scale subset, pedestrians are between 20 to 30 pixels. In the large subset, pedestrians are over 100 pixels. In the medium-scale subset, pedestrians are between 30 to 80 pixels. In the heavy occluded subset, pedestrians are 36% to 80% occluded.

The input size in KITTI dataset is 375 × 1242. The detection results are uploaded to KITTI website and the results are evaluated by mean Average Precision (mAP) which is the area under the Precision-Recall curve. There are three difficulty levels: easy, moderate and hard.

The heights of pedestrians used to train the small sub-network and large sub-network are below 50 pixels and larger than 30 pixels respectively.

4.2   Quantitative Comparison

Caltech Dataset. For comparison, we enlist here a group of nine algorithms, including HOG [1], VJ [2], SSD-resnet50 [28], SA-FastRCNN [14], YOLOv3 [9], SDS-RCNN [32], MS-CNN [6], AdaptFastRCNN [33], F-DNN+SS [24]. Evaluation results are measured in terms of the log-average miss rate for pedestrian instances of the six situations.

Figure 6(a) displays the quantitative results of reasonable. Our approach (16%) outperforms YOLOv3 [9] (20%) and reduce the FPPI by an average of 20%. Meanwhile, our method also outperforms the one stage method SSD-resnet50 [28] (20%). SDS-RCNN [32] and F-DNN+SS [24] achieve the lowest and second lowest log-average miss rate as segmentation methods are employed. AdaptFasterRCNN [33], SA-fastRCNN [14] and MS-CNN [6] performs slightly better than ours. These methods are two-stage RCNN methods which are slower than our method.

Further, for all (b), our approach achieves the second lowest missing rate of 53%, which results in substantially better performance than the existing results, e.g., 60% of AdaptFasterRCNN [33] and 61% of MS-CNN [6].

Far-scale (c). Our approach significantly outperforms all compared methods and achieves the lowest log-average miss rate of 72%, which exceeds the results 77% of F-DNN+SS [24]. As the amount of hard-to-detect far-scale instances dominates the overall pedestrian population of Caltech benchmark, our framework contributes an effective solution.

Medium-scale (e). Our method outperforms the other methods except F-DNN+SS [24] in a trend similar to that of (b).

Heavy occluded (f). Our method achieves the best results in FPPI (48%). [31] showed that nearly 70% of the pedestrians are occluded in realistic videos and the detection results degrades rapidly with heavy occlusion. Our method is able to locate pedestrians only partially visible.

KITTI Dataset. Table 1 shows the comparison of our method on pedestrian detection with other compared methods. Our approach outperforms the vanilla YOLOv3 method and improves 5.5% on hard condition. In addition, our detection time is comparable with YOLOv3and much faster than the other methods.

Efficiency is one of the advantages of our framework. Our method takes 11 frames per second (fps) with an input image of size 375 * 1242 on a single Nvidia Titan Xp GPU. Compared to the RPN+BF [7], our approach executes six times faster (fifth column of Table 1). Our method is slower than YOLOv3 as the structure of our network architecture while our method is more elaborated.

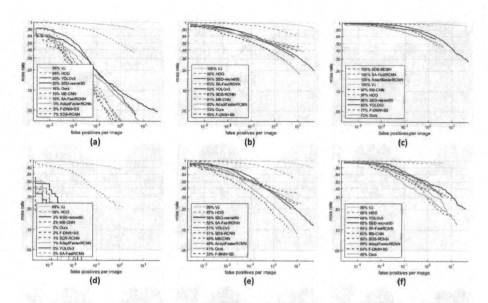

Fig. 6. Quantitative comparison results on the Caltech benchmark. (a) Reasonable. (b) All-scale. (c) Far-scale. (d) Large. (e) Medium-scale. (f) Heavy occluded.

Table 1. The comparison of our method on pedestrian detection with other compared methods on the KITTI dataset.

Method	AP on Easy	AP on Moderate	AP on Hard	Times (s)
RPN+BF [7]	75.58%	61.29%	56.08%	0.6
Faster R-CNN [23]	78.35%	65.91%	61.19%	2
YOLOv3 [9]	77.74%	64.3%	59.00%	0.043
Ours	77.88%	66.69%	62.22%	0.09

4.3 Qualitative Comparison

Figure 7 presents examples of detection results of YOLOv3 [9], SA FastRCNN [14] and our method on Caltech dataset to further demonstrate the superiority of our method in detecting small-scale instances. The three columns show the detection results by YOLOv3 [9] and SA FastRCNN [14] and our SA YOLOv3. The red rectangles represent ground-truth bounding boxes of pedestrians, and the detected instances by our SA YOLOv3 and the two baselines are annotated in green rectangles. One can observe that our method can successfully detect most of the small-scale pedestrian instances that YOLOv3 and SA FastRCNN have missed. It also shows that our method is robust to heavy occlusion of pedestrians, illumination and large background clutters.

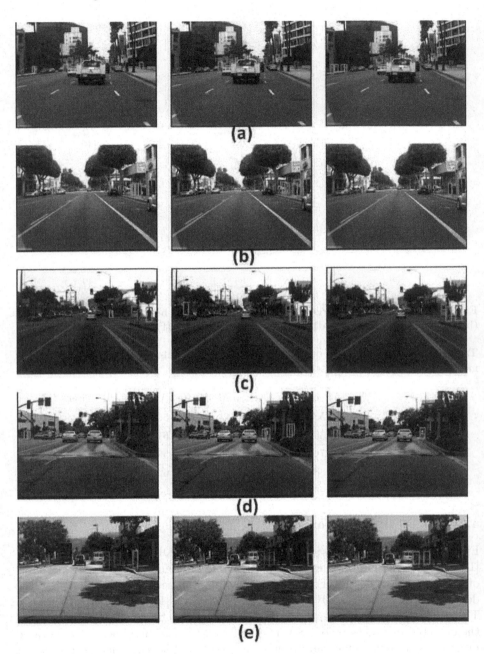

Fig. 7. Visual comparison of YOLOv3, SA Fast RCNN and our detection results on the Caltech benchmark dataset. The three columns sequentially show the detection results by YOLOv3 [9] and SA FastRCNN [14] and our SA YOLOv3. The red rectangles represent ground-truth bounding boxes of pedestrians, and the detected instances by our SA YOLOv3 and the two baselines are annotated in green rectangles. (Color figure online)

5 Conclusion

In this paper, we introduced SA YOLOv3, a new framework for the detection of small scale pedestrians. Although a set of state-of-the-art methods has been proposed, they have difficulty in detecting small pedestrians and often can not be used in real-time. Here, we made fully use of geometry property of input image and take advantage of the YOLOv3 framework to produce a network architecture. Our network consists of two sub-networks to handle two different pedestrian scales. Experimental results show that the proposed SA YOLOv3 framework can reduce the FPPI of the original YOLOv3 method by 20% on the reasonable condition of the Caltech dataset and 5.5% on the hard condition of the KITTI dataset.

References

1. Dalal, N., Triggs, B.: Histogram of oriented gradient for human detection. In: CVPR 2005, San Diego, California (2005)
2. Viola, P., Jones, M.: Robust real-time face detection. IJCV **57**, 137–154 (2004). https://doi.org/10.1023/B:VISI.0000013087.49260.fb
3. Geiger, A., Lenz, P., Urtasun, R.: Are we ready for autonomous driving? The kitti vision benchmark suite. In: IEEE Conference on Computer Vision and Pattern Recognition (CVPR) (2012)
4. Zhang, S., Benenson, R., Schiele, B.: CityPersons: a diverse dataset for pedestrian detection. In: The IEEE Conference on Computer Vision and Pattern Recognition (CVPR), vol. 1, no. 2, p. 3 (2017)
5. Wu, S., Wang, S., Laganiere, R., Liu, C., Wong, H.S., Xu, Y.: Exploiting target data to learn deep convolutional networks for scene-adapted human detection. IEEE Trans. Image Process. **27**(3), 1418–1432 (2018)
6. Cai, Z., Fan, Q., Feris, R.S., Vasconcelos, N.: A unified multi-scale deep convolutional neural network for fast object detection. In: Leibe, B., Matas, J., Sebe, N., Welling, M. (eds.) ECCV 2016. LNCS, vol. 9908, pp. 354–370. Springer, Cham (2016). https://doi.org/10.1007/978-3-319-46493-0_22
7. Zhang, L., Lin, L., Liang, X., He, K.: Is faster R-CNN doing well for pedestrian detection? In: Leibe, B., Matas, J., Sebe, N., Welling, M. (eds.) ECCV 2016. LNCS, vol. 9906, pp. 443–457. Springer, Cham (2016). https://doi.org/10.1007/978-3-319-46475-6_28
8. Redmon, J., Divvala, S., Girshick, R., Farhadi, A.: You only look once: unified, real-time object detection, In: Proceedings of the IEEE Conference on Computer Vision and Pattern Recognition, pp. 779–788 (2016)
9. Redmon, J., Farhadi, A.: Yolov3: an incremental improvement arXiv preprint arXiv:1804.02767 (2018)
10. Gong, Y., Wang, L., Guo, R., Lazebnik, S.: Multi-scale orderless pooling of deep convolutional activation features. In: Fleet, D., Pajdla, T., Schiele, B., Tuytelaars, T. (eds.) ECCV 2014. LNCS, vol. 8695, pp. 392–407. Springer, Cham (2014). https://doi.org/10.1007/978-3-319-10584-0_26
11. Xu, Y., Xiao, T., Zhang, J., Yang, K., Zhang, Z.: Scale-invariant convolutional neural networks. arXiv preprint arXiv:1411.6369 (2014)
12. Girshick, R.: Fast R-CNN. In: Proceedings of the IEEE International Conference on Computer Vision, pp. 1440–1448 (2015)

13. Girshick, R., Donahue, J., Darrell, T., Malik, J.: Rich feature hierarchies for accurate object detection and semantic segmentation. In: CVPR, pp. 580–587 (2014)
14. Li, J., Liang, X., Shen, S.M., Tingfa, X., Feng, J., Yan, S.: Scale-aware fast R-CNN for pedestrian detection. IEEE Trans. Multimed. **20**(4), 985–996 (2018)
15. Dollar, P., Appel, R., Belongie, S., Perona, P.: Fast feature pyramids for object detection. IEEE TPAMI **36**(8), 1532–45 (2014)
16. Chen, Y., Li, W., Sakaridis, C., Dai, D., Gool, L.V.: Domain adaptive faster R-CNN for object detection in the wild. In: Proceedings of the IEEE Conference on Computer Vision and Pattern Recognition, pp. 3339–3348 (2018)
17. Dollar, P., Tu, Z., Perona, P., Belongie, S.: Integral channel features. In: BMVC (2009)
18. Cai, Z., Saberian, M., Vasconcelos, N.: Learning complexity-aware cascades for deep pedestrian detection. In: ICCV (2015)
19. Hosang, J., Omran, M., Benenson, R., Schiele, B.: Taking a deeper look at pedestrians. In: CVPR (2015)
20. Tian, Y., Luo, P., Wang, X., Tang, X.: Deep learning strong parts for pedestrian detection. In: ICCV (2015)
21. Tian, Y., Luo, P., Wang, X., Tang, X.: Pedestrian detection aided by deep learning semantic tasks. In: CVPR (2015)
22. He, K., Zhang, X., Ren, S., Sun, J.: Spatial pyramid pooling in deep convolutional networks for visual recognition. In: Fleet, D., Pajdla, T., Schiele, B., Tuytelaars, T. (eds.) ECCV 2014. LNCS, vol. 8691, pp. 346–361. Springer, Cham (2014). https://doi.org/10.1007/978-3-319-10578-9_23
23. Ren, S., He, K., Girshick, R., Sun, J.: Faster R-CNN: towards real-time object detection with region proposal networks. In: NIPS (2015)
24. Du, X., El-Khamy, M., Lee, J., Davis, L.: Fused DNN: a deep neural network fusion approach to fast and robust pedestrian detection. In: 2017 IEEE Winter Conference on Applications of Computer Vision (WACV), pp. 953–961. IEEE (2017)
25. He, K., Zhang, X., Ren, S., Sun, J.: Deep residual learning for image recognition. In: Proceedings of the IEEE Conference on Computer Vision and Pattern Recognition, pp. 770–778 (2016)
26. Szegedy, C., et al.: Going deeper with convolutions. In: Proceedings of the IEEE Conference on Computer Vision and Pattern Recognition, pp. 1–9 (2015)
27. Sermanet, P., Kavukcuoglu, K., Chintala, S., LeCun, Y.: Pedestrian detection with unsupervised multi-stage feature learning. In: CVPR (2013)
28. Liu, W., et al.: SSD: single shot multibox detector. In: Leibe, B., Matas, J., Sebe, N., Welling, M. (eds.) ECCV 2016. LNCS, vol. 9905, pp. 21–37. Springer, Cham (2016). https://doi.org/10.1007/978-3-319-46448-0_2
29. Redmon, J., Farhadi, A.: YOLO9000: better, faster, stronger. arXiv preprint (2017)
30. Lin, T.-Y., Dollar, P., Girshick, R., He, K., Hariharan, B., Belongie, S.: Feature pyramid networks for object detection. In: Proceedings of the IEEE Conference on Computer Vision and Pattern Recognition, pp. 2117–2125 (2017)
31. Dollar, P., Wojek, C., Schiele, B., Perona, P.: Pedestrian detection: an evaluation of the state of the art. IEEE Trans. Pattern Anal. Mach. Intell. **34**(4), 743–761 (2012)
32. Brazil, G., Yin, X., Liu, X.: Illuminating pedestrians via simultaneous detection segmentation. arXiv preprint arXiv:1706.08564 (2017)

Image Categorization Using Agglomerative Clustering Based Smoothed Dirichlet Mixtures

Fatma Najar$^{(\boxtimes)}$ and Nizar Bouguila$^{(\boxtimes)}$

Concordia Institute for Information and Systems Engineering (CIISE),
Concordia University, Montreal, QC, Canada
`f_najar@encs.concordia.ca, nizar.bouguila@concordia.ca`

Abstract. With the rapid growth of multimedia data and the diversity
of the available image contents, it becomes necessary to develop advanced
machine learning algorithms for the purpose of categorizing and recognizing images. Hierarchical clustering methods have shown promising
results in computer vision applications. In this paper, we present a new
unsupervised image categorization technique in which we cluster images
using an agglomerative hierarchical procedure and a dissimilarity metric
is derived based on smoothed Dirichlet (SD) distribution. We propose a
mixture of SD distributions and a maximum-likelihood learning framework, from which we derive a Kulback-Leibler divergence between two
SD mixture models. Experiments on challenging images dataset that contains different indoor and outdoor places reveal the importance of the
hierarchical clustering when categorizing images. The conducted tests
prove the robustness of the proposed image categorization approach as
compared to the other related-works.

Keywords: Smoothed Dirichlet · Mixture models · Kulback-Leibler ·
Agglomerative clustering · Image categorization

1 Introduction

Image categorization is an action referring to assigning each image to the adequate category, group, or description. This arrangement could be an effortless
task for humans, but not as easy as it seems for machines. Doing so, huge efforts
have been devoted to propose several machine learning algorithms for image
classification [9], clustering [8,11,16], and online learning [14] as a key for plenty
applications such as multi-model summarization [6,15,19,39], super-resolution
[23,40], object detection [1], human action categorization [34], and image synthesis [42].

Image classification [30,38,41,43,44] which is based on pre-labeled data used
for training the model has emerged in numerous research works to address the
problem of categorization. Noting that even if those techniques have succeeded
in recognizing images, they are still limited to the fact that labeling images is

© Springer Nature Switzerland AG 2020
G. Bebis et al. (Eds.): ISVC 2020, LNCS 12510, pp. 27–38, 2020.
https://doi.org/10.1007/978-3-030-64559-5_3

such time and resources consuming task. Some of the classification algorithms are extended to online learning [32] which are more useful and adequate for real-time categorization since many observed images can be dynamically added. Meanwhile, clustering techniques [21,26,28] contribute to image categorization in an unsupervised fashion without the need to pre-label images. Unsupervised categorization approaches [2,3,10,13,22] such as mixture models, affinity propagation, and hierarchical clustering are based directly on the unlabeled data.

In this paper, the aim of the study is proposing a bottom-up hierarchical clustering algorithm known as agglomerative clustering. Commonly, these techniques employ as a metric the Euclidean distance which is not usually adequate to all cases. Euclidean distance ignores that image features could have non-linear structures which gives rise to the use of Riemannian metrics such as Fisher information, Kulback-Leibler divergence, and many more. Kulback-Leibler divergence is a dissimilarity metric defined in the probability distribution space. Usually, for the matter of calculating the KL, Gaussian distributions are the first choice taken by the majority of research works [24,25,27,37]. However, taking into consideration the well-known limitations of the Gaussian distribution [33], it is much effective to use non-Gaussian distributions for a better fitting [7,9]. Hence, we are considering the smoothed Dirichlet (SD) [35] distribution which is an approximation of the Dirichlet distribution defined in a subset of the simplex $\Delta = \{ \boldsymbol{X} = \{x_1, \ldots, x_D\} | \ \forall x_j > 0, \sum_{j=1}^{D} x_j = 1 \}$. The SD distribution is a trade-off between the multinomial distribution and the Dirichlet-Compound-Multinomial (DCM) [29,31] where the SD is as simple as the multinomial and as much robust as the DCM by way of capturing the term occurrence statistics and addressing the problem of word burstiness in such a combination between the multinomial and its conjugate prior namely the Dirichlet distribution.

To the best of our knowledge, there is no prior work on agglomerative clustering using KL-divergence based smoothed Dirichlet mixture model. Accordingly, our contributions in this work could be summarized as follows:

1. Propose a mixture model of SD and likelihood-based learning algorithm.
2. Introduce a new KL-divergence based SD for an agglomerative clustering approach.
3. Present an image categorization methodology and take advantage, for the first time, of the SD distribution in computer vision application.

The rest of the paper is organized as the following. We explain the proposed image categorization methodology in Sect. 2; where we present the mixture of smoothed Dirichlet distributions, the learning algorithm, the KL-divergence and the image categorization methodology. Section 3 is devoted to the experiments where we consider a challenging dataset: CAT2000, then we discuss the obtained results with comparison to the related clustering algorithms. We finalize this paper in Sect. 4 with concluding notes and relevant promising future works.

2   Methodology

In this section, we give a full description of our proposed model for image categorization. Since our framework is based on the smoothed Dirichlet, we provide a brief introduction to the SD distribution then we propose a mixture model and its parameters learning. Noting the proposed agglomerative clustering algorithm is based on KL-divergence between each pair of clusters, we define the proposed divergence that is derived from SD mixture models. After, we explain the image categorization methodology in accordance with the proposed agglomerative clustering based SD mixture model.

2.1   Mixture of Smoothed Dirichlet Distributions

Smoothed Dirichlet [35] is a probabilistic model proposed as a building block for generative topic models and proposed as an alternative distribution to the multinomial and the Dirichlet-Compound-Multinomial. The generative process of SD embodies two assumptions: (1) the documents are generated using a smoothed proportions representation, and (2) the smoothed proportions occupy only a subset of the whole simplex. Hence, the probability density function (pdf) for a D-dimentional vector $\boldsymbol{X} = \{x_1, \ldots, x_D\}$ under SD distribution is defined in a smoothing simplex $\Delta^s = \{\boldsymbol{X} = \lambda \, \boldsymbol{Y} + (1 - \lambda) \, \boldsymbol{Y}_{GE} | \boldsymbol{Y} \in \Delta\}$ where $\boldsymbol{Y}_{GE}$ is a general English proportion [35] and λ is a smoothing parameter:

$$p(\boldsymbol{X}|\boldsymbol{\alpha}) = \frac{S^S}{\prod_{j=1}^{D} \alpha_j^{\alpha_j}} \prod_{j=1}^{D} x_j^{\alpha_j - 1} \tag{1}$$

where $S = \sum_{j=1}^{D} \alpha_j$ and $\alpha_j > 0$, $j = 1, \ldots, D$ is the shape parameter that characterizes the distribution.

While data clustering using probabilistic models has received a lot of attention, mixture of distributions is the appropriate choice for fitting multimodal data. In this regard, we derive a mixture model of SD distributions with M components (SDMM):

$$P(\boldsymbol{X}|\Theta) = \sum_{k=1}^{M} \pi_k p(\boldsymbol{X}|\boldsymbol{\alpha}_k)$$

$$= \sum_{k=1}^{M} \pi_k \frac{S_k^{S_k}}{\prod_{j=1}^{D} (\alpha_{jk})^{\alpha_{jk}}} \prod_{j=1}^{D} x_j^{\alpha_{jk} - 1} \tag{2}$$

where $\Theta = \{\boldsymbol{\alpha}_k, \pi_k\}_{k=1}^{M}$ represents the mixture parameters, $S_k = \sum_{j=1}^{D} \alpha_{jk}$, and $\{\pi_k\}_{k=1}^{M}$ are the mixing weights coefficients subject to the constraints $\sum_{k=1}^{M} \pi_k = 1$ and $0 \leq \pi_k \leq 1$,

2.2 Model Learning

For the purpose of learning the mixture parameters, we consider a maximum-likelihood approach [12] on the basis of the Expectation-Maximization algorithm (EM) [20]. Let $\mathcal{X} = \{X_i\}_{i=1}^{N}$ be the observed data, we assume each X_i is independently drawn from a SDMM, the observed-data log-likelihood is:

$$\mathcal{L}(\mathcal{X}|\Theta) = \log \prod_{i=1}^{N} P(X_i|\Theta) \tag{3}$$

Considering the complete-data log-likelihood for the maximization process instead of the observed-data function, we introduce latent (hidden) variables $\mathcal{Z} = \{z_i\}_{i=1}^{N}$. Each $z_i = \{z_{ik}\}_{k=1}^{M}$ is associated with an observed vector X_i that illustrates the generation procedure conducted by the SD distribution of the mixture and displayed as an indicator variable as $z_{ik} = 1$ if X_i belongs to the k-th component otherwise it equals to 0. By using this latent variable, the log-likelihood of the complete-data is expressed as:

$$\mathcal{L}(\mathcal{X}, \mathcal{Z}|\Theta) = \log \prod_{i=1}^{N} \left(\sum_{k=1}^{M} \pi_k p(X_i|\alpha_k)^{z_{ik}} \right) \tag{4}$$

With EM algorithm, the heart of the matter comes with estimating the parameters based on the second derivative of the log-likelihood function with respect to each parameter. The E-step is about updating the posterior probabilities which are named also as responsibilities:

$$\hat{z}_{ik} = \frac{\pi_k p(X_i|\alpha_k)}{\sum_{k=1}^{M} \pi_k p(X_i|\alpha_k)} \tag{5}$$

In M-step, the update of SDMM parameters are obtained by setting the gradient of the complete-data log-likelihood function with respect to the parameters up to zero as following:

$$\frac{\partial \mathcal{L}(\mathcal{X}, \mathcal{Z}|\Theta)}{\partial \Theta_k} = 0 \tag{6}$$

Then, setting the above equation with respect to π_k, we obtain the update formula for the mixing weight ($k = 1, \ldots, M$) as:

$$\hat{\pi}_k = \frac{1}{N} \sum_{i=1}^{N} \hat{z}_{ik} \tag{7}$$

Regarding estimating the α_{jk} parameter, we expand the Eq. 4 to get:

$$\hat{\alpha}_{jk} = \sum_{i=1}^{N} \hat{z}_{ik} \frac{x_{ij}}{\zeta_k} \tag{8}$$

where ζ_k is a normalizer that ensures $\sum_{j=1}^{D} \alpha_{jk} = S_k$.

It is well-known that each EM-based algorithm should start with some initial parameters, where in our learning approach we initialize the mixing weights and the α parameters using the initialization process proposed in [17]. The complete learning approach is detailed in Algorithm 1.
for $k = 1, \ldots, M$

$$\alpha_{jk} = \frac{x'_{1j}(x'_{11} - x'_{21})}{x'_{21} - (x'_{11})^2}, \text{ for } j = 1, \ldots, D - 1 \tag{9}$$

$$\alpha_{jD} = \frac{(1 - \sum_{j=1}^{D-1} x'_{1j})(x'_{11} - x'_{21})}{x'_{21} - (x'_{11})^2} \tag{10}$$

where

$$x'_{1j} = \frac{1}{N} \sum_{i=1}^{N} x_{ij}, \ j = 1, \ldots, D \tag{11}$$

$$x'_{21} = \frac{1}{N} \sum_{i=1}^{N} x_{i1}^2 \tag{12}$$

Algorithm 1: SDMM learning algorithm

---

1 **Input:** Dataset $\mathcal{X} = \{X_1, \ldots, X_N\}$, number of components M ;
2 **Output:** Parameters Θ^*, ;
3 Initialize α_k and $\pi_k, k = 1, \ldots, M$;
4 **repeat**
5 | **foreach** *Component k* **do**
6 | **E-step:**;
7 | Estimate the posterior distribution $\hat{z}_{ik}$ $(i = 1, \ldots, N)$ using Eq. 5;
    | **M-step:**;
8 | Estimate the mixing weight components using Eq. 7;
9 | Update the $\hat{\alpha}_{jk}, j = 1, \ldots, D$ parameter using Eq. 8;
10 | **end**
11 **until** *Convergence of log-likelihood*;

2.3 KL-distance Based Smoothed Dirichlet Mixture Model

In this section, we propose a symmetric Kulback-Leibler divergence between two smoothed Dirichlet (SD) mixture models taken into consideration as a metric in our proposed hierarchical clustering framework. Hence, showing that SD distribution is a member of the exponential family, we simply can write the *pdf* as the following:

$$p(\boldsymbol{X}|\boldsymbol{\alpha}) = \exp\left(S\log S - \sum_{j=1}^{D}\alpha_j\log\alpha_j + \sum_{j=1}^{D}(\alpha_j - 1)\log x_j\right)$$

$$= \frac{1}{\prod_{j=1}^{D}x_j}\exp\left(\sum_{j=1}^{D}\alpha_j\log x_j + S\log S - \sum_{j=1}^{D}\alpha_j\log\alpha_j\right)$$

$$= H(\boldsymbol{X})\exp\left(G(\Theta)^{tr}T(\boldsymbol{X}) + \Phi(\Theta)\right)$$

where

$$\begin{cases} H(\boldsymbol{X}) = \frac{1}{\prod_{j=1}^{D}x_j} \\ G(\Theta) = (\alpha_1,\ldots,\alpha_D) \\ T(\boldsymbol{X}) = (\log x_1,\ldots,\log x_D) \\ \Phi(\Theta) = S\log S - \sum_{j=1}^{D}\alpha_j\log\alpha_j \end{cases} \tag{13}$$

Taking advantage of the exponential family properties [36], the KL divergence between two SD distributions is defined by:

$$KL(p(\boldsymbol{X}|\boldsymbol{\alpha}), p(\boldsymbol{X}|\boldsymbol{\alpha}')) = \Phi(\Theta) - \Phi(\Theta') + [G(\Theta) - G(\Theta')]^{tr}E_{\Theta}[T(\boldsymbol{X})] \tag{14}$$

where

$$E_{\Theta}[T(\boldsymbol{X})] = -\Phi'(\Theta)$$
$$= -(1 + \log S - \log\alpha_j - 1)$$
$$= \log\alpha_j - \log S, \text{ for } j = 1,\ldots,D \tag{15}$$

Following, using the log-normalizer and the natural parameters of the SD distribution, we obtain:

$$KL(p(\boldsymbol{X}|\boldsymbol{\alpha}), p(\boldsymbol{X}|\boldsymbol{\alpha}')) = \sum_{j=1}^{D}\alpha_j'\log\alpha_j' - \sum_{j=1}^{D}\alpha_j\log\alpha_j$$

$$+ \sum_{j=1}^{D}[\alpha_j - \alpha_j'](\log\alpha_j - \log S) \tag{16}$$

Taking into account that we consider the KL divergence in the domaine of mixture of SD distributions, we propose to use an upper approximation [25] given by:

$$KL_{upp}(P(\boldsymbol{X}|\Theta), P(\boldsymbol{X}|\Theta')) = \sum_{k=1}^{M}\pi_k\log\frac{\pi_k}{\pi_k'} + \sum_{k=1}^{M}\pi_k\mathcal{K}_{KL}(p(\boldsymbol{X}|\boldsymbol{\alpha}), p(\boldsymbol{X}|\boldsymbol{\alpha}'))$$

$$\tag{17}$$

where $\mathcal{K}_{KL}$ is the symmetric Kulback-Lebleir divergence:

$$\mathcal{K}_{KL}(p(\boldsymbol{X}|\boldsymbol{\alpha}), p(\boldsymbol{X}|\boldsymbol{\alpha}')) = e^{[-a(KL(p(\boldsymbol{X}|\boldsymbol{\alpha}), p(\boldsymbol{X}|\boldsymbol{\alpha}')) + KL(p(\boldsymbol{X}|\boldsymbol{\alpha}'), p(\boldsymbol{X}|\boldsymbol{\alpha})))]} \tag{18}$$

where a is a scale parameter.

2.4 Image Categorization Framework: Agglomerative Clustering

Agglomerative clustering is an unsupervised learning method. The strategy of this technique is to build a hierarchy of clusters based on their distances in a bottom-up fashion. Initially, features are extracted from images then each image is represented with its own cluster. At each level of the hierarchical approach, clusters that minimize the distance metric are merged together. In this paper, the distance between each two clusters is the KL-divergence (defined in Sect. 2.3) $D(C_i, C_j) = KL_{upp}(P(\boldsymbol{X}|\Theta_i), P(\boldsymbol{X}|\Theta_j))$ where the cluster C_i is represented with a mixture of SD distributions $P(\boldsymbol{X}|\Theta_i)$. This process is repeated untill all the images are categorized in the appropriate number of clusters. The complete image categorization methodology is graphically provided in Fig. 1.

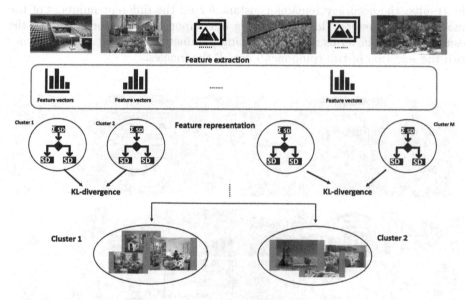

Fig. 1. Methodology adopted by the proposed agglomerative clustering-based SDMM

3 Experiments and Results

In this section, we evaluate our proposed approach through a challenging image dataset namely CAT2000 [4]. This dataset contains scenes from 20 different categories. For example, it includes objects, places, cartoon, and also satellite category where images have resolution of 1920×1080 pixels. In our paper, we select only images that contain places scenes: indoor that consists basically of closed spaces as houses, offices, and shops, and outdoor (natural and man made) that includes scenes from nature (mountains, forest, flowers) and open spaces as building and roads. Besides, each category could include some parts in common with the second one. As it is shown in Fig. 2, some of the indoor places contain plants which are for the greenhouse production that are similar to other landscape images. Indoor and outdoor categories do not contain only scenes, but also animals, foods, and human. For these reasons, in the first step of our framework, we consider the LBP descriptor [18] to extract robust features from images that lead to a better modeling. Following, we represent each image using a mixture of SD distributions where we consider different number of components ($M = 1, 2, 3$) to verify which is the best number of distributions that could better suits the image features. For this purpose, we studied the influence of the number of components of SD distributions on the categorization results. With regard to Fig. 3, when we consider only one component, the results are not efficient and the smoothing parameter of the SD distribution has no influence on the results, the accuracy remains constant for all the different numbers of the smoothing parameters. More the number of components is important, more the results fluctuate in terms of the smoothing parameter. The best result matches with the selection of two components for all the images.

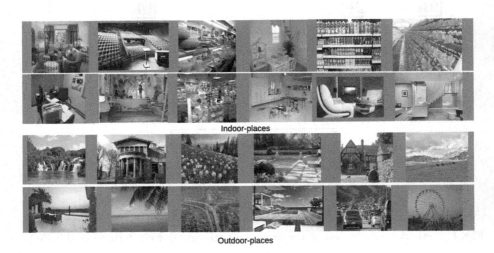

Indoor-places

Outdoor-places

Fig. 2. Samples images from CAT2000-places dataset

For the purpose of comparing our results to the other-related works, and for a fair comparison we applied the multinomial mixtures [5], Dirichlet-Compound-Multinomial mixtures [16], and smoothed Dirichlet mixtures for categorizing the places images. We constructed a bag-of-visual-words using the LBP features, and we made our tests on different vocabulary sizes (100, 200, 300) where the results displayed in Table 1 are for the 100 visual words. The results in Table 1 are in terms of categorization accuracies where the best accuracy is achieved in the case of agglomerative-KL based SDMM (66.50%) against SD with (56.16%), 55.16% when applying the DCM mixtures and 51.83% using multinomial mixture

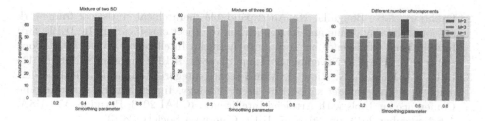

Fig. 3. Evaluation of the agglomerative clustering based-SDMM in terms of the smoothing parameter and the number of components

model. Comparing with SD mixtures where images are assigned to the class that maximizes more its log-likelihood, the agglomerative hierarchical clustering approach is shown to significantly improves the results.

Table 1. Evaluation results for categorizing CAT2000 dataset

Clustering methods	Accuracy
Multinomial mixture	51.83
Dirichlet-Compound-Multinomial	55.16
Smoothed Dirichlet	56.16
Agglomerative-KL+SDMM	66.50

4   Conclusion

In this paper, we addressed the problem of categorizing images. We proposed a mixture of SD distributions with its maximum-likelihood learning method and we derived the Kulback-Leibler divergence between SDMMs. This method showed high performance in dealing with image categorization in comparison with DCM and multinomial mixtures. Based on this distribution, we built an agglomerative hierarchical clustering approach where we consider the KL-divergence as a metric distance between clusters. Experiments on the challenging images dataset CAT2000 were presented to evaluate the proposed framework considering the places categories. Indeed, results prove the effectiveness of taking into account non-linear structures between image features and the robustness of the smoothed Dirichlet. To improve further the model accuracy, future research directions may consider others geometrical distances as a metric for merging the clusters and an alternative learning method to the maximum-likelihood.

References

1. Bakhtiari, A.S., Bouguila, N.: A hierarchical statistical model for object classification. In: 2010 IEEE International Workshop on Multimedia Signal Processing, MMSP 2010, Saint Malo, France, 4–6 October 2010, pp. 493–498. IEEE (2010)

2. Bakhtiari, A.S., Bouguila, N.: An expandable hierarchical statistical framework for count data modeling and its application to object classification. In: IEEE 23rd International Conference on Tools with Artificial Intelligence, ICTAI 2011, Boca Raton, FL, USA, 7–9 November 2011, pp. 817–824. IEEE Computer Society (2011)
3. Bdiri, T., Bouguila, N., Ziou, D.: Visual scenes categorization using a flexible hierarchical mixture model supporting users ontology. In: 25th IEEE International Conference on Tools with Artificial Intelligence, ICTAI 2013, Herndon, VA, USA, 4–6 November 2013, pp. 262–267. IEEE Computer Society (2013)
4. Borji, A., Itti, L.: Cat 2000: a large scale fixation dataset for boosting saliency research. arXiv preprint arXiv:1505.03581 (2015)
5. Bouguila, N., Ziou, D.: Improving content based image retrieval systems using finite multinomial Dirichlet mixture. In: Proceedings of the 2004 14th IEEE Signal Processing Society Workshop Machine Learning for Signal Processing, pp. 23–32 (2004)
6. Bouguila, N.: Spatial color image databases summarization. In: Proceedings of the IEEE International Conference on Acoustics, Speech, and Signal Processing, ICASSP 2007, Honolulu, Hawaii, USA, 15–20 April 2007, pp. 953–956. IEEE (2007)
7. Bouguila, N.: Clustering of count data using generalized Dirichlet multinomial distributions. IEEE Trans. Knowl. Data Eng. **20**(4), 462–474 (2008)
8. Bouguila, N.: A model-based approach for discrete data clustering and feature weighting using MAP and stochastic complexity. IEEE Trans. Knowl. Data Eng. **21**(12), 1649–1664 (2009)
9. Bouguila, N.: Count data modeling and classification using finite mixtures of distributions. IEEE Trans. Neural Netw. **22**(2), 186–198 (2011)
10. Bouguila, N., Amayri, O.: A discrete mixture-based kernel for SVMs: application to spam and image categorization. Inf. Process. Manag. **45**(6), 631–642 (2009)
11. Bouguila, N., ElGuebaly, W.: Discrete data clustering using finite mixture models. Pattern Recognit. **42**(1), 33–42 (2009)
12. Bouguila, N., Ghimire, M.N.: Discrete visual features modeling via leave-one-out likelihood estimation and applications. J. Vis. Commun. Image Represent. **21**(7), 613–626 (2010)
13. Bouguila, N., Ziou, D.: MML-based approach for finite Dirichlet mixture estimation and selection. In: Perner, P., Imiya, A. (eds.) MLDM 2005. LNCS (LNAI), vol. 3587, pp. 42–51. Springer, Heidelberg (2005). https://doi.org/10.1007/11510888_5
14. Bouguila, N., Ziou, D.: Using unsupervised learning of a finite Dirichlet mixture model to improve pattern recognition applications. Pattern Recognit. Lett. **26**(12), 1916–1925 (2005)
15. Bouguila, N., Ziou, D.: Unsupervised learning of a finite discrete mixture: applications to texture modeling and image databases summarization. J. Vis. Commun. Image Represent. **18**(4), 295–309 (2007)
16. Bouguila, N., Ziou, D., Vaillancourt, J.: Novel mixtures based on the Dirichlet distribution: application to data and image classification. In: Perner, P., Rosenfeld, A. (eds.) MLDM 2003. LNCS, vol. 2734, pp. 172–181. Springer, Heidelberg (2003). https://doi.org/10.1007/3-540-45065-3_15
17. Bouguila, N., Ziou, D., Vaillancourt, J.: Unsupervised learning of a finite mixture model based on the Dirichlet distribution and its application. IEEE Trans. Image Process. **13**(11), 1533–1543 (2004)
18. Bouwmans, T., Silva, C., Marghes, C., Zitouni, M.S., Bhaskar, H., Frelicot, C.: On the role and the importance of features for background modeling and foreground detection. Comput. Sci. Rev. **28**, 26–91 (2018)

19. Chen, J., Zhuge, H.: Abstractive text-image summarization using multi-modal attentional hierarchical RNN. In: Proceedings of the 2018 Conference on Empirical Methods in Natural Language Processing, pp. 4046–4056 (2018)

20. Dempster, A.P., Laird, N.M., Rubin, D.B.: Maximum likelihood from incomplete data via the EM algorithm. J. Roy. Stat. Soc.: Ser. B (Methodol.) **39**(1), 1–22 (1977)

21. Dueck, D., Frey, B.J.: Non-metric affinity propagation for unsupervised image categorization. In: 2007 IEEE 11th International Conference on Computer Vision, pp. 1–8. IEEE (2007)

22. Elguebaly, T., Bouguila, N.: Semantic scene classification with generalized gaussian mixture models. In: Kamel, M., Campilho, A. (eds.) ICIAR 2015. LNCS, vol. 9164, pp. 159–166. Springer, Cham (2015). https://doi.org/10.1007/978-3-319-20801-5_17

23. Ghassab, V.K., Bouguila, N.: Light field super-resolution using edge-preserved graph-based regularization. IEEE Trans. Multimed. **22**, 1447–1457 (2019)

24. Goldberger, J., Gordon, S., Greenspan, H.: An efficient image similarity measure based on approximations of KL-divergence between two gaussian mixtures. In: Null, p. 487. IEEE (2003)

25. Hershey, J.R., Olsen, P.A.: Approximating the Kullback Leibler divergence between Gaussian mixture models. In: 2007 IEEE International Conference on Acoustics, Speech and Signal Processing-ICASSP 2007, vol. 4, pp. IV-317. IEEE (2007)

26. Huang, Y., Liu, Q., Lv, F., Gong, Y., Metaxas, D.N.: Unsupervised image categorization by hypergraph partition. IEEE Trans. Pattern Anal. Mach. Intell. **33**(6), 1266–1273 (2011)

27. Kim, S.C., Kang, T.J.: Texture classification and segmentation using wavelet packet frame and Gaussian mixture model. Pattern Recogn. **40**(4), 1207–1221 (2007)

28. Liu, D., Chen, T.: Unsupervised image categorization and object localization using topic models and correspondences between images. In: 2007 IEEE 11th International Conference on Computer Vision, pp. 1–7. IEEE (2007)

29. Madsen, R.E., Kauchak, D., Elkan, C.: Modeling word burstiness using the Dirichlet distribution. In: Proceedings of the 22nd International Conference on Machine Learning, pp. 545–552 (2005)

30. Mensink, T., Verbeek, J., Perronnin, F., Csurka, G.: Distance-based image classification: generalizing to new classes at near-zero cost. IEEE Trans. Pattern Anal. Mach. Intell. **35**(11), 2624–2637 (2013)

31. Najar, F., Bouguila, N.: Happiness analysis with fisher information of Dirichlet-multinomial mixture model. In: Goutte, C., Zhu, X. (eds.) Canadian AI 2020. LNCS (LNAI), vol. 12109, pp. 438–444. Springer, Cham (2020). https://doi.org/10.1007/978-3-030-47358-7_45

32. Najar, F., Bourouis, S., Al-Azawi, R., Al-Badi, A.: Online recognition via a finite mixture of multivariate generalized Gaussian distributions. In: Bouguila, N., Fan, W. (eds.) Mixture Models and Applications. USL, pp. 81–106. Springer, Cham (2020). https://doi.org/10.1007/978-3-030-23876-6_5

33. Najar, F., Bourouis, S., Bouguila, N., Belghith, S.: A comparison between different gaussian-based mixture models. In: 2017 IEEE/ACS 14th International Conference on Computer Systems and Applications (AICCSA), pp. 704–708. IEEE (2017)

34. Najar, F., Bourouis, S., Zaguia, A., Bouguila, N., Belghith, S.: Unsupervised human action categorization using a Riemannian averaged fixed-point learning of multivariate GGMM. In: Campilho, A., Karray, F., ter Haar Romeny, B. (eds.) ICIAR 2018. LNCS, vol. 10882, pp. 408–415. Springer, Cham (2018). https://doi.org/10.1007/978-3-319-93000-8_46

35. Nallapati, R., Minka, T., Robertson, S.: The smoothed-Dirichlet distribution: a new building block for generative models. CIIR Technical Report (2006). http://www.cs.cmu.edu/nmramesh/sdtc.pdf

36. Nielsen, F., Garcia, V.: Statistical exponential families: a digest with flash cards. arXiv preprint arXiv:0911.4863 (2009)

37. Nielsen, F., Sun, K.: Guaranteed bounds on the Kullback-Leibler divergence of univariate mixtures. IEEE Signal Process. Lett. **23**(11), 1543–1546 (2016)

38. Rasiwasia, N., Vasconcelos, N.: Latent Dirichlet allocation models for image classification. IEEE Trans. Pattern Anal. Mach. Intell. **35**(11), 2665–2679 (2013)

39. Sharma, V., Kumar, A., Agrawal, N., Singh, P., Kulshreshtha, R.: Image summarization using topic modelling. In: 2015 IEEE International Conference on Signal and Image Processing Applications (ICSIPA), pp. 226–231. IEEE (2015)

40. Shechtman, E., Caspi, Y., Irani, M.: Space-time super-resolution. IEEE Trans. Pattern Anal. Mach. Intell. **27**(4), 531–545 (2005)

41. Vailaya, A., Figueiredo, M.A., Jain, A.K., Zhang, H.J.: Image classification for content-based indexing. IEEE Trans. Image Process. **10**(1), 117–130 (2001)

42. Vetter, T., Poggio, T.: Image synthesis from a single example image. In: Buxton, B., Cipolla, R. (eds.) ECCV 1996. LNCS, vol. 1064, pp. 652–659. Springer, Heidelberg (1996). https://doi.org/10.1007/BFb0015575

43. Yao, Y., Zhang, J., Shen, F., Hua, X., Yang, W., Tang, Z.: Refining image categorization by exploiting web images and general corpus. arXiv preprint arXiv:1703.05451 (2017)

44. Zhao, B., Li, F., Xing, E.P.: Large-scale category structure aware image categorization. In: Advances in Neural Information Processing Systems, pp. 1251–1259 (2011)

SAT-CNN: A Small Neural Network for Object Recognition from Satellite Imagery

Dustin K. Barnes, Sara R. Davis, and Emily M. Hand(✉)

University of Nevada, Reno, Reno, NV 89557, USA
{dkbarnes,sarad}@nevada.unr.edu, emhand@unr.edu

Abstract. Satellite imagery presents a number of challenges for object detection such as significant variation in object size (from small cars to airports) and low object resolution. In this work we focus on recognizing objects taken from the xView Satellite Imagery dataset. The xView dataset introduces its own set of challenges, the most prominent being the imbalance between the 60 classes present. xView also contains considerable label noise as well as both semantic and visual overlap between classes. In this work we focus on techniques to improve performance on an imbalanced, noisy dataset through data augmentation and balancing. We show that a very small convolutional neural network (SAT-CNN) with approximately three million parameters can outperform a deep pretrained classifier, VGG16 - which is used for many state-of-the-art tasks - with over 138 million parameters.

Keywords: Satellite imagery · CNN · Object recognition · Noisy data

1 Introduction

The amount of high quality satellite imagery available for public use has expanded considerably in recent years. With large datasets available, deep learning methods have become viable for use in tasks such as object detection, land classification and segmentation, and road identification in satellite imagery. The introduction of these datasets brings with it new challenges, disrupting conventional deep learning methodology. The large size of satellite images presents significant memory and processing challenges. One common method of addressing this is to break the image down into smaller sections, or chips, each of which may be processed individually. While this allows the images to be fed into a neural network, objects may be too large to fit into a single chip or may be split across multiple chips. Another challenge present is that the size of objects can vary greatly, from objects such as *cars* or *boats*, to *buildings* or large structures such as *airfields*. Additionally, there is often very little information available when attempting to discriminate between any two objects. Objects such as cars, trucks and tractors are all around the same size, approximately 15×6 pixels

© Springer Nature Switzerland AG 2020
G. Bebis et al. (Eds.): ISVC 2020, LNCS 12510, pp. 39–52, 2020.
https://doi.org/10.1007/978-3-030-64559-5_4

at 0.3 m resolution. Furthermore, the chips must usually also be resized before being fed into a network causing further distortions to the objects.

In this work we focus on discriminating between classes in the xView dataset [13], which demonstrates the difficulties inherent to object recognition in satellite imagery. We introduce a small CNN for object recognition from satellite imagery – SAT-CNN. We demonstrate through extensive experimentation that SAT-CNN outperforms the popular VGG16 architecture, even without pre-training. Our experiments and evaluation were able to identify significant issues with xView and provide a path forward for future use of the dataset.

2   Related Works

Despite the popularity of deep learning, classical methods are still both prominent in and effective at object detection and segmentation in satellite imagery. Edge detection, clustering and Hough transforms have proven reliable at identifying simple static objects like buildings [16,18,30]. More sophisticated methods including symmetry analysis and mean shift have shown promising results in identifying complex objects (e.g. vehicles and airplanes) [2,15], while tasks such as shadow and cloud detection have been thoroughly studied using thresholding and spectral ratios. [1,27].

With the release of large, publicly available, well-labelled datasets of high resolution satellite imagery, deep learning methods have been shown to be quite successful in this domain. Deep learning methods have been developed to solve a variety of tasks from classification of chipped images to segmentation of satellite imagery [10,14,23]. The large size of raw satellite data makes it a significant computational challenge for convolutional neural networks (CNNs) to process them in their entirety, and the extreme variance in object size makes it difficult for a network to identify a wide variety of objects. [29] and [8] both take a similar approach to solving this problem, specializing a portion of their model to detect objects at different scales. [23] also chooses to work with image chips, using an ensemble of deep CNNs whose output is concatenated with image metadata. [23] was trained and tested using the IARPA Functional Map of the World dataset [3].

2.1   Satellite Imagery Datasets

The open availability of satellite imagery data has exploded in the past few years, with datasets representing a wide array of tasks. Many datasets focus on classifying large regions of land, either by applying one or more tags for purposes such as land use, or by flagging the presence of certain points of interest within the region, such as a parking lot or shopping mall [26,34,36].

More commonly, datasets are geared towards the task of detection or segmentation of objects. These datasets are often highly specialized, focusing either on a single class or several closely related classes. Many focus on *building* [7,11,12,19,28,31,32], *vehicle* [20], agricultural classes such as crops

[4–6,21], or species of tree [22,33]. A small subset of these datasets catalogue a wide variety of classes with classes ranging from *airplanes* to *cars* to *stadiums* while also providing either ground truth bounding boxes or per-pixel instance segmentation.

xView, initially published as part of the DIUx 2018 Detection Challenge, consists of processed satellite imagery at 0.3 m resolution, with 846 images taken from across the world. The dataset features 60 unique classes with fine-grained labels, identified using axis-parallel bounding boxes. The degree to which xView distinguishes between it's classes is highly specific, in comparison to other datasets which tend to either focus on a specific task, such as detecting building footprints [7,12,31,33], cars [6,20,24], crop fields [4,5,21,34], or some combination thereof. xView provides a number of finely labeled vehicle classes, including *small car*, *bus*, *pickup truck*, *utility truck*, and 16 more. Other datasets either provide a single vehicle class [20] or distinguish between large and small vehicles [35]. xView also separates semi-trucks and train cars depending on what they are currently loaded with discriminating between *liquid containers*, *box containers*, *flatbeds*, and *tractors with no load*. These fine differences between classes are not only difficult for models to learn and properly classify, but also for labellers to identify.

Fig. 1. Example of ambiguity between *Building* and *Facility* classes.

Due to the fine-grained classes present in xView, label noise is extremely prominent. Additionally, some classes in xView are not very precisely defined. Figure 1 shows an example image from xView with ground truth bounding boxes shown for both the *building* and *facility* classes. There seems to be no visual difference between the two classes. Additionally, many classes are not mutually exclusive. For instance, a *semi truck tractor* is it's own class, however every instance of a *tractor with trailer* or *tractor with liquid trailer* will also contain the tractor itself. xView attempts to counteract the ambiguity and overlap by grouping classes together under overarching super-classes, such as *engineering vehicle* or *maritime vessel.* However, these super-classes are treated as their own unique class (making up a portion of the 60 total classes). They act as a catch-all for when a labeller is unsure which fine grained class a sample should belong to. This further obfuscates the boundaries between the sub-classes while providing no additional discriminatory power.

Finally, the distribution of classes is extremely imbalanced, with 87% of the dataset consisting of the *building* and *small car* classes. In stark comparison to this, classes such as *railway vehicle* only have 17 samples, representing approximately 0.002% of the dataset prior to any filtering. This imbalance is shown in Fig. 2.

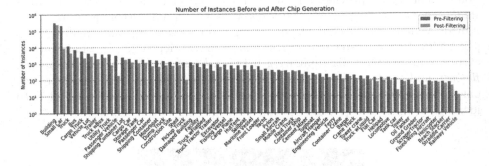

Fig. 2. Number of instances per class, before and after chip generation. Plotted on a logarithmic scale.

3   Methodology

In this work, we introduce a small CNN – SAT-CNN – capable of discriminating between objects in satellite imagery. In this section, we detail our methodology, including chip generation, data augmentation, balancing, and the network architecture.

3.1   Chip Generation

With the full satellite images provided by xView averaging approximately 3300 by 3000 pixels, and the objects occupying much smaller areas (33×38), it is necessary to crop the objects prior to training. We generate object *chips* by taking the bounding boxes provided with the xView dataset and expanding them to three times the original size in order to add context to each object.

If, at any point when generating chips, either the original bounding box or its context extends past the bounds of the original image, then that chip is discarded. In an effort to reduce the number of corrupted bounding boxes, chips where the original bounding box does not contain at least 16px in both dimensions are removed from consideration. Finally, two classes are provided in xView that are not documented, and have no label associated with them. All instances of these classes are removed. Full satellite images are excluded from chip generation if the source image is corrupt or the bounding boxes do not align with objects, determined by manual inspection. After filtering, 421,917 of the original 601,937 object instances across 846 images remained. Figure 2 shows the impact of filtering on the distribution of classes.

In addition to the chips generated using the labeled xView bounding boxes, we generated a set of *not-object* chips. These chips consist of regions in a satellite image which contain no labeled object. Up to 100 *not-object* chips are generated per satellite image.

After filtering the xView chips, we perform a stratified split of the dataset into a training, validation, and test partition. 70% of the dataset is used for training with 15% set aside for both validation and testing.

3.2 Data Augmentation

As xView contains many objects that have fewer than 100 samples, data augmentation is necessary to mitigate the effects of over-fitting. We experiment with two methods of data augmentation: random rotation and random cropping. When randomly rotating these crops, we often run into instances where the rotated region contains information that had been removed in the original crop. We use zero padding in these instances, and minimize the effect through use of random cropping. Because the chips are extracted with a significant amount of context, we are able to set a minimum cropping value such that it removes the majority of artifacts introduced by the rotation.

3.3 Balancing Methods

Due to the significant class imbalance in xView after filtering, a naively trained model would learn to always predict *building* as it would achieve a low loss and high accuracy. In order to remove the bias towards the over-represented classes, *building* and *small car* were only used for pre-training. Even after removing these two classes, the dataset is still severely imbalanced, with 32 of the 58 remaining classes each making up less than one percent of all chips.

In order to combat the class imbalance, we introduce two different methods for balancing the training data – AppendToBatch and CyclicBatch. AppendTo-Batch balancing involves appending samples from each class to a batch while training, with varying methods of choosing which samples are added. One method is to randomly choose a sample from each class, while the other is to iteratively append a sample from each class, ensuring that every instance of a class is sampled as uniformly as possible. This method ensures that each class is represented as at least 1.5% of the dataset when using a batch size of 64 or 0.7% with a batch size of 128, as opposed to the 0.004% which classes such as *railway vehicle* would receive without balancing.

CyclicBatch balancing builds each training batch from an equal number of each class. This can likewise be implemented using either random sampling from each class, or by iterating over samples from each class. CyclicBatch balancing seeks to give each class in the dataset exactly equal representation during training.

3.4 SAT-CNN Architecture

We introduce SAT-CNN, which has only five layers, and fewer than 3 million parameters. The architecture was chosen prioritizing the simplicity of the network, in order to reduce training time, and, ideally, to improve robustness to label noise. All convolutional filters, and max pooling have a stride of one. Each convolution layer is followed by a 2×2 max pooling and batch normalization. The convolution layers have 100 5×5, 200 3×3, 300 3×3, and 300 5×5 filters for layers one through four respectively. The final convolutional output is flattened and fed into a fully connected layer for the class predictions. We chose this architecture as it has been shown to work well in limited and noisy data settings [9]. No architecture search was performed, as initial results were comparable to VGG16 and this is not a work focusing on optimizing architecture.

4 Experiments and Results

We focus on analyzing the effectiveness of the proposed methods detailed in the previous section, as well as comparing the performance of the SAT-CNN and the very popular VGG16 network trained using transfer learning. Unless otherwise specified, all models are trained using the same set of randomly initialized weights, with no label balancing implemented. Models are trained using both random cropping and rotation.

4.1 Data Augmentation

While data augmentation resulted in minor improvements in overall performance, it made a considerable difference in helping the model generalize beyond the training set. Figure 3 shows the training and validation loss curves using no augmentation, cropping and rotation, cropping only and rotation only. The model trained with no augmentation very quickly over-fits to the training dataset. Adding either random rotation or random cropping improves the model's ability to avoid over-fitting considerably. Combining both augmentation methods provides diminishing returns. Data augmentation reduces the rate and degree to which our model over-fits to the training data, yet is not capable of completely preventing it.

This shows both the importance and effectiveness of simple data augmentation methodology in satellite imagery.

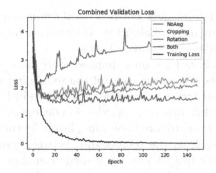

Fig. 3. Training losses vs Validation losses for different methods of image augmentation.

4.2 Balancing Methods

For the following experiments, we utilize two balancing methods: AppendTo-Batch and CyclicBatch balancing, both implemented using iterative sample selection. Figure 4 shows the results for batch balancing using F1 score. We can see from the figure that CyclicBatch balancing is of no use on the xView dataset. It is outperformed by the no balancing baseline using F1 score for all but one class – *pickup truck*. However, even for this class, CyclicBatch balancing is outperformed by AppendToBatch balancing.

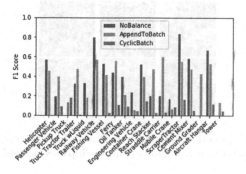

Fig. 4. Results for batch balancing using no balancing, AppendToBatch and Cyclic-Batch methods. All classes had a difference in F1 score of 0.1 or greater between no balance and AppendToBatch balancing.

AppendToBatch balancing is more promising, but the results are less clear at a glance. From Fig. 4, AppendToBatch appears to have somewhat random results, however it is worth inspecting the change in scores for different sets of classes, grouped by the number of samples each class contains. As expected, the classes which contain large portions of the dataset (>0.5% each) are only slightly impacted by balancing. Looking at less populated classes, a decrease in representation in the dataset does not necessarily represent a higher increase in F1 score from no balancing to balancing. However, a high change in F1 score (>0.1) is unique to under represented classes.

Of the 19 classes whose F1 scores changed more than 0.1, 18 of them make up less than 0.1% of the xView dataset. Of the remaining 18 classes, there does not appear to be a clear trend in increase or decrease in F1 score. Some classes see a major increase, while others a considerable decrease. These classes tend to be closely linked, either due to large bounding boxes featuring instances of other classes within them, such as the relationship between *pickup truck* and other vehicle classes. Another insight can be gained from how xView defines their classes. The super-classes such as *engineering vehicle*, contain some samples of all of their sub-classes. When training, items in this class are sometimes identified as the sub-class in which they belong, as opposed to the corresponding super-class. With balancing enabled, the sub-classes each become better at identifying samples, and so performance on these super-classes decreases. This effect can also be seen in chips which contain objects of multiple different classes. Due to the bounding boxes being drawn as axis-parallel squares, long objects that are rotated at an angle produce chips which may contain other objects. This is more common in vehicle, boat, and aircraft classes, as many of the instances occur in large lots. This can be seen in the decreased performance of *helicopter* and *scraper tractor*, which are parked next to classes such as *small aircraft* and *ground grader* as shown in Fig. 5.

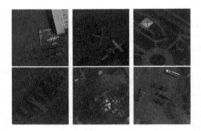

Fig. 5. Examples of chips containing multiple classes. The top row shows context chips for *helicopter* and the bottom row shows context chips for *ground grater*.

4.3   Transfer Learning

Our transfer learning experiments use only data augmentation, with no balancing in order to focus on what impact, if any, transfer learning has on both model performance and training time. Three pre-trained models are evaluated, in addition to a baseline using randomly initialized weights. Two models are trained using subsets of the xView chips. The first is trained on the binary task of *building* identification, and the second is trained on the task of identifying the

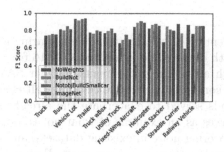

Fig. 6. F1 scores using SAT-CNN with different pre-trained weights.

building, *small car*, and *not object* classes. The third model is pre-trained on the ImageNet ILSVRC 2012 dataset.

Transfer learning using the SAT-CNN architecture seems to have little impact with regards to F1 score. Figure 6 shows how performance is roughly equivalent between different pre-trained weights. Interestingly, the model with randomly initialized weights – although it did not have the best accuracy or loss – was able to identify *some* instances across 57/58 classes, only failing to correctly identify a single instance of the *ground grader* class. No other model in our experiments could identify samples of *ground grader*. All other models failed to correctly identify any instances of 4 classes, although the models failed on different classes.

One final experiment was run using VGG16 pre-trained on Imagenet. We This model performs equivalent to our SAT-CNN on highly populated classes, however performance rapidly degrades as the number of samples decreases. VGG16 is unable to identify any instances of classes making up less than 0.1% of the dataset. Figure 7 shows this disparity in performance between class populations.

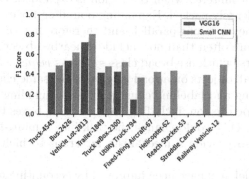

Fig. 7. F1 scores achieved by VGG16, with the number of samples in each class.

4.4   Evaluation

Through our experimentation, we uncovered some glaring issues with the xView dataset, that keep both our method as well as VGG16 from achieving improved performance. Through all of our experiments, neither SAT-CNN, nor VGG16 were able to achieve consistent performance across all classes in xView. Some aspects of our methods served to exacerbate the already ambiguous labels in xView. While this serves as an example of what not to do, these methods may also be useful in discovering noise in existing datasets, and explore the limits of what is possible given that there is noise present. Here we analyze some of the pitfalls of our method as well as xView.

Fig. 8. This ground-truth label shows why context is important with an incorrect label of a pick up truck in the middle of the ocean.

We present an analysis of how the proposed methods exacerbate existing noise within xView. First and foremost, our means of generating crops is somewhat naive. Using additional context to identify objects is necessary in some cases. Figure 8 shows a ground truth label of truck in the ocean. Neglecting the context in which an object is found can result in grossly mislabeled objects. Additionally, our method of expanding regions fails to take into account what objects might be encountered when the region is expanded. Objects in satellite imagery are often densely packed. Expanding bounding boxes which are already poorly fit (recall they are axis-parallel, and therefore not properly oriented to the objects) will more often than not include a nearby object. This is less of an issue in other datsets, which use broad classes such as *vehicle*. With xView's fine-grained labels, not all objects on a road may be of the same class. A more robust method of generating and labelling chips while still including context would be to expand the cropped region, including any bounding boxes that intersect with the expanded chip. This would change the task into a multi-label classification task, but would also provide a mechanism for crops to include other objects, reducing noise.

Finally, our model may have been improved by accounting for the hierarchical nature of xView by training to identify the super-class categories, and then using a more specialized classifier to identify the fine-grained classes to which the chip belongs. While this should improve performance on a hierarchical dataset such as xView, it provides no means of counteracting the noise present, nor does it account for other objects which are present in a given bounding box.

Fig. 9. An example of how axis-aligned bounding boxes capture irrelevant data. Additionally, this building is mislabelled as a small car.

While methodological approaches may improve performance in spite of noise present, there is only so much that can be done. xView represents an exceptionally noisy dataset, and there are numerous ways in which it needs to be improved. While the most obvious aspect is the noise present, the dataset also presents itself in a hierarchical manner, with super-classes acting as a catch-all in case of ambiguous labels. Both the labels as well as the evaluation methods used for the xView challenge act to turn any potential benefits gained by separating classes in such a manner into more noise. Rather than treating the super-classes as a combination of all sub-classes, both the labels and evaluation methods that currently exist treat them as unique classes, entirely separate from their sub-classes. This distinction forces the model to distinguish between objects of the same class, learning to recognize noise surrounding the object as opposed to the properties of the object itself.

When training without balancing, SAT-CNN is capable of achieving a perfect F1 score on the *railway vehicle* class. When balancing is introduced, the score decreases. Inspection of the training set, test set, and model predictions shows that all images present in super-class are in fact from a single sub-class, the *cargo car* class, and the decreased score is the result of the model making the correct classification. This decreases performance on not only the *railway vehicle* class, but also the *cargo car* class, as these count as false positive hits. As there are more *cargo car* samples than there are mislabeled *railway vehicles*, the model is still able to learn to identify them correctly despite the increase in loss. This is not the case for all classes. For example, *ground grader*, a class which performs poorly in every experiment, has only 45 samples, considerably less than its super-class of *engineering vehicle* which contains 126 instances. Visually inspecting chips labeled as *ground graders* shows that they often occur in the same chips as *front loaders*.

The noise present in xView is not the only confounding factor. As mentioned previously, the bounding boxes are all axis-parallel. While this aligns with the dimensions of some objects, many objects are not oriented along the image axes. This results in bounding boxes like that in Fig. 9, which encompass considerably more area than the object itself. While a pixel-wise segmentation is the ideal solution, this is considerably more intensive for labellers. A fair compromise would be to orient bounding boxes to the object, as is done in other datasets [35]. While unable to completely eliminate the problem of bounding boxes including nearby objects, it does reduce the likelihood that this will occur.

This is an assumption made in many other object detection datasets, beyond satellite imagery such as Pascal VOC and ImageNet [17, 25].

5   Conclusion

In this paper, we introduce a small CNN for object recognition from satellite imagery – SAT-CNN. We demonstrate through extensive experimentation that SAT-CNN outperforms the popular VGG16 architecture even without pre-training. This is an impressive accomplishment as SAT-CNN has fewer than 3 million parameters and is initialized randomly whereas VGG16 has 138 million parameters and is pre-trained on Imagenet. Through our experimentation, we uncovered some glaring issues with the xView dataset, that keep both our method as well as VGG16 from achieving improved performance. The evaluation of xView and the proposed methods highlighted issues with the dataset, provided insights as to potential solutions, and also noted problems that could not be over-come, including label and bounding box noise.

Our extensive evaluation of the xView dataset as well as the proposed methodology is a significant contribution of our work. xView is a very popular dataset for object detection and recognition in satellite imagery. Through our experiments and evaluation, we were able to identify significant issues with xView, and provide a path forward for future use of the dataset. Although we identify many problems with xView, we emphasize that it has significant value for the research community. Our work simply serves as a warning for future researchers as to the pitfalls of the dataset. Future work in object detection and recognition from satellite imagery using xView must focus on some combination of weakly-labeled, unsupervised, and noise-robust methods. xView provides a unique opportunity to learn from noisy hierarchical data.

References

1. Anoopa, S., Dhanya, V., Kizhakkethottam, J.J.: Shadow detection and removal using tri-class based thresholding and shadow matting technique. Procedia Technol. **24**, 1358–1365 (2016). https://doi.org/10.1016/j.protcy.2016.05.148
2. Chen, H., Chen, W., Gao, T., Lai, Z.: Efficient detection of intensively parked vehicles form satellite image with 0.5-meter spatial resolution. In: International Geoscience and Remote Sensing Symposium (IGARSS), July 2018, pp. 2487–2490 (2018). https://doi.org/10.1109/IGARSS.2018.8519107
3. Christie, G., Fendley, N., Wilson, J., Mukherjee, R.: Functional map of the world. In: Proceedings of the IEEE Computer Society Conference on Computer Vision and Pattern Recognition, vol. 2, pp. 6172–6180 (2018). https://doi.org/10.1109/CVPR.2018.00646
4. CrowdANALYTIX: Agricultural crop cover classification challenge (2018). https://crowdanalytix.com/contests/agricultural-crop-cover-classification-challenge
5. Denmark Department for Agriculture: Denmark LPIS Agricultural Field Boundaries (2018). https://kortdata.fvm.dk/download

6. DSTL: DSTL satellite imagery feature detection challenge (2017). https://www.kaggle.com/c/dstl-satellite-imagery-feature-detection

7. Gupta, R., et al.: Creating xBD : a dataset for assessing building damage from satellite imagery, pp. 10–17 (2019)

8. Hamaguchi, R., Hikosaka, S.: Building detection from satellite imagery using ensemble of size-specific detectors. In: IEEE Computer Society Conference on Computer Vision and Pattern Recognition Workshops June 2018, pp. 223–227 (2018). https://doi.org/10.1109/CVPRW.2018.00041

9. Hand, E., Castillo, C., Chellappa, R.: Predicting facial attributes in video using temporal coherence and motion-attention, pp. 84–92 (2018). https://doi.org/10.1109/WACV.2018.00017

10. He, Y., Sun, X., Gao, L., Zhang, B.: Ship detection without sea-land segmentation for large-scale high-resolution optical satellite images. In: International Geoscience and Remote Sensing Symposium (IGARSS) July 2018, pp. 717–720 (2018). https://doi.org/10.1109/IGARSS.2018.8519391

11. Humanity & Inclusion: CrowdAI mapping challenge (2018)

12. Inria: Inria aerial image labelling (2016). https://project.inria.fr/

13. Lam, D., et al.: xView: objects in context in overhead imagery (2018). http://arxiv.org/abs/1802.07856

14. Längkvist, M., Kiselev, A., Alirezaie, M., Loutfi, A.: Classification and segmentation of satellite orthoimagery using convolutional neural networks. Remote Sens. 8(4), 329 (2016). https://doi.org/10.3390/rs8040329

15. Li, W., Xiang, S., Wang, H., Pan, C.: Robust airplane detection in satellite images. In: Proceedings - International Conference on Image Processing, ICIP, vol. 60873161, pp. 2821–2824 (2011). https://doi.org/10.1109/ICIP.2011.6116259

16. Lin, C., Nevatia, R.: Building detection and description from a single intensity image. Comput. Vis. Image Underst. 72(2), 101–121 (1998). https://doi.org/10.1006/cviu.1998.0724

17. Everingham, M., Van Gool, L., Williams, C.K.I., et al.: The pascal visual object classes (VOC) challenge. Int. J. Comput. Vis. 88(2), 303–338 (2010). https://doi.org/10.1007/s11263-009-0275-4. http://www.flickr.com/

18. Mayer, H.: Automatic object extraction from aerial imagery - a survey focusing on buildings. Comput. Vis. Image Underst. 74(2), 138–149 (1999). https://doi.org/10.1006/cviu.1999.0750

19. Microsoft Corporation: Microsoft Building Footprints (2019). https://github.com/Microsoft/CanadianBuildingFootprints

20. Mundhenk, T.N., Konjevod, G., Sakla, W.A., Boakye, K.: A large contextual dataset for classification, detection and counting of cars with deep learning. In: Leibe, B., Matas, J., Sebe, N., Welling, M. (eds.) ECCV 2016. LNCS, vol. 9907, pp. 785–800. Springer, Cham (2016). https://doi.org/10.1007/978-3-319-46487-9_48

21. Netherlands Department for Economic Affairs: Netherlands LPIS agricultural field boundaries (2018). https://www.pdok.nl/introductie?articleid=1948958

22. NIST: NIST DSE plant identification with NEON remote sensing data (2017)

23. Pritt, M., Chern, G.: Satellite image classification with deep learning. In: Proceedings - Applied Imagery Pattern Recognition Workshop, October 2017, pp. 1–7 (2018). https://doi.org/10.1109/AIPR.2017.8457969

24. Robicquet, A., Sadeghian, A., Alahi, A., Savarese, S.: Learning social etiquette: human trajectory understanding in crowded scenes. In: Leibe, B., Matas, J., Sebe, N., Welling, M. (eds.) ECCV 2016. LNCS, vol. 9912, pp. 549–565. Springer, Cham (2016). https://doi.org/10.1007/978-3-319-46484-8_33

25. Russakovsky, O., et al.: ImageNet large scale visual recognition challenge. Int. J. Comput. Vision **115**(3), 211–252 (2015). https://doi.org/10.1007/s11263-015-0816-y

26. Sumbul, G., Charfuelan, M., Demir, B., Markl, V.: BigEarthNet: a large-scale benchmark archive for remote sensing image understanding, pp. 2–5 (2019). http://arxiv.org/abs/1902.06148

27. Tatar, N., Saadatseresht, M., Arefi, H., Hadavand, A.: A robust object-based shadow detection method for cloud-free high resolution satellite images over urban areas and water bodies. Adv. Space Res. **61**(11), 2787–2800 (2018). https://doi.org/10.1016/j.asr.2018.03.011

28. US-SOCOM: Urban 3D challenge. https://github.com/chrieke/awesome-satellite-imagery-datasets

29. Van Etten, A.: Satellite imagery multiscale rapid detection with windowed networks. In: Proceedings - 2019 IEEE Winter Conference on Applications of Computer Vision, WACV 2019, pp. 735–743 (2019). https://doi.org/10.1109/WACV.2019.00083

30. Wei, Y., Zhao, Z., Song, J.: Urban building extraction from high-resolution satellite panchromatic image using clustering and edge detection. In: IGARSS 2004, 2004 IEEE International Geoscience and Remote Sensing Symposium, pp. 2008–2010 (2008). https://doi.org/10.1109/IGARSS.2004.1370742

31. Weir, N., et al.: SpaceNet MVOI: a multi-view overhead imagery dataset (2019). http://arxiv.org/abs/1903.12239

32. WeRobotics, Worldbank: 2018 Open AI Tanzania building footprint segmentation challenge (2018). https://competitions.codalab.org/competitions/20100

33. WeRobotics, Worldbank: Automated feature detection of aerial imagery from South Pacific (2018)

34. Women in Data Science: WiDS Datathon 2019: Detection of oil palm plantations (2019). https://www.kaggle.com/c/widsdatathon2019

35. Xia, G.S., et al.: DOTA: a large-scale dataset for object detection in aerial images. In: Proceedings of the IEEE Computer Society Conference on Computer Vision and Pattern Recognition, pp. 3974–3983 (2018). https://doi.org/10.1109/CVPR.2018.00418

36. Yang, Y., Newsam, S.: Bag-of-visual-words and spatial extensions for land-use classification. In: GIS: Proceedings of the ACM International Symposium on Advances in Geographic Information Systems, pp. 270–279 (2010). https://doi.org/10.1145/1869790.1869829

Domain Adaptive Transfer Learning on Visual Attention Aware Data Augmentation for Fine-Grained Visual Categorization

Ashiq Imran[✉] and Vassilis Athitsos

Department of Computer Science and Engineering, University of Texas at Arlington, Arlington, TX, USA
ashiq.imran@mavs.uta.edu, athitsos@uta.edu

Abstract. Fine-Grained Visual Categorization (FGVC) is a challenging topic in computer vision. It is a problem characterized by large intra-class differences and subtle inter-class differences. In this paper, we tackle this problem in a weakly supervised manner, where neural network models are getting fed with additional data using a data augmentation technique through a visual attention mechanism. We perform domain adaptive knowledge transfer via fine-tuning on our base network model. We perform our experiment on six challenging and commonly used FGVC datasets, and we show competitive improvement on accuracies by using attention-aware data augmentation techniques with features derived from deep learning model InceptionV3, pre-trained on large scale datasets. Our method outperforms competitor methods on multiple FGVC datasets and showed competitive results on other datasets. Experimental studies show that transfer learning from large scale datasets can be utilized effectively with visual attention based data augmentation, which can obtain state-of-the-art results on several FGVC datasets. We present a comprehensive analysis of our experiments. Our method achieves state-of-the-art results in multiple fine-grained classification datasets including challenging CUB200-2011 bird, Flowers-102, and FGVC-Aircrafts datasets.

Keywords: Domain adaptation · Transfer learning · Fine-grained visual categorization · Visual attention

1 Introduction

Deep neural networks have provided state-of-the-art results in many domains in computer vision. However, having a big training set is very important for the performance of deep neural networks [7,15]. Data augmentation techniques have been gaining popularity in deep learning and are extensively used to address the scarcity of training data. Data augmentation has led to promising results in

© Springer Nature Switzerland AG 2020
G. Bebis et al. (Eds.): ISVC 2020, LNCS 12510, pp. 53–65, 2020.
https://doi.org/10.1007/978-3-030-64559-5_5

various computer vision tasks [15]. There are different data augmentation methods for deep models, like image flipping, cropping, scaling, rotation, translation, color distortion, adding Gaussian noise, and many more.

Previous methods mostly choose random images from the dataset and apply the above operations to enlarge the amount of training data. However, applying random cropping to generate new training examples can have undesirable consequences. For example, if the size of the cropped region is not large enough, it may consist entirely of background, and not contain any part of the labeled object. Moreover, this generated data might reduce accuracy and negatively affect the quality of the extracted features. Consequently, the disadvantages of random cropping might cancel out its advantages. More specific features need to be provided to the model to make data augmentation more productive.

In Fine-Grained Visual Categorization (FGVC), same-class items may have variation in the pose, scale, or rotation. FGVC contains subtle differences among classes in a sub-category of an object, which includes the model of the cars, type of the foods or the flowers, species of the birds or dogs, and type of the aircrafts. These differences are what make FGVC a challenging problem, as there are significant intra-class differences among the sub-categories, and at the same time, items from different classes may look similar. In contrast with regular object classification techniques, FGVC aims to solve the identification of particular subcategories from a given category [10,12].

Convolutional Neural Networks (CNNs) have been extensively used for various applications in computer vision. To achieve good performance with CNNs, typically we need large amounts of labeled data. However, it is a tedious process to collect labeled fine-grained datasets. That is why there are not many FGVC datasets, and existing datasets are not as large compared to standard image recognition datasets like ImageNet [7]. Normally, a model pre-trained on large scale datasets such as ImageNet is used, and that model is then fine-tuned using data from an FGVC dataset. Typically, FGVC datasets are not too big, so it becomes critical to design methods that can compensate for the limited amount of data. In this paper, we investigate some techniques that allow the model to learn features more effectively, and that perform well on large scale datasets with fine-grained categories.

Generally, there are two domains involved in fine-tuning a network. One is the source domain, which typically includes large scale image datasets like ImageNet [7], where initial models are pre-trained. Another is the target domain, where data is used to fine-tune the pre-trained models. In this paper, the target domain is FGVC datasets, and we are interested in developing techniques that can boost accuracy on these type of datasets. Modern FGVC methods use pre-trained networks with ImageNet dataset to a large extent. We explore the possibility of achieving better accuracy than what has been achieved so far using ImageNet. A model first learns useful features from a large amount of training data, and is then fine-tuned on a more evenly-distributed subset to balance the efforts of the network among different categories and transfer the already learned features.

In short, our research tries to address two questions: 1) What approaches beyond transfer learning do we need to take to boost the performance on FGVC datasets? 2) How can we determine which large scale source domain we choose, given that the target domain is FGVC?

We calculate the domain similarity score between the source and target domains. This score gives us a clear picture of selecting the source domain for transfer learning to achieve better accuracy in the target domain. Then, we focus on a visual attention guided network for data augmentation. As FGVC datasets are relatively smaller in size, we leverage the feature learning from fine-tuning as well as data augmentation to achieve better accuracy. The performance of the combination of these two strategies outperforms the baseline approach.

In summary, the main contributions of this work are:

1. We propose a simple yet effective improvement over the recently proposed Weakly Supervised Data Augmentation Network (WS-DAN) [12], which is used for generating attention maps to extract sequential local features to tackle the FGVC challenge. A domain similarity score can play a vital role before applying transfer learning. Based on the score, we decide which source domain is necessary to use for transfer learning. Then, we can employ WS-DAN [12] to achieve better results among FGVC datasets.
2. We demonstrate a domain adaptive transfer learning approach, that combines with visual attention based data augmentation, and that can achieve state-of-the-art results on CUB200-2011 [28], and Flowers-102 [20], and FGVC-Aircrafts [19] datasets. Additionally, we match the current state-of-the-art accuracy on Stanford Cars [14], Stanford Dogs [13] datasets.
3. We present the relationship of top-1 accuracy and domain score on six commonly used FGVC datasets. We illustrate the effect of image resolution in transfer learning in detail.

2 Related Work

In this section, we present a brief overview of data augmentation, fine-grained visual categorization, visual attention mechanism and transfer learning.

2.1 Data Augmentation

Machine learning theory suggests that a model can be more generalized and robust if it has been trained on a dataset with higher diversity. However, it is a very difficult and time-consuming task to collect and label all the images which involve these variations [33]. Data augmentation methods are proposed to address this issue by adding the amount and diversity of training samples. Various methods have been proposed focusing on random spatial image augmentation, specifically involving in rotation variation, scale variation, translation, and deformation, etc. [12]. Classical augmentation methods are widely adopted in deep learning techniques.

The main drawback of random data augmentation is low model accuracy. Additionally, it suffers from generating a lot of unavoidable noisy data. Various methods have been proposed to consider data distribution rather than random data augmentation. A search space based data augmentation method has been proposed [5]. It can automatically search for improving data augmentation policies in order to obtain better validation accuracy. In contrast, we leverage WS-DAN [12], which generates augmented data from visual attention features of the image. Peng *et al.* proposed a method for human pose estimation, by introducing an augmentation network whose task is to generate hard data online, thus improving the robustness of models [21]. Nevertheless, their augmentation system is complicated and less accurate compared to the network that we experimented with. Additionally, attention-aware data segmentation is more simple and proven effective in terms of accuracy.

2.2   Fine-Grained Visual Categorization

Fine-grained Visual Categorization (FGVC) is a challenging problem in the field of computer vision. Normally, object classification is used for categorize different objects in the image, such as humans, animals, cars, trees, etc. In contrast, fine-grained image classification concentrates more on detecting sub-categories of a given category, like various types of birds, dogs or cars. The purpose of FGVC is to find subtle differences among various categories of a dataset. It presents significant challenges for building a model that generalizes patterns. FGVC is useful in a wide range of applications such as image captioning [2], image generation [4], image search engines, and so on.

Various methods have been developed to differentiate fine-grained categories. Due to the remarkable success of deep learning, most of the recognition works depend on the powerful convolutional deep features. Several methods were proposed to solve large scale real problems [11,24,26]. However, it is relatively hard for the basic models to focus on very precise differences of an object's parts without adding special modules [12]. A weakly supervised learning-based approach was adapted to generate class-specific location maps by using pooling methods [18]. Adversarial Complementary Learning (ACoL) [34] is a weakly supervised approach to identify entire objects by training two adversarial complementary classifiers, which aims at locating several parts of objects and detects complementary regions of the same object. However, their method fails to accurately locate the parts of the objects due to having only two complementary regions. On the contrary, our proposed approach depends on attention-guided data augmentation and domain adaptive transfer learning. Our method extracts fine-grained discriminative features and provides a generalization of domain features to achieve state-of-the-art performance in terms of accuracy.

2.3   Attention

Attention mechanisms have been getting a lot of popularity in the deep learning area. Visual attention has been already used for FGVC. Xiao *et al.* proposed a two-way attention method (object-level attention and part-level attention) to train domain-specific deep networks [30]. Fu *et al.* proposed an approach that can predict the location of one attention area and extract corresponding features [9]. However, this method can only focus on a local object's parts at the same time. Zheng *et al.* addressed this issue and introduced Multi-Attention CNN (MA-CNN) [35], which can simultaneously focus on multiple body parts. However, selected parts of the object are limited and the number of selected parts is fixed (2 or 4), which might hamper accuracy.

The works mentioned above mostly focus on object localization. In contrast, our research concentrates more on data augmentation with visual attention, which has not been much explored. We use the attention mechanism for data augmentation purposes. Moreover, the benefit of guided attention based data augmentation [12] helps the network to locate object precisely, which helps our trained model learn about closer object details and hence, improve the predictions.

2.4 Transfer Learning

The purpose of transfer learning is to improve the performance of a learning algorithm by utilizing knowledge that is acquired from previously solved similar problems. CNNs have been widely used for transfer learning. They are mostly used in the form of pre-trained networks that serve as feature extractors [8,23].

Considerable amounts of effort have been made to understand transfer learning [3,25,31]. Initial weights for a certain network can be obtained from an already-trained network even if the network is used for different tasks [31]. Some prior work has shown some results on transfer learning and domain similarity [6]. Their contribution mostly addresses the effect of image resolution on large scale datasets and choosing different subsets of datasets to boost accuracy. In our work, we show that domain adaptive transfer learning can be useful if we also incorporate visual attention based data augmentation.

Unlike previous works, our proposed technique takes account of domain adaptive transfer learning between the source and target domains. Then, it incorporates the attention-driven approach for data augmentation. Our main goal is to guide the training model to learn relevant features from the source domain and augment data with the visual attention of the target domain. The combination of two processes can be useful to achieve better performance.

3   Domain Adaptive Transfer Learning (DATL)

In our work, we consider different types of large scale datasets to find out the similarity with FGVC datasets. We compute domain similarity score initially. Based on the domain similarity score we choose large scale datasets for transfer learning and then we perform WS-DAN [12] to train and evaluate the accuracy.

3.1 Domain Similarity

Generally, transfer learning performs better when using larger training datasets. Chen *et al.* showed that transfer learning performance increases logarithmically with the number of data [25]. In our work, we observe that using a bigger dataset does not always improve accuracy. Yosinski *et al.* [31] mentions that there is some correlation between the transferability of a network from the source task to the target task and the distance between the source and target tasks. Furthermore, they show that fine-tuning on a pre-trained network towards a target task can boost performance.

For measuring domain similarity, we use the approach of Cui *et al.* [6] who introduce a method which can calculate domain similarity by the Earth Mover's Distance (EMD) [22]. Furthermore, they show that transfer learning can be treated as moving image sets from the source domain S to the target domain T. The domain similarity [6] can be defined as

$$d(S,T) = EMD(S,T) = \frac{\sum_{i=1,j=1}^{m,n} f_{i,j} d_{i,j}}{\sum_{i=1,j=1}^{m,n} f_{i,j}} \tag{1}$$

where s_i is i-th category in S and t_j is j-th in T, $d_{i,j} = \|g(s_i) - g(t_j)\|$, feature extractor $g(.)$ of an image and the optimal flow $f_{i,j}$ computes total work as a EMD minimization problem. Finally, the similarity is calculated as:

$$sim(S,T) = e^{-\gamma d(S,T)} \tag{2}$$

where γ is a regularization constant of value 0.01.

The domain similarly score can be calculated between the source and target domains. In our approach, we use large scale datasets as source domains, and target domains are selected from six commonly used FGVC datasets.

3.2 Attention Aware Data Augmentation

In our method, we consider using the Weakly Supervised Data Augmentation Network (WS-DAN) [12]. Firstly, we extract features of the image I and feature maps $F \in R^{H \times W \times C}$, where H, W, and C correspond to height, width, and number of channels of a feature layer. Then, we generate attention maps $A \in R^{H \times W \times M}$ from feature maps, where M is the number of attention maps. One more critical component is bi-linear attention pooling, which is used to extract features from part objects. Element-wise multiplication between feature maps and attention maps is computed to get part-feature maps, followed by a pooling operation on part-feature maps.

Randomly generated data from augmentation can cause problems. However, attention maps can guide models to focus on essential parts of the data and augment those parts. With an augmentation map, a part's region can be zoomed, and detailed features can be extracted. This process is called attention cropping. Attention maps can represent parts of similar objects. Attention dropping can be applied to the network to distinguish parts of multiple objects. Both attention cropping and attention dropping are controlled through a threshold value.

During the training process, no bounding box or keypoints based annotation are available. For each particular training image, attention maps are generated to represent the distinguishable part of an object. The attention guided data augmentation component is responsible to select attention maps efficiently utilizing attention cropping and attention dropping. Bilinear Attention Pooling (BAP) is used to extract features from an object's parts. Element-wise multiplication between the feature maps and attention maps is used to generate the part feature matrix. Then, part features are extracted by a convolutional or pooling operation. In the last step, the original data along with attention generated augmented data are used as input training data.

During the testing process, the probability of the object's categories and attention maps are produced from input images. Then, the selected part of the object can be enlarged to refine the category's probability. The final prediction is evaluated as the average of those two probabilities.

4 Experiments

In this section, we show comprehensive experiments to verify the effectiveness of our approach. Firstly, we calculate the domain similarity score using EMD [22] to demonstrate the relationship between the source and target domains. Then, we compare our model with the state-of-the-art methods on six publicly available fine-grained visual categorization datasets. Furthermore, we perform additional experiments to demonstrate the effect of image resolution on transfer learning. We compare input images in the iNaturalist (iNat) dataset from 299×299 to 448×448 to observe the effect of image resolution in terms of accuracy. We train the baseline inceptionV3 model with iNat datasets for this experiment. Additionally, we combine both iNat and imageNet dataset to make a bigger dataset. We perform detailed experimental studies with different types of large scale datasets and apply the WS-DAN [12] method to observe the impact.

4.1 Datasets

We present a detailed overview of the datasets that we use for our experiments.

ImageNet: The ImageNet [7] contains 1.28 million training images and 50 thousand validation images along with 1,000 categories.

iNaturalist (iNat): The iNat dataset, introduced in 2017 [27], contains more than 665,000 training and around 10000 test images from more than 5000 natural fine-grained categories. Those categories include different types of mammals, birds, insects, plants, and more. This dataset is quite imbalanced and varies a lot in terms of the number of images per category.

Fine-Grained Object Classification Datasets: Table 1 summarizes the information of each dataset in detail.

4.2   Implementation Details

In our experiment, we used Tensorflow [1] to train all the models on multiple Nvidia Geforce GTX 1080Ti GPUs. The machine has Intel Core-i7-5930k CPU@ 3.50 GHz x 12 processors with 64 GB of memory. During training, we adopted Inception v3 [26] as the backbone network. We employed WS-DAN [12] technique to perform experiments to demonstrate the effectiveness of transfer learning. For all the datasets, we used Stochastic Gradient Descent (SGD) with a momentum of 0.9, the number of epoch 80, mini-batch size 12. The initial learning rate was set to 0.001, with exponential decay of 0.8 after every 2 epochs.

Table 1. Six commonly used FGVC datasets.

Datasets	Objects	Classes	Training	Test
CUB200-2011	Bird	200	5,994	5,794
FGVC-Aircraft	Aircraft	100	6,667	3,333
Stanford Cars	Car	196	8,144	8,041
Stanford Dogs	Dog	120	12,000	8,580
Flowers-102	Flowers	102	2,040	6,149
Food-101	Food	101	75,750	25,250

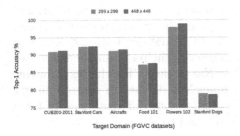

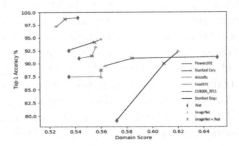

Fig. 1. Effect of transfer learning with different sizes of image resolution on iNat dataset.

Fig. 2. Correlation between transfer learning accuracy and domain similarity score between the source and target domain. Each colored line represents a target domain. (Color figure online)

5   Results

When training a CNN, input images are often preprocessed to match a specific size. Higher resolution images usually contain essential information and precise details that are important to visual recognition. We compare results on six FGVC datasets with different sizes of image resolution of the iNat dataset. In summary,

Table 2. Comparison to different types of FGVC datasets. Each row represents a network pre-trained on source domain for transfer learning and each column represents top-1 image classification accuracy by fine-tuning on the target domain.

Method	CUB200 2011	Stanford Cars	Aircrafts	Food 101	Flowers 102	Stanford Dogs
ImageNet	82.8	91.3	85.5	88.6	96.2	84.2
ImageNet on WS-DAN	89.3	**94.5**	**93.0**	87.2	97.1	**92.2**
iNat on WS-DAN	**91.2**	92.5	91.0	87.5	**98.9**	79.1
ImageNet + iNat on WS-DAN	91.0	94.1	91.5	**88.7**	98.7	90.0

images with higher resolution yields better accuracy except for the Stanford Dogs dataset. Figure 1 represents the effect of transfer learning with various sizes of image resolution on iNat dataset.

Table 3. Comparison in terms of accuracy with existing FGVC methods.

Method	CUB200 2011	Stanford Cars	Aircrafts	Food 101	Flowers 102	Stanford Dogs
Bilinear-CNN [18]	84.1	91.3	84.1	82.4	–	–
DLA [32]	85.1	94.1	92.6	89.7	–	–
RA-CNN [9]	85.4	92.5	–	–	–	87.3
Improved Bilinear-CNN [17]	85.8	92.0	88.5	–	–	–
GP-256 [35]	85.8	92.8	89.8	–	–	–
MA-CNN [9]	86.5	92.8	89.9	–	–	–
DFL-CNN [29]	87.4	93.8	92.0	–	–	–
MPN-COV [16]	88.7	93.3	91.4	–	–	–
Subset B [6]	89.6	93.5	90.7	90.4	–	88.0
WS-DAN [12]	89.4	94.5	93.0	87.2	97.1	92.2
DATL + WS-DAN	**91.2**	94.5	**93.1**	88.7	**98.9**	**92.2**

In Table 2, we present the top-1 accuracy of the target domains on various source domains. These results show the impact of transfer learning from a pretrained model. Large scale datasets are essential for getting improved accuracy when transfer learning is conducted. ImageNet dataset is much larger than iNat dataset; still, it shows worse accuracy in the CUB200-2011 dataset. So, we cannot conclude that using a bigger dataset with transfer learning can always yield better results. Moreover, the domain similarity score also supports this hypothesis. Hence, transfer learning can be effective if the target domain can be trained with similar source domain.

We compare our method with state-of-the-art baselines on six commonly used fine-grained categorization datasets. The summary of the comparison is presented in Table 3. We visually represent the relationship between the top-1 accuracy and the domain similarity score. We can observe from Fig. 2 that the domain similarity score positively correlated with transfer learning accuracy between large scale datasets and FGVC datasets. Each marker represents a source domain. With the right selection of source domain, better transfer learning performance can be achieved. For example, the domain similarity score between iNat and CUB200-2011 is around **0.65**, which is the reason it shows higher accuracy **(91.2)** when iNat is used as pre-training the source domain compared to others. For Flowers-102 dataset, the accuracy is **98.9** with iNat as the source domain which has the highest domain similarity score **0.54**, among other source domains. Similarly, Stanford Cars, Stanford Dogs and Aircrafts dataset show higher domain similarity score supports better accuracy. Only for the Food101 dataset, the accuracy from transfer learning remains similar while domain similarity changes. We believe this is due to having a large number of training images in Food101. Consequently, the target domain contains enough data and transfer learning is not as useful. We can observe that both ImageNet and iNat are highly biased, achieving dramatically different transfer learning accuracy on target datasets. Intriguingly, when we transfer networks trained on the combined ImageNet + iNat dataset and perform WS-DAN [12] method over it, we got better results in Food-101 dataset. The resulted accuracy of the combination of ImageNet and iNat, fell in-between ImageNet and iNat pre-trained model. It means that we cannot attain good accuracy on target domains by just using a larger (combined) source domain. Our work demonstrates that a domain similarity score can be useful for identifying which large scale dataset to employ. That way, the model can learn essential features for the target dataset from large source training sets. Furthermore, we can employ attention aware data augmentation techniques to achieve state-of-the-art accuracy on several FGVC datasets.

6   Conclusion

In this paper, we describe a simple technique that takes attention mechanism as a data augmentation technique. Attention maps are guided to focus on the object's parts and encourage multiple attention. We demonstrate that domain adaptive transfer learning plays a vital role in boosting performance. Depending on the domain similarity score, we can choose which source datasets to pre-train on to get better accuracy. We show that combining similarity-based selection of source datasets with attention-based augmentation technique can achieve state-of-the-art results in multiple fine-grained visual classification datasets. We also analyze the effect of image resolution on transfer learning between the source and target domains.

Acknowledgements. This work was partially supported by National Science Foundation grant IIS-1565328. Any opinions, findings, and conclusions or recommendations expressed in this publication are those of the authors, and do not necessarily reflect the views of the National Science Foundation.

References

1. Abadi, M., et al.: Tensorflow: a system for large-scale machine learning. In: 12th {USENIX} Symposium on Operating Systems Design and Implementation ({OSDI} 2016), pp. 265–283 (2016)
2. Anne Hendricks, L., Venugopalan, S., Rohrbach, M., Mooney, R., Saenko, K., Darrell, T.: Deep compositional captioning: describing novel object categories without paired training data. In: Proceedings of the IEEE Conference on Computer Vision and Pattern Recognition, pp. 1–10 (2016)
3. Azizpour, H., Razavian, A.S., Sullivan, J., Maki, A., Carlsson, S.: Factors of transferability for a generic convnet representation. IEEE Trans. Pattern Anal. Mach. Intell. **38**(9), 1790–1802 (2015)
4. Bao, J., Chen, D., Wen, F., Li, H., Hua, G.: CVAE-GAN: fine-grained image generation through asymmetric training. In: Proceedings of the IEEE International Conference on Computer Vision, pp. 2745–2754 (2017)
5. Cubuk, E.D., Zoph, B., Mane, D., Vasudevan, V., Le, Q.V.: Autoaugment: learning augmentation policies from data. arXiv preprint arXiv:1805.09501 (2018)
6. Cui, Y., Song, Y., Sun, C., Howard, A., Belongie, S.: Large scale fine-grained categorization and domain-specific transfer learning. In: Proceedings of the IEEE Conference on Computer Vision and Pattern Recognition, pp. 4109–4118 (2018)
7. Deng, J., Dong, W., Socher, R., Li, L.J., Li, K., Fei-Fei, L.: ImageNet: a large-scale hierarchical image database. In: 2009 IEEE Conference on Computer Vision and Pattern Recognition, pp. 248–255. IEEE (2009)
8. Donahue, J., et al.: DeCAF: a deep convolutional activation feature for generic visual recognition. In: International Conference on Machine Learning, pp. 647–655 (2014)
9. Fu, J., Zheng, H., Mei, T.: Look closer to see better: recurrent attention convolutional neural network for fine-grained image recognition. In: Proceedings of the IEEE Conference on Computer Vision and Pattern Recognition, pp. 4438–4446 (2017)
10. Ge, Z., Bewley, A., McCool, C., Corke, P., Upcroft, B., Sanderson, C.: Fine-grained classification via mixture of deep convolutional neural networks. In: 2016 IEEE Winter Conference on Applications of Computer Vision (WACV), pp. 1–6. IEEE (2016)
11. He, K., Zhang, X., Ren, S., Sun, J.: Deep residual learning for image recognition. In: Proceedings of the IEEE Conference on Computer Vision and Pattern Recognition, pp. 770–778 (2016)
12. Hu, T., Qi, H.: See better before looking closer: weakly supervised data augmentation network for fine-grained visual classification. arXiv preprint arXiv:1901.09891 (2019)
13. Khosla, A., Jayadevaprakash, N., Yao, B., Li, F.F.: Novel dataset for FGVC: stanford dogs. In: CVPR Workshop on FGVC, San Diego, vol. 1 (2011)
14. Krause, J., Stark, M., Deng, J., Fei-Fei, L.: 3D object representations for fine-grained categorization. In: Proceedings of the IEEE International Conference on Computer Vision Workshops, pp. 554–561 (2013)

15. Krizhevsky, A., Sutskever, I., Hinton, G.E.: ImageNet classification with deep convolutional neural networks. In: Advances in Neural Information Processing Systems, pp. 1097–1105 (2012)
16. Li, P., Xie, J., Wang, Q., Gao, Z.: Towards faster training of global covariance pooling networks by iterative matrix square root normalization. In: Proceedings of the IEEE Conference on Computer Vision and Pattern Recognition, pp. 947–955 (2018)
17. Lin, T.Y., Maji, S.: Improved bilinear pooling with CNNs. arXiv preprint arXiv:1707.06772 (2017)
18. Lin, T.Y., RoyChowdhury, A., Maji, S.: Bilinear CNN models for fine-grained visual recognition. In: Proceedings of the IEEE International Conference on Computer Vision, pp. 1449–1457 (2015)
19. Maji, S., Rahtu, E., Kannala, J., Blaschko, M., Vedaldi, A.: Fine-grained visual classification of aircraft. arXiv preprint arXiv:1306.5151 (2013)
20. Nilsback, M.E., Zisserman, A.: Automated flower classification over a large number of classes. In: 2008 Sixth Indian Conference on Computer Vision, Graphics & Image Processing, pp. 722–729. IEEE (2008)
21. Peng, X., Tang, Z., Yang, F., Feris, R.S., Metaxas, D.: Jointly optimize data augmentation and network training: adversarial data augmentation in human pose estimation. In: Proceedings of the IEEE Conference on Computer Vision and Pattern Recognition, pp. 2226–2234 (2018)
22. Rubner, Y., Tomasi, C., Guibas, L.J.: The earth mover's distance as a metric for image retrieval. Int. J. Comput. Vis. **40**(2), 99–121 (2000). https://doi.org/10.1023/A:1026543900054
23. Sharif Razavian, A., Azizpour, H., Sullivan, J., Carlsson, S.: CNN features off-the-shelf: an astounding baseline for recognition. In: Proceedings of the IEEE Conference on Computer Vision and Pattern Recognition Workshops, pp. 806–813 (2014)
24. Simon, M., Rodner, E.: Neural activation constellations: unsupervised part model discovery with convolutional networks. In: Proceedings of the IEEE International Conference on Computer Vision, pp. 1143–1151 (2015)
25. Sun, C., Shrivastava, A., Singh, S., Gupta, A.: Revisiting unreasonable effectiveness of data in deep learning era. In: Proceedings of the IEEE International Conference on Computer Vision, pp. 843–852 (2017)
26. Szegedy, C., Vanhoucke, V., Ioffe, S., Shlens, J., Wojna, Z.: Rethinking the inception architecture for computer vision. In: Proceedings of the IEEE Conference on Computer Vision and Pattern Recognition, pp. 2818–2826 (2016)
27. Van Horn, G., et al.: The inaturalist species classification and detection dataset. In: Proceedings of the IEEE Conference on Computer Vision and Pattern Recognition, pp. 8769–8778 (2018)
28. Wah, C., Branson, S., Welinder, P., Perona, P., Belongie, S.: The Caltech-UCSD birds-200-2011 dataset (2011)
29. Wang, Y., Morariu, V.I., Davis, L.S.: Learning a discriminative filter bank within a CNN for fine-grained recognition. In: Proceedings of the IEEE Conference on Computer Vision and Pattern Recognition, pp. 4148–4157 (2018)
30. Xiao, T., Xu, Y., Yang, K., Zhang, J., Peng, Y., Zhang, Z.: The application of two-level attention models in deep convolutional neural network for fine-grained image classification. In: Proceedings of the IEEE Conference on Computer Vision and Pattern Recognition, pp. 842–850 (2015)
31. Yosinski, J., Clune, J., Bengio, Y., Lipson, H.: How transferable are features in deep neural networks? In: Advances in Neural Information Processing Systems, pp. 3320–3328 (2014)

32. Yu, F., Wang, D., Shelhamer, E., Darrell, T.: Deep layer aggregation. In: Proceedings of the IEEE Conference on Computer Vision and Pattern Recognition, pp. 2403–2412 (2018)
33. Zhang, P., Zhong, Y., Deng, Y., Tang, X., Li, X.: A survey on deep learning of small sample in biomedical image analysis. arXiv preprint arXiv:1908.00473 (2019)
34. Zhang, X., Wei, Y., Feng, J., Yang, Y., Huang, T.S.: Adversarial complementary learning for weakly supervised object localization. In: Proceedings of the IEEE Conference on Computer Vision and Pattern Recognition, pp. 1325–1334 (2018)
35. Zheng, H., Fu, J., Mei, T., Luo, J.: Learning multi-attention convolutional neural network for fine-grained image recognition. In: Proceedings of the IEEE International Conference on Computer Vision, pp. 5209–5217 (2017)

3D Reconstruction

A Light-Weight Monocular Depth Estimation with Edge-Guided Occlusion Fading Reduction

Kuo-Shiuan Peng[1](✉), Gregory Ditzler[1], and Jerzy Rozenblit[1,2]

[1] Department of Electrical and Computer Engineering, University of Arizona,
Tucson, AZ 85721, USA
{kspeng,ditzler}@email.arizona.edu,
jerzyr@arizona.edu
[2] Department of Surgery, University of Arizona, Tucson, AZ 85721, USA

Abstract. Self-supervised monocular depth estimation methods suffer occlusion fading, which is a result of a lack of supervision by the ground truth pixels. A recent work introduced a post-processing method to reduce occlusion fading; however, the results have a severe halo effect. This work proposes a novel edge-guided post-processing method that reduces occlusion fading for self-supervised monocular depth estimation. We also introduce Atrous Spatial Pyramid Pooling with Forward-Path (ASPPF) into the network to reduce computational costs and improve inference performance. The proposed ASPPF-based network is lighter, faster, and better than current depth estimation networks. Our light-weight network only needs 7.6 million parameters and can achieve up to 67 frames per second for 256×512 inputs using a single nVIDIA GTX1080 GPU. The proposed network also outperforms the current state-of-the-art methods on the KITTI benchmark. The ASPPF-based network and edge-guided post-processing produces better results, both quantitatively and qualitatively than the competitors.

Keywords: Monocular depth estimation · Atrous Spatial Pyramid Pooling · Edge-Guided post-processing

1 Introduction

Depth estimation is a fundamental problem with a long history in computer vision, and it also serves as the cornerstone for many machine perception applications, such as 3D reconstruction, autonomous vehicles, industrial machine vision, robotic interactions, etc. Unfortunately, successful research in depth estimation is dependent on the availability of multiple observations in a target scene. The constraint of the multiple observations can be overcome by using supervised methods that are accelerated by deep learning [1]. These methods aim to directly predict the pixel depth from a single image by learning the given a large amount of ground truth depth data. Despite the promising results from monocular depth,

© Springer Nature Switzerland AG 2020
G. Bebis et al. (Eds.): ISVC 2020, LNCS 12510, pp. 69–81, 2020.
https://doi.org/10.1007/978-3-030-64559-5_6

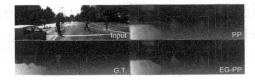

Fig. 1. Comparison between the conventional post-processing (PP) [2] and the proposed Edge-Guided post-processing (EG-PP) on KITTI dataset. Our method can reserve the sharp edge of the detected object depth and avoid the halo effect.

these methods suffer from the limitation of the quality and availability of ground truth pixel depth. Hence, self-supervised approaches that learn depth information from a single image have received increasing attention recently.

In the task of monocular depth estimation, self-supervised approaches only need supervision from stereo image pairs [2–4] or monocular video frames [5,6]. In monocular depth estimation, the disparity is used as an intermediate product for depth estimation which can be converted to reconstruct the images with the inverse warping transform [7]. Recent works have introduced novel objective functions, such as the left-right consistency [2], correlational consistency [8], and adaptive global and local error [4]. Further, the high solution input solution has also been evaluated by [9] and [6] to detect the fine objects in images. Unfortunately, one major challenges with self-supervision is reducing false detections by using a compact network. It was shown in [2] that the deeper networks (e.g., Resnet50) can yield better depth estimates compared to a more compact network (e.g., VGG14). However, very deep networks are inefficient for real-time usage. Hence, a high performance light-weight network design for a depth estimation network is needed for real-time systems.

There are only a few works that focus on optimization of the network structure for self-supervision in real-time. Recently, a Light-Weight RefineNet was proposed for joint semantic segmentation and depth estimation [10]. This method was designed for supervision method. We have tested it and found out that its performance is limited when applying to the self-supervision. When we studied the multi-task network, we realized that the depth estimation and semantic segmentation can share the same feature representation in the network. Based on this finding, we argue that the semantic segmentation network structure can be used in the depth estimation network. In this paper, we introduce Atrous Spatial Pyramid Pooling (ASPP) module into our depth network from Deeplab semantic segmentation network [11]. We add forward-paths into the ASPP module and reduce the layers numbers of each Atrous convolutional layers to further optimize the network structure. We successfully designed a Light-weight DispNet that has only 20% size of the conventional depth network [2] but up to 55% faster in prediction. The prediction time of the proposed model can achieve 68 frames per second (15 ms per frame) using a single nVIDIA GTX1080 GPU.

Another limitation of self-supervision is the stereo dis-occlusion effect. Self-supervision relies on stereo image pairs to calibrate the estimation without the ground truth data. This self-supervision method inherits the stereo dis-occlusion effect from the objective function that uses stereo image pairs. Disparity ramps happen in the stereo dis-occlusion area of the estimated disparity and largely downgrade the estimation quality both quantitatively and qualitatively. The early researches in the occlusion detection used handcrafted the features to proceed the machine learning algorithms [12]. Recently, learning-based methods left-right symmetry [13, 14] have been proposed to estimate occlusions using the convolutional network. Then a post-processing method has been proposed to compensate the occlusion shading using a flip prediction alignment method [2], the compensated output suffers severe halo effect as shown in Fig. 1(PP). None of the current methods can fit the need of reducing the occlusion fading for a self-supervised depth estimation task. To address the occluding fading issue, we proposed an Edge-Guided post-processing (EG-PP) method to eliminate the occluding fading and halo effects in inference stage shown in Fig. 1(EG-PP). The proposed method effectively improves both the quantitative and qualitative results and can be applied to all the other self-supervision-based methods.

The main contributions of this paper are as follows: (1) We propose a Lightweight DispNet that is smaller, faster, and more accurate than the conventional DispNet. We have also proved that the last few dense feature layers of the encoder in DispNet are less efficient in extracting long-range features in our setting. (2) We a propose a novel Edge-Guided post-processing method to improve the performance. The occlusion fading is largely reduced with a minimized halo effect after applying our method. We also experimentally show that EG-PP is universal and can be applied to any other self-supervised method. (3) We evaluate our approach compared to the state-of-the-art on the KITTI dataset [15]. We fairly compare our model with priors using same conventional post-processing method to demonstrate that our method has fundamentally improved the network performance. (4) The proposed method is generalized to other unseen benchmark datasets. We test our method with the Make3d dataset [16] compared with other current state-of-the-arts quantitatively and qualitatively.

2   Methodology

Our model is inspired by the works of [11] and [2]. We first introduce the ASPP module [11] into our network design and optimize the network structure from the multiple conventional backbones. Then the objective function is directly adopted from [2]. The proposed Edge-Guided post-processing is explained in the last section.

2.1   Light-Weight Disparity Network

Many recent works designed their network by starting with DispNet [17], which is an autoencoder-based architecture. The multi-scale features from DispNet are exploited from the encoder, and the spatial resolution is recovered from the decoder. The recovered multi-scale spatial resolutions are the estimated disparities.

Since it was shown that depth estimation and semantic segmentation have common feature representations, they can share the base-network to perform multi-task prediction [10]. Therefore, we use the network design concept of the semantic segmentation task. In the segmentation network, an effective module - Atrous Spatial Pyramid Pooling (ASPP) - was designed cascaded on top of the original network to detect long-range information [18]. We follow this design rule to modify the DispNet for depth estimation.

To further optimize our network, we analyzed the feature layers of the encoder, and we found that the last few convolutional blocks have a minor contribution to the estimation, especially after introducing the ASPP module shown in Fig. 2(b). Based on this observation, we simplify the DispNet by using the ASPP module to replace the last two convolutional blocks of the encoder. We also further use the maxpool to replace the convolutional block before the ASPP module. This design successfully reduces the network size of the network and produce a better performance than DispNet. We name this structure a Light-Weight DispNet. The proposed network structure is shown in Fig. 2(a). We here use [2] as a baseline example. If DispNet uses VGG14 as the backbone, the network parameters are about 31.6 million, and the inference time is about 19.11 ms. The corresponding Light-Weight DispNet only need 8.1 million (74% less) with inference time 14.74 ms (22.9% less).

Nevertheless, we further improve the network structure of the conventional ASPP module. Instead of using the Atrous Blocks in parallel, we add the forward-path for each Atrous Blocks (ASPPF) from the previous one which has the smaller dilation rate. The ASPPF can include more features from previous Atrous Block, but the computational cost would increase. Hence, we further reduce half of the number of the layers of each Atrous Block. A post convolutional block is also added after the concatenation of all the Atrous Blocks. We name this design as ASPP with Forward-Path (ASPPF) shown in Fig. 2(c). The proposed ASPPF modules has smaller size than the conventional ASPP module and the performance of the ASPPF design is better. The detailed analysis is elaborated in the section of Ablation Study.

2.2   Objective Function

We decide to adopt the objective function from [2] directly. There are several reasons. The most important consideration is that the aim of the left-right consistency function from [2] has demonstrated promising results among the recent works. The successors only have minor modifications. Besides, we would like to showcase that the proposed Light-Weight DispNet is substantially better than the conventional DispNet using the same objective function.

The objective function is a weighted sum of three terms: appearance (C_{ap}), disparity smoothness (C_{ds}), and left-right consistency (C_{cor}). The self-supervise total loss is defined as following:

$$C_s = \alpha_{ap} \times C_{ap} + \alpha_{ds} \times C_{ds} + \alpha_{lr} \times C_{cor} \tag{1}$$

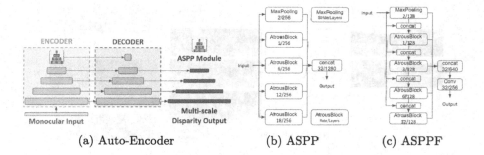

(a) Auto-Encoder   (b) ASPP   (c) ASPPF

Fig. 2. Light-Weight DispNet Structure, a) the proposed Auto-Encoder with ASPP module, b) the conventional ASPP module, and c) the proposed ASPPF module.

The weights $(\alpha_{ap}, \alpha_{ds}, \alpha_{lr})$ are determined before optimization and set as $(1.0, 0.1, 1.0)$. The definition of each term can be found in [2].

The stereo dis-occlusion effect is one limitation of self-supervision for monocular depth estimation. Stereo dis-occlusion creates disparity ramps (occlusion fading) on both the left side of the image and the occluders. [2] proposed a post-processing method to reduce this effect. This form of post-processing estimates the disparity map d_l and the flipped disparity map d'_l, which are from input image I and its horizontally flipped image I'. Then the flipped disparity map d'_l is flipped back as a d''_l that aligns with d_l but where the occlusion fading is on the right of occluders as well as on the right side of the image. The final result is an average of d_l and d''_l, but assigning the first 2% on the left of the image using d_l and the last 2% on the right to the disparities from d_l.

The post-processing uses a mirror to generate a well-aligned projected disparity d''_l that has right-side occlusion fading. The average of d_l and d''_l can reduce the left-side occlusion fading because d''_l has correct left-side estimation results. However, the right-side occlusion fading is also involved. This average process in the post-processing causes the halo effect in the final results, as shown in PP of Fig. 1. Instead of average, we propose an Edge-Guided weighted sum to suppress the occlusion fading of both d_l and d''_l in the combination to reduce the halo effect, as shown in EG-PP of Fig. 1.

2.3 Edge-Guided Post-Processing

The proposed Edge-Guided post-processing is depicted in Fig. 3. We follow the design concept of [2] to compute d_l and d''_l, but we add edge-aware weights (w, w'') in the final combination. Here we take w as an example to illustrate the algorithm. A right-edge detector is designed to extract the regional-edge confidence E. Instead of using Sobel detector, a wide-range horizontal gradient filter (f_{gx}) is used:

$$f_{gx} = \begin{bmatrix} 1 \dots 0 -1 \dots \\ 1 \dots 0 -1 \dots \\ 1 \dots 0 -1 \dots \end{bmatrix}_{3 \times (2N)} / (3 \times (2N)) \tag{2}$$

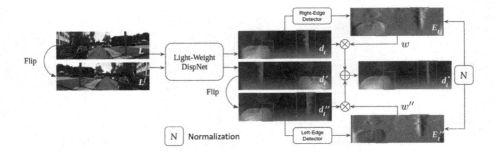

Fig. 3. Edge-Guided post processing

where N is the detection radius, whose default value is set to 10. After the
convolution process ($\otimes$) of d_l and f_{gx}, we add an offset (b) and a gain (a) on the
convolution result. Then a sigmoid function is applied:

$$E_l = \text{sigmoid}((d_l \otimes f_{gx} - b) * a) \tag{3}$$

where E_l is the right regional-edge confidence. The offset b and gain a are set
as 0.5 and 32 to maximize the E_l in the range [0, 1]. In this equation, the right
edge region has the confidence close to 1, while the left occlusion fading area
has the confidence close to 0. The confidence of the flat area keeps around 0.5.
The E_l'' is obtained in the same way but using the horizontal flipped f_{gx} as the
left-edge detector. The last step is to normalize E_l and E_l'' to obtain w and w''.
Then the final output $d_l^\star$ is a weighted sum of d_l and d_l'':

$$w = E_l/(E_l + E_l''), \qquad w'' = E_l''/(E_l + E_l'') \tag{4}$$

$$d_l^\star = wd_l + w''d_l'' \tag{5}$$

Normalization is required to prevent overlap detection between E_l and E_l''. It
ensures that the sum of w and w'' is 1 for each pixel and the final output $d_l^\star$ has
no overhead compared to d_l and d_l''. There are no learning parameters and the
computation cost is very low.

3   Experiments

Our benchmarks compare the performance of our approach to recent self-
supervised monocular depth estimation methods. We selected Godard et al.'s
work as our baseline and used the same benchmark configurations in [2]. We evaluated our approach on multiple aspects of KITTI dataset (i.e., both quantitative
and qualitative). The ablation study is first conducted to prove the effectiveness
of our approach using KITTI split. We then have a benchmark with the current
start-of-the-art on Eigen split. We showcase the improvement of optimized network with the ASPP module by comparing to the priors. For fair comparison,
we have all the methods with the conventional PP. In the last section of each

scenario, we add the results applying the proposed EG-PP to demonstrate the effectiveness of EG-PP. We also generalized our method to other popular unseen data – Make3d.

3.1   Datasets, Metrics and Implementation

We evaluate the performance of our method on the KITTI benchmark [15]. We use two different test splits, KITTI and Eigen Split [1], of KITTI data to perform the ablation study for our method and the benchmark compared with the existing works. We follow the approach of [2] that uses 29k image pairs as the training set. We train our models by 8 batches and 100 epochs on the KITTI data. Furthermore, it has been shown by Godard et al. that pre-training with Cityscapes dataset can improve the performance on KITTI benchmark [2,19]. We also include this strategy in the benchmark. In the combinational training on Cityscapes and KITTI dataset, we pre-train our models with an 8 batches and 50 epochs first on Cityscapes dataset and then on KITTI dataset. We use the evaluation metrics from Geiger et al. for depth estimation [15], which measures the error in meters from the ground truth and the percentage of depth that is within a threshold from the correct value. All of the reported error measurements represent the average error. Our methods were implemented in Tensorflow 1.15 [20] using Python 3.7 under the Ubuntu environment with a single NVIDIA GTX 1080 GPU. All input images are resized to 256 × 512 from the original size of the training image.

In the benchmarks, we show the experimental results of VGGASPPF (VGG8 Backbone) models. The VGGASPP (VGG14/VGG8 Backbone) model is included in the ablation study to show that the last three convolutional blocks are redundant. The computation costs of each backbone are also summarized in the Ablation section. We show that both our models have better performance than competitors in the benchmark studies. The our code for these experiments are publicly available [Github].

3.2   Results

Ablation Study. In the ablation study, we analyze the quantitative performance improvement and the computational costs of our various designs using KITTI split on the KITTI dataset. For the quantitative performance improvement, we use VGG14 of the prior work [2] as the baseline. We first apply PP and EG-PP on the baseline to show the effectiveness of EG-PP. Then we start from VGGASPP with VGG14 to check up the improvement and the optimized VGGASPP/VGGASPPF with VGG8 are evaluated. Last, we include the results of pretrain C+K cases.

In the first section of Table 1, we show that the proposed EG-PP is effective to not only our model but also the baseline method [2]. This is particularly evident in terms of RMSE(log) and $\delta < 1.25$, which are the most challenging parts. In the remaining of the sections in Table 1, we can see that the proposed ASPP models have better performance than the baseline among all

Table 1. Quantitative results for different variants of our approach on the KITTI Stereo 2015 test dataset. We use our prior [2] as our baseline is shown in the first section. The training scenario is based on the KITTI training set (K), while the last section shows the results which are pre-trained by Cityscapes training sets (C+K). The best result in each subsection is shown in bold.

Approach	Encoder	ASPP	PP	EG-PP	Train	ARD	SRD	RMSE	RMSE(log)	$\delta < 1.25$	$\delta < 1.25^2$	$\delta < 1.25^3$
						Lower is better.				Higher is better.		
Baseline	VGG14				K	0.1240	1.3880	6.125	0.217	0.841	0.936	0.975
Our ASPP	VGG14	v			K	0.1183	1.2671	6.070	0.209	0.848	0.941	0.977
Our ASPP	VGG8	v			K	0.1134	1.1636	5.734	0.201	0.853	0.945	0.979
Our ASPPF	VGG8	v			K	0.1112	1.1263	5.693	0.201	0.859	0.946	0.979
Our ASPPF w/ PP	VGG8	v	v		K	0.1068	1.0033	5.460	0.193	0.861	0.949	0.981
Our ASPPF w/ EG-PP	VGG8	v		v	K	0.1062	0.9924	5.365	0.188	0.864	0.952	0.983
Our ASPPF w/ EG-PP	VGG8	v		v	C+K	**0.0992**	**0.9196**	**5.035**	**0.175**	**0.883**	**0.961**	**0.986**

Table 2. Computational costs of different variants of our approach on the KITTI training dataset. The units of training of prediction are msec(ms)(lower is better) and frame per second(FPS) (Higher is better).

Approach	Blocks	Parameters	Predict(ms/FPS)
Baseline VGG	VGG14	31600072	19.11/52.32
Our VGGASPP	VGG14	38941384	22.03/45.4
Our VGGASPP	VGG8	8134344	14.74/67.83
Our VGGASPPF	VGG8	**7642440**	**14.5/68.97**
Baseline VGG+PP	VGG14	31600072	31.06/32.20
Our VGGASPPF+PP	VGG8	**7642440**	**21.93/45.6**
Our VGGASPPF+EGPP	VGG8	**7642440**	22.51/44.42

the metrics. The VGGASPP/VGG8 has an equivalent even better performance than VGGASPP/VGG14, which shows that the last few convolutional blocks in the VGG14 encoder are less effective when the ASPP module is applied. Last, VGGASPPF/VGG8 has better performance, although VGGASPP/VGG8 has a smaller computational cost.

In Table 2, we examine the computational costs of both our methods and the baseline. We included the VGG14 baseline to check the improvement rate. The results applying the post-processing are also included. The predictions happen in around 14.7ms/68FPS of the proposed VGGASPP/VGG8 model and 14.5ms/69 FPS of the proposed VGGASPPF/VGG8 model. Our VGGASPPF/VGG8 has only 24.2% of parameters but is 31.8% faster in the prediction compared to VGG14 model of the baseline. When the post-processing method is applied, the model's input becomes a batch of two images (left and flipped left images) and the prediction efficiency drops to around 22 ms/45.6 FPS of VGGASPPF/VGG8. When the proposed Edge-Guided post-processing is applied to the proposed VGGASPPF/VGG8 model, there is only 2.5% loss in computation time.

Table 3. This table shows the additional benchmark specifically compared with recent methods. All the results use the crop defined by Garg et al. [3]. In the PP column, Y means using the conventional PP, while Y+ means using the proposed EG-PP. The results which are pre-trained with Cityscapes (C) or ImageNet (I) are evaluated as well. The high resolution results are also included for the comparison with [6].

Approach	Train	Test	PP	ARD	SRD	RMSE	RMSE(log)	$\delta < 1.25$	$\delta < 1.25^2$	$\delta < 1.25^3$
				Lower is better.				Higher is better.		
Monodepth [2]	K	E - 80m	Y	0.1480	1.3440	5.927	0.247	0.803	0.922	0.964
Fei et al. [22]	K	E - 80m	Y	0.1390	1.2110	5.702	0.239	0.816	0.928	0.966
Monodepth2 [6]	K	E - 80m	Y	0.1300	1.1440	5.485	0.232	0.831	0.932	0.968
Wong et al. [4]	K	E - 80m	Y	0.1264	0.9935	5.282	0.222	0.831	0.939	0.973
Ours	K	E - 80m	Y+	**0.1072**	**0.9079**	**4.877**	**0.202**	**0.862**	**0.945**	**0.975**
Monodepth [2]	C+K	E - 80m	Y	0.1140	0.8980	4.935	0.206	0.861	0.949	0.976
Fei et al. [22]	C+K	E - 80m	Y	0.1120	0.8360	4.8920	0.204	0.862	0.950	0.977
Monodepth2 [6]	I+K	E - 80m	Y	0.1090	0.873	4.960	0.209	0.864	0.948	0.975
Ours	C+K	E - 80m	Y+	**0.1015**	**0.7966**	**4.633**	**0.193**	**0.876**	**0.953**	**0.979**
Monodepth2 [6] (1024×320)	I+K	E - 80m	Y	0.1070	0.8490	4.764	0.201	0.874	0.953	0.977
Ours (1024×320)	C+K	E - 80m	Y+	**0.0999**	**0.7665**	**4.455**	**0.189**	**0.881**	**0.956**	**0.980**
Monodepth [2]	K	E - 50m	Y	0.1400	0.9760	4.471	0.232	0.818	0.931	0.969
Fei et al. [22]	K	E - 50m	Y	0.1320	0.8910	4.3120	0.225	0.831	0.936	0.970
Wong et al. [4]	K	E - 50m	Y	0.1202	0.7432	4.022	0.209	0.845	0.946	0.976
Ours	K	E - 50m	Y+	**0.1009**	**0.6480**	**3.656**	**0.190**	**0.875**	**0.952**	**0.979**
Monodepth [2]	C+K	E - 50m	Y	0.1080	0.6570	3.729	0.194	0.873	0.954	0.979
Fei et al. [22]	C+K	E - 50m	Y	0.1060	0.6150	3.697	0.192	0.874	0.956	0.980
Ours	C+K	E - 50m	Y+	**0.0959**	**0.5853**	**3.486**	**0.181**	**0.887**	**0.958**	**0.981**

State-of-the-Art Comparison. In the benchmark, we include the post-processing in the comparison. We only include VGGASPPF/VGG8 in the evaluation. From the training aspect of view, there are K only and C+K cases. An exceptional case is that [6] has ImageNet [21] as the pre-train dataset. Another special case is the high resolution input case of [9] and [6]. We also implement the same resolution input on our model. In test cases, we use Eigen-split with full and near distance under Garg et al. crop shown in Table 3 [3]. Our results with conventional post-processing are still better than the recent priors. When we apply EG-PP, our results become significantly better, and only the last accuracy term is slightly behind.

The improved performance of our method is not only quantitative, but also qualitative. The results are shown in Fig. 4. Our results have a much better ability to reproduce clear object shapes and edges in any size, especially the signs and trunks in the test images. The halo effects around objects (e.g., cars, signs, trunks,etc.) are largely reduced using the proposed EG-PP. In the visual evaluation, we provide more accurate and visually appealing images to viewers.

Edge-Guided Post-process Generalization. The proposed EG-PP method is universal to be applied to any self-supervision depth estimation methods. We have prepared the experiment results of [2,4], and ours with non-PP, PP, and proposed EG-PP in Table 4. The performance of the quantitative results are improved for both of the two methods except the ARD and SRD terms of [2]

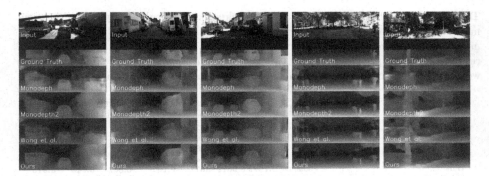

Fig. 4. Benchmark of qualitative results on KITTI dataset Eigen Split. We compare Ours with the priors - Monodepth [2], Monodepth2 [6], and Wong et al. [4]. Our VGGASPPF has applied the proposed Edge-Guided post-processing. Our results can capture much more clear object shapes, such as signs, cars, and trunks than priors. The halo effects are also effectively reduced in our results.

Table 4. Quantitative results for proposed Edge-Guided Post-Processing method on the KITTI Stereo 2015 test dataset. The PP means using post-processing. N is no PP, Y is the conventional PP proposed by [2], and Y+ is the proposed Edge-Guided PP. The best performance of each metric in each section is bolded. The proposed Edge-Guided PP can effectively improve the performance especially the most challenging accuracy metric $\delta < 1.25$.

Approach	Train	PP	ARD	SRD	RMSE	RMSE(log)	$\delta < 1.25$	$\delta < 1.25^2$	$\delta < 1.25^3$
			Lower is better				Higher is better		
Monodepth [2]	K	N	0.1240	1.3880	6.125	0.217	0.841	0.936	0.975
Monodepth [2]	K	Y	**0.1170**	**1.1773**	5.811	0.206	0.847	0.942	0.977
Monodepth [2]	K	Y+	**0.1170**	1.1873	**5.766**	**0.204**	**0.850**	**0.944**	**0.978**
Wong et al. [4]	K	N	0.1112	1.1350	5.682	0.202	0.854	0.946	0.979
Wong et al. [4]	K	Y	**0.1058**	**0.9811**	5.424	0.193	0.857	0.949	0.981
Wong et al. [4]	K	Y+	0.1074	1.0394	**5.417**	**0.191**	**0.861**	**0.950**	**0.982**
Ours	K	N	0.1112	1.1263	5.693	0.201	0.859	0.946	0.979
Ours	K	Y	0.1068	1.0033	5.460	0.193	0.861	0.949	0.981
Ours	K	Y+	**0.1062**	**0.9924**	**5.365**	**0.188**	**0.864**	**0.952**	**0.983**

and [4]. Thus, this result shows that the proposed EG-PP method can be applied to other self-supervision methods to improve the performance.

Dataset Generalization. We further apply our method to another unseen dataset to verify the ability of the generalization. We follow the idea of [2] and [6] to evaluate Make3d dataset [16]. We use the same setting as these two priors that Cityscapes Dataset only trains our model, and we only consider less than 70 m depth in evaluation. We also used the same evaluation code from [2] to generate the final results. The quantitative results are shown in Table 5. We have shown that our model has better results using stereo supervision. On the other hand,

Table 5. Quantitative results on Make3d.

Approach	abs_rel	sq_rel	rmse	rmse_log
Monodepth [2]	0.544	10.94	11.76	0.193
Fei et al. [22]	0.458	8.681	12.335	0.164
Wong et al. [4]	0.427	8.183	11.781	**0.156**
Ours	**0.365**	**5.073**	**8.135**	0.174

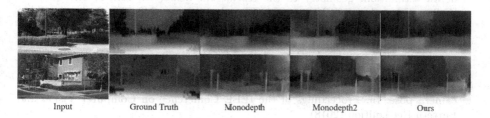

Input   Ground Truth   Monodepth   Monodepth2   Ours

Fig. 5. Qualitative results of Make3d Dataset. We compare our method with monodepth [2] and monodepth2 [6]. The results of two references come from the source papers and codes.

Fig. 5 shows the qualitative results. We compare our results to monodepth [2] and monodepth2 [6], where monodepth2 [6] is supervised by the monocular sequence. Our model provides better visual performance than monodepth [2] in clarity and competitive compared to monodepth2 [6].

4 Conclusion

We proposed a Light-weight DispNet and a novel Edge-Guided post-processing method to improve a self-supervised monocular depth estimator's performance. Our primary contribution is that the proposed Light-weight DispNet demonstrates the inherent capability to capture long-range features to estimate better the depth map with a much smaller network structure than the current commonly used DispNet. Another contribution of this work is that the Edge-Guided post-processing can resolve most occlusion fading effect of self-supervision methods. It can effectively reduce the halo effect that comes from the conventional post-processing to yield the object shape. The proposed EdgeGuided post-processing is suitable for all the self-supervised monocular depth estimators.

Acknowledgment. K. Peng and J. Rozenblit were supported by the National Science Foundation under #1622589. G. Ditzler was supported by the Department of Energy #DE-NA0003946 and National Science Foundation CAREER #1943552.

References

1. Eigen, D., Puhrsch, C., Fergus, R.: Depth map prediction from a single image using a multi-scale deep network. In: Neural Information Processing Systems (2014)
2. Godard, C., Mac Aodha, O., Brostow, G.J.: Unsupervised monocular depth estimation with left-right consistency. In: IEEE Conference on Computer Vision and Pattern Recognition (2017)
3. Garg, R., B.G., V.K., Carneiro, G., Reid, I.: Unsupervised CNN for single view depth estimation: geometry to the rescue. In: Leibe, B., Matas, J., Sebe, N., Welling, M. (eds.) ECCV 2016. LNCS, vol. 9912, pp. 740–756. Springer, Cham (2016). https://doi.org/10.1007/978-3-319-46484-8_45
4. Wong, A., Soatto, S.: Bilateral cyclic constraint and adaptive regularization for unsupervised monocular depth prediction. In: Proceedings of the IEEE Conference on Computer Vision and Pattern Recognition (2019)
5. Yin, Z., Shi, J.: Geonet: unsupervised learning of dense depth, optical flow and camera pose. In: Proceedings of the IEEE Conference on Computer Vision and Pattern Recognition (2018)
6. Godard, C., Mac Aodha, O., Firman, M., Brostow, G.J.: Digging into self-supervised monocular depth estimation. In: Proceedings of the IEEE International Conference on Computer Vision, pp. 3828–3838 (2019)
7. Jaderberg, M., Simonyan, K., Zisserman, A.: Spatial transformer networks. In: Neural Information Processing Systems (2015)
8. Peng, K.-S., Ditzler, G., Rozenblit, J. W.: Self-supervised correlational monocular depth estimation using ResVGG network. In: 7th IIAE International Conference on Intelligent Systems and Image Processing, pp. 93–102, 2019
9. Pillai, S., Ambrus, R., Gaidon, A.: Superdepth: self-supervised, super-resolved monocular depth estimation. In: 2019 International Conference on Robotics and Automation (ICRA) 2019
10. VNekrasov, V., Dharmasiri, T., Spek, A., Drummond, T., Shen, C., Reid, I.: Real-time joint semantic segmentation and depth estimation using asymmetric annotations. In: 2019 International Conference on Robotics and Automation (ICRA), pp. 7101–7107 (2019)
11. Chen, L.C., Papandreou, G., Schroff, F., Adam, H.: Rethinking atrous convolution for semantic image segmentation. arXiv:1706.05587, 2017
12. Humayun, A., Mac Aodha, O., Brostow, G.J.: Learning to find occlusion regions. In: 2011 IEEE Computer Society Conference on Computer Vision and Pattern Recognition, pp. 2161–2168 (2011)
13. Li, A., Yuan, Z.: Symmnet: a symmetric convolutional neural network for occlusion detection. arXiv preprint arXiv:1807.00959, 2018
14. Ilg, E., Saikia, T., Keuper, M., Brox, T.:Occlusions and motion and depth boundaries with a generic network for disparity and optical flow or scene flow estimation. In: European Conference on Computer Vision, pp. 614–630 (2018)
15. Geiger, A., Lenz, P., Urtasun, R.: Are we ready for autonomous driving? The KITTI vision benchmark suite. In: IEEE Conference on Computer Vision and Pattern Recognition (2012)
16. Saxena, A., Sun, M., Ng, A.: Make3D: learning 3D scene structure from a single still image. IEEE Trans. Pattern Anal. Mach. Intell. **31**(5), 824–840 (2009)
17. Mayer, N., et al.: A large dataset to train convolutional networks for disparity, optical flow, and scene flow estimation. In: IEEE Conference on Computer Vision and Pattern Recognition (2016)

18. Chen, L.C., Zhu, Y., Papandreou, G., Schroff, F., Adam, H.: Encoder-decoder with atrous separable convolution for semantic image segmentation. In: Proceedings of the European Conference on Computer Vision, pp. 801–818 (2018)
19. Cordts, M., et al.: The cityscapes dataset for semantic urban scene understanding. In: IEEE conference on computer vision and pattern recognition (2016)
20. Abadi, M., et al.: TensorFlow: large-scale machine learning on heterogeneous systems (2015)
21. Russakovsky, O., et al.: ImageNet large scale visual recognition challenge. Int. J. Comput. Vis. **115**(3), 211–252 (2015). https://doi.org/10.1007/s11263-015-0816-y
22. Fei, X., Wong, A., Soatto, S.: Geo-supervised visual depth prediction. IEEE Robot. Autom. Lett. **4**(2), 1661–1668 (2019)

Iterative Closest Point with Minimal Free Space Constraints

Simen Haugo$^{(\boxtimes)}$ and Annette Stahl

Department of Engineering Cybernetics,
Norwegian University of Science and Technology, Trondheim, Norway
{simen.haugo,annette.stahl}@ntnu.no

Abstract. The Iterative Closest Point (ICP) method is widely used for fitting geometric models to sensor data. By formulating the problem as a minimization of distances evaluated at observed surface points, the method is computationally efficient and applicable to a rich variety of model representations. However, when the scene surface is only partially visible, the model can be ill-constrained by surface observations alone. Existing methods that penalize free space violations may resolve this issue, but require that the explicit model surface is available or can be computed quickly, to remain efficient. We introduce an extension of ICP that integrates free space constraints, while the number of distance computations remains linear in the scene's surface area. We support arbitrary shape spaces, requiring only that the distance to the model surface can be computed at a given point. We describe an implementation for range images and validate our method on implicit model fitting problems that benefit from the use of free space constraints.

Keywords: 3D registration · Implicit modeling · Visibility constraints

1 Introduction

Iterative Closest Point (ICP) [1] is commonly used for fitting geometric models to sensor data. At its core is a local optimization, requiring only computation of data-to-model distances at observed surface points. This makes ICP computationally efficient and applicable to any model representation where the distance to the surface can be computed. However, when the scene surface is only partially visible, the model's shape and pose may be ill-constrained by surface observations alone. A common solution is to impose constraints or penalties on the parameters [2], but this is a model-specific intervention. Alternatively, one can integrate free space constraints (space observed to be empty) that vision systems often provide, but which is not used by ICP. This introduces a new challenge of managing computational complexity, as free space is inherently volumetric [3]. While efficient methods have been proposed when the model surface (or a bound) is available in explicit form [4–7], these are not applicable when the explicit surface is unavailable or prohibitively expensive to compute.

© Springer Nature Switzerland AG 2020
G. Bebis et al. (Eds.): ISVC 2020, LNCS 12510, pp. 82–95, 2020.
https://doi.org/10.1007/978-3-030-64559-5_7

We propose an extension of ICP for implicit models that integrates free space constraints, while retaining the computational complexity of the original method, *i.e.* the number of distance computations scales linearly by the surface area of the scene. Our method supports arbitrary shape spaces, requiring only that the distance to the model surface can be computed at a given point. We demonstrate on range data that our method is amenable to off-the-shelf optimizers, and can resolve parameters which are ill-constrained by surface observations alone.

2   Related Work

Geometric model fitting has been extensively studied over several decades (see [8] for a survey). Notably, we now have efficient methods that are highly robust against outliers and provide strong optimality guarantees [9–11]. To achieve such performance, state-of-the-art methods exploit the structure of the domain (*e.g.* SE3) and/or rely on the ability to match invariant features between the model and the data. These methods work very well for explicit representations, such as static point sets obtained from laser scanners [9,10] or deformable landmark models [11,12]. Unfortunately, they are incompatible with representations where the domain does not allow for easily-exploited structure or invariant features that can be detected and matched.

In this work, we focus on models represented as (parameterized) distance functions. Distance functions have been derived exactly or approximately for several primitives and implicit modeling operations, thereby enabling constructive modeling of objects [13–15]. In robotics and computer vision, distance functions are a natural representation for scene reconstruction and planning [16–18], and have recently fueled research as a neural shape representation in machine learning [19]. The ability to efficiently fit models, using only their distance function, to (incomplete) sensor data, would enrich each of these application areas. We therefore review related work on implicit model fitting, where the explicit surface is not directly maintained and where the implicit function itself may be expensive to evaluate.

The Iterative Closest Point (ICP) method [1,20–24] can be applied to any model representation, requiring only that the distance to the model surface can be computed at each point on the observed surface. This makes ICP efficient, as the computational cost scales linearly by the observed surface area. However, the model can be ill-constrained when the scene's surface is only partially observed (see Fig. 1), e.g. due to capturing data from predominantly one viewpoint or due to noise and specular reflections. Regularization strategies [8], such as penalizing description length [25,26], minimizing volume or surface area [2,27] or imposing constraints on the model parameters [2] can alleviate this problem, but are model-specific interventions that do not generalize.

Alternatively, the fitting method can use visibility information provided by the vision system; *e.g.* a finite range value from a laser scanner indicates not only that there is a surface at that distance from the sensor, but also that there are no surfaces in-between. Visibility information plays a central role in 3D

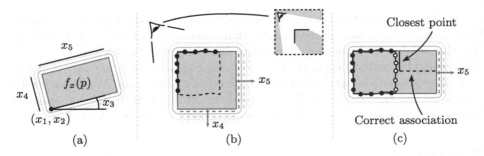

Fig. 1. Illustration of cases where a volume-aware method has advantages over Iterative Closest Point (ICP). Given a model (a) represented by a distance function (f_x), we seek to estimate the parameters x such that the resulting solid fits to a partially observed scene. When using ICP, a subset of parameters (x_4, x_5) can be ill-constrained due to (b) missing data (despite being wrong, the model fits all the observed points) and (c) poor initialization (closest point association leads to uninformative gradients).

reconstruction [28], *e.g.* in space carving [3, 16], and has also been used in model fitting, *e.g.* in volume matching [29–31], minimizing reprojection error [32–37] and matching of occluding contours or silhouettes [6, 7, 38–41]. These methods can be said to be *volume-aware* [42] and have the ability to resolve ill-constrained models by requiring the model to be consistent with free space.

However, existing methods can be prohibitively expensive for implicit models where the associated implicit function is expensive to evaluate. Volume matching (*e.g.* of density, distance or binary occupancy) supports any implicit representation, but is based on densely sampling the volumetric domain. Computing reprojection error or the model silhouette requires the extraction of visible points on the surface. Extraction can be done using accelerated ray casting for distance function models [13], but still requires multiple samples along rays. Extraction can also be done using spatial subdivision schemes [43], but requires an initial resolution that contains sampling points from every connected component of the model's interior and exterior. The availability of the explicit surface (or a close bound) has been used to derive efficient volume-aware methods [4–7]. For implicit models, the explicit surface must in general be recomputed each time the model changes. For small deformations, a set of points can be made to track the implicit surface as the model parameters are optimized [44]. However, efficiently maintaining such an approximation for general domains is an open problem.

Following this line of work, we propose a novel volume-aware method that integrates free space constraints. Similar to ICP, our method only requires the ability to compute the distance to the model at a given point. Unlike previous volume-aware methods, our method does not require the explicit surface or dense volumetric sampling. Instead, our method retains the computational complexity of ICP, in that the required number of distance computations scales linearly by the scene's surface area.

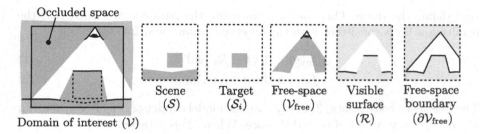

Fig. 2. Notation applied to an example scene containing a target object and outliers.

3 Theory and Method

This section describes our volume-aware extension of the ICP method. We first formalize volume-aware model fitting based on *volume- and surface-consistency* conditions. We then show how these conditions can be expressed in a constrained optimization problem which retains the computational complexity of ICP.

3.1 Notation

Here we introduce notation used in the following sections (see also Fig. 2). A scene, assumed to be some unknown solid $\mathcal{S}$, is observed by a vision system, *e.g.* a range sensor. We consider a domain of interest $\mathcal{V}$ that contains a subset of $\mathcal{S}$, *e.g.* a user-defined box region. The scene is assumed to be decomposed into target and outlier solids, $\mathcal{S}_i$ and $\mathcal{S}_o$, with respective boundaries $\partial\mathcal{S}_i$ and $\partial\mathcal{S}_o$.

Free space $\mathcal{V}_{\text{free}}$ is a closed subset of $\mathcal{V}$, determined by the vision system, which does not intersect the interior of $\mathcal{S}$ (*i.e.* $\mathcal{V}_{\text{free}} \subseteq \mathcal{V}$ and $\mathcal{V}_{\text{free}} \cap \text{int } \mathcal{S} = \emptyset$). Occluded space is the complement of free space inside the domain of interest. The free space boundary $\partial\mathcal{V}_{\text{free}}$ is the boundary between free and occluded space. The visible surface $\mathcal{R}$ is a subset of $\partial\mathcal{V}_{\text{free}}$, determined by the vision system, which also belongs to the physical scene boundary $\partial\mathcal{S}$. If the scene contains outliers, we assume that the visible surface has been segmented into respective target and outlier surfaces $\mathcal{R}_i \subseteq \partial\mathcal{S}_i$ and $\mathcal{R}_o \subseteq \partial\mathcal{S}_o$. The signed Euclidean distance to a solid $\mathcal{D}$ is denoted $d_{\mathcal{D}}(p) := \pm \min_{q \in \partial\mathcal{D}} ||p - q||_2$, where the sign is negative for p inside $\mathcal{D}$ and positive outside.

3.2 Problem Formulation and Volume-Aware Model Fitting

We assume a geometric model of the target object is given as a real-valued function $f_x(p) : \mathbb{R}^3 \times \mathcal{X} \to \mathbb{R}$ defining the solid $\mathcal{M}_x = \{p \in \mathbb{R}^3 : f_x(p) \leq 0\}$. We assume that f_x is the Euclidean distance function $d_{\mathcal{M}_x}$. The model parameters $x \in \mathcal{X}$ may include the object's pose (SE3 $\subseteq \mathcal{X}$), as in rigid registration, but here we assume x can also include any real-valued, discrete or symbolic parameters that define the shape. Our goal is to estimate the parameters x such that the resulting solid is consistent with the observed surface and free space, *i.e.*

$$f_x(p) = 0, \forall p \in \mathcal{R}_i \text{ and} \tag{1}$$

$$f_x(p) > 0, \forall p \in \text{int } \mathcal{V}_{\text{free}}. \tag{2}$$

The free space constraints (2) imply that the model cannot occupy free space, but can occupy any subset of occluded space. When (2) is satisfied, we say that $\mathcal{M}_x$ is *volume-consistent* with $\mathcal{V}_{\text{free}}$. When (1) is satisfied, we say that $\mathcal{M}_x$ is *surface-consistent* with $\mathcal{R}_i$. When both are satisfied, we say that $\mathcal{M}_x$ is *consistent*. For brevity, we will say that a solid is volume- or surface-consistent and leave it understood that volume consistency refers to $\mathcal{V}_{\text{free}}$ and that surface consistency refers to the visible surface $\mathcal{R}_i$.

3.3   Distance Constraints for Volume- and Surface-Consistency

When f_x is the Euclidean distance function, free space implies the existence of a set of inequality constraints bounding the distance from below:

$$f_x(p) \geq \min_{q \in \partial \mathcal{V}_{\text{free}}} ||p - q||_2, \forall p \in \mathcal{V}_{\text{free}}. \tag{3}$$

If the closest point $q \in \partial \mathcal{V}_{\text{free}}$ in (3) also belongs to $\partial \mathcal{S}$, the inequality is replaced by an equality. In practice, we do not know $\partial \mathcal{S}$ and therefore cannot identify everywhere that this holds. However, we do know the visible surface $\mathcal{R} \subseteq \partial \mathcal{S}$. Hence, we can identify the subset of equality constraints:

$$f_x(p) = \min_{q \in \mathcal{R} \cap \partial \mathcal{V}_{\text{free}}} ||p - q||_2, \forall p \in \mathcal{V}_{\text{free}}. \tag{4}$$

If the scene contains outliers, $\mathcal{R}$ in (4) is replaced by the target surface $\mathcal{R}_i$. The constraints (3)–(4) are sufficient conditions for the solid $\mathcal{M}_x$ of a feasible solution x to be volume- and surface-consistent. In the next sections, we address how to turn these constraints into a tractable optimization problem.

Comparison with Implicit-to-Implicit Methods. Before continuing, it may be helpful to compare the constraints (3)–(4) against the related class of implicit-to-implicit methods [31]. These methods penalize the difference between the distance function of the model and the scene, at each point in a volumetric domain of interest $\mathcal{V}$. Assume for simplicity that $\mathcal{S}_i = \mathcal{S}$. An implicit-to-implicit method can then be viewed as imposing the constraints

$$f_x(p) = \hat{d}_\mathcal{S}(p), \forall p \in \mathcal{V}, \tag{5}$$

where $\hat{d}_\mathcal{S}$ is an estimate of the unknown true scene distance function $d_\mathcal{S}$. One choice for $\hat{d}_\mathcal{S}$ is the distance transform of free space [31]. However, the resulting constraints either cannot guarantee volume-consistency or do not admit the distance function to the true solid as a feasible solution.

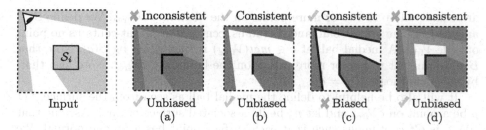

Fig. 3. Comparison between the set of feasible solids for different constraints: surface-consistency (a), surface- and volume-consistency (b), Eq. (5) with $\mathcal{V}$ as $\mathcal{V}_{\text{free}}$ (c) or truncated as described in the text (d). The shaded (resp. white) region in (a)–(d) is the region of space that can (resp. must not) be occupied by a feasible solid (*i.e.* a solid whose associated distance function satisfies the constraints). The thick lines indicate where the solid is required to have a boundary according to the constraints. A feasible set is consistent if it does not contain any solid that occupies free space. A feasible set is unbiased if it contains the target solid ($\mathcal{S}_i$). (Color figure online)

To see this, consider a point $p \in \mathcal{V}_{\text{free}}$ and the boundary point $q \in \partial \mathcal{V}_{\text{free}}$ closest to p. At p, the distance transform $d_{\mathcal{V}_{\text{free}}}(p)$ and the true distance function $d_{\mathcal{S}}(p)$ are equal if and only if $q \in \partial \mathcal{V}_{\text{free}} \cap \partial \mathcal{S}$. Where this is not the case, the equality constraint may require the boundary of the model solid to erroneously fit to a non-physical boundary, *e.g.* the boundary of the shadow behind the box in Fig. 3. Therefore, depending on the domain $\mathcal{V}$, the equality constraints (5) may not all be correct. If $\mathcal{V}$ is truncated to exclude the subset of $\mathcal{V}_{\text{free}}$ where $q \notin \partial \mathcal{V}_{\text{free}} \cap \partial \mathcal{S}$, the constraints (5) are all correct, but insufficient.

A comparison of the set of feasible solids for different constraints is illustrated in Fig. 3. The surface-consistency constraints (1) alone do not prevent a solid from occupying free space. We therefore say that the feasible set in Fig. 3(a) is inconsistent. However, because the true solid ($\mathcal{S}_i$) is contained by the feasible set, we say that the feasible set is unbiased. If we include the volume-consistency constraints (2), the feasible set (Fig. 3(b)) is both consistent and unbiased.

In comparison, the equality constraints (5) cannot produce a feasible set that is both consistent and unbiased. If $\mathcal{V} = \mathcal{V}_{\text{free}}$, a feasible solid is required to have a boundary where there may not be a physical scene boundary, as indicated by the thick lines in Fig. 3(c). If $\mathcal{V}$ is truncated as described above, the feasible set (Fig. 3(d)) is no longer biased, but has become inconsistent, as a feasible solid may occupy regions of free space where there are no constraints.

3.4 Optimization Problem Formulation

To turn the constraints (3)–(4) into a tractable optimization problem, we will use the geometric structure known as the *medial axis transform* of a solid, which is the locus of centers of balls which are maximal within the solid, along with their associated radii [45, 46]. These are also called *medial balls*. We will use the medial axis of free space, $mat(\mathcal{V}_{\text{free}})$, which is the set of points $c \in \mathcal{V}_{\text{free}}$ that are equally close to two or more points on the boundary $\partial \mathcal{V}_{\text{free}}$. We define $\mathcal{B}(p)$ and $r_{\mathcal{B}(p)}$ as the largest ball, and its radius, centered at p that contains no point outside $\mathcal{V}_{\text{free}}$. A medial ball at $c \in mat(\mathcal{V}_{\text{free}})$ is then given by $\mathcal{B}(c)$. Note that $\mathcal{B}(p)$ is tangent to one or more points on the boundary $\partial \mathcal{V}_{\text{free}}$. Note also that, by this definition, $r_{\mathcal{B}(p)} = d_{\mathcal{V}_{\text{free}}}(p)$.

It will also be helpful to define the medial ball as seen from the surface. Let p be a point on $\partial \mathcal{V}_{\text{free}}$ and let n_p be its associated surface normal. Assume that $\partial \mathcal{V}_{\text{free}}$ is C^2-continuous such that each surface point has a unique normal. We then define c_p as the point on the medial axis which also lies on the positive extension of n_p. Note that the medial ball $\mathcal{B}(c_p)$ is tangent to p and that $r_{\mathcal{B}(c_p)}$ is the distance along n_p from p to c_p, i.e. $c_p = p + r_{\mathcal{B}(c_p)} n_p$.

The following results relate the medial axis to the constraints from the previous section.

Proposition 1. *If $f_x(c) \geq r_{\mathcal{B}(c)}$ for all $c \in \mathrm{mat}(\mathcal{V}_{free})$ then $\mathcal{M}_x$ is volume-consistent with $\mathcal{V}_{free}$.*

Proposition 2. *Let $\partial \mathcal{V}_{free}$ be C^2-continuous and let $\mathcal{M}_x$ be volume-consistent with $\mathcal{V}_{free}$. If $f_x(p + t_p n_p) = t_p$ for all $p \in \mathcal{R}_i$ and some $t_p \in [0, r_{\mathcal{B}(c_p)})$, then $\mathcal{M}_x$ is surface-consistent with $\mathcal{R}_i$.*

Intuitively, these results imply that volume-consistency can be determined simply by comparing f_x against the radii of the medial balls in free space, *i.e.* without densely sampling the volume. Furthermore, given volume-consistency, surface-consistency can be determined by sampling one or more points along each surface normal. This suggests the following constrained optimization problem:

$$\min_{x} \quad E(x) = \sum_{p \in \mathcal{R}_i} (f_x(p + t_p n_p) - t_p)^2 \tag{6}$$

$$\text{subject to} \quad f_x(c) \geq r_{\mathcal{B}(c)}, \forall c \in mat(\mathcal{V}_{\text{free}}) . \tag{7}$$

Before we describe how this can be solved in practice, we want to highlight some key properties.

Proposition 3. *If x^* is a feasible solution to (6)–(7) and $E(x^*) = 0$, then $\mathcal{M}_{x^*}$ is volume-consistent with $\mathcal{V}_{free}$ and surface-consistent with $\mathcal{R}_i$.*

Proposition 4. *The number of distance computations per iteration scales linearly by the surface area of the scene.*

The objective function and the constraints require evaluating f_x only on the visible surface $\mathcal{R}_i$ and the medial axis $mat(\mathcal{V}_{\text{free}})$. Since the medial axis is a deformation retract of $\partial \mathcal{V}_{\text{free}}$ when $\partial \mathcal{V}_{\text{free}}$ is C^2-continuous [47], the complexity of the latter scales linearly by the surface area of $\partial \mathcal{V}_{\text{free}}$. The objective function is the sum of squared data-to-model distances, but taken at different level sets as determined by t_p, and likewise scales linearly by the surface area of $\mathcal{R}_i$. The number of distance computations per iteration therefore scales linearly by the surface area of the scene rather than the domain volume.

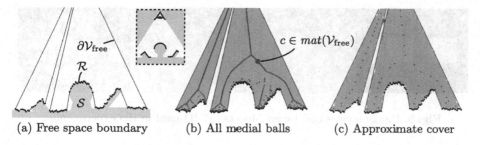

<table>
<tr><td>(a) Free space boundary</td><td>(b) All medial balls</td><td>(c) Approximate cover</td></tr>
</table>

Fig. 4. A 2D example of computing an approximate cover of free space. (a): Point samples on free space boundary from a noisy range image; the "spike" represents missing range values that are treated as zero. (b): The centres of all medial balls. (c): The centres of the medial balls remaining in the approximate cover.

Proposition 5. *Volumetric data structures are not required.*

Evaluating the objective function and constraints (6)–(7) requires the centers and radii of the medial balls. It also requires that these can be parameterized by a scalar (t_p) associated with each point on the visible surface. Importantly, this information can be stored without volumetric data structures, *e.g.* by associating each point on the free space boundary with a single floating point number, representing the distance to the medial axis along the normal.

Choosing t_p. Although t_p can be non-zero, we will in the remainder assume that $t_p = 0$. Thus, (6) becomes

$$E(x) = \sum_{p \in \mathcal{R}_i} f_x^2(p) \, , \tag{8}$$

which is recognized as the point-to-implicit ICP objective function [1, 21–23]. We show experimentally that this is sufficient to resolve ill-constrained parameters.

3.5 Approximate Cover

While the described method avoids a dense volumetric sampling of free space, the medial axis can still contain prohibitively many balls. We can greatly reduce the computational cost if we only need to check if the model is consistent with an approximation of free space—an approximate cover. To obtain this, we use the heuristic of [48], and detect if a ball is redundant by checking if it can be completely covered by slightly enlargening any of its neighboring balls by an amount δ. We greedily build a simplified medial axis by iteratively selecting the ball that covers the most uncovered balls when its radius is increased by δ. An example approximate cover is shown in Fig. 4.

Fig. 5. Range images and target objects (a)–(f) used in the experiments.

4   Experiments

We experimentally verify the following. First, that our volume-aware method constrains more parameters in partially observed scenes than the original ICP method (*i.e.* the optimization of (8) alone). Second, that our proposed optimization problem can be solved using off-the-shelf solvers. Third, that the approximate cover reduces computational cost.

4.1   Datasets and Implementation Details

As input we consider single-view range images from real and synthetic datasets. The scenes (Fig. 5) contain one or more target objects, labelled (a)–(f), which have a corresponding distance function model. The model for (a) and (b) is a cuboid with 9 parameters (pose and side lengths). The model for (c) is a discretized distance field with 7 parameters (similarity transform). The model for (d)–(f) is defined using constructive solid geometry and has 13 parameters. Parameters were standardized such that a unit change in any single parameter visually affected the shape with similar magnitude.

Our method requires the set of points on $\mathcal{R}_i$ and medial balls in $\mathcal{V}_{\text{free}}$. We implemented a pre-processing pipeline to obtain these quantities from single-view range images. For the former, backprojected range pixels provide a point sampling of the visible surface $\mathcal{R}$, from which we manually segment the subset of target points $\mathcal{R}_i$. Many methods have been proposed for estimating the medial axis from various inputs [49]. A fast and precise method is the shrinking ball method of Ma *et al.* [48], which operates on oriented point sets and computes the distance to the medial axis along each point's normal. To apply their method, we need a sufficiently dense and oriented point sampling of the free space boundary. We obtain this by connecting adjacent backprojected pixels into a piecewise linear mesh. This is similar to [50], but we include triangles at jump edges, as the shrinking ball method requires the surface to be a 2-manifold; otherwise balls may protrude into occluded space. We sample evenly-distributed points from the surface. We estimate their normals using [51] and impose a consistent orientation using the viewing direction. We apply a bilateral filter and a median filter to smoothen the range image and fill in small, isolated regions of missing values. To prevent erroneous constraints, larger missing regions are conservatively set to zero, which can cause "spikes" as seen in Fig. 6.

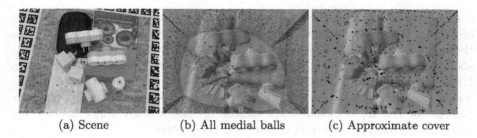

(a) Scene   (b) All medial balls   (c) Approximate cover

Fig. 6. (a): Scene used for Fig. 5 (e, f) from [52]. (b, c): Free space boundary and medial balls in original and approximate cover. The "spikes" are due to missing range values.

Table 1. Top row pair: estimated number of constrained parameters (higher is better) and sum of singular values in parenthesis (lower is better). Bottom four row pairs: Success rate using standard deviation 0.1, 0.25, 0.5 and 1.0 (top to bottom) as initialization uncertainty.

	Box (a)	Box (b)	Head (c)	Plug (d)	Plug (e)	Plug (f)
ICP	5/9 (4.4)	3/9 (9.9)	7/7 (0.0)	7/13 (7.1)	7/13 (14.4)	7/13 (12.7)
Our	9/9 (0.0)	8/9 (2.1)	7/7 (0.0)	9/13 (4.0)	9/13 (5.6)	9/13 (6.0)
ICP	100%	100%	100%	87%	98%	77%
Our	100%	100%	100%	100%	100%	100%
ICP	100%	100%	89%	54%	69%	55%
Our	100%	100%	98%	87%	90%	92%
ICP	86%	88%	48%	22%	26%	22%
Our	99%	100%	74%	39%	58%	42%
ICP	62%	47%	9%	3%	5%	1%
Our	100%	100%	26%	15%	16%	8%

Table 2. Number of surface points and number of medial balls, before and after computing the approximate cover, for the scenes shown in Fig. 5.

	(a,b)	(c)	(d)	(e,f)
Surface points ($|\mathcal{R}|$)	686	15 806	6 827	8 730
Medial balls (all)	48 386	32 019	42 013	40 193
Medial balls (approximate cover)	432	272	320	479

4.2 Ability to Resolve Ill-Constrained Parameters

We quantify how constrained the model parameters are at the global solution. We acquire an initial fit using a global search method. We then perform a random walk of length $k = 50$, where at each step $i = 1...k$ the current parameters are perturbed by a uniformly drawn vector $\delta \in [-\sigma, \sigma]^{|\mathcal{X}|}$, $\sigma = 0.1$, and re-optimized from the perturbed position. We perform $N = 100$ random walks, which gives a matrix of solutions $X = [x_1 \cdots x_N]$ from each random walk. As a measure of the number of constrained parameters, we use the rank of X, estimated as the number of singular values less than σ. If a parameter is well-constrained, it should return to its original value after re-optimization. Hence, singular values larger than σ indicates that one or more parameters are not constrained. The results in Table 1 (top) show that our method constrained more parameters (except for the Head model), thus indicating that it successfully utilizes free space information to resolve ill-constrained parameters.

4.3   Ability to Use Off-the-Shelf Solvers

We compare the success rate of our method against ICP, using an off-the-shelf solver. For both methods, we use Matlab's Sequential Quadratic Programming (SQP) implementation. As a proxy for success, we use the rotational parameters at the end of optimization compared with ground-truth, taking possible symmetries into account. If the trace of the relative rotation matrix for a given solution is higher than a threshold (2.99), it is considered successful. We count successful runs among 100 independent trials, drawing initial parameters from a uniform distribution around ground-truth parameters, repeated for four different standard deviations. The results in Table 1 show that our method had equal or higher success rate, indicating that our optimization problem is amenable to off-the-shelf solvers.

4.4   Reduction of Computational Cost by the Approximate Cover

Table 2 shows the number of surface points $|\mathcal{R}|$ and the number of inequality constraints, before and after computing the approximate cover. We set the ball enlargement parameter δ equal to 10 times the shortest distance between any pair of neighboring point samples of $\mathcal{R}$. The approximate cover decreased the number of inequality constraints (and thereby the number of evaluations of f_x per iteration) by 98.8%–99.2%, or about two orders of magnitude. The results in Table 1, which were obtained using the approximate cover, shows that the simplified constraints were still sufficient to resolve ill-constrained parameters.

5   Conclusion

We have presented a method for efficiently incorporating free space constraints in the classical Iterative Closest Point algorithm. It is able to resolve parameters that are ill-constrained by partial surface observations and supports any implicit model for which the distance to its surface can be computed.

Presently, our method only allows for outliers in the form of alternate structures or corrupt range values (which can be set to zero). Such outliers decrease the extent of utilizable free space. How to handle incorrect free space observations, which introduces bias, is an important question for future work.

Acknowledgments. This work is partly supported by the Research Council of Norway through the Centre of Excellence funding scheme, project number 223254, NTNU AMOS.

References

1. Besl, P.J., McKay, N.D.: A method for registration of 3-D shapes. IEEE Trans. Pattern Anal. Mach. Intell. **14**, 239–256 (1992)
2. Solina, F., Bajcsy, R.: Recovery of parametric models from range images: the case for superquadrics with global deformations. IEEE Trans. Pattern Anal. Mach. Intell. **12**, 131–147 (1990)
3. Kutulakos, K.N., Seitz, S.M.: A theory of shape by space carving. Int. J. Comput. Vis. **38**, 199–218 (2000)
4. Ganapathi, V., Plagemann, C., Koller, D., Thrun, S.: Real-time human pose tracking from range data. In: Fitzgibbon, A., Lazebnik, S., Perona, P., Sato, Y., Schmid, C. (eds.) ECCV 2012. LNCS, vol. 7577, pp. 738–751. Springer, Heidelberg (2012). https://doi.org/10.1007/978-3-642-33783-3_53
5. Schmidt, T., Newcombe, R.A., Fox, D.: DART: dense articulated real-time tracking. In: Robotics: Science and Systems (2014)
6. Tagliasacchi, A., Schröder, M., Tkach, A., Bouaziz, S., Botsch, M., Pauly, M.: Robust articulated-ICP for real-time hand tracking. In: Computer Graphics Forum, Vol. 34, pp. 101–114. Wiley Online Library (2015)
7. Tkach, A., Pauly, M., Tagliasacchi, A.: Sphere-meshes for real-time hand modeling and tracking. ACM Trans. Graph. (ToG) **35**, 1–11 (2016)
8. Tam, G.K., et al.: Registration of 3D point clouds and meshes: a survey from rigid to nonrigid. IEEE Trans. Visual. Comput. Graph. **19**, 1199–1217 (2012)
9. Zhou, Q.-Y., Park, J., Koltun, V.: Fast global registration. In: Leibe, B., Matas, J., Sebe, N., Welling, M. (eds.) ECCV 2016. LNCS, vol. 9906, pp. 766–782. Springer, Cham (2016). https://doi.org/10.1007/978-3-319-46475-6_47
10. Yang, J., Li, H., Campbell, D., Jia, Y.: Go-ICP: a globally optimal solution to 3D ICP point-set registration. IEEE Trans. Pattern Anal. Mach. Intell. **38**, 2241–2254 (2016)
11. Yang, H., Carlone, L.: In perfect shape: certifiably optimal 3D shape reconstruction from 2d landmarks. In: IEEE Conference on Computer Vision and Pattern Recognition, pp. 621–630 (2020)
12. Zhou, X., Zhu, M., Leonardos, S., Daniilidis, K.: Sparse representation for 3D shape estimation: a convex relaxation approach. IEEE Trans. Pattern Anal. Mach. Intell. **39**, 1648–1661 (2016)
13. Hart, J.C.: Sphere tracing: a geometric method for the antialiased ray tracing of implicit surfaces. Visual Comput. **12**, 527–545 (1996)
14. Barr, A.H.: Global and local deformations of solid primitives. In: SIGGRAPH, pp. 21–30. ACM (1984)
15. Pasko, A., Adzhiev, V., Sourin, A., Savchenko, V.: Function representation in geometric modeling: concepts, implementation and applications. Visual Comput. **11**, 429–446 (1995)
16. Curless, B., Levoy, M.: A volumetric method for building complex models from range images. In: SIGGRAPH, pp. 303–312. ACM (1996)
17. Newcombe, R.A., et al.: Kinectfusion: real-time dense surface mapping and tracking. In: ISMAR, pp. 127–136. IEEE (2011)

18. Jones, M.W., Baerentzen, J.A., Sramek, M.: 3D distance fields: a survey of techniques and applications. IEEE Trans. Visual. Comput. Graph. **12**, 581–599 (2006)
19. Park, J.J., Florence, P., Straub, J., Newcombe, R., Lovegrove, S.: Deepsdf: learning continuous signed distance functions for shape representation. In: IEEE Conference on Computer Vision and Pattern Recognition, pp. 165–174 (2019)
20. Chen, Y., Medioni, G.: Object modelling by registration of multiple range images. Image Vis. Comput. **10**, 145–155 (1992)
21. Fitzgibbon, A.W.: Robust registration of 2D and 3D point sets. Image Vis. Comput. **21**, 1145–1153 (2003)
22. Mitra, N.J., Gelfand, N., Pottmann, H., Guibas, L.: Registration of point cloud data from a geometric optimization perspective. In: Symposium on Geometry Processing, pp. 22–31. ACM (2004)
23. Pottmann, H., Huang, Q.X., Yang, Y.L., Hu, S.M.: Geometry and convergence analysis of algorithms for registration of 3D shapes. Int. J. Comput. Vis. **67**, 277–296 (2006)
24. Rusinkiewicz, S., Levoy, M.: Efficient variants of the ICP algorithm. In: International Conference on 3D Digital Imaging and Modeling, pp. 145–152 (2001)
25. Pentland, A.: Recognition by parts. In: Technical Report 406, SRI International. (1986)
26. Fayolle, P.A., Pasko, A.: An evolutionary approach to the extraction of object construction trees from 3D point clouds. Comput.-Aided Des. **74**, 1–17 (2016)
27. Yezzi, A., Soatto, S.: Stereoscopic segmentation. Int. J. Comput. Vis. **53**, 31–43 (2003)
28. Berger, M., et al.: A survey of surface reconstruction from point clouds. In: Computer Graphics Forum, pp. 301–329. Wiley Online Library (2017)
29. Xiao, J., Furukawa, Y.: Reconstructing the world's museums. Int. J. Comput. Vis. **110**, 243–258 (2014)
30. Du, T., et al.: InverseCSG: automatic conversion of 3D models to CSG trees. In: SIGGRAPH Asia 2018 Technical Papers, p. 213. ACM (2018)
31. Slavcheva, M., Kehl, W., Navab, N., Ilic, S.: SDF-2-SDF registration for real-time 3D reconstruction from RGB-D data. Int. J. Comput. Vis. **126**, 615–636 (2018)
32. Whitaker, R.T., Gregor, J.: A maximum-likelihood surface estimator for dense range data. IEEE Trans. Pattern Anal. Mach. Intell. **24**, 1372–1387 (2002)
33. Gargallo, P., Prados, E., Sturm, P.: Minimizing the reprojection error in surface reconstruction from images. In: IEEE International Conference on Computer Vision, pp. 1–8 (2007)
34. Ganapathi, V., Plagemann, C., Koller, D., Thrun, S.: Real time motion capture using a single time-of-flight camera. In: IEEE Conference on Computer Vision and Pattern Recognition, pp. 755–762 (2010)
35. Qian, C., Sun, X., Wei, Y., Tang, X., Sun, J.: Realtime and robust hand tracking from depth. In: IEEE Conference on Computer Vision and Pattern Recognition, pp. 1106–1113 (2014)
36. Niemeyer, M., Mescheder, L., Oechsle, M., Geiger, A.: Differentiable volumetric rendering: Learning implicit 3D representations without 3d supervision. In: IEEE Conference on Computer Vision and Pattern Recognition, pp. 3504–3515 (2020)
37. Loper, M.M., Black, M.J.: OpenDR: an approximate differentiable renderer. In: Fleet, D., Pajdla, T., Schiele, B., Tuytelaars, T. (eds.) ECCV 2014. LNCS, vol. 8695, pp. 154–169. Springer, Cham (2014). https://doi.org/10.1007/978-3-319-10584-0_11
38. Terzopoulos, D., Witkin, A., Kass, M.: Constraints on deformable models: Recovering 3D shape and nonrigid motion. Artif. Intell. **36**, 91–123 (1988)

39. Prisacariu, V.A., Segal, A.V., Reid, I.: Simultaneous monocular 2D segmentation, 3D pose recovery and 3D reconstruction. In: Lee, K.M., Matsushita, Y., Rehg, J.M., Hu, Z. (eds.) ACCV 2012. LNCS, vol. 7724, pp. 593–606. Springer, Heidelberg (2013). https://doi.org/10.1007/978-3-642-37331-2_45
40. Tsai, A., et al.: A shape-based approach to the segmentation of medical imagery using level sets. IEEE Trans. Med. Imaging **22**, 137–154 (2003)
41. Liu, S., Zhang, Y., Peng, S., Shi, B., Pollefeys, M., Cui, Z.: Dist: rendering deep implicit signed distance function with differentiable sphere tracing. In: IEEE Conference on Computer Vision and Pattern Recognition, pp. 2019–2028 (2020)
42. Tagliasacchi, A., Olson, M., Zhang, H., Hamarneh, G., Cohen-Or, D.: Vase: volume-aware surface evolution for surface reconstruction from incomplete point clouds. In: Computer Graphics Forum, vol. 30, pp. 1563–1571. Wiley Online Library (2011)
43. Mescheder, L., Oechsle, M., Niemeyer, M., Nowozin, S., Geiger, A.: Occupancy networks: learning 3D reconstruction in function space. In: IEEE Conference on Computer Vision and Pattern Recognition, pp. 4460–4470 (2019)
44. Witkin, A.P., Heckbert, P.S.: Using particles to sample and control implicit surfaces. In: SIGGRAPH, pp. 269–277. ACM (1994)
45. Siddiqi, K., Pizer, S.: Medial Representations: Mathematics, Algorithms and Applications, vol. 37. Springer, Heidelberg (2008). https://doi.org/10.1007/978-1-4020-8658-8
46. Blum, H.: A transformation for extracting new descriptors of shape. In: Models for the Perception of Speech and Visual Form. MIT Press (1967)
47. Wolter, F.E.: Cut locus and medial axis in global shape interrogation and representation. In: MIT Design Laboratory Memorandum 92-2 and MIT Sea Grant Report.(1992)
48. Ma, J., Bae, S.W., Choi, S.: 3D medial axis point approximation using nearest neighbors and the normal field. Visual Comput. **28**, 7–19 (2012)
49. Tagliasacchi, A., Delame, T., Spagnuolo, M., Amenta, N., Telea, A.: 3D skeletons: a state-of-the-art report. In: Computer Graphics Forum, vol. 35, pp. 573–597. Wiley Online Library (2016)
50. Turk, G., Levoy, M.: Zippered polygon meshes from range images. In: SIGGRAPH, pp. 311–318. ACM (1994)
51. Hoppe, H., DeRose, T., Duchamp, T., McDonald, J., Stuetzle, W.: Surface reconstruction from unorganized points. In: SIGGRAPH, pp. 71–78. ACM (1992)
52. Hodan, T., Haluza, P., Obdržálek, Š., Matas, J., Lourakis, M., Zabulis, X.: T-LESS: an RGB-D dataset for 6D pose estimation of texture-less objects. In: IEEE Winter Conference on Applications of Computer Vision, pp. 880–888. IEEE (2017)

Minimal Free Space Constraints
for Implicit Distance Bounds

Simen Haugo$^{(\boxtimes)}$ and Annette Stahl

Department of Engineering Cybernetics,
Norwegian University of Science and Technology, Trondheim, Norway
{simen.haugo,annette.stahl}@ntnu.no

Abstract. A general approach for fitting implicit models to sensor data
is to optimize an objective function measuring the quality of the fit. The
objective function often involves evaluating the model's implicit function
at several points in space. When the model is expensive to evaluate, the
number of points can become a bottleneck, making the use of volumetric
information, such as free space constraints, challenging. When the model
is the Euclidean distance function to its surface, previous work has been
able to integrate free space constraints in the optimization problem, such
that the number of distance computations is linear in the scene's surface
area. Here, we extend this work to only require the model's implicit
function to be a bound of the Euclidean distance. We derive necessary
and sufficient conditions for the model to be consistent with free space.
We validate the correctness of the derived constraints on implicit model
fitting problems that benefit from the use of free space constraints.

Keywords: 3D registration · Implicit modeling · Visibility constraints

1 Introduction

Infinite resolution, trivial support for constructive modeling operations and the
existence of closed-form expressions for a rich variety of primitives, has sparked
interest in the use of implicit models as a representation of scenes and objects.
However, the lack of an explicit surface and the open-ended domain (which may
be non-rigid and even non-differentiable) poses major challenges for their use
in model fitting. A general approach, based on optimizing an objective function
measuring the quality of the fit, often involves evaluating the associated implicit
function at multiple points in space. When the implicit function is expensive to
evaluate, the number of evaluations can become a bottleneck, making the use of
volumetric free space constraints (space observed to be empty) [1] impractical.

When the model is the Euclidean distance function to its surface, recent
work has been able to integrate free space constraints while ensuring that the
number of function evaluations remains linear in the scene's surface area [2].
Often, the Euclidean distance function is too expensive to compute efficiently,
and a distance bound is used instead [3].

© Springer Nature Switzerland AG 2020
G. Bebis et al. (Eds.): ISVC 2020, LNCS 12510, pp. 96–109, 2020.
https://doi.org/10.1007/978-3-030-64559-5_8

Contribution. We present an extension of [2] that only requires the model's implicit function to be a bound of the Euclidean distance to its surface. We derive a minimal set of necessary and sufficient conditions for the model to be consistent with free space. We validate the correctness of the derived constraints on implicit model fitting problems that benefit from the use of free space information.

2   Related Work

Distance Functions. Implicit models represent geometric objects indirectly by a function $f(p)$, which maps a given point $p \in \mathbb{R}^3$ to a scalar that, in the simplest case, indicates whether p is inside or outside the object. These have numerous applications in solid modeling [4–9], robotics [10,11], graphics [3,12], reverse engineering [13,14] and machine learning [15–17]. A special case is when $f(p)$ is equal to, or approximates, the (signed) Euclidean distance function $d(p)$, which is the distance from p to the closest point on the surface, with the sign indicating whether p is inside or outside. Discretized distance functions stored in volumetric grids are widely used in 3D reconstruction [1,18] and can easily be computed from explicit models using a distance transform [19]. Neurally-defined distance functions have recently received interest in the machine learning community as a compact and end-to-end learnable shape representation [20]. The Euclidean distance can be computed from an arbitrary implicit function by solving a constrained optimization problem, although this requires an initial estimate of the closest point on the surface to guarantee convergence [21].

A rich set of modeling operations and primitives have also been proposed for constructively defining distance-like functions [3,4]. Although the Euclidean distance function is challenging to define constructively, a bounding function can often be obtained instead [3]. In graphics, a desirable condition on the bounding function is that it does not overestimate the true distance. When f is Lipschitz, this can be ensured by identifying a Lipschitz constant, $\lambda > 0$, such that $|f| \leq \lambda |d|$. The resulting "signed distance bound", $\lambda^{-1} f$, defines everywhere an "unbounding sphere" which is guaranteed to be intersection-free. Lipschitz functions and constants have been derived for various modeling operations and primitives [3,22]. Our work uses Lipschitz functions, but we identify the additional condition that $\lambda^{-1} |f|$ should be bounded from below by a non-decreasing function of $|d|$. This lets us also avoid the error caused by underestimation of the true distance, which we use together with the Lipschitz condition to derive a minimal set of necessary and sufficient free space constraints.

Free Space Constraints. Besides points on the scene's surface, vision systems may also provide information about visibility. For example, a range measurement from a laser scanner says that not only is there a surface that far from the sensor, but also that there can be no surface in-between. The resulting "free space constraints" play a central role in 3D reconstruction [1,23–25], and are used in articulated and non-rigid model fitting to resolve model parameters that are ill-constrained from surface measurements alone [26–34].

Several works have addressed the computational challenges involved in the use of free space constraints for model fitting. When the model surface or a bound is available in explicit form, previous works have formulated efficient silhouette-based or symmetric objective functions [29,31,33,34]. For implicit models, when the model is equal to the Euclidean distance function to its surface, recent work [2] has been able to integrate free space constraints, while keeping the number of function evaluations linear in the scene's surface area. We extend the previous work [2] to only require a distance bound, thus enabling the use of more diverse implicit models without the need to compute the exact Euclidean distance.

3   Theory and Method

Our work builds on results from [2]. We summarize their main findings in Sect. 3.1. We present our extension in the subsequent sections.

3.1   Notation and Problem Formulation

Let S be a solid representing the scene and let V be a domain of interest. Free space V_{free} is a closed subset of V that is observed to be empty. The free space boundary ∂V_{free} is the boundary between free and unobserved space. The visible surface R is the observed subset of the physical scene boundary ∂S. Points in $\mathbb{R}^3$ are denoted c, p and q. A ball with center c and radius r is denoted (c, r). The signed Euclidean distance to a solid D is denoted $d_D(p) := \pm \min_{q \in \partial D} ||p - q||_2$, where the sign is negative for p inside D and positive outside.

A geometric model is given as a function $f_x(p) : \mathbb{R}^3 \times X \to \mathbb{R}$ and we seek to estimate the parameters $x \in X$ such that the solid $M_x = \{p \in \mathbb{R}^3 : f_x(p) \leq 0\}$ is consistent with the visible surface and with free space. Formally:

$$f_x(p) = 0, \quad \forall p \in R, \tag{1}$$

$$f_x(p) > 0, \quad \forall p \in \text{int } V_{\text{free}}. \tag{2}$$

These conditions can be turned into a constrained optimization problem [2]

$$\min_{x} \quad E(x) = \sum_{p \in R} f_x(p)^2 \tag{3}$$

$$\text{subject to } f_x(c) \geq r(c), \quad \forall c \in I, \tag{4}$$

where I is a set of points in V_{free} and $r(c)$ is the radius of the largest ball at c that is empty with respect to V_{free} (*i.e.* its interior contains no point of ∂V_{free}). Thus, each constraint in (4) defines a ball $(c, r(c))$ which M_x must not intersect. When $f_x = d_{M_x}$, previous work [2] has shown that the medial axis [35] of V_{free} is a minimal set of necessary and sufficient constraints I to ensure that a feasible solution of (3)–(4) is consistent with free space, *i.e.* satisfies (2).

3.2 Free Space Constraints for Distance Bounds

When $f_x \neq d_{\mathcal{M}_x}$, the constraints (4) are neither sufficient nor necessary. To resolve this, we will assume that f_x satisfies upper and lower bounds of the form

$$g(d_{\mathcal{M}_x}(c)) \leq \lambda^{-1} f_x(c) \leq d_{\mathcal{M}_x}(c), \quad \forall (c, x) \in (\mathbb{R}^3, \mathcal{X}) : f_x(c) > 0, \qquad (5)$$

where λ is a Lipschitz constant of f_x over the domain $\mathbb{R}^3 \times \mathcal{X}$ and $g(d) : \mathbb{R} \to \mathbb{R}$ is a non-decreasing function with $g(d) > 0$ for $d > 0$. We motivate the use and existence of bounds of this form in Sect. 3.4. In this section, we derive a set of necessary and sufficient free space constraints when the true distance $d_{\mathcal{M}_x}$ is unavailable, but f_x, g and λ are known. For simplicity in the derivation we will omit subscripts and write $f = f_x$, $d = d_{\mathcal{M}_x}$ and $\mathcal{M} = \mathcal{M}_x$.

Intuition. Consider the constraint $\lambda^{-1} f(c) \geq r(c)$. Observe that its satisfaction implies $d(c) \geq r(c)$. Hence, its satisfaction is a sufficient condition for $\mathcal{M}$ to not intersect the ball $(c, r(c))$. However, as f may underestimate the true distance, its violation does not imply $d(c) < r(c)$. Its satisfaction is therefore not a necessary condition. Suppose there exists a function g, such that $g(d) \leq \lambda^{-1} f$. Consider the constraint $\lambda^{-1} f(c) \geq g(r(c))$, obtained by "shrinking" the ball according to g. Observe that its satisfaction implies $d(c) \geq g(r(c))$. Hence, the "shrunk" ball $(c, g(r(c)))$ is intersection-free. Observe also that violation of the constraint implies $g(d(c)) < g(r(c))$ which, if g is non-decreasing, implies $d(c) < r(c)$. Hence, $\mathcal{M}$ intersects the "original" ball $(c, r(c))$.

Thus, if the constraint $\lambda^{-1} f(c) \geq g(r(c))$ is satisfied, the model is guaranteed to be outside the shrunk ball $(c, g(r(c)))$. If the constraint is violated, the model intersects the original ball $(c, r(c))$, though not necessarily the shrunk ball. This observation leads to Proposition 1.

Proposition 1. *Let $f_x : \mathbb{R}^3 \times \mathcal{X} \to \mathbb{R}$ be Lipschitz over the domain $\mathbb{R}^3 \times \mathcal{X}$ and let $\lambda > 0$ be an associated Lipschitz constant. Let $g : \mathbb{R} \to \mathbb{R}$ be a non-decreasing function, with $g(d) > 0$ for $d > 0$, such that $\forall (x, c) \in (\mathcal{X}, \mathcal{V}_{free}) : g(d_{\mathcal{M}_x}(c)) \leq \lambda^{-1} f_x(c)$. Let $r(c)$ be the radius of the largest ball at $c \in \mathcal{V}_{free}$ that is empty with respect to $\mathcal{V}_{free}$. Then*

$$\lambda^{-1} f_x(c) \geq g(r(c)), \quad \forall c \in \mathcal{V}_{free}, \qquad (6)$$

are necessary and sufficient conditions for f_x to satisfy the free space consistency conditions (2).

3.3 Minimal Set of Necessary and Sufficient Constraints

While the constraints (6) are necessary and sufficient, many of the associated balls can be fully contained by a larger ball. The constraints are thereby highly redundant. To obtain a minimal set of constraints, we consider each line segment connecting a point $p \in \partial \mathcal{V}_{free}$ with the point c_p that lies on the intersection of the boundary normal n_p and the medial axis of $\mathcal{V}_{free}$. That is, c_p is the point on the medial axis of $\mathcal{V}_{\text{free}}$ closest to p along n_p. We generate the shortest sequence of (shrunk) balls that cover the line segment without overlapping, by letting $c_{p,i} = p + t_{p,i} n_p$ and solving

$$t_{p,i} + g(r(c_{p,i})) = t_{p,i-1} - g(r(c_{p,i-1})), \quad i = 1, 2, ..., \tag{7}$$

successively for $t_{p,i}$ starting with $t_{p,0} = r(c_p)$. This equation requires ball i in the sequence to be tangent to ball $i - 1$. Depending on g, this may produce an infinite sequence of balls, which may be truncated in different ways. For example, by stopping or setting $t_{p,i}$ to its limit value (0) once below a desired tolerance t_{min}. If $g(d) = d$, the sequence has a length of one, as expected. When the sequences for all points $p \in \partial \mathcal{V}_{\text{free}}$ are combined, we obtain a minimal set of necessary and sufficient constraints.

Comparison with Sphere Tracing. The reader may notice a resemblence between the above and a technique used for rendering implicit surfaces known as sphere tracing [3]. One difference is that sphere tracing generates sample points based on evaluating the model, whereas the above generates sample points based on the input data. When sphere tracing is used for model fitting, it produces different sample points depending on the current model parameters. The above sample points remain the same during the optimization process. This observation enables further improvements, which we describe below (approximate cover). Sphere tracing requires the upper bound $\lambda^{-1} f \leq d$, while we also require the lower bound $g(d) \leq \lambda^{-1} f$. If $g(d) = d$, we only generate a single sample point, while sphere tracing may still take multiple steps to converge.

Approximate Cover. The minimal set may still exhibit substantial overlap between the constraints, which can lead to unnecessary computations. Because of our formulation of the bounds (5), the free space constraints are fully determined by the input data. Similar to [2], we can therefore pre-compute an "approximate cover" of free space—a simplified set of constraints that check for consistency with an approximation of free space. We may use the same heuristic as in [2] and [36], in which redundant balls are identified by checking if a given ball can be completely covered by slightly enlargening any of its neighboring balls. Like [2], we can greedily build an approximate cover by iteratively selecting the ball which covers the most uncovered balls, when its radius is increased by δ.

3.4 Upper and Lower Bounds for Some Implicit Models

The upper bound in (5) requires that f can be scaled to not overestimate the true distance d. Such functions are called signed distance bounds [3], although we only require the bound to hold when $f > 0$. When f is Lipschitz, dividing by a Lipschitz constant provides a distance bound. Several primitives and constructive modeling operations that yield functions satisfying this property, along with associated Lipschitz constants, have been described in the literature, including set operations, linear transformations, tapering and twisting [3,22].

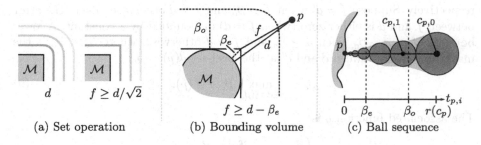

(a) Set operation   (b) Bounding volume   (c) Ball sequence

Fig. 1. (a, b): Examples of the lower bound $f \geq g(d)$ for a max-based intersection and a bounding volume. (c): Sequence of balls produced by (7) for an example bound $g(d)$.

Below, we describe two general forms of the function g required for the lower bound, based on a consideration of two common implicit modeling techniques: set operations and bounding volume hierarchies.

Set Operations. In constructive geometry, solids can be defined by successively applying set operations (union, intersection, difference) to primitives. Given the distance functions to two solids, a cheap distance-like function to their union, intersection or difference can be computed by the min and max operators [37]. While these do not yield the Euclidean distance to the resulting solid everywhere, they are guaranteed to not overestimate it [3]. As an example, the intersection between two planes is shown in Fig. 1(a), along with isolines of the Euclidean distance d and its max-based approximation f. Here, f and d are equal everywhere except when the closest point on $\partial \mathcal{M}$ is at the corner. The error between f and d grows proportionally to d, with largest growth on the diagonal extending away from the corner, where $d = \sqrt{2}f$. This gives a lower bound of the form

$$g(d) = \alpha d \tag{8}$$

with $\alpha = 1/\sqrt{2}$.

Bounding Volume Hierarchies. Bounding volumes are often used to avoid computation of geometric details when the evaluation point is sufficiently far away from the surface [3]. Figure 1(b) shows a single-stage bounding volume hierarchy, where the object $\mathcal{M}$ is bounded by a box. A bounding volume hierarchy first computes the distance to the box. If the result is greater than a threshold β_o, it is returned, terminating the computation of f. Otherwise, computation proceeds with the distance to $\mathcal{M}$. The threshold β_o is typically chosen by the model designer to be at the point where the distance to the bounding volume where it ceases to be a good approximation of the distance to the bounded object.

Consider a single-stage bounding volume hierarchy. Let d' and d be the Euclidean distance function to the bounding volume and the bounded object, respectively. Suppose $f = d'$ when $d' > \beta_o$ and $f = d$ otherwise. Then, the error between f and d is either zero (when $f = d$) or bounded by a constant. A lower bound is $f \geq d - \beta_e$ when $d \geq \beta_o$ and $f = d$ otherwise, where $\beta_e < \beta_o$ is the maximum error between d and d' at the level-set $d(p) = \beta_o$:

$$\beta_e = \max_{p \in d^{-1}(\beta_o)} \beta_o - d'(p). \tag{9}$$

The associated function g is

$$g(d) = \begin{cases} d & \text{if } d < \beta_o - \beta_e, \\ \beta_o - \beta_e & \text{if } \beta_o - \beta_e \leq d < \beta_o, \\ d - \beta_e & \text{otherwise,} \end{cases} \tag{10}$$

where the constant value in the transition region $\beta_o - \beta_e \leq d < \beta_o$ is used to ensure that g is non-decreasing.

Proportional or Constant Error. We observe that the error between f and d grew proportionally in the case of a set operation and was bounded by a constant in the case of a bounding volume hierarchy. This lead to two general forms of the function g. These can naturally be combined. An example sequence of balls produced by (7) for a function g that combines both of the above is shown in Fig. 1(c).

4   Experiments

We experimentally validate the proposed constraints. First, we show that the solution obtained using the "uncorrected" free space constraints of [2] is incorrect when $f_x \neq d_{\mathcal{M}_x}$. Second, we show that the use of the proposed "corrected" constraints (6) can resolve ill-constrained parameters when the bounds (5) are available. Finally, we study the computational cost of the proposed minimal set of constraints and the approximate cover.

Datasets and Pre-processing. We use the dataset in [2], comprised of single-view range images of objects with corresponding Euclidean distance functions. To obtain the necessary quantities ($\mathcal{R}$ and $\mathcal{I}$) for the constrained optimization problem (3)–(4), we use a pre-processing pipeline similar to [2]. For the corrected constraints, $\mathcal{I}$ is generated as described in Sect. 3.3. All results use an approximate cover for both methods. To solve the constrained optimization problem, we consider Matlab's implementation of Sequential Quadratic Programming (SQP). We also consider a non-smooth exact penalty method that replaces the constrained problem by the unconstrained problem

$$\min_x \quad \sum_{p \in \mathcal{R}} f_x(p)^2 + \mu \sum_{(c,r) \in \mathcal{I}} (\min(0, f_x(c) - r))^2 \,, \tag{11}$$

which we solve using a derivative-free (DF) solver.

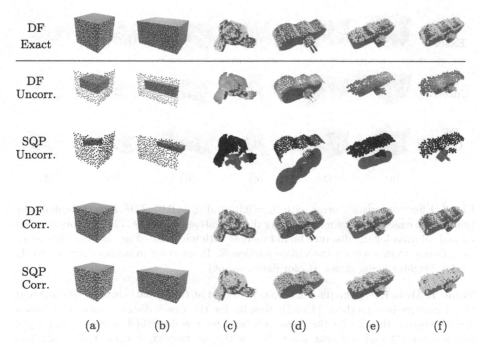

Fig. 2. Effect of proportional error with $\alpha = 0.7$. (*DF Exact*): Global solution for the exact distance models using the derivative-free solver. (*DF/SQP Uncorr./Corr.*): Global solution for the distance bound models with uncorrected or corrected free space constraints. Points are on the visible surface $\mathcal{R}$. Point color indicates distance to the model, brighter being closer. (Color figure online)

4.1 Effect of Error Between f_x and $d_{\mathcal{M}_x}$

Proportional Error. We study how a proportional error between f_x and $d_{\mathcal{M}_x}$ affects the global solution. We simulate a proportional error by replacing each model's distance function by $f_x' = \alpha f_x(p)$, for $\alpha < 1$. We compare the global solution of both solvers (DF and SQP) with and without corrected free space constraints. To find the global solution, we initialize x at ground-truth with a small random offset and run the given solver until convergence. We pick the solution with the best objective function value over 100 trials.

Constant Error. We repeat the above experiment, adding instead a single-stage bounding volume hierarchy such that $f_x'(p) = f_{x,\text{bound}}(p)$ if $f_{x,\text{bound}}(p) > \beta_o$ and $f_x'(p) = f_x(p)$ otherwise, where $f_{x,\text{bound}}$ is taken as the distance to a constant offset surface: $f_{x,\text{bound}} = f_x(p) - \beta_e$. Because the switch statement makes the model non-differentiable, we only report results using the derivative-free solver.

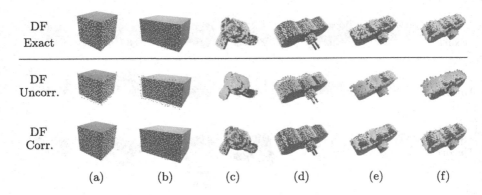

<table>
<tr><td>DF
Exact</td></tr>
<tr><td>DF
Uncorr.</td></tr>
<tr><td>DF
Corr.</td></tr>
</table>

(a)	(b)	(c)	(d)	(e)	(f)

Fig. 3. Effect of constant error with $\beta_o = 0.03$ and $\beta_e = 0.01$. (*DF Exact*): Global solution for the exact distance models using the derivative-free solver. (*DF Uncorr./Corr.*): Global solution for the distance bound models with uncorrected or corrected free space constraints. Points are on the visible surface $\mathcal{R}$. Point color indicates distance to the model, brighter being closer. (Color figure online)

Table 1. Mean Euclidean distance from $\mathcal{R}$ to $\partial\mathcal{M}$ at the global solution obtained with the derivative-free method. (*Exact*): Results for the exact distance models. (*Bound, uncorr./corr.*): Results for the distance bound models described in Sect. 4.1: proportional error (*) and constant error (**), with uncorrected or corrected constraints.

	Box (a)	Box (b)	Head (c)	Plug (d)	Plug (e)	Plug (f)
Exact	0.38	0.18	0.27	0.28	1.67	1.27
Bound*, uncorr.	17.79	18.29	10.44	11.38	16.37	17.24
Bound*, corr.	0.40	0.21	0.25	0.27	1.37	1.30
Bound**, uncorr.	2.33	3.09	2.29	2.35	2.78	3.12
Bound**, corr.	0.29	0.24	0.19	0.24	1.24	1.21

Results. The results in Fig. 2 and Fig. 3 show that when $f_x \neq d_{\mathcal{M}_x}$, uncorrected free space constraints lead to a global solution that is different from the true solution obtained using the exact distance models ($f_x = d_{\mathcal{M}_x}$). They also show that the correction with the distance bound models yields a global solution that is visually similar to the true solution. Table 1 quantifies the difference using the mean Euclidean distance from the visible surface to the model. It shows that the mean distance is one or two orders of magnitude greater without the correction and within 5–20% of true solution with the correction.

4.2 Ability to Resolve Ill-Constrained Parameters

We quantify how constrained the model parameters are at the global solution. Initializing x to ground-truth, we perform a random walk of length $k = 50$, where at each step $i = 1...k$ the current parameters are perturbed by a uniformly drawn

Table 2. Estimated number of constrained parameters out of all parameters and sum of singular values in parenthesis. (*Exact*): Results for the exact distance models. (*Bound, corr.*): Results for the distance bound models with corrected constraints.

	Box (a)	Box (b)	Head (c)	Plug (d)	Plug (e)	Plug (f)
Exact	9/9 (0.0)	8/9 (2.1)	7/7 (0.0)	9/13 (4.0)	9/13 (5.6)	9/13 (6.0)
Bound, corr.	9/9 (0.0)	8/9 (2.2)	7/7 (0.0)	9/13 (3.6)	9/13 (5.9)	9/13 (5.8)

vector $\delta \in [-\sigma, \sigma]^{|\mathcal{X}|}$, $\sigma = 0.1$, and re-optimized (using the derivative-free solver) from the perturbed position. We perform $N = 100$ random walks, which gives a matrix of solutions $X = [x_1 \cdots x_N]$ from each random walk. As a measure of the number of constrained parameters, we use the rank of X, estimated as the number of singular values less than σ. If a parameter is well-constrained, it should return to its original value after re-optimization. Singular values larger than σ indicates that one or more parameters were not constrained.

Results. Table 2 shows that the number of constrained parameters at the global solution for the distance bound models, with corrected constraints, is the same as for the exact distance models. This supports the visual results in Fig. 2 and Fig. 3 (bottom rows), where the solution is seen to acquire a fit that is only possible by the use of free space constraints (*e.g.* the dimensions of the Box (a) are correctly estimated, despite only two out the six faces being visible).

4.3 Computational Cost

Table 3 reports the number of free space constraints used by [2] and our method. It can be seen that our extension yields an increase in the number of constraints. The number of constraints produced by [2] scales linearly by the scene's surface area. A natural question is how our method scales as the scene volume grows.

To quantify this, we characterize the scale of the scene by the length r of the longest line segment pc_p between $\partial \mathcal{V}_{\text{free}}$ and the medial axis (*c.f.* Sect. 3.3). The algorithm described in Sect. 3.3 will generate the longest sequence along this line segment. Hence, an upper bound of the number of constraints is the length of the longest sequence multiplied by $|\partial \mathcal{V}_{\text{free}}|$. Figure 4 shows the sequence length as a function of r, for the proportional lower bound (8) with different values of α. We observe that the number of balls increases logarithmically as a function of r.

Therefore, our method does not scale linearly, since r may increase as the scene increases in volume. However, if the increase in r can be bounded by an appropriate factor, our method can achieve linear scaling. For example, when $\alpha = 0.8$, the number of balls along the longest line segment is constant within approximately each 10-fold increase in r. Thus, if the scene growth is bounded such that r grows by no more than a factor of 10, the number of constraints produced by our method will be linear in the scene's surface area.

Table 3. Number of surface points and (un)corrected free space constraints for the distance bound models described in Sect. 4.1: proportional error (*) and constant error (**), with (*approx.*) and without (*all*) the approximate cover.

	(a, b)	(c)	(d)	(e, f)
Surface points $|\mathcal{R}|$	686	15 806	6 827	8 730
Constraints $|\mathcal{I}|$ (all), uncorr	48 386	32 019	42 013	40 193
Constraints $|\mathcal{I}|$ (all), corr.*	118 950	93 826	98 768	99 116
Constraints $|\mathcal{I}|$ (all), corr.**	83 421	69 036	71 017	71 727
Constraints $|\mathcal{I}|$ (approx), uncorr.	432	272	320	479
Constraints $|\mathcal{I}|$ (approx), corr.*	2 722	1 046	1 776	2 646
Constraints $|\mathcal{I}|$ (approx), corr.**	1 240	493	793	1 289

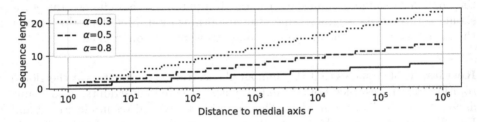

Fig. 4. Number of balls produced by the sequence (7) along a single line segment, as a function of the distance to the medial axis $r = r(c_p)$, for different α, using $t_{\min} = 1$.

Analysis of the Lower Bound for Some Implicit Models. The number of constraints added by our method depends on the lower bound g. Here, we analyze g for the implicit models shown in Fig. 5. These models are defined using min/max set operations on primitives with closed-form expressions for the Euclidean distance function. Therefore, a suitable form of the lower bound g is the form (8), parameterized by the constant α. Figure 5 (bottom) shows, for each model, the value of α and the cumulative histogram of local point-wise estimates $\hat{\alpha}(p)$ in a box region twice the size of the model. The histograms show that α is approximately 0.45, 0.09, 0.71 and 0.71, for the respective models.

For example, in Model A, $\hat{\alpha}(p) = 1/\sqrt{2}$ on the corner diagonals and $\hat{\alpha}(p) \approx 0.45$ inside the subtracted disk. The value of α is the minimum of these. The cumulative histogram for Model A shows that $\hat{\alpha}$ was less than $1/\sqrt{2}$ for only 0.5% of the points, indicating that the subset of points affected by the error between f_x and $d_{\mathcal{M}_x}$, caused by the disk subtraction, is very small. This is a shortcoming of our formulation of the lower bound, as a large error locally affects the lower bound globally. This is also seen in Model B and Model C. These models define identical solids, but Model B subtracts a closed primitive while Model C subtracts an open primitive. In Model B, the subtracted primitive's proximity near the top of the cavity causes f_x to be very small relative to $d_{\mathcal{M}_x}$, which in

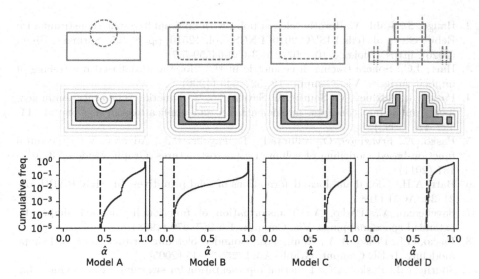

Fig. 5. Analysis of the constant α in the lower bound (8) for four models A–D. **Top:** Construction diagram of model. A dashed outline indicates that the shape is subtracted. **Middle:** Cross section of the model solid and isolines of f_x. **Bottom:** Cumulative histogram of point-wise estimates $\hat{\alpha}(p) = f_x(p)/d_{\mathcal{M}_x}(p)$ where p is taken over a region twice the size of the model and $f_x(p) > 0$. The dashed line indicates $\alpha = \min \hat{\alpha}$.

turn causes a long tail in the histogram. This is improved by the subtraction in Model C, which yields a smaller error between f_x and $d_{\mathcal{M}_x}$.

5 Conclusion

We have presented a method for integrating free space constraints in the classical Iterative Closest Point algorithm, requiring only that a bound of the distance to the model surface can be computed at a given point. Our method supports arbitrary shape spaces and provides a minimal set of sampling locations to ensure that the model is consistent with surface- and free space measurements.

Although our method does not retain the linear complexity compared to previous work [2], we do achieve linear complexity if the scene growth is bounded in terms of the largest distance to the medial axis. A relevant direction for future research is to investigate methods for further reducing the computational cost.

Acknowledgments. This work is partly supported by the Research Council of Norway through the Centre of Excellence funding scheme, project number 223254, NTNU AMOS.

References

1. Curless, B., Levoy, M.: A volumetric method for building complex models from range images. In: SIGGRAPH, pp. 303–312. ACM (1996)

2. Haugo, S., Stahl, A.: Iterative closest point with minimal free space constraints. In: Bebis, G., et al. (eds.) ISVC 2020. LNCS, vol. 12510, pp. 82–95. Springer, Cham (2020). https://doi.org/10.1007/978-3-030-64559-5_7
3. Hart, J.C.: Sphere tracing: a geometric method for the antialiased ray tracing of implicit surfaces. Vis. Comput. **12**, 527–545 (1996)
4. Pasko, A., Adzhiev, V., Sourin, A., Savchenko, V.: Function representation in geometric modeling: concepts, implementation and applications. Vis. Comput. **11**, 429–446 (1995)
5. Pasko, A., Fryazinov, O., Vilbrandt, T., Fayolle, P.A., Adzhiev, V.: Procedural function-based modelling of volumetric microstructures. Graph. Models **73**, 165–181 (2011)
6. Barr, A.H.: Global and local deformations of solid primitives. In: SIGGRAPH, pp. 21–30. ACM (1984)
7. Savchenko, V., Pasko, A.: Transformation of functionally defined shapes by extended space mappings. Vis. Comput. **14**, 257–270 (1998)
8. Pasko, G.I., Pasko, A.A., Kunii, T.L.: Bounded blending for function-based shape modeling. IEEE Comput. Graph. Appl. **25**, 36–45 (2005)
9. Sourin, A.I., Pasko, A.A.: Function representation for sweeping by a moving solid. IEEE Trans. Visual. Comput. Graph. **2**, 11–18 (1996)
10. Elfes, A.: Using occupancy grids for mobile robot perception and navigation. Computer **22**, 46–57 (1989)
11. Dragiev, S., Toussaint, M., Gienger, M.: Gaussian process implicit surfaces for shape estimation and grasping. In: IEEE International Conference on Robotics and Automation, pp. 2845–2850 (2011)
12. Seyb, D., Jacobson, A., Nowrouzezahrai, D., Jarosz, W.: Non-linear sphere tracing for rendering deformed signed distance fields. ACM Trans. Graph. (TOG) **38**, 1–12 (2019)
13. Fayolle, P.A., Pasko, A.: An evolutionary approach to the extraction of object construction trees from 3D point clouds. Comput.-Aided Des. **74**, 1–17 (2016)
14. Du, T., et al.: InverseCSG: automatic conversion of 3D models to CSG trees. In: SIGGRAPH Asia 2018 Technical Papers, p. 213. ACM (2018)
15. Mescheder, L., Oechsle, M., Niemeyer, M., Nowozin, S., Geiger, A.: Occupancy networks: learning 3D reconstruction in function space. In: IEEE Conference on Computer Vision and Pattern Recognition, pp. 4460–4470 (2019)
16. Niemeyer, M., Mescheder, L., Oechsle, M., Geiger, A.: Differentiable volumetric rendering: learning implicit 3D representations without 3D supervision. In: IEEE Conference on Computer Vision and Pattern Recognition, pp. 3504–3515 (2020)
17. Liu, S., Zhang, Y., Peng, S., Shi, B., Pollefeys, M., Cui, Z.: Dist: rendering deep implicit signed distance function with differentiable sphere tracing. In: IEEE Conference on Computer Vision and Pattern Recognition, pp. 2019–2028 (2020)
18. Newcombe, R.A., et al.: Kinectfusion: real-time dense surface mapping and tracking. In: ISMAR, pp. 127–136. IEEE (2011)
19. Jones, M.W., Baerentzen, J.A., Sramek, M.: 3D distance fields: a survey of techniques and applications. IEEE Trans. Visual. Comput. Graph. **12**, 581–599 (2006)
20. Park, J.J., Florence, P., Straub, J., Newcombe, R., Lovegrove, S.: Deepsdf: learning continuous signed distance functions for shape representation. In: IEEE Conference on Computer Vision and Pattern Recognition, pp. 165–174 (2019)
21. Besl, P.J., McKay, N.D.: A method for registration of 3-D shapes. IEEE Trans. Pattern Anal. Mach. Intell. **14**, 239–256 (1992)
22. Kalra, D., Barr, A.H.: Guaranteed ray intersections with implicit surfaces. In: SIGGRAPH, pp. 297–306 (1989)

23. Kutulakos, K.N., Seitz, S.M.: A theory of shape by space carving. Int. J. Comput. Vision **38**, 199–218 (2000)
24. Tagliasacchi, A., Olson, M., Zhang, H., Hamarneh, G., Cohen-Or, D.: Vase: volume-aware surface evolution for surface reconstruction from incomplete point clouds. In: Computer Graphics Forum, vol. 30, pp. 1563–1571. Wiley Online Library (2011)
25. Berger, M., et al.: A survey of surface reconstruction from point clouds. In: Computer Graphics Forum, pp. 301–329. Wiley Online Library (2017)
26. Gargallo, P., Prados, E., Sturm, P.: Minimizing the reprojection error in surface reconstruction from images. In: IEEE International Conference on Computer Vision, pp. 1–8 (2007)
27. Delaunoy, A., Prados, E.: Gradient flows for optimizing triangular mesh-based surfaces: applications to 3D reconstruction problems dealing with visibility. Int. J. Comput. Vision **95**, 100–123 (2011)
28. Ganapathi, V., Plagemann, C., Koller, D., Thrun, S.: Real time motion capture using a single time-of-flight camera. In: IEEE Conference on Computer Vision and Pattern Recognition, pp. 755–762 (2010)
29. Ganapathi, V., Plagemann, C., Koller, D., Thrun, S.: Real-time human pose tracking from range data. In: Fitzgibbon, A., Lazebnik, S., Perona, P., Sato, Y., Schmid, C. (eds.) ECCV 2012. LNCS, vol. 7577, pp. 738–751. Springer, Heidelberg (2012). https://doi.org/10.1007/978-3-642-33783-3_53
30. Qian, C., Sun, X., Wei, Y., Tang, X., Sun, J.: Realtime and robust hand tracking from depth. In: IEEE Conference on Computer Vision and Pattern Recognition, pp. 1106–1113 (2014)
31. Schmidt, T., Newcombe, R.A., Fox, D.: DART: dense articulated real-time tracking. In: Robotics: Science and Systems (2014)
32. Xiao, J., Furukawa, Y.: Reconstructing the world's museums. Int. J. Comput. Vision **110**, 243–258 (2014)
33. Tagliasacchi, A., Schröder, M., Tkach, A., Bouaziz, S., Botsch, M., Pauly, M.: Robust articulated-ICP for real-time hand tracking. In: Computer Graphics Forum, vol. 34, pp. 101–114. Wiley Online Library (2015)
34. Tkach, A., Pauly, M., Tagliasacchi, A.: Sphere-meshes for real-time hand modeling and tracking. ACM Trans. Graph. (ToG) **35**, 1–11 (2016)
35. Siddiqi, K., Pizer, S.: Medial Representations: Mathematics, Algorithms and Applications, vol. 37. Springer, Heidelberg (2008). https://doi.org/10.1007/978-1-4020-8658-8
36. Ma, J., Bae, S.W., Choi, S.: 3D medial axis point approximation using nearest neighbors and the normal field. Visual Comput. **28**, 7–19 (2012)
37. Ricci, A.: A constructive geometry for computer graphics. Comput. J. **16**, 157–160 (1973)

Medical Image Analysis

Fetal Brain Segmentation Using Convolutional Neural Networks with Fusion Strategies

Andrik Rampun$^{(\boxtimes)}$, Deborah Jarvis, Paul Griffiths, and Paul Armitage

Academic Unit of Radiology, Department of Infection,
Immunity and Cardiovascular Disease,
University of Sheffield, S10 2RX Sheffield, UK
{y.rampun,p.armitage}@sheffield.ac.uk

Abstract. Most of the Convolutional Neural Network (CNN) architectures are based on a single prediction map when optimising the loss function. This may lead to the following consequences; firstly, the model may not be optimised, and secondly the model may be prone to noise hence more sensitive to false positives/negatives, both resulting in poorer results. In this paper, we propose four fusion strategies to promote ensemble learning within a network architecture by combining its main prediction map with its side outputs. The architectures combine multi-source, multi-scale and multi-level local and global information collectively together with spatial information. To evaluate the performance of the proposed fusion strategies, we integrated each of them into three baseline architectures namely the classical U-Net, attention U-Net and recurrent residual U-net. Subsequently, we evaluate each model by conducting two experiments; firstly, we train all models on 200 normal fetal brain cases and test them on 74 abnormal cases, and secondly we train and test all models on 200 normal cases using a 4-fold cross validation strategy. Experimental results show that all fusion strategies consistently improve the performance of the baseline models and outperformed existing methods in the literature.

Keywords: Fetal brain segmentation · U-Net · Brain MRI · MRI · Ensemble learning

1 Introduction

Automated fetal brain segmentation is an important first step towards providing a detailed neuroimaging assessment, yet it is a challenging task due to the boundary of the fetus being indistinct, particularly towards the bottom and top slices, which can lead to under-segmentation. Furthermore, in fetal MRI, the brain often occupies a relatively small portion of the imaging field of view (FOV) and its location and orientation within the FOV can be highly variable. A recent review conducted in 2018 by Makropoulos *et al.* [1], suggests that the majority

© Springer Nature Switzerland AG 2020
G. Bebis et al. (Eds.): ISVC 2020, LNCS 12510, pp. 113–124, 2020.
https://doi.org/10.1007/978-3-030-64559-5_9

of existing studies in the literature are based on conventional image processing, such as superpixel and region growing techniques [2,3] combined with conventional classifiers such as the Support Vector Machine or Random Forests. In the last few years, several studies have developed CNN architectures for fetal brain segmentation and reported promising results.

The U-Net architecture was developed in 2015 by Ronneberger *et al.* [4] specifically for biomedical image segmentation and designed to provide accurate segmentation with a small amount of training data. In the last three years, several studies have proposed modifications to improve its performance. The most common modification is the addition of more convolutional layers. Salehi *et al.* [5] proposed a deep U-Net architecture consisting of 3-pathways which represent the coronal, axial and sagittal views. The network consists of 11-level convolutional layers in downsampling and upsampling paths. Each pathway receives different patch sizes as well as different kernel sizes to collect local and global context information. Alternatively, Schlemper *et al.* [6] developed an attention gate (AG) mechanism. They incorporated the AG mechanism into the skip connections path of the classical U-Net (attention U-Net). The AG mechanism enables the network to focus on target regions of interest by highlighting salient features, while disambiguating irrelevant and noisy responses. Experimental results show that the U-Net with AG mechanism improves the prediction performance of the classical U-Net across different datasets. Another alternative is to combine two network architectures, which enables the combined network to utilise the advantages of both networks. Alom *et al.* [7] proposed a recurrent residual (R2) U-Net by incorporating the R2 convolutional units into the classical U-Net. The main advantage is that the feature accumulation with recurrent residual convolutional layers ensures better feature representation for segmentation tasks. Experimental results demonstrate that their proposed models show superior performance compared to the classical U-Net.

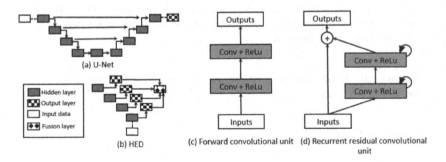

Fig. 1. A high level view of the U-Net and HED architectures and a graphical representation between forward convolutional (FC) and recurrent residual (R2) convolutional units.

In this paper, we propose four fusion strategies exploiting the network's side outputs to promote ensemble learning. Our work is motivated by the

U-Net [4] and Holistically-Nested Edge Detection (HED) [8] architectures. The U-Net architecture combines both location and contextual information, but it solely relies on a single feature map derived from previous layers. As a result, the model may not be optimised and be prone to false positives/negatives. On the other hand, the HED network combines several multi-scale and multi-level feature maps via an averaging fusion procedure, but it is less accurate in storing spatial and contextual information together, which is essential in semantic segmentation. Combining these two architectures allows us to utilise the advantages of both networks. It collectively combines multi-source, multi-scale and multi-level local and global information without loss of spatial information. Figure 1(a) and (b) shows a high level view of the U-Net and HED architectures. The U-Net architecture produces only one output layer derived from previous layers whereas the HED architecture produced several output layers before combining them via a fusion procedure.

This study has the following contributions: (a) We propose a hybrid network inspired from the classical U-Net [4] and HED [8] architectures which combines multi-scale and multi-level local and global information collectively together with spatial information. (b) In the hybrid network, we propose to use the U-Net's side outputs to promote feature fusion. Subsequently, we introduce four fusion strategies which enable the network to combine features via a fusion procedure. (c) To the best of our knowledge, our study is the largest fetal brain segmentation study in the literature, covering 274 fetal brains consisting of over 17,000 2D images. (d) We evaluate the performance of each fusion approach by training the network on 200 normal cases and testing it on 74 abnormal cases. This evaluation strategy truly challenges the model, due to the information differences between normal and abnormal cases. By comparison, all of the studies for fetal brain segmentation in the literature include normal and abnormal cases in their training dataset.

2   Methodology

Figure 2 shows two network architectures ((a) and (b)) where the classical U- Net is incorporated with the AG and R2 mechanisms, namely the attention U-Net (Att-U-Net) and recurrent residual U-Net (R2-U-Net), respectively.

Attention Gate: The AG mechanism [6] enables the model to automatically identify salient image regions and collect useful feature responses, so that only relevant activation units can be preserved. This can be done by computing the coefficients (c) for each feature map (m). Let $m^l = \{m_i^l\}_{i=1}^n$ be the feature map of the lth hidden layer where $l \in \{l, ..., L\}$), each m_i^l represents the pixel-wise feature vector of the number of channels. Therefore, for each m_i^l, its coefficient value is denoted as $c^l = \{c_i^l\}_{i=1}^n$ with a value range 0 to 1. The attention coefficients are computed as follow

$$c_i^l = \psi^T(\alpha_1(W_x^T x_i^l + W_g^T g + b_{xg})) + b_\psi \tag{1}$$

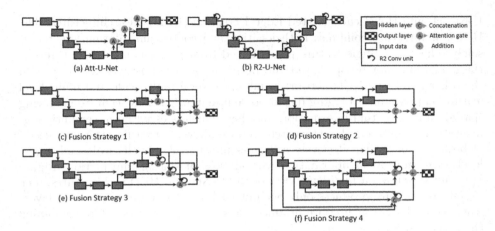

Fig. 2. Top row represents U-Net architectures combined with the AG and R2 mechanisms. Middle and bottom rows are our fusion strategies incorporated with the classical U-Net architecture.

$$c^l = \alpha_2(c_i^l(x^l, g)) \tag{2}$$

where W_x^T, W_g^T and ψ^T are linear transformations which are computed using channel-wise $1 \times 1 \times 1$ convolutions, b_ψ, b_{xg} are bias terms and g is a global feature vector (from the downsampling path).

Recurrent Residual (R2) Convolutional Unit: Schlemper *et al.* [7] incorporate a recurrent residual (R2) convolutional unit into the classical U-Net architecture instead of using the regular forward convolutional (FC) unit. Figure 1(c) and (d) show a graphical representation indicating the differences between FC and R2 units, respectively. The R2 convolutional unit has three stages. In the first stage, m_i^l is convolved with a 3×3 kernel (followed by ReLu) resulting o_i^l. The next step is performing an element-wise additive operation between these two feature maps, yielding mo_i^l. Subsequently, mo_i^l is once again convolved with a 3×3 kernel (followed by ReLu). In the second phase, the same procedure is applied to the final output obtained from the first stage. In the third stage, an element-wise additive operation is performed between m_i^l and the final output from the second stage. The main differences between FC and R2 convolutional units are; firstly the R2 unit contains four convolutional operations whereas the FC unit has only two convolutional operations and secondly the R2 unit performs an element wise additive operation between input and output whereas the FC unit does not. ***Side output:*** We employed the side output generation procedure from the original HED architecture [8]. Each m_i^l in the upsampling and downsampling paths is convolved with a 1×1 kernel with the same padding followed by the '*Conv2DTranspose*' operation with a $2f \times 2f$ kernel where f is the upsampling factor and s^l is the side output of the lth hidden layer.

Fusion Strategies (FS): Figure 2 shows four FS strategies (c, d, e and f) proposed in this study which can be incorporated into the classical U-Net architecture as well as the Att-U-Net and R2-U-Net architectures. **FS$_1$** : In Fig. 2(c), we incorporate the AG mechanism for each s^l in the upsampling path with s^L followed by an element-wise averaging procedure and 1×1 convolutional operation with the Sigmoid activation function. We apply the same strategy (element-wise averaging and 1×1 convolutional operation) to all four approaches proposed in this study. **FS$_2$** : In Fig. 2(d) we concatenate all s^l from the upsampling path of the network (except s^L) by adding each s^l in the third dimension. **FS$_3$** : In Fig. 2(e) a similar procedure to (c) was applied but the difference is that we further applied the R2 mechanism to each side output after the attention gate. **FS$_4$** : In Fig. 2(f) all s^l from the downsampling and upsampling (except s^L) paths were concatenated separately followed by the R2 mechanism. Subsequently, both outputs were averaged with s^L.

2.1 Experimental Setup

Data Augmentation: We applied the following data augmentation: i) random rotation range of up to 180°, ii) zooming in and out with a range of 0.1 to 2.0, and iii) horizontal and vertical flips.

Network Architectures: We employed the classical U-Net [4], Att-U-Net [6] and R2-U-Net [7] as baseline architectures (hence, the implementation is the same). Subsequently, we incorporate each FS approach into the baseline architectures.

Experiment Setting: All primary networks (e.g. U-net, Att-U-Net and R2-U-Net) were trained from scratch including the networks when the FS approaches are incorporated. The implementation is based on the Keras platform using the Tensorflow backend. The training and testing bed was performed on a high performance computer server with Nvidia DGX-1 graphics cards 8x Tesla P100 GPUs (16 GB RAM each), dual 20-core Intel Xeon E5-2698 2.2 GHz and 512 GB System RAM.

The network was trained with Adam optimisation with learning rate (lr) is 0.0001 and batch size (B) of 16. The number of iterations used per epoch (E) is based on the number of training samples divided by batch size $(\frac{\#n}{B})$. We monitor the Dice and Jaccard coefficients, set $E = 500$ and employ the *'EarlyStopping'* strategy on the validation set to automatically stop the training when the loss function value did not change after 50 epochs. The loss function is computed as a combination of binary cross-entropy and dice coefficient, which is described as:

$$\mathcal{L}(I_b, T_b) = -\frac{1}{B} \sum_{b=1}^{B} \left(\frac{1}{2} \cdot I_b \cdot \log T_b + \frac{2 \cdot I_b \cdot T_b}{I_b + T_b} \right) \qquad (3)$$

where I and T are the predicted probabilities and the ground truth of the bth image respectively, and B indicates the batch size.

3   Experimental Results

3.1   Data Descriptions

Our first dataset consisted of MR images of 200 healthy fetuses (over 10,000 images) with gestational age (GA) ranging between 18 and 37 weeks. Our second dataset consisted of MR images of 74 abnormal fetuses (over 6,000 images) with GA between 20 to 34 weeks. The abnormal cases consisted of the following abnormalities: agenesis of corpus callosum (ACC), mild ventriculomegaly (MV) and structurally deformed.

For each image, the brain was manually segmented by an expert radiographer with over 10 years experience (trained by an expert neuro-radiologist) using the '3D Slicer' software. All studies were performed on 1.5 T whole body scanner (Signa HDx, GE Healthcare) with an 8-channel cardiac coil positioned over the maternal abdomen. All images were acquired using a 3D FIESTA sequence, which is a 3D gradient echo steady state free precision sequence (TR = 5.1 ms, TE = 2.5 ms, α = 60°), slice thickness used varies according to gestational age/size of fetal head so can range 2.0 mm and 2.6 mm, and acquisition time = 20 s.

The following metrics are used to quantitatively evaluate the performance of the method: Jaccard $(J) = \frac{TP}{TP+FN+FP}$, Dice $(D) = \frac{2 \times TP}{FN+(2 \times TP)+FP}$, Accuracy $(Acc) = \frac{TN+TP}{TN+FN+TP+FP}$, Sensitivity $(Sn) = \frac{TP}{FN+TP}$ and Precision $(Pr) = \frac{TP}{TP+FP}$. These are the most common evaluation metrics used in previous fetal brain segmentation studies [5,7,9–11]. The TP, TN, FP and FN represent true positive, true negative, false positive and false negative, respectively.

3.2   Quantitative Results

In this study, we employed the classical U-Net [4], R2-U-Net [7] and Att-U-Net [6] as the baseline models. For experiment one, we trained each network architecture with 200 healthy fetal brains (80% training and 20% validation) and tested it on 74 abnormal fetal brains.

Table 1 shows that the FS_4 improved the performance of the original U-Net in terms of J (↑ 1.21%), D (↑ 0.85%), and Sn (↑ 1.34%) metrics (the ↑ indicates an improvement value). This strategy truly challenged the robustness of the model because it can only learn features from normal cases without any information from abnormal cases. It should be noted that the abnormal cases are different to the normal cases in terms of geometrical information. The FS_3 improved the accuracy of the original U-Net by 0.02%, while the FS_1 improved the original U-Net performance on Pr by 0.31%. Moreover, the FS_4 improved the performance of the R2-U-Net in most metrics. The R2-U-Net produced $J = 75.98\%$, $D = 84.15\%$ and $Sn = 82.61\%$ whereas the FS_4-R2-U-Net produced $J = 78.37\%(2.39\%)$, $D = 86.16\%(2.01\%)$ and $Sn = 86.70\%(4.09\%)$. For the Att-U-Net baseline model, once again the fusion strategies improved its performance across different evaluation metrics. The FS_4 produced the best results for

Table 1. Experiment 1 (abnormal cases): Each network was trained with 200 healthy cases and tested on 74 abnormal cases. The number of parameters (complexity) and training time indicated as C_X (millions) and t (hours), respectively.

Model	C_X	t	$J(\%)$	$D(\%)$	$A(\%)$	$Sn(\%)$	$Pr(\%)$
U-Net [4]	31.38 M	38	75.55 ± 7.81	83.69 ± 5.51	99.76 ± 0.89	83.56 ± 5.31	86.73 ± 4.81
FS$_1$-U-Net	31.39 M	34	75.31 ± 7.82	83.41 ± 5.64	99.75 ± 0.89	82.61 ± 5.51	**87.04 ± 4.74**
FS$_2$-U-Net	31.60 M	28	75.79 ± 7.61	83.74 ± 5.11	99.77 ± 0.89	83.95 ± 5.22	86.03 ± 4.82
FS$_3$-U-Net	32.06 M	34	75.95 ± 7.51	83.92 ± 4.96	**99.78 ± 0.89**	84.79 ± 5.08	85.72 ± 4.93
FS$_4$-U-Net	31.82 M	31	**76.76 ± 7.42**	**84.54 ± 4.82**	99.77 ± 0.90	**84.90 ± 5.13**	85.75 ± 4.23
R2-U-Net [7]	24.16 M	35	75.98 ± 7.78	84.15 ± 5.32	99.75 ± 0.90	82.61 ± 5.86	87.04 ± 3.98
FS$_1$-R2-U-Net	24.17 M	30	78.29 ± 7.56	85.86 ± 5.28	99.80 ± 0.89	85.54 ± 5.13	88.22 ± 3.88
FS$_2$-R2-U-Net	24.23 M	30	77.33 ± 7.67	84.93 ± 5.50	99.80 ± 0.89	83.98 ± 5.54	88.13 ± 3.79
FS$_3$-R2-U-Net	24.34 M	30	77.34 ± 7.67	85.09 ± 5.49	99.80 ± 0.90	83.70 ± 5.55	**88.79 ± 3.67**
FS$_4$-R2-U-Net	24.28 M	32	**78.37 ± 7.52**	**86.16 ± 5.46**	**99.81 ± 0.89**	**86.70 ± 5.29**	87.45 ± 3.88
Att-U-Net [6]	31.90 M	28	76.01 ± 7.79	84.18 ± 5.32	99.78 ± 0.89	83.71 ± 5.54	87.36 ± 3.87
FS$_1$-Att-U-Net	31.91 M	30	77.38 ± 7.76	85.01 ± 5.30	99.80 ± 0.90	85.45 ± 5.23	87.55 ± 3.76
FS$_2$-Att-U-Net	32.12 M	38	77.06 ± 7.81	84.71 ± 5.51	99.79 ± 0.89	86.61 ± 5.17	85.61 ± 4.06
FS$_3$-Att-U-Net	31.91 M	28	77.78 ± 7.71	85.65 ± 5.22	99.80 ± 0.89	86.01 ± 5.15	**87.79 ± 3.87**
FS$_4$-Att-U-Net	31.91 M	30	**78.61 ± 7.52**	**86.21 ± 5.24**	**99.81 ± 0.92**	**86.85 ± 5.18**	87.50 ± 3.83

Table 2. Experiment 2 (normal cases): Each network was trained using the 4-fold cross validation strategy based on 200 healthy cases. The number of parameters (complexity) and training time indicated as C_X (millions) and t (hours), respectively.

Model	C_X	t	$J(\%)$	$D(\%)$	$A(\%)$	$Sn(\%)$	$Pr(\%)$
U-Net [4]	31.38 M	32	77.62 ± 7.34	85.42 ± 5.76	99.71 ± 0.81	94.04 ± 5.79	80.37 ± 5.61
FS$_1$-U-Net	31.39 M	27	80.45 ± 6.91	87.75 ± 5.41	99.77 ± 0.79	93.09 ± 5.43	84.39 ± 4.98
FS$_2$-U-Net	31.60 M	24	80.01 ± 7.01	87.32 ± 5.57	99.76 ± 0.87	**94.81 ± 5.34**	82.47 ± 4.22
FS$_3$-U-Net	32.06 M	26	**81.08 ± 6.11**	**88.14 ± 4.23**	99.77 ± 0.89	94.13 ± 5.81	**84.43 ± 4.07**
FS$_4$-U-Net	31.82 M	27	80.84 ± 6.62	88.12 ± 4.23	**99.78 ± 0.87**	94.43 ± 5.73	83.97 ± 4.06
R2-U-Net [7]	24.16 M	30	81.13 ± 7.05	88.21 ± 4.96	**99.80 ± 0.89**	94.74 ± 5.04	84.92 ± 4.29
FS$_1$-R2-U-Net	24.17 M	24	81.98 ± 7.56	88.91 ± 5.28	99.78 ± 0.97	94.61 ± 5.13	85.12 ± 4.28
FS$_2$-R2-U-Net	24.23 M	25	82.31 ± 6.25	89.31 ± 4.96	**99.80 ± 0.89**	94.58 ± 5.34	85.52 ± 4.29
FS$_3$-R2-U-Net	24.34 M	24	**82.56 ± 6.68**	**89.41 ± 5.12**	99.78 ± 0.96	94.58 ± 5.16	**85.79 ± 4.01**
FS$_4$-R2-U-Net	24.28 M	27	81.57 ± 6.11	88.71 ± 5.36	**99.80 ± 0.87**	**94.87 ± 4.99**	84.32 ± 3.67
Att-U-Net [6]	31.90 M	23	79.37 ± 6.98	87.13 ± 4.32	99.75 ± 0.91	93.96 ± 5.32	82.87 ± 5.87
FS$_1$-Att-U-Net	31.91 M	25	80.46 ± 6.87	87.99 ± 4.30	**99.80 ± 0.90**	94.09 ± 5.27	83.89 ± 5.66
FS$_2$-Att-U-Net	32.12 M	30	**81.13 ± 7.05**	**88.21 ± 4.96**	**99.80 ± 0.89**	94.74 ± 5.04	84.92 ± 4.29
FS$_3$-Att-U-Net	31.91 M	24	80.21 ± 6.99	88.01 ± 5.12	**99.80 ± 0.89**	94.54 ± 5.05	83.98 ± 5.01
FS$_4$-Att-U-Net	31.91 M	26	80.41 ± 7.32	87.83 ± 5.46	**99.79 ± 0.86**	94.45 ± 5.52	83.35 ± 3.89

$J = 78.61\%$, $D = 86.21\%$, $A = 99.81\%$ and $Sn = 86.85\%$, whereas the FS$_3$-Att-U-Net produced best results for $Pr = 87.79\%$. The FS$_3$ approach improved the R2-U-Net performances on Pr by 1.75%.

Experiment two aims to evaluate the performance of our fusion strategies using a 4-fold cross validation strategy. For this purpose, we used the first dataset (200 healthy cases). Experimental results in Table 2 once again suggest that our fusion strategies improved the baseline models (U-Net, R2-U-Net and Att-U-Net) across different evaluation metrics. The most noticeable improvement is by the FS$_3$-U-Net boosting the J value of the classical U-Net [4] by 3.46%. The same fusion model also produced the highest improvement of the same baseline model in terms of D metric by 2.72%. The performances of the other baseline models (R2-U-Net [7] and Att-U-Net [6]) slightly improved when integrated with the fusion strategies. For example, the Pr and Sn metrics of the FS_2-Att-U-Net and FS_4-R2-U-Net models improved by 2.05% and 0.13%, respectively. On the other hand, all models produced similar results for accuracy.

In terms of model complexity (C_X) and training time (t), both are measured based on the number of trainable parameters and time taken (hours) for the model to converge. Tables 1 and 2 show that the fusion strategies add a very small number of trainable parameters (0.01 to 0.68 million) to the baseline models. The attention gate introduced by Schlemper et $al.$ [6] increased the number of trainable parameters of the classical U-Net [4] by 0.52 million. By comparison, the R2 convolution units decreased the number of trainable parameters of the U-Net [4] by over six millions. For training time, we found that integrating a fusion strategy into the baseline model (e.g. U-Net) reduced the training time, therefore the model tended to converge faster. Our explanation is due to ensemble learning mechanism within the network which tend to optimise the model faster by reducing the variance of predictions and generalisation error. For example, the U-Net model took 38 and 32 h to converge in experiment one and two respectively. Integrating any of the fusion strategies decreased the convergence time by four to ten hours for both experiments. However, the Att-U-Net converged faster than its FS variants by approximately 2 to 7 h. Our explanation for this is due to the AG mechanism. From our experience, we found that in some cases the AG mechanism focuses multiple regions of interests (more priority to train the model based on these regions) within the image, particularly at the higher spatial levels in the downsampling part. Unfortunately, one or two of them are false positives. This means the side outputs also contains these false positive regions. In the fusion layer, these false positive regions contribute to the model error, hence taking more time for the model to converge (i.e. minimise the loss function).

Figure 3 shows examples of segmentation results randomly selected from the first and second datasets. For case A, it can be clearly observed that the classical U-Net model over-segments the region outside the fetal brain (red line) resulting in a large number of false positives. The FS_3-U-Net improved the segmentation result in terms of dice similarity coefficient from 89.80% to 94.91% ($\uparrow$ 5.11%). The FS_1-U-Net and FS_4-U-Net produced similar dice score of 89.07% and 88.32%, respectively. For case B, the brain is structurally distorted which makes the shape of the brain completely different compared to normal/healthy brains. The R2-U-Net and FS_2-R2-U-Net failed to segment one part the brain (red line) completely. However, the segmentation is improved by the FS_1-R2-U-Net producing a dice score of 91.66% followed by the FS_4-R2-U-Net with a dice score of 89.37%. Case C represents a healthy brain with a ghosting artifact (red arrow). It can be observed that the Att-U-Net, FS_1-Att-U-Net and FS_4-Att-U-Net models are affected by this noise. However, the FS_2-Att-U-Net and FS_3-Att-U-Net successfully segment this region as a part of the brain, improving the segmentation of the baseline model (e.g. Att-U-Net) by 0.88% and 1.19%, respectively.

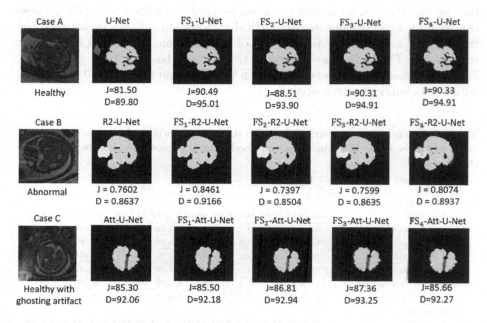

Fig. 3. Examples of segmentation for healthy, abnormal and noisy cases. TP (cyan), TN (black), FP (red) and FN (yellow). (Color figure online)

3.3 Quantitative Comparison

Table 3 shows quantitative comparisons between the best performing fusion models against other methods in the literature. The same training/testing strategy was employed as in experiment one and two. For normal/healthy cases, the FS_3-R2-U-Net outperformed the other methods in terms of Jaccard coefficient (82.56%), dice score (89.41%) and precision (85.79%). However, the R2-U-Net [7] produced the best results in terms of accuracy (99.80%) and sensitivity (94.74%). The HED network architecture is the fastest model to converge with approximately 15 h training time (14.86 millions trainable parameters) but produced the worst results across different metrics. The 3U-Net [5] model has the highest number of trainable parameters (68.82 millions) taking approximately 36 h to train. The model produced Jaccard and dice scores of 78.31% and 87.11%, respectively. The baseline models employed in this study (e.g. Att-U-net and R2-U-Net) produced very similar results to our proposed fusion model (FS_3-R2-U-Net) across different evaluation metrics with less than 2% difference.

For abnormal cases, our fusion model with the attention gate mechanism (FS_4-Att-U-Net) outperformed the other methods except for accuracy which is only 0.01% lower than the 3U-Net [5]. The R2-U-Net [7], Att-U-Net [6], and 3U-Net [5] share similar dice score of just over 84%. The HED model once again produced the worst results across different metrics. It should be noted that for this dataset, all models produced Jaccard coefficients below 79%. These results were expected due to geometrical information differences between the training and testing datasets. In terms of training time, all models took longer to converge. This is because they were trained on a larger dataset (200 cases). For normal cases, models were trained on 150 cases and tested on 50 cases using 4-fold cross validation strategy.

Table 3. Quantitative comparison between the best performing fusion models against other methods in the literature. Each method is ranked based on J score followed by the D score.

Model (Year)	C_X	t	$J(\%)$	$D(\%)$	$Sn(\%)$	$Pr(\%)$
Normal cases						
FS$_3$-R2-U-Net	24.34 M	24	**82.56 ± 6.68**	**89.41 ± 5.12**	94.58 ± 5.16	**85.79 ± 4.01**
Alom et al. (2018) [7]	24.16 M	30	81.13 ± 7.05	88.21 ± 4.96	**94.74 ± 5.04**	84.92 ± 4.29
Schlemper et al. (2019) [6]	31.91 M	23	79.37 ± 6.98	87.13 ± 4.32	93.96 ± 5.32	82.87 ± 5.87
Salehi et al. (2017) [5]	68.82 M	36	78.31 ± 7.91	87.11 ± 4.32	93.89 ± 5.32	81.29 ± 5.58
Badrinarayanan et al. (2017) [12]	27.62 M	31	77.64 ± 7.66	85.98 ± 5.76	94.04 ± 5.79	80.40 ± 5.59
Ronneberger et al. (2015) [4]	31.38 M	32	77.62 ± 7.34	85.42 ± 5.76	94.04 ± 5.79	80.37 ± 5.61
Xie and Tu (2015) [8]	14.86 M	15	75.42 ± 7.46	82.62 ± 5.92	92.11 ± 5.52	79.95 ± 5.91
Abnormal cases						
FS$_4$-Att-U-Net	31.91 M	30	**78.61 ± 7.52**	**86.21 ± 5.24**	**86.85 ± 5.18**	**87.50 ± 3.83**
Schlemper et al. (2019) [6]	31.91 M	28	76.01 ± 7.79	84.18 ± 5.32	83.71 ± 5.54	87.36 ± 3.87
Salehi et al. (2017) [5]	68.82 M	41	76.51 ± 7.82	84.12 ± 4.99	84.89 ± 5.12	87.39 ± 4.78
Alom et al. (2018) [7]	24.16 M	35	75.98 ± 7.78	84.15 ± 5.32	82.61 ± 5.86	87.04 ± 3.98
Ronneberger et al. (2015) [4]	31.38 M	38	75.55 ± 7.81	83.69 ± 5.51	83.56 ± 5.31	86.73 ± 4.81
Badrinarayanan et al. (2017) [12]	27.62 M	38	75.21 ± 8.96	82.18 ± 5.76	82.14 ± 5.39	84.41 ± 5.19
Xie and Tu (2015) [8]	14.86 M	19	71.23 ± 10.71	79.26 ± 9.32	81.11 ± 5.52	73.76 ± 5.61

4   Discussion and Conclusion

In this study, we thoroughly evaluate the robustness of each proposed fusion strategy. Firstly, by training them on normal cases followed by testing on abnormal cases. Secondly, we tested them on 200 healthy brain fetuses using a 4-fold cross validation strategy. Both experimental results suggest that our fusion strategies consistently improved the performance (e.g. Jaccard coefficient and dice score) of the baseline models such as the classical U-Net [4], R2-U-Net [7] and Att-U-Net [6]. When comparing with the state-of-the-art, our models outperformed some of the latest deep learning models in the literature particularly in terms of Jaccard coefficient, dice score and precision metrics. In fact, the FS$_4$-Att-U-Net produced the highest sensitivity score of 86.85% for abnormal cases.

Although the fusion strategies increase the number of trainable parameters by 0.01 up to 0.68 million, they decrease the training time whilst increasing the performance of the baseline models by up to 4.09%. By comparison to the other models in Table 3, the number of trainable parameters of our models are considered 'medium' yet capable of producing competitive results.

The main advantage of using a fusion strategy is that it optimises the model by averaging several prediction maps, reducing false positives/negatives. Furthermore, this strategy promotes ensemble learning to the network which reduces the variance of predictions and generalization errors. Finally, fusion strategies also allow the network to recover important cues that might disappear due to repetitive convolution operations. For example, some cues might only be available at a certain spatial level of the network. These cues might disappear after many convolutions. In this case the fusion strategy recovers these cues from both paths of the network via side outputs. Therefore, instead of optimising the loss function solely based on a single prediction map, the fusion strategy combines several activation/prediction maps.

In conclusion, we have presented four fusion strategies inspired by a combination of the classical U-Net and HED architectures. Each of the proposed fusion approaches can be easily integrated into other network architectures such as the SegNet [12] and V-Net [13]. Experimental results suggest that incorporating these fusion strategies into the classical U-Net, R2-U-Net and Att-U-Net improved the performance across different models. The FS_4 approach tends to improve the performance of most evaluation metrics, particularly J, D, A and Sn. For future work, we plan to evaluate the methods on different datasets such as liver, breast, lung, prostate, etc., as well as incorporating the fusion strategies into different backbone architectures, such as the SegNet [12] and V-Net [13].

References

1. Makropoulos, A., Counsell, S.J., Rueckert, D.: A review on automatic fetal and neonatal brain MRI segmentation. NeuroImage **170**, 231–248 (2018)
2. Alansary, A., et al.: Automatic brain localization in fetal MRI using superpixel graphs. In: Proceedings of Machine Learning Meets Medical Imaging, pp. 13–22 (2015)
3. Achanta, R., Shaji, A., Smith, K., Lucchi, A., Fua, P., Susstrunk, S.: SLIC superpixels compared to state-of-the-art superpixel methods. IEEE Trans. Pattern Anal. Mach. Intell. **34**(11), 2274–2281 (2012)
4. Ronneberger, O., Fischer, P., Brox, T.: U-Net: convolutional networks for biomedical image segmentation. In: Navab, N., Hornegger, J., Wells, W.M., Frangi, A.F. (eds.) MICCAI 2015. LNCS, vol. 9351, pp. 234–241. Springer, Cham (2015). https://doi.org/10.1007/978-3-319-24574-4_28
5. Salehi, S.S.M., Erdogmus, D., Gholipour, A.: Auto-context convolutional neural network (Auto-Net) for brain extraction in magnetic resonance imaging. IEEE Trans. Med. Imaging **36**(11), 2319–2330 (2017)
6. Schlemper, J., et al.: Learning to leverage salient regions in medical images: attention gated networks. Med. Image Anal. **53**, 197–207 (2019)

7. Alom, M.Z., Hasan, M., Yakopcic, C., Taha, T.M., Asari., V.K.: Recurrent Residual Convolutional Neural Network based on U-Net (R2U-Net) for Medical Image Segmentation in medical images, arXiv preprint arXiv:1802.06955 (2018)
8. Xie, S., Tu, Z.: Holistically-nested edge detection. In: Proceedings of IEEE International Conference on Computer Vision and Pattern Recognition, pp. 1395–1403 (2015)
9. Link, D., et al.: Automatic measurement of fetal brain development from magnetic resonance imaging: new reference data. Fetal Diagn. Ther. **43**(2), 113–122 (2018)
10. Kainz, B., Keraudren, K., Kyriakopoulou, V., Rutherford, M., Hajnal, J.V., Rueckert, D.: Fast fully automatic brain detection in fetal MRI using dense rotation invariant image descriptors. In: 2014 IEEE 11th International Symposium on Biomedical Imaging (ISBI), Beijing, pp. 1230–1233 (2014). https://doi.org/10.1109/ISBI.2014.6868098
11. Rajchl, M., et al.: DeepCut: object segmentation from bounding box annotations using convolutional neural networks. IEEE Trans. Med. Imaging **36**(2), 674–683 (2017). https://doi.org/10.1109/TMI.2016.2621185
12. Badrinarayanan, V., Kendall, A., Cipolla, R.: SegNet: a deep convolutional encoder-decoder architecture for image segmentation. IEEE Trans. Pattern Anal. Mach. Intell. **39**(12), 2481–2495 (2017)
13. Milletari, F., Navab, N., Ahmadi, S.-A.: V-Net: fully convolutional neural networks for volumetric medical image segmentation. In: Medical Image Computing and Computer Assisted Interventions- MICCAI. Springer, Cham, October 2016. http://arxiv.org/abs/1606.04797

Fundus2Angio: A Conditional GAN Architecture for Generating Fluorescein Angiography Images from Retinal Fundus Photography

Sharif Amit Kamran[1(✉)], Khondker Fariha Hossain[2], Alireza Tavakkoli[1], Stewart Zuckerbrod[3], Salah A. Baker[4], and Kenton M. Sanders[4]

[1] University of Nevada, Reno, NV 89557, USA
skamran@nevada.unr.edu
[2] Deakin University, Melbourne, Australia
[3] Houston Eye Associates, Houston, TX 77801, USA
[4] University of Nevada School of Medicine, Reno, NV 89557, USA

Abstract. Carrying out clinical diagnosis of retinal vascular degeneration using Fluorescein Angiography (FA) is a time consuming process and can pose significant adverse effects on the patient. Angiography requires insertion of a dye that may cause severe adverse effects and can even be fatal. Currently, there are no non-invasive systems capable of generating Fluorescein Angiography images. However, retinal fundus photography is a non-invasive imaging technique that can be completed in a few seconds. In order to eliminate the need for FA, we propose a conditional generative adversarial network (GAN) to translate fundus images to FA images. The proposed GAN consists of a novel residual block capable of generating high quality FA images. These images are important tools in the differential diagnosis of retinal diseases without the need for invasive procedure with possible side effects. Our experiments show that the proposed architecture achieves a low FID score of 30.3 and outperforms other state-of-the-art generative networks. Furthermore, our proposed model achieves better qualitative results indistinguishable from real angiograms.

Keywords: Generative adversarial networks · Image-to-image translation · Fluorescein Angiography · Retinal fundoscopy

1 Introduction

For a long time Fluorescein Angiography (FA) combined with Retinal Funduscopy have been used for diagnosing retinal vascular and pigment epithelial-choroidal diseases [18]. The process requires the injection of a fluorescent dye which appears in the optic vein within 8–12 s depending on the age and cardio-vascular structure of the eye and stays up to 10 min [16]. Although generally

© Springer Nature Switzerland AG 2020
G. Bebis et al. (Eds.): ISVC 2020, LNCS 12510, pp. 125–138, 2020.
https://doi.org/10.1007/978-3-030-64559-5_10

considered safe, there have been reports of mild to severe complications due to allergic reactions to the dye [1]. Frequent side effects can range from nausea, vomiting, anaphylaxis, heart attack, to anaphylactic shock and death [15]. In addition, leakage of fluorescein in intravaneous area is common. However, the concentration of fluorescein solutions don't have any direct impact on adverse effects mentioned above [24].

Given the complications and the risks associated with this procedure, a non-invasive, affordable, and computationally effective procedure is quite imperative. The only current alternatives to flourecein angigraphy (FA) is carried out by Optical Coherence Tomography and basic image processing technique. These systems are generally quite expensive. Without a computationally effective and financially viable mechanism to generate reliable and reproducible flourecein angiograms, the only alternative is to utilize retina funduscopy for differential diagnosis. Although automated systems consisting of image processing and machine learning algorithms have been proposed for diagnosing underlying conditions and diseases from fundus images [20], there has not been an effective effort to generate FA images from retina photographs. In this paper, we propose a novel conditional Generative Adversarial Network (GAN) called Fundus2Angio, capable of synthesizing fluorescein angiograms from retinal fundus images. The procedure is completely automated and does not require any human intervention. We use both qualitative and quantitative metrics for testing the proposed architecture. We compare the proposed architecture with other state-of-the-art conditional GANs [10,23,26]. Our model outperforms these networks in terms of quantitative measurement. For qualitative results, expert ophthalmologists were asked to distinguish fake angiograms from a random set of balanced real and fake angiograms over two trials. Results show that the angiograms generated by the proposed network are quite indistinguishable from real FA images.

2   Literature Review

Generative adversarial networks have revolutionized many image manipulation tasks such as image editing [25], image styling [4], and image style transfer [23,26]. Multi-resolution architectures are common practice in computer vision, while coupled architectures have the capability to combine fine and coarse information from images [2]. Recently, techniques on Conditional [9] and Unconditional GANs [3] have explored the idea of combined-resolutions within the architecture for domain specific tasks. Inspired by this, we propose an architecture that extract features at different scales.

Some approaches also used multi-scale discriminators for style-transfer [23]. However, they only attached discriminators with generator that deals with fine features while ignoring discriminators for coarse generator completely. In order to learn useful features at coarsest scale, separate multi-scale discriminators are necessary. Our proposed architecture employs this for both coarse and fine generators.

For high quality image synthesis, a pyramid network with multiple pairs of discriminators and generators has also been proposed, termed SinGAN [21].

Though it produces high quality synthesized images, the model works only on unpaired images. To add to this problem, each generator's input is the synthesized output produced by the previous generator. As a result, it can't be employed for pair-wise image training that satisfies a condition. To alleviate from this problem, a connection needs to be established that can propagate feature from coarse to fine generator. In this paper, we propose such an architecture that has a feature appending mechanism between the coarse and fine generators, making it a two level pyramid network with multi-scale discriminators as illustrated in Fig. 1.

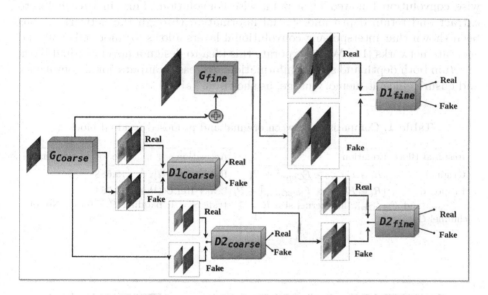

Fig. 1. Proposed Generative Adversarial Network consisting of two Generators G_{coarse}, G_{fine}, and four discriminators $D1_{coarse}$, $D1_{fine}$, $D2_{fine}$, $D2_{coarse}$. The generators take Fundus image as input and outputs FA image. Whereas, the discriminators take both Fundus and FA images as input and outputs if the pairs are real or fake.

3   The Proposed Methodology

This paper introduces a new conditional generative adversarial network (GAN) comprising of a novel residual block for producing realistic FA from retinal fundus images. First, we introduce the residual block in Sect. 3.1. We then delve into the proposed conditional GAN encompassing of fine and coarse generators and four multi-scale discriminators in Sects. 3.2 and 3.3. Lastly, in Sect. 3.4, we discuss the objective function and loss weight distributions for each of the architectures that form the proposed architecture.

3.1   Novel Residual Block

Recently, residual blocks have become the norm for implementing many image classification, detection and segmentation architectures [7]. Generative architectures have employed these blocks in interesting applications ranging from image-to-image translation to super-resolution [11,23]. In its atomic form, a residual unit consists of two consecutive convolution layers. The output of the second layers is added to the input, allowing for deeper networks. Computationally, regular convolution layers are expensive compared to a newer convolution variant, called separable convolution [5]. Separable convolution performs a depth-wise convolution followed by a point-wise convolution. This, in turn helps to extract and retain depth and spatial information through the network. It has been shown that interspersing convolutional layers allows for more efficient and accurate networks [12]. We incorporate this idea to design a novel residual block to retain both depth and spatial information, decrease computational complexity and ensure efficient memory usage, as shown in Table 1.

Table 1. Comparison between original and proposed residual block

Residual Block	Equation	Activation	No. of parameters[a]
Original	$\left[R_i \circledast F_{Conv} \circledast F_{Conv}\right] + R_i$	ReLU (Pre) [7]	18,688
Proposed	$\left[R_i \circledast F_{Conv} \circledast F_{SepConv}\right] + R_i$	Leaky-ReLU (Post)	10,784

[a] F_{Conv} and $F_{SepConv}$ has kernel size $K = 3$, stride $S = 1$, padding $P = 0$ and No. of channel $C = 32$.

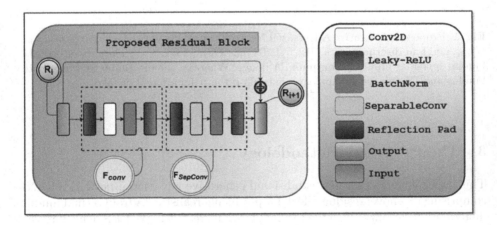

Fig. 2. Proposed Residual Block consisting of two residual units F_{conv} and $F_{SepConv}$. First one cosists of Reflection padding, Convolution, Batch-Normalization and Leaky-ReLU layers. The second one has some layers except has Separable Convolution instead of Vanilla Convolution. R_i and R_{i+1} signifies input and output of the residual block

As illustrated in Fig. 2, we replace the last convolution operation with a separable convolution. We also use Batch-normalization and Leaky-ReLU as post activation mechanism after both convolution and separable Convolution layers. For better results, we incorporate reflection padding as opposed to zero-padding before each convolution operation. The entire operation can be formulated as shown in Eq. 1:

$$R_{i+1} = \left[R_i \circledast F_{Conv} \circledast F_{SepConv} \right] + R_i$$
$$= F(R_i) + R_i \tag{1}$$

Here, $\circledast$ refers to convolution operation while F_{conv} and $F_{SepConv}$ signify the back-to-back convolution and separable convolution operations. By exploiting convolution and separable convolution layer with Leaky-ReLU, we ensure that two distinct feature maps (spatial & depth information) can be combined to generate fine fluorescein angiograms.

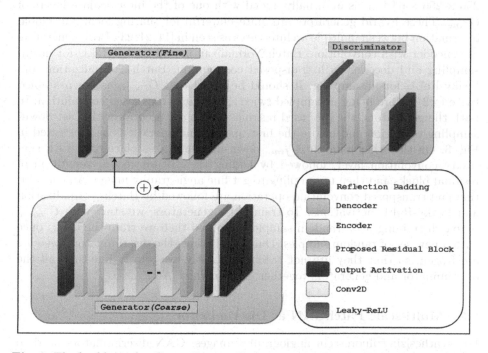

Fig. 3. The backbone for G_{fine}, G_{coarse} Generators and $D1$, $D2$ Discriminator Architectures. The G_{fine} consists of two encoding blocks (light green), followed by three residual blocks (purple) and one decoding block (orange). The G_{coarse} consists of four encoding blocks (light green), followed by nine residual blocks (purple) and three decoding blocks (orange). The discriminator consists of three encoding block (light green). Both the generators have intermediate Conv2D, Reflection padding layer and TanH as output activation function. Whereas, discriminators have intermediate Conv2D, Leaky-ReLU layers and Sigmoid as output activation. (Color figure online)

3.2   Coarse and Fine Generators

Using a coarse-to-fine generator for both conditional and unconditional GANs results in very high quality image generation, as observed in recent architectures, such as pix2pixHD [23] and SinGan [21]. Inspired by this idea, we use two generators (G_{fine} and G_{coarse}) in the proposed network, as illustrated in Fig. 3. The generator G_{fine} synthesizes fine angiograms from fundus images by learning local information, including retinal venules, arterioles, hemorrhages, exudates and microaneurysms. On the other hand, the generator G_{coarse} tries to extract and preserve global information, such as the structures of the macula, optic disc, color, contrast and brightness, while producing coarse angiograms.

The generator G_{fine} takes input images of size 512×512 and produces output images with the same resolution. Similarly, the generator G_{coarse} network takes an image with half the size (256×256) and outputs an image of the same size as the input. In addition, the G_{coarse} outputs a feature vector of the size $256 \times 256 \times 64$ that is eventually added with one of the intermediate layers of G_{fine}. These hybrid generators are quite powerful for sharing local and global information between multiple architectures as seen in [11,21,23]. Both generators use encoder with convolution, Batch-Normalizaiton and Leaky-ReLU for downsampling and decoder wtih transposed convolution, Batch-Normalization and Leaky-ReLU for upsampling. It should be noted that G_{coarse} is downsampled twice ($\times 2$) before being upsampled twice again with transposed convolution. In both the generators, the proposed residual blocks are used after the last downsampling operation and before the first upsampling operations as illustrated in Fig. 3. On the other hand, in G_{fine}, downsampling takes place once with necessary convolution layer, followed by adding the feature vector, repetition of residual blocks and then upsampling to get fine angiography image. All convolution and transposed convolution operation are followed by Batch-Normalization and Leaky-ReLU activations. To train these generators, we start with G_{coarse} by batch-training it on random samples once and then we train the G_{fine} once with a new set of random samples. During this time, the discriminator's weights are frozen, so that they are not trainable. Lastly, we jointly fine-tune all the discriminator and generators together to train the GAN.

3.3   Multi-scale PatchGAN as Discriminator

For synthesizing fluorescein angiography images, GAN discriminators need to adapt to coarse and fine generated images for distinguishing between real and fake images. To alleviate this problem, we either need a deeper architecture or, a kernel with wider receptive field. Both these solutions result in over fitting and increase the number of parameters. Additionally, a large amount of processing power will be required for computing all the parameters. To address this issue, we exploit the idea of using two Markovian discriminators, first introduced in a technique called PatchGAN [14]. This technique takes input from different scales as previously seen in [21,23].

We use four discriminators that have a similar network structure but operate at different image scales. Particularly, we downsample the real and generated angiograms by a factor of 2 using the Lanczos sampling to create an image pyramid of three scales (original and 2×downsampled and 4× downsampled). We group the four discriminators into two, $D_{fine} = [D1_{fine}, D2_{fine}]$ and $D_{coarse} = [D1_{coarse}, D2_{coarse}]$ as seen in Fig. 1. The discriminators are then trained to distinguish between real and generated angiography images at the three distinct resolutions respectively.

The outputs of the PatchGAN for D_{fine} are 64×64 and 32×32 and for D_{coarse} are 32×32 and 16×16. With the given discriminators, the loss function can be formulated as given in Eq. 2. It's a multi-task problem of maximizing the loss of the discriminators while minimizing the loss of the generators.

$$\min_{G_{fine}, G_{coarse}} \max_{D_{fine}, D_{coarse}} \mathcal{L}_{cGAN}(G_{fine}, G_{coarse}, D_{fine}, D_{coarse}) \qquad (2)$$

Despite discriminators having similar network structure, the one that learns feature at a lower resolution has the wider receptive field. It tries to extract and retain more global features such as macula, optic disc, color and brightness etc to generate better coarse images. In contrast, the discriminator that learns feature at original resolution dictates the generator to produce fine features such as retinal veins and arteries, exudates etc. By doing this we combine feature information of global and local scale while training the generators independently with their paired multi-scale discriminators.

3.4   Weighted Object Function and Adversarial Loss

We use LSGAN [17] for calculating the loss and training our conditional GAN. The objective function for our conditional GAN is given in Eq. 3.

$$\mathcal{L}_{cGAN}(G, D) = \mathbb{E}_{x,y}\big[(D(x,y) - 1)^2 \big] + \mathbb{E}_x\big[(D(x, G(x)) + 1))^2 \big] \qquad (3)$$

where the discriminators are first trained on the real fundus, x and real angiography image, y and then trained on the the real fundus, x and fake angiography image, $G(x)$. We start with training the discriminators D_{fine} and D_{coarse} for couple of iterations on random batches of images. Next, we train the G_{coarse} while keeping the weights of the discriminators frozen. Following that, we train the the G_{fine} on a batch of random samples in a similar fashion. We use Mean-Squared-Error (MSE) for calculating the individual loss of the generators as shown in Eq. 4.

$$\mathcal{L}_{L2}(G) = \mathbb{E}_{x,y}\|G(x) - y\|^2 \qquad (4)$$

where, $\mathcal{L}_{L2}$ is the reconstruction loss for a real angiogram, y, given a generated angiogram, $G(x)$. We use this loss for both G_{fine} and G_{coarse} so that the model can generate high quality angiograms of different scales. Previous techniques have also exploited this idea of combining basic GAN objective with a

MSE loss [19]. From Eq. 3 and 4 we can formulate our final objective function as given in Eq. 5.

$$\min_{G_{fine}, G_{coarse}} \max_{D_{fine}, D_{coarse}} \mathcal{L}_{cGAN}(G_{fine}, G_{coarse}, D_{fine}, D_{coarse})$$
$$+\lambda\big[\ \mathcal{L}_{L2}(G_{fine}) + \mathcal{L}_{L2}(G_{coarse})\big] \tag{5}$$

Here, λ dictates either to prioritize the discriminators or the generators. For our architecture, more weight is given to the reconstruction loss of the generators and thus we pick a large λ value.

4   Experiments

In the following section, different experimentation and evaluation is provided for our proposed architecture. First we elaborate about the data preparation and pre-prossessing scheme in Sect. 4.1. We then define our hyper-parameter settings in Sect. 4.2. Following that, different architectures are compared based on some quantitative and qualitative evaluation metrics in Sect. 4.3. Lastly, and Sect. 4.4,

4.1   Dataset

For training, we use the funuds and angiography data-set provided by Hajeb et al. [6]. The data-set consists of 30 pairs of diabetic retinopathy and 29 pairs normal of angiography and fundus images from 59 patients. Because, not all of the pairs are perfectly aligned, we select 17 pairs for our experiment based on alignment. The images are either perfectly aligned or nearly aligned. The resolution for fundus and angiograms are as follows 576×720. Fundus photographs are in RGB format, whereas angiograms are in Gray-scale format. Due to shortage of data, we take 50 random crops of size 512×512 from each images for training our model. So, the total number of training sample is 850 (17×50).

4.2   Hyper-parameter Tuning

LSGAN [17] was found to be effective for generating desired synthetic images for our tasks. We picked $\lambda = 10$ (Eq. 5). For optimizer, we used Adam with learning rate $\alpha = 0.0002$, $\beta_1 = 0.5$ and $\beta_2 = 0.999$. We train with mini-batches with batch size, $b = 4$ for 100 epochs. It took approximately 10 h to train our model on an NVIDIA RTX2070 GPU.

4.3   Qualitative Evaluation

For evaluating the performance of the network, we took 14 images and cropped 4 sections from each quadrant of the image with a size of 512×512. We conducted two sets of experiments to evaluate both the network's robustness to global

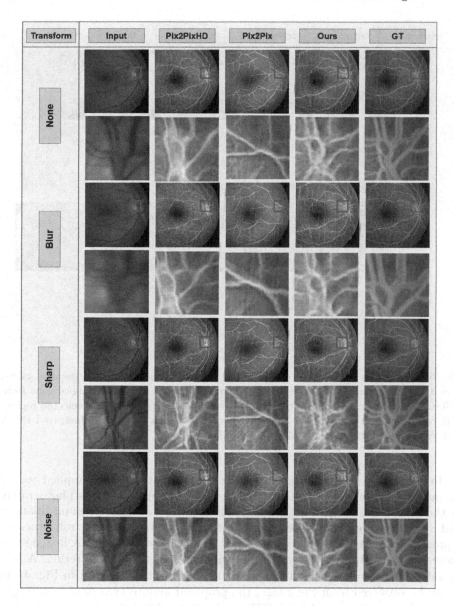

Fig. 4. Angiogram generated from transformed Fundus images. The first row shows the original image, ground truth and generated angiograms from different architectures. The second row shows the closed-up version of a selected region. The red bounding box signifies that specific region. Each row pairs illustrated None, Blur, Sharp and Noise transformations.

changes to the imaging modes and its ability to adapt to structural changes to the vascular patterns and structure of the eye. We used GNU Image Manipulation Program (GIMP) [22] for transforming and distorting images.

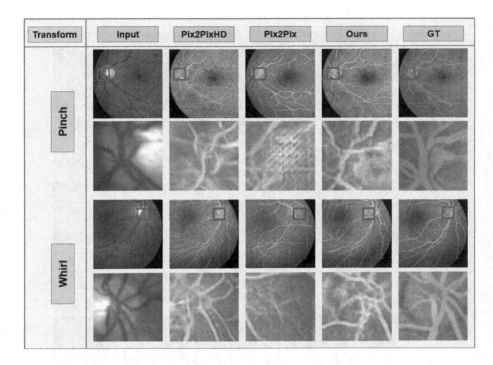

Fig. 5. Angiogram generated from distorted Fundus images with biological markers. The first row shows the original image, ground truth and generated angiograms from different architectures. The second row shows the closed-up version of a selected region. The red bounding box signifies that specific region. Each row pairs illustrated Pinch and Whirl transformations. (Color figure online)

In the first set of experiments, three transformations were applied to the images: 1) blurring to represent out of focus funduscopy or fundus photography in the presence of severe cataracts, 2) sharpening to represent pupil dilation, and 3) noise to represent interference during photography. Good robustness is represented by the generated angiograms similarity to the real FA image since these transformation do not affect the vascular structure of the retina. A side by side comparison of different architecture's prediction is shown in Fig. 4. As it can be observed from the image, the proposed architecture produces images very similar to the ground-truth (GT) under these global changes applied to the fundus image.

In the case of **blurred** fundus images, our model is less affected compared to other architectures, as seen in the second row of Fig. 4– structure of smaller veins are preserved better compared to Pix2Pix and Pix2PixHD.

In the case of **sharpened** images, the angiogram produced by Pix2Pix and Pix2PixHD show vein-like structures introduced in the back, which are not present in our prediction. These are seen in the third row of Fig. 4.

In the case of **noisy** images, as seen in the last row of Fig. 4 our prediction is still unaffected with this pixel level alteration. However, both Pix2Pix and Pix2PixHD fails to generate thin and small vessel structures by failing to extract low level features.

In the second set of experiments we modified the vascular pattern of the retina and the fundus images. These structural changes are represented by two different types of distortions: 1) pinch, representing the flattening of the retina resulting in the pulled/pushed retinal structure, and 2) whirl, representing retina distortions caused by increased intra-ocular pressure (IOP). Good adaptation to structural changes in the retina is achieved if the generated angiograms are similar to the angiograms with changed vascular structure. The effects of Pinch and Whirl on predicted angiogram is illustrated in Fig. 5.

Pinch represents the globe flattening condition, manifesting vascular changes on the retina as a result of distortions of retinal subspace. This experiment shows the adaptability and reproduciblity of the proposed network to uncover the changes in vascular structure. From the first row in Fig. 5 it is evident that our model can effectively locates the retinal vessels compared to other proposed techniques.

Whirl represented changes in the IOP or vitreous changes in the eye that may result in twists in the vascular structure. Similar to pinch, the network's ability to adapt to this structural change can be measured if the generated FA image is similar to the real angiogram showing the changed vascular structure. As seen in the last row of Fig. 5 our network encodes the feature information vessel structures, and is much less affected this kind of distortion. The other architectures failed to generate micro vessel structure as it can be seen in Fig. 5.

4.4 Quantitative Evaluations

For quantitative evaluation, we also performed two experiments. In the first experiment we use the Fréchet inception distance (FID) [8] that has been used to evaluate similar style-transfer GANs [13]. We computed the FID scores for different architectures on the generated FA image and original angiogram, and those generated from the changed fundus images by the five global and structural changes –i.e., blurring, sharpening, noise, pinch, and whirl. The results are reported in Table 2. It should be noted that, lower FID score means better results.

Table 2. Fréchet inception distance (FID) for different architectures

Architecture	Orig.	Noise	Blur	Sharp	Whirl	Pinch
Ours	**30.3**	**41.5** (11.2↑)	**32.3** (2.0↑)	**34.3** (4.0↑)	**38.2** (7.9↑)	**33.1** (2.8↑)
Pix2PixHD [23]	42.8	53.0 (10.2↑)	43.7 (1.1↑)	47.5 (4.7↑)	45.9 (3.1↑)	39.2 (3.6↓)
Pix2Pix [10]	48.6	46.8 (1.8 ↓)	50.8 (2.2↑)	47.1 (1.5↓)	43.0 (5.6↓)	43.7 (4.9↓)

From Table 2, using the original fundus image, the FID of our network angiogrm is 30.3, while other techniques are at least 10 points worse, Pix2PixHD (42.8) and Pix2Pix (48.6). For the case of noisy images, the FID for Pix2Pix dropped slightly but increased for both Pix2PixHD and our technique. Notice that the FID for our technique is still better than both Pix2Pix and Pix2PixHD. For all other changes, the FID score of our technique increased slightly but still outperformed Pix2Pix and Pix2PixHD in both robustness and adaptation to the structural changes.

Table 3. Results of qualitative with undisclosed portion of fake/real experiment

	Results		Average		
	Correct	Incorrect	Missed	Found	Confusion
Fake	15%	85%	53%	48%	**52.5%**
Real	80%	20%			

In the next experiment we evaluate the quality of the generated angiograms by asking experts (e.g. ophthalmologists) to identify fake angiograms among a collection of 40 balanced (50%, 50%) and randomly mixed angiograms. For this experiment, the experts were not told how many of the images are real and how many are fake. The non-disclosed ratio of fake and real images was a significant design choice for this experiment, as it will allow us to evaluate three metrics: 1) incorrectly labeled fake images representing how real the generated images look, 2) correctly labeled real images representing how accurate the experts recognized angiogram salient features, and 3) the confusion metric representing how effective the overall performance of our proposed method was in confusing the expert in the overall experiment. The results are shown in Table 3.

As it can be seen from Table 3, experts assigned 85% of the fake angiogams as real. This result shows that experts had difficulty in identifying fake images, while they easily identified real angiograms with 80% accuracy. Overall, the experts misclassified 53% of all images. This resulted in a confusion factor of 52.5%. This is significant, as the confusion factor of 50% is the best achievable result.

5   Conclusion

In this paper, we introduced Fundus2Angio, a novel conditional generative architecture that capable of generating angiograms from retinal fundus images. We further demonstrated its robustness, adaptability, and reproducibility by synthesizing high quality angiograms from transformed and distorted fundus images. Additionally, we illustrated how changes in biological markers do not affect the adaptability and reproducibility of synthesizing angiograms by using our technique. This ensures that the proposed architecture effectively preserves known biological markers (e.g. vascular patterns and structures). As a result, the proposed network can be effectively utilized to produce accurate FA images for the same patient from his or her fundus images over time. This allows for a better control on patient's disease progression monitoring or to help uncover newly developed diseases or conditions. One future direction to this work is to improve upon this work to incorporate retinal vessel segmentation and exudate localization.

References

1. Brockow, K., Sánchez-Borges, M.: Hypersensitivity to contrast media and dyes. Immunol. Allergy Clin. **34**(3), 547–564 (2014)
2. Brown, M., Lowe, D.G., et al.: Recognising panoramas. In: ICCV, vol. 3, p. 1218 (2003)
3. Chen, Q., Koltun, V.: Photographic image synthesis with cascaded refinement networks. In: Proceedings of the IEEE International Conference on Computer Vision. pp. 1511–1520 (2017)
4. Chen, W., Hays, J.: Sketchygan: towards diverse and realistic sketch to image synthesis. In: Proceedings of the IEEE Conference on Computer Vision and Pattern Recognition, pp. 9416–9425 (2018)
5. Chollet, F.: Xception: Deep learning with depthwise separable convolutions. In: Proceedings of the IEEE Conference on Computer Vision and Pattern Recognition. pp. 1251–1258 (2017)
6. Hajeb Mohammad Alipour, S., Rabbani, H., Akhlaghi, M.R.: Diabetic retinopathy grading by digital curvelet transform. Comput. Math. Methods Med. **2012**, 761901 (2012)
7. He, K., Zhang, X., Ren, S., Sun, J.: Identity mappings in deep residual networks. In: Leibe, B., Matas, J., Sebe, N., Welling, M. (eds.) ECCV 2016. LNCS, vol. 9908, pp. 630–645. Springer, Cham (2016). https://doi.org/10.1007/978-3-319-46493-0_38
8. Heusel, M., Ramsauer, H., Unterthiner, T., Nessler, B., Hochreiter, S.: Gans trained by a two time-scale update rule converge to a local nash equilibrium. In: Advances in Neural Information Processing Systems, pp. 6626–6637 (2017)
9. Huang, X., Li, Y., Poursaeed, O., Hopcroft, J., Belongie, S.: Stacked generative adversarial networks. In: Proceedings of the IEEE Conference on Computer Vision and Pattern Recognition, pp. 5077–5086 (2017)
10. Isola, P., Zhu, J.Y., Zhou, T., Efros, A.A.: Image-to-image translation with conditional adversarial networks. In: Proceedings of the IEEE Conference on Computer Vision and Pattern Recognition, pp. 1125–1134 (2017)
11. Johnson, J., Alahi, A., Fei-Fei, L.: Perceptual losses for real-time style transfer and super-resolution. In: Leibe, B., Matas, J., Sebe, N., Welling, M. (eds.) ECCV 2016. LNCS, vol. 9906, pp. 694–711. Springer, Cham (2016). https://doi.org/10.1007/978-3-319-46475-6_43
12. Kamran, S.A., Saha, S., Sabbir, A.S., Tavakkoli, A.: Optic-net: a novel convolutional neural network for diagnosis of retinal diseases from optical tomography images. In: 2019 18th IEEE International Conference on Machine Learning and Applications (ICMLA), pp. 964–971 (2019)
13. Karras, T., Laine, S., Aila, T.: A style-based generator architecture for generative adversarial networks. In: Proceedings of the IEEE Conference on Computer Vision and Pattern Recognition, pp. 4401–4410 (2019)

14. Li, C., Wand, M.: Precomputed real-time texture synthesis with Markovian generative adversarial networks. In: Leibe, B., Matas, J., Sebe, N., Welling, M. (eds.) ECCV 2016. LNCS, vol. 9907, pp. 702–716. Springer, Cham (2016). https://doi.org/10.1007/978-3-319-46487-9_43
15. Lira, R.P.C., Oliveira, C.L.D.A., Marques, M.V.R.B., Silva, A.R., Pessoa, C.D.C.: Adverse reactions of fluorescein angiography: a prospective study. Arquivos brasileiros de oftalmologia 70(4), 615–618 (2007)
16. Mandava, N., Reichel, E., Guyer, D., et al.: Fluorescein and ICG angiography. St. Louis: Mosby 106, 800–808 (2004)
17. Mao, X., Li, Q., Xie, H., Lau, R.Y., Wang, Z., Paul Smolley, S.: Least squares generative adversarial networks. In: Proceedings of the IEEE International Conference on Computer Vision, pp. 2794–2802 (2017)
18. Mary, V.S., Rajsingh, E.B., Naik, G.R.: Retinal fundus image analysis for diagnosis of glaucoma: a comprehensive survey. IEEE Access 4, 4327–4354 (2016)
19. Pathak, D., Krahenbuhl, P., Donahue, J., Darrell, T., Efros, A.A.: Context encoders: feature learning by inpainting. In: Proceedings of the IEEE Conference on Computer Vision and Pattern Recognition, pp. 2536–2544 (2016)
20. Poplin, R., et al.: Prediction of cardiovascular risk factors from retinal fundus photographs via deep learning. Nat. Biomed. Eng. 2(3), 158 (2018)
21. Shaham, T.R., Dekel, T., Michaeli, T.: Singan: Learning a generative model from a single natural image. In: Proceedings of the IEEE International Conference on Computer Vision, pp. 4570–4580 (2019)
22. Team, G., et al.: GIMP: GNU Image Manipulation Program. GIMP Team (2019)
23. Wang, T.C., Liu, M.Y., Zhu, J.Y., Tao, A., Kautz, J., Catanzaro, B.: High-resolution image synthesis and semantic manipulation with conditional gans. In: Proceedings of the IEEE Conference on Computer Vision and Pattern Recognition, pp. 8798–8807 (2018)
24. Yannuzzi, L.A., et al.: Fluorescein angiography complication survey. Ophthalmology 93(5), 611–617 (1986)
25. Zhu, J.-Y., Krähenbühl, P., Shechtman, E., Efros, A.A.: Generative visual manipulation on the natural image manifold. In: Leibe, B., Matas, J., Sebe, N., Welling, M. (eds.) ECCV 2016. LNCS, vol. 9909, pp. 597–613. Springer, Cham (2016). https://doi.org/10.1007/978-3-319-46454-1_36
26. Zhu, J.Y., Park, T., Isola, P., Efros, A.A.: Unpaired image-to-image translation using cycle-consistent adversarial networks. In: Proceedings of the IEEE International Conference on Computer Vision, pp. 2223–2232 (2017)

Multiscale Detection of Cancerous Tissue in High Resolution Slide Scans

Qingchao Zhang(ID), Coy D. Heldermon(ID), and Corey Toler-Franklin(✉)(ID)

University of Florida, Gainesville, FL 32611, USA
ctoler@cise.ufl.edu
https://www.cise.ufl.edu

Abstract. We present an algorithm for multi-scale tumor (chimeric cell) detection in high resolution slide scans. The broad range of tumor sizes in our dataset pose a challenge for current Convolutional Neural Networks (CNN) which often fail when image features are very small (8 pixels). Our approach modifies the effective receptive field at different layers in a CNN so that objects with a broad range of varying scales can be detected in a single forward pass. We define rules for computing adaptive prior anchor boxes which we show are solvable under the equal proportion interval principle. Two mechanisms in our CNN architecture alleviate the effects of non-discriminative features prevalent in our data - a foveal detection algorithm that incorporates a cascade residual-inception module and a deconvolution module with additional context information. When integrated into a Single Shot MultiBox Detector (SSD), these additions permit more accurate detection of small-scale objects. The results permit efficient real-time analysis of medical images in pathology and related biomedical research fields.

Keywords: Deep learning · Convolutional neural networks · Tumor tissue · Classification · Digital pathology

1 Introduction

Deep learning algorithms have been effective for detecting and classifying metastatic cancer in medical images. Breast cancer detection in histopathology images [1] and pulmonary lung cancer classification in CT scans [26] are examples which are essential for cancer diagnosis, staging and treatment [24]. CNN models are at the forefront of image-based classification methods that analyze high-resolution slide scans to detect tumors in tissue [5,17,40,42]. These automated approaches are more efficient than manual methods or traditional supervised machine learning techniques that require hand-labeled annotations from practitioners with specialized expertise.

We address challenges with CNN-based tumor (chimeric cell) detection and classification in medical datasets where tumor sizes vary significantly, and may be as small 8 pixels. We propose a method to optimize the size and distribution of SSD [29] priors (anchor boxes) and adjust the receptive field to include

© Springer Nature Switzerland AG 2020
G. Bebis et al. (Eds.): ISVC 2020, LNCS 12510, pp. 139–153, 2020.
https://doi.org/10.1007/978-3-030-64559-5_11

more context. SSD is suited for tumor detection because it identifies multi-scale objects in one shot using information from multiple CNN layers. Priors, pre-computed bounding boxes that closely match the distribution of ground truth boxes, are used to define effective detection regions across scales. However, limitations with SSD make it less effective on microscopic scans in our domain. The range of prior anchor box sizes is fixed and limited. It is difficult to select the most effective prior anchor box parameters for a given dataset. Moreover, results are inconsistent for less discriminating features (a known characteristic of pathology datasets). Our approach increases the number of detectable scales by adaptively changing the aspect ratio of prior anchor boxes and modifying the receptive field to include a broader range of context and background information. Although additional context information has improved detection performance at deeper CNN layers in spatial recurrent neural networks [2,9,22], the results have only been tested on nature scenes [7]. We incorporate an iterative anchor box refinement algorithm [45] that enhances performance. The result is an effective small object detector [3,31] capable of locating tiny features. Compared to prior methods, our approach achieves higher detection rates for a broader range of object sizes in a single session. Our contributions include:

- Adaptive prior anchor boxes which we demonstrate are solvable under an equal proportion interval principle.
- A foveal detection module that incorporates local context using cascade residual-inception modules.
- A deconvolution module that incorporates a broader range of background information.

2 Related Work

Object detection approaches related to our work can be divided into proposal-based and proposal-free frameworks.

Proposal-based methods are composed of proposal generation and classification stages. R-CNN [12] is an example that uses selective search [39] and edge boxes [50] for computing detection probabilities. Several modifications have been proposed to improve speed. Fast R-CNN [11] incorporates shared convolutional layers [14]. Faster R-CNN further increases accuracy and speed by replacing traditional proposal generation with proposal subnetworks [35]. R-FCN [6] uses all convolutional layers and score maps for improved prediction results. Sematic segmentation-aware [10,49] and Mask R-CNN [13] approaches showed that context and segmentation integration improves detection accuracy. FPN [28] used pyramidal features to detect multi-scale objects. HyperNet and Relation Networks utilize object relationships to improve accuracy [18,23].

Proposal-free methods are faster than two-stage proposal-based methods. The first successful proposal-free detector, YOLO [33,34], applies a single neural network to the entire image. The image is automatically divided into regions for computing bounding box predictions. SSH [32] uses integrated context information for face detection. SSD [29] is another example that utilizes multi-scale information to boost both accuracy and speed in a single framework. SSD has been particularly successful for face detection [46]. One key advantage of adopting SSD for tumor detection in medical images is it's ability to identify multiple size tumors in one session using multi-layer information. For this reason, SSD is extensively used to detect cancer in CT [27], endoscopic [16] and ultrasound images [4]. Several SSD variants integrate context information to increase accuracy [2,3,9,15]. We include pyramidal structures and adaptive prior anchors in a proposal-free approach. Although modifying SSD prior anchor boxes have been explored [22,47], and refinements proposed for better detection performance [45–47], our approach is unique because we adaptively adjust prior anchor box aspect ratios, and provide anchor box distribution rules that increase accuracy in microscopic slide scans. We also focus on optimizations for very small objects (which are often not detectable).

3   Adaptive Prior Anchors

We choose SSD as a starting point for our algorithm because, unlike scale-normalized detectors, it is better at detecting objects of multiple sizes. Figure 1 depicts the range of image-based feature sizes in our dataset of patches. In this section, we present details of our CNN architecture and SSD modifications.

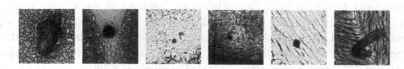

Fig. 1. The size of image-based features in our patch samples range from 8–300 pixels. Chimeric maternal cell clusters in offspring. Patch size: 300 × 300.

High-Resolution Detection Layers: Our base convolutional network is VGG16 [37]. The stride and receptive field size of layers in VGG16 increases with higher layers [43]. However, the resolution decreases as shown in Fig. 2. The smaller objects in deeper layers will have much less information. For example, an object of size 32 × 32 pixels will only have an effective region of 2 × 2 pixles in *conv5_3*. Therefore, we must rely on the shallow but high-resolution layers to detect small tumors. In our work, we add additional high-resolution *conv3_3* and *conv5_3* layers and remove SSD layers with strides that are too large. The details of our implementation are summarized in Table 1.

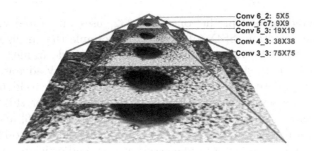

Fig. 2. Our multiple feature maps and detection layers.

Table 1. Implementation parameters: detection layer, stride, anchor size, aspect ratio (AR) and receptive field (RF)

Detection layer	Stride	Anchor size	Anchor AR	RF
$conv3\_3$	4	16	$1, 2, \frac{1}{2}$	48
$conv4\_3$	8	32	$1, \frac{3}{2}, 3, \frac{2}{3}, \frac{1}{3}$	108
$conv5\_3$	16	64	$1, \frac{3}{2}, 3, \frac{2}{3}, \frac{1}{3}$	228
$conv\_fc\_7$	32	128	$1, \frac{3}{2}, 3, \frac{2}{3}, \frac{1}{3}$	340
$conv6\_2$	64	256	$1, \frac{3}{2}, \frac{2}{3}$	468

Equal-Proportion Interval Aanchors: The effective receptive field is smaller than the theoretical receptive field [30]. Therefore, anchors in each layer should be smaller than the responding theoretical receptive field. We adopt the equal-proportion interval principle [46] which insures that anchors possess equal density compared to other methods (like the regular-space method in SSD). Comparing Fig. 3(a) and 3(b), equal-proportion interval anchors are better suited for multi-scale detection given the distribution of tumors in our images (more anchors at smaller but denser tumor regions). In addition, anchors that conform to the equal-proportion rule are more easily integrated into the receptive field and stride. This is because the receptive field and stride in SSD detection layers increase at a near proportional rate. Table 1 shows our anchor design.

Aspect Ratio Design: The aspect ratio (AR) defines the anchor profile. Here we adopt the width and height relationship:

$$W_{anchor} = size \cdot \sqrt{AR} \qquad (1)$$

$$H_{anchor} = \frac{size}{\sqrt{AR}} \qquad (2)$$

All previous anchor-based object detection frameworks [29, 36, 46] use a subjective *rule of thumb* to determine AR. **We propose an AR design criterion.** (1) AR values should be as small as possible to reduce the total number of anchors. (2) AR values must be large enough to cover almost every object (at least 99%)

to have a good recall. (3) AR values may differ from layer-to-layer depending on the detection criteria of the layer. In Sect. 4, we give a mathematical proof that the maximum AR (mAR) of anchors is only relevant to the threshold of intersection-over-union (IoU) and mAR of objects if the anchor of different layers are designed by the equal-proportion interval principle. The maximum anchors' AR (mAR_{anchor}) in each layer shall be chosen by Eq. 3

$$mAR_{anchor} =$$

$$mAR_{obj} \cdot max\{(\frac{2}{1 + \frac{1}{IoU}})^2, \frac{IoU}{2 - 2IoU}, IoU\} \qquad (3)$$

where $mAR_{obj} = sup_{i \in \Omega}\{AR_{obj}^i\}$, AR_{obj} is the objects' AR.

According to our statistics, 99% of the AR of the samples in our tumor datasets are less than 6 pixels. Most of the exceeding 1% of samples result from bad cropping (i.e. only cutting edges of the stained region). Therefore, we select the mAR_{obj} as 6. We choose IoU as 0.5 which is standard in prior work [12, 29, 36]. According to Eq. 3, we select $mAR_{anchor} = 3$. Having more anchors often weakens performance [41]. Thus, we just choose a discrete $AR_{anchor} \in \{1, 1.5, 3\}$ to control the number of anchors. Compared to SSD ($AR_{anchor} \in \{1, 2, 3\}$) [29] depicted in Fig. 3(a), our AR design covers more objects in Fig. 3(b) and has a better recall. We also observed that smaller tumor regions tend to be round (with smaller AR_{obj}). Thus the AR_{anchor} of the first layer can be chosen to be smaller, to decrease the total number of anchors and reduce computation cost. The AR_{anchor} of the last layer must not exceed the size of the whole slide image. Finally, the AR_{anchor} of the conv3_3 and conv6_2 are chosen as $\{1, 2\}$ and $\{1, 1.5\}$ respectively. The above calculation only considers the $width \geq height$ case due to symmetry. The final design params are in Table 1.

Double Sets of Anchors: Although our anchors cover almost all ground truth (GT) boxes in the above analysis, different box sizes still correspond to different

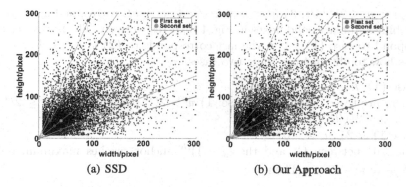

(a) SSD   (b) Our Approach

Fig. 3. The point cloud (black) represents the distribution of the tumor width and height. The colored dots denote the width and height of detection anchors. The colored lines connect anchors with the same AR but different scale. (Color figure online)

numbers of anchors. Statistics [46] show tiny outer objects are less likely to have a suitable anchor match. In order to alleviate this problem, we adopt double sets of anchors. We denote $\{S_1, ...S_k, ...\}$ as the first set anchors and $\{S'_1, ...S'_k, ...\}$ as the second set anchors. The size and AR values of the first set of anchors are shown in Table 1. The second set of anchors are $S'_k = \sqrt{S_k \cdot S_{k+1}}$ with aspect ratio 1, except for S'_{conv6_2} which is equal to the image-patch size 300 [29]. The final anchor sizes are depicted in Fig. 3(b).

4   Adaptive Aspect Ratio

Anchor Boxes: Figure 4 illustrates an example of anchor boxes in a layer j. Anchor boxes are rotation-invariant. The center of each box is aligned at a distance δ, where $\delta = S_j$, the stride of jth layer. We define a dominant area $C_x \pm \frac{1}{2}S_j, C_y \pm \frac{1}{2}S_j$ where (C_x, C_y) is the center of each anchor. The highest IoU for an object occurs where the anchor is centered closest to it's ground truth center [48]. This means that the IoU will reach a maximum for objects with GT boxes in the dominant region of the anchor while objects with centers outside the dominant region will be matched with a neighboring anchor. As shown in Table 1, S_j is much smaller than the anchor box size. For simplicity, we presume the object and anchor are concentric if matched.

The size of the anchor is chosen by the equal-proportion interval principle $\{2^f, 2^{f+1}, ..., 2^j, ..., 2^l\}$, where f is the first detection layer and l the last. For convenience, we only consider symmetrical cases where $width \geq height$. Here, we denote t as the maximum AR of anchors in the jth layer. We presume the width (w) and height (h) of objects follows ($w \leq kh$), where k is the maximum object AR, i.e. $k = sup\{\frac{w_i}{h_i}\}$. Note that IoU satisfies $IoU \geq T$, where T is a constant threshold. In our analysis, we only consider objects where AR ($w = kh$). By satisfying the maximum AR, we satisfy all remaining objects and conditions.

We set h to lie in the interval between $(j-1)^{th}$ and j^{th} set anchor (i.e. $\frac{2^{j-1}}{\sqrt{t}} < h \leq \frac{2^j}{\sqrt{t}}$), as shown in Fig. 4 *right*. There are only four cases of w: **1)** $w > 2^{j+1}\sqrt{t}$; **2)** $2^j\sqrt{t} < w \leq 2^{j+1}\sqrt{t}$; **3)** $ht < w \leq 2^j\sqrt{t}$; **4)** $w \leq ht$, corresponding to yellow, green, blue and black solid boxes in Fig. 4 *right* respectively. The first three cases correspond to case **(1)** $k \geq t$, the last corresponds to **(2)** $k < t$. Below we will discuss how to obtain t per these two cases.

Case **(1)**, $k \geq t$.
There are three cases in first case: **1)** $w > 2^{j+1}\sqrt{t}$; **2)** $2^j\sqrt{t} < w \leq 2^{j+1}\sqrt{t}$; **3)** $ht < w \leq 2^j\sqrt{t}$.
Case 1) & 2): $w > 2^j\sqrt{t}$
The IoU between Gt and the $(j-1)^{th}$ anchor reaches maximum only if $h \to \frac{2^{j-1}}{\sqrt{t}}$ & $w \to 2^j\sqrt{t}$. Then

$$max(IoU_{j-1}) \to \frac{\frac{2^{j-1}}{\sqrt{t}} \cdot 2^{j-1}\sqrt{t}}{\frac{2^{j-1}}{\sqrt{t}} \cdot 2^j\sqrt{t}} = \frac{1}{2} \tag{4}$$

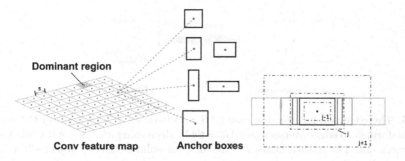

Fig. 4. Left: (left) Feature map (*conv_fc_7*). Boxes in the grid (cyan) are dominant regions with side length equal to stride S. The dotted red lines connect to anchor boxes on this feature layer. (right) The layout of homocentric GT boxes and anchors. Dashed boxes are equal-proportion anchors with equal AR. Solid boxes are GT boxes where the red one has the same AR as the anchors. (Color figure online)

Simultaneously,

$$IoU_j \rightarrow \frac{\frac{2^{j-1}}{\sqrt{t}} \cdot 2^j \sqrt{t}}{\frac{2^j}{\sqrt{t}} \cdot 2^j \sqrt{t}} = \frac{1}{2} \tag{5}$$

Therefore, we conclude $IoU_{j-1} \leq IoU_j$ under Case **1)** & **2)**. Similarly, we know $IoU_{j+1} \leq IoU_j$. Thus, IoU_j is the largest one under this condition.

Case **3)**: $ht < w \leq 2^j \sqrt{t}$

In this case, the GT box is totally enclosed by the jth anchor, as the edge non-intersection in Fig. 5. We can transform Case **3)** to Case **1)** & **2)** by replacing t by a smaller t' while keeping size, as illustrated in Fig. 5. Note that t' is a better solution as $t' < t$.

Given the above analysis, we conclude that IoU_j is the largest under **Case (1)**. Consequently, we assign the ground truth box ($w \times h$) to anchors in the jth layer if $\frac{2^{j-1}}{\sqrt{t}} < h \leq \frac{2^j}{\sqrt{t}}$. Otherwise, if $h \leq \frac{2^{j-1}}{\sqrt{t}}$, it will be assigned to the $(j-1)^{th}$ layer, else if $h > \frac{2^j}{\sqrt{t}}$, it will be assigned to the $(j+1)^{th}$ layer.

According to the above analysis, we can formulate the following equations:

$$IoU = \frac{I}{U} \geq T \tag{6}$$

$$I = h \cdot 2^j \sqrt{t} \tag{7}$$

$$U = (w - 2^j \sqrt{t})h + 2^j \sqrt{t} \cdot \frac{2^j}{\sqrt{t}} \tag{8}$$

$$w = kh \tag{9}$$

where the I denotes the intersection and U denotes the union.

Solving the above array produces Eq. (10)

$$Tkh^2 - (T+1)2^j \sqrt{t}h + T2^{2j} \leq 0 \tag{10}$$

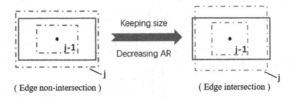

(Edge non-intersection)   (Edge intersection)

Fig. 5. The edge non-intersection case ($AR = t$) between j^{th} anchor and GT box can be transformed to edge-intersection ($AR = t'$) by decreasing anchors' AR while keeping size consistent. The dashed boxes are anchors, the solid boxes are object GT boxes.

If Eq. (10) has a solution, it must satisfy $\Delta \geq 0$, where Δ is

$$\Delta = 2^{2j}[(T + 1)^2 t - 4T^2 k] \tag{11}$$

From Eq. (11), we can generate the range of t:

$$t \geq (\frac{2}{1 + \frac{1}{T}})^2 \cdot k \tag{12}$$

Equation (10) can be written in form:

$$f(h) \leq 0, \qquad f(h) = Tkh^2 - (T + 1)2^j \sqrt{t} h + T2^{2j} \tag{13}$$

Because $f(h)$ is a convex function and $h \in (\frac{2^{j-1}}{\sqrt{t}}, \frac{2^j}{\sqrt{t}}]$, the necessary condition of Eq. (13) is $f(\frac{2^{j-1}}{\sqrt{t}}) \leq 0$ and $f(\frac{2^j}{\sqrt{t}}) \leq 0$:

$$f(\frac{2^{j-1}}{\sqrt{t}}) = Tk\frac{2^{2j-2}}{t} - (T + 1)2^j \sqrt{t} \cdot \frac{2^{j-1}}{\sqrt{t}} + T2^{2j} \leq 0 \tag{14}$$

$$f(\frac{2^j}{\sqrt{t}}) = Tk\frac{2^{2j}}{t} - (T + 1)2^j \sqrt{t} \cdot \frac{2^j}{\sqrt{t}} + T2^{2j} \leq 0 \tag{15}$$

Solving Eqs. (14) (15) respectively results in:

$$t \geq \frac{Tk}{2 - 2T} \tag{16}$$

and

$$t \geq Tk \tag{17}$$

We would like t to be as small as possible to reduce the total number of anchors, and from Eqs. (12), (16) and (17), we formulate:

$$t = max\{(\frac{2}{1 + \frac{1}{T}})^2 k, \frac{Tk}{2 - 2T}, Tk\} \tag{18}$$

We can see that because $T \in [0, 1]$, so $t \in (0, k]$. The condition $k \geq t$ always holds.

From our statistics, we can find that $k = 6$. If T is simply chosen to be 0.5, we can find that $t = 3$ from Eq. (18).

Case (2)$k < t$.
From the analysis in (1), we draw that for any $T \in [0, 1]$, there exist a t' satisfy Eq. (12) and $t' \leq k < t$. Just replacing t with t', we can produce a better result, as illustrated in Fig. 5. Here, for our specific problem (i.e. $k = 6$, $T = 0.5$), we use another simpler method to prove it.

From $\frac{2^{j-1}}{\sqrt{t}} < h \leq \frac{2^j}{\sqrt{t}}$ and $k < t$, results in:

$$w = kh < th \leq t \cdot \frac{2^j}{\sqrt{t}} = 2^j \sqrt{t} \tag{19}$$

where $2^j \sqrt{t}$ is the anchor width. Thus, both w and h are less than the width and height in j^{th} layer, which we denote as W_j and H_j respectively. Similarly, we have $w > W_{j-1}$ and $h > H_{j-1}$. So, we have

$$W_{j-1} < w < W_j \tag{20}$$

$$H_{j-1} < h < H_j \tag{21}$$

where, from the anchor equal-proportion interval principle, $W_j = 2W_{j-1}$ and $H_j = 2H_{j-1}$. Equation (20) $\times$ Equation (21), we can generate:

$$A_{j-1} < a < A_j \tag{22}$$

where, A_{j-1} and A_j are areas of anchor $j-1$ and j, and $a = h \cdot w$. This results in $A_j = 4A_{j-1}$. Now, if $A_{j-1} < a \leq 2A_{j-1}$, the *IoU* between the GT and $(j-1)^{th}$ layer anchor will be $\frac{A_{j-1}}{a} \geq 0.5$. Similarly, we find $\frac{a}{A_j} > 0.5$ if $2A_{j-1} < a < A_j$. Therefore, the ground truth box will have a *IoU* not less than 0.5 with anchors either in $(j-1)^{th}$ or j^{th} layer. Thus, we claim that the GT boxes will always have an anchor to match, if the condition $k < t$ holds. Actually, this claim holds for any Edge non-intersection cases (i.e. $w \leq 2^j \sqrt{t}$) with j^{th} layer in Fig. 4 *right*.

5   Foveal Context-Integrated Detection

Tumor detection in medical images is often more challenging than applications like face detection which rely on color and texture patterns that are more discriminative. As shown in Fig. 1, there is a broad variation in feature types (scale, shape, color). Moreover, tumor (chimeric cell) detection depends on a number of factors which are not limited to image-based features like color. Background context is important, particularly for dense features with little to no color variations. To address these challenges, we now introduce a context integrated detection module, similar to a foveal structure [44].

Cascade Residual-Inception Module: The Inception block [21] provides multiple receptive fields per chosen convolutional kernel size [38]. Inspired by work in this area [9,25], we make a separate residual-inception prediction module instead of predicting directly on the feature layer (Fig. 6(a)). Residual-inception is an effective combination of the inception module and the residual block [15]. We achieve improvement over prior examples [25,38] by altering the parallel convolutional layers of the inception module to form a cascade structure. Each convolutional layer in the cascade shares computation instructions and memory. Figure 6(c) outlines our implementation. We have $1 \times 1, 3 \times 3$ and 5×5 (by 2 cascade 3×3) conv kernels. The first 1×1 kernel reduces the dimension of feature map (i.e. the channel number). The cascade residual-inception module generates multiple receptive fields at lower computational cost. Our performance is similar to current inception modules [38] with only 25% of the parameters. Experimental results show that this design converges faster and produces a higher accuracy rate.

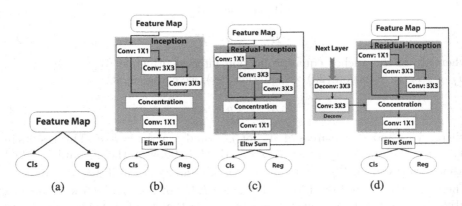

Fig. 6. Multiple prediction modules. Cls: classification. Reg: localization regression. (a) SSD, SSD adaptive: (b) inception, (c) residual-inception (d), residual-deconvolution.

Deconvolution Module with Context Information: To utilize broader context information, we adopt the deconvolution shown in Fig. 6(d). Other approaches like DSSD [9] incorporate context elements naively by adding or multiplying elements in the deconvolution feature map with the original feature map. This does not work well with our residual-inception structure because it reduces performance. We adopt the feature-fusion concatenation method [3]. This permits the convolutional layer to effectively learn useful background information while decreasing interference from noise. We concatenate the deconvolution module into the inception module as shown in Fig. 6(d). This design integrates hierarchical context information. The inception module provides local context while the deconvolution module provides broader context information.

In our implementation, we only add the foveal context-integrated module on the first three SSD detection layers where there is a small receptive field and higher resolutions. These shallow layers are mainly responsible for detecting small objects [46]. Large objects rely much less on context compared to small objects [19]. Thus, we only add the foveal detection module to shallow layers so that small objects are more recognizable.

6 Experimental Evaluation

We evaluate our system on a dataset of 30, 000 patches extracted from microscopic scans (Fig. 1). Each patch is 300×300 pixels. Tumor sizes in our scans range from 8–300 pixels. We separate patches into training and testing sets (9 : 1 respectively). We generate precision recall and average precision values by comparing the detected tumor regions with hand-labeled ground truth images. Our code is implemented using the *Caffe* toolbox [20] on a *Windows 10* system. We trained using a NVIDIA GTX 1080Ti GPU for 3 days with 2 additional days for finetuning. Training and finetuning was performed for 180, 000 and 100, 000 iterations respectively.

Table 2 compares our approach with R-CNN and traditional SSD. Our modifications - SSD adaptive, SSD adaptive foveal residual-inception and SSD adaptive foveal deconvolution - have a higher recall (0.699, 0.699, 0.702 respectively) compared to R-CNN and traditional SSD (0.713 and 0.608 respectively) as we detect small tumors that are undetectable in other methods. Figures 3(a) and 3(b) show tumor and anchor box size distributions for SSD and our method. Our adaptive prior anchors produce higher average precision rates [8] (0.747, 0.7485 and 0.7497 respectively) compared to R-CNN and traditional SSD (0.175 and 0.726 respectively). The precision-recall curves in Fig. 7 show that SSD-based approaches have a higher precision for a longer recall than R-CNN. Our modifications outperform traditional SSD. Although proposal-based R-CNN has a high recall, it's precision is low as most candidate boxes are ineffective in our domain. The two-stage process is also inefficient. SSD has been shown to outperform faster R-CNN while Mask R-CNN requires segmentation and is not popular for pure bounding box object detection. Our reliance on patch extraction to resolve GPU memory restrictions is a limitation which increases total computation time. Although SSD is more efficient with higher precision, there is no built-in guarantee anchor distributions will be optimal, and no mechanism to tackle non-discriminative tumors.

Table 2. Comparing R-CNN, SSD and our modified SSD (adaptive, adaptive foveal residual-inception and adaptive foveal deconvolution). Our design yields the best results per average precision (AP). (precision recall threshold = 0.5)

Method	Precision	Recall	AP
R-CNN	0.065	0.713	0.175
SSD	0.826	0.644	0.726
SSD-adaptive	0.808	0.699	0.747
SSD-adaptive foveal residual-inception	0.809	0.699	0.7485
SSD-adaptive foveal deconvolution	0.809	0.702	0.7497

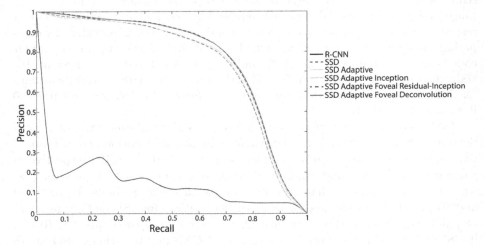

Fig. 7. Our SSD modifications produce higher precision for a longer recall when detecting multi-scale tumors in high resolution slide scans.

7   Conclusion

We presented a multiscale detection algorithm that augments SSD for successful detection of small tumors (chimeric cells) in patches extracted from high-resolution slide scans. Our approach includes a modified SSD deconvolution module that integrates background information and a foveal context module with a cascade residual inception module for local context integration. We introduced rules for computing adaptive prior anchor boxes with aspect ratios and distributions that are more suitable for detecting small-scale objects (8 pixels). Our evaluation methods show that our approach produces a higher precision recall when compared with traditional SSD. Our method is also effective for non-discriminative feature sets.

Acknowledgements. We thank K08 DK085141 and the American Cancer Society Chris DiMarco Institutional Research Grant (CDH) for funding support. This work was conducted at the UF Graphics Imaging and Light Measurement Lab (GILMLab).

References

1. Bejnordi, B.E., et al.: Deep learning-based assessment of tumor-associated stroma for diagnosing breast cancer in histopathology images. CoRR abs/1702.05803 (2017). http://arxiv.org/abs/1702.05803
2. Bell, S., Lawrence Zitnick, C., Bala, K., Girshick, R.: Inside-outside net: detecting objects in context with skip pooling and recurrent neural networks. In: IEEE Conference on Computer Vision and Pattern Recognition, vol. 1, pp. 2874–2883 (2016)
3. Cao, G., Xie, X., Yang, W., Liao, Q., Shi, G., Wu, J.: Feature-fused SSD: fast detection for small objects. In: Ninth International Conference on Graphic and Image Processing (ICGIP 2017), vol. 10615, p. 106151E. International Society for Optics and Photonics (2018)
4. Cao, Z., et al.: Breast tumor detection in ultrasound images using deep learning. In: Wu, G., Munsell, B.C., Zhan, Y., Bai, W., Sanroma, G., Coupé, P. (eds.) PatchMI 2017. LNCS, vol. 10530, pp. 121–128. Springer, Cham (2017). https://doi.org/10.1007/978-3-319-67434-6_14
5. Cruz-Roa, A., Gilmore, H., Basavanhally, A., Feldman, M.: Accurate and reproducible invasive breast cancer detection in whole-slide images: a deep learning approach for quantifying tumor extent. Sci. Rep. **7**, 46450 (2017)
6. Dai, J., Li, Y., He, K., Sun, J.: R-FCN: object detection via region-based fully convolutional networks. In: Lee, D.D., Sugiyama, M., Luxburg, U.V., Guyon, I., Garnett, R. (eds.) Advances in Neural Information Processing Systems, vol. 29, pp. 379–387. Curran Associates, Inc. (2016). http://papers.nips.cc/paper/6465-r-fcn-object-detection-via-region-based-fully-convolutional-networks.pdf
7. Deng, J., Dong, W., Socher, R., Li, L.J., Li, K., Fei-Fei, L.: ImageNet: a large-scale hierarchical image database. In: CVPR 2009 (2009)
8. Everingham, M., Eslami, S.M.A., Van Gool, L., Williams, C.K.L, Winn, J., Zisserman, A.: The pascal visual object classes challenge: a retrospective. Int. J. Comput. Vis. **111**(1), 98–136 (2015)
9. Fu, C.Y., Liu, W., Ranga, A., Tyagi, A., Berg, A.C.: DSSD: deconvolutional single shot detector. arXiv preprint arXiv:1701.06659 (2017)
10. Gidaris, S., Komodakis, N.: Object detection via a multi-region and semantic segmentation-aware CNN model. In: Proceedings of the IEEE International Conference on Computer Vision, pp. 1134–1142 (2015)
11. Girshick, R.: Fast R-CNN. In: Proceedings of the International Conference on Computer Vision (ICCV) (2015)
12. Girshick, R., Donahue, J., Darrell, T., Malik, J.: Rich feature hierarchies for accurate object detection and semantic segmentation. In: Proceedings of the IEEE Conference on Computer Vision and Pattern Recognition (CVPR) (2014)
13. He, K., Gkioxari, G., Dollár, P., Girshick, R.: Mask R-CNN. In: Proceedings of the International Conference on Computer Vision (ICCV) (2017)
14. He, K., Zhang, X., Ren, S., Sun, J.: Spatial pyramid pooling in deep convolutional networks for visual recognition. IEEE Trans. Pattern Anal. Mach. Intell. **37**(9), 1904–1916 (2015)

15. He, K., Zhang, X., Ren, S., Sun, J.: Deep residual learning for image recognition. In: Proceedings of the IEEE Conference on Computer Vision and Pattern Recognition, pp. 770–778 (2016)
16. Hirasawa, T., et al.: Application of artificial intelligence using a convolutional neural network for detecting gastric cancer in endoscopic images. Gastr. Cancer 21(4), 653–660 (2018). https://doi.org/10.1007/s10120-018-0793-2
17. Hou, L., Samaras, D., Kurc, T.M., Gao, Y., Davis, J.E., Saltz, J.H.: Patch-based convolutional neural network for whole slide tissue image classification. In: 2016 IEEE Conference on Computer Vision and Pattern Recognition (CVPR), pp. 2424–2433 (2016)
18. Hu, H., Gu, J., Zhang, Z., Dai, J., Wei, Y.: Relation networks for object detection. arXiv preprint arXiv:1711.11575 (2017)
19. Hu, P., Ramanan, D.: Finding tiny faces. In: 2017 IEEE Conference on Computer Vision and Pattern Recognition (CVPR), pp. 1522–1530. IEEE (2017)
20. Jia, Y., et al.: Caffe: convolutional architecture for fast feature embedding. arXiv preprint arXiv:1408.5093 (2014)
21. Kim, K., Cheon, Y., Hong, S., Roh, B., Park, M.: PVANET: deep but lightweight neural networks for real-time object detection. CoRR abs/1608.08021 (2016). http://arxiv.org/abs/1608.08021
22. Kong, T., Sun, F., Yao, A., Liu, H., Lu, M., Chen, Y.: RON: reverse connection with objectness prior networks for object detection. In: IEEE Conference on Computer Vision and Pattern Recognition, vol. 1, p. 2 (2017)
23. Kong, T., Yao, A., Chen, Y., Sun, F.: HyperNet: towards accurate region proposal generation and joint object detection. In: Proceedings of the IEEE Conference on Computer Vision and Pattern Recognition, pp. 845–853 (2016)
24. Kourou, K., Exarchos, T.P., Exarchos, K.P., Karamouzis, M.V., Fotiadis, D.I.: Machine learning applications in cancer prognosis and prediction. Comput. Struct. Biotechnol. J. 13(C), 8–17 (2015)
25. Lee, Y., Kim, H., Park, E., Cui, X., Kim, H.: Wide-residual-inception networks for real-time object detection. In: 2017 IEEE Intelligent Vehicles Symposium (IV), pp. 758–764. IEEE (2017)
26. Li, N., et al.: Detection and attention: diagnosing pulmonary lung cancer from CT by imitating physicians. CoRR abs/1712.05114 (2017). http://arxiv.org/abs/1712.05114
27. Li, N., et al.: Detection and attention: diagnosing pulmonary lung cancer from CT by imitating physicians. arXiv preprint arXiv:1712.05114 (2017)
28. Lin, T., Dollár, P., Girshick, R.B., He, K., Hariharan, B., Belongie, S.J.: Feature pyramid networks for object detection. CoRR abs/1612.03144 (2016). http://arxiv.org/abs/1612.03144
29. Liu, W., et al.: SSD: single shot multibox detector. In: Leibe, B., Matas, J., Sebe, N., Welling, M. (eds.) ECCV 2016. LNCS, vol. 9905, pp. 21–37. Springer, Cham (2016). https://doi.org/10.1007/978-3-319-46448-0_2
30. Luo, W., Li, Y., Urtasun, R., Zemel, R.: Understanding the effective receptive field in deep convolutional neural networks. In: Advances in Neural Information Processing Systems (NIPS), pp. 4898–4906 (2016)
31. Meng, Z., Fan, X., Chen, X., Chen, M., Tong, Y.: Detecting small signs from large images. CoRR abs/1706.08574 (2017). http://arxiv.org/abs/1706.08574
32. Najibi, M., Samangouei, P., Chellappa, R., Davis, L.S.: SSH: single stage headless face detector. In: ICCV, pp. 4885–4894 (2017)

33. Redmon, J., Farhadi, A.: YOLO9000: better, faster, stronger. In: 2017 IEEE Conference on Computer Vision and Pattern Recognition (CVPR), pp. 6517–6525, July 2017
34. Redmon, J., Divvala, S., Girshick, R., Farhadi, A.: You only look once: unified, real-time object detection, pp. 779–788, June 2016. https://doi.org/10.1109/CVPR.2016.91
35. Ren, S., He, K., Girshick, R., Sun, J.: Faster R-CNN: towards real-time object detection with region proposal networks. In: Neural Information Processing Systems (NIPS) (2015)
36. Ren, S., He, K., Girshick, R., Sun, J.: Faster R-CNN: towards real-time object detection with region proposal networks. In: Proceedings of the 28th International Conference on Neural Information Processing Systems, NIPS 2015, vol. 1, pp. 91–99. MIT Press, Cambridge (2015). http://dl.acm.org/citation.cfm?id=2969239.2969250
37. Simonyan, K., Zisserman, A.: Very deep convolutional networks for large-scale image recognition. arXiv preprint arXiv:1409.1556 (2014)
38. Szegedy, C., et al.: Going deeper with convolutions. In: Proceedings of the IEEE Conference on Computer Vision and Pattern Recognition, pp. 1–9 (2015)
39. Uijlings, J., van de Sande, K., Gevers, T., Smeulders, A.: Selective search for object recognition. Int. J. Comput. Vis. (2013). https://doi.org/10.1007/s11263-013-0620-5. http://www.huppelen.nl/publications/selectiveSearchDraft.pdf
40. Wang, D., Khosla, A., Gargeya, R., Irshad, H., Beck, A.H.: Deep learning for identifying metastatic breast cancer. arXiv preprint arXiv:1606.05718 (2016)
41. Weng, X.: The study of setting region proposals of object detection network SSD. master thesis in Electromechanical Science and Technology, Xidian University, June 2017
42. Yang, X., et al.: A deep learning approach for tumor tissue image classification, February 2016
43. Yu, W., Yang, K., Bai, Y., Xiao, T., Yao, H., Rui, Y.: Visualizing and comparing AlexNet and VGG using deconvolutional layers. In: Proceedings of the 33rd International Conference on Machine Learning (2016)
44. Zagoruyko, S., et al.: A multipath network for object detection. arXiv preprint arXiv:1604.02135 (2016)
45. Zhang, S., Wen, L., Bian, X., Lei, Z., Li, S.Z.: Single-shot refinement neural network for object detection. In: CVPR (2018)
46. Zhang, S., Zhu, X., Lei, Z., Shi, H., Wang, X., Li, S.Z.: S3FD: single shot scale-invariant face detector. In: 2017 IEEE International Conference on Computer Vision (ICCV), pp. 192–201. IEEE (2017)
47. Zhu, C., Tao, R., Luu, K., Savvides, M.: Seeing small faces from robust anchor's perspective. In: IEEE Conference on Computer Vision and Pattern Recognition (2018)
48. Zhu, C., Tao, R., Luu, K., Savvides, M.: Seeing small faces from robust anchor's perspective. CoRR abs/1802.09058 (2018). http://arxiv.org/abs/1802.09058
49. Zhu, C., Zheng, Y., Luu, K., Savvides, M.: CMS-RCNN: contextual multi-scale region-based CNN for unconstrained face detection. CoRR abs/1606.05413 (2016). http://arxiv.org/abs/1606.05413
50. Zitnick, C.L., Dollár, P.: Edge boxes: locating object proposals from edges. In: Fleet, D., Pajdla, T., Schiele, B., Tuytelaars, T. (eds.) ECCV 2014. LNCS, vol. 8693, pp. 391–405. Springer, Cham (2014). https://doi.org/10.1007/978-3-319-10602-1_26. https://www.microsoft.com/en-us/research/publication/edge-boxes-locating-object-proposals-from-edges/

DeepTKAClassifier: Brand Classification of Total Knee Arthroplasty Implants Using Explainable Deep Convolutional Neural Networks

Shi Yan[1,2](✉), Taghi Ramazanian[1](✉), Elham Sagheb[1], Sunyang Fu[1],
Sunghwan Sohn[2], David G. Lewallen[3], Hongfang Liu[1], Walter K. Kremers[1],
Vipin Chaudhary[2], Michael Taunton[3], Hilal Maradit Kremers[1](✉),
and Ahmad P. Tafti[1](✉)

[1] Department of Health Sciences Research, Mayo Clinic, Rochester, USA
{ramazanian.taghi,maradit,Tafti.Ahmad}@mayo.edu
[2] Department of Computer Science and Engineering,
The State University of New York at Buffalo, Buffalo, NY, USA
shiyan@buffalo.edu
[3] Department of Orthopedics, Mayo Clinic, Rochester, MN, USA

Abstract. Total knee arthroplasty (TKA) is one of the most successful surgical procedures worldwide. It improves quality of life, mobility, and functionality for the vast majority of patients. However, a TKA surgery may fail over time for several reasons, thus it requires a revision arthroplasty surgery. Identifying TKA implants is a critical consideration in preoperative planning of revision surgery. This study aims to develop, train, and validate deep convolutional neural network models to precisely classify four widely-used TKA implants based on only plain knee radiographs. Using 9,052 computationally annotated knee radiographs, we achieved weighted average precision, recall, and F1-score of 0.97, 0.97, and 0.97, respectively, with Cohen Kappa of 0.96.

Keywords: Deep learning · Knee radiographs · Total knee arthroplasty

1 Introduction

Total knee arthroplasty (TKA) is one of the most common inpatient surgical procedures [1]. Over 700,000 TKA procedures are performed each year in the United States, and approximately 4.7 million Americans are currently living with TKA implants [2].

Although TKA is an efficacious and cost-effective intervention [3–5], there has been a steady rise in the volume of revision TKA procedures in the United States in recent years [6]. With a much larger population of patients having undergone primary TKA, the number of patients requiring revision arthroplasty will also

© Springer Nature Switzerland AG 2020
G. Bebis et al. (Eds.): ISVC 2020, LNCS 12510, pp. 154–165, 2020.
https://doi.org/10.1007/978-3-030-64559-5_12

rise, despite improvements in technique, implant design, and biomaterials [7]. Available 2010 data indicate an estimated revision burden 7.5% for TKA [8,9].

Preoperative planning is essential for a successful revision surgery. One of the critical parts of preoperative planning is the identification of previously implanted knee implants. Implant-specific information, including manufacturer, design, and size are essential for a successful revision TKA [10]. Patient x-rays, hospital operative records and hospital implant sheet/labels are the common methods used by orthopedic surgeons and staff to find failed implant components. Inadequacy of documentation of implant information makes preoperative planning for revision surgery difficult and is a major barrier in identifying components of the failed implant. An estimated 41 h of physician and staff time annually is used to identify failed implants and still 10% of failed implant components could not be identified pre-operatively and 2% could not be identified intra-operatively. Inability to identify a failed implant results in more components replaced, increased blood loss, increased bone loss and increased recovery time [8].

The current contribution aims to develop and utilize deep learning computational vision mechanisms to first learn from computationally-annotated knee radiographs, and then automatically detect and understand TKA implant brands. We briefly summarize the **main significance** of the work as follows:

- **Clinical Significance:** Although the durability of TKA with current techniques and implants is well established, failure still happens due to several reasons, including infection, component loosening, instability and more. With the rise in annual number of primary TKA, numbers of patients who need revision TKA will also dramatically go up. Revision TKA is a complex procedure and needs precise preoperative planning. Identification of the prosthesis brand is one of the critical steps of preoperative planning, and it has a significant impact on the success of revision surgery. With the current advances in artificial intelligence (AI) components and the variety of clinical problems that the AI-powered methods have already demonstrated successful solutions [31–35], in this work, and with the use of deep learning computational vision strategies, we have developed an AI-powered system to assist surgeons to identify TKA implant brands in an autonomous fashion, where it is possible to use plain knee radiographs to precisely classify four different TKA implant types.
- **Technical Significance:** First, we proposed a non-intrusive automated AI-powered pipeline that fits well in TKA setting to identify TKA implants brand based on only knee radiographs. Second, we computationally assembled a fully-annotated knee radiographs dataset with different X-ray views, which includes AP view and lateral view, to train and validate deep learning methods for autonomous classification of TKA implants brand. Third, we implemented deep convolutional neural network models that effectively learn features from knee radiographs and detect four different TKA implants, from three manufactures *Depuy*, *Howmedica*, and *Zimmer*. Finally, this work is the first that combined realistic multiple-view of TKA radiographs with deep convolutional neural networks to tackle the problem of TKA implant brand classification, assisting preoperative planning for a successful revision surgery.

The present study was reviewed and approved by the Mayo Clinic institutional review board (IRB). The rest of the paper is organized as follows. Section II explains the materials and methods, including the fully-annotated knee radiographs dataset and the AI-powered pipeline to cope with the problem. Experimental validations are illustrated in Section III. Section IV provides further discussion and it concludes the study with drawing several research avenues for future work.

2   Materials and Methods

This section first describes our dataset, and compare the current dataset with others in the literature to illustrate the advantages along with the existing limitations. After that, the details of the deep learning model(s) are described.

2.1   Dataset

Following IRB approval, we conducted this study with knee radiographs at Mayo Clinic, which includes anteroposterior (AP) view, bilateral AP view, and lateral view TKA radiographs. Figure 1 shows some examples of TKA radiographs. The current dataset includes 3,903 patients (2,308 females and 1,595 males), with 9,052 radiographs in total. After pre-processing, we got 9,052 ROIs as it can be seen in Fig. 1(c), in which the TKA types vary in three different manufacturers, *Depuy*, *Howmedica*, and *Zimmer* and four specific brands, as *Depuy Attune*, *Depuy Sigma*, *Howmedica Triathlon*, and *Zimmer Persona* with number of images of 826, 5,002, 2,456, and 768, respectively.

In the process of data preparation, we first used our previous work to detect and localize the knee joint area and automatically provide bounding boxes of knee joint area. Then, by applying a threshold, we filtered the wrong bounding boxes. After that, we calculated the maximum width and height of the bounding boxes. Based on the maximum values, we cropped the ROIs from the original radiographs. Next, we did resize the cropped ROIs with the resolution of 224 × 224. Finally, we applied 5-fold cross validation based on the patient ID, and did generate the training and validation datasets.

In comparison to similar work in the literature [11], we have had several advantages on dataset preparation. First, we have a large amount of high quality radiographs, which has been divided into 4 specific brands to classify, while at [11] they only have two brands with small number of images to train and validate the deep learning method. Second, our method can be applied on different views of knee radiographs, not just for only knee AP view, but also for bilateral knee AP view and knee lateral view as well. That being said, our proposed method is tackling the problem of utilizing different X-ray view images. Third, after data pre-processing step in our method, the ROIs are focused on knee implant area, which can avoid the model to learn useless features from the images and reduce computation complexity at the same time. Lastly, we proposed our own deep learning model, which can be applied on TKA type classification. In the future

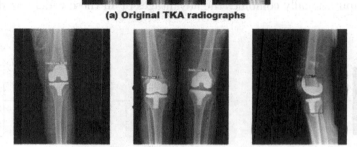

(a) Original TKA radiographs

(b) TKA detection and localization done by our previous work

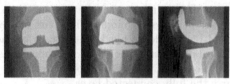

(c) Region of interest (ROI)

Fig. 1. (a) Samples of the original TKA radiographs within our dataset, which are basically converted from DICOM files. (b) It visually illustrates the detection and localization of the TKA region by using our previous works in the literature, which was able to precisely detect and localize the knee joint area including AP view, bilateral AP view, and lateral view radiographs. (c) It presents the input data (ROIs) to our deep learning methods, which is only consisting the ROIs of the TKA, and then normalized them with the resolution of 224 × 224 to feed to the convolutional neural nets.

work, we plan to try our model on osteoarthritis grading problem. Despite several advantages, our method also comes with limitations on the data processing. First, we excluded the radiographs including long-stem implant (Fig. 4). Currently, the number of radiographs with long-stem prosthesis is small, thus to avoid over-fitting, we removed these radiographs. In our future study, with more data injected into our dataset, we will add long-stem implants. Second, we only have had four specific implants. In real environment, there exist more than four types of implants, hence we will also add more brands in, and solve the problem to cover more diverse implants in our future study.

2.2   Deep Convolutional Neural Network Models

Deep learning is demonstrating successful applications in a variety of different problems in recent years, which benefits from the development of high performance computing devices and also a huge amount of fully-annotated large-scale data or even data with less-labels. Our proposed computational method and implementation was inspired by DenseNet [12], Inception [13,14,19], and dilation convolution [14,15,20]. In the following parts, we will briefly introduce DenseNet, Inception, and dilation convolution with their advantages just to make our work as self-contained. We implemented our own deep learning architecture which computationally combines the advantages of all these widely-used models (Fig. 2).

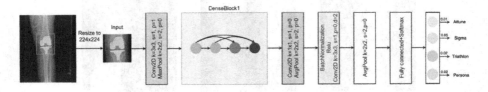

Fig. 2. Network architecture. We utilized our previous work to detect and localize the knee joint area, and then applied filter operation and resized the image into 224×224. After that, the images were put into the model. First part of the model is convolution and max pooling. Second part is dense block, the details of each point inside dense block shows on Fig. 3. Third part is transition layer which includes batch normalization, convolution, and pooling layer followed by dilation convolution and average pooling. The last part is of course the fully connected layer.

Dilation Convolution: Dilation convolution was originally proposed for the purpose of semantic segmentation, to combine multi-scale contextual information without any failure in resolution. As Fisher et al. declared at [14], the architectural model is designed and developed on the fact that dilated convolutions is backing exponential expansion of the receptive field without loss of coverage or even resolution. Thus, by using dilation convolution, the model could have larger receptive field with same computation strategy. The current paper does not have enough space to cover dilated convolutions applications, therefore we encourage interested readers to refer to [21–24] for further reading.

Densely Connected Convolutional Networks: DenseNet [12] is a well-known and widely-used deep convolutional network which can achieve an excellent classification score with fewer parameters. The following components of DenseNet contribute to it impressing results: (a) dense block, (b) transition layer, and (c) bottle neck. The building blocks of the dense block are composite functions, which represents three consecutive operations, batch normalization (BN), rectified linear unit (ReLU), and a 3×3 convolution (Conv). In contrast to ResNets [16,17], DenseNet introduced the dense connectivity to extract more information or important image features among different layers, which means the current layers are connected with all previous layer. After the input data went through dense block layer, a lot of feature map will be generated. DenseNet proposed growth rate to control the number of feature maps, and reduce the number of parameters. The growth rate controls how many information contribute to the next layer. In transition part, instead of summing up all output features, DenseNet is concatenating the feature maps, and deployed compression operation to reduce feature maps, when compression parameter was set as 1, which means no compression happened. Bottle neck part includes 1×1 convolution, which could be applied to reduce the number of parameters, just in case. Further details on the DenseNet applications can be found at [25–27].

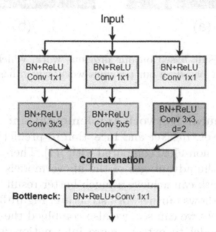

Fig. 3. Details of inception module of our model, which represents a basic point inside the denseblock. Our inception module concatenates different feature maps and utilize dilation convolution to obtain large receptive field with same computation.

Inception: GoogLeNet [13] was proposed on ILSVRC (ImageNet Large Scale Visual Recognition Competition) 2014, and won the game. Deep learning models came with many layers which can cause over-fitting, so the idea was to make the network wider instead of deeper. Based on this idea, GoogLeNet proposed the Inception model to make the network wider and extract more information at the same layer. As we can see in Fig. 4, an image of the implant can be either of (a) or (b). The object in the image has a large variation in size. In convolution neural network, the selection of kernel size is important, but due to the variation of the object models, it is tough to select the correct kernel size. Hence, we just used multiple kernel sizes at the same layer, and then let the network itself to decide which kernel size works better. GoogLeNet proposed the above method to address the problem of kernel size selection, which makes the model more robust and reliable. On GoogLeNet, the 1×1 convolution was also applied before next convolution operation to reduce the number of parameters of the model. More applications on the GoogLeNet can be found at [28–30].

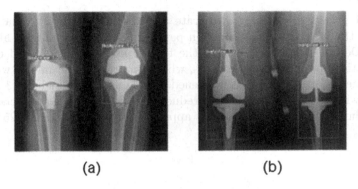

(a)   (b)

Fig. 4. (a) Detection result based on our previous work, which has normal implant size. (b) Detection result based on our previous work, which has long stem.

Our Own Deep Neural Network Implementation: At first, we tried to directly utilize DenseNet, ResNet and Inception to predict the implant brands, but the performance is non-ideal compared with [11]. Then we proposed our own method to aggregate the advantages of the above models and proves that our own deep neural network can achieve a much better result, as shown in Table 1 and Table 2. Figure 2 shows our network structure. Figure 3 shows the inception module of our model. As we can see, we also combined the Dilation convolution with the Inception model to extract more information without adding more computational complexity. By applying the Inception, our method gains the ability to obtain more useful features from input, which will contribute to long stem implant brand classification in future study. In the current work, we only apply one dense block, with more images of different brands joined in the future, we will add more dense blocks to learn more complicated features.

3 Experiment Validation and Results

This section will further describe the experimental setting and the results. We will also compare the prediction results between our own model and other famous deep learning architectures to show the effectiveness of our model.

In the experiment, we utilized a high performance server equipped with 2 Tesla V-100 GPUs with 6.21G main memory in total to run the model. All implementations were made by using PyTorch framework. We found the best hyper-parameters that fit our model well after we tried several extensive experiments. The hyper-parameter settings were the epochs number of 48, batch size of 16, and use Adam optimizer with the learning rate of 0.000001. The dataset is divided in some cases by image ID to avoid data leaking, while we divided the dataset based on the patient ID.

To evaluate the performance of our deep learning model and compare ours with other famous networks, we applied 5-fold cross validation to train and validate the models. For all models, we did use the default method in PyTorch

Table 1. Average precision and recall of each model based on 5-fold cross validation.

Model type	Precision				Recall			
	Attune	Sigma	Triathlon	Persona	Attune	Sigma	Triathlon	Persona
Inception	0.77	0.81	0.81	0.86	0.34	0.96	0.75	0.54
ResNet	0.79	0.91	0.83	0.81	0.58	0.94	0.87	0.77
DenseNet	0.79	0.89	0.84	0.88	0.55	0.95	0.87	0.70
Our implementation	0.96	0.98	0.98	0.96	0.94	0.99	0.97	0.95

Table 2. Average F1-score and accuracy of each model based on 5-fold cross validation.

Model type	F1 score				Accuracy	Cohen kappa
	Attune	Sigma	Triathlon	Persona		
Inception	0.47	0.88	0.78	0.66	0.81	0.66
ResNet	0.67	0.93	0.85	0.79	0.87	0.79
DenseNet	0.65	0.92	0.86	0.78	0.87	0.78
Our implementation	0.95	0.99	0.97	0.95	0.98	0.96

to initialize the parameters. We trained all models from scratch, meaning that we didn't use pre-trained model components. Then, we experimentally evaluated the performance of the models based on 5-cross validation.

Our evaluation metrics included Cohen Kappa score [17], accuracy, precision, recall and F1 score. Our model achieved 0.96, 0.98, 0.97, 0.97, and 0.97 with above evaluation methods. By the current results, we can see that our proposed model can get a much better performance on TKA implant brands classification with high recall score. Table 1 and Table 2 illustrate the precision, recall, F1-score, accuracy and Cohen Kappa results predicted by our model in comparison with other models. Figure 5 shows the ROC curve when k = 1, where k is the k-fold cross validation. We also calculated the ROC curve when k = 2, 3, 4, 5, however, due to page limitation, we only put one ROC curve in the presented results due to the page limit. By reviewing the ROC curves, we can also see that our model can achieve an excellent performance. In our model, we did combine the dense connection, bottle neck layer, transition layer, inception module, and dilation convolution. One of the possible reason that we can achieve a better result than other networks is we combined their advantages together and make them available in an integrated fashion. By leveraging their advantages, our model could extract more useful information, resulting in a better and reliable results.

Of late, the research area of interpretability of deep learning models and explainable AI is in high demand. Researchers, particularly those who are coming from different scientific disciplines rather than the computer science, often think deep learning technique is somehow a black box, meaning that no one knows what happened inside. In this work, we utilized the state-of-the art approach, Grad-CAM algorithm [18], to plot the class activation mapping. Thus, we could have a

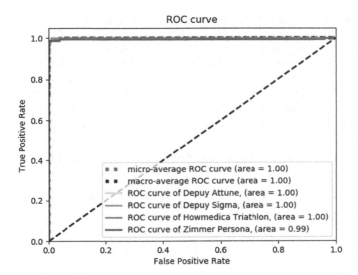

Fig. 5. The ROC curves are obtained by our own model. It compares the ROC for four different classes, including *Depuy Attune, Depuy Sigma, Howmedica Triathlon,* and *Zimmer Persona.* One can see is the proposed model is able to achieve a promising AUC for almost all classes.

better understanding of what happened in our proposed leaning model to classify brand of TKA Implants using deep convolutional neural networks, and how the model make the predictions. We plot the class activation mapping at different layer for each brand. As shown in Fig. 6, our model did learn some shape features from the image to classify different brands (e.g. Fig. 6(b) and (f)). However, our

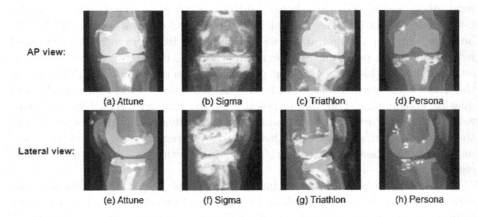

Fig. 6. The Class Activation Mapping (CAM) by utilizing Grad-CAM algorithm [18]. From the image, we can see that our model did learn the shape information from the image.

implementation still carries some shortcomings as our class activation mapping on Fig. 6(a), (d), and (h) are not very intuitive to explain such that the model learns the shape features from the images. The class activation mapping not only helped us to accurately analyze the model, but also increased the interpretation ability and helped to make an explainable deep learning model which can also help physicians, radiologists, and practitioners to understand and trust the deep learning model and the way it works.

4   Discussion, Conclusion, and Outlook

In this work, we proposed a deep neural network architectural model to precisely classify the brand of TKA implants in different views of plain knee radiographs. In this pilot study, a multi-view computationally annotated radiography dataset was used to classify four TKA implant types from three manufacturers, *Depuy*, *Howmedica*, and *Zimmer*, within four specific brands, namely *Depuy Attune*, *Depuy Sigma*, *Howmedica Triathlon*, and *Zimmer Persona*. Preliminary results demonstrate that we were able to build a feasible AI-powered component to precisely classify those TKA implants using only plain knee radiographs. From a clinical perspective, automatic and accurate identification of the design of a TKA implant is a principle step in preoperative planning of any TKA revision surgery, while any failure to identify the TKA implant type in a preoperative fashion may lead to prolonged hospitalization, a more complicated surgery, and additional healthcare costs, where it can be considered as a burden to healthcare providers. Thus, such a feasible, reliable, and explainable AI-powered tool would be a huge leap in orthopedic practice. We believe, more accurate and broader classification model(s) can be constructed with the use of combined medical images (data modality: *image*) with clinical and operative notes (data modality: *text*), rather than each data source individually. As part of our future work, we will integrate wealth of data from clinical data sources to build more accurate model(s) and also cover more diverse range of TKA implant types.

Acknowledgment. This work was supported by the National Institutes of Health (NIH) grants R01AR73147 and P30AR76312.

References

1. Kurtz, S.M., Ong, K.L., Lau, E., Bozic, K.J.: Impact of the economic downturn on total joint replacement demand in the United States: updated projections to 2021. JBJS **96**(8), 624–30 (2014)
2. Kremers, H.M., et al.: Prevalence of total hip and knee replacement in the United States. J. Bone Joint Surg. Am. Vol. **97**(17), 1386 (2015)
3. Losina, E., et al.: Cost-effectiveness of total knee arthroplasty in the United States: patient risk and hospital volume. Arch. Intern. Med. **169**(12), 1113–21 (2009)
4. Kremers, H.M., et al.: Comparative survivorship of different tibial designs in primary total knee arthroplasty. J. Bone Joint Surg. Am. **96**(14), e121 (2014)
5. Price, A.J., et al.: Knee replacement. Lancet **392**(10158), 1672–1682 (2018)

6. Bozic, K.J., et al.: The epidemiology of revision total knee arthroplasty in the United States. Clin. Orthop. Relat. Res.® **468**(1), 45–51 (2010)
7. Kurtz, S., Ong, K., Lau, E., Mowat, F., Halpern, M.: Projections of primary and revision hip and knee arthroplasty in the United States from 2005 to 2030. Jbjs **89**(4), 780–5 (2007)
8. Wilson, N.A., Jehn, M., York, S., Davis III, C.M.: Revision total hip and knee arthroplasty implant identification: implications for use of unique device identification 2012 AAHKS member survey results. J. Arthroplasty **29**(2), 251–5 (2014)
9. Steiner, C., Andrews, R., Barrett, M., Weiss, A.: HCUP projections: mobility/orthopedic procedures 2003 to 2012. US agency for healthcare research and quality (2012)
10. Scuderi, G.R.: Revision total knee arthroplasty: how much constraint is enough? Clin. Orthop. Relat. Res.® **392**, 300–305 (2001)
11. Paul, H.Y., et al.: Automated detection & classification of knee arthroplasty using deep learning. Knee **27**, 535–542 (2019)
12. Huang, G., Liu, Z., Van Der Maaten, L., Weinberger, K.Q.: Densely connected convolutional networks. In: Proceedings of the IEEE Conference on Computer Vision and Pattern Recognition, pp. 4700–4708 (2017)
13. Szegedy, C., et al.: Going deeper with convolutions. In: Proceedings of the IEEE Conference on Computer Vision and Pattern Recognition, pp. 1–9 (2015)
14. Yu, F., Koltun, V., Funkhouser, T.: Dilated residual networks. In: Proceedings of the IEEE Conference on Computer Vision and Pattern Recognition, pp. 472–480 (2017)
15. Yu, F., Koltun, V.: Multi-scale context aggregation by dilated convolutions. arXiv preprint arXiv:1511.07122, 23 November 2015
16. He, K., Zhang, X., Ren, S., Sun, J.: Deep residual learning for image recognition. In: Proceedings of the IEEE Conference on Computer Vision and Pattern Recognition, pp. 770–778 (2016)
17. Cohen, J.: A coefficient of agreement for nominal scales. Educ. Psychol. Meas. **20**(1), 37–46 (1960)
18. Selvaraju, R.R., Cogswell, M., Das, A., Vedantam, R., Parikh, D., Batra, D.: Grad-CAM: visual explanations from deep networks via gradient-based localization. In: Proceedings of the IEEE International Conference on Computer Vision, pp. 618–626 (2017)
19. Szegedy, C., Ioffe, S., Vanhoucke, V., Alemi, A.A.: Inception-v4, inception-ResNet and the impact of residual connections on learning. In: Thirty-first AAAI conference on artificial intelligence, 12 February 2017
20. Strubell, E., Verga, P., Belanger, D., McCallum, A.: Fast and accurate entity recognition with iterated dilated convolutions. arXiv preprint arXiv:1702.02098, 7 February 2017
21. Zhou, L., Zhang, C., Wu, M.: D-LinkNet: LinkNet with pretrained encoder and dilated convolution for high resolution satellite imagery road extraction. In: CVPR Workshops, 18 June 2018, pp. 182–186 (2018)
22. Wang, Y., Hu, S., Wang, G., Chen, C., Pan, Z.: Multi-scale dilated convolution of convolutional neural network for crowd counting. Multimed. Tools Appl. **79**, 1057–1073 (2019). https://doi.org/10.1007/s11042-019-08208-6
23. Liu, S., Xu, H., Liu, Y., Xie, H.: Improving brain tumor segmentation with dilated pseudo-3D convolution and multi-direction fusion. In: Ro, Y.M., et al. (eds.) MMM 2020. LNCS, vol. 11961, pp. 727–738. Springer, Cham (2020). https://doi.org/10.1007/978-3-030-37731-1_59

24. Wang, B., Zhang, X., Zhou, X., Li, J.: A gated dilated convolution with attention model for clinical cloze-style reading comprehension. Int. J. Environ. Res. Public Health **17**(4), 1323 (2020)
25. Rafi A.M., et al.: Application of DenseNet in camera model identification and post-processing detection. In: Proceedings of the IEEE Conference on Computer Vision and Pattern Recognition Workshops, pp. 19–28 (2019)
26. Chen, X., Du, J., Zhang, H.: Lipreading with DenseNet and resBi-LSTM. SIViP **14**(5), 981–989 (2020). https://doi.org/10.1007/s11760-019-01630-1
27. Chen, Y., Christodoulou, A.G., Zhou, Z., Shi, F., Xie, Y., Li, D.: MRI super-resolution with GAN and 3D multi-level DenseNet: smaller, faster, and better. arXiv preprint arXiv:2003.01217, 2 March 2020
28. Zhang, X., Pan, W., Bontozoglou, C., Chirikhina, E., Chen, D., Xiao, P.: Skin capacitive imaging analysis using deep learning GoogLeNet. In: Advances in Intelligent Systems and Computing, 16 July 2020
29. Balagourouchetty, L., Pragatheeswaran, J.K., Pottakkat, B., Ramkumar, G.: GoogLeNet based ensemble FCNet classifier for focal liver lesion diagnosis. IEEE J. Biomed. Health Inform. **24**(6), 1686–1694 (2020). https://ieeexplore.ieee.org/abstract/document/8845663
30. Kim, J.H., Seo, S.Y., Song, C.G., Kim, K.S.: Assessment of electrocardiogram rhythms by GoogLeNet deep neural network architecture. J. Healthc. Eng. **2019**, 1–10 (2019). https://www.ncbi.nlm.nih.gov/pmc/articles/PMC6512052/
31. Litjens, G., et al.: A survey on deep learning in medical image analysis. Med. Image Anal. **1**(42), 60–88 (2017)
32. Xu, Y., et al.: Deep learning of feature representation with multiple instance learning for medical image analysis. In: 2014 IEEE International Conference on Acoustics, Speech and Signal Processing (ICASSP), pp. 1626–1630. IEEE, 4 May 2014
33. López-Linares Román, K., García Ocaña, M.I., Lete Urzelai, N., González Ballester, M.Á., Macía Oliver, I.: Medical image segmentation using deep learning. In: Chen, Y.-W., Jain, L.C. (eds.) Deep Learning in Healthcare. ISRL, vol. 171, pp. 17–31. Springer, Cham (2020). https://doi.org/10.1007/978-3-030-32606-7_2
34. Tafti, A.P., Bashiri, F.S., LaRose, E., Peissig, P.: Diagnostic classification of lung CT images using deep 3D multi-scale convolutional neural network. In: 2018 IEEE International Conference on Healthcare Informatics (ICHI), pp. 412–414. IEEE, 4 June 2018
35. Abbas, A., Abdelsamea, M.M., Gaber, M.M.: Classification of COVID-19 in chest X-ray images using DeTraC deep convolutional neural network. arXiv preprint arXiv:2003.13815, 26 March 2020

Multi-modal Image Fusion Based on Weight Local Features and Novel Sum-Modified-Laplacian in Non-subsampled Shearlet Transform Domain

Hajer Ouerghi$^{(\boxtimes)}$, Olfa Mourali, and Ezzeddine Zagrouba

Université de Tunis El Manar, Institut Supérieur d'Informatique El Manar, Research Team SIIVA, LR16ES06, Laboratoire de recherche en Informatique, Modélisation et Traitement de l'Information et de la Connaissance (LIMTIC), 2 Rue Abou Rayhane Bayrouni, Ariana 2080, Tunisia
`hajer.ouerghi@fst.utm.tn, olfa.mourali@isi.utm.tn,`
`ezzeddine.zagrouba@uvt.tn`

Abstract. Multi-modal medical image fusion plays a significant role in clinical applications like noninvasive diagnosis and image-guided surgery. However, designing an efficient image fusion technique is still a challenging task. In this paper, we propose an improved multi-modal medical image fusion method to enhance the visual quality and contrast of the fused image. To achieve this work, the registered source images are firstly decomposed into low-frequency (LF) and several high-frequency (HF) sub-images via non-subsampled shearlet transform (NSST). Afterward, LF sub-images are combined using the proposed weight local features fusion rule based on local energy and standard deviation, while HF sub-images are fused based on the novel sum-modified-laplacien (NSML) technique. Finally, inversed NSST is applied to reconstruct the fused image. Furthermore, the proposed method is extended to color multi-modal image fusion that effectively restrains color distortion and enhances spatial and spectral resolutions. To evaluate the performance, various experiments conducted on different datasets of gray-scale and color images. Experimental results show that the proposed scheme achieves better performance than other state-of-art proposed algorithms in both visual effects and objective criteria.

Keywords: Medical image fusion · NSST · NSML · YIQ color space

1 Introduction

Nowadays, multi-modal medical image fusion has been emerging as a crucial area for clinical diagnosis and analysis. The target of multi-modal image fusion is to integrate complementary information of multi-modal source images into one comprehensive image, with the aim to improve visual quality, preserves more content information and decrease computational task [1]. In general, modern medical imaging modalities are

© Springer Nature Switzerland AG 2020
G. Bebis et al. (Eds.): ISVC 2020, LNCS 12510, pp. 166–179, 2020.
https://doi.org/10.1007/978-3-030-64559-5_13

available to guide doctors and radiologist in specific medical applications. These modalities are broadly classified into structural and functional [1]. Magnetic resonance imaging (MRI) and computed tomography (CT) reflect the structural information of an organ with high spatial resolution, therefore represented structural modalities. Where, functional MRI (fMRI), positron emission tomography (PET) and single-photon emission CT (SPECT) images give functional information with low spatial resolution, so grouped as functional modalities. Based on [1, 2], it is hard to obtain accurate information about specified organ from a single modality. For example, MRIs provide detailed information about pathological soft tissues, while CT images can clearly give the information of bone structures. Likewise, PET images can be utilized for the quantitative and dynamic detection of metabolic substances in the human body, while SPECT images show clinically variations in metabolism. Therefore, we need to create an effective multi-modal fusion method to facilitate the aided diagnosis and treatment planning. In the literature, image fusion algorithms are mainly developed at three levels: pixel [2], feature [3] and decision [4]. Usually, pixel-level fusion is used in the medical field because of its several advantages [2]. It is divided into spatial-domain and transform-domain. The spatial-domain fusion methods like principal component analysis (PCA) [5] and intensity-hue-saturation (IHS) [6] are broadly suitable for mono-modal image fusion, but they often suffer from block or region artifacts and spectral distortion. In the transform domain, different kinds of transforms have achieved great success, such as pyramid transform [7], wavelet transform [5], curvelet transform [8], contourlet transform [9] and shearlet transform [10]. Recently, Easley et al. [11] have proposed the NSST transform that has been successfully adopted in the medical fusion field.

On the other hand, the design of fusion rules for decomposed coefficients is the key factor that influences the image fusion quality. So far, a variety of fusion methods have been proposed. In the transform domain, sparse representation (SR) [11] and fuzzy logical [12] have successfully used for medical image fusion. In the similarity, pulse-coupled neuronal network (PCNN) and its modified versions have been widely adopted for medical fusion domain [13]. We have proposed a simplified PCNN model for fusing MRI and PET images in [14]. However, the major limitation of these models is time-consuming due to several parameters and complicated function mechanisms [14, 15]. In a similar vein, deep learning is a recent machine learning used for image fusion, but it not been widely applied in the medical fusion field due to the high time-consuming limitation and the significant demand for computational power [16]. Recently, sum-modified-laplacian (SML) is one of the obvious tools that can well-reflect the feature information about contours and edges of the image. At the beginning, Huang et al. [17] have employed SML for multi-focus image fusion and they achieved good results. Then, a new fusion scheme based on a novel SML (NSML) was proposed by Yin et al. [18] and used for capturing all salient features [19].

Inspired by the transform-domain algorithms, we proposed a pixel-based fusion method for multi-modal medical images. The core contribution of the proposed fusion method is the weight local features rules implementation for approximated coefficients based on local energies and standard deviation that significantly enhance visual appearance and reduce blurring effects. Besides, NSML is used for capturing all salient features from detailed coefficients. The proposed algorithm is further extended to color medical image fusion based on YIQ transformation. The rest of this paper is organized as follows. Section 2 briefly introduces related theories of NSST. Section 3 explains the proposed method in detail. Section 4 describes the extensive experimental results and discussions. Finally, Sect. 5 concludes the paper.

2 Non-subsampled Shearlet Transform

The NSST is a shift-invariant version of the shearlet transforms [11]. It has several advantages like shift-invariance, multi-directionality and computational simplicity. In two dimensions (2D), the affine system with composite dilation defined by [11]:

$$\psi_{j,k,m}(x) = |\det A|^{\frac{j}{2}} \psi\left(S^K A^j x - m\right) : j, k \in \mathbb{Z}^2 \tag{1}$$

A denotes the scaling matrix. S stands for the shear matrix. j, k, m are the scale, direction and shift parameters, respectively. For each d > 0 and s ∈ R,

$$A = \begin{bmatrix} d & 0 \\ 0 & d^{\frac{1}{2}} \end{bmatrix} \text{ and } S = \begin{bmatrix} 1 & s \\ 0 & 1 \end{bmatrix} \tag{2}$$

For any $\xi = (\xi_1, \xi_2) \in \mathbb{R}^2, \xi_1 \neq 0$, the shearlet function is defined as:

$$\widehat{\psi}^{(0)}(\xi) = \widehat{\psi}^{(0)}(\xi_1, \xi_2) = \widehat{\psi}_1(\xi_1)\widehat{\psi}_2\left(\frac{\xi_2}{\xi_1}\right) \tag{3}$$

Where $\widehat{\psi}$ is the Fourier transform of ψ, $\psi_1 \in C^\infty(R)$ and $\psi_2 \in C^\infty(R)$ are both wavelet and supp $\psi_1 \subset [-1/2, -1/16] \sqcup [1/16, 1/2]$, supp $\psi_2 \subset [-1, 1]$. This indicates that $\psi_0 \in C^\infty(R)$ and supp $\psi_0 \subset [-1/2, 1/2]^2$. Subsequently, we suppose that:

$$\sum_{j\geq 0} |\widehat{\psi}_1(2^{-2j}\omega)|^2 = 1, |\omega| \geq 18 \tag{4}$$

For each j ≥ 0, ψ_2 satisfies that:

$$\sum_{l=-2^j}^{2^j-1} |\widehat{\psi}_2(2^j\omega - 1)|^2 = 1, |\omega| \leq 1 \tag{5}$$

Based on several examples of ψ_1 and ψ_2, Eq. 4 and Eq. 5 notice that:

$$\sum_{j\geq 0}\sum_{l=-2^j}^{2^j-1} |\widehat{\psi}^{(0)}(\xi A_0^{-j}S_0^{-1}|^2 = \sum_{j\geq 0}\sum_{l=-2^j}^{2^j-1} \left|\widehat{\psi}_1\left(2^{-j}\xi_1\right)\right|^2 \left|\widehat{\psi}_2\left(2^j\frac{\xi_2}{\xi_1}\right)\right|^2 = 1 \tag{6}$$

The discrete NSST transform can be obtained from the different equations mentioned above. More theoretical background can be found in [11, 18].

3 Proposed Fusion Method

Let A and B denote the input images. In the beginning, we confirm that image registration is not related to the entire system. The input images are selected from a registered medical source. A schematic diagram of the proposed method is illustrated in Fig. 1. First, the input images were normalized and then decomposed up to three levels into LF and HF sub-bands by applying the NSST to separate the principal information and the edge details of the source image. The direction numbers from finer to coarser levels are set at [3, 4]. The 'maxflat' pyramidal filter is used and the size of the shearing window is set at 32, 32, and 16. After that, proposed fusion rules are adopted to integrate coefficients. Finally, inversed NSST is applied to get the fused image.

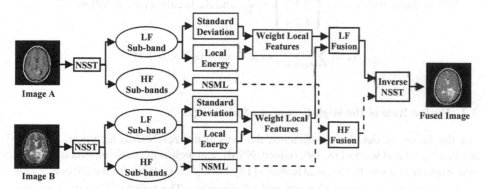

Fig. 1. Block diagram of the proposed fusion method.

3.1 Fusion Rule of the Low Frequency Sub-images

Approximated coefficients are very important for the visual quality of the fused image. Traditional ways for fusing LF sub-bands are by taking the weighted average or the maximum of the coefficient, but they directly affect the contrast and resolution of the output image [18].Therefore, a new fusion rule is given based on local energy and standard deviation, which are frequently used for fusing salient features [14, 19].

The local energy features enable us to describe the inherent texture of the image by analyzing the grade of associated information [9]. Besides, the local texture features of an image have a strong connection with the variation of the image coefficients, as well as its neighborhood [14]. The variation can be depicted by the regional standard deviation. Let $C_F(a, b)$ denotes the LF coefficient located at (a, b). The proposed fusion method is described as follows:

$$C_F(a, b) = \begin{cases} |C_A(a, b)|, & \delta_A \geq \delta_B \text{ and } \varepsilon_A \geq \varepsilon_B \\ |C_B(a, b)|, & \text{otherwise} \end{cases} \tag{7}$$

Where δ_μ is the weight for the standard deviation D_μ while ε_μ is the weight of the local energy E_μ. A and B are the input image, and $\mu = A,B$. They are calculated in the 3×3 neighborhood as follows:

$$\delta_\mu = \frac{D_\mu(a, b)}{D_A(a, b) + D_B(a, b)} \tag{8}$$

$$\varepsilon_\mu = \frac{E_\mu(a, b)}{E_A(a, b) + E_B(a, b)} \tag{9}$$

The regional standard deviation D_μ and the local energy E_μ are calculated as:

$$D_\mu = \sqrt{\sum_{s \in S, t \in T} \omega(s, t) \times \left[C_\mu(a + s, b + t) - S_\mu(a, b)\right]^2} \tag{10}$$

$$E_\mu = \sum_{s \in S, t \in T} \omega(s, t) \times \left[C_\mu(a + s, b + t)\right]^2 \tag{11}$$

Where the template $\omega = \begin{Bmatrix} 1 & 2 & 1 \\ 2 & 4 & 2 \\ 1 & 2 & 1 \end{Bmatrix} \times \frac{1}{16}$, and S_μ is calculated as follows:

$$S_\mu = \sum_{s \in S, t \in T} \omega(s, t) \times C_\mu(a + s, b + t) \tag{12}$$

3.2 Fusion Rule of the High Frequency Sub-images

For the fusion of detailed coefficients, the system utilizes NSML technique recently applied by several works [18, 19]. Indeed, NSML can well-reflect the important features and properly assesses the focused features [19]. Let $C_F^{l,k}(i, j)$ stands for the HF coefficient in the position (i, j) in the lth scale and k^{th} direction. The fused $C_F^{l,k}$ coefficients are selected by computing and comparing NSML. The coefficient $C_F^{l,k}(i, j)$ with maximum NSML value is selected as follows:

$$C_F^{l,k}(i, j) = \begin{cases} C_A^{l,k}(i, j), & NSML_A^{l,k}(i, j) \geq NSML_B^{l,k}(i, j) \\ C_B^{l,k}(i, j), & otherwise \end{cases} \tag{13}$$

The NSML is defined as:

$$NSML^{l,k}(i, j) = \sum_{m=-P}^{P} \sum_{n=-Q}^{Q} w(m, n) \left[ML^{l,k}(i + m, j + n)\right]^2 \tag{14}$$

$$ML^{l,k}(i, j) = \left|2MP^{l,k}(i, j) - MP^{l,k}(i - step, j) - MP^{l,k}(i + step, j)\right| + |2MP^{l,k}(i, j) - MP^{l,k}(i, j - step) - MP^{l,k}(i, j + step)| \tag{15}$$

Where $MP^{l,k}(i, j)$ denotes the directional band-pass, sub-band coefficient located at the pixel (i, j) in the lth sub-band at the kth decomposition level. While computing the derivative, step denoted the variable spacing between pixels, typically equal to 1. P and Q are the parameters that determine the window with a size of $(2P + 1)(2Q + 1)$, $w(m, n)$ represents the weights of the $ML^{l,k}(i + m, j + n)$, and must satisfying the normalization rules i.e. $\sum_m \sum_n (m, n) = 1$. Therefore, we choose $P = Q = 1$ and the same weighed window used for fusing LF coefficients.

3.3 Color Image Fusion

In recent years, fusion of structural and functional images has been an interesting hybrid tool that brings an important revolution in the medical field [1]. Usually, color images are in RGB (Red, Green, Blue) color space, which contains almost all the basic colors that can be perceived by human vision. Nevertheless, the three colors are treated equally and their components are strongly correlated. So, it makes the RGB color space very difficult to determine what color of the image will be changed if a component changes. To overcome this problem, several color transformations, such as YIQ, HSV, and IHS are proposed. In YIQ, image data consists of three components. The first component luminance (Y) represents the grayscale information, while the last two components hue (I) and saturation (Q) denote the chrominance information.

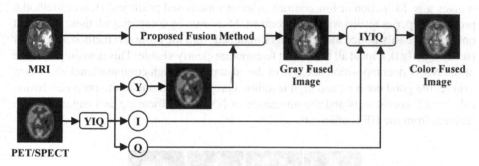

Fig. 2. Block diagram of the proposed color fusion scheme.

In this study, the color inputs are transformed from RGB to YIQ, which provides better spectral and spatial characteristics and reduces color distortion. The proposed scheme for color image fusion is illustrated in Fig. 2 and described as follows: First, the input PET/SPECT image perfectly registered and normalized in advance is transformed into the YIQ independent components. Second, the proposed gray fusion method is applied. The final output is obtained using the inversed YIQ by exploiting the new intensity and the original I and Q components of the color image.

4   Experimental Results and Discussion

To determine the overall performance of the proposed fusion method, extensive experiments are conducted on different types of pre-registered dataset images. All used images were frequently taken from the Website of Medical School of Harvard University "http://www.med.harvard.edu/AANLIB/" and from the fusion website "http://www.imagefusion.org". In this study, five objective image quality metrics are adopted [20]: (i) Entropy (E) that evaluates the quantity of information in the fused image. (ii) Feature Mutual Information (FMI) that measures the amount of feature information. (iii) Fusion Quality index ($Q^{AB/F}$) that gives valuable information about edge preservation. (iv) Standard Deviation (SD) that reflects the contrast information in the fused images. (v) Structural Similarity Index Measure (SSIM), which determines the structural similarity between two images.

4.1 Experiment-1: Gray-Scale Image Fusion

For the first section of experiments, four different datasets of CT and MRI images of the size 256×256 are selected as shown in Fig. 3. To verify the effectiveness of the proposed approach, the following existing state-of-art fusion methods are considered: Method.1 [12], Method.2 [21], Method.3 [18], Method.4 [13], Method.5 [22] and Method.6 [19].

Visual Analysis. Fusion results produced by the above techniques are shown in Fig. 4. Images (a) in every set are clearly noted blurred and having brightness issues and high noise. From images (b) and (c), a loss of contours and edges information can easily be noted as compared to images (g). The implementation of the modified MPCNN model in the MSVD domain gives better results, as can be shown by images (d). Method.5 provided clear results (see images (e)), but due to direct averaging of the LF coefficients, it gives less distinction or low contrast in some superposed positions. Hence, Method.6 produces superior results with good contrast. Moreover, by comparing all these images at once, it can easily notice that the images obtained from the proposed method are clearer (see images (g)), almost all the salient features are clearly visible. This is mainly because of the NSST decomposition because of the advantage of high computational efficiency. Where, the good contrast and high resolution are preserved due to the proposed fusion rule for LF coefficients and the utilization of NSML for focusing and capturing high features from the HF coefficients.

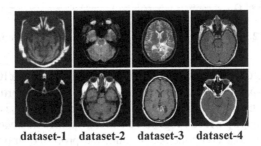

dataset-1   dataset-2   dataset-3   dataset-4

Fig. 3. Multi-modal source images. (a) dataset-1. top: MRI, bottom: CT (b) dataset-2. top: MRI-T2, bottom: MRI-T1 (c) dataset-3. top: MRI-T2, bottom: MRI-GAD (d) dataset-4. top: MRI-PD, bottom: CT.

Quantitative Analysis. Table 1, 2, 3, 4 provide quantitative performance. It should be noted that a larger measure implies better quality. First, through the significant results obtained for E given in Table 1, it can be clearly concluded that the proposed method gains the highest E for almost all the datasets, which shows that maximum structural information is present in the fused image. Second, the FMI results listed in Table 2 shows that the proposed method gives higher FMI for all datasets. It shows that maximum information about the edge strength, texture and contrast from the source images is retained in the fused image. Third, almost all datasets preserved the highest values of the $Q^{AB/F}$ (Table 3) except for dataset-1 in Method. 6, which indicates that more edge details are provided by our algorithm. Finally, results obtained for SD are given Table 4. The proposed technique produces higher contrast for all sets except dataSet-1 in Method.6.

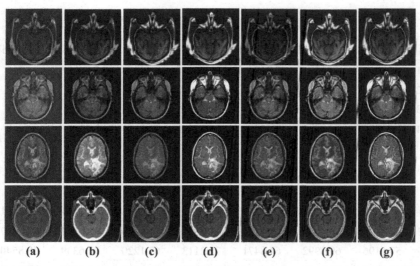

(a)   (b)   (c)   (d)   (e)   (f)   (g)

Fig. 4. Comparative visual results obtained from different fusion methods applied to multi-modal images. (a) Method.1, (b) Method.2, (c) Method.3, (d) Method.4, (e) Method.5, (f) Method.6, (g) Proposed.

From these results, it can be observed that the proposed method provides an efficient fusion tool compared with other mainstream algorithms.

Table 1. Entropy (E) comparison of different fusion methods

Data	Method.1	Method.2	Method.3	Method.4	Method.5	Method.6	Method.7
Set-1	6.3252	6.2564	6.4575	6.7454	6.4179	6.6257	**6.9276**
Set-2	5.2372	5.1190	5.2354	4.5308	5.3299	5.3810	**5.6103**
Set-3	4.5448	3.9737	4.2431	4.3084	4.2951	4.7046	**5.2872**
Set-4	5.6420	5.2750	5.1542	4.7685	5.9869	5.8250	**5.8601**

Table 2. Feature Mutual Information (FMI) comparison of different fusion methods

Data	Method.1	Method.2	Method.3	Method.4	Method.5	Method.6	Method.7
Set-1	0.9665	0.8758	0.9031	0.8869	0.8973	0.9157	**0.9689**
Set-2	0.8630	0.7812	0.8619	0.8581	0.8565	0.8752	**0.8774**
Set-3	0.8425	0.8342	0.8452	0.8659	0.8459	0.8794	**0.8845**
Set-4	0.8500	0.8792	0.8298	0.8607	0.8612	0.8679	**0.8805**

Table 3. Quality Index ($Q^{AB/F}$) comparison of different fusion methods

Data	Method.1	Method.2	Method.3	Method.4	Method.5	Method.6	Method.7
Set-1	0.8805	0.7051	0.7275	0.6771	0.6585	**0.6890**	0.6795
Set-2	0.4893	0.6527	0.4984	0.5110	0.5112	0.5196	**0.6053**
Set-3	0.4979	0.6285	0.4949	0.5267	0.5179	0.5415	**0.6137**
Set-4	0.4699	0.5288	0.4590	0.4827	0.5216	0.5586	**0.5609**

Table 4. Standard Deviation (SD) comparison of different fusion methods

Data	Method.1	Method.2	Method.3	Method.4	Method.5	Method.6	Method.7
Set-1	62.5335	56.6646	64.5731	61.2030	53.2106	**70.8927**	69.0667
Set-2	57.6196	69.3992	64.8471	72.2113	67.1220	77.6339	**78.8540**
Set-3	59.3623	71.5558	61.5954	74.7389	63.6425	69.3794	**72.6415**
Set-4	55.5056	61.1031	59.9547	76.7698	61.6975	68.3625	**72.0792**

4.2 Experiment-2: Color Image Fusion

For this section of experiments, five data-sets of MRI, PET and SPECT images having a size of 256×256 are selected as shown in Fig. 5. The following state-of-art schemes are selected to verify the effectiveness of the proposed color fusion method: Scheme.1 [12], Scheme.2 [15], Scheme.3 [23], Scheme.4 [14] and Scheme.5 [19].

Visual Analysis. Fused results are given in Fig. 6. Images (a) produced by Scheme.1 preserve both structural and functional information, but the approach works in grayscale space. From images (b), it can be observed that most of the information of brain structures in the non-functional area is lost. Furthermore, these images suffer from color distortion and contrast reduction. We expect more satisfactory results from Scheme.3 (see images (c)) because of the advantages of implementing fusion rules on every channel separately after each local Laplacian filtering (LLF) decomposition level. Although, the images obtained through this scheme contain some noise and are showing deficiency in edge strength. In general, more visual superiority is retained by Scheme.4 and Scheme.5, where the fused outputs have good resolution and contrast as well (see images (d)) and images (e)). Compare to these existing methods, it can be easily recognized in the images obtained by the proposed scheme (see images (f)) that problem of color and contrast reduction is highly improved.

Quantitative Analysis. In order to support the visual quality of the proposed scheme, the quantitative matrices FMI, $Q^{AB/F}$, SSIM and SD for the previously mentioned schemes are also computed. Results obtained from these matrices for all the five sets are plotted in Fig. 7, 8, 9, 10. In general, the proposed scheme gives the highest values for almost every set. Furthermore, our fused images show more visual superiority and effectiveness in

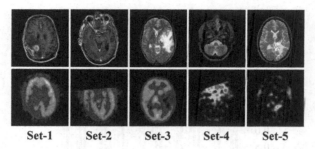

Fig. 5. Multi-modal color source images. Set-1, Set-2& Set-3.top: MRI, bottom: PET. Set-4 & Set-5.top: MRI, bottom: SPECT. (Color figure online)

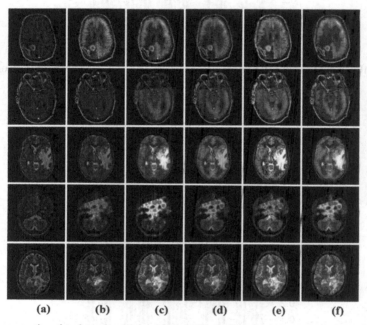

Fig. 6. Comparative visual results obtained from different fusion schemes applied to color images. (a) Scheme.1, (b) Scheme.2, (c) Scheme.3, (d) Scheme.4, (e) Scheme.5, (f) Proposed. (Color figure online)

contrast with excellent spatial and spectral resolutions. Hence, from the visual and quantitative analysis, we conclude that the proposed algorithm has successfully injected the anatomical information of the high-resolution MRI image into the metabolic information of the PET/SPECT image.

Computational Efficiency. In pursuit of the clear comparison, time costs of the compared algorithms are illustrated in Table 5. It can be observed that methods [21] and [14] consume lot more time (83 s and 180 s) compare to others. This is because these methods are based on learning algorithms like SR and PCNN. The method [23] provides advantageous results, but it was taking also important time 135 s due to the LLF

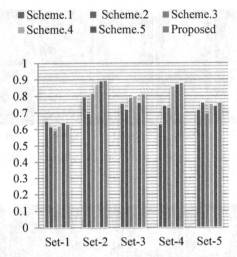

Fig. 7. FMI comparisons of color images, for the existing fusion schemes results. (Color figure online)

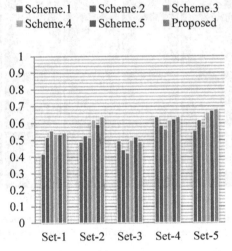

Fig. 8. $Q^{AB/F}$ comparisons of color images, for the existing fusion schemes results. (Color figure online)

decomposition process. The proposed method is taking less time about 6 s to produce one fusion image of size 256×256 from two input images on the platform implemented in Matlab2018b on a PC with Intel core2 Duo CPU and 4 GB of RAM. To conclude, the proposed fusion method is light-weight and efficient. Thus it can be dedicated to real time-aided diagnosis and treatment planning systems without consuming too many computational resources.

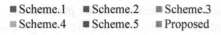

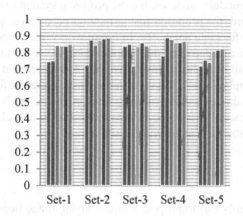

Fig. 9. SSIM comparisons of color images, for the existing fusion schemes results. (Color figure online)

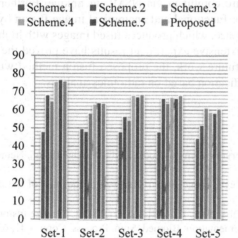

Fig. 10. SD comparisons of color images, for the existing fusion schemes results. (Color figure online)

Table 5. Time cost comparison (Time unit: second)

Algorithm	[12]	[21]	[13]	[22]	[23]	[14]	[19]	Proposed
Time cost	20	83	12	16	135	180	40	6

Although the proposed method achieves better performance, it has two limitations. Firstly, the proposed method is designed to fuse the pre-registered images, thus adding an image registration module might enable the proposed system to deal with the unregistered datasets. Second, the proposed fusion method needs more ground truth data to prove more efficiency for large databases. In future works, the proposed method can be extended to other medical aided diagnostic applications like segmentation and classification. Specifically, it will be dedicated for classifying low-grade and high-grade gliomas based on radiomics analysis [24]. Indeed, glioma classification before surgery is of the utmost important in clinical decision making and prognosis prediction. Therefore, an aided diagnosis framework composed of two parts, fusion and classification, will be proposed to assist radiologists in glioma classification.

5 Conclusion

The purpose of this study was to propose a multi-modal image fusion method based on an adopted weight local features and NSML fusion rules in the NSST domain. First, NSST has been applied on pre-registered source images. Subsequently, we design an adapted weight local features fusion rule for fusing the approximated sub-images, while detailed coefficients are combined via NSML technique. Furthermore, the proposed method is extended for functional and anatomical image fusion by transforming color images to YIQ color space, which produces fused images with high spatial and spectral resolutions. Overall, extensive experiment results have proved the effectiveness of the proposed method. In future work, the proposed fusion method will be adopted for an accurate glioma classification based on radiomics analysis.

References

1. Du, F., et al.: An overview of multi-modal medical image fusion. Neurocomputing **215**, 3–20 (2016)
2. Li, S., et al.: Pixel-level image fusion: a survey of the state of the art. Inform. Fusion **33**, 100–112 (2017)
3. Shahdoosti, H.R., Tabatabaei, Z.: MRI and PET/SPECT image fusion at feature level using ant colony based segmentation. Biomed. Sign. Process. Control **47**, 63–74 (2019)
4. Mangai, U.G., et al.: A survey of decision fusion and feature fusion strategies for pattern classification. IETE Tech. Rev. **27**(4), 293–307 (2010)
5. Reena Benjamin, J., Jayasree, T.: Improved medical image fusion based on cascaded PCA and shift invariant wavelet transforms. Int. J. Comput. Assist. Radiol. Surg. **13**(2), 229–240 (2017). https://doi.org/10.1007/s11548-017-1692-4
6. He, C., et al.: Multimodal medical image fusion based on IHS and PCA. Procedia Eng. **7**, 280–285 (2010)
7. Wang, W., Chang, F.: A multi-focus image fusion method based on laplacian pyramid. JCP **6**(12), 2559–2566 (2011)
8. Ali, F.E., et al.: Curvelet fusion of MR and CT images. Prog. Electromagn. Res. **3**, 215–224 (2008)
9. Yang, L., Guo, B.L., Ni, W.: Multimodality medical image fusion based on multiscale geometric analysis of contourlet transform. Neurocomputing **72**(1–3), 203–211 (2008)

10. Miao, Q.G., Shi, C., Xu, P.F., Yang, M., Shi, Y.B.: A novel algorithm of image fusion using shearlets. Opt. Commun. **284**(6), 1540–1547 (2011)
11. Easley, G., Labate, D., Lim, W.Q.: Sparse directional image representations using the discrete shearlet transform. Appl. Comput. Harmonic Anal. **25**(1), 25–46 (2008)
12. Manchanda, M., Sharma, R.: An improved multimodal medical image fusion algorithm based on fuzzy transform. J. Vis. Commun. Image Represent. **51**, 76–94 (2018)
13. Ouerghi, H., Mourali, O., Zagrouba, E.: Multimodal medical image fusion using modified PCNN based on linking strength estimation by MSVD transform. Int. J. Comput. Commun. Eng. **6**(3), 201–211 (2017)
14. Ouerghi, H., Mourali, O., Zagrouba, E.: Non-subsampled shearlet transform based MRI and PET brain image fusion using simplified pulse coupled neural network and weight local features in YIQ colour space. IET Image Proc. **12**(10), 1873–1880 (2018)
15. Ganasala, P., Kumar, V.: Feature-motivated simplified adaptive PCNN-based medical image fusion algorithm in NSST domain. J. Digit. Imaging **29**(1), 73–85 (2016)
16. Zhang, Y., et al.: IFCNN: A general image fusion framework based on convolutional neural network. Inform. Fusion **54**, 99–118 (2020)
17. Huang, W., Jing, Z.: Evaluation of focus measures in multi-focus image fusion. Pattern Recogn. Lett. **28**(4), 493–500 (2007)
18. Yin, M., et al.: A novel image fusion algorithm based on nonsubsampled shearlet transform. Optik **125**(10), 2274–2282 (2014)
19. Ullah, H., et al.: Multi-modality medical images fusion based on local-features fuzzy sets and novel sum-modified-Laplacian in non-subsampled shearlet transform domain. Biomed. Signal Process. Control **57**, 101724 (2020)
20. Jagalingam, P., Hegde, A.V.: A review of quality metrics for fused image. Aquatic Procedia 4. Icwrcoe 133–142 (2015)
21. Mohammed, A., Nisha, A.KL., Sathidevi, P.S.: A novel medical image fusion scheme employing sparse representation and dual PCNN in the NSCT domain. In: IEEE Region 10 Conference (TENCON). pp. 2147–2151. IEEE, Singapore (2016)
22. Liu, X., Mei, W., Du, H.: Multi-modality medical image fusion based on image decomposition framework and nonsubsampled shearlet transform. Biomed. Signal Process. Control **40**, 343–350 (2018)
23. Du, J., Li, W., Xiao, B.: Anatomical-functional image fusion by information of interest in local Laplacian filtering domain. IEEE Trans. Image Process. **26**(12), 5855–5866 (2017)
24. Lotan, E., et al.: State of the art: Machine learning applications in glioma imaging. Am. J. Roentgenol. **212**(1), 26–37 (2019)

Robust Prostate Cancer Classification with Siamese Neural Networks

Alberto Rossi[1,2](✉) (iD), Monica Bianchini[2] (iD), and Franco Scarselli[2] (iD)

[1] University of Florence, Via di S. Marta 3, 50139 Firenze, Italy
alberto.rossi@unifi.it
[2] University of Siena, Via Roma 56, 53100 Siena, Italy
https://sailab.diism.unisi.it/

Abstract. Nuclear magnetic resonance (NMR) is a powerful and non–invasive diagnostic tool. However, NMR scanned images are often noisy due to patient motions or breathing. Although modern Computer Aided Diagnosis (CAD) systems, mainly based on Deep Learning (DL), together with expert radiologists, can obtain very accurate predictions, working with noisy data can induce a wrong diagnose or require a new acquisition, spending time and exposing the patient to an extra dose of radiation. In this paper, we propose a new DL model, based on a Siamese neural network, able to withstand random noise perturbations. We use data coming from the ProstateX challenge and demonstrate the superior robustness of our model to random noise compared to a similar architecture, albeit deprived of the Siamese branch. In addition, our approach is also resistant to adversarial attacks and shows overall better AUC performance.

Keywords: Prostate cancer · Nuclear magnetic resonance · Siamese neural network · Deep learning

1 Introduction

According to cancer statistics for the year 2019 [18], prostate cancer is the most common cancer in the United States and the second most deadly for men. The GLOBOCAN [3] report focuses on 20 different countries to study the incidence of various forms of cancer and their mortality rate. The reported result is in line with the United States, as prostate lesions are the second most diagnosed form of cancer, ranking fifth for the mortality rate. There are some likely circumstances that have proven to be influential in the development of prostate cancer, such as obesity and ethnicity (South African and Caribbean people are more prone to the disease).

Fortunately, in the past two decades, advances in medical diagnostics have led to the establishment of a common procedure for early detection of prostate cancer, drastically reducing the mortality rate. In fact, the first marker is the Prostate Specific Antigen (PSA) [21], which can be detected with a simple blood

© Springer Nature Switzerland AG 2020
G. Bebis et al. (Eds.): ISVC 2020, LNCS 12510, pp. 180–189, 2020.
https://doi.org/10.1007/978-3-030-64559-5_14

test. Anyway, in case of suspected tumor, a biopsy is required, in order to establish the real presence of a malignant lesion. The biopsy outcome can be assessed quantitatively based on the Gleason score [17]. However, a biopsy is a very invasive test—during which complications may occur [15]—, which should only be prescribed if strictly necessary, in order to avoid over–treatment.

A valid aid for diagnosis can also come from the use of multi–parametric magnetic resonance imaging (mp–MRI), a fast and non–invasive test, aimed at avoiding or, at least, reducing the need for surgery, like in biopsy. The obtained images are evaluated based on a scaling system called PIRADS [25]. Along with this innovation in the field of physics, the great advances in computer science and, in particular, in artificial intelligence, have also provided new tools to automate the diagnosis and support radiologists in their decisions. This approach is called Computer Aided Diagnosis (CAD) [13] and, in general, allows the localization and automatic classification of NMR images of the prostate.

The impressive results recently obtained by deep learning in image analysis, particularly by convolutional neural networks (CNNs) [7,11,19], have contributed in improving conventional feature–based CAD systems. Indeed, state–of–the–art CNN models can achieve performance comparable to that of expert radiologists [12,16,20,24,26] for prostate lesion classification. However, although CNNs' performance is indisputable, they can suffer from perturbations in the input images , which can be random or produced by an algorithm designed to deceive the classifier [5,22]. The reason of this lack in robustness was initially supposed to be the non–linearity of the separation surfaces traced by CNNs but, in [5], it has been shown that such a problem can also occur when linearity is imposed. What happens in practice is that the separation surfaces are so close and so complex in shape that a small perturbation can actually cause the class boundary to be crossed, resulting in an incorrect classification.

DL approaches for classification tasks are usually defined as optimization problems, where the function to be minimized is the cross–entropy loss. Unfortunately, even if efficient separation surfaces can be obtained, they are based on known samples, i.e. those used for training, while noisy data can actually be misclassified. Unlike the cross–entropy loss, the contrastive loss function [6] is aimed at learning similarities between pairs of patterns, regardless of their class. The contrastive loss consists of two terms applied separately, so that if two patterns are considered similar, the loss encourages their closeness, spreading them in the feature space in case of dissimilarity. In this way, some robustness is added to the network behavior in case of noise.

A convenient neural network model to deal with the contrastive loss is the Siamese network [4]. In this architecture, a single set of shared weights are used for two input streams, producing two separate embeddings, processed in the last layers to express whether the related pair of objects is similar or not. Siamese networks are particularly effective for one–shot learning [10]—which aims to learn information on object categories from one, or a few, training images—but they have proven to be useful also for verification tasks or to compare groups of objects (see, f. i. [8], where a three–stream architecture is employed). More interesting for the scope of this paper is the use of Siamese networks to achieve metric learning based on contrastive loss [1,23,27,28], which means that two samples are compared and a similarity measure is evaluated.

Based on the results reported in [2], in which a Siamese network trained with a composite loss (cross–entropy plus a customized Euclidean distance) is used to improve the robustness for the recognition of facial expressions, we propose a hybrid Siamese network equipped with a combined cross–entropy/contrastive loss, to implement a robust prostate lesion classifier. To show the potential of our model, a set of experiments was conducted, comparing the Siamese performance with a standard ResNet classifier. For the sake of fairness, the hybrid Siamese network is made up of a ResNet backbone, so that only the loss function is changed. The two architectures have been evaluated on a validation set injected with random noise, calculating the corresponding decrease in performance in terms of AUC. Finally, to get a more comprehensive analysis, we also applied adversarial attacks to the models. The results clearly reveal a substantial increase in robustness for the hybrid network for both tests, along with better performance.

The rest of the paper is organized as follows. Section 2.1 reports details on the used dataset, while Sect. 2.2 provides information about image preprocessing. In Sect. 2.3, our proposed Siamese architecture is presented, whereas the following Sect. 2.4 describes the experimental setup. The obtained results are reported in Sect. 3. Finally, Sect. 4 outlines some conclusion and future prospects.

2   Materials and Methods

In this section, the hybrid Siamese network is described in detail along with the data employed for the experiments. The data preprocessing procedure and the experimental setup are also explained.

2.1   The Dataset

The images used for this study comes from the ProstateX challenge [13], hosted in the 2017 SPIE Medical Imaging Symposium. The dataset is composed by NMR images acquired in different modalities, namely T2–weighted (T2W), proton density–weighted (PD–W), dynamic contrast–enhanced (DCE), and diffusion–weighted (DWI), providing both High b–Value images and ADC maps. The training collection is composed by 330 lesions coming from 203 patients. For each lesion, the clinical significance (yes/no), the position of the lesion in physical coordinates and the voxel identifier are reported, together with the affected prostate zone, namely apical (AS), peripheral (PZ) and transition (TZ). The corresponding zonal distribution is reported in Table 1. Instead, the test set collects 208 images, coming from 141 patients, with attached coordinates and prostate zone for each lesion, but without the target. Therefore, any classification method can be evaluated only by submitting the obtained results to the challenge web page[1].

---

[1] https://prostatex.grand-challenge.org/.

Table 1. The dataset distribution with respect to the lesion prostate zone and clinical significance.

Prostate zone	Number	% not Significant	% Significant
Apical (AS)	55	44	56
Peripheral (PZ)	191	81	19
Transition (TZ)	82	89	11

2.2 Image Preprocessing

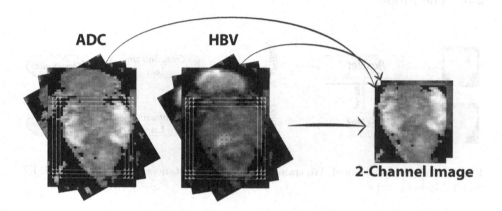

Fig. 1. Image augmentation and composition.

The standard radiological procedure employs three different modalities to correctly evaluate a prostate lesion, namely T2W, ADC and High b–Value [25]. Of all the models evaluated on ProstateX, one of the few with an associated paper is [14]. Here, in fact, maximum performance on the validation set was achieved by using a combination of T2W, ADC and High b–Value. Instead, the best test AUC (equal to 0.84) was obtained from an ensemble model, where also other modalities, with a low score on the validation set, were combined. Still in [14], a time–consuming normalization and registration procedure was used to resize and align images correctly. In this paper, for the sake of simplicity and to demonstrate how the improved robustness is due to our model and not to the parameter choice, we decided to use only DWI images, i.e. High b–Value and ADC formats. This set of data does not require any registration or normalization, since all images are acquired in the same physical space. Finally, while in [14] images considered not adequate for a good training were discarded, we use the entire dataset.

From both the selected modalities, we crop a $32 \times 32 \times 1$ square ROI containing the lesion, according to the coordinate points available in the dataset. Since the dataset is very small, we extract 297 variants for each lesion, cropping the image with 11 different rotation values $[0, \pm 10, \pm 15, \pm 20, \pm 30, \pm 40]$ and shifting its center point in the range $[-2, 0, 2]$ for each of the three axes, as shown in Fig. 1. ADC and High b–Value ROI are then concatenated to obtain a 2–channel image, on which per–channel normalization and mean subtraction are applied. Finally, online image augmentation, consisting of random flip, shear and zoom, is used to further improve training performance. During the evaluation phase, the 297 variants are averaged to obtain the final prediction, as in [14].

2.3   The Model

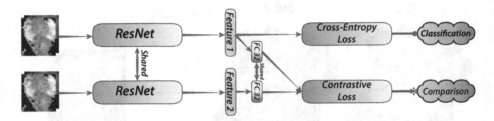

Fig. 2. The proposed model. We train three different instances for each of the AS, PZ and TZ lesion groups.

$$L_e = \sum_{i}^{n} \sum_{k}^{K} -y_i^k log(\tilde{y}_i^k) \tag{1}$$

Our proposed architecture is a Siamese network [4,10] that accepts pairs of input images and learns by comparing them. This network has a shared set of weights, which means that both images are processed with the same weights to produce two embeddings. Then, the obtained representations are compared to evaluate their similarity. The Siamese network has a ResNet [7] backbone, which, thanks to the presence of skip connections, has proven to be one of the most effective models in image classification. Siamese networks can be trained based on different losses, depending on the problem to be solved. For example, in one–shot learning [10], the cross–entropy loss defined in Eq. 1, where n are the dataset dimension, K the model classes, y_i the target, $\tilde{y}_i$ the prediction, is used. Instead, in metric learning [1,23,27,28], the contrastive loss [6] is employed to provide a real metric. The contrastive loss is defined as:

$$L_c(W, Y, X_1, X_2) = (1 - Y)(D_W)^2 + Y(\max\{0, m - D_W\})^2 \tag{2}$$

where W denotes the set of trainable weights, Y is the target (1 for dissimilar patterns, and 0 otherwise), X_1, X_2 represent the embeddings extracted from the backbone network, D_W is the Euclidean distance between X_1 and X_2, and $m > 0$ is a margin used to let a pair contribute to the loss only if its distance D_W belongs to $(0, m)$. Roughly speaking, this loss allows to spread patterns that are dissimilar, gradually approaching similar ones.

In our model, we combine the cross–entropy L_e and the contrastive loss L_c as follows:

$$L(W, X_1, X_2, C_1) = \alpha L_c(W, Y, X_1, X_2) + \beta L_e(W, X_1, C_1) \tag{3}$$

with α and β weighting the relative importance of the two losses. In Eq. (3), C_1 is the class of the query image X_1 and Y is the target for the contrastive loss, defining the similarity between two images, based on the class correspondence.

As far as we know, there are no examples in the literature of the combined use of cross–entropy and contrastive loss, although a related approach is presented in [2], where two loss functions—i.e. the standard cross–entropy and a customized loss based on the Euclidean distance—are blended for training a Siamese network for facial expression recognition.

In this paper, we prove that the property of moving patterns across the feature space, making them closer or farther depending on their similarity, can improve the robustness of a prostate lesion classifier with respect to input perturbations. The proposed architecture is shown in Fig. 2.

2.4 Experimental Setup

In our experiments, which aim to asses the robustness of the proposed model, the Siamese neural network trained on the combined loss function is compared with a standard ResNet [7] (able to process one input at a time), having the same architecture and exploiting the cross–entropy loss function. After training, we performed two different tests. The first experiment was based on applying Gaussian noise, with zero mean and standard deviation varying in the range of $[0, 0.025, 0.05, 0.075, 0.1, 0.2]$, to the inputs. This allows to measure the drop in performance in order to evaluate the network robustness. Subsequently, a test was performed by applying an FGSM adversarial attack [5] to the network and measuring how much the image has to be perturbed in order to change the predicted class. The results are evaluated measuring the $\| \cdot \|_\infty$ between the original image and the corresponding adversarial example.

Since lesions located in different positions of the prostate have different appearance and class distribution, we build three different models, one for each zone, i.e. AS, PZ and TZ, to better address the three cases. Relevant features of the three different ResNet architectures can be found in Table 2 (while more details about the ResNet can be derived from the original paper [7]).

All hyperparameters were instantiated by splitting the validation set with respect to each of the three cases (AS, PZ and TZ), maintaining the same class distribution as in the training set. Learning is carried out with the Adam optimizer [9], with an initial learning rate of 10^{-4}, decreased by a factor 0.5 after 5 epochs with no improvement in the loss. The training is terminated based on an

Table 2. Details of the ResNet architectures used in the experiments.

Prostate zone	ResNet version	# of filter in the first block
Aphical (AS)	8	12
Peripheral (PZ)	20	16
Transition (TZ)	14	12

early stopping procedure, with a patience of 20 epochs, saving the best model according to the validation loss. Parameters α and β are set to 0.25 and 1 respectively, maintaining predominant the classification performance. We trained the networks on 25 instances for each of the three zones on an NVidia GTX 1080TI. The code was implemented in Keras.

3   Results

We have run 25 experiments for each of the three prostate areas, for a more reliable model assessment. For each zonal architecture, the corresponding performance reduction on the validation set is calculated, by varying the variance of the Gaussian noise added to the input. The obtained results, concerning the AUC and the accuracy, are plotted in Fig. 3, reporting the mean (horizontal line), the quartiles (boxes), the rest of the distribution (whiskers) and outliers (diamond) for the 25 run of each configuration. This figure show how hybrid models achieve better performance with respect to the ResNet case, particularly for the AUC metric, independently from the noise injection level. Next, we tried to cheat our model (and the baseline) using the FGSM [5] adversarial attack, computing the ∞–norm between the original image and the one produced by FGSM. This gives us a measure of how easy is to make the classifier change the predicted class by modifying the input. The average of this distance, together with its maximum, is shown in Fig. 4 on a logarithmic scale. The high number of circles in the top-right part of the figure reveals how the hybrid model needs more FGSM iterations to be cheated than the corresponding ResNet, meaning that the hybrid model reports large average and maximum distances between the original image and the corrupted. Averaging the output of the 5 best models according to validation set for each of the prostate zone, and letting the three ensembles respond for the corresponding test lesion zone, the hybrid Siamese network got an AUC of 0.8, improving the ResNet (ensembled in the same way) by 0.05.

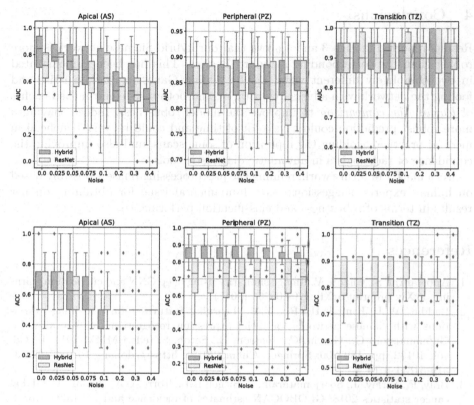

Fig. 3. Difference in AUC (a) and accuracy (b) when the noise increases.

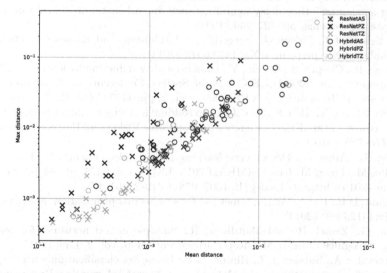

Fig. 4. Average and maximum distance returned by the FGSM adversarial attack, for the 25 training runs.

4   Conclusions

Results reported in Figs. 3 and 4 prove that our hybrid Siamese network is more robust than the corresponding standard ResNet. This has been demonstrated in two completely different ways, i.e. by adding Gaussian random noise and fooling the network with adversarial attacks, and both tests confirm the benefits of *learning by comparison* to improve the model robustness. Indeed, having a more robust prediction could save a lot of time and could be very beneficial in medical practice, avoiding the repetition of some scans, and also improving the confidence of radiologists in automatic diagnostic tools.

As a matter of future work, refining the pre–processing phase—possibly based on human experts' suggestions—is a fundamental issue for obtaining further results in terms of robustness and classification performance.

References

1. Appalaraju, S., Chaoji, V.: Image similarity using deep CNN and curriculum learning. arXiv preprint arXiv:1709.08761 (2017)
2. Baddar, W.J., Kim, D.H., Ro, Y.M.: Learning features robust to image variations with siamese networks for facial expression recognition. In: Amsaleg, L., Guðmundsson, G., Gurrin, C., Jónsson, B., Satoh, S. (eds.) MMM 2017. LNCS, vol. 10132, pp. 189–200. Springer, Cham (2017). https://doi.org/10.1007/978-3-319-51811-4_16
3. Bray, F., Ferlay, J., Soerjomataram, I., Siegel, R.L., Torre, L.A., Jemal, A.: Global cancer statistics 2018: GLOBOCAN estimates of incidence and mortality worldwide for 36 cancers in 185 countries. CA: Cancer J. Clin. **68**(6), 394–424 (2018)
4. Bromley, J., Guyon, I., LeCun, Y., Säckinger, E., Shah, R.: Signature verification using a "siamese" time delay neural network. In: Advances in Neural Information Processing Systems, pp. 737–744 (1994)
5. Goodfellow, I.J., Shlens, J., Szegedy, C.: Explaining and harnessing adversarial examples. arXiv preprint arXiv:1412.6572 (2014)
6. Hadsell, R., Chopra, S., LeCun, Y.: Dimensionality reduction by learning an invariant mapping. In: 2006 IEEE Computer Society Conference on Computer Vision and Pattern Recognition (CVPR 2006), vol. 2, pp. 1735–1742. IEEE (2006)
7. He, K., Zhang, X., Ren, S., Sun, J.: Deep residual learning for image recognition. In: Proceedings of the IEEE Conference on Computer Vision and Pattern Recognition, pp. 770–778 (2016)
8. Hoffer, E., Ailon, N.: Deep metric learning using triplet network. In: Feragen, A., Pelillo, M., Loog, M. (eds.) SIMBAD 2015. LNCS, vol. 9370, pp. 84–92. Springer, Cham (2015). https://doi.org/10.1007/978-3-319-24261-3_7
9. Kingma, D.P., Ba, J.: Adam: a method for stochastic optimization. arXiv preprint arXiv:1412.6980 (2014)
10. Koch, G., Zemel, R., Salakhutdinov, R.: Siamese neural networks for one-shot image recognition. In: ICML deep learning workshop, vol. 2, Lille (2015)
11. Krizhevsky, A., Sutskever, I., Hinton, G.E.: ImageNet classification with deep convolutional neural networks. In: Advances in Neural Information Processing Systems, pp. 1097–1105 (2012)

12. Le, M.H., et al.: Automated diagnosis of prostate cancer in multi-parametric MRI based on multimodal convolutional neural networks. Phys. Med. Biol. **62**(16), 6497 (2017)
13. Litjens, G., Debats, O., Barentsz, J., Karssemeijer, N., Huisman, H.: Computer-aided detection of prostate cancer in MRI. IEEE Trans. Med. Imaging **33**(5), 1083–1092 (2014)
14. Liu, S., Zheng, H., Feng, Y., Li, W.: Prostate cancer diagnosis using deep learning with 3D multiparametric MRI. In: Medical Imaging 2017: Computer-Aided Diagnosis, vol. 10134, p. 1013428. International Society for Optics and Photonics (2017)
15. Loeb, S., Carter, H.B., Berndt, S.I., Ricker, W., Schaeffer, E.M.: Complications after prostate biopsy: data from seer-medicare. J. Urol. **186**(5), 1830–1834 (2011)
16. Schelb, P., et al.: Classification of cancer at prostate MRI: deep learning versus clinical PI-RADS assessment. Radiology **293**(3), 607–617 (2019)
17. Schröder, F.H., et al.: Screening and prostate-cancer mortality in a randomized european study. N. Engl. J. Med. **360**(13), 1320–1328 (2009)
18. Siegel, R.L., Miller, K.D., Jemal, A.: Cancer statistics, 2019. CA: Cancer J. Clin. **69**(1), 7–34 (2019)
19. Simonyan, K., Zisserman, A.: Very deep convolutional networks for large-scale image recognition. arXiv preprint arXiv:1409.1556 (2014)
20. Song, Y., et al.: Computer-aided diagnosis of prostate cancer using a deep convolutional neural network from multiparametric MRI. J. Magn. Reson. Imaging **48**(6), 1570–1577 (2018)
21. Stamey, T.A., Yang, N., Hay, A.R., McNeal, J.E., Freiha, F.S., Redwine, E.: Prostate-specific antigen as a serum marker for adenocarcinoma of the prostate. N. Engl. J. Med. **317**(15), 909–916 (1987)
22. Szegedy, C., et al.: Intriguing properties of neural networks. arXiv preprint arXiv:1312.6199 (2013)
23. Wang, J., et al.: Learning fine-grained image similarity with deep ranking. In: Proceedings of the IEEE Conference on Computer Vision and Pattern Recognition, pp. 1386–1393 (2014)
24. Wang, Z., Liu, C., Cheng, D., Wang, L., Yang, X., Cheng, K.T.: Automated detection of clinically significant prostate cancer in MP-MRI images based on an end-to-end deep neural network. IEEE Trans. Med. Imaging **37**(5), 1127–1139 (2018)
25. Weinreb, J.C., et al.: PI-RADS prostate imaging-reporting and data system: 2015, version 2. Eur. Urol. **69**(1), 16–40 (2016)
26. Yang, X., et al.: Co-trained convolutional neural networks for automated detection of prostate cancer in multi-parametric MRI. Med. Image Anal. **42**, 212–227 (2017)
27. Zagoruyko, S., Komodakis, N.: Learning to compare image patches via convolutional neural networks. In: Proceedings of the IEEE Conference on Computer Vision and Pattern Recognition, pp. 4353–4361 (2015)
28. Zhang, C., Liu, W., Ma, H., Fu, H.: Siamese neural network based gait recognition for human identification. In: 2016 IEEE International Conference on Acoustics, Speech and Signal Processing (ICASSP), pp. 2832–2836. IEEE (2016)

Vision for Robotics

Simple Camera-to-2D-LiDAR Calibration Method for General Use

Andrew H. Palmer[(⊠)], Chris Peterson, Janelle Blankenburg, David Feil-Seifer, and Monica Nicolescu

University of Nevada, Reno, Reno, NV 89557, USA
{ahpalmer,chrispeterson,jjblankenburg}@nevada.unr.edu,
{dave,monica}@cse.unr.edu

Abstract. As systems that utilize computer vision move into the public domain, methods of calibration need to become easier to use. Though multi-plane LiDAR systems have proven to be useful for vehicles and large robotic platforms, many smaller platforms and low-cost solutions still require 2D LiDAR combined with RGB cameras. Current methods of calibrating these sensors make assumptions about camera and laser placement and/or require complex calibration routines. In this paper we propose a new method of feature correspondence in the two sensors and an optimization method capable of using a calibration target with unknown lengths in its geometry. Our system is designed with an inexperienced layperson as the intended user, which has led us to remove as many assumptions about both the target and laser as possible. We show that our system is capable of calibrating the 2-sensor system from a single sample in configurations other methods are unable to handle.

Keywords: Extrinsic calibration · 2D LiDAR · Optical camera · Gradient descent

1 Introduction

Multi-plane LiDAR works for vehicle platforms due to their ability to carry around the computers capable of processing the data quickly; however, other platforms do not have the same capabilities. Searching through a large point cloud is costly in terms of processing time. For these less capable systems, using a 2D LiDAR with an optical camera gets both the detection and distance information a robot needs to navigate and interact with the world.

Calibration is key to determining which points in the image correspond to which indices in the laser. Several systems, such as [1,7,16,18], exist to derive these transformation values. However, when it comes to applications laypeople are capable of using, these methods require exact target geometries or multiple samples (which take time to position). Some methods, such as [3,11,12], have been designed to make calibration easier by either limiting the number of samples

This work has been supported by NSF Awards #IIS-1719027 and #IIS-1757929.

© Springer Nature Switzerland AG 2020
G. Bebis et al. (Eds.): ISVC 2020, LNCS 12510, pp. 193–206, 2020.
https://doi.org/10.1007/978-3-030-64559-5_15

to one or two, using simpler target shapes, or allowing for wider varieties of configurations between the camera and laser. All of these are improvements over prior systems, yet they too lack the simplicity a calibration system meant for non-experts requires.

A system designed around the ease of use for non-experts should at least have the following traits: 1) the calibration target should be easy to construct and detect, 2) the system should be able to find transformation values from only a single sample, and 3) the system should be able to handle cases where the camera and laser are not aligned in the same relative direction. Current systems of calibrating a 2D LiDAR and an intrinsically calibrated optical camera do not achieve all three of these properties. Therefore, developing a user-friendly system to find the calibration between these sensors is necessary.

The rest of the paper is structured as follows. Section 2 provides background information; Sect. 3 discusses our target geometry and setup; Sect. 4 discusses the derivatives used in our method; Sect. 5 discusses our simulation setup; Sect. 6 discusses our experimental results; Sect. 7 discusses our results and future work; and Sect. 8 presents our conclusions.

2   Background

To perform a calibration, two elements are needed: detected points of correspondence between sensors and an optimization approach that computes a geometric transformation between these points. Determining this correspondence has led to a vast array of calibration targets with specialized properties.

Prior methods for obtaining points of correspondence between an optical camera and 2D LiDAR such as [1,7,16,18] have relied on detecting checkerboards in images and lines in the laser reading. However, with such flat surfaces detecting displacement in the Z-axis is difficult. This led to methods using trihedrons to determine at what height the laser intersects the target [5,8,12,14].

However, there are rotational problems with these targets that led to methods like [3]. That method also has the benefit of calibrating from a single sample. Unfortunately, these prior methods rely on the laser and camera to have relatively the same forward-facing view of the target, which limits the use of those for contexts where the camera and laser have significantly different views of the target.

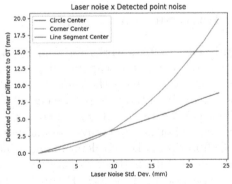

Once the correspondence is known, methods such as [10,13,17]

Fig. 1. Comparison of laser noise to detections.

are used to find the optimal transformation parameters. Most methods of calibration have used either the Levenberg-Marquardt optimization [13] or EPnP [10] after data has been cleaned up with RANSAC [4]. This leads to many systems of calibration requiring multiple samples.

To understand how different target shapes can be detected in the laser, we examined the noise in the laser sensor and its effect on the detection of centers of line segments, corners, and circle centers. We examined 13 noise settings from 0 to 24 mm in increments of 2 mm. This noise was applied to the sensor depths as a Gaussian noise. Figure 1 shows the results of this analysis. 1000 samples were collected at each noise level. As is evident from Fig. 1, circle fitting is more robust at high levels of noise. This suggests that circle fitting is preferred for setups in large areas.

3   Setup

Our setup for finding a calibration in the real world uses a target made out of spheres. We color the spheres to stand out against the background and show an image with correspondence assigned to the target for validation by the user. Currently we manually place the spheres at laser height. A sphere allows us to calibrate with viewing directions where the camera is on opposite sides of the target from the laser. Our set up in the real world is shown in Fig. 2a.

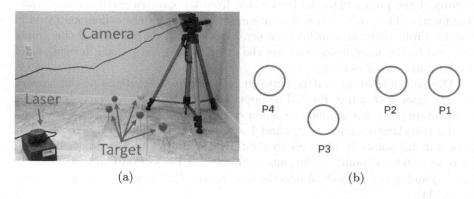

(a)   (b)

Fig. 2. (a) A real world setup of our laser, camera, and target. (b) Top down view of calibration target shape.

To have a target with unknown dimensions, we needed to define a shape that could be detected from relative positions alone. We defined our target as follows. Points 1, 2, and 4 lie on a line within the plane. Point 1 is closer than point 4 to point 2. Point 3 resides outside of the line formed by the other points, and its projection onto that line resides between points 2 and 4. A top down of points 1, 2, 3, and 4 is shown in Fig. 2b. Point 5 has the same (x, y) position as point 2 with a displacement in the Z-axis.

Because we did not want to rely on fixed dimensions for the target, we had to develop a method to estimate the height of point 5 for the purposes of both the camera projection and the laser frame. We cover this process in Sect. 4.

Our system can handle undefined lengths for the distances between target points; thus, it is possible to make a target out of common household materials such as ping pong balls, skewers, and paint. To detect the target, we determine which point corresponds to point 2 and then determine points 1, 3, and 4 based on the geometry of the target. Point 5 is above point 2; for the laser this makes it easier to determine the (x, y) location of point 5. To make it simple to detect the non-planar point, we used a different color as our identifier for point 5.

We also rotated the camera around the Z axis to have it face back toward the laser when the random initial guess put the camera in front of the laser. For cases with the camera behind the target this second initial guess should reduce the burden of modifying the rotation components.

The Euclidean distance is the best error metric suited to our method because the camera points should be perfectly projected onto the laser plane at the detected laser locations with correct transform values.

4   Derivations

Due to the unknown Z-coordinate of point 5, choosing gradient descent allows us to update an estimate at each iteration. To derive this gradient, we need to project the points onto the laser plane from the camera given a transformation matrix. The projection and rotation between the frames is demonstrated in Fig. 3a. From there we can find the error between those points and the points detected in the laser frame and use the error to find the partial derivatives of the transformation matrix.

The transformation matrix between the coordinate systems of the camera and the laser is shown in Eq. 1. The upper left nine values, $r_{11}, r_{12}, \dots r_{33}$, allow us to rotate the point around the center of the camera frame before we translate by the translation values, t_x, t_y, and t_z. We have to include a fourth element, 1, in our 3D points to allow us to multiply the matrix to the point. In Eq. 1, cp is an extended point in the camera frame (P5 Projection Camera Frame in Fig. 3a) and lp is a projection into the laser frame (P5 Projection in Laser Frame in Fig. 3a).

To get a 3D point for transformation, we take a target detection camera pixel and extend it forward from the image plane to get an x, y, and z location in the camera frame. This is done by applying the inverse projection matrix defined by the camera properties found prior to calibration. Applying the inverse is shown in Eq. 2. The pixel locations are specified

$$
\begin{bmatrix} r_{11} & r_{12} & r_{13} & t_x \\ r_{21} & r_{22} & r_{23} & t_y \\ r_{31} & r_{32} & r_{33} & t_z \\ 0 & 0 & 0 & 1 \end{bmatrix} \begin{bmatrix} x_{cp} \\ y_{cp} \\ z_{cp} \\ 1 \end{bmatrix} = \begin{bmatrix} x_{lp} \\ y_{lp} \\ z_{lp} \\ 1 \end{bmatrix} \quad (1)
$$

$$
\begin{bmatrix} 0 & 0 & 1 \\ -1 & 0 & 0 \\ 0 & -1 & 0 \end{bmatrix} \begin{bmatrix} f_x & 0 & p_x \\ 0 & f_y & p_y \\ 0 & 0 & 1 \end{bmatrix}^{-1} \begin{bmatrix} i_x \\ i_y \\ 1 \end{bmatrix} = \begin{bmatrix} x_{cp} \\ y_{cp} \\ z_{cp} \end{bmatrix} \quad (2)
$$

$$
\begin{bmatrix} x_{lp} \\ y_{lp} \\ z_{lp} \\ 1 \end{bmatrix} = \begin{bmatrix} r_{11}x_{cp} + r_{12}y_{cp} + r_{13}z_{cp} + t_x \\ r_{21}x_{cp} + r_{22}y_{cp} + r_{23}z_{cp} + t_x \\ r_{31}x_{cp} + r_{32}y_{cp} + r_{13}z_{3p} + t_x \\ 1 \end{bmatrix} \quad (3)
$$

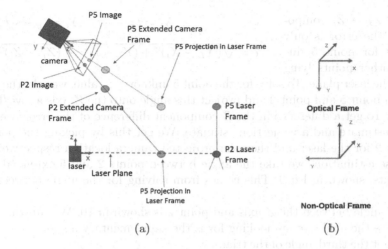

Fig. 3. (a) Diagram of camera and laser with projections and detections of point 2 and point 5 into the laser frame. (b) Axis representations of optical and non-optical frames.

by i_x, i_y. The f_x, f_y correspond to the focal distance in pixels with respect to the x and y directions of the image. The p_x, p_y represent the principal point of the image, most often the center of the image.

The first matrix in Eq. 2 applies a rotation to adjust our axis representations from the optical frame to the non-optical frame. The rotation is shown in Fig. 3b. This rotation transforms the X axis into the negative Y axis, the Y axis into the negative Z axis, and the Z axis into the X axis. We can examine the correctness of the transformation matrix once the points have been extended into 3D and transformed into the laser frame. The transformation is restated differently in Eq. 3 to demonstrate how the projection onto the laser plane functions.

The camera center, when transformed to $[x_c, y_c, z_c, 1] \rightarrow [t_x, t_y, t_z, 1]$, resolves to the camera position in the laser frame, or just the translation values. Forming a line through the camera center and the transformed extended camera point we can find the projection onto the laser plane as seen in Fig. 3a.

The changes of x, y, and z for each point relative to the camera center are shown in Eqs. 4, 5, and 6. This is a vector from the camera center to

$$\chi = x_{lp} - x_c = r_{11}x_{cp} + r_{12}y_{cp} + r_{13}z_{cp} \quad (4)$$

$$\gamma = y_{lp} - y_c = r_{21}x_{cp} + r_{22}y_{cp} + r_{23}z_{cp} \quad (5)$$

$$\zeta = z_{lp} - z_c = r_{31}x_{cp} + r_{32}y_{cp} + r_{33}z_{cp} \quad (6)$$

the transformed extended point. χ, γ, and ζ represent the changes in the three axes directions. The line can be described by x and y in terms of z. This is shown in the equations in 7, where we solved for the x and y values of the intersection, X_i and Y_i, of the line with the plane.

As stated above, we use the Euclidean distance between the projection onto the plane and the laser detection as the value of our error. This is shown in Eq. 8, where X_i, Y_i, and Z_i are the camera projection points.

The $Z_L - Z_i$ component of the error is only relevant for point 5 due to the other points lying

$$X_i = t_x - \frac{\chi}{\zeta}t_z \quad Y_i = t_y - \frac{\gamma}{\zeta}t_z \quad (7)$$

$$e = \sqrt{(X_L - X_i)^2 + (Y_L - Y_i)^2 + (Z_L - Z_i)^2} \quad (8)$$

within the laser plane. To solve for the point 5 unknown z value, we take the angle between point 5 and point 2 and project this angle onto the Z-axis above/below point 2. To get a difference in the Z component difference of the error, we need a laser estimate and a projection estimate. We get this by picking the position of point 2 for the laser and then the projected camera location respectively. To get these estimations we take the angle between points 2 and 5 extended camera points, shown in Eq. 9. This comes from solving for the angle between two vectors.

The angle between the Z axis and point 2 is shown in 10. We subtract from π because the angle we are looking for is the supplementary angle.

We get the third angle of the triangle by Eq. 11. Using the Law of Sines we can solve for the point 5 Z shown in Eq. 12. The distance from the camera center to point 2 is d_1. We can call these z estimations using point 2 from the laser detection and from camera projection z_{lp5} and z_{cp5} respectively. We perform this estimation in each iteration of gradient descent.

$$\theta_1 = \cos^{-1}\left(\frac{p_5 \cdot p_2}{||p_5||||p_2||}\right) \quad (9)$$

$$\theta_2 = \pi - \cos^{-1}\left(\frac{[0,0,1] \cdot p_2}{||p_2||}\right) \quad (10)$$

$$\theta_3 = \pi - (\theta_1 + \theta_2) \quad (11)$$

$$z_{p5} = \frac{\sin(\theta_1)d_1}{\sin(\theta_3)} \quad (12)$$

The (x, y) position of point 5 from the laser detection does not change at each iteration, but the position of point 5 from the camera projection completely changes each iteration. Thus, we also update point 5's x, y, and z coordinates at each iteration, as shown in Eq. 13.

The projected location of point 5 is established by replacing the estimated height into the equations of x and y in terms of z for the projected line.

All of the above leads to an expanded error equation, shown in 14.

$$p_5 = \begin{bmatrix} z_{cp5}\frac{\chi_5}{\zeta_5} + x_{ip5} \\ z_{cp5}\frac{\gamma_5}{\zeta_5} + y_{ip5} \\ z_{cp5} \\ 1 \end{bmatrix} \quad (13)$$

$$e = \sqrt{\left(X_L - (t_x - \frac{\chi}{\zeta}t_z)\right)^2 + \left(Y_L - (t_y - \frac{\gamma}{\zeta}t_z)\right)^2 + (z_l - z_c)^2} \quad (14)$$

We solve for the derivatives in steps. First, we find the changes in distance to the camera, d_1, shown in 15.

$$\frac{\partial d_1}{\partial t_x} = \frac{-(X_{p2l} - t_x)}{d_1} \quad \frac{\partial d_1}{\partial t_y} = \frac{-(Y_{p2l} - t_y)}{d_1} \quad \frac{\partial d_1}{\partial t_z} = \frac{-(Z_{p2l} - t_z)}{d_1} \quad (15)$$

However, because the height of the laser detection of point 2 is 0, the t_z equation of 15 becomes 16. Since there is no z component to any of the other points except point 5, we can get the derivatives of z_{p5}, shown in 17.

$$\frac{\partial d_1}{\partial t_z} = \frac{t_z}{d_1} \tag{16}$$

$$\frac{\partial z_{p5}}{\partial t_x} = z_{p5}\frac{-(X_{p2l} - t_x)}{d_1^2} \quad \frac{\partial z_{p5}}{\partial t_y} = z_{p5}\frac{-(Y_{p2l} - t_y)}{d_1^2} \quad \frac{\partial z_{p5}}{\partial t_z} = z_{p5}\frac{t_z}{d_1^2} \tag{17}$$

Now that we have finished the first two sets of derivatives, we can take the derivatives of the error with respect to the translation. To make the equations slightly more readable, we use the convention $\bar{X} = X_L - X_i$ and $\bar{Y} = Y_L - Y_i$. We get the partial derivatives of the translation elements as in 18, 19, and 20.

$$\frac{\partial e}{\partial t_x} = \frac{-\bar{X}}{e} + \frac{z_l - z_c}{e}\left(\frac{-z_l(X_{p2l} - t_x)}{d_{1l}^2} - \frac{-z_c(X_{p2c} - t_x)}{d_{1c}^2}\right) \tag{18}$$

$$\frac{\partial e}{\partial t_y} = \frac{-\bar{Y}}{e} + \frac{z_l - z_c}{e}\left(\frac{-z_l(Y_{p2l} - t_y)}{d_{1l}^2} - \frac{-z_c(Y_{p2c} - t_y)}{d_{1c}^2}\right) \tag{19}$$

$$\frac{\partial e}{\partial t_z} = -\left(\frac{\chi\frac{\partial e}{\partial t_x} + \gamma\frac{\partial e}{\partial t_y}}{\zeta}\right) + \frac{z_l - z_c}{e}\left(\frac{z_l t_z}{d_{1l}^2} - \frac{z_c t_z}{d_{1c}^2}\right) \tag{20}$$

Knowing that the height is 0 for the points 1–4, we can change 18, 19, and 20 to the equations in 21 for all points other than point 5.

$$\frac{\partial e}{\partial t_x} = \frac{-\bar{X}}{e} \quad \frac{\partial e}{\partial t_y} = \frac{-\bar{Y}}{e} \quad \frac{\partial e}{\partial t_z} = -\left(\frac{\chi\frac{\partial e}{\partial t_x} + \gamma\frac{\partial e}{\partial t_y}}{\zeta}\right) \tag{21}$$

Solving for the derivatives of the vector components in the transformed extended points, we get 22 for $\chi, \gamma,$ and ζ respectively.

$$\frac{\partial e}{\partial \chi} = \frac{t_z \bar{X}}{\zeta e} \quad \frac{\partial e}{\partial \gamma} = \frac{t_z \bar{Y}}{\zeta e} \quad \frac{\partial e}{\partial \zeta} = \frac{-t_z}{\zeta^2 e}(\bar{X}\chi + \bar{Y}\gamma) \tag{22}$$

The remaining derivatives of the rotation components, shown in 23, are found using the vector component derivatives from 22.

$$
\begin{aligned}
\frac{\partial e}{\partial r_{11}} &= x_{cp}\frac{\partial e}{\partial \chi} & \frac{\partial e}{\partial r_{12}} &= y_{cp}\frac{\partial e}{\partial \chi} & \frac{\partial e}{\partial r_{13}} &= z_{cp}\frac{\partial e}{\partial \chi} \\
\frac{\partial e}{\partial r_{21}} &= x_{cp}\frac{\partial e}{\partial \gamma} & \frac{\partial e}{\partial r_{22}} &= y_{cp}\frac{\partial e}{\partial \gamma} & \frac{\partial e}{\partial r_{23}} &= z_{cp}\frac{\partial e}{\partial \gamma} \\
\frac{\partial e}{\partial r_{31}} &= x_{cp}\frac{\partial e}{\partial \zeta} & \frac{\partial e}{\partial r_{32}} &= y_{cp}\frac{\partial e}{\partial \zeta} & \frac{\partial e}{\partial r_{33}} &= z_{cp}\frac{\partial e}{\partial \zeta}
\end{aligned} \tag{23}
$$

This results in the gradient for our transformation matrix shown in 24.

This gradient is used to update our transformation matrix at each iteration in gradient descent. We augmented RMSProp [15] by adding a maximum history to the equation. This is represented by the indexing of the sum in Eq. 26. We chose 1000 for this max history value because it appeared to work well. We used 1×10^{-5} for the value of δ as a way to prevent division by zero. The ϵ term in Eq. 26 represents how much we either rely on the history or the new gradient for our expected value. We initially adjusted this as a confound and determined that 0.1 worked well.

$$\nabla F = \begin{bmatrix} \frac{\partial e}{\partial r_{11}} & \frac{\partial e}{\partial r_{12}} & \frac{\partial e}{\partial r_{13}} & \frac{\partial e}{\partial t_x} \\ \frac{\partial e}{\partial r_{21}} & \frac{\partial e}{\partial r_{22}} & \frac{\partial e}{\partial r_{33}} & \frac{\partial e}{\partial t_y} \\ \frac{\partial e}{\partial r_{31}} & \frac{\partial e}{\partial r_{32}} & \frac{\partial e}{\partial r_{33}} & \frac{\partial e}{\partial t_z} \\ 0 & 0 & 0 & 0 \end{bmatrix} \qquad (24)$$

$$F_{t+1} = F_t - \frac{\ell}{G}\nabla F \quad G = \sqrt{E[g^2]_t + \delta} \qquad (25)$$

$$E[g^2]_t = \epsilon \sum_{i=t-1}^{t-n} \frac{g_i^2}{n} + (1 - \epsilon)|\nabla F|^2 : n = min(history, 1000) \qquad (26)$$

Since all the points together make the sample, taking the average of the gradients over all the points per update is more meaningful. Thus, we average the gradients of all points together before updating. But the division by e in all the derivatives has the effect of normalizing the gradients. Therefore, if a single point is causing issues, say point 3, then all the other points could overshadow the significance of that point and keep the camera matrix from moving toward a smaller error. To avoid this, we introduce a weighted sum of the gradients for each point proportional to the magnitude of the error at that point. This means that for $t_x, t_y, t_z, \chi, \gamma$, and ζ gradients we multiply by the error. This adjustment results in the updated gradients below, Eqs. 27–30.

$$\frac{\partial e}{\partial t_x} = -\bar{X} + (z_l - z_c)\left(\frac{-z_l(X_{p2l} - t_x)}{d_{1l}^2} - \frac{-z_c(X_{p2c} - t_x)}{d_{1c}^2}\right) \qquad (27)$$

$$\frac{\partial e}{\partial t_y} = -\bar{Y} + (z_l - z_c)\left(\frac{-z_l(Y_{p2l} - t_y)}{d_{1l}^2} - \frac{-z_c(Y_{p2c} - t_y)}{d_{1c}^2}\right) \qquad (28)$$

$$\frac{\partial e}{\partial t_z} = -\left(\frac{\chi\frac{\partial e}{\partial t_x} + \gamma\frac{\partial e}{\partial t_y}}{\zeta}\right) + (z_l - z_c)\left(\frac{z_l t_z}{d_{1l}^2} - \frac{z_c t_z}{d_{1c}^2}\right) \qquad (29)$$

$$\frac{\partial e}{\partial \chi} = \frac{t_z \bar{X}}{\zeta} \quad \frac{\partial e}{\partial \gamma} = \frac{t_z \bar{Y}}{\zeta} \quad \frac{\partial e}{\partial \zeta} = \frac{-t_z}{\zeta^2}(\bar{X}\chi + \bar{Y}\gamma) \qquad (30)$$

The same simplification for points 1–4 can be applied to 27, 28, and 29 as they were above to get 21 from 18, 19, and 20 respectively.

During the averaging process of all the points we need to also divide by the sum of errors in addition to the number of points. This correction for a weighted sum provides a much faster convergence.

5   Simulated Environment

We used Gazebo [9] to simulate an environment where we generated different target configurations and camera positions. Figure 4 shows the base target used for points 1, 3, and 4 in addition to the 4 different height settings between points 2 and 5.

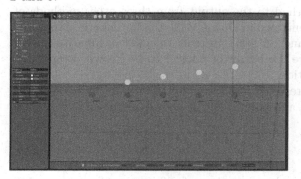

The target has colored spheres for visual detection differences between point 5 and the other points. The center of the sphere is the point of correspondence between the laser and the camera.

Fig. 4. Simulated targets with transparency. Left to right: base target, point 5 location at 9 cm, 13 cm, 16 cm, and 20 cm.

We tested orientations of the camera both below and above the laser plane. Each target configuration had random lengths within the target geometry. The height of point 5 was also randomly chosen from a pool of models having either a 0.09, 0.13, 0.16, or 0.20 m distance between points 2 and 5. We randomly placed point 3 on either side of the 1-2-4 points line.

We checked each target placement and configuration to see if the laser could get 4 detected points and the camera 5 detected points. In the same way a user can make sure the real world detections matched in the sensor display, we checked to see if the assignments matched the actual target when projected with the ground truth transformation. If the assignments did not match we generated a new configuration and placement. As soon as both sensors had a detection of the target, we ran our gradient descent method on the detected points. The laser stayed stationary at the origin across all configurations. We generated new target configurations and positions as well as camera locations for each group of samples.

The camera positions were random within a rectangular prism of size 5.5 m × 3 m × 4 m centered on a point 1.25 m in front of the laser to generate possible positions behind the target. The orientation of our camera was semi-random. We oriented the camera toward the target in each configuration.

We measured the distance of our resulting transformation matrix to our ground truth (GT) by the Euclidean distance. To evaluate the
$$\theta = 2sin^{-1}\left(\frac{1}{2\sqrt{2}}||\hat{R} - R_{GT}||_{\mathcal{F}}\right) \quad (31)$$
difference in angle, we used the chord distance to evaluate the difference in rotation angle defined in [6].

The chord distance is shown in Eq. 31, where $\hat{R}$ is the found rotational matrix, R_{GT} is the rotation matrix of the ground truth, and $\mathcal{F}$ refers to the Frobenius Norm, or Euclidean Norm, of the matrices. We applied a Gaussian random value to the detected centers in each sensor to shift their locations in the image and the laser.

We also compared our method to the output from three other methods of solving the PnP problem implemented in OpenCV [2]; the Levenberg-Marquardt optimization [13], EPnP [10], and P3P [17]. In order to enable comparisons with these algorithms, which require the height of point 5 to be known, we provide this information in our evaluation.

Each target configuration resulted in 32 samples of output, 4 camera noise settings, 4 laser noise settings, and point 5 height known/unknown.

6   Results

We tested our calibration method on a variety of different configurations; 118 unique camera-laser positions. Approximately 42.3% (50 configurations) had the camera positioned behind the target (on the opposite side of the target from the laser). With our results as consistent as they are, we have shown that our system can handle both forward- and rear-facing target calibration.

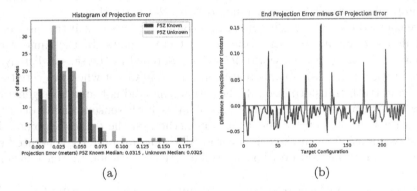

$$(a) \qquad\qquad\qquad (b)$$

Fig. 5. (a) Histogram of projection errors. (b) Comparison of projection error and GT error per sample.

We examined the distribution of projection error for samples without noise in both point 5 Z known and unknown cases, Fig. 5a. We can see from this histogram that the error values are centered on 0.018. There is no significant difference in the distributions of point 5 Z known and unknown.

We also compared the GT error to the resulting projection error of solutions from our method, Fig. 5b. For most of the configurations we have negative values in this difference, with most found transformations having a smaller error than the GT. This is an example of how noise in the detection of point centers effects our projections.

Our method's average distance to the GT is 0.0361 m, with a median value of 0.0180 m. The average rotational error is 0.7515°, with a median value of 0.4149°. Figure 6 shows the distribution of angular and distance to GT values.

We also examined how other methods implemented in OpenCV [2] compare in solving the Perspective-n-Point problem on our samples. The results are shown in Table 1. The correction for optical to non-optical rotations was applied to the other methods for comparison. When we look at the other methods

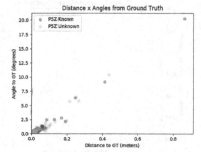

Fig. 6. Translation vs rotational error.

of solving the Perspective-n-Point problem, it becomes clear that the OpenCV methods suffer greatly without the knowledge about point 5's Z value. This issue is because they cannot use a point with partially unknown location in the world space.

Table 1. Our method of solving the Perspective-n-Point problem compared to Levenberg-Marquardt [13], EPnP [10], and P3P [17] for both point 5 height known and unknown.

Method	No Point 5 Translation (m)	Rotation (deg)	Point 5 Translation (m)	Rotation (deg)
Levenberg-Marquardt	3.7858	122.11	1.2251×10^9	118.42
EPnP	1.0027×10^{92}	113.35	3.5279	112.98
P3P	3.4361	115.39	3.4003	115.24
Our Method	0.0361	0.7515	0.0396	0.8269

We evaluated our system with different levels of noise. We used 4 settings of camera Gaussian noise to shift the camera detection locations in both x and y location: 0, 1, 2, and 3 pixels standard deviation. We also used 4 settings for laser Gaussian noise to shift the detected centers in both x and y: 0, 3, 6, and 9 mm standard deviation. The translation error is shown in Fig. 7b, and the rotation error in Fig. 7b.

Table 2. Averages and standard deviation of point 5 height estimated error for each target with and without known height by the laser a priori.

Target	Known result	SD	Unknown result	SD
1 (9 cm)	0.000396 m	0.002251	−0.000098 m	0.002058
2 (13 cm)	−0.000023 m	0.002273	0.000066 m	0.002012
3 (16 cm)	−0.001080 m	0.003715	−0.001712 m	0.003464
4 (20 cm)	0.000577 m	0.001723	0.000491 m	0.001450

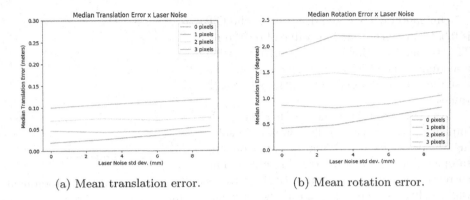

(a) Mean translation error.   (b) Mean rotation error.

Fig. 7. Mean translation (a) and rotation (b) error for different modes of laser and camera noise.

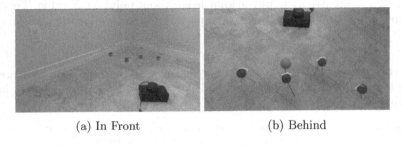

(a) In Front   (b) Behind

Fig. 8. Camera above the laser plane observing the calibration target from the front (a) and behind (b) with laser visualization applying our method's calibration result.

Our method relies on estimating the height of point 5 during its iterative process. The average error and standard deviation for each target's estimated height with height known and unknown in the laser frame points are shown in Table 2 (height of each target specified next to target number).

Additionally, we tested our method on a real-world situation with colored ping-pong balls, kebab skewers, a Logitech C920 (resolution of 640 × 360), and a Slamtec RPLIDAR A3. The results for both front and back facing are shown in Fig. 8. From these images we can see that our method is capable of calibrating in the real world in addition to a simulated environment.

7   Discussion and Future Work

The results from our real-world configurations show that our calibration system is capable of using everyday materials in a flexible geometry, which leads us to believe that users not skilled in calibration can reconstruct targets without feeling intimidated.

Through all configurations both in simulation and in the real world, our system found a calibration with a single image and laser sample. The above results indicate that each of the qualities that make a system user friendly were achieved: 1) simple to construct target, 2) single sample calibration, and 3) diverse camera-to-laser positions.

One limitation for our calibration process is a camera position that places the camera at the same height as the laser plane. This results in an indistinguishable target assignment in the camera for the target. We plan to address this in the future.

Currently our system still requires the user to specify on which side of the laser plane the camera resides. In the future, we plan to add checks into the calibration process to remove this limitation.

In future work, we will add a graphical interface to allow the user to specify the colors of the spheres instead of defaulting to red-green or red-yellow.

8   Conclusions

We developed a novel routine for calibrating a camera and 2D LiDAR using gradient descent. In order to find a gradient capable of adjusting the camera's height, we proposed a method of estimating a point's height off the laser plane to keep the camera from finding a solution that places the image plane parallel to the laser plane. We also showed that our estimations are close to the actual ground truth height of that point. We showed that our method is robust to laser noise and to a lesser extent camera noise.

We developed a system that could solve for the transformation matrix using only a single sample and a target with unknown dimensions. We showed that our method is one of only three that is capable of generating calibration parameters from a single sample, and our method is one of two that can calibrate while not viewing the target from the same general direction. Most importantly, our method is the only one that can do both. In addition, we showed that our method works with everyday materials, making it easier for users to remake targets without a large degree of expertise.

References

1. Ahmad Yousef, K., Mohd, B., Al-Widyan, K., Hayajneh, T.: Extrinsic calibration of camera and 2D laser sensors without overlap. Sensors 17(10), 2346 (2017). https://doi.org/10.3390/s17102346. http://dx.doi.org/10.3390/s17102346
2. Bradski, G.: The OpenCV Library. Dr. Dobb's J. Softw. Tools (2000)
3. Dong, W., Isler, V.: A novel method for the extrinsic calibration of a 2D laser rangefinder and a camera. IEEE Sens. J. 18(10), 4200–4211 (2018)
4. Fischler, M.A., Bolles, R.C.: Random sample consensus: a paradigm for model fitting with applications to image analysis and automated cartography. Commun. ACM 24(6), 381–395 (1981). https://doi.org/10.1145/358669.358692
5. Gomez-Ojeda, R., Briales, J., Fernandez-Moral, E., Gonzalez-Jimenez, J.: Extrinsic calibration of a 2D laser-rangefinder and a camera based on scene corners. In: 2015 IEEE International Conference on Robotics and Automation (ICRA), pp. 3611–3616 (2015)

6. Hartley, R.I., Trumpf, J., Dai, Y., Li, H.: Rotation averaging. Int. J. Comput. Vis. **103**, 267–305 (2012)
7. Hillemann, M., Jutzi, B.: Ucalmicel - unified intrinsic and extrinsic calibration of a multi-camera-system and a laserscanner. ISPRS Ann. Photogr. Remote Sens. Spat. Inf. Sci. **IV–2/W3**, 17–24 (2017). https://doi.org/10.5194/isprs-annals-IV-2-W3-17-2017
8. Hu, Z., Li, Y., Li, N., Zhao, B.: Extrinsic calibration of 2-D laser rangefinder and camera from single shot based on minimal solution. IEEE Trans. Instrum. Meas. **65**(4), 915–929 (2016)
9. Koenig, N., Howard, A.: Design and use paradigms for gazebo, an open-source multi-robot simulator. In: IEEE/RSJ International Conference on Intelligent Robots and Systems, Sendai, Japan, pp. 2149–2154, September 2004
10. Lepetit, V., Moreno-Noguer, F., Fua, P.: EPnP: An accurate o(n) solution to the PnP problem. Int. J. Comput. Vis. **81**, 155–166 (2009). https://doi.org/10.1007/s11263-008-0152-6. http://infoscience.epfl.ch/record/160138
11. Li, N., Hu, Z., Zhao, B.: Flexible extrinsic calibration of a camera and a two-dimensional laser rangefinder with a folding pattern. Appl. Opt. **55**, 2270 (2016). https://doi.org/10.1364/AO.55.002270
12. Li, Y., Hu, Z., Li, Z., Cai, Y., Sun, S., Zhou, J.: A single-shot pose estimation approach for a 2D laser rangefinder. Meas. Sci. Technol. **31**(2), 025105 (2019). https://doi.org/10.1088/1361-6501/ab455a
13. Moré, J.J.: The Levenberg-Marquardt algorithm: implementation and theory. In: Watson, G.A. (ed.) Numerical Analysis. LNM, vol. 630, pp. 105–116. Springer, Heidelberg (1978). https://doi.org/10.1007/BFb0067700
14. Tian, Z., Huang, Y., Zhu, F., Ma, Y.: The extrinsic calibration of area-scan camera and 2D laser rangefinder (LRF) using checkerboard trihedron. IEEE Access **8**, 36166–36179 (2020)
15. Tieleman, T., Hinton, G.: Lecture 6.5-RmsProp: divide the gradient by a running average of its recent magnitude. COURSERA: Neural Netw. Mach. Learn. **4**, 26–31 (2012)
16. Vasconcelos, F., Barreto, J.P., Nunes, U.: A minimal solution for the extrinsic calibration of a camera and a laser-rangefinder. IEEE Trans. Pattern Anal. Mach. Intell. **34**, 2097–2107 (2012). https://doi.org/10.1109/TPAMI.2012.18
17. Gao, X.-S., Hou, X.-R., Tang, J., Cheng, H.-F.: Complete solution classification for the perspective-three-point problem. IEEE Trans. Pattern Anal. Mach. Intell. **25**(8), 930–943 (2003)
18. Zhou, L.: A new minimal solution for the extrinsic calibration of a 2D lidar and a camera using three plane-line correspondences. IEEE Sens. J. **14**(2), 442–454 (2014)

SalsaNext: Fast, Uncertainty-Aware Semantic Segmentation of LiDAR Point Clouds

Tiago Cortinhal[1]($\boxtimes$), George Tzelepis[2], and Eren Erdal Aksoy[1,2]

[1] School of Information Technology, Halmstad University, Halmstad, Sweden
tiago.cortinhal@hh.se
[2] Volvo Group Trucks Technology, Volvo Technology AB, Gothenburg, Sweden

Abstract. In this paper, we introduce *SalsaNext* for the uncertainty-aware semantic segmentation of a full 3D LiDAR point cloud in real-time. *SalsaNext* is the *next* version of *SalsaNet* [1] which has an encoder-decoder architecture where the encoder unit has a set of ResNet blocks and the decoder part combines upsampled features from the residual blocks. In contrast to *SalsaNet,* we introduce a new context module, replace the ResNet encoder blocks with a new residual dilated convolution stack with gradually increasing receptive fields and add the *pixel-shuffle* layer in the decoder. Additionally, we switch from stride convolution to average pooling and also apply central dropout treatment. To directly optimize the Jaccard index, we further combine the weighted cross entropy loss with *Lovász-Softmax* loss [4]. We finally inject a Bayesian treatment to compute the *epistemic* and *aleatoric* uncertainties for each point in the cloud. We provide a thorough quantitative evaluation on the Semantic-KITTI dataset [3], which demonstrates that the proposed *SalsaNext* outperforms other published semantic segmentation networks and achieves 3.6% more accuracy over the previous state-of-the-art method. We also release our source code (https://github.com/TiagoCortinhal/SalsaNext).

Keywords: Semantic segmentation · LiDAR Point Clouds · Deep learning

1 Introduction

Scene understanding is an essential prerequisite for autonomous vehicles. Semantic segmentation helps gaining a rich understanding of the scene by predicting a meaningful class label for each individual sensory data point. Achieving such a fine-grained semantic prediction in real-time accelerates reaching the full autonomy to a great extent.

Safety-critical systems, such as self-driving vehicles, however, require not only highly accurate but also reliable predictions with a consistent measure of uncertainty. This is because the quantitative uncertainty measures can be propagated to the subsequent units, such as decision making modules to lead to safe

© Springer Nature Switzerland AG 2020
G. Bebis et al. (Eds.): ISVC 2020, LNCS 12510, pp. 207–222, 2020.
https://doi.org/10.1007/978-3-030-64559-5_16

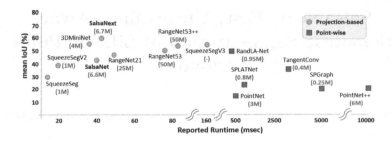

Fig. 1. Mean IoU versus runtime plot for the state-of-the-art 3D point cloud semantic segmentation networks on the Semantic-KITTI dataset [3]. Inside parentheses are given the total number of network parameters in Millions. All deep networks visualized here use only 3D LiDAR point cloud data as input. Note that only the published methods are considered.

manoeuvre planning or emergency braking, which is of utmost importance in safety-critical systems. Therefore, semantic segmentation predictions integrated with reliable confidence estimates can significantly reinforce the concept of safe autonomy.

Advanced deep neural networks recently had a quantum jump in generating accurate and reliable semantic segmentation with real-time performance. Most of these approaches, however, rely on the camera images [13], whereas relatively fewer contributions have discussed the semantic segmentation of 3D LiDAR data [18,25]. The main reason is that unlike camera images, LiDAR point clouds are relatively sparse, unstructured, and have non-uniform sampling, although LiDAR scanners have a wider field of view and return more accurate distance measurements.

As comprehensively described in [9], there exists two mainstream deep learning approaches addressing the semantic segmentation of 3D LiDAR data only: point-wise and projection-based neural networks (see Fig. 1). The former approach operates directly on the raw 3D points without requiring any pre-processing step, whereas the latter projects the point cloud into various formats such as 2D image view or high-dimensional volumetric representation. As illustrated in Fig. 1, there is a clear split between these two approaches in terms of accuracy, runtime and memory consumption. Projection-based approaches (shown in green circles in Fig. 1) achieve the state-of-the-art accuracy while running significantly faster. Although point-wise networks (red squares) have slightly lower number of parameters, they cannot efficiently scale up to large point sets due to the limited processing capacity, thus, they take a longer runtime. Note also that both point-wise and projection-based approaches in the literature lack uncertainty measures, i.e.confidence scores, for their predictions.

We here introduce a novel neural network architecture to perform uncertainty-aware semantic segmentation of a full 3D LiDAR point cloud in real-time. Our proposed network is built upon the *SalsaNet* model [1], hence, named *SalsaNext*. The *SalsaNet* model has an encoder-decoder skeleton where the encoder unit consists of a series of ResNet blocks and the decoder part upsamples and fuses features extracted in the residual blocks. In the proposed *SalsaNext,* our contributions lie in the following aspects:

- To capture the global context information in the full 360° LiDAR scan, we introduce a new context module before encoder, which has a residual dilated convolution stack fusing receptive fields at various scales.
- To increase the receptive field, we replaced the ResNet block in the encoder with a novel combination of a set of dilated convolutions (with a rate of 2) each of which has different kernel sizes $(3, 5, 7)$. We further concatenated the convolution outputs and combined with residual connections yielding a branch-like structure.
- To avoid any checkerboard artifacts in upsampling, we replaced the transposed convolution layer in the *SalsaNet* decoder with a *pixel-shuffle* layer [22] which directly leverages on the feature maps to upsample the input with less computation.
- To boost the roles of very basic features (e.g.edges and curves) in the segmentation process, the dropout treatment was altered by omitting the first and last network layers in the dropout process.
- To have a lighter model, average pooling was employed instead of stride convolutions in the encoder.
- To enhance the segmentation accuracy by optimizing the mean intersection-over-union score, i.e.the Jaccard index, the weighted cross entropy loss in *SalsaNet* was combined with the *Lovász-Softmax* loss [4].
- To further estimate the *epistemic* (model) and *aleatoric* (observation) uncertainties for each 3D LiDAR point, the deterministic *SalsaNet* model was transformed into a stochastic format by applying the Bayesian treatment.

The input of *SalsaNext* is the rasterized image of the full LiDAR scan, where each image channel stores position, depth, and intensity cues in the panoramic view format. The final network output is the point-wise classification scores together with uncertainty measures. To the best of our knowledge, this is the first work showing the both *epistemic* and *aleatoric* uncertainty estimation on the LiDAR point cloud segmentation task. Computing both uncertainties is of utmost importance in safe autonomous driving since the *epistemic* uncertainty can indicate the limitation of the segmentation model while the *aleatoric* one highlights the sensor observation noises for segmentation.

Quantitative and qualitative experiments on the Semantic-KITTI dataset [3] show that the proposed *SalsaNext* significantly outperforms other published state-of-the-art networks in terms of pixel-wise segmentation accuracy while having much fewer parameters, thus requiring less computation time. Note that we also release our source code and trained model to encourage further research on the subject.

2   Related Work

Regarding the processing of unstructured 3D LiDAR points, there are two common methods as depicted in Fig. 1: point-wise representation and projection-based rendering. We refer the interested readers to [9] for more details.

Point-wise methods [19, 20] directly process the raw irregular 3D points without applying any additional transformation or pre-processing. Shared multi-layer perceptron-based PointNet [19], the subsequent work PointNet++ [20], and *superpoint* graph SPG networks [14] are considered in this group. Although such methods are powerful on small point clouds, their processing capacity and memory requirement, unfortunately, becomes inefficient when it comes to the full 360° LiDAR scans.

Projection-based methods instead transform the 3D point cloud into various formats such as voxel cells [30], multi-view representation [15], lattice structure [21, 23], and rasterized images [1, 25–27]. In the multi-view representation, a 3D point cloud is projected onto multiple 2D surfaces from various virtual camera viewpoints. Each view is then processed by a multi-stream network as in [15]. In the lattice structure, the raw unorganized point cloud is interpolated to a permutohedral sparse lattice where bilateral convolutions are applied to occupied lattice sectors only [23]. Methods relying on the voxel representation discretize the 3D space into 3D volumetric space (i.e.voxels) and assign each point to the corresponding voxel [30]. Sparsity and irregularity in point clouds, however, yield redundant computations in voxelized data since many voxel cells may stay empty. A common attempt to overcome the sparsity in LiDAR data is to project 3D point clouds into 2D image space either in the top-down [1, 28] or spherical Range-View (RV) (i.e.panoramic view) [2, 18, 25–27] formats. Unlike point-wise and other projection-based approaches, such 2D rendered image representations are more compact, dense and computationally cheaper as they can be processed by standard 2D convolutional layers. Therefore, our *SalsaNext* model projects the LiDAR point cloud into 2D RV image generated by mapping each 3D point onto a spherical surface.

When it comes to the uncertainty estimation, Bayesian Neural Networks (BNNs) are the dominant approach. BNNs learn approximate distribution on the weights to further generate uncertainty estimates, i.e.prediction confidences. There are two types of uncertainties: *Aleatoric* which can quantify the intrinsic uncertainty coming from the observed data, and *epistemic* where the model uncertainty is estimated by inferring with the posterior weight distribution, usually through Monte Carlo sampling. Unlike *aleatoric* uncertainty, which captures the irreducible noise in the data, *epistemic* uncertainty can be reduced by gathering more training data. For instance, segmenting out an object that has relatively fewer training samples in the dataset may lead to high *epistemic* uncertainty, whereas high *aleatoric* uncertainty may rather occur on segment boundaries or distant and occluded objects due to noisy sensor readings inherent in sensors. Bayesian modelling helps estimating both uncertainties.

Gal *et al.* [7] proved that dropout can be used as a Bayesian approximation to estimate the uncertainty in classification, regression and reinforcement learning tasks while this idea was also extended to semantic segmentation of RGB images by Kendall *et al.* [13]. Loquercio *et al.* [17] proposed a framework which extends the dropout approach by propagating the uncertainty that is produced from the sensors through the activation functions without the need of retraining. Recently, both uncertainty types were applied to 3D point cloud object detection [6] and optical flow estimation [12] tasks. To the best of our knowledge, BNNs have not been employed in modeling the uncertainty of semantic segmentation of 3D LiDAR point clouds, which is one of the main contributions in this work.

In this context, the closest work to ours is [29] which introduces a probabilistic embedding space for point cloud instance segmentation. This approach, however, captures neither the aleatoric nor the epistemic uncertainty but rather predicts the uncertainty between the point cloud embeddings. Unlike our method, it has also not been shown how the aforementioned work can scale up to large and complex LiDAR point clouds.

3   Method

In this section, we give a detailed description of our method including the point cloud representation, network architecture, uncertainty estimation, and training details.

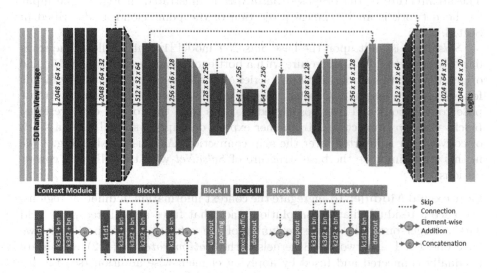

Fig. 2. Architecture of the proposed *SalsaNext* model. Blocks with dashed edges indicate those that do not employ the dropout. The layer elements k, d, and bn represent the kernel size, dilation rate and batch normalization, respectively.

3.1   LiDAR Point Cloud Representation

As in [18], we project the unstructed 3D LiDAR point cloud onto a spherical surface to generate the LIDAR's native Range View (RV) image. This process leads to dense and compact point cloud representation which allows standard convolution operations.

In the 2D RV image, each raw LiDAR point (x, y, z) is mapped to an image coordinate (u, v) as

$$\begin{pmatrix} u \\ v \end{pmatrix} = \begin{pmatrix} \frac{1}{2}[1 - \arctan(y, x)\pi^{-1}]w \\ [1 - (\arcsin(z, r^{-1}) + f_{down})f^{-1}]h \end{pmatrix} \quad ,$$

where h and w denote the height and width of the projected image, r represents the range of each point as $r = \sqrt{x^2 + y^2 + z^2}$ and f defines the sensor vertical field of view as $f = |f_{down}| + |f_{up}|$.

Following the work of [18], we considered the full 360° field-of-view in the projection process. During the projection, 3D point coordinates (x, y, z), the intensity value (i) and the range index (r) are stored as separate RV image channels. This yields a $[w \times h \times 5]$ image to be fed to the network.

3.2   Network Architecture

The architecture of the proposed *SalsaNext* is illustrated in Fig. 2. The input to the network is an RV image projection of the point cloud as described in Sect. 3.1.

SalsaNext is built upon the base *SalsaNet* model [1] which follows the standard encoder-decoder architecture with a bottleneck compression rate of 16. The original *SalsaNet* encoder contains a series of ResNet blocks [10] each of which is followed by dropout and downsampling layers. The decoder blocks apply transpose convolutions and fuse upsampled features with that of the early residual blocks via skip connections. To further exploit descriptive spatial cues, a stack of convolution is inserted after the skip connection. As illustrated in Fig. 2, we in this study improve the base structure of *SalsaNet* with the following contributions:

Contextual Module: To aggregate the context information in different regions, we place a residual dilated convolution stack that fuses a small receptive field with a larger one right at the beginning of the network. More specifically, we have one 1×1 and two 3×3 kernels with *dilation rates* $= (1, 2)$, which are residually connected and fused by applying element-wise addition (see Fig. 2). Starting with relatively small 1×1 kernel helps aggregate channel-wise local spatial features while having 3×3 kernels with different dilation rates captures various complex correlations between different segment classes. This helps focusing on more contextual information alongside with more detailed global spatial information via pyramid pooling similar to [5].

Dilated Convolution: Receptive fields play a crucial role in extracting spatial features. A straightforward approach to capture more descriptive spatial features would be to enlarge the kernel size. This has, however, a drawback of increasing the number of parameters drastically. Instead, we replace the ResNet blocks in the original *SalsaNet* encoder with a novel combination of a set of dilated convolutions having effective receptive fields of $3, 5$ and 7 (see Block I in Fig. 2). We further concatenate each dilated convolution output and apply a 1×1 convolution followed by a residual connection in order to let the network exploit more information from the fused features coming from various depths in the receptive field. Each of these new residual dilated convolution blocks (i.e.Block I) is followed by dropout and pooling layers (Block II in Fig. 2).

Pixel-Shuffle Layer: The original *SalsaNet* decoder involves transpose convolutions which are computationally expensive layers in terms of number of parameters. We replace these standard transpose convolutions with the *pixel-shuffle* layer [22] (see Block III in Fig. 2) which leverages on the learnt feature maps to produce the upsampled feature maps by shuffling the pixels from the channel dimension to the spatial dimension. More precisely, the *pixel-shuffle* operator reshapes the elements of $(H \times W \times Cr^2)$ feature map to a form of $(Hr \times Wr \times C)$, where H, W, C, and r represent the height, width, channel number and upscaling ratio, respectively.

We additionally double the filters in the decoder side and concatenate the *pixel-shuffle* outputs with the skip connection (Block IV in Fig. 2) before feeding them to the dilated convolutional blocks (Block V in Fig. 2) in the decoder.

Central Encoder-Decoder Dropout: As quantitative experiments in [13] show, inserting dropout only to the central encoder and decoder layers results in better segmentation performance. It is because the lower network layers extract basic features such as edges and corners which are consistent over the data distribution and dropping out these layers will prevent the network to properly form the higher level features in the deeper layers. Central dropout approach eventually leads to higher network performance. We, therefore, insert dropout in every encoder-decoder layer except the first and last one highlighted by dashed edges in Fig. 2.

Average Pooling: In the base *SalsaNet* model the downsampling was performed via a strided convolution which introduces additional learning parameters. Given that the down-sampling process is relatively straightforward, we hypothesize that learning at this level would not be needed. Thus, to allocate less memory *SalsaNext* switches to average pooling for the downsampling.

All these contributions from the proposed *SalsaNext* network. Furthermore, we applied a 1×1 convolution after the decoder unit to make the channel numbers the same with the total number of semantic classes. The final feature map is finally passed to a soft-max classifier to compute pixel-wise classification scores. Note that each convolution layer in the *SalsaNext* model employs a leaky-ReLU activation function and is followed by batch normalization to solve the internal covariant shift. Dropout is then placed after the batch normalization. It can, otherwise, result in a shift in the weight distribution which can minimize the batch normalization effect during training [16].

3.3   Uncertainty Estimation

Heteroscedastic Aleatoric Uncertainty. We can define *aleatoric* uncertainty as being of two kinds: *homoscedastic* and *heteroscedastic*. The former defines the type of *aleatoric* uncertainty that remains constant given different input types, whereas the later may rather differ for different types of input. In the LiDAR semantic segmentation task, distant points might introduce a *heteroscedastic* uncertainty as it is increasingly difficult to assign them to a single class. The same kind of uncertainty is also observable in the object edges when performing semantic segmentation, especially when the gradient between the object and the background is not sharp enough.

LiDAR observations are usually corrupted by noise and thus the input that a neural network is processing is a noisy version of the real world. Assuming that the sensor's noise characteristic is known (e.g.available in the sensor data sheet), the input data distribution can be expressed by the normal $\mathcal{N}(\mathbf{x}, \mathbf{v})$, where $\mathbf{x}$ represents the observations and $\mathbf{v}$ the sensor's noise. In this case, the aleatoric uncertainty can be computed by propagating the noise through the network via Assumed Density Filtering (ADF). This approach was initially applied by Gast *et al.* [8], where the network's activation functions including input and output were replaced by probability distributions. A forward pass in this ADF-based modified neural network finally generates output predictions μ with their respective aleatoric uncertainties σ_A.

Epistemic Uncertainty. In *SalsaNext*, the *epistemic* uncertainty is computed using the weight's posterior $p(\mathbf{W}|\mathbf{X}, \mathbf{Y})$ which is intractable and thus impossible to present analytically. However, the work in [7] showed that dropout can be used as an approximation to the intractable posterior. More specifically, dropout is an approximating distribution $q_\theta(\omega)$ to the posterior in a BNN with L layers, $\omega = [\mathbf{W}_l]_{l=1}^{L}$ where θ is a set of variational parameters. The optimization objective function can be written as:

$$\hat{\mathcal{L}}_{MC}(\theta) = -\frac{1}{M} \sum_{i \in S} \log p(y_i | f^\omega(x_i)) + \frac{1}{N} \mathbf{KL}(q_\theta || p(\omega))$$

where the **KL** denotes the regularization from the Kullback-Leibler divergence, N is the number of data samples, S holds a random set of M data samples, y_i denotes the ground-truth, $f^\omega(x_i)$ is the output of the network for x_i input with weight parameters ω and $p(y_i | f^\omega(x_i))$ likelihood. The **KL** term can be approximated as:

$$KL(q_M(\mathbf{W}) || p(\mathbf{W})) \propto \frac{i^2(1-p)}{2} ||\mathbf{M}||^2 - K\mathcal{H}(p)$$

where

$$\mathcal{H}(p) := -p \log(p) - (1-p) \log(1-p)$$

represents the entropy of a Bernoulli random variable with probability p and K is a constant to balance the regularization term with the predictive term.

For example, the negative log likelihood in this case will be estimated as

$$- \log p(y_i | f^\omega(x_i)) \propto \frac{1}{2} \log \sigma + \frac{1}{2\sigma} ||y_i - f^\omega(x_i)||^2$$

for a Gaussian likelihood with σ model's uncertainty.

To be able to measure the *epistemic* uncertainty, we employ a Monte Carlo sampling during inference: we run n trials and compute the average of the variance of the n predicted outputs:

$$\mathrm{Var}_{p(y|f^\omega(x))}^{epistemic} = \sigma_{epistemic} = \frac{1}{n} \sum_{i=1}^{n} (y_i - \hat{y})^2.$$

As introduced in [17], the optimal dropout rate p which minimizes the **KL** divergence, is estimated for an *already trained network* by applying a grid search on a log-range of a certain number of possible rates in the range $[0, 1]$. In practice, it means that the optimal dropout rates p will minimize:

$$p = arg\,min_{\hat{p}} \sum_{d \in D} \frac{1}{2} \log(\sigma_{tot}^d) + \frac{1}{2\sigma_{tot}^d}(y^d - y_{pred}^d(\hat{p}))^2,$$

where σ_{tot} denotes the total uncertainty by summing the aleatoric and the epistemic uncertainty, D is the input data, $y_{pred}^d(\hat{p})$ and y^d are the predictions and labels.

3.4   Loss Function

Datasets with imbalanced classes introduce a challenge for neural networks. Take an example of a bicycle or traffic sign which appears much less compared to the vehicles in the autonomous driving scenarios. This makes the network more biased towards to the classes that emerge more in the training data and thus yields significantly poor network performance.

To cope with the imbalanced class problem, we follow the same strategy in *SalsaNet* and add more value to the under-represented classes by weighting the softmax cross-entropy loss $\mathcal{L}_{wce}$ with the inverse square root of class frequency as

$$\mathcal{L}_{wce}(y, \hat{y}) = -\sum_i \alpha_i p(y_i) log(p(\hat{y}_i)) \quad with \quad \alpha_i = 1/\sqrt{f_i},$$

where y_i and $\hat{y}_i$ define the true and predicted class labels and f_i stands for the frequency, i.e.the number of points, of the ith class. This reinforces the network response to the classes appearing less in the dataset.

In contrast to *SalsaNet*, we here also incorporate the *Lovász-Softmax* loss [4] in the learning procedure to maximize the intersection-over-union (IoU) score, i.e.the Jaccard index. The IoU metric (see Sect. 4) is the most commonly used metric to evaluate the segmentation performance. Nevertheless, IoU is a discrete and not derivable metric that does not have a direct way to be employed as a loss. In [4], the authors adopt this metric with the help of the Lovász extension for submodular functions. Considering the IoU as a hypercube where each vertex is a possible combination of the class labels, we relax the IoU score to be defined everywhere inside of the hypercube. In this respect, the *Lovász-Softmax* loss ($\mathcal{L}_{ls}$) can be formulated as follows:

$$\mathcal{L}_{ls} = \frac{1}{|C|} \sum_{c \in C} \overline{\Delta_{J_c}}(m(c)), \quad and \quad m_i(c) = \begin{cases} 1 - x_i(c) & \text{if } c = y_i(c) \\ x_i(c) & \text{otherwise} \end{cases},$$

where $|C|$ represents the class number, $\overline{\Delta_{J_c}}$ defines the Lovász extension of the Jaccard index, $x_i(c) \in [0, 1]$ and $y_i(c) \in \{-1, 1\}$ hold the predicted probability and ground truth label of pixel i for class c, respectively.

Finally, the total loss function of *SalsaNext* is a linear combination of both weighted cross-entropy and *Lovász-Softmax* losses as follows: $\mathcal{L} = \mathcal{L}_{wce} + \mathcal{L}_{ls}$.

3.5   Optimizer and Regularization

As an optimizer, we employed stochastic gradient descent with an initial learning rate of 0.01 which is decayed by 0.01 after each epoch. We also applied an L2 penalty with $\lambda = 0.0001$ and a momentum of 0.9. The batch size and spatial dropout probability were fixed at 24 and 0.2. To prevent overfitting, we augmented the data by applying a random rotation and translation, flipping randomly around the y-axis and randomly dropping points before creating the projection. Every augmentation is applied independently of each other with a probability of 0.5.

3.6   Post-processing

The main drawback of the projection-based point cloud representation is the information loss due to discretization errors and blurry convolutional layer responses. This problem emerges when, for instance, the RV image is re-projected back to the original 3D space. The reason is that during the image rendering process, multiple LiDAR points may get assigned to the very same image pixel which leads to misclassification of, in particular, the object edges. This effect becomes more obvious, for instance, when the objects cast a shadow in the background scene.

To cope with these back-projection related issues, we employ the kNN-based post-processing technique introduced in [18]. The post-processing is applied to every LIDAR point by using a window around each corresponding image pixel, that will be translated into a subset of point clouds. Next, a set of closest neighbors is selected with the help of kNN. The assumption behind using the range instead of the Euclidian distances lies in the fact that a small window is applied, making the range of close (u, v) points serve as a good proxy for the Euclidian distance in the 3D space.

Table 1. Quantitative comparison on Semantic-KITTI test set (sequences 11 to 21). IoU scores are given in percentage (%). Note that only the published methods are considered.

Approach	Size	car	bicycle	motorcycle	truck	other-vehicle	person	bicyclist	motorcyclist	road	parking	sidewalk	other-ground	building	fence	vegetation	trunk	terrain	pole	traffic-sign	mean-IoU
Pointnet [19]		46.3	1.3	0.3	0.1	0.8	0.2	0.2	0.0	61.6	15.8	35.7	1.4	41.4	12.9	31.0	4.6	17.6	2.4	3.7	14.6
Pointnet++ [20]		53.7	1.9	0.2	0.9	0.2	0.9	1.0	0.0	72.0	18.7	41.8	5.6	62.3	16.9	46.5	13.8	30.0	6.0	8.9	20.1
SPGraph [14]	50K pts	68.3	0.9	4.5	0.9	0.8	1.0	6.0	0.0	49.5	1.7	24.2	0.3	68.2	22.5	59.2	27.2	17.0	18.3	10.5	20.0
SPLATNet [23]		66.6	0.0	0.0	0.0	0.0	0.0	0.0	0.0	70.4	0.8	41.5	0.0	68.7	27.8	72.3	35.9	35.8	13.8	0.0	22.8
TangentConv [24]		86.8	1.3	12.7	11.6	10.2	17.1	20.2	0.5	82.9	15.2	61.7	9.0	82.8	44.2	75.5	42.5	55.5	30.2	22.2	35.9
RandLa-Net [11]		94.2	26.0	25.8	40.1	38.9	49.2	48.2	7.2	90.7	60.3	73.7	38.9	86.9	56.3	81.4	61.3	66.8	49.2	47.7	53.9
LatticeNet [21]		92.9	16.6	22.2	26.6	21.4	35.6	43.0	46.0	90.0	59.4	74.1	22.0	88.2	58.8	81.7	63.6	63.1	51.9	48.4	52.9
SqueezeSeg [25]		68.8	16.0	4.1	3.3	3.6	12.9	13.1	0.9	85.4	26.9	54.3	4.5	57.4	29.0	60.0	24.3	53.7	17.5	24.5	29.5
SqueezeSeg-CRF [25]		68.3	18.1	5.1	4.1	4.8	16.5	17.3	1.2	84.9	28.4	54.7	4.6	61.5	29.2	59.5	25.5	54.7	11.2	36.3	30.8
SqueezeSegV2 [26]		81.8	18.5	17.9	13.4	14.0	20.1	25.1	3.9	88.6	45.8	67.6	17.7	73.7	41.1	71.8	35.8	60.2	20.2	36.3	39.7
SqueezeSegV2-CRF [26]	64 × 2048 pixels	82.7	21.0	22.6	14.5	15.9	20.2	24.3	2.9	88.5	42.4	65.5	18.7	73.8	41.0	68.5	36.9	58.9	12.9	41.0	39.6
RangeNet21 [18]		85.4	26.2	26.5	18.6	15.6	31.8	33.6	4.0	91.4	57.0	74.0	26.4	81.9	52.3	77.6	48.4	63.6	36.0	50.0	47.4
RangeNet53 [18]		86.4	24.5	32.7	25.5	22.6	36.2	33.6	4.7	91.8	64.8	74.6	27.9	84.1	55.0	78.3	50.1	64.0	38.9	52.2	49.9
RangeNet53++ [18]		91.4	25.7	34.4	25.7	23.0	38.3	38.8	4.8	91.8	65.0	75.2	27.8	87.4	58.6	80.5	55.1	64.6	47.9	55.9	52.2
3D-MiniNet [2]		90.5	42.3	42.1	28.5	29.4	47.8	44.1	14.5	91.6	64.2	74.5	25.4	89.4	60.8	82.8	60.8	66.7	48.0	56.6	55.8
SqueezeSegV3 [27]		92.5	38.7	36.5	29.6	33.0	45.6	46.2	20.1	91.7	63.4	74.8	26.4	89.0	59.4	82.0	58.7	65.4	49.6	58.9	55.9
SalsaNet [1]	64 × 2048 pixels	87.5	26.2	24.6	24.0	17.5	33.2	31.1	8.4	89.7	51.7	70.7	19.7	82.8	48.0	73.0	40.0	61.7	31.3	41.9	45.4
SalsaNext [Ours]		91.9	48.3	38.6	38.9	31.9	60.2	59.0	19.4	91.7	63.7	75.8	29.1	90.2	64.2	81.8	63.6	66.5	54.3	62.1	59.5

4   Experiments

We evaluate the performance of *SalsaNext* and compare with the other state-of-the-art semantic segmentation methods on the large-scale challenging Semantic-KITTI dataset [3] which provides over 43K point-wise annotated full 3D LiDAR scans. We follow exactly the same protocol in [18] and divide the dataset into training, validation, and test splits. Over 21K scans (sequences between 00 and 10) are used for training, where scans from sequence 08 are particularly dedicated to validation. The remaining scans (between sequences 11 and 21) are used as test split. The dataset has in total 22 classes 19 of which are evaluated on the test set by the official online benchmark platform. We implement our model in PyTorch and release the code for public use[1].

To evaluate the results, we use the Jaccard Index, i.e.mean intersection-over-union (IoU) over all classes given by $mIoU = \frac{1}{C}\sum_{i=1}^{C} \frac{|\mathcal{P}_i \cap \mathcal{G}_i|}{|\mathcal{P}_i \cup \mathcal{G}_i|}$, where $\mathcal{P}_i$ is the set of point with a class prediction i, $\mathcal{G}_i$ the labelled set for class i and $|\cdot|$ the cardinality of the set.

4.1   Quantitative and Qualitative Results

Table 1 reports obtained quantitative results compared to other published point-wise and projection-based approaches. Our proposed model *SalsaNext* considerably outperforms the others by leading to the highest mean IoU score (59.5%)

---

[1] https://github.com/TiagoCortinhal/SalsaNext.

which is +3.6% over the previous state-of-the-art method [27]. In contrast to the original *SalsaNet,* we also obtain more than 14% improvement in the accuracy. When it comes to the performance of each individual category, *SalsaNext* performs the best in 9 out of 19 categories. Note that in most of these remaining 10 categories (e.g. road, vegetation, and terrain) *SalsaNext* has a comparable performance with the other approaches.

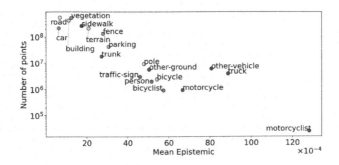

Fig. 3. The relationship between the *epistemic* (model) uncertainty and the number of points (in log scale) that each class has in the entire test dataset.

Following the work of [17], we further computed the *epistemic* and *aleatoric* uncertainty without retraining *SalsaNext* (see sect. 3.3). Figure 3 depicts the quantitative relationship between the *epistemic* (model) uncertainty and the number of points that each class has in the entire Semantic-KITTI test dataset. This plot has diagonally distributed samples, which clearly shows that the network becomes less certain about rare classes represented by low number of points (e.g.motorcyclist and motorcycle). There is, to some degree, an inverse correlation between the obtained uncertainty and the segmentation accuracy: when the network predicts an incorrect label, the uncertainty becomes high as in the case of motorcyclist which has the lowest IoU score (19.4%) in Table 1.

For the qualitative evaluation, Fig. 4 shows some sample semantic segmentation and uncertainty results generated by *SalsaNext* on the Semantic-KITTI test set. In this figure, only for visualization purposes, segmented object points are also projected back to the respective camera image. We, here, emphasize that these camera images have not been used for training of *SalsaNext.* As depicted in Fig. 4, *SalsaNext* can, to a great extent, distinguish road, car, and other object points. In Fig. 4, we additionally show the estimated *epistemic* and *aleatoric* uncertainty values projected on the camera image for the sake of clarity. Here, the light blue points indicate the highest uncertainty whereas darker points represent more certain predictions. In line with Fig. 3, we obtain high

Fig. 4. Sample qualitative results of *SalsaNext* [best view in color]. At the bottom of each scene, the range-view image of the network response is shown. Note that the corresponding camera images on the right are only for visualization purposes and have not been used in the training. The top camera image on the right shows the projected segments whereas the middle and bottom images depict the projected *epistemic* and *aleatoric* uncertainties, respectively. Note that the lighter the color is, the more uncertain the network becomes.

epistemic uncertainty for rare classes such as other-ground as shown in the last frame in Fig. 4. We also observe that high level of *aleatoric* uncertainty mainly appears around segment boundaries (see the second frame in Fig. 4) and on distant objects (e.g.last frame in Fig. 4). In the supplementary video[2], we provide more qualitative results.

4.2 Ablation Study

Table 2 shows the total number of model parameters and FLOPs (Floating Point Operations) with the obtained mIoU scores on the Semantic-KITTI validation set before and after applying the kNN-based post processing (see Sect. 3.6). As depicted in this table, each of our contributions on *SalsaNet* has a unique improvement in the accuracy. The post processing step leads to a certain jump (around 2%) in the accuracy. The peak in the model parameters is observed when dilated convolution stack is introduced in the encoder, which is vastly reduced after adding the *pixel-shuffle* layers in the decoder. Switching to the *pixel-shuffle* layers yields 1.0% more accuracy while having 2.52M less parameters and 22% less FLOPs. Recall that pixel shuffle is a differentiable process which rearranges elements from depth dimension to spatial domain in a deterministic way. Therefore, shuffling pixels in the decoder leads to more accurate image reconstruction as it introduces fewer checkerboard artifacts with a vastly reduced number of parameters. Combining the weighted cross-entropy loss with *Lovász-Softmax* leads to the highest increment in the accuracy. This is mainly

---

[2] https://www.youtube.com/watch?v=MlSaIcD9ItU.

because the Jaccard index which is the main metric to measure the segmentation accuracy is directly optimized as a part of the loss function. We can achieve the highest accuracy score of 59.9% by having only 2.2% (i.e.0.15M) extra parameters compared to the original *SalsaNet* model. Table 2 also shows that the number of FLOPs is correlated with the number of parameters. We note that adding the *epistemic* and *aleatoric* uncertainty computations do not introduce any additional training parameter since they are computed after the network is trained.

Table 2. Ablative analysis on the validation set

	Mean IoU (w/o kNN)	Mean IoU (+kNN)	Number of parameters	FLOPs
SalsaNet [1]	43.2	44.4	6.58 M	51.60 G
+ context module	45.0	46.4	6.64 M	69.20 G
+ central dropout	48.5	50.8	6.64 M	69.20 G
+ average pooling	48.9	51.2	5.85 M	66.78 G
+ dilated convolution	50.6	52.3	9.25 M	161.60 G
+ Pixel-Shuffle	51.2	53.3	6.73 M	125.68 G
+ *Lovász-Softmax* loss	**56.4**	**59.9**	6.73 M	125.68 G

Table 3. Runtime performance on the Semantic-KITTI test set

	Processing time (msec)					
	CNN	kNN	Total	Speed (fps)	Parameters	FLOPs
RangeNet++ [18]	63.51	2.89	66.41	15 Hz	50 M	720.96 G
SalsaNet [1]	35.78	2.62	38.40	26 Hz	6.58 M	51.60 G
SalsaNext [Ours]	38.61	2.65	41.26	24 Hz	6.73 M	125.68 G

4.3 Runtime Evaluation

Table 3 reports the total runtime performance for the CNN backbone network and post-processing module of *SalsaNext* in contrast to other networks. To obtain fair statistics, all measurements are performed using the entire Semantic-KITTI dataset on the same single NVIDIA Quadro RTX 6000 - 24 GB card. *SalsaNext* clearly exhibits better performance compared to RangeNet++ [18] while having 7× less parameters. *SalsaNext* can run at 24 Hz when the uncertainty computation is excluded for a fair comparison with deterministic models.

This achieved high speed is significantly faster than the sampling rate of mainstream LiDAR sensors which is typically 10 Hz. Figure 1 also compares the overall performance of *SalsaNext* with the other state-of-the-art semantic segmentation networks in terms of runtime, accuracy, and memory consumption.

5   Conclusion

We introduced *SalsaNext* as a new uncertainty-aware semantic segmentation network that can process the full 360° LiDAR scan in real-time. *SalsaNext* builds up on the *SalsaNet* model and achieves over 14% more accuracy. In contrast to other published state-of-the-art methods, *SalsaNext* returns +3.6% better mIoU score. Our method differs in that *SalsaNext* can also estimate both data and model-based uncertainty.

References

1. Aksoy, E.E., Baci, S., Cavdar, S.: Salsanet: Fast road and vehicle segmentation in lidar point clouds for autonomous driving. In IEEE IV, (2020)
2. Alonso, I., Riazuelo, L., Montesano, L., Murillo, A.C.: 3d-mininet: Learning a 2d representation from point clouds for fast and efficient 3d lidar semantic segmentation. RA-L, (2020)
3. Behley, J., Garbade, M., Milioto, A., Quenzel, J., Behnke, S., Stachniss, C., Gall, J.: SemanticKITTI: A Dataset for Semantic Scene Understanding of LiDAR Sequences. In ICCV, (2019)
4. Berman, M., Triki, A.R., Blaschko, M.: The lovász-softmax loss: A tractable surrogate for the optimization of the intersection-over-union measure in neural networks. In CVPR, (2018)
5. Chen, L.C., Papandreou, G., Schroff, F., Adam, H.: Rethinking atrous convolution for semantic image segmentation. In arXiv, (2017)
6. Feng, D., Rosenbaum, L., Dietmayer, K.: Towards safe autonomous driving: Capture uncertainty in the deep neural network for lidar 3d vehicle detection. In ITSC, (2018)
7. Gal, Y., Ghahramani, Z.: Dropout as a bayesian approximation: Representing model uncertainty in deep learning. In ICML, (2016)
8. Gast, J., Roth, S.: Lightweight probabilistic deep networks. In CVPR, (2018)
9. Guo, Y., Wang, H., Hu, Q., Liu, H., Liu, L., Bennamoun, M.: Deep learning for 3d point clouds: A survey. IEEE TPAMI, (2019)
10. He, K., Zhang, X., Ren, S., Sun, J.: Deep residual learning for image recognition. In CVPR, pages 770–778, (2016)
11. Hu, Q., Yang, B., Xie, L., Rosa, S., Guo, Y., Wang, Z., Trigoni, N., Markham, A.: Randla-net: Efficient semantic segmentation of large-scale point clouds. In CVPR, (2020)
12. Ilg, E., Cicek, O., Galesso, S., Klein, A., Makansi, O., Hutter, F., Brox, T.: Uncertainty estimates and multi-hypotheses networks for optical flow. In ECCV, pages 652–667, (2018)
13. Kendall, A., Badrinarayanan, V., Cipolla, R.: Bayesian segnet: Model uncertainty in deep convolutional encoder-decoder architectures for scene understanding. In BMVC, (2017)

14. Landrieu L., Simonovsky, M.: Large-scale point cloud semantic segmentation with superpoint graphs. In CVPR, (2018)
15. Lawin, F.J., Danelljan, M., Tosteberg, P., Bhat, G., Khan, F.S., Felsberg, M.: Deep projective 3d semantic segmentation. In CAIP, (2017)
16. Li, X., Chen, S., Hu, X., Yang, J.: Understanding the disharmony between dropout and batch normalization by variance shift. In CVPR, (2019)
17. Loquercio, A., Segu, M., Scaramuzza, D.: A general framework for uncertainty estimation in deep learning. IEEE RA-L **5**(2), 3153–3160 (2020)
18. Milioto, A., Vizzo, I., Behley, J., Stachniss, C.: RangeNet++: Fast and Accurate LiDAR Semantic Segmentation. In IROS, (2019)
19. Qi, C.R., Su, H., Mo, K., Guibas, L.J.: Pointnet: Deep learning on point sets for 3d classification and segmentation. In CVPR, (2017)
20. Qi, C.R., Yi, L., Su, H., Guibas, L.j.: Pointnet++: Deep hierarchical feature learning on point sets in a metric space. In NIPS, (2017)
21. Rosu, A.R., Schütt, P., Quenzel, J., Behnke, S.: LatticeNet: Fast Point Cloud Segmentation Using Permutohedral Lattices. In RSS, (2020)
22. Shi, W., Caballero, J., Huszar, F., Totz, J., Aitken, A.P., Bishop, R., Rueckert, D., Wang, Z.: Real-time single image and video super-resolution using an efficient sub-pixel convolutional neural network. In CVPR, pages 1874–1883, (2016)
23. Su, H., Jampani, V., Sun, D., Maji, S., Kalogerakis, E., Yang, M.H., Kautz, J.: Splatnet: Sparse lattice networks for point cloud processing. In CVPR, (2018)
24. Tatarchenko, M., Park, J., Koltun, V., Zhou, Q.Y.: Tangent convolutions for dense prediction in 3d. In CVPR, (2018)
25. Wu, B., Wan, A., Yue, X., Keutzer, K.: Squeezeseg: Convolutional neural nets with recurrent crf for real-time road-object segmentation from 3d lidar point cloud. In ICRA, (2018)
26. Wu, B., Zhou, X., Zhao, S., Yue, X., Keutzer, K.: Squeezesegv 2: Improved model structure and unsupervised domain adaptation for road-object segmentation from a lidar point cloud. In ICRA, (2019)
27. Xu, C., Wu, B., Wang, Z., Zhan, W., Vajda, P., Keutzer, K. and Tomizuka, M.: Squeezesegv3: Spatially-adaptive convolution for efficient point-cloud segmentation. In arXiv, (2020)
28. Zeng, Y., Hu, Y., Liu, S., Ye, J., Han, Y., Li, X., Sun, N.: Rt3d: Real-time 3-d vehicle detection in lidar point cloud for autonomous driving. IEEE RAL **3**(4), 3434–3440 (2018)
29. Zhang, B., Wonka, P.: Point cloud instance segmentation using probabilistic embeddings. In CoRR, (2019)
30. Zhou, Y., Tuzel, O.: Voxelnet: End-to-end learning for point cloud based 3d object detection. In CVPR, (2018)

Mobile Manipulator Robot Visual Servoing and Guidance for Dynamic Target Grasping

Prateek Arora and Christos Papachristos(✉)

Robotic Workers Lab, University of Nevada, Reno,
1664 N. Virginia, Reno, NV 89557, USA
prateeka@nevada.unr.edu, cpapachristos@unr.edu

Abstract. This paper deals with the problem of real time closed loop tracking and grasping of a dynamic target by a mobile manipulation robot. Dynamic object tracking and manipulation is crucial for robotic system that intend to physically interact with the real world. The robot considered corresponds to an eye-in-hand gripper-and-arm combination mounted on a four-wheel base. The proposed policy is inspired by the principles of visual servoing, and leverages a computationally simple paradigm of virtual force-based formulation, due to the intended deployment for real-time closed loop control. The main objective of our strategy is to align a dynamic target frame to the onboard gripper, while respecting the constraints of the mobile manipulator system. The algorithm was implemented on a real robot and evaluated across multiple diverse real time experimental studies, detailed within this paper.

Keywords: Visual servoing · Mobile manipulation · Dynamic target tracking · Dynamic grasping

1 Introduction

Recent years have witnessed a rise in the use of robotic manipulation in industry, and a vast expansion of applicable domains for field robotics. Furthermore, manipulators end specialized end-effectors are actively combined with diverse robotic vehicles, showcasing their effectiveness in mobile manipulation applications including grasping, pick and place, generic object manipulation, and technical activities execution [6,13,14,21]. This commonly entails the use of a visual system onboard that allows to detect and localize the objects of interest; visual servoing [20] i.e. the use of visual information for closed loop control in such operations, is widespread among many works that deal with mobile manipulation [2,18].

This material is based upon work supported by Governor's Office of Economic Development of the State of Nevada under the Construction Robotics Award.

© Springer Nature Switzerland AG 2020
G. Bebis et al. (Eds.): ISVC 2020, LNCS 12510, pp. 223–235, 2020.
https://doi.org/10.1007/978-3-030-64559-5_17

In this work, we deal with the challenge of dynamic target tracking and grasping using a mobile manipulation system, via a real-time closed loop execution policy. The employed eye-in-hand mobile manipulation robot is equipped with onboard perception systems and algorithms enabling its operational autonomy. The proposed method relies on visual-servoing and leverages the paradigm of virtual forces to achieve the tasks of "hunting" down and grasping dynamic targets via motion-controlled tracking and guidance. Additionally, The problem of tracking is formulated to exhibit a unified behaviour of mobile base and the manipulator, ensuring that the mobile base navigates towards the object when it is out of reach, and that the arm grasps the object it becomes feasible while avoiding singular configurations. Figure 1 illustrates the system in operation; a video demonstration is available at: https://www.youtube.com/watch?v=UpREPxifF8I.

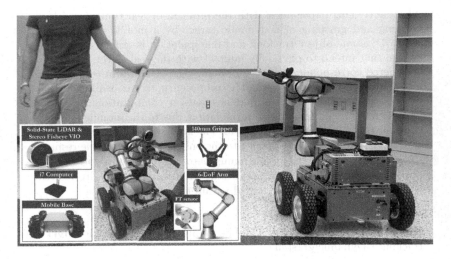

Fig. 1. The *Beaver* mobile manipulation robot performing dynamic target tracking and grasping (video online at: https://www.youtube.com/watch?v=UpREPxifF8I).

This paper comprises the following Sections: Sect. 2 presents the mobile manipulation robot system architecture and the employed nomenclature, Sect. 3 elaborates the proposed visual servoing policy for dynamic target tracking and grasping, Sect. 4 details the experimental verification studies, and finally Sect. 5 concludes the article.

2   Mobile Manipulation Robot

The mobile manipulation robot that is used for the development and demonstration of the proposed guidance scheme is overviewed within this Section.

2.1 Beaver Robot

Beaver represents an autonomous physical interaction robot, equipped with the required perception, navigation, and planning pipelines that enable fundamental capabilities including multi-modal SLAM [8–11], volumetric mapping [7], exploration [5,15–17], guidance [19], and manipulation [4]. Its onboard perception incorporates a custom "eye–in–hand" multi-modal sensor module that enables autonomy in the aforementioned contexts. Figure 2 illustrates the specific embodiment including a breakdown of its main components and subsystems. The robot comprises:

Fig. 2. *Beaver* system architecture.

- A differential 4-wheel drive mobile base with 0.85 [m] wheelbase, > 120 [kg] payload capacity, and 4 wheel encoders providing direct wheel odometry.
- An industrial-grade 6–DoF manipulator arm with 0.85 [m] reach and $\simeq$ 5 [kg] manipulation payload capacity, rigidly mounted onto the mobile base.
- An Force/Torque sensor integrated with the arm, providing force and torque feedback at ranges of up to 50 [N] and 10 [Nm] respectively.
- A 2–$Finger$ gripper with 140 [mm] opening and 125 [N] holding force.
- An Intel $i7$–$9750H$ (6-core) and NVIDIA RTX–2070 GPU based onboard computer with $WiFi$ connectivity.
- An Intel Realsense $L515$ sensor integrating a solid-state 860 [nm] LiDAR sensor and a 6–DoF IMU with 400 [Hz] update rate, as well as an RGB color camera (rolling shutter).
- An Intel Realsense $T265$ sensor providing on-chip Visual Inertial Odometry (VIO) and 2 fisheye-lens (173°–FoV) monochrome camera image streams.

The software architecture relies on a fully preemptible real-time build of a state-of-the-art Linux kernel. Additionally the framework of the Robot Operating System (ROS) acts as the middleware solution for the required inter-process communication between a collection of modules including device drivers to high-level algorithmic pipelines.

2.2   Reference Frames

Figure 3 illustrates the *Beaver* robot alongside the corresponding coordinate system frames of reference utilized within this paper's nomenclature. Onwards, we will be using the following notations:

- A reference frame A is denoted as $\mathcal{F}_A$.
- A translation vector between 2 reference frames $\mathcal{F}_A$ and $\mathcal{F}_B$ expressed in the $\mathcal{F}_A$ frame is denoted as $_A r_{AB}$.
- A rotation matrix between 2 reference frames $\mathcal{F}_A$ and $\mathcal{F}_B$ is denoted as $\mathcal{R}_{AB}$ ($\in SO_3$).
- As a result, the $\mathcal{T}_{AB}$ ($\in \mathbb{R}^{4 \times 4}$) rigid body transformation matrix between the 2 aforementioned reference frames is given as:

$$\mathcal{T}_{AB} = \begin{bmatrix} \mathcal{R}_{AB} & _A r_{AB} \\ \mathbf{0}^{\times 3} & 1 \end{bmatrix} \ (\in SE_3)$$

- A q_{AB} quaternion denotes another possible representation of the equivalent rotation represented by $\mathcal{R}_{AB}$ (and encapsulated in $\mathcal{T}_{AB}$).

The indicated frames of interest are:

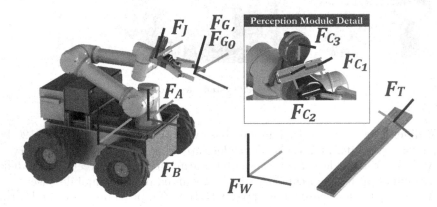

Fig. 3. *Beaver* reference frames.

- $\mathcal{F}_W$ represents an inertial frame of reference, i.e. a "flat world" coordinate frame which is arbitrarily chosen to be gravitationally-aligned, and coincident with the virtual footprint of the mobile base at the beginning of an experiment (the centroid of all four wheels' ground contact points).
- $\mathcal{F}_{C_i}$ represents the i-th camera optical frame. As intuitively noted in the illustration, the $i \in [1,3]$ indices correspond to the camera frames:

$$\begin{bmatrix} \mathcal{F}_{C_1} \rightarrow \text{T265 left fisheye camera} \\ \mathcal{F}_{C_2} \rightarrow \text{T265 right fisheye camera} \\ \mathcal{F}_{C_3} \rightarrow \text{L515 RGB camera} \end{bmatrix}$$

- $\mathcal{F}_G$ represents the gripper grasping virtual end-effector configuration, i.e. the centroid of the closed finger pads, and is aligned per the fingers' axes.
- $\mathcal{F}_J$ represents the force-torque sensor coordinate frame. This is where
- $\mathcal{F}_A$ represents the arm base coordinate frame, i.e. the frame of reference for calculation of the joint forward kinematic solution to derive the $\mathcal{T}_{AJ}$ and the $\mathcal{T}_{GJ}$ transformations.
- $\mathcal{F}_B$ represents the mobile base coordinate frame, which is continuously varying as the robot employs differential drive Wheel locomotion to move within its environment.
- $\mathcal{F}_T$ represents the dynamic target coordinate frame, and is aligned and coincident with the desired grasp pose for the gripper $\mathcal{F}_G^{ref}$. It is also possible to continuously varying in pose over time as a human freely carries it around.

Finally, $\mathcal{F}_{G^0}$ signifies a "resting" pose for the manipulator gripper. It represents a desired nominal configuration for the times that the system is not using the arm to actively track and reach out to grasp the target.

2.3 Notes

It is highlighted here that while the robot's autonomy pipeline includes Simultaneous Localization and Mapping alongside volumetric 3D reconstruction and obstacle-aware wheeled navigation, for the purposes of the proposed scheme that addresses the vision based mobile grasping of dynamic targets, we focus on a policy that is inspired by the principles of direct visual servoing. The motivation behind this lies in its well-established ability to handle dynamic grasping objectives and scenes in real-time.

As a result, the coordinate frame $\mathcal{F}_W$ is not involved in the developed guidance policy as it will subsequently be elaborated, and therefore neither is a full Simultaneous Localization And Mapping solution a prerequisite for its execution. However, in the experimental studies we present results that are "world"-transformed to facilitate the intuitive understanding of the derived behaviors; results which in fact leverage the robot's autonomous SLAM pipeline.

3   Guidance for Dynamic Target Grasping

As stressed above, the proposed approach is inspired by direct visual servoing and computationally lightweight approaches to dynamic environment robotic navigation that leverage attractive and repulsive forces to represent follow and avoid objectives respectively.

3.1   Nomenclature

This scheme was developed on the basis of correlating objectives to virtual force/torque components and modifiers. In the following nomenclature we will refer with:

– $\mathbf{f}_{AB}$ to an attractive or repulsive virtual force between two frames $\mathcal{F}_A$ and $\mathcal{F}_B$ and expressed in (assumed to be acting on) the former. An attractive force is aligned per the $\hat{u}_{AB} = \frac{{}^{A}r_{AB}}{||{}^{A}r_{AB}||}$ translation unit vector. A repulsive force is conversely aligned with the reverse direction.

– $\mathbf{t}_{AB}$ to a virtual attractive or repulsive virtual torque between two frames $\mathcal{F}_A$ and $\mathcal{F}_B$ and assumed to be acting on the former. An attractive torque represents a twist aligned per the rotation axis $\hat{\omega}_{AB} = \frac{q_{AB_{ijk}}}{||q_{AB_{ijk}}||}$ of the rotation quaternion. A repulsive torque is analogously reversely aligned.

3.2 Objectives

The main objective of the dynamic target grasping scheme is to align and match the gripper end-effector to the target frame, a goal represented as $\mathcal{F}_G^{ref} \equiv \mathcal{F}_T$. At the same time however, taking into consideration the robotic intended operation as a mobile manipulation system, as well as the distinct flexibility given by the robotic arm which can act as a $6\text{–}DoF$ orientation mechanism for the mounted perception module cameras, we propose the following formulation:

Global Objective. The global objective being to reach and grasp the dynamically moving target, we calculate an attractive force/torque combination:

$$\mathbf{f}_{GT} = W_f \frac{1}{||{}^{G}r_{GT}||} \hat{u}_{AB} \tag{1}$$

$$\mathbf{t}_{GT} = \begin{cases} [W_t \theta_{GrGT} \hat{\omega}_{GrGT}]_\times & \text{if: } ||{}^{A}r_{AB}|| > d_{lunge} \\ [W_t \theta_{GT} \hat{\omega}_{GT}]_\times & \text{otherwise} \end{cases} \tag{2}$$

In (1) the virtual force magnitude (with the direction is always towards the target for an attractive case) is in inverse-distance form, intending to make the system more aggressive as it approaches the target. The desired behavior is to "lunge" in the final grasping approach to ensure that the dynamic target has little opportunity to move around. Similarly, in (2) the torque is designed along this "lunging" grasp approach, by distinguishing 2 behavioral regions, namely

– While the distance $||{}_{A}r_{AB}||$ to the target remains larger than a threshold value d_{lunge}, the end-effector aligning torque given in axis-angle formulation $([\theta\ \hat{\omega}]_\times)$ is driven by the bearing vector ${}_{G}r_{GT}$ between the gripper and the target. This aim to orient the gripper towards the target in a tracking-like fashion, which effectively ensures that visual feedback is maintained until the end-effector reaches close enough to grasp.

– When the distance $||{}_{A}r_{AB}||$ reaches below the "lunging" threshold d_{lunge}, the orientation objective is modified into aligning the gripper to the reference frame $F_G^{ref} \equiv F_T$, to ensure an effective physical grasp. Hence, the attractive torque t_{GT} becomes driven by the full $\mathcal{T}_{GT}$ rotational transformation.

It is finally mentioned that W_f and W_t are scalars representing control scaling factors.

Arm Sub–objectives. The force/torque global objective (1, 2) formulation aims to track the pose of the target while it is away, and "lunge" to assume a final grasping pose when it is close enough. If left unchecked to directly act on frame $\mathcal{F}_G$ while the target is very far away, it would eventually drive the arm to extend as far as possible leading into singular configurations [3].

This would in one part impede the tracking objective due to the kinematic "lock" of the available Degrees of Freedom of the manipulator, and it would also become dangerous for the mobile base to drive around with a fully extended arm. Motivated by the intuition of reserving kinematic flexibility, we propose to condition the attractive force by a penalizing exponential decay factor λ_{rest} as follows:

Let $\hat{u}_{G^0 G} = \frac{{}_{G^0} r_{G^0 G}}{\|{}_{G^0} r_{G^0 G}\|}$ be the unit vector of the $\mathcal{T}_{G^0 G}$ transformation between the end-effector "resting" pose and the current gripper frame (which continuously varies in time). Also, let $\mathcal{R}_{G \hat{u}_{G^0 G}}$ represent the rotational transformation between the gripper frame and that "resting–to–gripper" unit vector. The transformed virtual force by this rotation:

$$\hat{u}_{G^0 G} \mathbf{f}_{GT} = \mathcal{R}_{G \hat{u}_{G^0 G}} \mathbf{f}_{GT} \tag{3}$$

represents the "resting–to–gripper" bearing vector $(\hat{u}_{G^0 G})$-aligned projection of the $\mathbf{f}_{GT}$ attractive force. We follow by conditioning the longitudinal (transverse in a spherical coordinate sense) component by the aforementioned exponential decay penalty factor λ_{rest} multiplied by the bearing vector magnitude $\|{}_{G^0} r_{G^0 G}\|$ as in (4):

$$\hat{u}_{G^0 G} \mathbf{f}'_{GT} = \begin{bmatrix} e^{-\lambda_{rest}} \|{}_{G^0} r_{G^0 G}\| & 0 & 0 \\ 0 & 1 & 0 \\ 0 & 0 & 1 \end{bmatrix} \hat{u}_{G^0 G} \mathbf{f}_{GT} \tag{4}$$

$$\mathbf{f}'_{GT} = \mathcal{R}^T_{G \hat{u}_{G^0 G}} \, \hat{u}_{G^0 G} \mathbf{f}'_{GT}, \tag{5}$$

and then by transforming back to the original gripper frame we get the conditioned attractive force $\mathbf{f}'_{GT}$.

The effect of this conditioning is that the magnitude of attraction as the end-effector moves away from the resting frame $\mathcal{F}_{G^0}$ phases out, until the end-effector degrades to behave as if "sliding" on the manifold of a sphere centered around $\mathcal{F}_{G^0}$. This allows target tracking to continue even if the target remains out of reach for a long time.

Arm Control Frame. In Sect. 2 the $\mathcal{F}_J$ frame of the force/torque sensor is mentioned. Control takes place in this frame by transforming the conditioned attractive force and accounting for measured external force/torque disturbances:

$$\begin{bmatrix} {}_J \mathbf{f}_{GT} \\ {}_J \mathbf{t}_{GT} \end{bmatrix} = \mathcal{T}_{GJ} \begin{bmatrix} \mathbf{f}'_{GT} \\ \mathbf{t}_{GT} \end{bmatrix} - \begin{bmatrix} \mathbf{f}_J \\ \mathbf{t}_J \end{bmatrix}, \tag{6}$$

as the corresponding (real) mechanical wrench $[\mathbf{f}_J \, \mathbf{t}_J]^T$ is measured by the sensor. Effectively, this allows the arm to behave in a compliant manner in case there is contact with another dynamically moving agent (e.g. a human) present in the environment, or in case of small collisions during the grasping approach.

Consistently with approaches relying on real-time kinematic motion planning for dynamic environment adaptation and closed-loop grasping [12], and leveraging the high update rates of force/torque feedback and target detection loops, we perform continuous cartesian jogging [1] control of the manipulator arm according to the reference conditioned $\mathbf{f}'_{GT}$ wrench.

Figure 4 summarizes the aforementioned policy.

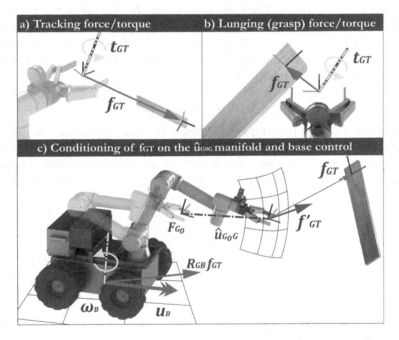

Fig. 4. Forces and moments summary for dynamic target grasping with a mobile manipulator robot: a) the torque orients the gripper towards the target achieving tracking, b) in the final "lunge" phase the attractive torque aligns the gripper with the grasping pose, c) the gripper attractive force progressively degrades to motion on a spherical manifold away from the "resting" pose.

Base Sub–objectives and Control Frame. The mobile base employs a classic wheeled robot paradigm of bearing-based navigation [22]. Although in contrast to a 6–DoF arm grasping motion planning, a model predictive non-holonomic guidance scheme [19] for this differential drive platform is feasible to be executed at rates comparable to the robot dynamics, in this work we intentionally present a unified behavior relying on a collective virtual force/torque-driven approach.

A spring-model virtual attractive force is used for the base

$$\mathbf{f}_{GT}^{S} = W_f^{S} \; \|_G r_{GT}\| \; \hat{u}_{AB}; \tag{7}$$

after transformation to the base frame by: $\mathcal{R}_{BG} \, [\mathbf{f}_{GT} \; \mathbf{t}_{GT}]^T$, its 2D xy–planar projection $\mathbf{f}_{BT}^{2\times1}$ is used to drive the robot kinematics $[u_B \; \omega_B]^T$:

$$u_B = W_u \; \|\mathbf{f}_{BT}\| \tag{8}$$
$$\omega_B = W_\omega \; arctan2(\mathbf{f}_{BT}^y, \mathbf{f}_{BT}^x) \tag{9}$$

as per classical formulations, and with W_u and W_ω scalars that represent control scaling factors. Figure 4-c) illustrates this straightforward policy.

4   Experimental Studies

For the experimental evaluation of the proposed strategy we used the *Beaver* robot presented in Sect. 2, and the target was a wooden plank with width $\simeq0.85$ [m] and mass $\simeq1.5$ [kg]. For the evaluation of the proposed policy, the target detection and grasping pose computation are assumed to be known and are therefore encoded by attaching a known Apriltag marker on the plank.

4.1   Arm-Only Grasping

We fist show the result of the policies elaborated in Sect. 3.2 by showcasing an arm-only operation.

Simple Case. The first case corresponds to a simple static pose for the target, with the robot positioned such that it is within the arm's reach. As observed in Fig. 5, visually-servoed continuous jogging seamlessly leads to the grasping of the plank.

Significant Target Pose Twist. The second case shows the behavior when the grasping pose is significantly twisted ($>90°$ rotated in this sequence). As shown in Fig. 6 grasping is successful, while it is also visible how the eventual grasping pose alignment takes place during the final "lunging" phase.

Dynamic Target. The third case illustrated in Fig. 7 examines the behavior during dynamic motion of the target. Based on our policy, the eye-in-hand system tracks the target as it moves and never extends too far from the "resting" pose, while when the grasping becomes feasible it manages to complete the objective.

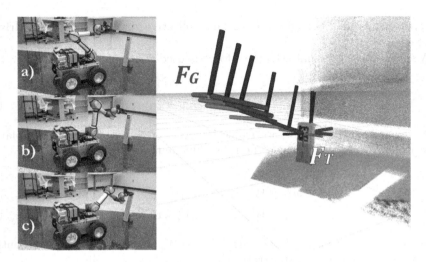

Fig. 5. Arm-only (fixed base) grasping with a simple target.

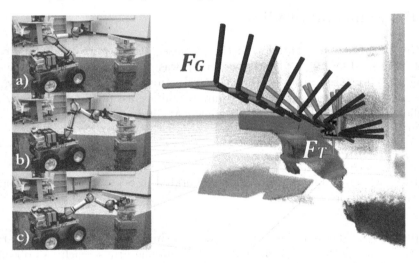

Fig. 6. Arm-only (fixed base) grasping with a twisted grasp-pose target.

4.2   Mobile Base Grasping

We subsequently demonstrate the full policy with the mobile base actively participating in the tracking and grasping approach objectives.

Static Target. The first case visualized in Fig. 8 corresponds to a static target that is placed away from the robot, but the mobile base can move the arm to grasp it. The collective system accurately performs the desired operation.

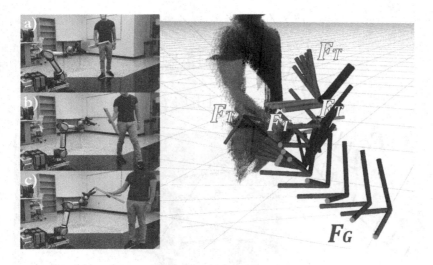

Fig. 7. Arm-only (fixed base) grasping with a dynamically moving target.

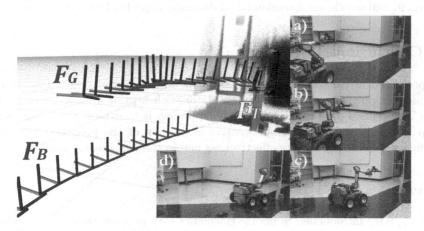

Fig. 8. Full mobile manipulation-based grasping of a static target.

Dynamic Target. For the final case presented in Fig. 9, we dynamically move with the target in-hand, which effectively leads to the desired set of behaviors of our policy: a) maintain tracking of the dynamic target though collective mobile base guidance and arm motion planning, b) approach the target while maintaining a kinematically efficient boundary for the manipulator arm, c) grasp the target once the lunging distance is achieved. It is mentioned that the indicated dynamic motion of the human is selected at random as the *Beaver* robot effectively "hunts" after the target.

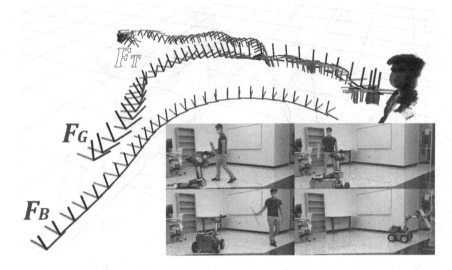

Fig. 9. Full mobile manipulation-based dynamic target tracking and grasping.

5   Conclusions

We presented a real time closed loop implementation of dynamic object tracking and grasping using a mobile manipulator with a prior knowledge of target pose. The central philosophy behind our approach is to exploit the eye-in-hand setup by visual servoing. Comprehensive evaluation of the proposed approach conclusively demonstrates its effectiveness across the considered cases.

References

1. Buss, S.R.: Introduction to inverse kinematics with jacobian transpose, pseudoinverse and damped least squares methods. IEEE J. Robot. Autom. **17**(1–19), 16 (2004)
2. Calli, B., Dollar, A.M.: Robust precision manipulation with simple process models using visual servoing techniques with disturbance rejection. IEEE Trans. Autom. Sci. Eng. **16**(4), 406–419 (2018)
3. Chiaverini, S.: Singularity-robust task-priority redundancy resolution for real-time kinematic control of robot manipulators. IEEE Trans. Robot. Autom. **13**(3), 398–410 (1997)
4. Chitta, S., Sucan, I., Cousins, S.: Moveit! [ROS topics]. IEEE Robot. Autom. Mag. **19**(1), 18–19 (2012)
5. Dang, T., Mascarich, F., Khattak, S., Papachristos, C., Alexis, K.: Graph-based path planning for autonomous robotic exploration in subterranean environments. In: 2019 IEEE/RSJ International Conference on Intelligent Robots and Systems (IROS), pp. 3105–3112. IEEE (2019)
6. Hebert, P., et al.: Mobile manipulation and mobility as manipulation-design and algorithms of robosimian. J. Field Robot. **32**(2), 255–274 (2015)

7. Hornung, A., Wurm, K.M., Bennewitz, M., Stachniss, C., Burgard, W.: OctoMap: an efficient probabilistic 3D mapping framework based on octrees. Auton. Robot. **34**(3), 189–206 (2013)
8. Khattak, S., Papachristos, C., Alexis, K.: Keyframe-based direct thermal-inertial odometry. In: 2019 International Conference on Robotics and Automation (ICRA), pp. 3563–3569. IEEE (2019)
9. Khattak, S., Papachristos, C., Alexis, K.: Keyframe-based thermal-inertial odometry. J. Field Robot. **37**(4), 552–579 (2020)
10. Labbé, M., Michaud, F.: Rtab-map as an open-source lidar and visual simultaneous localization and mapping library for large-scale and long-term online operation. J. Field Robot. **36**(2), 416–446 (2019)
11. Mascarich, F., Khattak, S., Papachristos, C., Alexis, K.: A multi-modal mapping unit for autonomous exploration and mapping of underground tunnels. In: 2018 IEEE Aerospace Conference, pp. 1–7. IEEE (2018)
12. Morrison, D., Corke, P., Leitner, J.: Closing the loop for robotic grasping: a real-time, generative grasp synthesis approach. Robot. Sci. Syst. **XIV**, 1–10 (2018)
13. Papachristos, C., Alexis, K., Tzes, A.: Efficient force exertion for aerial robotic manipulation: exploiting the thrust-vectoring authority of a tri-tiltrotor UAV. In: 2014 IEEE international conference on robotics and automation (ICRA), pp. 4500–4505. IEEE (2014)
14. Papachristos, C., Alexis, K., Tzes, A.: Technical activities execution with a tiltrotor UAS employing explicit model predictive control. IFAC Proc. Vol. **47**(3), 11036–11042 (2014)
15. Papachristos, C., et al.: Autonomous exploration and inspection path planning for aerial robots using the robot operating system. In: Koubaa, A. (ed.) Robot Operating System (ROS). SCI, vol. 778, pp. 67–111. Springer, Cham (2019). https://doi.org/10.1007/978-3-319-91590-6_3
16. Papachristos, C., Khattak, S., Alexis, K.: Uncertainty-aware receding horizon exploration and mapping using aerial robots. In: 2017 IEEE International Conference on Robotics and Automation (ICRA), pp. 4568–4575. IEEE (2017)
17. Papachristos, C., Mascarich, F., Khattak, S., Dang, T., Alexis, K.: Localization uncertainty-aware autonomous exploration and mapping with aerial robots using receding horizon path-planning. Auton. Robot. **43**(8), 2131–2161 (2019). https://doi.org/10.1007/s10514-019-09864-1
18. Pasteau, F., Narayanan, V.K., Babel, M., Chaumette, F.: A visual servoing approach for autonomous corridor following and doorway passing in a wheelchair. Robot. Auton. Syst. **75**, 28–40 (2016)
19. Rösmann, C., Hoffmann, F., Bertram, T.: Timed-elastic-bands for time-optimal point-to-point nonlinear model predictive control. In: 2015 European Control Conference (ECC), pp. 3352–3357 (2015)
20. Shirai, Y., Inoue, H.: Guiding a robot by visual feedback in assembling tasks. Pattern Recogn. **5**(1), 99–108 (1973)
21. Siam, M., Singh, A., Perez, C., Jagersand, M.: 4-DoF tracking for robot fine manipulation tasks. In: 2017 14th Conference on Computer and Robot Vision (CRV), pp. 329–336. IEEE (2017)
22. Siegwart, R., Nourbakhsh, I.R., Scaramuzza, D.: Introduction to Autonomous Mobile Robots. MIT Press, Cambridge (2011)

Statistical Pattern Recognition

Structural Pattern Recognition

Interpreting Galaxy Deblender GAN from the Discriminator's Perspective

Heyi Li[1(✉)], Yuewei Lin[2], Klaus Mueller[1], and Wei Xu[2]

[1] Stony Brook University, Stony Brook, NY 11790, USA
{heyli,mueller}@cs.stonybrook.edu
[2] Brookhaven National Laboratory, Upton, NY 11973, USA
{ywlin,xuw}@bnl.gov

Abstract. In large galaxy surveys it can be difficult to separate overlapping galaxies, a process called *deblending*. Generative adversarial networks (GANs) have shown great potential in addressing this fundamental problem. However, it remains a significant challenge to comprehend how the network works, which is particularly difficult for non-expert users. This research focuses on understanding the behaviors of one of the network's major components, the Discriminator, which plays a vital role but is often overlooked. Specifically, we propose an enhanced Layer-wise Relevance Propagation (LRP) algorithm called Polarized-LRP. It generates a heatmap-based visualization highlighting the area in the input image that contributes to the network decision. It consists of two parts i.e. a positive contribution heatmap for the images classified as ground truth and a negative contribution heatmap for the ones classified as generated. As a use case, we have chosen the deblending of two overlapping galaxy images via a branched GAN model. Using the Galaxy Zoo dataset we demonstrate that our method clearly reveals the attention areas of the Discriminator to differentiate generated galaxy images from ground truth images, and outperforms the original LRP method. To connect the Discriminator's impact on the Generator, we also visualize the attention shift of the Generator across the training process. An interesting result we have achieved is the detection of a problematic data augmentation procedure that would else have remained hidden. We find that our proposed method serves as a useful visual analytical tool for more effective training and a deeper understanding of GAN models.

Keywords: Explainable AI · Galaxy image deblending · Generative adversarial network · Layer-wise relevance propagation

1 Introduction

Astronomical researchers routinely assume the strict isolation of the targeted celestial body and so their objective is simplified into evaluating the properties of a single object. However, galactic overlapping is ubiquitous in current surveys due to projection effects and source interactions. This introduces bias to

© Springer Nature Switzerland AG 2020
G. Bebis et al. (Eds.): ISVC 2020, LNCS 12510, pp. 239–250, 2020.
https://doi.org/10.1007/978-3-030-64559-5_18

multiple physical traits such as photometric redshifts and weak lensing at levels beyond requirements. With the arrival of the next generation of ground-based galaxy surveys such as the Large Synoptic Survey Telescope (LSST) [7] which is expected to begin operation in 2023, this issue becomes more urgent. Specifically, the increase of both depth and sensitivity will cause the number of blended galaxy images to grow exponentially. Dawson [4] predicts that around 50% of galaxies captured in LSST images encounter overlapping with a 3" center-to-center distance. This leads to immense quantities of imaging data warranted as unusable. According to the estimation in [18], up to 200 Million galaxy images could be discarded each year if the blending issue is not effectively addressed throughout the ten year period of the LSST survey. However, the task of galaxy deblending remains an open problem in the field of astronomy and no gold standard solution exists in the processing pipeline. Recently, a GAN model called Galaxy Deblender GAN [18] has been applied in solving the galaxy deblending problem and has yielded promising results in separating confirmed blends of two galaxies. During our discussions with domain scientists, we noticed two facts: (1) a visual explanation can help them understand model behavior without machine learning expertise, and (2) the behavior of the Discriminator is most perplexing to astronomers.

The generative adversarial network (GAN) was first proposed by Goodfellow [5] that consists of two major components, the Discriminator and the Generator. It has achieved state-of-the-art performance in many computer vision applications, especially in face generation [8,9]. Many GAN variants [2,17] have been proposed to improve the training stability and to increase image diversity. However, the discrepancy of a thorough understanding of GANs makes building and training GAN models extremely challenging for non-expert users. This prohibits a wide utilization of these models and potentially prevents them from reaching optimum performance. More importantly, the lack of interpretation directly results in less trustworthiness in images generated by GANs.

Different visualization algorithms have been proposed to increase the interpretability of convolutional neural networks (CNNs). Among them, the heatmap-based approach that connects the input features to the classification or prediction output is an emerging trend. For instance, class activation mapping (CAM) based methods [19,20] directly use the activation of the last convolutional layer to infer the downsampled relevance of the input pixels. But such methods are only applicable to specific architectures which use the average pooling layer. The layer-wise relevance propagation (LRP) algorithm [16] is proposed to address this issue. For each image, LRP propagates the classification score backward through the model and calculates relevance intensities over all pixels. Although successful in interpreting discriminative classifiers [13], the LRP algorithm does not cover network structures like GAN models.

In this work, we propose a Polarized-LRP method extending the original LRP in its explanation of GAN models from the Discriminator's perspective with the Galaxy Deblender GAN as the use case. Our method backpropagates the single probability value given by the Discriminator to the input layer, during which it calculates the positive or negative contributions depending on the classification of the input image. The generated heatmaps called *relevance maps* highlight the important pixels in the input image. By comparing relevance maps of the same input at different training stages, our method clearly reveals the gradual changes of the Generator in response to the direct feedback from the Discriminator. Moreover, we demonstrate the role of our method in model refinement by uncovering a problematic step in data augmentation which was previously unknown to astronomers. To the best of our knowledge, our Polarized-LRP is the first method in the literature which can effectively visualize the behavior of the Discriminator and its impact on the Generator.

The major contributions of our work are threefold.

- An innovative LRP algorithm i.e. Polarized-LRP to enhance the original LRP is proposed and its superiority is demonstrated with comparison experiments.
- The first work extending the LRP algorithm to explain GAN models is presented and applied to a real-world scientific problem.
- The effectiveness of our method in both training understanding and model debugging is demonstrated with experiment results.

The remainder of this paper is organized as follows. Related works are introduced in Sect. 2. Our new LRP method is presented in Sect. 3. Extensive experiments validating the effectiveness of our method are shown in Sect. 4. The conclusions and future work discussions are followed in Sect. 5.

2   Related Works

In this section, a detailed literature review of papers on GAN model understanding is first presented. Then the Galaxy Deblender GAN is introduced serving as our use case for the demonstration.

2.1   GAN Model Understanding

To thoroughly understand the literature, we searched all accepted papers in the top machine learning, computer vision, and visualization conferences from Year 2017 to Year 2019 using related keywords including but not limited to "explain/explanation", "visual/visualization", and "neural network". Then we narrowed down our selections by examining the abstracts and excluding those irrelevant. Table 1 summarizes our findings that there are only 44 papers focusing on explaining deep neural networks. Table 2 further shows a detailed categorization of those found papers, where there are only two works in GAN interpretation.

Among the limited works explaining GANs, Liu [15] designed a graphic user interface to display connections between neurons of neighboring layers in the model. Unfortunately, their tool is intended only for machine learning experts and hence not supportive for non-domain researchers. Most recently, Bau [3] presented a dissecting framework that examines the causal relationship between

Table 1. The total number of accepted papers in the top ML, CV, and VIS conferences from Year 2017 to Year 2019. The last column shows the number of papers from each conference that falls in the area of deep learning understanding. Papers are filtered using keywords in titles and abstracts.

Conference	2017	2018	2019	Focus on XAI
CVPR	783	979	1294	**10**
ICCV/ECCV	621	776	1077	8
NeuralIPS	678	1011	1428	8
ICML	434	621	773	9
VIS	143	197	253	9
Total	2659	3584	4825	**44**

network units and object concepts. However, the Discriminator is completely omitted in their work. Although not being used to generate images during the inference stage, the Discriminator significantly affects the performance of the Generator, which is important to investigate.

Table 2. A detailed categorization of all selected papers on deep learning understanding from Table 1. A majority of the papers focus only on CNN models. Research on visual understanding of GAN models is largely lacking.

Network structure	Number of papers
CNN	30
RNN/LSTM	5
GNN	2
GAN	**2**
Others	5
Total	44

2.2 The Galaxy Deblender GAN

The design of the Galaxy Deblender GAN is based on the super resolution GAN (SRGAN) [12]. The Generator consists of two branches because of the assumption that only two galaxies co-appear in one blended image. Each branch integrates many residual blocks and skip connections [6]. The two branches share the first M residual blocks but hold N more distinctive residual blocks each, where $(M, N) = (10, 6)$. The Discriminator outputs a probability score, where 0 means a generated image and 1 represents a ground truth image captured by the telescope.

We follow the detailed Galaxy Deblender GAN architecture in [18], build and re-train it from scratch due to no publicly available pre-trained network. Raw galaxy images are open-sourced from the Kaggle Galaxy Zoo classification challenge [14]. Both the Generator and the Discriminator are optimized using the Adam optimizer [10]. The learning rate is initialized as 10^{-4} and decreased by an order of magnitude to 10^{-5} after $100,000$ iterations. Then the training stage continues for another $100,000$ iterations. One single Tesla V100 graphics card was used for the training.

Table 3. The replication results shown as the mean values of PSNR and SSIM metrics

Mean	PSNR (dB)	SSIM
Reported	34.61	0.92
Replicated	33.47	0.89

Table 3 shows the reported peak noise-to-signal ratio (PSNR) value and structural similarity index (SSIM) value along with ours. Although our values are slightly lower than their reported ones, they are within a reasonable shift range. Figure 1 includes one example generated using our reproduced model.

Fig. 1. One example of inputs and outputs of our replicated galaxy deblender GAN model. The pair of ground truth images is on the left. The blended image is in the middle. The pair of the generated images is on the right. The PSNR ratio for each pair of the ground truth image and the generated image is shown at the bottom left corner.

3   Our Method

3.1   Polarized-LRP

As mentioned in Sect. 1, the LRP algorithm has not been applied to generative models before. The root of this limitation lies in the structure of the relevance input. The multi-class classifier's output consists of the predicted probability for each class. All elements in this vector are adjusted to zero except the highest one which represents the target class. This one-hot vector then serves as the relevance input. In this way, only neurons connected to the non-zero elements are activated during the backpropagation. In the original LRP algorithm, only positive contributions are considered, which makes sense for multi-class classifications. However, the Discriminator of a GAN model only returns one probability value indicating whether this is a generated image. Applying the LRP algorithm directly renders all output heatmaps meaninglessly. An example showing the limitation of the original LRP will be presented in Sect. 4.1.

To address this issue, our method calculates two relevance maps from the same probability value i.e. the positive and the negative maps. The positive relevance map displays only positive contributions from the pixels in the input image to the probability value, while the negative relevance map shows only negative contributions. If the image is classified as generated by the Discriminator, the negative contributions from input pixels dominate and thus decrease the probability score. In this case, the negative relevance map is adopted automatically to represent and convey the decision of the Discriminator. On the contrary, the positive relevance map is chosen if the image is classified as ground truth. By polarizing the relevance into positive and negative, our algorithm creates two "virtual" classes from the Discriminator's output probability. Equation 1 shows the relevance computation of our proposed method.

$$R_{j\rightarrow i}^{(l+1)\rightarrow(l)} = \begin{cases} \frac{[w_{ij}x_i]^+}{\sum_k[w_{kj}x_k]^+ + b_k^+}R_j^{(l+1)}, & \text{if is Ground Truth} \\ \frac{[w_{ij}x_i]^-}{\sum_k[w_{kj}x_k]^- + b_k^-}R_j^{(l+1)}, & \text{if is Generated} \end{cases} \quad (1)$$

The weights and biases are denoted by w_{ij} and b_k respectively. $[]^+$ and $[]^-$ represent value truncation at zero.

3.2   Demonstration Examples

We present two cases as examples of our method. The first row in Fig. 2 shows the positive relevance map for a ground truth image. We choose the viridis colormap to show the relevance map where blue indicates smaller importance and yellow indicates higher importance. From the map on the right, we can see that the Discriminator focuses on the interior of the galaxy ellipse. Pixels in the attention area make strong positive contributions to the probability score, which explains why the Discriminator classifies this image as ground truth. The second row in Fig. 2 exhibits the negative relevance map for a generated image. The map indicates that the Discriminator makes its decision based on pixels on the periphery of the central area, which has the most noticeable artifacts in the image. These results are consistent with the visual inspection between the ground truth image and the generated image by a domain expert.

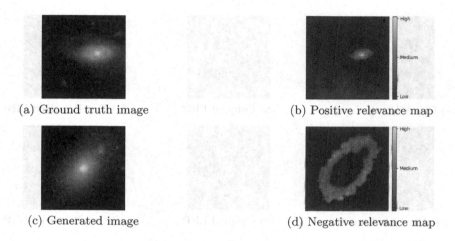

(a) Ground truth image   (b) Positive relevance map

(c) Generated image   (d) Negative relevance map

Fig. 2. The exemplar results. The first row includes an example of the positive relevance map and the second row contains an example of the negative relevance map. All images are enlarged to 256 × 256 for a better illustration.

4   Experiment Results

To demonstrate the effectiveness, we first compare our algorithm with the original LRP method. Next, we compare the relevance maps of the same input at different training stages for the training understanding. Finally, as the usage for the model debugging, we discover an unusual pattern that leads to the successful diagnosis of an erroneous data augmentation procedure.

4.1   Comparison with the Original LRP

The original LRP method has been compared with other existing heatmap-based methods such as SmoothGrad, Deconvnet, and PatternAttribution by iNNvestigate [1], and DeepSHAP by [13]. Both works have shown the exceeding performance of LRP in explaining model predictions. Therefore, to evaluate our Polarized-LRP algorithm, we only focus on the comparison with the original LRP method in explaining the Discriminator of a GAN model.

Specifically, we compare relevance maps produced using Polarized-LRP and original LRP [11] for both the ground truth image and the generated image. Figure 3 shows one example of a ground truth image in the first row and one example of a generated image in the second row. In the case of a ground truth image, the relevance map from our Polarized-LRP presents more contrast between dominant pixels of the galaxy area and less relevant pixels in the background compared to the relevance map from the original LRP.

The drawback of the original LRP is more obvious in the latter case. As is explained in Sect. 3.1, the original LRP method only shows pixels that contribute "positively" to the prediction score. For a generated image, as shown in the second row of Fig. 3, the relevance map of the original LRP (Fig. 3(e)) is almost

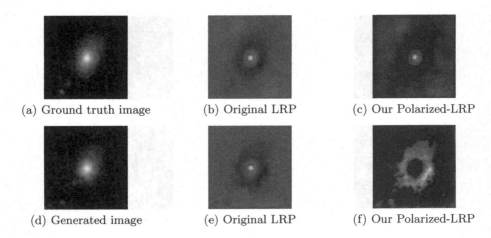

(a) Ground truth image   (b) Original LRP   (c) Our Polarized-LRP

(d) Generated image   (e) Original LRP   (f) Our Polarized-LRP

Fig. 3. The comparative study with the original LRP method. The first row displays an example of the ground truth image and the second row includes an example of a generated image. Each relevance map image is normalized before the visualization. All images are enlarged to 256×256 for a better illustration.

identical to the map of the ground truth (Fig. 3(b)), which does not make sense to the users. The failure has twofold. On the one hand, such a score is close to zero, which simply fails to provide meaningful feedback. On the other hand, even with the limited feedback, the highlighted pixels indicate where the model is based on to label the image as ground truth. Apparently, to evaluate the decision for a generated image, we instead want to learn the locations of the unrealistic pixels that make the model prediction as generated. In contrast, our Polarized-LRP algorithm calculates the relevance map of a generated image based on the negative contributions as in Eq. 1. Therefore, it highlights the periphery of a galaxy where most salient artifacts can be observed. Thus our method is clearly superior in explaining the GAN discriminators.

4.2 Training Understanding

Model weights are saved during training at an interval of 1000 iterations. Afterwards, weights at the recorded iterations are used to create complete relevance maps for comparison.

An example of a high-quality generation is shown in Fig. 4. Three iterations are selected correspondingly at an early stage, at an approximate mid-point, and near the end when the model converges. For the three generated images, the Discriminator gave a score of 0.001, 0.001, 0.003. We plot their relevance maps as to indicate why they are identified as generated. From the central image in the first row, we can see that the Generator only manages to replicate the inner bright spot. In the Discriminator's relevance map, this corresponds to the small hole in the middle. Furthermore, our relevance map on the left clearly reveals that the low probability score by the Discriminator is mostly due to the unrealistic-looking pixels in the surrounding areas. This information is then passed on to the Generator as the adversarial loss penalty. As is shown in the images in the subsequent rows, the ring structure in our relevance map grows thinner and darker. Along with the expansion of the central hole (meaning the confidence area in the center of galaxy enlarges), the generated image slowly transforms towards the ground truth image. One interesting finding is that the Generator learns the glaring spot first and then incrementally apprehends the surroundings. This is comprehensible because the Generator is first trained with only the style loss from VGG19. During this so-called "burn-in" period, features such as salient spots are expected to be grasped by the Generator. The benefit of the style loss during the "burn-in" period is easily visualized in our relevance map. How the Generator changes during training under the guidance of the Discriminator is also revealed.

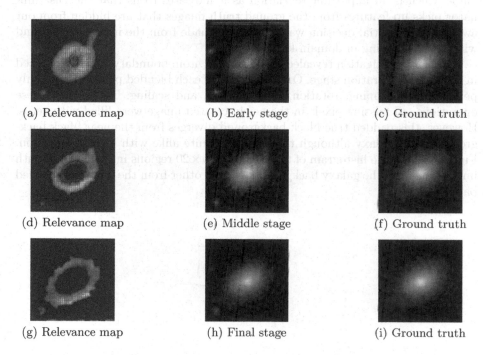

(a) Relevance map   (b) Early stage   (c) Ground truth

(d) Relevance map   (e) Middle stage   (f) Ground truth

(g) Relevance map   (h) Final stage   (i) Ground truth

Fig. 4. Three representative stages: early, middle and near-end stages are shown in rows. The relevance maps, generated images, and grounth truth images are shown in columns. All images are enlarged to 256 × 256 for a better illustration.

4.3   Model Debugging

While analyzing the Galaxy Deblender GAN using our method, we noticed a strange phenomenon consistently appearing in the positive relevance maps.

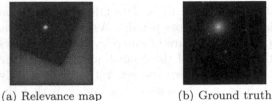

(a) Relevance map   (b) Ground truth   (c) Contrast increased

Fig. 5. The "phantom boundary" becomes apparent when the contrast of the ground truth image is increased. All images are enlarged to 256×256 for a better illustration.

Figure 5(a) shows the boundary of a rectangular shape in the positive relevance map of a ground truth image. This shape only appears in the positive relevance maps which is an important revelation as it indicates to us that the Discriminator picks up features from the ground truth images that are hidden from our awareness. A partial decision was mistakenly made from the image background without any footing in domain knowledge.

Further investigation revealed that this "phantom boundary" was introduced in the data preparation stage. One image out of each blended pair was randomly perturbed by flipping, rotation, displacement, and scaling. Then, after these operations, all missing pixels in the newly created image were filled with zeros. However, this padded true black background diverges from the near black background of the galaxy although the two seem quite alike with visual inspection. Figure 6 shows the histogram of two different 20×20 regions in the ground truth image, one from the galaxy background and the other from the manually padded background.

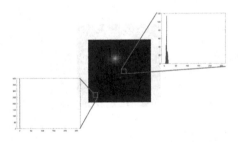

Fig. 6. Two 20×20 background regions randomly selected from the ground truth image. While they look alike visually, these two regions have very different histograms. The ground truth image is enlarged to 256×256 for a better illustration.

This problem had a large impact as it crippled our Galaxy Deblender GAN model from reaching its optimum performance. Instead of capturing features of real celestial bodies, the Discriminator learned a much simpler strategy to manipulate the equilibrium system utilizing the "phantom boundary". No matter how realistic the generated images look like, the Discriminator can easily differentiates them as long as phantom boundaries are absent in the results. Although the Generator might eventually learn to generate phantom boundaries when provided with sufficient training data and adequate update iterations, a huge amount of efforts is wasted to chase this lost cause.

While zero-padding is a frequently used technique in image processing, many non-domain experts are unaware of its shortcoming. Fortunately, with the help of our proposed algorithm this problem could be detected. It can be resolved by replacing the zero-padding with a random noise distribution obtained from physics statistics.

5   Conclusion

Motivated by the deficiency of GAN model understanding, we propose a Polarized-LRP technique to interpret the GAN's Discriminator with relevance maps highlighting the contributing pixels in the input image. We adopt the Galaxy Deblender GAN as a use case to demonstrate our method. By unifying the positive and negative contributions in a single formula and visualizing according to the prediction, our algorithm successfully reveals the decision making of the Discriminator. A training understanding is demonstrated to show the Discriminator's role on affecting the Generator, with the connection to loss function design. A model debugging example in uncovering a hidden mistake in the data preparation of the galaxy images is also included.

Although designed for the galaxy deblending problem, Polarized-LRP is not restricted to this network by any means. In the future, we plan to apply our method to interpret other well-established GAN models. In addition, we will apply LRP to the Generator as well for a complete understanding of both GAN components. Finally, a visual analytics system is also considered so as to facilitate direct user interaction.

Acknowledgement. This work was supported by BNL LDRD grant 18-009 and ECP CODAR project 17-SC-20-SC.

References

1. Alber, M., et al.: Innvestigate neural networks!. J. Mach. Learn. Res. **20**(93), 1–8 (2019)
2. Arjovsky, M., Chintala, S., Bottou, L.: Wasserstein generative adversarial networks. In: International Conference on Machine Learning, pp. 214–223 (2017)
3. Bau, D., et al.: GAN dissection: visualizing and understanding generative adversarial networks. In: International Conference on Learning Representations (2019)
4. Dawson, W.A., Schneider, M.D., Tyson, J.A., Jee, M.J.: The ellipticity distribution of ambiguously blended objects. Astrophys. J. **816**(1), 11 (2015)
5. Goodfellow, I., et al.: Generative adversarial nets. In: Advances in Neural Information Processing Systems, pp. 2672–2680 (2014)
6. He, K., Zhang, X., Ren, S., Sun, J.: Deep residual learning for image recognition. In: Proceedings of the IEEE Conference on Computer Vision and Pattern Recognition, pp. 770–778 (2016)

7. Ivezić, Ž., et al.: LSST: from science drivers to reference design and anticipated data products. Astrophys. J. **873**(2), 111 (2019)

8. Karras, T., Aila, T., Laine, S., Lehtinen, J.: Progressive growing of GANs for improved quality, stability, and variation. In: International Conference on Learning Representations (2018)

9. Karras, T., Laine, S., Aila, T.: A style-based generator architecture for generative adversarial networks. In: Proceedings of the IEEE Conference on Computer Vision and Pattern Recognition, pp. 4401–4410 (2019)

10. Kingma, D.P., Ba, J.: Adam: a method for stochastic optimization. In: International Conference on Learning Representations (2015)

11. Lapuschkin, S., Binder, A., Montavon, G., Müller, K.R., Samek, W.: The lrp toolbox for artificial neural networks. J. Mach. Learn. Res. **17**(1), 3938–3942 (2016)

12. Ledig, C., et al.: Photo-realistic single image super-resolution using a generative adversarial network. In: Proceedings of the IEEE Conference on Computer Vision and Pattern Recognition, pp. 4681–4690 (2017)

13. Li, H., Tian, Y., Mueller, K., Chen, X.: Beyond saliency: understanding convolutional neural networks from saliency prediction on layer-wise relevance propagation. Image Vis. Comput. **83**, 70–86 (2019)

14. Lintott, C., et al.: Galaxy zoo 1: data release of morphological classifications for nearly 900 000 galaxies. Mon. Not. R. Astron. Soc. **410**(1), 166–178 (2010)

15. Liu, M., Shi, J., Cao, K., Zhu, J., Liu, S.: Analyzing the training processes of deep generative models. IEEE Trans. Visual Comput. Graph. **24**(1), 77–87 (2017)

16. Montavon, G., Binder, A., Lapuschkin, S., Samek, W., Müller, K.-R.: Layer-wise relevance propagation: an overview. In: Samek, W., Montavon, G., Vedaldi, A., Hansen, L.K., Müller, K.-R. (eds.) Explainable AI: Interpreting, Explaining and Visualizing Deep Learning. LNCS (LNAI), vol. 11700, pp. 193–209. Springer, Cham (2019). https://doi.org/10.1007/978-3-030-28954-6_10

17. Radford, A., Metz, L., Chintala, S.: Progressive growing of GANs for improved quality, stability, and variation. In: International Conference on Learning Representations (2016)

18. Reiman, D.M., Göhre, B.E.: Deblending galaxy superpositions with branched generative adversarial networks. Mon. Not. R. Astron. Soc. **485**(2), 2617–2627 (2019)

19. Selvaraju, R.R., Cogswell, M., Das, A., Vedantam, R., Parikh, D., Batra, D.: Grad-CAM: visual explanations from deep networks via gradient-based localization. In: Proceedings of the IEEE International Conference on Computer Vision, pp. 618–626 (2017)

20. Zhou, B., Khosla, A., Lapedriza, A., Oliva, A., Torralba, A.: Learning deep features for discriminative localization. In: Proceedings of the IEEE Conference on Computer Vision and Pattern Recognition, pp. 2921–2929 (2016)

Variational Bayesian Sequence-to-Sequence Networks for Memory-Efficient Sign Language Translation

Harris Partaourides[1]([✉]), Andreas Voskou[1], Dimitrios Kosmopoulos[2], Sotirios Chatzis[1], and Dimitris N. Metaxas[3]

[1] Cyprus University of Technology, Limassol, Cyprus
{c.partaourides,sotirios.chatzis}@cut.ac.cy, ai.voskou@edu.cut.ac.cy
[2] University of Patras, Patras, Greece
dkosmo@upatras.gr
[3] Rutgers University, New Brunswick, NJ, USA
dnm@cs.rutgers.edu

Abstract. Memory-efficient continuous Sign Language Translation is a significant challenge for the development of assisted technologies with real-time applicability for the deaf. In this work, we introduce a paradigm of designing recurrent deep networks whereby the output of the recurrent layer is derived from appropriate arguments from nonparametric statistics. A novel variational Bayesian sequence-to-sequence network architecture is proposed that consists of a) a full Gaussian posterior distribution for data-driven memory compression and b) a nonparametric Indian Buffet Process prior for regularization applied on the Gated Recurrent Unit non-gate weights. We dub our approach Stick-Breaking Recurrent network and show that it can achieve a substantial weight compression without diminishing modeling performance.

Keywords: Deep learning · Weight compression · Sign Language Translation · Gloss to Text

1 Introduction

National Sign Languages (SLs) are an important part of the European and the world cultural diversity. In Europe, there are 30 official SLs, 750 thousand deaf sign language users but only 12 thousand interpreters. This shortage undermines the right for equal education, employment, information, health services [11] and in some cases endangers the lives of deaf people [25]. The scientific community has long been interested in developing assistive technologies for deaf users, but their broad applicability is yet to be achieved.

Sign Language Recognition (SLR) applications have achieved satisfactory performance on recognizing distinct signs by means of computer vision models. In

© Springer Nature Switzerland AG 2020
G. Bebis et al. (Eds.): ISVC 2020, LNCS 12510, pp. 251–262, 2020.
https://doi.org/10.1007/978-3-030-64559-5_19

contrast, a more demanding and useful in real-life scenarios task is the translation of sign language sentences i.e. continuous Sign Language Translation (SLT). Efficient continuous SLT requires the seamless combination of computer vision and Neural Machine Translation (NMT) architectures. Moreover, the task has an inherent difficulty due to the fact that we are translating between two different mediums of communication. In other words, SLs are visual languages, while written languages are auditory. Currently, the state-of-the-art approaches for SLT utilize the encoder-decoder sequence-to-sequence architectures [10]. The encoder extracts the salient information from a signer's video by means of deep convolutional neural networks, and the decoder utilizes the extracted sequential information to produce full-fledged sentences. Researchers consider SLT a two-fold process, where the first fold considers SLR as an intermediate tokenization component that extracts glosses (signs notations) from video namely Sign2Gloss. The second part utilizes glosses to perform NMT; the Gloss to Text task namely Gloss2Text. In this paper, we focus on the latter.

Currently, SLT is considered an open problem with many challenges, especially on the domain of real-time applicability. The current state-of-the-art approaches entail millions of parameters and suffer from a common issue in Deep Neural Networks (DNNs), namely overparameterization. This is observed when a large fraction of the network parameters is redundant for modeling performance, and inflicts an unnecessary computational burden that hinders real-time operation on consumer-grade hardware devices, such as mobile phones and laptops. Moreover, parameter redundancy renders DNNs susceptible to overfitting hence sub-optimal generalization.

Numerous approaches have been developed by the deep learning community to address overfitting in DNNs, such as ℓ_2 regularization, Dropout, DropConnect and variational variants thereof [12,30]. To effectively train the network weights, these approaches tackle overfitting through the scope of regularization. However, since they retain the network weights in their entirety, they do not directly address memory efficiency. One popular approach that achieves memory efficient networks is teacher-student networks, where a condensed network (student) is trained by leveraging a larger network (teacher) [2,16]. However, this approach has two main drawbacks a) the joint computational costs of training two networks and b) the increased number of heuristics for effective teacher distillation. Alternatively, several authors have proposed data-driven weight compression and regularization on a single trained network.

In this context, Bayesian Neural Networks (BNNs) provide a solid inferential framework to achieve effective regularization of DNNs [13]. A fully probabilistic paradigm is obtained by imposing a prior distribution over the network components, inferring the appropriate posteriors, and obtaining predictive distributions via marginalization in a Bayesian sense. Since Bayesian inference requires drawing samples from the posterior distribution, we can additionally utilize the posterior variance magnitude to adjust floating-point precision. This stems from the insight that higher variance implies that lower floating-point precision is required to retain accuracy at the time of Bayesian averaging [22,28]. Additionally, as it has been shown in [5], the use of an additional set of auxiliary Bernoulli latent variables can obtain a sparsity-inducing behavior. This can be achieved by imposing appropriate stick-breaking priors [18] over the postulated auxiliary latent variables to explicitly indicate the utility of each component and perform data-driven regularization.

Drawing upon these insights, we propose a principled approach to reduce the network memory footprint by employing nonparametric statistics on the recurrent component of the sequence-to-sequence networks employed for SLT. We achieve this by imposing a full Gaussian posterior distribution on the Gated Recurrent Unit (GRU) non-gate weights that offers a natural way for weight compression. Additionally, we impose a nonparametric Bayesian Indian Buffet Process (IBP) prior [14] again on the GRU non-gate weights for regularization. For efficient training and inference of the network, we rely on stochastic gradient variational Bayes. We dub our approach Stick-Breaking Recurrent (SB-GRU) network, and evaluate its effectiveness on the Gloss-to-Text SLT task, making use of the PHOENIX-2014T benchmark dataset [10].

We provide a number of quantitative results that exhibit the ability of our approach to yield improved predictive accuracy, in parallel with appropriate data-driven schemes to perform weight compression and regularization. Furthermore, our approach produces faster inference thus taking SLT a step closer to real-time applicability on memory constrictive devices.

The rest of this paper is organized as follows: In Sect. 2, we introduce the necessary theoretical background. In Sect. 3, we introduce the proposed approach and describe the training and inference algorithms of the model. In Sect. 4, we perform experimental evaluations of our approach and provide insights into its functionality. Finally, in the concluding Section, we summarize the contribution of this work, and discuss directions for further research.

2   Related Work

In this paper, we investigate memory-efficient translation of sign language to text. We therefore first review recent advancements in the field of NMT. Thereafter, we briefly present a core methodological component used in this work, namely the (nonparametric) Indian Buffet Process process.

2.1   Neural Machine Translation

NMT utilizes sequence-to-sequence architectures built upon Recurrent Neural Network (RNN) variants to learn the statistical model for efficient translations. In the seminal papers of [8,31] the authors showed the effectiveness of these types of model architectures in translating different languages. Initially, simple RNNs were used to learn the translation of a source sequence to a target sequence. They were soon followed by variations of RNNs that tackle the limited temporal attention span of RNNs e.g. Long Short-Term Memory [17] and GRU [9]. These approaches have managed to improve translation performance and achieve longer temporal horizons. A complementary approach that uses attention mechanisms [3] between the encoder and the decoder allows the network to better focus on certain sequences of the input. This is achieved by a similarity measure between the state of the decoder and the input. The most used variation of the attention mechanism is the one proposed by Luong et al. [23]. Finally, recent works replace the whole RNN architecture with purely attention-based architectures [34].

Typically, sequence-to-sequence models include an initial embedding layer for vector representation of input words. This representation of words lies in a high-dimensional plane where similar words are placed closer together. This approach is preferred than the simplistic one-hot encoding procedure. However, in the context of SLT, and in order to accommodate visual features, this embedding is replaced with a feature extraction process from video using Convolutional Neural Networks (CNNs) [4]. To better capture spatio-temporal relationships, 3D CNNs [15] can be further utilized. Additionally, several research works have taken advantage of glosses information pertinent to SLT to facilitate model training. This is placed after the computer vision component (e.g. CNN component) as an auxiliary source of information.

2.2 The Indian Buffet Process

The Indian Buffet Process (IBP) [14] is a probability distribution over infinite sparse binary matrices. It is a stochastic process suitable to be used as a flexible prior, allowing the number of considered features to increase as more data points are made available. Using the IBP, we can infer in a data-driven fashion a finite number of features for modeling a finite set of observations, in a way that ensures sparse representations [33]. These features can be expanded as new observations appear. To be used in Variational Inference the authors in [32] presented a stick-breaking construction for the IBP.

Let us consider N observations, $\boldsymbol{Z} = [z_{j,k}]_{j,k=1}^{N,K}$ denotes a binary matrix where j an observation and k a feature. The binary matrix indicates the existence of the features in the observations. As features approach infinity, $K \to \infty$, we arrive at the following hierarchical representation for the IBP [32]:

$$u_k \sim \text{Beta}(\alpha, 1) \qquad \pi_k = \prod_{j=1}^{k} u_j \qquad z_{jk} \sim \text{Bernoulli}(\pi_k) \qquad (1)$$

where u the stick variables and $\alpha > 0$ is the innovation (or strength) hyperparameter of the process, a non-negative parameter that controls the magnitude of the induced sparsity. In practice, we limit K to the input dimensionality to avoid overcomplete representation of the observed data.

3 Proposed Approach

Let us assume an input dataset $\{\boldsymbol{x}_n\}_{n=1}^{N} \in \mathbb{R}^J$, where N the observations and J the features of each observation. Deep networks perform input representation to extract informative features from the raw input data by means of hidden layers with nonlinear units. To produce layer outputs $\{y_n\}_{n=1}^N \in \mathbb{R}^K$, the model performs affine transformations via the inner product of the input with the layer weights $W \in \mathbb{R}^{J \times K}$, where K the number of output units of the layer. In each example n, the derived input representation yields $y_n = \sigma(x_n W + b)$ where $b \in \mathbb{R}^K$ the bias and $\sigma(\cdot)$ a non-linear activation function. These outputs are used as inputs to the next layer.

For data-driven weight compression and regularization, we adopt concepts from Bayesian nonparametrics. For regularization, we retain the needed synaptic weights by employing a matrix of binary latent variables $Z \in \{0,1\}^{J \times K}$, where each entry therein is $z_{j,k} = 1$, if the synaptic connection between the jth dimension of the input and the kth feature is retained, and $z_{j,k} = 0$ otherwise. To perform inference, we impose the sparsity-inducing IBP prior over the binary latent variables Z. The corresponding posterior distribution is independently drawn from $q(z_{j,k}) = \text{Bernoulli}(z_{j,k}|\tilde{\pi}_{j,k})$. This promotes retention of the barely needed connections based on the theory detailed in Sect. 2.2. For weight compression, we define a distribution over the synaptic weight matrices, W. A spherical prior $W \sim \prod_{j,k} \mathcal{N}(w_{j,k}|0,1)$ is imposed for simplicity purposes and the corresponding posterior distribution to be inferred $q(W) = \prod_{j,k} \mathcal{N}(w_{j,k}|\mu_{j,k}, \sigma_{j,k}^2)$. The resulting dense layer output takes the following form:

$$[y_n]_k = \sigma(\sum_{j=1}^{J}(w_{j,k} \cdot z_{j,k}) \cdot [x_n]_j + b_j) \in \mathbb{R} \qquad (2)$$

This concludes the formulation of a dense layer with IBP prior over the utility indicators and spherical prior over the synaptic weights. We employ this mechanism to effect data-driven weight compression and regularization, as we show below.

3.1   A Recurrent Variant

To accommodate architectures that utilize recurrent connections, we adopt the following rationale. Let us assume an input tensor $\{X_n\}_{n=1}^N \in \mathbb{R}^{T \times J}$ where N the observations, T the timesteps and J the features of each observation. At each timestep, the recurrent layer output $\{y_n\}_{n=1}^N \in \mathbb{R}^K$ is derived by means of the input $x_{t,n}$ and the previous output y_{t-1}, where K is the number of output units of the layer. Hence, for each example n, at each timestep t, the input representation yields: $y_{t,n} = \sigma(x_{t,n} W_{input} + y_{t-1} W_{rec} + b)$ with weights $W_{input} \in \mathbb{R}^{J \times K}$, $W_{rec} \in \mathbb{R}^{K \times K}$, bias $b \in \mathbb{R}^K$ and $\sigma(\cdot)$ a non-linear activation function. We can, then, employ the utility latent indicator variables, z, and a distribution over the synaptic weight matrices over any weight matrix, via a procedure similar to the aforementioned dense-layer formulation.

In this paper, we consider the Gated-Recurrent Unit (GRU) [7] that reads:

$$m_t = \sigma([y_{t-1}, x_t] W_{J+K, K} + b_m) \qquad (3)$$

$$r_t = \sigma([y_{t-1}, x_t] \boldsymbol{W}_{J+K,K} + b_r) \tag{4}$$

$$\widetilde{y}_t = \tanh([r_t \odot y_{t-1}, x_t] \boldsymbol{W}_{J+K,K} + b_y) \tag{5}$$

$$y_t = (1 - m_t) \odot y_{t-1} + m_t \odot \widetilde{y}_t \tag{6}$$

where $[\cdot, \cdot]$ the concatenation between two vectors, $\odot$ the Hadamard product and $\boldsymbol{W}_{J+K,K}$ the concatenation between $\boldsymbol{W}_{input}$ and $\boldsymbol{W}_{rec}$. We apply our proposed modeling principles and rationale only on the non-gate related weights. We dub our recurrent layer variant the Stick-Breaking Gated Recurrent Unit (SB-GRU). Equation 5 now reads:

$$\widetilde{y}_t = \tanh([r_t \odot y_{t-1}, x_t] \boldsymbol{W}_{J+K,K} \boldsymbol{Z}_{J+K,K} + b_y) \tag{7}$$

3.2   Model Training

The proposed model can be trained by using Stochastic Gradient Variational Bayes (SGVB) to maximize its Evidence Lower Bound (ELBO). As the resulting ELBO expression cannot be computed analytically, we resort to Monte-Carlo sampling techniques that ensure low-variance estimation. These comprise the standard reparameterization trick, the Gumbel-SoftMax relaxation trick [24], and the Kumaraswamy reparameterization trick [21], applied to the postulated Gaussian weights $\boldsymbol{W}$, the discrete latent indicator variables $\boldsymbol{Z}$, and the stick variables $\boldsymbol{u}$, respectively. The standard reparameterization trick applied on the Gaussian weights cannot be used for the IBP prior Beta-distributed stick variables. Thus, one can approximate the variational posteriors $q(u_k) = \text{Beta}(u_k | a_k, b_k)$ via the Kumaraswamy distribution [21] that reads:

$$q(u_k; a_k, b_k) = a_k b_k u_k^{a_k - 1} (1 - u_k^{a_k})^{b_k - 1} \tag{8}$$

where samples from $q(u_k; a_k, b_k)$ can be reparametrized as follows [26]:

$$u_k = \left(1 - (1 - X)^{\frac{1}{b_k}}\right)^{\frac{1}{a_k}}, \; X \sim U(0, 1) \tag{9}$$

We know turn to the case of the Discrete Bernoulli latent variables of our model. Performing back-propagation through reparametrized drawn samples is infeasible, hence recent solutions introduced appropriate continuous relaxations [19,24]. Let us assume a Discrete distribution $\boldsymbol{X} = [X_k]_{k=1}^K$. The drawn samples are of the form:

$$X_k = \frac{\exp(\log \eta_k + G_k)/\lambda)}{\sum_{i=1}^K \exp((\log \eta_i + G_i)/\lambda)}, \tag{10}$$

$$G_k = -\log(-\log U_k), \; U_k \sim \text{Uniform}(0, 1) \tag{11}$$

where $\boldsymbol{\eta} \in (0, \infty)^K$ the *unnormalized* probabilities and $\lambda \in (0, \infty)$ the *temperature* of the relaxation of the differentiable functions. In this paper, we anneal the values of the hyperparameter λ similar to [19]. We further consider posterior independence a) across layers and, b) among the latent variables $\boldsymbol{Z}$ in each layer. All the posterior expectations in the ELBO are computed by drawing MC samples under the Normal, Gumbel-SoftMax and Kumaraswamy reparameterization tricks, respectively. Hence, the resulting ELBO is of the form:

$$
\begin{aligned}
\mathcal{L}(\phi) = \mathbb{E}_{q(\cdot)} \Big[&\log p(\mathcal{D}|\boldsymbol{Z}, \boldsymbol{u}, \boldsymbol{W}) - \Big(KL\big[q(\{\boldsymbol{Z}\})\|p(\{\boldsymbol{Z}|\boldsymbol{u}\})\big] \\
&+ KL\big[q(\{\boldsymbol{u}\})\|p(\{\boldsymbol{u}\})\big] \\
&+ KL\big[q(\{\boldsymbol{W}\})\|p(\{\boldsymbol{W}\})\big]\Big)\Big]
\end{aligned}
\tag{12}
$$

where the KL divergences of the stick-variables u_k, weight utility indicators $z_{j,k}$, and Gaussian weights can be obtained by:

$$
\begin{aligned}
KL[q(u_k)|p(u_k)] &= \mathbb{E}_{q(u_k)}[\log p(u_k) - \log q(u_k)] \\
&\approx \log p(\hat{u}_k) - \log q(\hat{u}_k), \ \forall k
\end{aligned}
\tag{13}
$$

$$
\begin{aligned}
KL[q(z_{j,k})|p(z_{j,k})] &= \mathbb{E}_{q(z_{j,k}),q(u_k)}[\log p(z_{j,k}|\pi_k) - \log q(z_{j,k})] \\
&\approx \log p(\hat{z}_{j,k}| \prod_{i=1}^{k} \hat{u}_i) - \log q(\hat{z}_{j,k}), \ \forall j, k
\end{aligned}
\tag{14}
$$

$$
\begin{aligned}
KL[(q(w_{j,k,u})|p(w_{j,k,u})] &= \mathbb{E}_{q(w_{j,k,u})}[\log p(w_{j,k,u}) - \log q(w_{j,k,u})] \\
&\approx \log p(\hat{w}_{j,k,u}) - \log q(\hat{w}_{j,k,u}), \ \forall j, k, u
\end{aligned}
\tag{15}
$$

We can then employ standard off-the-self stochastic gradient techniques to maximize the ELBO. In our experiments, we adopt ADAM [20].

3.3   Inference Algorithm

Having trained our SBR model, we can now use the posteriors to perform inference for unseen data. Our model exhibits two advantages compared to conventional techniques. First, exploiting the inferred weight utility latent indicator variables, we can omit the contribution of weights that are effectively deemed unnecessary in a data-driven fashion. Specifically, we employ a *cut-off threshold*, τ to omit any weight with inferred corresponding posterior $q(z)$ below τ. Typically, in Bayesian Neural Networks literature the utility is only *implicitly inferred* by means of *thresholding higher-order moments*. These thresholds are derived on the hierarchical densities of the *network weights themselves*, $\boldsymbol{W}$ and require extensive heuristics for the selection of the hyperparameter values in each network layer. Our approach is in direct contrast to these techniques where we only need to specify the global innovation hyperparameter α and global truncation threshold τ. Moreover, our model formulation is robust to small fluctuations of their values.

Second, exploiting the inferred variance of the Gaussian posterior distribution employed over the network weights, $\boldsymbol{W}$, we can reduce the weights floating-point bit precision level in a data-driven fashion. Specifically, we employ a unit round off to limit the memory requirements for representing the network weights. This is achieved by means of the mean of the weight variance [22]. In principle, the higher the level of uncertainty present on the Gaussian posterior the less bits are actively contributing to inference since their approximate posterior sampling fluctuates too much. In contrast to [22], we disentangle the two procedures (bit-precision and omission) by imposing *different posteriors*. This alleviates the tendency to underestimate posterior variance, therefore better retaining predictive performance while performing stronger network compression.

In a proper Bayesian setting, at the prediction generation stage we need to perform averaging of multiple samples which is inefficient. Without losing generality, a common approximation is the replacement of weight values with their weight posterior means during forward propagation [22,27]. To achieve weight compression, we replace the trained weights with their bit-precision counterparts.

4   Experimental Evaluation

To exhibit the efficacy and effectiveness of our approach, we perform a thorough experimental evaluation in the context of an SLT task. We use the model architecture from [10], which consists of 4 layers in the encoder and 4 in the decoder, with 1000 units in each layer; we replace the last layer of the encoder with our proposed recurrent layer variant. The task we consider for our experiments is the Gloss to Text Translation. To this end, we utilize the primary benchmark for SLT, namely "RWTH-PHOENIX-Weather 2014T" dataset [10]. Additionally, we also evaluate the Gloss2Text GRU model without attention, from the reference paper, as a baseline. In all cases, we perform stochastic gradient descent by means of Adam [20], with learning rate 0.00001, batch size 128 and dropout 0.2, until convergence. The performance metrics used in our experiments are BLUE and ROUGE. We implement our model in TensorFlow [1].

4.1   RWTH-PHOENIX-Weather 2014T Dataset

PHOENIX14T is a collection of weather forecast videos in German sign language, annotated with the corresponding glosses and fully translated in German text. This annotation process makes it directly applicable to Sign to Text, Sign to Gloss and Gloss to Text translation. The glosses annotation procedure has been done manually by deaf experts, and the text has been automatically transcribed via available Speech to Text software, directly applied on the spoken weather forecast.

In this paper, we consider the Gloss to Text subset of the dataset. This includes 8257 pairs of gloss to text sentences where 7096 are used for training, 519 for validation and 642 for testing. Glosses represent the discrete gestures of the sign language in textual form. Additionally, auxiliary words are used to stand for non-manual information that go with the signs. This results in a simplified sign language vocabulary compared to the spoken language counterpart, but augmented with auxiliary words. In the specific corpus, we have a glosses vocabulary size of 1066 (337 singletons) and a German vocabulary of 2887 (1077 singletons).

4.2   Quantitative Study

The SB-GRU model architecture comprises of two new processes: weight reparameterization and stick-breaking process. We perform an ablation study on these components to exhibit the effectiveness of each mechanism on the model performance. In this context, we run our experiments with the mechanisms separately and in conjunction. We dub GRU_{repar} and GRU_{BP} the reparameterization and stick-breaking only process model variant and compare with the Gloss2Text GRU model without attention used in [10]. Moreover, we include the performance of the models when applied with weight compression, $GRU_{repar,wc}$ and $SB\text{-}GRU_{wc}$ The results are shown in Table 1.

Table 1. Performance metrics

Model	Dev		Test	
	Bleu-4	Rouge	Bleu-4	Rouge
Baseline	16.3	40.3	16.3	40.7
GRU_{repar}	16.7	41.1	17.0	41.5
$GRU_{repar,wc}$	16.2	40.6	16.7	40.7
GRU_{bp}	18.4	43.9	17.0	43.1
SB-GRU	17.9	43.0	18.1	43.5
$SB\text{-}GRU_{wc}$	17.7	43.0	17.8	42.8

We observe that utilizing an IBP prior over the utility indicators and a spherical prior over the synaptic weights leads to a solid performance increase. Separately applied, the two schemes present similar performance improvements; in both cases, the GRU_{bp} exhibit some overfitting. However, when used in conjunction in the context of the proposed SB-GRU network, we yield a significant performance increase in terms of both the considered performance metrics. In addition, by performing weight posterior inference, we can reduce the weight memory footprint by a factor of 16, with a required bit precision of 1, without losing significant performance. Regarding computational complexity, the baseline model performs a training step in 0.3 s, GRU_{repar} in 0.33 s (+12%), GRU_{bp} in 0.44 s (+46%) and SB-GRU in 0.48 s (+59%).

4.3   Qualitative Results

To provide some qualitative insights on the Gloss2Text task, in Table 2 we present few examples from the test set ground truth (glosses + translation), along with the translation samples generated from our various networks.

Table 2. Predictive performance on the Test set

Gloss	jetzt wetter wie-aussehen morgen samstag zweite april
Text	und nun die wettervorhersage für morgen samstag den zweiten april
Text(eng)	and now the weatherforecast for tomorrow saturday the second april
GRU_{repar}	und nun die wettervorhersage für morgen samstag den zweiten april
$GRU_{repar,wc}$	und nun die wettervorhersage für morgen samstag den zweiten april
GRU_{bp}	und nun die wettervorhersage für morgen samstag den zweiten april
SB-GRU	und nun die wettervorhersage für morgen samstag den zweiten april
$SB\text{-}GRU_{wc}$	und nun die wettervorhersage für morgen samstag den zweiten april
Gloss	montag anfang wechselhaft mehr kuehl
Text	die neue woche beginnt wechselhaft und kuhler
Text(eng)	the new week starts unpredictable and cooler
GRU_{repar}	am montag wieder wechselhaft und kühler
$GRU_{repar,wc}$	auch am montag wechselhaft und wechselhaft
GRU_{bp}	die neue woche beginnt wechselhaft und wieder kühler
SB-GRU	die neue woche beginnt wechselhaft und wieder kuhler
$SB\text{-}GRU_{wc}$	am montag wieder wechselhaft und kühler
Gloss	sonntag regen teil gewitter
Text	am sonntag ab und an regenschauer teilweise auch gewitter
Text(eng)	on sunday from time to time rain showers sometimes also thunderstorms
GRU_{repar}	am sonntag regnet es ab und an
$GRU_{repar,wc}$	am sonntag regnet es ab und an
GRU_{bp}	am sonntag regnet es im nordwesten einzelne gewitter
SB-GRU	am sonntag verbreitet regen oder gewitter
$SB\text{-}GRU_{wc}$	am sonntag verbreitet regen oder gewitter

To facilitate understanding, we also include the English translation of these examples.

We observe that the overall grammar of the translation is coherent with major errors present at the translation of places, numbers, and dates. This is a direct effect of the infrequent words and singletons that exist in the specific dataset.

5   Conclusions

Memory-efficient continuous sign language translation is a significant challenge for the development of assisted technologies with real-time applicability. In this paper, we introduced a novel variational Bayesian sequence-to-sequence network architecture that consists of a) a full Gaussian posterior distribution on the GRU non-gate weights for data-driven memory compression and b) a nonparametric IBP prior on the same weights for regularization. We dubbed our approach Stick-Breaking Recurrent network and showed that we can achieve a substantial weight compression without diminishing modeling performance/accuracy. These findings motivate us to further examine the efficacy of these principles when applied to the more challenging Sign to Text task, specifically their applicability to the convolutional layers of the network, as well as the complete model structure. We also intend to investigate the usefulness of applying asymmetric densities to the weights [29]. Finally, another focus area for future work is the employment of quantum-statistical principles for model training [6], that may facilitate better handling of the uncertainty that stems from the limited availability of training data.

Acknowledgments. This research was partially supported by the Research Promotion Foundation of Cyprus, through the grant: INTERNATIONAL/USA/0118/0037.

References

1. Abadi, M., et al.: TensorFlow: large-scale machine learning on heterogeneous systems (2015). Software http://tensorflow.org
2. Ba, J., Caruana, R.: Do deep nets really need to be deep? In: Advances in Neural Information Processing Systems, pp. 2654–2662 (2014)
3. Bahdanau, D., Cho, K., Bengio, Y.: Neural machine translation by jointly learning to align and translate. In: 3rd International Conference on Learning Representations, ICLR 2015 (2015)
4. Camgoz, N.C., Hadfield, S., Koller, O., Bowden, R.: SubUNets: end-to-end hand shape and continuous sign language recognition. In: 2017 IEEE International Conference on Computer Vision (ICCV), pp. 3075–3084. IEEE (2017)
5. Chatzis, S.: Indian buffet process deep generative models for semi-supervised classification. In: IEEE ICASSP (2018)
6. Chatzis, S.P., Korkinof, D., Demiris, Y.: A quantum-statistical approach toward robot learning by demonstration. IEEE Trans. Rob. **28**(6), 1371–1381 (2012)
7. Cho, K., van Merrienboer, B., Gulcehre, C., Bougares, F., Schwenk, H., Bengio, Y.: Learning phrase representations using RNN encoder-decoder for statistical machine translation. EMNLP (2014)
8. Cho, K., Van Merriënboer, B., Bahdanau, D., Bengio, Y.: On the properties of neural machine translation: encoder-decoder approaches. arXiv preprint arXiv:1409.1259 (2014)
9. Chung, J., Gulcehre, C., Cho, K., Bengio, Y.: Empirical evaluation of gated recurrent neural networks on sequence modeling. In: NIPS 2014 Workshop on Deep Learning, December 2014 (2014)
10. Cihan Camgoz, N., Hadfield, S., Koller, O., Ney, H., Bowden, R.: Neural sign language translation. In: Proceedings of the IEEE Conference on Computer Vision and Pattern Recognition, pp. 7784–7793 (2018)
11. Dreuw, P., et al.: The signspeak project-bridging the gap between signers and speakers. In: Proceedings of the Seventh International Conference on Language Resources and Evaluation (LREC 2010) (2010)
12. Gal, Y., Ghahramani, Z.: Dropout as a Bayesian approximation: representing model uncertainty in deep learning. arXiv:1506.02142 (2015)
13. Graves, A.: Practical variational inference for neural networks. In: Proceedings of the NIPS (2011)
14. Griffiths, T.L., Ghahramani, Z.: Infinite latent feature models and the Indian buffet process. In: Proceedings of the NIPS (2005)

15. Guo, D., Zhou, W., Li, H., Wang, M.: Hierarchical LSTM for sign language translation. In: Thirty-Second AAAI Conference on Artificial Intelligence (2018)
16. Hinton, G., Vinyals, O., Dean, J.: Distilling the knowledge in a neural network. In: NIPS Deep Learning and Representation Learning Workshop (2015)
17. Hochreiter, S., Schmidhuber, J.: Long short-term memory. Neural Comput. **9**(8), 1735–1780 (1997)
18. Ishwaran, H., James, L.F.: Gibbs sampling methods for stick-breaking priors. J. Am. Stat. Assoc. **96**, 161–173 (2001)
19. Jang, E., Gu, S., Poole, B.: Categorical reparameterization using Gumbel-Softmax. In: Proceedings of the ICLR (2017)
20. Kingma, D.P., Ba, J.: Adam: a method for stochastic optimization. arXiv preprint arXiv:1412.6980 (2014)
21. Kumaraswamy, P.: A generalized probability density function for double-bounded random processes. J. Hydrol. **46**(1–2), 79–88 (1980)
22. Louizos, C., Ullrich, K., Welling, M.: Bayesian compression for deep learning. In: Proceedings of the NIPS (2017)
23. Luong, M.T., Brevdo, E., Zhao, R.: Neural machine translation (seq2seq) tutorial (2017)
24. Maddison, C., Mnih, A., Teh, Y.: The concrete distribution: a continuous relaxation of discrete random variables. In: International Conference on Learning Representations (2017)
25. Murray, K.: Lack of British sign language interpreters putting deaf people at risk. Guardian **8** (2013)
26. Nalisnick, E., Smyth, P.: Stick-breaking variational autoencoders. In: Proceedings of the ICLR (2016)
27. Neklyudov, K., Molchanov, D., Ashukha, A., Vetrov, D.P.: Structured Bayesian pruning via log-normal multiplicative noise. In: Advances in Neural Information Processing Systems, pp. 6775–6784 (2017)
28. Panousis, K., Chatzis, S., Theodoridis, S.: Nonparametric Bayesian deep networks with local competition. In: International Conference on Machine Learning, pp. 4980–4988 (2019)
29. Partaourides, H., Chatzis, S.P.: Asymmetric deep generative models. Neurocomputing **241**, 90–96 (2017)
30. Partaourides, H., Chatzis, S.P.: Deep network regularization via Bayesian inference of synaptic connectivity. In: Kim, J., Shim, K., Cao, L., Lee, J.-G., Lin, X., Moon, Y.-S. (eds.) PAKDD 2017. LNCS (LNAI), vol. 10234, pp. 30–41. Springer, Cham (2017). https://doi.org/10.1007/978-3-319-57454-7_3
31. Sutskever, I., Vinyals, O., Le, Q.V.: Sequence to sequence learning with neural networks. In: Advances in Neural Information Processing Systems, pp. 3104–3112 (2014)
32. Teh, Y.W., Görür, D., Ghahramani, Z.: Stick-breaking construction for the Indian buffet process. In: Proceedings of the AISTATS (2007)
33. Theodoridis, S.: Machine Learning: A Bayesian and Optimization Perspective. Academic Press, Cambridge (2015)
34. Vaswani, A., et al.: Attention is all you need. In: Advances in Neural Information Processing Systems, pp. 5998–6008 (2017)

A Gaussian Process Upsampling Model for Improvements in Optical Character Recognition

Steven I. Reeves[1]([⊠]), Dongwook Lee[1], Anurag Singh[2], and Kunal Verma[2]

[1] University of California, Santa Cruz, Santa Cruz, USA
steven.reeves@amd.com
[2] AppZen Inc., San Jose, USA

Abstract. The automatic evaluation and extraction of financial documents is a key process in business efficiency. Most of the extraction relies on the Optical Character Recognition (OCR), whose outcome is dependent on the quality of the document image. The image data fed to the automated systems can be of unreliable quality, inherently low-resolution or downsampled and compressed by a transmitting program. In this paper, we illustrate a novel Gaussian Process (GP) upsampling model for the purposes of improving OCR process and extraction through upsampling low resolution documents.

1 Introduction

The retrieval of textual information from images of the document is a very important and hard computer vision task. It has applications in search engines, accessibility tools for the visually impaired, and for processing of financial and legal documents. In general, the technology to do this is known as OCR engines. The OCR capabilities have come a long way with increased training data, better machine learning algorithms and improved image processing techniques. Despite these advances most of the OCR engines expect well formed images, which are noise free and of high resolution for high accuracy. In many cases, the resolution of the document image plays a role in how well the characters are extracted. In this paper we present a novel GP Modeling based algorithm to upsample the low resolution document images which shows improvement in the increased performance. For the study and experiments done in this paper we have used the popular open-source OCR framework Tesseract.

This manuscript is organized in the following sections, we begin with an introduction of the state-of-the-art OCR extraction software Tesseract. Next, the GP based upsampling method is discussed, along with a brief study on the choice of covariance kernels and the use of a maximum likelihood estimate for the mean. Finally, we summarize the results by comparing our algorithms with a baseline (the bicubic upsampling technique), for measurement we analyze the produced OCR accuracy resulting from these upsampled images.

© Springer Nature Switzerland AG 2020
G. Bebis et al. (Eds.): ISVC 2020, LNCS 12510, pp. 263–274, 2020.
https://doi.org/10.1007/978-3-030-64559-5_20

2   Background

2.1   OCR

Optical Character Recognition is the conversion of pixel represented words and characters within images into machine-encoded text. As previously mentioned, the OCR framework Tesseract [11] is used to extract text in the document images used in this manuscript. Tesseract was originally formulated by HP research between 1984 and 1994. Since then it has changed hands and now is an open-source software package managed by Google [5] – under the Apache 2.0 License. We use Tesseract 4.1.1, which generates text based utilizing a Long-Short Term Memory (LSTM) network. Tesseract ingests single-channel images and generates feature-maps based on these images. Then these feature maps are embedded into an input for the LSTM [5,11].

2.2   The GP Upsampling Algorithm

This interpolation method has taken inspiration from a new interpolation method for computation fluid dynamics proposed in [8], an evolution of the algorithms shown in [9,10]. The authors used a windowed GP method to upsample simulation data from coarse to fine computational meshes. For our application we define text in single-channel document images by pixels with low intensity values (close to 0 or black), surrounded by pixels of high intensity (closer to 255 or white in an 8 bit context). Specifically, pixel values are low in the interior of a character, and pixel values are comparatively high outside of characters. Because of this specific structure, the type of GP modeling will change. Instead of modeling the raw values, the deviation from a mean intensity will be modeled. This allows the upsampling algorithm to better maintain these intensities in the presence of characters. This structure is discussed in more detail in Subsects. 2.2 and 3. Mathematically, we define the upsampling operator to be

$$f_* = f_0 + \mathbf{k}_*^T \mathbf{K}^{-1} \left(\mathbf{f} - \bar{\mathbf{f}} \right) \tag{1}$$

which follows the formula for the posterior mean [7]. In Eq. (1), $\mathbf{k}_*$ is a vector of covariances between the sample pixel locations and the location of the pixel we wish to interpolate. Furthermore $\mathbf{K}$ is a matrix of pairwise covariances between sample points. The term f_0 is the estimate for the prior mean pixel intensity over the sample, and $\bar{\mathbf{f}} = f_0 \mathbf{1}$, calculation of these terms is found in Subsect. 2.2. In Subsect. 2.2, we discuss the choice of covariance kernel to generate $\mathbf{k}_*$ and $\mathbf{K}$.

Choice of Covariance Kernel. The commonly used squared exponential kernel [7] is often used when the underlying function is continuous and is the de-facto covariance function when building a GP. Image data on the other hand, is inherently discontinuous and is comprised of 8 or 16 bit integers. So instead of the SE kernel, a member of Matérn family of kernels is used. In the Matérn family of covariance functions, there are three hyper-parameters that dictate their character – as indicated in Eq. (2).

$$K_{mat}(\mathbf{x}, \mathbf{y}) = \Sigma^2 \frac{2^{1-\nu}}{\Gamma(\nu)} \left(\sqrt{2\nu} \frac{||\mathbf{x} - \mathbf{y}||}{\ell} \right)^\nu K_\nu \left(\sqrt{2\nu} \frac{||\mathbf{x} - \mathbf{y}||}{\ell} \right) \qquad (2)$$

For the Matérn kernels, there are three hyper-parameters Σ, ℓ, and ν. The hyper-parameter Σ related to the output variance function, and is widely used for uncertainty quantification. The term ℓ is the inherent length scale of covariance in for the underlying function space. The hyper-parameter ν on the other hand, relates the level of "continuousness" of the functions that are sampled. The function K_ν is the modified Bessel function of the second kind of order ν. The Matérn family of covariance functions give continuity properties ranging infinitely differentiable functions, as produced by the SE kernel, and nowhere differentiable – such as those generated by the Ornstein-Uhlenbeck covariance kernel.

Consideration of the input and output datatypes of the GP are key when choosing or building a covariance function. The datatype for this application are document images, which contain sharp contrasts that are handled better by a low ν Matérn kernel. The Matérn kernel with $\nu = 3/2$ is used in this algorithm. For this specific value, Eq. (2) can be simplified. By setting $\nu = 3/2$,

$$K_{3/2}(\mathbf{x}, \mathbf{y}) = \Sigma^2 \left(1 + \sqrt{3} \frac{||\mathbf{x} - \mathbf{y}||}{\ell} \right) \exp \left(-\sqrt{3} \frac{||\mathbf{x} - \mathbf{y}||}{\ell} \right). \qquad (3)$$

We choose $\Sigma = 1$ as the uncertainty portion of GP modeling will not be used for this application.

In order to discuss the practical difference between the Matérn 3/2 kernel and the Squared Exponential, Figs. 1a and 1b are generated utilizing functions from the Scikit Learn framework [6]. These figures contain prior and posterior mean functions of the GP generated using the aforementioned covariance kernels. The prior mean functions sampled from the GP offer illustrations of typical functions that "live" in the function spaces that the covariance kernels expect. The sampled response variable follows the formula $Y = \sin\left((X - 2.5)^2\right)$, with 10 independent variable samples that follow $X \sim \mathcal{U}(0, 5)$. Figure 1a contains the prior and posterior mean functions generated from GP with the SE Kernel using these response and independent variables. The gray space represents the uncertainty of the GP models. For Fig. 1b the above process is repeated utilizing the Matérn 3/2 kernel instead of SE. Note that in Fig. 1a, the prior and posterior mean functions are much smoother than the functions sampled from and produced by the GP with the Matérn kernel, as represented in Fig. 1b.

Maximum Likelihood Estimate for the Prior Mean. The prior mean function that will be used is the *maximum likelihood estimate for the prior mean*, calculated over the 5×5 square patch of pixels. This is done to change the character of the upsampling model so the model predicts the variation about the mean intensity in each sample. Typically, non-zero mean functions are used

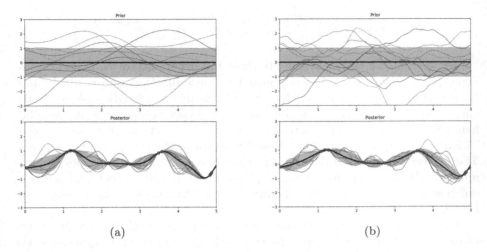

Fig. 1. Two GP models fit to 10 samples. Left: GP model with Squared Exponential Kernel, Right: GP model with Matèrn.

when there is an observed or assumed trend in the data. In the case of document images, pixel data is expected to retain certain intensities when inside a character or in the white space of a document. Because of these characteristics, a constant non-zero mean is chosen. Note that the derived prior mean functions is only constant over a single window, the prior mean will be constructed over each sample varies over the image.

To calculate the maximum likelihood estimate (MLE) for a constant prior mean, $\bar{\mathbf{f}} = f_0\mathbf{1}$, the Gaussian log-likelihood function is optimized with respect to f_0. The log-likelihood is

$$\ln \mathcal{L} = -\frac{1}{2}\left(\mathbf{f} - \bar{\mathbf{f}}\right)^T \mathbf{K}^T \left(\mathbf{f} - \bar{\mathbf{f}}\right) - \frac{1}{2}\ln(\det|\mathbf{K}|) - \frac{N}{2}\ln(2\pi). \qquad (4)$$

The maximum is calculated by setting the derivative of Eq. 4 with respect to f_0 and solving for f_0. Therefore the maximum likelihood estimate for the prior mean is:

$$f_0 = \frac{\mathbf{1}^T\mathbf{K}^{-1}\mathbf{f}}{\mathbf{1}^T\mathbf{K}^{-1}\mathbf{1}}. \qquad (5)$$

Also, this maximum likelihood estimate for the prior mean can be recast as

$$f_0 = \frac{\left(\sum_i \mathbf{K}^{-1}_{[i]}\right)\cdot\mathbf{f}}{\sum_{i,j}\mathbf{K}^{-1}_{[i,j]}}.$$

This interpretation is simply a weighted average with respect to the GP model.

3   Algorithm

In this upsampling algorithm, single channel grayscale document images are used. The GP upsampling algorithm begins with the construction of the model weights with a length scale parameter derived from the original resolution of the image – $\ell = 20\min(1/h, 1/w)$. The upsampling ratio dictates the number of weight vectors needed, for example, when upsampling 4×, 16 new pixels are generated and therefore 16 weight vectors are needed. These vectors are generated by utilizing the Cholesky factorization of $\mathbf{K}$ and then applying back substitution to calculate each $\mathbf{k}_*^T\mathbf{K}^{-1}$. The key factor is that the covariance kernel utilized in this methodology is isotropic– it only depends on the distance between samples. Since a sliding window is used, the upsampling weights only need to be calculated once and can be used throughout the image. This is because the distance between sample pixels are related to their pixel index (i, j) and the distance between each of the upsampled pixels and the rest of the window is identical for every window.

When performing upsampling over the document image, a sliding 5×5 pixel window is used as the sample for the GP model. Figure 2 helps illustrate the sliding window GP method. The figure contains 3 grids of pixels. The first grid represents the constant maximum likelihood estimate for the prior mean over this pixel grid. The second grid represents the deviation of the sampled pixel values from the MLE. Together, these grids combine to interpolate 16 new pixels, replacing the pixel in the (i, j) location.

In the implementation of this algorithm, the maximum likelihood estimate for the prior mean is generated when the 5×5 sample is loaded. Then each GP weight vector $\mathbf{k}_*^T\mathbf{K}^{-1}$ is applied to the residual between the MLE and pixels in the sampled window to model the deviation. The deviation and the MLE are combined to generate each new pixel f_*.

As an example, Fig. 3 is used to illustrate the upsampling results utilizing this GP algorithm. The top image in the figure is the low resolution image (resized by copying the nearest pixels to be the same size as the GP image), and bottom text is from the GP upsampled image. When Tesseract is used on these images, it yields the following texts. The low resolution image Tesseract output is:

"*desigm £rédacimice en fiflanEm, Et le chiet*",

which is not an accurate representation of the ground truth. However, for the GP upsampled image, Tesseract generates

"*design et regactnce en << Azzmuts >>. est le chef*".

It is clear that the GP upsampled version is much closer to the ground truth text of

"*design et rédactrice en << Azimuts >>, est le chef*".

Tesseract works best when used on near-binary images as an input. In this case, near binary means that the majority of the pixels in the image are close to 0 if they are within a character, or 255 otherwise. However, sometimes the single channel images are calculated from RGB images that yield other shades of gray. In this case some images processing techniques can be used to better "binarize" these images. Aside from binarization, images can contain noise or

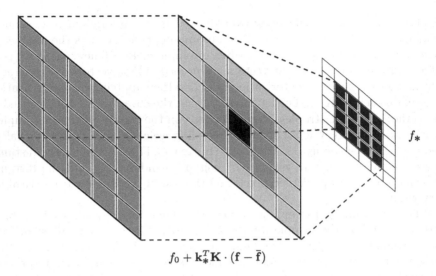

$$f_0 + \mathbf{k}_*^T \mathbf{K} \cdot (\mathbf{f} - \bar{\mathbf{f}})$$

Fig. 2. Schematic for the 5×5 GP model for four times upsampling. The dark gray grid (left) illustrates the computation of f_0 over the sample, while the GP model combination on the middle grid. The fine grid on the right, illustrates the 16 new f_* generated by combining the two, effectively replacing the pixel (i, j)

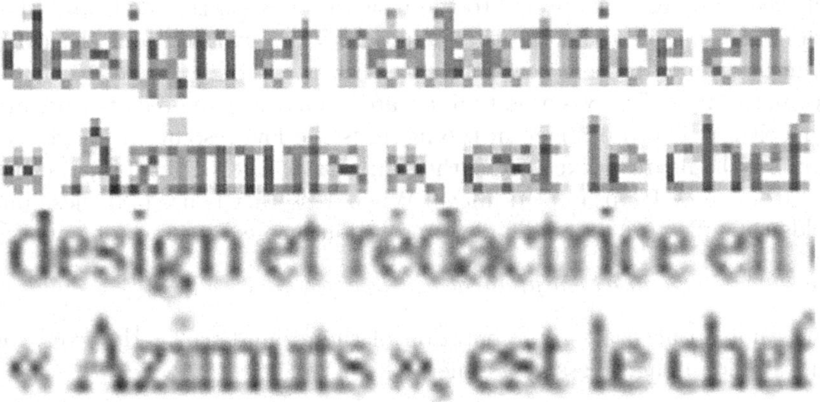

design et rédactrice en

« Azimuts », est le chef
design et rédactrice en

« Azimuts », est le chef

Fig. 3. Section of Page 154 of the LRDE dataset. Top: Four times downsampled image crop. Bottom: Four times GP upsampled.

textures within them, which can negatively effect the detection of characters. A common way to handle excess noise and textures is to use a blurring operation to smooth out those regions. However, utilizing these blur convolutions can lead to unwanted removal of edges.

To remove noise and textures without compromising edges the bilateral filtering approach illustrated by Tomasi and Manduchi is used [12]. Bilateral filters reduce noise and textures without compromising edges, that is, without compromising the upsampled edges generated in the GP upsampling.

If the image is not approximately binary, a thresholding technique can be used to force the text to be truly black. An adaptive Gaussian threshold process is used to generate binary images. Thresholding utilizes a set intensity value and replaces all pixels below that value to black and all pixels above the threshold to white. If there are shadows in the image, global thresholding can lead to large portions of the image to be blacked out. This could result in the majority of words in a document image to become inaccessible. An adaptive-thresholding technique utilizes a neighborhood of pixels and calculates the threshold value locally to perform binarization. With Adaptive Gaussian thresholding, the threshold value is the weighted sum of neighborhood pixels in a Gaussian window [1,2].

Figure 4 contains the results of the pipeline for processing low resolution images and is a visual explanation why filtering is necessary, especially when performing binarization. The top image is a GP upsampled version of a noisy low resolution image. The middle image is a thresholded version of the noisy image without using the bilateral image filter. Binarization, in this case, enhances the inherent noise, resulting in Tesseract to detect no characters. The bottom image is the noisy input image with bilateral filtering applied, and then thresholded. With the last image the Tesseract engine can detect every character.

The OCR pipeline used is as follows. First, a low resolution image is upsampled using the GP model presented earlier. Then, noise and unwanted textures from the high resolution image are removed while preserving edges by utilizing bilateral filtering. After the GP upsampled image is filtered, if the image is not approximately binary, an adaptive thresholding technique is used to convert the filtered high resolution image into a binary image to be ingested by the Tesseract OCR engine. For clarity, Fig. 5 contains an algorithmic diagram with each process.

4   Experiments

In order to test the methodology, the EPITA Research and Development Laboratory (LRDE) dataset from [4] is used. This dataset is publicly available but is copyrighted, ©2012 EPITA Research and Development Laboratory (LRDE) with permission from Le Nouvel Observateur. This dataset is based on the French magazine Le Nouvel Observateur, issue 2402, November 18th-2th, 2010. The original images come from this magazine, and LRDE has generated the ground truth OCR from these images. This dataset is free for research, evaluation, and illustration and can be downloaded from LRDE's website.

To test the proposed GP upsampling algorithm, the original images' resolution is downsampled four times in width and height. Then these low resolution representations are combined with Gaussian noise. Next, the noisy low resolution images are upsampled using the GP method illustrated in this manuscript. Finally, the upsampled images are then passed through the image processing pipeline illustrated in Fig. 5, to extract detected characters.

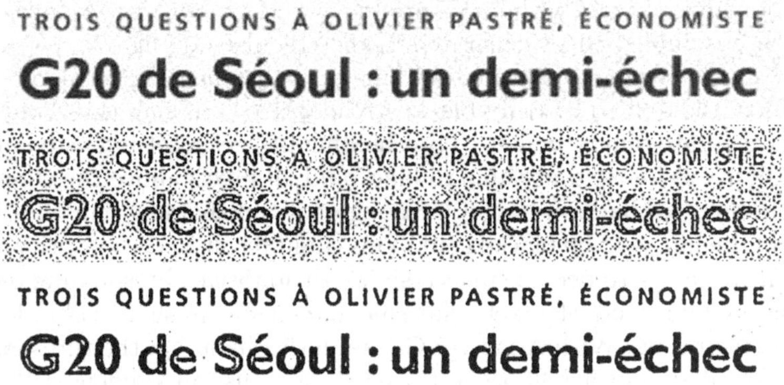

TROIS QUESTIONS À OLIVIER PASTRÉ, ÉCONOMISTE
G20 de Séoul : un demi-échec
TROIS QUESTIONS À OLIVIER PASTRÉ, ÉCONOMISTE
G20 de Séoul : un demi-échec
TROIS QUESTIONS À OLIVIER PASTRÉ, ÉCONOMISTE
G20 de Séoul : un demi-échec

Fig. 4. Top: Noisy grayscale GP upsampled text block. Middle: Adaptive thresholding with no filter. Bottom: GP upsampled image with bilateral filter and adaptive thresholding.

Low Resolution Image
GP Upsampling
High Resolution GrayScale Image
Deniosing
Bilateral Filtering
Is Approximate Binary
No
Adaptive Threshold
Yes
High Resolution Input Image
High Quality OCR Text

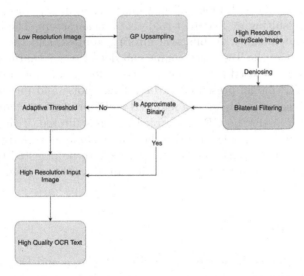

Fig. 5. The image processing pipeline used for higher quality OCR.

For this purpose, accuracy is calculated by comparing the number of words detected in the upsampled document to those that are present in the ground truth text. This is a fairly conservative measure, as increased accuracy in upsampling can lead to increased similarity in generated words with the true words. However, in this case, number of true words matched is a more direct measurement of accuracy that will effect applications that utilize image extracted text.

First, the accuracy of the GP method is compared to the OCR extracted utilizing the low resolution images. Figure 6 contains a graph comparing the accuracy of OCR obtained from the GP upsampled images against OCR from the low resolution images, for each image in the dataset. In the figure, the blue line represents the OCR accuracy for each GP upsampled image, whereas the red line is the OCR accuracy of the low resolution images. Flat dashed lines are included to illustrate the mean accuracy of each set. There are several dips in the graph where both the upsampled accuracy and the low resolution accuracy are very low, these pages of the magazine are comprised of mostly images where text is not the dominant feature. The extraneous information limits the capabilities of the Tesseract OCR engine.

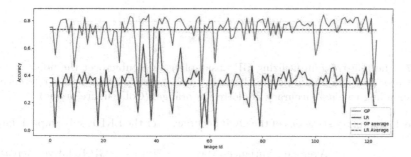

Fig. 6. GP upsampled OCR accuracy vs. the Low Resolution accuracy with dashed lines denoting average accuracies.

Most applications that require OCR will upsample sufficiently low resolution images. So, naturally, the GP algorithm is compared against the bicubic interpolation method, a common baseline in upsampling algorithms. For this implementation the bicubic method used is contained in the Python Image Library [3]. In this test, the text generated by the GP based pipeline is compared against an analogous bicubic interpolation based pipeline. Figure 7 contains a plot of the relative gain in accuracy when utilizing GP over bicubic interpolation over the LRDE dataset. In the figure, the relative gain is depicted by the blue dots for each image in the dataset. Additionally, a line denoting equal performance is plotted as an orange line for reference. For the majority of images, the proposed algorithm's extracted text better matches the ground truth text over the baseline interpolation. Some summary statistics are included in Table 1. The GP algorithm performs the best over the base low resolution images, and the bicubic interpolation based pipeline. The GP algorithm had the highest average accuracy, lowest variance and the highest minimum and maximum accuracy out of the three tests. The last column in the table is the relative gain in OCR accuracy by using the GP algorithm instead of Bicubic or just using the low resolution image. There is a 6.26% increase in character recognition against the bicubic upsampling.

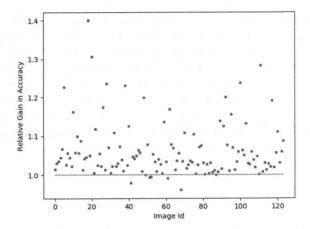

Fig. 7. The relative gain utilizing GP upsampling vs bicubic over the noisy low resolution test set. The blue dots are the individual accuracy gains, and a reference line corresponding to equal accuracy is plotted in orange. (Color figure online)

Table 1. Summary statistics of the OCR accuracy over the LRDE subsampled dataset.

	Average	Variance	Max	Min	GP Relative Increase
GP	0.735020	0.012018	0.844515	0.214765	N/A
Bicubic	0.695874	0.013746	0.835996	0.175597	6.26%
Low Resolution	0.345170	0.014018	0.725663	0.003584	195%

5   Conclusion

In this paper, a new GP based interpolation model was produced for the explicit purpose of upsampling single-channel document images. Evaluation over a real-word data set revealed an increase in OCR accuracy over the baseline upsampling method, bicubic interpolation, when used in conjunction with the Tesseract OCR engine.

GP model could be built over the entire low resolution image which could generate new pixels with inputs in a non-local sense. This provides issues in multiple areas. The kernel utilized in this context decay rapidly as distance is increased, so the new information gained will become less of a contribution than a hinderance when it comes to computation. Even though the weights are calculated using the Cholesky Factorization of the covariance matrix $\mathbf{K}$, the computational complexity of factorization is still $n^3/3$ where n is the size of row and column size of $\mathbf{K}$ [13]. So even on a relatively small resolution image, say 500×500, $\mathbf{K}$ will have size 250,000, which will require 5.208×10^{15} operations. This is realistically infeasible, which leads well into the approach described in this paper. The windowed GP model can be reinterpreted as a Sparse Gaussian

Processes that only utilizes information that is local to the interpolation pixels, which will have the most relevant information in both models.

Some minor improvements could be gained by optimizing the length scale parameter, which could be found by maximizing the log-likelihood with respect to ℓ. However, each window may have a different optimal length scale, which again, leads to an unwanted increase in computational complexity. Additionally, one can tune ℓ for the dataset, but the value in this paper appears to be general, as it depends on the size of the low resolution image. As mentioned previously, we use an ℓ that is proportional to the initial resolution. This allows for a characteristic length scale to mostly take into acount the pixels used by the convolution kernel, while allowing invertibility of the covariance kernel matrix.

Utilizing the proposed GP algorithm as an upsampling method for OCR yields on average a positive gain in accuracy versus a more traditional bicubic method when used to upsample the images for inputs to the Tesseract OCR engine. The GP algorithm uses a sliding window of 5×5 pixel sampled across the image. The yield in accuracy against bicubic can help text based Natural Language Processing (NLP) models perform better when placed in an end-to-end environment, like in financial applications, or for accessibility of documents and scanned images for people who are visually impaired. We further believe that image enhancement through this method can be beneficial to many types of pre-trained object recognition problems, and is a subject of research of the primary authors.

References

1. Bradski, G.: The OpenCV library. Dr. Dobb's J. Softw. Tools **25**, 120–125 (2000)
2. Smith III, J.O.: Spectral audio signal processing (2011)
3. Keys, R.: Cubic convolution interpolation for digital image processing. IEEE Trans. Acoustics Speech Signal Process. **29**, 1153–1160 (1981)
4. Lazzara, G., Levillain, R., Géraud, T., Jacquelet, Y., Marquegnies, J., Crepin-Leblond, A.: The SCRIBO module of the Olena platform: a free software framework for document image analysis. In: 2011 International Conference on Document Analysis and Recognition, pp. 252–258 (2011)
5. Patel, C.I., Patel, A., Patel, D.T.: Optical character recognition by open source OCR tool tesseract: a case study (2012)
6. Pedregosa, F., et al.: Scikit-learn: machine learning in Python. J. Mach. Learn. Res. **12**, 2825–2830 (2011)
7. Rasmussen, C., Williams, C.: Gaussian Processes for Machine Learning. Adaptive Computation and Machine Learning. MIT Press, Cambridge (2005)
8. Reeves, S.I., Lee, D., Reyes, A., Graziani, C., Tzeferacos, P.: An application of Gaussian process modeling for high-order accurate adaptive mesh refinement prolongation (2020)
9. Reyes, A., Lee, D., Grasiani, C., Tzeferacos, P.: A new class of high-order methods for fluid dynamics simulation using Gaussian process modeling. J. Comput. Phys. **76**, 443–480 (2017)
10. Reyes, A., Lee, D., Graziani, C., Tzeferacos, P.: A variable high-order shock-capturing finite difference method with GP-WENO. J. Comput. Phys. **381**, 189–217 (2019)

11. Smith, R.: An overview of the tesseract OCR engine. In: Proceedings of the Ninth International Conference on Document Analysis and Recognition (ICDAR), pp. 629–633 (2007)
12. Tomasi, C., Manduchi, R.: Bilateral filtering for gray and color images, pp. 839–846 (1998)
13. Trefethen, L., Bau, D.: Numerical Linear Algebra. Society for Industrial and Applied Mathematics (1997)

Posters

Video Based Fire Detection Using Xception and Conv-LSTM

Tanmay T. Verlekar$^{(\boxtimes)}$ and Alexandre Bernardino

ISR - Instituto de Sistemas e Robótica, Av. Rovisco Pais 1, 1049-001 Lisbon, Portugal
tverlekar@isr.tecnico.ulisboa.pt

Abstract. Immediate detection of wildfires can aid firefighters in saving lives. The research community has invested a lot of their efforts in detecting fires using vision-based systems, due to their ability to monitor vast open spaces. Most of the state-of-the-art vision-based fire detection systems operate on individual images, limiting them to only spatial features. This paper presents a novel system that explores the spatio-temporal information available within a video sequence to perform classification of a scene into fire or non-fire category. The system, in its initial step, selects 15 key frames from an input video sequence. The frame selection step allows the system to capture the entire movement available in a video sequence regardless of the duration. The spatio-temporal information among those frames can then be captured using a deep convolutional neural network (CNN) called Xception, which is pre-trained on the ImageNet, and a convolutional long short term memory network (ConvLSTM). The system is evaluated on a challenging new dataset, presented in this paper, containing 70 fire and 70 non-fire sequences. The dataset contains aerial shots of fire and fire-like sequences, such as fog, sunrise and bright flashing objects, captured using a dynamic/moving camera for an average duration of 13 s. The classification accuracy of 95.83% highlights the effectiveness of the proposed system in tackling such challenging scenarios.

Keywords: Fire detection · Video processing · Deep learning

1 Introduction

A series of wildfires erupting across a country can result in a large number of deaths, injuries and destruction of properties. In recent years, an increase in heat waves, droughts, climate variabilities and changes in regional weather patterns has dramatically increased the risk of wildfires. Human activities, demographics, territorial and forest management changes have also contributed to this increase. A large number of firefighters risk their lives to mitigate the destruction caused by such fires. Thus, immediate detection of wildfires can play a significant role in the response of the firefighters in combating and controlling its spread.

Conventional systems for fire detection rely on sensors that detect an increase in temperature or smoke to trigger an alarm [1]. Such systems are designed to operate in closed environments, where sufficient heat or particles can reach their sensors. Since

© Springer Nature Switzerland AG 2020
G. Bebis et al. (Eds.): ISVC 2020, LNCS 12510, pp. 277–285, 2020.
https://doi.org/10.1007/978-3-030-64559-5_21

closed proximity to fire and smoke is not possible in open spaces, the conventional sensor-based systems are ineffective in tackling wildfires. Conversely, the ability of vision-based systems to monitor vast open spaces has allowed the research community to develop several fire detection systems using a simple 2D camera [2].

Traditional vision-based fire detection systems rely on colour cues [3, 4] and image contours [5] to classify an image into a fire or non-fire category. The use of static features allows such systems to perform successful classification, only when the flames are prominently displayed in the image. The classification accuracy of the vision-based fire detection systems can be improved by using dynamic features such as motion [6] or dynamic textures [7] obtained from a video sequence. The best results among such systems are obtained by combining all available features into a multi-feature fusion system [8].

The field of computer vision has seen a significant improvement in its classification ability with the introduction of deep convolutional neural networks (CNN) [9]. Some of the state-of-the-art vision-based fire detection systems fine-tune popular CNNs, such as VGG16 and Resnet50 [10] to classify an image into fire or non-fire category. Such systems perform significantly better than the traditional vision-based fire detection systems, detecting fire even in small areas of an image while also being robust against objects having color or intensity similar to a fire in the scene. Some novel CNN based architectures, such as the densely dilated convolutional network, designed specifically to perform fire detection, perform even better than the fine-tuned CNNs, while also being lighter than them [11]. Apart from detecting, some CNNs allow segmenting the fire in an image using a bounding box [12] or pixel precision [13]. Other state-of-the-art systems rely on spatio-temporal information available from the entire video sequence to perform classification. The system presented in [14] stacks 64 frames to generate a tensor and uses it as an input to a deep convolutional generative adversarial neural network. The system presented in [15] uses a CNN to detect spatial features within a frame and then accumulates them across a video sequence using a Long Short Term Memory (LSTM) network. Although effective, these systems rely on a fixed duration video sequence for their input. They also process every available frame, which may contain a lot of redundant information, making them computationally expensive. And finally, they rely on a static camera setup to produce reliable results.

This paper presents a novel system to classify a video sequence into a fire or non-fire category using a CNN called Xception and a convolutional long short term memory network (ConvLSTM). It also presents a frame selection step which allows the system to process video sequences of varying duration. The system is evaluated on a challenging new dataset containing 70 fire and 70 non-fire sequences. The dataset contains video sequences of fog, intense sunshine, very small areas under fire and others, captured using a dynamic/moving camera. The proposed architecture allows the system to correctly classify sequences captured under such challenging scenarios.

2 Proposed System

The proposed system performs binary classification of an input video sequence into fire or non-fire category. The system operates in 4 steps, as illustrated by the system architecture presented in Fig. 1.

- During the first step the proposed system selects 15 key frames from an input video sequence;
- Each frame is processed using a CNN called Xception, pre-trained on the ImageNet dataset [9] to obtain static features;
- Spatio-temporal features across frames can then be obtained using a ConvLSTM;
- Final classification is performed using a fully connected (FC) network.

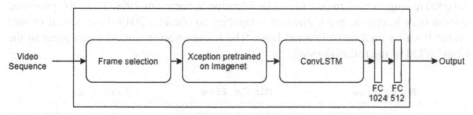

Fig. 1. Proposed system architecture.

2.1 Frame Selection

Due to advancements in camera technology, even a simple inexpensive camera can capture 30 frames per second. A high frame rate can capture a lot of redundant information, especially when observing fire sequences. To avoid processing similar looking frames, the proposed system automatically selects 15 frames uniformly distributed over the entire video sequence. The frame selection step allows the system to:

- Avoid all the starting/ending frames where the video might not contain any significant information;
- Capture the entire movement available in a video sequence;
- Operate on video sequences with varying duration.

However, in its current implementation the proposed system operates under the following assumptions for an input sequence:

- At least one frame is selected for each second;
- Positive sequences contain fire in majority of their frames, while negatives sequences are without fires;
- In dynamic sequences the camera movement isn't abrupt.

The selected frames are then resized to 299 × 299 pixels, so that they can be used as input to Xception.

2.2 Xception

Xception is a CNN architecture based entirely on depthwise separable convolution layers as illustrated in Fig. 2. The network consists of repeated pointwise convolution followed by a depthwise convolution [9]. A pointwise convolution is a 1 × 1 convolution used to change input dimensions, and a depthwise convolution is a channel-wise n × n spatial convolution. The two types of convolutions reduce the number of connections in Xception, making it lighter than most other CNNs. Xception is also one of the best CNNs in classifying the ImageNet [9]. ImageNet is a dataset of over 15 million labeled high-resolution images with around 22,000 categories. Xception uses a subset of ImageNet of 1000 categories with roughly 1.3 million training images, 50,000 validation images and 100,000 testing images to provide a classification accuracy of 79%. Thus, the proposed system uses Xception, pre-trained on ImageNet, to obtain a 2048-dimensional feature vector from its final convolutional layer. The feature vector is used as an input to the ConvLSTM in the following step.

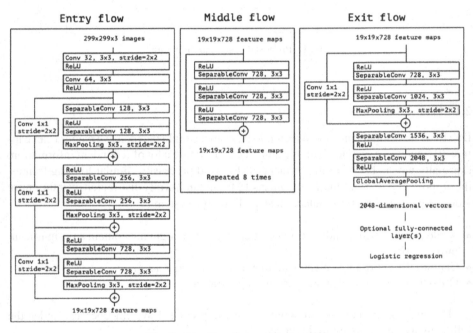

Fig. 2. The Xception architecture [9].

2.3 ConvLSTM

LSTM is a deep recurrent neural network (RNN) explicitly designed to remember information for long periods of time [16]. It is configured as a chain of repeating cells connected to each other using a cell state (C), as illustrated in Fig. 3. Each cell has four neural network layers interacting with each other to decide on what information must be discarded from the cell state, what new information must be added to the cell state, and the output of each cell. A ConvLSTM is a LSTM architecture specifically designed for sequence prediction problems with spatial inputs, like images or video sequences. It operates similar to a LSTM, but the internal matrix multiplications are replaced with convolution operations, illustrated with red colour in Fig. 3. As a result, the information flowing through the ConvLSTM cells maintains the input dimension, allowing the network to obtain better spatio-temporal correlations [16].

The proposed system uses a single layer of ConvLSTM, with 15 ConvLSTM cells. The number of output filters in the convolution is set to 64, with a kernel size of 7×7 and strides of 2×2.

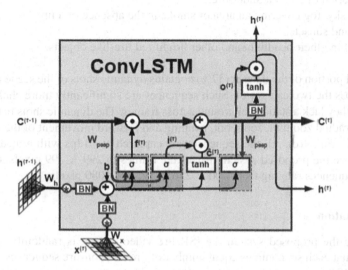

Fig. 3. A ConvLSTM cell [17].

2.4 FC Network

The output obtained from the final ConvLSTM cell is used as an input to the FC network. The FC network of the proposed system consists of two FC layers of dimensions 1024 and 512 respectively, with a dropout of 0.2 between them to prevent overfitting. It also contains a SoftMax layer to perform classification.

3 Experimental Results

The scarceness of publicly available video-based fire detection datasets prevents a thorough evaluation of most state-of-the-art vision-based fire detection systems. The largest video dataset currently available (to our best knowledge) is MIVIA [18] with only 14 fire and 17 non-fire video sequences.

3.1 ISR Fire Video Dataset

To evaluate the proposed system a novel dataset is collected containing 70 fire and 70 non-fire video sequences, called the ISR fire video dataset. The video sequences for the dataset are acquired by segmenting videos from You-tube. To make the classification process challenging, and effective in tackling wildfires, the dataset is populated with sequences such as - see Fig. 4:

- Aerial shots of trees, houses and fields on fire;
- Flames occluded by heavy smoke;
- Small section of an area under fire.
- Clouded sky, fog covering an area or smoke in the absence of a fire;
- Sunrise and sunsets;
- Cars flashing their headlight and other bright red fire-like objects.

A small portion of the dataset (37%) contains dynamic shots of the scene distributed evenly across the two categories. Such sequences are significantly more challenging to classify as they lack a static background across frames. The dynamic shots in the dataset include a gradual zoom in, zoom out, panning and forward movement of the camera, as illustrated in Fig. 4(c). All the sequences are captured at 30 fps with a mean duration of 13 s. Since the proposed system resizes the frames to 299×299 pixels, the dataset includes sequences ranging from 400×256 to 1920×1080 pixels.

3.2 Evaluation

To evaluate the proposed system the ISR fire video dataset is randomly split into 3 sets, such that each set contains equal number of fire and non-fire sequences. Out of the available 140 sequences, 44 sequences are selected for testing, 68 sequences are selected for training and remaining 28 sequences are selected for validation. The training set is augmented using shift, zoom and rotate to further increase the size of the training set to 204 sequence. The proposed system is trained using an Intel® Core™ i7-9700 CPU with GeForce RTX 2080 Ti. Training is performed using the cross-entropy loss function. The batch size is set to 5 and the number of epochs is set to 50, with the early stopping criteria set to monitor accuracy. To assess variance, the evaluation is repeated 3 times by randomly selecting new training, validation and test sets for each iteration. The results of the evaluation are reported in Table 1.

The classification accuracy and the corresponding loss of the proposed system is illustrated in Fig. 5. From the figure it can be seen that the classification accuracy of the system over the training set is at 100%, suggesting that the proposed system is effective in learning to classify fire and non-fire sequences. The validation accuracy of the proposed system reduces marginally across the three iterations with a mean score of 98.66%. The ability of the system to classify new sequences can be inferred from its performance over the test set. As reported in Table 1, the proposed system performs remarkably with a mean classification accuracy of 95.83%. The classification accuracy is significantly better than the VGG16+LSTM architecture, employed by the state-of-the-art systems, such as [15]. The classification accuracy improves with the use of Xception in place of VGG16 and ConvLSTM in place of LSTM, with the proposed system providing the best results. Thus, the quality of features obtained using Xception can be considered better than VGG16. While the improvement in performance using ConvLSTM suggests

Fig. 4. Dataset samples, (a) fire, (b) non-fire, (c) dynamic shot.

that there exists a strong spatio-temporal correlation between features obtained from sequential frames.

Table 1. Classification accuracy of the proposed system (%).

Systems	Train	Validation	Test
Proposed (Xception+ConvLSTM)	100.0 ± 0.0	98.7 ± 1.9	95.8 ± 1.2
Xception+LSTM	100.0 ± 0.0	94.7 ± 4.9	90.0 ± 0.0
VGG16+ConvLSTM	100.0 ± 0.0	90.7 ± 4.9	85.0 ± 0.0
VGG16+LSTM [15]	98.3 ± 0.2	89.3 ± 1.9	78.3 ± 3.1

It should also be noted that the state-of-the-art system presented in [14] uses all available frames from a video sequence. Thus, for a 15 s video sequence captured at 30 fps, it will process 450 frames. The proposed system provides equivalent results using just 15 frames, making it computationally inexpensive.

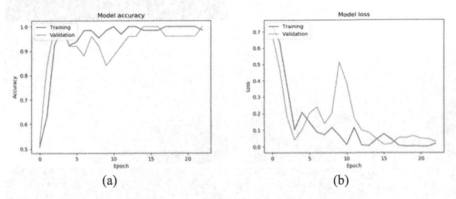

(a)   (b)

Fig. 5. Plots representing (a) accuracy and (b) loss.

4 Conclusion

This paper presents a novel system that explores the spatio-temporal information available in a video sequence to perform fire detection. The proposed system can operate on video sequences of varying duration using the frame selection step. The spatial features are obtained using a popular CNN called Xception pre-trained on ImageNet. It then uses a ConvLSTM which performs significantly better than most RNNs in obtaining spatio-temporal correlations between frames. The system operates on a challenging dataset presented in this paper containing 70 fire and 70 non-fire video sequences captured using a dynamic camera. The results suggest that the proposed system is effective in classifying fire and non-fire sequences in challenging scenarios. Thus, the proposed system can be mounted on drones to aid firefighters in detecting wildfires.

One limiting factor of this paper that can be improved further, is the size of the dataset used. As a future work, the dataset can be populated with more dynamic shots of fire and non-fire scenes, along with more difficult to classify sequences. The system can be improved to provide frame by frame decisions, while exploring the spatio-temporal information available in a video sequence.

Acknowledgement. This work was supported by FCT with the LARSyS - FCT Project UIDB/50009/202 and project FIREFRONT (PCIF/SSI/0096/2017).

References

1. Fonollosa, J., Solórzano, A., Santiago, M.: Chemical sensor systems and associated algorithms for fire detection: a review. Sensors **18**(2), 553 (2018)
2. Bu, F., Gharajeh, M.: Intelligent and vision-based fire detection systems: a survey. Image Vision Comput. **91**, 103803 (2019)
3. Chen, T., Wu, P., Chiou, Y.: An early fire-detection method based on image processing. In: International Conference on Image Processing (2004)
4. Seebamrungsat, J., Suphachai, P., Riyamongkol, P.: Fire detection in the buildings using image processing. In: Third ICT International Student Project Conference (2014)
5. Poobalan, K., Liew, S.: Fire detection algorithm using image processing techniques. In: International Conference on Artificial Intelligence and Computer Science (2015)
6. Chunyu, Y., Jun, F., Jinjun, W., Yongming, Z.: Video fire smoke detection using motion and color features. Fire Technol. **46**(3), 651–663 (2010)
7. Ye, W., Zhao, J., Wang, S., Wang, Y., Zhang, D., Yuan, Z.: Dynamic texture-based smoke detection using Surfacelet transform and HMT model. Fire Saf. J. **73**, 91–101 (2015)
8. Gong, F., et al.: A real-time fire detection method from video with multifeature fusion. Comput. Intell. Neurosci. **2019**(1), 1–17 (2019)
9. Chollet, F.: Xception: deep learning with depthwise separable convolutions. In: IEEE conference on computer vision and pattern recognition (2017)
10. Sharma, J., Granmo, O., Goodwin, M., Fidje, J.: Deep convolutional neural networks for fire detection in images. In: International Conference on Engineering Applications of Neural Networks (2017)
11. Li, T., Zhao, E., Zhang, J., Hu, C.: Detection of wildfire smoke images based on a densely dilated convolutional network. Electronics **8**(10), 1131 (2019)
12. Kang, L., Wang, I., Chou, K., Chen, S., Chang, C.: Image-based real-time fire detection using deep learning with data augmentation for vision-based surveillance applications. In: IEEE International Conference on Advanced Video and Signal Based Surveillance (2019)
13. Xu, Z., Wanguo, W., Xinrui, L., Bin, L., Yuan T.: Flame and smoke detection in substation based on wavelet analysis and convolution neural network. In: 3rd International Conference on Innovation in Artificial Intelligence (2019)
14. Aslan, S., Güdükbay, U., Töreyin, B., Çetin A.: Deep convolutional generative adversarial networks-based flame detection in video. arXiv:1902.01824 (2019)
15. Kim, B., Lee J.: A video-based fire detection using deep learning models. Appl. Sci. **9**(14), 2862 (2019)
16. Xingjian, S., Chen, Z., Wang, H., Yeung, D., Wong, W., Woo, W.: Convolutional LSTM network: a machine learning approach for precipitation nowcasting. Adv. Neural Inform. Process. Syst. **28**, 802–810 (2015)
17. https://medium.com/neuronio/an-introduction-to-convlstm-55c9025563a7
18. https://mivia.unisa.it/datasets/video-analysis-datasets/fire-detection-dataset/

Highway Traffic Classification for the Perception Level of Situation Awareness

Julkar Nine[1]([⊠]), Shanmugapriyan Manoharan[2], Manoj Sapkota[3], Shadi Saleh[1], and Wolfram Hardt[1]

[1] Department of Computer Engineering, Technische Universität Chemnitz, Straße der Nationen 62, 09111 Chemnitz, Germany
`julkar.nine@informatik.tu-chemnitz.de`
[2] Embedded Systems, Technische Universität Chemnitz, Straße der Nationen 62, 09111 Chemnitz, Germany
[3] Automotive Software Engineering, Technische Universität Chemnitz, Straße der Nationen 62, 09111 Chemnitz, Germany
`https://www.tu-chemnitz.de/`

Abstract. The automotive industry is rapidly moving towards the highest level of autonomy. However, one of the major challenges for highly autonomous vehicles is the differentiation between driving modes according to different driving situations. Different driving zones have different driving safety regulations. For example, German traffic regulations require a higher degree of safety measurements for highway driving. Therefore, a classification of the different driving scenarios on a highway is necessary to regulate these safety assessments. This paper presents a novel vision-based approach to the classification of German highway driving scenarios. We develop three different and precise algorithms utilizing image processing and machine learning approaches to recognize speed signs, traffic lights, and highway traffic signs. Based on the results of these algorithms, a weight-based classification process is performed, which determines the current driving situation either as a highway driving mode or not. The main goal of this research work is to maintain and to ensure the high safety specifications required for the German highway. Finally, the result of this classification process is provided as an extracted driving scenario-based feature on the perceptual level of a system known as situation awareness to provide a high level of driving safety. This study was realized on a custom-made hardware unit called "CE-Box", which was developed at the Department of Computer Engineering at TU Chemnitz as an automotive test solution for testing automotive software applications on an embedded hardware unit.

Keywords: Situation awareness · German highway · Traffic light · Speed limit signs · Computer vision · Machine learning

© Springer Nature Switzerland AG 2020
G. Bebis et al. (Eds.): ISVC 2020, LNCS 12510, pp. 286–297, 2020.
https://doi.org/10.1007/978-3-030-64559-5_22

1   Introduction

The issue of accurate driving scenario perception plays a significant role in the avoidance of accidents and traffic control. Driving scenarios differ with the change of driving modes. Safety rules and regulations also have a distinct level of priorities based on various driving modes. The different countries enforce distinct rules and regulations in order to establish the safe driving situations. For the purpose of the research of this study, the German Highway traffic system has been considered. The German highway system, having permission for high driving speeds is a more critical location than others [2]. According to the German Statistics portal [3], around 90% of accidents involving passenger cars happened in the location of German highways and Motorways. This is happening even after the German highway is considered as one of the safest in the whole world [4]. This highlights the significance of understanding the driving scenarios as we move towards higher levels of autonomy. An accurate classification system to classify German highway driving scenarios could be essential for highly autonomous vehicles to automate the safety measurements and maintain a low level of accidents.

Vision-based approaches are becoming an impressive area for more and more researchers to co-operate with the automotive industry to make traffic environments safer. The classification of the German highway is a very special problem due to the reason of not having a standard definition. German traffic rules and regulations have some specifications for different driving locations and modes [2]. Based on these specifications, a classification system is proposed in this research work, which consists of three sub-systems. These different sub-systems were created based on the recognition of traffic lights and traffic speed signs. An additional recognition system was developed to detect some German highway specific signs.

Due to the lack of standardized specifications regarding traffic lights, perception becomes a very special problem. Although generalizing traffic lights becomes difficult, it is possible to recognize using specific techniques. Recognition of Traffic signs on the other hand comes with different challenges due to the variety of traffic signs. This problem could also be solved when machine learning or deep learning techniques are applied. With the emergence of image based system, this paper focuses on the camera sensor, using image processing and machine learning techniques to recognize traffic speed signs and lights.

German highway driving scenarios have also consisted of several highway specific traffic signs. These signs are specific to the German highways. Hence, a custom image processing algorithm is additionally developed to recognize some of these specific signs which detected the German highway route numbers and the direction of the route.

In recent times, the term situation awareness is attaining a lot of popularity in the automotive industry [16]. According to the pioneer of situation awareness, Endsley M.R., situation awareness means to extract and perceive information as features from both internal and external environments, provide understanding towards the perceived information, take actions and predict states based on the taken actions [1]. The classification system proposed in this paper is provided to the perception level of situation awareness to analyze the overall situation.

In this paper, a weight-based classification system is proposed to classify the German highway driving scenarios. Although the deep learning techniques like SSD, FRCNN, YOLO capable in providing the accurate results, they also requires high level processing unit as well. Hence, keeping the target hardware into consideration the implementation of three sub-systems was carried out using machine learning and image processing approaches. It focuses on the contours-based ellipse fitting technique to detect the circles of speed limit signs, blob detection technique for detecting the traffic light shapes, contours, and scan line method for detecting the German highway route numbers and Hough line transformation for detecting the directional signs. The "CE-Box" was one of the hardware units from TU Chemnitz that was used for the testing of the implementation [6].

2   State of the Art

2.1   Situational Awareness

The major concern in the system operation is situation awareness which plays a significant part in making decisions based on the persuasive view of the diverse state [1]. Primarily consider the factor from the environment which helps to bring awareness of the current situation. The situation awareness model does the sorting of errors and then the design effects are created to enhance the operations. It consists of three levels and the first level is perception, where features are extracted from the surrounding environment. The second level called comprehension gives meaning to these extracted features and can take actions on them [1,6]. Whereas the third level works around predicting states based on the actions taken in the comprehensive levels.

2.2   Traffic Light Detection and Recognition

Philipsen M. P. et al. [7], used a learning-based method and spotlight intensity-based method to detect the traffic light. The Learning-based method involves the modified Adaboost classifier and sliding window techniques. The former method performs better concerning precision and recall. C. Chiang et al. [8], proposed a method for segmenting the traffic lights. The pixel extraction using HLS Color transformation and shape extraction using the ellipse detector of the traffic light. R. de Charette et al. [9], proposed a template matching method which classifies the traffic light with the confidence of the match with the template. Julkar Nine et al. [10], presented a method to recognize the traffic light using a monocular camera with "CE-Box" setup and "BlackPearl". Reducing the noise in the captured image, detecting the traffic light using a Laplacian edge detector, and finally, Hough Circle Transformation is used to distinguish the traffic light.

2.3 Speed Limit Sign Detection and Recognition

W. Li et al. [11], have used this RGB color space for detecting the boundary of the speed limit signs. The method extracts the individual R, G, B components from the image and then used the median filter to remove the noise from them and finally combined the components. Torresen J. et al. [12], use the image filtering process based on an RGB color model for their speed limit sign detection system. Ardianto S. et al. [13], uses this HSV color space for the segmentation of the outer boundary of the sign. But before using color thresholding, the paper uses histogram equalization so that the quality of the image is improved and contrast is increased. This method is accomplished by converting the original image to YCrCb color space and then using the histogram equalization method to equalize only the luminance portion of the image. The image is eventually transformed into HSV color space for the segmentation process. And also used the SVM classifier with Histogram of Oriented Gradients (HOG) features for the recognition of limit signs. The suggested method utilizes the multiple linear SVMs for the classification purpose and also reduces the number of feature vectors to increase the speed of recognition. Miyata S. [14], also use the HSV color model for extracting the outer ring of the speed limit signs. The method uses a machine learning algorithm known as the AdaBoost classifier to find the limit signs using the features extracted from the image. The features were extracted using Local Binary Pattern (LBP) features. The benefit of using these patterns is that the features could be locally extracted from the image. Another advantage is that the features are less prone to change in the illumination conditions. Pon A. D. et al. [15] proposed an approach to train the deep learning model in a mini-batch selection mechanism to detect the traffic light and sign. One network architecture improves detection performance. However, the model does not achieve good accuracy or recall.

3 System Design

3.1 System Architecture

The sub-systems for the classification system aim to develop applications for the recognition of traffic objects in given input videos. The videos are given as the input for the system architecture layer, whereas the processed data will be provided as output from the application layer. Several algorithms are performed simultaneously to detect the German highway specific traffic signs, speed limit signs, and traffic lights. Once the algorithm detects any of these signs, it stores the detection output and provides the result to the classification system. There is an additional option available in the system to send the output as a CAN message with unique identifiers for future implementation purposes. The system architecture is presented in Fig. 1.

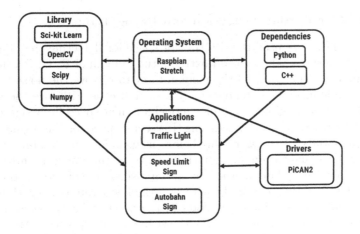

Fig. 1. System Architecture

3.2 Software

"CE-Box" contains manifold racks of Raspberry Pi embedded with PiCAN 2 modules. The operating system used in each of the Raspberry Pi was Raspbian Stretch. Several libraries are installed such as scikit-learn, skimage, scipy, numpy, OpenCV along Python to run and test the algorithm in the "CE-Box". For the execution of computer vision application and image processing, C++ dependencies are used.

3.3 Hardware

Julkar Nine et al. [10], have made use of a hardware component called "CE-Box" developed under the Department of Computer Engineering of TU Chemnitz for the application as shown in Fig. 2. The hardware unit consists of several racks. Each of the racks is powered by Raspberry Pi 3b+ models with embedded

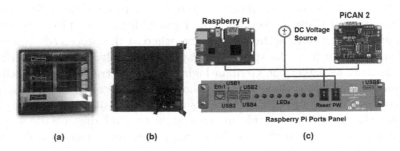

Fig. 2. System Setup: (a) CE-Box Top View, (b) CE-Box Rack, (c) CE-Box Connection (Front Panel) [10]

PiCan2 module. The racks can communicate with each other via CAN communication. This hardware setup is used to test the proposed algorithm. The input videos are processed by the algorithm in the Raspberry Pi. Then, the output of the algorithm is stored and forwarded to the classification system. It can also be provided as a CAN message with unique identifiers to PiCAN 2 for future implementation purposes. The PiCAN 2 can communicate with ECU through CAN message. Through the screw terminal or DB9 connector, PiCAN 2 is powered and Python is used as the programming language.

4 Implementation

The German highway is classified based on the information gathered from three different detection systems. Therefore, one of the major contributions of this work is recognizing these three different objects: speed limit signs, the traffic lights, and the German highway specific signs which consist of highway route number signs along with the advance directional signs presented on the billboards of the German highway from the images captured with the camera mounted on the front of a vehicle.

The frames of the videos are sent to a pipeline which has a set of three algorithms each working for the recognition of different signs as mentioned above. The initial phase of each algorithm contains some pre-processing techniques such as color conversion, thresholding, grayscale conversion, and noise reduction. The YCbCr color space is used for the detection of the speed limit sign, and HSV color space for traffic light since they are less sensitive to illumination changes and give better results during the implementation.

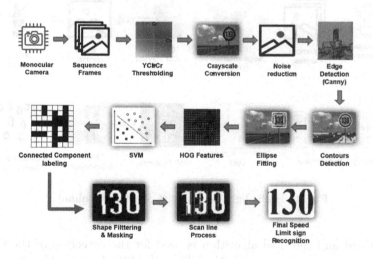

Fig. 3. Speed limit sign detection

One of the algorithms is dedicated to the recognition of a speed limit sign which is based on contours. The contour-based detection gave better results with edge information. So, canny edge detection is used before finding contours. Finally, the ellipse fitting technique has been used to find the speed limit signs as shown in Fig. 3. This technique has successfully detected a range of limit signs including the misshaped ones which are warped from the regular round shapes. Even though a successful detection of signs had been generated, a significant quantity of false positives still existed. To reduce these, a linear SVM classifier is used which was trained using the HOG features. The BelgiumTS Dataset [16] had been used for this purpose. The recognition of the speed limit is done using the connected component labeling technique followed by some shape-based filtering and then the scan-line process. The technique can recognize any speed limit signs captured from the camera under suitable light conditions.

The second algorithm is used for the detection of traffic lights. The blob detection technique is used for this purpose. The input to this technique is a binary image which is a result of a sequence of pre-processing steps as shown in Fig. 4. In the color thresholding stage, three different ranges are used for extracting the red, green, and yellow color information. This led to the detection of the number of blobs (red, green, and yellow) present in the frames as a result of the blob detection technique. After that, contour properties and some shape adjustment techniques are used which could extract the traffic light box present in the frame that contains the detected blobs. Lastly, for the accurate detection and recognition of the traffic lights, three different SVM classifiers are used, one for each traffic color using the histogram of oriented features. As a result, the algorithm effectively recognized the traffic lights taken from the camera.

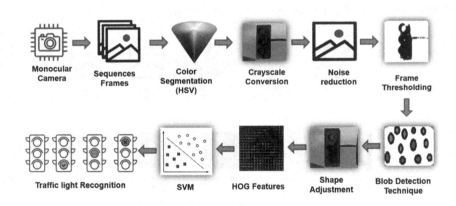

Fig. 4. Traffic light detection (Color figure online)

The third and the final algorithm is used for the detection of the German highway route numbers present in the billboards of the German highway. Firstly, the image is grayscaled, and then the bilateral filter is used for the reduction of noise. After that, the Canny edge detector is used for extracting edge information. The results are improved by using a bilateral filter before using the edge detector, as contrary to previous detection methods, in which the Gaussian filter

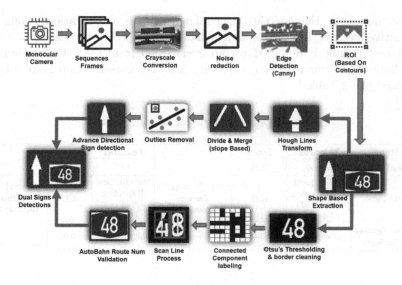

Fig. 5. German highway Specific Sign Detection

was used. The focus of this algorithm is to find the shapes inside the billboard signs. Therefore, a Region Of Interest (ROI) is created using the edge information and then finding the boundaries of the billboards using the contours. After the ROI is extracted, a shape-based filtration is applied using the contour properties yet again that could extract the relevant shapes that look similar to advance directional and the German highway route number signs as shown in Fig. 5. Now, the German highway route number and the advance directional signs are detected using the two separate procedures.

The advance directional sign is detected based on the presence of a pointed arrowhead. The relevant portion of the arrowhead sign is cropped and then the Hough transform is used to detect the lines. Left and right slanting lines are used to recognize the arrowheads. And for the detection of the German highway route number signs, the cropped region is cleaned at first using Otsu's thresholding and border segmentation. After that, connected component labeling is used followed by the scan-line process for the effective recognition of the digits present inside the sign. The route number sign is validated by the recognition of the digits inside the sign. The successful detection of both the German highway route number and the advance directional signs are strong candidates that are useful for classifying the German highway.

A weight-based classification system is proposed based on the recognition result of the three sub-systems. Traffic speed limit signs which are in the range of 80–150 km/h is provided with a weight of 0.35, whereas the absence of a traffic light in every 1500 frames is provided with a weight of 0.25, the most weight is provided to the German highway specific signs with 0.4. If one of thee sub-systems generate a result within the classification boundaries, the German highway driving scenario is detected. Subsequent outputs from the sub-systems would increase the weight, thus increase the confidence of the classification. Along with the positive weights, a negative weight is also provided in the case when more than 1 traffic light is detected within every 1500 frames as the frequency of traffic lights in German highways are very low. The classification system is also showcased using Table 1.

Table 1. Design criteria for classifier system

Criteria	Features	Score		Features	Score	
Speed Sign	80-150	0.35		< 80	0.0	
Traffic Light	Less frequent [Not Repeating within 1500 frames]	0.25	$0.8 \geq \sum(\text{Score}) \leq 1$ German Highway -> Yes	More frequent [Repeating within 1500 frames]	0.35	$\sum(\text{Score}) < 0.8$ German Highway-> No
German Highway Specific Signs	Detected	0.4		Not Detected	0.0	

5   Result and Evaluation

The evaluation of the results achieved was evaluated based on three criteria. These were the recognition accuracy of the three sub-systems, the computation time for each of the algorithms both individually and merged, and the correctness of the weighted confidence of the classifier. Implemented algorithms were tested in a total of 62,800 frames which were extracted from several videos for recognizing traffic speed signs and traffic lights and provide an average accuracy of approximately 99%.

(a) Speed Limit Sign   (b) Traffic Light

Fig. 6. Recognition of speed limit sign and traffic light

The analysis showcased in Fig. 6a and Fig. 6b indicates that the algorithms detect the speed limit sign and traffic light as expected and the outcomes were drawn on the images. Similarly, the German highway detection algorithm was tested on several custom made videos with a total of 20,361 frames and generates a recognition rate of approximately 99%.

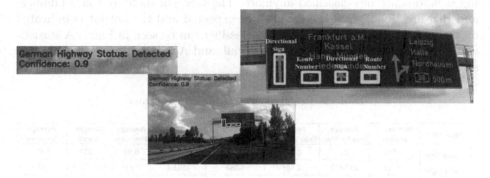

Fig. 7. The German highway specific sign recognition

Due to the algorithms being developed and tested under the Raspberry Pi 3b+ models of "CE-Box", the computation was always a bottleneck of this research. Hence, two different evaluation were carried out. First, the algorithms were allowed to be run on different Raspberry Pis simultaneously. Later, all three algorithms were merged and ran under the same Raspberry Pi. The results showcased the difference in computation time for all the algorithms when it comes to detecting the object. It took almost twice the amount of time to compute the same object from the same video for the combined algorithm. Details can be seen in Fig. 8.

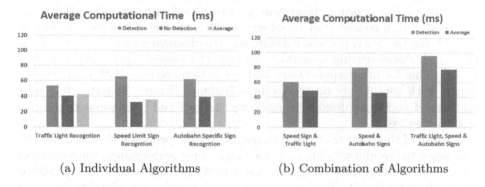

(a) Individual Algorithms   (b) Combination of Algorithms

Fig. 8. Average computational time (in seconds)

With the generation of results from any of the three sub-systems, it is provided to the classifier. Depending on the generated result, the classifier provides a confidence weight based on which the German highway driving scenarios are classified. The confidence weight will keep on increasing as long as any of the sub-systems generate information that falls within the classification criteria. If the sub-systems do not generate any result or generate a result that is out of bounds of the classifier, the confidence keeps on losing weight until German highway driving scenarios are not classified anymore. The German highway route numbers and the directional signs are detected as expected and the output is indicated on the image and also the result of the classifier can be seen in Fig. 7. A statistical overview regarding the Precision, Recall, and Accuracy of the algorithms is shown in Table 2.

Table 2. Results & evaluation of algorithms

Algorithms	Number of Frames	Average True Positives	Average False Positives	Average False Negatives	Average True Negatives	Average Precision	Average Recall	Average Accuracy
Speed Sign	29238	27	0.133	1.4	1920.67	0.99	0.949	0.999
Traffic Light	33562	247.467	2.533	6.067	1981.4	0.941	0.967	0.996
German Highway Specific Signs	20361	20.4	0.4	2.333	1334.27	0.878	0.982	0.998
Merged Algorithms	20790	98.289	1.022	3.267	1745.44	0.936	0.966	0.998

6   Conclusions and Future Aspects

In this paper, three algorithms were developed to recognize the speed limit sign, the traffic light, and the highway traffic sign. Our solution is evaluated using the German Traffic Sign Recognition Benchmark [17]. The proposed solution is implemented using computer vision and machine learning approaches to achieve a high perception level for situation awareness. As these objects are recognized, the driving mode will be classified as a high driving mode or city driving mode. For testing and evaluating the system, a custom hardware unit called "CE-Box" was used, which consisted of Raspberry Pi 3b+ models. The research demonstrated that the newly proposed classification mechanism is capable of classifying German highway driving scenarios with respect to some aspects and that it is also scalable for other applications and perception systems. Although the presented work concentrate on the German Highway Driving Scenario. It can be customized and generalized by considering the rule and regulations from other countries as well.

Inspite of the number of sub-systems used in the proposed classification system generated results with high accuracy and robust performance, the confidence weights of the classification system itself could be improved a lot by adding more sub-systems to it. German highway entrance and exit traffic signs were not considered for this research project. Including more traffic signs could also be beneficial. Classification of other driving traffic modes can also be implemented and evaluated with the proposed work. Hardware used in the "CE-Box" can also be updated and evaluated for better performance feedback improving the computation time of the algorithms.

References

1. Endsley, M.R.: Toward a theory of situation awareness in dynamic systems. Hum. Factors J. Hum. Factors Ergon. Soc. **37**(1), 32–64 (1995)
2. German Road Traffic Rules and Regulations. https://www.stvo.de/strassenverkehrsordnung. Accessed 01 Apr 2020
3. German Statistics Portal. https://www.destatis.de/EN/Themes/Society-Environment/Traffic-Accidents/_node.html. Accessed 01 Apr 2020
4. German Highway. https://www.thelocal.de/20190201/are-germanys-autobahns-really-the-safest-highways-in-the-world. Accessed 01 May 2020
5. Endsley, M.R.: Situation awareness in future autonomous vehicles: beware of the unexpected. In: Bagnara, S., Tartaglia, R., Albolino, S., Alexander, T., Fujita, Y. (eds.) IEA 2018. AISC, vol. 824, pp. 303–309. Springer, Cham (2019). https://doi.org/10.1007/978-3-319-96071-5_32
6. Nine, J., Manoharan, S., Hardt, W.: Concept of the comprehension level of situation awareness using an expert system. In: 14th International Forum on Strategic Technology (IFOST), Tomsk, Russian Federation (2019)
7. Philipsen, M.P., Jensen, M.B., Mogelmose, A., Moeslund, T.B., Trivedi, M.M.: Traffic light detection: a learning algorithm and evaluations on challenging dataset. In: IEEE 18th International Conference on Intelligent Transportation System (ITSC), pp. 2341–2345 (2015)
8. Chiang, C.C., Ho, M.C., Liao, H.S., Pratama, A., Syu, W.C.: Detecting and recognizing traffic lights by genetic approximate ellipse detection and spatial texture layouts. Int. J. Innov. Comput. Inf. Control **7**(12), 6919–6934 (2011)
9. Charette, R.D., Nashashibi, F.: Real time visual traffic lights recognition based on spot light detection and adaptive traffic lights templates. In: IEEE Intelligent Vehicles Symposium, pp. 358–363 (2009)
10. Nine, J., Saleh, S., Khan, O., Hardt, W.: Traffic light sign recognition for situation awareness using monocular camera. In: Symposium International Symposium on Computer Science, Computer Engineering and Educational Technology (ISCSET), Laubusch, Germany (2019)
11. Li, W., Li, H., Dong, T., Yao, J., Wei, L.: Improved traffic signs detection based on significant color extraction and geometric features. In: 8th International Congress on Image and Signal Processing (CISP), pp. 616–620 (2015)
12. Torresen, J., Bakke, J.W., Yang, Y.: A camera based speed limit sign recognition system. In: Proceedings of 13th ITS World Congress and Exhibition, pp. 115–129 (2006)
13. Ardianto, S., Chen, C.J., Hang, H.M.: Real-time traffic sign recognition using color segmentation and SVM. In: International Conference on Systems, Signals and Image Processing, pp. 1–5 (2017)
14. Miyata, S.: Automatic recognition of speed limits on speed-limit signs by using machine learning. J. Imaging **3**, 25 (2017)
15. Pon, A.D., Andrienko, O., Harakeh, A., Waslander, S.L.: A hierarchical deep architecture and mini-batch selection method for joint traffic sign and light detection. arXiv:1806.07987 (2018)
16. BelgiumTS - Belgian Traffic Sign Dataset for training of Speed Limit Sign. https://btsd.ethz.ch/shareddata/. Accessed 01 May 2020
17. Stallkamp, J., Schlipsing, M., Salmen, J., Igel, C.: The German traffic sign recognition benchmark: a multi-class classification competition. In: The 2011 International Joint Conference on Neural Networks, pp. 1453–1460, July 2011

3D-CNN for Facial Emotion Recognition in Videos

Jad Haddad[1,2]([✉]), Olivier Lezoray[1]([✉]), and Philippe Hamel[2]

[1] Normandie Univ, UNICAEN, ENSICAEN, CNRS, GREYC, 14000 Caen, France
{jad.haddad,olivier.lezoray}@unicaen.fr
[2] Zero To One Technology, Campus Effiscience, Colombelles, France

Abstract. In this paper, we present a video-based emotion recognition neural network operating on three dimensions. We show that 3D convolutional neural networks (3D-CNN) can be very good for predicting facial emotions that are expressed over a sequence of frames. We optimize the 3D-CNN architecture through hyper-parameters search, and prove that this has a very strong influence on the results, even if architecture tuning of 3D CNNs has not been much addressed in the literature. Our proposed resulting architecture improves over the results of the state-of-the-art techniques when tested on the CK+ and Oulu-CASIA datasets. We compare the results with cross-validation methods. The designed 3D-CNN yields a 97.56% using Leave-One-Subject-Out cross-validation, and 100% using 10-fold cross-validation on the CK+ dataset, and 84.17% using 10-fold cross-validation on the Oulu-CASIA dataset.

Keywords: Facial emotion recognition · Video · 3D-CNN · CK+ · Oulu-CASIA

1 Introduction

Facial emotion recognition has been gaining a lot of attention over the past decades with applications in cognitive sciences and affective computing. Ekman et al. have identified six basic facial expressions (anger, disgust, fear, happiness, sadness, and surprise) as basic emotional expressions that are universal and common among human beings [1]. Human emotions are complex to interpret, and building recognition systems is essential in human-computer interaction since affective information is a major component of human communication. Many approaches have been proposed for automatic facial expression recognition [2]. Most of the traditional non-deep approaches have focused on analyzing static images independently, thus ignoring the temporal relations of sequence frames in videos. However this temporal information is essential for tracking small changes in the face throughout the expression of an emotion. Recently, with the surge of deep learning, more promising results have been reported [3–7] tackling the automatic facial emotion recognition task using both geometric and photometric features.

© Springer Nature Switzerland AG 2020
G. Bebis et al. (Eds.): ISVC 2020, LNCS 12510, pp. 298–309, 2020.
https://doi.org/10.1007/978-3-030-64559-5_23

2   Emotion Recognition in Videos

Predicting dynamic facial emotion expressions in videos has received a lot of attention. Many previous works have explored tracking geometric features of the face relying on the evolution of facial landmarks across frames [8], or have used e.g., the LBP-TOP approach [9]. Recently, deep learning techniques have emerged as they can provide enormous performance gains [7]. Several deep techniques can be considered for analyzing sequential data, the most prominents being Recurrent Neural Networks (RNN) [10], and Long Short-Term Memories (LSTM) [11]. Many works have been led on the combination of classical 2D Convolutional Neural Networks with RNNs or LTSMs to cope with the temporal aspect in emotion recognition in videos [12,13]. In these approaches, a RNN (or LSTM) takes the features extracted by a CNN over individual frames as inputs and encodes the temporal dynamics. Few works have been led on the use of 3D-CNN [14,15] as compared to the combination CNN-LSTM in the facial emotion recognition domain. However convolutional neural networks with 3D kernels (3D-CNNs) can have a superior ability to extract spatio-temporal features within video frames, as compared to 2D CNNs, even if combined with temporal networks. This is the line of the work we propose and we aim at designing an efficient 3D-CNN for emotion recognition in videos [3,16].

3   Our Approach

We consider 3D-CNNs to perform facial emotion recognition in videos. We base our study on [14], and regularize the feature extraction part of the network with batch normalization because of its success in reducing internal covariate shift [17]. We explore how we can optimize the structure and parameters of the network to obtain better performances. Unlike 2D convolution, when a 3D convolution is applied on a video sequence, the output is a 3D tensor. Therefore, 3D convolutions preserve the temporal aspect of a video sequence. In video contexts, facial expressions do not manifest themselves instantly, but instead, they are built up gradually across time until they reach their peak. Thus, a static approach would result in predictions that can vary a lot across the frames and lead to uninterpretable results. A 3D-CNN solves this issue since by nature it takes as input a group of sequential frames and analyzes them together to predict an emotion.

3.1   Deep 3D CNN

The full architecture of our proposed model to be optimized is presented in Fig. 1, such that the white components are fixed, and the red components are to be explored. We suppose that an expression can be detected in 10 consecutive frames as in the state of the art. Our model takes as input a window of 10 RGB frames of size 112×112. We use the Adam optimizer and we set the learning rate to 0.0001, and set the maximum number of epochs to 16. We process batches

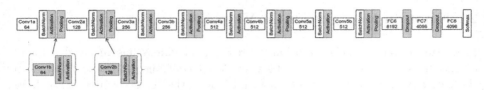

Fig. 1. Full architecture to optimize. Number of filters is denoted in each Conv box.

of size 30, and we report the results of the best epoch. The momentum of batch normalization layers is set to 0.1. We denote the kernel dimensions as (f, w, h) where f represents the temporal dimension, w represents the width dimension, and h represents the height dimension. All convolutional layers have a kernel of size (3, 3, 3), and a padding of (1, 1, 1). However, we will search in the following sections for the best temporal dimension size of the convolutional kernel. All pooling layers have a kernel size of (2, 2, 2) and a stride of (2, 2, 2), except for the first pooling layer, which has a kernel size of (1, 2, 2) and a stride of (1, 2, 2), and for the last pooling layer which has a kernel size of (1, 2, 2), a stride of (2, 2, 2), and a padding of (0, 1, 1).

3.2 Data Augmentation

Data augmentations have proved to increase the task performance of neural networks [18]. When a deep network has many parameteres, it can easily overfit when the size of the training dataset is small. Data augmentation overcomes this issue by artificially creating new samples by applying transformations to the training set. We explore two geometric and one photometric augmentation techniques:

1. **Flip:** flip horizontally.
2. **Rotation:** rotate by a random angle $\alpha \in [-30, 30]$.
3. **Linear contrast:** adjust contrast by scaling each pixel to $127 + \alpha * (v - 127)$ where v is the pixel value and α is a random multiplier $\in [0.22, 2.2]$.

3.3 Architecture Optimization

To find the best combination of all the options that we want to explore, we can do a grid search to explore every possible combination. Even though this technique yields the most accurate results, we would be facing a combinatorial explosion, which is computationally expensive. To tackle this problem, we used the Optuna[1] framework [19] to search for the best hyper-parameters combination. Optuna uses by default Tree-structured Parzen Estimator (TPE) [20], which is more efficient and much less computationally expensive than a grid search. TPE is a sequential model-based optimization (SMBO) approach. SMBO methods

---

[1] http://optuna.org/.

sequentially construct models to approximate the performance of hyperparameters based on previous measurements, and then choose new hyperparameters to test, based on this model. On each trial, TPE fits for each parameter one Gaussian Mixture Model (GMM) $l(x)$ to the set of parameter values associated with the best objective values, and another GMM $g(x)$ to the remaining parameter values. Then it chooses the parameter value x that maximizes the ratio $l(x)/g(x)$. We're interested in exploring the following parameters:

- Type of pooling layer.
- Type of activation function.
- Optimizing using Lookahead (k = 5, alpha = 0.5) [21].
- Applying CLAHE [22] on input images with $clipLimit = 2$ and $tileGridSize = (8,8)$, as illumination can vary a lot which can result in large intra-class variances, which we want to minimize [7].
- Normalizing images so that each pixel value $\in [-1, 1]$. Normalization increases the robustness of the training efficacy of a neural network [23]
- Size of the temporal dimension in convolutional kernels and modifying the padding of the kernel so that we preserve the same shape of the temporal dimension.
- Weights initialization [24].
- Regularization using dropout between fully connected layers.
- Adding a second convolutional block in first two layer groups.
- Assigning weight to each class and pass it to cross-entropy loss.

The details of the hyper-parameters search are shown in Table 1.

Table 1. Hyper-parameters to explore.

Parameter	Options
Optimization	Lookahead+Adam/Adam
CLAHE	True/false
Normalization	True/false
Activation	ReLU/ELU/pReLU/leaky ReLU/Mish [25]
Loss weights	True/false
Temporal size	1/3/5/7/9
Initializer	Xavier uniform/Xavier normal
Pooling layer	AvgPooling/MaxPooling
Second ConvLayer	True/false
Dropout	[0, 1]

Optuna offers pruning functionality for early stopping trials that are not promising. In this experiment, we prune trials that will yield a LOSO cross-validation accuracy less than 96.5%, allowing us to iterate faster on the different combinations generated by the estimator.

4 Experiments

In this section we consider two state-of-the-art databases and show that a 3D-CNN with an efficient hyper-paprameter search can lead to very good results.

4.1 Evaluation on CK+

CK+ [26] contains 593 video sequences from 123 subjects. Among these videos, 327 sequences from 118 subjects are labeled with seven basic expression labels, i.e., anger, contempt, disgust, fear, happiness, sadness, and surprise. 266 of these video sequences are not annotated, and are discarded for the rest of the experiment. CK+ does not provide training/testing splits, therefore to compare our model's performance, we adopt the cross-validation technique. We use Leave-One-Subject-Out (LOSO) cross-validation technique as a metric to construct and optimize our network's architecture. However, to compare our results with previous works done on this dataset, we use 10-fold subject-independent cross-validation experiments as most of the state-of-the-art algorithms were evaluated in such a way. We constructed 10 subsets as described in several previous works [3,27], and compute the overall accuracy over 10 folds.

Preprocessing. We process the last 10 frames of each sequence by extracting the face using OpenCV's deep learning model for face detection. We then resize the cropped faces to the scale of 112×112, and rescale the pixels values so that each pixel $\in [0,1]$. The majority of the video sequences are grayscale, therefore, we convert the few colored video sequences to grayscale RGB to preserve the consistency of the dataset.

Data Augmentation. We perform different image augmentations empirically according to the representability of each class, knowing that geometric augmentations outperform photometric methods [18], we obtain a quasi-balanced dataset:

- Contempt: $1 \times$ Flip, $7 \times$ Rotation, $4 \times$ Linear contrast.
- Fear: $1 \times$ Flip, $4 \times$ Rotation, $4 \times$ Linear contrast.
- Sadness: $1 \times$ Flip, $4 \times$ Rotation, $3 \times$ Linear contrast.
- Anger: $1 \times$ Flip, $2 \times$ Rotation, $1 \times$ Linear contrast.
- Happy: $1 \times$ Flip, $1 \times$ Rotation, $1 \times$ Linear contrast.
- Disgust: $1 \times$ Flip, $1 \times$ Rotation, $1 \times$ Linear contrast.
- Surprise: $1 \times$ Flip, $1 \times$ Rotation, $0 \times$ Linear contrast.

Furthermore, we duplicate the last frame for video sequences having less than 10 frames.

Hyper-parameters Optimization. More than 800 different configuration have been tested, we show the ones that have their LOSO above the pruning threshold and the best results are in the top right corner. After 600 trials, the

TPE starts converging as shown in Fig. 2, we observe that certain parameters contribute much in increasing the model's performance (e.g., CLAHE, Xavier uniform, *temporal_size* = 3) and other parameters lower the model's performance (e.g. normalization, *temporal_size* ∈ {1; 7; 9}, *dropout* ∈ [0.5, 1], adding a second convolutional layer to the first two layer groups).

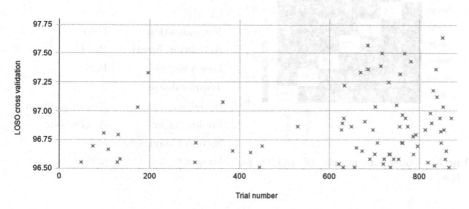

Fig. 2. Hyper-parameters search on CK+. Each red cross represents a different configuration.

Results. The best trial of LOSO cross-validation on CK+ yielded **97.56%**. The hyper-parameters combination proposed by the TPE for this accuracy is illustrated in Table 2 along with its confusion matrix in Fig. 5, and the resulting architecture is illustrated in Fig. 3.

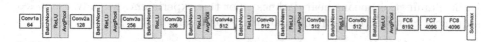

Fig. 3. Resulting architecture for CK+, number of filters is denoted in each Conv box.

We use the resulting architecture to evaluate the 10-fold subject-independent cross-validation, we achieve **100%**. This is so far the best result obtained on this dataset.

Fig. 4. Resulting architecture for Oulu CASIA, number of filters is denoted in each Conv box.

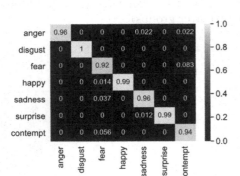

Fig. 5. Confusion matrix of LOSO for CK+.

Table 2. Hyper-parameters of the best CK+ LOSO trial.

Hyper-parameter	Value
Optimization	Adam
CLAHE	True
Normalization	False
Activation function	ReLU
Loss weights	False
Temporal size	3
Initializer	Xavier uniform
Pooling layer	AvgPooling
Second ConvLayer	False
Dropout	0.2511

4.2   Evaluation on Oulu-CASIA

We perform hyper-parameter tuning of the full architecture to obtain the optimized 3D-CNN architecture for the Oulu-CASIA dataset.

Oulu-CASIA [28] consists of six expressions (surprise, happiness, sadness, anger, fear and disgust) from 80 people between 23 to 58 years old. 73.8% of the subjects are males. Subjects were filmed by an NIR camera and a VIS camera which capture the same facial expression. All expressions are captured in three different illumination conditions: normal, weak and dark. Normal illumination means that good normal lighting is used. Weak illumination means that only computer display is on and subject sits on the chair in front of the computer. Dark illumination means near darkness. For this experiment, we only use video sequences captured in normal illumination condition.

Preprocessing. We process the last 10 frames of each sequence by extracting the face using OpenCV's deep learning model for face detection. We then resize the cropped faces to the scale of 112×112, and rescale the pixels values so that each pixel $\in [0, 1]$.

Data Augmentation. We augment all the video sequences using $1 \times$ Flip, $5 \times$ Rotation, $2 \times$ Linear contrast. Furthermore, we duplicate the last frame for video sequences having less than 10 frames.

Results. The best trial of 10-fold cross-validation on Oulu CASIA yielded **84.17%**. The hyper-parameters combination proposed by the TPE for this accuray is illustrated in Table 3 along with its confusion matrix in Fig. 6, and the resulting architecture is illustrated in Fig. 3.

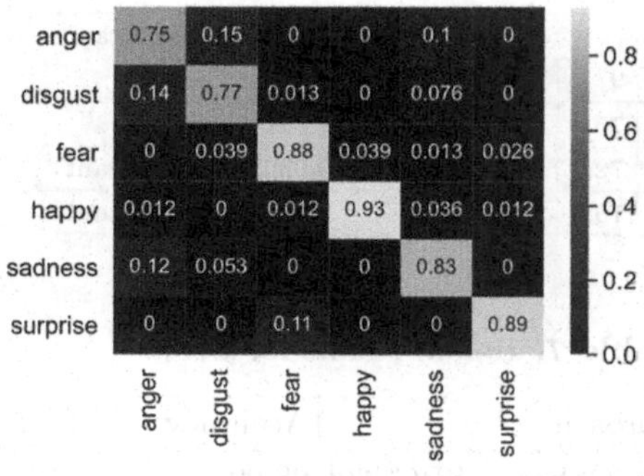

Table 3. Hyper-parameters of the best Oulu-CASIA 10-fold trial.

Fig. 6. Confusion matrix of 10-fold for Oulu-CASIA.

Hyper-parameter	Value
Optimization	Lookahead + Adam
CLAHE	False
Normalization	True
Activation function	Leaky ReLU
Loss weights	False
Temporal size	3
Initializer	None
Pooling layer	MaxPooling
Second ConvLayer	False
Dropout	0.4233

4.3 Importance of Meta Optimization

We evaluate the optimized architecture of CK+ on Oulu-CASIA and vice-versa to see the importance of having an architecture that is optimized to the dataset in question as opposed to having one architecture for both datasets. The p-value is used to determine the significance between the two architectures and therefore, the importance of having a different architecture optimized to each dataset. Tables 4 and 5 show that the p-value is significant. Thus, having an optimized architecture for each dataset is necessary to have a better accuracy.

Table 4. P-value comparisons between architecture for the CK+ dataset. With **c1** being the optimized architecture for CK+ Fig. 3, **c2** the optimized architecture for Oulu-CASIA Fig. 4, and **c3** the optimized architecture for Oulu-CASIA Fig. 4 pretrained on the Oulu-CASIA dataset

Fold										Average	P-value	Significance
	1	2	3	4	5	6	7	8	9	10			
c1	100	100	100	100	100	100	100	100	100	100	100		
c2	93.9	100	84.8	78.7	87.8	93.9	93.9	96.8	87.5	90	90.76	0.00057	Significant
c3	96.8	96.8	84.8	93.9	87.8	93.9	78.7	96.8	87.5	93.9	91.14	0.00067	Significant

4.4 Comparison with the State-of-the-Art

We evaluate the accuracy of our proposed network architecture. Our approach improves the results of the state-of-the-art on CK+ according to [7] using

Table 5. P-value comparisons between architecture for the Oulu-CASIA dataset. With **c1** being the optimized architecture for CK+ Fig. 3, **c2** the optimized architecture for Oulu-CASIA Fig. 4, and **c4** the optimized architecture for CK+ Fig. 3 pre-trained on the CK+ dataset

	Fold										Average	P-value	Significance
	1	2	3	4	5	6	7	8	9	10			
c2	97.5	97.5	80	82.5	82.5	80	72.5	97.5	75	77.5	84.25		
c1	81.2	81.2	70.8	75	72.9	72.9	83.3	72.9	72.9	87.5	77.08	0.03650	Significant
c4	85	97.5	75	82.5	77.5	70	65	97.5	75	72.5	79.75	0.00597	Significant

Table 6. LOSO results for CK+.

Approach	Accuracy (%)
CNN (AlexNet) [30]	94.4
DAE (DSAE) [31]	95.79
Our approach	**97.56**

Table 7. 10-fold results for CK+.

Approach	Accuracy (%)
LBP/Gabor + SRC [32]	98.09
DBN + MLP [33]	98.57
CNN [34]	98.62
FAN [27]	99.69
Our approach	**100**

Table 8. 10-fold results for Oulu-CASIA.

Approach	Accuracy (%)
FLT [3]	74.17
C3D [3]	74.38
FLT+C3D [3]	81.49
Our approach	84.17
STC [29]	84.72
LSTM (STC-NLSTM) [29]	**93.45**

Leave-One-Subject-Out cross-validation as shown in Table 6. The results of the state-of-the-art according to [2] using 10-fold cross-validation as shown in Table 7. Our approach yields to the best state-of-the-art results so far obtained on this dataset. Our model yields results in the range of the state-of-the-art on Oulu-CASIA using 10-fold cross-validation are shown in Table 8. Our model surpasses the results of [3], and yields similar results as the Spatio-temporal convolutional (STC) used in [29]. We believe that better results could be obtained on this dataset with our approach by focusing more on the temporal aspect by using an additional LSTM, as done in [29]. Finally, our results show the benefits of: (i) using 3D-CNNs over traditional CNN or CNN-LSTM approaches, (ii) an efficient hyper-parameter search for a considered 3D-CNN architecture.

Regarding this last point, if one looks at the final architectures shown in Fig. 3 and 4, one can see that they look very similar. However the best hyper-parameters are very different (see Tables 2 and 3). This is favor of our proposal that considers an efficient hyper-parameter space exploration.

5 Conclusion

We have proposed 3D-CNNs for video-based facial expression recognition. 3D-CNNs can extract very subtle temporal features that enables to go beyond 2D-CNNs. However their design can be delicate and we have proposed to use an efficient hyper-parameter search to address this issue. The experiments have confirmed the benefit of our approach. The results on CK+ show that our network surpasses the actual state-of-the-art results on CK+ with 97.56% for Leave-One-Subject-Out cross-validation and 100% for 10-fold subject-independent cross-validation. Similarly, a rate of 84.17% on Oulu-CASIA for 10-fold subject-independent cross-validation. In future works we plan to combine the video modality with audio recording.

References

1. Ekman, P., Friesen, W.V.: Constants across cultures in the face and emotion. J. Pers. Soc. Psychol. **17**(2), 124–129 (1971)
2. Huang, Y., Chen, F., Lv, S., Wang, X.: Facial expression recognition: a survey. Symmetry **11**(10) (2019)
3. Jung, H., Lee, S., Yim, J., Park, S., Kim, J.: Joint fine-tuning in deep neural networks for facial expression recognition. In: Proceedings of the IEEE International Conference on Computer Vision 2015 Inter, pp. 2983–2991 (2015)
4. Hasani, B., Mahoor, M.H.: Facial expression recognition using enhanced deep 3D convolutional neural networks, pp. 30–40, May 2017
5. Sharma, G., Singh, L., Gautam, S.: Automatic facial expression recognition using combined geometric features. 3D Res. **10**(2) (2019)
6. Mollahosseini, A., Chan, D., Mahoor, M.H.: Going deeper in facial expression recognition using deep neural networks. In: 2016 IEEE Winter Conference on Applications of Computer Vision, WACV 2016 (2016)
7. Li, S., Deng, W.: Deep facial expression recognition: a survey, pp. 1–25 (2018)
8. Ghimire, D., Lee, J., Li, Z.-N., Jeong, S.: Recognition of facial expressions based on salient geometric features and support vector machines. Multimed. Tools Appl. **76**(6), 7921–7946 (2016). https://doi.org/10.1007/s11042-016-3428-9
9. Nigam, S., Singh, R., Misra, A.K.: Local binary patterns based facial expression recognition for efficient smart applications. In: Hassanien, A.E., Elhoseny, M., Ahmed, S.H., Singh, A.K. (eds.) Security in Smart Cities: Models, Applications, and Challenges. LNITI, pp. 297–322. Springer, Cham (2019). https://doi.org/10.1007/978-3-030-01560-2_13
10. Graves, A., Liwicki, M., Fernández, S., Bertolami, R., Bunke, H., Schmidhuber, J.: A novel connectionist system for unconstrained handwriting recognition. IEEE Trans. Pattern Anal. Mach. Intell. **31**(5), 855–868 (2009)

11. Hochreiter, S., Schmidhuber, J.: Long short-term memory. Neural Comput. **9**(8), 1735–1780 (1997)
12. Li, T.H.S., Kuo, P.H., Tsai, T.N., Luan, P.C.: CNN and LSTM based facial expression analysis model for a humanoid robot. IEEE Access **7**, 93998–94011 (2019)
13. Jain, N., Kumar, S., Kumar, A., Shamsolmoali, P., Zareapoor, M.: Hybrid deep neural networks for face emotion recognition. Pattern Recogn. Lett. **115**, 101–106 (2018)
14. Tran, D., Bourdev, L., Fergus, R., Torresani, L., Paluri, M.: Learning spatiotemporal features with 3D convolutional networks. In: Proceedings of the IEEE International Conference on Computer Vision 2015 International Conference on Computer Vision, ICCV 2015, pp. 4489–4497 (2015)
15. Zhao, J., Mao, X., Zhang, J.: Learning deep facial expression features from image and optical flow sequences using 3D CNN. Vis. Comput. **34**(10), 1461–1475 (2018). https://doi.org/10.1007/s00371-018-1477-y
16. Teja Reddy, S.P., Teja Karri, S., Dubey, S.R., Mukherjee, S.: Spontaneous facial micro-expression recognition using 3D spatiotemporal convolutional neural networks. In: 2019 International Joint Conference on Neural Networks (IJCNN), vol. 2019-July, pp. 1–8. IEEE, July 2019
17. Ioffe, S., Szegedy, C.: Batch normalization: accelerating deep network training by reducing internal covariate shift. In: 32nd International Conference on Machine Learning, ICML 2015, vol. 1, pp. 448–456 (2015)
18. Taylor, L., Nitschke, G.: Improving deep learning using generic data augmentation (2017)
19. Akiba, T., Sano, S., Yanase, T., Ohta, T., Koyama, M.: Optuna: a next-generation hyperparameter optimization framework. In: Proceedings of the ACM SIGKDD International Conference on Knowledge Discovery and Data Mining, pp. 2623–2631 (2019)
20. Bergstra, J., Bardenet, R., Bengio, Y., Kégl, B.: Algorithms for hyper-parameter optimization. In: Advances in Neural Information Processing Systems 24: 25th Annual Conference on Neural Information Processing Systems 2011, NIPS 2011, pp. 1–9 (2011)
21. Zhang, M.R., Lucas, J., Hinton, G., Ba, J.: Lookahead optimizer: k steps forward, 1 step back, pp. 1–16, July 2019
22. Reza, A.M.: Realization of the contrast limited adaptive histogram equalization (CLAHE) for real-time image enhancement. J. VLSI Signal Process. Syst. Signal Image Video Technol. **38**(1), 35–44 (2004)
23. Nawi, N.M., Atomi, W.H., Rehman, M.: The effect of data pre-processing on optimized training of artificial neural networks. Procedia Technol. **11**(Iceei), 32–39 (2013)
24. Glorot, X., Bengio, Y.: Understanding the difficulty of training deep feedforward neural networks. J. Mach. Learn. Res. **9**, 249–256 (2010)
25. Misra, D.: Mish: a self regularized non-monotonic neural activation function (1), August 2019
26. Lucey, P., Cohn, J.F., Kanade, T., Saragih, J., Ambadar, Z., Matthews, I.: The extended Cohn-Kanade dataset (CK+): a complete dataset for action unit and emotion-specified expression. In: 2010 IEEE Computer Society Conference on Computer Vision and Pattern Recognition - Workshops, pp. 94–101, no. July, IEEE, June 2010
27. Meng, D., Peng, X., Wang, K., Qiao, Y.: Frame attention networks for facial expression recognition in videos. In: Proceedings - International Conference on Image Processing, ICIP 2019-Septe(September), pp. 3866–3870 (2019)

28. Zhao, G., Huang, X., Taini, M., Li, S.Z., Pietikäinen, M.: Facial expression recognition from near-infrared videos. Image Vis. Comput. **29**(9), 607–619 (2011)
29. Yu, Z., Liu, G., Liu, Q., Deng, J.: Spatio-temporal convolutional features with nested LSTM for facial expression recognition. Neurocomputing **317**, 50–57 (2018)
30. Ouellet, S.: Real-time emotion recognition for gaming using deep convolutional network features, pp. 1–6 (2014)
31. Zeng, N., Zhang, H., Song, B., Liu, W., Li, Y., Dobaie, A.M.: Facial expression recognition via learning deep sparse autoencoders. Neurocomputing **273**, 643–649 (2018)
32. Zhang, S., Zhao, X., Lei, B.: Facial expression recognition using sparse representation. WSEAS Trans. Syst. **11**(8), 440–452 (2012)
33. Zhao, X., Shi, X., Zhang, S.: Facial expression recognition via deep learning. IETE Tech. Rev. (Inst. Electron. Telecommun. Eng. India) **32**(5), 347–355 (2015)
34. Breuer, R., Kimmel, R.: A deep learning perspective on the origin of facial expressions, pp. 1–16 (2017)

Reducing Triangle Inequality Violations with Deep Learning and Its Application to Image Retrieval

Izat Khamiyev[✉], Magzhan Gabidolla, Alisher Iskakov, and M. Fatih Demirci

Department of Computer Science, Nazarbayev University, Nur-Sultan, Kazakhstan
`izat.khamiyev@nu.edu.kz`

Abstract. Given a distance matrix with triangular inequality violations, the metric nearness problem requires to find the closest matrix that satisfies the triangle inequality. It has been experimentally shown that deep neural networks can be used to efficiently produce close matrices with a fewer number of triangular inequality violations. This paper further extends the deep learning approach to the metric nearness problem by applying it to the content-based image retrieval. Since vantage space representation of an image database requires distances to satisfy triangle inequalities, applying deep learning to the matrices in the vantage space with triangular inequality violations produces distance matrices with a fewer number of violations. Experiments performed on the Corel-1k dataset demonstrate that fully convolutional autoencoders considerably reduce triangular inequality violations on distance matrices. Overall, the image retrieval accuracy based on the distance matrices generated by the deep learning model is better than that based on the original matrices in 91.16% of the time.

Keywords: Deep learning · Convolutional neural networks · Image retrieval · Metric nearness

1 Introduction

Content-based image retrieval methods, as well as other methods in computer vision, usually rely on distance functions, which satisfy metric properties. The distance function of any two images incorporates a notion of similarity and is often computed from image representations, such as shape and texture. Formally, a distance function defined for objects in an arbitrary set X is a metric if it satisfies the following conditions for all $x, y, z \in X$:

1. $d(x, y) \geq 0$
2. $d(x, y) = 0 \Leftrightarrow x = y$
3. $d(x, y) = d(y, x)$
4. $d(x, z) \leq d(x, y) + d(y, z)$

G. Bebis et al. (Eds.): ISVC 2020, LNCS 12510, pp. 310–318, 2020.
https://doi.org/10.1007/978-3-030-64559-5_24

The last condition is triangle inequality, which states that for any three objects in a set, the distance between any two of them is not larger than the sum of distances between these two objects and intermediate objects. The triangle inequality property is also required in many image retrieval techniques. However, this condition is often violated due to the noise in the real-world data. Moreover, as shown in [2], human similarity judgment does not obey this property. Intuitively, a mermaid is looking similar to both a human and a fish, but a human is much different from a fish, as can be seen in Fig. 1.

Fig. 1. Human similarity judgment do not obey triangle inequality.

As mentioned before, some image retrieval methods require distances to obey all the properties of a metric. For example, a method proposed by [13], which utilizes vantage objects for image retrieval, specifically employs the triangle inequality property to calculate the resemblance of any two objects based on their similarity to a vantage object. More specifically, this method embeds objects into a k-dimensional vector space, which represents a resemblance of that object to each of the k vantage objects (see Fig. 2). Demirci [3] employed the algorithm proposed in [12] to restore the triangle inequality property between the entries in a distance matrix and greatly improved the computation time of the vantage object retrieval with a small trade-off in accuracy. The algorithm [12] removes triangle inequality violations (TIVs) in a distance matrix by finding another distance matrix closest to the input but with no violations. More formally, given an input distance matrix D, the algorithm searches for M such that:

$$M \in \arg\min_{X} \|X - D\| \tag{1}$$

Gabidolla et al. [4] showed that it is possible to train a deep learning model that removes most of the TIVs by finding a very close distance matrix. The proposed work, which builds upon [4] shows that our deep learning-based TIV fixing model can greatly improve the performance of the image retrieval framework using vantage objects. We experiment with image retrieval with natural images and implement a model for removing TIVs in a distance matrix employed

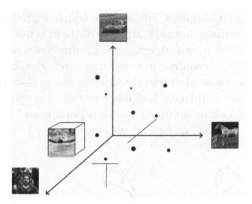

Fig. 2. Vantage space with 3 dimensions. A swimmer is more similar to a human vantage image than the other two.

in image retrieval. Using the distance matrix produced by our model yields a far better retrieval accuracy when compared to the one using the original distance matrix. An overview of our framework is shown in Fig. 3.

The next section discusses the related work in image retrieval. After that, we describe our methodology, dataset, and how we generated data for training our model in Sect. 3. The results of our experiments are presented in Sect. 4, and then we proceed to discussion. The last section contains a conclusion of our work.

2   Related Work

Gabidolla et al. [4] for the first time proposed a deep learning approach to solve the metric nearness problem. The authors created synthetic data with TIVs and used the triangle fixing algorithm [12] to produce ground truth target matrices. They performed a number of experiments with different deep learning architectures to empirically find which models work better for this task. According to the results, the best working models were fully convolutional networks in the form of autoencoders.

After the success of convolutional neural networks (CNN) in image classification [6], the features of CNNs were applied to content-based image retrieval [1]. In spite of being trained on different tasks, CNN features showed improved results in image retrieval. Gordo et al. [5] train CNNs specifically for image retrieval using a three-stream Siamese network to extract region-based features, and achieves superior performance. Liu et al. [7] utilize deep features to produce hashing based image retrieval. To mitigate the need for a large amount of hand-labeled training data, Radenovic et al. [9] use the output of reconstructed 3D models in the training of CNNs for image retrieval, and experimentally show better results. Song et al. [11] leverage generative adversarial networks to produce binary codes from images in an unsupervised way for more effective binary

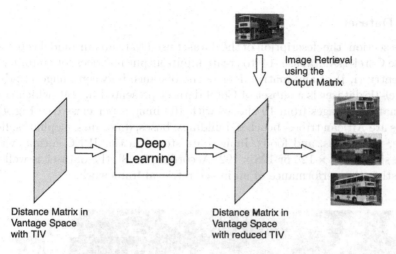

Fig. 3. An overview diagram of the proposed framework. After reducing the TIVs using deep learning, we perform image retrieval.

hashing. Zhang et al. [15] build a zero-shot hashing framework using orthogonal projection of both images and semantic information to produce image retrieval on unseen classes. The reader is referred to Zhou et al. [16] for a recent extensive review of content-based image retrieval.

Vleugels and Veltkamp proposed the idea of representing images in vantage space for efficient image retrieval [13]. After choosing some m number of pre-determined vantage images, all the images in a database are represented as m dimensional vector of distances to the vantage objects. Using an efficient nearest neighbor search algorithm in the vantage space for a query image, the authors experimentally demonstrated an efficient image retrieval scheme. However, the main requirement for this approach is that the distance function used to measure the image similarity must satisfy metric properties, particularly the triangle inequality property.

3 Methodology

Our main goal is to offer a deep neural network trained with input matrices containing TIVs and with the target of metric matrices so that TIVs are reduced with the restriction that the output matrix should be as close as possible to the input matrix. Given a distance (or, dissimilarity) matrix as input, we then reduce TIVs and generate an output matrix using the deep learning model. Finally, we show that image retrieval based on this output yields superior results over the one obtained from the input matrix.

3.1 Dataset

In this section, the description of the dataset used to train our model is presented. We use Corel-1k database [14] to create input-output matrices for training, where each entry (i, j) of any matrix depicts the distance between image i and image j. Corel-1k dataset is a subset of Corel dataset presented in [14], which contains 1000 natural images from 10 classes with 100 images per class (see Fig. 4). The classes are African tribes, beaches, buildings, buses, dinosaurs, elephants, flowers, horses, mountains, and foods. Images are stored in the JPEG format with the image size of 192 × 128 or 128 × 192. According to [8], the dataset is well suited for testing the performance of an image retrieval framework.

Fig. 4. Representative view of each category in Corel-1k database

3.2 Data Generation for Deep Learning

As mentioned before, each entry of the input matrix is the distance between the corresponding images. Given a pair of images i and j, we first represent each image using its deep features and find the distance between their features to compute the value located in the matrix entry (i, j). More specifically, we use *vgg11_bn* model [10] and take the last fully connected layer of size 1 × 4096 as the feature vector. We then calculate the Euclidean distance between two such feature vectors. However, because the Euclidean distance satisfies metric properties by definition, the distance calculation was modified to create matrices with TIVs in order to train the deep neural network. Since our goal is to apply efficient image retrieval using vantage objects, the matrices were created as discussed in [13]. In particular, one random image of each class in Corel-1k was chosen to be the vantage object and the remaining 29 images from each class were used to create the vantage space. Hence, one vantage space can be viewed as a 10 × 290 matrix, where each entry is the Euclidean distance between the feature vectors of the corresponding images. In order to simulate triangular inequalities within the matrix, the following modification was performed.

Firstly, two random pairs of vantage objects were chosen and combined together, thus reducing the dimensionality of the vantage space from 10 to 8. Secondly, when calculating the distance between query q and the combined vantage object $(v_i v_j)$, the distance was obtained as $min(d(q, v_i), d(q, v_j))$, where

$d(q, v_i)$ (or, $d(q, v_j)$) represent the Euclidean distance between the feature vectors of images q and v_i (or, q and v_j). Here, calculating the distance between the query image and any of the vantage objects that were not combined remained as before. Since the resulting matrix did not satisfy the metric properties, it was used as an input matrix to train. In this setup, the target matrix was created by randomly deleting one object from vantage objects that were paired. The target matrix contained no TIVs due to the fact that its distances were obtained using the Euclidean distances. For training, we created 50000 such matrices with the average 39.45 TIVs per input matrix.

3.3 Model

The training and testing of the deep networks were performed on Nvidia Quadro P2000 GPU with 5 GB GDDR5 memory. We initially proposed two models. The first one was the feed-forward neural network, however, training the model required too many layers and therefore could not fit in memory. Hence, convolutional neural networks came to handle this problem. According to [4], it was experimentally shown that fully convolutional autoencoders perform well in solving the metric nearness problem. Therefore, we experimented with a number of convolutional autoencoders with different hyperparameters (see Fig. 5). The model was constructed so that it takes a matrix of size 8×290 and produces a matrix of the same dimensions. The dataset consisted of 50000 input-target objects and it was split into 30000 matrices for training, 10000 matrices for validation, and 10000 matrices for testing. From validation, the loss function that showed the best performance was the mean squared error loss (MSELoss) function, and the optimizer was Stochastic Gradient Descent (SGD) with a learning rate 0.01.

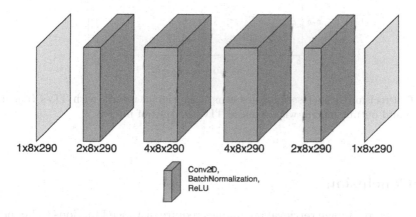

1x8x290   2x8x290   4x8x290   4x8x290   2x8x290   1x8x290

Conv2D,
BatchNormalization,
ReLU

Fig. 5. Fully convolutional autoencoder

4   Results

According to the results, the proposed deep neural network reduced TIVs by 97% on average. Moreover, the output matrices were relatively close to the input matrices in terms of Mean Squared Error (MSE), with an average MSE of 2.83% per entry.

To evaluate the performance of image retrieval using the output matrices generated by the deep learning model, 300 images (30 images from each class of Corel-1k) that were not used in training were selected for testing. The perturbed matrix with TIVs was created using the methodology presented in the previous section. For each query image, its k-closest images were obtained from the vantage space through the range-search algorithm. For comparison, we performed the same range-search for each query using the input matrices with TIVs.

In this experimental setup, we calculated the precision as the percentage of retrieved images that had the same class as the query. Figure 6 shows the average precision as a function of k-closest images. The results reveal that in 91.16% of the time, the image retrieval performed on the output matrices with reduced TIVs yields superior results over the one obtained from the original matrices. Although TIVs were not completely removed, the results still demonstrate the importance of the proposed framework yielding improved performance when applied to image retrieval.

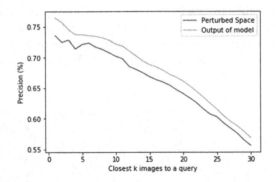

Fig. 6. Precision vs k-closest images using the original matrix with TIVs (perturbed space) and output matrix with reduced TIVs (output of model).

5   Conclusion

Many effective image retrieval techniques require distance functions to be metric. On the other hand, it is well known that partial image matching yields distance matrices with triangle inequality violations (TIVs). In this paper, we used a deep learning framework for reducing TIVs in a distance matrix and successfully applied the resulting matrix for improved image retrieval. Although the proposed framework originated from metric nearness, the way the ground truth target matrices were generated diverged the proposed methodology from the original metric nearness problem. The metric nearness problem requires that the output matrix is the closest matrix with zero TIVs. Our future work will focus on completely removing TIVs, while obtaining better image retrieval accuracy.

Acknowledgements. This work has been funded in part by the Nazarbayev University faculty development grant project "Forming Reliable Feature Correspondences and Distortion-free Graph Embedding with Deep Learning". Project PI - M.F. Demirci, Grant 110119FD4530.

References

1. Babenko, A., Slesarev, A., Chigorin, A., Lempitsky, V.: Neural codes for image retrieval. In: Fleet, D., Pajdla, T., Schiele, B., Tuytelaars, T. (eds.) ECCV 2014. LNCS, vol. 8689, pp. 584–599. Springer, Cham (2014). https://doi.org/10.1007/978-3-319-10590-1_38
2. Bronstein, A.M., Bronstein, M.M., Bruckstein, A.M., Kimmel, R.: Partial similarity of objects, or how to compare a centaur to a horse. Int. J. Comput. Vis. **84**(2), 163 (2008)
3. Demirci, M.F.: Efficient shape retrieval under partial matching. In: 2010 20th International Conference on Pattern Recognition, pp. 3057–3060, August 2010
4. Gabidolla, M., Iskakov, A., Demirci, M.F., Yazici, A.: On approximating metric nearness through deep learning. In: Rutkowski, L., Scherer, R., Korytkowski, M., Pedrycz, W., Tadeusiewicz, R., Zurada, J.M. (eds.) ICAISC 2019. LNCS (LNAI), vol. 11508, pp. 62–72. Springer, Cham (2019). https://doi.org/10.1007/978-3-030-20912-4_6
5. Gordo, A., Almazán, J., Revaud, J., Larlus, D.: Deep image retrieval: learning global representations for image search. In: Leibe, B., Matas, J., Sebe, N., Welling, M. (eds.) ECCV 2016. LNCS, vol. 9910, pp. 241–257. Springer, Cham (2016). https://doi.org/10.1007/978-3-319-46466-4_15
6. Krizhevsky, A., Sutskever, I., Hinton, G.E.: ImageNet classification with deep convolutional neural networks. Commun. ACM **60**(6), 84–90 (2017)
7. Liu, H., Wang, R., Shan, S., Chen, X.: Deep supervised hashing for fast image retrieval. In: The IEEE Conference on Computer Vision and Pattern Recognition (CVPR), June 2016
8. Murala, S., Maheshwari, R., Balasubramanian, R.: Directional local extrema patterns: a new descriptor for content based image retrieval. Int. J. Multimed. Inf. Retrieval **1**(3), 191–203 (2012)
9. Radenovic, F., Tolias, G., Chum, O.: Fine-tuning CNN image retrieval with no human annotation. CoRR abs/1711.02512 (2017). http://arxiv.org/abs/1711.02512
10. Simonyan, K., Zisserman, A.: Very deep convolutional networks for large-scale image recognition. arXiv preprint arXiv:1409.1556 (2014)
11. Song, J.: Binary generative adversarial networks for image retrieval. CoRR abs/1708.04150 (2017). http://arxiv.org/abs/1708.04150
12. Sra, S., Tropp, J., Dhillon, I.S.: Triangle fixing algorithms for the metric nearness problem. In: Saul, L.K., Weiss, Y., Bottou, L. (eds.) Advances in Neural Information Processing Systems 17, pp. 361–368. MIT Press (2005)

13. Vleugels, J., Veltkamp, R.C.: Efficient image retrieval through vantage objects. Pattern Recogn. **35**(1), 69–80 (2002)
14. Wang, J.Z., Li, J., Wiederhold, G.: Simplicity: semantics-sensitive integrated matching for picture libraries. IEEE Trans. Pattern Anal. Mach. Intell. **9**, 947–963 (2001)
15. Zhang, H., Long, Y., Shao, L.: Zero-shot hashing with orthogonal projection for image retrieval. Pattern Recogn. Lett. **117** (2018). https://doi.org/10.1016/j.patrec.2018.04.011
16. Zhou, W., Li, H., Tian, Q.: Recent advance in content-based image retrieval: a literature survey. CoRR abs/1706.06064 (2017). http://arxiv.org/abs/1706.06064

A Driver Guidance System to Support the Stationary Wireless Charging of Electric Vehicles

Bijan Shahbaz Nejad[✉], Peter Roch, Marcus Handte, and Pedro José Marrón

University of Duisburg-Essen, Essen, Germany
bijan.shahbaz-nejad@uni-due.de

Abstract. Air pollution is a problem in many cities. Although it is possible to mitigate this problem by replacing combustion with electric engines, at the time of writing, electric vehicles are still a rarity in European cities. Reasons for not buying an electric vehicle are not only the high purchase costs but also the uncomfortable initiation of the charging process. A more convenient alternative is wireless charging, which is enabled by integrating an induction plate into the floor and installing a charging interface at the vehicle. To maximize efficiency, the vehicle's charging interface must be positioned accurately above the induction plate which is integrated into the floor. Since the driver cannot perceive the region below the vehicle, it is difficult to precisely align the position of the charging interface by maneuvering the vehicle. In this paper, we first discuss the requirements for driver guidance systems that help drivers to accurately position their vehicle and thus, enables them to maximize the charging efficiency. Thereafter, we present a prototypical implementation of such a system. To minimize the deployment cost for charging station operators, our prototype uses an inexpensive off-the-shelf camera system to localize the vehicles that are approaching the station. To simplify the retrofitting of existing vehicles, the prototype uses a smartphone app to generate navigation visualizations. To validate the approach, we present experiments indicating that, despite its low cost, the prototype can technically achieve the necessary precision.

Keywords: Human-computer interaction · Visualization · Computer vision · Pose estimation · Driver guidance

1 Introduction

Electric vehicles can help to reduce air pollution in cities. Although many governments subsidize electric vehicles, they are not often bought. The reasons for this are, besides the high purchase costs, the short-range due to the battery capacity and the necessary planning of the charging intervals. For a vehicle to be charged, it must be manually connected to the charging station. This requires the driver to get out of the vehicle and physically connect the car to a charging station,

© Springer Nature Switzerland AG 2020
G. Bebis et al. (Eds.): ISVC 2020, LNCS 12510, pp. 319–331, 2020.
https://doi.org/10.1007/978-3-030-64559-5_25

which can be tedious. Wireless charging can help to make the process more comfortable but requires additional charging components. As described in [20], an induction plate is typically integrated into the floor and a compatible charging interface is installed on a vehicle's underbody. To maximize the efficiency of the charging process, the charging components must be accurately aligned [6]. This includes that the air gap between the charging components does not exceed a certain threshold. Moreover, there is the problem that both charging components must be aligned by moving the vehicle into the correct position. In terms of precision, the vehicle must be positioned an order of magnitude more accurate than it is required for parking. It is difficult for a driver to accurately align the charging components because they are out of the driver's field of vision. In [2], two studies show that only 5% of the vehicles were positioned precisely enough to enable efficient wireless charging. To mitigate the problem, a driver guidance system can be used to support the driver when positioning the vehicle. In this paper, we discuss the requirements for driver guidance systems to enable efficient wireless charging. We present a prototype that extends a wireless charging station with an inexpensive off-the-shelf camera system to determine the position of a nearby vehicle. Furthermore, we use a smartphone app to minimize the vehicle's retrofitting effort which visualizes supportive feedback inside of the car. A wireless charging station is being deployed as part of the TALAKO-project ("Taxi Charging Concept for Public Spaces") [1]. Since the construction work has not yet been completed, we validate the precision and usability of the prototype from a technical point of view. As soon as the charging station has been built, we will analyze whether our driver guidance system is also suitable for practical use under real conditions.

2   Wireless Charging

Wired charging of an electric vehicle encompasses several steps. The driver must park, get out of the vehicle, and use a cable to establish a physical connection between the car and the charging station. For this, a parking lot with a charging station is needed. In contrast to most gas stations, many charging stations do not have a roof to protect the driver from environmental influences such as rain or snow, which can make wired charging in bad weather a cumbersome experience. When charging wirelessly, the driver does not have to get out of the car. This means that exposition to environmental influences is comparable to regular parking and the driver can save the time that would be required to initialize the charging process. A wireless charger for electric vehicles consists of a transmitting coil and a receiving coil, compensation network, and power electronics converters [15]. Since electric vehicles and charging stations produced by many manufacturers do not support wireless charging, retrofitting may be necessary. To quickly charge vehicles, high field strengths are needed, which can be dangerous [10]. To mitigate this problem, the transmitter coil is usually integrated into the floor and the receiver coil is attached to the underbody of the vehicle. This way, the chassis can shield nearby persons from most of the radiation.

Efficient wireless charging can only take place if the vehicle's charging interface is precisely aligned above the induction plate that is integrated into the floor. To do this, the driver must maneuver the vehicle manually into an appropriate position. In comparison to regular parking, this is more complicated, because the charging interface is located under the vehicle and thus out of the driver's field of vision. When parking, it is usually sufficient to achieve a positioning accuracy in the range of a few decimeters. For efficient wireless charging, the required accuracy is in the range of a few centimeters and thus, an order of magnitude higher. It is unlikely that drivers can achieve this without further support. Thus, a driver guidance system becomes a fundamental prerequisite to enable the efficient wireless charging of electric vehicles.

3   Requirements for Driver Guidance Systems

The goal is to enable the driver to precisely align the charging interface of the vehicle above the plate that is integrated into the floor. Various approaches could be taken to reach this goal. For example, markings on the ground could be used, which can serve as an orientation during the positioning. Moreover, parking stoppers that protrude from the floor can serve as physical limitations. Alternatively, mechanical systems can be used, which automatically bring both charging components into an aligned position. The problem of markers and parking stoppers is that they are not applicable when multiple vehicle types with various dimensions should be charged. A dimension specific marker- or parking stopper setup for each vehicle type would be required. In addition, the driver's sitting position and vehicle's dimensions differ, there is no guarantee that the markings will be fully visible from the driver's perspective. Dirt or changing weather conditions such as rain or snow might also influence the visibility of the markings. On the one hand, the parking stoppers' advantage is that they are usually more visible than markings and are not quickly covered by dirt or snow because they protrude from the ground. Yet, parking stoppers can cause injuries if people trip over them. The advantage of a mechanical system is that it can be used for different types of vehicles, for example by using multiple configurations. However, buying and installing a mechanical system is expensive. In addition, complicated maintenance work may be required since vandalism or street cleaning can cause damage if, for example, parts protrude from the floor. If several vehicle types should be supported and expensive mechanical systems are to be avoided, an orientation system is required to help the driver to align the charging components. The driver cannot achieve this accuracy without any guidance. Therefore, we derive the following requirements for a driver guidance system to support wireless charging of electric vehicles:

Generic. The dimensions of vehicles can vary depending on the vehicle type. Moreover, the position of the charging interface can be attached to various positions on the underbody of the vehicle. It is necessary that the driver guidance system can be used independently of these properties so that ideally all drivers can be supported.

Cost Efficient. Adjustments of existing components or the installation of new components for driver guidance can be expensive. Hence it is necessary to minimize the number of components required to realize the system and to rely on off-the-shelf components, if possible.

Robust. Since it is difficult for a driver to properly align the charging interface by maneuvering the car, the driver guidance system is a critical part of the charging station whose down times severely affect the station's availability. As a result, it is necessary to ensure that the system is robust with respect to external factors such as vandalism or bad weather and that it relies on components that do not induce additional maintenance effort.

Precise. Efficient wireless charging can only take place, if the charging interface of the electric vehicle is aligned accurately over the induction plate which is integrated into the floor. Although, the acceptable tolerances may vary depending on the coil configuration, the accuracy requirements of current systems usually range around 10 cm.

Usable. Ideally, using the driver guidance system to initiate the charging process should be as convenient and quick as parking a vehicle with an internal combustion engine. In addition, the interactions with the driver guidance system should not distract the driver.

4   Prototype

In the following, we present a prototype for a driver guidance system that we developed based on the requirements described previously. First, we motivate the system architecture and then discuss the individual system components. An overview of the architecture is depicted in Fig. 1.

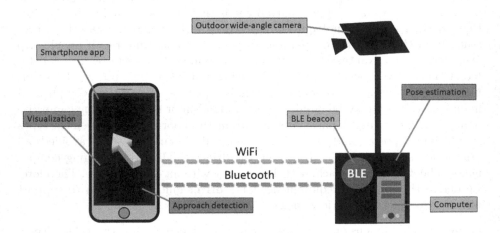

Fig. 1. Architecture of the driver guidance system. Blue squares indicate components and green squares indicate their primary functions. (Color figure online)

4.1   System Architecture

To automatically assist a driver in the alignment process, the relative position of the charging plate integrated into the floor and the charging interface installed on the underbody of the vehicle must be determined. This requires a positioning mechanism. Based on the determined positions, the driver must be informed about the current positioning situation so that the driver can counteract if misalignments occur. There are various technologies with which positioning can be carried out, such as GPS (Global Positioning System) or RFID (Radio-frequency identification). We use a camera because high accuracy can be achieved if the resolution of the captured images is sufficiently high. Cameras are inexpensive and do not require maintenance. Moreover, due to their ubiquitous use in surveillance applications, ruggedized variants, that are weather- and vandal-proof are widely available. Conceptually, there are two ways to attach the camera. The camera can either be mounted on the vehicle or attached to the charging station. When attaching a camera to a vehicle several issues must be addressed. First, without further precautions, the camera can become dirty while driving. Also, the induction plate is only visible when the camera is pointed at it. For this reason, multiple cameras may be required to be installed around the vehicle, which can lead to higher costs. If the location of the induction plate is visually not differing from the surrounding floor, additional markings may be required on it. To avoid the issues resulting from a vehicle integration and to minimize the cost, our system extends the charging station with a single wide-angle camera. To minimize the effect of environmental factors, we use a ruggedized and weather-proof case and propose to mount the camera at the top of the station so that it cannot be manipulated easily by people that are passing by. Besides from increasing the robustness, this mounting position also ensures that the

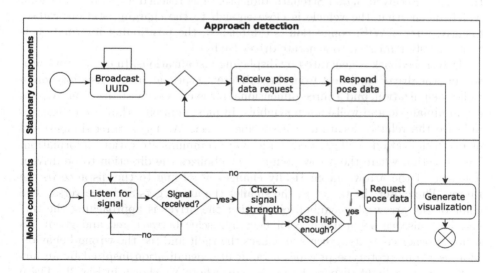

Fig. 2. Abstract overview of the approach detection process.

camera can easily detect vehicles that are approaching. Like the camera setup, there are also many possibilities to provide the driver with feedback on the current positioning situation. As with the positioning system, we pay attention to the aspect of cost-efficiency. Instead of integrating additional components into the vehicle, we propose to use a smartphone app to generate feedback for the driver using visualizations. In terms of usability, there is also the advantage that most drivers can already operate a smartphone and do not need to acclimate to new hardware devices. However, due to this combination of decisions, we have a distributed system design where the location detected by the camera on the charging station must be transmitted to the smartphone of the driver. To do this, it is necessary to establish a connection between the camera system and the smartphone app. Since this connection must be reliable and exhibit a low latency, our system does not use the cellular network but instead relies on a WiFi connection that is established, when the car approaches the station. To ensure that the driver does not have to interact with the phone while driving, our prototype fully automates the setup process.

4.2   Mobile Components

One of the two primary functions of the smartphone app is an approach detection mechanism. It automatically recognizes via a background service whether the vehicle is near the charging station to start the driver guidance. An overview of the procedure is illustrated in Fig. 2. A separate BLE (Bluetooth Low Energy) beacon in the camera system continuously broadcasts a signal with a charging station specific UUID (Universally Unique Identifier). At the same time, a background process of the smartphone app listens to whether a nearby charging station is sending a signal. If a signal is received, it is checked whether the RSSI (Received Signal Strength Indicator) has reached a certain threshold, which means that the vehicle is close enough to the charging station. Subsequently, after a WiFi connection is established, the positioning information is continuously requested to generate driver feedback.

Driver feedback is generated by displaying visualizations. In our current prototype, the driver can select from three different types, an arrow-visualization, a radar visualization, and a three-dimensional birds-eye view visualization. Arrows are minimalistic and well-known symbols. In most contexts, they are utilized to indicate the relative location of a specific object. We use a three-dimensional arrow visualization as illustrated in Fig. 3a to communicate various information. The direction where the arrow points to symbolizes the direction to be driven. The size of the arrow automatically changes according to the distance to the target. The closer the target is, the smaller the arrow gets and vice versa. The color of the arrow also symbolizes whether the driver is approaching the target. For this, we use a linear color encoding scale between red and green. As usual in other contexts, green symbolizes the right and red the wrong behavior. Moreover, our prototype provides a radar-like visualization inspired by an aircraft's primary flight display. Example screenshots are shown in Fig. 3b. There is a circular area with various distance markings and two moving red lines. The horizontal line symbolizes the distance from the vehicle's charging interface to the induction plate which is integrated into the floor. The vertical line shows the offset in the left or right direction. The goal of the driver is to arrange both lines as centrally as possible in the middle of the circle so that they cross in the green area. Our third visualization imitates the positioning area from a birds-eye view using 3D graphics. The amount of information presented has been reduced to the bare minimum. An example is shown in Fig. 3c. The location of the induction plate is indicated by a hollow cylinder, which is also delimited by a circular area. There is a circle on the vehicle that symbolizes the location of the vehicle's charging interface. The charging components are aligned if the vehicle's circle is completely inside the induction plate's hollow cylinder. To increase the level of detail, there is the possibility to change the zoom level.

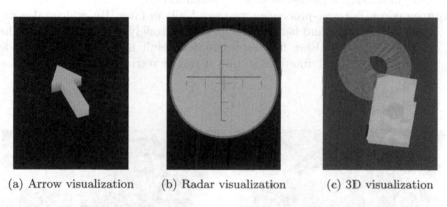

(a) Arrow visualization   (b) Radar visualization   (c) 3D visualization

Fig. 3. Driver feedback visualizations. (Color figure online)

4.3 Stationary Components

Our camera system is composed of a ruggedized outdoor wide-angle camera that is connected to a computer, and a separate BLE beacon for the approach detection mechanism. The camera is installed at the charging station so that at least the entire positioning area can be recorded. In this way, the vehicle can already be perceived when it is several meters away from the induction plate. The captured images are retrieved by a computer vision software which is implemented using OpenCV [11] to estimate the pose of the electric vehicle. We define the pose as the three-dimensional rotation and the translation relative to the camera's position. Some preparation steps are necessary for this. The camera needs to be calibrated by determining the camera matrix and the distortion coefficients so that the recorded frames can be undistorted. Besides, the position of the induction plate, which is integrated into the floor, must be specified. Moreover, vehicle type-specific dimensions, as well as the relative offset from the car's origin of the receiver coil must be specified. Given this configuration, the steps to estimate the pose are:

Preprocessing. The image is undistorted, and it is semantically divided into foreground and background using Background Subtraction [21]. We assume that the probability is high that vehicles get classified as part of the foreground. The remaining computations are then solely performed on the foreground image.

Estimation. The vehicle's pose is determined using a wheel detection algorithm, which detects the wheels of the vehicle based on their circular shape, as illustrated in Fig. 4a. At the beginning various filters are applied to reduce noise in the image. Then the Hough circle transformation [13] is utilized to find circles that represent the wheels. To filter false positives, we reject circles that are outside of reasonable limits. Then four points of a resulting wheel pair are used to compute the object pose from 3D-2D point correspondences, using infinitesimal plane-based pose estimation [4].

Aggregation. For post-processing, we use a Kalman-filter [19], which takes past poses into account and helps to compensate strongly deviating poses. When aggregation step finishes the last computed result is continuously provided via WiFi on a REST interface so that it can be retrieved by the smartphone app.

(a) Wheels detected by Wheel Detection Estimator.

(b) ArUco markers detected by Marker-based Estimator.

Fig. 4. Illustration of the techniques being applied to estimate the pose.

5 Validation

The design of our prototype system described in the previous section is geared towards achieving a low cost and a high robustness. For the latter, we refrain from requiring any mechanical components and instead leverage a camera system that is mounted on the station. For the former, we do not require any components to be installed in the car and we solely rely on a single off-the-shelf camera with an associated computer and a BLE beacon. Given a configuration of different car models with their position of wireless charging interfaces, it is also trivial to achieve the desired genericity. To rigorously evaluate the usability and precision, measurements must be carried out under real conditions. As part of the TALAKO-project, we are deploying a wireless charging station that will be tested under realistic conditions by taxi drivers. However, since the construction work is still ongoing, we present an experimental validation which indicates that the system can achieve the necessary precision and usability from a technical point of view.

5.1 Precision

In this section, we experimentally investigate whether the precision of the camera system's pose estimation technically fulfills the precision requirement. To put the results in perspective, we compare the pose estimation through wheel detection with pose estimation based on a board of five ArUco [7] markers depicted in Fig. 4b. ArUco markers are specifically designed to facilitate a fast and precise detection, however, due to esthetic reasons, we think that they are ill-suited for practical deployments. To achieve natural illumination and reflections, the experiment is conducted in an outdoor parking area. An illustration of the experimental setup is presented in Fig. 5. For the experiment the vehicle, which is illustrated in Fig. 4, is positioned sideways at the angles of 0° and 10° at the distances of 3, 4, and 5 m in front of the system's camera. A marker board composed of five ArUco markers with different IDs each having a side length of 15 cm is being attached to the vehicle, as illustrated in Fig. 4a. A video with a resolution of 1280 × 720 is recorded for each pose, of which 30 images are used by the background subtractor and 20 frames are forwarded to the pose estimators to determine the distance as well as the rotation of the vehicle. We examine the Wheel Detection Estimator as well as the Marker-based Estimator which is utilizing the entire marker board as well as using the single markers individually. Table 1 shows how accurate the estimators can detect the wheels and the markers, and Fig. 6 visualizes the error in estimating the pose by each estimator. The marker board and its individual markers are found in almost all cases, but inaccurately recognized corner points lead to imprecise pose estimation. Reasons for the inaccurate detection of the corner points can be the marker size which might be too small, as well as the resolution of the recorded frames, which might be too low. Although the measurements of the Marker-based Estimator exhibit a low precision, the marker detection works consistently, even when the vehicle's rotation changes. Using bigger markers might increase the precision, but at the same time further reduces their practical applicability. In contrast to the markers, the wheels can be detected in 75.8% of all frames. In the case of the experiment at 3 m distance and 10° of rotation, no wheels were detected

Fig. 5. Illustration of the pose estimation experiment setup.

on any frame, and therefore no pose was estimated. Due to the rotation of the vehicle, the circular shape of the wheels is distorted so that the wheels cannot be identified as circles by the Hough Circle Transform. However, when wheels are detected, the Wheel Detection Estimator can deliver a precision that meets our 10 cm requirement in most of the cases.

Table 1. Accuracy of the wheel and the marker detection. We describe the distance and rotation of the vehicle in the notation of ⟨distance⟩m ⟨rotation⟩°, e.g. 3 m 10°, meaning a distance of 3 m and a rotation of 10°.

	3 m 0°	3 m 10°	4 m 0°	4 m 10°	5 m 0°	5 m 10°	∅
Marker Board	100%	100%	100%	100%	100%	100%	100%
Single Marker	100%	100%	100%	100%	100%	99%	99.8%
Wheel Detection	100%	0%	95%	80%	100%	80%	75.8%

5.2   Usability

To ensure that the system's usability is not prevented by technical limitations, it is necessary that the driver guidance is activated in a timely manner, so that driver can be supported when approaching. To validate this, we analyze the required time in the approach detection until the smartphone can retrieve the positioning information from the camera system. When entering the Bluetooth range of a BLE Beacon, it takes between 7 and 12 s for a Samsung Galaxy S7 Edge to detect the BLE advertisement and report it to the application. It takes approximately 5 s to establish the WiFi connection, which means that a total time of 12 to 17 s is required. Assuming the vehicle is approaching at a moderate speed, the overall time is acceptable. When the connection is established, it is also ideal if there is no perceivable latency in the driver feedback. We therefore analyze the update rate at which the positioning information is provided by the camera system. Our prototype system is installed on a Dell G7 Laptop with an Intel Core i7-9750H CPU and 16 GB RAM. We measure the sliding average of frames per second for a minute that will be processed and the average over the whole experiment. The resolution of the image data is 1920 × 1080. When executing the pose estimation the system can process approximately 7–8 frames per second. We would argue that this is sufficient because a driver's reaction time is in the range of 200–300. As a result, we would assume that the driver will usually not maneuver at a speed that would require more than a couple of frames per second.

6   Related Work

There are two categories of wireless charging, stationary as described in this paper or dynamic, whereby a vehicle is charged while it is in motion. To solve the

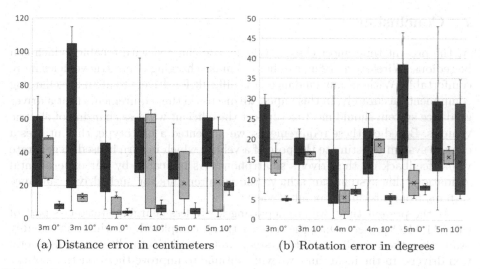

(a) Distance error in centimeters   (b) Rotation error in degrees

Fig. 6. Box plots that visualize the error, which is the difference between the ground truth and the measurement achieved by each pose estimator. The whiskers represent the maximum and minimum values and the colored boxes show the first and third quartile. The cross stands for the average error and the horizontal bar indicates the median. Blue: Single markers; Green: Marker board; Red: Wheel Detection; (Color figure online)

misalignment problem with dynamic charging, there is a camera-based system in [14], which uses computer vision to recognize the deviation from the charging route and visualizes it to the user. An alternative approach is presented in [9], in which lateral misalignments are recognized by voltage differences, whereupon steering commands are generated for the electric power steering system to control the lateral position of the vehicle. In addition to the lateral position alignment, the air gap between the charging components is also relevant for efficient charging. For this purpose, a mechanical positioning mechanism is presented in [12] which can adjust the distance between the charging components. There are also approaches for stationary charging that use mechanical systems to adjust the position of the charging components. In [18] the misalignment of both coils is determined using wireless sensors, whereupon an electromechanical system automatically adjusts the position of the coil which is integrated into the floor. There are approaches for stationary charging that enable positioning for short distances using RFID [17] or magnetic systems [5] or combine both [3]. However, in addition to RFID, [8] also installs a camera on the vehicle to enable positioning from further distances, to visualize based on the current driving situation an optimal trajectory. In contrast to the approaches that use several hardware components for positioning, we use exactly one camera to save costs. Furthermore, the camera is installed on the charging station and not on the vehicle because we want to avoid vehicle-specific integration efforts.

7   Conclusion

At the present time, most electric vehicles are charged with a cable, which can be tedious. Wireless charging can help to make charging of electric vehicles more comfortable. Without any guidance, it is difficult for drivers to align the charging components accurately. In this paper, we discussed the requirements that a driver guidance system should meet to support the efficient wireless charging of electric vehicles. Based on these requirements, we presented a prototype, that utilizes a camera system to estimate the pose of a vehicle which in turn is used to generate visual feedback on the driver's smartphone. As indicated by our experimental validation, this system can achieve the requirements for such driver guidance systems from a technical point of view.

At the present time, we are deploying a wireless charging station as part of the TALAKO-project. Once the construction is completed, we will be thoroughly evaluating the overall usability system under realistic conditions with several taxi drivers. In the meantime, we will continue to improve the robustness of the system, e.g. by extending the wheel detection algorithm to support ellipses [16]. In addition, we are working on additional visualizations that augment the images taken by the camera with instructions for the driver.

Acknowledgment. This paper was funded by the TALAKO-project ("Tax-iladekonzept für Elektrotaxis im öffentlichen Raum" tr. "Taxi Charging Concept for Public Spaces").

References

1. Taxiladekonzept für Elektrotaxis im öffentlichen Raum. https://talako.uni-due.de/
2. Birrell, S.A., Wilson, D., Yang, C.P., Dhadyalla, G., Jennings, P.: How driver behaviour and parking alignment affects inductive charging systems for electric vehicles. Transp. Res. Part C: Emerg. Technol. **58**, 721–731 (2015). Technologies to support green driving
3. Chen, S., Liao, C., Wang, L.: Research on positioning technique of wireless power transfer system for electric vehicles. In: 2014 IEEE Conference and Expo Transportation Electrification Asia-Pacific (ITEC Asia-Pacific), pp. 1–4 (2014)
4. Collins, T., Bartoli, A.: Infinitesimal plane-based pose estimation. Int. J. Comput. Vis. **109**, 252–286 (2014)
5. Gao, Y., Duan, C., Oliveira, A.A., Ginart, A., Farley, K.B., Tse, Z.T.H.: 3-D coil positioning based on magnetic sensing for wireless EV charging. IEEE Trans. Transp. Electrification **3**(3), 578–588 (2017)
6. Gao, Y., Ginart, A., Farley, K.B., Tse, Z.T.H.: Misalignment effect on efficiency of wireless power transfer for electric vehicles. In: 2016 IEEE Applied Power Electronics Conference and Exposition (APEC), pp. 3526–3528 (2016)
7. Garrido-Jurado, S., Muñoz-Salinas, R., Madrid-Cuevas, F., Marín-Jiméenez, M.: Automatic generation and detection of highly reliable fiducial markers under occlusion. Pattern Recogn. **47**, 2280–2292 (2014)
8. Hudecek, J., Küfen, J., Langen, O., Dankert, J., Eckstein, L.: A system for precise positioning of vehicles aiming at increased inductive charging efficiency. MedPower **2014**, 1–6 (2014)

9. Hwang, K., et al.: Autonomous coil alignment system using fuzzy steering control for electric vehicles with dynamic wireless charging. Math. Probl. Eng. **2015**, 1–14 (2015)

10. Jiang, H., Brazis, P., Tabaddor, M., Bablo, J.: Safety considerations of wireless charger for electric vehicles - a review paper. In: 2012 IEEE Symposium on Product Compliance Engineering Proceedings, pp. 1–6 (2012)

11. Kaehler, A., Bradski, G.: Learning OpenCV 3: Computer Vision in C++ with the OpenCV Library, 1st edn. O'Reilly Media Inc. (2016)

12. Karakitsios, I., et al.: An integrated approach for dynamic charging of electric vehicles by wireless power transfer - lessons learned from real-life implementation. SAE Int. J. Altern. Powertrains **6**, 15–24 (2017)

13. Kerbyson, D.J., Atherton, T.J.: Circle detection using Hough transform filters. In: Fifth International Conference on Image Processing and its Applications, pp. 370–374 (1995)

14. Kobeissi, A.H., Bellotti, F., Berta, R., De Gloria, A.: IoT grid alignment assistant system for dynamic wireless charging of electric vehicles. In: 2018 Fifth International Conference on Internet of Things: Systems, Management and Security, pp. 274–279 (2018)

15. Li, S., Mi, C.C.: Wireless power transfer for electric vehicle applications. IEEE J. Emerg. Sel. Top. Power Electron. **3**(1), 4–17 (2015)

16. Libuda, L., Grothues, I., Kraiss, K.-F.: Ellipse detection in digital image data using geometric features. In: Braz, J., Ranchordas, A., Araújo, H., Jorge, J. (eds.) GRAPP/VISAPP -2006. CCIS, vol. 4, pp. 229–239. Springer, Heidelberg (2007). https://doi.org/10.1007/978-3-540-75274-5_15

17. Loewel, T., Lange, C., Noack, F.: Identification and positioning system for inductive charging systems. In: 2013 3rd International Electric Drives Production Conference (EDPC), pp. 1–5 (2013)

18. Ni, W., et al.: Radio alignment for inductive charging of electric vehicles. IEEE Trans. Ind. Inform. **11**, 1 (2015)

19. Welch, G., Bishop, G.: An Introduction to the Kalman Filter (1995)

20. Wu, H.H., Gilchrist, A., Sealy, K.D., Israelsen, P., Muhs, J.M.: A review on inductive charging for electric vehicles. In: 2011 IEEE International Electric Machines & Drives Conference (IEMDC), pp. 143–147 (2011)

21. Zivkovic, Z., van der Heijden, F.: Efficient adaptive density estimation per image pixel for the task of background subtraction. Pattern Recogn. Lett. **27**(7), 773–780 (2006)

An Efficient Tiny Feature Map Network for Real-Time Semantic Segmentation

Hang Huang[1], Peng Zhi[1], Haoran Zhou[1], Yujin Zhang[1], Qiang Wu[1], Binbin Yong[1], Weijun Tan[2], and Qingguo Zhou[1(✉)]

[1] Lanzhou University, Lanzhou, China
{huangh2018,zhip13,zhouhr19,yjzhang19,wuq17,yongbb,zhouqg}@lzu.edu.cn
[2] Linksprite Technologies, Longmont, USA
weijun.tan@linksprite.com

Abstract. In this paper, we propose an efficient semantic segmentation network named Tiny Feature Map Network (TFMNet). This network significantly improves the running speed while achieves good accuracy. Our scheme uses a lightweight backbone network to extract primary features from input images of particular sizes. The hybrid dilated convolution framework and the DenseASPP module are used to alleviate the gridding problem. We evaluate the proposed network on the Cityscapes and CamVid datasets, and obtain performance comparable with the existing state-of-the-art real-time semantic segmentation methods. Specifically, it achieves 72.9% mIoU on the Cityscapes *test* dataset with only 2.4M parameters and a speed of 113 FPS on NVIDIA GTX 1080 Ti without pre-training on the ImageNet dataset.

Keywords: Semantic segmentation · Tiny feature maps · DenseASPP

1 Introduction

Semantic segmentation is a key technology in computer vision. It is used to infer pixel-wise or point-wise semantic categories from input images or point clouds. It is widely used in various fields, such as autonomous driving, robot sensing. Many of such applications rely heavily on the efficiency of the model. Especially in the scenario of autonomous driving, a more efficient model means prompt and safer manipulation of vehicles.

Recent real-time semantic segmentation models have made great progresses in the tradeoff between speed and accuracy [11,20,22,24]. Some studies have already got promising results on the benchmark [7,12], but it is far from the best. For example, Some methods increase the speed by restricting the resolution of the input image, which leads to a significant accuracy loss due to the loss of detailed information [20]. Some adopt different branches to extract features from the original image [22]. However, the features extracted at the bottom of neural network are usually low-level features of edges, corners and colors, which are universal. Multiple extractions reduce the speed of the model. DenseASPP [21]

© Springer Nature Switzerland AG 2020
G. Bebis et al. (Eds.): ISVC 2020, LNCS 12510, pp. 332–343, 2020.
https://doi.org/10.1007/978-3-030-64559-5_26

realizes feature reuse and multi-scale feature extraction by combining DenseNet [9] and ASPP [2], but its speed is very slow.

In the field of pure pursuit of semantic segmentation accuracy, the final feature size in [10, 25] is 1/8 of the input image size. This shows that the 1/8 feature map has the potential to achieve good precision. In this paper, a $1/k$ feature map means that the size of the feature map is $1/k$ of the original image size.

Based on above observations, we propose the TFMNet to further improve the performance of real-time semantic segmentation. The proposed network uses a *Fast Downsample Module* (FDM) to extract 1/8 feature map quickly, and all the subsequent modules are based on the 1/8 feature map. Then, an *Improved DenseASPP Module* (IDAM) is applied to the smaller feature map, which can significantly improve the accuracy while pertaining the competitive speed.

In addition, we note that the size of the input images in [3,4] was odd, but the authors of these studies did not explain the reasons. Many researchers are confused about this problem and wonder whether it is necessary. We have investigated this problem and herein we can propose a novel and easy to understand explanation, and design experiments to verify its necessity (Fig. 1).

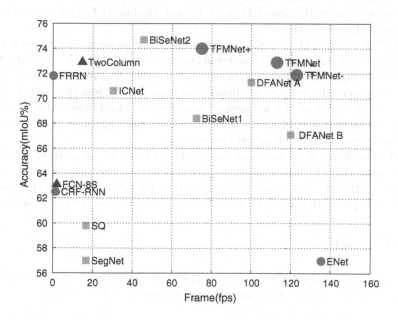

Fig. 1. Performance of existing methods on Cityscapes *test* set, including FRRN [17], FCN-8s [14], CRF-RNN [26], TwoColumn [20], SQ [18], SegNet [1], ICNet [24], BiSeNet [22], ENet [15], DFANet [11]. The three shapes of circle, square and triangle respectively represent training without or with ImageNet [8], or not mentioned in paper.

2   Related Work

Fully Convolutional Networks (FCN) [14] extended image-level classification to pixel-wise classification, which lays the foundation for pixel-wise segmentation. After that, many approaches [3,5,10,13,23,25] were proposed to pursue higher accuracy. Differently, the goal of real-time semantic segmentation is to achieve more efficient, or faster implementation with good enough accuracy. Many networks [1,11,15,17,22,24] have been proposed to achieve this goal.

ICNet (2018) [24] utilized deep network to capture high-level semantic information from low resolution inputs and got details from high resolution inputs using a shallow network. And then, a cascade network was use to fuse the features from different resolution inputs. By doing so, it achieved good efficiency.

With a similar idea, BiSeNet (2018) [22] created a spatial path, a three-layer convolutional network, to preserve the spatial information and to generate high-resolution features. Meanwhile, with BiSeNet, a context path with global average pooling was use to reduce the computation complexity and obtain a sufficient receptive field. In the context path, an attention refinement module was included to compute the attention vector to optimize the output features. In addition, a convolutional network named Feature Fusion Module (FFM) was used to fuse features of the two paths.

DFANet (2019) [11] designed a lightweight backbone network based on the Xception [6] model. It uses concatenation units to cascade the output of each layer as the input of subsequent layers. Because the features extracted by each layer are reused, the number of channels in each layer is less than other models, therefore the speed of the network is accelerated. In addition, this method of feature extraction can promote the interaction and aggregation of features in different layers, thereby elevating the accuracy.

Different from these methods, we apply all complex structures to the tiny feature map. Firstly, we propose a FDM to reduce the size of input images, which is a strategy that can increase speed remarkably. Then, we propose the IDAM to improve the accuracy by aggregating multi-scale features densely.

3   TFMNet

In this section, we first present an overview of the network architecture, then elaborate on the main approaches to improve speed and accuracy.

3.1   Overview

The network structure is illustrated in Fig. 2, where the size of the input image is set according to Sect. 3.4.

The numbers $H \times W \times C$ in each module box indicates the dimension of the output layer. For example, $129 \times 129 \times 128$ in the FDM block indicates that feature map output by FDM contains 128 channels, and the width and height of

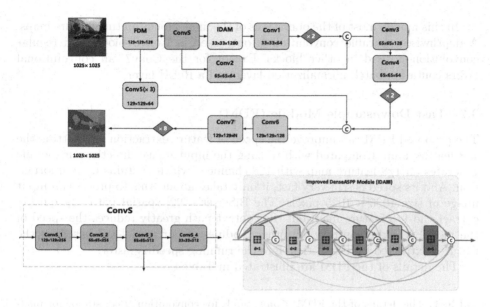

Fig. 2. Overview of our network: ×k means a k times upsampling, C means concatenation. d in IDAM means dilation rate.

the feature map channel are 129. The symbol ×k means a k times upsampling. The symbol C means a fusion by concatenation.

The FDM is used to aggregate the 1/8 feature map. The details are shown in Table 1. The Conv5 block contains 3 convolutional layers whose 1/8 feature map output is fused with the 2× upsampled Conv4 output.

The ConvS block further downsamples the feature map to 1/32. The details of ConvS block are in the left bottom of Fig. 2, where ConvS_3 output is the input to the Conv2 block, whose output is concatenated with the 2× upsampled Conv1 output.

The IDAM is used to extract multi-scale features. The IDAM details are illustrated in the right bottom of Fig. 2. It contains six densely connected dilated convolutions with dilation rates of (1, 2, 5, 1, 2, 5). The dilation rate is indicated by d in the Fig. 2. The Conv1 compresses the multi-scale features extracted by IDAM to reduce the number of channels and speed up the model. Then the 1/32 feature map is upsampled to a 1/16 feature map using bilinear interpolation and is fused with the underlying 1/16 feature map from the Conv2. The Conv3 and Conv4 further extract the feature of the fused features. Then bilinear interpolation is used to restore the 1/16 feature map to the 1/8 feature map, which is concatenated with the output of the Conv5. The Conv6 extracts the feature map from the fused feature, and then uses a convolution layer with N 1 × 1 filters(Conv7) to get the 1/8 feature map, where N represents the number of categories in the dataset. At the end, the 1/8 feature map is upsampled by a factor of eight to get feature map of full resolution.

In this model, most of the operations of the model focus on tiny feature maps. A depthwise separable convolution is only used in ConvS block, and regular convolution is used in other blocks. Except for the Conv7, all convolutional layers contain a batch normalization layer and a ReLU layer.

3.2 Fast Downsample Module (FDM)

The proposed FDM can improve the speed of feature extraction and getting the 1/8 feature map. Compared with resizing the input image directly, our module generates an 1/8 feature map with 128 channels, which contains more information. And its speed is still very fast, it only takes about 3 ms to process an input image of size 1025 × 1025 pixels. The BiSeNet's [22] spatial path can quickly extract the 1/8 feature map, but the context path greatly reduces the speed of the model. On the contrary, all other modules of our model are based on the features extracted by FDM, therefore the running speed is faster.

The details of the FDM are illustrated in Table 1.

Table 1. The details of the FDM. *Conv* stands for convolution. *Pool* stands for maximum pooling.

Type	Filter shape	Input size	Output size	Stride
Conv	$7 \times 7 \times 3 \times 32$	$1025 \times 1025 \times 3$	$513 \times 513 \times 32$	2
Pool	$3 \times 3 \times 32$	$513 \times 513 \times 32$	$257 \times 257 \times 32$	2
Conv	$3 \times 3 \times 32 \times 64$	$257 \times 257 \times 32$	$257 \times 257 \times 64$	1
Conv	$3 \times 3 \times 64 \times 128$	$257 \times 257 \times 64$	$129 \times 129 \times 128$	2

3.3 Improved DenseASPP Module

In non-real-time semantic segmentation, the DenseASPP module proposed in [21] can effectively integrate multi-scale features, thus improving the accuracy of the model. However, the calculation complexity of the DenseASPP module is very high. In order to take advantage of this module without reducing the inferring speed substantially, we modify this module for the 1/32 feature map. The original DenseASPP module has a set of dilation rates with a value of $(3, 6, 12, 18, 24)$. It is too large for a tiny feature map and obviously needs to be adjusted down.

The research on HDC [19] showed that, the setting of dilation rate should meet three requirements. The first requirement is that the dilation rate in the continuous convolution cannot have a common factor greater than 1. Secondly, it is required to set the dilation rate to zigzag, such as $(1, 2, 5, 1, 2, 5)$ cyclic pattern. The third requirement is to meet the following equation:

$$M_i = max\left[M_{i+1} - 2r_i, M_{i+1} - 2\left(M_{i+1} - r_i\right), r_i\right] \tag{1}$$

where r_i is the dilation rate of the i layer and M_i is the maximum dilation rate at the i layer. If the total number of layers is n, then $M_n = r_n$. If we apply it to a kernel of $k \times k$, the goal of Eq. 1 is to make $M_2 < k$. Therefore, we can at least cover all the holes in the way to set the dilation rate to 1.

We apply the HDC [19] principles to improve the DenseASPP module. We increase the number of layers of the module to six, and set the dilation rate to $(1, 2, 5, 1, 2, 5)$. The improved module is called IDAM.

3.4   Size of the Input Image

Usually, the input size of the image satisfies the Eq. 2 [1,2,11,15,22,24], which makes the model morbid.

$$L = k \times 2^m \tag{2}$$

where L is the height or width of the input image, k is a positive integer and m represents the number of downsampling in the network with stride 2.

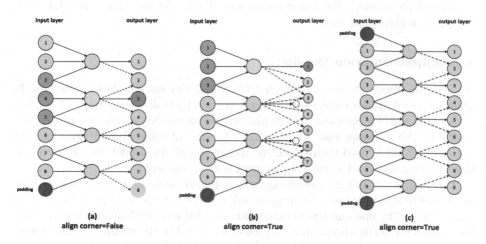

Fig. 3. Description of the receptive field shifting problem. The network uses bilinear interpolation to get full-resolution inference results from the label map.

To describe the problem intuitively, we simplify the network to include only one down-sampling layer and one up-sampling layer, as shown in Fig. 3. In Fig. 3, *align corners* represents the alignment type in upsampling, and the numbers in the circles represent the position of the pixel.

In Fig. 3(a), the first column represents the input image, and the third column represents the output of the upsampling layer. As you can see, the category of pixel 3 depends on the values of pixels 3, 4, and 5 instead of the values of pixels 2, 3, and 4. It is apparent that the original pixel and the center of the corresponding receptive field are mismatched. The same problem exists in Fig. 3(b). To solve this problem, we change Eq. 2 to Eq. 3, and the parameters in Eq. 3 have the same meaning as the parameters in Eq. 2.

$$L = k \times 2^m + 1 \tag{3}$$

In this case, the workflow of the model is shown in Fig. 3(c). The category of pixel 3 depends on the values of pixels 2, 3, 4. By optimizing the size of the input image, the problem of skewing can be effectively solved.

4 Experiments

In this section, we describe the implementation details of the TFMNet, and then present our experiments designed to verify the efficiency of the model. We compare the speed and accuracy with the current state-of-the-art real-time semantic segmentation models on the challenging **Cityscapes** *test* set and **CamVid** *test* set. During the evaluation, we do not use any testing augmentation, such as multi-scale testing. For fair comparison, We do not use the TensorRT optimization in the speed test.

4.1 Implementation Details

All tests on speed are conducted on a GTX 1080 Ti and the batch size is 1. In order to speed up our experiment, the main training task is done on a TPU v3-8, with batch size 64, momentum 0.9 and weight decay $2e-4$. We use the "poly" policy in the learning rate with an initial value of 0.04. Exponential moving average (EMA) is used to enhance the robustness of the model. In addition, the loss function used in the training process is cross entropy.

Cityscapes dataset is a challenging benchmark including 19 classes. It contains 5,000 finely annotated images, all of which have a high resolution of 1024×2048. The fine annotated images are divided into 2975 images for training, 500 images for verification and 1525 images for test. Firstly, we use the Cityscapes dataset for the qualitative analysis of the experiments. In the training process, we randomly scale the picture, and the range is $0.5, 1.0, 1.25, 1.5, 1.75, 2.0$. Then the image is cropped into the size of 513×513 for training.

4.2 Performance Results

In Table 2 we report quantitative results compared with the main baseline. The proposed method achieves 72.9% mIoU with only 2.4M parameters and a speed of 113FPS. Compared with the previous state-of-the-art model DFANet A, TFM-Net obtains 1.6% improvement of mIoU with only 1/3 as many parameters at a 1.13× speed acceleration. Compared with the DFANet B, TFMNet- obtains 4.8% improvement of mIoU at a faster speed. We also want to emphasize that DFANet uses ImageNet dataset for pretraining, but our model does not. Compared with the speed-seeking BiSeNet1, the proposed TFMNet has 1.56× speed acceleration and only 1/2 as many parameters, with 4.5% improvement of mIoU. Compared with the BiSeNet2, TFMNet+ achieves a 1.65× speed acceleration with only a loss of 0.7% mIoU. ENet has the fastest speed, but its mIoU is only 57%.

Table 2. Inference Speed and accuracy analysis on Cityscapes *test* dataset. "–" represents the parameter is not mentioned in the corresponding paper. "TFMNet-" and "TFMNet+" are from Sect. 4.7.

Model	InputSize	ImageNet	Params	Time (ms)	Frame (fps)	mIoU (%)
SegNet [1]	640 × 360	yes	29.5M	16	16.7	57
ENet [15]	640 × 360	no	0.4M	7	135.4	57
SQ [18]	1024 × 2048	yes	–	60	16.7	59.8
FRRN [17]	512 × 1024	no	–	469	0.25	71.8
ICNet [24]	1024 × 2048	yes	26.5M	33	30.3	70.6
TwoColumn [20]	1024 × 2048	–	–	68	14.7	72.9
BiSeNet1 [22]	768 × 1536	yes	5.8M	13	72.3	68.4
BiSeNet2 [22]	768 × 1536	yes	49M	21	45.7	**74.7**
DFANet A [11]	1024 × 1024	yes	7.8M	10	100	71.3
DFANet B [11]	1024 × 1024	yes	4.8M	8.3	120	67.1
TFMNet	1025 × 1025	no	2.4M	8.8	113	72.9
TFMNet-	1025 × 1025	no	2.3M	8.1	123	71.9
TFMNet+	1025 × 1025	no	2.9M	13.3	75	74.0

4.3 Comparison on Other Datasets

The TFMNet is also evaluated on CamVid dataset. CamVid contains 701 finely annotated images of street scenes with a size of 960 × 720 × 3, in which there are 367 images for training, 101 images for validation and 233 images for testing. The image resolution for training is cropped into the size of 513 × 513, and the resolution for evaluation is 961 × 737. Other than that, we adopt the same setting as [16]. The results are reported in Table 3. As can be observed, while the accuracy performance of the proposed method is significantly better than the state-of-the-art methods, the inference speed remains comparable. It should also be emphasized that only the 367 images in the training set are used for training, and no other data are used.

4.4 Speed Test

We test the speed of our model in various sizes and compare it with the current state-of-the-art real-time semantic segmentation models. According to Sect. 3.4, we fill the image from 1024 × 1024 to 1025 × 1025 in the actual test of TFMNet. The same processing method is used for other sizes.

The experimental results are illustrated in Table 4. As can be observed, compared with all methods, the proposed model is faster with the sizes they use.

Table 3. Results on CamVid *test* set.

Model	Time (ms)	Frame (fps)	mIoU (%)
ENet [15]	–	–	51.3
ICNet [24]	36	27.8	67.1
BiSeNet1 [22]	–	–	65.6
BiSeNet2 [22]	–	–	68.7
DFANet A [11]	8	120	64.7
DFANet B [11]	**6**	**160**	59.3
TFMNet (Ours)	6.4	156	**69.4**

Table 4. Comparison with state-of-the-art real-time semantic segmentation models. The unit of the number in the table is FPS. "–" represents that there is no experimental result of the model at the corresponding input size.

Model	Size			
	1024×2048	1024×1024	512×1024	768×1536
ICNet	30.03	–	–	–
BiSeNet1	–	–	–	72.3
BiSeNet2	–	–	–	45.7
DFANet	–	100	160	–
TFMNet	**63.9**	**113.1**	**183.8**	**103.9**

4.5 Ablation Study: Skewing Problem

In this section, we conduct three groups of comparison experiments to verify the theoretical analysis in Sect. 3.4. Because TPU does not support bilinear interpolation with $align\,corners = False$, experiments in this section are carried on a single RTX 2080 Ti GPU.

Table 5. The inference performance on Cityscapes *validation* dataset of models trained with different processing methods.

Input size	512×512	512×512	513×513
Equation	(2)	(2)	(3)
Align corners	False	True	True
mIoU(%)	71.0	70.9	**71.4**

The training of the three groups of experiments is carried on the same GPU. We set batch size to 32, training step to 100k. We use Cityscapes validation set for evaluation. The experiment results are shown in Table 5. According to the experiment results, higher accuracy can be obtained by satisfying the input dimension of Eq. 3.

4.6   Ablation Study: Improved DenseASPP Module

In this section, we use Cityscapes validation set to verify the validity of IDAM. We set batch size to 64, training step to 300k. The experimental results are shown in Table 6. As can be observed, the accuracy of IDAM is improved by 1.6% mIoU compared with DenseASPP. In order to further verify the validity of IDAM, we modify the dilation rate in IDAM to (1, 2, 3, 4, 5, 6), which does not meet the HDC [19] principle, and name the new module IDAM-. Experiments show that IDAM is significantly better than IDAM-. In addition, experimental results show that IDAM is also better than the DenseNet and ASPP.

Table 6. The inference performance of different modules on Cityscapes *validation* dataset. IDAM- means that the dilation rate in IDAM is replaced with (1, 2, 3, 4, 5, 6).

module	DenseASPP	IDAM	IDAM-	DenseNet	ASPP
mIoU(%)	71.9	**73.5**	72.5	70.7	69.8

4.7   Ablation Study: FDM Scaling

In this section, we scale the FDM to meet the needs of different scenarios in real-time semantic segmentation. We name the model after deleting the third layer in FDM as TFMNet-. And we name the model of adding a new layer after the third layer in FDM as TFMNet+. The number of convolution kernels of the newly added convolutional layer is 256. The size of the input image is 1025*1025.

The experimental results are shown in Table 7. It can be seen from the table that the TFMNet can achieve an accuracy of 71.9 mIoU at a speed of 123 fps. And the TFMNet+ can achieve an accuracy of 74.0 mIoU at 75 fps.

Table 7. The performance on Cityscapes *test* dataset of models with different FDM.

Model	TFMNet	TFMNet-	TFMNet+
Frame (fps)	113	**123**	75
mIoU (%)	72.9	71.9	**74.0**

5   Conclusion

Our TFMNet uses FDM to extract small feature map fast, and a complex IDAM is applied to the small feature map. According to the comparative experiments, the proposed method achieves better results than the state-of-the-art methods on Cityscapes and CamVid while achieving comparable speed.

References

1. Badrinarayanan, V., Kendall, A., Cipolla, R.: SegNet: a deep convolutional encoder-decoder architecture for image segmentation. IEEE Trans. Pattern Anal. Mach. Intell. **39**(12), 2481–2495 (2017)
2. Chen, L.C., Papandreou, G., Kokkinos, I., Murphy, K., Yuille, A.L.: DeepLab: semantic image segmentation with deep convolutional nets, atrous convolution, and fully connected CRFs. IEEE Trans. Pattern Anal. Mach. Intell. **40**(4), 834–848 (2017)
3. Chen, L.C., Papandreou, G., Schroff, F., Adam, H.: Rethinking atrous convolution for semantic image segmentation. arXiv preprint arXiv:1706.05587 (2017)
4. Chen, L.C., Zhu, Y., Papandreou, G., Schroff, F., Adam, H.: Encoder-decoder with atrous separable convolution for semantic image segmentation. In: Proceedings of the European Conference on Computer Vision (ECCV), pp. 801–818 (2018)
5. Choi, S., Kim, J.T., Choo, J.: Cars can't fly up in the sky: improving urban-scene segmentation via height-driven attention networks. In: Proceedings of the IEEE/CVF Conference on Computer Vision and Pattern Recognition (CVPR), June 2020
6. Chollet, F.: Xception: deep learning with depthwise separable convolutions. In: Proceedings of the IEEE Conference on Computer Vision and Pattern Recognition, pp. 1251–1258 (2017)
7. Cordts, M., et al.: The cityscapes dataset for semantic urban scene understanding. In: Proceedings of the IEEE Conference on Computer Vision and Pattern Recognition, pp. 3213–3223 (2016)
8. Deng, J., Dong, W., Socher, R., Li, L.J., Li, K., Fei-Fei, L.: ImageNet: a large-scale hierarchical image database. In: 2009 IEEE Conference on Computer Vision and Pattern Recognition, pp. 248–255. IEEE (2009)
9. Huang, G., Liu, Z., Van Der Maaten, L., Weinberger, K.Q.: Densely connected convolutional networks. In: Proceedings of the IEEE Conference on Computer Vision and Pattern Recognition, pp. 4700–4708 (2017)
10. Huang, Z., Wang, X., Huang, L., Huang, C., Wei, Y., Liu, W.: CCNet: criss-cross attention for semantic segmentation. arXiv preprint arXiv:1811.11721 (2018)
11. Li, H., Xiong, P., Fan, H., Sun, J.: DFANet: deep feature aggregation for real-time semantic segmentation. In: Proceedings of the IEEE Conference on Computer Vision and Pattern Recognition, pp. 9522–9531 (2019)
12. Lin, T.-Y., et al.: Microsoft COCO: common objects in context. In: Fleet, D., Pajdla, T., Schiele, B., Tuytelaars, T. (eds.) ECCV 2014. LNCS, vol. 8693, pp. 740–755. Springer, Cham (2014). https://doi.org/10.1007/978-3-319-10602-1_48
13. Liu, C., et al.: Auto-deeplab: hierarchical neural architecture search for semantic image segmentation, pp. 82–92 (2019). https://doi.org/10.1109/CVPR.2019.00017
14. Long, J., Shelhamer, E., Darrell, T.: Fully convolutional networks for semantic segmentation. In: Proceedings of the IEEE Conference on Computer Vision and Pattern Recognition, pp. 3431–3440 (2015)

15. Paszke, A., Chaurasia, A., Kim, S., Culurciello, E.: ENet: a deep neural network architecture for real-time semantic segmentation. arXiv preprint arXiv:1606.02147 (2016)
16. Sturgess, P., Alahari, K., Ladicky, L., Torr, P.H.: Combining appearance and structure from motion features for road scene understanding. In: The British Machine Vision Conference (BMVC) (2009)
17. Pohlen, T., Hermans, A., Mathias, M., Leibe, B.: Full-resolution residual networks for semantic segmentation in street scenes. In: Proceedings of the IEEE Conference on Computer Vision and Pattern Recognition, pp. 4151–4160 (2017)
18. Treml, M., et al.: Speeding up semantic segmentation for autonomous driving. In: MLITS, NIPS Workshop, vol. 2, p. 7 (2016)
19. Wang, P., et al.: Understanding convolution for semantic segmentation. In: 2018 IEEE Winter Conference on Applications of Computer Vision (WACV), pp. 1451–1460. IEEE (2018)
20. Wu, Z., Shen, C., van den Hengel, A.: Real-time semantic image segmentation via spatial sparsity. arXiv preprint arXiv:1712.00213 (2017)
21. Yang, M., Yu, K., Zhang, C., Li, Z., Yang, K.: DenseASPP for semantic segmentation in street scenes. In: Proceedings of the IEEE Conference on Computer Vision and Pattern Recognition, pp. 3684–3692 (2018)
22. Yu, C., Wang, J., Peng, C., Gao, C., Yu, G., Sang, N.: BiseNet: bilateral segmentation network for real-time semantic segmentation. In: Proceedings of the European Conference on Computer Vision (ECCV), pp. 325–341 (2018)
23. Yuan, Y., Chen, X., Wang, J.: Object-contextual representations for semantic segmentation. In: 16th European Conference Computer Vision (ECCV 2020), August 2020. https://www.microsoft.com/en-us/research/publication/object-contextual-representations-for-semantic-segmentation/
24. Zhao, H., Qi, X., Shen, X., Shi, J., Jia, J.: ICNet for real-time semantic segmentation on high-resolution images. In: Proceedings of the European Conference on Computer Vision (ECCV), pp. 405–420 (2018)
25. Zhao, H., Shi, J., Qi, X., Wang, X., Jia, J.: Pyramid scene parsing network. In: Proceedings of the IEEE Conference on Computer Vision and Pattern Recognition, pp. 2881–2890 (2017)
26. Zheng, S., et al.: Conditional random fields as recurrent neural networks. In: Proceedings of the IEEE International Conference on Computer Vision, pp. 1529–1537 (2015)

A Modified Syn2Real Network for Nighttime Rainy Image Restoration

Qunfang Tang[1,2], Jie Yang[1(✉)], Haibo Liu[2], and Zhiqiang Guo[1]

[1] Hubei Key Laboratory of Broadband Wireless Communication and Sensor
Networks, Wuhan University of Technology, Wuhan, China
seainlost81@126.com, jieyang509@163.com
[2] School of Electrical Information Engineering, Hunan Institute of Technology,
Hengyang, China

Abstract. The restoration or enhancement of rainy images at nighttime
is of great significance to outdoor computer vision applications such as
self-driving and traffic surveillance. While image deraining has drawn
increasingly research attention currently and the majority of deraining
methods are able to achieve satisfying performance for daytime image
rain removal, there are few related studies for nighttime image deraining,
as the conditions of nighttime rainy scenes are more complicated and
challenging. To address the nighttime image deraining issues, we designed
an improved model based on the Syn2Real network, called NIRR. In
order to obtain good rain removal and visual effect under the nighttime
rainy scene, we propose a new refined loss function for the supervised
learning phase, which combines the perceptual loss and SSIM loss. The
qualitative and quantitative experimental results show that our proposed
method outperforms the state-of-the-arts whether it is on the synthetic
nighttime rainy image or on the real-world nighttime rainy image.

Keywords: Nighttime image deraining · Semi-supervised network ·
Gaussian processes

1 Introduction

Rainy images acquired at outdoor environments during daytime and nighttime,
often suffer from a series of visibility degradations, e.g. obstructing and blurring background scenes, altering the object content and changing contrast and
color of images, etc. Due to detail loss and signal distortion, these undesirable
degradations cause visual unpleasure and seriously influence the accuracy of
many outdoor computer vision applications, such as video surveillance [1,11,22],
autonomous navigation [15], object detection and tracking [3,18,26]. Hence, it is
important to develop effective methods that can restore or enhance rainy images.

In recent years, the issue of single image deraining has drawn increasingly
research attention. Many algorithms have been developed, including the model-
driven and the data-driven methods [28]. Although some satisfying performances

© Springer Nature Switzerland AG 2020
G. Bebis et al. (Eds.): ISVC 2020, LNCS 12510, pp. 344–356, 2020.
https://doi.org/10.1007/978-3-030-64559-5_27

have been achieved when dealing with daytime rainy images, but they are not suitable for night rainy scenes, as the characteristics of daytime and nighttime rainy scene are very different, the conditions of nighttime scenes are more complicated. For example, on the one hand, the nighttime image itself suffers from visibility degradation due to low ambient lighting, and the presence of rain will further seriously affect its visual quality, lead to low contrast, and limited color information. On the other hand, nighttime scenes usually have active light sources, such as street lights, car lights, and building lights. These active light sources can cause uneven lighting distribution, leading to the failure of many rain removal methods. Therefore, nighttime rainy image restoration or enhancement is more challenging.

As is known to all, the restoration or enhancement of rainy images at nighttime is of great significance to the applications such as self-driving and traffic surveillance. However, to the best of our knowledge, there is few related studies, excepting literature [20], in which Shi et al. developed a rainy image model to describe rainy scenes at night with low illumination and proposed a joint deep neural network-based method for single nighttime rainy image enhancement. This method achieves promising results on synthetic rainy images, but it has problems such as over-enhancement, lack of fidelity and rain residual on real-world nighttime rainy images. In the other words, it lacks the generalization capabilities to real-world image deraining. This is because, firstly, it is a fully-supervised network and it can only use fully labeled data to train, obtaining labeled real-world training data is quite challenging. Secondly, only modeling the light rainy condition might not be enough, the synthetic nighttime rainy images should contain multiple variants of nighttime rainy conditions, such as variations in scale, density and orientation of the rain streaks, to model the complex conditions of real-world nighttime rain.

Recently, Yasarla et al. [29] proposed a Gaussian Process-based semi-supervised learning framework (Syn2Real network) which enabled the network in learning to derain using synthetic dataset while generalizing better using unlabeled real-world images. Inspired by the success of the Syn2Real network in removing rain from images during the daytime, we improve the Syn2Real network, called NIRR, to solve the aforementioned problem of rain removal at nighttime. Similar to the Syn2Real network, our network uses semi-supervised learning, which can use unlabeled real-world rainy images for training to improve the generalization ability of real-world image deraining task. In our NIRR, we designed a new loss function composed of perceptual loss and SSIM loss for the supervised learning stage, aiming to obtain good rain removal and visual effect under nighttime rainy scenes. We have also established a new synthetic nighttime rain dataset, which contains light and heavy nighttime rain conditions, and 7 rain streak directions to simulate the complex conditions of real-world rain. Experimental results show that our method is able to effectively remove rain from nighttime rainy images.

To summarize, this paper makes the following contributions:

- An improved network based on Syn2Real network and a new synthetic night-time rain dataset are established to address the nighttime rain removal issues.
- We adopt perceptual loss to improve the visual quality of deraining image, rather than concentrating only on the characterization of rain streaks. By simply adding SSIM loss, our method can effectively improve the overall similarity in deraining results, and it is also readily trained.
- Extensive experiments on synthetic and real rainy images demonstrate the superiority of our method in both qualitative and quantitative measures.

The rest of the paper is organized as follows. Related work is presented in Sect. 2. Section 3 details the proposed approach. We present the experiments and results in Sect. 4. Finally, Sect. 5 concludes the paper.

2   Related Work

In this section, we divide the single image rain removal methods into two categories: model-driven(non-deep learning) and data-driven(deep learning) ones, and discuss the existing methods of the two class in detail in the following subsections.

2.1   Model-Driven Methods

Before 2017, the conventional methods are model-driven approaches, which decompose the rainy image into the rain-free background scene and the rain streaks layer, and different prior terms are designed to describe and separate the rain streak from the background layer. The major developments in the model-based approach are driven by the following ideas: sparse coding, and priors based Gaussian mixture models.

Sparse Coding. Kang et al. [8] firstly proposed a single image deraining method that decomposed an input image into the low/high- frequency component using dictionary learning and sparse coding. Luo et al. [13] presented a discriminative sparse coding (DSC) over a learned dictionary for separating rain streaks from the background image based on image patches. Zhu et al. [31] constructed a joint optimization process to remove rain-streak details from the estimated background, as well as to remove non-streak details from the estimated rain streak layer using layer-specific priors. Deng et al. [4] formulated a directional group sparse model (DGSM) to model rain streak directions and sparsity, and effectively removed blurred rain streaks.

Gaussian Mixture Models. Li et al. [10] utilized the Gaussian mixture models (GMM) as a prior to decompose the input image into the rain streaks and the rain-free background layer. The traditional model-based method can achieve success in certain scenarios, however, it tends to be degenerated when applicating complicated and diverse practical rain types. Therefore, it is critical to explore more powerful coding manner for fitting general rains in real-world.

2.2   Data-Driven Methods

Since 2017, the data-driven single-image rain removal method has developed rapidly and made great progress. Its development process can be summarized as: deep convolutional networks, generative adversarial networks and semi/unsupervised methods.

Deep Convolutional Networks. Yang et al. [27] firstly used deep learning ideas to image deraining, they constructed a joint rain detection and removal network to detect rain locations by predicting the binary rain mask, and took a recurrent framework to remove rain streaks and clear up rain accumulation progressively. Fu et al. [5] proposed a deep detail network (DetailNet), which took only the high frequency details as input, and predicted the residue of the rain and clean images. Using the latest smoothed dilation technique and a gated subnetwork, Chen et al. [2] proposed a new end-to-end gated context aggregation network, which was initially designed for dehazing, and applied for deraining task and achieved great performance.

Generative Adversarial Networks. Qian et al. [16] injected visual attention into both the generative and discriminative networks for learning to attend raindrop regions and percept their surroundings. Zhang et al. [30] directly used the multi-scale conditional generative adversarial network (CGAN) to solve single image de-raining task and obtain good results. Li et al. [9] built a two-stage single-image deraining network that combined the physics-driven network and adversarial learning refinement network.

Semi/Unsupervised Learning Methods. Wei et al. [25] firstly proposed a semi-supervised learning method toward single image rain removal, which formulated the residual as a specific parametrized rain streak distribution between an input rainy image and its expected network output. Yasarla et al. [29] proposed a Gaussian Process-based semi-supervised learning framework which enabled the network in learning to derain using synthetic dataset while generalizing better using unlabeled real-world images.

In this paper, we use semi-supervised learning method to solve the problem of nighttime image rain removal because of the excellent ability to learn from synthetic and real world data.

3   Proposed Approach

Inspired by the success of Syn2Real network [29] on daytime deraining, we first adopt Syn2Real network to address the nighttime rain removal issues. In order to obtain good visual effect and quantitative scores under nighttime rainy scene, we modify the loss function for the supervised learning phase and this is the major improvement. This section presents the details of our proposed approach.

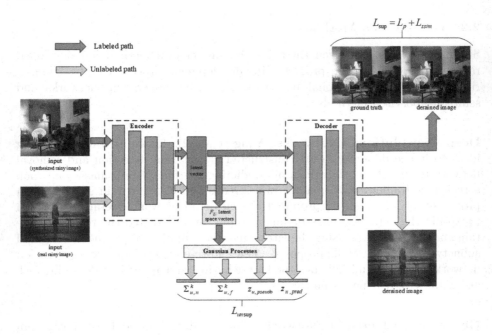

Fig. 1. The architecture of our NIRR.

3.1 Framework

As shown in Fig. 1, our approach consists of a CNN based on the UNet structure [19], where each block is constructed using a Res2Block [6]. The same as Syn2Real network [29], the Gaussian Process (GP) is a critical step in the framework to involve iteratively training on the labeled and unlabeled data. A Gaussian Process $f(v)$ can be denoted as follows

$$f(v) \sim GP(m(v), K(v, v') + \sigma_\epsilon^2 I), \tag{1}$$

where $m(v)$ and $K(v, v')$ are the mean function and covariance function of $f(v)$, I is the identity matrix and σ_ϵ^2 is the variance of the additive noise. In Eq. 1, $v, v' \in V$ denote the possible inputs that index the GP. So, any collection of function values is then jointly Gaussian as follows

$$f(V) = [f(v_1), ..., f(v_n)]^T \sim N(\mu, K(V, V') + \sigma_\epsilon^2 I). \tag{2}$$

In our paper, a Gaussian posterior distribution in closed form is computed by conditioning on the observed data to make predictions at unlabeled points. The detailed review on GP can be found in [17,29].

Figure 1 shows that our NIRR is divided into two phases: labeled training phase and unlabeled training phase. The goal of our NIRR is to learn the network parameters by minimizing the supervised loss function (L_{sup}) in the labeled training phase and the unsupervised loss function (L_{unsup}) in the unlabeled training phase.

During the labeled training phase, the intermediate feature vectors z_l^i's for all the labeled training images z_l^i's are stored in a matrix F_{zl}, which is also used to generate the pseudo-GT for the unlabeled data in the unlabeled training phase. In the unlabeled training phase, GP formulation is used to generate pseudo-GT, which is used in L_{unsup}.

3.2 Loss Function

In our paper, the overall loss function used for training the network is defined as follows

$$L_{total} = L_{sup} + \lambda_{unsup} L_{unsup}, \tag{3}$$

where λ_{unsup} is a predefined weight that controls the contribution from L_{sup} and L_{unsup}. And the value of λ_{unsup} is 0.0015.

From Fig. 1, L_{unsup} is a function of $z_{u,pred}$, $z_{u,pseudo}$, $\sum_{u,f}^k$ and $\sum_{u,n}^k$, as defined below

$$L_{unsup} = \|z_{u,pred}^k - z_{u,pseudo}^k\|_2 + log\Sigma_{u,n}^k + log(1 - \Sigma_{u,f}^k), \tag{4}$$

where $z_{u,pred}^k$ is the latent vector obtained by forwarding an unlabeled input image x_u^k through the encoder, $z_{u,pseudo}^k$ is the pseudo-GT latent space vector, $\Sigma_{u,n}^k$ and $\Sigma_{u,f}^k$ are the variances obtained by using F_{zl}. For their expressions and specific meanings, see in [29]. The unsupervised loss function L_{unsup} in our paper is the same as in [29], and we mainly modify the supervised loss function L_{sup}.

Nighttime rainy images usually have characteristics of low contrast, uneven lighting distribution, limited color information and visual unpleasure, making the task of rain removal more challenging. The SSIM loss [24] is measured based on local image characteristics (such as local contrast, luminance and details), which are also the characteristics of rain streaks. Therefore, in our nighttime rain removal network, using SSIM loss as a part of the loss function is beneficial to the training of the supervised learning part and produces better rain removal effect. Johnson et al. [7] have shown that training with a perceptual loss measured on the early layers of VGG-16 [21] can make the model to preserve better reconstruct fine details like color, texture and shape, leading to pleasing visual result. So, in order to make our network perform well in the task of nighttime rain removal, we combine the above two loss functions into a new refined loss function L_{sup}, defined as follows

$$L_{sup} = L_p + L_{ssim}, \tag{5}$$

where L_p is the perceptual loss and L_{ssim} is the SSIM loss. L_p is the feature loss from the layer relu1_2 and relu2_2 of the VGG-16 [21]. In order to obtain more edge details from deraining image, L_1 norm is adopted in the perceptual loss L_p to minimize the distance between adjacent feature layers. Different from the negative SSIM loss in other papers, our SSIM loss L_{ssim} only needs to calculate the similarity between the deraining image B_{dr} and the corresponding ground-truth clean image B. It is defined as follows

$$L_{ssim} = 1 - SSIM(B_{dr}, B), \qquad (6)$$

where $SSIM(\cdot)$ is regarded as the similarity function.

4   Experiments and Results

In this section, we present the experiments and results, including the dataset used for training and testing, evaluation metrics, and evaluation results on synthetic and real-world data.

4.1   Datasets and Metrics

Datasets. The data-driven rain removal method requires a large number of training samples to obtain good performance, and the existing published datasets are used for training and testing of the daytime rain removal network. Therefore, we make a new dataset to adapt to the nighttime rainy scenes. First, we select 1200 nighttime images from ExDark [12], which has 7363 exclusively low-light images with 12 object classes captured in different time of day (e.g. twilight, nighttime), different location (e.g. indoor, outdoor), and different type of light sources (e.g. the sun, man-made lights). Then, we add rain to these images using Photoshop. Each image is synthesized into 14 nighttime rainy images with two intensities (e.g. light and heavy) and 7 different orientations (e.g. 60°, 70°, 80°, 90°, 100°, 110° and 120°) respectively. So the synthesized dataset called **NiRain** contains a total of 16800 nighttime rainy images. In this synthesized dataset, we sample 9800 images as a train set, 700 images as a test set and 700 images as a validation set. Samples of synthesized images under these 14 conditions are shown in Fig. 2. In addition, we have downloaded 120 real-world nighttime rainy images from the internet as a train set to better the generalization capability of our network. Fig. 3 shows the samples of real-world images.

Evaluation Metrics. In our experiments, two widely used metrics, namely, PSNR (Peak Single to Noise Ratio) and SSIM (Structural Similarity) [23], are adopted as the quality metrics. Generally speaking, the higher the values of PSNR and SSIM, the better the rain removal effect.

4.2   Implementation Details

In order to show the performance of our method, we implement a series of experiments on synthetic and real-world images, and compare our method with the state-of-the-art methods, such as the Discriminative Sparse Coding based method (DSC) [13] (ICCV'15), Gaussian Mixture Model (GMM) based method [10] (CVPR'16), Gated Context Aggregation Network (GCANet) [2]

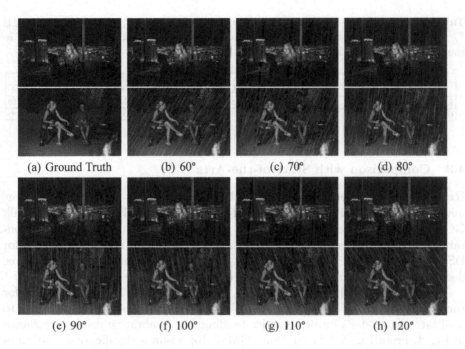

| | | | |
| (a) Ground Truth | (b) 60° | (c) 70° | (d) 80° |

| | | | |
| (e) 90° | (f) 100° | (g) 110° | (h) 120° |

Fig. 2. Samples of synthesized images. In the sub-picture (b)–(h), the upper picture of each image group is a synthesized light rain scene, and the lower picture is a synthesized heavy rain scene, and the orientations of the rain streaks are 60°, 70°, 80°, 90°, 100°, 110°, 120° respectively.

Fig. 3. Samples of real-world nighttime rainy images.

(WACV'19), Semi-supervised Learning method (SIRR) [25] (CVPR'19), Gaussian Process-based Semi-supervised Learning framework (Syn2Real) [29] (CVPR'20).

The proposed NIRR is implemented using Pytorch [14], and is trained on a PC with Intel Core i7 CPU 3.6 GHz, 16GB RAM and NVIDIA TITAN Xp. In our experiments, the images are randomly cropped to the size of 128 × 128, and the batch size is 4. Adam is used as the optimization algorithm and the models are trained for a total of 105 epochs. The learning rate starts from 0.001 and is decayed by a factor of 0.5 at every 25 epochs.

Table 1. Average PSNR and SSIM comparison (PSNR/SSIM) on the validation set. First and second best results are highlighted in color. The results of some images in the validation set are shown in Fig. 4.

Name	DSC [13]		GMM [10]		GCANet [2]		SIRR [25]		Syn2Real [29]		NIRR	
	PSNR	SSIM	PSNR	SSIM	PSNR	SSIM	PSNR	SSIM	PSNR	SSIM	PSNR	SSIM
Light rain	32.0388	0.90590	35.7851	0.94773	38.9273	0.97244	36.6823	0.95881	37.2401	0.96792	38.4586	0.97768
Heavy rain	30.3937	0.81014	30.6587	0.82775	36.8971	0.95286	35.4616	0.93770	37.5588	0.96648	37.9454	0.97199

4.3 Comparison with State-of-the-Arts

Results on Synthetic Images. In this subsection, we compare the performance of our method and other state-of-the-arts, such as DSC [13], GMM [10], GCANet [2], SIRR [25] and Syn2Real [29], on the validation set, which contains 350 synthetic rainy images at nighttime. We should note that, except for DSC [13] and GMM [10], GCANet [2], SIRR [25] and Syn2Real [29] are three deep learning methods, and are retrained with the default settings.

Quantitative results are tabulated in Table 1. As shown in Table 1, except for the PSNR in light rain condition, our NIRR obtains the best results. In order to facilitate the reader's intuitive understanding, the qualitative results are shown in Fig. 4. From Fig. 4, DSC [13] and GMM [10] retain a signification portion of rain traces after rain removal. GCANet [2] and SIRR [25] can remove majority of the rain streaks, but they still leave some rain residual. Syn2Real [29] can get a good deraining effect, but if you zoom in on Fig. 4, you can see that the first image in the sixth row still has slightly rain residual. However, our NIRR is able to preserve the details while effectively removing the rain streaks on all the testing rainy images. We also display the PSNR and SSIM values under each derained image separately, it can also be seen that our NIRR almost achieves the highest PSNR and SSIM. So, in a conclusion, our NIRR outperforms the other state-of-the-arts, and obtains the best results on synthetic images.

Results on Real-World Images. In this subsection, two real-world rainy images in Fig. 5 are used to illustrate the effectiveness of different methods. It can be seen that the DSC [13], GMM [10] and GCANet [2] all get undesirable rain removal effects because the traditional and supervised-learning methods are difficult to deal with the rain streaks with different scales and directions contained in real-world nighttime rainy images. Among the other three semi-supervised learning methods, the SIRR [25] method has excessive rain removal. For the real rainy image 'Restaurant', Syn2Real [29] achieves the rain removal result as good as our NIRR. However, it leaves some traces after rain removal in the image 'Riverside'. In general, our NIRR achieves the best results and image detail preservation for nighttime rain removal in real-world images.

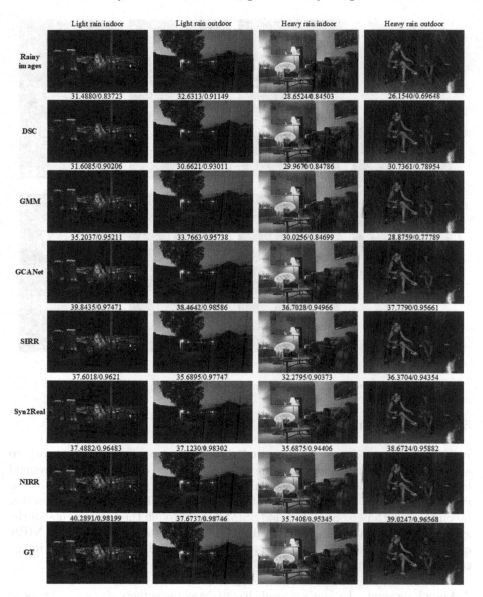

Fig. 4. Qualitative comparison and PSNR/SSIM of different methods, from the first row to the last row, the displayed pictures are the synthetic rainy images, the derained results of DSC, GMM, GCANet, SIRR, Syn2Real, our NIRR and the ground truth, respectively.

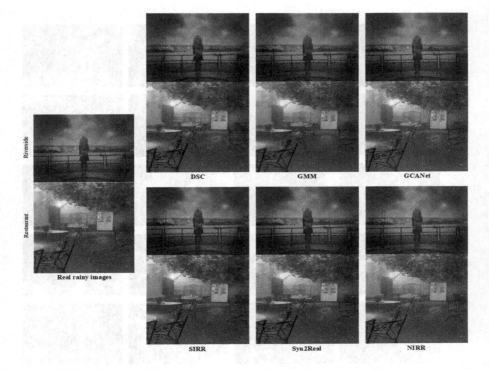

Fig. 5. Deraining results of real-world nighttime rainy images.

5   Conclusions

In this paper, we design an improved model based on Syn2Real network to address the problem of nighttime image rain removal. In our NIRR, a new refined loss function for the supervised learning phase is proposed to obtain good rain removal and visual effect under nighttime rainy scene. The refined loss function is combined with perceptual loss and SSIM loss. Through the experiments on the synthesized dataset **NiRain** and real-world nighttime rainy images, our NIRR can effectively remove the rain streaks and preserve the details of deraining image compared to the state-of-the-arts.

Acknowledgment. The authors would like to thank the authors of compared papers, who provided the original codes, and the anonymous reviewers for their insightful comments and valuable suggestions. This work was supported by National Natural Science Foundation of China (No. 51879211), Hunan Provincial Natural Science Foundation of China (No. 2017JJ3053), and Hunan Provincial Science Research Project of China (Nos. 17A051).

References

1. Bahnsen, C.H., Moeslund, T.B.: Rain removal in traffic surveillance: does it matter? IEEE Trans. Intell. Transp. Syst. **20**(8), 2802–2819 (2018)

2. Chen, D., et al.: Gated context aggregation network for image dehazing and deraining. In: 2019 IEEE Winter Conference on Applications of Computer Vision (WACV), pp. 1375–1383. IEEE (2019)
3. Chen, Y., Li, W., Sakaridis, C., Dai, D., Van Gool, L.: Domain adaptive faster R-CNN for object detection in the wild. In: Proceedings of the IEEE Conference on Computer Vision and Pattern Recognition, pp. 3339–3348 (2018)
4. Deng, L.J., Huang, T.Z., Zhao, X.L., Jiang, T.X.: A directional global sparse model for single image rain removal. Appl. Math. Model. **59**, 662–679 (2018)
5. Fu, X., Huang, J., Zeng, D., Huang, Y., Ding, X., Paisley, J.: Removing rain from single images via a deep detail network. In: Proceedings of the IEEE Conference on Computer Vision and Pattern Recognition, pp. 3855–3863 (2017)
6. Gao, S., Cheng, M.M., Zhao, K., Zhang, X.Y., Yang, M.H., Torr, P.H.: Res2Net: a new multi-scale backbone architecture. IEEE Trans. Pattern Anal. Mach. Intell., 1 (2019)
7. Johnson, J., Alahi, A., Fei-Fei, L.: Perceptual losses for real-time style transfer and super-resolution. In: Leibe, B., Matas, J., Sebe, N., Welling, M. (eds.) ECCV 2016. LNCS, vol. 9906, pp. 694–711. Springer, Cham (2016). https://doi.org/10.1007/978-3-319-46475-6_43
8. Kang, L.W., Lin, C.W., Fu, Y.H.: Automatic single-image-based rain streaks removal via image decomposition. IEEE Trans. Image Process. **21**(4), 1742–1755 (2011)
9. Li, R., Cheong, L.F., Tan, R.T.: Heavy rain image restoration: integrating physics model and conditional adversarial learning. In: Proceedings of the IEEE Conference on Computer Vision and Pattern Recognition, pp. 1633–1642 (2019)
10. Li, Y., Tan, R.T., Guo, X., Lu, J., Brown, M.S.: Rain streak removal using layer priors. In: Proceedings of the IEEE Conference on Computer Vision and Pattern Recognition, pp. 2736–2744 (2016)
11. Liang, M., Yang, B., Wang, S., Urtasun, R.: Deep continuous fusion for multi-sensor 3D object detection. In: Proceedings of the European Conference on Computer Vision (ECCV), pp. 641–656 (2018)
12. Loh, Y.P., Chan, C.S.: Getting to know low-light images with the exclusively dark dataset. Comput. Vis. Image Underst. **178**, 30–42 (2019)
13. Luo, Y., Xu, Y., Ji, H.: Removing rain from a single image via discriminative sparse coding. In: Proceedings of the IEEE International Conference on Computer Vision, pp. 3397–3405 (2015)
14. Paszke, A., et al.: Pytorch: an imperative style, high-performance deep learning library. In: Advances in Neural Information Processing Systems, pp. 8026–8037 (2019)
15. Perera, A.G., Wei Law, Y., Chahl, J.: UAV-gesture: a dataset for UAV control and gesture recognition. In: Proceedings of the European Conference on Computer Vision (ECCV) (2018)
16. Qian, R., Tan, R.T., Yang, W., Su, J., Liu, J.: Attentive generative adversarial network for raindrop removal from a single image. In: Proceedings of the IEEE Conference on Computer Vision and Pattern Recognition, pp. 2482–2491 (2018)
17. Rasmussen, C.E.: Gaussian processes in machine learning. In: Bousquet, O., von Luxburg, U., Rätsch, G. (eds.) ML -2003. LNCS (LNAI), vol. 3176, pp. 63–71. Springer, Heidelberg (2004). https://doi.org/10.1007/978-3-540-28650-9_4
18. Ren, S., He, K., Girshick, R., Sun, J.: Faster R-CNN: towards real-time object detection with region proposal networks. In: Advances in Neural Information Processing Systems, pp. 91–99 (2015)

19. Ronneberger, O., Fischer, P., Brox, T.: U-Net: convolutional networks for biomedical image segmentation. In: Navab, N., Hornegger, J., Wells, W.M., Frangi, A.F. (eds.) MICCAI 2015. LNCS, vol. 9351, pp. 234–241. Springer, Cham (2015). https://doi.org/10.1007/978-3-319-24574-4_28

20. Shi, Z., Feng, Y., Zhao, M., He, L.: A joint deep neural networks-based method for single nighttime rainy image enhancement. Neural Comput. Appl., 1–14 (2019)

21. Simonyan, K., Zisserman, A.: Very deep convolutional networks for large-scale image recognition. arXiv preprint arXiv:1409.1556 (2014)

22. Sultani, W., Chen, C., Shah, M.: Real-world anomaly detection in surveillance videos. In: Proceedings of the IEEE Conference on Computer Vision and Pattern Recognition, pp. 6479–6488 (2018)

23. Sun, S.H., Fan, S.P., Wang, Y.C.F.: Exploiting image structural similarity for single image rain removal. In: 2014 IEEE International Conference on Image Processing (ICIP), pp. 4482–4486. IEEE (2014)

24. Wang, Z., Bovik, A.C., Sheikh, H.R., Simoncelli, E.P.: Image quality assessment: from error visibility to structural similarity. IEEE Trans. Image Process. **13**(4), 600–612 (2004)

25. Wei, W., Meng, D., Zhao, Q., Xu, Z., Wu, Y.: Semi-supervised transfer learning for image rain removal. In: Proceedings of the IEEE Conference on Computer Vision and Pattern Recognition, pp. 3877–3886 (2019)

26. Wu, Y., Lim, J., Yang, M.H.: Online object tracking: a benchmark. In: Proceedings of the IEEE Conference on Computer Vision and Pattern Recognition, pp. 2411–2418 (2013)

27. Yang, W., Tan, R.T., Feng, J., Liu, J., Guo, Z., Yan, S.: Deep joint rain detection and removal from a single image. In: Proceedings of the IEEE Conference on Computer Vision and Pattern Recognition, pp. 1357–1366 (2017)

28. Yang, W., Tan, R.T., Wang, S., Fang, Y., Liu, J.: Single image deraining: from model-based to data-driven and beyond. IEEE Trans. Pattern Anal. Mach. Intell. (2020)

29. Yasarla, R., Sindagi, V.A., Patel, V.M.: Syn2Real transfer learning for image deraining using gaussian processes. In: Proceedings of the IEEE/CVF Conference on Computer Vision and Pattern Recognition, pp. 2726–2736 (2020)

30. Zhang, H., Sindagi, V., Patel, V.M.: Image de-raining using a conditional generative adversarial network. IEEE Trans. Circ. Syst. Video Technol., 3943–3956 (2019)

31. Zhu, L., Fu, C.W., Lischinski, D., Heng, P.A.: Joint bi-layer optimization for single-image rain streak removal. In: Proceedings of the IEEE International Conference on Computer Vision, pp. 2526–2534 (2017)

Unsupervised Domain Adaptation for Person Re-Identification with Few and Unlabeled Target Data

George Galanakis[1,2]([✉]), Xenophon Zabulis[2], and Antonis A. Argyros[1,2]

[1] Computer Science Department, University of Crete, Rethymno, Greece
{ggalan,argyros}@csd.uoc.gr
[2] Institute of Computer Science, FORTH, Heraklion, Greece
{ggalan,zabulis,argyros}@ics.forth.gr

Abstract. Existing, fully supervised methods for person re-identification (ReID) require annotated data acquired in the target domain in which the method is expected to operate. This includes the IDs as well as images of persons in that domain. This is an obstacle in the deployment of ReID methods in novel settings. For solving this problem, semi-supervised or even unsupervised ReID methods have been proposed. Still, due to their assumptions and operational requirements, such methods are not easily deployable and/or prove less performant to novel domains/settings, especially those related to small person galleries. In this paper, we propose a novel approach for person ReID that alleviates these problems. This is achieved by proposing a completely unsupervised method for fine tuning the ReID performance of models learned in prior, auxiliary domains, to new, completely different ones. The proposed model adaptation is achieved based on only few and unlabeled target persons' data. Extensive experiments investigate several aspects of the proposed method in an ablative study. Moreover, we show that the proposed method is able to improve considerably the performance of state-of-the-art ReID methods in state-of-the-art datasets.

Keywords: Person re-identification · Unsupervised domain adaptation · Agglomerative clustering

1 Introduction

During the recent years, person re-identification (ReID) has received a lot of attention in the computer vision research community [30]. This is especially due to the increased interest in surveillance applications related to security, crime prevention and crowd analytics. The goal of person ReID, is to match people across non-overlapping camera views at different times. In an effort towards more accurate person identification, modern solutions propose learning discriminative, appearance-based features with increased robustness against illumination and pose variations, but also tolerant to missing information, such as occlusions.

© Springer Nature Switzerland AG 2020
G. Bebis et al. (Eds.): ISVC 2020, LNCS 12510, pp. 357–373, 2020.
https://doi.org/10.1007/978-3-030-64559-5_28

Table 1. Comparison of ReID methods according to their type and level of supervision. Rows: requirements of the methods due to their supervision type and the resulting suitability in real world settings (see text for details).

Supervision level → / Properties ↓	Fully-sup.	Unsup.	Semi-sup.	UFT-reID
Requires auxiliary non-target dataset	-	optional	optional	✓
Uses target training dataset	✓	✓	✓	-
Requires ID annotations in target dataset	✓	-	partial	-
Uses views from all cameras in target dataset	✓	✓	✓	optional
Easy to deploy in new settings	×	✓	×	✓
Suitable for small galleries	×	×	×	✓

These features are learned in a supervised, semi-supervised or unsupervised manner, based on several public surveillance data.

Table 1 summarizes the requirements and properties of the person ReID methods with respect to their type of supervision. *Supervised learning* is the most prominent methodology, as it incorporates a lot of information from the target domain in which these methods will need to operate. Such information includes images depicting persons from multiple cameras, paired with the corresponding person ids. The outcome of the learning process is a model capable of extracting features to represent persons. The hope is that the training set contains enough variability, therefore it is expressive and generalizes well. The model is afterwards evaluated on images of unseen persons, while the cameras and other conditions (e.g., illumination conditions) remain the same. As it is often demonstrated [13], supervised models do not generalize well to new domains. This means that even if two datasets are obtained in visually similar conditions training in one of them (source) and directly using the model on the other (target) dataset, results in very significant ReID performance degradation.

To overcome the expense of labeling requirements in the target domain, *semi-supervised* transfer learning techniques have been developed. These techniques incorporate labeled data from an auxiliary (source, non-target) domain and partially labeled data from the new (target) domain. Other techniques, also referred to as *unsupervised* domain adaptation, require no labelled data from the new domain. Moreover, some recent unsupervised techniques such as the one proposed in [18] depend only on unlabeled auxiliary data from the target domain. The common ground of these techniques is their dependence on the availability of a substantially large set of auxiliary data from the new, target domain.

In real world applications, enough amounts of data (even unlabeled) from the target domain may be few, hard to obtain, or even unavailable. This holds especially for places where, within a specific time-frame, passers-by are in the dozens rather than in the hundreds. This situation makes most of the existing ReID methods inadequate, due to limited input for learning. For this reason, we argue that effective, real-world solutions must require no same-domain auxiliary data.

In that direction, we propose UFT-ReID, a novel ReID method that is unsupervised with respect to the target domain and operates directly on unlabeled, test target data, without requiring a training target dataset. Moreover, contrary to existing approaches that use training input from all available cameras of the target domain, the proposed ReID method is demonstrated in situations were part of the viewpoints are not available. Due to its loose supervision requirements, UFT-ReID can be applicable even in small person galleries. Indeed, extensive experiments with UFT-ReID prove that the proposed approach is very effective even in such constrained settings.

2   Related Work

Modern person ReID approaches learn robust person representations by incorporating appropriate *CNN architectures* and objective functions that result from different *training and supervision objectives*. Below, we discuss these two components separately as usually, they are independent to each other.

2.1   CNN Architectures

Initial ReID approaches, including [1,11,16] borrowed or got inspired by CNN models that were designed specifically for object classification. This trend is followed by current works [10,15,18], too. Recent efforts in CNN architecture design incorporate methods which take into account that person images are constrained, i.e., they only contain standing persons rather than generic object classes. Towards this direction, some methods propose rough segmentation of a person's body into parts [26,27,33,39]. Other methods directly integrate pose estimation [23,25,32] or dense part correspondence [40] for extracting part-aware features. In contrast to competing works, [21,38,45] do not adopt an ordinary backbone network, but propose their own. Finally, some recent works proposed modified architectures that better generalize to new domains [14,44].

2.2   Training Objectives

CNN models are trained by minimizing some properly designed loss objective function. In order to express and quantify the loss, this function may (or may not) utilize the ground truth person IDs. In this light, approaches may be classified to supervised, semi-supervised or unsupervised.

Supervised Methods: The majority of proposed works present supervised methods, while most common losses are classification and metric loss. Classification loss is inspired by object classification and is usually implemented as cross-entropy loss. In this case, each person is regarded as a different object class. Approaches which adopt the classification loss include [9,17,23,45]. More interestingly [34] measured separate classification loss for each body part. Metric loss is inspired by the distance metric learning framework. Its objective is

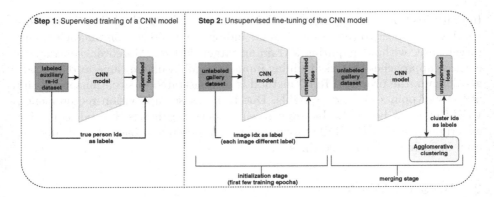

Fig. 1. Overview of the two-step approach followed by the proposed UFT-ReID method.

twofold; to simultaneously minimize intra-class and maximize inter-class distance. Variances of this loss, also referred to as triplet loss, are adopted by the methods in [4,11,22,24,37]. Some works proposed novel loss functions [8,38]. Finally, combinations of losses are incorporated in [2,21,38,40].

Unsupervised Methods: Methods that do not use any supervision with respect to target domain fall into two subcategories. First, domain adaptation methods, aim at adapting well-performing models that are trained on auxiliary data, to a different target domain. Recent methods which follow this approach are [6,7,33,35,36]. Completely unsupervised methods, including [5,18] do not include supervision at any stage of training. Some of these works propose generating pseudo-labels [7,18,35] or pseudo-positive samples [33] that can be utilized as previously within classification or metric losses, respectively. The notion of such pseudo labels has been effectively explored in other visual tasks such as [3,20], too. Other methods propose more appropriate unsupervised objectives [28,35].

Semi-supervised Methods: Semi-supervised approaches require that only a part of target data is labeled. These works borrow and combine methodologies from both supervised and unsupervised settings. Some recent works in this domain are [19,29].

Our Approach and Contribution: The proposed UFT-ReID method corresponds to domain adaptation techniques, while it is achieved by unsupervised fine-tuning on the target domain. In contrast to other works, UFT-ReID operates directly on target persons' data. This is a novel formulation that is more relevant to real-world situations, where the requirement for same-domain auxiliary data is hard or even impossible-to-fulfill. We demonstrate that this setting is feasible and that our approach is very effective, especially for small person galleries. Our work adopts the pseudo-label generation approach and corresponding loss function from [18], however it deviates from them as follows. Firstly and most importantly, our method and corresponding evaluation scheme do not require same-domain auxiliary person data. Such data are extensively utilized by [18] to facilitate learning in a completely unsupervised way. Instead, we pre-train on auxiliary domain dataset (domain adaptation). We argue that for real deployment one should always perform supervised pre-training on existing re-id datasets, since this results to already capable baselines [45]. Finally, our architectures are specially designed for the ReID task, in contrast to the general ResNet utilized in [18].

3   The UFT-ReID Method

The workflow of UFT-ReID (Fig. 1) consists of two steps: (1) supervised model training and (2) unsupervised model fine-tuning. In both cases, model refers to the same deep neural network. Supervised training is accomplished using an auxiliary domain data, while fine-tuning is performed directly on the target domain and especially on target persons; those of ReID interest.

3.1   Supervised Model Training

Given a labeled person dataset from a particular domain, our goal is to learn a mapping from the original image space, to a feature space in which, images of the same person are close, while images of different persons are more distant. This mapping can be effectively structured by typical supervised learning approaches, using conventional or problem-specific CNN architectures, loss functions and training methodologies. The outcome of learning is a feature extraction model, robust for unseen persons in this particular domain, though limited for other domains. For this step we utilized and experimented with two modern architectures as described in Sect. 4.2.

3.2   Unsupervised Model Fine-Tuning

Unsupervised training techniques are naturally more suitable for real-world applications where we are not aware of the identity of each person in a gallery and live manual annotation is highly undesirable, as it is costly or even impossible. Instead of training from scratch, we propose to refine the model of the previous (supervised model training) step, solely in an unsupervised fashion. This model has been trained on a separate domain; different cameras, lighting conditions etc, but on the same task (person ReID). It is expected that a tuning to the new domain should be sufficient to adapt the model to the new persons' appearances, without mitigating its generalizability.

Model fine-tuning is a well known technique for transfer learning. Given a pre-trained CNN, the common practice is (a) to modify its output layer to contain the new classes and (b) train the rest of the model according to some initial, relatively small learning rate. Note that, depending on the model architecture, it may be useful to define different learning rates for groups of layers. This is explained by the structure of CNNs, where first convolutional layers represent primitive information, which is a common base across different datasets and even tasks.

Traditional fine-tuning depends on availability of class labels (supervision). As previously posed, supervised methods require resource-intensive identity annotation, therefore they are not easily applicable to new domains. In this work we are interested in the unsupervised setting which is more suitable for our task. Lack of person ids guided us to seek for an unsupervised solution with respect to target domain. In this light, we are inspired by a recent unsupervised framework [18], also employed for person ReID, however for a different setting. More specifically, our approach relies on the use of pseudo-labels. A common method for proposing pseudo-labels during learning is clustering. This approach is followed for example in [7,18,35]. However, in [18] clustering is naturally integrated with training. A bottom-up clustering approach is proposed, for jointly optimizing the CNN and the relationship between individual samples (images).

In UFT-ReID we utilize this framework as follows. At first, we initialize our CNN with weights pre-trained from the previous, supervised step. We also prepare the model for the unsupervised task, by keeping only relevant layers and assign unique labels to each training sample. This is because initially, all training samples are considered as independent clusters. At each training stage, cluster numbers are utilized as pseudo-labels for optimizing the CNN. However, the number of clusters is not constant, but gradually lowers as clusters merge. In more detail, the training scheme operates as follows:

1. **Initialization stage:** All training samples are regarded as unique clusters. The CNN is trained for e_i epochs, with respect to minimization of the repelled loss.
2. **Merging stage:** The current state of the CNN is utilized for features extraction. Afterwards, according to a merging criterion, m clusters are merged and CNN is trained for another e_m epochs.
3. **Stopping criterion:** Training stops when the number of clusters due to several merges reaches m.

The repelled loss is defined as the negative log probability (cross-entropy) that a sample belongs to the correct cluster. For a single sample x_i it corresponds to:

$$\mathcal{L} = -log(p(\hat{y_i}|x_i, \mathbf{V})), \tag{1}$$

where p is defined as:

$$p(c|x, \mathbf{V}) = \frac{exp(\mathbf{V}_c^{\mathrm{T}} \mathbf{v}/\tau)}{\sum_{j=1}^{C} exp(\mathbf{V}_j^{\mathrm{T}} \mathbf{v}/\tau)}. \tag{2}$$

In the above equations, x corresponds to the input samples within the batch, $\mathbf{v}$ are the $L2$-normalized features of these samples as extracted by the CNN at the current state, C is the current number of clusters, $\mathbf{V}$ is a lookup table which maintains the features of the centroid of each cluster, and τ is a temperature parameter which controls the softness of the probability distribution [12]. The contribution of repelled loss is that it computes probabilities based on feature

Table 2. Choices of learning rate (lr) parameter for step 2 (fine-tuning). For each case, lr is 10x smaller for all layers up to and including top base layer.

Model	#IDs	lr	Top base layer	Model	#IDs	lr	Top base layer
	10-33	1e-3			10-83	1.5e-4	
PCB	45-282	1e-4	ResNet-50.layer3	OSNet	113-282	1.5e-5	OSNet.conv4
	383-702	1e-5			383 - 702	1.5e-6	

similarity and simultaneously trades off intra-cluster similarity and inter-cluster diversity, over the whole training set.

Cluster merging is based on the minimum distance criterion. This criterion takes the shortest Euclidean distance between samples in two clusters as the dissimilarity measure. In order to ensure that all clusters contain approximately the same number of samples, a diversity regularization term is introduced. This boosts merging smaller clusters. The overall dissimilarity merging score is computed as a sum of the minimum distance criterion and the regularization term, whose impact is controlled by a parameter λ. For more details about bottom-up clustering, we refer the reader to [18].

In UFT-ReID we utilize a pre-trained CNN on an auxiliary source domain and we fine-tune it using the above framework. Fine-tuning is performed in fewer data, containing only target persons. With respect to the CNN itself, we choose and experiment with modern architectures (PCB [26] and OSNet [45], see Sect. 4.2) specifically designed for the ReID task. These architectures take into account that the image belongs to a person, therefore they are able to exploit contextual information. Furthermore, the experimentation with different architectures essentially reveals that our approach is capable of applying successfully transfer learning via unsupervised fine-tuning that is irrelevant to the backbone architecture.

4 Experiments and Discussion

Our experiments where conducted on a PC equipped with Intel Core i7 CPU, 16GB RAM and an NVIDIA GTX1080 GPU. We re-implemented [18] as extension to Torchreid framework [43], based on the original reference code and appropriate modifications for supporting additional features related to our training and evaluation strategies.

4.1 Datasets

To evaluate UFT-ReID we employ two recent datasets, Market1501 [41] and DukeMTMC-reid [42] which comprise of multiple persons and multiple views per person. Both datasets are utilized either as auxiliary/source or as target, in different experiments. Let $M \rightarrow D$ denote fine-tuning on DukeMTMC-reid,

Table 3. $M \rightarrow D$ fine-tuning results using the proposed UFT-ReID method for different target gallery sizes.

Architecture		10	13	18	24	33	45	61	83	113	153	208	282	382	518	702
PCB	Baseline	70.9	66.3	61.9	59.8	56.0	52.7	49.8	46.5	43.8	41.1	38.3	35.6	32.7	30.2	27.6
	With UFT-ReID	78.6	74.3	73.5	70.8	68.1	64.7	62.9	60.5	57.6	55.2	51.7	47.5	40.5	38.6	35.6
	% Benefit	7.6	8.0	11.6	11.0	12.1	12.0	13.1	14.0	13.8	14.1	13.4	11.9	7.9	8.4	8.0
OSNet	Baseline	77.8	73.6	71.9	68.5	64.5	61.2	58.1	55.4	52.8	50.4	47.6	45.0	42.0	39.1	36.0
	With UFT-ReID	75.1	75.3	76.0	79.4	78.5	76.2	72.3	66.5	64.9	62.8	60.3	56.4	48.9	46.9	43.9
	% Benefit	−2.8	1.7	4.0	11.0	14.0	15.1	14.1	11.1	12.1	12.4	12.7	11.3	7.0	7.9	7.9

Table 4. Left: $D \rightarrow M$ fine-tuning results using the proposed UFT-ReID method. Fewer target gallery sizes have been tested because of the size of the target dataset (Market1501). Right: $M \rightarrow D_r$ UFT-ReID results.

Architecture		20	30	50
	Baseline	79.2	76.4	71.7
PCB	With UFT-ReID	83.8	82.3	75.3
	% Benefit	4.6	5.9	3.7
	Baseline	81.5	78.7	75.3
OSNet	With UFT-ReID	85.9	83.1	79.8
	% Benefit	4.4	4.4	4.5

Architecture		33	45	61
	Baseline	63.2	58.9	55.1
PCB	With UFT-ReID	65.4	64.4	57.1
	% Benefit	2.1	5.5	2.0
	Baseline	71.8	67.8	66.0
OSNet	With UFT-ReID	77.0	74.9	71.6
	% Benefit	5.2	7.1	5.6

based on a model which is pre-trained on Market1501, and $D \rightarrow M$ the opposite. We point out that $M \rightarrow D$ is a more difficult task because Market1501 contains fewer images observed from less viewpoints, i.e., it is less general. As a consequence, the pre-trained model is less expressive.

In our work we experiment with person galleries of varying size. In order to simulate such galleries, we generate random subsets for each target dataset. Let P be the number of persons contained in the test part of the target dataset and k the number of persons in the subset. In this work we focus on galleries containing $k \geq 10$ persons. In order to simulate diverse scenarios, we choose 15 values of k spaced evenly on a logarithmic scale in the range $[10, P]$. We randomly select k person ids and we repeat 20 times. In total, 300 random galleries of varying ids and sizes are generated. We do such randomization once and prior to all our experiments and store the galleries for further utilization. We further refer to a gallery sized x as G_x, e.g. G_{30} denotes gallery containing 30 persons.

It should be noted that in both Market1501 and DukeMTMC-reid datasets, the original gallery and query subsets contain person images obtained from the same cameras. However, this comes in contrast to a more realistic, cross-camera evaluation setting. Some person ReID methods [31,43] address this issue, but only during evaluation, where images from same cameras are discarded during pairwise matching. In contrast, in a separate experiment we purposely utilized images from only two cameras from DukeMTMC-reid's gallery during fine-tuning, while leaving the rest six cameras for query. We refer to this reduced

Table 5. Left: comparison with [33], standard eval. protocol. Right: comparison with [33], our eval. protocol and gallery type G_{33}.

Method	% rank-1	Method	% rank-1
PatchnetUn	65.7	PatchnetUn	88.33
PatchnetUn w. Pedal + Ipfl ([33])	72.0	PatchnetUn w. Pedal + Ipfl ([33])	**89.95**
OSNet	68.1	OSNet	89.08
OSNet w. repelled (UFT-ReID)	69.6	OSNet w. repelled (UFT-ReID)	89.50
		OSNet w. repelled + Pedal + Ipfl (UFT-ReID)	**90.47**

dataset as D_r. This setting is more challenging, as refinement is based on images captured by part of the cameras which are different to those used to capture the test images.

4.2 Settings

CNN Architectures: We utilize two recently proposed person ReID architectures named PCB [26] and OSNet [45]. PCB mainly aims at learning discriminative part-informed features, without the need for exact part/pose estimation. It is based on ResNet-50 architecture and augmented with additional layers. These layers are parallel for each body subdivision, while the final descriptor is the concatenation of the feature vectors from the separate layers. OSNet is a novel architecture, capable for multi-scale feature learning at each level of the architecture. The core of this architecture is an omni-scale residual block which allows the propagation of smaller scale features to higher layers. For both architectures we used the implementations provided by [43]. We trained models on source datasets using the default training parameters (Fig. 1, step 1).

Fine-Tuning Parameters: In the second step, we utilize the trained CNN model, apart from its output layer (classifier). Batch size is chosen to be small (16). Experiments with larger values are provided in Sect. 4.4. Learning rate is also chosen to be small so that the original model does not alter much. During preliminary experiments we found out that it is more beneficial to lower the learning rate as the number of persons grows. Thus, we choose variable learning rates, depending on the number of persons in the gallery. Furthermore, we choose smaller learning rates for the base layers of the network. Detailed learning rate settings are given in Table 2. The number of training epochs is not predefined, but dependent on the total number of samples and clustering algorithm parameters, as explained below.

Unsupervised Algorithm Parameters: As explained in Sect. 3.2, during the first e_i fine-tuning epochs, the number of clusters is equal to the number of gallery samples. Afterwards, and every e_m epochs, the number of clusters is reduced by m, due to merges. This is an iterative process which stops when the total number of clusters reaches m. In our experiments we set $e_i = 20$

Table 6. Comparison with OSNet variants [44,45] using our eval. protocol. Gallery type: G_{33}.

Architecture	Baseline	+UFT-reid	% Benefit
OSNet (original)	64.5	78.5	14.0
OSNet-IBN [45]	74.5	77.6	3.1
OSNet-AIN [44]	76.5	**80.0**	3.5

Table 7. Average fine-tuning training duration in minutes (OSNet architecture).

Auxiliary source → Target	33	45	61
$M \rightarrow D$	07:46	10:55	15:03
$M \rightarrow D_r$	06:01	08.16	11:17

and $e_m = 2$. Nevertheless, we realized that by increasing e_m we obtain a clear performance gain, at the cost of more time-consuming training. m is set to the number of gallery ids. Finally, we experimentally confirmed that the optimal value for the diversity regularization parameter λ is 0.05, as suggested in [18]. Section 4.4 presents additional experiments using various options for e_m and λ.

4.3   Experimental Results

Tables 3, 4 demonstrate the effectiveness of our method in various settings. In all experiments we report the rank-1 accuracy, obtained by the CMC curve. More specifically, Table 3 shows the impact of UFT-ReID fine-tuning for a wide range of gallery persons. The particular experiment is conducted using a CNN model pre-trained on Market1501, while galleries are sampled from DukeMTMC-reid ($M \rightarrow D$). It is shown that fine-tuning using UFT-ReID achieves considerably better rank-1 accuracy, increasing the baseline up to 14% and 15.1% for PCB and OSNet architectures, respectively. For both architectures, higher accuracy is obtained in the case of mid-sized galleries. This may indicate that a mid-sized gallery is a good balance for appearance diversity. Too small diversity encountered in smaller galleries is not enough for generalized learning. On the other hand, too large diversity, encountered in larger galleries may encompass persons that are similar to each other, negatively affecting the overall accuracy.

In Table 4 (left) we present similar results for fine-tuning models pre-trained on DukeMTMC-reid using some random Market1501 galleries ($D \rightarrow M$). In this case, the benefit is smaller on average. This is expected, because base models are trained on a larger dataset, (DukeMTMC-reid), therefore better equipped against a smaller dataset.

Finally, Table 4 (right) shows experimental results using the reduced DukeMTMC-reid gallery dataset which, as explained in Sect. 4.1, contains images from cameras that were not used for the unsupervised fine tuning step ($M \rightarrow$

D_r). Even in this case, UFT-ReID increases the accuracy of the baseline methods, although as expected, the benefit is on average smaller compared to the
$M \rightarrow D$ experiment.

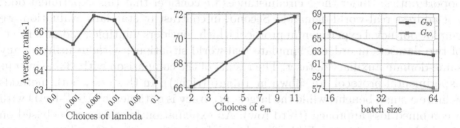

Fig. 2. Left: effect of diversity regularization parameter λ on average rank-1 accuracy.
Middle: effect of merging epochs e_m on accuracy. Right: accuracy for variable batch
size, G_{30} and G_{50}.

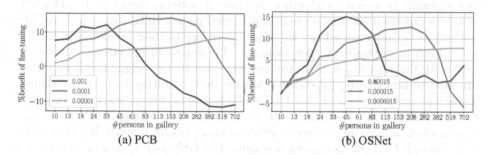

Fig. 3. Average % benefit of fine-tuning with respect to rank-1 accuracy. The experiment includes variable gallery sizes and variable learning rates using PCB and OSNet
architectures.

Comparison to State-of-the-Art: We compare our approach to that of [33]
which considers MSMT17 as source, while supervised training is conducted in a
combined train + test dataset. MSMT17 is the largest ReID dataset containing
4101 persons captured from up to 15 views, much larger than Market1501 and
DukeMTMC-reid. For fairness, we also utilized MSMT17 as the source dataset.
To perform the aforementioned comparison, we conducted two types of experiments. First, we evaluated our work using the standard protocol they also use.
Corresponding results are presented in Table 5 (left). Our method is able to
obtain some benefit with respect to the baseline model, however smaller than
the one of [33]. We stress that this experiment regards a very large dataset
(MSMT17) as source. This captures a wide variety of appearance characteristics, letting the supervised training to generalize better. Subsequently, impact

of fine-tuning on the target domain is smaller. In a real-world scenario however, such suitable source dataset will not always be available. We also note that the particular experiment incorporates imagery of auxiliary persons from the same domain (DukeMTMC-reid, train); a hard requirement which limits deployment opportunities. Under these circumstances we consider that this experiment does not address real-world demands. Second, in contrast to standard evaluation, we employ our novel experimental protocol which considers multiple random subsets of two datasets in order to simulate real-world situations, *without* utilizing any same-domain auxiliary dataset. The results of the comparison with [33] using our experimental protocol are shown in Table 5 (right)). In this case, both methods achieve a small benefit, while the largest accuracy is obtained by UFT-ReID with a combined loss approach (third row). An explanation for this can be based on the evidence provided in Tables 3 and 5 (right) for the case of G_{33}. The accuracy of the Market1501-trained base model is much lower than the MSMT17-trained base model for the same (OSNet) architecture, i.e. 64.5% vs. 89.08%. Thus, the MSMT17 dataset results in an already capable baseline model, therefore fine-tuning is left with less room for substantial improvement (Table 5 (right)).

Comparison to OSNet Variants: In all previous experiments, OSNet refers to the originally proposed architecture, precisely denoted as "osnet_x1_0". This version was proposed for same-domain supervised person ReID. More recently, the authors of OSNet released two subsequent versions of their architecture [44,45], specialized to generalize to new domains. These new architectures, denoted as OSNet-IBN, and OSNet-AIN, are modifications to the original, however they are able to address the substantial domain shift, resulting to better baselines. Table 6 presents the benefit that UFT-ReID is able to achieve starting from these new baselines, in an experiment with a G_{33} gallery. The original OSNet architecture achieves a fairly low average rank-1 accuracy (64.5%), which is increased by 14% through UFT-ReID-based refinement. The OSNet-IBN variant sets a much better baseline performance (74.5%) than the original OSNet, which is again further improved by UFT-ReID by 3.1%. Interestingly, UFT-ReID refinement of the original OSNet, results in better accuracy (78.5%) compared to either the baseline or the refined OSNet-IBN variants. OSNET-AIN starts with an even better baseline (76.5%). Still, UFT-ReID improves it further by 3.5%, achieving the best result among the three variants.

Training Execution Time: Table 7 shows average training execution times of UFT-ReID in a couple of experimental settings involving the OSNet architecture. Duration varies, depending on the amount of training images contained in the gallery. We notice that such durations are acceptable for some non time-critical applications , such as for crowd analytics or cross-camera person tracking in smart spaces.

We also compare the execution time of UFT-ReID to that of [33]. For a fair comparison, we measured parts of the training process that are relevant to each method, i.e. initializations, computations of losses and clustering. A G_{33} experiment has shown that the execution time of [33] is 2.5× the execution time of UFT-ReID. This is attributed mainly to the heavy computations required within the Ipfl loss.

4.4 Ablation Study

We now show how different parameters affect the performance of our framework. In most cases we chose small galleries, which is the main focus of our work. In all following experiments we used the Market1501 as the source dataset and the DukeMTMC-reid as the target dataset.

Internal Parameters: At first we experimented with two internal parameters of the bottom-up clustering algorithm; the diversity regularization λ and the number of merging epochs e_m. Experimentation on different values of λ is also conducted by [18]. Our motivation for repeating the experiment, is both due to the different formulation of the problem, as well as the utilization of fewer data. More specifically, the chance that two persons share similar appearance is smaller in the case of small-sized galleries. Experimentation was conducted on 20 random galleries containing 30 persons.

Figure 2 (left) demonstrates the effect of altering λ while keeping all other parameters fixed. We confirmed that the optimal value for λ is 0.005.

Next, we experimented with the effect of increasing e_m. Our motivation is to let the CNN stabilize between two cluster merging operations where the state pseudo-labels remain the same. Our experiments included the following options for e_m: $\{2, 3, 4, 5, 7, 11\}$.

Figure 2 (middle) shows the average rank-1 accuracy for these options. It turns out that by increasing e_m, we obtain better accuracy. However, this is at the cost of a more time-consuming fine-tuning, as training time increases considerably. More specifically, in our experiments the training time when using $e_m = 11$ was about three times more, compared to using $e_m = 2$. In all other experiments, for achieving reasonable training duration, we kept $e_m = 2$.

Batch Size: We conducted experiments using random 30- and 50-person galleries. Figure 2 (right) depicts a negative trend on the average rank-1 accuracy when using batch sizes larger than 16. Therefore, we chose $b = 16$ for subsequent experiments.

Data Augmentation: Typical CNN optimization requires lots of training images in an effort to generalize to diverse scenarios. To compensate for lack of such images, various online or offline data augmentation methods have been proposed.

In [18] images are randomly cropped and horizontally flipped, in an online fashion. We further experimented with randomly altering the color properties of images, including brightness, contrast, hue and saturation. The motivation is that our method is evaluated on smaller galleries, therefore lack of appearance diversity is expected as opposed to the case of a complete dataset. We conducted an experiment of random 30-person galleries to investigate the impact of augmentation based on color jittering. Using such augmentation, rank-1 accuracy increased from 65.7% to 68.1% in the particular experiment. Its impact was quite small, however it was used in subsequent experiments.

Learning Rate: As discussed in Sect. 3.2, lr is a crucial parameter for fine-tuning, as it balances the adaptation to the new domain and the preservation of the already learned knowledge. Preliminary experiments with small galleries (20–50 persons) shown that the initial learning rate should be fixed around 10% of the final value of a stepped learning rate reduce approach during supervised training. Our experiments in the full-scale experiment and dataset ranges (Sect. 4.1) confirmed that such choice for learning rate is satisfactory for galleries with few persons. For larger gallery sizes performance degraded significantly, and even worsens the original trained model. For this case we experimented with lower lr.

Figure 3 demonstrates the benefit of fine-tuning for variable gallery sizes and three options of lr. The outcome of the experiment is that larger gallery sizes require smaller learning rates. As shown in Fig. 3, this happens regardless of the choice of architectures (i.e., PCB or OSNet). We interpret this result as follows. The original model is trained on a large variety of person appearances. By fine-tuning we want to extend the model to new persons (i.e. appearances) from the target domain. In traditional supervised training, the choice of learning rate controls how large of a step to take in the direction of the negative gradient of the loss function. The original model correctly represents such appearance diversity, therefore smaller learning rates are required for not moving too far from the initial solution. On the other hand, in the case of smaller gallery sizes we want to mitigate the expressiveness of the model. This is achieved by adapting to fewer data while using larger learning rates.

5 Summary and Discussion

We presented UFT-ReID, a novel method for person re-identification. UFT-ReID performs fine-tuning and adaptation of a model already learned on an auxiliary, source dataset to a new, target one. It does so, with no requirement for training data on the target domain. Thus, it is compatible with real-world applications that require easy deployment of ReID methods in novel settings.

We also presented a new evaluation protocol, that is more suitable for real-world demands. Several experiments were conducted, demonstrating that UFT-ReID is able to adjust models and improve their accuracy, bringing them above state-of-the-art performance. Additionally, a number of experiments explored the parameter space of UFT-ReID, providing evidence on proper parameter settings and relevant justifications.

Ongoing work considers the extension of UFT-ReID by incorporating other unsupervised losses, training methodologies including early stop, as well as experimentation with novel optimizers. Another important topic of ongoing research considers the improvement of the cluster merging criterion described in Sect. 3.2. The selection of this criterion is crucial because it relates to the pseudo-labels generated during the fine-tuning. Errors due to false cluster merges, eventually propagate as errors within the objective function. Indicatively, in [5], another merging criterion is proposed, exploiting feature affinities within and between clusters. Preliminary experiments with a G_{33} gallery using the PCB architecture shows that the use of this criterion increases further the rank-1 accuracy of UFT-ReID by 6.6%.

Acknowledgments. This work is partially funded by the H2020 project CONNEX-IONs (GA 786731) and the FORTH-ICS internal RTD Programme "Ambient Intelligence and Smart Environments".

References

1. Ahmed, E., Jones, M., Marks, T.K.: An improved deep learning architecture for person re-identification. In: CVPR (2015)
2. Bai, X., Yang, M., Huang, T., Dou, Z., Yu, R., Xu, Y.: Deep-person: learning discriminative deep features for person re-identification. Pattern Recogn. **98**, 107036 (2020)
3. Caron, M., Bojanowski, P., Joulin, A., Douze, M.: Deep clustering for unsupervised learning of visual features. In: ECCV (2018)
4. Chen, W., Chen, X., Zhang, J., Huang, K.: Beyond triplet loss: a deep quadruplet network for person re-identification. In: CVPR (2017)
5. Ding, G., Khan, S.H., Tang, Z.: Dispersion based clustering for unsupervised person re-identification. In: BMVC, p. 264 (2019)
6. Ding, Y., Fan, H., Xu, M., Yang, Y.: Adaptive exploration for unsupervised person re-identification. ACM TOMM **16**(1), 3:1–3:19 (2020)
7. Fan, H., Zheng, L., Yan, C., Yang, Y.: Unsupervised person re-identification: clustering and fine-tuning. ACM TOMM **14**(4), 83 (2018)
8. Fan, X., Jiang, W., Luo, H., Fei, M.: Spherereid: deep hypersphere manifold embedding for person re-identification. Vis. Commun. Image Represent. **60**, 51–58 (2019)
9. Fu, Y., et al.: Horizontal pyramid matching for person re-identification. In: AAAI, vol. 33 (2019)
10. Guo, Y., Cheung, N.M.: Efficient and deep person re-identification using multi-level similarity. In: CVPR (2018)
11. Hermans, A., Beyer, L., Leibe, B.: In defense of the triplet loss for person re-identification. arXiv preprint arXiv:1703.07737 (2017)
12. Hinton, G., Vinyals, O., Dean, J.: Distilling the knowledge in a neural network. arXiv preprint arXiv:1503.02531 (2015)
13. Hsu, H.K., et al.: Progressive domain adaptation for object detection (2019)
14. Jia, J., Ruan, Q., Hospedales, T.M.: Frustratingly easy person re-identification: generalizing person re-id in practice. arXiv preprint arXiv:1905.03422 (2019)
15. Kalayeh, M.M., Basaran, E., Gökmen, M., Kamasak, M.E., Shah, M.: Human semantic parsing for person re-identification. In: CVPR (2018)
16. Li, W., Zhao, R., Xiao, T., Wang, X.: DeepReID: deep filter pairing neural network for person re-identification. In: CVPR (2014)
17. Li, W., Zhu, X., Gong, S.: Harmonious attention network for person re-identification. In: CVPR (2018)
18. Lin, Y., Dong, X., Zheng, L., Yan, Y., Yang, Y.: A bottom-up clustering approach to unsupervised person re-identification. In: AAAI (2019)
19. Liu, W., Chang, X., Chen, L., Yang, Y.: Semi-supervised Bayesian attribute learning for person re-identification. In: AAAI (2018)

20. Lucic, M., Tschannen, M., Ritter, M., Zhai, X., Bachem, O., Gelly, S.: High-fidelity image generation with fewer labels. arXiv preprint arXiv:1903.02271 (2019)
21. Quan, R., Dong, X., Wu, Y., Zhu, L., Yang, Y.: Auto-ReID: searching for a part-aware convnet for person re-identification. arXiv preprint arXiv:1903.09776 (2019)
22. Ristani, E., Tomasi, C.: Features for multi-target multi-camera tracking and re-identification. In: CVPR (2018)
23. Saquib Sarfraz, M., Schumann, A., Eberle, A., Stiefelhagen, R.: A pose-sensitive embedding for person re-identification with expanded cross neighborhood re-ranking. In: CVPR (2018)
24. Shen, C., et al.: Sharp attention network via adaptive sampling for person re-identification. IEEE CAS (2018)
25. Su, C., Li, J., Zhang, S., Xing, J., Gao, W., Tian, Q.: Pose-driven deep convolutional model for person re-identification. In: ICCV (2017)
26. Sun, Y., Zheng, L., Yang, Y., Tian, Q., Wang, S.: Beyond part models: Person retrieval with refined part pooling (and a strong convolutional baseline). In: ECCV (2018)
27. Wang, G., Yuan, Y., Chen, X., Li, J., Zhou, X.: Learning discriminative features with multiple granularities for person re-identification. In: ACM Multimedia Conference. ACM (2018)
28. Wang, J., Zhu, X., Gong, S., Li, W.: Transferable joint attribute-identity deep learning for unsupervised person re-identification. In: CVPR (2018)
29. Wu, A., Zheng, W.S., Lai, J.H.: Distilled camera-aware self training for semi-supervised person re-identification. IEEE Access **7**, 156752–156763 (2019)
30. Wu, D., et al.: Deep learning-based methods for person re-identification: a comprehensive review. Neurocomputing **337**, 354–371 (2019)
31. Xiao, T.: Open-ReID framework (2016). https://github.com/Cysu/open-reid
32. Xu, J., Zhao, R., Zhu, F., Wang, H., Ouyang, W.: Attention-aware compositional network for person re-identification. In: CVPR (2018)
33. Yang, Q., Yu, H.X., Wu, A., Zheng, W.S.: Patch-based discriminative feature learning for unsupervised person re-identification. In: CVPR (2019)
34. Yao, H., Zhang, S., Hong, R., Zhang, Y., Xu, C., Tian, Q.: Deep representation learning with part loss for person re-identification. IEEE Trans. Image Process. **28**(6), 2860–2871 (2019)
35. Yu, H.X., Wu, A., Zheng, W.S.: Unsupervised person re-identification by deep asymmetric metric embedding. TPAMI (2019)
36. Yu, H.X., Zheng, W.S., Wu, A., Guo, X., Gong, S., Lai, J.H.: Unsupervised person re-identification by soft multilabel learning. In: CVPR (2019)
37. Yu, R., Dou, Z., Bai, S., Zhang, Z., Xu, Y., Bai, X.: Hard-aware point-to-set deep metric for person re-identification. In: ECCV (2018)
38. Yu, T., Li, D., Yang, Y., Hospedales, T.M., Xiang, T.: Robust person re-identification by modelling feature uncertainty. In: ICCV (2019)
39. Zhang, X., et al.: AlignedReID: surpassing human-level performance in person re-identification. arXiv preprint arXiv:1711.08184 (2017)
40. Zhang, Z., Lan, C., Zeng, W., Chen, Z.: Densely semantically aligned person re-identification. In: CVPR, June 2019
41. Zheng, L., Shen, L., Tian, L., Wang, S., Wang, J., Tian, Q.: Scalable person re-identification: a benchmark. In: ICCV (2015)
42. Zheng, Z., Zheng, L., Yang, Y.: Unlabeled samples generated by GAN improve the person re-identification baseline in vitro. In: ICCV (2017)
43. Zhou, K., Xiang, T.: Torchreid: a library for deep learning person re-identification in pytorch. arXiv preprint arXiv:1910.10093 (2019)

44. Zhou, K., Yang, Y., Cavallaro, A., Xiang, T.: Learning generalisable omni-scale representations for person re-identification. arXiv preprint arXiv:1910.06827 (2019)
45. Zhou, K., Yang, Y., Cavallaro, A., Xiang, T.: Omni-scale feature learning for person re-identification. In: ICCV (2019)

How Does Computer Animation Affect Our Perception of Emotions in Video Summarization?

Camila Kolling[1,2]([✉]), Victor Araujo[1], Rodrigo C. Barros[1],
and Soraia Raupp Musse[1]

[1] Pontifical Catholic University of Rio Grande do Sul, Porto Alegre, RS, Brazil
{camila.kolling,victor.flavio}@edu.pucrs.br,
{rodrigo.barros,soraia.musse}@pucrs.br
[2] Kunumi, Belo Horizonte, MG, Brazil
camila@kunumi.com

Abstract. With the exponential growth of film productions and the popularization of the web, the summary of films has become a useful and important resource. Movies data specifically has become one of the most entertaining sources for viewers, especially during quarantine. However, browsing a movie in enormous collections and searching for a desired scene within a complete movie is a tedious and time-consuming task. As a result, automatic and personalized movie summarization has become a common research topic. In this paper, we focus on emotion summarization for videos with one shot and apply three independent methods for its summarization. We provide two different ways to visualize the main emotions of the generated summary and compare both approaches. The first one uses the original frames of the video and the other uses an open source facial animation tool to create a virtual assistant that provides the emotion summarization. For evaluation, we conducted an extrinsic evaluation using a questionnaire to measure the quality of each generated video summary. Experimental results show that even though both videos had similar answers, a different technique for each video had the most satisfying and informative summary.

Keywords: Movie summarization · Emotion recognition · Computer animation

1 Introduction

Video data is exponentially increasing over the internet, including social networks, surveillance, and movies due to advances and easy access to capturing technologies. However, searching for a specific scene within a complete movie is a time-consuming task. Movie summarization (MS) techniques have tried to tackle this problem by producing a short video sequence from the movie, which contains the most important events or scenes [3]. Hence, the viewers may have

© Springer Nature Switzerland AG 2020
G. Bebis et al. (Eds.): ISVC 2020, LNCS 12510, pp. 374–385, 2020.
https://doi.org/10.1007/978-3-030-64559-5_29

an idea about the context and the semantics of the movie by watching only the important scenes.

The challenge in video summarization lies in the definition of "important" video segments to be included in a summary and their extraction [14]. Recently, many MS techniques have been presented by researchers that can be broadly categorized into automatic MS techniques [3,6,8,13,16] and user-preference based MS techniques [5,10]. In the first one, shots and scenes for a given movie are automatically detected and their high-level features are semi-automatically annotated, while for the later the user preferences are generated by means of a query.

In other words, in automatic MS techniques, there is no direct preference from the users to generate a summary. These techniques rely on multiple clues. For instance, Ngo et al. [13] represent a video as a complete undirected graph and use the normalized cut algorithm to partition the graph into video clusters. In order to remove redundant and non informative shots, at most one shot is retained from each cluster. Hesham et al. [8] introduced Smart-Trailer, which generates a short summary as a trailer using the subtitles of the movie. Another text based approach is from Sang et al. [16], which incorporates character analysis into semantic movie summarization. In Otani et al. [14], they used neural networks to map videos as well as its descriptions to a common semantic space. To generate the summary of the videos, they extract the deep features from each segment of the original video and apply a clustering-based summarization technique. Potapov et al. [15] proposed to summarize a video focusing on a specific event and used as the importance of a video segment the classifier's confidence.

Some approaches use hierarchical video summarization, which usually can be obtained from key frames. That is the case for Evangelopoulos et al. [6], which proposes a multimodal saliency representation of audiovisual streams, in which signal (audio and visual) and semantic (linguistic/textual) cues are integrated hierarchically. Also, Taskiran et al. [17] cluster key frames extracted from shots using color, edge, and texture features and present them in a hierarchical fashion using a similarity pyramid. In Do et al. [3] they introduce a method to index characters and extract a shortened version of a movie using character's co-appearances. Social network analysis was used to find the importance during movie segmentation to summarize and index the movie.

In this paper, we implemented three methods for extracting the summary of emotions in videos composed of a single shot using automatic MS, where one of them is proposed by Ul Haq et al. [18]. Using each technique, we decided to test two different approaches to visualize the generated summary: using the original frames of the video or using an open source framework of facial animation to provide a virtual assistant. In addition, we applied an online questionnaire to validate our methods through human perception. The main contributions of this work are summarized as follows:

- We present a framework for automatically generating summary of videos for three methods.
- We propose two new approaches for video summarization.

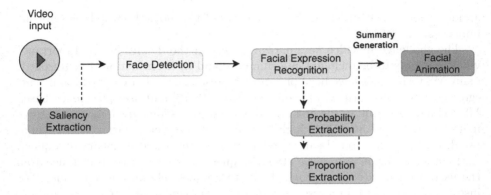

Fig. 1. Framework of the movie summarization methodology.

- We adapted the summarization of the emotions to an open source facial animation tool to visualize the summarization of the main emotions of each video.

2   Methodology

An overview of the proposed framework is illustrated in Fig. 1. Our pipeline, without any emotion summarization mechanism, has the following steps: *1)* original video as input, shown in gray; *2)* face detection, depicted in the yellow rectangle; *3)* facial expression recognition, visualized on the orange rectangle; and, as an option, the *4)* facial animation tool, shown on the red rectangle. From this, we can add three different approaches for automatic MS: *(a) Saliency Extraction*, based on the work of Ul Haq et al. [18], which is encapsulated between the video input and the face detection steps, shown in green. Also, both the *(b) Probability Extraction*, in blue, and *(c) Proportion Extraction*, in purple, attached between the facial expression recognition and, optionally, the facial animation tool. It is important to notice that each approach is applied independently, *i.e.*, we do not combine the summary generation methods. All these methods are discussed in subsequent sections in detail.

2.1   Saliency Extraction

Based on recent work [18], this approach uses a saliency extraction technique before the face recognition step. Saliency of an image/frame is used to extract the foreground information, which can also be used for predicting the amount of information on it [19]. We first obtain the saliency map and then take the average saliency score for each frame. This average is calculated by taking the sum of all nonzero pixels and dividing it by the total number of image pixels. This average saliency score is compared with a predefined threshold to select the most salient shots. If the saliency score is greater than this threshold, we pass this frame to the face recognition step. Otherwise, we discard it. In this work, we conducted a test and we empirically found that the value of 0.78 worked best.

2.2   Face Detection

For each frame of the video input, we run an algorithm that detects one or more human faces. From this detection, we obtain bounding boxes around each face in the collected frames. For this step, we used OpenCV face detection tool. OpenCV's deep learning face detector is based on the Single Shot Detector (SSD) [12] framework with a ResNet [7] base network.

2.3   Facial Expression Recognition

We used a pretrained neural network [1] that classifies the emotion based on a person's face. The model was trained on the Facial Expression Recognition 2013 (FER-2013) dataset [9]. This dataset consists of $35,887$ grayscale, 48×48 sized face images with seven emotions, i.e., angry, disgusted, fearful, happy, neutral, sad and surprised. Considering the size of the images used to train this model, we decided to use only the bounding boxes described in Sect. 2.2. In order to remove possible outliers captured by the network and add temporal consistency, we discarded frames which have a frequency less than 10% of the total length of the video.

2.4   Probability Extractor

The neural network [1] that we used in this work classify a person's face within seven emotions: angry, disgusted, fearful, happy, neutral, sad and surprised, as mentioned in Sect. 2.3. The output of this neural network is a probability distribution over these seven categories, i.e., each one of them has a probability associated with it, and they all sum to one. In this module, we extract the highest probability, which in theory represents the emotion which was classified by the model and it should express a person's current emotion. Finally, we compare it with a predefined threshold T, which has a value of 0.99. We select only the frames which have $P > T$, i.e., the probability P greater than this threshold. Otherwise, we discard it.

2.5   Proportion Extractor

Here we describe a novel approach to summary generation, which we called *proportion*. It extracts the distribution of the emotions detected throughout the original video maintaining this same distribution for the summary. We opted for discarding emotions that were detected in less than 10% of the total video

Fig. 2. Open-source facial animation tool used in this work [2].

(a) Video 1 (filmed more closely).   (b) Video 2 (filmed more distant).

Fig. 3. Frame of both videos showing the emotion "happiness".

frames, to avoid using emotions that were mispredicted by the neural network described in Sect. 2.3. Also, in this work, we used the number of summary frames as half the number of frames on the original video.

2.6   Facial Animation

After recovering the main emotions of the video, we pass this list of emotions to an open source FACS-based 3D face animation system. OpenFACS [2], shown in Fig. 2, is a software that allows the simulation of realistic facial expressions through the manipulation of specific Action Units (AUs) as defined in the Facial Action Coding System [4]. OpenFACS has been developed together with an API which is suitable to generate real-time dynamic facial expressions for a three-dimensional character. It is easily embedded in existing systems without any prior experience in Computer Graphics.

3   Experimental Results

This section introduces the setup used for our experiments. Also, we describe in more details the videos and metrics used in this work.

3.1 Video Setup

In this work, we shot two different videos with the same person. The difference between both videos is the distance from the camera: the first video was filmed more closely, while the second was filmed more distant, as shown in Fig. 3. Also, both videos had the same emotion distribution and a total length of 1 min and 25 s. Each emotion have a duration of ≈20 s, i.e., ≈100 frames.

3.2 Evaluation of Generated Summary

One of the challenges in evaluating the generated movie is the lack of metrics and standards. Again we follow the steps of recent work [18], and use extrinsic evaluation, *i.e.*, the performance is evaluated as information retrieval problem using a multiple choice questionnaire, and the quality of the generated summary is then measured by the increase in quiz scores. The participants were chosen randomly and voluntarily responded to the online survey, which was distributed using Google Forms tool. All the participants of the questionnaire were instructed to watch the selected movies before the evaluation and asked to rate the following three questions after watching the summary generated by the three methods:

1. How satisfied are you with the emotion summary of the video?
2. What is the level of information for the emotion summary of the video?
3. How useful is the facial animation for the emotion summary of the video?

   This last question was always placed after presenting both summaries of original frames and computer facial animation. We randomly placed the questions about each technique in the questionnaire and the corresponding generated summary, so we could minimize the participants bias. We evaluated the answers using the Likert Scale [11], which is a psychometric scale commonly involved in research that employs questionnaires. When responding to a question using this scale, respondents specify their level of agreement or disagreement on a symmetric agree-disagree scale for a series of statements. It is composed of five possible answers: very negative, negative, neutral, positive and very positive.

3.3 Results

In our experiments, a total of 45 subjects participated in the subjective evaluation, having age in the range from 18 to 55 years, in which most of them were 22 years old (15.6%). Figure 4 shows the percentage of answers for all metrics and both videos using the original frames of the video to generate the summary. We can visualize that, for the first video (Fig. 4(a)), the techniques that had the highest values for Very Positive responses were Saliency and Proportion, especially, for the informative part, while Probability had higher values for Positive responses. In general, the techniques were rated positively, *i.e.*, having high values for Very Positive and Positive responses.

   As for the second video (Fig. 4(b)), we can infer that a similar distribution of answers was achieved for Positive and Very Positive answers, w.r.t all summary

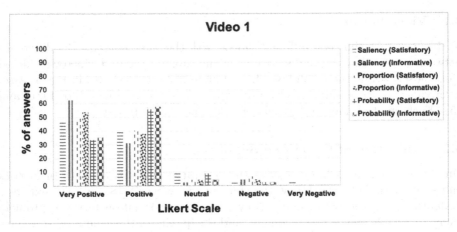

(a) Video 1 (filmed more closely).

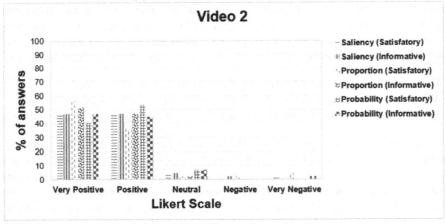

(b) Video 2 (filmed more distant).

Fig. 4. Using original frames of the video to visualize the generated summary.

algorithms. However, in this case, the Proportion technique had higher values for Very Positive responses. To compare the values between the two graphs (Fig. 4(a) and (b)), we performed a statistical analysis using a paired T-test[1], with a significance level of 5%. For example, we compared the percentage of Very Positive values in Fig. 4(a) (46.66%) with the percentage of Very Positive values in Fig. 4(b) (47.77%), however the comparison did not result in a significant p-value. In all other cases, only when comparing the Negative responses that the p-value was significant ($<.001$), with the percentage for Video 1 being higher than Video 2 (respectively, 3.70% and 0.74%), i.e., the first had more Negative responses than the second video.

---

[1] excel-easy.com/examples/t-test.html.

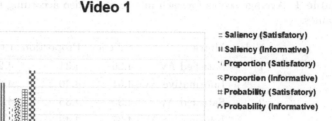

(a) Video 1 (filmed more closely).

(b) Video 2 (filmed more distant).

Fig. 5. Using computer animation to visualize the generated summary.

The results using 3D facial animation system, as described in Sect. 2.6, are depicted in Fig. 5. We can infer that using the facial animation systems, the answers tend to be more negative. In this sense, we can see that, for both videos, the graphs of Fig. 5 are more scattered than of Fig. 4. In other words, we can see that there are more Neutral and Negative answers and less Positive responses using OpenFACS compared to the approach illustrated in Fig. 4. To compare these behaviors of the graphs of the two Figures (4 and 5) we used the independent T-test. Firstly, we compared the results of the graph in Fig. 4(a) with the results of the graph in Fig. 5(a), since the two referring to Video 1. Regarding the Very Positive responses, the video with the original frames had a higher percentage than the video with the animation (46.66% and 10.74%, respectively), resulting in a very significant p-value ($<.001$). Regarding the Positive, Neutral

Table 1. Average scores for each metric and video according to scores using original frames.

Video	Metric	Saliency	Proportion	Probability
1	Satisfied AV	4.26	4.31	4.20
	Informative AV	4.51	4.40	4.26
2	Satisfied AV	4.35	4.35	4.31
	Informative AV	4.37	4.48	4.42

Table 2. Average scores for each metric and video according to scores using computer animation.

Video	Metric	Saliency	Proportion	Probability
1	Satisfied AV	3.51	3.68	3.48
	Informative AV	3.57	3.66	3.64
2	Satisfied AV	3.66	3.57	3.64
	Informative AV	3.66	3.73	3.64

and Negative responses, they also resulted in significant p-values (respectively, .02, .001 and $<.001$). Therefore, the percentages values were higher for the animation than for the original frames (respectively, 57.40%, 13.70% and 16.66% for the animation, 43.70%, 5.55% and 3.70% for the original frames). For the Very Negative responses, the p-value was not significant. In the comparison of Fig. 4(b) with Fig. 5(b), referring to Video 2, it was also similar, with significant p-values for Very Positive ($<.001$), Positive ($<.001$), Neutral ($<.001$) and Negative ($<.001$), the first being higher for the video with the original frames and the others were higher for the video containing the animation. Specifically, we can visualize in Fig. 5 that the first video had more positive responses than the second video. Nonetheless, in both cases, few of the answers are concentrated in the Very Positive side of the graph. We performed a paired T-test to compare the values of the responses of (a) and (b). However, unlike the result of the analysis in Fig. 4, no p-value was significant.

Since both graphs share a lot of information, we opted for constructing a table which summarizes all of the aforementioned charts. To build this table, we used an average score for each Likert level, $e.g.$, Very Positive with score 5, Positive with score 4, and so on. Tables 1 and 2 illustrate the results of the generated summary using original frames and computer animation system, respectively, for both videos. The maximum average score is 4.51 and the minimum average score is 3.48. Visually, Table 1 shows that the Saliency method had the highest average score value (Informative - 4.51) than the other methods in video 1, while for video 2 it was the Proportion method (Informative - 4.48). So, for the two videos containing the original frames, Saliency had the highest value among the methods. In this case, to analyze the three methods we performed

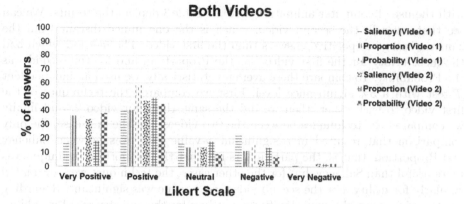

Fig. 6. Utility of the facial animation system for both videos.

Table 3. Utility average score using OPENFacs for both videos.

Video	Saliency	Proportion	Probability
1	3.48	4.0	3.68
2	4.04	3.66	4.08

a statistical analysis using the one-factor ANOVA[2], also with a 5% significance level. However, the resulting p-value was not significant. In Table 2 we can see that, for the first video, the method which had the best satisfaction average score was Proportion (3.68), and also for information (3.66). As for the second video, Proportion was the best method considering the amount of information (3.73) and Saliency was the best approach considering satisfaction (3.66). We also used one-factor ANOVA for this case, however, the p-value was also not significant.

Regarding information and satisfaction, Figs. 4 and 5 depict that these two variables are related. We used Pearson's correlation to evaluate the relationship of these two variables in all cases (using the values of Table 1 and 2), and we obtained a value of 0.98, that is, the information is highly correlated to satisfaction. We also analyzed the comparison of satisfaction and information between Tables and using the independent T-test with a 5% significance level. Thus, we obtained significant p-values ($<.001$ and $<.001$, respectively). Therefore, we can conclude that the participants perceived the videos with original frames more informative (average of 4.41) and satisfactory (average of 4.30) than the videos with the animations (respectively the averages of 3.65 and 3.59).

The last question for each method on the questionnaire was about the utility of the facial animation system to visualize the emotion summary. Figure 6 shows the results for both videos. Most of the answers are concentrated on the Very Positive and Positive answer. Following the same methodology, we opted to use the average scores to check which technique was considered the most useful

---

[2] excel-easy.com/examples/anova.html.

with the use of computer animation system. Table 3 depicts the results. We can see that, overall, the second video, which is the one filmed distant from the camera, had more positive answers than the first video. The method which had the most utility for the first video was the Proportion, and for the second was the Probability. To compare these averages statistically, we used an independent T-test with a 5% significance level. First we compared the techniques of the first video to each other, then we did the same thing for video 2, and finally we compared the techniques between the two videos. For the first case, the only comparison that resulted in a significant p-value (.02) was between Saliency and Proportion, that is, the participants felt that the Proportion technique was more useful than Saliency, but for the other cases, the techniques were evaluated similarly for utility. For the second video, no p-value was significant. Regarding the two videos, we obtained significant p-values for the Saliency and Probability comparisons (respectively, .01 and .04), and not significant for Proportion (.11). With that, we can say that, for Saliency and Probability, video 2 was more useful for the participants, but for Proportion, both video 1 and video 2 are similar.

4   Conclusion

In this work we have provided a framework for video summarization. We have studied two methods, namely (1) Saliency Extraction and (2) Probability Extraction, and introduced the technique (3) Proportion Extraction. Furthermore, we have conducted a series of experiments in form of a questionnaire.

From this work, we can conclude that the best overall results was achieved using the original frames from the video. This could be related to the lack of expressiveness of the facial animation system used, which some participants commented about. Both videos had similar results, even though in the first video the best technique was Saliency, and in the second video Proportion had more positive answers. Since both videos had the same emotion distribution, both videos were very alike, hence this could have motivated this similarity reflected on the results. In most cases the facial animation system was not useful to visualize the main emotions of the generated summary.

For future work, we would like to test different pretrained models for emotion recognition. We would like to test each technique in a movie with high quality frames. Also, we would like to test the methods combined, and not just individually as done in this work. Finally, following the suggestions of the participants, we would like to test different facial animation systems.

Acknowledgment. The authors would like to thank CNPq and CAPES for partially funding this work.

References

1. Correa, E., Jonker, A., Ozo, M., Stolk, R.: Emotion recognition using deep convolutional neural networks. Technical report IN4015 (2016)

2. Cuculo, V., D'Amelio, A.: OpenFACS: an open source FACS-based 3D face animation system. In: Zhao, Y., Barnes, N., Chen, B., Westermann, R., Kong, X., Lin, C. (eds.) ICIG 2019. LNCS, vol. 11902, pp. 232–242. Springer, Cham (2019). https://doi.org/10.1007/978-3-030-34110-7_20
3. Do, T.T.H., Tran, Q.H.B., Tran, Q.D.: Movie indexing and summarization using social network techniques. Vietnam J. Comput. Sci. 5(2), 157–164 (2018). https://doi.org/10.1007/s40595-018-0111-2
4. Ekman, P., Friesen, W.V.: Facial action coding system: a technique for the measurement of facial movement. Consulting Psychologists Press, Palo Alto (1978)
5. Ellouze, M., Boujemaa, N., Alimi, A.M.: Im (s) 2: interactive movie summarization system. J. Vis. Commun. Image Represent. 21(4), 283–294 (2010)
6. Evangelopoulos, G., et al.: Multimodal saliency and fusion for movie summarization based on aural, visual, and textual attention. IEEE Trans. Multimedia 15(7), 1553–1568 (2013)
7. He, K., Zhang, X., Ren, S., Sun, J.: Deep residual learning for image recognition. In: Proceedings of the IEEE Conference on Computer Vision and Pattern Recognition, pp. 770–778 (2016)
8. Hesham, M., Hani, B., Fouad, N., Amer, E.: Smart trailer: automatic generation of movie trailer using only subtitles. In: 2018 First International Workshop on Deep and Representation Learning (IWDRL), pp. 26–30. IEEE (2018)
9. Kaggle: Challenges in representation learning: facial expression recognition challenge (2012). https://www.kaggle.com/c/challenges-in-representation-learning-facial-expression-recognition-challenge
10. Kannan, R., Ghinea, G., Swaminathan, S.: What do you wish to see? a summarization system for movies based on user preferences. Inf. Process. Manag. 51(3), 286–305 (2015)
11. Likert, R.: A technique for the measurement of attitudes. Arch. Psychol. (1932)
12. Liu, W., Anguelov, D., Erhan, D., Szegedy, C., Reed, S., Fu, C.-Y., Berg, A.C.: SSD: single shot multibox detector. In: Leibe, B., Matas, J., Sebe, N., Welling, M. (eds.) ECCV 2016. LNCS, vol. 9905, pp. 21–37. Springer, Cham (2016). https://doi.org/10.1007/978-3-319-46448-0_2
13. Ngo, C.W., Ma, Y.F., Zhang, H.J.: Video summarization and scene detection by graph modeling. IEEE Trans. Circ. Syst. Video Technol. 15(2), 296–305 (2005)
14. Otani, M., Nakashima, Y., Rahtu, E., Heikkilä, J., Yokoya, N.: Video summarization using deep semantic features. In: Lai, S.-H., Lepetit, V., Nishino, K., Sato, Y. (eds.) ACCV 2016. LNCS, vol. 10115, pp. 361–377. Springer, Cham (2017). https://doi.org/10.1007/978-3-319-54193-8_23
15. Potapov, D., Douze, M., Harchaoui, Z., Schmid, C.: Category-specific video summarization. In: Fleet, D., Pajdla, T., Schiele, B., Tuytelaars, T. (eds.) ECCV 2014. LNCS, vol. 8694, pp. 540–555. Springer, Cham (2014). https://doi.org/10.1007/978-3-319-10599-4_35
16. Sang, J., Xu, C.: Character-based movie summarization. In: Proceedings of the 18th ACM International Conference on Multimedia, pp. 855–858 (2010)
17. Taskiran, C., Chen, J.Y., Albiol, A., Torres, L., Bouman, C.A., Delp, E.J.: Vibe: a compressed video database structured for active browsing and search. IEEE Trans. Multimedia 6(1), 103–118 (2004)
18. Ul Haq, I., Ullah, A., Muhammad, K., Lee, M.Y., Baik, S.W.: Personalized movie summarization using deep CNN-assisted facial expression recognition. Complexity 2019 (2019)
19. Zhang, D., Han, J., Jiang, L., Ye, S., Chang, X.: Revealing event saliency in unconstrained video collection. IEEE Trans. Image Process. 26(4), 1746–1758 (2017)

Where's Wally: A Gigapixel Image Study for Face Recognition in Crowds

Cristiane B. R. Ferreira[1], Helio Pedrini[2], Wanderley de Souza Alencar[1],
William D. Ferreira[1], Thyago Peres Carvalho[1], Naiane Sousa[1],
and Fabrizzio Soares[1,3(✉)]

[1] Instituto de Informática, Universidade Federal de Goiás, Goiania, GO, Brazil
{cristianebrf,wanderleyalencar,wferreira7}@ufg.br,
thyagopcarvalho@gmail.com,
naianesousa@discente.ufg.br
[2] Institute of Computing, University of Campinas, Campinas, SP, Brazil
helio@ic.unicamp.br
[3] Department of Computer Science, Southern Oregon University, Ashland, OR, USA
soaresf@sou.edu
https://www.inf.ufg.br
https://www.ic.unicamp.br
https://www.sou.edu

Abstract. Several devices are capable of capturing images with a large
number of people, including those of high resolution known as gigapixel
images. These images can be helpful for studies and investigations, such
as finding people in a crowd. Although they can provide more details,
the task of identifying someone in the crowd is quite challenging and
complex. In this paper, we aim to assist the work of a human observer
with larger images with crowds by reducing the search space for several
images to a ranking of ten images related to a specific person. Our model
collects faces in a crowded gigapixel image and then searches for people
using three different poses (front, right and left). We built a handcraft
dataset with 42 people to evaluate our method, achieving a recognition
rate of 69% in the complete dataset. We highlight that, from the 31% "not
found" among the top ten in the ranking, many of them are very close
to this boundary and, in addition, 92% of non-matched are occluded
by some accessory or another face. Experimental results showed great
potential for our method to support a human observer to find people in
the crowd, especially cluttered images, providing her/him with a reduced
search space.

Keywords: Gigapixel image · Face detection · Face recognition ·
Crowd visualization

1 Introduction

A crowd of people is a common situation in which people agglomerate around
an event for some reason. For instance, people usually gather in places for a

G. Bebis et al. (Eds.): ISVC 2020, LNCS 12510, pp. 386–397, 2020.
https://doi.org/10.1007/978-3-030-64559-5_30

common interest, such as outdoors, theaters, stadiums, shopping malls and airports. Port Authority of New York and New Jersey [8] reports that airports, such as the Hartsfield–Jackson Atlanta International Airport, had about 103,902,992 passengers only in 2017, which is approximately 284,665 per day or 11,861 per hour.

Fig. 1. Where's Wally (Where's Wally books are also known as Where's Waldo in North America.) concept of our proposed study (Adapted from CNN).

When there are hundreds or even thousands of people together, there may be situations where it is important and necessary to detect and identify people at the scene, such as a missing child or a crime suspect. In this way, equipment can capture images or videos of scenes typically populated by a large number of people and the identification of people on site is required for several reasons, including the occurrence of a crime and the search for a possible suspect, considering her/his facial identification. Identifying multiple faces in a crowd is not a simple task because it requires prior face separation and subsequent identification and classification of an already trained facial database.

Figure 1 represents part of President Donald Trump's inauguration speech as the President of the United States. This image is known as a gigapixel image. Gigapixel images belong to a category that contains a very large amount of information, since their sizes can vary from 0.3 to 300 gigapixels or more. Generally, these images have hundreds of single pictures stitched together to create a huge, unique image.

Some studies show that the use of visual scenes that approximate the detail and complexity of natural scenes helps to understand the properties of a complex visual scene and influences its complete understanding, as shown by Clarke et al. [4]. Thus, human beings have great difficulties in finding patterns in images overloaded with information, such as images of crowds. Considering this, in our work we present a visual aid model for a human observer to work with crowded gigapixel images by reducing the search space for several images to a ranking of ten images related to a specific person. Our approach is able to separate faces in these images, as well as the search and recognition of people through a test dataset, considering a set of three different poses for each person to be found and identified in the gigapixel image. Our model contributes to a better visualization and search space reduction for an observer's analysis.

Our text is organized as follows. Section 2 presents a short literature review related to gigapixel images and crowded gigapixel images. Section 3 describes the datasets used in our experiments to validate our method, described in Sect. 4. Section 5 reports and analyzes the experimental results. Finally, Sect. 6 concludes our work and presents directions for future work.

2   Literature Review

Some advances have been made in the field of gigapixel images. Yang et al. [11] used a deep convolutional network to discover responses of facial parts from arbitrary uncropped face images. Part detectors emerged within CNN trained to classify attributes from uncropped face images.

Bai et al. [2] presented a convolutional neural network architecture for face detection, where super-resolution and refinement network were used to generate real and sharp high-resolution images and a discriminator network was introduced to classify faces vs. non-faces. Furthermore, a loss was introduced to promote the discriminator network to distinguish the real/fake image and face/non-face simultaneously.

Zhang et al. [12] proposed a method that performs pedestrian counting on a gigapixel image. Pedestrian detection is performed using Exemplar Support Vector Machines running on a GPU-based architecture, and object-oriented histograms are used for the object characterization. Cao et al. [3] introduced a gigapixel crowd counting method. They used Dilated Convolution Neural Network and they performed the count on 3 different scales and weighted the results.

Wang et al. [10] presented a gigaPixel-level humAN-centric viDeo dAtaset, for large-scale, long-term and multi-object visual analysis, comparing human detection and tracking tasks and aiming to assist in the analysis of human behavior and interactions in large-scale real-world scenarios.

Ferreira et al. [5] presented a study and method to deal with pedestrian detection in gigapixel images by reducing their dimensions and associated computational effort. In their work, a multiresolution analysis was performed on gigapixel images to evaluate the required time processing and its impacts caused by the person detection algorithm.

Ferreira et al. [6] presented an impact analysis of the resolution reduction in the detection of people on gigapixel images. People detectors were trained with the INRIA and CALTECH data sets and results showed that, although gigapixel images provided a huge rate of false positives, the resolution reduction significantly decreased the number of bounding boxes and false positives, however, increased the rate of missing people.

3   Dataset Description

In our work, we used two datasets for combined experiments. The first one is a gigapixel image from Trump's inauguration, discussed in Subsect. 3.1. The second one is a handcrafted dataset of different poses from different events of Trump's inauguration special guests, presented in Subsect. 3.2.

3.1   Gigapixel Image Dataset

The gigapixel picture that we evaluated in our approach is named *The Inauguration of Donald Trump*, taken by CNN[1]. It was taken in Washington DC on January 20, 2017 at 3:00 PM GMT-2 and an estimated 300,000 to 600,000 people attended the public ceremony. Although, there is no information available on the equipment used to take the picture, in a StackExchange photography forum [9], there is a discussion speculating that it was taken with a Gigapan Epic Pro. However, more details on how CNN captured Trump's inauguration can be found in [1]. The image is stored in a cube face representation, where each cube face means a camera targeting direction. We extracted the image from www.fanpic.co with a Python script, via URL presented as follows:

http://europe.tiles.fanpic.co/749-2017-cnn/mres_s/ll/v/ll_s_v_h.jpg

where {s} is the cube face composed of f, b, u, d, l and r, which are front, back, up, down, left and right, respectively, {l} is the resolution level, where 1 is the lowest and 7 is the highest resolution, and {v} and {h} are the vertical and horizontal position of the camera, respectively, ranging from 1 to 125 at the highest resolution.

We downloaded the image of all cube faces at level 7, which is the highest resolution, and provides RGB tiles with 512×512 pixels and a total of 93,750 tiles. However, we used a small portion of the gigapixel image that corresponds to the surrounding location of the president's speech stage, where authorities sit, such as Supreme Court judges, Senators and Deputies, former presidents and first ladies, religious leaders, family and closer friends, and so on. We consider columns from 92 to 124 on the left cube face, columns from 00 to 30 on the front cube face and lines from 73 to 90 on both cube faces, therefore, resulting in a total of 1,152 tiles.

The tiles are designed to avoid spherical effect of the picture acquisition process and already stitched. However, there is no information about the software and algorithms used for that. In addition, we observed that, in several cases, flattening of the image occurs, which can bring some effects of radial distortion of people's faces and hinder the process of facial recognition.

It is also important to mention that, in the construction of this gigapixel image, several problems hinder the process of identifying and recognizing people, due to factors such as their position in the scene, for example. Several people appear from behind, others from the side and others with their faces hidden. Thus, there are several problems such as the variance of people's pose, occlusion, which are major challenges to be solved.

We created a strategy to go through the gigapixel image that will be detailed in Sect. 4 and we obtained a total of 432 face images with this approach after discarding a few non-faces detected images. Figure 2 shows these faces and Table 1 shows some statistics for this face dataset.

---

[1] Available at https://edition.cnn.com/interactive/2017/01/politics/trump-inaugurat ion-gigapixel. (Access was unstable when finishing this text).

Fig. 2. Gigapixel image samples to construct the gigapixel face dataset.

Table 1. Statistics for the gigapixel image dataset.

Images	Total	Face position				Occlusion by	Occlusion by	No
		Frontal	Right	Left	Backface	Accessories	Other Faces	Occlusion
All	432	111	284	11	26	123	41	268
Selected	42	12	25	1	4	7	9	26

Table 1 groups faces based on two main criteria: face position and face visibility. For the first case, we observed four frequent positions in these images: front, right, left and back. In the second one, we observed images with accessory occlusion, images with face occlusion and no occlusion. Using part of the gigapixel image, our model found 432 faces. From this total and considering the first criterion, 111 faces were found in the front position, 283 faces turned to the right, 11 faces to the left and 26 with backface. Since there are many people present in the image who are not known authorities or public people, 42 people from this total were known (authorities, religious leaders, family members, among others). Thus, considering this new total, we have 12 of them who appear with their faces in the front position, 25 with faces turned to the right, 1 with a face turned to the left and 4 with backface. When considering the second criterion, we are concerned with seeing if the faces are occluded. Most faces were not occluded (26) and 16 faces were occluded by accessories (7) or by another face (9).

Figure 3 shows some of the problems found and which make it difficult to recognize the faces extracted from the gigapixel image. In Fig. 3(a), we can see a backface. In Fig. 3(b) to 3(f), we can observe that the faces are occluded by various accessories, such as hat, glasses, raincoat and hand on the face. In Fig. 3(g), (h) and (i), we have occlusion by other faces. In Fig. 3(j), we have a complex problem caused by gigapixel stitching distortion.

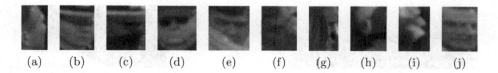

(a)   (b)   (c)   (d)   (e)   (f)   (g)   (h)   (i)   (j)

Fig. 3. Gigapixel dataset samples: (a) backface; (b) to (f) accessory occlusion; (g) to (i) occlusion by other faces and (j) gigapixel stitching distortion.

3.2 Handcrafted Dataset

This dataset was created from images downloaded from people who were at Trump's inauguration, such as member of the U.S. Supreme Court, former presidents and first ladies, President Donald Trump and his family members, some religious celebrities, representatives and senators.

We use the images of the front, left and right poses of each individual's face, in different situations and dates, as shown in Fig. 4. In the handcrafted database, we have 42 different individuals, with 3 images of each, resulting in a total of 126 images.

We searched several websites for a complete list of all authorities, family, friends, religious leaders, Supreme court judges, speaker of the house representatives, among others, who were present at President Trump's inauguration. Since we have not found this complete document, we conducted searches on several sites, such as BBC, Wikipedia and U.S. Supreme Court, to find some names of people invited and who attended the event.

In addition, as President Trump's inauguration was not just attended by officials, we had difficulty finding a public dataset to collect images of everyone present at the ceremony. We found a dataset of images of members of the American Congress[2], but it consists of images only in the frontal pose of each member. However, in the image gigapixel, several people appear with their faces hidden or in a side pose due to the positioning of the equipment that captured the images. Thus, we chose to build our database considering the criteria of the three positions: front, right and left, as well as the issue of copyright of the images. The dataset construction was a very challenging task, as not all images available on the Internet are available for public use.

Left   Frontal   Right

Fig. 4. Example of Obama's faces in the handcrafted dataset.

---

[2] https://github.com/unitedstates/contact-congress.

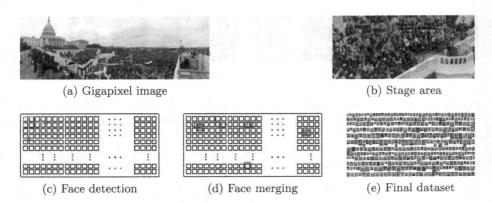

(a) Gigapixel image

(b) Stage area

(c) Face detection

(d) Face merging

(e) Final dataset

Fig. 5. Face detection steps in the gigapixel image.

4   Proposed Method

In our model, we developed two stages, both using the DLIB library for face detection and matching. The first is related to the detection of faces in the region of interest from President Trump's inauguration. The second is related to the use of 126 images of the dataset built with images of people known in three different poses and the attempt to locate these people on the faces detected in the gigapixel image. In Subsects. 4.1 and 4.2, we describe details of our approach.

4.1   Face Detection in Gigapixel Image

At this stage, we first select a small portion of the gigapixel image that corresponds to the location surrounding the president stage. Figure 5(a) shows an entire gigapixel image and Fig. 5(b) shows the portion of the gigapixel image that we are considering in this work. Thus, we construct a model to scroll a sliding window through it, with 2 columns × 2 rows of tile images with 512 × 512 RGB pixels each, resulting in a 1024 × 1024 pixel sliding window, as seen in Fig. 5(c). This measurement was used considering the average face size in the gigapixel image.

We proceed to face detection by scanning the portion of the gigapixel image with the sliding window. As the stride adopted for the sliding window approach is 1 tile, the scanning process may find more bounding boxes than necessary, since many of them are overlapping. Although we could adopt strides larger than 1 tile, this could cause data loss, since we did not use any previous information about the faces in the images. Thus, in order to reduce unnecessary bounding boxes and face redundancy, we performed a merging process by calculating the intersection over union (IoU) based on a non-maximum suppression criterion and we adopted a similar approach developed by Ferreira et al. [5,6]. If the IoU ratio is greater than a defined value, we merge the bounding boxes. In this study, we chose a threshold value of 0.9 for the fusion.

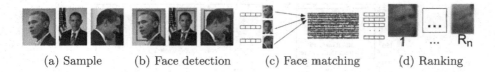

| (a) Sample | (b) Face detection | (c) Face matching | (d) Ranking |

Fig. 6. Matching between the handcrafted dataset and gigapixel face images.

To find each bounding box that contains a face, we use the DLIB library in each window. This library uses the Histogram of Oriented Gradients (HOG) and considers the score of how many gradients points there are in each direction (up, right, etc.). Then, the HOG method searches for the most similar to a known HOG pattern that was extracted from several other training faces. This approach uses the Face Landmark Estimation, proposed by Kazemi and Sullivan [7], whose main idea is to calculate 68 facial landmarks. Then, a machine learning algorithm is trained to find these 68 specific points on any face. This model trains a Deep Convectional Neural Network to generate an array of 128 measurements for each face. This embedding process is illustrated in Fig. 5(c) and 5(d). Figure 5(e) shows a sample of 432 face images detected in a small portion of the gigapixel image that corresponds to the location around the president's speech stage, where former presidents, former first ladies, senators, among other guests, were at the ceremony.

4.2 Matching Between the Handcrafted Dataset and Gigapixel Face Images

In this step, we use a set of images of public people that include authorities and known people, who were present at the ceremony, considering 3 poses of each one (front, right and left). We built the image dataset shown in Sect. 3.2. An image sample is shown in Fig. 6a). Similar to the previous stage, we also performed a face detection step in the handcrafted dataset images through DLIB, as shown in Fig. 6a), and extracted an array of 128 landmark features for each one. For face matching, we calculate the Euclidean distance (Eq. 1) between the landmark feature array of each image to be tested and all landmark feature arrays of face images extracted from a small portion of the gigapixel image considered, as shown in Fig. 6c). Finally, we build a distance ranking using Eq. 2 to be used as a measure to conclude whether a face was correctly recognized or not.

$$Distance_{i,j} = \sqrt{\left(\sum_{k=1}^{n}\left(fperson_i^p(k) - fgiga_j(k)\right)\right)^2}, \tag{1}$$

where $fperson_i$ and $fgiga_j$ are landmark feature sets of images i and j in the handcrafted and gigapixel datasets, respectively, p is a person pose (left, right, frontal), k is a landmark feature, n is the total amount of features ($n = 128$), and $Distance_{i,p,j}$ is the Euclidean distance between the landmark features.

$$Rank_i = \min\left(Distance_{i,j}\right), \tag{2}$$

where $Rank_i$ is the least distance of person i against gigapixel dataset images.

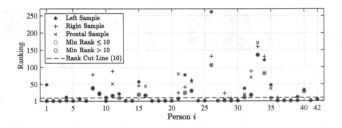

Fig. 7. Ranking of people found in our experiments.

5   Experimental Results

We conducted our experiments to find people in the crowd considering only the president's speech surrounding area, which is reserved for the new president, vice president and their family and friends, former presidents, first ladies and former ones, Supreme Court judges, speaker of the House of Representatives, party leader, special authorities, invited guests, among others. For each person, we search for them using a frontal, left and right face pose. However, due to the camera's position, most people posed in right face. Since our goal is not to find an exact match, but to reduce an observer's effort, we considered the first 10 faces based on a measured distance ranking. We present our results in Table 2, which summarizes the results by total, by face pose and also grouped by occlusion.

Table 2. Result by minimum ranking.

	Ranking total	Ranking by face pose				Occlusion by	Occlusion by	No
		Front	Right	Left	Back	Accessories	Other faces	Occlusion
≤10	69%	83%	64%	100%	25%	57%	44%	92%
>10	31%	17%	36%	0%	75%	43%	56%	8%

As we can see from our results, 69% were found, while 31% were considered not found. Although the most expressive problem is with backface, they have only 4 people and, also, the backface does not provide enough landmark points to be matched, but one person (25%) was found. The second most expressive result is the right face pose, in which a third is the person is not found. This is the largest group, because of the audience and camera's position. It is possible to observe that the most common reason for not finding someone's face is occlusion by accessory or by another face, since only 8% without occlusion are not found. Figure 7 illustrates our experimental results.

We represent the pose of the person ranked bellow and above the top-10 (Rank Cut Line) as green and red circles, respectively. We can observe that, although there is group of people who did not rank among the first ten, many of them were very close. Moreover, many people have all poses ranked in close positions. It is important to note that, while ≈60% of the faces in the gigapixel

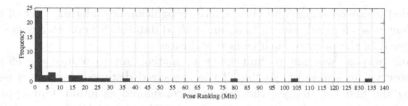

Fig. 8. Histogram of minimum ranking of person poses.

dataset are right poses, only ≈41% of the matched faces are in fact right pose, whereas ≈33% and ≈26% matches are left and front poses, respectively. This shows that different poses are useful in the dataset, even if a specific pose is dominant in the crowd. Figure 8 illustrates a histogram of the minimum ranking per person.

We can see that most of the images are at zero ranking and a minimum ranking of 10 is able to obtain an image cluster. If we increased the ranking to 12, 13, 14, 15 and so on, we could get one or two more images in each increment. However, that would increase the number of images to be inspected by an observer. We can also notice that some images are far from the defined boundary (10), for instance, there are images with a minimum ranking between 35 to 135.

Figure 9 shows some interesting results achieved in our experiments. For example, in Fig. 9(a), a person is one of the faces ranked as first position for all three poses, but a large part of his face is occluded by another face in the gigapixel image. Another more complex case, shown in Fig. 9(b), is a person who corresponds to only one of the three poses, even though his face was almost completely occluded by someone else. In addition, a challenging case due to backface is presented in Fig. 9(c), where the person falls in the first ten images in the face ranking, greatly reducing the amount of faces to be analyzed by an expert.

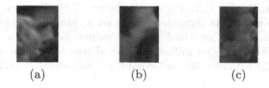

(a)　　　　　　　(b)　　　　　　　(c)

Fig. 9. Backface and occluded face samples recognized in our approach.

6 Conclusions

In this work, we present a model to assist a human observer in finding people in large images of crowds, reducing the search space for several images to a ranking of ten images related to a specific person. We conducted a face detection on a crowded gigapixel image and then a face recognition considering a set of three different poses for each person in a handcrafted dataset. Several challenges were addressed in the process, such as face occlusion.

Our purpose was not to find an exact match, but to reduce the effort of the observer or specialist, so that if the measured distance classifies a person among the first ten images, the person is considered as found. Our approach showed promising results, as we achieved recognition rates of 69% in total. When considering images with a ranking higher than 10 for all three poses, 92% of them have occlusions. The proposed method has great potential to help a human observer to find people in the crowd, especially in cluttered images, through a reduced search space.

Acknowledgment. The authors thank CAPES-Brazil (Coordination for the Improvement of Higher Education Personnel) for this study's partial support.

References

1. Arthur, K.E.: How CNN Captured the Gigapixel Image of Trump's Inauguration (2017). http://www.afd-techtalk.com/gigapixel-trump/. Accessed 3 Aug 2020
2. Bai, Y., Zhang, Y., Ding, M., Ghanem, B.: Finding tiny faces in the wild with generative adversarial network. In: IEEE Conference on Computer Vision and Pattern Recognition, pp. 21–30. Salt Lake City, June 2018
3. Cao, Z., Yan, R., Huang, Y., Shi, Z.: Gigapixel-level image crowd counting using csrnet. In: IEEE International Conference on Multimedia Expo Workshops, pp. 426–428 (2019)
4. Clarke, A.D.F., Elsner, M., Rohde, H.: Where's Wally: the influence of visual salience on referring expression generation. Front. Psychol. **4**, 329 (2013)
5. Ferreira, C., Soares, F., Pedrini, H., Bruce, N., Ferreira, W., Cruz Junior, G.: Multiresolution Analysis on searching for people in gigapixel images. In: IEEE Canadian Conference on Electrical Computer Engineering, pp. 1–4, Quebec City, May 2018
6. Ferreira, C.B.R., Soares, F.A., Pedrini, H., Bruce, N.M., Ferreira, W., Junior, G.C.: A study of dimensionality reduction impact on an approach to people detection in gigapixel image. IEEE Can. Conf. Electr. Comput. Eng. **43**(3), 122–128 (2020)
7. Kazemi, V., Sullivan, J.: One millisecond face alignment with an ensemble of regression trees. In: IEEE Conference on Computer Vision and Pattern Recognition, June 2014
8. Port Authority of New York and New Jersey: 2017 Annual Airport Traffic Report, April 2018. Accessed 21 Feb 2019
9. StackExchange: How did CNN take that Gigapixel Photo for Trump's Inauguration? (2017). https://photo.stackexchange.com/questions/86489/how-did-cnn-take-that-gigapixel-photo-for-trumps-inauguration. Accessed 3 Aug 2020
10. Wang, X.,et al.: PANDA: a gigapixel-level human-centric video dataset. In: IEEE/CVF Conference on Computer Vision and Pattern Recognition, pp. 3265–3275 (2020)

11. Yang, S., Luo, P., Loy, C.C., Tang, X.: From facial parts responses to face detection: a deep learning approach. In: IEEE International Conference on Computer Vision, pp. 3676–3684. Santiago, December 2015
12. Zhang, S., et al.: Pedestrian counting for a large scene using a GigaPan panorama and exemplar-SVMs. In: 9th International Conference on Computational Intelligence and Security, pp. 229–235. IEEE (2013)

Optical Flow Based Background Subtraction with a Moving Camera: Application to Autonomous Driving

Sotirios Diamantas[1](✉) and Kostas Alexis[2]

[1] Department of Engineering and Computer Science, Tarleton State University,
Texas A&M University System, Box T-0390, Stephenville, TX 76402, USA
diamantas@tarleton.edu
[2] Autonomous Robots Lab, Department of Computer Science and Engineering,
University of Nevada, Reno, 1664 N. Virginia St., Reno, NV 89557, USA
kalexis@unr.edu

Abstract. In this research we present a novel algorithm for background subtraction using a moving camera. Our algorithm is based purely on visual information obtained from a camera mounted on an electric bus, operating in downtown Reno which automatically detects moving objects of interest with the view to provide information for collision avoidance and number of vehicles for an autonomous vehicle. In our approach we exploit the optical flow vectors generated by the motion of the camera on the bus while keeping parameter assumptions at a minimum. At first, we estimate the Focus of Expansion which is used to model and simulate 3D points given the intrinsic parameters of the camera and perform multiple linear regression to estimate the regression equation parameters and implement on the real data set of every frame to identify moving objects. We validated our algorithm using data taken from a common bus route in the city of Reno.

Keywords: Optical flow · Background subtraction · Moving camera · Motion detection · Autonomous vehicles

1 Introduction

Background subtraction is a fundamental problem in the field of computer vision and it has a number of applications relating to object detection and tracking, object segmentation and classification, change detection identification, among others [1]. Background subtraction relates to the identification of objects that

---

This material is based upon work supported by the "Intelligent Mobility: Living Labs" project funded by the Nevada Governor's Office for Economic Development.
S. Diamantas—This research was carried out while the author was a postdoctoral fellow at the Autonomous Robots Lab, Department of Computer Science & Engineering, University of Nevada, Reno.

G. Bebis et al. (Eds.): ISVC 2020, LNCS 12510, pp. 398–409, 2020.
https://doi.org/10.1007/978-3-030-64559-5_31

Fig. 1. Electric bus with camera sensors and IMU onboard operated in the city of Reno. Upper left corner: Cameras and IMU sensor onboard bus; Lower left corner: Notation for optical flow vectors: Green vectors denote static objects, blue vectors denote moving objects, red vectors denote outliers. (Color figure online)

are moving in a scene while the images perceived are obtained from a static camera. Although significant contributions have enabled background subtraction algorithms to efficiently deal with the problem of background subtraction using a fixed, non-moving camera, little has been done to tackle the problem of background subtraction using a moving camera. In this paper, we propose a new algorithm for moving object detection using a single moving camera without the need to use supplementary sensors such as Inertial Measurement Units (IMU), stereo vision, or depth sensors.

The algorithm we present in this paper has been tested in real-world environment and the results obtained show its robustness in terms of accuracy in spite of the high speed camera motion due to the motion of the vehicle. A multi-camera rig consisting of three cameras and an IMU has been mounted on an electric bus and images are obtained in average traffic conditions in the area between campus and downtown Reno. The employed vehicle platform, namely a Proterra EcoRide BE35 electric bus, is depicted alongside the developed camera rig. The data from one of these cameras are employed to verify the proposed method for optical flow-based background subtraction with a moving camera. Figure 1 provides a pictorial representation of the electric bus along with the sensors onboard. Traditional methods model pixel intensities over time and detect when a scene changes over time [6]. On the other hand, background subtraction from a moving camera is a problem that has risen during the past few years especially due to the emergence of autonomous vehicles whose guidance requires the detection of moving objects in their field of view to avoid collisions and plan a safe path.

The paper consists of five sections. In the next section, a background literature review is presented relating to research on background subtraction. In Sect. 3, we present the methodology followed and the various steps involved in our proposed algorithm. In Sect. 4, the results from this research are presented along with real world examples. Finally, in the last part of this paper, a conclusions section is presented along with a discussion on the results obtained.

2   Background Work

Optical flow has been extensively utilized in a number of research works related to robot motion for tackling problems of scene recognition and robot homing using the optical flow *fingerprint* of landmarks [5,7] as well as to estimate the speed of unknown moving objects [8]. Optical flow has also been used in tracking multiple objects in road scenes using foreground blobs from background subtraction [2]. In [17] the authors employ semantic segmentation for autonomous driving using optical flow.

In contrast to the traditional methods for background subtraction which employ Gaussian Mixture Models (GMMs) [10,20,21] these usually apply to cases where the camera is static. For moving cameras different methodologies, however, are adopted. Following are examples of implementations that have been carried out using moving cameras. In [9] an online method is presented that makes use of long term trajectories along with a Bayesian filtering framework to segment background from the foreground in each frame. In [18] the authors exploit the fact that all trajectories to static areas in a scene lie in a three dimensional subspace and is used to differentiate between foreground and background objects. No 3D reconstruction of the scene is required but rather a sparse model of the background is created from feature trajectories.

In a different setting, the problem of moving camera background subtraction is not approached as binary problem but rather as a multi-label segmentation problem by modeling different foreground objects in different layers [19]. In addition, Bayesian filtering is employed to infer a probability map and a multi-label graph-cut based on Markov Random Field is used for labeling. Finally, in [12] a saliency based method is presented using the SIFT flow field of moving objects.

3   Methodology

In this section a description is given about the methods followed to tackle the problem of background subtraction with a moving camera. At first, the camera rig with the sensors is mounted on an electric bus manufactured by Proterra and operated by the Regional Transportation Commission (RTC) which is employed in the city of Reno. The data was collected during the normal operation hours of the bus following the standard route. The cameras used are *FLIR PointGrey Chameleon3* (sensor: ON Semi PYTHON 1300 CMOS, 1/2″) with a resolution of 1280 × 1024 set at 20 fps. Two cameras are gray scale and the third one is a color one. The IMU unit is an *um7* which is not used for the purpose of this

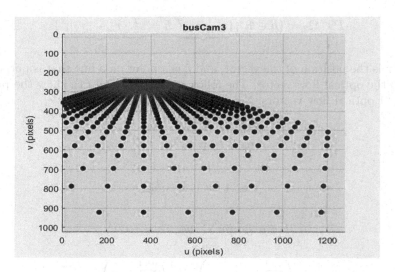

Fig. 2. Projection of 3D points based on camera intrinsic parameters and Focus of Expansion for each frame. FOE at current Figure is FOE = (368,216)

research. For recording camera data we have used the Robot Operating System (ROS).

First, the camera used for the background subtraction problem was calibrated and the intrinsic parameters were obtained. Optical flow vectors from the camera motion produce the so-called Focus of Expansion (FOE). FOE is calculated using the Lucas-Kanade (LK) algorithm [13]. Based on the intrinsic parameters of the camera, a series of 3D points are simulated and projected onto a simulated image plane like the one used by the camera sensor. The camera height from the ground plane is fixed and thus is used to simulate as accurately as possible moving objects that lie on the ground plane, i.e., the road. In total, 2000 3D points have been modeled and simulated with a constant distance from the principal point of the camera with the view to represent flat terrain 3D points. Figure 2 shows a pictorial representation of the projected 3D points with an example FOE = (368, 216).

The LK algorithm is applied to two time adjacent image frames and the *leave-one-out* resampling method is used to estimate the FOE. Subsequently, a mathematical description of the *leave-one-out* method used to estimate the FOE point from optical flow vectors is presented.

The convergence of optical flow vectors at point P occurs when a system of linear equations is minimized. Vectors, therefore, serve as linear equations. Equations (1) and (2) present an example of two vectors,

$$P \in \Omega_1 = \{h \in \Re^2 | \underbrace{(v_1 - r_1)^T}_{\alpha_1} h = \underbrace{v_1^T \cdot r_1 - ||r_1||^2}_{\beta_1}\} \tag{1}$$

$$P \in \Omega_2 = \{h \in \Re^2 |\ \underbrace{(v_2 - r_2)^T}_{\alpha_2}\ h = \underbrace{v_2^T \cdot r_2 - ||r_2||^2}_{\beta_2}\} \tag{2}$$

where r is the position of the vector, and v is a point on a line that is perpendicular to the optical flow vector. The following Eqs. (3) and (4), show the process for $n - 1$ optical flow vectors. Noise in the system is denoted by ϵ_i.

$$\begin{aligned} h\alpha_1 + \epsilon_1 &= \beta_1 \\ h\alpha_2 + \epsilon_2 &= \beta_2 \\ &\vdots \\ h\alpha_{n-1} + \epsilon_{n-1} &= \beta_{n-1} \end{aligned} \tag{3}$$

$$h \in argmin \sum_{i=1}^{n-1} (h\alpha_i - \beta_i + \epsilon_i)^2 \tag{4}$$

$$\underbrace{\left(\sum_{i=1}^{n-1} \alpha_i \alpha_i^T + \epsilon_i \right)}_{C} h = \underbrace{\left(\sum_{i=1}^{n-1} \alpha_i \beta_i \right)}_{\gamma} \tag{5}$$

$$h = C^{-1}\gamma \tag{6}$$

The *leave-one-out* sampling works by taking out one optical flow vector from the sample while estimating point P using the remaining $n - 1$. The Euclidean distance, $d(p_j, P_i)$, is then calculated between point p_j of the removed vector and the convergence point, P_i. The process is repeated n times, which is the number of optical flow vectors. This results in a set of n distances. The optical flow vectors that fall above a certain threshold, in this case, beyond the 90th percentile, are considered as outliers. Using the inliers and the *leave-one-out*, Eqs. (3)–(6) are used to find the convergence point. The convergence point, P, is thus, denoted by h, in Eq. (6)

The purpose of estimating the FOE and camera intrinsic parameters is to, as accurately as possible, model and simulate the set of 3D points. The set of 3D points are projected onto the image plane and an optical flow pattern is obtained using a constant-velocity camera model. The optical flow vector magnitudes at twice the velocity, i.e., 100 km/h (from 50 km/h) produce vectors at twice the magnitude, thus a linear relationship can be realized. A multiple linear regression is performed between two explanatory variables (x_1 and x_2; which are pixel values along the x- and y-axis) and a response variable (y; magnitude of optical flow vectors) which is used to fit a linear equation to observed data (Eq. 7); in our case the magnitude of optical flow vectors between two consecutive time stamps is given with a camera velocity of 50 km/h. Uniform sampling is performed in the optical flow vector data set from the camera with the view to estimate the linear fit model. Given the linear relationship between the different camera velocities we can even estimate the speed of the vehicle by using the ratio between the predicted linear model and the observed one derived from the uniform sample space.

$$y = \beta + \beta_1 x_1 + \beta_2 x_2 \tag{7}$$

For this research we used OpenCV and the C++ programming language to implement the LK optical flow algorithm, and the Machine Vision Toolbox [3] for modeling and simulating feature points and estimating the parameters of multiple linear regression. Modeling accurately feature points based on the FOE of the camera motion and camera intrinsics, and implementing multiple linear regression is critical in obtaining accurate results.

4   Results

Figures 4 and 5 depict the results obtained from the moving camera onboard the electric bus. Figures 4 (a)–(d) show the raw images while Figs. 4 (e)–(h) show the estimated moving and non-moving features in the image plane. The same arrangement appears in Fig. 5 and in Fig. 6. RGB color coding denotes outliers, inliers, and moving objects, respectively. Although the velocity of the bus is not constant and at the same time unknown, the results obtained are quite accurate with the exception of some few individual false moving vector detections. In Fig. 4 a series of moving vehicles on the left hand side of the images are correctly identified. The algorithm provides best results for moving objects whose optical flow magnitude is large enough to denote motion. Objects with little motion, thus insignificant optical flow magnitude, are considered static.

Similarly, in Fig. 5, a number of moving vehicles are identified and denoted with the blue optical flow vectors. In Figs. 6 and 7, a single moving vehicle is shown. The output of the algorithm is quite accurate given the unknown speed of the moving camera as well as that of the incoming vehicles[1]. Erroneous estimates

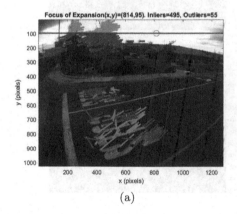
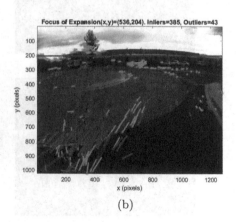

(a)   (b)

Fig. 3. (a)–(b) Two images where the proposed algorithm provides false positives in spite of the fact there are no moving vehicles. Sharp turns of the moving bus with the onboard camera result in erroneous output.

---

[1] A video of results can be found at: https://www.youtube.com/watch?v=JtNTe0 GWivs.

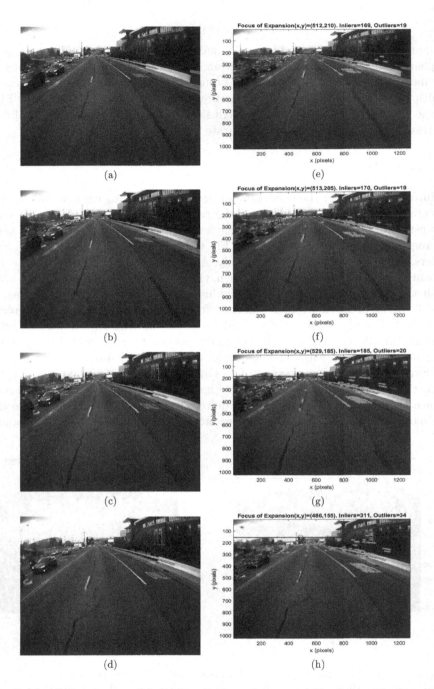

Fig. 4. (a)–(d) Raw images; (e)–(h) Results from the proposed background subtraction method. Red vectors denote outliers; Green vectors denote inliers; Blue vectors denote moving objects. A number of moving vehicles are correctly identified and denoted with blue vectors. Static features are also correctly identified. (Color figure online)

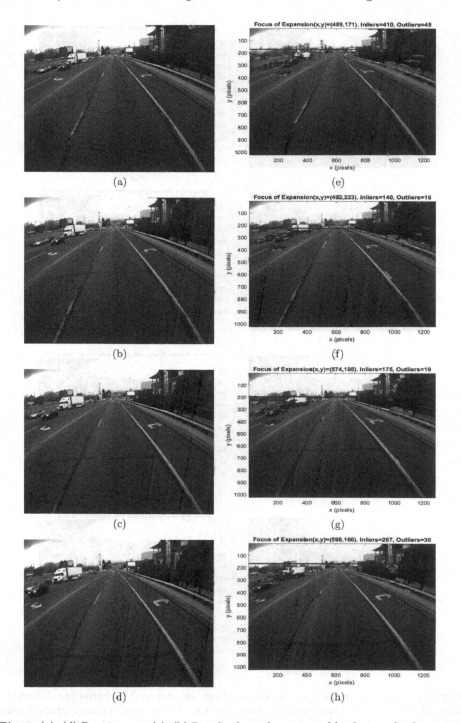

Fig. 5. (a)–(d) Raw images; (e)–(h) Results from the proposed background subtraction method. Red vectors denote outliers; Green vectors denote inliers; Blue vectors denote moving objects. (Color figure online)

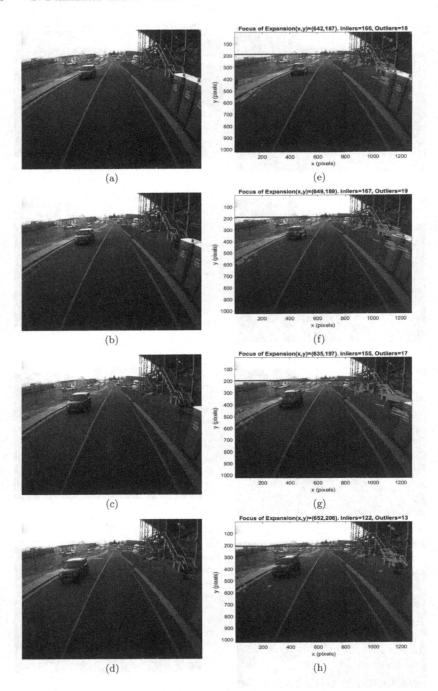

Fig. 6. (a)–(d) Raw images; (e)–(h) Results from the proposed background subtraction method. Red vectors denote outliers; Green vectors denote inliers; Blue vectors denote moving objects. A single moving vehicle is correctly detected on the left hand side of the image. (Color figure online)

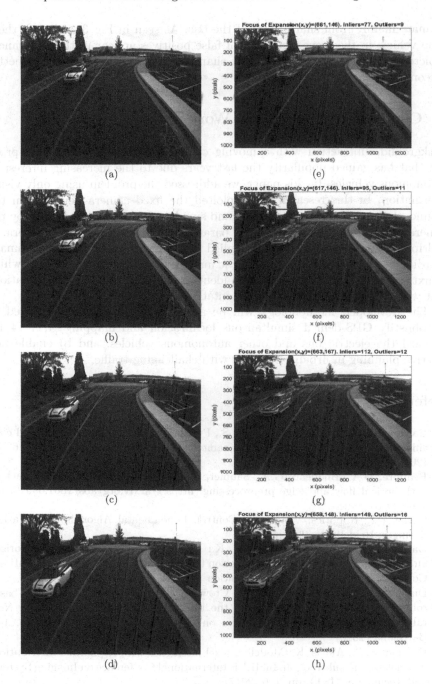

Fig. 7. (a)–(d) Raw images; (e)–(h) Results from the proposed background subtraction method. Red vectors denote outliers; Green vectors denote inliers; Blue vectors denote moving objects. A second moving vehicle is correctly detected in the image. A small number of blue vectors appears on the upper part of the image possibly denoting background motion from trees or branches. (Color figure online)

emanate mainly from sharp turns of the bus. As seen in Fig. 3, although there is no vehicle in the scene a number of false positives appear in these instances depicted with blue vectors. Modeling sharp turns would likely result in better outcomes.

5   Conclusions and Future Work

Background subtraction with a moving camera is a highly challenging problem that has gained popularity the last years due to the increasing interest in autonomous vehicles. In this paper, we addressed the problem using only visual information. In this research, we exploited the fixed camera height from the ground plane with the view to model and simulate feature points as seen by the camera sensor based on the intrinsic parameters obtained from the camera. A multiple linear regression model is applied to the synthetic data given the image coordinates of the features as well as the magnitude of optical flow vectors which is juxtaposed against the real data to identify significant optical flow variations that will signify moving object representations.

The developed methodology will be a core module that will be used to a) robustify GPS-denied simultaneous localization and mapping [4,11,14–16] onboard the electric bus and other autonomous vehicles, and b) enable fast reactive planning in urban conditions with challenging traffic.

References

1. Bardas, G., Astaras, S., Diamantas, S., Pnevmatikakis, A.: 3D tracking and classification system using a monocular camera. Wirel. Pers. Commun. **92**(1), 63–85 (2017)
2. Beaupré, D.A., Bilodeau, G.A., Saunier, N.: Improving multiple object tracking with optical flow and edge preprocessing. https://arxiv.org/abs/1801.09646, pp. 1–6 (2018)
3. Corke, P.I.: Robotics, Vision and Control: Fundamental Algorithms in Matlab. Springer, Heidelberg (2011)
4. Dang, T., Papachristos, C., Alexis, K.: Visual saliency-aware receding horizon autonomous exploration with application to aerial robotics. In: IEEE International Conference on Robotics and Automation (ICRA), pp. 2526–2533 (2018)
5. Diamantas, S.C., Oikonomidis, A., Crowder, R.M.: Towards optical flow-based robotic homing. In: Proceedings of the International Joint Conference on Neural Networks (IEEE World Congress on Computational Intelligence), pp. 1–9. Barcelona (2010)
6. Diamantas, S., Alexis, K.: Modeling pixel intensities with log-normal distributions for background subtraction. In: IEEE International Conference on Imaging Systems and Techniques (IST), pp. 1–6 (2017)
7. Diamantas, S.C.: Biological and Metric Maps Applied to Robot Homing. Ph.D. Thesis, School of Electronics and Computer Science, University of Southampton (2010)

8. Diamantas, S.C., Dasgupta, P.: Active vision speed estimation from optical flow. In: Natraj, A., Cameron, S., Melhuish, C., Witkowski, M. (eds.) TAROS 2013. LNCS (LNAI), vol. 8069, pp. 173–184. Springer, Heidelberg (2014). https://doi.org/10.1007/978-3-662-43645-5_18

9. Elqursh, A., Elgammal, A.: Online moving camera background subtraction. In: Fitzgibbon, A., Lazebnik, S., Perona, P., Sato, Y., Schmid, C. (eds.) ECCV 2012. LNCS, vol. 7577, pp. 228–241. Springer, Heidelberg (2012). https://doi.org/10.1007/978-3-642-33783-3_17

10. KaewTraKulPong, P., Bowden, R.: An improved adaptive background mixture model for real-time tracking with shadow detection. In: Remagnino, P., Jones, G.A., Paragios, N., Regazzoni, C.S. (eds.) Video-Based Surveillance Systems, chap. 11, pp. 135–144. Springer, Boston (2002). https://doi.org/10.1007/978-1-4615-0913-4_11

11. Leutenegger, S., Melzer, A., Alexis, K., Siegwart, R.: Robust state estimation for small unmanned airplanes. In: IEEE Multiconference on Systems and Control (MSC), pp. 1003–1010 (2014)

12. Li, J., Guo, J., Fan, H.: Video background subtraction algorithm for a moving camera. Int. J. Multimedia Ubiquit. Eng. **10**(8), 83–96 (2015)

13. Lucas, B.D., Kanade, T.: An iterative image registration technique with an application to stereo vision. In: Proceedings of the 7th International Joint Conference on Artificial Intelligence (IJCAI), 24–28. pp. 674–679, August 1981

14. Mascarich, F., Khattak, S., Papachristos, C., Alexis, K.: A multi-modal mapping unit for autonomous exploration and mapping of underground tunnels. In: IEEE Aerospace Conference (AeroConf), pp. 1–7 (2018)

15. Papachristos, C., Khattak, S., Alexis, K.: Autonomous exploration of visually-degraded environments using aerial robots. In: International Conference on Unmanned Aircraft Systems (ICUAS), pp. 775–780 (2017)

16. Papachristos, C., Khattak, S., Alexis, K.: Uncertainty-aware receding horizon exploration and mapping using aerial robots. In: IEEE International Conference on Robotics and Automation (ICRA), pp. 4568–4575 (2017)

17. Rashed, H., Yogamani, S., El-Sallab, A., Krizek, P., El-Helw, M.: Optical flow augmented semantic segmentation networks for automated driving. https://arxiv.org/abs/1901.07355, pp. 1–8 (2019)

18. Sheikh, Y., Javed, O., Kanade, T.: Background subtraction for freely moving cameras. In: Proceedings of the IEEE 12th International Conference on Computer Vision (2009)

19. Zhu, Y., Elgammal, A.: A multilayer-based framework for online background subtraction with freely moving cameras. https://arxiv.org/abs/1709.01140. pp. 4321–4330 (2017)

20. Zivkovic, Z.: Improved adaptive gaussian mixture model for background subtraction. In: 17th International Conference on Pattern Recognition, ICPR 2004, Cambridge, UK, August 23–26 2004, pp. 28–31 (2004)

21. Zivkovic, Z., van der Heijden, F.: Efficient adaptive density estimation per image pixel for the task of background subtraction. Pattern Recogn. Lett. **27**(7), 773–780 (2006)

Deep Facial Expression Recognition with Occlusion Regularization

Nikul Pandya, Philipp Werner$^{(\boxtimes)}$, and Ayoub Al-Hamadi

Neuro-Information Technology, Otto von Guericke University Magdeburg,
Magdeburg, Germany
{nikulbhai.pandya,philipp.werner,ayoub.al-hamadi}@ovgu.de,
http://www.iikt.ovgu.de/nit.html

Abstract. In computer vision, occlusions are mainly known as a challenge to cope with. For instance, partial occlusions of the face may lower the performance of facial expression recognition systems. However, when incorporated into the training, occlusions can be also helpful in improving the overall performance. In this paper, we propose and evaluate occlusion augmentation as a simple but effective regularizing tool for improving the general performance of deep learning based facial expression and action unit recognition systems, even if no occlusion is present in the test data. In our experiments we consistently found significant performance improvements on three databases (Bosphorus, RAF-DB, and AffectNet) and three CNN architectures (Xception, MobileNet, and a custom model), suggesting that occlusion regularization works independently of the dataset and architecture. Based on our clear results, we strongly recommend to integrate occlusion regularization into the training of all CNN-based facial expression recognition systems, because it promises performance gains at very low cost.

Keywords: Facial expression recognition · Facial action unit intensity estimation · Occlusion regularization · Data augmentation · CNN

1 Introduction

Deep learning methods, especially CNNs, outperform previous state of the art in nearly all computer vision tasks, e.g. object detection, image classification, and facial expression recognition. Facial expression recognition attracts researchers' attention because of its many applications in human-machine interaction, social robotics, medical diagnosis and treatment, and semi-automated driving.

Regularization is one of the key elements of deep learning, allowing to generalize well to unseen data, even when training on a limited training set or with an imperfect optimization procedure [8]. Some widely and successfully used regularization techniques are data augmentation, drop-out, batch normalization, and weight decay, which are also common in expression recognition [11,22]. In addition to these methods, this paper proposes an occlusion-based regularization

© Springer Nature Switzerland AG 2020
G. Bebis et al. (Eds.): ISVC 2020, LNCS 12510, pp. 410–420, 2020.
https://doi.org/10.1007/978-3-030-64559-5_32

technique, which consistently improves performance in facial expression recognition and can be combined with any existing regularization technique and network architecture. Occlusion regularization is a specific form of data augmentation and very easy to implement: Training images are synthetically occluded by random black bars or objects at random locations.

The work's main contributions are:

1. We propose to apply occlusion augmentation in facial expression recognition tasks, such as recognition of emotion categories and recognition of facial action unit intensities. Occlusion augmentation is a simple and effective regularizer, which can be applied with any CNN approach. It is beneficial even if the test data does *not* contain occlusions.
2. We experimentally show the resulting performance improvements using three datasets with different expression recognition tasks (RAF [12], AffectNet [16], and Bosphorus [18] databases) and three CNN architectures (pre-trained Xception [2] and MobileNet [6] as well as a custom architecture).
3. We compare our results with state-of-the-art results. We clearly outperform prior work on the Bosphorus dataset. On the RAF dataset we reach comparable results with our simple approach, which may also be applied to further improve results of more sophisticated state-of-the-art approaches.

2   Related Work

Most of the work related to occlusion in facial expression recognition intended to improve performance on partially occluded images. In contrast, our work addresses performance improvements on all face images, including occlusion-free images. For a general overview on facial expression recognition and on expression recognition under partial occlusion, the reader is referred to Li et al. [11] and Zhang et al. [24], respectively. A recent approach on occlusion-aware expression recognition is the CNN network with an attention mechanism proposed by Li et al. [13]. They combined multiple representations from facial regions of interest by weighting via a proposed gate unit, which computes an adaptive weight from the region itself according to the unobstructedness and importance. This way they improved performance on both occluded and occlusion-free face images.

Kukačka et al. [8] review and classify the literature on regularization. Among the most widely used methods are data augmentation, batch normalization, and drop-out. There are lots of works on using data augmentation to improve the performance of a deep learning network in general, which includes facial expression recognition tasks. Bengio et al. [1] showed that the performance of a deep neural network can be improved by data augmentation in the image classification problem. Even before, back in 1998, LeCun et al. [9] used various affine transformation for data augmentation for training LeNet. Lemley et al. [10] proposed a smart data augmentation technique to optimize data augmentation during training. Lin et al. [14] used data augmentation and compact feature learning to improve the performance of the facial expression recognition model. Sarandi

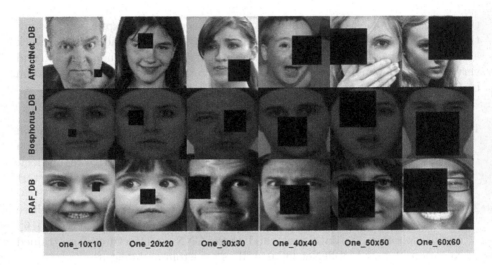

Fig. 1. Example images of the used databases with synthetic random black-bar occlusions of the used sizes. The occlusions are only augmented during training. Testing is done with the original (mostly occlusion-free) images.

et al. [17] used synthetic object occlusion for 3D body pose estimation performance improvements, which inspired our work on occlusion-based regularization in the facial expression domain.

Ioffe and Szegedy [7] showed how batch normalization can improve training time and the performance of deep learning networks. Batch normalization has a regularizing effect, because mean and standard deviation used for normalization vary between the randomly composed mini-batches. This introduces additional variation and teaches the layers to be robust to a lot of variation in their input. Another widely used concept of regularization in deep learning networks is drop-out, which was introduced by Hinton et al. [5]. Drop-out randomly removes hidden neurons during the training of a deep network. By doing so, the network does not depends on a specific activation during training, which reduces overfitting.

3 Approach

We propose to augment synthetic occlusions on the images that are used to train expression recognition models. The position of the occlusion mask in pixel coordinates is randomly selected for each sample (and epoch) in a way that it is always completely within the image. Two types of occlusions are considered in this work:

Black-Bar Occlusions: We use square occlusion masks of the sizes 10×10 to 60×60 pixels for all the experiments and set all pixels to zero. Some examples of random black bar occlusion can be seen in Fig. 1.

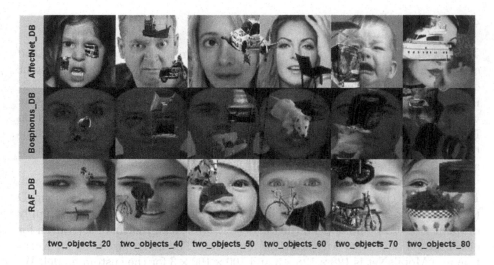

Fig. 2. Example images of the used databases with synthetic random object occlusions of the used sizes. The occlusions are only augmented during training. Testing is done with the original (mostly occlusion-free) images.

Object Occlusions: The PASCAL VOC 2011 [4] dataset is used to augment real objects (excluding faces) on face images. After several experiments, we selected to occlude each training image with two objects, because this resulted in better performance than using one object. Some exemplary occlusion masks and how much occlusion they create on training images can be seen in Fig. 2.

The occlusions do *not* resemble realistic occlusions, such as occlusions by hands, glasses, or other objects, because our goal is providing a simple regularization technique. Synthesizing realistic occlusions is a complex task, hard to implement, and – as our experiments show – not necessary for improving the performance.

Similar to other data augmentation techniques and batch normalization, occlusion augmentation increases the variance of the input and teaches the network to be more robust to variations. It encourages the network not to base its decisions exclusively on few local activations, but to combine multiple indicating activations globally. The size of the occlusion is a critical parameter: Occluding more pixels increases the variation of the training images and thus the regularization effect. However, occluding more pixels also hides more information that may be needed for a correct prediction.

The occlusion augmentation can be used with any CNN architecture and training loss. Further, it can be combined with any other regularization technique and be implemented as an extension of an arbitrary data augmentation pipeline. Although it is a simple approach, it is effective in improving the performance, as we will see in the following experiments.

4   Experiments and Results

To show the regularization effect of occlusion augmentation we use three facial expression datasets: Bosphorus [18], RAF [12], and AffectNet [16]. We present experiments on varying the degree of occlusion augmentation using three CNN models: Xception [2], MobileNet [6], and a custom architecture. This way we verify occlusion regularization with both, standard models pre-trained on ImageNet [3] and a custom model with random (Xavier) weight initialization. All three models are trained using both black-bar and object occlusion augmentation.

The custom model architecture contains six convolution layers (kernel 3×3, 16/32/.../512 channels, ReLU), all except the first followed by MaxPoolig2D (pool size 2×2). After the convolution part, we flatten the features, apply dropout ($p = 0.2$), and append the final dense layer, using softmax activation for classification and linear activation for regression. The image size used for Xception and MobileNet is $128 \times 128 \times 3$ and $100 \times 100 \times 3$ for the custom model. We conduct the experiments with the Keras deep learning framework. The occlusions are augmented with custom Python source code (using OpenCV).

4.1   Black-Bar Occlusion Regularization

The **Bosphorus Database** [18] contains 2,902 images, each with 26 facial action unit (AU) intensity labels. The images of 87 subjects (2,470 samples) are used for training and 17 subjects' faces (432 samples) are used as test images. We align all the training and test images with a similarity transform using facial landmarks provided with the database. The Xception and MobileNet networks are trained with classification loss (categorical cross-entropy) and the custom model with regression loss (mean squared error), because we want to verify that occlusion regularization works with both classification and regression. Figure 3 illustrates the performance improvements using black-bar occlusion regularization. The baselines (occlusion size of zero, i.e. no occlusion) are the average of three runs for each of the models. The y-axis in the plot presents the average of the 26 AUs' ICC(3,1) values [19] of the models on the test data (0 corresponds to chance level and 1 to error-free prediction) and the x-axis presents different occlusion sizes used in the respective training runs. It can be clearly seen from the plots that the performance of the models improves as the size of the occlusion mask increases until some range. Then, it starts to decline again. This is as to be expected, because at some occlusion size the negative impact of hiding information starts to outweigh the positive effect of regularization.

The **Real-World Affective Faces** Database (RAF-DB) [12] is a large database with around 30,000 diverse real-world face images downloaded from the internet. All images were annotated with basic or compound emotions by 40 trained annotators. Images with basic emotion expressions were used for experiments (including 12,271 training images and 3,068 test images). The RAF database provides both original images and aligned images; we use aligned face images for our experiments. Figure 4 shows the model performance improvements

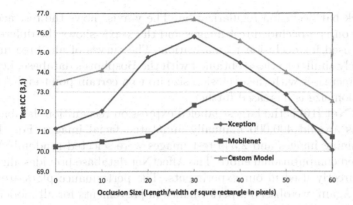

Fig. 3. Performance on Bosphorus (black-bar occlusion). An occlusion size of 0 corresponds to baseline results, which are outperformed by augmenting mid-size occlusions.

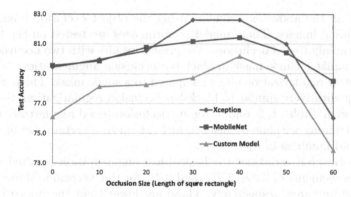

Fig. 4. Performance on RAF (black-bar occlusion). An occlusion size of 0 corresponds to baseline results, which are outperformed by augmenting mid-size occlusions.

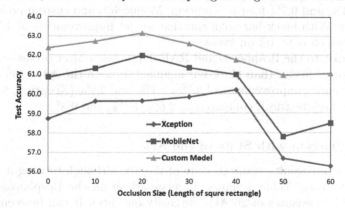

Fig. 5. Performance on AffectNet (black-bar occlusion). An occlusion size of 0 corresponds to baseline results, which are outperformed by augmenting mid-size occlusions.

using black bar occlusion regularization. The y-axis shows the test accuracy of the model on non-occluded test images and the x-axis shows the different occlusion sizes used for occlusion regularization. The curves of all three models are qualitatively similar to those obtained with the Bosphorus database, i.e. the performance increases with the occlusion size up to a certain point and decreases if the occlusion size is increased further.

AffectNet [16] is the largest labeled expression recognition database by far: It contains around 400,000 manually annotated facial images. For this work, 99,852 training images and 2,549 test images were selected randomly to reduce the required computational effort. The AffectNet database provides aligned faces that we directly used in our experiments. The performance plots are depicted in Fig. 5. Again, we observed performance improvements for all models up to a tipping point, after which performance decreases again.

4.2   Object Occlusion Regularization

We repeat all the above experiments using the object occlusion augmentation on the training images. Then, model performances are tested on the test data, which are mainly free of occlusions. We present results with two occlusion masks per image unlike a single mask in black bar occlusion augmentation, because we found a better regularization effect compared to a single mask. The performance plots are qualitatively similar to black-bar occlusion regularization. So we show the numbers in Tables 1, 2, and 3. Again, occlusion-based regularization outperforms the training without occlusions, at least up to a certain size of occlusion (see the bold numbers in the tables).

On the Bosphorus dataset the best object augmentation resulted in performance improvements of 3.3%, 3.7%, and 0.7% for the Xception, MobileNet, and custom architectures, respectively. These are lower than the improvements of the best black-bar augmentation, which are 5.6%, 4.3%, and 3.2%.

On RAF the performance improvements of the best object augmentation are 2.3%, 3%, and 0.7% for the Xception, MobileNet, and custom architectures, respectively. With black-bar augmentation we get improvements of 4.7%, 1.7%, and 1.6%, which is better on average.

In contrast to the Bosphorus and RAF databases, object occlusion augmentation performs better than black-bar augmentation on the AffectNet database, with performance improvements of 2.7%, 1.7%, and 2.9% (Xception, MobileNet, and custom architecture), compared to 2.6%, 1.1%, and 0.8%.

4.3   Comparison with State of the Art

We compare our results with the state of the art, although beating it is not the focus of our work. Table 4 shows the comparison on the Bosphorus database (mean of ICC measures of 26 AUs' intensity outputs). It can be seen from the table that we outperform the previous state of the art on this database clearly.

We also compare our best test accuracy on the RAF dataset with the existing state of the art. Table 5 shows that we obtain comparable results. Since occlusion

Table 1. Test performance achieved on Bosphorus datasets with different CNN models (columns) by augmenting the training data with synthetic **object occlusions** (rows).

Training	Bosphorus Database (ICC(3,1))		
Occlusions	Xception	MobileNet	Custom
No Occlusions	0.712	0.702	0.735
Two 10 × 10	**0.745**	**0.724**	**0.736**
Two 20 × 20	**0.715**	**0.739**	**0.739**
Two 30 × 30	**0.721**	**0.703**	**0.742**
Two 40 × 40	0.675	0.660	0.721
Two 50 × 50	0.608	0.569	0.698

Table 2. Test performance achieved on RAF datasets with different CNN models (columns) by augmenting the training data with synthetic **object occlusions** (rows).

Training	RAF Database (Accuracy in %)		
Occlusions	Xception	MobileNet	Custom
No Occlusions	79.5	79.6	76.1
Two 10 × 10	**80.0**	**78.8**	**76.3**
Two 20 × 20	**80.4**	**81.3**	**76.2**
Two 30 × 30	**81.0**	**81.2**	**76.8**
Two 40 × 40	**81.1**	**82.6**	**76.6**
Two 50 × 50	**81.8**	**80.9**	75.4

Table 3. Test performance achieved on AffectNet datasets with different CNN models (columns) by augmenting the training data with synthetic **object occlusions** (rows).

Training	AffectNet Database (Accuracy in %)		
Occlusions	Xception	MobileNet	Custom
No Occlusions	58.8	60.9	62.4
Two 10 × 10	**61.2**	**61.8**	**63.8**
Two 20 × 20	**60.3**	**61.2**	**63.3**
Two 30 × 30	**63.5**	**61.1**	**63.4**
Two 40 × 40	**63.3**	**62.6**	**64.1**
Two 50 × 50	58.4	**61.3**	62.1

Table 4. State of the art on Bosphorus database.

Model	Test ICC(3,1)
Easy Ensemble [15,21]	0.340
SVR Ensemble imbalanced [21]	0.553
SVR Ensemble balanced [21]	0.533
SVR Ensemble MIDRUS [21]	0.603
Custom model with black-bar occlusion regularization	**0.767**

Table 5. State of the art on RAF database.

Model	Test Accuracy in %
VGG16 [20]	80.96
DLP-CNN [25]	80.89
pCNN [13]	81.64
GAN-Inpainting [23]	81.87
Xception [2]	79.45
Xception with black-bar occlusion regularization	**82.61**
gCNN [13]	83.05
gACNN [13]	85.07

regularization is working for all different datasets and models used in this work, we think that gCNN and gACNN can be further improved if these models are trained with additional occlusion regularization. For the AffectNet we did not use the full dataset, so comparison with other works is not fair.

5   Conclusion

We proposed and evaluated the idea of using occlusion augmentation for regularization in order to improve performance in facial expression recognition. Two types of occlusion augmentation were considered: black-bar occlusion and object occlusion. With both we found significant performance improvements (compared to not using occlusion augmentation) on three databases, three CNN architectures, two recognition tasks (basic emotions and AU intensities), and two loss functions (softmax cross-entropy and mean squared error). On the Bosphorus and RAF databases we observe greater performance improvements using black-bar than object occlusion regularization. On the AffectNet database it was vice versa. Due to the consistent improvements, we strongly recommend to integrate occlusion regularization into the training of all CNN-based facial expression recognition systems. We propose to use black-bar regularization (which is easy to implement and yields good results) with a square size in range of about 20–40% of the CNN input image size.

Future work should investigate occlusion augmentation and occlusion regularization in further experiments. Adding more randomization (e.g. regarding size and aspect ratio) may be a promising direction. Another approach is to randomly select for each image, whether the occlusion augmentation should be applied (leaving a subset of the images occlusion-free). Moreover, an algorithm may be developed which can automatically find the best occlusion augmentation for a particular database by searching the parameter space.

Acknowledgments. This work was funded by the German Federal Ministry of Education and Research (BMBF), project HuBA (03ZZ0470). The sole responsibility for the content lies with the authors.

References

1. Bengio, Y., et al.: Deep learners benefit more from out-of-distribution examples. In: Proceedings of the Fourteenth International Conference on Artificial Intelligence and Statistics, pp. 164–172 (2011)
2. Chollet, F.: Xception: deep learning with depthwise separable convolutions. In: Proceedings of the IEEE Conference on Computer Vision and Pattern Recognition, pp. 1251–1258 (2017)
3. Deng, J., Dong, W., Socher, R., Li, L.J., Li, K., Fei-Fei, L.: Imagenet: a large-scale hierarchical image database. In: 2009 IEEE Conference on Computer Vision and Pattern Recognition, pp. 248–255. IEEE (2009)
4. Everingham, M., Eslami, S.M.A., Van Gool, L., Williams, C.K.I., Winn, J., Zisserman, A.: The pascal visual object classes challenge: a retrospective. Int. J. Comput. Vis. **111**(1), 98–136 (2015)
5. Hinton, G.E., Srivastava, N., Krizhevsky, A., Sutskever, I., Salakhutdinov, R.R.: Improving neural networks by preventing co-adaptation of feature detectors. arXiv: 1207.0580 (2012)
6. Howard, A.G., et al.: Mobilenets: Efficient convolutional neural networks for mobile vision applications. arXiv: 1704.04861 [cs.CV] (2017)
7. Ioffe, S., Szegedy, C.: Batch normalization: Accelerating deep network training by reducing internal covariate shift. arXiv: 1502.03167 (2015)
8. Kukacka, J., Golkov, V., Cremers, D.: Regularization for deep learning: A taxonomy. arXiv: 1710.10686 [cs.LG] (2017)
9. LeCun, Y., Bottou, L., Bengio, Y., Haffner, P., et al.: Gradient-based learning applied to document recognition. Proc. IEEE **86**(11), 2278–2324 (1998)
10. Lemley, J., Bazrafkan, S., Corcoran, P.: Smart augmentation learning an optimal data augmentation strategy. IEEE Access **5**, 5858–5869 (2017)
11. Li, S., Deng, W.: Deep facial expression recognition: A survey. arXiv: 1804.08348 [cs.CV] (2018)
12. Li, S., Deng, W., Du, J.: Reliable crowdsourcing and deep locality-preserving learning for expression recognition in the wild. In: Proceedings of the IEEE Conference on Computer Vision and Pattern Recognition, pp. 2852–2861 (2017)
13. Li, Y., Zeng, J., Shan, S., Chen, X.: Occlusion aware facial expression recognition using CNN with attention mechanism. IEEE Trans. Image Process. **28**(5), 2439–2450 (2018)

14. Lin, F., Hong, R., Zhou, W., Li, H.: Facial expression recognition with data augmentation and compact feature learning. In: 2018 25th IEEE International Conference on Image Processing (ICIP), pp. 1957–1961. IEEE (2018)
15. Liu, X.Y., Wu, J., Zhou, Z.H.: Exploratory undersampling for class-imbalance learning. IEEE Trans. Syst. Man Cybern. **39**(2), 539–550 (2009)
16. Mollahosseini, A., Hasani, B., Mahoor, M.H.: Affectnet: a database for facial expression, valence, and arousal computing in the wild. IEEE Trans. Affective Comput. **10**(1), 18–31 (2017)
17. Sárándi, I., Linder, T., Arras, K.O., Leibe, B.: Synthetic occlusion augmentation with volumetric heatmaps for the 2018 ECCV posetrack challenge on 3D human pose estimation. arXiv: 1809.04987 (2018)
18. Savran, A., Alyüz, N., Dibeklioğlu, H., Çeliktutan, O., Gökberk, B., Sankur, B., Akarun, L.: Bosphorus database for 3D face analysis. In: Schouten, B., Juul, N.C., Drygajlo, A., Tistarelli, M. (eds.) BioID 2008. LNCS, vol. 5372, pp. 47–56. Springer, Heidelberg (2008). https://doi.org/10.1007/978-3-540-89991-4_6
19. Shrout, P.E., Fleiss, J.L.: Intraclass correlations: uses in assessing rater reliability. Psychol. Bull. **86**(2), 420 (1979)
20. Simonyan, K., Zisserman, A.: Very deep convolutional networks for large-scale image recognition. arXiv: 1409.1556 (2014)
21. Werner, P., Saxen, F., Al-Hamadi, A.: Handling data imbalance in automatic facial action intensity estimation. In: British Machine Vision Conference (BMVC), pp. 124.1–124.12 (2015)
22. Werner, P., Saxen, F., Al-Hamadi, A., Yu, H.: Generalizing to unseen head poses in facial expression recognition and action unit intensity estimation. In: IEEE International Conference on Automatic Face and Gesture Recognition (FG) (2019)
23. Yu, J., Lin, Z., Yang, J., Shen, X., Lu, X., Huang, T.S.: Generative image inpainting with contextual attention. In: Proceedings of the IEEE Conference on Computer Vision and Pattern Recognition, pp. 5505–5514 (2018)
24. Zhang, L., Verma, B., Tjondronegoro, D., Chandran, V.: Facial expression analysis under partial occlusion: a survey. ACM Comput. Surv. **51**(2) (2018). https://doi.org/10.1145/3158369
25. Zhao, L., Li, X., Zhuang, Y., Wang, J.: Deeply-learned part-aligned representations for person re-identification. In: Proceedings of the IEEE International Conference on Computer Vision, pp. 3219–3228 (2017)

Semantic Segmentation with Peripheral Vision

M. Hamed Mozaffari$^{(\boxtimes)}$ (iD) and Won-Sook Lee

School of Electrical Engineering and Computer Science, University of Ottawa,
Ottawa, Canada
{mmoza102,wslee}@uottawa.ca

Abstract. Deep convolutional neural networks exhibit exceptional performance on many computer vision tasks, including image semantic segmentation. Pre-trained networks trained on a relevant and large benchmark have a notable impact on these successful achievements. However, confronting a domain shift, usage of pre-trained deep encoders cannot boost the performance of those models. In general, transfer learning is not a general solution for various computer vision applications with small accessible image databases. An alternative approach is to develop stronger deep network models applicable to any problem rather than encouraging scientists to explore available pre-trained encoders for their computer vision tasks. To deviate the direction of the research trend in image semantic segmentation toward more effective models, we proposed an innovative convolutional module simulating the peripheral ability of the human eyes. By utilizing our module in an encoder-decoder configuration, after extensive experiments, we achieved acceptable outcomes on several challenging benchmarks, including PASCAL VOC2012 and CamVid.

Keywords: Semantic segmentation · Convolutional Neural Networks · Dilated convolution · Deep learning · Peripheral vision · Encoder-Decoders · Image processing

1   Introduction

Semantic segmentation is a fundamental step in a large group of applications, from scene understanding in self-driving vehicles to delineation of lesions in medical image analysis [19]. The aim of semantic segmentation is to assign one label for multiple objects of the same type. The main complication of semantic segmentation is closely related to scene and label variety [30] as well as the requirement of laborious works for manual labelling. However, in recent years, several groundbreaking deep learning methods based on Fully Convolutional Networks (FCNs) [21] have been exploited for the problem of semantic segmentation with astonishing advancements in several benchmarks [19] over systems relying on hand-crafted features [7].

© Springer Nature Switzerland AG 2020
G. Bebis et al. (Eds.): ISVC 2020, LNCS 12510, pp. 421–429, 2020.
https://doi.org/10.1007/978-3-030-64559-5_33

Researchers conclude that the crucial elements for success of semantic segmentation methods are one of the two factors [4, 7, 30] of using multi-scale features, where features concatenated from intermediate layers using skip connections (e.g. spatial pyramid pooling) [30] or utilizing multi-scale input images to a shared network [4, 16]. Moreover, embedding different Convolutional Neural Networks (CNNs) in "cascade" (deeper [11]) and "cascode" (shallower [7, 30]) configurations have boosted the performance of CNN models. Recently, combinations of encoder-decoder architectures [25] and other techniques such as spatial pyramid pooling [30] architectures with dilated convolution [6, 7, 22], and also post-processing methods [5] provide sharper object boundaries for several image segmentation benchmarks.

The major success of deep learning models in computer vision area owes to domain adaptation [12] where weights of a pre-trained model [13, 28] employed for fine-tuning of another model [29]. In designing almost all state-of-the-art image semantic segmentation models, the default routine is to adopt a publicly available classification encoder [1, 3], trained on a large database such as ImageNet [8]. Although this approach demonstrates considerable improvement in both accuracy [7, 14, 30] and speed [27], the impact of elaborating a model pre-trained on the current task as a relevant feature extractor is always ignored in many studies [27]. Moreover, using a model designed for classification tasks, pre-trained on a large dataset, cannot be a reliable approach for fine-tuning of another model which designed for image semantic segmentation task. This issue becomes even more critical when the target domain is entirely different from the source domain [18] (e.g. Pre-trained VGG16 model [28] on ImageNet [8], fine-tuned for medical image segmentation).

On the other hand, publicly available encoders are trained for specific tasks, and there are usually restrictions for using available pre-trained weights [18]. For instance, a non-modifiable network structure with a fixed-sized input image (e.g. PSPNet [30], DeepLabV3+ [7], and VGG16 [28] require squared sized images of 384×384, 513×513, and 224×224, respectively), forces researchers to manipulate (crop or interpolation) training data. An alternative technique is optimizing network architectures and improving their effectiveness [18]. For example, variants of U-net [25] model are optimized, dominated and applied in many medical image analysis tasks with outstanding results [10], even without using pre-trained encoders.

In this work, we demonstrate that the performance of recent scene parsing frameworks strongly depends on their pre-trained encoder block despite their outstanding results in many studies. At the same time, we demonstrate that for small-sized networks, pre-trained models cannot even boost the performance [24]. As a result of this dependency, there is not yet one prevailing deep learning model applicable to different types of databases. Towards designing a general deep learning model for semantic segmentation task, we proposed a new convolutional module inspired by human peripheral vision [26] (named RetinaConv), embedded into a new deep convolutional encoder-decoder architecture called Iris-Net. Several novel scenes parsing framework [3, 21, 22, 25, 30] and IrisNet model evaluated on different databases, PASCAL VOC 2012 [9] and CAMVID [2] without employing any pre-trained model. Experimental results demonstrate that our proposed model can predict similar or even better instances in comparison with other techniques.

2   Methodology and Network Architecture

The human brain can process different scenes in a fraction of a second, and it can detect objects and movements outside of the direct line of sight, away from the center of gaze (known as peripheral vision [26]). With the aid of this ability, we can detect and sense objects without turning our heads or eyes, resulting in fewer computations for our brain. Moreover, the human eye has a limited field of view, whereas the scene is sharper in the center and more blurry around edges [26]. Simulating the peripheral vision property of the human eye, we designed a new convolutional module called RetinaConv. RetinaConv module is presented in Fig. 1, where the center of the filter (mimicking center of the human eye gaze) is stronger than neighbours. A RetinaConv kernel is created by adding two convolutional kernels, one standard and another dilated type. Similar to a Gaussian filter, RetinaConv can have different standard deviations with varying dilation and stride rates in both type of kernels.

For the implementation of RetinaConv, we benefit from the distributivity property of convolution operators $f * (g + h) = f * g + g * h$, where f is input feature, g and h are standard and dilated convolutional kernels, respectively. Different concentrations of peripheral vision can be generated by changing the hyper-parameters of RetinaConv. One advantage of RetinaConv is that it has two different effective receptive fields simultaneously. With the RetinaConv block, we propose our end-to-end IrisNet model (see Fig. 2) for solving semantic segmentation tasks. IrisNet detects and emphases the core features of an input image easier than individual convolutional block due to the use of both standards and dilated convolutions in each RetinConv block. The minimum performance of the IrisNet is guaranteed at least to the extent of the U-net [25] network using unit dilation rates.

Due to the particular configuration of the RetinaConv block, IrisNet benefits from the receptive filed of both standard and dilated convolution. For instance, applying two times a standard convolutional kernel to an input image with a filter size of 3×3, padding size of 1, and stride of 2×2, the effective receptive field [20] for each feature is 3×3 and 7×7 for the first and second time, respectively. On the other hand, using a RetinaConv with a dilation rate of 2 and the same settings as the previous example, corresponding effective receptive filed is 5×5 and 13×13 with more concentration on features near to the center of the receptive fields. Stacking several layers of RetinaConv mimics the peripheral vision ability of the human brain (see Fig. 1).

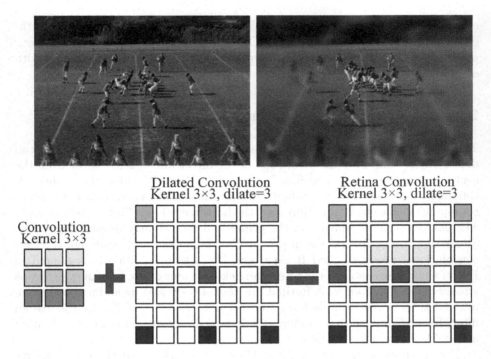

Fig. 1. Peripheral vision in the human eye. The center of gaze is sharper due to more light detectors on Retina (dense kernel) and around is blurry because of fewer detectors on Retina (sparse kernel).

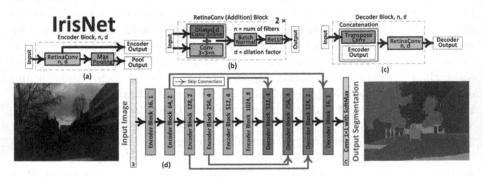

Fig. 2. Network architecture of IrisNet with different embedded blocks.

3   Experimental Evaluations

Our proposed method is successful on scene parsing and semantic segmentation of different database types. One strength capacity of our model is its ability to train on different types of image data with acceptable results without employing any pre-trained model. We evaluate the proposed method in this section on two different databases, including PASCAL VOC 2012 or general semantic segmentation [9] and CamVid for pedestrian and vehicle segmentation [2].

We implemented RetinaConv and IrisNet on the public platform Tensorflow. All models in this study were optimized using categorical cross-entropy loss by Adam optimization method with first (β_1) and second (β_2) momentum of 0.9 and 0.999, respectively. In the last layer of all networks, we used "Softmax" activation functions. The learning rate value for all models was exponentially variable with iterations, initially set by 0.001 with the decay factor of 10^{-6}. The performance might be slightly improved by increasing the epoch number, which is set by 100 for CamVid and 150 for PASCAL VOC. For data augmentation, we adopt horizontal flipping, scaling between 0.5 to 1.5, and shift with 10% in all directions, randomly.

Furthermore, for the CamVid dataset, we added a random Gaussian blurring filter with a variance noise ranges of 0.2. We cropped images during our online data augmentation process to 320×320 for CamVid and 224×224 for PASCAL VOC. Following [15], we employed batch normalization instead of drop-out layers between each convolutional layer. For network configuration and hyperparameter-tuning of our model, we used default values from each publication or publicly available codes. For IrisNet, we followed the configuration of common encoder-decoders [1,6,23,25] in the literature for a fair comparison between models. Activation function for IrisNet was ReLU, and due to the limited computational resources (GPU power), we selected the "batch-size" to 20 during training. The ratio of train, validation, and test sets are 90%, 5%, and 5%, respectively. For the comparison study, we keep the best models by saving checkpoints during the training and validation stage. In the test step, raw data are fed to each network with their original sizes.

IrisNet works satisfyingly on scene parsing challenge of PASCAL VOC 2012 benchmark where the dataset has 20 objects categories and one background. Online augmentation of the PASCAL VOC dataset results in $7,863K$, $438K$, and $438K$ images, cropped by 224×224 for training, validation, and testing. Table 1 shows the comparison results of IrisNet with several advanced methods on each benchmark.

Table 1. Performance of models in evaluation study on the PASCAL VOC 2012 test set in terms of IOU and mean IOU. The number of trainable parameters for each model is in millions.

Model	parameters	Airplane	Bicycle	Bird	Boat	Bottle	Bus	Car	Cat	Chair	Cow	Table	Dog	Horse	Motor	Person	Plant	Sheep	Sofa	Train	TV	mIOU
BowNet	0.92	**62.7**	**41.5**	16.3	17.6	**53.8**	35.6	41.9	67.2	13.8	67.8	12.9	**85.4**	63.2	49.1	38.4	51.7	67.2	23.8	27.6	21.9	51.2
UNET [25]	23.7	61.8	39.6	56.8	27.3	53.5	74.6	48.6	**73.8**	18.3	**74.9**	10.2	84.3	**65.3**	53.0	79.0	**70.4**	**72.5**	70.6	31.4	17.8	55.7
FCN8 [21]	13.2	56.9	40.2	23.9	34.2	40.6	42.6	50.2	64.8	20.9	59.9	13.8	79.2	52.1	54.9	68.2	69.1	60.9	59.4	29.7	20.6	55.1
LinkNet [3]	20.3	55.2	32.1	34.2	**35.0**	35.2	68.5	39.1	53.6	38.9	49.6	20.3	30.2	30.6	52.6	56.8	59.7	55.8	22.7	22.0	13.9	55.8
FPN [17]	17.5	38.4	28.7	62.6	42.1	36.8	60.0	23.8	36.1	21.3	32.7	13.4	75.8	50.7	49.9	55.7	49.8	48.7	35.9	28.1	12.2	53.5
IrisNet	71.7	44.9	30.2	**66.3**	24.3	44.5	**75.6**	**52.4**	65.8	**43.5**	72.1	**42.8**	80.3	51.6	**80.3**	**82.7**	51.8	55.5	62.6	**42.6**	**27.8**	**57.2**

From Table 1, IrisNet outperforms other methods in terms of mean intersection over union (mIOU). The number of trainable parameters for each model is also reported in this table. As can be seen, models such as BowNet and UNET with fewer parameters can predict acceptable results due to their efficient structures. For this reason, optimizing all sections of a network structure (even encoder block) is just as crucial as investigating other Influential aspects, such as decoder block. Several instances predicted by each encoder-decoder network are illustrated in Fig. 3. Although the results for all models are not considerable, IrisNet predicted instances with more details. For instance, the tail of the "cat" and ears/grass for "cow" have more details than other models.

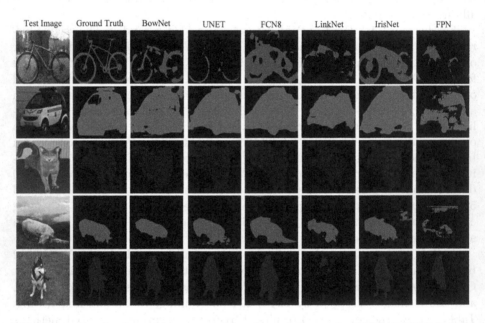

Fig. 3. Results of each model in terms of per-class results on the PASCAL VOC 2012 [9] testing set. All models are trained on the dataset with random weight initialization (no pre-trained encoder).

CamVid dataset has 32 semantic classes for urban scene understanding. To compare each model on a more straightforward dataset, we employed a subset of CamVid contains three classes of "background", "car", and "pedestrian". In our evaluation study, there were 367, 101, and 233 annotated images for training, validation, and testing sets, while after online augmentation, training and validation sets were increased to $734K$ and $202K$ images, respectively. All models except PSPNet (384×384) were trained with cropping sizes of 320×320.

Table 2 reports our assessment results of six networks on the CamVid dataset in three configurations (random initialization, initializing with pre-trained weights, and fine-tuning by freezing encoder parameters) while, except

Table 2. Quantitative results of the CamVid test set. Methods without available pre-trained models are indicated by n/a. None means the network could not train features from the dataset, without providing any predicted instance.

Method	Backbone	Random initial			Pre-trained weights			Fine-tuning		
	ImNet	mIOU	F1	Loss	mIOU	F1	Loss	mIOU	F1	Loss
BowNet [22]	n/a	50.52	0.58	0.48	n/a	n/a	n/a	n/a	n/a	n/a
UNET [25]	VGG16	35.80	0.38	0.87	37.58	0.41	0.86	0.40	0.43	0.81
PSPNet [30]	VGG16	32.18	0.33	0.93	**46.50**	**0.54**	**0.65**	54.80	0.63	0.50
LinkNet [3]	VGG16	38.83	0.44	0.80	39.19	0.44	0.80	65.06	0.73	0.36
FPN [17]	VGG16	None	None	None	None	None	None	**68.44**	**0.76**	**0.32**
IrisNet	n/a	**55.77**	**0.61**	**0.45**	n/a	n/a	n/a	n/a	n/a	n/a

BowNet and IrisNet, the backbone network is VGG16 encoder network pre-trained on ImageNet dataset. For each configuration, we presented three evaluation criteria mIOU, F1, and Categorical Cross-Entropy. From the table, IrisNet could predict better instances than other models, while random initialization was used for each model. Definitely, all models might achieve better results by optimizing all aspects of the experiment and training for more epochs. Some examples of this evaluation study are displayed in Fig. 4. From the figure can be seen that although IrisNet performs better in comparison with other models, it is weak in dealing with large objects in the scene.

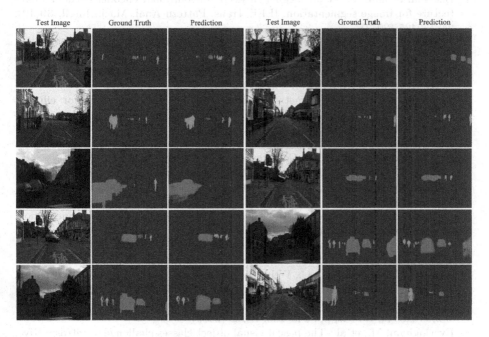

Fig. 4. Results of assessment of each model on CamVid test set.

4   Conclusion

Our proposed encoder-decoder model (IrisNet) employs a new convolutional module (RetinaConv) to mimic the nature of peripheral vision in human eyes. Specifically, benefits from the effective receptive field of RetinaConv, IrisNet encodes multi-scale information superior to other cutting-edge deep learning models. The primary motivation behind IrisNet architecture using the Reti- naConv module was the need to implement an efficient deep learning model for semantic segmentation, which works independently from pre-trained models while capable of applying on several types of datasets. To address this desired model, we improved the feature extraction ability of a ubiquitous encoder- decoder model (UNET) by employing RetinaConv. Our experimental results show that the dependency of the proposed method from using pre-trained encoder blocks is significant, and it achieves comparable performance with other state-of-the-art models in similar configurations on several challenging bench- marks. Generalization capability of the IrisNet in image segmentation task on datasets with different distributions and context was evaluated with an accept- able achievements. We believe that optimized, universal, and efficient deep net- work architectures will stay longer in literature than models with just higher accuracy and performance.

References

1. Badrinarayanan, V., et al.: Segnet: a deep convolutional encoder-decoder archi- tecture for image segmentation. IEEE Trans. Pattern Anal. Mach. Intell. **39**(12), 2481–2495 (2017)
2. Brostow, G.J., Shotton, J., Fauqueur, J., Cipolla, R.: Segmentation and recognition using structure from motion point clouds. In: Forsyth, D., Torr, P., Zisserman, A. (eds.) ECCV 2008. LNCS, vol. 5302, pp. 44–57. Springer, Heidelberg (2008). https://doi.org/10.1007/978-3-540-88682-2_5
3. Chaurasia, A., et al.: Linknet: exploiting encoder representations for efficient semantic segmentation. In: 2017 IEEE Visual Communications and Image Pro- cessing (VCIP), pp. 1–4. IEEE (2017)
4. Chen, L.C., et al.: Attention to scale: scale-aware semantic image segmentation. In: Proceedings of the IEEE Conference on CVPR, pp. 3640–3649 (2016)
5. Chen, L.C., et al.: Deeplab: Semantic image segmentation with deep convolutional nets, atrous convolution, and fully connected CRFs. IEEE Trans. Pattern Anal. Mach. Intell. **40**(4), 834–848 (2017)
6. Chen, L.C., et al.: Rethinking atrous convolution for semantic image segmentation. arXiv preprint arXiv:1706.05587 (2017)
7. Chen, L.-C., Zhu, Y., Papandreou, G., Schroff, F., Adam, H.: Encoder-decoder with atrous separable convolution for semantic image segmentation. In: Ferrari, V., Hebert, M., Sminchisescu, C., Weiss, Y. (eds.) ECCV 2018. LNCS, vol. 11211, pp. 833–851. Springer, Cham (2018). https://doi.org/10.1007/978-3-030-01234-2_49
8. Deng, J., et al.: Imagenet: a large-scale hierarchical image database. In: 2009 IEEE Conference on CVPR, pp. 248–255. IEEE (2009)
9. Everingham, M., et al.: The pascal visual object classes challenge: a retrospective. Int. J. Comput. Vis. **111**(1), 98–136 (2015)

10. Falk, T., et al.: U-net: deep learning for cell counting, detection, and morphometry. Nat. Methods **16**(1), 67 (2019)
11. Fu, J., et al.: Stacked deconvolutional network for semantic segmentation. IEEE Trans. Image Process. (2019)
12. Hamed Mozaffari, M., Lee, W.S.: Domain adaptation for ultrasound tongue contour extraction using transfer learning: a deep learning approach. J. Acoust. Soc. Am. **146**(5), EL431–EL437 (2019)
13. He, K., et al.: Deep residual learning for image recognition. In: Proceedings of the IEEE Conference on CVPR, pp. 770–778 (2016)
14. He, K., et al.: Mask R-CNN. In: Proceedings of the IEEE ICCV, pp. 2961–2969 (2017)
15. Ioffe, S., et al.: Batch normalization: Accelerating deep network training by reducing internal covariate shift. arXiv preprint arXiv:1502.03167 (2015)
16. Lin, G., et al.: Refinenet: multi-path refinement networks for high-resolution semantic segmentation. In: Proceedings of the IEEE Conference on CVPR, pp. 1925–1934 (2017)
17. Lin, T.Y., et al.: Feature pyramid networks for object detection. In: Proceedings of the IEEE Conference on CVPR, pp. 2117–2125 (2017)
18. Liu, S., et al.: Deep learning in medical ultrasound analysis: a review. Engineering (2019)
19. Liu, X., Deng, Z., Yang, Y.: Recent progress in semantic image segmentation. Artif. Intell. Rev. **52**(2), 1089–1106 (2018). https://doi.org/10.1007/s10462-018-9641-3
20. Liu, Y., Yu, J., Han, Y.: Understanding the effective receptive field in semantic image segmentation. Multimedia Tools Appl. **77**(17), 22159–22171 (2018). https://doi.org/10.1007/s11042-018-5704-3
21. Long, J., et al.: Fully convolutional networks for semantic segmentation. In: Proceedings of the IEEE Conference on CVPR, pp. 3431–3440 (2015)
22. Mozaffari, M.H., Lee, W.S.: Encoder-decoder CNN models for automatic tracking of tongue contours in real-time ultrasound data. Methods (2020)
23. Noh, H., et al.: Learning deconvolution network for semantic segmentation. In: Proceedings of the IEEE ICCV, pp. 1520–1528 (2015)
24. Poudel, R.P., et al.: Fast-SCNN: fast semantic segmentation network. arXiv preprint arXiv:1902.04502 (2019)
25. Ronneberger, O., Fischer, P., Brox, T.: U-Net: convolutional networks for biomedical image segmentation. In: Navab, N., Hornegger, J., Wells, W.M., Frangi, A.F. (eds.) MICCAI 2015. LNCS, vol. 9351, pp. 234–241. Springer, Cham (2015). https://doi.org/10.1007/978-3-319-24574-4_28
26. Rosenholtz, R.: Capabilities and limitations of peripheral vision. Ann. Rev. Vis. Sci. **2**, 437–457 (2016)
27. Siam, M., et al.: RTSeg: real-time semantic segmentation comparative study. In: 2018 25th IEEE International Conference on Image Processing (ICIP), pp. 1603–1607. IEEE (2018)
28. Simonyan, K., et al.: Very deep convolutional networks for large-scale image recognition. arXiv preprint arXiv:1409.1556 (2014)
29. Tan, C., Sun, F., Kong, T., Zhang, W., Yang, C., Liu, C.: A survey on deep transfer learning. In: Kůrková, V., Manolopoulos, Y., Hammer, B., Iliadis, L., Maglogiannis, I. (eds.) ICANN 2018. LNCS, vol. 11141, pp. 270–279. Springer, Cham (2018). https://doi.org/10.1007/978-3-030-01424-7_27
30. Zhao, H., et al.: Pyramid scene parsing network. In: Proceedings of the IEEE conference on CVPR, pp. 2881–2890 (2017)

Generator from Edges: Reconstruction of Facial Images

Nao Takano[✉] and Gita Alaghband

Computer Science and Engineering, University of Colorado Denver, Denver, USA
{nao.takano,gita.alaghband}@ucdenver.edu

Abstract. Applications that involve supervised training require paired images. Researchers of single image super-resolution (SISR) create such images by artificially generating blurry input images from the corresponding ground truth. Similarly we can create paired images with the canny edge. We propose Generator From Edges (GFE) [Fig. 1]. Our aim is to determine the best architecture for GFE, along with reviews of perceptual loss [1,2]. To this end, we conducted three experiments. First, we explored the effects of the adversarial loss often used in SISR. In particular, we uncovered that it is not an essential component to form a perceptual loss. Eliminating adversarial loss will lead to a more effective architecture from the perspective of hardware resource. It also means that considerations for the problems pertaining to generative adversarial network (GAN) [3], such as mode collapse, are not necessary. Second, we reexamined VGG loss and found that the mid-layers yield the best results. By extracting the full potential of VGG loss, the overall performance of perceptual loss improves significantly. Third, based on the findings of the first two experiments, we reevaluated the dense network to construct GFE. Using GFE as an intermediate process, reconstructing a facial image from a pencil sketch can become an easy task.

1 Introduction

While there have been quite a few methods and proposals for single image super-resolution (SISR), few applications exist for reconstructing an original face from the corresponding edge image. The techniques used in our Generator From Edges (GFE) are variations of those used in SISR. In SISR, there are roughly two categories. The first is by way of the perceptual loss that includes adversarial loss, which requires a generative adversarial network. The second omits adversarial loss. GFE belongs to the second category.

We focus on three perceptual losses that have large impact on the overall performance; adversarial loss, MSE loss, and VGG loss. Removing adversarial loss results in a simpler architecture, enabling us to eliminate the discriminator used in GAN. Figure 2a depicts the differences between SRGAN [2], one of the most influential works for SISR, and our proposed GFE.

In general, the larger the neural network model is, the better the outcome we expect. This is true in the accuracy of classification as well as in the synthesis of

© Springer Nature Switzerland AG 2020
G. Bebis et al. (Eds.): ISVC 2020, LNCS 12510, pp. 430–443, 2020.
https://doi.org/10.1007/978-3-030-64559-5_34

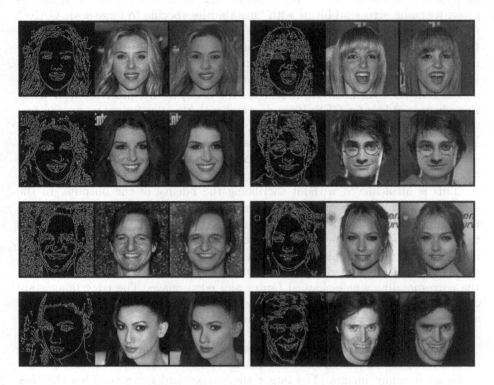

Fig. 1. From Left: Input, Ground Truth, Output; With CelebA-HQ [5], we used 28,998 for training and 1,000 for testing. These are sample outcomes from the testing set.

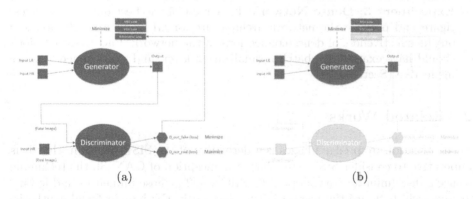

Fig. 2. (a): SRGAN diagram, (b): GFE, the proposed architecture – many of the elements go away

images. But as the size of the input image and the complexity of the synthesis grow, we come across problems with "instabilities specific to large-scale GANs" [4] and the rate of contribution by the discriminator diminishes. In addition, the discriminator requires a large memory footprint. In order to use a large network for training with the limited amount of memory for hardware such as GPU, the question arises as to how much the discriminator contributes to the outcome of the synthesis. We observed very little, if any, positive effect using the adversarial loss for GFE. If we do away with the discriminator, we can free up its otherwise occupied GPU memory, making it possible to construct a larger generator. Moreover, using only two loss functions (image loss and VGG loss – Sect. 3) permits easier settings for hyper-parameters. We attempt to measure the effect of the discriminator and perform image synthesis without it.

This is all achieved without sacrificing the fidelity of the outputs. In the sections that follow, we present our contributions by describing details for the three experiments conducted in this study. We define Generator From Edges to be a generator (in the same sense as the one used in GAN, but without discriminator) for an application that restores images from their corresponding canny edge. All the experiments train with pairs of images; a ground truth and the corresponding single-channel (grayscale) edge image. The edge images are created by running the OpenCV Canny function from CelebA (Experiment 1) and CelebA-HQ [5] datasets (Experiments 2 and 3).

- **Experiment 1: Effect of Adversarial Loss.** Using CelebA dataset, we measured the effectiveness of adversarial loss for both SISR and the synthesis from canny images. The larger the images and more complex the task becomes, the less adversarial loss contributes to the outcome (Sect. 4).
- **Experiment 2: VGG loss.** VGG loss is another element of perceptual loss. The absence of adversarial loss leaves our perceptual loss more reliant on the VGG loss [2,6]. We used CelebA-HQ dataset with the image size 224×224. Using middle layers is more effective than using the last layers (Sect. 5).
- **Experiment 3: Dense Network.** In pursuit of the best quality, we investigate and propose the network architecture for GFE. The specific focus is on the effectiveness of dense connections in the network. Each residual block should have exactly one batch normalization layer, and skip connections are ineffective (Sect. 6).

2   Related Works

Reconstruction from edge images is a derivative of the SISR problem, thus it is imperative to consider SISR first. Since the inception of GAN [3], the technique to use a discriminator was adopted by SRGAN [2], whose influences and follow-up research [6–9] are the inspiration for our work. For human facial synthesis, whereas we generate a photo from edges (sketch), other research generates a sketch from an input photo [10–12]. Huang et al. [13] made a frontal view synthesis from profile images. Li et al. [14] as well as Jo and Park [15] generated facial images with a partial reconstruction from sketches. In terms of application, our work is related to Lu et al. [16] and Yu et al. [17]. The former uses Contextual GAN, where input photos and images are trained in semi-supervised fashion. The latter uses a Conditional CycleGAN to address the heterogeneous nature of photos and sketches. StarGAN [18] offers an impressive multi-domain image-to-image translation on human faces. Liu et al. [19] uses SR for human faces. In the general domains to generate images from sketches other than human faces, substantial advancements have been made [20–25]. More recently, Mask based image synthesis on human faces [26,27] is gaining attention. Also, Qian et al. [28] propose Additive Focal Variational Auto-encoder (AF-VAE) for facial manipulation.

Going back a few years, a wide applicability of image-to-image translation in the supervised setting was proposed by Isola et al. [29] with GAN. Our work follows this line of research; but instead of adversarial loss, we use VGG loss.

Chen et al. [30] demonstrated a similar applicability to [29] but with a Cascaded Refinement Network, which starts with a low resolution module and doubles its size for consecutive modules. For SISR, VDSR [31] and SRResNet [2] were notable architectures prior to SRGAN. Lim et al. [32] used a multi-scale model (EDSR) that enables flexible input image size, which also reduces the number of parameters. Tong et al. [33] applied dense skip connections in a very deep network to boost the SR reconstruction. Mei et al. [34] used a multi-frame network to generate more than one output and fused them into a single output. Ma, et al. [35] replaced simple skip connections with the connection nodes and proposed a multi-level aggregated network (MLAN). The research presented in these papers successfully synthesized images without using a GAN, which led us to ask ourselves: If we can create images without GAN, then how much does a GAN contribute to the outcome? If we drop it from our system altogether, what would be gained? We examine these topics in the context of the synthesis/reconstruction of an image of a human face.

3 Perceptual Loss Functions

Perceptual loss functions were first defined by Johnson, et al. [1] and adopted by Ledig, et al. [2]. They are per-pixel loss functions used in feed-forward image transformations. In SRGAN [2] and its variants, three loss functions are used. Empirically, none of the loss functions among the three can generate a convincing image alone. In our study, we use at least two losses in various combinations to determine if and how they contribute to the overall outcome.

- Image Loss (I): also referred to as per-pixel loss [1], or MSE loss [2]. This is a pixel-wise L2 loss between the output of the generator and the ground truth. We call it image loss in order to distinguish it from the mean squared error used in VGG loss. The resources required to calculate the image loss are the least expensive among the three. We used L2 in this paper, but it is also possible to use L1.

$$L_I(G) = \sum_{x=1}^{W} \sum_{y=1}^{H} (I_{x,y}^{target} - G(I^{Input})_{x,y})^2 \tag{1}$$

- VGG loss (V): Using a pre-trained VGG Network [36] (available in [37]) plays a crucial role for training the generator. The network has been trained with ImageNet and already knows what real-world images look like, delivering the results for object classification/identification as well as synthesis. Given ϕ is a VGG network, the loss function is defined to be

$$L_V(G) = \sum_{x=1}^{W} \sum_{y=1}^{H} [\phi_{i,j}(I^{target})_{x,y} - \phi_{i,j}(G(I^{Input}))_{x,y}]^2 \tag{2}$$

where $\phi_{i,j}$ refers to the feature maps obtained from the j-th Convolution/ReLU pair before the i-th maxpooling layer within the VGG-19 network, the same notation used in [2,6].
- Adversarial Loss (A): which is calculated with the discriminator, is what makes the system a GAN. In other words, in the absence of this loss, there is no need for a discriminator, and the resulting framework is no longer designated as a generative adversarial network. The resources required for computing the adversarial loss and how impactful it is in our image reconstruction deserves attention.

$$L_A(G) = \sum_{n=1}^{N} -\log D(G(I^{Input})) \tag{3}$$

The total loss, L, is calculated as

$$L = \lambda_0 I + \lambda_1 V + \lambda_2 A \tag{4}$$

where I, V, A represent image loss (L_I), VGG loss (L_V), and adversarial loss (L_A), respectively. In the actual calculation, we set $\lambda_0 = 1$, so that only two parameters λ_1 and λ_2 are considered to determine the portion of each loss influencing the computation. In Sects. 4 and 5, we examine these losses more closely.

4   Experiment 1. – Impact of Adversarial Loss

In the realm of supervised training, there are quite a few papers that report successful reconstruction of images without adversarial loss [30–35]. Prior to the architecture of GFE described in Sect. 6, this section analyzes the value of adversarial loss with the degree of its effect on both super-resolution (SR) and canny edge (Canny). In this experiment, we used smaller image sizes as well as a shallower network than those used in the experiments 2 and 3.

4.1   Architecture

The generator consists of 16 layers of residual blocks, each with 64 feature maps. This is the structure used in [2]. We used it for both SISR and image reconstruction from edges (Canny) for the experiment. The discriminator has eight convolutional layers with an increasing number of feature maps; 64-64-128-128-256-256-512-512, followed by two dense layers and a sigmoid activation function. In search of a suitable implementation we turn off VGG loss, if any, and run only in adversarial loss to see how the network converges. We selected a few implementations published in Github [38,39] among those that converge with adversarial loss only, and plugged them into our implementation so that fair comparisons can be made. The sizes of input and output images are the same; we experimented on 3 sizes – 96×96, 128×128, and 176×176 for both SR and Canny.

4.2   Methods

Since the image loss has the minimum overhead to calculate, we leave it in all three scenarios listed below. In all three cases, we set $\lambda_0 = 1$ in Eq. (4). We ran 20 epochs and took the best Fréchet Inception Distance (FID) [40,41]. FID uses a pre-trained Inception network and calculates the Fréchet distance between two multivariate Gaussian distributions with mean μ and covariance Σ,

$$\text{FID}(x, g) = ||\mu_x - \mu_g||^2 + \text{Tr}(\Sigma_x + \Sigma_g - 2(\Sigma_x \Sigma_g)^{1/2})$$

where x, g are the activations of the pool_3 layer of the Inception-v3 net for real samples and generated samples, respectively.

- Image loss + VGG loss [I + V] ($\lambda_1 > 0$ and $\lambda_2 = 0$)
- Image loss + Adversarial loss [I + A] ($\lambda_1 = 0$ and $\lambda_2 > 0$)
- Image loss + VGG loss + Adv. loss [I + V + A] ($\lambda_1 > 0$ and $\lambda_2 > 0$)

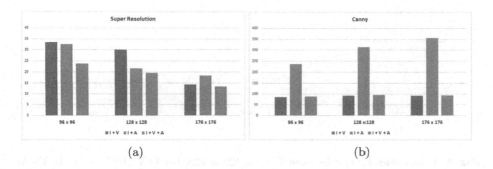

Fig. 3. FID scores (lower is better) – combinations of losses for SR and Canny

4.3   Discussion

As commonly seen, the more complex the task is, the more difficult it is for the generative adversarial network to converge. For SISR, Fig. 3a clearly shows its contribution by adversarial loss to the image quality, especially in lower resolutions. However, for synthesis from canny images, a task more complex than SR, adversarial loss does not show any positive effect to the outcome. In fact, we could not successfully generate convincing images at all if VGG loss is not included (the case [I + A] in Fig. 3b). SISR is easier for image reconstruction, where adversarial loss can be incorporated into a part of the perceptual loss more naturally, than the reconstruction from canny edges.

We recorded the loss values as the training continued at each epoch. Figure 4 shows sample loss values over the course of training for the size of 128×128 of Figs. 3a and 3b. While image loss and VGG loss show a typical, oscillating yet steady decrease in values, adversarial loss converges rather quickly to a constant value after several hundred iterations. This raises a few interesting theoretical points: First, if we knew the constant value in advance, we could use it in lieu of the adversarial loss and save computer resources. Second, if we could come up with a method to decrease the adversarial loss throughout the training, we could take full advantage of the power of the generative adversarial network. For now, however, these are left for future research, and we conclude that adversarial loss does not contribute to the synthesis of images from canny edge, and that the resource is better used for a larger generator. Consequently at this point, GAN is not used in our study. Unless otherwise noted, the remainder of this paper uses only image loss and VGG loss.

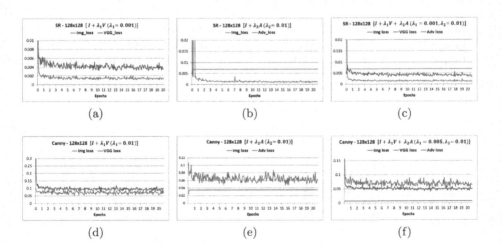

Fig. 4. Loss values by epochs from Fig. 3a [128×128] (a) I+V (b) I+A (c) I+V+A, and Loss values from Fig. 3b [128×128] (d) I+V (e) I+A (f) I+V+A

5   Experiment 2. – Optimizing VGG Loss

VGG-19 consists of 16 Convolution layers, each followed by ReLU activation. Between the last (16th) ReLU layer and the output softmax layer, there are three fully connected layers, which are not used for perceptual loss. For perceptual loss, both aforementioned papers used the last pair (16th layer, $\phi_{5,4}$); while Ledig et al. [2] used the activation layer, Wang et al. [6] claims it is more effective to use the convolutional layer before the activation, which we confirm to be true. In this experiment, we further analyze using VGG loss computed from various layers and recommend an optimized VGG loss for our image reconstruction application.

5.1   Architecture and Dataset

We used VGG-19 along with image loss as part of the perceptual loss in the generator (GFE). As we established in Sect. 4.3, adversarial loss is not used and we can eliminate the discriminator. The architecture of the generator is the same as the one used in Sect. 4, but with the CelebA-HQ dataset—it consists of 30,000 high-resolution images with the size 1024×1024 (We resize them to 224×224). Removing 2 outliers (imgHQ00070 and imgHQ02815), and setting aside 1,000 images for validation/testing, we have 28,998 images for training.

5.2   Result

Contrary to common usage of how VGG loss is applied, our study shows using middle layers is more effective than using later layers, either the convolutional layer or the activation layer. Discarding the later layers also saves the memory space in the hardware. Fig. 5 shows that the convolutional layers of $\phi_{4,2}$ and $\phi_{4,3}$, (10th and 11th convolutional layers, respectively) show the best FID scores (lower is better – Yellow bars are convolutional, Blue is ReLU, and Black is Pool Layer).

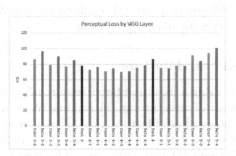

Fig. 5. VGG loss – layer by layer analysis

5.3   Multiple Layers of VGG Loss

More than one layer can be used as part of perceptual loss. Without the assistance of adversarial loss, we have $\lambda_2 = 0$, and assuming $\lambda_0 = 1$, Eq. (4) becomes

$$L = I + \lambda_{1_1} V + \lambda_{1_2} V + \cdots + \lambda_{1_n} V \tag{5}$$

where n is the number of VGG layers to be used for perceptual loss. Starting with Conv $\phi_{4,3}$, we selected the best 4 layers and added new layers one by one (see Fig. 5 for reference to layers).

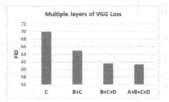

Figure 6 shows a sample of FID scores for $n = \{1, 2, 3, 4\}$ in our experiments with 16 block layers of generator ([A] Conv4-1; [B] Conv4-2; [C] Conv4-3; [D] ReLu4-3). Using two layers ($n = 2$) is better than using a single layer ($n = 1$), and $n = 3$ is better than $n = 2$. But for $n > 3$, the effect of adding extra layers diminishes.

Fig. 6. VGG loss – using multiple layers

Most of our experiments in Sect. 6 use 2 layers of Conv $\phi_{4,2}$ and Conv $\phi_{4,3}$.

6   Experiment 3. – Generator from Edges

We form GFE based on the results obtained from Sects. 4 and 5. Increasing the size of the network is effective up to a certain point due to the vanishing gradient problem, and residual blocks along with skip connections are notable solutions for large networks [42]. In SISR, making the residual block denser (more connections within the block), as well as having more skip connections between blocks is reported to improve performance. For GFE, however, dense networks are not an effective solution when making the network larger.

In this section, we describe the experiments in pursuit of the best architecture for GFE with the network in a monolithic structure, which has a constant number of feature maps (64) throughout the generator, adapted by SRGAN [2] and other models for image generation.

6.1   Architecture

By using a fixed number of feature maps at every block layer, we can focus on the study of structures in the residual block and skip connections for a large network. The number of feature maps at each layer is 64, and the kernel sizes are all 3×3. Starting with 16, we increase the number of block layers at increments of 8. Without the discriminator, we have more memory available for the construction of GFE. All experiments were conducted in a single GPU with 11GB of memory, and it is worth noting that the image size we generate (224×224) is mainly determined by the capacity of the GPU memory for training. The same dataset as Sect. 5 (Experiment 2) is used. Also, we used L2 (MSE) loss for perceptual loss calculation throughout our study. Despite certain claims that L1 loss gives a better result, in our experiments FID scores are consistently better using L2.

6.2   Sketch to Photo

Figure 7 shows some potential practical applications with GFE. We took some pencil sketches from CUHK [43] as well as from the internet. Note that since we trained with the canny transformation, we first have to convert the sketch image to canny, and then make an inference with the trained network. Not just as a simple coloring exercise, in the output images we can see the depth of textures of human face that commonly appear in every person, which shows a great potential for an image translation from a pencil sketch to a photo.

Fig. 7. From Left: (Top) GT, Sketch, Canny, Output (Bottom) Sketch, Canny, Output

6.3 Residual Block

The base unit of the construction, often called the residual block, is illustrated in Fig. 8a. The input is followed by a convolutional layer, followed by a ParametricReLU and another convolutional layer. Then a batch normalization (BN) is added before the output that is combined with the input as a single dense connection. This is very similar to SRGAN [2]; the difference being the omission of the first BN layer. This omission is crucial for reducing the memory footprint.

The batch normalization layers consume the same amount of memory as the preceding convolutional layers, and removing a BN layer from the unit block saves us approximately 20% of the memory space in our model. If we had removed both BN layers, we would have saved 40% of the memory usage [32], but our experiments show that leaving in one BN layer yields better results than none at all. Comparing a single BN layer with two BN layers, we found no noticeable differences.

Several studies in SISR propose dense residual blocks [6,33], but a generator with such dense residual units requires considerably more GPU memory, forcing us to train the network with smaller batch sizes (mini-batches). For GFE, dense residual blocks are inadequate; a large network with 32 or more block layers negatively impact the outcome.

Thus, we use one connection within the block, between the input and the BN layer. Even with just one connection at each block, when a generator is constructed by having residual blocks stacked multiple times, the entire network is connected in such a way that the gradient vanishing problem is dramatically reduced.

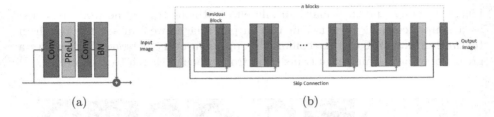

(a)   (b)

Fig. 8. Residual block (base unit) and skip connection type 1

6.4 Skip Connections and Large Networks

Let the number of basic blocks (residual blocks in the middle, and blocks for
Conv + PReLU at the beginning and end of the network) be n [Fig. 8b]. We
define the skip connection type as follows:

- Type 0: No skip connection
- Type 1: Connect with layer 1 and layer $n - 1$
- Type 2: Connect with layer 1 and layer $n/2$, as well as $n/2$ and $n - 1$
- Type 3: Connect with layer 1 and layer $n - 1$, as well as layer $n/2$ and $n - 1$
- Type 4: Connect with Type 1 and Type 2 combined

Figure 8b shows skip connection Type
1. By going deeper in the generator, the
output of synthesized images becomes
better, and we found that forming 48
block layers (with each block consisting
of 4 sub-layers [Fig. 8a]) achieves the
best result. We tested with the above
5 skip connections to see which type is
best using the residual block defined in
Sect. 6.3. None of the connection types
has a positive effect for our application

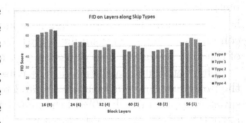

Fig. 9. Lower the better. (Numbers in
parentheses indicate batch size)

[Fig. 9], thus, we conclude that no skip connection is necessary for our monolithic
architecture of GFE.

6.5 The Limit of Depth in the Generator

Larger networks are not necessarily better than smaller ones. We started out
our experiment with 16 layers of residual blocks, with a batch size of 9 (nine
images are processed in the GPU at once in a single iteration). As we increased
layers, we had to decrease the batch size due to the limitation of GPU memory.
Initially the image quality improved but soon it saturated in improvement.

We observed some degradation for a network whose block size is greater than
48, where the mini-batch size needs to be 1 (one) to fit in our GPU [Fig. 9]. At
this point we suspect that batch normalization is no longer in effect, and in fact

the training is somewhat unstable (consecutive epochs have FID values in a wide swing). Although we attempted to tweak hyper parameters such as learning rate, we were unable to improve image quality.

7   Conclusion and Discussion

We demonstrated the Generator From Edges (GFE) for image translation on human faces, from edges to photo, without a generative adversarial network. This was led by the analysis of architectural features that unnecessarily consume GPU memory, such as a discriminator and extra batch normalization layers. We also reviewed a dense network and observed that skip connections are not effective if the basic unit is densely connected.

Although the trained network can restore facial images even when the edges are not drawn precisely in the input [44], the nature of supervised training commands deterministic outputs. For a practical application in mind, however, removing the GAN loses stochasticity in the inference mechanism, in which when an incomplete image is fed to the network, the outcome would also be less than ideal. This could be addressed with an unsupervised training in such a way that incomplete input leads to more convincing output. At the same time, as mentioned in Sect. 2, we are seeing rapid advancements in research—such as mask-guided (with GAN) or geometry-guided (with VAE) settings—to fill in the gap where nondeterministic outcomes are desired.

References

1. Johnson, J., Alahi, A., Fei-Fei, L.: Perceptual losses for real-time style transfer and super-resolution. In: Leibe, B., Matas, J., Sebe, N., Welling, M. (eds.) ECCV 2016. LNCS, vol. 9906, pp. 694–711. Springer, Cham (2016). https://doi.org/10.1007/978-3-319-46475-6_43
2. Ledig, C., et al.: Photo-realistic single image super-resolution using a generative adversarial network. In: IEEE Conference on CVPR (2017)
3. Goodfellow, I.J.: Generative adversarial nets. In: Advances in Neural Information Processing Systems, vol. 27 (2014)
4. Brock, A., Donahue, J., Simonyan, K.: Large Scale GAN Training for High Fidelity Natural Image Synthesis. ArXiv (2018)
5. Karras, T., Aila, T., Laine, S., Lehtinen, J.: Stability, and Variation. ICLR, Progressive Growing of GANs for Improved Quality (2018)
6. Wang, X., et al.: Enhanced super-resolution generative adversarial networks. In: ECCV Workshops, ESRGAN (2018)
7. Vu, T., Luu, T.M., Yoo, C.D.: Perception-enhanced image super-resolution via relativistic generative adversarial networks. In: ECCV Workshops (2018)
8. Liu, Y., et al.: An attention-based approach for single image super resolution. In: 2018 24th International Conference on Pattern Recognition (ICPR) (2018)
9. Feng, R., Gu, J., Qiao, Y., Dong, C.: Suppressing model overfitting for image super-resolution networks (2019)
10. Yu, J., Shi, S., Gao, F., Tao, D., Huang, Q.: Towards realistic face photo-sketch synthesis via composition-aided GANs (2017)

11. Zhang, S., Ji, R., Hu, J., Gao, Y., Lin, C.-W.: Robust face sketch synthesis via generative adversarial fusion of priors and parametric sigmoid. In: IJCAI (2018)
12. Zhu, M., Wang, N., Gao, X., Li, J.: Deep graphical feature learning for face sketch synthesis. In: IJCAI (2017)
13. Huang, R., Zhang, S., Li, T., He, R.: Beyond face rotation: global and local perception GAN for photorealistic and identity preserving frontal view synthesis. In: 2017 IEEE International Conference on Computer Vision (ICCV) (2017)
14. Li, Y., Liu, S., Yang, J., Yang, M.-H.: Generative face completion. In: 2017 IEEE Conference on Computer Vision and Pattern Recognition (CVPR) (2017)
15. Jo, Y., Park, J.: SC-FEGAN: Face Editing Generative Adversarial Network with User's Sketch and Color. ArXiv (2019)
16. Lu, Y., Wu, S., Tai, Y.-W., Tang,C.-K.: Image generation from sketch constraint using contextual GAN. In: ECCV (2017)
17. Yu, S., Han, H., Shan, S., Dantcheva, A., Chen, X.: Improving face sketch recognition via adversarial sketch-photo transformation. In: 2019 14th IEEE International Conference on Automatic Face and Gesture Recognition (2019)
18. Choi, Y., Choi, M.-J., Kim, M., Ha, J.-W., Kim, S., Choo, J.: StarGAN: unified generative adversarial networks for multi-domain image-to-image translation. In: 2018 IEEE/CVF Conference on Computer Vision and Pattern Recognition (2017)
19. Liu, L., Wang, S., Wan, L.: Component semantic prior guided generative adversarial network for face super-resolution. IEEE Access **7**, 77027–77036 (2019)
20. Pathak, D., Krähenbühl, P., Donahue, J., Darrell, T., Efros, A.A.: Context encoders: feature learning by inpainting. In: 2016 IEEE Conference on Computer Vision and Pattern Recognition (CVPR) (2016)
21. Chen, W., Hays, J.: SketchyGAN: towards diverse and realistic sketch to image synthesis. In: 2018 IEEE/CVF Conference on Computer Vision and Pattern Recognition (2018)
22. Wu, H., Zheng, S., Zhang, J., Huang, K.: GP-GAN: Towards realistic high-resolution image blending. In: MM 2019 (2017)
23. Zhao, Y., Price, B.L., Cohen, S., Gurari, D.: Guided image inpainting: replacing an image region by pulling content from another image. In: 2019 IEEE Winter Conference on Applications of Computer Vision (WACV) (2018)
24. Yu, J., Lin, Z.L., Yang, J., Shen, X., Lu, X., Huang, T.S.: Free-Form Image Inpainting with Gated Convolution. ArXiv (2018)
25. Wang, Z., Wang, N., Shi, J., Li, J.-J., Yang, H.: Multi-instance sketch to image synthesis with progressive generative adversarial networks. IEEE Access **7**, 56683–56693 (2019)
26. Gu, S., Bao, J., Yang, H., Chen, D., Wen, F., Yuan, L.: Mask-guided portrait editing with conditional GANs. In: CVPR (2019)
27. Lee, C.-H., Liu, Z., Lingyun, W., Luo, P.: MaskGAN: Towards Diverse and Interactive Facial Image Manipulation. ArXiv (2019)
28. Qian, S., et al.: Make a face: towards arbitrary high fidelity face manipulation. In: ICCV (2019)
29. Isola, P., Zhu, J.-Y., Zhou, T., Efros, A.A.: Image-to-image translation with conditional adversarial networks. In: CVPR (2017)
30. Chen, Q., Koltun, V.: Photographic image synthesis with cascaded refinement networks (2017)
31. Kim, J., Lee, J.K., Lee, K.M.: Accurate image super-resolution using very deep convolutional networks. In: 2016 IEEE Conference on Computer Vision and Pattern Recognition (CVPR) (2015)

32. Lim, B., Son, S., Kim, H., Nah, S., Lee, K.M.: Enhanced deep residual networks for single imawge super-resolution. In: IEEE Conference on Computer Vision and Pattern Recognition Workshops (CVPRW) (2017)
33. Tong, T., Li, G., Liu, X., Gao, Q.: Image super-resolution using dense skip connections (2017)
34. Mei, K., Jiang, A., Li, J., Liu, B., Ye, J., Wang, M.: Deep residual refining based pseudo-multi-frame network for effective single image super-resolution. IET Image Process. **13**(4), 591–599 (2019)
35. Ma, C., Tan, W., Bare, B., Yan, B.: A multi-level aggregated network for image restoration. In: 2019 IEEE International Conference on Multimedia and Expo (ICME) (2019)
36. Simonyan, K., Zisserman, A.: Very deep convolutional networks for large-scale image recognition (2015)
37. https://pytorch.org/docs/stable/torchvision/models.html
38. https://github.com/david-gpu/srez
39. https://github.com/twhui/SRGAN-PyTorch
40. Heusel, M., Ramsauer, H., Unterthiner, T., Nessler, B., Hochreiter, S.: GANs trained by a two time-scale update rule converge to a local Nash equilibrium. In: Advances in Neural Information Processing Systems (2017)
41. https://github.com/bioinf-jku/TTUR
42. He, K., Zhang, X., Ren, S., Sun, J.: Deep residual learning for image recognition. In: 2016 IEEE Conference on Computer Vision and Pattern Recognition (CVPR) (2015)
43. http://mmlab.ie.cuhk.edu.hk/archive/facesketch.html
44. Takano, N., Alaghband, G.: SRGAN: training dataset matters. In: International Conference on Image Processing, Computer Vision, and Pattern Recognition (IPCV) (2019)

CD²: Combined Distances of Contrast Distributions for Image Quality Analysis

Sascha Xu[1](✉), Jan Bauer[2], Benjamin Axmann[3], and Wolfgang Maass[4]

[1] X-Motive, Saarbrücken, Germany
sascha.xu@xmotive.de
[2] Hochschule Karlsruhe, Karlsruhe, Germany
jan.bauer@hs-karlsruhe.de
[3] Mercedes-Benz, Stuttgart, Germany
benjamin.axmann@daimler.com
[4] DFKI, Saarbrücken, Germany
wolfgang.maass@dfki.de

Abstract. The quality of visual input impacts both human and machine perception. Consequently many processing techniques exist that deal with different distortions. Usually they are applied freely and unsupervised. We propose a novel method called CD^2 to protect against errors that arise during image processing. It is based on distributions of image contrast and custom distance functions which capture the effect of noise, compression, etc. CD^2 achieves excellent performance on image quality analysis benchmarks and in a separate user test with only a small data and computation overhead.

Keywords: Image quality analysis · Image processing · RR-IQA

1 Introduction

Modern cars have up to 8 cameras giving full coverage of the traffic situation. Their video data is relevant to both human drivers and autonomous driving agents. In accordance with automotive functional safety guidelines [8] we propose a novel method for guarded image transmission and processing. The perceptual differences between an original image and a processed version have to be assessed. The goal is to detect safety hazards that hinder the extraction of information about items in the scene. Image processing explicitly changes pixel values thus methods such as the CRC-checksum are not applicable. Instead a perceptual comparison has to be conducted for the image pair: Where and what kind of changes have been applied to the image? Have objects been obscured or even lost? Is the image still perceptually similar to the reference?

Safety hazards shall be detected so that warning and countermeasures can be taken. A manifestation of safety hazards in image processing is displayed in Fig. 1. Because of a contrast enhancement operation, the pedestrians in the red box have become poorly visible. In the blue box image augmentation covers up

© Springer Nature Switzerland AG 2020
G. Bebis et al. (Eds.): ISVC 2020, LNCS 12510, pp. 444–457, 2020.
https://doi.org/10.1007/978-3-030-64559-5_35

(a) Street with Pedestrians and Cars   (b) Processed Street Scene

Fig. 1. Safety hazard: misused image processing

a vehicle and could cause the driver to overlook it. In general wrong processing in wrong moments may lead to accidents by hindering/misleading the driver.

Algorithms are affected by this as well: Dodge and Karam [5] examine the effect of noise, blur and compression distortions on neural networks. They show that widely used networks perform much worse on the Imagenet [4] challenge when faced with distorted images. Thus on the one hand there is the need to process blurry and noisy camera data for driver assistance systems. On the other hand it must be ensured that the image processing itself does not become a source of error.

1.1 Related Work

This task fits very well into the domain of image quality assessment (IQA). There exist three modi operandi for IQA: Full-reference IQA (FR-IQA) has access to the complete reference and result image. The structural similarity index (SSIM) by Wang et al. [21] is the most prominent FR-IQA index. SSIM assesses image similarity with pixel statistics about luminosity, contrast and structure. Since visual perception is illumination invariant and instead relies on luminance differences and patterns, subsequent methods such as the Gradient-SSIM of Chen et al. [2] operate on gradient maps. Sampat et al. [15] utilize the Wavelet transformation to represent structures of an image and create their variant Wavelet-SSIM. Finally the latest FR-IQA indices such as FSIM by Zhang et al. [25] are built on a combination of Wavelet and gradient similarity measures which are pooled together into one quality index.

Blind IQA aims to judge the quality of an individual image. There is no reference image, only the result image is available. Traditionally this was approached similar to full-reference methods using features from the frequency and gradient domain [14,24]. With the rise of neural networks CNN architectures have been utilized for blind IQA as well [9]. For the evaluation of image augmentation however blind IQA is not suitable. To make a qualified statement about what parts of the image are covered up, the content of the reference image must be taken into account.

The middle ground between full-reference and blind IQA is occupied by reduced-reference IQA (RR-IQA). Here the use of natural scene statistics and distributions to represent images is widespread [12,18,22]. By applying statistical distances on the distributions of reference and processed image RR-IQA requires only limited data.

The goal of this paper is to develop a method to safeguard and control results of image processing and transmission. Therefore the reference image should be taken into account. A full-reference method is costly in bandwidth and often not feasible for implementation. Consequently we opt for a reduced reference approach.

1.2   Guarded Image Processing

The layout of the proposed method is displayed in Fig. 2. An image source (e.g. rear-view camera) produces the reference image which is to be processed and transmitted to its destination, typically a display or a driver assistance system. The reference image is represented through a feature set. The feature set acts as a signature for the image, which should contain sufficient information but in much reduced size. Motivated by the affinity of the human visual system for contrast we utilize histograms to capture the distribution of contrast in local regions of the image. The features are sent along the image stream and travel through the processing pipeline to the destination.

At the destination the feature set of the processed image is compared to the features of the reference. CD^2 stands for the combined use of distance functions that measure general and distortion specific similarity of the contrast distributions. In the end a detailed map for local distortion as well as an accurate global indicator is obtained. This allows to diagnose and locate dangerous image processing safety hazards and create a strong, resilient system. CD^2 offers the following advantages compared to current RR-IQA methods:

1. *Improved Perceptual Modelling*: RR-IQA methods rely on statistics of known factors like gradients and wavelets. We further explore the connection of their distributions to perception by incorporating them into a hierarchical model for the different stages of visual perception.

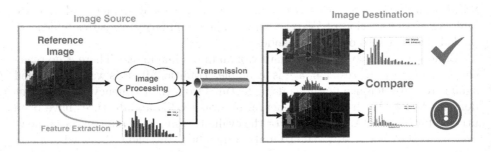

Fig. 2. Layout of a guarded image processing system

2. *Local Predictions*: Telltales affect only a small region of the image, but IQA methods are designed for entire images. We design our method to make precise local comparisons.
3. *Efficiency*: In real world application hardware requirements should be low. The FPGA prototype of CD^2 is able to operate on pixel streams without frame buffering and allows real time inference at 60 fps.

Evaluation is carried out through a user test on automotive displays focusing on distortion of street scenes. It is complemented by benchmark tests on the LIVE [16], TID [13] and CSIQ [11] IQA databases. In the end we find that the proposed method performs better than competing RR-IQA methods at a very low time and hardware complexity. The rest of the paper is organized as follows: Sect. 2 introduces our features. Section 3 focuses on the distance functions used to compare to images. Section 4 details the experiments and the user test. Section 5 describes the FPGA prototype and gives closing remarks.

2   Contrast Distribution as Features

To ensure safety of image processing we impose the following requirement: Objects which were visible in the reference image must be visible in the altered image. Therefore the main focus lays on the early stages of visual perception when the shapes and contours of objects are detected. Tschechne and Neumann [19] propose a hierarchical approach to model the process of shape recognition in the visual cortex. We employ a simplified feedforward model which models the factors that allow our visual system to detect objects, but not the specific shapes themselves. Our three stage model tries to account for pixel scale contrast stimuli, intermediate stage grouping of stimuli and a global weighting of regions into a complete picture.

Image contrast as a visual property is closely associated to stimulus strength for our visual system. During the detection of objects these contrasts in the form of edges and shadows play a major role [1]. Algorithmic edge detection commonly employs image gradients, which are also a great indicator of blur. Therefore they serve as the contrast measure of our choice. The gradients will be computed on the luminance channel of the CIELAB color space. For an image $I(x, y)$ consisting of luminance integers between 0 and 255, the image gradient $\nabla I(x, y)$ may be approximated with a number of kernels. In the following 3×3 Sobel kernels are used to filter an image. The resulting pixelmap of contrast stimuli/gradients usually amounts to millions of values per image.

$$\nabla I(x, y) = [\frac{\delta I(x, y)}{\delta x}, \frac{\delta I(x, y)}{\delta y}] = [g_x(x, y), g_y(x, y)] \qquad (1)$$

Objects span over larger areas and thus many, many pixels. The visual system scans over areas and searches for evidence of objects which manifest themselves through edges and shadows. One local gradient value alone may not mean much unless it is put into context with surrounding gradients. Therefore the image is

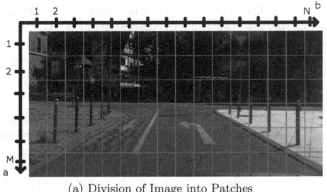

(a) Division of Image into Patches

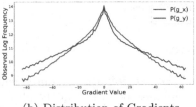

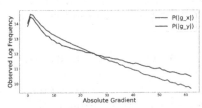

(b) Distribution of Gradients   (c) Distribution of Absolute Gradients

Fig. 3. Empirical gradient distributions for reference image

divided up into an evenly spaced grid of MxN patches shown in Fig. 3a. Each image patch in row a, column b is analyzed by its gradient distributions $P_{ab}(g_x)$ and $P_{ab}(g_y)$. They contain vital information regarding edges, surfaces, shadows and allow to detect distortions like noise or compression through comparisons (topic of Sect. 3). The sign of the gradients is dropped based on the assumption that natural image gradients are zero symmetric distributed (see Fig. 3b and [7]). This natural scene statistics approach condenses the gradients into a much more compact form while retaining sufficient information to make a qualitative prediction about differences and deterioration of image quality.

2.1   Gradient Distributions to Contrast Histograms

The gradient distribution is defined for all possible unsigned Sobel gradients. This makes it hard to process and unnecessary large in size. Histograms help categorize gradients into similar segments and shrink down the domain of the distribution. Here the challenge lies in dividing up the domain into segments of similarly perceived stimuli. Though we deal with gamma encoded pixel values, a linear division of the domain does not seem appropriate. As seen in Fig. 3b the gradients have a center heavy distribution. Huang et al. [7] explain this phenomenon with the prevalence of homogeneous surfaces and sparsity of edges

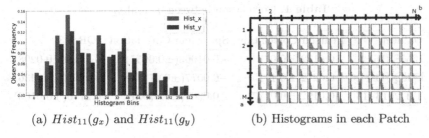

(a) $Hist_{11}(g_x)$ and $Hist_{11}(g_y)$ (b) Histograms in each Patch

Fig. 4. Feature representation for image 3b

in natural scenes, resulting in an exponentially decreasing probability for linearly increasing gradient.

The gradient value is set as stimulus intensity and categorized according to the Fechner law [6]. The Fechner law postulates that the actual and perceived change of stimulus intensity scales logarithmically. The domain of [0,1020] is split into bins using powers of 2 as thresholds. Each bin edge represents approximately a linear increase in the perceived strength of a gradient stimulus. 5 intermediate thresholds are added in the middle of the domain to increase resolution to a total of 16 bins. In this fashion all gradient distributions $P_{ab}(g_x)$ are transformed into histograms $Hist_{ab}(g_x)$ (likewise $Hist_{ab}(g_y)$). The result of such a binning is displayed in Fig. 4. For each patch in the grid the histogram of gradients is collected. It gives an indication of the amount of strong edges, smooth surfaces, shadows and visible content in that image patch.

2.2 Interaction Between Gradients

Until now the marginal distributions $P_{ab}(g_x)$ and $P_{ab}(g_y)$ were viewed independently. A dependency between g_x and g_y is however expected since they are partly computed on the same pixels. Some IQA methods therefore utilize the gradient magnitude and orientation to take the information of the joint distribution $P_{ab}(g_x, g_y)$ into account [2,25].

To assess the gains of transmitting the joint distribution we examined the dependency of g_x and g_y in three IQA databases. Table 1 shows the median Pearson and Spearman correlation coefficients observed for the gradients g_x and g_y. The correlations deviate around zero. This implies that there likely is no linear or monotone relationship between g_x and g_y. Due to the discrete nature of the histograms, mutual information is another tool to assess the information contained in the joint distribution $P(g_x, g_y)$. The Information Quality Ratio (IQR [23]) of 0.3 implies that there is relatively little information in the joint histogram compared to the marginals (MI: Mutual Information, H: Entropy).

$$IQR(g_x, g_y) = \frac{MI(Hist(g_x), Hist(g_y))}{H(Hist(g_x), Hist(g_y))} \qquad (2)$$

Sending over a joint histogram $Hist_{ab}(g_x, g_y)$ with $16^2 = 256$ bins would cause a lot of extra overhead. However it contains only a modest amount of

Table 1. Correlation between g_x and g_y

Dataset	Pearson Correlation	Spearman Correlation	IQR [23]
LIVE [16]	$-0.0132(\pm0.0773)$	$-0.01063(\pm0.0651)$	$0.2713(\pm0.0208)$
CSIQ [11]	$-0.0212(\pm0.1115)$	$-0.0077(\pm0.0714)$	$0.2799(\pm0.0436)$
TID2013 [13]	$-0.0192(\pm0.0777)$	$-0.0207(\pm0.0792)$	$0.2756(\pm0.0163)$

mutual information (30% of marginals information). Therefore we restrict ourselves to transmitting the two marginal distribution histograms $Hist_{ab}(g_x)$ and $_{ab}Hist(g_y)$ for together $2*16 = 32$ bins.

The complete feature set for an image consists of M × N patches containing two 16-bin histograms $Hist_{ab}(g_x)$ and $Hist_{ab}(g_y)$ of the Sobel-X/Y gradient distributions. For lossless histogram transmission of an image with s pixels the bins must have $\lceil log_2(s) \rceil$ bits. In an automotive HD-image (1920×720) divided into 6×16 patches our features use $6 * 16 * 32 * 14\text{Bit} \approx 5kB$, compared to the full image with $1920 * 720 * 3 * 8\text{Bit} \approx 4MB$. Such feature data can easily be transmitted alongside a pixel stream. The histogram itself is a compact image signature that acts as a logarithmically contrast response model for gradients.

3   Distances for Contrast Distributions

In the previous section we have looked extensively at the design of the histogram features. This section aims to use the histogram grid for a perceptual comparison of images in regards to safety hazards. Given the features of the *reference* image $Histr_{ab}(g_x)$ and $Histr_{ab}(g_y)$ and the features of a *processed* image $Histp_{ab}(g_x)$ and $Histp_{ab}(g_y)$, the goal is to detect and evaluate safety hazards resulting in a deterioration of quality. The distance functions presented in the following are executed once each on the g_x and g_y histograms.

3.1   Perceptual Dissimilarity

When objects or pedestrians vanish from perception due to a faulty processing operation, a safety hazard has occurred and is to be detected. Figure 5 shows an overly contrast stretched version of the image from Fig. 3a. In particular in the upper part of the image details are clipped away due to the processing. A look at the computed distance map in Fig. 5c highlights the advantages of our approach. It clearly identifies the areas where most of the content was lost and the areas which are still similar to the reference. Although the pixel values in the lower image half differ a lot from the reference, which would alarm PSNR for example, the gradient histograms are similar. Thus our algorithm can infer that the lower image half is still perceptually similar.

Any significant change in the perception of the scene will result in an altered gradient distribution, may it be a vanishing of objects, the injection of noise or

(a) Distorted Image

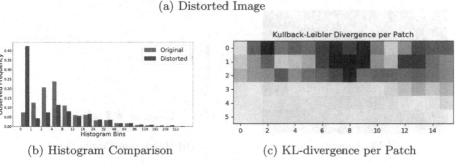

(b) Histogram Comparison   (c) KL-divergence per Patch

Fig. 5. Effects of image distortion on $Hist(g_x)$

compression related artifacts. To quantify these distortions, distance functions of probabilistic background are picked and designed.

In diagram 5c the Kullback-Leibler divergence is used. It provides an information-theoretic quantification of the difference between two histograms $Histr_{ab}$ and $Histp_{ab}$ of an image patch. A successful contrast enhancement would sharpen only existing boundaries and clip away no details. Since KL is weighted by the probability in each bin and edges are sparse, the resulting KL-divergence is negligible. Another useful indicator is the Earth-Movers-Distance (Emd). It describes the amount of contrast that needs to be shifted to transform the histogram of the reference image to the result. The set of distances is rounded out with the Histogram Intersection and the Total-Variation distance, which simply describes the maximum bin difference between $Histr_{ab}$ and

Table 2. Histogram distances ($Hist(i)$: value of i-th histogram bin)

Kullback-Leibler$_{ab}$: $\sum_{i=1}^{16} Histr_{ab}(i) * log(\frac{Histr_{ab}(i)}{Histp_{ab}(i)})$
Emd$_{ab}$: $\sum_{i=1}^{16} |Emd_i|, Emd_{i+1} = Histr_{ab}(i) + Emd_i - Histp_{ab}(i)$
Intersection$_{ab}$: $\sum_{i=1}^{16} min(Histr_{ab}(i), Histp_{ab}(i))$
TotalVariation$_{ab}$: $max(|Histr_{ab}(i) - Histp_{ab}(i)|)$

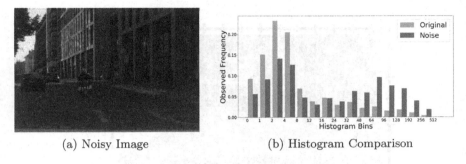

(a) Noisy Image   (b) Histogram Comparison

Fig. 6. Effects of white noise on $Hist(g_x)$

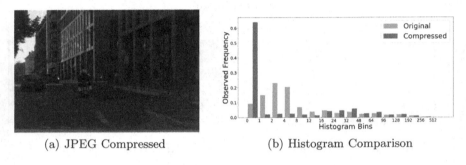

(a) JPEG Compressed   (b) Histogram Comparison

Fig. 7. Effects of JPEG compression on $Hist(g_x)$

$Histp_{ab}$. Together these distances give different estimates of perceptual similarity or degradation.

3.2 Noise Artifacts

The distances from Table 2 treat each bin equally. However some distortions mainly affect the specific lower/higher ranges of the histogram, which motivates to design custom distance functions. When noise appears on a previously homogeneous surface, it produces strong, non-natural edges and gradients. Figure 6 shows the change after noise is introduced. There is a significant increase in the high contrast proportion of the histogram.

Due to its commonness, a custom distance function targeted at noise is added. Insertion of noise is gauged by thresholding and comparing the amount of large gradients. The upper t bins of each histogram are summed up. Two t values (4 and 6) are applied for the sake of robustness.

$$NoiseInc = \sum_{i=16-t}^{16} Hist_{ref}(i) - \sum_{i=16-t}^{16} Hist_{pro}(i) \tag{3}$$

3.3   Compression Artifacts

Compression, specifically JPEG compression also has a special effect on our gradient histograms. The JPEG [20] standard uses the discrete cosine transform (DCT) to encode 8×8 pixel blocks. DCT is widespread and also used by video coding schemes like MPEG. JPEG compression causes blocking: Small DCT coefficients are quantized to zero resulting in many blocks of same pixel values and zero gradients. Figure 7 shows the histogram shift caused by JPEG compression. The amount of blocking is strongly reflected in an increased proportion of zero gradients. They are contained in the first histogram bin.

$$Blocking = Histr_{ab}(1) - Histp_{ab}(1) \tag{4}$$

Furthermore it is also visible that the gradients are very unevenly distributed in the compressed image. The variety and range of contrast can be represented by the Shannon entropy of a histogram. By comparing the respective entropy before and after processing, a shrink in the range of contrasts is detected which is often associated with visual distortion and artifacts.

$$EntropyGap = \sum_{i=1}^{16} Histr_{ab}(i) - \sum_{i=1}^{16} Histp_{ab}(i) \tag{5}$$

All presented distance functions capture different aspects important for distortions such as loss of detail or noise. Two variants of combining these distances into a system which predicts the strength of error in an image are explored:

1. *Spatial combination*: The distances obtained by computing the KL-divergence on each patch separately are aggregated into a global distortion score forming the method **CD^2-A**.

$$\sum_{a=1}^{M} \sum_{b=1}^{N} Kl_{ab}(g_x) + Kl_{ab}(g_y) \tag{6}$$

2. *Functional combination*: The set of all presented distance functions d_i is to be transformed by a function f into a quality score. The distances are computed only once per image on the global histograms for g_x and g_y. f is modelled through gradient tree boosting from the Lightgbm framework [10]. This model (called **CD^2-B**) is trained with the help of IQA datasets and evaluated in the next section. An approach involving both a spatial and functional combination of distances is intriguing but left to future work.

$$f(d_1, ..., d_{16}) = \sum_i \gamma_i * tree_i(subset_i(d_1, ..., d_{16})) \tag{7}$$

4   Experiments

The proposed methods are tested on the LIVE [16], CSIQ [11] and TID2013 [13] datasets. These datasets contain pairs of a reference and a processed image subject to different levels of compression, noise, etc. Human subjects give opinions

Table 3. Performance on IQA-datasets

		CD^2-A	CD^2-B	WNISM	RRED	PSNR	SSIM	FSIM
TID2013 [13]	RMSE	0.9804	**0.5659**	1.0042	0.7134	1.0890	0.9027	0.5967
	PLCC	0.6125	**0.8962**	0.5851	0.8180	0.4784	0.6868	0.8767
	SROCC	0.5342	**0.8891**	0.5155	0.7633	0.6391	0.6264	0.8511
LIVE [16]	RMSE	14.6130	7.8534	18.4173	9.4880	13.3790	11.6272	**7.5718**
	PLCC	0.8455	0.9595	0.7371	0.9383	0.8715	0.9056	**0.9612**
	SROCC	0.8546	0.9582	0.7407	0.9397	0.8728	0.9098	**0.9608**
CSIQ [11]	RMSE	0.1673	**0.0925**	0.1934	0.1223	0.1736	0.1510	0.1092
	PLCC	0.7684	**0.9376**	0.6760	0.8837	0.7509	0.8176	0.9091
	SROCC	0.7943	**0.9339**	0.6821	0.9073	0.8023	0.8353	0.9212

about image quality that are transformed to difference-in-mean-opinion-score (DMOS) to quantify distortion.

CD^2-A/B is compared against the FR-IQA metrics PSNR, SSIM [21] and FSIM [25] as well as the RR-IQA indices RRED [17] and WNISM [22]. CD^2 is implemented in Python, for the other methods their original Matlab source code was used. The DMOS prediction is tested with 5-fold cross validation. Reported are the mean root mean-square error (RMSE), Pearson linear correlation coefficient (PLCC) and Spearman rank-order correlation coefficient (SROCC).

4.1   DMOS Prediction Performance

Table 3 shows the DMOS prediction performance across the benchmarks. The best method is highlighted in each row. CD^2-A posts a competitive performance in comparison with other RR-IQA methods. It outmatches WNISM, though a significant gap exists to RRED. RRED however requires $n * \frac{32}{36}$ Bit of feature data for n pixels and drops down to a similar level when its feature data is reduced [17]. CD^2-A performs comparable to the FR-IQA baseline PSNR. In addition the method brings along a number of advantages in computational and data efficiency and offers local interpretability (see Fig. 5c).

The CD^2-B boosting model performs great across the board. It posts the best performance for TID2013 and CSIQ. It surpasses its competitor RR-IQA methods and is on par with the FR-IQA state of the art FSIM. This performance edge may be based in the ability to adapt to the specific distortions of each dataset through training on all distances. While indices like SSIM or CD^2-A score identically for different datasets, CD^2-B adapts its scoring to the current benchmark and gains over its static competitors.

4.2   User Test

In addition an automotive application-oriented user test was carried out. The goal of the test is to determine a threshold for CD^2-A at which an image distortion is deemed dangerous. The subjects are set up in front of an automotive

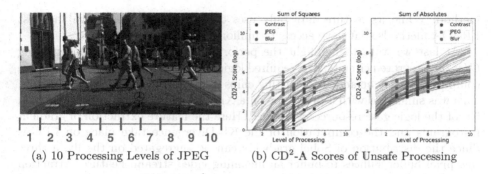

(a) 10 Processing Levels of JPEG   (b) CD^2-A Scores of Unsafe Processing

Fig. 8. Results of user test

head-unit display producing 400 nits. On the display street scenes from the Cityscapes dataset [3] are shown. The participants can adjust the strength of a processing operation (contrast, JPEG and gaussian blur) between ten levels, illustrated in Fig. 8a. The task is to input the lowest level, where the subject is no longer able to perceive all important details of the scene.

In total 7 subjects (age 19–59, 2 female, 4 non-expert) participated in the study annotating 25 images per category. The selected processing levels for each image were averaged to create pairs of original scene and unsafely processed scene. Figure 8b shows the results of the test: Each point represents an image (X: average level, Y-value: CD^2-A score). The lines visualize the CD^2-A score for all 10 levels. Our first observation is that the level of dangerous processing varies based on content which justifies the approach of perceptual assessment instead.

The perfect perceptual score provides a threshold τ dividing safe from unsafe processing. In the plot this would be a horizontal line $Y = \tau$ on which all points lie. The two subplots of Fig. 8b compare taking the sum of squares of the KL-divergence grid (left) against the sum of absolutes (right). The sum of absolutes provides a clearer vertical divide and was thus chosen for the CD^2-A method. Per category the border between acceptable and dangerous levels of processing approximates a horizontal line, though the thresholds differ for different operations. Therefore we see CD^2-A fit for use focused on assessing image processing if provided information about the type of the operation.

5 Conclusion

We presented the CD^2 method for the perceptual assessment of image processing with regard to safety. Based on local contrast histograms that categorize and compress contrast stimuli, a compact image signature is created. At the image destination the quality of the altered image is verified with help of the original image signature. Through a selection of statistical distances an accurate assessment about levels of noise, compression and detail loss can be made. Tests on IQA benchmarks and a user study showcase the strong performance of our method. While its feature data only uses $5\,\text{kB}$, CD^2 is on par with the best FR-IQA methods that have access to millions of pixels.

At last we want to highlight the performance advantages when deploying CD^2 on integrated circuits. The required logic for feature extraction and distance computation may be added to existing chips in cameras or displays for example. This was simulated with a prototype on a Xilinx Artix-7 FPGA where less than 5% of the logic gate resources were used. Here the feature extraction of gradient histograms and the computation of the KL-Divergence take place on FPGA. Since the distribution of Sobel gradients can be aggregated on the fly, a three row pixel-buffer suffices to buffer an incoming video stream. Feature extraction is finished $10\,\mu s$ after the entire image is received and the feature distances may be computed in even less time. Deployed in modern automobiles, CD^2 is able to provide instant inference about image safety and hazards with modest means, even for 60 fps HD-video.

References

1. Avidan, G., Harel, M., Hendler, T., Ben-Bashat, D., Zohary, E., Malach, R.: Contrast sensitivity in human visual areas and its relationship to object recognition. J. Neurophysiol. **87**(6), 3102–3116 (2002)
2. Chen, G.H., Yang, C.L., Xie, S.L.: Gradient-based structural similarity for image quality assessment. In: 2006 International Conference on Image Processing, pp. 2929–2932. IEEE (2006)
3. Cordts, M., et al.: The cityscapes dataset for semantic urban scene understanding. In: Proceedings of the IEEE Conference on Computer Vision and Pattern Recognition, pp. 3213–3223 (2016)
4. Deng, J., Dong, W., Socher, R., Li, L.J., Li, K., Fei-Fei, L.: Imagenet: a large-scale hierarchical image database. In: 2009 IEEE Conference on Computer Vision and Pattern Recognition, pp. 248–255. IEEE (2009)
5. Dodge, S., Karam, L.: A study and comparison of human and deep learning recognition performance under visual distortions. In: 2017 26th International Conference on Computer Communication and Networks (ICCCN), pp. 1–7. IEEE (2017)
6. Hecht, S.: The visual discrimination of intensity and the Weber-Fechner law. J. General Physiol. **7**(2), 235–267 (1924)
7. Huang, J., Mumford, D.: Statistics of natural images and models. In: Proceedings. 1999 IEEE Computer Society Conference on Computer Vision and Pattern Recognition (Cat. No PR00149), vol. 1, pp. 541–547. IEEE (1999)
8. ISO: Road vehicles - Functional safety (2011)
9. Kang, L., Ye, P., Li, Y., Doermann, D.: Convolutional neural networks for no-reference image quality assessment. In: Proceedings of the IEEE Conference on Computer Vision and Pattern Recognition, pp. 1733–1740 (2014)
10. Ke, G., et al.: LightGBM: a highly efficient gradient boosting decision tree. In: Advances in Neural Information Processing Systems, pp. 3146–3154 (2017)
11. Larson, E.C., Chandler, D.M.: Most apparent distortion: full-reference image quality assessment and the role of strategy. J. Electron. Imaging **19**(1), 011006 (2010)
12. Li, Q., Wang, Z.: Reduced-reference image quality assessment using divisive normalization-based image representation. IEEE J Sel. Topics Sig. Process. **3**(2), 202–211 (2009)

13. Ponomarenko, N., et al.: Image database tid2013: peculiarities, results and perspectives. Sig. Process.: Image Commun. **30**, 57–77 (2015)
14. Saad, M.A., Bovik, A.C., Charrier, C.: Blind image quality assessment: a natural scene statistics approach in the DCT domain. IEEE Trans. Image Process. **21**(8), 3339–3352 (2012)
15. Sampat, M.P., Wang, Z., Gupta, S., Bovik, A.C., Markey, M.K.: Complex wavelet structural similarity: a new image similarity index. IEEE Trans. Image Process. **18**(11), 2385–2401 (2009)
16. Sheikh, H.: Live image quality assessment database release 2 (2005). http://live. ece.utexas.edu/research/quality
17. Soundararajan, R., Bovik, A.C.: Rred indices: reduced reference entropic differencing for image quality assessment. IEEE Trans. Image Process. **21**(2), 517–526 (2011)
18. Tao, D., Li, X., Lu, W., Gao, X.: Reduced-reference IQA in contourlet domain. IEEE Trans. Syst. Man Cybern. Part B (Cybern.) **39**(6), 1623–1627 (2009)
19. Tschechne, S., Neumann, H.: Hierarchical representation of shapes in visual cortex-from localized features to figural shape segregation. Frontiers Comput. Neurosci. **8**, 93 (2014)
20. Wallace, G.K.: The jpeg still picture compression standard. IEEE Trans. Consumer Electron. **38**(1), xviii–xxxiv (1992)
21. Wang, Z., Bovik, A.C., Sheikh, H.R., Simoncelli, E.P., et al.: Image quality assessment: from error visibility to structural similarity. IEEE Trans. Image Process. **13**(4), 600–612 (2004)
22. Wang, Z., Simoncelli, E.P.: Reduced-reference image quality assessment using a wavelet-domain natural image statistic model. In: Human Vision and Electronic Imaging X, vol. 5666, pp. 149–159. International Society for Optics and Photonics (2005)
23. Wijaya, D.R., Sarno, R., Zulaika, E.: Information quality ratio as a novel metric for mother wavelet selection. Chem. Intell. Lab. Syst. **160**, 59–71 (2017)
24. Xue, W., Mou, X., Zhang, L., Bovik, A.C., Feng, X.: Blind image quality assessment using joint statistics of gradient magnitude and Laplacian features. IEEE Trans. Image Process. **23**(11), 4850–4862 (2014)
25. Zhang, L., Zhang, L., Mou, X., Zhang, D.: FSIM: a feature similarity index for image quality assessment. IEEE Trans. Image Process. **20**(8), 2378–2386 (2011)

Real-Time Person Tracking and Association on Doorbell Cameras

Sung Chun Lee[✉], Gang Qian, and Allison Beach

ObjectVideo Labs, Tysons, VA 22102, USA
{slee,gqian,abeach}@objectvideo.com

Abstract. This paper presents key techniques for real-time, multi-person tracking and association on doorbell surveillance cameras at the edge. The challenges for this task are: significant person size changes during tracking caused by person approaching or departing from the doorbell camera, person occlusions due to limited camera field and occluding objects in the camera view, and the requirement for a lightweight algorithm that can run in real time on the doorbell camera at the edge. To address these challenges, we propose a multi-person tracker that uses a detect-track-associate strategy to achieve good performance in speed and accuracy. The person detector only runs at every n-th frame, and between person detection frames a low-cost point-based tracker is used to track the subjects. To maintain subject tracking accuracy, at each person detection frame, a person association algorithm is used to associate persons detected in the current frame to the current and recently tracked subjects and identify any new subjects. To improve the performance of the point-based tracker, human-shaped masks are used to filter out background points. Further, to address the challenge of drastic target scale change during the tracking we introduced an adaptive image resizing strategy to dynamically adjust the tracker input image size to allow the point-based tracker to operate at the optimal image resolution given a fixed number of feature points. For fast and accurate person association, we introduced the Sped-Up LOMO, a fast version of the popular local maximal occurrence (LOMO) person descriptor. The experimental results on doorbell surveillance videos illustrate the efficacy of the proposed person tracking and association framework.

Keywords: Human tracker · Edge computing · Feature descriptor

1 Introduction

Person detection and tracking are important for video surveillance applications. Once a person is detected by a person detector, a tracker is invoked to track the subject in the video. There are several factors that make this task highly challenging in the doorbell camera surveillance system. Firstly, most human motion is approaching toward the door or departing from the house, which cause significant human size changes. Secondly, due to small field of view of the doorbell camera, there exists human occlusion, which makes the tracking problem harder. In addition, a subject may disappear from the camera view for a short period of time, and then reappear. To maintain the correct tracking identity of

© Springer Nature Switzerland AG 2020
G. Bebis et al. (Eds.): ISVC 2020, LNCS 12510, pp. 458–469, 2020.
https://doi.org/10.1007/978-3-030-64559-5_36

the same subject through such temporary disappearance is another challenge. Thirdly, our use case requires a human tracking system running inside the doorbell camera, which requires light weight and real-time processing algorithm.

To address these challenges, in this paper, we present a lightweight multi-person tracker that runs in real time on the camera at the edge. The proposed tracking framework uses a detect-track-associate strategy to achieve good performance in both speed and accuracy. Our person detector is a lightweight deep model similar to the tiny YOLOv3 [19, 20] trained using inhouse data. To obtain high tracking frame rate, the person detection only runs at every n-th frame, and a low-cost feature-based tracker is used to track the subjects in intermediate frames between person detection frames. To maintain subject tracking accuracy, at each person detection frame, a person association algorithm is used to associate persons detected in the current frame to the current and recently tracked subjects and identify any new subjects.

2 Related Work

Early approach of tracking was to use a template matching. It uses an example image of an object as a template and searches for a new location of the template in the next frame image. It conducts per-pixel comparison of the template and image fragment with image distance metric such as normalized cross correlation.

Some approaches exploit the color information to track the object. color is a powerful feature. It selects rectangular bounding box for an object and its neighboring background region if object color is different from its immediate surroundings. In [1], they selected discriminative tracking features by computing color and brightness histograms for object ROI (Region Of Interest) and background region. For each feature value, it computes the likelihood ratio of the object or the background and selects the region which maximize object likelihood. In [2], authors later improved this approach by exploiting that object of interest can have similar appearance to other objects in the scene. The visual tracker tends to drift and can switch to tracking of similar objects. Authors can directly suppress objects of similar appearance if any. Fusing both template and pixel-wise approach was also proposed [2]. Color distribution relies on pixel values to discriminate target from background. It is robust to the shape changes because it has no concept of locality, but it is very sensitive to blur and poor illumination changes. Meanwhile, a template-based model relies on spatial configurations, which is robust to blur and poor illumination, but sensitive to shape changes.

Recently, deep learning-based tracking approaches have been introduced. There are two main categories; online and offline learning approaches. In online learning approach, they tried to build an object vs background classifier to apply the sampled candidate regions and to select region with highest score for next tracking bounding box. In [4], authors tried to train a neural network to distinguish "object" and "background" regions and treat each video as new domain. They divided neural network into shared and domain-specific layers. They applied online training of domain-specific component (binary classifier and bounding box regressor). The drawback of this approach is that the computation time is very high, and it is not feasible to use for the edge device. *GOTURN* (Generic Object Tracking Using Regression Networks) algorithm was introduced, which is an offline-based approach [5]. They trained a neural network using a collection of videos and images with bounding box labels and applied this network at the inference time without fine-tuning. By avoiding fine-tuning, this network can reach 100 FPS (with GPU).

The hybrid of online and offline approaches has been attempted. In [6], they used a Siamese Network with RPN for Visual Object Tracking in offline fashion. The Siamese network consists of two identical fully connected CNNs with same weights to generate the similarity score of the two inputs. They also adapted online learning approach as local one-shot detection task. This approach was evolved to discriminate and track the similar objects in the same frame [7]. This approach ranked the 1st in VOT-2018 real time challenge and the 2nd in VOT-2018 long term challenge.

In [8], authors proposed a simple online real time tracking (SORT) with Deep Association. They used a CNN-based object detector (e.g. Faster RCNN) and applied the Kalman filter for prediction of the object position in the next frame. They also used the Hungarian algorithm for matching new detections and the existing trajectories. Finally, deep association metric is used as affinity measure.

3   Overview

We developed a doorbell camera surveillance system that detects and tracks multiple humans in front of the doorbell camera. In this paper, we will describe a lightweight multiple human tracker that can run in real time on the camera at the edge.

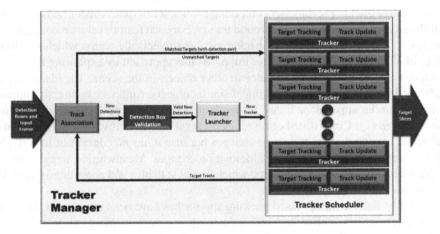

Fig. 1. The overview of the multiple human tracker manager.

The system runs the human detection periodically (e.g. every $5th$ frame) and the human tracker in every frame because the human detection requires more computation time than the tracker. As shown in Fig. 1, human detection bounding boxes are given at every $5th$ frame from the doorbell surveillance camera. The proposed system first connects new human detection boxes with the already initiated human targets if any. If the new detection boxes are associated with the existing targets, then the system updates the human target with additional features from the new human detection box. The system initiates tracking of new human target for unassociated human detection boxes. In frames between the human detection operations, the system tracks the image bounding boxes of existing human targets until human detections become available by human detection operation in the next *5th* frame.

Our approach follows the similar flow of the work of [8], but we proposed a novel and fast algorithm for each step to be able to run on a doorbell camera in real time. We assumed the human detection boxes are given in every *5th* frame. In [8], they used the Faster RCNN network to detect humans, but in our framework, we developed in-house human detector that can run in near real time in the doorbell camera. The scope of this paper is about the tracker, not the human detector. The evaluation of this work was focused only on the tracking performance. The human detector's performance does not influence the tracking evaluation which will be described in the Sect. 4.2 and Sect. 5.1. In this paper, we propose a multi-scale adaptive human tracker running on the doorbell camera in real time.

4   Tracking Approach

In this paper, we tried to improve the tracking work of [9] so that we can track humans efficiently in real time for the doorbell camera surveillance system.

4.1   Feature Selection

In order to predict the next position and size of the human target box in the next frame, we need to search the candidate area in the next frame and to match features between the current and the next frames.

The previous approach [9] used uniform grid points inside the bounding box to search and match as a generic object tracker. Tracker accepts a pair of images I_t, I_{t+1} and a bounding box b_t and outputs the bounding box b_{t+1}. A set of points is initialized on a rectangular grid within the bounding box *bt*. These points are then tracked by Lucas-Kanade tracker which generates a sparse motion. The uniform feature points are good for general objects and moving cameras which we are unable to extract the object shape information. However, they are not useful for static camera and human object target because many noisy background points can be selected within the bounding box, which prevents from predicting the target more reliably. Because we are using the static doorbell camera and our target object is human, we select features using human shape mask as shown in Fig. 2.

The selected feature points using human shape masks are used to match between the current and next frames to predict the location and size of the human target box in the next frame.

4.2   Efficient Human Tracker with Adaptive Image Scale

The fixed number of the selected feature points is fixed for faster tracking. It is suitable for target to move from left and right (not much scale changes during tracking), but it

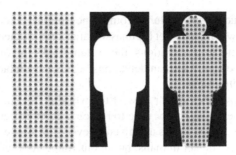

Fig. 2. Left: uniformly selected feature points, Center: human shape mask, Right: selected feature points using human shape masks.

is not advantageous for human target to move forward and backward from the doorbell camera, which generates significant bounding box size changes. Tracking large size bounding box using the fixed number of feature points implies that the selected feature points are very sparse, which causes missing feature matches and tracking failure. On the contrary, tracking small size box bounding box using the fixed number of feature points implies that the selected feature points are very dense within the small target box, which may cause false feature matches. To address this issue, we propose to dynamically rescale the input image frames for tracking depending on the size of the target box to be tracked.

At every frame, the system generates a set of scaled (e.g. downsize) images from the original resolution frame image. For example, the proposed system keeps 4 scaled images such as 1/2, 1/4, 1/8, 1/16 scales. Each scaled image is used for a group of similar size bounding boxes. There are 4 size groups based on the width range of the bounding box (in the original image) [0, 140], [140, 280], [280, 560], [560, 10000] respectively. For example, when the bounding box width is under 140 (pixels), we track these targets in the 1/2 scaled image. To do this, we first downscale the target bounding box to half size (e.g. 140 becomes 70) and run the tracker with the downsized bounding box on the half size image. Larger size bounding boxes are applied to the smaller scaled image. For example, if the bounding box width size is 560, then the system downsized the box into 1/8 (e.g. 560 becomes 70) and adaptively selects 1/8 scaled image to track the resized bounding box. This way we can exploit the fix number of feature points within the same size bounding box (e.g. approximately its width is 70).

We select this good width size (=70) of the bounding box for the tracker based on our experiments. The tracking performance is measured by 'robustness' which implies how many times the tracker failed, *i.e.* drifted from the target, and had to be reinitialized. The robustness is computed as follow [10, 11]:

$$R = e^{-\frac{SF}{N_{frames}}}$$

where 'N_{frames}' is the total length of the video. 'S' is the length of tracking experiment. 'F' is the total number of tracking fails during the entire frames 'N_{frames}'.

Table 1 shows the robustness of the tracking based on the bounding box size (width). For example, $S = 10$ means that the probability of successful tracking the target for *10* frames without tracking fails. As shown in Table 1, the highest robustness score was produced when the width of the bounding box is '70'.

Table 1. Robustness score per bounding box size.

Bounding box size (width)	Robustness: $e^{\frac{-SF}{N_{frames}}}$			
	S = 5	S = 10	S = 15	S = 20
40	0.823	0.677	0.557	0.459
50	0.825	0.681	0.562	0.464
60	0.829	0.686	0.569	0.471
70	**0.829**	**0.688**	**0.571**	**0.473**
80	0.825	0.680	0.561	0.463
90	0.820	0.673	0.552	0.453
100	0.816	0.666	0.544	0.444
110	0.814	0.663	0.540	0.440
120	0.820	0.673	0.552	0.453

We collected 222 evaluation videos from 11 different doorbell cameras. The resolution of the doorbell video is 1440 × 1920. Some example snapshots captured from the evaluation doorbell cameras are shown in Fig. 3.

Fig. 3. Example scenes of the evaluation doorbell cameras.

We compared with previous person tracking approaches. Because these previous approaches are already implemented in OpenCV contribution library, we used these methods through OpenCV functions. Table 2 shows the comparison on the robustness as described in Table 2 and the processing time. We tested the evaluation on the machine with Intel(R) Xeon(R) CPU E5-2698 v4 @ 2.20 GHz. The highest robustness method is 'CSRT' [17]. The proposed method achieved 22 times faster than CSRT with 3% loss of the robustness.

Table 2. Comparison on robustness and processing time.

Image descriptors	Processing time (fps)	Robustness			
		S = 5	S = 10	S = 15	S = 20
MedianFlow [9]	30.5	0.41	0.17	0.07	0.03
TLD [14]	6.0	0.63	0.40	0.25	0.16
KCF [15]	17.6	0.83	0.69	0.58	0.48
MIL [16]	9.8	0.88	0.77	0.67	0.59
CSRT [17]	7.3	0.89	0.79	0.71	0.63
Ours	161.7	0.86	0.74	0.64	0.55

5 Human Track Association

In [12], authors introduced an image feature descriptor that is an effective feature representation called Local Maximal Occurrence ($LOMO$), and a subspace and metric learning method called Cross-view Quadratic Discriminant Analysis ($XQDA$) was proposed for person re-identification. The $LOMO$ feature analyzes the horizontal occurrence of local feature and maximizes the occurrence to make a stable representation against viewpoint changes. However, its size is too big, and the computation time of the $LOMO$ is way too high to run on the doorbell camera. We are proposing the modified version of the local maximal occurrence descriptor that is very small and fast computing so that we can run it on the edge.

5.1 Fast and Small Size Image Descriptor

In this paper, we propose an image descriptor to associate newly detected human bounding boxes and the previously tracked humans, which it is fast and small enough to run on the doorbell camera.

Faster Image Feature Descriptor
We re-configured the $LOMO$ descriptor so that we can run in small computation time. The main idea is that we simplified the block image feature computation and at the same time we enhanced the histogram descriptor so that we can save computation time but, at the same time we can keep the quality of the image descriptor. Table 3 shows pseudo code comparison between $LOMO$ and the proposed descriptor ($LOMO\_SPD$). The main differences are as followings:

- The original version assumes that the actual human in the human detection box may have various sizes. For example, the actual human can be very small inside the detected human bounding box. In order to be size invariant, they applied three scale image pyramids to compute the $LOMO$ descriptor. However, we compute the image feature from only one scale image (48×128) because the human detector generates the well-fitted human size bounding boxes.

Table 3. Code Comparison between the *LOMO* and the speedup version (*LOMO_SPD*)

```
LOMO (image) # input image: (48×128)
    for pool in range (3) # Three pyramid scales (48×128, 24×64, 12×32)
        # 10 × 10 image block with 5 overlapping steps (b_sz = 10, b_st = 5)
        h_t, w_d = image.shape
        r_n = (h_t - (b_sz - b_st)) / b_st
        c_n = (w_d - (b_sz - b_st)) / b_st
        for r in range(r_n):
            for c in range(c_n):
                i_b = image[r*b_st : r*b_st+b_sz, c*b_st : c*b_st+b_sz]
                #Compute 'SILTP' descriptor as s_ht
                #Compute HSV histogram as h_ht for 'i_b' (bin size: [8, 8, 8])
                if c == 0:
                    s_fc = s_ht
                    h_fc = h_ht
                else:
                    s_fc = max(s_fc, s_ht)
                    h_fc = max(h_fc, h_ht)
                s_ft = Concatenate(s_ft, s_fc)
                h_ft = Concatenate(h_ft, h_fc)
        image = DownSizeImageByHalf (image)
    Normalize(s_ft)
    Normalize(h_ft)
    lomo = Concatenate(s_ft, h_ft)

    return lomo


LOMO_SPD (image) # input image: (48×128)
    # 30 × 30 image block with 15 overlapping steps (b_sz = 30, b_st = 15)
    h_t, w_d = image.shape
    r_n = (h_t - (b_sz - b_st)) / b_st
    c_n = (w_d - (b_sz - b_st)) / b_st
    for r in range(r_n):
        for c in range(c_n):
            i_b = image[r*b_st : r*b_st+b_sz, c*b_st : c*b_st+b_sz]
            #Compute HS histogram as hs_ht for i_b (bin size: [30, 48])
            if c == 0:
                hs_fc = hs_ht
            else:
                hs_fc = max(hs_fc, hs_ht)
            hs_ft = Concatenate(hs_ft, hs_fc)
    Normalize(hs_ft)
    lomo = hs_ft

    return lomo
```

- The original *LOMO* additionally uses '*SILTP*' [13] feature descriptor for illumination invariant texture description. However, we skipped the computation of '*SILTP*' descriptor, instead we apply '*HS* (Hue and Saturation)' histogram descriptor later. We intentionally removed '*V* (value, *i.e.* lightness)' channel to be robust to illumination changes.

- We used the larger size image block to reduce the computation time, but at the same time we enhanced the histogram bin size so that we can keep the quality of the image descriptor.

We evaluated two descriptors using a doorbell dataset. The dataset consists of 28 people and each person has 15 image bounding boxes to be matched each other. Table 4 shows the comparison between the original *LOMO* and the speedup version of *LOMO* regards to feature size and computation time. Because the experiment was evaluated in the same workstation computer, the relative comparison tells us very significant improvement in terms of computation time. 'Rank1 Matching Percentage' implies that the probability of the finding the correct human association at the first ranked result. The proposed descriptor can increase the order of magnitude of the computation speed of the original one with little loss in image association accuracy.

Table 4. Comparison between the original *LOMO* and the speedup version (*LOMO_SPD*).

	Feature size (Feature vector dimension)	Computation time (milliseconds)	Rank1 matching percentage
LOMO	26,960	116.2	90.29%
LOMO_SPD	10,080	0.7	89.67%

Faster Distance Computation Between Image Feature Descriptors

The original *LOMO* used a metric learning-based method (*QDA: Quadratic Determinant Analysis*). It tries to reduce feature vector dimension and learn a metric kernel such that we can minimize the ratio between the inter-covariance and extra-covariance [12]. Authors suggests two kernel computations during the training stage. They first reduce the input vector space by projecting the high dimensional vectors into the *QR* decomposed space. The *QR* decomposition is a decomposition of a matrix into a product where Q is an orthogonal matrix and R is an upper triangular matrix. If the input matrix has n linearly independent columns, then the first n columns of Q form an orthogonal basis for the column space of the matrix. During the kernel learning process, the space projection kernel W is obtained from the first n columns of Q. The number n is decided by the number of the column basis whose eigenvalue is higher or equal to '1.0'. The second leant kernel is a matrix, M, which is a Mahalonobis distance kernel to compute the distance between a feature vector and a distribution of feature vectors.

Given two *LOMO*-Speedup descriptors (1×10080), g, p, first we reduce the vector by applying W to each vector:

$$g \times W = (1 \times 10080) \times (10080 \times 52) = g' (1 \times 52)$$
$$p \times W = (1 \times 10080) \times (10080 \times 52) = p' (1 \times 52)$$

In this approach, we save this vector to compute Mahalonobis Distance (one per each box). The Mahalonobis Distance between g' and p' is computed by applying the learnt kernel M as following:

$$g' \times M \times p'^T = (1 \times 52) \times (52 \times 52) \times (52 \times 1) = (1 \times 1) => \text{distance value}$$

Because we compute the Mahalonobis Distance for every pairs in tracking time, we want to save this computation time by decomposing M through *Cholesky decomposition*:

$M = L \times L^H$ *(when M is positive definite)* ➔ $W \times L = D$

After we apply new kernel D, we can obtain new feature vector g'', p'' as following:

$$g \times D = (1 \times 10080) \times (10080 \times 52) = g''(1 \times 52) ==> \text{we save this vector}$$
$$p \times D = (1 \times 10080) \times (10080 \times 52) = p''(1 \times 52) ==> \text{we save this vector}$$

The main difference between the original *LOMO* distance computation and the speed up version of the *LOMO* with applying the learnt kernel D instead of W is the improvement of the computation time. The original *LOMO* descriptor computes the Mahalonobis distance computation (multiplication of the matrix, M) while the proposed method computes the distance by a Euclidean distance of $|g'' - p''|$, which is much faster than the original computation involving matrix computation of M.

Table 5 shows that the expected computation time for human association during an example of human tracking scenario in a frame. In this scenario, there are previously tracking five human tracks and three newly human detection boxes appeared. Each track has 50 bounding boxes (image descriptors) to compare. The expected computation time is estimated as following:

*(descriptor computation + **projection** (**W**))* $\times$ *(# of new Probs)* +
*(**Mahalonobis distance computation**)* $\times$ *(# of galleries)* $\times$ *(# of descriptors in gallery)* $\times$ *(# of probs)*

As shown in Table 5, the expected computation in this scenario is 162 ms. In order to save the computation time, we propose to compute the decomposition of the two kernels during descriptor computation. This way, we can not only reduce a significant amount of vector dimension to save, but we can also reduce the computation time for distance computation as show in Table 5. New expected computation time is:

*(descriptor computation + **projection** (**D**))* $\times$ *(# of new Probs)* +
*(**Euclidean distance computation**)* $\times$ *(# of galleries)* $\times$ *(# of descriptors in gallery)* $\times$ *(# of probs)*

As shown in Table 5, the new expected computation in the same scenario is now 7.0 ms, which is such a big improvement in the computation time.

Occlusion Reasoning Among Multiple People

To associate new human detection boxes and the existing human target boxes, we apply a human shape mask instead of the entire bounding box region to extract colors more accurately. When there are multiple people in front of the doorbell camera, some people may be occluded by others, which can generate inaccurate *LOMO_SPD* for the occluded human target. The proposed system analyzes the occlusion reasoning test to extract more accurate human shape mask. The occlusion test is done by comparing the foot location of the bounding box (y axis in image). The higher y value means the closer to the doorbell camera, which will be the occluding human.

Table 5. Expected computation time comparison between two different methods.

	LOMO_SPD with W and M	LOMO_SPD with D
Feature size to save (Vector Dim)	52	52
Descriptor computation time (ms)	0.70	0.70
Projection time (W or D) (ms)	0.45	0.35
Expected new detections in frame	3	3
Descriptor distance computation time (ms)	0.061	0.005
Maximum testing gallery size	50	50
Maximum number of tracks	5	5
Total computation time per frame (ms)	161.90	7.08

6 Conclusion

We proposed a real-time person tracking and association method for doorbell cameras. The proposed image descriptor is good fit to run on a doorbell camera because it is not only the smaller size image descriptor, but it also takes a very fast processing time. In addition, we derived a feature projection kernel so that the distance computation time for image descriptors becomes very fast. We have shown the efficiency and speed improvement through the experiments of doorbell surveillance videos.

References

1. Collins, R.T., Liu, Y., Leordeanu, M.: Online selection of discriminative tracking features. IEEE Trans. Pattern Anal. Mach. Intell. **27**(10), 1631–1643 (2005)
2. Possegger, H., Mauthner, T., Bischof, H.: In defense of color-based model-free tracking, CVPR (2015)
3. Bertinetto, L., Valmadre, J., Golodetz, S., Miksik, O., Torr, P.H.S.: Staple: Complementary Learners for Real-Time Tracking, CVP (2016)
4. Nam, H., Han, B.: Learning Multi-domain Convolutional Neural Networks for Visual Tracking, CVPR (2016)
5. Held, D., Thrun, S., Savarese, S.: Learning to Track at 100 FPS with Deep Regression Networks, ECCV (2016)
6. Li, B., Yan, J., Wu, W., Zhu, Z., Hu, X.: High Performance Visual Tracking with Siamese Region Proposal Network, CVPR (2018)
7. Zhu, Z., Wang, Q., Li, B., Wu, W., Yan, J., Hu, W.: Distractor-aware siamese networks for visual object tracking. ECC (2018)
8. Wojke, N., Bewley, A., Paulus, D.: Simple Online and Realtime Tracking with a Deep Association Metric, ICIP (2017)
9. Kalal, Z., Mikolajczyk, K., Matas, J.: Forward-Backward Error: Automatic Detection of Tracking Failures, ICPR (2010)
10. Kristan, M., et al.: A novel performance evaluation methodology for single-target trackers. IEEE Trans. Pattern Anal. Mach. Intell. **99**(11) (2016)

11. Ester, M., et al. (eds.). A density-based algorithm for discovering clusters in large spatial databases with noise. In: Proceedings of the Second International Conference on Knowledge Discovery and Data Mining (KDD-96), pp. 226–231. AAAI Press (1996)
12. Liao, S., Hu, Y., Zhu, X., Li, S.Z.: Person re-identification by Local Maximal Occurrence representation and metric learning, CVPR (2015)
13. Liao, S., Zhao, G., Kellokumpu, V., Pietikainen, M., Li, S.Z.: Modeling pixel process with scale invariant local patterns for background subtraction in complex scenes, CVPR (2010)
14. Kalal, Z., Mikolajczyk, K., Matas, J.: Tracking-learning-detection. IEEE Trans. Pattern Anal. Mach. Intell. 34(7), 1409–1422 (2012)
15. Danelljan, M., Khan, F.S., Felsberg, M., van de Weijer, J.: Adaptive color attributes for real-time visual tracking, CVPR (2014)
16. Babenko, B., Yang, M.-H., Belongie, S.: Visual tracking with online multiple instance learning, CVPR (2009)
17. Lukezic, A., Voj'ir, T., Cehovin Zajc, L., Matas, J., Kristan, M.: Discriminative correlation filter tracker with channel and spatial reliability Int. J. Comput. Vis. 126(8) (2018)
18. Bewley, A., Zongyuan, G., Ramos, F., Upcroft, B.: Simple online and realtime tracking, ICIP (2016)
19. Redmon, J., Farhadi, A.: YOLO9000: better, faster, stronger, CVPR (2017)
20. Redmon, J., Farhadi, A.: YOLOv3: An incremental improvement. arXiv:1804.02767 (2018)

MySnapFoodLog: Culturally Sensitive Food Photo-Logging App for Dietary Biculturalism Studies

Paul Stanik III[1]([✉]), Brendan Tran Morris[1][iD], Reimund Serafica[1][iD], and Kelly Harmon Webber[2]

[1] University of Nevada, Las Vegas, Las Vegas, NV 89154, USA
stanik@unlv.nevada.edu, {brendan.morris,reimund.serafica}@unlv.edu
[2] University of Arkansas, Fayetteville, AR 72701, USA
khwebber@uark.edu

Abstract. It is believed that immigrants to the U.S. have increased rates of chronic diseases due to their adoption of the Western diet. There is a need to better understand the dietary intake of these immigrants. Tracking food consumption can be easily done by using a food app, but there is currently no culturally-appropriate food tracking app that is relatively easy for participants and the research community to use. The MySnapFoodLog app was developed using the cross-platform Flutter framework to track users' food consumption with the goal of using AI to recognize Filipino foods and determine if a meal is healthy or unhealthy. A pilot study demonstrates the feasibility of the app alpha release and the need for further data collection and training to improve the Filipino food recognition system.

Keywords: Food recognition · Food detection · Photo-logging

1 Introduction

U.S. immigrants experience biculturalism which changes the way they live by adopting the Western culture, e.g., beliefs, attire, and diet. This can give rise to dietary biculturalism by incorporating foods from the Western diet along with ethnic foods [20]. U.S. immigrants become at risk for developing chronic diseases by adopting the Western diet, which typically neglects fruits and vegetables and is high in saturated fat and added sugar [6,15]. Based on previous studies, it is believed that the development of chronic diseases in immigrant populations is due to unhealthy Western food consumption [5,17,23]. However, these studies did not give enough attention to the potential unhealthy ethnic foods that immigrants may also be consuming.

In order to better understand eating behaviors, nutritionist and health practitioners have generally relied on food journaling where detailed notes must be recorded at every meal. While the food journals provide necessary records, they are known to only be effective over short periods due to excessive effort

© Springer Nature Switzerland AG 2020
G. Bebis et al. (Eds.): ISVC 2020, LNCS 12510, pp. 470–482, 2020.
https://doi.org/10.1007/978-3-030-64559-5_37

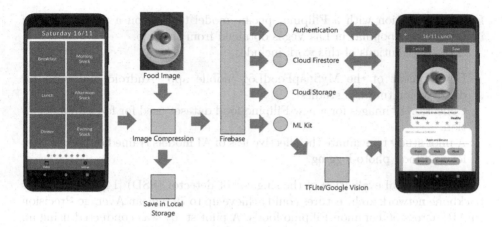

Fig. 1. MySnapFoodLog architecture overview and design diagram

[7,21]. With improved technology, photo-logging has become more popular since it reduces participant efforts and food images have become an integral part of social media. In addition, photo-logging results in more accurate recall when reviewing images. One study found between 10–18% higher caloric intake with images over manually recorded food diary [16]. The photo-logging process itself has shown health benefits – 55% increase in fruit and vegetable consumption with 39% decrease in sweet and chocolate consumption [18].

A photo-logging food app, called MySnapFoodLog, was specifically developed for dietary biculturalism studies (Fig. 1). The app allows users to take pictures of and label their food and presents a daily photo log view for mindfulness. The app is built around a cloud backend to facilitate researcher access to data and in-app export. Beyond improved accessibility with photos, the app was designed to use artificial intelligence (AI) technology to further reduce the barrier of compliance and sustained usage by providing automatic recognition of food items. As a research tool the app functionality needed to include the ability to (1) take and store pictures of food, (2) indicate when the food was eaten, (3) log a description of the food, and (4) easily access the back-end data of the users. AI food recognition was used to save users time when logging description. While many food apps on the market feature some of the required functions, none allow full access of the back-end data.

Further, no existing app is culturally appropriate for dietary biculturalism studies. Food apps are designed for common Western foods and are not able to reliably recognize food of ethnic cultures. This work specifically targets the Filipino American population since they are the second largest subgroup of Asian Americans, one of the fastest growing immigrant populations, the largest Asian population in Nevada, and cardio vascular disease, including hypertension, is disproportionally high among them [8,19,22]. This work develops a culturally-appropriate food tracking app which replaces Google ML Kit's image labeling for food detection with a Filipino specific model trained on a new dataset of images of food popular in Las Vegas obtained from the web.

The contributions of this work include:

- Development of the MySnapFoodLog mobile app (Android and iOS) for dietary biculturalism studies.
- Collection of images for a new Filipino food dataset used for food item detection.
- A pilot study to evaluate the effectiveness of AI models trained on web images for real food photo-logging.

Experimental evaluation of the single-shot detector (SSD) [14] using various backbone network architectures could achieve up to 79.0 mean Average Precision (mAP) across 56 common Filipino foods. A pilot study was conducted using an alpha version of MySnapFoodLog to track Western and Ethnic food consumption as well as healthy vs. unhealthy meals. Food recognition in the real-use scenario was only 31.8 mAP over 31 foods indicating plenty of room for detector improvement.

2   MySnapFoodLog App

The MySnapFoodLog application was designed specifically for use in dietary biculturalism studies to be conducted by researchers at the University of Nevada, Las Vegas. The app was designed to provide a simple interface with minimal effort for a user since food journaling is known to be challenging for sustained usage [7,21]. An overview of the current beta design is presented in Fig. 1 which shows how the application is built around users taking pictures in the app frontend and the backend handles the application authentication, storage, and AI operations.

2.1   Application Frontend

The alpha release of MySnapFoodLog was a native Android app, however, the Android only implementation limited user participation in a pilot study (Sect. 5). A large number of potential participants used iOS devices and had to use a third-party app which did not provide convenient means for recovering user data. To overcome this issue, MySnapFoodLog was completely redesigned for the beta release using Google's Flutter software development kit (SDK) [2] and Dart language for cross platform deployment from a single codebase.

The main page of MySnapFoodLog features a 3 × 2 grid of all the meals logged for a given day, and the six categories of food are Breakfast, Morning Snack, Lunch, Afternoon Snack, Dinner, and Evening Snack (Fig. 2a). This daily food view for mindfulness was inspired by the "See How You Eat" app [10] and avoids calorie counting and emphasizes awareness of food choice.

Users can log food consumption by going to a specified day and tapping on one of the six meal categories which fits best for the food. The user is given the choice of using the device's camera to take a picture of their food or to select a photo from the device's photo gallery. An efficient cache system was designed for performance with picture on the user's device and cloud storage. Images are only downloaded and cached from the cloud if not found on the device. All images are saved to the cloud for easy researcher use even if a user were to delete the images or log entries. Besides native caching, an additional image caching mechanism was implemented for improved performance by storing about a week's worth of images in app memory.

After an image is saved, the user has the opportunity to provide a descriptive food annotation. Generally, this is one reason people do not continue using food logs since annotation takes extra time. MySnapFoodLog uses ML Kit's image labeling services to provide five automatically generated suggestions as buttons for what the application thinks the food is (Fig. 2c). Tapping on one of the buttons fills in the description of the food, saving users time and making it easier to log food consumption. The user can also manually type in the description of the food and make changes to the description at a later time. A health rating system, as seen in Fig. 2c, was also implemented so users could rate how healthy they think their food is out of five stars (with one star representing unhealthy and five stars representing healthy).

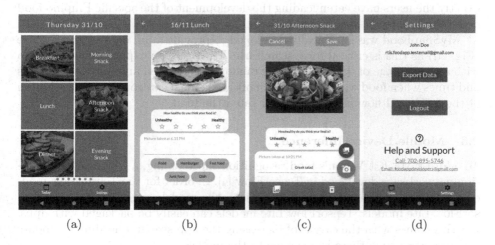

(a)   (b)   (c)   (d)

Fig. 2. MySnapFoodLog Application View. (a) Mindfulness inspired daily meal view. (b) Photo logging page with image of food, and text field to record food name, showing the top-5 results from ML Kit's Image Labeling. (c) Logging page with added star healthy/unhealthy assessment (d) Page for data export tool.

2.2   Application Backend

MySnapFoodLog's backend is managed using Firebase. The application uses Firebase Authentication for sign-in and secure data transfer. Firebase's Cloud Firestore serves as the NoSQL cloud database for the application and Firebase's

Cloud Storage is used to store user images. Both Cloud Firestore and Cloud Storage use Firebase Authentication.

Images are compressed to less than 1MB to efficiently store them in the database and users' devices. Since image compression can be an expensive operation, applications typically use a separate thread for the operation to prevent performance issues of the user interface (UI). However, the Dart is a single threaded language and required the use of Isolates. Isolates are similar to threads, but they do not share memory. They communicate with each other through ports by sending messages [1]. The UI for a typical application in Dart is run on a single isolate, so several are spawned for the image compression operation.

Once an image is compressed and stored, it is processed by Firebase's ML Kit SDK which provides Google's machine learning processes, like Google Cloud Vision API, for mobile applications [3]. MySnapFoodLog uses ML Kit's Vision for object detection and image labeling. The application retrieves the top five results for image labels and provides those results to the user as buttons. ML Kit's Vision is a general purpose image recognition system and not a dedicated food image detector. Typical outputs include "dish," "food," "cuisine," and "ingredient" as suggestions for the user. While these results are accurate in describing the image, they do not precisely describe what the food is as required for health classification. In regards to research use, it is critical to know what exactly the users have eaten leading the development of the specific Filipino food detector.

MySnapFood was specifically developed to provide a full data export feature (Fig. 2d) as this is critical for research use. The user can export/email the data with a given range of dates, the user's randomly generated anonymous ID, dates and times when food was logged, which of the six meal categories, the description of the food, and how healthy the user rated the food.

2.3   Mobile Device Inference

To address ML Kit Vision's food recognition shortcoming, a custom food detection network was developed in TensorFlow [4]. In order for the TensorFlow models to perform inferences on mobile devices, the models were converted to TensorFlow Lite models. TensorFlow Lite models can easily be packaged with apps, but this comes with the caveat of increasing the app size and needing to update the app every time there is a change to the models.

Instead of packaging a food detection model directly with the app, the model can be hosted remotely on ML Kit. ML Kit has the option to host TensorFlow Lite models with a 40 MB size limit. Hosting a model instead of packaging it with the app can eliminate the need for an update of the app when there are changes made to the model. The models that were trained on the Filipino food dataset (Sect. 3) exceeded the 40 MB limit and required quantization to convert floating point model weights to integers to significantly reduce model size. While it is possible to do quantization during training, post-training quatization through TensorFlow Lite conversion was used for ease. The quantization resulted in between 74–85% reduction in model size without significant impact on performance (Table 2).

3   Filipino Food Dataset

A new Filipino food dataset was collected for this project since no other dataset currently exists. Since the use case was for Las Vegas participants, the dataset was localized to the Las Vegas area by collecting images from of Filipino and Asian Fusion restaurants, social media, and review websites.

Fig. 3. Filipino food dataset classes.

The dataset consists of 2887 images and 3723 bounding boxes for food item instances. A total of 56 food classes (Fig. 3) were extracted by requiring greater than 38 total instances of each food item. Only images with popular food were retrieved. Food were considered popular based on number of images uploaded by customers on social media and if the same food was served in different restaurants. Figure 4 gives example images of some of the Filipino food classes. Since the images are taken from restaurant websites and social media, they tend to be of high quality in image resolution/detail, lighting, and framing. Images were collected from restaurant websites (59), the restaurant Yelp account (2455), restaurant reviews on Google (118), Instagram [restaurant account and tagged images] (161), and the restaurant Facebook account (94) where available. The dataset will be made available at http://rtis.oit.unlv.edu/datasets.html.

4   Experimental Evaluation

The Filipino food dataset was split into 90% training and 10% validation for evaluation of the detector performance. Given the small dataset size, data augmentation (e.g., flipping images horizontally, rotating images, image translations) was used to double the effective database size. TensorFlow v1.14.0 was used for transfer learning training of various convolutional neural networks backbones for object detection.

4.1   Network Architectures and Evaluation Criteria

With a relatively small dataset, transfer learning was used to modify pre-trained detection models from the TensorFlow Object Detection API [9]. Faster R-CNN

Fig. 4. Filipino food dataset example images. Top row are professional images while images in the middle two rows come from social media. Bottom row are images with annotated bounding boxes.

with Inception-v2, SSD ResNet-50 v1 FPN, and SSD MobileNet v1 FPN models which were pre-trained on MS COCO [13] were selected for evaluation due to low computation time. Different transfer learning experiments were performed to compare performance of retraining the entire model (full retrain) and freezing the first convolution layer during training (fine-tune). The final model was hosted online in Google Firebase to reduce the binary size of the app and to ensure the most-up-to-date model is always available without requiring app updates from users.

The COCO API [12] performance evaluation metrics are considered for object detection. These metrics evaluated mAP@[0.5:0.95] – the average of mean average precision (mAP) with intersection over union (IOU) thresholds 0.5 to 0.95 by increments of 0.05 – in addition to mAP@0.5 (Pascal VOC metric) and mAP@0.75.

Table 1. Filipino food detection results

Model	Method	$mAP_{50:95}$	mAP_{50}	mAP_{75}
SSD ResNet-50 v1 FPN	Full Retrain	79.0	81.8	81.6
SSD ResNet-50 v1 FPN	Fine-Tune	77.6	79.6	79.6
SSD MobileNet v1 FPN	Full Retrain	74.8	81.8	81.7
SSD MobileNet v1 FPN	Fine-Tune	75.2	83.8	83.7
Faster R-CNN Inception v2	Full Retrain	46.6	63.6	55.7
Faster R-CNN Inception v2	Fine-Tune	41.8	58.6	49.3

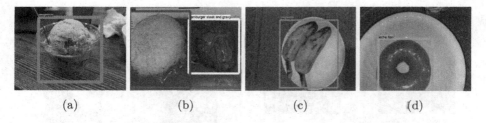

(a)   (b)   (c)   (d)

Fig. 5. Sample Filipino food detections: (a) single well-framed item [buko pandan] (b) multiple items [rice, hamburger steak and gravy], (c) major misclassification [plantain], and (d) misclassification of similar looking food [leche flan]. Note: misclassifications come from foods not part of Filipino training labels.

4.2 Food Detection Results

The full experimental results are compiled in Table 1. Overall, the SSD detectors outperformed the Faster R-CNN architecture by a large margin. The SSD object detector variants achieved mAP in the 70s while Faster R-CNN only in the 40s. Full-retrain performed better than the fine-tune, except for SSD MobileNet, though this likely was a result of overfitting to the small dataset (see pilot results in Sect. 5).

Some sample MobileNet outputs are provided in Fig. 5. (a) and (b) are examples of correctly detected foods which are well framed – large and centered in the single food case or large and well separated in the multiple item. (c) shows misclassified *plantains* since it was not considered as part of the Filipino dataset. (d) is a donut misclassified as the visually similar Filipino dessert *leche flan*.

An in-app comparison between MobileNet (left) and ML Kit's Image Labeling (right) is provided in Fig. 6. ML Kit's Image Labeling does not recognize Filipino staples. It recognizes the *buko pandan* as a type of ice cream dish but completely misses on the *rice* and *hamburger steak and gravy*. Cultural sensitivity – recognizing app users' ethnic food culture – is important as it is believed that it will both reduce effort in food logging and will result in more user satisfaction and prolonged use.

While there is room for improvement, these results show that standard object detection architectures should work well for culturally-appropriate food recognition.

5 Pilot Study

An alpha release, without automated food recognition, of MySnapFoodLog was used in a pilot by Nursing and Nutrition researchers to study acculturation and eating habits of 50 Filipino adults in Las Vegas and to assess the efficacy the photo-logging app [24]. (At the time of the pilot, only an Android version of MySnapFoodLog existed so images were collected using the BiteSnap App [11] for iPhone users). Each participant was instructed to take pictures of their food

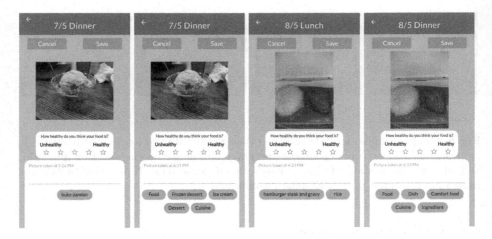

Fig. 6. Results comparison between (left) MobileNet and (right) ML Kit's Image Labeling highlights the need for culturally sensitive app able to recognize Filipino foods.

(breakfast, lunch, dinner, and two snacks) for five days and provided detailed instructions on how to use the app to take pictures. A typical day for each user would include 3–6 recorded pictures which resulted in a total of 980 pictures in the pilot study (examples in Fig. 7). Each participant was also required to meet with the research team after five days for an exit survey.

5.1   Image Collection Overview

The main goal for the pilot was to understand how often Las Vegas Filipinos were eating Western vs. Ethnic foods and healthy vs. unhealthy. Out of 980 pictures, 40% (n = 392) were classified as unhealthy (ethnic) traditional food, and 35% (n = 343) were classified as unhealthy Western food by two independent nutrition coders. The large percentage of unhealthy foods highlights the population risks. A total of 55% (n = 539) of the images were of ethnic food. In the 980 images, there were 138 unique food labels with only 22% overlap with the web-based Filipino training dataset which resulted in 274 pilot test labels.

5.2   Real Filipino Food Recognition

While not part of the original pilot study, the Filipino food detection system was tested on the pilot data to characterize performance in realistic use cases. A summary of results in shown in Table 2. Since the pilot dataset did not contain food item bounding boxes, the detection labels were compared with the image labels without regard for location (considering only recognition).

On real user images, people used the app exclusively for the food study, rather than taking pictures for social media, and there was a significant drop in recognition performance. A 35% confidence threshold was required just to

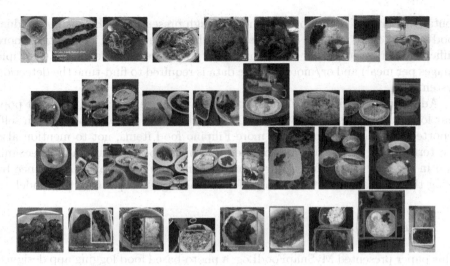

Fig. 7. Filipino foods from pilot study. First row: good images, Second row: poor quality (blurry), Third row: poor framing (too close, too far, too many small items in image), Fourth row: detection bounding boxes.

Table 2. Pilot Filipino food detection results

Model	Confidence		
	35%	50%	75%
SSD ResNet-50 v1 FPN full	29.2	18.4	5.8
SSD ResNet-50 v1 FPN fine-tune	6.99	4.0	1.8
SSD ResNet-50 v1 FPN fine-tune quantized	6.18	4.0	1.8
SSD MobileNet v1 FPN full	28.2	15.7	4.8
SSD MobileNet v1 FPN fine-tune	32.2	19.9	6.2
SSD MobileNet v1 FPN fine-tune quantized	32.1	20.6	6.1

have reasonable recognition rate. Interestingly, MobileNet performed better than ResNet on the real pilot images unlike the training dataset. The ResNet fine-tune was by far the worst despite being the top performer in the Filipino food dataset validation for mAP@[0.5:0.95]. Even though participants received some training on how to use the app, the quality of images from pilot participants were often poor for recognition (Fig. 7). Images were blurry and out of focus (second row), too-close or too-far, or had too many plates in a single image which resulted in small food items (third row). The fourth row shows bounding boxes which highlights how detected foods were generally large in size.

It is important to note that the Filipino training dataset contains images retrieved from social media, restaurant reviews, and restaurant websites with single food item professionally plated pr prominently displayed in the center of the image. Pilot food was mostly homemade (or left-overs), stored in plastic containers, or plated with other dishes in rough presentation. Here an individual food item did not occupy a large area in the image making recognition more difficult. Users need further education in how to take reasonable images (multiple images per meal) and or/more realistic data is required to find-tune the detection system.

Additionally, while the Filipino food training dataset retrieved the most popular local food items, there was only 22% overlap with the pilot population self-reported labels. There are many more Filipino food items, not to mention also Western items, that should be considered in-order to make automated recognition in the wild successful. Future work will improve detection performance by using the natural pilot study images for re-training and updating the model.

6   Conclusion

This paper presented MySnapFoodLog, a photo-based food logging app designed specifically for research into the phenomena of dietary biculturalism. The app was designed to provide users a simple interface to log eating habits by snapping a photo of a meal and labeling the contents without complicated details. The app is built on Google's Flutter framework for cross platform (Android and iOS) deployment and utilizes Google Firebase to archive data for researcher use. The app facilitates longer-term usage by using the ML Kit's Image Labeling to automatically recognize the food content in images to minimize user logging effort. Pilot testing demonstrated the feasibility of culturally sensitive food recognition yet highlighted the need for additional large scale testing to handle the diversity of food items and realistic food images of poorer quality.

Acknowledgment. Student pilot data coders Denise Warner, Tanya Cooper, and Natasha Lishing. Alpha release developers Aditya Rajuladevi, Jenny Yao, Yuria Mann, and Xinyu Wang.

References

1. Isolate class - dart:isolate class - Dart API, November 2019. https://api.dartlang.org/stable/2.6.1/dart-isolate/Isolate-class.html
2. Technical overview - Flutter, November 2019. https://flutter.dev/docs/resources/technical-overview
3. ML Kit for Firebase, July 2020. https://firebase.google.com/docs/ml-kit
4. TensorFlow, July 2020. https://www.tensorflow.org/
5. Azar, K.M.J., Chen, E., Holland, A.T., Palaniappan, L.P.: Festival foods in the immigrant diet. J. Immigrant Minority Health **15**(5), 953–960 (2013). https://doi.org/10.1007/s10903-012-9705-4
6. Brug, J., Glanz, K., Kok, G.: The relationship between self-efficacy, attitudes, intake compared to others, consumption, and stages of change related to fruit and vegetables. Am. J. Health Promotion **12**(1), 25–30 (1997). https://doi.org/10.4278/0890-1171-12.1.25, pMID: 10170431

7. Cordeiro, F., et al.: Barriers and negative nudges: exploring challenges in food journaling. In: Proceedings of ACM Conference on Human Factors in Computing Systems, pp. 1159–1162. ACM, Seoul, Republic of Korea, April 2015. https://doi.org/10.1145/2702123.2702155

8. Dela Cruz, F.A., Galang, C.B.: The illness beliefs, perceptions, and practices of Filipino Americans with hypertension. J. Am. Acad. Nurse Practitioners 20(3), 118–127 (2008). https://doi.org/10.1111/j.1745-7599.2007.00301.x

9. Huang, J., et al.: Speed/accuracy trade-offs for modern convolutional object detectors. In: 2017 IEEE Conference on Computer Vision and Pattern Recognition (CVPR), pp. 3296–3297, July 2017. https://doi.org/10.1109/CVPR.2017.351

10. Karlsson, M.: Simple app for balanced eating — see how you eat coach 80/20 diet rule app, November 2019. https://seehowyoueat.com/

11. Karlsson, M.: Bitesnap - photo food journal, June 2020. https://getbitesnap.com/

12. Lin, T.Y., Dollar, P.: MS COCO API (2016). https://github.com/pdollar/coco

13. Lin, T., et al.: Microsoft COCO: common objects in context. CoRR abs/1405.0312 (2014). http://arxiv.org/abs/1405.0312

14. Liu, W., et al.: SSD: single shot multibox detector. In: Leibe, B., Matas, J., Sebe, N., Welling, M. (eds.) ECCV 2016. LNCS, vol. 9905, pp. 21–37. Springer, Cham (2016). https://doi.org/10.1007/978-3-319-46448-0_2

15. Mummah, S.A., Mathur, M., King, A.C., Gardner, C.D., Sutton, S.: Mobile technology for vegetable consumption: a randomized controlled pilot study in overweight adults. JMIR mHealth uHealth 4(2), e51 (2016). https://doi.org/10.2196/mhealth.5146, http://mhealth.jmir.org/2016/2/e51/

16. O'Loughlin, G., et al.: Using a wearable camera to increase the accuracy of dietary analysis. Am. J. Preventive Med. 44(3), 297–301 (2013). https://doi.org/10.1016/j.amepre.2012.11.007, http://www.sciencedirect.com/science/article/pii/S074937971200863X

17. Rothman, A.J., Sheeran, P., Wood, W.: Reflective and automatic processes in the initiation and maintenance of dietary change. Ann. Behav. Med. 38(suppl_1), s4–s17 (2009). https://doi.org/10.1007/s12160-009-9118-3

18. Salmenius-Suominen, H., Lehtovirta, M., Vepsäläinen, H., Konttinen, H., Erkkola, M.: Visual food diary for social support, dietary changes and weight loss. iproc 2(1), e38 (2016). https://doi.org/10.2196/iproc.6135, http://www.iproc.org/2016/1/e38/

19. Serafica, R., Angosta, A.D.: Acculturation and changes in body mass index, waist circumference, and waist-hip ratio among Filipino Americans with hypertension. J. Am. Soc. Hypertension 10(9), 733–740 (2016). https://doi.org/10.1016/j.jash.2016.07.002, http://www.sciencedirect.com/science/article/pii/S1933171116304430

20. Serafica, R., Knurick, J., Morris, B.T.: Concept analysis of dietary biculturalism in Filipino immigrants within the context of cardiovascular risk. Nursing Forum 53(2), 241–247 (2018). https://doi.org/10.1111/nuf.12232, https://onlinelibrary.wiley.com/doi/abs/10.1111/nuf.12232

21. Serafica, R., Lukkahatai, N., Morris, B.T., Webber, K.: The use of social media and mEMA technology in comparing compliance rate among users. Asian/Pacific Island Nurs. J. 3(4) (2019). https://doi.org/10.31372/20180304.1019, https://dx.doi.org/10.31372%2F20180304.1019

22. Serafica, R.C., Lane, S.H., Ceria-Ulep, C.D.: Dietary acculturation and predictors of anthropometric indicators among Filipino Americans. SAGE Open 3(3) (2013). https://doi.org/10.1177/2158244013495543

23. Sodjinou, R., Agueh, V., Fayomi, B., Delisle, H.: Dietary patterns of urban adults in Benin: relationship with overall diet quality and socio-demographic characteristics. Eur. J. Clin. Nutr. **63**, 222–228 (2009). https://doi.org/10.1038/sj.ejcn.1602906
24. Webber, K., Serafica, R., Morris, B., Warner, D., Cooper, T.: Dietary habits and chronic disease risk of Filipino immigrants in Las Vegas, NV. In: Annual Meeting of The Obesity Society. Las Vegas, NV (Nov 2019), poster

Hand Gesture Recognition Based on the Fusion of Visual and Touch Sensing Data

F. T. Timbane, S. Du[✉], and R. Aylward

Department of Electrical Engineering, Tshwane University of Technology,
Gauteng, Pretoria, South Africa
203900783@tut4life.ac.za, dushengzhi@gmail.com,
AylwardRC@tut.ac.za

Abstract. The use of computers has evolved so rapidly that our daily lives revolve around it. With the advancement of computer science and technology, the interaction between humans and computers is not limited to mice and keyboards. The whole-body interaction is the trend supported by the newest techniques. Hand gesture becomes more and more common, however, is challenged by lighting conditions, limited hand movements, and the occlusion of the hand images. The objective of this paper is to reduce those challenges by fusing vision and touch sensing data to accommodate the requirements of advanced human-computer interaction. In the development of this system, vision and touchpad sensing data were used to detect the fingertips using machine learning. The fingertips detection results were fused by a K-nearest neighbor classifier to form the proposed hybrid hand gesture recognition system. The classifier is then trained to classify four hand gestures. The classifier was tested in three different scenarios with static, slow motion, and fast movement of the hand. The overall performance of the system on both static and slow-moving hand are 100% precision for both training and testing sets, and 0% false-positive rate. In the fast-moving hand scenario, the system got a 95.25% accuracy, 94.59% precision, 96% recall, and 5.41% false-positive rate. Finally, using the proposed classifier, a real-time, simple, accurate, reliable, and cost-effective system was realised to control the Windows media player. The outcome of fusing the two input sensors offered better precision and recall performance of the system.

Keywords: Static hand gesture · Hybrid hand gesture recognition · Human-computer interface · Human-machine interface · Touchpad

1 Introduction

Computers have evolved rapidly and are used to connect people around the world. Individuals, organisations, industries, and schools relies on computers to function in terms of communications, to provide services, production, and education. In many ways, it has become an integral part of our lives; in fact, people can undeniably use them to do almost anything they want to do. In the past, the only way one could interact with a computer

© Springer Nature Switzerland AG 2020
G. Bebis et al. (Eds.): ISVC 2020, LNCS 12510, pp. 483–493, 2020.
https://doi.org/10.1007/978-3-030-64559-5_38

was using devices such mouse, keyboard, and joystick [1]. With the development of technology and computer vision, those traditional computer interactions are no longer satisfactory for applications such as interactive games and virtual reality. Much research has been conducted on how humans can interact with computers. Hence, Human-Computer Interaction (HCI) has become a trend of technological evolution towards making life more convenient and easier.

Gesture recognition is one of the approaches employed to focus on accommodating the advanced application of HCI. Also, in circumstances where a person's hands cannot touch, such as in a medical environment, in the industry where there is too much noise, or when giving commands in a military operation, gesture recognition is a solution that can be applied [2, 3]. Gesture recognition became one of the very important fields of research for HCI. It provides the basis for recognising the body, head, and hand movement or posture, and facial expression. This research study mainly focused on hand gesture recognition. Hand gestures offer a means to expressively interact between people using hand postures and dynamic hand movements for communication [4, 5]. Hand gesture recognition is popularly applied to the recognition of sign language [6].

There are various technologies for hand gesture recognition such as vision-based [7] and instrument-based hand gesture recognition [8]. A vision-based hand gesture has been the most common and natural way for people to interact and communicate with one another [9]. Vision-based hand gesture recognition is one of the most challenging tasks in computer vision and pattern recognition. It uses image acquisition, image segmentation, feature extraction, and classification methodology to give the machine the ability to detect and recognise human gestures to convey certain information and to control devices [10]. There are different types of vision-based approaches such as the 3D model, the colour glove, and appearance-based hand gesture recognition [9].

The existing vision-based hand gesture recognition systems have inherent challenges such as lighting conditions, and occlusion, which limit the reliability and accuracy of the systems [11]. The instrument-based approach is the only technology that satisfies the advanced requirements of a hand gesture system [12]. However, this method consists of sensors attached to the glove, which convert the flexion of the fingers into an electrical signal for the determination of the hand gesture. There are several disadvantages that render this technology unpopular. The main concerns include the loss of the naturalness when sensors cables are attached to the hand, rendering it inconvenient, a lot of hardware required, and costly.

The above-mentioned information motivated us to also play a part in solving the challenges faced by the existing vision-based hand gesture recognition. This research aims to design and implement a real-time vision-based hand gesture recognition, by fusing vision and the touch sensing data with the hope of achieving a low cost, accurate and reliable system. The two approaches were developed and tested separately, then combined to realise the proposed system. A machine-learning algorithm was used to train and test the system. Four (Play, Pause, Continue, and Stop) gestures were trained to control a Windows media player for demonstration purposes. The outcome of fusing the two input sensors offered a better precision and recall performance of the hand gesture recognition system.

This system can be very helpful to physically impaired people because they can define gestures and train them according to their needs. The hand gesture recognition system can also improve the HMI to the joystick dependent system to allow people who cannot grab with their hands to be able to operate those systems. Furthermore, the system can also use only the touchpad to recognise gestures during bad lighting conditions or occlusion on the vision side.

2 Related Works

2.1 Hand Gesture Recognition Systems

Parul et al. [13] got 82% of success by using three axial accelerometers to monitor the orientation of the hand. The results are displayed in an application that also converts text to speech to enable those who cannot see or hear. Rikem et al. [14] presented the Micro-Electromechanical System (MEMS) accelerometer-based embedded system for gesture recognition. The overall recognition rate for both modes was 98.5%.

Rohit et al. [15] proposed a data glove-based system to interpret hand gestures for disabled people and to convert those gestures to a meaningful message displayed them on a screen. The approach used IR sensors attached to the glove to translate finger and hand movements to words. Kammari et al. [16] proposed a gesture recognition system using a surface electromyography sensor. The results suggest that the system responds to every gesture on the mobile phone within 300 ms, with an average user-dependent testing accuracy of 95.0% and in user-independent testing 89%. The instrument-based gesture recognition system is one of the best approaches that produce good results on hand gesture recognition. However, the sensors that are used in this approach offer some drawbacks; such as computational expensive, costly, and the wearing of sensors makes people lose their naturalness.

Gotkar et al. [17] designed a dynamic hand gesture recognition for Indian Sign Language (ISL) words to accommodate hearing-impaired people. The results indicated an average accuracy of 89.25%. Laskar et al. [18] proposed the stereo vision-based hand gesture recognition under the 3D environment to recognise the forward and backward movement of the hand as well as the 0-9 Arabic numerals. The results indicated that an average accuracy of 88% of the proposed method for detecting Arabic numerals and forward/backward movements.

2.2 Classifiers for Hand Gesture Recognition

Shroffe et al. [19] presented a hand gesture recognition technique based on electromyography (EMG) signals to classify pre-defined gestures using the artificial neural network (ANN) as the classifier. The average success rate of the overall training was found to be 83.5%. Sharmar et al. [20] developed the handwritten digit recognition based on the neural network to control examination scores in the paper-based test. The proposed method based on the neural network yielded about 90% accuracy of the results. Chethenas et al. [21] presented the design of a static gesture recognition system using a vision-based approach to recognise hand gestures in real-time. The approach followed three stages:

image acquisition, feature extraction, and recognition. The K-curvature algorithm is applied to the proposed system.

Senthamizh et al. [22] presented a real-time human face detection and face recognition. The approach implements the Haar Cascade algorithm for recognition, which was organised by an OpenCV using Python language. The results indicated that 90% to 98% of the recognition rate was achieved. The results varied because of distance, camera resolution, and lighting conditions.

Goel et al. [23] conducted a comparison study of KNN and SVM algorithms. The system recognises 26 letters of the alphabet. It was shown that the KNN classifies data based on the distance metrics, while the SVM needs a proper training stage. The KNN and SVM are used as multi-class classifiers in which binary data belonging to either class is segregated. The comparison results for the two classifiers are shown in Table 1.

Table 1. Comparison between SVM and KNN [22]

Classifier	Training set	Test set	Accuracy rate (%)
SVM	10 000	10 000	98.9
KNN	10 000	10 000	96.47

The results and observations, however, indicate that the SVM is more reliable than the KNN. However, the KNN is less computational than the SVM.

3   Methodology

This section describes the approaches and procedures that are followed to develop and test the prototype. The approach followed by the stages is depicted in Fig. 1.

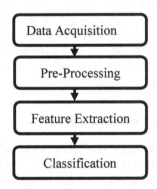

Fig. 1. Flow diagram of hand gesture approach

Data acquisition enables the acquisition of images or video frames from a webcam into MATLAB. In this system, a Logitech webcam is used to capture 2D images and save them in jpg format.

Pre-processing can be defined as the method to eliminate the unnecessary elements of noise in an image. The primary objective of the pre-processing procedure is to transform data into a form that can be more effectively and easily processed by the stages that follows.

The extraction of features is a stage after pre-processing where the success of the gesture recognition system depends on it. The feature extraction stage gives the gesture recognition system the most effective features. An image analysis feature extraction element seeks to identify the inherent features or characteristics of objects found within an image. Upon extracting the correct features from the image and choosing a suitable data set, a machine learning technique can be used to identify the gesture.

Classification is the mechanism of discrimination between different classes. KNN algorithm is used on our proposed system to train and classify different gestures. The KNN method is illustrated in Fig. 2.

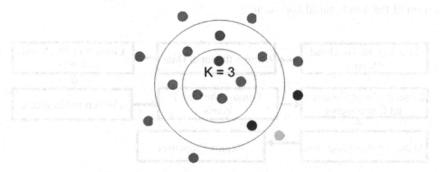

Fig. 2. KNN classification

3.1 Vision-Based Approach

A vision-based hand gesture recognition approach consists of one or more cameras to capture gestures that are then interpreted by a computer using vision techniques. The detailed method of the proposed vision-based system is shown in Fig. 3.

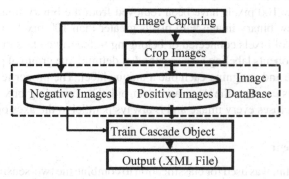

Fig. 3. Flow diagram of vision based approach

The images are captured using an 8 Megapixel Logitech USB webcam. All images containing the ROI (positive images) with different angles and sizes were cropped to form a positive image database. The image database consists of a positive image folder with cropped images and a negative image folder, where 8 000 positive cropped images are stored in the positive image folder and 20 000 negative images are stored in a negative image folder. TrainCascadeObjectDetector is a MATLAB function that is used to train the object detector. An object detection algorithm typically takes a raw image as an input and outputs the most important features in the form of an XML file.

3.2 Touch-Based Approach

This approach follows the mathematical morphology for image segmentation for recognising the touched surface. The analysis of image characteristics and the detection of the touched areas will be done using the morphological method. Figure 4 shows the flow diagram of the touch-based approach.

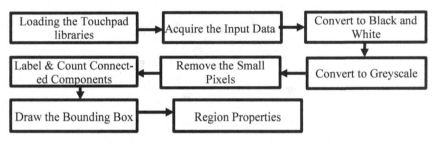

Fig. 4. Flow diagram of touch-based approach

The first step of processing data using the touchpad with MATLAB is to import the touchpad necessary libraries into the MATLAB directory, as well as establish communication between the touchpad and MATLAB. Image acquisition in this situation is the process of applying a touch to the touchpad and output the image in a matrix format. When the image is converted to greyscale, the low-intensity values in an image are displayed as black, whereas the high-intensity values will be displayed as white. The intensity of black and white or binary ranges from 0 to 1. All connected components with pixels below 100 pixels have been removed from the binary image in this study, producing the new binary image with pixels greater than 100 pixels. Connected components are a set of pixels connected or belonging to the same class in a binary image. Connected components labeling is the method of defining the group of pixels connected in a binary image and assigning each one a unique label. The properties that have been considered in this case are the Area and Centroid. The bounding box is an imaginary rectangle that encloses every image and is always parallel to the axes on its sides.

3.3 Fused System

The KNN algorithm was used for classification to combine the two-sensing data. Figure 5 represents the flow diagram of the fused system. The system is divided into phases of training and testing; Sect. 4 discusses the test phase. During the training phase, the two-sensing data will receive gestures simultaneously at the input. The gesture goes through different stages to output two bounding boxes. The two bounding boxes are then connected, trained using the KNN algorithm, and saved as trained samples.

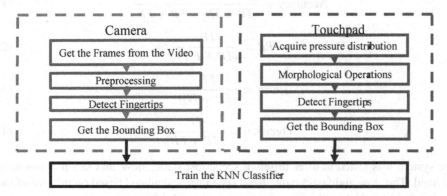

Fig. 5. Flow diagram of the Fused System

The trained samples are saved through a class ID and sample features. Choosing k is one of the most important factors when training the KNN algorithm. The gesture is defined by the number of bounding boxes captured by both sensing data. The class ID is then assigned to the extracted features from each gesture and forms the feature vector. For each gesture, the features are extracted, so that any gesture will have several feature vectors depending on the number of bounding boxes that the gesture has. Therefore, each gesture will have a unique number of feature vectors. In this study, only four gestures were trained as per Fig. 6; therefore, the data set consisted of 400 samples, where each sample had a class of either Play, Pause, Resume, or Stop. Every class had 100 trained samples.

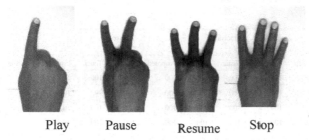

Play   Pause   Resume   Stop

Fig. 6. Controling gestures

4 Results and Analysis

The system was tested to verify the results, where real-time data from both sensing devices as input were applied. The performance of the system was based on its ability to recognize the input gesture correctly [24]. The metric that was used to accomplish this is called the recognition rate. Each gesture recognition result was evaluated based on the following equations:

$$Accuracy = \frac{TP + TN}{(TP + TN + FP + FN)} \tag{1}$$

$$TPR = \frac{TP}{(TP + FN)} \tag{2}$$

$$FPR = \frac{FP}{(FP + TP)} \tag{3}$$

$$Precision = \frac{TP}{(TP + FP)} \tag{4}$$

The system was tested in three different scenarios: static, slow, and fast movement of the hand. The slow and fast-moving hand speed was calculated based on the size of the touchpad (420×310 pixels) since the finger was swiped from one end to another end of the touchpad. The calculations were conducted as follows: During the slow-motion, it took 2 s from one end of the touchpad to another end, resulting in a speed of 210 pixels per second. The movement was about 12.7 pixels between two frames. During the fast motion, it took 1 s from one end of the touchpad to another end, which resulted in a speed of 420 pixels per second. The movement was about 19.3 pixels between frames.

The tests were done on both the individual systems (Vision and Touchpad) and fused system, testing three scenarios: static, slow motion, and fast movement of the hand, using the above-mentioned equations. Table 2 shows the comparative performance on static and slow scenarios for the four gestures on vision, touchpad, and fused gesture recognition systems. Due to the size of the touchpad, only two gestures were checked

Table 2. The Performance comparison of vision, touchpad, and fusion methods

Static

	Accuracy (%)			Precision (%)			TPR recall (%)			FPR (%)		
	Vision	Touch	Proposed	Vision	Touch	Proposed	Vision	Touch	Proposed	Vision	Touch	Proposed
Play	100	100	100	100	100	100	100	100	100	0	0	0
Pause	100	99.94	100	100	100	100	100	99	100	0	0	0
Resume	100	100	100	100	100	100	100	100	100	0	0	0
Stop	100	100	100	100	100	100	100	100	100	0	0	0

Slow motion

	Vision	Touch	Proposed	Vision	Touch	Proposed	Vision	Touch	Proposed	Vision	Touch	Proposed
Play	100	100	100	100	100	100	100	100	100	0	0	0
Pause	100	100	100	100	100	100	100	100	100	0	0	0
Resume	100	100	100	100	100	100	100	100	100	0	0	0
Stop	100	100	100	100	100	100	100	100	100	0	0	0

Fast motion

	Vision	Touch	Proposed	Vision	Touch	Proposed	Vision	Touch	Proposed	Vision	Touch	Proposed
Play	88.5	95.75	96.5	81.30	95.75	96.04	100	90	97	18.75	4.26	3.96
Pause	78.5	91.58	94	73.95	91.58	93.14	88	87	95	26.05	8.42	6.87

on fast scenarios. The findings in the table indicate that in all scenarios all systems performed very well in terms of the accuracies, precisions, recalls, and false-positive rates. It means that since the precision and recall performed so well and balanced, the systems are reliable.

The bar graphs in Fig. 7 shows the average recognition performance on static and slow-moving gesture scenarios for the four gestures on vision, touchpad, and fused systems. For the four movements in three scenarios, the bar graphs represent the average accuracy, precision, recall, and false-positive rate of recognition. For both static and slow-moving gesture scenarios, the vision-based system achieved 100% performance on precision, accuracy, recall, and 0% false-positive rate.

The vision-based system achieved an 83.5% accuracy, 77.63% precision, 94% recall, and 22.8% false-positive rate for the fast-moving gesture scenario. The decrease of the performance for the fast-moving gesture scenario is believed to be related to the poor image quality, for instance, the impact of blurring when objects move fast.

The touch-based system obtained 100% on the accuracy, precision, recall, and 0% on false-positive rates of slow-moving gesture scenarios. For the fast-moving gesture scenario, the touch-based system obtained 95.25% accuracy, 94.59% precision, 96%, recall, and 5.41% false-positive rate performance.

The proposed fusion system achieved 100% performance in both static and slow-moving gesture scenarios on the accuracy, precision, recall, and 0% false-positive rate. In the fast-moving gesture scenario, the proposed system achieved 95.25% accuracy, 94.59% precision, 96% recall, and 5.41% false-positive rate.

It can be seen that all scenarios, all systems performed very well in terms of accuracy, precisions, recalls, and false-positive rates, however, the fused system performs better than the individual systems on the fast-moving gesture. This shows that the fused system has enhanced the performance of vision and touchpad systems.

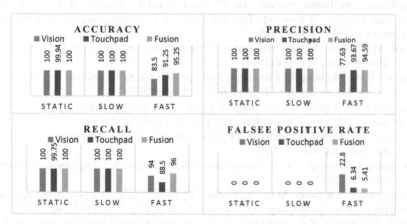

Fig. 7. The average results for vision, touchpad and fused systems

5 Conclusion and Future Work

To overcome the challenges faced by a vision-based hand gesture recognition system, this research developed a prototype for a hybrid hand gesture recognition system by fusing heterogeneous sensing data and video. The objective was achieved by implementing the vision-based method and interpretations of the touch data provided by a touchpad. The system used a KNN classifier to trained and classify four hand gestures to control the Windows media player. The outcome of the fused system offered better precision and recall performance. For future work, more attempts could be made to improve the model. Multiple hands for gesture recognition need to be considered. Furthermore, the method developed in this research will be extended to a dynamic hand gesture recognition which is more acceptable to human operators.

References

1. Shah, N., Patel, J.: Gesture recognition technique: a review. Int. J. Recent Trends Eng. Res. **3**(4), 550–558 (2017)
2. Rao, S., Rajasekhar, C.H.: Password-based gesture controlled robot. Int. J. Eng. Res. Appl. **6**(4), 63–69 (2016)
3. Prabhu, R.R., Sreevidya, R.: Design of robotic arm based on hand gesture control system using wireless sensor networks. Int. Res. J. Eng. Technol. **4**(3), 617–621 (2017)
4. Liu, K., Chen, C., Jafari, R., Kehtarnavaz, N.: Fusion of inertia and depth sensor data for robust hand gesture recognition. IEEE Sens. J. **14**(6), 1898–1903 (2014)
5. Zhang, Q., Lu, J., Wei, H., Zhang, M., Duan, H.: Dynamic hand gesture segmentation method based on unequal-probabilities background difference and improved fcm algorithm. Int. J. Innov. Comput. Inform. Control **11**(5), 1823–1834 (2015)
6. Malik, M., Vishnoi, K.: Gesture recognition technology: a comprehensive review of its application and future prospects. In: 4th International Conference on System Modelling and Advancement in Research Trends College of Computing Science and Information Technology, pp 355 – 361 (2015)
7. Joshi, M., Patil, S.: Vision-based gesture recognition system – a survey. Int. J. Appl. Innov. Eng. Manage. **3**(5), 321–324 (2014)
8. Yuvaraju, M., Priyanka, R.: Flex sensor based gesture control wheelchair for stroke and SCI patients. Int. J. Eng. Sci. Res. Technol. **6**(5), 543–549 (2017)
9. Itkarkar, R.R., Nandy, A.K.: A study of vision-based hand gesture recognition for human machine interface. Int. J. Innov. Res. Adv. Eng. **1**(12), 48–52 (2014)
10. Kumar, S., Balyan, A., Chawla, M.: Object detection and recognition in images. Int. J. Eng. Dev. Res. **5**(4), 1029–1034 (2017)
11. Meshram, A.P., Rojatkar, D.V.: Gesture recognition technology. J. Eng. Technol. Innov. Res. **4**(1), 135–138 (2017)
12. Krishmaraj, N., Kavitha, M.G., Jayasankar, T., Kumar, K.V.: A glove based approach to recognize indian sign language. Int. J. Recent Technol. Eng. **7**(6), 1419–1425 (2019)
13. Parul, W., Sanjana, K.K., Sushmitha, M.A., Suraksha, C.: Sign language recognition using a smart hand device with sensor combination. Int. J. Res. Appl. Sci. Eng. Technol. **6**(4), 4507–4511 (2018)
14. Riken, M., Ponnammal, P.: MEMS accelerometer based 3D mouse and handwritten recognition system. Int. J. Innov. Res. Comput. Commun. Eng. **2**(3), 3333–3339 (2014)

15. Rohit, H.R., Gowthman, S., Sharath, C.A.S.: Hand gesture recognition in real-time using IR sensor. Int. J. Pure Appl. Math. **114**(7), 111–121 (2017)
16. Kammari, R., Basha, S.M.: A hand gesture recognition framework and wearable gesture-based interaction prototype for mobile devices. Int. J. Innov. Technol. **3**(8), 1412–1417 (2015)
17. Ghotkar, A., Vidap, P., Deo, K.: Dynamic hand gesture recognition using hidden markov model by microsoft kinect sensor. Int. J. Comput. Appl. **150**(5), 5–9 (2016)
18. Lskar, M.A., Das, A.J., Talukdar, A.K., Kumar, K.: "Stereo vision-based hand gesture recognition under 3D environment", second international symposium on computer vision and the internet. Procedia Comput. Sci. **58**, 194–201 (2015)
19. Shroffe, E.H.D., Manimegalai, P.: Hand gesture recognition based on EMG signal using ANN. Int. J. Comput. Appl. **3**(2), 31–39 (2013)
20. Sharma, A., Barole, Y., Kerhalkar, K., Prabhu, K.R.: Neural network-based handwritten digit recognition for managing examination score in paper based test. Int. J. Adv. Res. Electric. Electron. Instrum. Eng. **5**(3), 1682–1685 (2016)
21. Chethanas, N.S., Divya, P., Kurian, M.Z.: Static hand gesture recognition system for device control. Int. J. Electric. Electron. Data Commun. **3**(4), 27–29 (2015)
22. Senthamizh, S.R, Sivakumar, D., Sandhya, J.S., Ramya, S., Kanaga, S., Rajs, S.: Face recognition using haar – cascade classifier for criminal identification. Int. J. Recent Technol. Eng. **7**(6S5), 1871–1876 (2019)
23. Goel, A., Mahajan, S.: Comparison: KNN & SVM algorithm. Int. J. Res. Appl. Sci. Eng. Technol. **5**(12), 165–168 (2017)
24. Kaur, J., Kaur, P.: Shape-based object detection in digital images. Int. J. Res. Appl. Sci. Eng. Technol. **5**(12), 332–339 (2017)

Gastrointestinal Tract Anomaly Detection from Endoscopic Videos Using Object Detection Approach

Tejas Chheda[✉], Rithvika Iyer, Soumya Koppaka, and Dhananjay Kalbande

Sardar Patel Institute of Technology, Mumbai, India
{tejas.chheda,rithvika.iyer,soumya.koppaka,drkalbande}@spit.ac.in

Abstract. Endoscopy is a medical procedure used for the imaging and examination of our internal body organs for detecting, visualizing and localising anomalies to facilitate their further treatment. Currently, the medical practitioners expertise is vastly relied upon to analyse these endoscopic videos. This can be a bottleneck in rural areas where specialized medical practitioners are scarce. By learning from and improving upon existing research, the proposed system leverages object detection methods to achieve an automated detection mechanism to provide real-time annotations to assist medical professionals performing endoscopy and provide insights for educational purposes. It works by extracting video frames and processing it using a real-time object detection deep learning model trained on a standard dataset to detect two anomalies namely: Esophagitis and Polyps. The output is in the form of an annotated video. Using Intersection over Union metric (IOU), the model is observed to be performing accurately on the training set but shows a lesser accuracy on the test set of images. This however can be improved using alternate metrics which are more suited to irregular shaped multiclass, multiple object detection and can better explain the observed results.

Keywords: Endoscopic videos · Object detection · Real-time video annotations · Anomaly detection

1 Introduction

Endoscopy is a non-surgical procedure used to investigate a person's gastrointestinal tract. Using an endoscope, an instrument attached to a light and camera, medical practitioners can probe and observe internal tract images on a screen. It is utilized to recognize and detect different ailments like irritations, tumors, polyps, ulcers, and numerous gastrointestinal tract related diseases.

There is a lack of application of object detection methods like You Only Look Once (YOLO) and Regional Convolutional Neural Network (R-CNN) to the domain of endoscopic video analysis, despite having given promising results in other medical domains and object detection in general. A proposed method

© Springer Nature Switzerland AG 2020
G. Bebis et al. (Eds.): ISVC 2020, LNCS 12510, pp. 494–505, 2020.
https://doi.org/10.1007/978-3-030-64559-5_39

should give good results while being computationally less expensive with a lower latency compared to current existing methodologies. It also should not lag when trying to identify numerous classes of anomalies simultaneously. Hence, there is an acute requirement for the use of object detection methods to localise anomalies like esophagitis, polyps, etc. in an endoscopic video to perform analysis. This project has a tremendous social potential, in rural areas specially there is a scarcity of specialized doctors. Thus, this is quite beneficial for medical professionals to annotate and analyse videos not only for endoscopies but in various other medical procedures too. It also can be used as an effective tool for educating medical students and amateurs using visual representation for better understanding thus, increasing its social impact further.

The proposed GI Anomaly Detection System is an automated annotation method for an endoscopic video of the infected gastrointestinal tract in a real-time video using object detection without human intervention. The application uses the YOLO methodology to perform real-time object detection. YOLO object detection method was selected because of it was real time, fast and accurate. The methodology then processes the video to localise anomalies and outputs the annotated video of the same procedure. Anomalies are flagged by passing the video frames to a deep learning model which is trained using a standard dataset. The two anomalies that the system can detect are esophagitis and polyps.

2   Literature Survey

Object detection domain has seen significant progress and improvements in recent years. The scope of this domain extends to various fields where classification and localising of target objects is of critical value especially in real-time applications. The paper [8] explains a hybrid approach for organ detection in real time from X-ray images using faster region-based CNN and regional proposal networks (RPN). It employs a sliding window approach on the input and has lesser processing time.

Certain methods use unsupervised approach for object detection. The paper [6] uses gaussian mixture model and Markov random field (MRF) for performing object localisation. It consists of three steps - spatiotemporal saliency map generation, centroid-based object segmentation and feature learning for object detection.

The paper [14] adopts a methodology to classify every pixel in the image as lesion or background point and localising the defect by locating center of the lesion. After evaluating different deep neural networks the paper establishes that AlbuNet34 is the most accurate as compared to others. Similarly, the paper [17] detects colon cancer and inflammation in colonoscopy videos by texture analysis using kernel filters. It focuses on improving the computation speed and accuracy for real-time application. The paper [4] uses weakly annotated images for detecting and localising gastrointestinal anomalies from endoscopic videos. It performs automatic feature detection using weakly supervised convolutional neural network (WCNN).

There are two types of object detection methods currently being used widely - single stage and two stage modelling approaches. YOLO and Single shot multibox detector (SSD) methodologies are single stage approaches. Given an input image these are trained to output only the object predictions associated with it. They are less accurate in result prediction but are computationally efficient and suited for real-time applications. R-CNN, Fast Regional, Faster Regional and Masked Regional Convolutional Neural Network (MR-CNN) are two stage models. These models predict the object in the first pass and improve on localising the object with more precise boundaries in the second pass. They are more accurate than single stage models but are computationally slower [13].

R-CNN is a convolutional neural network working on feature extraction and classification technique. It employs bounding box approach by iterating the same over the entire input image [3]. These configurations cover all possible regions of the input image and detect objects of various sizes in any region. Owing to this, it generally gives better classification performance however it is computationally expensive and not suited for real-time applications. Hence, improvements to R-CNN - the Fast R-CNN and the Faster R-CNN were proposed with comparable accuracies and reduced inference times [2].

The paper [10] employs the Faster R-CNN approach to detect potentially carcinogenic polyp lesions on endoscopic images. The methodology uses features extracted from VGG-16 architecture of given image, and inputs it to a RPN network that can predict and localise the target objects using bounding boxes. The approach was tested on three datasets of images and had an average F1 score of 0.92 which showed that this approach could be employed for endoscopy video object detection.

YOLO is the most suited approach for object detection in most applications. It finds its usage in the medical sphere as well. It comprises of a single neural network, capable of directly predicting the bounding boxes and class labels of the associated detections. Since it processes given image region-wise using numerous bounding boxes in each region, it is different from other traditional object detection techniques. It is generally assumed to have lower accuracy but being computationally faster, it finds application in most of the real-time detection use cases [12].

The paper [15] employs YOLO for detecting polyps. The methodology works on 7×7 grids and detects 2 bounding boxes for each such grid. The bounding boxes containing the polyp detection are subjected to thresholding operation to remove predictions having low target object detection confidence score. The model is tested from five distinct datasets and the results suggest that model yields accurate results on four of the five datasets in consideration. The resultant F1 score of 0.70 suggests that the methodology can be extended to endoscopic images for performing object detection.

SSD is another kind of network used for object detection. SSD is a single shot approach requiring only single pass to identify the region of object and identify the target object present in the particular region. Since it is not a two shot approach as R-CNN, it requires much less computation resources than other such RPN based approaches with accuracy generally higher or comparable to such approaches [7].

The paper [5] increases the count of feature maps to improve the prediction accuracy of object detection methodology by replacing the VGG-Net convolutional neural network architecture with ResNet architecture. It was noticed at a mean average precision of 79% was achieved at 35 frames per second (FPS) for 300 X 300 input data which has a better performance than SSD .

3 GI Anomaly Detection System

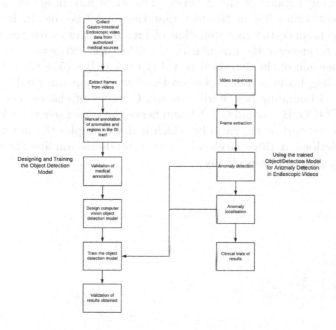

Fig. 1. Methodology diagram for the GI Anomaly Detection System

3.1 Architecture of the Model

In order to develop the Computer Vision model for the object detection task, we decided to train our own implementation of the You Only Look Once (YOLOv3) object detection model. YOLO is a neural network that performs the task of detecting objects in images as well as localising it to a particular region. It creates bounding boxes around the objects detected and has the ability to detect multiple objects in an image. It uses the principle of regression wherein it predicts bounding boxes along with the probability measure of each class in a single pass of the network. This is a big advantage as compared to other object detection models like RCNN which require multiple passes of an image and hence YOLO is approx thousand times faster than an RCNN and approx 100 times faster than a Fast-RCNN. This speed is essential since we require the anomaly detection in realtime. We have leveraged the use of Darknet, a framework to train these neural networks which serves as the fundamental basis for YOLO. We chose YOLO using Darknet framework since this combination is the most powerful in terms of speed and accuracy of results since Darknet is built in C and YOLO runs approx 500 times faster on a GPU as Darknet leverages CUDA. The highlight of the YOLOv3 model specifically is that it conducts object detection at three different scales. YOLO is a Full CNN and the final output is obtained by applying unit two dimensional detection kernels on feature maps of 3 different sizes at 3 non-intersecting regions of the network. The main advantage of detection at three different scales lies in the fact that the model is able to better detect smaller objects since the concatenation of previous layers with the upsampled layers helps to preserve the granularity of the features extracted.

The dimension of the detection kernel is $1 \times 1 \times (B \times (5 + C))$. Where B = No of bounding boxes a unit region on the feature map can predict, 5=object confidence+ 4 bounding box attributes and C = No. of classes. For our model trained on COCO, $B = 3$ and $C = 80$, and hence the kernel size is $1 \times 1 \times 255$. The stride of the network is the ratio by which it downsamples the input. YOLOv3 makes predictions at three levels which work by downsampling the input by a factor of 32, 16 and 8 respectively.

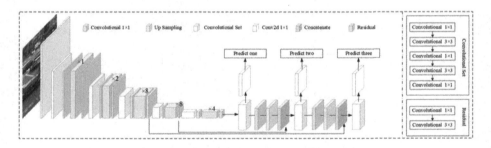

Fig. 2. YOLOv3 architecture of the GI anomaly detection system [9]

3.2　Training the Object Detection Model

This is the most crucial step which determines the ability of our system to accurately detect and localise the anomalies in the gastrointestinal Tract. This can be further subdivided into the following steps:

– Collection of gastrointestinal endoscopic videos and images from authenticated medical sources. This data was accurately analyzed by leading medical experts and the insights were thoroughly understood

- Following the extraction of frames from endoscopic video data, these frames were manually annotated to localise anomalies in the GI tract. These annotations were verified by qualified medical professionals.
- Once we annotate the images we then trained our own weights using Darknet. Our training set consists of 723 esophagitis images and 770 polyps. This training is time intensive but by leveraging the GPU we can speed up the process. As seen in the graphs below, once we reach a stage of minimum loss and relatively static precision and recall, we save the trained weights.

3.3 Developing Accurate Testing Metrics for Evaluating the Performance of the Model

Our model makes use of intersection over union (IOU) metric as a means to evaluate the performance. Intersection over union measures the overlap between the actual boundary and the predicted boundary of the object detected. It uses an IOU threshold to classify the prediction as either a true or false positive. In case of multiple multi-class objects, IOU counts the first occurrence as positive and the rest as negative. However, there are various other metrics for object detection that can give us a more accurate analysis of the predictions.

3.4 Extraction and Annotation of Frames from the Video in Real-Time for Anomaly Detection

Frames are extracted from the video at a rate of 25 frames per second. They are then subjected to background subtraction, resizing to make the image suitable for the object detection model and a spatio-temporal filter. Finally the annotations are generated using the object detection model. The resulting annotated frames are then consolidated into an output video at the same frame rate of 25 frames per second in real-time. One of the key issues we face here include dealing with memory issues for capturing and storing relatively longer videos at high frame rates. In order to tackle this issue for certain videos we also extracted only key frames. Key frames are those which represent a meaningful difference from all other previous frames and capture elements that could potentially be useful for the task of object detection. This helps to solve the issue of insufficient memory for the storage of extracted frames.

4   Results and Discussion

The dataset used for training our system is the Kvasir Dataset which comprises of various landmarks and anomalies pertaining to the gastrointestinal endoscopy video data [11]. Our system was trained on kvasir version 2 dataset having 8 classes with 1000 images each out of which two classes were esophagitis and polyps. Other classes described landmarks and medically operated anomalies which were not relevant to our system.

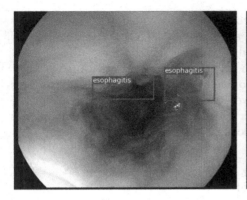 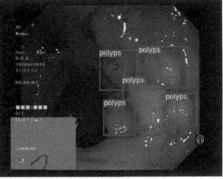

Fig. 3. GI anomaly detection system - esophagitis and polpys detection

The detection results can be seen in the Fig. 3. For our use case, false negatives are more critical failures as compared to false positives. This is because not being able to detect an anomaly possess greater system failure threat than being able to detect normal region as anomaly. Hence biasing model for better recall with comparable precision is a good trade-off to achieve in our system. Although over emphasis on betterment of recall rate could in turn lead to too many false positive detections which should also be avoided.

While tuning our model we consider two parameters - the confidence threshold and the IOU threshold. The confidence threshold inversely affects the false positive detections. By increasing the confidence threshold the recall rate drops considerably. This is because the false positive detections is negatively correlated with the confidence threshold. The false positive detections decreases when confidence threshold increases as the model only makes those detections that have confidence parameter greater than the threshold. By numerous iterations as discussed in Table 1 0.8 was found to be a good threshold for achieving a reasonable trade-off between precision and recall rate with respect to change in confidence threshold.

IOU serves as the metric to determine the true positive detections. By increasing IOU threshold true positive detections shall decrease as model would only consider those detections as true positive whose IOU value with ground truth is greater than this threshold. It serves as the most important metric in evaluating our model as by correctly tuning IOU we are able to drastically wary precision rates that our model shall output. Very high precision could in turn result in lower recall rate and vice-versa, making it important for this parameter to be fine tuned. Table 1 shows the various values of IOU thresholds and their corresponding results. The Fig. 6 shows the variation of precision, recall and F1 score with respect to varying IOU threshold class-wise.

Our training set comprised of 723 esophagitis images and 770 polpys images. The results from training phase are summarized in Table 1. Additionally Fig. 4 shows the loss curve, Fig. 5 shows the precision and the recall curve for the

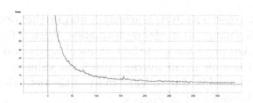

Fig. 4. GI anomaly detection system - training phase loss curve

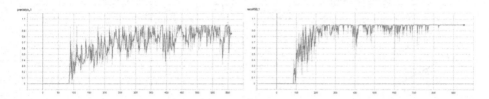

Fig. 5. GI anomaly detection system - training phase - precision and recall curve

training phase. During training phase, the constantly decreasing loss value on every step indicates that model is continuously improving its performance. The increasing precision and recall curves corroborate the same.

Table 1. Training and testing phase - average precision Metrics.

Parameters		Train Set			Test Set		
IOU	Confidence	Esophagitis	Polyps	Model (mAP)	Esophagitis	Polyps	Model (mAP)
0.5	0.001	0.8619	0.9776	0.9198	0.0353	0.7135	0.3744
0.5	0.8	0.8133	0.9677	0.8905	0.0170	0.6248	0.3209
0.5	0.9	0.7771	0.9493	0.8632	0.0168	0.5880	0.3024
0.8	0.8	0.0509	0.3587	0.2048	0.0001	0.0917	0.0459
0.7	0.8	0.3120	0.8104	0.5612	0.0030	0.2995	0.1516
0.6	0.8	0.6356	0.9382	0.7869	0.0084	0.4852	0.2468
0.4	0.8	0.8939	0.9782	0.9360	0.0431	0.6791	0.3611
0.3	0.8	0.9092	0.9815	0.9453	0.0660	0.7044	0.3852
0.2	0.8	0.9129	0.9817	0.9473	0.1115	0.7475	0.4295
0.1	0.8	0.9152	0.9822	0.9487	0.1779	0.7496	0.4638
0.01	0.8	0.9153	0.9814	0.9484	0.2439	0.7517	0.4978

As seen in the train set results in Table 1, the average precision metric for both classes esophagitis and polyps increases continuously with decreasing IOU threshold. It should however be noted at after a certain threshold, the increase in value slows down as compared to earlier. From the table it is evident that by decreasing IOU threshold below 0.4 there is not much significant increase in the average precision values. This denotes that most of the true positives detected by the model are detected once IOU reaches 0.4 and further decreasing this value cannot cause drastic change in model performance. With IOU at 0.4, the model performs with average precision of 0.8939 on esophagitis and 0.9782 on polyps class leading to an overall mean average precision value to be 0.9360. These values indicate that model is able to learn most of the detection and localisation output present in the train set of images.

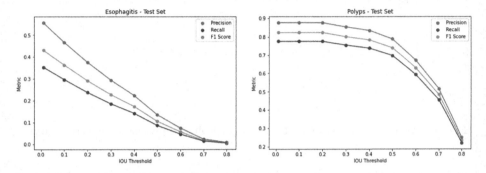

Fig. 6. GI anomaly detection system - esophagitis and polyps test set evaluation curve

Our test set comprised of 181 esophagitis images and 193 polyps images. The results from testing phase are also summarized in Table 1. Additionally Fig. 6 shows the precision, recall and F1 scores for each of the classes in consideration. In the test set, it is observed that the curve in Fig. 6 for esophagitis is concave in nature whereas the curve for polyps is convex in nature. This suggests that for equal increase in IOU threshold the rate of decrease in true positive rate is higher for esophagitis class than the polyps class. It can be inferred from this observation that the true positive detection detections for esophagitis are not as constant as polyps class when change in IOU threshold is made. It is also noticed that for the polyps class, the curve in Fig. 6 remains stable for substantial lower range values of IOU threshold, indicating that true positive detections are high and constant and false negative detections are low and constant in given range which yields greater overall detection rate. These results suggest that the model performs better on polyps class as compared to esophagitis class as is also indicated by the average precision parameter for test set in Table 1.

As seen in the test set results in Table 1, the average precision metric for both classes esophagitis and polyps increases continuously with decreasing IOU threshold. It can be noticed that for IOU 0.3 and lower, there is much less increases in average precision for polyps class indicating that not many more true positive detections are being made even by further decreasing the IOU threshold. However for the esophagitis class, the average precision value constantly increases with decrease in IOU threshold, indicating that even with small change in IOU threshold the number of true positive detections are increasing significantly. On the contrary, the output detections of esophagitis class in turn show much accurate detections. This disparity in observed and mathematical results can be attributed to the complexity of the esophagitis class and the evaluation metric being used. As discussed earlier, esophagitis class consists of irregular protrusions which are difficult to annotate and localise as they would require point-based annotation than a boxed-based annotation method, which is the requirement for using YOLO method itself. Due to this the evaluation result of esophagitis class does not accurately represent the model accuracy on the same using test images with manually checked detections. Using an evaluation metric other than IOU would in this case yield more accurate evaluation results for esophagitis which currently has average precision of 0.1115 for IOU threshold of 0.2. This includes methods like bipartite graph matching, calculating hoover index and other multi-object overlap matching methods which overcome the limitations of IOU in case of irregular objects and multiple detections in the same frame [16]. These were found to be better performance evaluation metrics that were sensitive to the shape, geometry and boundary of the object and produced an evaluation which was consistent with the inspected visual output. Polyps class comprises of regular round-shaped outgrowth which can be effectively annotated using box-based annotation method. The results on this class with 0.7475 average precision for IOU threshold of 0.2 accurately depicts the better performance of model as evident from the manually checked detections on the test set. The test set has a mean average precision of 0.4295 with IOU threshold of 0.2.

Overall it can be inferred that the model performance in train set is high and acceptable as indicated by the mean average precision parameter in Table 1 for both the classes - esophagitis and polyps. Model performance in test set is high for polyps and low for esophagitis, indicating the current model has high variance and is overfitted especially for esophagitis class.

5   Conclusion

The fact an object detection approach could be successfully applied to the specific task of anomaly detection on endoscopy videos makes this approach a new implementation for the same task that was earlier accomplished using image processing techniques with lower accuracy. By this method we can make more accurate detections and obtain better localisation of the anomaly. The results obtained, depicted in the output images also corroborate our assumptions. It should however be noted that the greater detection accuracy on polyps class as compared to esophagitis class can be attributed to the fact that polyps are distinct objects visible to the human eye whereas esophagitis comprises irregular shaped protrusions. Since we evaluate our results based on an IOU metric, getting lower accuracy on this class can be justified by the above reason. In this regard, it can be identified that there exists a need to evaluate such irregular shaped classes better using the same object detection approach. There is scope for improvement in this regard as although the detections are considered valid by human practitioners, its mathematical justification could be made more thorough and representative of ground truth results. The evaluation measure can be made more in tune with the observed annotated images using alternative metrics [1] which can better represent the performance metrics in irregular shaped multi-class object detection approaches.

6 Future Scope

The annotations obtained on the test set indicate that object detection approach yields accurate results on detecting and localising the anomaly in gastrointestinal tract videos. We can extend this approach to accommodate more anomalies and also extend it to other applications of object localisation in videos. Also as discussed earlier, the need for a better evaluation metric than IOU could be developed and tested for application to irregular sized object detection use cases. Such metrics will ease the assessment mechanism of object detection domain in general and lead to better insights into model performance.

References

1. Bernardin, K., Elbs, A., Stiefelhagen, R.: Multiple object tracking performance metrics and evaluation in a smart room environment. In: Proceedings of IEEE International Workshop on Visual Surveillance (2006)
2. Girshick, R.: Fast R-CNN. In: 2015 IEEE International Conference on Computer Vision (ICCV), pp. 1440–1448 (2015). https://doi.org/10.1109/ICCV.2015.169
3. Girshick, R.B., Donahue, J., Darrell, T., Malik, J.: Rich feature hierarchies for accurate object detection and semantic segmentation. CoRR abs/1311.2524 (2013). http://arxiv.org/abs/1311.2524
4. Iakovidis, D.K., Georgakopoulos, S.V., Vasilakakis, M., Koulaouzidis, A., Plagianakos, V.P.: Detecting and locating gastrointestinal anomalies using deep learning and iterative cluster unification. IEEE Trans. Med. Imaging 37(10), 2196–2210 (2018). https://doi.org/10.1109/TMI.2018.2837002
5. Jeong, J., Park, H., Kwak, N.: Enhancement of SSD by concatenating feature maps for object detection (2017)
6. Lin, G., Fan, W.: Unsupervised video object segmentation based on mixture models and saliency detection. Neural Process. Lett. (2019). https://doi.org/10.1007/s11063-019-10110-z
7. Liu, W., et al.: SSD: single shot multibox detector. In: Leibe, B., Matas, J., Sebe, N., Welling, M. (eds.) ECCV 2016. LNCS, vol. 9905, pp. 21–37. Springer, Cham (2016). https://doi.org/10.1007/978-3-319-46448-0_2
8. Mansoor, A., Porras, A.R., Linguraru, M.G.: Region proposal networks with contextual selective attention for real-time organ detection. In: 2019 IEEE 16th International Symposium on Biomedical Imaging (ISBI 2019), pp. 1193–1196, April 2019. https://doi.org/10.1109/ISBI.2019.8759480
9. Mao, Q.C., Sun, H.M., Liu, Y.B., Jia, R.S.: Mini-YOLOv3: real-time object detector for embedded applications. IEEE Access PP, 1 (2019). https://doi.org/10.1109/ACCESS.2019.2941547
10. Mo, X., Tao, K., Wang, Q., Wang, G.: An efficient approach for polyps detection in endoscopic videos based on faster R-CNN (2018)

11. Pogorelov, K., et al.: Efficient disease detection in gastrointestinal videos - global features versus neural networks. Multimedia Tools App. **76**(21), 22493–22525 (2017). https://doi.org/10.1007/s11042-017-4989-y
12. Redmon, J., Divvala, S.K., Girshick, R.B., Farhadi, A.: You only look once: Unified, real-time object detection. CoRR abs/1506.02640 (2015). http://arxiv.org/abs/1506.02640
13. Shetty, J., Jogi, P.S.: Study on different region-based object detection models applied to live video stream and images using deep learning. In: Pandian, D., Fernando, X., Baig, Z., Shi, F. (eds.) ISMAC 2018. LNCVB, vol. 30, pp. 51–60. Springer, Cham (2019). https://doi.org/10.1007/978-3-030-00665-5_6
14. Shvets, A.A., Iglovikov, V.I., Rakhlin, A., Kalinin, A.A.: Angiodysplasia detection and localization using deep convolutional neural networks. In: 2018 17th IEEE International Conference on Machine Learning and Applications (ICMLA), pp. 612–617, December 2018. https://doi.org/10.1109/ICMLA.2018.00098
15. Zheng, Y., et al.: Localisation of colorectal polyps by convolutional neural network features learnt from white light and narrow band endoscopic images of multiple databases. In: 2018 40th Annual International Conference of the IEEE Engineering in Medicine and Biology Society (EMBC), pp. 4142–4145, July 2018. https://doi.org/10.1109/EMBC.2018.8513337
16. Özdemir, B., Aksoy, S., Eckert, S., Pesaresi, M., Ehrlich, D.: Performance measures for object detection evaluation. Pattern Recogn. Lett. **31**, 1128–1137 (2010). https://doi.org/10.1016/j.patrec.2009.10.016
17. Sevo, I., Avramovic, A., Balasingham, I., Elle, O., Bergsland, J., Aabakken, L.: Edge density based automatic detection of inflammation in colonoscopy videos. Comput. Bio. Med. **72**, 138–150 (2016). https://doi.org/10.1016/j.compbiomed.2016.03.017, http://www.sciencedirect.com/science/article/pii/S0010482516300713

A Multimodal High Level Video Segmentation for Content Targeted Online Advertising

Bogdan Mocanu[1,2], Ruxandra Tapu[1,2(✉)], and Titus Zaharia[1]

[1] ARTEMIS Department, Institut Polytechnique de Paris, Télécom SudParis, Laboratoire SAMOVAR, 9 rue Charles Fourier, 91000 Évry, France
{bogdan.mocanu,ruxandra.tapu,titus.zaharia}@telecomsudparis.eu
[2] Telecommunication Department, Faculty of ETTI, University "Politehnica" of Bucharest, Splaiul Independentei 313, 060042 Bucharest, Romania

Abstract. In this paper we introduce a novel advertisement system, dedicated to multimedia documents broadcasted over the Internet. The proposed approach takes into account the consumer's perspective and inserts contextual relevant ads at the level of the scenes boundaries, while reducing the degree of intrusiveness. From the methodological point of view, the major contribution of the paper concerns a temporal video segmentation method into scenes based on a multimodal (visual, audio and semantic) fusion of information. The experimental evaluation, carried out on a large dataset with more than 30 video documents validates the proposed methodology with average F1 scores superior to 85% .

Keywords: Advertisement insertion · Temporal video segmentation · Multimodal video analysis · Story detection

1 Introduction

With the development of broadband Internet access, we have witness the rapid and constantly increasing popularity of the real-time entertainment. According to the Live Video Streaming survey [1] more than 78% of the users consume online video streams at least once a day. In addition, people of ages between 13 and 34 have indicated that the primary types of online video content they watch are full length movies, TV shows and sport videos.

The online video advertising market is fast and continuously growing. The major objective of the advertisements insertion systems is to automatically associate the most relevant ads with video content, such that they appeal the maximum interest of the targeted consumers. In addition, the ads insertion points should be selected in a way that can minimize the related degree of intrusiveness.

Some online multimedia advertisement systems, such as: Google's AdSense [2] or YouTube [3] correlate the ads with the video content based on textual metadata. The ads insertion points are set at a fixed timing (at the beginning or the end of the online video stream). Other strategy, adopted by the TV broadcasters is to place the ads at a fixed

© Springer Nature Switzerland AG 2020
G. Bebis et al. (Eds.): ISVC 2020, LNCS 12510, pp. 506–517, 2020.
https://doi.org/10.1007/978-3-030-64559-5_40

temporal location within the video stream. However, such approaches show quickly its limitation being considered highly invasive.

In this paper, we introduce a novel framework dedicated to advertising insertion in online videos streams. The proposed methodology ensures the ads relevance, while minimizing the degree of intrusiveness. In addition, by adopting a temporal video segmentation strategy into video scenes the ads insertion locations are uniformly distributed along the video timeline.

The major contributions of this work can be summarized as follows:

(1). A novel multimodal video temporal segmentation algorithm into stories. The proposed method jointly combines two channels of information: visual and audio in order to construct semantically correlated clusters of video shots. The major steps of the method involves: video segmentation into shots, shot clustering based on both low and high level (*i.e.*, faces and objects) visual features, shot grouping based on voice pattern analysis and speaker re-identification.

(2). A novel advertisement insertion strategy based on semantic criteria. The ads insertion locations are established using a cost function that takes into consideration the following parameters: the temporal distribution, the ads commercial relevance and the degree of intrusiveness.

The rest of the paper is organized as follows. Section 2 reviews the state of the art literature dedicated to online video advertisement. Section 3 details the proposed ad insertion method. The experimental results are presented in Sect. 4. Finally, Sect. 5 concludes the papers and opens some perspectives of further developments.

2 Related Work

The key objective of any online video advertisement platform is to determine the contextual relationship between the proposed ad and the video content, in order to increase the degree of receptiveness of the consumers, while avoiding intrusiveness.

A first class of methods denoted, textual video advertising approaches, such as AdSense [2] or AdWords [3] rely on matching the textual content of an online video stream with the ad associated metadata. Although such systems are today popular, the methods are usually unable to provide an accurate and complete description over the video document and to perform an efficient matching.

A different family of methods attempt to determine the optimal ads insertion positions based on a semantic analysis of the video content and to insert the ads at the level of the scene boundaries. Within this context, the following part of this section is dedicated to the topic of high level temporal video segmentation for ads positioning.

In [4], the vADeo system is introduced. vADeo propose to segment the video stream into stories by analyzing the multimedia signal (audio and video) in order to extract color/texture histograms and mel-frequency cepstral coefficients at multiple scales. The approach provides robust temporal video segmentation results but is unable to establish any correlation between the ad and the video content.

An advertisement system for online video so-called VideoSense, is proposed in [5]. Three major components are here proposed: a back-end for building the ad keywords from the associated metadata, a multimedia processing that detects the ads insertion points using visual information and a front-end for online matching ads with the detected insertion points.

The AdOn system introduced in [6] divides the video stream in shots and extracts for each shot a key-frame. Then, using the set of key-frames, a video caption is obtained using text detection and OCR algorithms. The ads locations are established using two parameters: the shot temporal length and the motion vectors global magnitude computed at the level of the video shot.

The VideoAder system introduced in [7] is based on content-based object retrieval techniques in order to identify the relevant ads and their potential embedding positions. Different from the VideoSense [5] or AdOn [6] frameworks that rely on the video associated metadata, the VideoAder uses directly the detect products (objects) extracted from the entire video corpus in order to prioritize between various ads. The objects are identified based on the Laplacian of Gaussian [8] and SIFT [9] feature points in an agglomerative clustering context. A similar method adopting an object recognition framework is proposed in [10].

The ActiveAd framework [11] is designed to improve the effectiveness of the advertising by combining online shopping information with online video advertising. With the development of deep convolutional neural networks architectures a human clothing advertisements system is further proposed in [12]. The method includes the following components: video shot segmentation using HOG features [13], human body part detection and alignment using discriminatively trained part-based models and ads selection based on cloth retrieval method. A content targeting video advertisement system has been recently introduced in [14]. The video shot segmentation is performed first. Then, using the video shots, the scenes boundaries are detected and used as candidate locations for the ads insertion. The ads possible locations are ranked based on their relevance by considering the visual similarity obtained between the key-frames extracted from the video shots and from the ads segments.

After reviewing the state-of-the-art the following conclusion can be highlighted: the performance of the video advertisement is highly dependent on the quality of the temporal video segmentation algorithm. Methods based solely on low level visual features fail to accurately determine the scene boundaries, notably in the case of complex videos streams (*e.g.,* for videos containing adjacent scenes with similar visual patterns, but performed by different characters).

In this paper, we propose a novel temporal video segmentation method that jointly exploits a multimodal fusion of information (visual, audio and semantic) in order to perform the video segmentation into scenes. The propose method is able to determine the scene boundaries with a frame-level precision. Moreover, by recognizing the semantic labels of the different objects that are present in the video scenes the system automatically selects correlated, relevant ads.

3 Proposed Approach

Figure 1 presents an overview of the proposed framework, which includes three major components that are: shot boundary detection, video segmentation into stories and advertisement insertion.

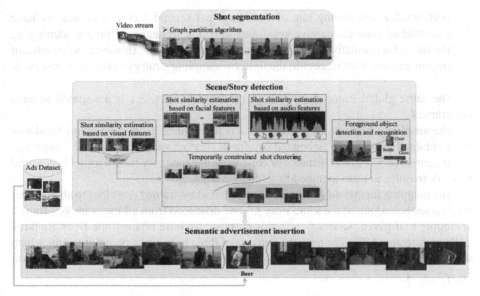

Fig. 1. The proposed advertisement insertion framework

Let us now detail each of the modules involved, by starting with the shot segmentation approach.

3.1 Shot Segmentation

The video segmentation into shots adopts the graph partition strategy introduced in [15]. For each video frame, a global frame descriptor is defined as the direct concatenation of the HSV color histogram with the low level feature vector extracted from the last layer (prior to classification) of the ResNet50 [16] CNN architecture. Here, the weights of the graph are defined as the cosine distance between global frame descriptors (*i.e.,* the video frames represent nodes in the graph spanning structure). The shots boundaries are established with the help of a graph partition algorithm.

3.2 Scene/Story Detection

The video segmentation into stories is based on a multimodal agglomerative clustering technique that jointly exploits visual, audio and semantic (objects) features.

A. **Scene detection based on visual features.** The video shot is characterized by a uniform variation of the visual content and in general its associated frames are highly correlated. In this context, we have decided to represent the shot as a sequence of key-frames selected depending on the visual content variation and on the shot temporal duration. The first key-frame selected is situated one second away after the shot boundary. We have adopted this strategy in order to avoid selecting as key-frames images belonging to gradual transitions. Then, a uniform shot sampling is performed at a sampling rate of one image per second. Let us note that we have also studied content-adaptive key-frame selection strategies, aiming at identifying the most discriminative frames based on color histograms. However, no significant improvements, with respect to the uniform sampling strategy, have been observed.

The same global frame descriptor (f_k) defined in Sect. 3.1 is associated to each key-frame k.

The similarity between two video shots is determined as the maximum similarity score obtained between the associated key-frames feature vectors. Instead of using traditional metrics (*e.g.*, cosines distance or chi-square distance), we train a triplet loss neural network in order to learn a embedding function $d(f)$.

The mapping function $d(\cdot)$ is learned such that a key-frame f_k. is close to all the other key-frames belonging to the same story f_i^+ and distanced from all the other key-frames belonging to different scenes f_j^-. To this purpose, we have retained the Deep Ranking CNN architecture [17]. The network consists of three base network architectures which share the same parameters, each taking as input an image from the triplets of the form $\left(f_k, f_i^+, f_j^-\right)$.

The CNN loss is defined over triplets of features $\left(f_k, f_i^+, f_j^-\right)$ using the Hinge loss:

$$L = \max\left(0, d(f_k) - d(f_i^+)^2 + \left(d(f_k) - d(f_i^+)^2\right)\right),\tag{1}$$

In the testing phase, a similarity score $\sigma(f_k, f_i)$ between pairs of key-frames features (f_k and f_i) is determined. The measure $p_{k,i}$ can be interpreted as the probability of features f_k and f_i to be similar and takes values within the [0, 1] interval. Finally, the *visual similarity VS* between two video shots s_m and s_n is computed as described in the following equation:

$$VS(s_m, s_n) = \max_{\substack{k = 1, \ldots, K(s_m) \\ i = 1, \ldots, K(s_n)}} (\sigma(f_k, f_i)),\tag{2}$$

where $K(s)$ represents the total number of key-frames retained for shot s.

Next, an agglomerative clustering procedure is applied in order to group together video shots satisfying the visual similarity constraint. To this purpose, we first impose a natural constraint: the video shots within a scene to be temporally continuous. Then, we compute the visual similarity only between the video shots situated within a temporal sliding window of 60 s.

Two video shots are clustered into the same story if the *VS* score is above a pre-established threshold (Th_1). In our experiments, the value of Th_1 has been set to 0.9. A high value for the Th_1 parameter will guarantee that all shots assigned to the same cluster are visually similar. However, some video shots will not be assigned to any scene. In order to deal with the remaining shots we introduce an additional analysis, based on global facial features.

B. **Scene detection based on global facial features.** The shot clustering using face descriptors involves the following processes: face detection, multiple face tracking and person re-identification.

The face detection, performed on each frame of the video stream, is based on the Faster R-CNN [18] approach, extended with the Region Proposal Networks [19].

The face tracking is performed using the ATLAS algorithm [20] and extended to the case of multiple moving faces. The face tracking plays an essential role in the person re-identification process, notably when a simple, per-frame face detection and matching approach would fail, such in the case where similar faces are situated in the vicinity of the target one, when the face expression and pose change, or in the presence of abrupt variations in color/lighting conditions.

The face re-identification is based on a global face descriptor $g(F)$ that is able to aggregate, within a video shot, all the face instances belonging to the same character. The global face descriptor is defined as described in Eq. (3):

$$g(F) = \sum_k \alpha_k \cdot v_k, \tag{3}$$

where $\{\alpha_k\}_{k=1}^N$ is a set of real-valued, positive and unitary-normalized weights and v_k is a descriptor associated to each face instance and defined as the activation map of the last layer (before the classification stage) of the VGG16 CNN.

The weights α_k are determined using a learning-based optimization scheme that adaptively computes them, depending on the frame's degree of noise/motion, the face pose or the viewing angle. To this purpose, we have trained the VGG16 CNN with only two categories. The first class contains relevant, frontal, un-blurred and un-occluded face instances, while in the second class we have included noisy/blurred/profile face instances. The CNN will return as output the weight α for each face instance as the probability to belong to the relevant class.

Finally, the *face similarity* FS between two video shots s_m and s_n is computed as described in the following equation:

$$FS(s_m, s_n) = \max_{\substack{i = 1, \ldots, F(s_n) \\ j = 1, \ldots, F(s_m)}} \left(d\big(g(F_i), g(F_j)\big)\right), \tag{4}$$

where $F(s)$ represents the total number of faces detected in the video shot s and $d(\cdot)$ is the cosine distance between the individual face descriptors.

In order to obtain the video scenes, the shots are clustered into groups with the help of the clustering technique presented in Sect. 3.2.A.

Based on the global visual descriptors and on the face descriptors, we obtain two sets of different scenes. In order to combine them, we merge into a single cluster the video scenes from both sets that share at least one common video shot.

C. **Scene detection based on audio features.** The audio module receives as input the video partition into shots and performs an analysis over the audio channel in order to cluster together shots that share similar audio features.

The audio stream, associated to the entire video document, is spitted into smaller audio segments (*audio chunks*) based on the timestamps associated to video shots boundaries. On these audio chunks we apply traditional speech processing techniques, including silence removal, music identification, voice activity detection (with further differentiation into female/male voice) and noise removal [21].

The audio pattern re-identification task is treated as a multi-category classification problem. In this context, the voice audio segments are converted into spectrograms. In order to deal with spectrograms input we used a modified version of the ResNet50 CNN architecture [16]. The CNN is able to cope with variable length audio signals and returns as output a fixed-size descriptor (a_i). Finally, the *audio similarity AS* between two video shots s_m and s_n is computed as described in the following equation:

$$AS(s_n, s_m) = \max_{\substack{i = 1, \ldots, A(s_n) \\ j = 1, \ldots, A(s_m)}} \left(d\left(a_i, a_j \right) \right), \tag{5}$$

where $A(s)$ represents the total number of voice audio segments detected in the video shot s and $d(\cdot)$ is the cosine distance between the audio descriptors.

In order to obtain the audio scenes, the shots are clustered into groups based on the clustering technique presented in Sect. 3.2.A. Finally, the scenes provided by the visual and audio modules are merged into a single cluster if they share at least one common video shot.

D. **Shot clustering using semantic criterions.** For the remaining singular video shots (*i.e.*, not assigned to any scene using the visual and audio descriptors) we construct their semantic representation. To this purpose, on each key-frame of the video shot we apply an object detection and recognition algorithm. In our work, we have used YOLOv3 [22] trained on the COCO [23] dataset. The semantic description a video shot/scene is defined as the union of the semantic labels of the corresponding objects that are detected and recognized in the considered shot/scene.

Singular shots sharing the same objects with temporally adjacent scenes are clustered together. Otherwise, a new scene is formed containing a single video shot.

3.3 Ads Insertion Based on Semantic Criteria

The scenes boundaries represent good candidates as advertisement insertion points. In order to prioritize between various positions, we have considered the following set of parameters:

(1). *The average time length of successive frames (ATL)* – simply defined as the average time duration of two successive scenes S_i and S_{i+1}, normalized by the duration of the entire video. Ideally, the ads locations should be evenly distributed within the video stream. By using the scenes boundaries as potential insertion points this constraint is automatically satisfied due to the intrinsic structure of a multimedia document. The *ATL* parameter is computed for each pair of successive scenes ($ATL_{i, i+1}$) and used in order to privilege the ads insertion between longer scenes.

(2). *The ads commercial relevance (CR)* – a video scene is semantically described by its associated set of recognized objects. Similarly, each advertisement can be semantically described by the list of its associated objects. The ads commercial relevance ($CR_{i,i+1}$) is defined as the number of common objects between the scene S_i and the advertisement k, normalized to the maximum number of common objects that can be found between a scene and an advertisement, over the whole video and over the whole set of ads.

(3). *The ads degree of intrusiveness (DI)* – the degree of intrusiveness is determined based on length of the silence interval computed within each pair of video scenes (S_i, S_{i+1}). The optimal location maximizes the silence length. In order to be consistent with the above parameters, the silence intervals are also normalized.

Based on the *ATL*, *CR* and *DI* parameters a global score is assigned to each pair of two successive video scenes (S_i, S_{i+1}), defined as:

$$Score_{(S_i,S_{i+1})} = ATL_{i,i+1} + CR_{i,i+1} + DI_{i,i+1}, \tag{6}$$

Finally, the scenes boundaries are ranked using the associated scores in decreasing order. The highest values correspond to the most optimal ads insertion locations.

4 Experimental Evaluation

The proposed advertisement insertion framework has been tested on a dataset of 30 movies, with the average duration of 25 min. The videos were selected from the France Télévisions TV series "*Plus belle la vie*" and "*Un si grand soleil*" and from classical Hollywoodian series "*Big Bang Theory*", "*Friends*" and "*Ally McBeal*". The videos are recorded at a resolution of 1024 x 576 pixels, at a frame rate of 25 fps.

The video database is characterized by 9700 shots and 544 video scenes. The groundtruth labels for the scenes boundaries have been obtained manually using a set of five human annotators.

The temporal video segmentation algorithm has been evaluated using traditional objective metrics, such as: the recall (R), the precision (P) and F1 score (F1).

First, we have evaluated the influence each stage involved in the temporal video segmentation framework, has on the overall system performance. We have considered for comparison the following scenarios:

(1). A video segmentation into scenes performed solely based on low level visual descriptors (the visual features extracted from the last layer before the classification of a CNN concatenated with the HSV color histograms);

(2). A video scene segmentation strategy based solely on visual features that jointly combines low level descriptors and facial information (*cf.* Section 3.2.B);

(3). A video scene identification strategy based on a multimodal approach that combines visual and audio features (*cf.* Section 3.2.C);

(4). The semantic video segmentation framework proposed in this paper that combines visual, audio and semantic features (*cf.* Section 3.2.D).

The experimental results obtained are presented in Table 1. The analysis of the experimental results highlights the following observations:

(1). The video segmentation into stories using low-level visual features is useful to cluster highly similar video shots and to extract the core of the video scene. However, for precise boundaries (determined at the frame level) the approach usually shows its limitations.

Table 1. Experimental evaluation of the proposed temporal segmentation method.

Method	Ground Truth	P	R	F1
(1) Video segmentation based on low-level visual descriptors	544	0.37	0.95	0.54
(2) Video segmentation based on low-level and facial features		0.61	0.90	0.73
(3) Video segmentation based on visual and audio features		0.71	0.89	0.78
(4) The semantic video segmentation framework proposed in this paper		**0.82**	**0.89**	**0.85**

(2). The person re-identification strategy improves the system performance (with gains of more than 19% in terms of F1 score). This behavior can be explained by the robustness of the global face descriptor that is invariant to various types of noises, compression artifacts or movement. In addition, the system is able to develop a fix size representation of the human face that is independent to the face track length.

(3). The shot clustering into scenes based on audio features proves to be effective in grouping video shots sharing similar audio patterns. The audio descriptors are useful in merging video shots, for which the visual descriptors usually fail (*e.g.*, for the introduction shots with low visual similarity or when the personages' face is not visible).

(4). The video segmentation method proposed in this paper returns the best results in terms of F1 scores. By adopting a multimodal analysis that combines the visual, audio and semantic information the system is able determine the scene boundaries with a frame-level precision.

In addition to this evaluation, we have compared our temporal video segmentation framework against two state of the art methods, presented in [4] and [14] that propose to insert the ads at the level of the scene boundaries. The parameters involved in various methods have been selected such that to maximize the performance scores. The results obtained are summarized in Table 2.

We can observe that the proposed approach returns the highest scores, with gains in precision and recall of more than 15%. This behavior can be explained by the complexity and robustness of various CNN modules involved as well as by their combination within a unified workflow.

Finally, in Fig. 2 we give some illustrations of the proposed temporal segmentation framework with the different stages involved and the selected ads.

Table 2. Comparative experimental evaluation

Method	P	R	F1
(1) Sengamedu [4]	0.54	0.67	0.59
(2) Wang [14]	0.67	0.72	0.69
(3) Proposed approach	**0.82**	**0.89**	**0.85**

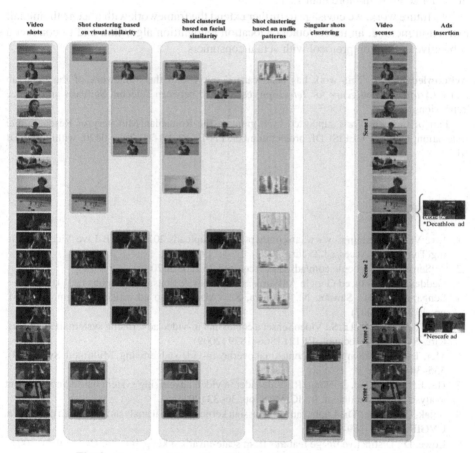

Fig. 2. Experimental results of the ads insertion strategy proposed

5 Conclusion and Perspectives

In this paper we have introduced a novel, content targeted advertisement system dedicated to online video platforms. The proposed framework exploits various CNN architectures in order to identify the optimal insertion points by taking into account the ad temporal distribution, commercial relevance and degree of intrusiveness.

The video scenes boundaries represent good candidates as advertisement insertion locations. In this regard, we have introduced a novel temporal video segmentation framework that jointly exploits a multimodal fusion of information (visual, audio and semantic). The method is able to determine the scene boundaries with a frame-level precision. The experimental evaluation, performed on a set of 30 video documents selected from the France Télévisions TV series and from classical Hollywoodian soap operas, validate the approach with average precision and recall scores superior to 82%. When compared with other state of the art methods [4] and [14] the proposed approach shows an increase in the F1 score with more than 15%.

As future work, we envisage to further extend the framework with a scene thumbnail extraction method, an indoor/outdoor location recognition algorithm and to conduct a subjective evaluation protocol with actual consumers.

Acknowledgement. This work has been carried out within the framework of the joint lab AITV (*Artificial Intelligence for Television*) established between Télécom SudParis and France Télévisions.

Part of this work was supported by a grant of the Romanian Ministery of Research and Innovation, CNCS – UEFISCDI, project number: PN-III-P1-1.1-TE-2019-0420, within PNCDI III.

References

1. Live Video Streaming - www.iab.com/wp-content/uploads/2018/06/IAB-Live-Video-Streaming-Trends.pdf. Accessed 25 June 2020
2. AdSense - www.google.com/adsense. Accessed 25 June 2020
3. Geddes, B.: Advanced Google AdWords. John Wiley & Sons, Indianapolis (2014)
4. Sengamedu, S.H., Sawant, N., Wadhwa, S.: vADeo: video advertising system. In: ICM, pp. 455–456 (2007)
5. Mei, T., Hua, X.S., Li, S.: VideoSense: a contextual in-video advertising system. IEEE Trans. Circ. Syst. Video Technol. **19**(12) 1866–1879 (2009)
6. Mei, T., et al.: AdOn: toward contextual overlay in-video advertising. Multimed. Syst. **16**(4), 335–344 (2010)
7. Hu, J., Li, G., Xiao, J., Hong, R.: Videoader: a video advertising system based on intelligent analysis of visual content. In: ICIMCS, pp. 30–33 (2011)
8. Sotak, G.E., et al.: The Laplacian-of-Gaussian kernel: a formal analysis and design procedure. CVGIP **48**, 147–189 (1989)
9. Lowe, D.: Distinctive image features from scale-invariant keypoints. In: IJCV, **60**(2) (2004)
10. Wang, J., Wang, B., Duan, L., Tian, Q., Lu, H.: Interactive ads recommendation with contextual search on product topic space. Multimed. Tools Appl. **70**(2), 799–820 (2011). https://doi.org/10.1007/s11042-011-0866-2
11. Wang, J., et al.: ActiveAd: a novel framework of linking ad videos to online products. Neurocomput. **185**, 82–92 (2016)
12. Zhang, H., Cao, X., Ho, J.K.L., Chow, T.W.S.: Object-level video advertising: an optimization framework. IEEE TII **13**(2), 520–531 (2017)
13. Dalal, N., Triggs, B.: Histograms of oriented gradients for human detection. In: IEEE CVPR, San Diego, CA, USA, vol. 1, pp. 886–893 (2005)

14. Wang, G., Zhuo, L., Li, J., Ren, D., Zhang, J.: An efficient method of content-targeted online video advertising. JVCIR **50**, 40–48 (2018)
15. Tapu, R., Zaharia, T., Prêteux, F.: A scale-space filtering-based shot detection algorithm. In: 26th Convention of Electrical and Electronics Engineers in Israel, pp. 919–923 (2010)
16. He, K., Zhang, X., Ren, S., Sun, J.: Deep residual learning for image recognition. In: CVPR, Las Vegas, NV, pp. 770-778 (2016)
17. Wang, J., et al.: Learning fine-grained image similarity with deep ranking. In: CVPR, pp. 1386–1393 (2014)
18. Ren, S., He, K., Girshick, R., Sun, J.: Faster R-CNN: towards real- time object detection with region proposal networks. In: NIPS (2015)
19. Jiang, H., Learned-Miller, E.G.: Face detection with the faster R-CNN. In: 12th IEEE International Conference on Automatic Face & Gesture Recognition, pp. 650–657 (2017)
20. Mocanu, B., Tapu, R., Zaharia, T.: Single object tracking using offline trained deep regression networks. In: IPTA, pp. 1–6 (2017)
21. Doukhan, D., et al.: An open-source speaker gender detection framework for monitoring gender equality. In: ICASSP, pp. 5214–5218 (2018)
22. Redmon, J., Farhadi, A.: YOLOv3, An incremental improvement (2018). arXiv:1804.02767
23. Lin, Y., et al.: Microsoft COCO: common objects in context. In: ECCV (2014)

AI Playground: Unreal Engine-Based Data Ablation Tool for Deep Learning

Mehdi Mousavi⑩, Aashis Khanal⑩, and Rolando Estrada⁽✉⁾⑩

Department of Computer Science, Georgia State University, Atlanta, GA 30303, USA
{smousavi2,akhanal1}@student.gsu.com, restrada1@gsu.edu

Abstract. Machine learning requires data, but acquiring and labeling real-world data is challenging, expensive, and time-consuming. More importantly, it is nearly impossible to alter real data post-acquisition (e.g., change the illumination of a room), making it very difficult to measure how specific properties of the data affect performance. In this paper, we present AI Playground (AIP), an open-source, Unreal Engine-based tool for generating and labeling virtual image data. With AIP, it is trivial to capture the same image under different conditions (e.g., fidelity, lighting, etc.) and with different ground truths (e.g., depth or surface normal values). AIP is easily extendable and can be used with or without code. To validate our proposed tool, we generated eight datasets of otherwise identical but varying lighting and fidelity conditions. We then trained deep neural networks to predict (1) depth values, (2) surface normals, or (3) object labels and assessed each network's intra- and cross-dataset performance. Among other insights, we verified that sensitivity to different settings is problem-dependent. We confirmed the findings of other studies that segmentation models are very sensitive to fidelity, but we also found that they are just as sensitive to lighting. In contrast, depth and normal estimation models seem to be less sensitive to fidelity or lighting, and more sensitive to the structure of the image. Finally, we tested our trained depth-estimation networks on two real-world datasets and obtained results comparable to training on real data alone, confirming that our virtual environments are realistic enough for real-world tasks.

Keywords: Synthetic data · Deep learning · Virtual environment

1 Introduction

The remarkable success of deep learning in recent years would not have been possible without large, high-quality datasets [8]. Deep neural networks have thousands or even millions of parameters, which require vast numbers of training examples to tune. However, producing a high-quality dataset of real data is very challenging. First, one has to acquire the raw data, an often laborious task. Second, the training data must either be labeled manually—which is slow, subjective and may require significant expertise—or with expensive, specialized equipment. Finally, errors can occur in both the acquisition and labeling phases.

ⓒ Springer Nature Switzerland AG 2020
G. Bebis et al. (Eds.): ISVC 2020, LNCS 12510, pp. 518–532, 2020.
https://doi.org/10.1007/978-3-030-64559-5_41

Fig. 1. Virtual environments: Sample screenshots from our annotated virtual environments. From left to right: depth, surface normals, and semantic labels

A subtle limitation of real world datasets is its static nature. For instance, once an image has been taken, one cannot change its illumination from day to night or replace one object for another[1]. The best way to achieve these effects is by manipulating the source of the data before acquisition; however, this approach requires a controlled environment and precise measurements. For example, to change the color of a couch one would need to swap out two otherwise identical couches and place them in the same, exact location. Aside from its difficulty, this approach is not feasible for natural scenes or crowd-sourced data.

The above limitation makes it difficult to isolate the impact of individual features on a system's performance. For example, if we want to assess how an object's texture affects our system's ability to segment it, we would need to compare our system's output across different objects and hope that the impact of other features, e.g., lighting or shape, cancels out across the samples. As such, data ablation studies are rare in machine learning. Most ablation analyses add/remove either (1) components of the model [10] or (2) secondary features computed from the data [9]. The latter is close in spirit to data ablation but is more limited, since secondary features are dependent on the raw, unchangeable data.

To address this gap, we developed AI Playground, a user-friendly tool based on the Unreal Engine (Epic Games, USA) [4] that supports data ablation studies in computer vision.[2] Our system allows researchers to easily capture synthetic data from fully customizable virtual environments; this data can then be used to train or test an AI system. Virtual data is free from acquisition errors or labeling bias and is ideal for the data ablation studies discussed above, e.g., capturing the same image under multiple lighting conditions. More importantly, as our experiments confirm, today's high-resolution computer graphics are realistic enough to be used for training deep neural networks on real-world tasks.

---

[1] Photo-manipulation techniques can be used to alter images, but their effects are either non-specific (e.g., reducing brightness) or introduce unwanted artifacts. They also require significant human effort.

[2] Source code, documentation, images, and high-definition figures are available on our GitHub page: https://git.io/JJkhQ.

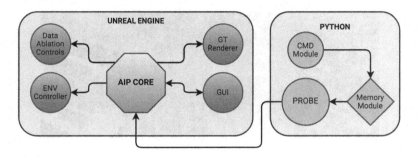

Fig. 2. AI Playground: Our tool has two main modules: the *AIP Core* within UE4 and *Probe*, a Python module that communicates with the Core. Probe receives instructions generated by the Command module, and saves its state in its own dedicated memory. This allows changing settings inside the engine while AIP is running. Manually changing components is also possible via the GUI.

As we detail in Sect. 3, AI Playground is an open-source UE project with four main components: (1) a set of high-resolution environments; (2) multiple ground-truth annotations (e.g., depth, surface normals, etc.); (3) built-in tools for data ablation (e.g., for adjusting lighting, polygon resolution, etc.); and (4) a user-friendly, graphical interface. Users can either run our system as a pre-built application or import it as a regular UE project. In the latter case, users can extend their local version of AIPlayground or copy parts of it (e.g., scripts) to use in their own projects. It is easy to add custom environments or ground-truth annotations without writing any code. We have provided sample code and necessary documentation to enable more data ablation extensions to AIPlayground. Figure 2 provides a flowchart of our tool.

We used AIP to carry out a series of data ablation studies to validate its usefulness. As detailed in Sect. 4, we trained and tested deep networks on (1) monocular depth estimation, (2) surface normal estimation, and (3) semantic segmentation. AIP allowed us to draw novel insights about feature importance (Sect. 5), and we also confirmed that networks trained on depth estimation via AI Playground achieve good performance on real-world datasets.

2   Related Work

Data-hungry models like DCNN (Deep Convolutional Neural Networks) have generated newfound interest in virtual data [5,6,14]. One popular approach is to use modded old video games (e.g., Atari games [11]). However, this approach lacks customizability and photo-realism. This data cannot be customized to fit a more specific problem and using old video games introduces a lack of photo-realism that has been proven beneficial for virtual data[10,18]. In contrast, Veeravasarapu *et al.* [18] used probabilistic generative models to create random environments in Blender (Blender Foundation, The Netherlands) [2]. However, these probabilistic models need to be manually adapted for each type of desired environment. For example, the probabilistic model of an outdoor street scene varies significantly from one of an interior environment. Also, while randomness is useful for quickly creating novel environments, these environments may not be faithful to reality. For example, a random probabilistic model might decide to put a couch on a table, which never happens in the real world. Furthermore, depending on hardware, rendering an image in Blender using ray-tracing can take up to a minute or more; the same level of fidelity can be achieved in game engines in real-time. As mentioned in [18], generating a Path-traced image in Blender takes up to 9 min (547 s), and ray-tracing based rendering for a single image can take 20 s or more.

In another study, researchers used 3D reconstruction to generate a photo-realistic 3D scene that allows limited interaction such as walking around [16]. This method requires expensive equipment and complex calculations to generate the pixel-wise ground-truth for tasks like *depth estimation* and *surface normal estimation*. The generated ground-truth and 3D environment are subject to arti-facts and estimation errors appearing as black spots in the images. Also, these environments are extremely hard to expand as they require costly specialized equipment for measurement.

The work most similar to our proposed system is UnrealCV—an Unreal Engine 4 (UE4) plugin that has been used in a number of research projects. UnrealCV provides an interface to communicate with the Unreal Engine for com-puter vision and robotics research [13]. However, UnrealCV requires command-line-based interaction and C++ coding. As such, it has a high barrier of entry and can be discouraging for computer vision researchers who are unfamiliar with game engines. It also lacks intuitive dials and knobs for dynamic interaction with the environment. More importantly, it is not built for data ablation; any sys-tematic changes in fidelity, lighting, etc. have to be coded from scratch by the researcher.

In contrast, our goal is to reduce the skill level need to obtain virtual pixel-perfect data. Our approach is accessible, user-friendly, and has many intuitive ways to interact with the environment. We use the high quality renderer inte-grated in Unreal Engine to produce lifelike synthetic images, and AIP does not require any knowledge of UE4 programming. As we detail in the following section, our companion Python module (Probe) communicates with the UE4 application to control the environment and take samples while keeping a record of every step for image re-creation.

3   AIPlayground

AIPlayground is a UE4-based tool for data ablation studies in computer vision. Unreal Engine is the engine of choice for video games with high-resolution, real-time 3D graphics. It is free for both commercial and non-commercial use and its source code is publicly available (though not fully open source). As illustrated in Fig. 2, our system has four components: (1) high-resolution 3D environments; (2) multiple ground-truth annotations; (3) data ablation controls; and (4) a

Fig. 3. Sample images captured by Probe. Left to right: brown room day, brown room night, blue room day, blue room night (all high settings) (Colour figure online)

user-friendly, graphical interface. We use Blueprint, Unreal's visual scripting language, for the ground-truth annotations and data ablation controls. We use a separate Python interaction module—Probe—for data collection. The key contributions of AIP are: **1.** Portable data ablation tools for UE4 Environments, **2.** Multimodal, accurate ground-truth generation for visual tasks, and **3.** Python and UE4 interplay for data acquisition.

3.1 Three-Dimensional Environments

In addition to being a game engine, Unreal Engine provides powerful tools for realistic architectural visualization. As such, we developed two environments based on UE4's built-in "Realistic Rendering" scene, dubbed Brown Room and Blue Room in our experiments. Each environment has two general lighting profiles, Day and Night, as illustrated in Fig. 3. To mimic existing real-world datasets, the environments are static (i.e., no movement of the components aside from the probe character). AIP currently uses static (i.e., baked) lighting to illuminate the scene. Baking light-maps is a commonly used method to simulate high-fidelity lighting on lower-capacity hardware. It uses ray-tracing to determine dark and light spots in the scene and paints the textures on those areas to look accordingly. The result is a very realistic environment that is rendered rapidly with little to no extra computation required at run-time. This means AIP supports very high frame-rates, which allow for fast data acquisition. We can switch between different ground-truth annotations in fractions of a second without causing artifacts such as blur, fuzziness on the edges, or motion-blur.

3.2 Ground-Truth Annotations

One of the main advantages of virtual environments is that obtaining ground-truth annotations is trivial relative to real-world environments. Specifically, we use Unreal Blueprint (an internal scripting language) to calculate the ground-truth properties listed below. AIP includes Blueprint scripts for estimating depth, surface normals, and object classes, and can be readily extended by adding additional scripts. We use post-processing shaders, called materials in UE4, to

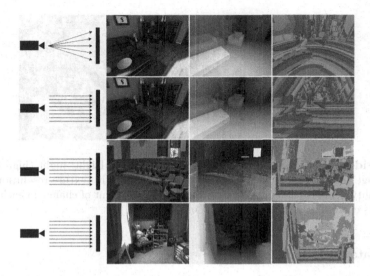

Fig. 4. Depth estimation: AIP uses perspective projection (first row), which is more accurate than orthographic projection (second row). The third column uses color banding to highlight the differences between these two approaches. The bottom rows show examples from the DIODE and NYUv2 datasets. Note the lack of artifacts in the virtual ground truth.

overlay these properties over the image, enabling pixel-perfect alignment between the data and the ground-truth labels (see Fig. 1 for examples).

Depth Estimation: We calculate the normalized distance between each pixel that belongs to a specific object and the camera. We set the real-life range of depth to 10 m, which covers the entire environment and does not clip between any corners of the room. We define the depth using *perspective projection* relative to the viewer's POV, which is significantly more accurate than orthographic methods. In perspective depth, each light ray is traced to the exact pixel from the object its coming from; in orthographic depth, on the other hand, light-rays are assumed to be coming from *infinity* (see Fig. 4). In real-world datasets, e.g., NYUv2 [12] and DIODE [17], depth is registered based on orthographic projection because of physical limitations in the sensor.

Surface Normals: We estimate the normal vector w.r.t to each 3D surface, then color each pixel to indicate the vector's direction. We use 6 main colors to show 6 axis of direction (positive and negative xyz, as shown in Fig. 1).

Semantic Segmentation: In UE4, it is easy to map visible pixels to their corresponding 3D objects. Our Blueprint script uses this mapping to overlay pixel-perfect semantic labels on the various objects in the scene (e.g., couch, table, lamp, etc.).

Fig. 5. Fidelity Comparison: Left: day (high fidelity), Right: night (high fidelity). Each image snippet of low fidelity indicates the difference in texture resolution, reflections quality, render scaling and shadow quality. The amount of change in each of these settings is customizable through AIP's Core.

3.3   Data Ablation Controls

Similar to the ground-truth, we use Blueprint to dynamically alter properties of the environment. We can access and isolate specific properties in different objects. For example, we can isolate metallic objects or rough surfaces with a pixel-perfect binary ground truth. We can also change the fidelity of reflections, lighting, mesh level of detail (LOD), render resolution (either localized to an object or globally), anti-aliasing algorithms (or toggle on and off), or render scaling. Figure 5 illustrates the same scene rendered under different fidelity settings. Our scripts are reusable, in the sense that they do not require adaptation to other environments and are also easily portable to other UE projects.

3.4   User Interface

The AIP Core can be opened as a project in UE4, giving access to all its assets and scripts. Alternatively, we provide a pre-compiled version which can be run as an independent program. AIP has intuitive user menus and keyboard shortcuts. Our Python Probe script uses the latter to collect data (see Sect. 4 for details).

4   Experiments and Results

We carried out multiple experiments to validate the usefulness of our proposed system. Specifically, we tested AIP in two ways. First, we verified its viability as a data ablation tool. As we detail below, we captured the same images under different fidelity and lighting settings (which we refer to as a *scenario*), then trained deep neural networks on each scenario to assess the impact of the various environmental features. We carried out both same- and cross-scenario testing (e.g., a Brown/Day/High network on Brown/Night/High). Table 1 summarizes the scenarios used. For each scenario, we tested our networks on (1) monocular depth and (2) surface normal estimation, as well as (3) semantic segmentation.

Table 1. Scenarios used in experiments[a]

Default maps	Settings		
	Lighting	Fidelity	Anti-Aliasing
Brown room	Day	High	Temporal AA
Brown room	Night	High	Temporal AA
Brown room	Day	Low	Temporal AA
Brown room	Night	Low	Temporal AA
Blue room	Day	High	Temporal AA
Blue room	Night	High	Temporal AA
Blue room	Day	Low	Temporal AA
Blue room	Night	Low	Temporal AA
Abstract shapes	Day	High	Temporal AA
Unlit[b] brown room	N/A	High	Temporal AA
Unlit blue room	N/A	High	Temporal AA

[a]shows settings used, not indicative of all settings available.
[b]diffuse shading.

Fig. 6. Sample results: Sample images, ground truth, and predictions for semantic segmentation (first three columns), depth estimation (middle columns), and surface normal estimation (last three columns). Figure best viewed onscreen.

Second, to validate that our virtual data is realistic enough, we tested networks trained with AIP on real-world depth-estimation datasets, achieving results comparable to training on real data alone. Below, we first detail our experimental setup, then discuss each experiment.

4.1 Experimental Setup

Hardware: We conducted all our experiments in a Dell Precision 7920R server with two Intel Xeon Silver 4110 CPUs, two GeForce GTX 1080 Ti graphics cards, and 128 GBs of RAM.

Image Acquisition: Our Probe script can control the viewpoint by simulating keystrokes. It can move and look freely (yaw and pitch) in the environment. Probe can also send specific commands and can gather images with high overlap (in groups) or low overlap (completely random). Probe's step size, look sensitivity, randomness of image acquisition (group capture), and number of images to gather are all customizable and can be saved for reproduction across all different scenarios. For our depth estimation experiments, we randomly collected 8265, 640×480 synthetic color images. We collected the same images, by replicating the same camera positions and rotations, across different lighting and fidelity scenarios (Table 2). We split these images into 80% for training, and 20% for testing. Similarly, for semantic segmentation and surface normal estimation, we gathered 3000 images for each scenario and split in the same ratio.

Deep Neural Networks: We used a encoder-decoder architecture, and loss function from [12] for depth estimation, and an implementation of U-net [15] from [7] for surface normal estimation and semantic segmentation. We use smooth L1 loss function for Surface Normal Estimation, and Cross-Entropy loss for segmentation task. We use a *mini-batch size* of 16, *learning rate* of 0.001, and trained for 51 *epochs* for all experiments.

Table 2. Depth estimation: Data ablation test results. Metrics are threshold accuracy ($\delta_i < 1.25^i$), average relative error (REL), root mean squared error (RMS), and average (log10) error. Arrows indicate if higher or lower values are better. For space, we included only some of the conducted experiments; results shown are indicative of the behavior of the trained models in other scenarios. **SC:** Sanity Check. **L:** Change in lighting. **M:** Change in maps. **F:** Positive change in fidelity

Training Scenario/Fidelity	Test/Fidelity	Goal	$\delta_1 \uparrow$	$\delta_2 \uparrow$	$\delta_3 \uparrow$	REL↓	RMS↓	log10↓
Brown/Day/High	Brown/Day/High	SC	0.7992	0.9113	0.9474	0.1426	0.0278	0.0740
Blue/Day/Low	Blue/Day/Low	SC	0.7609	0.8980	0.9278	0.1643	0.0366	0.0858
Brown/Night/High	Brown/Night/High	SC	0.8333	0.9248	0.9509	0.1327	0.0278	0.0689
Brown/Day/Low	Brown/Day/Low	SC	0.7719	0.8945	0.9388	0.1544	0.0289	0.0798
Brown/Day/High	Brown/Night/High	L	0.7616	0.8928	0.9315	0.1711	0.0398	0.0875
Brown/Night/High	Brown/ Day/High	L	0.7366	0.8942	0.9420	0.1904	0.0351	0.0939
Blue/Day /Low	Blue/Day/High	F	0.7817	0.9062	0.9329	0.1587	0.0370	0.0822
Brown/Day/Low	Brown/Day/High	F	0.8010	0.9113	0.9475	0.1426	0.0273	0.0731
Brown/Night/High	Blue/Night/High	M	0.5959	0.8632	0.9079	0.3415	0.0671	0.1193
Brown/Day/High	Blue Day/High	M	0.6420	0.8528	0.9223	0.2220	0.0433	0.1067

4.2   Monocular Depth Estimation Experiments

Data Ablation: Table 2 shows a representative sample of the data ablation experiments we conducted using our depth ground truth. For these experiments, we initialized our deep networks using the weights from a network trained on NYUv2. For evaluation, we used the same metrics as those used in [3]: average relative error (REL), root mean squared error (RMS), average log10 error, and threshold accuracy ($\delta_i < 1.25^i$ for $i = [1, 2, 3]$). As we discuss further in Sect. 5, models trained in higher fidelity data generally tend to yield higher scores, even on lower-fidelity scenarios.

Table 3. Depth estimation: Results on real-world datasets.

Train/Fidelity	Test	$\delta_1 \uparrow$	$\delta_2 \uparrow$	$\delta_3 \uparrow$	REL↓	RMS↓	log10↓
Brown/Day/High	NYUv2	0.3666	0.6012	0.7586	0.5044	0.2014	0.1938
Brown/Day/Low	NYUv2	0.3720	0.6062	0.7627	0.5010	0.2010	0.1921
Brown/Night/High	DIODE	0.3563	0.5948	0.7945	0.7659	3.6897	0.2148
Brown/Night/Low	DIODE	0.3163	0.5647	0.7345	0.7743	3.7898	0.2149
Brown/Night/High	DIODE - Filtered	0.6546	0.7725	0.8371	0.6608	2.9765	0.1458
Brown/Day/High	NYUv2 - Filtered	0.5996	0.8405	0.9308	0.2835	0.1232	0.1054
DIODE/Indoor[17]	DIODE/Indoor	0.4919	0.7159	0.8256	0.3306	1.6948	0.1775
NYUv2[1]	NYUv2	0.895	0.980	0.9960	0.1030	0.390	0.0430
NYUv2[1]	DIODE/Indoor	0.2869	0.5097	0.6730	0.6599	2.8854	0.2573

Real-World Validation: To demonstrate the transferability of learned features from a synthetic dataset, we tested our best-performing models on the real-world DIODE and NYUv2 datasets. In addition to the full test set, we also evaluated our networks on a filtered subset that only contained scenes structurally similar to our virtual environments, i.e., indoor scenes of a living room, with objects such as couches, beds, TVs, etc. As Table 3 shows, our high-fidelity trained model had better threshold accuracy on DIODE than a model trained only on NYUv2 [17], confirming that the features learned on our environments are transferable to real-world data. In addition, our model trained on Night lighting, high-fidelity settings achieved 31% δ_1 vs 28% δ_1 of NYUv2 model—59% δ_2 vs 50% δ_2 of NYUv2 model—79.4% δ_3 vs 67.3% of δ_3 of NYUv2 model. These results further confirm that our photo-realistic data can match and even exceed real-life training. Furthermore, these models achieved a much higher score in our filtered test set, suggesting that depth estimation is more sensitive to the structure of the input image than to lighting or fidelity. We also believe our models would have performed even better had DIODE used perspective depth (Fig. 4).

4.3 Surface Normal Estimation Experiments

We carried out a similar set of data ablation experiments as above, but using surface normal data as the ground truth. Here, we trained each model from scratch, i.e., without pre-trained weights, and used the same evaluation metrics as in [19]: mean (average L1 loss), median (average L2 loss), and percentage of pixels that differ by 11.5°, 22.5°, and 30° relative to the true surface normal. Surface normal estimation is a promising use case for AIP because it is very challenging to capture surface normal information for real scenes. One needs expensive equipment to measure the angles, and these sensors are extremely hard to calibrate. As Table 4 shows, we can successfully train deep networks using AIP (see Fig. 6). Overall, surface normal models seem to be less sensitive to photo-realistic features and higher fidelity settings compared to depth estimation or segmentation. Models trained on high fidelity settings perform 2% better than ones trained on low fidelity, a point we discuss further in Sect. 5.

Table 4. Surface normal estimation: Metrics are percentage of pixels that differ by 11.5°, 22.5°, and 30° from the true normal, and mean and median errors. Mean and median are higher than [19] because our loss function did not implement hybrid measures to reduce them. This wasn't necessary since our ground-truth data does not suffer from the problem mentioned in [19]. **SC:** Sanity Check. **L:** Change in Lighting. **M:** Change in Maps. **F:** Positive Change in Fidelity

Scenario/Fidelity	Test/Fidelity	Goal	11.5° ↑	22.5° ↑	30° ↑	Mean↓	Median↓
Brown/Day/High	Brown/Day/High	**SC**	0.9014	0.9566	0.9727	24.4575	88.2878
Blue/Day/Low	Blue/Day/Low	**SC**	0.9274	0.9746	0.989	30.5607	94.9516
Blue/Night/High	Blue/Night/High	**SC**	0.865	0.9224	0.9401	28.2409	69.2181
Brown/Day/Low	Brown/Day/Low	**SC**	0.8883	0.9443	0.961	25.3718	81.4871
Brown/Day/High	Brown/Night/High	**L**	0.052145	0.2238	0.3464	106.70	121.26
Brown/Night/High	Brown/Day/High	**L**	0.050291	0.2135	0.4253	115.82	119.86
Blue/Day/Low	Blue/Day/High	**F**	0.195269	0.2683	0.3015	97.832	113.57
Brown/Day/Low	Brown/Day/High	**F**	0.028247	0.2102	0.368	109.14	118.08

Table 5. Semantic segmentation: Mean intersection over union (IOU) of all classes for different scenarios. Higher values are better. **SC:** Sanity Check. **L:** Change in Lighting. **M:** Change in Maps. **F:** Positive Change in Fidelity

Scenario/Fidelity	Test/Fidelity	Goal	Global IOU↑
Brown/Day/High	Brown/Day/High	**SC**	0.8984
Blue/Day/Low	Blue/Day/Low	**SC**	0.4119
Blue/Night/High	Blue/Night/High	**SC**	0.8335
Brown/Day/Low	Brown/Day/Low	**SC**	0.4714
Brown/Day/High	Brown/Night/High	**L**	0.6932
Brown/Night/High	Brown/Day/High	**L**	0.6418
Blue/Day/Low	Blue/Day/High	**F**	0.3862
Brown/Day/Low	Brown/Day/High	**F**	0.4188

4.4 Semantic Segmentation Experiments

Semantic segmentation involves assigning a class label to every pixel on the image. The built-in environments in AIP have fifteen classes, all of which corresponds to regular household objects, e.g., *wall, couch, table, TV, plant*, etc. We use a label of *other* for miscellaneous items. As with the surface normals, we trained different networks from scratch on each scenario. We used mean intersection over union (IOU) of all classes as our evaluation metric. As we can see in Table 5, model performance is directly linked to a scenario's fidelity (see Fig. 6). Semantic segmentation seems to depend heavily on the render scaling and resolution. At lower settings, borders of the objects are blurry, as is their texture. This causes the model to label them as *other* since it cannot surely ascertain their object class, thus lowering the global IOU (see Fig. 7 for an example).

5   Discussion

Below, we discuss some insights from our data ablation experiments that serve as examples of the kind of analyses that AIP makes possible.

Sensitivity to Lighting: Changes in lighting are a result of the environment, so they cannot be "fixed" by a better acquisition device. As such, a general-purpose model should be robust to them. However, objects can appear in drastically different ways under different lighting conditions, which did affect performance across all experiments. More specifically, segmentation models are particularly sensitive to differences in lighting. In Fig. 7 both models labeled the top part of the *TV* as *Wall* since they have almost the same color. However, the model trained on a Day setting was much less accurate on the Night image than its counterpart, presumably because the Night setting is darker overall and has more pronounced reflections. The opposite effect is visible in the reverse case (bottom Fig. 7), where the reflection in the lamp confused the model because that level of reflection from sunlight does not exist in the Night lighting.

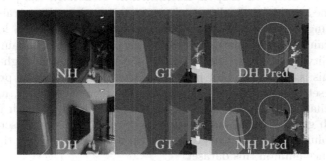

Fig. 7. Semantic segmentation: (Image, Ground Truth, Prediction). Top: A model trained on Brown Day High (DH) images segmenting a Brown Night High (NH) image. Bottom: a model trained on Brown Night High tested on Brown Day High. Note the impact of lighting on the final result.

Our surface normal models are also sensitive to changes in lighting. However, for depth estimation, performance drops only slightly when the lighting is changed, suggesting that local contrast is less important for this problem.

The Impact of Fidelity on Surface Normals vs. Segmentation: Semantic segmentation is very sensitive to changes in fidelity. When objects are blurred due to lower rendering resolution and lower texture clarity, the model appears to be indecisive about picking an object's class in its border regions. As shown in Fig. 6, we see that the model incorrectly classified border regions as *Other*.

In contrast, surface normal estimation is more robust to these kinds of changes. This difference between these two problems highlights the importance of using data ablation tools. Previous studies, e.g., [5,6,18], mainly focus on the effects of fidelity on their segmentation experiments. Our findings with surface normals, on the other hand, suggest that fidelity as a general feature of the image might not be enough to draw conclusions about the quality of the data. AIP's tools allow us to study other aspects of data, such as texture, structure complexity, lighting and more.

Perspective vs. Orthographic Depth: Orthographic depth projection is when light-rays coming to the camera are assumed to be coming from *infinity*. In calculating the depth ground-truth, this simplification introduces errors to the measurement. We have seen the effects of this assumption on the NYUv2 and DIODE dataset (Fig. 4). Specifically, our models' performance on DIODE was lower in part due to them being trained on perspective depth, which is different from the GT used in DIODE. Although orthographic measurements are currently widely used, we argue that perspective depth, which AIP supports, is the *correct* way to measure depth.

Impact of Fidelity on Depth Estimation: Generally, the performance of models trained on higher fidelity settings are better than those trained in lower fidelity settings (Table 2). However, one exception is when the lower fidelity setting in training better matches the features of the target domain. In Table 3, our low fidelity model does slightly better on NYUv2 than the high-fidelity one. We argue this is due to the blur present in NYUv2, which is also present in our low fidelity settings training set due to its lower render settings, making them visually similar. The DIODE dataset, on the other hand, is much more recent, so the depth ground truth was measured with a more accurate sensor. Due to the lack of blur and fuzz on the ground-truth, we did not observe the same kind of performance gain on this dataset.

6   Conclusion and Future Work

Using AIP, we generated different image datasets and conducted experiments that are nearly impossible with real data, thus demonstrating that AIP is a viable tool for data ablation studies in computer vision. We also verified that our high-fidelity trained models can match or exceed the scores achieved by training with real-data. As suggested by other studies [5,6,14,18], we found that higher-fidelity data is linked to better performance in segmentation, but we also found that sensitivity to scene structure, fidelity and lighting scenario of training data varies from task to task. For example, our surface normal and depth estimation models were not as sensitive to fidelity as our segmentation models were. AIP enables us to change individual features, e.g., quality of shadows, quality of reflections, quality of lighting or resolution of textures, and assess their impact on different models based on the current task. More generally, AIP can help researchers find sensitive points in their models and aid them in creating high-quality data for training neural networks for a specific computer vision task.

AIP environments can be expanded to include more indoor scenes, outdoor scenes and fully interactive environments allowing individual interaction with objects. Additionally, we'll be providing support for reinforcement learning studies and real-time ray-tracing. Another exciting avenue is that UE4 allows fast change of the lighting profile by using HDRI maps. This opens the possibility of adding more specific lighting scenarios like rainy, overcast and foggy. In our future updates, we'll be adding support to introduce intentional camera artifacts such as chromatic aberration, penumbra, lens flares and distortions to help study the effects of using small sensors in capturing data. This is especially useful in robotics since consumer-grade robots rarely come with expensive capture equipment; fine-tuning training to the exact specifications of the camera is a very exciting avenue for future work. Furthermore, we are refining our ground-truth options, including removing texture and changing colors and properties of shaders. These enhancements will enable us to manipulate the scene even further, e.g., changing the pattern in a fabric or changing smoothness of a stone. We believe that AIP will open new and exciting avenues in synthetic data and machine learning.

References

1. Alhashim, I., Wonka, P.: High quality monocular depth estimation via transfer learning. arXiv e-prints arXiv:1812.11941 (2018)
2. Community, B.O.: Blender - a 3D modelling and rendering package. Blender Foundation, Stichting Blender Foundation, Amsterdam (2018). http://www.blender.org
3. Eigen, D., Puhrsch, C., Fergus, R.: Depth map prediction from a single image using a multi-scale deep network. CoRR abs/1406.2283 (2014)
4. Epic Games: Unreal engine. https://www.unrealengine.com
5. Gaidon, A., Wang, Q., Cabon, Y., Vig, E.: Virtual worlds as proxy for multi-object tracking analysis (2016)
6. Haltakov, V., Unger, C., Ilic, S.: Framework for generation of synthetic ground truth data for driver assistance applications. In: Weickert, J., Hein, M., Schiele, B. (eds.) GCPR 2013. LNCS, vol. 8142, pp. 323–332. Springer, Heidelberg (2013). https://doi.org/10.1007/978-3-642-40602-7_35
7. Khanal, A., Estrada, R.: Dynamic deep networks for retinal vessel segmentation. CoRR abs/1903.07803 (2019)
8. LeCun, Y., Bengio, Y., Hinton, G.: Deep learning. Nature **521**(7553), 436–444 (2015). https://doi.org/10.1038/nature14539
9. Merrick, L.: Randomized ablation feature importance. arXiv e-prints arXiv:1910.00174 (2019)
10. Meyes, R., Lu, M., Waubert de Puiseau, C., Meisen, T.: Ablation studies in artificial neural networks. arXiv e-prints arXiv:1901.08644 (2019)
11. Mnih, V., et al.: Playing atari with deep reinforcement learning. arXiv e-prints arXiv:1312.5602 (2013)
12. Silberman, N., Hoiem, D., Kohli, P., Fergus, R.: Indoor segmentation and support inference from RGBD images. In: Fitzgibbon, A., Lazebnik, S., Perona, P., Sato, Y., Schmid, C. (eds.) ECCV 2012. LNCS, vol. 7576, pp. 746–760. Springer, Heidelberg (2012). https://doi.org/10.1007/978-3-642-33715-4_54

13. Qiu, W., et al.: UnrealCV: virtual worlds for computer vision. ACM Multimedia Open Source Software Competition (2017)
14. Richter, S.R., Vineet, V., Roth, S., Koltun, V.: Playing for data: ground truth from computer games. In: Leibe, B., Matas, J., Sebe, N., Welling, M. (eds.) ECCV 2016. LNCS, vol. 9906, pp. 102–118. Springer, Cham (2016). https://doi.org/10.1007/978-3-319-46475-6_7
15. Ronneberger, O., Fischer, P., Brox, T.: U-Net: convolutional networks for biomedical image segmentation. In: Navab, N., Hornegger, J., Wells, W.M., Frangi, A.F. (eds.) MICCAI 2015. LNCS, vol. 9351, pp. 234–241. Springer, Cham (2015). https://doi.org/10.1007/978-3-319-24574-4_28
16. Savva, M., et al.: Habitat: a platform for embodied AI research. In: Proceedings of the IEEE/CVF International Conference on Computer Vision (ICCV) (2019)
17. Vasiljevic, I., et al.: DIODE: a dense indoor and outdoor DEpth dataset. CoRR abs/1908.00463 (2019)
18. Veeravasarapu, V., Rothkopf, C., Visvanathan, R.: Model-driven simulations for computer vision. In: 2017 IEEE Winter Conference on Applications of Computer Vision (WACV), pp. 1063–1071 (2017)
19. Zeng, J., et al.: Deep surface normal estimation with hierarchical RGB-D fusion. CoRR abs/1904.03405 (2019)

Homework Helper: Providing Valuable Feedback on Math Mistakes

Sara R. Davis, Carli DeCapito, Eugene Nelson, Karun Sharma,
and Emily M. Hand(✉)

University of Nevada, Reno, Reno, NV 89557, USA
{sarad,cdecapito,enelson,karuns}@nevada.unr.edu, emhand@unr.edu

Abstract. Many parents feel uncomfortable helping their children with homework, with only 66% of parents consistently checking their child's homework [22]. Because of this, many turn to math games and problem solvers as they have become widely available in recent years [12,21]. Many of these applications rely on multiple choice or keyboard entry submission of answers, limiting their adoption. Auto graders and applications, such as PhotoMath, deprive students of the opportunity to correct their own mistakes, automatically generating a solution with no explanation [19]. This work introduces a novel homework assistant – Homework Helper (HWHelper) – that is capable of determining mathematical errors in order to provide meaningful feedback to students without solutions. In this paper, we focus on simple arithmetic calculations, specifically multi-digit addition, introducing 2D-Add, a new dataset of worked addition problems. We design a system that acts as a guided learning tool for students allowing them to learn from and correct their mistakes. HWHelper segments a sheet of math problems, identifies the student's answer, performs arithmetic and pinpoints mistakes made, providing feedback to the student. HWHelper fills a significant gap in the current state-of-the-art for student math homework feedback.

Keywords: Math education · Intelligent tutoring systems · Computer uses in education · Automated student feedback

1 Introduction

Timely feedback is critical to student achievement [17]. However, class sizes are increasing in most U.S. public schools [1] which makes it difficult for students to receive timely, individualized feedback. Compounding this problem, more than 60% of parents are not able to help their children with homework, either due to a lack of understanding or due to time constraints [22]. Students who do not receive feedback at home or in the classroom may turn to the use of applications like Photomath [19] to quickly complete assignments as it is portable and easy to use. These type of applications do not provide students with any feedback on their mistakes, opting to simply solve the problem for them [19].

© Springer Nature Switzerland AG 2020
G. Bebis et al. (Eds.): ISVC 2020, LNCS 12510, pp. 533–544, 2020.
https://doi.org/10.1007/978-3-030-64559-5_42

In this work, we introduce the HWHelper application, capable of analyzing student handwritten math problems for correctness, and providing relevant feedback to the student so that they can correct their work, never giving them the solution. Ultimately, learning from their own mistakes and generating their own procedure to fix their mistakes in a guided manner should lead to better content retention [5]. The HWHelper pipeline is shown in Fig. 1.

The contributions of this work are as follows:

1. 2D-Add, a two-digit addition dataset consisting of 2010 worked problems, hand-labeled with problem and digit bounding boxes, digit values, solutions and errors.
2. HWHelper, an android application to provide automated feedback on freeform two-digit addition problems.

Fig. 1. The HWHelper system work flow. Problems and digits are first segmented. Digits are then grouped into terms and the addition is performed. The student answer is compared to the solution. All incorrect problems are highlighted for the student, and the student can select problems for review. If HWHelper misidentifies any digit, the student can manually enter digits to correct the system. Error messages are then displayed, providing feedback for improvement.

2   Related Work

This paper focuses on providing feedback to students for answer adjustment. This involves two tasks: recognizing and solving math problems, and providing feedback. We review the relevant literature in the following sections.

2.1   Recognizing Math Problems

Digit identification belongs to the field of optical character recognition (OCR) [15], and has been widely studied for its ability to automate many tasks, such as license plate recognition [7], postal code sorting [18], and language translation [16]. Convolutional neural networks (CNNs) are used in most state-of-the-art systems involving image processing [2], with OCR [7,16,18], and digit classification and segmentation being no exception [15]. Handwritten characters are more difficult to recognize than printed characters [9]. Handwritten character recognition improves when samples are collected in real time using technology such as a smartpen, likely due to the added information from pen stroke [4].

Applying character recognition to the problem of math education, past research has successfully extracted math symbols from documents for the purpose of document analysis [25]. Most previous work in applying character recognition to math education has utilized real-time collection methods to improve the accuracy of student sample collection [3,11,12]. In these systems, the pen's movement is tracked in order to determine the digit being drawn by the student [3]. In terms of freedom of expression and application, the use of a static CNN-based OCR system is typically less accurate, but more flexible for student use [8]. Since the basic structure of a math problem in our dataset is consistent, the problem of recognizing multiple math problems at once can be solved using traditional segmentation methods through the application of a CNN [2].

While work in the area of intelligent tutoring systems has existed for years [23], the application of lightweight CNN-based techniques to the problem of math problem recognition is less researched, and is explored in this work.

2.2   Providing Feedback to Students for Answer Adjustment

Software in the area of math education is abundant with most programs relying on multiple choice, keyed entry, or answer selection with the mouse [21]. While this software can be useful, it does not provide a way for students to show their work and receive guided feedback [21]. Students who visualize their errors are more likely to correct themselves and retain the knowledge about how to solve that type of problem in the future [5,13]. Despite research showing that feedback must be appropriate for student age range and background knowledge, math education software may not always provide age appropriate feedback [20]. The strategies for problem solving and recognition of how the student made the mistake differs by age group, and has a significant impact on student retention [14]. Applications such as Photomath [19] and Wolfram Alpha [24] simply provide students with a solution to a math problem, without context, which does not give students the opportunity to learn from their mistakes [14]. Although these sites may provide outside resources for additional help [24], they often require a higher reading level, so many of the linked sites are not content appropriate for young students or those who are developmentally delayed [14]. Introducing problem solving skills, such as review and reflection on errors, is imperative for learning and retention [6,13]. [8] creates a platform for teachers to reflect on common student errors, but does not provide a system to interact with students and prompt them to correct their mistakes. HWHelper builds on prior work by utilizing well established arithmetic rules to provide students with feedback that allows them to properly solve a math problem without giving them the solution (Fig. 1).

Other works have studied automatic grading, and step by step problem solving [8,12,21]. [21] uses multiple choice assessment, while [12] utilizes online data gathering techniques to analyze pen stroke rather than the actual handwritten digit, making their works inconvenient for student homework use. [8] uses keyboard entry rather than handwritten work and focuses on teacher identification of student errors, rather than prompting students to correct their own errors.

Our work primarily differs from prior automatic grading work in that it focuses on providing students with:

1. age appropriate, automated feedback to correct their own mistakes **without giving them an explicit answer** [19,24], rather than providing teachers with feedback on student learning target accomplishment [8].
2. a handwritten free response platform for students to **flexibly record their submissions and mistakes**, rather than keyboard [8], multiple choice [5], or pen stroke entry [3].
3. a portable, computationally inexpensive framework **capable of running on most devices**, rather than on desktops only [8].

3   HWHelper Application

In this section, we detail the HWHelper application, including the data collection, math problem and digit segmentation, term grouping, arithmetic and logic for error identification and reporting.

3.1   Data Collection

We introduce a new dataset, 2D-Add, consisting of 2010 problems of multi-digit addition. Each sheet contains up to six problems with three rows and two columns (Fig. 2).

The terms in each problem range from 1 to 49, so that no solution is greater than two digits in length, for the sake of simplicity. Problems are not repeated, but flipping of terms is allowed. That means that $1 + 12$ is in the set, as is $12 + 1$, but neither of those patterns are repeated.

The sheets were randomly divided among five labelers, aged 20–28. Before filling out the sheets, the participants were instructed to "write like a first grader" to simulate the challenges that HWHelper might encounter in a classroom setting. They were also told to make at least 30% of their answers incorrect. This exercise generated 340 sheets of math problems, and 2010 individual problems, which make up the 2D-Add dataset. Seven possible mistakes are identified from the data collected.

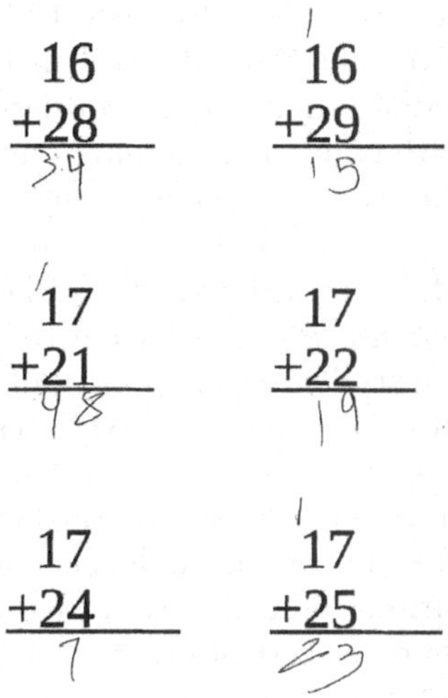

Fig. 2. An example of a worked math sheet in 2D-Add.

There are seven consistent addition errors found in the 2D-Add dataset. They can be seen in Fig. 3, and are listed below:

1. Drop down first and second term answer.
2. Ones place added incorrectly.
3. Tens place added incorrectly.
4. Carried when a carry was not necessary.
5. Carried incorrectly.
6. Did not carry when a carry was necessary.
7. Other – Typically non-numeric.

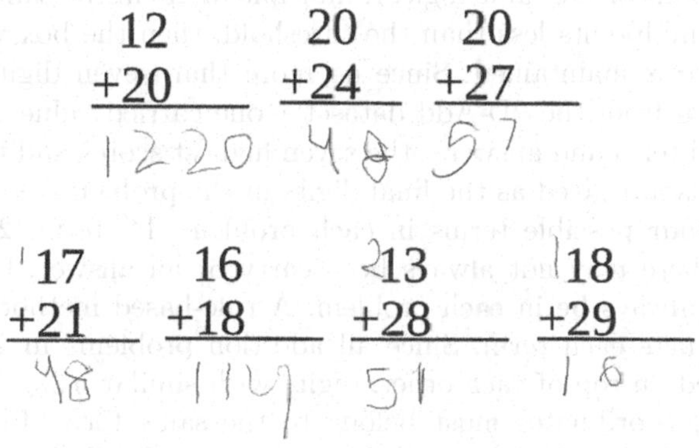

$$\begin{array}{r} 12 \\ +20 \\ \hline \end{array} \qquad \begin{array}{r} 20 \\ +24 \\ \hline \end{array} \qquad \begin{array}{r} 20 \\ +27 \\ \hline \end{array}$$

1220   48   57

$$\begin{array}{r} {}^{1}17 \\ +21 \\ \hline \end{array} \qquad \begin{array}{r} 16 \\ +18 \\ \hline \end{array} \qquad \begin{array}{r} {}^{1}13 \\ +28 \\ \hline \end{array} \qquad \begin{array}{r} {}^{1}18 \\ +29 \\ \hline \end{array}$$

48   114   51   16

Fig. 3. Examples of each of the seven mistakes. Errors 1, 2, 3, 4, 5, 6 and 7 are shown from left to right, top to bottom.

3.2   Problem and Digit Identification

We utilize a deep convolutional neural network (CNN) as our model for problem and digit segmentation. HWHelper is a mobile application and needs to provide real-time feedback to students. With this in mind, we utilize a light-weight model capable of segmenting problems and terms in real time. While 2D-Add is composed of consistently spaced math problems, we do not want to rely on this format in the future, and so we use a CNN to segment problems rather than simply dividing the sheets into segments. This allows HWHelper to be more versatile.

In contrast to problem detection, where there is only a single class, digit identification requires that all digits (0 to 9) be both localized and recognized. Both of these steps are essential, as the precise location and value of each digit is needed in order to perform the arithmetic properly, and for HWHelper to reason about the mistakes that are made. The digit detector must be capable of identifying typed digits as well as hand-written digits in a variety of locations within the problem. Young student handwriting can be very messy, so the digit recognition must be robust to different types of handwriting.

3.3 Term Grouping

Once all digits have been localized and recognized, they can be grouped together to form terms in the math problem. First, all duplicate digit detections are removed, which results in the final of digits for a math problem. This is accomplished by taking the digits with the top ten confidence scores from the model. All confidence scores are values between 0 and 1. The x and y midpoints of each pair of boxes are compared, and if their difference is greater than a threshold, they are added to the final list of digits in the problem. This removes multiple detections of the same digit. If multiple digits in the same position have a difference in midpoints less than the threshold, then the box with the higher confidence score is maintained. Since no more than seven digits should be in a single problem from the 2D-Add dataset – one carried value, and two in the first and second term and answer – the seven highest scores and their associated boxes and labels are saved as the final digits in the problem.

There are four possible terms in each problem: 1st term, 2nd term, carry and answer. There may not always be a carry or an answer, but the 1st and 2nd terms will always be in each problem. A rule-based method utilizing digit position constructs each term. Since all addition problems in 2D-Add consist of terms stacked on top of each other, digits with similar y_{min} coordinates and dissimilar x_{min} coordinates must belong to the same term. In cases where a single digit has multiple neighboring digits within a threshold, the closest digit is selected as belonging to the same term. Digits with similar y_{min} and dissimilar x_{min} values are grouped into a term with two digits. Digits without a similar y_{min} and x_{min} are kept as single digit terms.

The terms are then ordered into *carry*, 1st, 2nd and *answer* by comparing each term's y_{min} values. If only two terms are detected, then the *carry* and *answer* are left empty. If four terms are detected then all terms are present. If only three terms are detected, we must determine whether the *carry* or the *answer* is present. If there is no term detected in the bottom $\frac{1}{4}$ of the image, then we assume there is a carry and no answer, and vice-versa.

3.4 Answer and Solution Comparison

The seven errors present in 2D-Add are detailed in Sect. 3.1. The algorithm below demonstrates how each error is identified.

HWHelper performs the arithmetic, adding the 1st and 2nd terms to find the solution to the problem. The solution is compared to the student's answer. If the student's answer does not match the solution, the specific error is determined and then feedback is provided to the student. Figure 3 shows an example of each of the 7 errors in the 2D-Add dataset.

Algorithm 1: HWHelper Error Generation

Result: Error

if $answer == concat(1^{st}, 2^{nd})$ **then**
  | report Error 1
else if $answer[0] \; ! = solution[0]$ **then**
  | // First digit of answer is not correct.
  | report Error 2
else if $1^{st}[0] + 2^{nd}[0] > 9$ **then**
  | $expected\_carry = 1^{st}[0] + 2^{nd}[0] - 9$
  | // The solution requires a carry.
  | **if** $\exists \; carry \; \& \; expected\_carry \; ! = carry$ **then**
    | // Expected carry and carry do not match.
    | report Error 5
  | **else if** $\neg\exists \; carry$ **then**
    | // No carry when there should have been.
    | report Error 6

else if $\exists \; carry$ **then**
  | // Carry when there should not have been one.
  | report Error 4
else if $answer[0] == solution[0]$ **then**
  | **if** $answer[1] \; != solution[1]$ **then**
    | // Carry is correct, but second digit of answer is
       incorrect.
    | report Error 3

else
  | // Catchall for any other errors.
  | report Error 7

---

4 Experiments

In this section, we detail the experiments conducted to evaluate the efficacy of the HWHelper application. For both problem detection and digit recognition experiments, 80% of the 2D-Add dataset is reserved for training, and the other 20% is set aside for validation and testing. The TensorFlow object detection API – specifically the SSD Mobilenet pre-trained on COCO – is used to segment individual problems as well as digits [10]. Our experiments are separated into problem and digit segmentation, and error reporting and prompting.

4.1   Problem and Digit Segmentation

For problem detection, we utilize the SSD Mobilenet pre-trained on COCO. For training, we use a learning rate of 0.01, batch size of 15, with images of size 600×600. Problem segmentation creates bounding boxes around each problem (see Fig. 4). HWHelper achieves 100% accuracy on problem detection on 2D-Add. This indicates that given a specific template for problem location, the HWHelper system is capable of identifying the locations of each individual problem in a practice sheet. The segmented problems are then fed to a second model for digit segmentation.

For digit segmentation, we again utilize an SSD Mobilenet model pre-trained on the COCO dataset. We modify the configuration for 10-class classification (digits 0–9). In training, we again use a learning rate of 0.01 and a batch size of 15. Our model achieves an average accuracy of 95.3% accuracy on digit segmentation and recognition.

The majority of misclassifications were made on handwritten digits, with 110 of the 118 misclassified digits being handwritten. The 8 misclassified typed digits are covered by handwritten digits or scribbles, resulting in their misclassification.

We implemented a user check within HWHelper to determine if a digit had been identified correctly, as outlined in Sect. 4.2.

Both the problem and digit segmentation models are converted to TensorFlow Lite for integration into HWHelper. TensorFlow Lite offers the fastest method of detection. Since HWHelper is a mobile application, it is important to utilize models with as few parameters as possible to avoid slow response times due to low computational power.

4.2   User Interface

The generated codes are compared to a list of hand-labeled errors for each problem. The accuracy for error reporting is 63.2% on the test set. To determine if the mistakes made by the error message production are due to the error messaging system or the detected digits, the same experiment was repeated using the ground truth values for first term, second term, carry, and answer. This resulted in a accuracy of 100%. This indicates that the 63.2% accuracy using detected digits is due to inaccurate digit identification, which can be prevented with manual digit entry.

HWHelper is implemented as an Android application. Students can take a photo of their homework using their android tablet or phone. HWHelper then performs all of the problem and digit segmentation, term grouping, and mathematical computations in its backend. Correct problems are shown in a green box while incorrect problems are shown in a red box, as shown in Fig. 4. The user may then select a problem that has been identified as incorrectly solved. The application outputs which of the seven math errors outlined in Sect. 3.1 has been found by the application, and prompts the user with an age appropriate message to try again. This process is shown in Fig. 5.

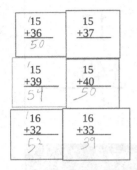

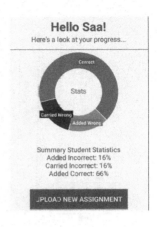

Fig. 4. A correctly segmented arithmetic calculation sheet with color coding, where all problems except one in the sample have been incorrectly solved. (Color figure online)

Fig. 5. An incorrectly solved arithmetic calculation, and its associated error message.

Fig. 6. The statistics screen presented to students after uploading assignments.

In order to use the application, teachers and students need to create and register for an account. Once registered, students can upload sheets of two-digit addition problems for evaluation. After the student has evaluated a sheet of problems, the application presents them with a cumulative pie chart for all problems ever completed by the student. This pie chart is found on the home page and describes the relative percentages of different mistakes and the percent of problems completed correctly. An example is shown in Fig. 6. This allows the student to reflect on their previous mistakes and assess the improvement of their skills over time.

If multiple answers are detected in a problem, HWHelper prompts the user to enter the values found on the sheet (see Fig. 8) to ensure that the application can correctly assess the math problem. Even when the application does not detect multiple responses, it is possible that model incorrectly identified an individual digit. To ensure that the application is as user friendly as possible, the application always outputs the message "Does something seem wrong?". This is shown in Fig. 9, where the output is particularly useful since a number has been misidentified by the system. Selecting "click here" brings the user to a screen where they can manually input the problem information (Fig. 7), after which the application will display an error message with feedback if necessary. The user may also opt to simply retake the picture if the image appears blurry to them.

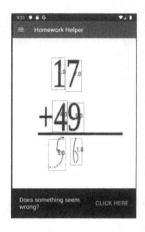

Fig. 7. The screen that the application pulls up when the user selects "click here" after being prompted with "Does something seem wrong?"

Fig. 8. The prompt output by the Android application when multiple answers are detected in a problem.

Fig. 9. The screen shown to the user after all digits have been identified; in this particular example, not all digits have been correctly identified and the user should select "click here" to correct the misidentification.

5   Conclusions and Future Work

In this work, we introduce the HWHelper application, providing automated feedback to students. With 100% accuracy on problem segmentation, HWHelper performs very well when provided with sheets of math problems that conform to a standard format like those in 2D-Add and most homework assignments. HWHelper is also capable of identifying individual digits with high accuracy – 95.3% on average. The proposed algorithms to group digits into terms are robust enough to handle a variety of inputs. HWHelper is capable of overcoming errors in digit and term detection as it allows for user input to fix such mistakes.

HWHelper shows that it is possible to use technology to provide automatic feedback to free response student work. Along with the HWHelper application, we introduce 2D-Add, a dataset of worked two-digit addition problems, which we will make available for future research in this direction.

Future research will explore variations in problem layout, such as side by side addition, to accommodate a wider classroom audience. Additionally, the framework will be expanded to include the capability to perform different arithmetic calculations, such as subtraction and multiplication, which could be accomplished by detecting arithmetic symbols in addition to digits. The modularity of the current HWHelper will make the addition of other operators (subtraction and multiplication) very reasonable. We will collect additional data from students in the classroom working with local K-12 schools. This additional data will improve digit recognition and the HWHelper system overall. We will also perform usability testing within the target population, to identify areas for improvement in the user interface and feedback portions of HWHelper.

References

1. National center for education statistics. https://nces.ed.gov/fastfacts/display.asp?id=28
2. Aloysius, N., Geetha, M.: A review on deep convolutional neural networks. In: Proceedings of the International Conference on Communication and Signal Processing (ICCSP 2017), pp. 0588–0592 (2017). https://doi.org/10.1109/ICCSP.2017.8286426
3. Anthony, L., Yang, J., Koedinger, K.R.: A paradigm for handwriting-based intelligent tutors. Int. J. Hum. Comput. Stud. **70**(11), 866–887 (2012)
4. Batuwita, K.B.M.R., Bandara, G.E.M.D.C.: An improved segmentation algorithm for individual offline handwritten character segmentation. In: International Conference on Computational Intelligence for Modelling, Control and Automation and International Conference on Intelligent Agents, Web Technologies and Internet Commerce (CIMCA-IAWTIC 2006), vol. 2, pp. 982–988 (2005). https://doi.org/10.1109/CIMCA.2005.1631596
5. Borasi, R.: Capitalizing on errors as "springboards for inquiry": a teaching experiment. J. Res. Math. Educ. **25**(2), 166–208 (1994). http://www.jstor.org/stable/749507
6. Butler, A.C., Karpicke, J.D., Roediger, H.: Correcting a metacognitive error: feedback increases retention of low-confidence correct responses. J. Exp. Psychol. Learn. Mem. Cogn. **34**(4), 918–928 (2008)
7. Chuang, C., Tsai, L., Deng, M., Hsieh, J., Fan, K.: Vehicle licence plate recognition using super-resolution technique. In: Proceedings of the 11th IEEE International Conference on Advanced Video and Signal Based Surveillance (AVSS 2014), pp. 411–416 (2014). https://doi.org/10.1109/AVSS.2014.6918703
8. Feldman, M.Q., Cho, J.Y., Ong, M., Gulwani, S., Popović, Z., Andersen, E.: Automatic diagnosis of students' misconceptions in K-8 mathematics. In: Proceedings of the 2018 CHI Conference on Human Factors in Computing Systems, pp. 1–12 (2018)
9. Gader, P.D., Keller, J.M., Krishnapuram, R., Chiang, J.-H., Mohamed, M.A.: Neural and fuzzy methods in handwriting recognition. Computer **30**(2), 79–86 (1997). https://doi.org/10.1109/2.566164
10. Howard, A.G., et al.: MobileNets: efficient convolutional neural networks for mobile vision applications. arXiv abs/1704.04861 (2017)
11. Huang, X., Craig, S.D., Xie, J., Graesser, A., Hu, X.: Intelligent tutoring systems work as a math gap reducer in 6th grade after-school program. Learn. Individ. Differ. **47**, 258–265 (2016)
12. Hwang, G.J., Chang, H.F.: A formative assessment-based mobile learning approach to improving the learning attitudes and achievements of students. Comput. Educ. **56**(4), 1023–1031 (2011). https://doi.org/10.1016/j.compedu.2010.12.002
13. Isotani, S., Adams, D., Mayer, R.E., Durkin, K., Rittle-Johnson, B., McLaren, B.M.: Can erroneous examples help middle-school students learn decimals? In: Kloos, C.D., Gillet, D., Crespo García, R.M., Wild, F., Wolpers, M. (eds.) EC-TEL 2011. LNCS, vol. 6964, pp. 181–195. Springer, Heidelberg (2011). https://doi.org/10.1007/978-3-642-23985-4_15

14. Kapur, M.: Productive failure in learning math. Cogn. Sci. **38**(5), 1008–1022 (2014)
15. Kir, B., Oz, C., Gulbag, A.: The application of optical character recognition for mobile device via artificial neural networks with negative correlation learning algorithm. In: Proceedings of the International Conference on Electronics, Computer and Computation (ICECCO 2013), pp. 220–223 (2013). https://doi.org/10.1109/ICECCO.2013.6718268
16. Koga, M., Mine, R., Kameyama, T., Takahashi, T., Yamazaki, M., Yamaguchi, T.: Camera-based kanji OCR for mobile-phones: practical issues. In: Proceedings of the Eighth International Conference on Document Analysis and Recognition (ICDAR 2005), pp. 635–639. IEEE (2005)
17. Marzano, R.J., Pickering, D.J., Pollock, J.E.: Classroom instruction that works: research-based strategies for increasing student achievement. Gale Virtual Reference Library, Association for Supervision and Curriculum Development (2001). https://books.google.com/books?id=c25kDO0adxwC
18. Ni, D.X.: Application of neural networks to character recognition. In: Proceedings of Students/Faculty Research Day, CSIS, Pace University (2007)
19. Photomath, Inc.: Photomath (2019). https://photomath.net/
20. Rittle-Johnson, B., Schneider, M., Star, J.R.: Not a one-way street: bidirectional relations between procedural and conceptual knowledge of mathematics. Educ. Psychol. Rev. **27**(4), 587–597 (2015). Document feature
21. Sung, H.Y., Hwang, G.J.: A collaborative game-based learning approach to improving students' learning performance in science courses. Comput. Educ. **63**, 43–51 (2013). https://doi.org/10.1016/j.compedu.2012.11.019
22. U.S. Department of Education: Parent and family involvement in education: results from the national household education surveys program of 2016 (2016). https://nces.ed.gov/pubs2017/2017102.pdf
23. Vanlehn, K.: The relative effectiveness of human tutoring, intelligent tutoring systems, and other tutoring systems. Educ. Psychol. **46**(4), 197–221 (2011). https://doi.org/10.1080/00461520.2011.611369
24. Wolfram Research Inc: Mathematica, Version 12.0, Champaign (2019)
25. Zanibbi, R., Yu, L.: Math spotting: retrieving math in technical documents using handwritten query images. In: Proceedings of the 2011 International Conference on Document Analysis and Recognition, pp. 446–451 (2011). https://doi.org/10.1109/ICDAR.2011.96

Interface Design for HCI Classroom: From Learners' Perspective

Huyen N. Nguyen(✉), Vinh T. Nguyen, and Tommy Dang

Texas Tech University, Lubbock, TX 79409, USA
{huyen.nguyen,vinh.nguyen,tommy.dang}@ttu.edu

Abstract. Having a good Human-Computer Interaction (HCI) design is challenging. Previous works have contributed significantly to fostering HCI, including design principle with report study from the instructor view. The questions of how and to what extent students perceive the design principles are still left open. To answer this question, this paper conducts a study of HCI adoption in the classroom. The studio-based learning method is adapted to teach 83 graduate and undergraduate students in 16 weeks long with four activities. A standalone presentation tool for instant online peer feedback during the presentation session is developed to help students justify and critique other's work. Our tool provides a sandbox, which supports multiple application types, including Web-applications, Object Detection, Web-based Virtual Reality (VR), and Augmented Reality (AR). After presenting one assignment and two projects, our results shows that students acquired a better understanding of the Golden Rules principle over time, which is demonstrated by the development of visual interface design. The Wordcloud reveals the primary focus was on the user interface and sheds light on students' interest in user experience. The inter-rater score indicates the agreement among students that they have the same level of understanding of the principles. The results show a high level of guideline compliance with HCI principles, in which we witness variations in visual cognitive styles. Regardless of diversity in visual preference, the students present high consistency and a similar perspective on adopting HCI design principles. The results also elicit suggestions into the development of the HCI curriculum in the future.

Keywords: Human-Computer Interaction · Instant online peer feedback · Interface design · Learners' perspective · User study design · Inter-rater measurement

1 Introduction

HCI has a long, rich history, and its origin can be dated back to the 1980s with the advent of personal computing. As such, computers were no longer considered an expensive tool, and room-sized dedicated to experts in a given domain. Consequently, the need to have an easy and efficient interaction for general and

© Springer Nature Switzerland AG 2020
G. Bebis et al. (Eds.): ISVC 2020, LNCS 12510, pp. 545–557, 2020.
https://doi.org/10.1007/978-3-030-64559-5_43

untrained users became increasingly vital for technology adoption. In recent years, along with the presence of new devices (e.g., smartphones, tablets), HCI has expanded its perceptual concept from interaction with a computer to that of any target device, and it has been incorporated into multiple disciplines, such as computer science, cognitive science, and human-factors engineering.

Having a good HCI design is a challenging task since it not only has to cope with "more than just a computer now... but considerable awareness that touch, speech, and gesture-based interfaces" [4] but also requires a substantial cognitive effort to think and make the product that encompassed the aspects of *useful, usable*, and ultimately *used* by the public [13], such as user interfaces assisting monitoring and system operational tasks [7,15]. Literature work has contributed significantly to fostering HCI from imposing design principles, processes, guidelines to teaching. For example, the ACM SIGCHI Executive Committee [12] developed a set of curriculum recommendations for HCI in education, or Ben Shneiderman [22] suggested eight golden rules of interface design. Adopting the existing guidelines, teachers/instructors have attributed an abundance of efforts to support students in understanding the concept, developing, and creating a good interaction design in classrooms [4,10]. In line with instructing learners, curriculum, teaching/learning methods, project outputs, tools/techniques are reported to share with the HCI community. In this regard, findings are often observed from the instructors' perspectives, the questions of *how*, and *to what extent* students perceive the design principles are unexplored.

Having the answers to these questions would play an essential indicator for both educators and learners as it allows them to reshape their perceptual thinking on how HCI is being taught and learned. For instructors, looking at HCI from students' perspectives enables them to reorganize teaching materials and methods so that learning performance can be best achieved. For learners, the opportunity of having their point of view to justify or being justified by instructors/peers would allow them to develop the critical thinking skills prepared for their future careers.

To the best of our knowledge, no work in the literature exploits these questions in the HCI domain, making this research a unique contribution. In this study, we seek to answer the aforementioned questions by decomposing them into sub-questions as 1) Given a set of design principles/guidelines, to what extents students follow them, 2) Which part of the HCI design the learners focus on, and 3) Do they have the same perspectives on adopting design principles and are these views consistent? By addressing these research questions qualitatively and quantitatively, the contributions of our paper can be laid out as:

- it reports the instructional methods and instruments used for teaching and learning HCI in the classroom.
- it provides an analysis of the qualitative method for student peer-review project assessment.
- it extracts insights of HCI design principles adoption in the classroom.

The rest of this paper is organized as follows: Section 2 summarizes existing research that is close to our paper. Section 3 presents study design methods for collecting students' information. Section 4 analyzes data and provide insights in detail. Section 5 concludes our paper with future work direction.

2   Related Work

Numerous researches on teaching HCI guidelines have been studied: from the general design of the course, major topics should be covered to the incorporation of user-centered design. One of the fundamental literature in designing the HCI curriculum is presented in 1992 by Hewett et al. [12], "ACM SIGCHI Curricula for Human-Computer Interaction". The report provided "a blueprint for early HCI courses" [4], which concentrated on the concept of "HCI-oriented," not "HCI-centered," programs. Therefore, it is beneficial to frame the problem of HCI broadly enough to aid learners and practitioners to avoid the classic pitfall of design separated from the context of the problem [12]. Regarding the in-class setting, PeerPresents [21] introduced a peer feedback tool using online Google docs on student presentations. With this approach, students receive qualitative feedback by the end of class. To encourage immediacy in the discussion, our system provides feedback on-the-fly: the presenters receive feedback and questions as they are submitted to the system, the presenters can start the discussion right after their presentation session. Instant Online Feedback [8] demonstrates the use of instant online feedback on face-to-face presentations. Besides the similar feedback form containing quantitative and qualitative aspects, we include the demo of the final interface within the form so that the audience can directly perform testing. Online feedback demonstrates its advantages in terms of engagement, anonymity, and diversity. Online Feedback System [11] facilitates students' motivation and engagement in the feedback process. Compared to the face-to-face setting, the establishment of anonymity encourages more students to participate and contributes to balanced participation in the feedback process [8]. Along with a higher quantity, diversity in the feedback elicits novel perspectives and reveals unique insights [16]. For a classroom setting, time is often limited within a class session. With such time restriction, the time frame dedicated to giving feedback should be held rather low [8]. Peer feedback should be delivered in a timely manner [14]: for online classes, the feedback only demonstrates its efficiency if provided within 24 h. Another study shows that instant feedback helps enhance accuracy estimate than that received at the end of a study because of its immediacy [17].

3   Materials and Methods

3.1   Teaching Method and Activities

The main goal of our study is to investigate the adoption of HCI design principles in the classroom setting from the learners' perspective. It is a daunting task for instructors to justify the adoption level due to variations in visual cognitive styles. For example, teachers may like bright and high contrast design, whereas students prefer a colorful dashboard. Thus, a teaching method and assessment should be carefully designed to help motivate and engage students and adequately reflect their performance level. Literature work has proposed several teaching methods [3], such as inquiry-based learning, situated-based learning, project-based learning, and studio-based learning. As such, we chose the studio-based learning approach due to its characteristics, encompassed our critical factors. These characteristics can be laid out as follows:

- Students should be engaged in project-based assignments (**C1**).
- Student learning outcomes should be iteratively assessed in formal and informal fashion through design critiques (**C2**).
- Students are required to engage in critiquing the work of their peers (**C3**).
- Design critiques should revolve around the artifacts typically created by the domains (**C4**).

Based on the above criteria, we divided the entire course work into four main activities spanning over 16-week long, including 1) Introduction to HCI, 2) Homework assignment, 3) Projects engagement: Throughout the course, students were actively involved in two projects (characteristic **C1**), and 4) Evaluation and design critiques: In each assignment/projects both instructors and students were engaged for evaluations (characteristics **C2**, **C4**), this process not only helps to avoid bias in the results but also allows learners to reflect their learning for justifying their peers (characteristic **C3**). The assignment's purpose is to give students some practice in the design of everyday things. In the first project, we incorporated the problem-based learning method on the problem extended from the assignment. The second project had a different approach by adapting the computational thinking-based method, where students can explore a real-life problem and then solve it on their own.

3.2 Participants

The present study was conducted with university students enrolled in the Human-Computer Interaction course in computer science. There was a total of 83 students, of which 62 students are undergraduate, 13 masters, and eight doctoral students. There were 64 males and 19 females.

3.3 Assessment Tool

Aalberg and Lors [1] indicated that 'the lack of technology support for peer assessment is one likely cause for the lack of systematic use in education.' To address these issues, many assessment tools have been introduced [8,9,21]. However, no such a comprehensive tool enables instructors to carry out a new task that has not been presented. Particularly, in our study, the evaluation requires features such as instant feedback, timing control, list preview, or even 3D objects embedded applications. We developed a standalone tool to facilitate peer evaluation and data collection, supporting multiple application types, including webpage, web-based VR, and AR. The tool is expected to serve these goals:

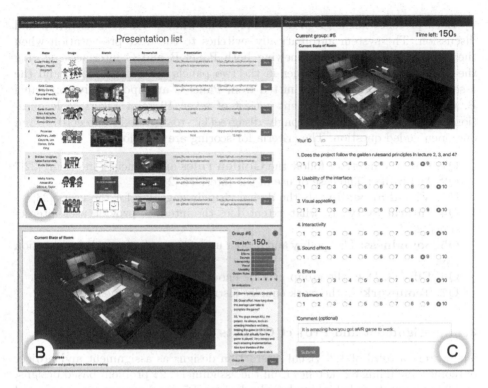

Fig. 1. User interface of the web presentation application in various contexts. A) List of presentations from the instructor's view, B) Presenter's view, C) Audience's view.

- **G1** From the presenter's perspective: Each presenter (group or individual) demonstrates their interface design within their session. The presenter can see the feedback and evaluation visualization within their session.
- **G2** From the audience's perspective: The audience can give comments and evaluations for the current design presented [9]. Authentication for the in-class audience is necessary for input validity.
- **G3** The system presents online, instant evaluation from the audience (anonymously) to the presenter without interrupting the presentation.

User Interface. Figure 1 describes our web presentation system according to three perspectives. Panel A shows the presenter list (student names and group members' images have been customized for demonstration purposes). This view allows the instructors to manage students' turn to present, each group has two thumbnail images for sketch and final design, indicating the development process. Panel B is the presenter's view with live comments on the right-hand side, updated on-the-fly. The average scores and evaluation are updated live in the presenter's view – visualized in an interactive, dynamic chart. Panel C is the audience's view for providing scores and feedback on the presenting project.

Each presentation is given a bounded time window for demonstration and discussion. The system automatically switches to the next presentation when the current session is over, renewing both Panel B and C interfaces. During the presentation, the clock timer in the two panels are synchronized, and the assessment and comments submitted from Panel C are updated live on Panel B. Questions for peer assessment consist of seven 10-point Likert scale questions (which ranged from "strongly disagree(1)" to "strongly agree(10)") and one open-ended question. The criteria for scoring are as follows.

- **Q1**, Does the interface follow the **Golden rules** and principle in design [22]?
- **Q2**, **Usability**: The ease of use of the interface [24].
- **Q3**, **Visual appealing**: Is the design visually engaging for the users [23]?
- **Q4**, **Interactivity**: To what extent does the interface provide user interactions [23]?
- **Q5**, **Soundness**: The quality and proper use of the audio from the application [23].
- **Q6**, **Efforts**: Does the group provide enough effort for the work?
- **Q7**, **Teamwork**: Is the work equally distributed to team members?

3.4   Assignment and Project Outputs

There were a total of 126 visual interaction designs as assignment and project outcomes, including 82 sketches from the assignment, 21 problem-based designs, and 22 computational thinking based solutions. Figure 2 presents some selected work corresponding to the assignment, project 1, project 2, respectively.

Previous work showed that there was some ambiguity in the results when students gave scores to their peers. Part of the issue is that they wanted to be 'nice' or aimed to get the job done. To alleviate these issues, unusual score patterns will be excluded, and evaluators (students) will be notified anonymously through their alias names. Examples of good grading and inadequate grading are presented in Fig. 3. Good grading is illustrated via the diversity in assessment outcome among different criteria, opposite to inadequate examples.

4   Results

4.1   R1: Given a Set of Design Principles/guidelines, to What Extents Students Follow Them?

In order to tackle the first research question, we are looking for an indication among the students that reflects the overall level of guideline compliance. To measure the extent that the learners follow the guidelines, we use the typical statistic measures mean and standard deviation, where each record is a quantitative assessment from a user to a presenter, spreading on the provided criteria.

Table 1 presents the mean and standard deviation on the peer assessment score for project 1 and project 2. In both projects, *Efforts* criterion always has the highest mean value, indicating that the students highly appreciate the

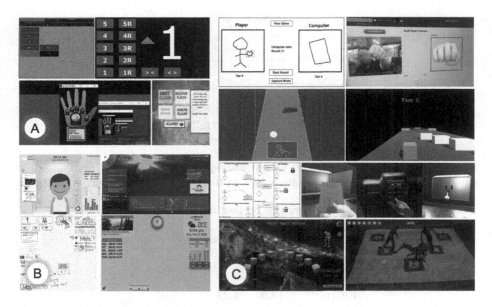

Fig. 2. Selected work on interface design for the individual assignment (A), project 1 (B), project 2 (C). For each project 1 and 2, sketches are on the left, and final designs are on the right. Our study covers a variety of applications, including Object Detection (as a Computer Vision application), Web-based 3D application, VR, and AR. The interdisciplinary nature is presented in the final result.

efforts their peers put in. Regarding project 1, *Visual Design* has the lowest mean (8.20) and also the highest standard deviation (1.48), showing variation visual cognitive styles and diverse individual opinions on what should be considered "visually engaging". In project 2, *Golden Rules* criterion has the mean increased and became the criterion with the lowest standard deviation (1.12), meaning that there is less difference between the perception of Golden Rules among the students, demonstrating that the students present better compliance to the guidelines. As an experience learned from project 1, *Sounds* was introduced in project 2 as a channel for feedback interactions. *Sounds* having the lowest mean (7.33) and highest standard deviation (2.30), setting it apart from other standard deviations (around 1.1 1.2), indicating that the students had difficulty incorporating this feature on their projects. Overall, the other criteria have their mean values increased from project 1 to project 2, showing a better presentation and understanding of the guidelines.

4.2 R2: Which Part of the HCI Design the Learners Focus On?

We answer this question using a qualitative method for analysis; we take inputs from students' comments for each project. We expected that the majority of the captured keywords would be centered around UI design, as indicated in previous literature that most of the HCI class focus on UI design [10,12].

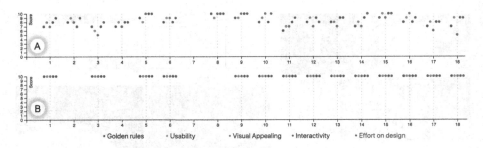

Fig. 3. Examples of good (panel A) and inadequate (panel B) peer grading for 18 students. Each dot represents grade (from 1 to 10), corresponds to five criteria above.

Table 1. Mean and standard deviation on peer assessment score for project 1 and 2

Criteria	Mean	Standard deviation
Project 1		
Golden rules	8.39	1.30
Efforts	8.90	1.23
Interactivity	8.56	1.27
Usability	8.45	1.31
Visual design	8.20	1.48
Project 2		
Golden rules	8.52	1.12
Efforts	8.78	1.24
Interactivity	8.60	1.23
Usability	8.54	1.17
Visual design	8.30	1.36
Sounds	7.33	2.30

We constructed a wordcloud of the most frequent words in regards to course content, with stop words removed. Figure 4 presents the most frequent words used in the project 1 – interface design for a smart mirror. Bigger font size in the wordcloud indicates more frequent occurrences, hence more common use of the words. Essentially, wordcloud gives an engaging visualization, which can be extended with a time dimension to maximize its use in characterizing subject development [6], being able to provide insights within an interactive, comprehensive dashboard [19]. Hereafter, the number in parentheses following a word indicates the word's frequency. In terms of dominant keywords, besides the design topic such as *mirror* (72), *design* (40), *interface* (33), the students were interested in the service that the interface provides: *widget* (34) and *feature* (23), then *color* (24), *text* (20) *button* (19) – the expectation on fundamental visual components aligned, with *cluttered* (16) and *consistent* (16) – highlighting the most common pitfall and standard that the design should pay close attention.

Functionality in design are taken into account: *touch* (4), *draggable* (8), *facial recognition* (6), *voice command* (3). As such, when looking at an application, students focused primarily on UI design, hence our study confirmed existing research [10,12].

Furthermore, user experience (UX) concerns are demonstrated through the students' perspective. By exploring more uncommon terms, user's experience is indicated by: *understandable* (4), *usability* (2), *helpful* (2). Users' emotions and attitudes towards the product are expressed: *easy* (8), *love* (5) and *enjoy* (2) (positive), in contrast to *hard* (15), *distracting* (5), *difficult* (3), *confusing* (2) (negative). Indeed, the comments reflect the views of students: *"The mirror is well done. The entire thing looks very consistent and I enjoy the speaking commands that lets you know what you are doing."* (compliment), *"Accessing the bottom menu to access dark mode could be a little confusing for some users as no icons are listed on the screen."* (suggestion). The findings on UX can complement existing work in ways that emphasize the need to integrate UX subjects in the HCI curriculum. HCI principles can be considered a crucial instrument for UX development; these results validated that HCI is the forerunner to UX design [13].

Overall, we can classify the keywords into three groups: UI, UX and Implementation. Besides UI and UX discussed above, the Implementation aspect is viewed through *data* (10), *implementation* (8), *api* (6), *function* (5), and *coding* (2). Compared to the expectation, there is a minimal amount of terminologies to the principle used, such as *golden rule* (2) – with only two occurrences, as opposed to the large number of visual elements mentioned in practical development. Some students even suggested *wheelchair* (3), as they consider the design for a variety of users. This pattern demonstrates that the focus shifts from theoretical design to direct visual aesthetics, as the students perceived and adopted the HCI principles effectively to apply them in the empirical application. To sum up, the keywords retrieved from the wordcloud cover primarily UI and UX interests from the students' perspective in the process of adopting HCI into interface design, demonstrating the diversity and broad coverage that peer assessment outcomes can provide. The method can be scaled to other disciplines that regard crowd wisdom in the development process.

4.3 R3: Do They Have the Same Perspectives on Adopting the Design Principles and Are These Views Consistent?

To answer the third question, we are looking for an agreement among students when they evaluated their peers. We hypothesize that the HCI principles are adopted when the scores provided by learners are *agreed*, and this agreement may imply that students have the same level of understanding of the principles.

To measure the level of agreement among learners, we use the intraclass correlation coefficient (ICC) [18], where each student is considered a rater, the project is the subject of being measured. ICC is widely used in the literature because it is easy to understand, can be used to assess both relative and absolute agreement, and the ability to accommodate a broad array of research scenarios compared to other measurements such as Cohen's Kappa or Fleiss Kappa [20].

Fig. 4. Wordcloud constructed from students' comments about the design for project 1. This is the top 150 most common words used, distributed in three categories: UI, UX, and Implementation.

Table 2. Inter-rater agreement measures for project 1 and project 2.

Subjects	Raters	Type	Agreement	Consistency	ICC scale [5]
Project 1					
19	77	Golden rules	0.963	0.972	Excellent
19	77	Efforts	0.900	0.970	Excellent
19	77	Interactivity	0.955	0.962	Excellent
19	77	Usability	0.965	0.972	Excellent
19	77	Visual design	0.971	0.977	Excellent
Project 2					
21	75	Golden rules	0.922	0.947	Excellent
21	75	Efforts	0.932	0.952	Excellent
21	75	Interactivity	0.896	0.923	Excellent
21	75	Usability	0.879	0.886	Excellent
21	75	Visual design	0.964	0.971	Excellent
21	75	Sounds	0.970	0.977	Excellent

Cicchetti [5] provides a guideline for inter-rater agreement measures, which can be briefly described as poor (less than 0.40), fair (between 0.40 and 0.59), good (between 0.60 and 0.74), excellent (between 0.75 and 1.00).

Table 2 provides the results on the level of agreement and consistency when students evaluate their peers. There is a difference in the number of raters (83 students in total, 77 in project 1, and 75 in project 2); this is due to the exclusion of ambiguous responses, as noted in Subsect. 3.4 and Fig. 3. It can be seen from Table 2 that students tend to give the same score (agreement score = 0.963) given the principle guideline (or golden rules) in project 1, so do as in project 2 (agreement score = 0.922). These scores are considerably high (excellent) when mapped to the inter-rater agreement measure scales suggested by Cicchetti [5]. In addition, we also find a high consistency among students when evaluating the other aspects of the projects such as efforts, interactivity, usability, and visual design since consistency scores are all above 0.75.

5   Conclusion and Future Work

In this paper, we have presented the learners' perspective on the perception and adoption of HCI principles in a classroom setting. A standalone web presentation platform is utilized to gather instant online peer feedback from students throughout the course. The qualitative analysis of peer feedback demonstrated that the students primarily emphasize the design feature and then visual components and interactivity. This approach can be extended to present subject evolution and student development over time, providing a bigger context. The outcome also pointed out that the interests spread in both UI and UX, suggesting further incorporation of UX in the HCI curriculum, which is currently having a shortage in the existing literature. On the quantitative analysis, we have found that the students followed the guidelines by a large margin. The results indicated a high level of agreement among the students, determined by the inter-rater agreement measures. We also have found high consistency within the class regarding other aspects evaluated, such as efforts, interactivity, usability, and visually appealing.

This research, however, is subject to several limitations. The course duration in this study is short, with only 16 weeks; a more prolonged period can help reduce random errors. Another limitation is the sample size, with 83 students; we believe that a larger sample size could increase the generalizability of the result (nevertheless, our sample size meets the minimum requirement suggested by [2]). We will expand the study in the following semesters for future work, and we expect that researchers can conduct related studies to confirm our findings.

References

1. Aalberg, T., Lorås, M.: Active learning and student peer assessment in a web development course. In: Norsk IKT-konferanse for forskning og utdanning (2018)
2. Albano, A.: Introduction to educational and psychological measurement using R (2017)
3. Carter, A.S., Hundhausen, C.D.: A review of studio-based learning in computer science. J. Comput. Sci. Coll. **27**(1), 105–111 (2011)
4. Churchill, E.F., Bowser, A., Preece, J.: Teaching and learning human-computer interaction: past, present, and future. Interactions **20**(2), 44–53 (2013)

5. Cicchetti, D.V.: Guidelines, criteria, and rules of thumb for evaluating normed and standardized assessment instruments in psychology. Psychol. Assess. **6**(4), 284 (1994)
6. Dang, T., Nguyen, H.N., Pham, V.: WordStream: interactive visualization for topic evolution. In: Johansson, J., Sadlo, F., Marai, G.E. (eds.) EuroVis 2019 - Short Papers. The Eurographics Association (2019). https://doi.org/10.2312/evs.20191178
7. Dang, T., Pham, V., Nguyen, H.N., Nguyen, N.V.: AgasedViz: visualizing groundwater availability of Ogallala Aquifer, USA. Environ. Earth Sci. **79**(5), 1–12 (2020)
8. Figl, K., Bauer, C., Kriglstein, S.: Students' view on instant online feedback for presentations. In: Proceedings of the AMCIS 2009, p. 775 (2009)
9. Gehringer, E.F.: Electronic peer review and peer grading in computer-science courses. ACM SIGCSE Bull. **33**(1), 139–143 (2001)
10. Greenberg, S.: Teaching human computer interaction to programmers. Interactions **3**(4), 62–76 (1996)
11. Hatziapostolou, T., Paraskakis, I.: Enhancing the impact of formative feedback on student learning through an online feedback system. Electron. J. E-learn. **8**(2), 111–122 (2010)
12. Hewett, T.T., et al.: ACM SIGCHI Curricula for Human-Computer Interaction. ACM, New York (1992)
13. Interaction Design Foundation: What is Human-Computer Interaction (HCI)? (2019). https://www.interaction-design.org/literature/topics/human-computer-interaction. Accessed 1 July 2020
14. Kulkarni, C.E., Bernstein, M.S., Klemmer, S.R.: PeerStudio: rapid peer feedback emphasizes revision and improves performance. In: Proceedings of the Second (2015) ACM Conference on Learning@ Scale, pp. 75–84 (2015)
15. Le, D.D., Pham, V., Nguyen, H.N., Dang, T.: Visualization and explainable machine learning for efficient manufacturing and system operations. Smart Sustain. Manuf. Syst. **3**(2), 127–147 (2019)
16. Ma, X., Yu, L., Forlizzi, J.L., Dow, S.P.: Exiting the design studio: leveraging online participants for early-stage design feedback. In: Proceedings of the 18th ACM Conference on Computer Supported Cooperative Work & Social Computing, pp. 676–685 (2015)
17. Magrabi, F., Coiera, E.W., Westbrook, J.I., Gosling, A.S., Vickland, V.: General practitioners' use of online evidence during consultations. Int. J. Med. Inf. **74**(1), 1–12 (2005)
18. McGraw, K.O., Wong, S.P.: Forming inferences about some intraclass correlation coefficients. Psychol. Methods **1**(1), 30 (1996)
19. Nguyen, H.N., Dang, T.: EQSA: Earthquake situational analytics from social media. In: Proceedings of the IEEE Conference on Visual Analytics Science and Technology (VAST 2019), pp. 142–143 (2019). https://doi.org/10.1109/VAST47406.2019.8986947
20. Nichols, T.R., Wisner, P.M., Cripe, G., Gulabchand, L.: Putting the kappa statistic to use. Qual. Assur. J. **13**(3–4), 57–61 (2010)
21. Shannon, A., Hammer, J., Thurston, H., Diehl, N., Dow, S.: PeerPresents: A wab-based system for in-class peer feedback during student presentations. In: Proceedings of the 2016 ACM Conference on Designing Interactive Systems, DIS 2016, pp. 447–458. Association for Computing Machinery, New York (2016). https://doi.org/10.1145/2901790.2901816

22. Shneiderman, B., Plaisant, C., Cohen, M., Jacobs, S., Elmqvist, N., Diakopoulos, N.: Designing the User Interface: Strategies for Effective Human-Computer Interaction. Pearson, London (2016)
23. Sims, R.: Interactivity: a forgotten art? Comput. Hum. Behav. **13**(2), 157–180 (1997)
24. Nguyen, V.T., Hite, R., Dang, T.: Web-based virtual reality development in classroom: from learner's perspectives. In: Proceedings of the IEEE International Conference on Artificial Intelligence and Virtual Reality (AIVR 2018), pp. 11–18 (2018). https://doi.org/10.1109/AIVR.2018.00010

Pre-trained Convolutional Neural Network for the Diagnosis of Tuberculosis

Mustapha Oloko-Oba and Serestina Viriri[✉]

School of Mathematics, Statistics and Computer Sciences,
University of KwaZulu-Natal, Durban, South Africa
219098624@stu.ukzn.ac.za, viriris@ukzn.ac.za

Abstract. Tuberculosis (TB) is an infectious disease that claimed about 1.5 million lives in 2018. TB is most prevalent in developing regions. Even though TB disease is curable, it necessitates early detection to prevent its spread and casualties. Chest radiographs are one of the most reliable screening techniques; although, its accuracy is dependent on professional radiologists interpretation of the individual images. Consequently, we present a computer-aided detection system using a pre-trained convolutional neural network as features extractor and logistic regression classifier to automatically analyze the chest radiographs to provide a timely and accurate interpretation of multiple images. The chest radiographs were pre-processed before extracting distinctive features and then fed to the classifier to detect which image is infected. This work established the potential of implementing pre-trained Convolutional Neural Network models in the medical domain to obtained good results despite limited datasets.

Keywords: Tuberculosis · Chest radiograph · Pre-processing · Features extractor · Logistic regression · Convolutional neural network.

1 Introduction

Tuberculosis (TB) is ranked among the topmost ten deadly diseases that resulted in 1.5million deaths in 2018 from about 10 million people falling it globally. Tuberculosis is predominant in developing nations, which contributes to about 95(%) of infected cases and deaths [1]. Everyone is at risk of contracting Tuberculosis even though it is common in men, with about 5.7million cases reported in 2018. Tuberculosis is curable, and most of the causalities could be averted if only the disease is diagnosed early [1]. Traditional approaches employed in screening Tuberculosis includes Tuberculin Skin Test [2], Smear Microscopy [3], Interferon Gamma Release Assays [4], among others. Still, regrettably, most of these approaches have limitations, especially in developing countries ranging from high cost for general adoption, inadequate equipment, requires a stable power supply, inaccurate results because of low sensitivity, and inability to distinguish between latent and active Tuberculosis [5].

© Springer Nature Switzerland AG 2020
G. Bebis et al. (Eds.): ISVC 2020, LNCS 12510, pp. 558–569, 2020.
https://doi.org/10.1007/978-3-030-64559-5_44

More recently, Chest Radiograph (CXR) has been identified as a prominent and less expensive technique for detecting abnormalities in the lungs relating to Tuberculosis [6–8]. World Health Organization recommends the application of CXR as a screening tool for pulmonary diseases [9]. However, interpreting the CXR requires skilled and expert radiologists who are lacking in developing regions and usually results in delay and misdiagnosis [10, 11].

Over the years, Computer-aided classification tasks using Convolutional Neural Network (CNN), a Deep Learning technique, have become prominent for analyzing different pulmonary abnormalities in the medical domain. The application of an efficient classification tool is vital for improving the quality of diagnosis while reducing the time taken to diagnose a large volume of CXRs [12, 13]. This endeavor is to achieve the global decline in Tuberculosis incidence to about 4–5% annually compared to the current 2% yearly as part of the World Health Organization "End TB Strategy" [1].

Convolutional neural networks have demonstrated tremendous success for several computer vision tasks, including face detection, age and gender classification, object detection, autonomous cars, and even medical imaging analysis. Although, it still requires continuous effort to develop a sophisticated and efficient computer-aided detection system to assist the medical practitioner in the early diagnosis and treatment of deadly diseases such as Tuberculosis.

Application of a convolutional neural network can be made either by building the system from scratch or by using the weight of a pre-trained model, usually referred to as "Transfer Learning" [15]. In transfer learning, the weights of a pre-trained model can be used as features extractor upon which a classifier is trained, or the weights can be fine-tuned [14]. The former is the focus of this study, which is to employ a pre-trained model as a features extractor to train a more effective and accurate classifier.

This study aims to present VGG16 variants of VGGNet [25] pre-trained CNN architecture as features extractor then train a Logistic Regression (LR) [41] classifier to determine which images constitute Tuberculosis manifestations. To the best of our knowledge, only few research work has employed a pre-trained CNN models as a features extractor and trained a machine learning classifier to detect the presence of Tuberculosis. An example is [16].

2   Related Work

The possibilities and strength offered by deep learning and machine learning models have been tremendous in the last years. Their popularity, achievement, and interest in their application for object detection and classification task is partly as a result of the availability of large datasets for training models (either from scratch or transferring the weights of state-of-the art models available from ImageNet repository) [18] and sophisticated computing power infrastructures like GPUs, cloud services and other related frameworks [17, 19]. In this section, we will review most of the all-important study that employed transfer learning CNN architectures for detecting Tuberculosis on Chest Radiograph.

It is evident from [18,21] that a convolutional neural network built on the ImageNet extensive database can learn complicated and distinctive features. This capability makes it deployable as features extractor in different domains where large datasets are not readily available such as Remote Sensing [20], Maritime Vessels [21], Medical Field [16,22,23] to achieve competing outcomes or sometimes better performance.

One of the recent studies that employed a pre-trained convolutional neural network for classifying chest radiographs to identify TB abnormalities was [24]. The authors applied the VGG16 model for training 75% of the Shenzhen and Montgomery datasets, while 25% was used as a testing set. Two experiments were performed where augmentation was applied in one instance and not applied in the other case. The result for the example with augmentation achieved 81.25% accuracy, while 80% accuracy was obtained for the case without augmentation. These results prove that increased performance can be achieved by employing preprocessing techniques on the images. Although, only augmentation technique was applied in this case and yet shows an improvement of 1.25%.

The work presented in [16], applied three pre-trained CNNs models to extract features from chest radiographs to identify TB infection. The authors employed each of "Bag of CNN Features," "Simple Features Extractor," and "Ensembles" as proposals to evaluate the potential of GoogLeNet [28], VggNet [25], and, ResNet [29] as features extractor from Montgomery and Shenzhen datasets. The images were segmented and resized according to the original input size of the pre-trained models except for the implementation of "Bag of Features" where the images were not resized. The proposals were evaluated in terms of AUC and Accuracy, where either of GoogLeNet, ResNet, and VggNet shows improvement on different datasets and also at different performance metrics. For instance, under the implementation of "Simple Features" GoogLeNet obtained the best accuracy of 0.782% with 0.838% AUC on the Montgomery datasets meanwhile on the Shenzhen dataset, VggNet attained a higher AUC of 0.912% with Resent having the best accuracy at 0.834% still, the overall best accuracy and AUC stood at 0.847% and 0.926%, respectively. It was evident in this study that the size of datasets and class imbalance can impact the performance of a model.

GoogLeNet [28] architecture was used in [26] for training CXR to detect different TB manifestations. The authors classified the CXR as healthy or unhealthy with one or more of consolidation, cardiomegaly, pulmonary edema, pneumothorax, or pleural effusion. The input images were resized using the half-fill, half-crop technique to normalize the images with large dimensions. Then the images with shorter dimensions were padded with noise to deal with aspect ratio imbalance. The evaluation metric employed were sensitivity, specificity, and AUC with validation of 2 board-certified radiologists, each having 8 and 3 years of experience. The best performance of their experiments was achieved on the healthy class obtaining 91% sensitivity and specificity with 0.964% AUC higher than the unhealthy classes. The disparity could be as a result of the class and data imbalance since the datasets used is a private dataset that is not publicly available and might not have been appropriately labeled.

The authors in [27] are the first to apply deep convolutional neural networks on chest radiographs to diagnose TB. They adopt prominent AlexNet [17] architecture and tweak it by adding a new convolutional layer to handle the high-resolution image since the chest radiographs resolutions are higher than the input images applied in AlexNet as well as a minimum number of nodes in the classifier layer. The system was trained on large private datasets initially using random weight and later trained using AlexNet learned weights. The experiment with the random weight achieved 0.77% accuracy and 0.82% AUC. Meanwhile, the experiment conducted with AlexNet learned weights attained 0.90% accuracy with an AUC of 0.96%. Another experiment was then performed to classify two benchmark datasets (Montgomery and Shenzhen). The average class probabilities of the training were taking to attain ensemble outcomes on both datasets. The Montgomery produced an accuracy of 0.674% and AUC of 0.884%, while accuracy and AUC stand at 0.837% and 0.926% respectively for the Shenzhen dataset. A comparison to evaluate the performance of CNN with and without application of transfer learning is then performed. The result found that CNN with transfer learning outperformed having an accuracy of 0.903% and AUC of 0.964% against the 0.773% accuracy and 0.816% AUC obtained for the CNN without transfer learning.

The study conducted in [30] evaluates the performance of some pre-trained convolutional neural networks concerning localization and classification of different TB abnormalities from chest radiographs. The study used heatmap as a way of localization in the chest radiograph images. Experiments were performed on three public datasets and showed that the performance of a particular pre-trained CNN model across all the abnormalities. In other words, a model can perform better on some manifestations and act woefully on other manifestations. The study also found that for classification accuracy, shallow layers perform better than deeper layers and finally concludes that Ensemble [32] of different pre-trained CNN models attained better performance than a single one. The result of their system was evaluated in terms of accuracy, sensitivity, specificity, and AUC, where the best performance obtained for the detection of the cardiomegaly abnormalities saw VggNet achieved 92.00% accuracy, 0.94% AUC, 96.00% sensitivity. At the same time, ResNet got better at a specificity of 96.00%.

Another study that applied transfer learning to screen chest radiographs for the presence of TB is presented in [31]. The authors modified the AlexNet and VggNet architectures to classify chest radiograph images into healthy and unhealthy classes. The modified architecture was trained on Shenzhen and Montgomery datasets; the experimental results show AlexNet achieved 80.4% while VggNet slightly outperformed the AlexNet to obtain 81.6% classification accuracy. The study further concludes that having a large number of datasets will boost accuracy as the model will be able to learn more discriminative features.

In [33], pre-trained CNN models were fine-tuned to train chest radiograph images collected at the Yonsei University to detect TB automatically. The images obtained are accompanied by demographic information such as patients' height, weight, age, and gender. Before training the modified model, the lungs region in the images were segmented using U-Net [34], then resized to 256 256 pixels, and augmented as a way of pre-processing. The experiments performed to compare the performance of the model directly on the images and the performance of incorporating demographic information with the images. The authors used an equal number of image samples for the positive and negative classes for training the model. The results show the experiment which incorporates demographic information with the images obtained 0.9213% while the one based on the images alone achieved 0.9075% on the test set. The result clearly shows that incorporating demographic information like age, gender, height, and weight can slightly improve the performance of the model.

3 Methods and Techniques

In this section, we discussed the Chest Radiograph databases employed for the development of the Computer-aided detection system for identifying the presence of Tuberculosis.

3.1 Datasets

The following databases were used for the experiments done in this work. These databases are publicly available at: https://lhncbc.nlm.nih.gov/publication/pub9931 and have been utilized in many studies.

The Shenzhen database [35, 36] is explicit to TB disease and is publicly available for research. The database is made up of 336 unhealthy samples and 326 healthy samples. The identification of each image ends either with a "0" signifying healthy sample or a "1" meaning unhealthy sample. All images are approximately 3000 × 3000 pixels in resolution. This database also contains clinical readings that give demographic details about each of the samples with respect to age, sex, and diagnosis. The chest radiographs in this database were collected at the Guandong Hospital in Shenzhen, China, and saved in (png) format. See Fig. 1 for samples of chest radiographs in this database.

The Montgomery County chest radiograph database [35, 36] is a TB-specific database collected by the Department of Health Services, Maryland, U.S.A for research intent. This database is composed of 58 unhealthy samples and 80 healthy samples. The naming convention of each image ends either with "0" denoting a healthy sample or "1" indicating an unhealthy sample. All samples are of the size 4892 × 4020 pixels or 4020 × 4892 pixels available as (png) format. This database is also accompanied by clinical readings that give demographic details about each of the samples with respect to sex, age, and manifestations. Additionally, the database contains manually generated left and right mask segmentation of the chest radiographs. See Fig. 2 for samples of chest radiographs in this database.

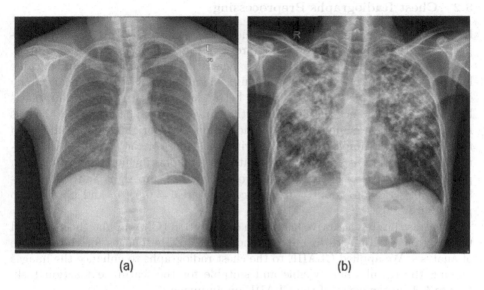

Fig. 1. Sample in the Shenzhen Database. **(a)** is a healthy chest radiograph of a 60 years old male patient while **(b)** is an unhealthy chest radiograph of a 36 years old male patient diagnosed with "bilateral pulmonary TB".

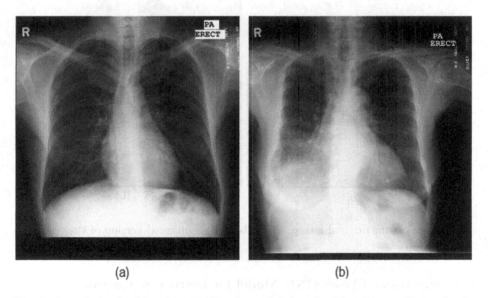

Fig. 2. Sample in the Montgomery Database. **(a)** is a healthy chest radiograph of a 33 years old male patient while **(b)** is an unhealthy chest radiograph of an 84 years old female patient diagnosed with "bilateral miliary nodules diffusely with right middle lobe and right pleural effusion".

3.2   Chest Radiographs Preprocessing

In this study, we applied "Data Augmentation [38], and CLAHE [39] as pre-processing techniques to boost and improve the quality of the chest radiographs.

Augmentation is an artificial data generation technique used in machine learning to control overfitting, improving generalization as well as the accuracy of the network. CNN models perform better when the size of the datasets is large [31,40], and since the number of the chest radiographs in our database is not large enough, we applied data augmentation to the original chest radiograph to generate new samples while preserving the labels of the samples. The augmentation operations applied to generate new samples includes: "rotation with probability = 1, max left and right probability = 2, flip right and left probability = 0.1, random zoom = 0.2, percentage area = 0.5 top and bottom flip probability of 0.2.

Contrast limited adaptive histogram equalization (CLAHE) has been applied to many medical images to improve the quality of the images for the purpose of analysis. We applied CLAHE to the chest radiographs to enhance the images making the details more visible and suitable for the feature extraction task. Figure 3 show the effect of the CLAHE on an image.

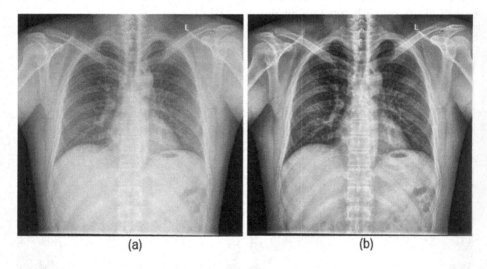

(a)   (b)

Fig. 3. (a) is the original image, while (b) is the enhanced version of the original.

3.3   Pre-trained Deep CNN Model for Feature Extraction

The concept of Transfer Learning is actually to employ the weight of a model that is trained on perticular objects and transfer it to train a different object to eliminate the complexity of training a model from scratch. There are several benchmark deep CNN learning models trained on large datasets like ImageNet

[18] to recognize several objects. Example of these models that have performed excellently well includes AlexNet [17], VggNet [25], GoogLeNet [28], ResNet [29] among other prominent ones. In this present work, we treated the Vgg16 variant of VggNet as a feature extractor rather than as end-to-end network as the case of the original model.

We truncated the three fully convolutional layers in the original vgg16, which resulted in making the "max-pooling" the final and output layer, as presented in Fig. 4. The chest radiographs images are resized to $224 \times 224 \times 3$ to conform to the input dimension of Vgg16 and then propagated through the network until the last max-pooling layer, which now serves as the output layer having a $7 \times 7 \times 512$ shape that is flattened into a vector map and fed as input to the classifier. Of course, the output can be extracted at any random layer, but we decided to output at the pooling layer, this is with respect to the analysis presented in [37].

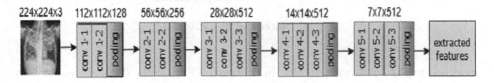

Fig. 4. Truncated Vgg16 where "Max-pooling layer" is employed as the output layer.

After extracting features from the chest radiographs, these features are then fed as input to the Logistic Regression classifier for training to obtain classification details, as illustrated in Fig. 5. The LR classifier is powerful and efficient for binary classification. Its relation to exponential probability distribution makes them perform well in medical domain because it allows the dependence of class labels on features and gives room to carry out sensitivity analysis.

As a tradition, we split the dataset into training and validation set prior to training the classifier such that an indicator is configured as [:q] and [q:] specifying that all the images prior to ":q" are included in the training set while the images after "q:" are reserved for validation. The system 'C' parameters range between "0.0001 to 1000", the optimum parameter for the classifier is then selected by employing a grid search. Once the optimum parameter is established, the model is then evaluated against the testing data to determine the performance of the classifier in detecting whether an image is infected with TB or not.

4   Result and Discussion

This section presents the experimental results performed on both Montgomery and Shenzhen benchmark datasets. These datasets were split into 70(%) used for training the logistic regression classifier on the extracted features from the

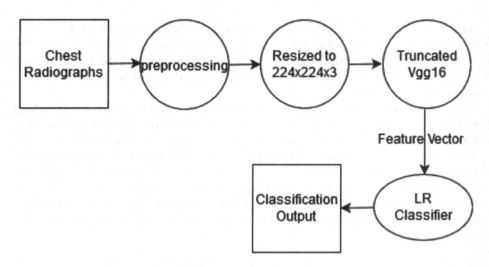

Fig. 5. Procedural flow diagram.

modified pre-trained vgg16 model. In contrast, 30(%) of the dataset was used to evaluate the performance of the classifier on both datasets.

In the first experiment carried out on the Montgomery set, the system obtained an accuracy of 89(%) and precision of 90.1(%) while on the Shenzhen set, the system performed at 95.8(%) accuracy with a precision of 96(%). Also, we took a step further to determine the Rank-1 accuracy of the system, which is the number of times where the predicted output conforms to the corresponding ground-truth. Hence, the Rank-1 accuracy obtained for both datasets is 92.40(%) and 99.25(%), respectively, as shown in Table 1.

Table 1. Results of the experiments

Database	Accuracy (%)	Precision (%)	Rank-1 (%)
Montgomery	89	90.1	92.40
Shenzhen	95.8	96	99.25

It can be observed from Table 1 that the result obtained in the experiment on the Montgomery set is lower compared to the Shenzhen set, as reported in related work. This outcome is mostly as a result of lesser dataset and class imbalance, Although, in this case since we performed augmentation on the dataset, we can say only class imbalance where the ratio of healthy to unhealthy samples is about "60 : 40" in the Montgomery set is the factor responsible for it (Table 2).

Table 2. Comparison of the proposed model with related work. The performance metrics are measured in (%)

Ref	Model	Accuracy	Precision
24	VggNet	81.25	0.80
16	GoogLeNet, VggNet, ResNet	0.847	-
27	AlexNet	90.03	-
30	AlexNet, VggNet, ResNet	92.00	-
31	VggNet, Inception, ResNet, DensNet	81.60	-
Proposed	**VggNet**	**95.80**	**96.00**

5   Conclusion

In this work, we explored pre-trained CNN and implemented Vgg16 as a features extractor. Logistic Regression classifier was then trained on the extracted features to detect Tuberculosis. This study and other related work have shown characteristics such as eliminating "training complexity, expenses, high computing power, and large datasets' that made implementing pre-trained CNN models powerful and relevant to medical and other fields where dataset are limited for classification. Although the approach applied in this work has obtained excellent results, but a better computer-aided detection system can still be developed if a large amount of annotated chest radiographs dataset can be created. These annotated datasets can then be utilized in building deeper models from the scratch to identify various pulmonary diseases.

References

1. World Health Organization.: Global status report on alcohol and health 2018. World Health Organization (2019)
2. Cohn, D.L., O'Brien, R.J., Geiter, L.J., Gordin, F., Hershfield, E., Horsburgh, C.: Targeted tuberculin testing and treatment of latent tuberculosis infection. MMWR Morb Mortal Wkly Rep **49**(6), 1–54 (2000)
3. Desikan, P.: Sputum smear microscopy in tuberculosis: is it still relevant? Indian J. Med. Res. **137**(3), 442 (2013)
4. Zwerling, A., van den Hof, S., Scholten, J., Cobelens, F., Menzies, D., Pai, M.: Interferon-gamma release assays for tuberculosis screening of healthcare workers: a systematic review. Thorax **67**(1), 62–70 (2012)
5. Leung, C.C.: Reexamining the role of radiography in tuberculosis case finding. Int. J. Tuberc. Lung Dis.: Official J. Int. Union Against Tuberc. Lung Dis. **15**(10), 1279 (2011)
6. Jaeger, S., et al.: Automatic screening for tuberculosis in chest radiographs: a survey. Quant. Imaging Med. Surg. **3**(2), 89 (2013)
7. Naing, W.Y.N., Htike, Z.Z.: Advances in automatic tuberculosis detection in chest x-ray images. Signal Image Process. **5**(6), 41 (2014)

8. World Health Organization.: Tuberculosis prevalence surveys: a handbook. World Health Organization (2011)
9. World Health Organization.: Chest radiography in tuberculosis detection: summary of current WHO recommendations and guidance on programmatic approaches (No.WHO/HTM/TB/2016.20). World Health Organization (2016)
10. Noor, N.M., Rijal, O.M., Yunus, A., Mahayiddin, A.A., Peng, G.C., Abu-Bakar, S.A.R.: A statistical interpretation of the chest radiograph for the detection of pulmonary tuberculosis. In: 2010 IEEE EMBS Conference on Biomedical Engineering and Sciences (IECBES), pp. 47–51 (2010)
11. Pedrazzoli, D., Lalli, M., Boccia, D., Houben, R., Kranzer, K.: Can tuberculosis patients in resource-constrained settings afford chest radiography? Eur. Respir. J. 49(3), 1601877 (2017)
12. Schmidhuber, J.: Deep learning in neural networks: an overview. Neural Networks 61, 85–117 (2015)
13. Livieris, I.E., Kanavos, A., Tampakas, V., Pintelas, P.: A weighted voting ensemble self-labeled algorithm for the detection of lung abnormalities from X-rays. Algorithms 12(3), 64 (2019)
14. Al Hadhrami, E., Al Mufti, M., Taha, B., Werghi, N.: Transfer learning with convolutional neural networks for moving target classification with micro-Doppler radar spectrograms. In: IEEE International Conference on Artificial Intelligence and Big Data (ICAIBD), pp. 148–154 (2018)
15. Nogueira, K., Penatti, O.A., Dos Santos, J.A.: Towards better exploiting convolutional neural networks for remote sensing scene classification. Pattern Recogn. 61, 539–556 (2017)
16. Lopes, U.K., Valiati, J.F.: Pre-trained convolutional neural networks as feature extractors for tuberculosis detection. Comput. Biol. Med. 89, 135–143 (2017)
17. Krizhevsky, A., Sutskever, I., Hinton, G. E.: Imagenet classification with deep convolutional neural networks. In: Advances in Neural Information Processing Systems, pp. 1097–1105 (2012)
18. Deng, J., Dong, W., Socher, R., Li, L.J., Li, K., Fei-Fei, L.: Imagenet: a large-scale hierarchical image database. In: IEEE Conference on Computer Vision and Pattern Recognition, pp. 248–255 (2009)
19. Dean, J., et al.: Large scale distributed deep networks. In: Advances in Neural Information Processing Systems, pp. 1223–1231 (2012)
20. Xie, M., Jean, N., Burke, M., Lobell, D., Ermon, S.: Transfer learning from deep features for remote sensing and poverty mapping. In: Thirtieth AAAI Conference on Artificial Intelligence (2016)
21. Bousetouane, F., Morris, B.: Off-the-shelf CNN features for fine-grained classification of vessels in a maritime environment. In: Bebis, G., et al. (eds.) ISVC 2015. LNCS, vol. 9475, pp. 379–388. Springer, Cham (2015). https://doi.org/10.1007/978-3-319-27863-6_35
22. Liu, T., Xie, S., Yu, J., Niu, L., Sun, W.: Classification of thyroid nodules in ultrasound images using deep model based transfer learning and hybrid features. In: 2017 IEEE International Conference on Acoustics, Speech and Signal Processing (ICASSP), pp. 919–923 (2017)
23. Ribeiro, E., Uhl, A., Wimmer, G., Häfner, M.: Exploring deep learning and transfer learning for colonic polyp classification. Comput. Math. Methods Med. (2016)
24. Ahsan, M., Gomes, R., Denton, A.: Application of a Convolutional Neural Network using transfer learning for tuberculosis detection. In: IEEE International Conference on Electro Information Technology (EIT), pp. 427–433 (2019)

25. Simonyan, K., Zisserman, A.: Very deep convolutional networks for large-scale image recognition. arXiv preprint arXiv:1409.1556 (2014)
26. Cicero, M., et al.: Training and validating a deep convolutional neural network for computer-aided detection and classification of abnormalities on frontal chest radiographs. Invest. Radiol. **52**(5), 281–287 (2017)
27. Hwang, S., Kim, H. E., Jeong, J., Kim, H.J.: A novel approach for tuberculosis screening based on deep convolutional neural networks. In: International Society for Optics and Photonics.: Computer-Aided Diagnosis, vol. 9785, p. 97852W (2016)
28. Szegedy, C., et al.: Going deeper with convolutions. In: Proceedings of the IEEE Conference on Computer Vision and Pattern Recognition, pp. 1–9 (2015)
29. He, K., Zhang, X., Ren, S., Sun, J.: Deep residual learning for image recognition. In: Proceedings of the IEEE Conference on Computer Vision and Pattern Recognition, pp. 770–778 (2016)
30. Islam, M.T., Aowal, M.A., Minhaz, A.T., Ashraf, K.: Abnormality detection and localization in chest x-rays using deep convolutional neural networks. arXiv preprint arXiv:1705.09850 (2017)
31. Rohilla, A., Hooda, R., Mittal, A.: Tb detection in chest radiograph using deep learning architecture. In: ICETETSM-17, pp. 136–147 (2017)
32. Rokach, L.: Ensemble-based classifiers. Artif. Intell. Rev. **33**(1–2), 1–39 (2010)
33. Heo, S.J., et al.: Deep learning algorithms with demographic information help to detect tuberculosis in chest radiographs in annual workers' health examination data. Int. J. Environ. Rese. Public Health **16**(2), 250 (2019)
34. Ronneberger, O., Fischer, P., Brox, T.: U-Net: convolutional networks for biomedical image segmentation. In: Navab, N., Hornegger, J., Wells, W.M., Frangi, A.F. (eds.) MICCAI 2015. LNCS, vol. 9351, pp. 234–241. Springer, Cham (2015). https://doi.org/10.1007/978-3-319-24574-4_28
35. Jaeger, S., et al.: Automatic tuberculosis screening using chest radiographs. IEEE Trans. Med. Imaging **33**(2), 233–245 (2013)
36. Candemir, S., et al.: Lung segmentation in chest radiographs using anatomical atlases with nonrigid registration. IEEE Trans. Med. Imaging **33**(2), 577–590 (2013)
37. Sharif Razavian, A., Azizpour, H., Sullivan, J., Carlsson, S.: CNN features off-the-shelf: an astounding baseline for recognition. In: Proceedings of the IEEE conference on Computer Vision and Pattern Recognition Workshops, pp. 806–813 (2014)
38. Bloice, M.D., Stocker, C., Holzinger, A.: Augmentor: an image augmentation library for machine learning. arXiv preprint arXiv:1708.04680 (2017)
39. Kurt, B., Nabiyev, V.V., Turhan, K.: Medical images enhancement by using anisotropic filter and clahe. In: IEEE International Symposium on Innovations in Intelligent Systems and Applications, pp. 1–4 (2012)
40. Tajbakhsh, N., et al.: Convolutional neural networks for medical image analysis: full training or fine tuning? IEEE Trans. Med. Imaging **35**(5), 1299–1312 (2016)
41. Hosmer Jr., D.W., Lemeshow, S., Sturdivant, R.X.: Applied logistic regression, vol. 398. John Wiley and Sons, New York (2013)

Near-Optimal Concentric Circles Layout

Prabhakar V. Vemavarapu, Mehmet Engin Tozal$^{(\boxtimes)}$, and Christoph W. Borst

School of Computing and Informatics, University of Louisiana at Lafayette,
Lafayette, LA 70504, USA
{C00255627,metozal,cxb9999}@louisiana.edu

Abstract. The majority of graph visualization algorithms emphasize improving the readability of graphs by focusing on various vertex and edge rendering techniques. However, revealing the global connectivity structure of a graph by identifying significant vertices is an important and useful part of any graph analytics system. Centrality measures reveal the "most important" vertices of a graph, commonly referred to as central or influential vertices. Hence, a centrality-oriented visualization may highlight these important vertices and give deep insights into graph data. This paper proposes a mathematical optimization-based clustered graph layout called Near-Optimal Concentric Circles (NOCC) layout to visualize medium to large scale-free graphs. We cluster the vertices by their betweenness values and optimally place them on concentric circles to reveal the extensive connectivity structure of the graph while achieving aesthetically pleasing layouts. Besides, we incorporate different edge rendering techniques to improve graph readability and interaction.

Keywords: Graph visualization · Connectivity · Layout algorithm · Scale-free networks.

1 Introduction

Recent advancements in data collection have been producing big complex data modeled as graphs (entities (vertices/nodes) and their relationships (edges/links)). Effective analysis of medium-to-large graphs is gaining popularity in many application domains, including social sciences, engineering, and natural sciences. Human ability to identify and comprehend visual patterns makes visualization a critical tool to understand graphs, and many studies used it as an effective tool to improve perception in graph exploration [14,15,19,26]. A reasonably well-drawn graph visualization will help users to quickly get deeper insights into the data by highlighting existing patterns and revealing hidden patterns.

Many visualization algorithms such as force-based for large-scale graphs result in space-filling, cluttered visualization like a hairball [11]. This visual clutter, due to overlapping vertices and a large number of edge-crossings, makes visualizations hard to read and interpret. Rendering a large number of vertices in a small space increases vertex overlaps and aggravates the visual clutter. A variety of methods have been proposed to address this problem and the

© Springer Nature Switzerland AG 2020
G. Bebis et al. (Eds.): ISVC 2020, LNCS 12510, pp. 570–580, 2020.
https://doi.org/10.1007/978-3-030-64559-5_45

most promising solution is attribute-based clustering of the vertices for visualization [18]. Vertex clustering creates simpler visualizations by grouping vertices with similar attributes to organize the graph in a presentable way. The majority of the vertex-cluster based graph layout algorithms focus on graph readability by reducing vertex overlaps, increasing intra-cluster edges, reducing inter-cluster edges, and rendering only a portion of the edges [18,25]. They do not attempt to highlight the intrinsic structures of graphs - which is the main focus of our work.

Another solution for clutter reduction is to consider the layout generation as a mathematical optimization problem [30]. An objective function with constraints is defined on the vertex positions based on certain graph drawing aesthetics such as constant edge length. Layout generation algorithms consider these constraints and try to minimize a cost function to produce the final layout. Finding an optimal solution for this minimization cost function is NP-hard in most of the cases. Therefore, heuristics are employed to attain a *"near-optimal"* or an approximate solution for the immediate goal of clutter reduction in graph drawings.

In this paper, we present a novel *scale-free* graph visualization technique that features *centrality-based* clustering of the vertices, called Near-Optimal Concentric Circles (NOCC) layout. Large, scale-free graphs appear in many real-world systems including social, computer and biological networks [8,12,20,28,32,34]. These graphs exhibit a power-law vertex degree distribution $P(k) \sim k^{-\gamma}$ where $P(k)$ is the probability that a vertex has k links, and γ is the degree exponent which is typically in the range (2, 3) [24]. This indicates that a small portion of the vertices in these graphs have very high degrees while many vertices have low degrees. Centrality measures contextually identify influential vertices, and highlighting these vertices is useful in analyzing the topological structures of graphs. There are many centrality measures defined on graphs. Choosing the appropriate one depends on the problem at hand. In our approach, we choose the *betweenness* centrality to generate the vertex clusters as betweenness reveals the critical vertices that effectively connect other pairs of vertices in a graph.

After clustering the vertices based on their betweenness values, we present a concentric circle layout generation algorithm using mathematical optimization that places the vertices on circles representing the clusters. Finally, we combine graph coloring and partial edges to show that our algorithm generates aesthetically pleasing layouts.

Our main contribution in this study is a novel betweenness-based central-vertex graph layout algorithm for scale-free graphs using mathematical optimization that naturally shows the intrinsic connectivity structure by highlighting influential vertices. We use polar coordinates to enforce the constraints strictly rather than in a lazy manner [6].

2   Related Work

The history of graph visualization can be traced back over centuries. One of the earliest and the most fundamental visualizations of graphs is a node-link diagram, where vertices are represented as dots and relations between vertices as lines. Knuth's flowchart drawing paper [23] is considered one of the seminal works on graph visualization algorithms.

Ahmed et al. [1] present a variation of a fast-force-directed layout to visualize scale-free graphs in three dimensions. Vertices are constrained to parallel planes or on the surface of a sphere to minimize occlusion. Jia et al. [21] present a better interactive layout for large scale-free graphs that filters a large portion of less important edges while preserving other important features of the graph. Andersen et al. [2] present an algorithm that focuses on partitioning edges into local and global sets. Local or global edges are defined by the size of the maximum short flow between the edges' endpoints. These sets are visualized using a force-directed method emphasizing local edges. Baur et al. [3] describe a 2.5D method where the core hierarchy is partitioned into k-cores and these cores are used to visualize the graph structure. Cores are represented by 2D layouts. The interdependence for increasing k value is the third dimension, drawn using spectral layout starting with cores with the maximum value. Chan et al. [7] present Out-Degree Layout (ODL) by separating the vertices into multiple hierarchical layers based on the outdegree of each vertex. They demonstrate that their algorithm can produce aesthetically pleasing layouts by naturally drawing related vertices closer to each other. Giot et al. [16] present a layout algorithm that emphasizes cores of very large graphs. They use a combination of the hierarchical coreness decomposition with existing layout algorithms according to cluster topologies to produce vertex-overlap-free drawings. Takac et al. [27] propose a scalable, fast, and easy graph visualization layout called radius degree layout (RDL). Vertices are randomly placed on the circle arc and the distance from the center of the visualization to the vertex is inversely proportional to its degree.

Concentric circle-based visualization is a popular layout in visualizing rooted trees [13]. The root vertex of the tree is at the center and the descendant vertices are placed on subsequent rings (circles), similar to a concentric circle layout. It is used in other layouts like [9] and [6] to reflect the distance between entities of a graph. Chou et al. [9] visualizes the closest neighbors of a selected paper (vertex). The selected vertex is shown at the center and vertices (papers) related to the selected one are shown on a number of concentric discs according to their distance. Vertices are binned into categories, and each ring (circle) represents a bin. Castermans et al. also present a concentric circle based visualization of the closest neighbors of a selected entity [6]. The distances represent the *"near-exact"* distances between the neighbors and the selected vertex. Although [9] and [6] are concentric circle-based layouts, they focus on showing only a small portion of a graph: the vertex of interest and its neighborhood. This is different from our work, where we focus on revealing the extensive connectivity structure of a scale-free graph by identifying the important vertices based on betweenness.

Most of the discussed related work presents layout techniques to improve the readability of scale-free graphs via an existing layout algorithm or showing only a small portion of the graph. In [1,2,17] the authors present the results on small to medium-size graphs and the scalabilities of these algorithms are not discussed. In [21], the authors present vertex filtering to avoid rendering all vertices. Interested readers can find more related works in [4] and [10].

In this work, we present a novel concentric circle based graph layout algorithm that emphasizes relatively important vertices based on the betweenness centrality. In this process, we use the benefit of global optimization - not dependent on initial positions or points.

3   Near-Optimal Concentric Circles Layout

NOCC places vertices in a 2-dimensional space, with position depending on betweenness. NOCC uses the betweenness centrality - an indicator to identify relatively important vertices emphasizing extensive connectivity structure of scale-free graphs. Removal of a vertex with high betweenness can potentially disconnect a graph. For example, in router-level Internet topology graphs, failure of a router with high betweenness centrality will cause significant service disruptions until recovery processes occur.

Vertex betweenness gives the scale to which a vertex is present on the shortest paths between pairs of other vertices using the following formula:

$$C_b(v) = \sum_{\substack{s \neq v \neq t \\ s,v,t \in V}} \frac{\sigma_{st}(v)}{\sigma_{st}} \tag{1}$$

where σ_{st} is the total number of shortest paths from vertex s to t and $\sigma_{st}(v)$ is the total number of these paths through v.

We used the ck-means algorithm [29] to cluster the vertices using different centralities - degree, stress, betweenness, closeness, and variations of eigencentrality, to study the inter-cluster relations. We define *Edgehop* as the difference in the cluster number of the two endpoints of an edge. For example, an edge from a vertex in cluster 2 to a vertex in cluster 4 has edgehop of $4 - 2 = 2$. Edgehop is used to identify patterns in inter-cluster and intra-cluster edges. We used the ck-means algorithm [29] to cluster the vertices using betweenness centrality to study the *Edgehop* relations and found a pattern as shown in Fig. 1 to visualize graphs in small display areas. These figures indicate that:

(i) Most of the edges are between the vertices in the outermost cluster that is congruent with the number of vertices at the edge of the scale-free graphs.
(ii) Very few edges span from the outermost toward the innermost clusters.
(iii) Significant number of edges are between the vertices in the same cluster (edgehop = 0) or in the immediately neighboring cluster (edgehop = 1), or in the clusters that are close to each other (edgehop = 2 or 3).

To visualize the clusters in the final layout, we use a concentric circles layout, as it naturally highlights the important vertices relevant to the connectivity structure of a graph while conveying the hierarchy of importance. Vertices with high betweenness values are drawn on circles closer to the common center and vice-versa. Vertices having similar importance are visualized on the same circle. The main idea in generating the NOCC layout are:

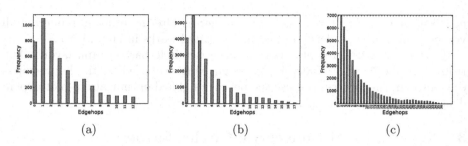

Fig. 1. Charts showing the edgehop histograms. Edgehop histogram for graphs with (a) $|V| = 1000$, (b) $|V| = 5000$ (c) $|V| = 10000$.

(i)   For each cluster, generate random vertex positions.
(ii) Generate final vertex positions by minimizing the total edge length.
(iii) Render the final layout to place the vertices in an optimal way.

Therefore, cluster 1 has the vertices with the highest betweenness.

3.1 Global Optimization Function

The next challenge is to place vertices on their respective circles to achieve an aesthetically pleasing visualization to convey the connectivity information. Note that a particular placement of vertices on their circles affects the placement of their neighboring vertices cascadingly. We modeled the layout calculation step as a global minimization (optimization) problem with constraints to produce easily readable layouts.

After generating vertex clusters, $\{c_1, c_2, c_3, \ldots, c_m\}$, the vertices are placed on concentric circles according to the clusters that they belong to. We aim for a near-optimal placement of the vertices of a graph $G(V, E)$ on these circles. We calculate the length of each edge and minimize the total edge length of the graph. This will also reduce a considerable amount of long edges, which will, in turn, reduce edge-crossings.

The coordinates of a vertex $v_i \in V$, denoted by denoted by $(x_i, y_i) \in \mathbb{R}^2$, are represented using the Polar coordinates, (r, θ). Vertices are placed on concentric circles/rings, $\{c_1, c_2, c_3, \ldots, c_m\}$, centered at the origin. As all the circles in the visualization are origin-centered, the coordinates of a vertex v_i on a circle of radius r_i at an angle θ_i are given by:

$$x_i = r_i \cos(\theta_i)$$
$$y_i = r_i \sin(\theta_i)$$

$$(2)$$

The distance between two points i, j at equal distance from the center, r is given by:

$$d = 2r \sin(\frac{\theta_j - \theta_i}{2})$$

$$(3)$$

The following optimization will meet the rationale of placing the neighboring vertices closer to each other by minimizing the total edge length:

$$\text{minimize} \quad \sum_{(v_i,v_j)\in E} r_i^2 + r_j^2 - 2r_i r_j \cos(\theta_j - \theta_i)$$

subject to   (4)

$$2\pi r_k \frac{\theta_{k'} - \theta_k}{2\pi} \geq 2a, \quad \forall v_k, v_{k'} \in c_k$$

where r_k is the radius of the circle for cluster c_k and a is the radius of the filled circles representing the vertices. The constraint ensures that the vertices on the same cluster circle do not overlap. Specifically, the distance between any two vertices of a cluster is at least two times the radius of a vertex.

For each edge, the endpoint vertices are constant throughout the optimization process and thus the radii are constant. The optimization problem is a non-linear optimization problem with a linear inequality constraint as presented in 4.

3.2 Generating Vertex Positions

We use the NLOPT[1] library, and specifically its Improved Stochastic Ranking Evolution Strategy (ISRES). The original algorithm can be found here[2].

The layout generation is a two-step process shown in Algorithm 1. The first step generates the layout for the vertices in the innermost cluster. The second step generates the layout for the vertices in the remaining clusters.

Algorithm 1. Layout Generation Algorithm

Require: Graph Vertex Clusters
Require: Radii of the concentric circles (rings)
Ensure: Graph layout Set the positions of the vertices in cluster 1
1: Place cluster 1 vertices at equal angles on ring 1 Run the optimization for the vertices on ring 1
2: Optimization Algorithm: ISRES
3: Set the objective function and inequality constraints
4: Set the termination condition
5: Place the vertices in each cluster
6: **for** *each cluster from 2 to m* **do**
7:     Place the vertices at equal angles on their rings
8:     **for** *each vertex(v) belongsto i* **do**
9:         Set position bounds to [0,2π]
10:     **end for**
11: **end for**
12:
        Run the optimization for all vertices on rings 2 to m
13: Set the objective function and inequality constraints
14: Set the termination condition
15: Run the algorithm to produce the final layout

---

[1] http://ab-initio.mit.edu/wiki/index.php/NLopt.
[2] http://www3.hi.is/~tpr/papers/RuYa05.pdf.

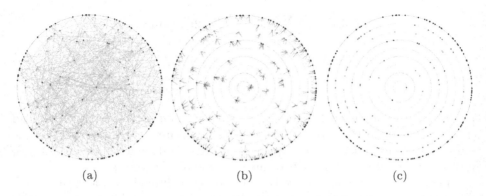

(a)   (b)   (c)

Fig. 2. NOCC Layout for a computer-generated graph with 200 vertices and 597 edges (a) Complete edges, (b) Partial Edges, (c) Just the vertices without edges.

Graph vertex clusters and the concentric circle radii are inputs to Algorithm 1 and graph layout is the output. Line 1 places the vertices of the innermost cluster equi-angularly, which are fixed throughout the next steps. The vertices in the innermost cluster are placed at equal arc distances as they are the most important vertices in terms of connectivity and we want to highlight them for easy viewing and interactions using a mouse. Moreover, they serve as the invariants between multiple runs of the optimization algorithm. Line 2 will set the optimization algorithm to ISRES. Line 3 sets the objective function along with its constraints. Line 4 will set the termination threshold which is 0.001 in our experiments. Lines 6 to 15 define the second step in the process that will generate the final layout. Line 6 to 11 place the vertices of rings 2 to m equi-angularly on the rings and set the bounds for the position of each vertex. The optimization procedure described at lines 13 to 15 is similar to the procedure described at lines 2 to 4. Finally, line 15 runs the optimization function with all the above parameters to produce the final layout.

Since the algorithm runs for a limited number of iterations to reach the termination threshold, the output of the vertex placement is not necessarily optimal, so we call it "near-optimal".

3.3   Graph Rendering

Size and Colors of Vertices. Vertex colors are assigned according to their corresponding clusters. Colors are chosen in-order from a list to distinguish the vertices of a cluster from its two immediate neighboring clusters to improve the visual clarity. The cluster ring has the same color as its vertices.

Cluster Radius. For the radius of each cluster, we tested various radii options and concluded that the visualization is aesthetically pleasing with a constant increment of the cluster radii. If the radius of a ring is too large to fit the display screen, we can re-space rings, re-cluster the vertices on a ring, or allow vertex overlapping.

Edge Rendering. We render two edge styles. The first is a line segment between two vertices drawn in grey color. Figure 2a hows a synthetic graph with all the vertices and complete edges rendered. The second edge style is partial edge rendering (PED), similar to [25] and [5], drawn to improve the readibility of the NOCC layout visualizations. A partial edge is an edge that is drawn only around its incident vertices. It has become a popular style to curtail edge-crossings for clutter reduction [5]. The default partial edge length is 10% of the actual edge length. At each vertex, a partial edge is drawn with the same color of the vertex it is connected to and the direction pointing towards the connected vertex. Figure 2b shows the same layout from Fig. 2a with partial edges as described. This rendering will give the user an idea of the degree of each vertex and the clusters of its neighbors through the partial edge colors. Lastly, Fig. 2c shows only the vertex positions generated by NOCC without any edges. Users can interactively switch between the three types of visualizations.

The main features of the layout are:

(i) A concentric circle-based 2D layout where each circle represents a cluster.
(ii) Clusters are based on the betweenness values of vertices. The cluster with the smallest radius has the vertices with the highest betweenness. As we move away from the center, the betweenness' of vertices decreases.
(iii) All edges are rendered and PED of each vertex show the directions to the connected vertices. Lengths of partial edges can be tuned.
(iv) All vertices are the same size, and vertices of a cluster have the same color.

4 Case Study - Human Protein-Protein Interactions

We present the visualization of a real-world graph: the Human Binary Protein-Protein Interactions (PPI) dataset, freely available from Koblenz Network Collection[3]. Proteins rarely function in isolation and their interactions are of great interest to the biological research community. Protein-Protein Interactions (PPI) are crucial for understanding protein functions, analyzing biological processes, and examining diseases. PPI networks enable study of the characteristics of proteins and their interactions by representing proteins as nodes and their interactions as edges.

In [33] the authors identify bottleneck proteins, which have high betweenness and low degree centralities in PPI networks. These proteins are more likely to be essential for crucial functional and dynamic properties [22,33]. It is reported that drug-target proteins have high degree and/or betweenness [31]. Therefore, identifying and visualizing the bottleneck proteins will help biologists to examine (i) if these proteins are the targets of various pathogens and (ii) if they can target these proteins to treat certain diseases.

Figure 3c presents the Human Binary Protein-Protein Interactions graph consisting of 2217 vertices and 6418 edges drawn using the NOCC layout with partial edges as a case study. The vertices (proteins) on the center rings (clusters)

---

[3] http://konect.uni-koblenz.de/networks/maayan-figeys.

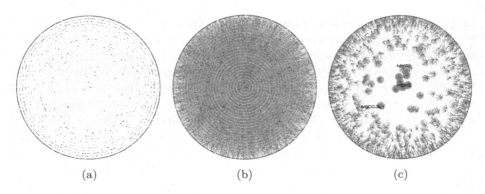

(a)   (b)   (c)

Fig. 3. NOCC Layout of Human Binary Protein-Protein Interactions graph consisting of 2217 vertices and 6418 edges (a) Complete graph without the edges (b) Complete graph with edges (c) Complete graph with partial edges.

are the vertices with higher betweenness values. These are the major influential proteins such as IKBKE, MYC and ASCC3L1 through which a lot of communication takes place. In Fig. 3, the contextual importance of the vertices decreases as we move away from the center toward the outer circles. Yu et al. divide proteins into four categories based on their degree and betweenness centralities [33]: (i) nonhub-nonbottlenecks, (ii) hub-nonbottlenecks, (iii) nonhub-bottlenecks and (iv) hub-bottlenecks. The NOCC layout naturally demonstrates those important bottleneck proteins that need to be studied further by domain experts. IKBKE in Fig. 3c is one of the very important proteins in treating cancer and inflammatory diseases. This is a hub-bottleneck protein with degree 314 and betweenness 295061. Another significant protein naturally revealed in Fig. 3c is MYC and it is a nonhub-bottleneck protein. MYC has a relatively low degree of 115 with a high betweenness value of 122303. Similarly, ASCC3L1 in Fig. 3c plays an essential role in pre-mRNA splicing. It has a very low degree of 14 with a high betweenness value of 34333.2.

5   Conclusions and Future Work

We summarized a visualization model that generates a central-vertex based layout while reducing the visual clutter and improving the visual information. We described a graph layout algorithm that reveals the extensive connectivity structures of scale-free graphs by naturally highlighting relatively important vertices with a tightly connected core vertex group. The NOCC layout can also be used in graph resilience analysis under targeted vertex failures. It naturally highlights the vertices that play the key role in graph connectivity. Although previous works attempted to generate better layouts to reduce the visual clutter, they weren't successful in highlighting the intrinsic connectivity structures of graphs.

Future work include formal comparison of NOCC with similar concentric circle and large graph visualization layouts to study its usefulness in terms of visual quality, layout generation speed and interactivity.

Acknowledgements. This work was supported by the National Science Foundation under Grant Number 1429526 and by the Louisiana Board of Regents Support Fund under contract LEQSF(2019-20)-ENH-DE-22.

References

1. Ahmed, A., Dwyer, T., Hong, S.H., Murray, C., Song, L., Wu, Y.X.: Visualisation and analysis of large and complex scale-free networks. In: EuroGraphics/IEEE EuroVis (2005)
2. Andersen, R., Chung, F., Lu, L.: Drawing power law graphs. In: Pach, J. (ed.) GD 2004. LNCS, vol. 3383, pp. 12–17. Springer, Heidelberg (2005). https://doi.org/10.1007/978-3-540-31843-9_2
3. Baur, M., Brandes, U., Gaertler, M., Wagner, D.: Drawing the AS graph in 2.5 dimensions. In: Pach, J. (ed.) GD 2004. LNCS, vol. 3383, pp. 43–48. Springer, Heidelberg (2005). https://doi.org/10.1007/978-3-540-31843-9_6
4. Bertini, E.: Social networks visualization: a brief survey (2005)
5. Binucci, C., Liotta, G., Montecchiani, F., Tappini, A.: Partial edge drawing: homogeneity is more important than crossings and ink. In: 2016 7th International Conference on Information, Intelligence, Systems and Applications (IISA), pp. 1–6 (2016)
6. Castermans, T., et al.: Solarview: low distortion radial embedding with a focus. IEEE Trans. Visual Comput. Graphics **25**, 2969–2982 (2018)
7. Chan, D.S.M., Chua, K.S., Leckie, C., Parhar, A.: Visualisation of power-law network topologies. In: IEEE International Conference on Networks, pp. 69–74. Sydney, Australia (2003)
8. Chiasserini, C.F., Garetto, M., Leonardi, E.: Social network de-anonymization under scale-free user relations. IEEE/ACM Trans. Netw. **24**(6), 3756–3769 (2016). http://dblp.uni-trier.de/db/journals/ton/ton24.html#ChiasseriniGL16
9. Chou, J.K., Yang, C.K.: PaperVis: literature review made easy. Comput. Graphics Forum (2011). https://doi.org/10.1111/j.1467-8659.2011.01921.x
10. Correa, C.D., Ma, K.L.: Visualizing Social Networks, pp. 307–326. Springer, US, Boston, MA (2011)
11. Dianati, N.: Unwinding the hairball graph: pruning algorithms for weighted complex networks. Phys. Rev. E **93**, 012304 (2016)
12. Ding, Y., Li, X., Tian, Y., Ledwich, G., Mishra, Y., Zhou, C.: Generating scale-free topology for wireless neighbourhood area networks in smart grid. IEEE Trans. Smart Grid **10**, 4245–4252 (2018). https://doi.org/10.1109/TSG.2018.2854645
13. Eades, P.: Drawing Free Trees. IIAS-RR, International Institute for Advanced Study of Social Information Science, Fujitsu Limited (1991)
14. Etemad, K., Samavati, F., Carpendale, S.: Daisy visualization for graphs. In: Proceedings of the Joint Symposium on Computational Aesthetics and Sketch Based Interfaces and Modeling and Non-Photorealistic Animation and Rendering, pp. 103–112. Expresive 2016, Eurographics Association, Aire-la-Ville, Switzerland, Switzerland (2016). http://dl.acm.org/citation.cfm?id=2981324.2981340
15. Fujita, Y., Fujiwara, Y., Souma, W.: Visualizing large-scale structure of a million-firms economic network. In: SIGGRAPH Asia 2015 Visualization in High Performance Computing (SA 2015), pp. 13:1–13:4. ACM, New York, NY, USA (2015). https://doi.org/10.1145/2818517.2818525, http://doi.acm.org/10.1145/2818517.2818525

16. Giot, R., Bourqui, R.: Fast graph drawing algorithm revealing networks cores. In: International Conference on Information Visualisation, pp. 259–264. Barcelona, Spain (2015)
17. Guo, X., Chen, H., Liu, X., Xu, X., Chen, Z.: The scale-free network of passwords : visualization and estimation of empirical passwords. CoRR abs/1511.08324 (2015)
18. Ho, J., Hong, S.-H.: Drawing clustered graphs in three dimensions. In: Healy, P., Nikolov, N.S. (eds.) GD 2005. LNCS, vol. 3843, pp. 492–502. Springer, Heidelberg (2006). https://doi.org/10.1007/11618058_44
19. Itoh, T., Klein, K.: Key-node-separated graph clustering and layouts for human relationship graph visualization. IEEE Comput. Graphics Appl. **35**(6), 30–40 (2015). http://dblp.uni-trier.de/db/journals/cga/cga35.html#ItohK15
20. Jeong, H., Mason, S., Barabási, A.L., Oltvai, Z.: Lethality and centrality in protein networks. Nature **411**, 41–42 (2001)
21. Jia, Y., Hoberock, J., Garland, M., Hart, J.: On the visualization of social and other scale-free networks. IEEE Trans. Visual Comput. Graphics **14**(6), 1285–1292 (2008)
22. Joy, M., Brock, A., Ingber, D.E., Huang, S.: High-betweenness proteins in the yeast protein interaction network. J. Biomed. Biotech. **2005**, 96–103 (2005)
23. Knuth, D.E.: Computer-drawn flowcharts. Commun. ACM **6**(9), 555–563 (1963)
24. Newman, M.: Power laws, Pareto distributions and Zipf's law. Contemp. Phys. **46**(5), 323–351 (2005)
25. Sathiyanarayanan, M., Pirozzi, D.: Social network visualization: Does partial edges affect user comprehension? In: International Conference on Communication Systems and Networks, pp. 570–575 (2017)
26. Schulz, C., Nocaj, A., Görtler, J., Deussen, O., Brandes, U., Weiskopf, D.: Probabilistic graph layout for uncertain network visualization. IEEE Trans. Vis. Comput. Graph. **23**(1), 531–540 (2017). http://dblp.uni-trier.de/db/journals/tvcg/tvcg23.html#SchulzNGDBW17
27. Takac, L., Zabovsky, M.: Radius degree layout—fast and easy graph visualization layout. In: International Conference on Digital Technologies, pp. 338–343. Zilina, Slovakia (2014)
28. Verma, T., Araújo, N.A.M., Herrmann, H.J.: Revealing the structure of the world airline network. CoRR abs/1404.1368 (2014). http://dblp.uni-trier.de/db/journals/corr/corr1404.html#VermaAH14
29. Wang, H., Song, M.: Ckmeans. 1d.dp: optimal k-means clustering in one dimension by dynamic programming. R Found. Stat. Comput. **28**(17), 29 (2012)
30. Ware, C., Purchase, H., Colpoys, L., McGill, M.: Cognitive measurements of graph aesthetics. Inf. Vis. **1**(2), 103–110 (2002)
31. Yamada, T., Bork, P.: Evolution of biomolecular networks lessons from metabolic and protein interactions. Nat. Rev. Mol. Cell Biol. **10**, 791–803 (2009)
32. Yu, H., Greenbaum, D., Lu, H.X., Wei Zhu, X., Gerstein, M.: Genomic analysis of essentiality within protein networks. Trends in Genet. TIG **20**(6), 227–231 (2004)
33. Yu, H., Kim, P.M., Sprecher, E., Trifonov, V., Gerstein, M.: The importance of bottlenecks in protein networks: correlation with gene essentiality and expression dynamics. PLoS Comput. Biol. **3**(4), e59 (2007)
34. Zhang, B., Liu, R., Massey, D., Zhang, L.: Collecting the internet as-level topology. SIGCOMM Comput. Commun. Rev. **35**(1), 53–61 (2005). https://doi.org/10.1145/1052812.1052825

Facial Expression Recognition and Ordinal Intensity Estimation: A Multilabel Learning Approach

Olufisayo Ekundayo and Serestina Viriri[(✉)]

School of Mathematics, Statistics and Computer Sciences,
University of KwaZulu-Natal, Durban, South Africa
218085734@stu.ukza.ac.za, viriris@ukzn.ac.za

Abstract. Facial Expression Recognition has gained considerable attention in the field of affective computing, but only a few works considered
the intensity of emotion embedded in the expression. Even the available
studies on expression intensity estimation successfully assigned a nom-
inal/regression value or classified emotion in a range of intervals. The
approaches from multiclass and its extensions do not conform to man
heuristic manner of recognising emotion with the respective intensity.
This work is presenting a Multi-label CNN-based model which could
simultaneously recognise emotion and also provide ordinal metrics as
the intensity of the emotion. In the experiments conducted on BU-3DFE
and Cohn Kanade (CK+) datasets, we check how well our model could
adapt and generalise. Our model gives promising results with multilabel
evaluation metrics and generalise well when trained on BU-3DFE and
evaluated on CK+.

Keywords: FER · Multilabel · Ordinal · Intensity estimation

1 Introduction

Human face contains much information through which estimated parameters
like; identity, age, emotion, gender, status, race and so on about an individual
could be deduced. Facial expression as one of the non-verbal communication
channels contains the most substantial proportion of man's medium of communication [6,15]. The main goal of the facial expression recognition system is to
automate the inherent ability in human beings and detects the man affective
state directly from changes experienced in the face, as a result of the facial
muscular response to the affective state. The process of achieving this classification is known as Facial Expression Recognition (FER). Ekman and Friesen [3]
studies aided facial expression classification into their proposed emotion states.
Several techniques of achieving FER have been introduced in the literature. The
list is not limited to handcrafted methods, conventional machine learning methods, Neural Network and deep learning methods. Studies in affective computing

© Springer Nature Switzerland AG 2020
G. Bebis et al. (Eds.): ISVC 2020, LNCS 12510, pp. 581–592, 2020.
https://doi.org/10.1007/978-3-030-64559-5_46

considered expression recognition from a facial image in both static (controlled and uncontrolled) environment and dynamic environment. Automation of facial expression is vital in Human-Computer Interaction (HCI) and Computer Vision (CV). Areas of facial expression application keep evolving, and virtually applicable to every area where communication or human interaction with a system is involved.

Facial expression is subtle, [17,19,20] claimed that expression is often reflected as mixture of basic emotion in face. [25] emphasised that in the real world, the display of pure emotion is rare, and that emotion as a subjective notion should be assigned a relative value and not the absolute value of the standard classification algorithms. There is virtually no pure emotion because emotion is always accompanying by some other information that portrays its semantics. Limiting the recognition or detection of emotion subjectively to six basic emotion states (anger, disgust, fear, happy, sad and surprise) undermines the performance of facial expression recognition system.

One of the information that accompanies emotion is the degree or intensity of the expression displayed. It is undeniable that man recognizes emotion along with some ordinal metrics that depict the degree or the rate of expressing emotion in the face. To adequately capture the semantics of emotion, it is better to consider the ordinal information associated with it. Some of the research conducted on intensity estimation of facial expression images include [1,18]. Most of the existing approaches consider the task as a regression problem [22], which is far from man's concept of estimating emotion [15,25]. Man has a hierarchical structure perception about emotion and therefore estimate it using referenced base value, which allows its semantics preservation.

A man could identify the affective state with its accompanied relative intensity value from the face. Therefore, emotion intensity could appropriately be represented using ordinal metrics to the best of our knowledge non of the existing studies on emotion intensity estimation as regard facial expression considered ordinal metrics in their works. It is understandably, the lack of hierarchical or ordinal annotated data for facial expression intensity estimation task could be responsible for such limitation. Nevertheless, facial expression recognition should not be restricted to a multi-class problem. This argument is substantiated with the fact that more information about affect states are inferred from facial expression than the fundamental categorical values. This work considers facial expression recognition as a multi-label task, with the motive that an image of facial expression belongs to one of the six emotion states with an associated degree of intensity. The significance of this work is attributed to a relative based approach for emotion intensity estimation by using ordinal metrics. Another Uniqueness is the multi-label modelling and transformation of emotion recognition and intensity estimation, which has not been adopted for intensity estimation as far as our knowledge is concerned. This work is adapting CNN network to FER multilabel classification task, where both emotion and emotion intensity are simultaneously recognized.

The order of arrangement of this work is as follow; Sect. 2 is the review of some of the existing works on intensity estimation of facial expression recognition. It shall include a thorough elucidation of the methods and their respective limitations. Section 3 gives the general discussion of the deep learning classification model we are considering. Section 4 contains the description of the multilabel approach and the adaptation of CNN model to multilabel problem. Section 5 presented the description of the experiment and provides information of both the databases and the multilabel metrics for evaluation. Section 5.4 contains the result presentation and the discussion. Section 6 provides the conclusion of the work and the possible future works.

2 Related Works

Most of the research carried out on facial expression recognition, approach it from the perspective of multiclass problem [8,21]. [5,11,14] are recent review of different deep learning approaches on facial expression recognition, for any interested reader. Many successes in this field have been recorded with different machine learning algorithms and image processing techniques, especially with the state of the art method [4,16]. Regardless of the success, we cannot ignore the fact that facial expression image in most cases consists of more than one information about the affective state it is representing [20,25]. One of the extensions of facial expression recognition task is intensity estimation of facial expression recognition, and most of the studies in this regard are an extension of a multiclass or regression problem.

The popularly adopted techniques to facial expression intensity estimation are grouped into regression-based, distance-based, graphical-based and clustering-based model, as discussed in [9]. For instance Rudovic et al. [22] employed a manifold to modeled the topology of multidimensional continuous facial affect data by using a Supervised Locality Preserving Projection (SLPP) algorithm to encode the ordering of the expression class labels, to achieve smooth transitions between emotion intensities on the manifold. The topology was later incorporated into the Hidden Conditional Ordinal Random Field (H-CORF), and to ensure that the proposed dynamic ordinal regression is preserved, H-CORF parameters were constrained to lie on the ordinal manifold by forcing latent variables as a Gaussian Markov random field. The resulting model simultaneously achieved both dynamic recognition and intensity estimation of facial expressions of multiple emotions. Kimura and Yachida [23] proposed that facial expression recognition and degree estimation could be achieved through expressionless face referencing. They model the expressionless face with an elastic net model having the notion of obtaining any slight deformation caused by expression displayed in a face, with a motion vector of the deformed net. The motion vector of the node is mapped to low dimensional Eigenspace using K-L expansion, and estimation derived by the projection of the input image into the emotion space. Kamarol et al. [9] proposed a framework for facial expression recognition and intensity estimation with low computation. Feature extraction was carried-out using AAM (geometric feature), and the feature developed with KNN and weighting scheme; also the input video was represented by a weight vector that contained the most likely expression class of the input sequence and the expression intensity present in each frame in the sequence. HMM, as a classifier detects the emotion, and a change point detector encodes the expression intensity from the weight vector. The above mentioned compute intensity estimation using absolute value (quantitatively), this is not appropriate according to [25]. The goal of this work is to estimate facial expression intensity base on ordinal value and the emotion recognition simultaneously.

3   Convolution Neural Network

Convolution Neural Network is a deep learning model whose concept evolved from the Artificial Neural Network. It was first introduced by Lecun et al. [7]. CNN is an algorithm purposely designed for image processing and Computer vision tasks. Just like most deep learning networks, CNN performs an end to end learning, and the procedure executes in a hierarchy of layers. Each layer of CNN produces representation features ranging from low-level features of the image to a more abstractive concept. The process at which CNN automatically learns its representation features emulates the vision mechanism of an animal. That is, the animal visual cortex inspires CNN architectural design. CNN models are self-sufficient in extracting their representation features, and there is no need for any pre-calculated methods for features extraction. Its high performance contributes immensely to its popularity.

CNN could achieve end-to-end learning with the aid of the back-propagation algorithm and guided by loss function that leads the networks to the optimum result. Depending on the nature of the problem, softmax loss is mostly used in a multi-class problem where the chance of a class is dependent on the chances of occurrence of others. Recently sigmoid function initially meant for binary classification is adapted to multi-label tasks capitalising on its capability to generate a probability score of each available class independently. An instance of multi-label CNN network is discussed in [12] where the network adapted to the learning of topology preserved ordinal relationship and age difference information for age estimation and prediction task. DBCNN (Deep Bimodal Convolution Neural Network) proposed by Li and Deng [10] for facial expression recognition gives a promising result in the recognition of mixture or compound emotion from expression displayed in the face.

In this work, we are considering a multilabel CNN based network capable of learning the emotion features and the intensity of expression features for the prediction of emotion with its respective degree of intensity in an ordinal manner.

4   Multi-label Approach

In a multi-label classification problem, an image may belong to two or more categories of classes. The multi-label properties stated is evident in facial expression classification task; an expression image carries information of both the type of the emotion and the degree at which it is expressed. In this work, we considered a model transformation technique for the implementation of the facial expression recognition multi-label task.

4.1 Problem Description

Data description, Let $X = R^m$ represent the input space, and let $Y = y_1, \ldots\ldots y_c$ denote the complete sets of label where c is the number of possible label value, also $Z = z_1, \ldots\ldots, z_k$ is the complete set of the degree where $k \in K$ is the intensity of the label $y \in Y$. Then the possibility of sample $x \in X$ having c_{th} class Y_c with the associated k_{th} intensity estimation degree Z_k is expressed as a function; $F: X \rightarrow Y \times Z$. Figure 1 is the pictorial description of how emotion is mapped with the degree of intensity expression.

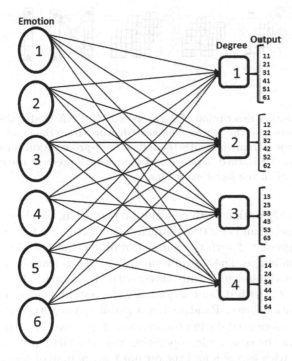

Fig. 1. The problem formulation of Multi-label Convolution Network showing the possible affective state with the respective degree of intensity of a facial expression sample. The nodes under emotion represent the six basic emotion classes Anger, Disgust, Fear, Happy, Sad, Surprise, the nodes under the degree Low, Normal, High, Very_High and the output is the possible result of the multi-label CNN classification.

This work employs a deep learning model to execute the multi-label task of facial expression recognition. The Convolution Neural Network architecture used is shown in the Fig. 2. The model is a variant of VGG-Network [24] in the arrangements of convolution layers. The model comprises of five convolution layers; the first convolution layer takes the input and convolutes it with a kernel of size 3×3 to give 32 filters as output. Max pooling with pooling 2×2 is applied for down-sampling after the first layer. Second convolution and third convolution layers output 64 filters each and likewise each of the forth and the fifth convolution layers output 128 filters. Down-sampling of the same pooling size is employed after the third and the fifth layer. The model has only one fully connected layer and the last layer, which is the sigmoid layer compute the likelihood of all the classes independently, which makes the FER multi-label implementation possible with CNN network. Some regularization techniques like drop-out and batch normalization are used at each layer in other to control the model from overfitting to the training samples.

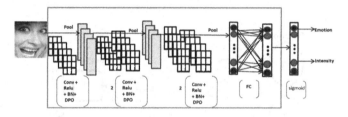

Fig. 2. The framework description of the proposed ML-CNN model: the network learns the emotion features and the degree of intensity features from the input image and make adjustments to the parameters with the aid of back-propagation during training. At the testing phase, the learned parameter of the network predicts the emotion and the respective intensity in the facial expression.

Convolution Operation: with convolution operation, patches from expression images are extracted and also transformed to generate a 3D feature map in which the depth is represented with the number of filters that encode the unique part of the expression image. The convolution operation can learn local patterns from the image when the image is convoluted with the kernel. This model uses the kernel of size 3×3 with default stride, and the output feature map is specified at each convolution layer. Padding (zero paddings) is introduced to minimize border effects experienced during convolution. Equation (1) is the mathematical representation of the convolution operation whereby the input expression image is f, convoluted with kernel h and the output feature map of x row and y column is computed.

$$G[x,y] = (f * h)[x,y] = \sum_{j}\sum_{k} h[j,k]f[x-j,y-k] \qquad (1)$$

And the dimension of the output feature map (F) as given in (2) is computed using the expression image size (M, N), number of strides and filter (f, f).

$$D(p,q) = [m,n,c] * [f,f,c] = \frac{m+2p-f}{s} + 1, \frac{n-2p-f}{s} + 1 \qquad (2)$$

Activation Operation: this module carries out the predictions base on the score generated from the feature map of each expression image. We use the ReLu activation function at each convolution layer of the network and the dense layer. We employed the sigmoid activation function in (3) for the final prediction at the fully connected layer and binary cross-entropy loss in (4) is used for the computation of the model loss.

$$S = \frac{1}{e^{-S}} \tag{3}$$

$$L(y, \overline{y}) = -\frac{1}{N} \sum_{i=1}^{N} (y \cdot log(\overline{y_i}) - (1 - y) \cdot log(1 - \overline{y_i})) \tag{4}$$

in (4) y is the actual class label while the $\overline{y}$ is the predicted label from the model. Max pooling Operation: this operation is conducted on the output of the convolution layer. The feature map is downsampled when it is convoluted with the kernel size used is 2×2 and with two strides.

Optimization Operation and the regularization: Stochastic gradient descent (SGD) with a learning rate of 0.0001 is used as the model optimizer. Drop out and data augmentation are the employed regularization techniques for the model.

5   Experiment

This section is a brief description of the affective databases used, the pre-processing techniques, the experiment discussion and the multilabel evaluation metrics used.

5.1   Database

Binghamton University-3D facial Expression (BU-3DFE) dataset was introduced at Binghamton University by [26]; it contains 100 subjects with 2500 facial expression models. Fifty-six of the subjects were female, and 44 were male, the age group ranges from 18 years to 70 years old, with a variety of ethnic/racial ancestries, including White, Black, East-Asian, Middle-east Asian, Indian, and Hispanic Latino. 3D face scanner was used to capture seven expressions from each subject; in the process, four intensity levels were captured alongside for each of the six basic prototypical expressions. Associated with each expression shape model, is a corresponding facial texture image captured at two views (about $+45°$ and $-45°$). As a result, the database consists of 2,500 two view's texture images and 2,500 geometric shape models. BU-3DFE dataset has been severally as a multi-label datasets [2, 10] To the best of our knowledge BU-3DFE dataset is the only available dataset that annotated intensity of facial expression images in ordinal hierarchies. The intensity annotation of BU-3DFE is given in Fig. 3. Another popularly used benchmark dataset for intensity estimation is Cohn Kanade extension (CK+) data [13] This dataset, unlike the BU-3DFE, is a sequence data collected in a controlled environment. To make the CK+ conformable to our proposed method we adopted the general annotation of Onset, peak and offset in a frame to categorise the data into Low, Normal and High as the degree of emotional intensity.

5.2   Data Pre-processing and Experiment Discussion

This work considered two major and important pre-processing techniques to improve the performance of the system. We used facial landmarking algorithm to detect the region of the face and also to remove background information which could subject the system to unnecessary computation. To make the system robust against over-fitting because of the small quantities of available data for CNN to learn, we employed data augmentation. Data augmentation was not used on the fly to ensure data balancing especially in CK+ dataset.

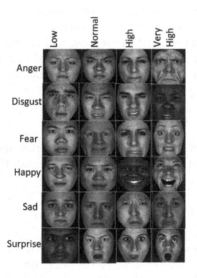

Fig. 3. This figure describes the hierarchical ordinal annotation of BU-3DFE, and provides information of six basic emotion states and their respective intensity estimation using relative value.

The experiment evaluated the proposed ML-CNN model on both BU-3DFE and CK+ datasets. After preprocessing, each of the raw data was scaled to a uniform size of 96 × 96. The datasets were first partitioned into the training set (70%), the validation set (20%) and the remaining 10% for the testing set. The training dataset was augmented and the pixel values were divided by 255 to ensure data scale normalization. We trained the proposed multi-label CNN network model on the training datasets. At each of the convolution layer of the network, we prevent over-fitting by using batch-normalization and dropout regularization techniques. We used Stochastic Gradient Descent with initial learning rate of 0.0003 for the network optimization. And Validation follows immediately using validation dataset. We made some investigations in the experiments. We observed the performance of our model on the raw data without augmentation, we likewise checked for the performance when face localization and augmentation were applied and lastly, we observed how well the model was able to generalise to unseen data samples by training the system with BU-3DFE and validate with CK+ data.

For each of our investigation, we conducted the model evaluation with the data testsets. The choice of our model performance metrics are the multilabel performance evaluation metrics; the hamming loss, coverage, ranking loss, and cross entropy loss. Brief discussion of the metrics are given in the next section.

5.3   Evaluation Metrics

Hamming loss computes the loss generated between the binary string of the actual label and the binary string of the predicted label with XOR operation for every instance of the test data. The average over all the sample is taking as given in (5) below

$$H = \frac{1}{|N| \cdot |L|} \sum_{i=1}^{|N|} \sum_{j=1}^{|J|} XOR(y_{i,j}, \hat{y_{i,j}}) \tag{5}$$

Ranking Loss: this metric is used to compute the average of numbers where the labels are incorrectly ordered. The smaller the ranking loss within the closed range between 0 and 1, the better our model performance. (6) is the mathematical illustration of ranking loss.

$$Rank_{loss}(y, \hat{f}) = \frac{1}{N} \sum_{1=0}^{N-1} ||y_i||_0 \frac{1}{k - ||y_i||_0} |Z| \tag{6}$$

where k is the number of labels and Z is (m, n): $\hat{f}_{i,m} \geq \hat{f}_{i,n}$, $y_{i,m} = 1$, $y_{i,n} = 0$.

Average Precision: this metric is employed to find the function of higher ranked that are true for each ground truth label. The higher the value within the closed range between 0 and 1 the better the performance of the model. Mathematical illustration of label ranking average precision is given in (7) below.

$$LRAP = \frac{1}{N} \sum_{i=0}^{N-1} \frac{1}{||y||_0} \sum_{j:y_{i,j}=1} \frac{|L_{i,j}|}{Ri,j} \tag{7}$$

where $L_{i,j}$ = K: $y_{i,k} = 1$, $\hat{f}_{i,k} \geq \hat{f}_{i,j}$ and |.| is the cardinality of the set. Coverage error: this metrics is used to evaluate on average the number of labels that should be included so that all the true labels would be predicted at the final prediction. The smaller its value the better the model performance. The mathematical illustration is shown in (8).

$$Coverage(y, \hat{f}) = \frac{1}{N} \sum_{i=0}^{N-1} maxrank_{i,j} \tag{8}$$

where $rank_{i,j}$ is $-\{k : \hat{f}_{i,k} \geq f_{i,k}-\}$.

5.4   Result and Discussion

We present a summary of the result obtained from four categories of the experiments in Table 1. The first experiment evaluates the proposed method on BU-3DFE without augmentation; the data contains 2400 samples. At the evaluation, we observed overfitting when the number of the epoch is 25, and as showed in Table 1. The coverage error 4.512 is high. The overfitting is traceable to insufficient data for the model to learn the representative features. In the other experiment that conducted augmentation on the training samples of BU-3DFE, no overfitting observed, and the values obtained for the metrics are promising. The result obtained from CK+ is relative to the BU-3DFE+Augmentation, which indicate the adaptability of the proposed method. The proposed method also generalised well when trained with BU-3DFE and tested with CK+, the value obtained for the hamming loss is 0.1668, the ranking loss is 0.1925, average precision is 0.7322, and the coverage error is 1.4810.

Table 1. The summary of the model performance evaluation using four multi-label metrics: ↑ indicates that the higher the value the better the model performance and ↓ indicates that the lower or smaller the value the better the performance.

Database	Hamming loss ↓	Ranking loss ↓	Average precision ↑	Coverage ↓
BU-3DFE	0.1521	0.4773	0.7353	4.512
BU-3DFE + AUG	0.0694	0.1911	0.8931	1.9457
CK+	0.1426	0.0581	0.8993	1.6473
Generalization	0.1668	0.1925	0.7322	1.4910

6   Conclusion

This work presented a novel approach which relied on the human unique means of detecting emotion and estimating the intensity simultaneously. Our proposed Ordinal multi-label deep learning based method gives a promising result on BU-3DFE- a multilabel benchmark dataset with intensity annotation in hierarchy of ordinal values. We extend the evaluation of our method also to a sequence dataset (CK+), the result was also a prospective one as indicated in Table 1. Our model was able to generalise well when it was trained with BU-3DFE and evaluated on CK+. The future work will tends towards model performance enhancement, and to consider the a dynamic/temporal and emotion in the wild environment using our reference based approach for emotion detection and intensity estimation.

References

1. Chang, K.Y., Chen, C.S., Hung, Y.P.: Intensity rank estimation of facial expressions based on a single image (2013). https://doi.org/10.1109/SMC.2013.538
2. Dhall, A., Goecke, R., Gedeon, T.: Automatic group happiness intensity analysis. IEEE Trans. Affect. Comput. **6**(1), 13–26 (2015). https://doi.org/10.1109/TAFFC.2015.2397456
3. Ekman, P., Friesen, W.V.: Constants across cultures in the face and emotion. J. Pers. Social Psychol. **17**(2), 124–129 (1971). https://doi.org/10.1037/h0030377
4. Georgescu, M.I., Ionescu, R.T., Popescu, M.: Local learning with deep and hand-crafted features for facial expression recognition. IEEE Access **7**, 64827–64836 (2019). https://doi.org/10.1109/ACCESS.2019.2917266
5. Ghayoumi, M.: A quick review of deep learning in facial expression. J. Commun. Comput. **14**, 34–38 (2017). https://doi.org/10.17265/1548-7709/2017.01.004
6. Ghimire, D., Lee, J.: Geometric feature-based facial expression recognition in image sequences using multi-class AdaBoost and support vector machines. Sensor **13**, 7714–7734 (2013). https://doi.org/10.3390/s130607714
7. Henderson, D., Howard, R.E., Hubbard, W., Jackel, L.D.: Backpropagation applied to handwritten zip code recognition. Neural Comput. **551**, 541–551 (1989). https://doi.org/10.1162/neco.1989.1.4.541
8. Huang, Y., Chen, F., Lv, S., Wang, X.: Facial expression recognition: a survey. SS Symmetry **11**, 1189 (2019). https://doi.org/10.3390/sym11101189
9. Khairuni, S., Kamarol, A., Hisham, M., Kälviäinen, H., Parkkinen, J., Parthiban, R.: Joint facial expression recognition and intensity estimation based on weighted votes of image sequences. Pattern Recogn. Lett. **92**, 25–32 (2017). https://doi.org/10.1016/j.patrec.2017.04.003
10. Li, S., Deng, W.: Blended emotion in-the-wild: multi-label facial expression recognition using crowdsourced annotations and deep locality feature learning. Int. J. Comput. Vis. **127**, 884–906 (2018). https://doi.org/10.1007/s11263-018-1131-1
11. Li, S., Deng, W.: Deep facial expression recognition: a survey. IEEE Trans. Affect. Comput. **3045**(c), 1–20 (2020). https://doi.org/10.1109/TAFFC.2020.2981446
12. Liu, H., Lu, J., Feng, J., Zhou, J.: Ordinal deep feature learning for facial age estimation. In: Proceedings - 12th IEEE International Conference on Automatic Face and Gesture Recognition, FG 2017–1st International Workshop on Adaptive Shot Learning for Gesture Understanding and Production, ASL4GUP 2017, Biometrics in the Wild, Bwild 2017, Heteroge, pp. 157–164 (2017). https://doi.org/10.1109/FG.2017.28
13. Lucey, P., Cohn, J.F., Kanade, T., Saragih, J., Ambadar, Z., Matthews, I.: The extended Cohn-Kanade dataset (CK+): a complete dataset for action unit and emotion-specified expression. In: 2010 IEEE Computer Society Conference on Computer Vision and Pattern Recognition - Workshops, CVPRW 2010, July, pp. 94–101 (2010). https://doi.org/10.1109/CVPRW.2010.5543262
14. Mahmood, Z., Muhammad, N.: A review on state-of-the-art face recognition approaches. Fractals **25**(2), 1–19 (2017). https://doi.org/10.1142/S0218348X17500256
15. Martinez, B., Valstar, M.F.: Advances, challenges, and opportunities in automatic facial expression recognition. In: Kawulok, M., Celebi, M.E., Smolka, B. (eds.) Advances in Face Detection and Facial Image Analysis, pp. 63–100. Springer, Cham (2016). https://doi.org/10.1007/978-3-319-25958-1_4

16. Mayya, V., Pai, R.M., Pai, M.M.: Automatic facial expression recognition using DCNN. Proc. - Proc. Comput. Sci. **93**(September), 453–461 (2016). https://doi.org/10.1016/j.procs.2016.07.233
17. Xia, X.: Facial expression recognition based on monogenic binary coding. Appl. Mech. Mater. **512**, 437–440 (2014). https://doi.org/10.4028/www.scientific.net/AMM.511-512.437. Scientific Net
18. Nomiya, H., Sakaue, S., Hochin, T.: Recognition and intensity estimation of facial expression using ensemble classifiers. In: 2016 IEEE/ACIS 15th International Conference on Computer and Information Science (ICIS), pp. 1–6 (2016). https://doi.org/10.1109/ICIS.2016.7550861
19. Ekman, P., Friesen, W.V.: Unmasking the Face: A Guide to Recognising Emotion from Facial Clue. Malor Books, San Jose (2003)
20. Plutchik, R., Bering, J.M., Descriptions, B.: Contents a phylogenetic approach to religious origins on the subcortical sources of basic human emotions and emergence of a unified mind science, vol. 08191 (2001)
21. Ramzan, M., Khan, H.U., Awan, S.M., Ismail, A., Ilyas, M., Mahmood, A.: A survey on state-of-the-art drowsiness detection techniques. IEEE Access **7**, 61904–61919 (2019). https://doi.org/10.1109/ACCESS.2019.2914373
22. Rudovic, O., Pavlovic, V., Pantic, M.: Multi-output Laplacian dynamic ordinal regression for facial expression recognition and intensity estimation. In: 2012 IEEE Conference on Computer Vision and Pattern Recognition, pp. 2634–2641 (2012). https://doi.org/10.1109/CVPR.2012.6247983
23. Kimura, S., Yachida, M.: Facial expression recognition and its degree estimation, pp. 295–300 (1997). https://doi.org/10.1109/CVPR.1997.609338
24. Simonyan, K., Zisserman, A.: Very deep convolutional networks for large-scale image recognition. In: 3rd International Conference on Learning Representations, ICLR 2015 - Conference Track Proceedings, pp. 1–14 (2015)
25. Yannakakis, G.N., Cowie, R., Busso, C.: The ordinal nature of emotions, pp. 248–255 (2017). https://doi.org/10.1109/ACII.2017.8273608
26. Yin, L., Wei, X., Sun, Y., Wang, J., Rosato, M.J.: A 3D facial expression database for facial behavior research. In: FGR 2006: Proceedings of the 7th International Conference on Automatic Face and Gesture Recognition, pp. 211–216 (2006). https://doi.org/10.1109/FGR.2006.6

Prostate MRI Registration Using Siamese Metric Learning

Alexander Lyons[1]([✉]) and Alberto Rossi[2,3]([✉]) [iD]

[1] Columbia Grammar and Preparatory School, New York, NY 10025, USA
alyons21@cgps.org
[2] Department of Information Engineering, University of Florence,
Via di Santa Marta, 50129 Florence, FI, Italy
alberto.rossi@unifi.it
[3] Department of Information Engineering and Mathematics, University of Siena,
Via Roma 56, 53100 Siena, Italy

Abstract. The process of registering intra-procedural prostate magnetic resonance images (MRI) with corresponding pre-procedural images
improves the accuracy of certain surgeries, such as a prostate biopsy.
Aligning the two images by means of rigid and elastic deformation may
permit more precise use of the needle during the operation. However,
gathering the necessary data and computing the ground truth is a problematic step. Currently, a single dataset is available and it is composed
of only a few cases, making the training of standard deep convolutional
neural networks difficult. To address this issue the moving image (intra-
procedural) is randomly augmented producing different copies, and a
convolutional siamese neural network tries to choose the best aligned
copy with respect to the reference image (pre-procedural). The results of
this research show that this method is superior to both a simple baseline
obtained with standard image processing techniques and a deep CNN
model. Furthermore, the best policy found for building the couple set
for the siamese neural network reveals that a rule based on the mutual
information that considers only the highest and the lowest value, representing similar and dissimilar cases, is the best option for training. The
use of mutual information allows the model to be unsupervised, since
the segmentation is no longer necessary. Finally, research on the size
of the augmented set is conducted, showing that producing 18 different
candidates is sufficient for a good performance.

Keywords: Image registration · MRI-guided biopsy · Prostate MRI ·
Siamese network

1 Introduction

Prostate cancer is one of the most common types of cancer in men, and is also
among the types with the highest mortality rate [2,14]. Fortunately, scientific

© Springer Nature Switzerland AG 2020
G. Bebis et al. (Eds.): ISVC 2020, LNCS 12510, pp. 593–603, 2020.
https://doi.org/10.1007/978-3-030-64559-5_47

and technological progress has drastically reduced the impact of this type of cancer in the last decades. Early diagnosis is an effective tool to lower the mortality rate. A measurement of Prostate Specific Antigen (PSA) [17] obtained through a simple blood analysis could be the first step for diagnosing the disease. Unfortunately, the accuracy of this process is not optimal, and so the most common diagnostic procedure requires a biopsy graded with a specific scale called the Gleason score. This process is invasive and can lead to overtreatment and complications for the patient, such as hemorrhages [11]. Progress in radiology has led to the implementation of MRI scanners to produce images of the prostate (as well as of many other organs) without the need of surgery. The scoring system and guidelines are available in a document called PIRADS [21]. This type of scan can also be used to guide the needle during a prostate biopsy [19] and brachytherapy. However, this task can be conducted in real time only with the acquisition of images at a lower resolution. Moreover, factors such as the presence of the needle and visual differences within each image due to patient position and motion can affect the process of comparing pre- and intra-procedural images. To this end, a registration algorithm is needed to correctly align images having different properties [4]. This process is particularly superior to the usage of ultrasound images [4]. Despite the effectiveness of convolutional neural network algorithms for many different tasks [6,12,13,16], such algorithms are often inefficient when the training dataset is small, even if this detrimental effect could be mitigated by the fine tuning process [18]. The question addressed in this research arises as a result of these considerations. How can an efficient algorithm for prostate MRI registration be built having just a few images available for training? To answer this question, the performance of a different learning scheme is evaluated, based on siamese neural networks. Proposed by Bromley et al. [3], this work introduces a new kind of network, which has two input streams being fed to the same set of weights, producing two separate embeddings used to assess whether or not the two samples are from the same class. This kind of network has proved to be particularly effective in the field of few-shot learning [9], where the dataset size is very small. It can also be used to address metric learning and to understand the similarity between two different objects [1,20,22,23]. When dealing with similarity, this process is simply done by applying a special type of loss, i.e. contrastive loss [5], which encourages the closeness of two similar objects while penalizing samples that are dissimilar. Given these tools, the first step in our research is to randomly augment (i.e. modify) the original intra-procedural prostate MRI, producing several variants of the same image. The siamese neural network equipped with contrastive loss is designed to choose the most similar pair of images between the reference image and all the images belonging to the set of augmented images. Results prove that this simple scheme achieves a better performance than a registration process based on the SimpleITKv4. We also prove that this model performs better than an available deep CNN developed by Kuang and Schmah [10] for registering brain MRI images from the MindBoggle-101 dataset [8]. Their model focuses on optimizing a deep neural network that directly outputs displacement fields. Three different ways of building couples for the siamese training are compared, based on Intersection over Union (IoU), Dice Score (DS), and Mutual Information (MI), and conclude that choosing similar and dissimilar samples for training based on MI is the best option. This fact is important since it eliminates the need for segmentations, leading to an unsupervised method. Furthermore, we shows in depth the effect of the size of the augmented set on performance, discovering that 18 variants is the optimal balance between sufficient choice and a feasible complexity of the choice. Lastly, this research tests the effect of the number of similar and dissimilar samples per slice, determining that the performances are not affected, and suggesting the use of just the most similar and dissimilar images. The rest of this paper is organized as follows: Sect. 2 provides details about the dataset used and the preprocessing procedure, while Sect. 3 describes the setup of the experiment, including the siamese network, the corresponding setup for the case of prostate MRI registration, the baseline used, and the research question addressed. Finally, Sect. 4 reports the results of the experimentation, while in Sect. 5 the conclusions are drawn.

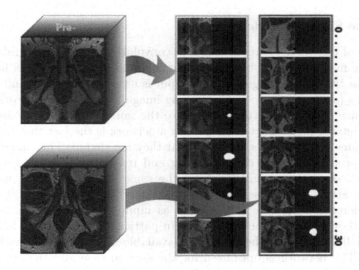

Fig. 1. Example of Pre- (yellow) and Intra-procedural (red) images (Color figure online)

2 Dataset and Image Preprocess

The dataset used is part of the work of Fedorov et al. [4]. It is composed of anonymized pre- and intra-procedural MRI images from 10 patients. Three sets of prostate gland segmentations are manually prepared by the same number of raters, two of whom have more than ten years of experience in MRI rating. Moreover, this dataset is also supplied with per-patient landmarks. The images are acquired in the axial position with the standard T2-Weighted (T2W) modalities. The original pre-procedural MRI images had a size of $512 \times 512 \times 30$. The voxel spacings were 0.3125, 0.3125, and 3, respectively. The original intra-procedural MRI images had a size of $320 \times 320 \times 40$. The voxel spacings were 0.5, 0.5, and 3, respectively. To normalize the images while maintaining as much information as possible, the images are resized to be $128 \times 128 \times 128$, with voxel spacings of 1.10021, 1.0021, and 0.856299, respectively. In addition, all of the voxel values within each segmentation image are converted to be either 0 or 1. For training the network, any pairs of pre-procedural and intra-procedural MRI slices that don't contain any segmentation information (i.e. images that contain only background) aren't considered. The first seven patients are used for training, patient 8 for validation, and the remaining two for testing the model. Figure 1 shows an example of pre-procedural and intra-procedural MRI images.

3   Experimental Setup

In this section, we describe the convolutional siamese network, the overall framework, the baseline used, and finally the research question answered.

3.1   The Siamese Model

The core of this model is represented by convolutional siamese neural networks [3,9]. The main difference between this model and a standard CNN is that the former has two inputs. In general, one input is used as a reference and the other as a query (also referred to as the moving image), so that the network is asked to recognize if the two patterns belong to the same class, i.e. they are similar. Another interesting characteristic of such a network is the fact that both inputs use the same set of weights, meaning that they are shared. This allows the network to produce versions of the moving and reference image that are always correlated, since they originated from the same agent. The most well-known implementations of siamese networks work exactly as described [3,9]. A query and a reference image are fed together as input and the network establishes whether they belong to the same class. In particular, this method is proved to be especially effective in the case of few available samples, as in few-shot learning [14]. The network is optimized for the general case and the cross-entropy loss function is responsible for guiding the training. Alternatively, by applying a contrastive loss function [5] to the siamese network, metric learning was implemented, as shown in several papers [1,20,22,23]. In the embedding space, it has the desirable property of bringing closer similar samples and distancing dissimilar samples.

$$L(W, Y, X_1, X_2) = (1 - Y)(D_W)^2 + Y max(0, m - D_W)^2 \tag{1}$$

The mathematical details of this loss function are shown in the Eq. 1 where W is the set of trainable weights, Y is the target (0 for similar samples and 1 for dissimilar samples), X_1 and X_2 are the two input images, D_W is the euclidean distance between the calculated embedding (using the set of weights W) of X_1 and X_2, and m is a margin used to let a pair contribute to the loss only if its

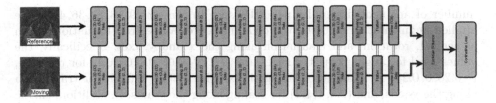

Fig. 2. The details of the network used. Blue lines mean that parameters are shared between the two branches. (Color figure online)

distance D_W belongs to $(0, m)$. The details of the network used are provided in Fig. 2. In particular, the parameters are shared for all the layers. At the end, for each of the two inputs, an embedding is created, and then the euclidean distance between them is used to evaluate the contrastive loss.

3.2 General Framework

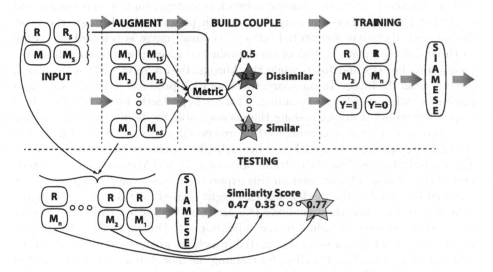

Fig. 3. Illustration of the overall method. There are three distinguished training phases: the moving image (M) (and the corresponding segmentation Ms) augmentation, the couple set formation, i.e. finding similar and dissimilar samples based on a metric, and the training. When testing, the network is asked to choose the best registered candidates from the set M.

The overall framework is composed of three different steps, and it is illustrated in Fig. 3. The first step consists of randomly producing augmented samples of the intra-procedural images. In particular, we evaluate the influence of the cardinality of the augmented samples on the performance of the model, varying the number of augmented samples per MRI slice in the set $(9, 18, 27, 36, 45)$. The applied augmentation consists of a combination of affine transformations, such as scaling, rotation, and translation along the x and y axes. Specifically, the values used for augmenting the slices are $(-0.1, -0.05, 0, 0.05, 0.1)$ for rotation, $(-0.25, 0, 0.25)$ for translation along the x-axis, $(-0.25, 0, 0.25)$ for translation along the y-axis, and $(0.8, 1, 1.2)$ for scaling along the y-axis. In addition, elastic distortion [15] is applied. The first step of this transformation is to produce a random displacement field $\Delta x(x, y) = rand(-1, 1)$ and $\Delta y(x, y) = rand(-1, 1)$, where $rand(-1, 1)$ means a random number in the range $(-1, 1)$. Those displacement fields are convolved with a gaussian of standard deviation σ and finally an intensity factor α controls the magnitude of the distortion. In particular we used $\alpha = 1.2$ and a $\sigma = 0.7$. Subsets of size $(9, 18, 27, 36, 45)$ of these augmented slices are grouped together randomly, creating the selection of images the model can choose from. In the training procedure, the same set of parameters is used to augment the corresponding intra-procedural segmentations (necessary for building couples based on DS and IoU) exactly in the same way as for the images from which they originated. The second step is only necessary for training and it is achieved by couple creation. Essentially, a set of informative pairs of samples are built to efficiently train the siamese network to distinguish between similar and dissimilar patterns. For this purpose, for each pre-procedural image the most similar and dissimilar augmented intra-procedural image is selected according to three different metrics, two of them evaluated given the corresponding segmentation (i.e. DS and IoU), while the Mutual Information (MI) is evaluated directly from the image. In summary, this operation produces a set of similar and dissimilar pairs used for the training. This set is perfectly balanced. The third step is the model training, making the network able to choose the most similar intra-procedural image according to the corresponding pre-procedural image. For the training process, the model goes through 100 epochs with a batch size of 64. The optimization is done with Adam optimizer [7] and learning rate of 0.0001. Out of the 10 cases of data used for this experiment, cases one through seven are assigned for training the model, and case eight is used for validating the model as it is trained, while the remaining two are used for testing. All the hyperparameters are chosen according to the validation set. During testing, for each of the two cases, individual slices are created, which are augmented by means of the same method as used for the slices for training the model. For each unaugmented intra-procedural slice, each set of augmented slices is inputted into the network, as well as its respective pre-procedural slice. The images reporting the highest similarity score are selected, and finally the model is evaluated based on different metrics comparing the pre-procedural slice segmentation and the segmentation of the slice the model deems as most accurately registered. Four different metrics are used for evaluating each pair of registered images. An ROI DS and ROI IoU score, as well as an DS and IoU score that includes every pixel within each slice. The ROI score only considers the overlap of the segmentation itself, while the other metric also considers the overlap of the background of each segmentation, not reducing it to an ROI.

3.3   Baselines

The first baseline model used to compare the siamese model's results comes from the SimpleITK python library, a toolkit commonly used for analyzing medical images, such as MRI images and CT scans. In addition to image augmentation operations, which are used to augment the data, the SimpleITK toolkit includes a registration method for 3D images. The model takes in a fixed and a moving image, and interpolates each of the images so that the model can accurately read the images and transfer them to a virtual domain. As a result, the moving image can be manipulated in a domain separate from the image it came from. From this virtual domain, a transformation is applied to the moving image, creating a registered image. Then, the transform is optimized based on how well the image was registered. This process of updating the transform and analyzing the results is repeated until the final (most accurately registered) image is formed. The instance of this model that is used on the prostate MRI data was trained for 2000 epochs with a learning rate of 0.05. The second baseline model comes from research done by Kuang and Schmah [10]. Their FAIM is a deep learning model trained using the Mindboggle-101 dataset [8], which contains 101 MRI images. The focus of their research was to create a model that had a low level of "foldings" within the deformation, caused by the fact that Jacobian determinants used to create the deformations were negative. To accomplish this, their model included a regularization method to increase the loss of displacement fields produced from the spatial deformation module where the Jacobian determinant was negative. To train their model, a pair of moving and reference images were inputted into the model. The moving image was fed into the spatial deformation module, performing the transformations created by the network on a sampled moving image. Finally, the loss was calculated using a cross correlation loss with two regularization methods, including the negative Jacobian determinant. To apply this model to the prostate MRI data, the siamese model is trained with the same number of epochs (10) and the same learning rate (10^{-4}). This model was chosen as a reference because it is one of the few with open access to the associated code. Even for this model, it is adapted so that single slices are inputted, and not the entire 3D volume.

3.4   Research Questions

The fundamental questions addressed in this paper are the following:

- Can a siamese network in a convenient to use environment outperform other common and deep learning algorithms in the task of prostate MRI interventional registration?
- Which is the best strategy to build the training couple necessary for the siamese network? Three policies are tested, consisting of selecting the most similar and dissimilar samples using DS, IoU and MI. While the latter policy allows us to have a complete unsupervised model, the other two require prostate segmentation.

- What is the best size of the augmented images set from which the siamese network can choose the best candidate to be the registered image? Each slice is augmented by means of five different values (9, 18, 27, 36, 45).
- Is it sufficient for the training to pick just the most similar and dissimilar images or should an extended set be considered? The selection of up to 5 similar and dissimilar images is tested.

4 Results

Table 1. Results from the siamese model and two baselines evaluated.

Model	IoU (roi)	DS (roi)	IoU (all)	DS (all)
SimpleItk	47.9	62.9	83.1	87.3
FAIM	37.5	50.8	92.1	92.1
Siamese	69.2	80.0	97.1	97.1

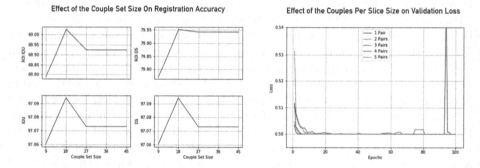

Fig. 4. The effect of the size of the couple set evaluated with all the four scores (left), and that of the pair per slice in validation loss (right).

The results reported in Table 1 show how the siamese model outperforms the two baselines by a large margin. The following discussion addresses the best policy for building the couple set. All the policies result in almost equal outcomes. In particular DS and IoU produce exactly the same couple set, while MI differs from the other two in some of the choices. This suggests that using MI is more advantageous, as it eliminates the need for segmentation, yielding a completely unsupervised method. Next, selecting from a total of 18 possible candidates for the best augmentation yields the best results. Increasing this number makes the decision too difficult for the network, reducing the performance. The left part of Fig. 4 reports the score for all the metrics according to the size of the couple set. The results show that considering more couples from each slice to be registered has no effect on the accuracy of the model. Even though more data is being used for training, any added pairs of images beyond the most accurately registered pair reduces the decisiveness of the siamese model. Therefore, when only one image is selected as the most accurately registered image during the evaluation process, the additional pairs for training don't have a significant impact on the model's decision. The validation loss reported in the right part of Fig. 4 reveals how selecting just the most similar and dissimilar samples for training produces the best validation loss, even if the difference is very low. Lastly, Fig. 5 shows an example in which the siamese network selects the correct candidate from among the set of 9 possible choices, together with the considered slice (odd row) the difference between its segmentation and that of the reference image is reported (even row).

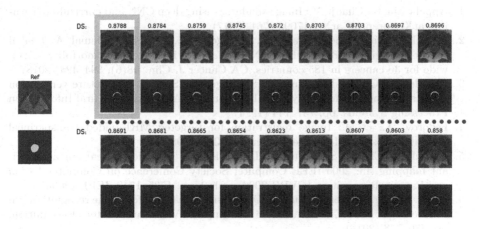

Fig. 5. Qualitative results from the siamese model. The DS is reported for each candidate, while yellow rectangles depict the augmentation selected by the network. For each candidate, the difference between its segmentation and the reference segmentation is reported (even row). (Color figure online)

5 Conclusion

This paper sheds light on the process of intra-procedural prostate MRI registration. This process is fundamental in clinical practice. Based on siamese neural networks, the model made in this research is able to outperform two competing baselines, demonstrating the power of siamese networks and metric learning for the case of a very restricted dataset as in prostate MRI registration. This research reveals how informative training couples can be created just through the use of mutual information, avoiding the use of segmentation required by the intersection over union or dice metric. This allows to have a completely unsupervised method. A large number of registration candidates is not necessary to achieve good performance. In fact, the best score was reached with 18 possible candidates. Finally, this experimentation shows that increasing the number of pairs of pre-procedural and intra-procedural images gained from a set of augmentations doesn't have an effect on the model's performance. This shows that this model is innovative in the field of radiology. Its simplicity together with low training time and accurate performance could help in the process of guiding biopsy or surgical intervention in general. It would be useful to test the model in a real surgical scenario gathering the feedback of experienced radiologists, which could help to further improve the model. Another interesting test would involve the use of a pre-trained neural network as a backbone to the siamese network, with further fine tuning to match the data's particular use.

References

1. Appalaraju, S., Chaoji, V.: Image similarity using deep CNN and curriculum learning. arXiv preprint arXiv:1709.08761 (2017)
2. Bray, F., Ferlay, J., Soerjomataram, I., Siegel, R.L., Torre, L.A., Jemal, A.: Global cancer statistics 2018: GLOBOCAN estimates of incidence and mortality worldwide for 36 cancers in 185 countries. CA Cancer J. Clin. **68**(6), 394–424 (2018)
3. Bromley, J., Guyon, I., LeCun, Y., Säckinger, E., Shah, R.: Signature verification using a "Siamese" time delay neural network. In: Advances in Neural Information Processing Systems, pp. 737–744 (1994)
4. Fedorov, A., et al.: Image registration for targeted MRI-guided transperineal prostate biopsy. J. Magn. Reson. Imaging **36**(4), 987–992 (2012)
5. Hadsell, R., Chopra, S., LeCun, Y.: Dimensionality reduction by learning an invariant mapping. In: 2006 IEEE Computer Society Conference on Computer Vision and Pattern Recognition (CVPR 2006), vol. 2, pp. 1735–1742. IEEE (2006)
6. He, K., Zhang, X., Ren, S., Sun, J.: Deep residual learning for image recognition. In: Proceedings of the IEEE Conference on Computer Vision and Pattern Recognition, pp. 770–778 (2016)
7. Kingma, D.P., Ba, J.: Adam: a method for stochastic optimization. arXiv preprint arXiv:1412.6980 (2014)
8. Klein, A., Tourville, J.: 101 labeled brain images and a consistent human cortical labeling protocol. Front. Neurosci. **6**, 171 (2012)
9. Koch, G., Zemel, R., Salakhutdinov, R.: Siamese neural networks for one-shot image recognition. In: ICML Deep Learning Workshop, vol. 2. Lille (2015)
10. Kuang, D., Schmah, T.: FAIM – a ConvNet method for unsupervised 3D medical image registration. In: Suk, H.-I., Liu, M., Yan, P., Lian, C. (eds.) MLMI 2019. LNCS, vol. 11861, pp. 646–654. Springer, Cham (2019). https://doi.org/10.1007/978-3-030-32692-0_74
11. Loeb, S., Carter, H.B., Berndt, S.I., Ricker, W., Schaeffer, E.M.: Complications after prostate biopsy: data from SEER-Medicare. J. Urol. **186**(5), 1830–1834 (2011)
12. Milletari, F., Navab, N., Ahmadi, S.A.: V-Net: fully convolutional neural networks for volumetric medical image segmentation. In: 2016 Fourth International Conference on 3D Vision (3DV), pp. 565–571. IEEE (2016)
13. Ronneberger, O., Fischer, P., Brox, T.: U-Net: convolutional networks for biomedical image segmentation. In: Navab, N., Hornegger, J., Wells, W.M., Frangi, A.F. (eds.) MICCAI 2015. LNCS, vol. 9351, pp. 234–241. Springer, Cham (2015). https://doi.org/10.1007/978-3-319-24574-4_28
14. Siegel, R.L., Miller, K.D., Jemal, A.: Cancer statistics, 2019. CA Cancer J. Clin. **69**(1), 7–34 (2019)

15. Simard, P.Y., Steinkraus, D., Platt, J.C., et al.: Best practices for convolutional neural networks applied to visual document analysis. In: ICDAR, vol. 3 (2003)
16. Simonyan, K., Zisserman, A.: Very deep convolutional networks for large-scale image recognition. arXiv preprint arXiv:1409.1556 (2014)
17. Stamey, T.A., Yang, N., Hay, A.R., McNeal, J.E., Freiha, F.S., Redwine, E.: Prostate-specific antigen as a serum marker for adenocarcinoma of the prostate. N. Engl. J. Med. **317**(15), 909–916 (1987)
18. Tajbakhsh, N., et al.: Convolutional neural networks for medical image analysis: full training or fine tuning? IEEE Trans. Med. Imaging **35**(5), 1299–1312 (2016)
19. Tempany, C., Straus, S., Hata, N., Haker, S.: MR-guided prostate interventions. J. Magn. Reson. Imaging: Official J. Int. Soc. Magn. Reson. Med. **27**(2), 356–367 (2008)
20. Wang, J., et al.: Learning fine-grained image similarity with deep ranking. In: Proceedings of the IEEE Conference on Computer Vision and Pattern Recognition, pp. 1386–1393 (2014)
21. Weinreb, J.C., et al.: PI-RADS prostate imaging-reporting and data system: 2015, version 2. Eur. Urol. **69**(1), 16–40 (2016)
22. Zagoruyko, S., Komodakis, N.: Learning to compare image patches via convolutional neural networks. In: Proceedings of the IEEE Conference on Computer Vision and Pattern Recognition, pp. 4353–4361 (2015)
23. Zhang, C., Liu, W., Ma, H., Fu, H.: Siamese neural network based gait recognition for human identification. In: 2016 IEEE International Conference on Acoustics, Speech and Signal Processing (ICASSP), pp. 2832–2836. IEEE (2016)

Unsupervised Anomaly Detection of the First Person in Gait from an Egocentric Camera

Mana Masuda[✉][iD], Ryo Hachiuma[✉][iD], Ryo Fujii[✉][iD], and Hideo Saito[✉][iD]

Keio University, Tokyo, Japan
{mana.smile,ryo-hachiuma,ryo.fujii0112,hs}@keio.jp

Abstract. Assistive technology is increasingly important as the senior population grows. The purpose of this study is to develop a means of preventing fatal injury by monitoring the movements of the elderly and sounding an alarm if an accident occurs. We present a method of detecting an anomaly in a first-person's gait from an egocentric video. Followed by the conventional anomaly detection methods, we train the model in an unsupervised manner. We use optical flow images to capture ego-motion information in the first person. To verify the effectiveness of our model, we introduced and conducted experiments with a novel first-person video anomaly detection dataset and showed that our model outperformed the baseline method.

Keywords: Assistive technology · Egocentric video · Unsupervised learning · Adversarial training · Optical flow

1 Introduction

As the population ages, remotely monitoring the elderly has become invaluable for providing independent living. As their physical and cognitive skills decrease, the older population faces increased risk for potentially life-threatening accidents while they walk, such as falling down and stumbling. Thus, the ability to monitor their mobility and be alerted of potential dangers (abnormalities) is extremely useful for caregivers in the prevention of injuries and the provision of swift emergency care (Fig. 1).

In the field of computer vision, the problem of detecting anomalous events in human activity has been extensively studied using surveillance cameras [6,14,18]. Unfortunately, this approach suffers from visual occlusions, difficulty handling multiple subjects, and the need to extrapolate spatio-temporal parameters when the full-body cannot be seen. Moreover, they are restricted to fixed areas. Considering that gait is characterized by moving the body from one location to another, daily-life data on gait are difficult to capture without using multiple cameras attached to the environment.

An alternative approach is to use wearable sensors attached to the subject's body. Particularly, anomaly detection systems using inertial measurement unit

© Springer Nature Switzerland AG 2020
G. Bebis et al. (Eds.): ISVC 2020, LNCS 12510, pp. 604–617, 2020.
https://doi.org/10.1007/978-3-030-64559-5_48

Fig. 1. The proposed method predicts the camera wearer's anomaly in gait from a chest-mounted egocentric camera. The images with blue frame shows the normal action (gait), and the images with red frames shows the abnormal action (falling down). (Color figure online)

(IMU) sensors for gait assessment [4] and fall detection [21] have been shown to be highly effective in the detection of anomalous activity. However, accelerometer values from IMU sensors cannot capture the spatial information of the environment [19].

It is reasonable to expect that wearable cameras, such as smart glass or a head-mounted display (HMD), will be readily available in the near future [26]. Based on this, egocentric video analysis has recently attracted increased attention in many applications in assistive technologies, such as personalized object recognition [11], object usage guidance [5], 3D pose estimation [29], and video summarization [7], in an attempt to understand human behavior from a first-person perspective.

In this paper, we aim to detect anomalies in gait from the perspective of the first person (the person wearing the camera) using an egocentric camera images. Note that the aim of our work differs from gait assessment studies that measure the potential risk of falling down. Rather, our work aims to detect any abnormal activity in gait, such as falling down, stumbling, or swaying.

Due to the difficulty of collecting a sufficient number of videos of anomalous activity, an anomaly detection model must be trained in an unsupervised manner. That is to say, the model should be trained to capture the distribution of the data (normal activity) and detect anomalous data as out-of-distribution during testing. Modern image-based anomaly detection systems [3,13,31] employ an autoencoder-based model to learn the manifold for the normal class at the time of training and calculate the difference between the input image and the reconstructed image to calculate the pixel-level anomaly score during testing.

This method, however, cannot be used directly in our task for several reasons. First, because the location in which the subject walks is always changing, it is difficult to model the distribution of normal data from a raw RGB image when it is being compared to the anomaly activity detected in the surveillance camera. Second, the anomaly score is usually computed using the difference between the Euclidean space in the reconstructed and original images; however, the anomaly is reflected in the image globally (if the person falls down, the camera will also fall down), not locally (pixel-level), and a pixel-wise anomaly calculation might detect novel objects in the image as anomalies.

Therefore, we present an anomaly detection method that uses a 2D Convolution Neural Network (CNN) and the input of optical flow images. Our network is inspired by GANomaly [1]. To more easily capture the distribution of normal data, our model calculates the dense optical flow of successive frames and used this as input instead of raw RGB images. The use of optical flow means our model involves time series data using a 2D CNN, allowing it to work with time-series data at a lower computational cost than if it were to use a 3D CNN. During testing, we calculated the anomaly score in the latent vector space instead of the image space to capture the anomaly of the image globally.

As there is no publicly available dataset that contains first-person videos of normal and anomalous gait, we introduced a novel dataset that consists of two-hour egocentric video sequences of normal gait and five types of anomalous activities: squatting, stumbling, staggering, falling down, and collision. The sequences were captured by cameras on three different individuals at different places. Unlike the conventional anomalous action detection dataset [14], this dataset focuses on the anomalous events that happen, not on the person themselves. The experiments were conducted using this dataset. Our codes and the dataset are available from our repository[1].

The contributions of this paper are summarized as follows:

- We aim to detect the anomalous events in the gait of the first-person (camera wearer) from an egocentric video. To the best of our knowledge, this is the first work tackling this problem. We present a 2D CNN-based anomaly detection network trained in an unsupervised manner with input in the form of optical flow images.
- We introduce a novel first-person video anomaly detection dataset that consists of normal gait and five different anomalous events using an egocentric camera, and the dataset is now publicly available. Unfortunately, we cannot provide the raw RGB images due to privacy issues. We will also make public the reproducible results, training, and evaluation code.
- We experiment with this anomaly detection dataset and show that our model outperforms the baseline method. Moreover, we conduct an ablation study on different hyperparameter settings to verify the effectiveness of our approach.

2   Related Work

2.1   Egocentric Vision

A typical problem in egocentric vision is the recognition of the activities of the first-person (the person wearing the camera). Recent works have primarily focused on action-forecasting [30] and person localization [27, 29]. [29] predicts the camera wearers place in a future frame, and [27] predicts the future locations

---

[1] https://github.com/llien30/ego-ad.

of people in first-person videos. To forecast first-person behavior, most models use pose prediction: [30] used 3D human pose prediction previously used for third-person pose estimation tasks. In contrast, our method does not need to estimate the pose to detect the abnormal behaviors of the first-person, reducing the time to inference.

2.2   Anomaly Detection

Anomaly detection is a well-known task within the field of machine learning, with the major areas of real-world application being fraud detection, biomedical, video surveillance, etc. Anomaly detection is also referred to in previous studies as "novelty-detection" and "out-of-distribution detection". The basic method of anomaly detection is to identify whether or not the data is out of normal data distribution. The traditional anomaly detection methods are distance-based, using the distance between the normal and abnormal data.

Recent studies on anomaly detection have involved the use of deep neural networks, with methods using auto-encoder and variational auto-encoders to train a model to reconstruct normal images and detect abnormal images as samples with high reconstruction errors. Since the adversarial-learning-based method was proposed in [24], many new methods using adversarial-learning have been used, and various methods have been introduced to the generative model. Efficient GAN [31] combines the auto-encoder to the generative model and reduces the inference time. AnoVAEGAN [3] introduces VAEGAN [13] as the generative model. In GANomaly [1], Akcay *et al.* proposed an adversarial network such that the generator comprises encoder–decoder–encoder sub-networks. The objective of our model is not only to minimize the distance between the original and reconstructed normal images, but also to minimize the difference between their latent vector representations. Skip-GANomaly [2] introduced skip connection to reconstruction, and the accuracy of anomaly detection was improved by reconstructing the image more precisely.

2.3   Video Anomaly Detection

Video anomaly detection has received considerable attention in computer vision and robotics. Many methods have been proposed for third-person video specifically. [9] proposed a 3D convolutional auto-encoder (Conv-AE) to model regular frames, and [15] proposed a stacked RNN for temporally-coherent sparse coding (TSC-sRNN). In [14], the generator was trained using an optical flow image to reconstruct the next frame image and detect anomalies by looking for differences between a predicted future frame and the actual frame. In [18], both the RGB image and optical flow image were reconstructed to calculate the anomaly score. When detecting anomalies from a first-person perspective, however, it is hard to reconstruct either the current or future RGB frames due to the first-person's motion. [28] localized the potential anomaly participants to detect traffic accidents from first-person videos under the assumption that the anomalous roadway event can be detected by looking for deviations between the predicted and actual locations of objects. However, the motion of the egocentric camera on a walking person, which is described by 6-Dof, is significantly more complex than that of a dash-cam, which can be determined using the forward velocity and yaw angle. Also, the abnormal event is only limited to the collision between objects (e.g., cars, bikes, pedestrians).

Previous approaches to person-centric anomaly detection and prediction relied on 2D pose estimation [17], such as in [10], where a method was proposed for predicting falls that consisted of a pose-prediction module and a falls classifier. To apply this to our scenario would require the pose of the first-person, which is not as readily available as the third person 2D pose estimation of a static camera. Therefore, we leverage optical flow containing the first-person's ego-motion information. Qiao *et al.* [22] reconstructed optical flow images to detect abnormal actions from third-person video; however, to the best of our knowledge, this is the first work that uses only optical-flow images to detect anomaly actions in the first person using a reconstruction-based approach.

3   Method

If the abnormal actions, such as falling down or struggling, should occur, the image of the first-person's view would drastically change. Therefore, we take into consideration that there should be some difference between the optical flow calculated from the egocentric video for normal behavior and the optical flow for abnormal behavior. For these reasons, we use optical flow to detect first-person incidents from the first-person video.

Also, we do not aim to detect anomalies of the image in the pixel-level but rather to use the entire image to determine the existence of an anomaly. Thus, we compare the feature vectors of the original and reconstructed images instead of comparing the original and reconstructed images themselves as in previous studies. To achieve this, we adopt a sub-network, named the reconstructor, with two encoders and one decoder. This structure is inspired by GANomaly [1]. The details of the structure of the reconstructor are described in detail in Sect. 3.1. We use PWC-Net [25] to generate the optical flow image from an egocentric video.

Problem Definition. Our objective is to train an unsupervised network that detects anomalies using optical flow images. The definition of our problem is as follows: The training dataset is denoted as $\mathcal{I}$ which is composed of m normal egocentric videos while the person is walking. From these videos, we calculate M optical flow images X_i, as in

$$\mathcal{I} = \{X_1, \cdots, X_M\}. \tag{1}$$

The test dataset is denoted as in $\hat{\mathcal{I}}$, which is composed of n normal and abnormal videos. From these videos, we calculated N optical flow images $\hat{X}_i$ and labeled $y_i \in [0, 1]$ for the evaluation, as in

$$\hat{\mathcal{I}} = \{(\hat{X}_1, y_1), \cdots, (\hat{X}_N, y_N)\}. \tag{2}$$

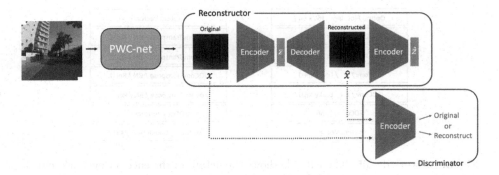

Fig. 2. Network overview. Our model consists of two networks: reconstructor R and discriminator D. The reconstructor consists of two encoders and a decoder.

To detect the abnormal events, the number of images in the training dataset is larger than the number in the testing dataset ($N \ll M$).

Using the dataset, our goal is to first model $\mathcal{I}$ to learn its manifold $\mathcal{X}$, then detect the abnormal samples that are not on the learned manifold $\mathcal{X}$ in $\hat{\mathcal{I}}$ as outliers during the inference stage. To detect the abnormal data in the feature vector space, the model learns the distribution of the normal data $\mathcal{X}$ and learns to encode the similar feature vector using two encoders.

Network Structure. The overview of the network is depicted in Fig. 2. Our network consists of two main networks—a reconstructor network and a discriminator network—and a PWC-Net that generates an optical flow image from two successive images. The reconstructor consists of two encoders and one decoder.

The first sub-network is the first encoder in the autoencoder network. The encoder network learns the input optical-flow representation in the latent space. This network input is $x \in \mathbb{R}^{w \times h \times 2}$ and downscales x by compressing it to a latent vector z with the use of 2d convolutional layers followed by batch-norm and LeakyReLU activation [16]. z is a bottleneck features of the reconstructor. The decoder consists of 2D conv-transpose layers followed by a batchnorm layer and a ReLU activation layer, except for the last layer that is only a 2D conv-transpose layer.

Network detail is shown in Fig. 3. The left side shows the detail of the encoder network and the right side shows the detail of the decoder network. The number of channels in the middle layer of the encoder was set to $\{2(input), 8, 16, 32, 64, z(output)\}$.

3.1 Reconstructor Network

We use a reconstructor to learn the manifold of normal samples and detect anomalies. To compare the feature vector of the original image to that of the reconstructed image, we adopt an encoder–decoder–encoder network for the reconstructor, as shown in Fig. 2. As with existing methods [1, 2, 24, 31], we train

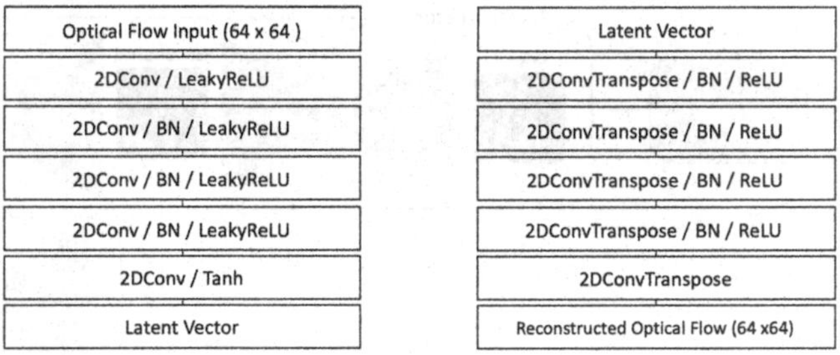

Optical Flow Input (64 x 64)
2DConv / LeakyReLU
2DConv / BN / LeakyReLU
2DConv / BN / LeakyReLU
2DConv / BN / LeakyReLU
2DConv / Tanh
Latent Vector

Latent Vector
2DConvTranspose / BN / ReLU
2DConvTranspose / BN / ReLU
2DConvTranspose / BN / ReLU
2DConvTranspose / BN / ReLU
2DConvTranspose
Reconstructed Optical Flow (64 x64)

Fig. 3. Network details. The left side shows the details of the encoder network and the right side shows the details of the decoder network.

the reconstructor to perform anomaly detection based on image reconstruction by training it to learn adversarially with the discriminator so that the reconstructor is able to reconstruct images that resemble the original image. To ensure that the feature vectors of the original and reconstructed images are different for the abnormal images, we train the network to make the feature vectors of the original and reconstructed images similar. Because of the structure of the reconstructor, we only need to put the image in the reconstructor once to perform the test.

3.2   Loss Functions

Similar to GANomaly [1], we use three losses—adversarial loss, contextual loss, and encoder loss—to train the reconstructor. We use adversarial loss for the loss function of the discriminator [8]. To explain the loss function, let m be the size of the latent vectors.

Adversarial Loss is the loss calculated from the output of the discriminator. We use "feature matching adversarial loss", which is often used in anomaly detection models [1,24,31]. To explain the loss function, let D_{feat} be a function that outputs just before the last layer of the discriminator D. We use MSELoss to calculate the adversarial loss. The adversarial loss function is defined as

$$L_{adv} = \frac{1}{m} \sum_{i=1}^{m} (D_{feat}(x) - D_{feat}(\hat{x}))^2. \tag{3}$$

Contextual Loss. Contextual loss is the loss calculated as the difference between the original image and the reconstructed image and is the loss used to train the autoencoder. We used L_1 distance between the original image and the deconstructed image. The contextual loss function is defined as

$$L_{con} = \frac{1}{m} \sum_{i=1}^{m} (x - \hat{x}). \tag{4}$$

Encoder Loss is the loss calculated as the difference between the original image's feature vector z and the reconstructed image's feature vector $\hat{z}$. This loss is especially important in our model because we employed this difference in feature space when computing the anomaly score. We use MSELoss to calculate the encoder loss. To explain the loss function, let $E_{original}$ be a function of the first encoder network and E_{recon} be a function of the second encoder network. The encoder loss function is defined as

$$L_{enc} = \frac{1}{m} \sum_{i=1}^{m} (E_{original}(x) - E_{recon}(\hat{x}))^2. \tag{5}$$

Our objective function for the reconstructor is defined as

$$L = \lambda_{adv} L_{adv} + \lambda_{con} L_{adv} + \lambda_{enc} L_{enc}, \tag{6}$$

where λ_{adv}, λ_{con}, and λ_{enc} are the weighting hyperparameters that adjust the impact of individual losses on the overall objective function.

3.3   Anomaly Action Detection

We score abnormalities using the difference between z and $\hat{z}$. The anomaly score $\mathcal{A}$ of the testing image x is defined as

$$\mathcal{A}(\mathrm{x}) = \frac{1}{m} \sum_{i=1}^{m} (E_{original}(\mathrm{x}) - E_{recon}(\hat{\mathrm{x}}))^2. \tag{7}$$

The evaluation criteria for the anomaly score $\mathcal{A}$ is to threshold (ϕ) the score, where $\mathcal{A}(\mathrm{x}) > \phi$ indicates an anomaly.

4   Experiments

4.1   Dataset

As there is no publicly available dataset that contains anomaly actions captured from an egocentric video, we created our own. Three people mounted a GoPro camera (60 FPS, 1920×1080 resolution) on their chest. For the training data, the video is recorded for about 30 min while each person walked in an outdoor environment, with each environment being different from the others. For the test data, they were asked to perform anomalous action in their gait. Five types of anomaly actions were used: squat down, stumble, stagger, fall down, and collision. Around five minutes of video was captured for each person. We annotated abnormal and normal labels for each frame in the test videos. The RGB images from the dataset with abnormal labels are shown in Fig. 4. To generate the optical flow images, we centered and cropped the RGB image to 1080×1080, then resized it to 224×224. We used PWC-Net to generate the optical flow images. An example of the annotation of a dataset is shown in Fig. 5. Images surrounded by blue are normal and images surrounded by red are abnormal.

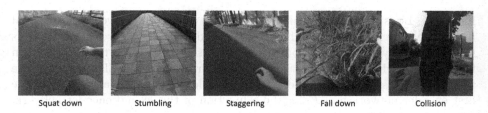

Squat down   Stumbling   Staggering   Fall down   Collision

Fig. 4. Examples of abnormal actions. From the left to right: squat down, stumble, stagger, fall down, and collision.

Fig. 5. Comparison of the optical flow and corresponding RGB images. The optical flow is color coded for better visualization. Images surrounded by blue are annotated as normal and images surrounded by red are annotated as abnormal. (Color figure online)

4.2 Baseline Method

In the experiment, we aimed to verify the effectiveness of detecting the anomaly from the optical flow instead of the raw RGB image. Since optical flow is generated from two successive RGB images, it is unreasonable to compare optical flow-based anomaly detection with single RGB-based anomaly detection. Therefore, we concatenated two consecutive RGB images in the channel direction and created a 6-channel image. We used the area under the curve (AUC) of the Receiver Operating Characteristic (ROC) as an evaluation metric.

4.3 Experimental Setups

We conducted the experiment in three setups to verify the robustness of our method. The setups are as follows:

- **Person-specific:** In this setup, the model is trained with and for a single person. Even though the person during training and test is the same, the place-captured training and test data are different.
- **Person-generic:** In this setup, the model is trained and tested with all three people.

- **Person-out:** In this setup, the model is trained using data from two people and then tested with data from the remaining person. This setup evaluates the model's robustness against an unknown person and place.

4.4 Network Training

The size of the feature vector was set to 64 through the experiments. Following the previous anomaly detection model [1,24,31], our adversarial training is also based on the standard Deep Convolutional GAN (DCGAN) approach [23]. We implement our approach in PyTorch [20] (v1.4.0+cu100, with python 3.8.0) and run it on NVIDIA quadoro GV100 or P6000 processing unit using CUDA 10.0. We optimize the network by using Adam [12] with an initial learning rate $2e^{-3}$ and the momentums $\beta_1 = 0.5$, $\beta_2 = 0.999$. Our model is optimized based on the loss L (defined in Eq. 6) using the weighted values $\lambda_{adv} = 1$, $\lambda_{con} = 50$, and $\lambda_{enc} = 1$. We train the model for under 150 epochs for all cases. Note that the weights of PWC-Net is fixed during the training. The pretrained weight is downloaded from the official repository[2].

5 Results

5.1 Qualitative Evaluation

The graph of the time series of anomaly scores is shown in the following Fig. 6. The upper graph shows the temporal transition of the anomaly score by RGB images and the lower graph shows the transition of anomaly score by optical flow image. The graph and images show that even if the image does not contain any abnormal objects (e.g., hands, feet, etc.) that do not appear in a normal image, the motion of the first person (camera wearer) is captured in the optical flow image and the anomal score is increased. Unlike the optical flow image, the anomaly scores by RGB images do not differ much between abnormal and normal. This shows that optical flow images can identify anomalies more accurately than RGB images.

5.2 Quantitative Evaluation

The results of this experiment are shown in Table 1. The results show that optical flow is better for detecting anomalies than using RGB images. We also found that the accuracy of the RGB images varied greatly between training with each data set and combining a few different data sets. When we used optical flow images, however, we were able to achieve an accuracy of over 0.9 for all conditions. Therefore, it can be said that optical flow images are more robust to domain changes than consecutive RGB images.

The comparison of the AUC for each abnormal behavior is also shown in Table 1. The size of the feature vector was set to 64 for all cases. The results are

---

[2] https://github.com/NVlabs/PWC-Net.

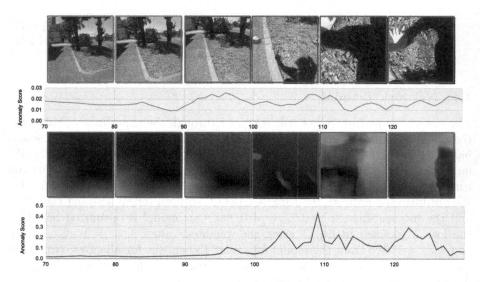

Fig. 6. The temporal transition of the anomaly score by RGB images and optical flow images. The x-axis shows the frame index and the y-axis shows predicted anomaly score. The upper graph shows the anomaly score by RGB images and the lower graph shows the anomaly score by optical flow images. Images surrounded by blue are annotated as normal and images surrounded by red are annotated as abnormal. (Color figure online)

the average of the three data sets except for the person-generic setup. This result shows the accuracy is higher when detecting fast-moving anomalies (stumbling), and lower when detecting slow-moving anomalies (staggering). Even if slow-moving anomalies, however, we were able to achieve an accuracy of over 0.91 on average.

5.3   Comparison of Feature Vector Size

The size of the feature vectors is very important because our method compares the feature vectors of the original and the reconstructed images to predict whether the first person is conducting a normal or abnormal action. Therefore, we gradually increased the vector size from 32 and performed comparative experiments for sizes 32, 64, 128, and 256.

The results of this experiment are in Table 2. The experimental results show that the small vector sizes of 32 and 64 outperformed the large vector sizes of 128 and 256. It can be seen that if the size of the feature vector is large, the feature vector represents the image in detail, whereas if the size of the feature vector is small, the feature vector represents the global information of the optical flow image. As we aim to detect the abnormal events of the first-person, the anomaly is referred to the image globally. Therefore, the small vector size is suitable for our task.

Table 1. AUC results for all setups.

Method	Person-specific					
	Squat down	Stumble	Stagger	Fall down	Collision	Average
Baseline	0.679	0.514	0.850	0.919	0.593	0.711
Ours	**0.981**	**0.915**	**0.831**	**0.969**	**0.951**	**0.929**
Method	Person-generic					
	Squat down	Stumble	Stagger	Fall down	Collision	Average
Baseline	0.639	0.589	0.593	0.813	0.697	0.666
Ours	**0.939**	**0.933**	**0.807**	**0.985**	**0.915**	**0.916**
Method	Person-out					
	Squat down	Stumble	Stagger	Fall down	Collision	Average
Baseline	0.659	0.813	0.689	0.850	0.409	0.684
Ours	**0.945**	**0.990**	**0.922**	**0.998**	**0.892**	**0.949**

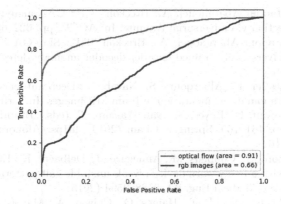

Fig. 7. Comparison of the ROC curve of an optical flow image and consecutive RGB image.

Table 2. Comparison of feature vector size. We compared the feature vectors with different sizes (32, 64, 128, and 256).

Feature vector dim.	Accuracy
32	0.927
64	**0.934**
128	0.908
256	0.877

6 Conclusion

We presented an anomaly detection model that detects first-person abnormalities in gait from an egocentric video. By employing an encoder–decoder–encoder network, we made a model that uses features extracted from an egocentric video and detects anomalies by comparing the features of the original with those of reconstructed images. We also produced a novel first-person video anomaly detection dataset using an egocentric camera. Experiments using our dataset showed that our model outperformed the baseline. The recording of our dataset, however, may have violated other people's privacy, and future work should consider models that more effectively support people in ways that do not violate the privacy of others. Future research should also be done on the possibility of forecasting an individual's abnormal actions using an egocentric camera.

References

1. Akçay, S., Atapour-Abarghouei, A., Breckon, T.P.: GANomaly: semi-supervised anomaly detection via adversarial training. In: ACCV, pp. 622–637 (2018)
2. Akçay, S., Atapour-Abarghouei, A., Breckon, T.P.: Skip-GANomaly: skip connected and adversarially trained encoder-decoder anomaly detection. In: IJCNN, pp. 1–8 (2019)
3. Baur, C., Wiestler, B., Albarqouni, S., Navab, N.: Deep autoencoding models for unsupervised anomaly segmentation in brain MR images. In: Crimi, A., Bakas, S., Kuijf, H., Keyvan, F., Reyes, M., van Walsum, T. (eds.) BrainLes 2018. LNCS, vol. 11383, pp. 161–169. Springer, Cham (2019). https://doi.org/10.1007/978-3-030-11723-8_16
4. Brodie, M., Lord, S., Coppens, M., Annegarn, J., Delbaere, K.: Eight-week remote monitoring using a freely worn device reveals unstable gait patterns in older fallers. IEEE Trans. Bio-Medical Eng. **62**, 2588–2594 (2015)
5. Damen, D., Leelasawassuk, T., Haines, O., Calway, A., Mayol-Cuevas, W.: You-do, i-learn: discovering task relevant objects and their modes of interaction from multi-user egocentric video. In: BMVC (2014)
6. Doshi, K., Yilmaz, Y.: Continual learning for anomaly detection in surveillance videos. In: CVPR Workshops (2020)
7. Furnari, A., Farinella, G.M., Battiato, S.: Recognizing personal contexts from egocentric images. In: ICCV Workshop, pp. 393–401 (2015)
8. Goodfellow, I., et al.: Generative adversarial nets. In: NeurIPS, pp. 2672–2680 (2014)
9. Hasan, M., Choi, J., Neumann, J., Roy-Chowdhury, A.K., Davis, L.S.: Learning temporal regularity in video sequences. In: CVPR, pp. 733–742 (2016)
10. Hua, M., Nan, Y., Lian, S.: Falls prediction based on body keypoints and seq2seq architecture. In: ICCV Workshop, pp. 1251–1259 (2019)
11. Kacorri, H., Kitani, K.M., Bigham, J.P., Asakawa, C.: People with visual impairment training personal object recognizers: feasibility and challenges. In: CHI Conference on Human Factors in Computing Systems, pp. 5839–5849 (2017)
12. Kingma, D.P., Ba, J.: Adam: a method for stochastic optimization. arXiv preprint arXiv:1412.6980 (2014)

13. Larsen, A.B.L., Sønderby, S.K., Larochelle, H., Winther, O.: Autoencoding beyond pixels using a learned similarity metric. In: International Conference on Machine Learning, pp. 1558–1566 (2016)
14. Liu, W., Luo, W., Lian, D., Gao, S.: Future frame prediction for anomaly detection-a new baseline. In: CVPR, pp. 6536–6545 (2018)
15. Luo, W., Liu, W., Gao, S.: A revisit of sparse coding based anomaly detection in stacked RNN framework. In: ICCV, pp. 341–349 (2017)
16. Maas, A., Hannun, A., Ng, A.: Rectifier nonlinearities improve neural network acoustic models. In: ICML (2013)
17. Morais, R., Le, V., Tran, T., Saha, B., Mansour, M., Venkatesh, S.: Learning regularity in skeleton trajectories for anomaly detection in videos. In: CVPR, pp. 11988–11996 (2019)
18. Nguyen, T.N., Meunier, J.: Anomaly detection in video sequence with appearance-motion correspondence. In: ICCV, pp. 1273–1283 (2019)
19. Nouredanesh, M., Li, A.W., Godfrey, A., Hoey, J., Tung, J.: Chasing feet in the wild: a proposed egocentric motion-aware gait assessment tool. In: Leal-Taixé, L., Roth, S. (eds.) ECCV 2018. LNCS, vol. 11134, pp. 176–192. Springer, Cham (2019). https://doi.org/10.1007/978-3-030-11024-6_12
20. Paszke, A., et al.: Automatic differentiation in PyTorch (2017)
21. Phillips, L., et al.: Using embedded sensors in independent living to predict gait changes and falls. West. J. Nurs. Res. **39**, 78–94 (2017)
22. Qiao, M., Wang, T., Li, J., Li, C., Lin, Z., Snoussi, H.: Abnormal event detection based on deep autoencoder fusing optical flow. In: Chinese Control Conference, pp. 11098–11103 (2017)
23. Radford, A., Metz, L., Chintala, S.: Unsupervised representation learning with deep convolutional generative adversarial networks. CoRR (2016)
24. Schlegl, T., Seeböck, P., Waldstein, S.M., Schmidt-Erfurth, U., Langs, G.: Unsupervised anomaly detection with generative adversarial networks to guide marker discovery. In: IPMI, pp. 146–157 (2017)
25. Sun, D., Yang, X., Liu, M.Y., Kautz, J.: PWC-Net: CNNs for optical flow using pyramid, warping, and cost volume. In: CVPR, pp. 8934–8943 (2018)
26. Tadesse, G.A., Cavallaro, A.: Visual features for ego-centric activity recognition: a survey. In: ACM Workshop on Wearable Systems and Applications, pp. 48–53 (2018)
27. Yagi, T., Mangalam, K., Yonetani, R., Sato, Y.: Future person localization in first-person videos. In: CVPR, pp. 7593–7602 (2018)
28. Yao, Y., Xu, M., Wang, Y., Crandall, D.J., Atkins, E.M.: Unsupervised traffic accident detection in first-person videos. In: IROS, pp. 273–280 (2019)
29. Yuan, Y., Kitani, K.: 3D ego-pose estimation via imitation learning. In: Ferrari, V., Hebert, M., Sminchisescu, C., Weiss, Y. (eds.) ECCV 2018. LNCS, vol. 11220, pp. 763–778. Springer, Cham (2018). https://doi.org/10.1007/978-3-030-01270-0_45
30. Yuan, Y., Kitani, K.: Ego-pose estimation and forecasting as real-time PD control. In: ICCV, pp. 10082–10092 (2019)
31. Zenati, H., Foo, C.S., Lecouat, B., Manek, G., Chandrasekhar, V.R.: Efficient GAN-based anomaly detection. arXiv preprint arXiv:1802.06222 (2018)

Emotion Categorization from Video-Frame Images Using a Novel Sequential Voting Technique

Harisu Abdullahi Shehu[1]([✉])(iD), Will Browne[1](iD), and Hedwig Eisenbarth[2](iD)

[1] School of Engineering and Computer Science, Victoria University of Wellington,
6012 Wellington, New Zealand
{harisushehu,will.browne}@ecs.vuw.ac.nz
[2] School of Psychology, Victoria University of Wellington,
6012 Wellington, New Zealand
hedwig.eisenbarth@vuw.ac.nz

Abstract. Emotion categorization can be the process of identifying different emotions in humans based on their facial expressions. It requires time and sometimes it is hard for human classifiers to agree with each other about an emotion category of a facial expression. However, machine learning classifiers have done well in classifying different emotions and have widely been used in recent years to facilitate the task of emotion categorization. Much research on emotion video databases uses a few frames from when emotion is expressed at peak to classify emotion, which might not give a good classification accuracy when predicting frames where the emotion is less intense. In this paper, using the CK+ emotion dataset as an example, we use more frames to analyze emotion from mid and peak frame images and compared our results to a method using fewer peak frames. Furthermore, we propose an approach based on sequential voting and apply it to more frames of the CK+ database. Our approach resulted in up to 85.9% accuracy for the mid frames and overall accuracy of 96.5% for the CK+ database compared with the accuracy of 73.4% and 93.8% from existing techniques.

Keywords: CK+ · Emotion categorization · K-nearest neighbors · Random forests · Sequential vote · Video-frame

1 Introduction

Significant effort has been made in developing emotion classification methods for human facial expressions. This is driven by the increasing number of intelligent systems where it is important to approximate an emotional state of mind, so as to improve their interaction with humans. Thus, emotion categorization becomes an increasingly important area of research in computer vision [1,2] as classification from facial expression is so far the most readily available way to estimate states of emotion.

© Springer Nature Switzerland AG 2020
G. Bebis et al. (Eds.): ISVC 2020, LNCS 12510, pp. 618–632, 2020.
https://doi.org/10.1007/978-3-030-64559-5_49

Emotion recognition is a common field of study. Here, we made the distinction between emotion recognition and emotion categorization as we contend that it is not possible to know the underlying emotion of a person because it can be superficially manipulated, e.g. bluffing in poker or business interactions.

Evidence has shown that human beings are not good at classifying emotion [3–5]. An image that will be classified to have a particular emotion by one person might be classified to have a different emotion by another person. This is due to the different perspectives we all have as a result of variation in neurobiological processes [6]. On the other hand, machine learning classifiers have done well in categorizing emotion when appropriate features are provided to the classifiers.

Researchers have used various methods to analyze emotion from posed and non-posed visual datasets [7,8]. A posed dataset is generated by capturing the picture of participants in a controlled environment based on instructions given to them by an experimenter. Alternatively, datasets with non-posed expressions are created without instruction where labeling is post stimuli by "emotion experts"[1].

The CK+ database [9], which is mainly based on posed expressions, is chosen to be used as an example of an emotion video database. As the videos in the CK+ database have already been converted to image frames, this made it readily available to be used compared to other emotion video databases such as the DISFA [10] and FAMED [11] dataset, etc., in which the videos will need to be converted to image frames. Overall, the CK+ database has a total of seven classes of expressions, which comprise of the 6 basic (anger, disgust, fear, happiness, sadness, and surprise) emotions defined by Ekman [12] plus contempt expression.

The CK+ database does not label frames as "peak" i.e. where the emotion is most vividly expressed. However, the term peak is often applied to frame(s) in this dataset. A number of researchers use the last frame [13,14] whereas others use the last three frames as peak frames [15,16]. Much research on the CK+ dataset uses a subset of the available frames where the emotion is considered at peak. This is anticipated to make the associated technique less effective in categorizing frames where the emotion is not expressed at peak.

The aim of this research is to use multiple frames of the CK+ database to analyze emotion labels from different image frames and compare our approach to that using just peak frames. Also to improve accuracy, a sequential voting technique that performs voting on each sequence of the video frames based on the prediction made will be applied.

The rest of the paper is organized as follows: Sect. 2 explains how people use video frame images for emotion categorization research using the CK+ database as an example. In Sect. 3, we explain the properties of the CK+ database and its emotion categories. In addition, we also explain our proposed method and introduce a sequential voting approach. Section 4 compares the use of more emotion video frames to fewer peak frames and shows the effectiveness of the sequential voting approach. In Sect. 5, we further discuss the obtained result and highlight

---

[1] People that are trained in emotion categorization. These people labeled these databases based on the assumption that people smile when happy, frown their faces when sad, and scowl when anger irrespective of their age, race, and ethnicity.

the shortcomings of the applied method. In Sect. 6, we conclude the paper and hint at certain limitations that could be addressed in future studies.

2 Related Work

Happy and Routray [17] proposed an approach based on Support Vector machine (SVM) multi-class classification. The face in each image is first detected followed by landmark detection of the region of interest such as the eyebrow corners, nose, eyes, and the lips corners. Also, active patch locations are defined with respect to the location of this landmark. All active patches are evaluated in the training phase and the ones with a maximum variation of features between the expressions are selected. A SVM multi-class classifier is used to classify the selected features after they are being projected into six different lower-dimensional (from 192 × 192 to 48 × 48 pixels) subspace on the CK+ database. The last images of every sequence of the six basic expressions where the expression is at its peak were selected resulting in a total of 329 images and the result was evaluated based on voting out two of the six different dimensions using 10-fold cross-validation, which lead to an accuracy of 94.09%. Although the CK+ has seven different facial expressions, Happy and Routray chose to analyze emotion from only six out of the seven expressions of the CK+ database as they consider the six basic expressions to be universal.

In contrast to [17], Elaiwat et al. [15] used all the seven expressions plus *neutral* provided by the CK+ database. They proposed an approach based on Restricted Boltzmann Machines (RBM) on the CK+ dataset in which voting is performed in the validation phase. Three image pairs were constructed from each of the 327 labeled sequences of the CK+ database in which the first image corresponded to neutral and the remaining two images corresponded to the strongest expression of that particular expression. Each image pair from the constructed pairs voted for one of the seven expressions and the expression class with the highest number of votes was considered to be the expression of the sequence. 10-fold cross-validation was used in the evaluation process, which leads to an accuracy of 95.66%. Surprisingly, the time it takes the method of Elaiwat et al. to train on a single epoch was significantly lower compared to the current-state-of-the-art approach as the training phase had been done off-line.

Similarly, Kim et al. [16] also used three frames from each sequence to analyze emotion labels from the CK+ database. They proposed an approach based on a hierarchical deep neural network. The first network performs feature extraction using a convolution neural network (CNN) whereas the second method extracts changes to the features and learns to identify all the six basic emotions. Adaptive weighing function is used to combine the result of the two features for the final result. Like [15], Kim et al. also used 10-fold cross-validation to evaluate their result and have achieved an accuracy of 96.46%. Unlike [17], the proposed method used dynamic features as opposed to static features and at the same time utilized a dual network instead of a single network.

Thus, all of the work by [15–17] used fewer frames than available of the CK+ database where the emotion is expressed at peak. However, a model trained with fewer frames where emotion is only expressed at peak might not perform well in recognizing frames where the emotion is not expressed at peak. Besides, peak expressions are rare in everyday life [18]. Therefore, we aim to address the issues of using fewer peak frames by using more frames of the CK+ database and compare the robustness of the two different approaches.

3   Methods

3.1   Dataset

In this research, we used the CK+ dataset [9] which is an extended version of the Cohn-Kanade database that was released in 2000 [19]. The CK+ was developed due to certain limitations on the CK dataset, including but not limited to non-validated emotion labels, lack of common performance metrics to evaluate new algorithms, and also the non-existence of a standard protocol for a common database. In the CK+ database, a sample of 201 adults between the ages of 18–

Angry   Contempt   Disgust   Fear   Happy   Neutral   Sad   Surprise

Fig. 1. Sample expressions from the CK+ database. Note that majority of the images from the videos are black and white

50 years that comprises of 69% female, 13% Afro-American, 81% Euro-American, and 6% from other groups were recorded using AG-7500 cameras. A series of 23 facial displays were instructed to the participants by the experimenter. Certain participants smile to the experimenter between the task, which are also included in the dataset and as a result, the CK+ does not only contain posed but at the same time, few non-posed expressions. Figure 1 shows examples of expressions from the CK+ database. As not all images in the CK+ database are labeled, only the labeled images are used. The image sequence in the CK+ varies from 10 to 60 frames starting from neutral to peak expressions and a total of 593 labeled sequences from 123 subjects.

3.2   Hardware Specification

A Dell computer with Intel(R) Core(TM) i7-8700 CPU @ 3.2 GHz processor, utilizing Windows 10 Education and 15.8 GB usable RAM is used in this research.

3.3   Proposed Methodology

There are several important factors such as resolution, illumination effects, and intensity of expressions to consider when classifying human facial expressions [20,21]. They are considered to be important because they are the primary information stored within pixels.

Visual inspection of randomly selected frame sequences lead to the decision to use the second-half of the frames for training. Thus, in this research, the second-half of frames from each sequence of the CK+ database are assigned the emotion label of the sequence. In cases where the number of frames is odd, the value of the least succeeding integer is taken. For instance, we assign disgust to frames starting from 6 to 11 in a given sequence where the number of frames is 11 and the decoded emotion is disgust as illustrated in Fig. 2.

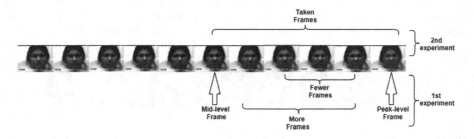

Fig. 2. Sample usage of the CK+ database. Note that the last-half of the frames of the CK+ are referred to as the taken frames, the first taken frame is referred to as the mid-level frame, the last taken frame is referred to as the peak-level frame, the last three frames preceding the peak-level frame are considered to be the fewer frames and finally, all frames between the mid-level frames and peak-level frames are referred as more frames of the CK+ database.

Figure 2 shows example changes of image frames of the CK+ database from neutral to peak expressions and also shows how the CK+ database is used in this research. Henceforth, we will refer to the first taken frame of each sequence where the emotion is not expressed at peak as the mid-level frame and the last taken frame of each sequence where the emotion is expressed at peak as the peak-level frame. As we aim to use more frames, all frames between the mid-level and peak-level frames are used for training a particular model.

To compare the advantage of using more frames over fewer frames, the last three frames before the peak-level frames of each sequence where the emotion is at peak are also used for training a separate model. After that, both models trained using more frames and fewer peak frames are tested with both mid-level and peak-level frames in the first experiment.

Figure 3 represents the flow chart of the novel method. Blocks represented in the flow chart are explained in this section.

- Pre-processing: Emotion labels were converted to integers and image pixel values to an array. Normalization has also been performed on the pixels of the raw images as a pre-processing technique to normalize all pixel values between the range of [0, 1] to enable fast computation.
- Feature-extraction: Many machine learning algorithms can accomplish the task of image classification [22–24], however, all algorithms require proper features for conducting the classification. In this research, image color information is split into three different (RGB) channels as shown in Fig. 3. Furthermore, since most of the video frames of the CK+ database are in grayscale, we know that all the RGB channels should have the same value. Therefore, to avoid having redundant features, two feature vectors of only the red (R) channel are extracted from each image. The first feature is the mean whereas the second feature is the standard deviation of the R channel. These features are later used for the classification of the images.
- Classification: After feature extraction has been performed on the data, both features extracted from mid-level and peak-level frames are classified by models train on more and fewer peak frames. Thereafter, in order to reflect generalized performance on the data, stratified 10-fold cross-validation is used to test the performance of the model before applying the voting technique.

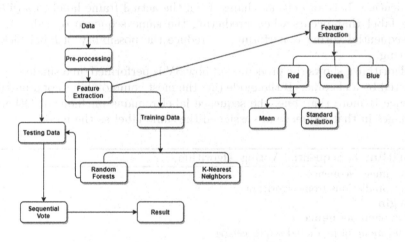

Fig. 3. Flow of the novel method.

3.4 Machine Learning Classifiers

Random Forest (RF) and K-Nearest Neighbour (KNN) are used in this research. RF is chosen to be used in this research because it is an ensemble technique that is averaged over many trees. Therefore, it has a higher chance of achieving a higher classification accuracy compared to other machine learning classification techniques such as decision tree (DT) that explore fewer decision boundaries

[25]. KNN is chosen to be used due to its simplicity as it requires no explicit training phase. Another reason why the algorithms are chosen to be used is based on their promising performance obtained in the research of [26] and [27] respectively.

Random forest is an extension of the decision tree (DT) algorithm [28], which uses control conditional statements to predict an outcome. It constructs multiple DTs during training and merges them into a single forest [29,30]. The goal is to rely on a collection of decisions from the multiple constructed DTs to improve accuracy [31]. The algorithm does not allow overfitting trees in the model, so maintains the prediction accuracy over a large proportion of data.

The K-nearest neighbor is often referred to as a lazy learner because it does not learn from the training data. In KNN, objects are classified based on the plurality vote of their neighbors [32].

3.5   Sequential Vote

The sequential voting (SV) process is a conditional statement, which is performed based on what the majority of images in a given sequence are predicted to be.

Since the CK+ database is a database of mainly posed video converted to image frames, it is assumed that all images in a single video sequence belong to a single class. Label flickering is a common problem that occurs in video classification. It is an unusual change from the actual frame label to a different frame label that occurs when predicting the same sequence of video frames. The sequential voting is performed to reduce the possibility of label flickering occurring.

Algorithm 1 shows the procedure of how SV is performed on a single sequence predicted by a classifier. If the mode (i.e. the most common label) of a particular sequence is more than one, the sequence label remains unchanged. Otherwise, all images in that sequence are assigned the same label as the mode.

Algorithm 1. Sequential Voting Algorithm.

1: Get image sequence
2: Get predictions from algorithm
   Begin
   For each sequence i
3: Find *mode* of predicted sequence$_{label}$
4: **if** len(sequence$_{mode}$) > 1 **then**
5:     continue
6: **end if**
7: **if** len(sequence$_{mode}$) $= 1$ **then**
8:     sequence$_{label}$ = *mode*
9: **end if**
        return sequence$_{label}$

Most research on the CK+ database is performed either on the six basic emotions or six basic emotions plus contempt expression provided by the CK+

database. For the sake of comparison, results are presented using both six basic expressions and also 6 basic plus contempt expression provided by the CK+ database.

4 Results

Table 1 shows the percentage accuracy obtained after testing a model trained with fewer frames with mid-level and peak-level frames of the CK+ database. The overall accuracy of 72.5% has been achieved when tested with mid-level frames whereas an accuracy of 93.3% has been achieved when tested with peak-level frames.

While the model trained with fewer frames is not able to achieve an accuracy of more than 83% on any of the classes when tested with mid-level frames, an accuracy of not less than 89% has been achieved on all classes when the same model is tested with peak-level images.

A k value of one is used for the KNN algorithm and the algorithm is deterministic on the CK+ database. Unlike KNN, as the RF algorithm is not deterministic, results achieved by the RF algorithm are presented with upper and lower bound with a 95% confidence interval.

* refers to mean accuracy across all categories in Table 1 and 2. In the expression section of Table 5, An represents anger, Di represents disgust, Fe represents fear, Ha represents happy, Sa represents sadness and Su represents surprise expression.

Table 1. Percentage of correctly classified classes by model trained on fewer frames and test with mid and peak level images using KNN

Testpoint	Anger	Disgust	Fear	Happy	Sad	Surprise
Mid-level	79	75	68	83	71	59
Peak-level	100	90	92	96	89	93

*$Mid\text{-}level = 72.5\%$, Peak-level $= 93.3\%$

Table 2 shows the percentage accuracy obtained after testing a model trained with more frames with mid-level and peak-level frames of the CK+ database respectively. An accuracy of 85.8% has been achieved when tested with mid-level frames whereas the achieved accuracy is up to 92% when the model is tested with peak-level images.

Although the accuracy achieved by the model trained with more frames is lower when tested with mid-level frames compared with the achieved accuracy on peak-level frames, the achieved accuracy is up to 13.3% higher than the accuracy achieved when the same frames are predicted by the model trained with fewer peak frames of the CK+ database.

In addition, the accuracy achieved in all the classes in Table 2 when predictions are made on the mid-level frames by a model trained with more frames is

Table 2. Percentage of correctly classified classes by model trained on more frames and test with mid and peak level images using KNN

Testpoint	Anger	Disgust	Fear	Happy	Sad	Surprise
Mid-level	93	86	88	93	82	73
Peak-level	98	86	84	94	100	90

*Mid-level = 85.8%, Peak-level = 92%

higher than the accuracy achieved in all the classes in Table 1 when the same mid-level frames are predicted by a model trained with fewer peak frames.

Table 3. Accuracy obtained from predictions on mid-level and peak-level images made by model trained on more and fewer frames

Algorithm	Classes	No. of training images	Testpoint	Accuracy
RF	6 basic	927	Mid-level	68.9 ± 0.3
			Peak-level	90.2 ± 0.3
KNN			Mid-level	72.5
			Peak-level	93.3
RF	6 basic + contempt	981	Mid-level	70.5 ± 0.3
			Peak-level	90.6 ± 0.2
KNN			Mid-level	73.4
			Peak-level	93.8
RF	6 basic	2132	Mid-level	79.9 ± 0.2
			Peak-level	90.0 ± 0.3
KNN			Mid-level	85.5
			Peak-level	92.0
RF	6 basic + contempt	2205	Mid-level	81.1 ± 0.2
			Peak-level	89.5 ± 0.2
KNN			Mid-level	85.9
			Peak-level	92.4

Table 3 shows the accuracy achieved by KNN and RF when the prediction is made on mid-level and peak-level images by both model trained with more and fewer frames. While the models trained on fewer frames are trained with less than a thousand images, more than two thousand images are used to train the model with more frames. Based on these results, the accuracy achieved by KNN is higher than the accuracy achieved by the RF algorithm in all of the cases.

From the results obtained, it can be seen that the use of fewer frames achieved only a slightly better accuracy when predictions are made on peak-level frames. However, a linear regression analysis predicting accuracy by *Testpoint* and *Framesize* resulted in a significant difference.

Table 4 presents the regression results of the statistical test performed. The test is performed after getting the result of 30 runs of each case when the mid-level and peak-level frames are classified by two different classifiers trained on fewer and more frames of the CK+ database. The test is performed across 120 samples using the *Least Squares* method. The *Accuracy* is used as the dependent variable across *Framesize* and *Testpoint* as independent variables.

Framesize species whether the model is trained with more or fewer frames and *Testpoint* indicates whether the classier is used to classify mid-level or peak-level frames.

Table 4. Regression results

	Coefficient	P	[0.025	0.975]
Intercept	0.6889	<.001	0.687	0.691
C(Testpoint)	0.2127	<.001	0.209	0.216
C(Framesize)	0.1079	<.001	0.105	0.111
C(Testpoint):C(Framesize)	−0.1207	<.001	−0.125	−0.116
Adjusted R^2	0.994			
F-statistics	6769			
AIC	−862.0	**BIC**	−850.8	

As can be seen from Table 4, a p-value of $p < .001$ of the t-statistic of the Ordinary Least Squares (OLS) method shows that the result obtained by the model trained with more frames was significantly better than the result obtained by the model trained with fewer frames specifically in the case of predicting the mid frames. Also, the overall *effect size* of 0.553 has been found for the factor Framesize.

These results suggest that the use of more frames provides a better performance compared with the use of fewer peak frames. Consequently, in order to apply sequential voting, we assigned all second-half (taken) frames of each sequence the emotion label of the sequence (see Fig. 2) in the second experiment.

Table 5 shows the accuracy achieved by RF and KNN from six basic emotions both before and after the sequential voting is performed. It can be seen clearly from the table that the result obtained after the sequential voting process increases the overall accuracy by 6% and 5.5% in RF and KNN algorithms respectively.

The accuracy in each class has also increased after the sequential voting. The sad class has seen the most increase with up to 8%, from 92% to 100%. This happens because most of the image frames in the sad class sequence are predicted correctly by the classifier and as a result, the sad class sequence always appears to have a single mode which the voting algorithm uses to correctly change the label of the wrongly predicted frames.

Table 5. Prediction accuracy on six basic emotions of the CK+ database before and after sequential voting (+SV)

Expressions	Algorithms			
	RF	RF + SV	KNN	KNN + SV
An	94	99	94	98
Di	88	95	90	93
Fe	90	96	92	95
Ha	95	98	95	98
Sa	92	100	93	99
Su	84	91	85	93
Standard dev.	0.18	0.21	0.0	0.0
Average acc.	90.5 ± 0.1	96.5 ± 0.1	91.5	96.0

Table 6 shows results achieved on CK+ database both before and after SV using KNN and RF algorithms. Surprisingly, before the SV is performed, the accuracy achieved by KNN is higher than the accuracy achieved by RF on both six basic and six basic plus contempt expression. However, after the SV, the result achieved by RF surpasses the result achieved by KNN on six basic emotions and equivalent to the result achieved by KNN on six basic plus contempt emotional expression.

Table 6. Sequential voting result from the CK+ database

Method	Classes	Accuracy
RF	6 basic	90.5 ± 0.1
RF + SV	6 basic	96.5 ± 0.1
KNN	6 basic	91.5
KNN + SV	6 basic	96.0
RF	6 basic + contempt	90.6 ± 0.1
RF + SV	6 basic + contempt	96.2 ± 0.1
KNN	6 basic + contempt	91.5
KNN + SV	6 basic + contempt	96.2

5 Discussion

This study set out with the aim of assessing the importance of using more frames of an emotion video database to categorize emotion from different image frames.

In reviewing the literature, many studies [15–17] are found to be using fewer frames of the CK+ database where the expression is at peak to predict emotion labels. Several other studies [13,14] recently conducted on the CK+ database using the state-of-the-art deep learning algorithms were also found to be using fewer (typically final frames) than the available frames of the CK+ database. While a high accuracy result is obtained on peak-level frames when fewer peak frames are used to train the model, the results were not very encouraging when the same model is used to predict emotion labels from mid-level frames. To the best of our knowledge, this is the first study to use more varied frames of sequential video images to predict emotion.

The model trained with more frames achieved an accuracy of up to 1.3% and 1.4% lower than the accuracy achieved by the model trained with fewer peak frames when the prediction is made for peak-level frames on the 6 basic and 6 basic plus contempt expression. However, the overall performance of the model is significantly better than that of the model trained with fewer frames.

RF algorithm has seen the strongest increase in accuracy when SV is applied in comparison to the result the algorithm achieved as SV increase the result with up to 6% and 5.6% compared to the increase of 4.5% and 4.7% on 6 basic and 6 basic plus contempt expression when the same SV technique is applied to KNN algorithm.

Overall, these results indicate that the application of SV to reduce label flickering increases the categorization accuracy achieved by both RF and KNN algorithms.

Several reports [33,34] have shown that the state-of-the-art deep learning algorithms take a very long time, ranging from hours to weeks to train on facial expression datasets even using Graphical Processing Units (GPU). We also know from our previous work [26] that deep learning methods such as the residual neural network (ResNet) takes over an hour to train on the CK+ database. Thus, compared to these state-of-the-art approaches, the evidence presented thus far supports the idea that our approach achieved a considerably lower execution time. It takes between 5.0 ± 0.04 to 5.4 ± 0.01 seconds to compute the result of the CK+ database when tested on both more frames and the sequential voting technique respectively.

Based on the results obtained, we can say that here, we have set a substandard for other researchers on how to use video-frames with facial expressions to perform emotion classification research based on emotion labels.

6   Conclusion and Future Work

This paper proposed an approach to use more, over fewer, peak frames where emotion is expressed at peak to analyze emotion classes in the CK+ database. We have compared our approach to an approach using fewer peak frames and have achieved a better accuracy result when the prediction is made on mid-level images. We have also found that the use of more frames to train the model gives a significantly better performance compared to when fewer peak frames are used. Furthermore, we have shown that performing sequential voting on the results obtained by RF and KNN classifiers increases the accuracy further.

This study is carried out on posed emotion video frames images of the CK+ database and therefore despite these promising results, questions remain on whether the same technique could be used on non-posed emotion video-frames as well as on other datasets. Future work should, therefore, apply this new approach to non-posed and other emotion video datasets.

References

1. Tian, Y.-L., Kanade, T., Cohn, J.F.: Facial expression analysis. In: Handbook of Face Recognition, pp. 247–275. Springer, New York (2005). https://doi.org/10.1007/0-387-27257-7_12
2. Martinez, B., Valstar, M.F.: Advances, challenges, and opportunities in automatic facial expression recognition. In: Kawulok, M., Celebi, M.E., Smolka, B. (eds.) Advances in Face Detection and Facial Image Analysis, pp. 63–100. Springer, Cham (2016). https://doi.org/10.1007/978-3-319-25958-1_4
3. Matsumoto, D., Hwang, H.S.: Evidence for training the ability to read microexpressions of emotion. Motiv. Emot. **35**(2), 181–191 (2011)
4. Krumhuber, E.G., Küster, D., Namba, S., Shah, D., Calvo, M.G.: Emotion recognition from posed and spontaneous dynamic expressions: human observers versus machine analysis. Emotion (2019)
5. Barrett, L.F., Adolphs, R., Marsella, S., Martinez, A.M., Pollak, S.D.: Emotional expressions reconsidered: challenges to inferring emotion from human facial movements. Psychol. Sci. Public Interest **20**(1), 1–68 (2019)
6. Chakravarti, A.: Perspectives on human variation through the lens of diversity and race. Cold Spring Harb. Perspect. Biol. **7**(9), a023358 (2015)
7. Islam, B., Mahmud, F., Hossain, A.: Facial region segmentation based emotion recognition using extreme learning machine. In: 2018 International Conference on Advancement in Electrical and Electronic Engineering, ICAEEE, pp. 1–4 (2019)
8. Mahmud, F., Islam, B., Hossain, A., Goala, P.B.: Facial region segmentation based emotion recognition using K-nearest neighbors. In: 2018 International Conference on Innovation in Engineering and Technology, ICIET 2018, pp. 1–5 (2019)
9. Lucey, P., Cohn, J.F., Kanade, T., Saragih, J., Ambadar, Z., Matthews, I.: The extended Cohn-Kanade dataset (CK+): a complete dataset for action unit and emotion-specified expression. In: 2010 IEEE Computer Society Conference on Computer Vision and Pattern Recognition - Workshops, CVPRW 2010, pp. 94–101 (2010)
10. Mavadati, S.M., Mahoor, M.H., Bartlett, K., Trinh, P., Cohn, J.F.: DISFA: a spontaneous facial action intensity database. IEEE Trans. Affect. Comput. **4**(2), 151–160 (2013)
11. Longmore, C.A., Tree, J.J.: Motion as a cue to face recognition: evidence from congenital prosopagnosia. Neuropsychologia **51**, 864–875 (2013)
12. Ekman, P., Friesen, W.V.: Constants across cultures in the face and emotion. J. Pers. Soc. Psychol. **17**(2), 124 (1971)
13. Mollahosseini, A., Chan, D., Mahoor, M.H.: Going deeper in facial expression recognition using deep neural networks. In: 2016 IEEE Winter Conference on Applications of Computer Vision (WACV), Lake Placid, NY, pp. 1–10 (2016)

14. Minaee, S., Abdolrashidi, A.: Deep-emotion: facial expression recognition using attentional convolutional network. arXiv preprint arXiv:1902.01019 (2019)
15. Elaiwat, S., Bennamoun, M., Boussaid, F.: A spatio-temporal RBM-based model for facial expression recognition. Pattern Recognit. **49**, 152–161 (2016)
16. Kim, J.H., Kim, B.G., Roy, P.P., Jeong, D.M.: Efficient facial expression recognition algorithm based on hierarchical deep neural network structure. IEEE Access **7**, 41273–41285 (2019)
17. Happy, S.L., Routray, A.: Automatic facial expression recognition using features of salient facial patches. IEEE Trans. Affect. Comput. **6**(1), 1–12 (2015)
18. Xiao, R., Li, X., Li, L., Wang, Y.: Can we distinguish emotions from faces? Investigation of implicit and explicit processes of peak facial expressions. Front. Psychol. **7**, 1330 (2016). (1664–1078)
19. Kanade, T., Cohn, J.F., Tian, Y.: Comprehensive database for facial expression analysis. In: Proceedings - 4th IEEE International Conference on Automatic Face and Gesture Recognition, FG 2000, March, pp. 46–53 (2000)
20. Ting, G., Moydin, K., Hamdulla, A.: An overview of feature extraction methods for handwritten image retrieval. In: Proceedings - 2018 3rd International Conference on Smart City and Systems Engineering, ICSCSE 2018, pp. 840–843 (2018)
21. Pisal, A., Sor, R., Kinage, K.S.: Facial feature extraction using hierarchical max(HMAX) method. In: 2017 International Conference on Computing, Communication, Control and Automation, ICCUBEA 2017, (figure 2), pp. 1–5 (2018)
22. Loussaief, S., Abdelkrim, A.: Machine learning framework for image classification. In: 2016 7th International Conference on Sciences of Electronics, Technologies of Information and Telecommunications, SETIT 2016, pp. 58–61 (2017)
23. Li, Y., Wang, S., Zhao, Y., Ji, Q.: Simultaneous facial feature tracking and facial expression recognition. IEEE Trans. Image Process. **22**(7), 2559–2573 (2013)
24. Cruz, A.C., Bhanu, B., Thakoor, N.S.: One shot emotion scores for facial emotion recognition. In: 2014 IEEE International Conference on Image Processing, ICIP 2014, (C), pp. 1376–1380 (2014)
25. Safavian, S.R., Landgrebe, D.: A survey of decision tree classifier methodology. IEEE Trans. Syst. Man Cybernet. **21**(3), 660–674 (1991)
26. Shehu, H.A., Browne, W., Eisenbarth, H.: An adversarial attacks resistance-based approach to emotion recognition from images using facial landmarks. In: 2020 IEEE International Conference on Robot and Human Interactive Communication (2020)
27. Sohail, A.S.M., Bhattacharya, P.: Classification of facial expressions using K-nearest neighbor classifier. In: Gagalowicz, A., Philips, W. (eds.) MIRAGE 2007. LNCS, vol. 4418, pp. 555–566. Springer, Heidelberg (2007). https://doi.org/10.1007/978-3-540-71457-6_51
28. Kamiński, B., Jakubczyk, M., Szufel, P.: A framework for sensitivity analysis of decision trees. Central Eur. J. Oper. Res. **26**(1), 135–159 (2017). https://doi.org/10.1007/s10100-017-0479-6
29. Shehu, H.A., Tokat, S., Sharif, M.H., Uyaver, S.: Sentiment analysis of Turkish Twitter data. In: AIP Conference Proceedings, vol. 2183, no. 1, p. 080004. AIP Publishing LLC, December 2019
30. Shehu, H.A., Tokat, S.: A hybrid approach for the sentiment analysis of Turkish Twitter data. In: Hemanth, D.J., Kose, U. (eds.) ICAIAME 2019. LNDECT, vol. 43, pp. 182–190. Springer, Cham (2020). https://doi.org/10.1007/978-3-030-36178-5_15
31. Breiman, L.: Random forests. Mach. Learn. **45**(1), 5–32 (2001)
32. Altman, N.S.: An introduction to kernel and nearest-neighbor non-parametric regression. Am. Stat. **46**(3), 175–185 (1992)

33. Fan, Y., Lam, J.C.K., Li, V.O.K.: Multi-region Ensemble Convolutional Neural Network for Facial Expression Recognition. In: Kůrková, V., Manolopoulos, Y., Hammer, B., Iliadis, L., Maglogiannis, I. (eds.) ICANN 2018. LNCS, vol. 11139, pp. 84–94. Springer, Cham (2018). https://doi.org/10.1007/978-3-030-01418-6_9
34. Chengeta, K., Viriri, S.: A review of local, holistic and deep learning approaches in facial expressions Recognition. In 2019 Conference on Information Communications Technology and Society (ICTAS), pp. 1–7. IEEE, March 2019

Systematic Optimization of Image Processing Pipelines Using GPUs

Peter Roch[✉], Bijan Shahbaz Nejad, Marcus Handte, and Pedro José Marrón

University of Duisburg-Essen, Essen, Germany
peter.roch@uni-due.de

Abstract. Real-time computer vision systems require fast and efficient image processing pipelines. Experiments have shown that GPUs are highly suited for image processing operations, since many tasks can be processed in parallel. However, calling GPU-accelerated functions requires uploading the input parameters to the GPU's memory, calling the function itself, and downloading the result afterwards. In addition, since not all functions benefit from an increase in parallelism, many pipelines cannot be implemented exclusively using GPU functions. As a result, the optimization of pipelines requires a careful analysis of the achievable function speedup and the cost of copying data. In this paper, we first define a mathematical model to estimate the performance of an image processing pipeline. Thereafter, we present a number of micro-benchmarks gathered using OpenCV which we use to validate the model and which quantify the cost and benefits for different classes of functions. Our experiments show that comparing the function speedup without considering the time for copying can overestimate the achievable performance gain of GPU acceleration by a factor of two. Finally, we present a tool that analyzes the possible combinations of CPU and GPU function implementations for a given pipeline and computes the most efficient composition. By using the tool on their target hardware, developers can easily apply our model to optimize their application performance systematically.

Keywords: Image processing · Performance evaluation · OpenCV · Computer vision · CUDA · Parallel processing

1 Introduction

Computer vision systems have been applied successfully in a broad spectrum of application areas, for example traffic surveillance [2,3], automatic attendance management [19] or tracking of human interactions [11]. These and other similar systems often have real-time constraints and require the image processing to run at high frame rates. As a result, their implementation must be fast and efficient.

In most applications, the image processing logic is structured as a pipeline of image processing functions that are executed sequentially. First, the image needs to be captured from a camera. Thereafter, the image runs through a sequence

© Springer Nature Switzerland AG 2020
G. Bebis et al. (Eds.): ISVC 2020, LNCS 12510, pp. 633–646, 2020.
https://doi.org/10.1007/978-3-030-64559-5_50

of pre-processing functions, which often include filtering noise, resizing or gray-scaling. The main task is then to extract the desired information by means of edge detection, feature-matching or stereo-correspondence matching, to name a few. Some applications may also require additional post-processing steps, e.g., to filter results or to overlay the extracted information onto the original image.

Since GPUs are capable of executing highly parallel code and since many image processing functions can significantly benefit from a parallel implementation, they can be a powerful tool to reduce the processing time. As a result, widely used libraries such as OpenCV [12] often provide alternative function implementations that can leverage a dedicated graphics card.

However, calling such a GPU-accelerated function requires uploading the input parameters to the GPU's memory, calling the function itself, and downloading the result afterwards. In addition, since not all functions benefit from an increase in parallelism, many pipelines cannot be implemented exclusively using GPU functions. As a result, the optimization of pipelines can become a non-trivial task which requires careful and thorough analysis of the achievable function speedup and the cost of copying data.

To support the optimization of image processing pipelines using GPUs in a systematic manner, this paper makes the following contributions:

1. First, the paper defines a mathematical model to compute the execution time of arbitrary pipelines that combine CPU and GPU functions.
2. Second, the paper studies the costs of GPU-acceleration and validates the analytical model using a number of benchmarks gathered with OpenCV.
3. Third, the paper presents a framework, which computes the optimal combination of CPU and GPU functions for a given image processing pipeline.

2   Analytical Model

NVIDIA CUDA [10] is a general purpose parallel computing platform and programming model to make use of NVIDIA GPUs. A GPU is organized into multi-dimensional *Grids* of *Thread-Blocks*, each containing multiple *Threads*. Every *Thread* has access to its own local memory as well as to the shared memory of its *Thread-Block*. Every *Grid*, and therefore every *Thread-Block* inside also has access to the GPU's global memory, often referred to as device-memory. This architecture is illustrated in Fig. 1. A *Kernel* is defined as a function, which is executed on one or more *Thread-Blocks*, hence each *Thread* inside the same *Thread-Block* will execute the same *Kernel*.

Since the GPU uses its own memory, data exchanged between the GPU and the host system needs to be copied between the device memory and the host memory. The operation of copying data to the device memory is commonly referred to as *uploading*, whereas copying data from device memory to host memory is called *downloading*. Since CUDA 6, it is possible to allocate data inside *unified memory*, where the CUDA software or hardware will manage uploading and downloading. Usually, host memory is pageable, meaning that the OS can

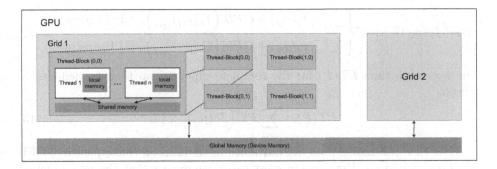

Fig. 1. GPU architecture

allocate memory not only inside the physical RAM, but also inside a swap-file located on the hard-drive. In contrast, page-locked memory cannot be moved to a swap-file and has to be kept always inside the physical RAM.

The GPU cannot access pageable host memory directly. If data has to be copied to the device memory, the CUDA driver will allocate a temporary buffer inside page-locked memory. This additional copy operation can be avoided if host memory is allocated as page-locked memory beforehand. However, this approach has to be used carefully, because physical RAM is limited. If an application allocates too much page-locked memory, the operating system is forced to use a swap-file for other processes, which can slow down the whole system.

Since most non-trivial applications will require the sequential execution of multiple image processing functions, we can mathematically describe the execution time of such a pipeline by summing up the processing times of all functions and adding time required for uploading and downloading the function parameters for each transition between CPU and GPU as follows:

Let P be an arbitrary pipeline containing N tasks, where $T_i(p_{i1}, p_{i2}, \ldots, p_{in})$, noted as $T_i\left(p_{ij}\right)_{j=1}^{n}$, is the i-th task in P accepting n parameters, with p_{ij} being the j-th parameter of Task i. Further, we define $u(p_{ij})$ and $d(p_{ij})$ as the time needed to upload or download the parameter p_{ij} and $t_{\uparrow}(p_{ij})$ and $t_{\downarrow}(p_{ij})$ as the time needed to make parameter p_{ij} available for GPU or CPU execution:

$$
\begin{aligned}
t_{\uparrow}(p_{ij}) &= \begin{cases} 0, & \text{if parameter } p_{ij} \text{ is stored in device memory} \\ u(p_{ij}), & \text{otherwise} \end{cases} \\
t_{\downarrow}(p_{ij}) &= \begin{cases} 0, & \text{if parameter } p_{ij} \text{ is stored in host memory} \\ d(p_{ij}), & \text{otherwise} \end{cases}
\end{aligned}
\tag{1}
$$

Moreover, we define $CPU\left(T_i\left(p_{ij}\right)_{j=1}^{n}\right)$ and $GPU\left(T_i\left(p_{ij}\right)_{j=1}^{n}\right)$ as the time needed to execute the OpenCV CPU or GPU function corresponding to task $T_i\left(p_{ij}\right)_{j=1}^{n}$. The processing time $PT\left(T_i\left(p_{ij}\right)_{j=1}^{n}\right)$ of task $T_i\left(p_{ij}\right)_{j=1}^{n}$ is calculated as shown in Eq. 2:

$$PT\left(T_i\left(p_{ij}\right)_{j=1}^n\right) = \begin{cases} \sum_{j=1}^n t_\downarrow(p_{ij}) + CPU\left(T_i\left(p_{ij}\right)_{j=1}^n\right), \text{ CPU execution} \\ \sum_{j=1}^n t_\uparrow(p_{ij}) + GPU\left(T_i\left(p_{ij}\right)_{j=1}^n\right), \text{ GPU execution} \end{cases} \quad (2)$$

The execution time $ET(P)$ for the complete pipeline can then be deduced as follows:

$$ET(P) = \sum_{i=1}^N PT\left(T_i\left(p_{ij}\right)_{j=1}^n\right) \quad (3)$$

Note that this model does not introduce restrictions on the sequence of CPU and GPU functions. However, in most cases, we expect that the first function (image acquisition) and the last function (usage of the results) cannot run on the GPU. Thus, even "fully" GPU-accelerated pipelines will usually require at least one parameter upload for the image and one download to use the final result.

3   Benchmarks and Validation

To estimate the performance of an image processing pipeline using the model defined in Sect. 2, it is necessary to determine the time required for executing each function on the CPU and GPU. In addition, it is also necessary to determine the time required for uploading and downloading of their respective parameters given a particular pipeline composition. Thus, to validate the model, we first measure the timings for representative functions using micro-benchmarks and then compare the model with actual measurements of two different pipelines.

3.1   Test Setup

For both, the micro-benchmarks and the validating measurements, we are using the widely used image processing library OpenCV. While OpenCV itself is written in C and C++, it offers bindings for Java, Python and MATLAB. Since Java is less error-prone and has a higher productivity compared to C++ [15], we are using OpenCV's Java interface for all measurements. The overhead of calling native methods from Java is provenly in the order of nanoseconds [8], so the experimental results detailed in this paper should be comparable to other interfaces as well. Since the official Java interface does not support GPU functions, we used the JavaCV [17] wrapper to invoke them.

As input data for the measurements, we use a skyscraper image of [5] and the left image of a stereo image pair of [18], showing a motorcycle, and resize them to different resolutions. To minimize timer effects during bench-marking, each measurement represents the total time taken by 100 executions of the respective function. Since we cannot control the OS scheduling, we repeat each measurement 100 times and we report the average processing time $\overline{time}$ in milliseconds as well as the standard deviation σ. To study the effects of different hardware, we repeat all measurements on three different computer system configurations:

– *L:* A high-end laptop with an Intel® Core™ i7-9750H CPU, an NVIDIA GeForce RTX 2070 with Max-Q Design GPU and 16 GB RAM

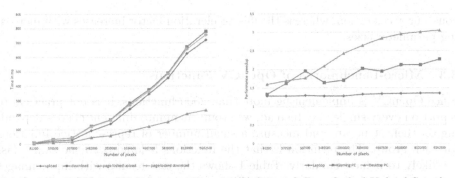

(a) Desktop PC Upload & Download Times   (b) Paged & Page-locked Upload Speedup

Fig. 2. Comparison of upload and download functions on different hardware

- *GPC:* A high-end gaming PC with an Intel® Core™ i7-7800X CPU, an NVIDIA GeForce GTX 1080 Ti GPU and 32 GB RAM
- *DPC:* A desktop PC with an Intel® Core™ i5-7500 CPU, an NVIDIA GeForce GTX 1050 Ti GPU and 8 GB RAM.

3.2   Micro-benchmarks for Uploading and Downloading

In OpenCV, larger parameter values, including images, are represented as instances of the class cv::Mat (i.e., matrix). The complementary GPU representation of this class is cv::cuda::GpuMat. OpenCV's implementation of GpuMat does not use the *unified memory* feature introduced in CUDA 6, so the programmer has to take care of uploading and downloading the data manually. This is done by the functions GpuMat.upload(Mat) and GpuMat.download(Mat), respectively.

Figure 2 shows the results of micro-benchmarks for uploading and downloading Mat parameters representing images of varying size using paged and page-locked memory. Figure 2a shows the timings of executing 100 operations per measurement on the desktop PC. The x-axis shows the number of pixels, whereas the y-axis denotes the processing time in ms. The average standard deviation σ across these measurements is 5% of the average processing time. The maximum is 20%.

As depicted in Fig. 2a, page-locked memory solely affects the upload operation and the remaining operations exhibit a similar overhead. Since this result is identical for the laptop and the gaming PC, we omit their figures for the sake of brevity. Instead, we focus on the difference between paged and page-locked uploads for all hardware configurations in Fig. 2b.

Interestingly, the laptop's i7-9750H processor shows only little benefit of page-locked memory, while the i5-7500 processor has the highest benefit of page-locked memory. This is probably due to internal memory handling of the different processor types. Furthermore, both i7 processors seem to have an approximately constant acceleration, whereas the i5's acceleration factor increases with increasing parameter sizes.

3.3 Micro-benchmarks of OpenCV Functions

Since OpenCV is implementing more than 2500 functions, it is not practical to report on every single one. Instead, we group them into different classes depending on their structure and measure a small number of representative functions for each group. The intuition is that the functions belonging to the same class are likely to behave similarly. Table 1 shows the test results with input images of different resolutions: 350 × 232, 1482 × 1000 and 3705 × 2500. The faster implementation of each CPU-GPU pair is highlighted.

Table 1. Micro-benchmarks for OpenCV Functions (100 Operations in ms)

Task	PC	350 × 232				1482 × 1000				3705 × 2500			
		CPU		GPU		CPU		GPU		CPU		GPU	
		time	σ	time	σ	time	σ	time	σ	time	σ	time	σ
T	L	< **0.1**	<0.1	4.9	2.2	**2.1**	0.4	5.3	0.9	54.8	3.1	**9.7**	1.3
	GPC	< **0.1**	<0.1	3.7	0.5	**3.0**	0.6	4.5	0.5	40.7	1.2	**9.1**	0.4
	DPC	< **0.1**	<0.1	4.2	0.5	**2.1**	0.3	8.0	1.2	153.7	2.5	**27.8**	1.7
G	L	**3.0**	<0.1	4.1	0.4	12.9	1.1	**6.9**	1.1	135.8	2.9	**24.0**	1.5
	GPC	**3.0**	<0.1	3.3	0.4	11.8	1.9	**7.9**	0.4	98.3	2.1	**17.2**	0.5
	DPC	**3.0**	<0.1	4.8	1.2	16.7	0.9	**14.4**	1.4	286.4	1.5	**66.2**	1.0
MF	L	259.6	4.8	**155.4**	11.0	4342.6	15.8	**2086.7**	3.0	26211.4	26.0	**12170.8**	13.7
	GPC	255.4	2.5	**210.8**	4.7	4349.1	18.8	**2913.5**	13.6	26281.9	63.7	**17366.4**	2.7
	DPC	**274.4**	1.0	390.2	4.0	4663.4	21.1	**4075.8**	9.1	28074.4	42.6	**22189.4**	2.6
GF	L	9.5	1.2	**8.5**	0.5	59.2	2.5	**21.2**	1.0	325.9	10.3	**98.8**	0.8
	GPC	**8.9**	2.4	11.9	0.8	**67.8**	3.2	101.2	1.5	**294.3**	8.7	524.5	1.0
	DPC	**11.7**	0.8	13.5	2.0	**87.7**	1.3	106.3	2.0	**474.9**	3.8	577.8	0.9
DIL	L	**9.1**	0.3	25.2	3.8	**52.0**	1.7	171.1	1.2	**310.5**	1.6	934.5	1.7
	GPC	**9.2**	1.6	80.6	2.3	**51.3**	0.7	849.9	1.8	**353.6**	6.6	4775.9	2.0
	DPC	**10.0**	<0.1	105.2	3.6	**54.4**	0.9	1112.7	2.6	**351.4**	1.9	6401.5	0.9
ERO	L	**9.1**	0.3	24.0	0.1	**51.0**	1.6	171.8	1.2	**310.9**	2.1	929.8	0.9
	GPC	**9.0**	0.1	80.2	1.0	**51.7**	2.5	859.0	1.4	**352.4**	6.2	4778.0	1.9
	DPC	**10.0**	<0.1	105.4	2.3	**53.8**	0.6	1119.3	3.5	**351.3**	3.5	6421.9	0.8
CAN	L	70.6	0.8	**46.4**	9.7	472.1	2.5	**85.5**	5.9	1717.1	16.0	**328.2**	2.8
	GPC	**50.6**	4.3	54.4	1.6	369.6	3.7	**85.9**	3.3	1693.5	16.3	**297.5**	3.3
	DPC	57.9	0.3	**54.1**	4.8	706.8	2.3	**245.6**	7.7	3050.3	10.1	**1108.6**	3.0
SKY	L	**245.1**	6.9	666.2	77.9	2341.0	6.6	**1191.1**	15.5	6436.7	9.3	**1982.1**	62.4
	GPC	**234.6**	3.1	661.2	95.6	3505.6	105.1	**1611.7**	22.6	8629.4	51.6	**3423.1**	30.3
	DPC	**248.4**	1.0	727.0	73.2	2463.6	9.6	**1523.4**	13.3	7366.0	10.7	**3840.0**	24.9
MOT	L	**296.2**	4.2	723.2	74.4	1975.5	5.0	**1187.3**	3.8	6712.7	16.4	**1987.3**	55.4
	GPC	**287.4**	2.0	895.5	18.1	2791.8	88.8	**1611.4**	11.4	8962.9	67.7	**3562.7**	50.1
	DPC	**305.2**	1.2	791.3	34.0	2092.2	3.6	**1519.9**	11.9	7643.2	10.4	**3943.4**	99.5
STR	L	173.8	2.8	**121.0**	11.3	4248.0	25.8	**895.2**	6.5	25060.6	213.9	**5710.3**	12.7
	GPC	**168.4**	4.4	241.1	12.5	4222.8	28.1	**711.0**	5.4	23213.5	207.6	**3889.5**	50.5
	DPC	**183.0**	1.3	264.5	7.3	5649.1	24.5	**2619.5**	8.7	40224.3	198.7	**18217.0**	1.6

Pixel-Wise Operations. These operations need to perform some function on every single pixel in the image. As a result, the image content does not affect the processing time for the task, instead the time is primarily determined by the image size. As representative functions for this category, we select thresholding ("T") and gray-scaling ("G"). Thresholding low resolution images is faster when executed on the CPU, with the GPU being faster only with higher resolution images as input. The same holds for gray-scaling. With small input images, these functions cannot be parallelized sufficiently to be accelerated by the GPU.

Kernel Operations. Kernel operations are functions which need to manipulate each pixel of the image by taking into account the pixel's neighborhood. The kernel can have any shape or size and is scanned over the whole image. The new value of the kernels anchor point is determined by a function applied to every pixel inside the kernels area. Kernel operations can be further categorized into two sub-categories: filtering and morphological operations.

To evaluate filtering operations, we use median filter ("MF") and gaussian filter ("GF"). The median filter is fundamentally slower than the gaussian filter. However, it can be accelerated by its GPU implementation on all tested hardware. The gaussian filter, while speeded up on the laptops graphics card, is slower on both other GPUs. We believe that this is caused by hardware differences.

Both morphological operations, dilation ("DIL") and erosion ("ERO"), need approximately the same amount of time. Interestingly, their GPU implementation is considerably slower. The CUDA implementation of OpenCV's morphological operations uses the NVIDIA Performance Primitives (NPP), which has a time complexity of $O(npq)$, with n image pixels and a rectangular kernel of size $p * q$, according to [21]. This makes the NPP implementation comparably slow. The authors describe a parallel implementation of the van Herk/Gil-Werman (vHGW) algorithm [4,7] using CUDA, which is significantly more efficient.

Geometric Information Retrieval Operations. Functions of this category extract geometric information out of the image. Common algorithms falling into this category are Canny edge detection, Hough line transform or Hough circle transform. To evaluate geometric information retrieval operations, we use the Canny edge detection function ("CAN"), since it has a broad range of applications. The laptop and gaming PC perform similar, while the desktop PC is notably slower. The GPU implementation is faster on all three systems.

Feature-Based Operations. Feature-based operations are functions which are used to compare two images. A feature is defined as some point in an image with information describing that point. A feature extractor can find points distinguishable from other points in the image and compute descriptors describing these points. A feature matcher can compare descriptors of different features and match corresponding features found in different images. A special case of feature detection and matching is stereo matching, where a stereo matcher has to find corresponding points in two images in horizontal lines in order to compute a disparity value, which in turn can be used to compute the physical distance to the observed objects.

From this category, we measure feature detection, feature matching and stereo matching. To test feature detection, we resize the skyscraper image ("SKY") and the motorcycle image ("MOT") to have the same resolutions. Despite the fact that the motorcycle image is more suitable for feature detection, the results show similar processing times on both images. Again, the GPU accelerates the feature detection process depending on the images resolution. For stereo matching ("STR") two horizontally aligned images from the same scene are needed. For this, we use a second image of the motorcycle, taken from a different perspective. Similar to feature detection, stereo matching is also accelerated by the GPU at higher resolutions.

Feature matching does not operate on images, but instead uses the computed descriptors to identify matches. Hence, the time required to match two images depends on the number of features rather than their resolution. Thus, instead of varying the image size, we vary the number of features when comparing feature matching implementations. Figure 3 shows the resulting GPU speedup.

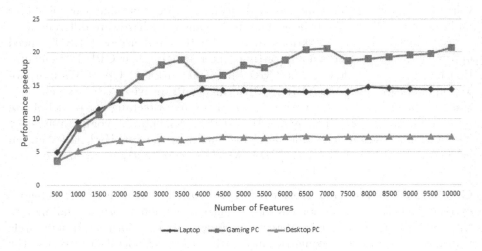

Fig. 3. Speedup of GPU-based feature matching

Structural Analysis Operations. Operations of this category are used to analyze structures in images. This covers different functions such as finding contours, finding the convex hull of an object or polygon approximation. Such operations are often unsuited for parallel programming, because parts of the image need to be analyzed in connection with other parts.

Typical OpenCV functions of this category like `findContours`, `convexHull` or `approxPolyDP` are only implemented using the CPU. Therefore, we don't discuss their timings. However, for a systematic optimization, the presence of such functions must be considered, since pipelines that include them will have to switch from GPU to CPU (and back), which can change the optimal composition.

3.4 Experimental Validation of the Analytical Model

To validate the model defined in Sect. 2, we discuss experiments with two image processing pipelines. The first pipeline performs edge detection and involves gray-scaling, noise reduction using a Gaussian filter and finally a Canny edge detector. The second pipeline computes a disparity map and it involves gray-scaling, a Gaussian filter as well as stereo-matching. For each pipeline, we create a CPU- and a GPU-based implementation and measure their execution time for different image sizes. Then, we use the analytical model described in Sect. 2 and the results of the micro-benchmarks to compute an estimate for the execution time, with and without considering the overhead for data transfer among GPU and CPU. Figure 4a shows the results for the lowest resolution and Fig. 4b shows the results for the highest resolution.

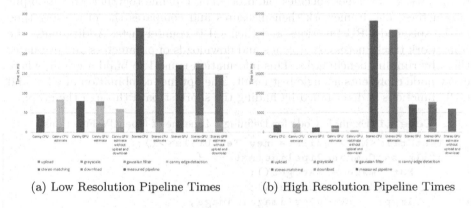

(a) Low Resolution Pipeline Times   (b) High Resolution Pipeline Times

Fig. 4. Comparison of model estimates and measurements for different pipelines

When comparing the measurements with the estimate gathered from applying the analytical model, we find that, in general, the model is able provide an estimate that lies within 10–20% of the measured time. Given that the micro-benchmarks used to compute the estimate are not perfect and given the fact that they cannot completely capture all effects such as caching, for example, we would argue that this result is sufficiently accurate. When simply comparing the time required to execute the CPU and GPU functions, as done when ignoring the time for uploading and downloading, the computed estimations get significantly worse. In fact, in all cases, this results in an overestimation of the speedup achievable by a GPU implementation and depending on the pipeline, the resulting error can become fairly large. For example, when looking at the edge detector pipeline with a resolution of 3705 × 2500, the actual time required by the GPU implementation exceeds the estimate by a factor of more than 2. This clearly indicates that the model presented in Sect. 2 is a more realistic and thus, better basis for performance optimizations.

4   Optimization Framework

Although the model presented in Sect. 2 is fairly simple, applying it in practice can be cumbersome. Since many functions can be executed on the GPU or CPU interchangeably, the number of possible pipeline compositions usually grows exponentially with its length. In addition, since the upload and download effort depends on the location of parameters, it is necessary to track the parameter location for each possible pipeline composition. Last but not least, as shown in Fig. 2 and Table 1, the effort for the individual components of the model can vary significantly based on the hardware configuration.

To mitigate these problems and to simplify the practical use of the model, we have developed an optimization framework that takes care of finding the optimal pipeline composition for a given hardware configuration. To use the framework, a developer specifies the processing pipeline together with its input parameters. The framework then measures and compares the processing time of the specified CPU functions and their GPU counterparts. Additionally, the framework tracks necessary uploads and downloads of parameters and evaluates them by running benchmarks. This information is used to build a graph, where every node represents a single test result. The optimal combination of CPU and GPU functions is determined by finding the shortest path through the graph.

Code 1.1. Example Code for Defining a Pipeline of OpenCV Functions

```
1   TestUtils<Mat> utils = new TestUtils<>();
2   utils.setCommandPipeline(mat -> {
3       Mat image = mat.get();
4       Mat edges = new Mat();
5       Imgproc.cvtColor(image, image,
6           Imgproc.COLOR_BGR2GRAY);
7       Imgproc.medianBlur(image, image, 15);
8       Imgproc.Canny(image, edges, 15, 45);
9   });
10  utils.setInput(new MatInput(theImage));
11  utils.initializeCommands(true);
12  utils.warmup(20);
13  utils.runTests(25);
14  utils.evaluate();
```

Code 1.1 shows exemplary usage of our framework. First, a `TestUtils` object has to be instantiated. The type argument specifies the type of the input parameter. The method `setCommandPipeline(Consumer<Input<T>>)` defines the pipeline which shall be evaluated. Inside the lambda expression, normal OpenCV function calls are made, except that the import statement should be changed. We implemented custom classes and methods matching the signatures of common OpenCV functions, but instead of computing something, they track invocations.

The remaining interaction is simple. The method `setInput(Input<T>)` sets the input parameter used for the command pipeline. Useful implementations for a single `Mat`, a 2-tuple of `Mats`, or an array of `Mats` are available, while custom implementations can be added. The method `initializeCommands(boolean)` initializes the pipeline and tracks method invocations. The boolean flag indicates whether all possible combinations of functions or only an efficient subset of them should be evaluated. It is likely that GPU functions are faster than their CPU counterparts. If the flag is set to false, the framework only compares paths with as few uploads and downloads as possible, which accelerates the testing time. Methods `warmup(int)` and `runTests(int)` are used to set the number of iterations, which are used to warm up the system and test every function, respectively. The method `evaluate()` starts the actual evaluation.

For this specific pipeline, 8 paths have to be evaluated. There are 3 different functions, each of them can be executed as a CPU or GPU function, which results in 8 different combinations. If the flag in `initializeCommands(boolean)` is set to `false`, only 2 paths (all functions only run on CPU or GPU) will be evaluated, which can significantly speed up the evaluation. The resulting graph is shown in Fig. 5. Rounded rectangles represent a single step in the pipeline, either as a CPU function or a GPU function. Circles represent the `Mat` parameters. The transition between CPU functions can be executed immediately. Paths switching between CPU and GPU functions need to upload or download the respective parameters, which increases the processing time. Uploading and downloading transitions are indicated by red or blue arrows, respectively. Based on previous experiments the fastest path would be either CPU-only execution or GPU-only execution, depending on the resolution of the input image.

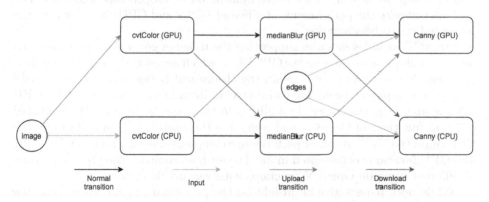

Fig. 5. The graph corresponding to the pipeline shown in Code 1.1

Internally, functions register implementations of the interface `Task` in a shared list. Every task can be converted to a `CpuTask` or a `GpuTask`, which will run the corresponding OpenCV function on the CPU or GPU, accordingly. A description is used to describe the task in the final output. The list of `Tasks` can be traversed to evaluate every combination of CPU and GPU functions. Necessary uploads and downloads of `Mats` are tracked and connected with the functions where they occurred.

The framework includes a range of implementations of the `Task` interface for a representative subset of the OpenCV functions, including thresholding, color conversion, resizing, morphology operations and some image filters. Custom implementations can be used to test any other function. If a GPU implementation is not available for a given function, the framework only tests the CPU implementation and automatically detects which `Mats` have to be downloaded.

Given the available task implementations, the extensible nature of the framework, and the algorithms to compute the optimal pipeline composition, we are convinced that the framework can serve as a solid basis to support the systematic optimization of image processing pipelines.

5   Related Work

There have been many different attempts to accelerate sophisticated algorithms by using hardware suited for parallel programming, such as GPUs or FPGAs. For instance, the performance of different random number generation algorithms [20] or image processing algorithms [1] was compared on such hardware. Two other algorithms, the push-relabel algorithm [13] and the "Vector Coherence Mapping" algorithm [14] were implemented using CUDA. Compared to equivalent CPU implementations, both are substantially faster, the former 15, the latter 22 times.

A micro-benchmark suite for OpenCL is presented in [22]. OpenCL is a vendor independent framework for computing on heterogeneous platforms. The authors compare the performance of different GPUs and CPUs in regards to the presented micro-benchmarks.

OpenCV includes modules supporting the usage of general-purpose computing on graphics processing units (GPGPUs), which are already used by previous research. The authors of [9] explain the theoretical background of many tasks related to computer vision. They also give an introduction into OpenCVs GPU module and its performance. In addition to that, the authors of [16] evaluated different functions of OpenCV and compared their processing time if run on the CPU or on the GPU. Another performance comparison between OpenCV's CPU and GPU functions is presented in [6]. The authors compare the processing time of different common OpenCV functions with varying image sizes.

While both papers give an insight on the performance gain when using the GPU module, they don't provide much information on uploading and downloading the data. The authors of [16] mention that programmers need to copy data between CPU and GPU and also explain some design considerations, but don't quantify the time needed to do so.

This paper not only quantifies the time needed to upload and download images, but also presents a mathematical model to estimate the execution time of any image processing pipeline. As shown, it is not sufficient to compare the processing time of functions themselves. Instead, it is necessary to take uploading and downloading of the data into consideration. Additionally, image processing functions are seldom executed in isolation. As more functions are added to the pipeline, the underlying model gains complexity, handled by the optimization framework. Developers can use it to compute the optimal combination of CPU and GPU functions.

6   Conclusion and Future Work

Computer vision systems require fast image processing pipelines. One way to reduce the execution time is to leverage the parallelism of modern GPUs to speed up individual image processing functions. However, since not all functions can benefit from a parallel execution and due to the fact that transitions between GPU and CPU code introduce overhead for uploading and downloading, optimizing the performance of image processing pipelines requires a careful analysis.

In this paper, we introduced a mathematical model that captures the relevant relationships as basis for the systematic optimization of image processing pipelines. Using micro-benchmarks collected with OpenCV, we analyzed different classes of image processing functions. The measurements show that not all of them will benefit equally. In addition, for simple filtering functions, functions with a sub-optimal implementation or applications operating on low resolution images, moving the computation from CPU to GPU can even increase the total execution time. As indicated by our validation, it is essential to account for the upload and download time when estimating the time required to execute a particular pipeline composition, since negligence can easily yield an estimation error that exceeds a factor of two. We hope that the model, measurements and optimization framework presented in this paper will help developers to find the optimal configuration for their application.

At the present time, we are currently analyzing the effects of asynchronous GPU calls which are supported by the class cv::cuda::Stream. Asynchronous calls can potentially increase the parallelism. However, when using streams for asynchronous calls it is necessary to allocate matrices in page-locked memory. In addition, some operations cannot be parallelized in all cases.

References

1. Asano, S., Maruyama, T., Yamaguchi, Y.: Performance comparison of FPGA, GPU and CPU in image processing. In: 2009 FPL, pp. 126–131, August 2009
2. Beymer, D., McLauchlan, P., Coifman, B., Malik, J.: A real-time computer vision system for measuring traffic parameters. In: Proceedings of IEEE CVPR, pp. 495–501, June 1997
3. Coifman, B., Beymer, D., McLauchlan, P., Malik, J.: A real-time computer vision system for vehicle tracking and traffic surveillance. Transp. Res. Part C Emerg. Technol. 6(4), 271–288 (1998)

4. Gil, J., Werman, M.: Computing 2-d min, median, and max filters. IEEE PAMI **15**(5), 504–507 (1993)
5. Griffin, G., Holub, A., Perona, P.: Caltech-256 object category dataset (2007, unpublished). https://resolver.caltech.edu/CaltechAUTHORS:CNS-TR-2007-001
6. Hangün, B., Eyecioğlu, Ö.: Performance comparison between OpenCV built in CPU and GPU functions on image processing operations. IJESA **1**, 34–41 (2017)
7. van Herk, M.: A fast algorithm for local minimum and maximum filters on rectangular and octagonal kernels. Pattern Recognit. Lett. **13**(7), 517–521 (1992)
8. Kurzyniec, D., Sunderam, V.: Efficient cooperation between Java and native codes - JNI performance benchmark. In: 2001 PDPTA (2001)
9. Marengoni, M., Stringhini, D.: High level computer vision using OpenCV. In: 2011 24th SIBGRAPI Conference on Graphics, Patterns, and Images Tutorials, pp. 11–24, August 2011
10. NVIDIA Corporation: CUDA C++ programming guide (2020). https://docs.nvidia.com/cuda/cuda-c-programming-guide/index.html. Accessed 22 Sept 2020
11. Oliver, N.M., Rosario, B., Pentland, A.P.: A Bayesian computer vision system for modeling human interactions. IEEE PAMI **22**(8), 831–843 (2000)
12. OpenCV team: OpenCV (2020). https://opencv.org/. Accessed 28 Feb 2020
13. Park, S.I., Ponce, S.P., Huang, J., Cao, Y., Quek, F.: Low-cost, high-speed computer vision using NVIDIA's CUDA architecture. In: 2008 37th IEEE AIPR Workshop, pp. 1–7, October 2008
14. Park, S.I., Ponce, S.P., Huang, J., Cao, Y., Quek, F.: Low-cost, high-speed computer vision using NVIDIA's CUDA architecture. In: 2008 37th IEEE AIPR Workshop, pp. 1–7, October 2008
15. Phipps, G.: Comparing observed bug and productivity rates for Java and C++. Softw. Pract. Exper. **29**(4), 345–358 (1999)
16. Pulli, K., Baksheev, A., Kornyakov, K., Eruhimov, V.: Real-time computer vision with OpenCV. Commun. ACM **55**(6), 61–69 (2012)
17. Samuel Audet: Java interface to OpenCV, FFmpeg, and more (2020). https://github.com/bytedeco/javacv. Accessed 28 Feb 2020
18. Scharstein, D., et al.: High-resolution stereo datasets with subpixel-accurate ground truth. In: Jiang, X., Hornegger, J., Koch, R. (eds.) GCPR 2014. LNCS, vol. 8753, pp. 31–42. Springer, Cham (2014). https://doi.org/10.1007/978-3-319-11752-2_3
19. Shehu, V., Dika, A.: Using real time computer vision algorithms in automatic attendance management systems. Proc. ITI **2010**, 397–402 (2010)
20. Thomas, D.B., Howes, L., Luk, W.: A comparison of CPUs, GPUs, FPGAs, and massively parallel processor arrays for random number generation. In: Proceedings of the ACM/SIGDA FPGA, FPGA 2009, pp. 63–72. Association for Computing Machinery, New York (2009)
21. Thurley, M.J., Danell, V.: Fast morphological image processing open-source extensions for GPU processing with CUDA. IEEE JSTSP **6**(7), 849–855 (2012)
22. Yan, X., Shi, X., Wang, L., Yang, H.: An OpenCL micro-benchmark suite for GPUs and CPUs. J. Supercomput. **69**(2), 693–713 (2014)

A Hybrid Approach for Improved Image Similarity Using Semantic Segmentation

Achref Ouni[✉], Eric Royer, Marc Chevaldonné, and Michel Dhome

Université Clermont Auvergne, CNRS, SIGMA Clermont, Institut Pascal,
63000 Clermont-Ferrand, France
Achref.EL_OUNI@uca.fr

Abstract. Content Based Image Retrieval (CBIR) is the task of finding the images from the datasets that consider similar to the input query based on its visual characteristics. Several methods from the state of the art based on visual methods (Bag of visual words, VLAD, ...) or recent deep leaning methods try to solve the CBIR problem. In particular, Deep learning is a new field and used for several vision applications including CBIR. But, even with the increase of the performance of deep learning algorithms, this problem is still a challenge in computer vision. To tackle this problem, we present in this paper an efficient CBIR framework based on incorporation between deep learning based semantic segmentation and visual features. We show experimentally that the incorporate leads to the increase of accuracy of our CBIR framework. We study the performance of the proposed approach on four different datasets (Wang, MSRC V1, MSRC V2, Linnaeus).

Keywords: CBIR · Semantic segmentation · Image representation · Features extraction

1 Introduction

Content Based Image Retrieval (CBIR) is a fundamental step in many computer vision applications such as pose estimation, virtual reality, Medical diagnosis, remote sensing, crime detection, video analysis and military surveillance. CBIR is the task of retrieving the images similar to the input query from the dataset based on their contents. CBIR system (see Fig. 1) based on three main steps: (1) Feature extraction (2) Signature construction (3) Retrieval. The performance of any proposed approach depends on the way in an image signature is constructed. Therefore, construction image signature is a key step and the core of CBIR system. State of the art mentions two main contributions used to retrieve the closest image: BoVW (Bag of Visual Words) and CNN (Convolutional Neural Networks) descriptors for image retrieval. Both contributions represent images as vector of valued features. This vector encodes the primitive image such as color, texture and shape.

In this paper, we present a new idea to improve the potential of recovering the relevant images. Our work incorporate the extracted visual features with the

© Springer Nature Switzerland AG 2020
G. Bebis et al. (Eds.): ISVC 2020, LNCS 12510, pp. 647–657, 2020.
https://doi.org/10.1007/978-3-030-64559-5_51

semantic information to build a robust semantic signature. Before computing the distance between the query and the datasets, we have proposed also an efficient test for checking the semantic similarity. This step keeps only the images with the same semantic content with the query and penalize the rest. Our results on different database highlight the power of our approach.

This article is structured as follows: we provide a brief overview of convolutional neural networks descriptors and bag of visual words related works in Sect. 2. We explain our proposals in Sect. 3. We present the experimental part on four different datasets and discuss the results of our work in Sect. 4. Section 5 conclusion.

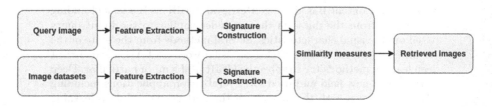

Fig. 1. Cbir system

2   State of the Art

Many CBIR systems have been proposed in last year [1, 9, 20, 28]. In the literature two main methods for retrieving the images by similarity: (1) methods based on visual features extracted from the image using visual descriptors (2) Learning methods based on deep learning architecture for construction a global signature extracted from the features layer. Let's start by describing the methods based visual features. Bag of visual words (BoVW) or Bag of visual features (BoF) [8] is the popular model used for image classification and image similarity. BoVW treated as following. For each image, the visual features detected then extracted using a visual descriptors such as SIFT [15]. This step will be repeated in a recursive way on all images dataset until collecting all visual descriptors dataset. Then a clustering step using K-MEANS [11] will be applied on the descriptors to build the visual vocabulary (visual words) from the center of each cluster. In order to obtain the visual words, the features query replaced by the index of the visual words that consider the nearest using euclidean distance. Finally, the image described as a histogram of the frequency of the visual phrase exist in the image. Inspired by BoVW, vector of locally aggregated descriptors (VlAD) [10] present an improvement which is assign to each visual feature its nearest visual word and accumulate this difference for each visual word. Fisher Vector encoding [19] uses GMM [21] to construct a visual word dictionary. VLAD and Fisher are similar but VLAD does not store second order information about the features and use K-MEANS instead GMM. Another inspiration from BoVW presented by Bag of visual phrase (BoVP) [2,17,18]. BoVP describe the image as a matrix of visual phrase occurrence instead of a vector in BoVW. The idea is to link two or more visual words by a criterion. Then the phrase can be constructed by different way (sliding windows, k-nearest neighbors, Graph). [2] Local regions are grouped by the method of clustering (single-linkage). [18] Group each key point with its closest spatial neighbors using L2 distance. In other side, deep learning has proven useful in computer vision application. In particular, convolutional neural network (CNN, or ConvNet) is the most commonly applied to analyzing the image by content. CNN algorithms based on architecture for analyzing the images. The architecture is composed by a set of layers. The major layers are: the input layer, hidden layers and the output layer. In CNN for computing the similarity between two images it is necessary to extract the features vector from the feature layer then calculating the distance using L2 metric. Many CNN models have been proposed, including AlexNet [12], VGGNet [23], GoogleNet [26] and ResNet [25]. The fully connected layer (feature layer) usually found towards the end of CNN architectures with vector size of 4096 of float which describe the feature image (color, shape, texture, ...). Similar to Local visual Feature approaches, after extracting all descriptors the retrieval accuracy computed using Euclidean distance between the images. NetVLAD [3] inspired from VLAD is a CNN architecture used for image retrieval. [4] reduce the training time and provides an average improvement in accuracy. Using ACP is frequently in CBIR application thanks to its ability to reduce the descriptor dimension without losing its accuracy. [22] using convolution neural network (CNN) to train the network and support vector machine (SVM) to train the hyperplane then compute the distance between the features image and the trained hyper-plane.

3   Contributions

In this section, we present a brief explanation of our framework. Our aim is to improve the image representation. The rentability and efficiency of any CBIR system depends on the robustness of the image signature. Figure 2 presents our global framework. Our framework starts with parallel process: extraction visual features and extraction semantic information for both query and datasets. Then, we exploit the extracted information for two main uses: (i) Creation semantic signature (ii) Creation semantic histogram. To build a semantic signature, we incorporate the semantic information with the visual descriptors. Then, we check the resemblance between two images based on their semantic histograms and we compute the distance between the query and the selected candidates using L2 metric.

3.1   Semantic Signature

The most CBIR system describe the image as a vector of N unit. Bag of visual [8] words represent the image as a frequency histogram of vocabulary that are in the image. In deep learning, the image signature is a vector of N float extracted

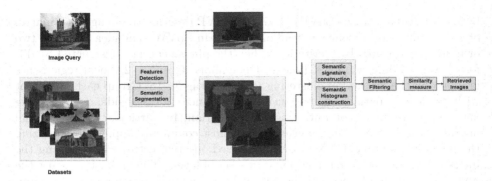

Fig. 2. Global framework

from the feature layer. In this work, we present a new idea to construct an image signature based on incorporation between semantic information and the visual features. We define the signature as a matrix of $N * M$ float where the width N corresponds to the size of descriptor (SIFT 128) and the height M corresponds to the number of classes on which the network was trained. Figure 3 and algorithm 1 describes the different steps of our approach. The process of construction composed of three different steps: (i) Detection and extraction the visual features (ii) Extraction of semantic information (iii) Regrouping the keypoints by class label and computing their center. To compute the center of classes, for each class label on the image we select the set of keypoints that belongs and we apply for them the clustering algorithm (K-MEANS). Consequently, each class label will be presented by a vector of N float. Finally the image signature is composed of N center of clusters that represent the existing classes label in the image. It is not necessarily that the image contains all classes during the prediction. In this case, we assign a null vector for the missing classes.

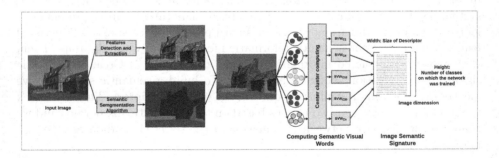

Fig. 3. Semantic signature construction

Algorithm 1 Create Image Signature

Require: Image I, Size N   ▷ number of classes on which the network was trained
  $Features$=DetectionExtractionFeatures(I)
  I_{seg}=SemanticSegmentationPrediction(I)
  For i = 1 to N **do**
    IF Exist($Class_i$ in I_{seg})
      SG=∅
      For j = 1 to Size($Features$) **do**
        IF Label($Features_j$)==$Class_i$
          SG= SG . $Features_j$ ▷ Concatenation
        EndIF
      EndFor
      SVW=Kmeans(SG,1)   ▷ Semantic visual words
    Else
      SVWs=∅
    EndIF
    Signature(i,:)=SVW
  EndFor
  Return Signature

3.2 Semantic Histogram

Except that the semantics provides us a class by label, we can also know the objects in the image and their proportion. We exploit this information to check the semantic similarity between the images. Then, we assume that if two images share the same classes label are then semantically similar otherwise the content of the images is different. Consequently, using the semantic information we can select the images which are similar in content with the query. In other side, we can neutral then penalize in the calculation step the dissimilar images with Sim $(I_{query}, I_{dataset}) \leq \epsilon$. To deal with this problem, we proposed to construct for each image a semantic histogram. As shown in Fig. 4, we define the image as a vector of N unit contains the proportion of each class in the image. Then, we measure the semantic similarity between two images using equation (1).

$$Sim(query, candidate) = \sum_{i=0}^{n} |P_{query_i} - P_{dataset_i}| \qquad (1)$$

where P are the the proportion of a class in the image.

The main advantage of the checking phase is makes us able to increase the CBIR accuracy by keeping only the images that have the same semantic content with the query and to penalize the rest that consider semantically different (Fig. 5).

4 Experimental Results

4.1 Benchmark Datasets for Retrieval.

In this section, we present the potential of our approach on four different datasets (Table 1). Our goal is to increase the CBIR accuracy and reduce the execution time. To evaluate our proposition, we test on the following datasets:

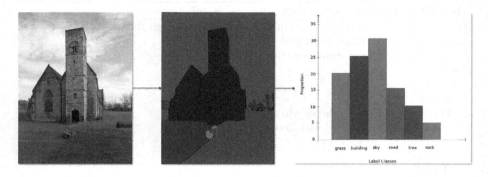

Fig. 4. Semantic histogram

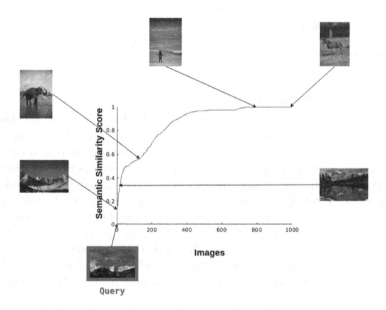

Fig. 5. Semantic similarity between the images

Table 1. Database used to evaluate of approach

Name	Size	Ground	Query mode
	DB/Queries	Truth	
MSRC v1	241/241	–	query-in-ground Truth
MSRC v2	591/591	–	query-in-ground Truth
Wang [27]	1000/1000	100	query-in-ground Truth
Linnaeus [6]	6000/2000	400	queries/dataset are disjoint

- MSRC v1[1] (Microsoft Research in Cambridge) which has been proposed by Microsoft Research team. MSRC v1 contains 241 images divided into 9 categories. The evaluation on MSRC v1 is based on MAP score (mean average precision)
- MSRC v2[2] (Microsoft Research in Cambridge) contains 591 images included MSRC v1 dataset and divided into 23 categories. The evaluation on MSRC v2 is based on MAP score (mean average precision)
- Corel 1000 [27] or Wang is a dataset of 1000 images divided into 10 categories and each category contains 100 image. The evaluation computed by the average precision of the first 100 nearest neighbors among 1000.
- Linnaeus [6] is a collection of 8000 images of 4 categories (berry, bird, dog, flower). The evaluation on Linnaeus is based on MAP score (mean average precision).

4.2   Performance Metrics

In content based image retrieval (CBIR) the most used evaluate measures is the precision. The precision P is the number of relevant images found compared to the total number of images proposed for a given query.

$$P(I_k) = \sum_{j=1}^{K} \frac{I_j}{K} \tag{2}$$

where k is the number of retrieved images.

In the multi-class case

$$A_v = \frac{1}{M_v} \sum_{k=1}^{M_v} P(I_k) \tag{3}$$

$$mAP = \frac{1}{S} \sum_{k=1}^{S} A_v \tag{4}$$

where M_v is the number of classes and S is the number of queries.

4.3   Benchmark Datasets for Semantic Segmentation

Many semantic segmentation datasets have been proposed in the last years such as Cityscapes [7], Mapillary [16], COCO [14], ADE20K [29], Coco-stuff [5], Mseg [13] and others. The semantic representation is divided into two main categories: Stuff and Things. Things objects have characteristic shapes like vehicle, dog, computer... . Stuff is the description of amorphous objects like sea, sky, tree,... . Therefore, the semantic segmentation datasets are divided into three main categories: (i) Stuff-only (ii) Thing-only (iii) Stuff and Things. To obtain

---

[1] https://pgram.com/dataset/msrc-v1/.
[2] https://pgram.com/dataset/msrc-v2/.

a robust prediction, we use the recent implementation HRNet-W48 [24] architecture trained on Coco-stuff [5] and Mseg [13] datasets. The main advantage of using Coco-stuff [5] and Mseg [13] datasets is that they are able to predict for both thing and stuff with high number of class predicted for an image.

Table 2. Details about semantic dataset used to predict the images

Dataset	Images	Merged classes	All classes	Stuff/Thing classes	Year
Coco-stuff [5]	164K	172	172	92/80	2018
Mseg [13]	220K	194	316	102/94	2020

Table 3. MAP evaluations using Mseg datasets

Retrieval Dataset	Descriptors		
	KAZE	SURF	HOG
MSRC v1	0.79	0.84	0.85
MSRC v2	0.61	0.58	0.60
Linnaeus [6]	0.71	0.73	0.71
Wang [27]	0.73	0.74	0.71
Using semantic filter			
MSRC v1	0.81	0.86	0.87
MSRC v2	0.74	0.73	0.71
Linnaeus [6]	0.73	0.75	0.74
Wang [27]	0.84	0.84	0.83

Table 4. MAP evaluations using Coco-stuff datasets

Retrieval Dataset	Descriptors		
	KAZE	SURF	HOG
MSRC v1	0.77	0.82	0.84
MSRC v2	0.57	0.55	0.61
Linnaeus [6]	0.67	0.68	0.66
Wang [27]	0.71	0.72	0.69
Using semantic filter			
MSRC v1	0.80	0.85	0.86
MSRC v2	0.71	0.72	0.71
Linnaeus [6]	0.72	0.75	0.73
Wang [27]	0.82	0.83	0.80

Table 5. Comparison of precision for top 20 retrieved images (Wang dataset)

Methods	Top 20
ElAlami [9]	0.76
Guo and Prasetyo [1]	0.77
Zeng et al. [28]	0.80
Jitesh Pradhan [20]	0.81
Proposed method	0.91

Table 6. Comparison of the accuracy of our approach with methods from the state of the art

Methods	MSRC v1	MSRC v2	Linnaeus	Wang
BoVW [8]	0,48	0.30	0,26	0.48
n-BoVW [17]	0.58	0.39	0.31	0.60
VLAD [10]	0.78	0.41	–	0.74
N-Gram [18]	–	–	–	0.37
AlexNet [12]	0.81	0.58	0,47	0.68
VGGNet [23]	0.76	0.63	0,48	0.76
ResNet [25]	0.83	0.70	0,69	0.82
Ruigang [22]	–	–	0.70	–
Ours (best)	**0.86**	**0.72**	**0.75**	**0.84**

4.4 Results on Benchmark Datasets for Retrieval

We conducted our experimentation on two different semantic dataset (Table 2) and four retrieval datasets (Table 1). We test our approach using three different descriptors (Kaze, Surf, Kaze). In addition, we compare there with two categories of methods: (i) Local visual Feature: methods that are based on local features like Surf, Sift included the inherited methods such as BoVW, Vlad, Fisher. (ii) Learning based features: methods that based on learning the features using deep learning algorithms. Tables 3, 4 present the performance of the retrieval on the 4 datasets with three different descriptors. Above, we show the map (mean average precision) scores using only the semantic signature (Fig. 3). Down, we present the results by adding the semantic filter. In experimentation we set epsilon (ϵ) at 0.9 to keep only the images that are considered semantically similar to the input query and we assign a negative score to the rest. It clearly indicates that adding the semantic filter improves the accuracy.

For the methods [1, 9, 20, 28] in Table 5, we compare the precision of the top 20 retrieved images for all categories for Wang dataset. In Table 6 we compare our results with a large state of the art methods. For [12, 23, 25] we extract from their architecture the features vector from the features layer then we evaluate the their performance on the datasets using L2 distance. As indicate the results our proposed present good performance for all datasets.

5   Conclusion

In this paper, we have presented an efficient CBIR approach based on incorporation between deep learning based semantic segmentation and visual features. We have presented two main uses of the semantic information: (i) Creation semantic signature (ii) Creation semantic histogram. We have proven that the use of the semantic information increase the CBIR accuracy. With different descriptors (KAZE, SURF, HOG) our approach achieve a better results in terms of accuracy compared to the state of the art methods.

References

1. Admile, N.S., Dhawan, R.R.: Content based image retrieval using feature extracted from dot diffusion block truncation coding. In: 2016 International Conference on Communication and Electronics Systems (ICCES), pp. 1–6. IEEE (2016)
2. Albatal, R., Mulhem, P., Chiaramella, Y.: Visual phrases for automatic images annotation. In: 2010 International Workshop on Content Based Multimedia Indexing (CBMI), pp. 1–6. IEEE (2010)
3. Arandjelović, R., Gronat, P., Torii, A., Pajdla, T., Sivic, J.: NetVLAD: CNN architecture for weakly supervised place recognition. In: IEEE Conference on Computer Vision and Pattern Recognition (2016)
4. Balaiah, T., Jeyadoss, T.J.T., Thirumurugan, S.S., Ravi, R.C.: A deep learning framework for automated transfer learning of neural networks. In: 2019 11th International Conference on Advanced Computing (ICoAC), pp. 428–432. IEEE (2019)
5. Caesar, H., Uijlings, J., Ferrari, V.: Coco-stuff: thing and stuff classes in context. In: Proceedings of the IEEE Conference on Computer Vision and Pattern Recognition, pp. 1209–1218 (2018)
6. Chaladze, G., Kalatozishvili, L.: Linnaeus 5 dataset for machine learning. Technical report (2017)
7. Cordts, M., et al.: The cityscapes dataset for semantic urban scene understanding. In: Proceedings of the IEEE Conference on Computer Vision and Pattern Recognition, pp. 3213–3223 (2016)
8. Csurka, G., Dance, C., Fan, L., Willamowski, J., Bray, C.: Visual categorization with bags of keypoints. In: Workshop on Statistical Learning in Computer Vision. ECCV, Prague, vol. 1, pp. 1–2 (2004)
9. ElAlami, M.E.: A new matching strategy for content based image retrieval system. Appl. Soft Comput. **14**, 407–418 (2014)
10. Jégou, H.,Douze, M., Schmid, C., Pérez, P.: Aggregating local descriptors into a compact image representation. In: 2010 IEEE Computer Society Conference on Computer Vision and Pattern Recognition, pp. 3304–3311. IEEE (2010)
11. Krishna, K., Narasimha Murty, M.: Genetic k-means algorithm. IEEE Trans. Syst. Man Cybern. Part B (Cybern.) **29**(3), 433–439 (1999)
12. Krizhevsky, A., Sutskever, I., Hinton, G.E.: ImageNet classification with deep convolutional neural networks. In: Advances in Neural Information Processing Systems, pp. 1097–1105 (2012)

13. Lambert, J., Zhuang, L., Sener, O., Hays, J., Koltun, V.: MSeg: a composite dataset for multi-domain semantic segmentation. In: Computer Vision and Pattern Recognition (CVPR) (2020)
14. Lin, T.-Y., et al.: Microsoft COCO: common objects in context. In: Fleet, D., Pajdla, T., Schiele, B., Tuytelaars, T. (eds.) ECCV 2014. LNCS, vol. 8693, pp. 740–755. Springer, Cham (2014). https://doi.org/10.1007/978-3-319-10602-1_48
15. Lindeberg, T.: Scale invariant feature transform (2012)
16. Neuhold, G., Ollmann, T., Bulo, S.R., Kontschieder, P.: The mapillary vistas dataset for semantic understanding of street scenes. In: Proceedings of the IEEE International Conference on Computer Vision, pp. 4990–4999 (2017)
17. Ouni, A., Urruty, T., Visani, M.: A robust CBIR framework in between bags of visual words and phrases models for specific image datasets. Multimed. Tools Appl. **77**(20), 26173–26189 (2018). https://doi.org/10.1007/s11042-018-5841-8
18. Pedrosa, G.V., Traina, A.J.M.: From bag-of-visual-words to bag-of-visual-phrases using n-grams. In: 2013 XXVI Conference on Graphics, Patterns and Images, pp. 304–311. IEEE (2013)
19. Perronnin, F., Dance, C.: Fisher kernels on visual vocabularies for image categorization. In: 2007 IEEE Conference on Computer Vision and Pattern Recognition, pp. 1–8. IEEE (2007)
20. Pradhan, J., Kumar, S., Pal, A.K., Banka, H.: Texture and color visual features based CBIR using 2D DT-CWT and histograms. In: Ghosh, D., Giri, D., Mohapatra, R.N., Savas, E., Sakurai, K., Singh, L.P. (eds.) ICMC 2018. CCIS, vol. 834, pp. 84–96. Springer, Singapore (2018). https://doi.org/10.1007/978-981-13-0023-3_9
21. Rasmussen, C.E.: The infinite gaussian mixture model. In: Advances in Neural Information Processing Systems, pp. 554–560 (2000)
22. Fu, R., Li, B., Gao, Y., Wang, P.: Content-based image retrieval based on CNN and SVM. In: 2016 2nd IEEE International Conference on Computer and Communications (ICCC), pp. 638–642 (2016)
23. Simonyan, K., Zisserman, A.: Very deep convolutional networks for large-scale image recognition. arXiv preprint arXiv:1409.1556 (2014)
24. Sun, K., et al.: High-resolution representations for labeling pixels and regions. arXiv preprint arXiv:1904.04514 (2019)
25. Szegedy, C., Ioffe, S., Vanhoucke, V., Alemi, A.A.: Inception-v4, inception-resnet and the impact of residual connections on learning. In: Thirty-First AAAI Conference on Artificial Intelligence (2017)
26. Szegedy, C., et al.: Going deeper with convolutions. In: Proceedings of the IEEE Conference on Computer Vision and Pattern Recognition, pp. 1–9 (2015)
27. Wang, J.Z., Li, J., Wiederhold, G.: Simplicity: semantics-sensitive integrated matching for picture libraries. IEEE Trans. Pattern Anal. Mach. Intell. **23**(9), 947–963 (2001)
28. Zeng, S., Huang, R., Wang, H., Kang, Z.: Image retrieval using spatiograms of colors quantized by Gaussian mixture models. Neurocomputing **171**, 673–684 (2016)
29. Zhou, B., Zhao, H., Puig, X., Fidler, S., Barriuso, A., Torralba, A.: Scene parsing through ade20k dataset. In: Proceedings of the IEEE Conference on Computer Vision and Pattern Recognition, pp. 633–641 (2017)

Automated Classification of Parkinson's Disease Using Diffusion Tensor Imaging Data

Harsh Sharma$^{(\boxtimes)}$, Sara Soltaninejad, and Irene Cheng

Department of Computing Science, University of Alberta, Edmonton, Canada
{hsharma,soltanin,locheng}@ualberta.ca

Abstract. Parkinson's Disease (PD) is one of the most common neurological disorders in the world, affecting over 6 million people globally. In recent years, Diffusion Tensor Imaging (DTI) biomarkers have been established as one of the leading techniques to help diagnose the disease. However, identifying patterns and deducing even preliminary results require a neurologist to automatically analyze the scan. In this paper, we propose a Machine Learning (ML) based algorithm that can analyze DTI data and predict if the person has PD. We were able to obtain a classification accuracy of 80% and an F1 score of 0.833 using our approach. The method proposed is expected to reduce the number of misdiagnosis by assisting the neurologists in making a decision.

Keywords: Parkinson's Disease · Diffusion Tensor Imaging · Image classification · Medical imaging

1 Introduction

Parkinson's disease (PD) is a neuro-degenerative disease that affects the Central Nervous System. It is usually characterized by motor symptoms like tremors, rigidity, akinesia and postural instability. However, non-motor symptoms like Autonomic dysfunction, Cognitive and neuro-behavioural abnormalities, sleep disorders and sensory abnormalities are also common [16]. Assessment of Parkinson's can be done by a neurologist based on the medical history and neurological examinations but there is no definitive test to avoid a high rate of misdiagnosis [28].

Magnetic Resonance Imaging (MRI) is a widely used imaging technique in detection of neurological abnormalities. The use of iron-sensitive T2* Weighted Imaging (T2* or "T2-Star") and Susceptibility Weighted Imaging (SWI) sequences at a magnetic field strength of at least 3T, has become more accurate in diagnosis of Parkinson's over time [34]. Development of newer techniques like Diffusion Tensor Imaging (DTI) has shown potential as a sensitive method to study PD pathophysiology and severity [4,24].

In this paper, we propose an automated method to classify subjects with PD by using raw Diffusion Weighted (DW) images. In the sections below, we first

G. Bebis et al. (Eds.): ISVC 2020, LNCS 12510, pp. 658–669, 2020.
https://doi.org/10.1007/978-3-030-64559-5_52

discuss the motivation behind the development and then the methods employed in preprocessing and classification are described. We have identified Fractional Anisotropy (FA) and Mean Diffusivity (MD) as accurate metrics for our classification algorithm. The results obtained and the limitations of the approach are discussed.

2 Motivation and Existing Methods

Diffusion is the process of movement of molecules from an area of high concentration to low concentration. Diffusion-Weighted Imaging (DWI) is a variant of conventional MRI based on the tissue water diffusion rate. It is a non-invasive method and requires no special equipment [37]. This technique can characterize water diffusion properties at each picture element (voxel) of an image.

The predominant application of DWI is in the areas of brain where the anisotropy, and orientation of tracts can be measured. These are primarily the white matter regions of the brain. The integrity of the region is determined using various metrics like diffusivity and anisotropy. The patterns in these metrics help in the diagnosis of various diseases like schizophrenia [8], Alzheimer's [38] and Parkinson's [21].

Several studies [11,32,39] have shown DTI as an effective and clinically relevant separation between PD and controls. In [11,39], it was found that compared to controls, PD patients exhibit significantly reduced fractional anisotropy (FA). This suggests that DTI can potentially be used an early trait PD biomarker.

To get a complete understanding of the advancements in the domain of automated classification of Parkinson's, we conducted a thorough literature review and observed that the use of DTI data is a relatively unexplored field. To the best of our knowledge only three papers have been published - by Haller et al. in 2012 [13], by Banerjee et al. in 2016 [5] and by Sivakumar and Quinn in 2019 [35].

In [13], the authors performed group level TBSS analysis and individual level SVM classification using the FA data. The study was conducted using 40 images (17 PD and 23 *Other*). At the group level, the authors observed that the candidates in the PD group had significant increase in FA and significant decrease in RD and MD, compared to the candidates in the *Other* group. For the individual level classification, the authors reported an accuracy of approximately 97%. As noted in the work, the accuracy measure was unexpectedly high and the method suffers from several limitations. The foremost being the small number of cases available for the study. The authors have also used the same data for training and testing which makes the results further more unreliable.

In [5], Banerjee et al. use an ensemble average propagator (EAP) to distinguish between PD and control. On a dataset of 22 control and 46 PD subjects, they have reported a classification accuracy of 98.53% with a sensitivity of 0.98 and specificity of 1. In the same study, they also report an accuracy of 76.47% using FA maps. Both the models are support vector machine based models and the data used has been dimensionally reduced using Principal Geodesic Analysis (PGA). We have provided comparison with the model in Sect. 4.1 below.

As mentioned earlier, DTI captures the movement of water molecules across the brain regions. This is done by capturing several images at fixed time intervals (roughly five seconds). In [35], the authors used raw DTI scans to analyze the movement of water across these time steps. The scans were subjected to dimensionality reduction techniques using tucker tensor decomposition and linear dynamical systems approach. The extracted features were then passed to a Random Forest (RF) classifier. The reported results show a high accuracy and a high F-measure but there are several constraints with these values. The dataset used for classification was highly skewed (421 PD vs 213 control) which would lead to a huge bias in the results [17]. Also, raw data was used for the study and the affect of noise in the scans was not accounted for while doing the analysis.

The dearth of research in the automated classification using DTI and the high number of misdiagnosis in PD, motivated the need to develop an algorithm that would assist a neurologist in accurate and early determination of the disease.

3   Proposed Method

The proposed method consists of three stages - preprocessing, tensor calculations, and classification. All these stages are described in details in the subsections below.

3.1   Dataset

We obtained 207 DWI - 68 Healthy Candidates and 139 PD - from the Parkinson's Progression Markers Initiative (PPMI) database. PPMI is a collaboration of researchers, funders and study participants working toward the goal of identifying progression biomarkers to improve PD therapeutics [28]. PPMI has clinical sites in the United States, Europe, Israel, and Australia and the data and samples provide a comprehensive database of Parkinson's patients. The images were downloaded in the Digital Imaging and Communications in Medicine (DICOM) format - a standard for the communication and management of medical imaging information and related data [29].

We randomly selected 20 images (10 from each class) from the dataset as our test dataset and used the remaining for training and validation. We will explain how to address the data imbalance issue in training in the Experimental Results section below.

3.2   Preprocessing

The preprocessing pipeline, shown in Fig. 1 begins with the conversion of the raw DICOM data to 4-dimensional NIfTI images. NIfTI-1 is a new Analyze-style data format, proposed by the NIfTI Data Format Working Group (DFWG) as a short-term measure to facilitate inter-operation of functional MRI data analysis software packages [1]. *dcm2niix* is a free open source tool that facilitates the conversion of the complicated DICOM format to the simpler NIfTI format [26].

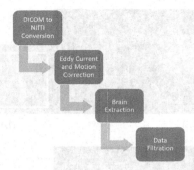

Fig. 1. Preprocessing pipeline - The steps involved in preprocessing the images as explained in Sect. 3.2

dcm2niix outputs the NIfTI file along with the bvec and bval files. The bvec and bval files are the metadata extracted from the DICOM that cannot be stored in the NIfTI headers. They contain the gradient directions and diffusion weighting values respectively. The dimensions of each NIfTI image were found to be $116 \times 116 \times 72 \times 65$, where 65 represents the number of DICOM images in the series and 72 is the number of slices.

After the conversion of data, the NIfTI files need to be processed further before they can be used for any calculations/classifications. Eddy currents are the distortion current generated due to a magnetic field. Diffusion Weighted Images have a high impact of eddy currents due to strong diffusion-sensitizing magnetic field gradients flanked by short ramp times [7]. The distortions caused by eddy currents and movement of the subject during the acquisition of the scan can be corrected by using the *eddy* command of the FMRIB Software Library (FSL) [3].

Diffusion weighted imaging data is acquired by applying a weighted gradient along a specific direction. The weighting is typically characterised by the b-values (strength of weighting) and a unit length vector v (for direction) [2,30]. The *eddy* tool models the diffusion signal as a Gaussian Process and assumes that the similarity in the signals of two acquisitions along two vectors varies proportionally with the angle between them and also that it is identical along vectors v and $-v$, where v is a unit vector in any random direction [2]. As evident from Fig. 2, the resultant images have lesser noise and are much more sharper than the raw scans. This helps in a better analysis of the scans.

The eddy corrected scans still contain a lot of unwanted regions which contribute no information for PD detection. The brain extraction tool, *BET*, from FSL helps to get rid of the non-brain tissues in the images. It generates a brain mask by generating the intensity histogram of the image to get a rough brain/non-brain threshold. It helps segregate the very bright parts (e.g., eyeballs and parts of the scalp), less bright parts (e.g., brain tissue), and the dark parts (including air and skull). An estimated skull region is then generated using

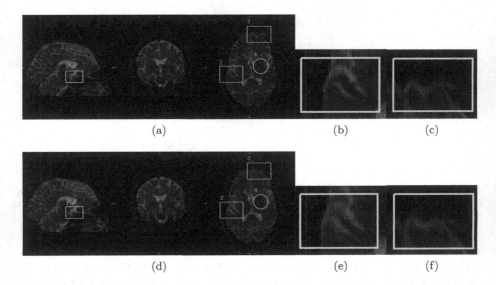

Fig. 2. Multiplanar views of the scans before (a) and after (d) eddy correction. Differences can be observed in the highlighted regions. (b) and (e) show zoomed in view of regions marked as 2 in (a) and (d) respectively while (c) and (f) show zoomed in view of regions marked as 3

triangular tessellation and iterating outwards from the center of gravity. More details on the flow can be found in [36].

As the final step of preprocessing, the brain extracted images were visualized manually using MRIcroGL, a free tool provided by the University of South Carolina [9]. During the visualization, two major problems were identified with a few of the scans. First, some of the scans were corrupted during acquisition and the brain was estimated as a sphere instead. Second, the dimensions of the images were not equal to the expected value of $116 \times 116 \times 72 \times 65$. Due to these inconsistency, these scans were removed from the study and the leftover data was used for tensor calculation and classification. A corrupted scan is shown in Fig. 3 for reference.

3.3 Tensor Calculation

The preprocessed DW images are then used to calculate the Fractional Anisotropy (FA) and Mean Diffusivity (MD) maps. In the DTI model, each DW image is used to calculate the gradient of water diffusion which is then represented as a tensor. FA and MD values represent the different properties of these tensors across voxels [22].

Fractional Anisotropy (FA). FA is a scalar value that measures the degree of asymmetry in a diffusion process. The value of FA lies between 0 and 1 where 0 corresponds to no anisotropy and 1 to perfectly anisotropic [12,33]. In terms

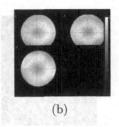

(a)   (b)

Fig. 3. (a) Rendered View, (b) Multiplanar view of corrupted scans in the original dataset

of the eigenvalues, $\lambda_1, \lambda_2, \lambda_3$, of the diffusion tensor, FA can be calculated by Eq. (1)

$$FA = \sqrt{\frac{(\lambda_1 - \lambda_2)^2 + (\lambda_2 - \lambda_3)^2 + (\lambda_3 - \lambda_3)^2)}{2(\lambda_1^2 + \lambda_2^2 + \lambda_3^2)}} \qquad (1)$$

For a perfectly isotropic diffusion $\lambda_1 = \lambda_2 = \lambda_3$ and FA = 0. With increased anisotropy, the λ values become more equal and value of FA approaches 1. Further details about calculation of the eigenvalues and eigenvectors can be found in [33], and [22].

Mean Diffusivity (MD). Trace is the sum of diffusivity along the three principal Cartesian axes and MD is average along the three axes and hence equal to trace divided by 3 (Eq. (2)) [12,25].

$$MD = \frac{\lambda_1 + \lambda_2 + \lambda_3}{3} \qquad (2)$$

FA and MD have been accurately used to identify the White Matter integrity of the brain tissues and have been established as two of the best DTI metrics to diagnose PD [4,27].

The *dtifit* tool provided with FSL calculates the eigenvectors, eigenvalues, Mean Diffusivity, and Fractional anisotropy by using the pre-processed Diffusion weighted data, binary brain mask, gradient directions, and bvalues. The FA and MD maps returned by the dtifit tool are shown in Fig. 4

3.4   Classification

After calculating the FA and MD maps for all the subjects, we shortlisted the following learning models for doing the classification and then compared the results for all of them.

– Support Vector Machine (SVM) - SVMs are a set of supervised learning methods that can used for efficient classification of data. SVMs classify data by estimating decision function parameters to distinguish between data points

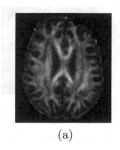 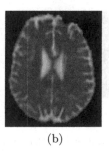

(a)   (b)

Fig. 4. Calculated (a) Fractional Anisotropy and (b) Mean Diffusivity maps

of various classes. They generally perform well for high dimensional data [31]. We used SVM with a linear kernel for MD data and a polynomial function of degree 6 for FA data.

- Stochastic Gradient Descent optimized linear SVM (SGD) - Stochastic gradient descent is a technique used for optimizing the decision functions for a learning method. Since we have only two classes, we used the SGD Classifier provided by scikit-learn which implements a regularized linear model with stochastic gradient descent learning [31]. We used squared hinge loss and l2 regularization for MD data and modified huber loss and elaticnet regularizer for FA data.
- Random Forests (RF) - RF is an ensemble classifier that uses decision trees to make prediction on the class of the input data. RF is generally not very sensitive to outlier data and are immune to overfitting [15].
- XGBoost (XGB) - XGBoost is an open source library that implements gradient boosted decision trees. It is designed to be fast and accurate and can provide better results than RF [10].

We used the *hyperopt* python library [6] to do an optimized search for the best parameters for each model. The reported results correspond to the models with the best performing parameters. Due to the small amount of data samples we did not employ any deep learning based solutions.

4   Experimental Results

As mentioned in the dataset section, we were able to obtain 139 PD and only 68 HC images. Over the years, it has been observed that such a huge mismatch in the number of samples often results in a bias towards the majority class. To prevent this bias, two popular techniques - undersampling and oversampling - are used [17]. For our dataset, we used undersampling by randomly selecting PD images in order to balance the number of subjects in each class.

After isolating the 20 test images, we created 7 different balanced training sets from the whole gamut of PD images. Random seed values were selected to ensure that same images are not repeated in two training sets. All the models were then trained and tested for each pair of dataset. To prevent overfitting we did not train any model on more than one training set.

Our input data contains a large number of features, $116 \times 116 \times 72$ points for each image. All these features might not be useful for distinguishing between the classes. Feature selection is a process in which only the most important features are selected and used for classification. Principal component analysis (PCA) is a commonly used technique for feature selection. It helps to reduce the dimensionality of data by creating new uncorrelated variables that maximize the variance of the given data [20]. To test our hypothesis, that all the input features might not be equally important, we use PCA to select a fixed number of features for each input image and used only those features for training the classification models.

We also used different cross-validation values to evaluate our models. Cross validation is a machine learning technique commonly used in cases where there is limited data available. In cross validation the data is first shuffled and then split into smaller groups. One of the groups is kept as a test set and the model is trained on the remaining. The process is repeated till all the groups have served as the test set. We tested regular as well as stratified cross-validation techniques and have reported the best parameters along with the values for evaluation metrics in Tables 1 and 2. Stratified cross validation is different from regular cross validation in the sense that while creating the subgroups, the percentage of samples for each class is preserved.

We evaluated our models for accuracy, precision and recall. Accuracy is the percent of correct predictions made by the classifier, precision reflects the ratio of number of subjects that were actually PD (and identified as PD) to the number of subjects were classified as PD and recall is ratio of the number of subjects that were identified as PD to the number of subjects that should have been identified as PD. We have also calculated and reported the F1-Score which is the harmonic mean of precision and recall.

It can be seen from the results that all the models perform well for the given data and have a good accuracy on the test dataset, with RF and XGB performing slightly better than SVM and SGD. All the models also have a high precision and recall values which further shows that the classifiers perform well on the dataset. It can also be seen that feature selection generally does not improve the results.

4.1 Comparison with Other Models

Haller S. et al. in [13] reported an accuracy of upto 97% using SVM model but we have not been able to replicate the same results using the parameters discussed in the paper. Compared to the results reported by Banerjee et al. in [5], our SVM model (for FA) performed slightly worse but we were able to obtain better results using other algorithms. Also, our dataset was more balanced and slightly bigger than the one used in [5]. We also compared, our finetuned models to the SVM models (default parameters) provided with SVM[light] [18], SVM[perf] [19], and WEKA [14]. In each of the three, our models outperformed the standard

Table 1. Test results using FA data for different models

	Cross val	Accuracy	Precision	Sensitivity (Recall)	F1 Score	Num of Features
SVM [13]	10	0.975	1	0.94	0.969	100
SVM [5]	–	0.76	–	0.78	–	67
SVM	3	0.70	0.83	0.50	0.625	All
SGD	0	0.70	0.64	0.90	0.750	All
RF	5	0.75	0.73	0.80	0.762	All
XGB	6	0.75	0.73	0.80	0.762	All
SVC+PCA	3	0.65	0.64	0.70	0.667	20
SGD+PCA	6[a]	0.70	0.70	0.70	0.700	8
RF+PCA	5	0.70	0.83	0.50	0.625	4
XGB+PCA	5[a]	0.75	0.73	0.80	0.762	20

[a]Stratified cross validation

Table 2. Test results using MD data for different models

	Cross val	Accuracy	Precision	Sensitivity (Recall)	F1 Score	Num of Features
SVM	3	0.70	0.67	0.80	0.727	All
SGD	6	0.70	0.67	0.80	0.727	All
RF	5	0.75	0.73	0.80	0.762	All
XGB	0	0.75	0.73	0.80	0.762	All
SVC+PCA	6[a]	0.70	0.67	0.80	0.727	12
SGD+PCA	6[a]	0.65	0.62	0.80	0.696	12
RF+PCA	6[a]	0.80	0.71	1.00	0.833	12
XGB+PCA	8[a]	0.75	0.73	0.80	0.762	16

[a]Stratified cross validation

model provided. Thus, the high accuracy reported in [13] can be deemed as an outlier and attributed to the less number of subjects and same data being used for training and testing.

The approach proposed by Sivakumar and Quinn in [35] is fundamentally different and cannot be compared with the proposed approach.

5   Limitations and Future Work

Machine Learning models tend to be "data-hungry" and it has been observed that same algorithms generally perform better when there are more data points to learn from [23,40]. The major limitation of the approach discussed is the availability of limited number of publicly DW scans. The low amount of data limits the ability of the models to classify results. Also, the architecture of the model used in the algorithm uses a flattened representation of the FA and MD maps to learn the features and classify the samples. However, the location of the voxels could contain some vital information that can help in a more accurate classification.

Further ahead lies the challenge of acquiring more data to improve the accuracies of the models. The input data contain a large number of features $(116 \times 116 \times 72)$ and we tried an automated feature selection using PCA but in future investigation into more feature selection algorithms will be helpful in improving the results.

6 Conclusions

We developed and tested various different models for classification of DTI data to determine patients who might be suffering from PD. DTI has been established as a good potential biomarker for diagonising PD and our results show that an automated classification of the scan is also possible. Our classification models have good accuracies and high values for precision and recall. The results are promising and with acquisition of more data, they can be improved further and made potentially clinically applicable.

References

1. NIfTI: Neuroimaging informatics technology initiative. https://nifti.nimh.nih.gov/. Accessed 30 Sept 2019
2. Andersson, J.L., Sotiropoulos, S.N.: Non-parametric representation and prediction of single-and multi-shell diffusion-weighted MRI data using gaussian processes. Neuroimage **122**, 166–176 (2015)
3. Andersson, J.L., Sotiropoulos, S.N.: An integrated approach to correction for off-resonance effects and subject movement in diffusion MR imaging. Neuroimage **125**, 1063–1078 (2016)
4. Atkinson-Clement, C., Pinto, S., Eusebio, A., Coulon, O.: Diffusion tensor imaging in Parkinson's disease: review and meta-analysis. NeuroImage Clin. **16**, 98–110 (2017)
5. Banerjee, M., Okun, M.S., Vaillancourt, D.E., Vemuri, B.C.: A method for automated classification of Parkinson's disease diagnosis using an ensemble average propagator template brain map estimated from diffusion MRI. PloS One **11**(6), e0155764 (2016)
6. Bergstra, J., Yamins, D., Cox, D.D.: Making a science of model search: hyperparameter optimization in hundreds of dimensions for vision architectures (2013)
7. Bodammer, N., Kaufmann, J., Kanowski, M., Tempelmann, C.: Eddy current correction in diffusion-weighted imaging using pairs of images acquired with opposite diffusion gradient polarity. Magn. Reson. Med.: Off. J. Int. Soc. Magn. Reson. Med. **51**(1), 188–193 (2004)
8. Bopp, M.H., Zöllner, R., Jansen, A., Dietsche, B., Krug, A., Kircher, T.T.: White matter integrity and symptom dimensions of schizophrenia: a diffusion tensor imaging study. Schizophrenia Res. **184**, 59–68 (2017)
9. for Brain Imaging MC: MRIcroGL. https://www.mccauslandcenter.sc.edu/mricrogl/home. Accessed 30 Sept 2019
10. Chen, T., Guestrin, C.: Xgboost: a scalable tree boosting system. In: Proceedings of the 22nd ACM SIGKDD International Conference on Knowledge Discovery and Data Mining, pp. 785–794. ACM (2016)

11. Du, G., et al.: Imaging nigral pathology and clinical progression in Parkinson's disease. Mov. Disorders **27**(13), 1636–1643 (2012)
12. Elster, A.D.: DTI. http://mriquestions.com/dti-tensor-imaging.html. Accessed 30 Sept 2019
13. Haller, S., Badoud, S., Nguyen, D., Garibotto, V., Lovblad, K., Burkhard, P.: Individual detection of patients with Parkinson disease using support vector machine analysis of diffusion tensor imaging data: initial results. Am. J. Neuroradiol. **33**(11), 2123–2128 (2012)
14. Holmes, G., Donkin, A., Witten, I.H.: Weka: a machine learning workbench (1994)
15. Horning, N.: Introduction to decision trees and random forests. Am. Mus. Nat. Hist **2**, 1–27 (2013)
16. Jankovic, J.: Parkinson's disease: clinical features and diagnosis. J. Neurol. Neurosurg. Psychiatry **79**(4), 368–376 (2008)
17. Japkowicz, N., Stephen, S.: The class imbalance problem: a systematic study. Intell. Data Anal. **6**(5), 429–449 (2002)
18. Joachims, T.: Making large-scale SVM learning practical. Advances in Kernel methods-support vector learning (1999). http://svmlight.joachims.org/
19. Joachims, T.: Training linear SVMs in linear time. In: Proceedings of the 12th ACM SIGKDD International Conference on Knowledge Discovery and Data Mining, pp. 217–226. ACM (2006)
20. Jolliffe, I.T., Cadima, J.: Principal component analysis: a review and recent developments. Philos. Trans. R. Soc.: Math. Phys. Eng. Sci. **374**(2065), 20150202 (2016)
21. Kim, H.J., et al.: Alterations of mean diffusivity in brain white matter and deep gray matter in Parkinson's disease. Neurosci. Lett. **550**, 64–68 (2013)
22. Kingsley, P.B.: Introduction to diffusion tensor imaging mathematics: part i. Tensors, rotations, and eigenvectors. Concepts Magn. Reson. Part A **28**(2), 101–122 (2006)
23. Klein, G.: Blinded by data (2016). https://www.edge.org/response-detail/26692. Accessed: 30 Sept 2019
24. Knossalla, F., et al.: High-resolution diffusion tensor-imaging indicates asymmetric microstructural disorganization within substantia nigra in early Parkinson's disease. J. Clin. Neurosci. **50**, 199–202 (2018)
25. Larvie, M., Fischl, B.: Volumetric and fiber-tracing MRI methods for gray and white matter. In: Handbook of Clinical Neurology, vol. 135, pp. 39–60. Elsevier (2016)
26. Li, X., Morgan, P.S., Ashburner, J., Smith, J., Rorden, C.: The first step for neuroimaging data analysis: DICOM to NIfTI conversion. J. Neurosci. Methods **264**, 47–56 (2016)
27. Liu, L., et al.: Detecting dopaminergic neuronal degeneration using diffusion tensor imaging in a rotenone-induced rat model of Parkinson's disease: fractional anisotropy and mean diffusivity values. Neural Regener. Res. **12**(9), 1485 (2017)
28. Marek, K., et al.: The Parkinson progression marker initiative (PPMI). Progr. Neurobiol. **95**(4), 629–635 (2011)
29. Digital Imaging and Communications in Medicine (DICOM) Standard: Standard, National Electrical Manufacturers Association, Rosslyn, VA, USA (2019). available free at http://medical.nema.org/
30. Papadakis, N.G., Xing, D., Huang, C.L.H., Hall, L.D., Carpenter, T.A.: A comparative study of acquisition schemes for diffusion tensor imaging using MRI. J. Magn. Reson. **137**(1), 67–82 (1999)
31. Pedregosa, F., et al.: Scikit-learn: machine learning in Python. J. Mach. Learn. Res. **12**, 2825–2830 (2011)

32. Prodoehl, J., et al.: Diffusion tensor imaging of Parkinson's disease, a typical parkinsonism, and essential tremor. Mov. Disorders, **28**(13), 1816–1822 (2013). https://doi.org/10.1002/mds.25491. https://onlinelibrary.wiley.com/doi/abs/10.1002/mds.25491

33. Rajagopalan, V., et al.: A basic introduction to diffusion tensor imaging mathematics and image processing steps. Brain Disord. Ther. **6**(229), 2 (2017)

34. Schwarz, S.T., Afzal, M., Morgan, P.S., Bajaj, N., Gowland, P.A., Auer, D.P.: The 'swallow tail' appearance of the healthy nigrosome-a new accurate test of Parkinson's disease: a case-control and retrospective cross-sectional MRI study at 3T. PloS One **9**(4), e93814 (2014)

35. Sivakumar, R., Quinn, S.: Parkinson's classification and feature extraction from diffusion tensor images (2019)

36. Smith, S.M.: Fast robust automated brain extraction. Human Brain Mapp. **17**(3), 143–155 (2002)

37. Soares, J., Marques, P., Alves, V., Sousa, N.: A Hitchhiker's guide to diffusion tensor imaging. Front. Neurosci. **7**, 31 (2013)

38. Tu, M.C., et al.: Effectiveness of diffusion tensor imaging in differentiating early-stage subcortical ischemic vascular disease, Alzheimer's disease and normal ageing. PloS One **12**(4), e0175143 (2017)

39. Vaillancourt, D., et al.: High-resolution diffusion tensor imaging in the substantia nigra of de novo Parkinson disease. Neurology **72**(16), 1378–1384 (2009)

40. Wissner-Gross, A.: Datasets over algorithms (2016). https://www.edge.org/response-detail/26587. Accessed 30 Sept 2019

Nonlocal Adaptive Biharmonic Regularizer for Image Restoration

Ying Wen[1]([⊠])(iD) and Luminita A. Vese[2]([⊠])(iD)

[1] School of Mathematics, Harbin Institute of Technology, Harbin, China
wenyinghitmath@gmail.com
[2] Department of Mathematics, University of California, Los Angeles, CA, USA
lvese@math.ucla.edu

Abstract. In this paper, we propose a nonlocal adaptive biharmonic regularization term for image denoising and restoration, combining the advantages of fourth order models (without the staircase effect while preserving slopes) and nonlocal methods (preserving texture). For its numerical solution, we employ the L^2 gradient descent and finite difference methods to design explicit, semi-implicit, and implicit schemes. Numerical results for denoising and restoration are shown on synthetic images, real images, and texture images. Comparisons with local fourth order regularizer and the nonlocal total variation are made, which help illustrate the advantages of the proposed model.

Keywords: Nonlocal method · Fourth order · Image restoration

1 Introduction

Image denoising and restoration (denoising-deblurring) has always been an essential and challenging task in the fields of image processing and computer vision. In this paper, we propose a nonlocal higher order model to denoise and deblur images corrupted by Gaussian noise. Until now, there is a variety of methods developed to deal with denoising and restoration problems in the variational setting. Rudin, Osher, and Fatemi proposed the total variation regularization [1] which is remarkably effective at simultaneously preserving edges whilst smoothing away noise in flat regions, and it is widely applied to various research fields of computer vision. Perona and Malik proposed a partial differential equation based model for image denoising [2] which consists of a forward-backward diffusion process controlled by a diffusion coefficient to smooth noise and preserve edges. To overcome the staircase effect of second order partial differential equation methods, fourth order equations for image denoising have been employed. We mention the earlier work of Chambolle and Lions [3], of Chan, Marquina, and Mulet [4], of You and Kaveh [5], of Lysaker et al. [6], and of Hajiaboli [7]. These models can better preserve smooth regions and ramps, thus diminishing the staircase effect. These image denoising and restoration methods are based on local image operators. However, texture is nonlocal in nature and requires

© Springer Nature Switzerland AG 2020
G. Bebis et al. (Eds.): ISVC 2020, LNCS 12510, pp. 670–681, 2020.
https://doi.org/10.1007/978-3-030-64559-5_53

nonlocal information for efficient noise removal and image restoration. Following the nonlocal means filter of Buades, Coll, and Morel [8], Gilboa and Osher proposed the nonlocal total variation regularization for image processing [9]. Their work utilized the nonlocal gradient and Laplacian to formulate variational-based methods for image denoising, inpainting, anomaly detection, and image-texture separation. In the work of Lou et al [10], the authors have extended the nonlocal total variation model to image restoration (simultaneous denoising and deblurring). Other second-order nonlocal methods for image restoration have been proposed in [11].

Here we propose a nonlocal fourth order model for image denoising and restoration. The model can be seen as a nonlocal version of the biharmonic operator. Also, two versions are considered, an isotropic and an anisotropic one. In the anisotropic case, an adaptive coefficient is used, depending on the input image, that helps preserve edges while smoothing out homogeneous regions. In terms of the numerical implementation, three finite difference schemes, explicit, semi-implicit, and implicit are investigated. Experiments of denoising and restoration of synthetic, natural, and texture images show the effectiveness of our model.

1.1   Local Fourth Order Models

We recall several local fourth order models previously introduced in [5, 6, 12]. Let $\Omega \subset \mathbb{R}^2$ be the image domain, $f : \Omega \to \mathbb{R}$ the given noisy image, and $u : \Omega \to \mathbb{R}$ the restored image.

The You-Kaveh regularizer [5] is

$$E^{YK}(u) = \int_\Omega g(|\Delta u|)\mathrm{d}x,$$

where the authors require $g(\cdot) \geq 0$, $g'(\cdot) > 0$, and its corresponding time-dependent Euler-Lagrange equation is

$$\frac{\partial u}{\partial t} = -\Delta(g'(|\Delta u|)\frac{\Delta u}{|\Delta u|}) = -\Delta(c(|\Delta u|)\Delta u).$$

Usually, set $c(\cdot) = \frac{1}{1+(\cdot/k)^2} = g'(\cdot)$ and k is a modulatory parameter, which is the edge-preserving function from [2] (the independent variable being now $|\Delta u|$ instead of $|\nabla u|$).

The Lysaker-Lundervold-Tai (LLT) regularizer [6] minimizes the total variation norm of $|\nabla u|$, and it is

$$E^{LLT}(u) = \int_\Omega (|u_{x_1 x_1}| + |u_{x_2 x_2}|)\mathrm{d}x.$$

Based on the LLT model, Wen et al. [12] proposed an adaptive LLT regularizer (ALLT) to better preserve structures in images. The ALLT fourth-order model is the time-dependent gradient descent of the energy

$$E^{ALLT}(u) = \int_\Omega \alpha(f)(|u_{x_1 x_1}| + |u_{x_2 x_2}|)\mathrm{d}x,$$

where $\alpha(f) = \frac{1}{1+(\nabla f_\sigma/k)^2}$ is a feature detection function based on the gradient of the noisy image, and $f_\sigma = G_\sigma * f$, with $G_\sigma = \frac{1}{2\pi\sigma^2}e^{-\frac{\|x\|^2}{2\sigma^2}}$. From [7] and [12], gradient-based edge detector is more effective than second order derivative based.

These fourth order models encourage piecewise planar solutions [5,12]. Thus, these models can preserve edges without the staircase effect.

1.2   Nonlocal Total Variation (NLTV)

Nonlocal methods are well adapted to texture preserving and denoising. Referred to [9], we first review nonlocal differential operators. The nonlocal gradient vector $\nabla_w u(x) : \Omega \to \Omega \times \Omega$, is defined by

$$(\nabla_{NL}u)(x,y) := (u(y) - u(x))\sqrt{w(x,y)},$$

where $w : \Omega \times \Omega \to \mathbb{R}$ is a nonnegative and symmetric weight function, such as $w(x,y) = \exp\left\{-\frac{G_\sigma * (\|u(x+\cdot)-u(y+\cdot)\|^2)(0)}{2h^2}\right\}$. And the magnitude of nonlocal gradient at $x \in \Omega$ is

$$|\nabla_{NL}u|(x) = \sqrt{\int_\Omega (u(y) - u(x))^2 w(x,y)dy}.$$

The nonlocal divergence $\text{div}_{NL}v : \Omega \times \Omega \to \Omega$ of the vector $v : \Omega \times \Omega \to \mathbb{R}$ is defined as the adjoint of the nonlocal gradient

$$(\text{div}_{NL}v)(x) := \int_\Omega (v(x,y) - v(y,x))\sqrt{w(x,y)}dy.$$

The nonlocal Laplacian $\Delta_{NL}u : \Omega \to \mathbb{R}$ of u can be defined by

$$\Delta_{NL}u(x) := \frac{1}{2}\text{div}_{NL}(\nabla_{NL}u(x)) = \int_\Omega (u(y) - u(x))w(x,y)dy.$$

Based on the above nonlocal operators, the NLTV regularization [9] is,

$$\min_u E^{NLTV}(u) = \int_\Omega |\nabla_{NL}u|,$$

and the associated time-dependent Euler-Lagrange equation is

$$\frac{\partial u}{\partial t} = \int_\Omega (u(y) - u(x))w(x,y)\left(\frac{1}{|\nabla_{NL}u(x)|} - \frac{1}{|\nabla_{NL}u(y)|}\right)dy,$$

which can also be expressed as

$$\frac{\partial u}{\partial t} = \text{div}_{NL}\left(\frac{\nabla_{NL}u}{|\nabla_{NL}u|}\right).$$

2   The Proposed Model

Inspired by the local fourth order models and the nonlocal gradient and Laplacian, we propose the following nonlocal second order functional for image restoration,

$$\inf_u E(u) = \int_\Omega \alpha_{NL}(f)|\Delta_{NL}u|^2 \mathrm{d}x + \frac{\lambda}{2}\int_\Omega (f - Ku)^2 \mathrm{d}x, \tag{1}$$

where $|\Delta_{NL}u(x)| = |\int_\Omega (u(y)-u(x))w(x,y)\mathrm{d}y|$, $\alpha_{NL}(f)$ is an adaptive coefficient function to distinguish edges and smooth areas and thus will adaptively guide the image restoration process. The first term in (1) is the regularization term, while the second term is the usual data fidelity term; $K : L^2(\Omega) \rightarrow L^2(\Omega)$ models the blur kernel which is a linear and continuous operator, $\Omega \subset \mathbb{R}^2$ is the image domain, $f \in L^2(\Omega)$ is the given noisy-blurry image, and $\lambda > 0$ is a coefficient that balances the regularization and data fidelity terms.

The corresponding Euler-Lagrange equation associated with (1), in a time-dependent fashion, is

$$\frac{\partial u}{\partial t} = -\Delta_{NL}(\alpha_{NL}(f)\Delta_{NL}u) + \lambda K^*(f - Ku). \tag{2}$$

In the following, two choices of $\alpha_{NL}(f)$ are given.

The first one is $\alpha_{NL}(f) = 1$. The model (1) is isotropic, and the regularization term becomes a nonlocal biharmonic model. Fourth order linear diffusion damps oscillations at high frequencies much faster than second-order diffusion [13]. At the same time, different from second order based methods, fourth order methods can efficiently overcome the staircase effect, while preserving slopes and creases in the image.

The second one is

$$\alpha_{NL}(f) = \frac{1}{1 + |\nabla_{NL}f_\sigma|^2/k^2}, \tag{3}$$

where k is a modulatory parameter, and as before, $f_\sigma = G_\sigma * f$ is a smoothed version of f. Using (3), model (1) becomes anisotropic, and $\alpha_{NL}(f)$ provides a guidance for the degree of diffusion. We use f_σ to first roughly removing the noise, and then utilize the nonlocal gradient $\nabla_{NL}f_\sigma$ as an edge detector. Thus, $\alpha_{NL}(f)$ has the ability of distinguishing edges and smooth areas of the original image. From the coefficient (3), $\alpha_{NL}(f) \in [0,1]$. On or near edges, $|\nabla_{NL}f_\sigma|$ is large and thus $\alpha_{NL}(f)$ is small approaching 0. On the contrary, on flat areas or away from edges, $|\nabla_{NL}f_\sigma|$ is small and $\alpha_{NL}(f)$ is large approaching 1. Using this coefficient (3) in the proposed high order functional (1), we have that $\alpha_{NL}(f)$ induces less diffusion when $|\nabla_{NL}f_\sigma|$ is large for preserving structures, and bigger diffusion when $|\nabla_{NL}f_\sigma|$ is small for smoothing out the noise.

Most of local fourth-order image restoration models use the second order derivatives (Laplace operator) to define the edge-preserving function to distinguish edges from homogeneous regions. Following [7] and [12], compared with the Laplace operator, the gradient operator has a better edge detection capability. It is the same in nonlocal situations, and that is why we employ the nonlocal gradient for designing the adaptive coefficient function α (and not the nonlocal Laplacian). In the following, we give a group of simulation experiments to verify the above phenomenon.

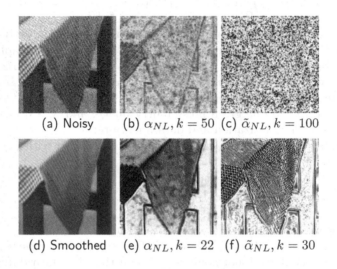

(a) Noisy   (b) $\alpha_{NL}, k = 50$ (c) $\tilde{\alpha}_{NL}, k = 100$

(d) Smoothed   (e) $\alpha_{NL}, k = 22$ (f) $\tilde{\alpha}_{NL}, k = 30$

Fig. 1. Comparison of the edge detection ability of nonlocal gradient and nonlocal Laplace operator. (a) an noisy image, (b) α_{NL} for image (a) with $k = 50$, (c) $\tilde{\alpha}_{NL}$ for image (a) with $k = 100$, (d) a smoothed image, (e) α_{NL} for image (d) with $k = 22$, (f) $\tilde{\alpha}_{NL}$ for image (d) with $k = 30$.

Define the nonlocal Laplace operator based adaptive function by

$$\tilde{\alpha}_{NL}(f) = \frac{1}{1 + |\Delta_{NL} f_\sigma|^2 / k^2}. \tag{4}$$

For a fair comparison, the parameter k for both (3) and (4) is turned to best show the edges. First, we start with a noisy image f, and use (3) and (4) to distinguish edges and homogeneous areas. In Fig. 1a, we show the noisy image. Correspondingly, Fig. 1b and Fig. 1c display the map of gradient-based and Laplace-based function, respectively. However, from Fig. 1c we can not find the roughly sharp edges of Fig. 1a. Thus, as in the case of the local Laplace operator, the nonlocal Laplace operator cannot detect edges for images with a lot of noise. Second, there is another group of experiment in the second row of Fig. 1. Different from the first row, we replace f_σ with a smooth and cleaner image in (3) and (4). The edge maps of (3) and (4) are shown in Fig. 1e and Fig. 1f, respectively. At the thick sharp edges, α_{NL} shows dark lines. On the contrary, as expected, $\tilde{\alpha}_{NL}$ shows two light lines at the boundary of edges. It verifies the bilateral effect of the nonlocal Laplace operator, which is the same as when using the local version. Also, the nonlocal Laplace based edge detector has a larger reaction of crease points (such as the table leg of Fig. 1f). Thus, the nonlocal gradient based function is more suitable for distinguishing edges and homogeneous areas.

3   Numerical Implementation

To numerically solve the proposed model (1), we design three different finite difference schemes. Before introducing these three schemes, we first give some notations.

Let u_i^n denote the value of a pixel i in the image ($1 \leq i \leq N$) with time level n, the time step is τ, $t = n\tau$, $n = 0, 1, ...$, and let $w_{i,j}$ be the sparsely discrete version of $w = w(x, y) : \Omega \times \Omega \to \mathbb{R}$. We use the neighbors set $j \in N_i$ defined by $j \in N_i := \{j : w_{i,j} > 0\}$. Then, as in [9], the discretizations of the nonlocal gradient $\nabla_{NLd}(u_i)$ and nonlocal Laplacian $\Delta_{NLd}(u_i)$ are

$$\nabla_{NLd}(u_i) := (u_j - u_i)\sqrt{w_{i,j}}, \quad j \in N_i,$$
$$\Delta_{NLd}(u_i) := \sum_{j \in N_i} (u_j - u_i)w_{i,j},$$

and the magnitude of the discrete nonlocal gradient is

$$|\nabla_{NLd}(u_i)| := \sqrt{\sum_{j \in N_i} (u_j - u_i)^2 w_{i,j}}. \tag{5}$$

We construct the weight function $w_{i,j}$ following the algorithm in [9,11].

Explicit Scheme. We first give the finite difference explicit scheme, as follows,

$$\frac{u_i^{n+1} - u_i^n}{\tau} = -\Delta_{NLd}(\alpha_{NL}(f_i)\Delta_{NLd}(u_i^n)) + K^*(f_i - Ku_i^n). \tag{6}$$

Implicit Scheme. The implicit scheme is

$$\frac{u_i^{n+1} - u_i^n}{\tau} = -\Delta_{NLd}(\alpha_{NL}(f_i)\Delta_{NLd}(u_i^{n+1})) + K^*(f_i - Ku_i^n). \tag{7}$$

Semi-implicit Scheme. For the semi-implicit scheme, we first expand the proposed fourth order regularizer as

$$-\Delta_{NL}(\alpha_{NL}(f)\Delta_{NL}u) = -\int_\Omega (\alpha_{NL}(f)(y)\Delta_{NL}u(y) - \alpha_{NL}(f)(x)\Delta_{NL}u(x))\, w(x,y)\mathrm{d}y,$$

where $\Delta_{NL}u(y) = \int_{\Omega}(u(z) - u(y))w(y,z)\mathrm{d}z$ and $\Delta_{NL}u(x) = \int_{\Omega}(u(z') - u(x))w(x,z')\mathrm{d}z'$. Thus, the regularization term equals to

$$-\int_{\Omega} \alpha_{NL}(f)(y) \cdot \int_{\Omega}(u(z) - u(y))w(y,z)\mathrm{d}z \cdot w(x,y)\mathrm{d}y$$

$$+\int_{\Omega} \alpha_{NL}(f)(x) \cdot \int_{\Omega} u(z')w(x,z')\mathrm{d}z' \cdot w(x,y)\mathrm{d}y$$

$$-\alpha_{NL}(f)(x) \cdot u(x) \int_{\Omega}\int_{\Omega} w(x,z')\mathrm{d}z' \cdot w(x,y)\mathrm{d}y.$$

Notice, the u in the last term of the above formula is independent of the integration, and we discretize it in the $n+1$ level. Therefore, the semi-implicit scheme is,

$$\frac{u_i^{n+1} - u_i^n}{\tau} + \alpha_{NL}(f_i) \cdot u_i^{n+1} \sum_{j \in N_j} \left(w_{i,j} \sum_{k \in N_k} w_{i,k}\right)$$

$$= -\sum_{j \in N_j} \alpha_{NL}(f_j)\Delta_{NLd}(u_j^n) + \alpha_{NL}(f_i) \sum_{j \in N_j}\sum_{k' \in N_k'} (u_{k'}^n w_{i,j} \cdot w_{i,k'}) + K^*(f_i - Ku_i^n).$$

$$(8)$$

For the explicit scheme (6) and semi-implicit scheme (8), u_i^{n+1} can be expressed explicitly. However, for the implicit scheme (7), the inverse of a very large matrix has to be calculated to solve for u_i^{n+1}.

4   Experiments

In order to quantify the denoising and restoration effect, for the original clean image u_o and its restored image u, the denoising performance is measured in terms of peak signal to noise ratio (PSNR),

$$\mathrm{PSNR} = 10\log_{10}\frac{M_1 N_1 |\mathrm{max}u_o - \mathrm{min}u_o|}{\|u - u_o\|_{L^2}^2}\mathrm{dB},$$

and mean absolute deviation error (MAE),

$$\mathrm{MAE} = \frac{\|u - u_o\|_{L^1}}{M_1 N_1},$$

where $M_1 \times N_1$ is the size of image. Besides, we also use the structural similarity (SSIM) [14].

4.1   Image Denoising

We apply our proposed model to image denoising, and thus this is when the blur kernel K is the identity. To study the performance of our method, we compare the proposed NLABH model (1) with ALLT [12] and NLTV [9]. For illustration, we test four images *synthetic, Lena, Barbara,* and *texture* (the original images are shown in Fig. 3 and Fig. 4). All the Denoising results obtained using the NLABH model are obtained using the semi-implicit scheme. The PSNR, MAE, and SSIM values of the Denoising results are listed in Table 1, where the best results are shown in boldface. Next, we report some of the numerical experiments for the original test images and the corresponding results are depicted in Fig. 3 and Fig. 4.

Table 1. Comparison of PSNR, MAE, and SSIM of the different models with Gaussian noise, and noise level $\sigma_n = 10, 20, 30$.

σ_n	PSNR			MAE			SSIM		
	10	20	30	10	20	30	10	20	30
				Synthetic					
ALLT	**43.820**	**38.548**	35.045	1.058	1.767	2.869	0.507	0.448	0.418
NLTV	42.074	36.921	35.042	0.964	1.906	2.419	**0.765**	**0.481**	**0.450**
NLABH	42.775	38.224	**35.323**	**0.824**	**1.531**	**2.273**	0.752	0.470	0.439
				Lena					
ALLT	33.611	29.892	27.953	3.748	5.506	6.820	0.744	0.630	0.552
NLTV	34.562	30.820	28.802	3.458	5.151	6.455	0.743	0.630	0.559
NLABH	**34.992**	**31.464**	**29.348**	**3.250**	**4.735**	**6.045**	**0.768**	**0.663**	**0.583**
				Barbara					
NLTV	34.371	30.377	28.575	3.633	5.648	6.863	0.724	0.601	0.521
NLABH	**35.046**	**31.729**	**29.619**	**3.359**	**4.803**	**6.164**	**0.757**	**0.661**	**0.572**
				Texture					
NLTV	**29.419**	**24.907**	22.671	**6.830**	**11.439**	14.868	0.950	0.859	0.774
NLABH	29.315	24.806	**22.689**	6.880	11.472	**14.567**	**0.951**	**0.866**	**0.792**

Figure 2 shows the energy (1) with time for two experiments, and $\lambda = 0.1$, $\tau = 0.001$. The energy values for both experiments are continuously decreasing and eventually stabilize, which illustrates the stability of our numerical scheme in practice.

For the synthetic image in first row of Fig. 3 containing smooth surfaces and sharp edges, the local fourth order model ALLT [12] can restore the smooth areas while preserve edges very well, which corresponds to the property of fourth order equations. Comparing the NLTV and NLABH, the first row of Fig. 3 and Table 1 show that NLABH can restore homogeneous regions smoothly, and the shape of edges is preserved sharply due to the adaptive function.

For the real image *Lena* (the second row of Fig. 3), the best denoised image is the one denoised by NLABH, both visually and by measurements. The NLABH model can better preserve both sharp and blunt lines in the image. Figure 4 shows denoising results of texture images (*Barbara* and *texture*). Because the local

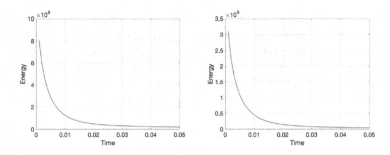

Fig. 2. Energy versus time for denoising experiments. (left) *Lena* with $\sigma_n = 20$, (right) *Barbara* with $\sigma_n = 10$.

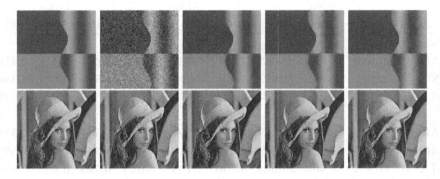

Fig. 3. Denoising results of *synthetic* and *Lena* images. The first column: (top) original image *synthetic*, (bottom) original image *Lena*. The second column: (top) noisy image for *synthetic* image, $\sigma_n = 20$, (bottom) *Lena* image, $\sigma_n = 10$. The third-fifth columns: denoised images using ALLT, NLTV, and NLABH methods.

method does not work well in textured regions, we only show the results of NLTV and NLABH. The denoised images by NLABH are smoother; simultaneously, texture and edges are preserved. Moreover, we can still see a little bit of the staircase effect in the denoised images using NLTV. From the second row of Fig. 4 (*Barbara*), compared with NLTV, NLABH can restore these blunt texture at the upper part of the tablecloth. All of these verify the effectiveness of NLABH.

4.2   Image Restoration

In this subsection, we compare the NLTV and NLABH models for image restoration. The algorithm details of NLTV for image restoration is given in [10]. As for the denoising experiments from Subsect. 4.1, we employ the semi-implicit scheme and give PSNR, MAE, and SSIM values for comparison.

Simulation experiment results are shown in Fig. 6. The corresponding comparison of PSNR, MAE, and SSIM is listed in Table 2. We show the energy (1) of time for two experiments. λ in Fig. 5 is 16 and 250 respectively, and $\tau = 0.1$. The energy values decrease with time, which shows that the algorithm for numeri-

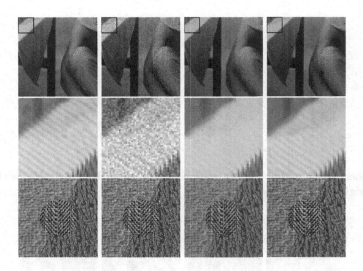

Fig. 4. Denoising results of *Barbara* and *texture* images. The first column: (top) original image *Barbara*, (middle) zoom in part of *Barbara* corresponding to the red box, (bottom) original image *texture*. The second column: (top) noisy image for *Barbara* image, $\sigma_n = 20$, (middle) zoom in part of noisy *Barbara* corresponding to the red box, (bottom) *texture* image, $\sigma_n = 30$. The third-fourth columns: denoised images using NLTV and NLABH methods.

cally solving our model ((1)) is stable in practice. From the first row of Fig. 6, we can see that the proposed NLABH model has a good performance at restoring the curved surface. Moreover, the restored images obtained using the NLABH model are cleaner than the ones obtained by the NLTV. From the second row of Fig. 6, the lines restored by NLABH are more fluent without serrated edges. At the same time, the third and fourth rows of Fig. 6 verify the effectiveness of preserving fluent lines.

Table 2. Comparison of PSNR, MAE, and SSIM of the different models with different blur and noise

	Gaussian blur σ_b	Gaussian noise σ_n	Model	PSNR	MAE	SSIM
Synthetic	2	7	NLTV	**35.023**	**1.876**	**0.858**
			NLABH	34.505	2.249	0.438
Lena	2	7	NLTV	**27.909**	6.347	0.565
			NLABH	27.897	**6.294**	**0.585**
Barbara-1	1	7	NLTV	21.211	17.263	**0.276**
			NLABH	**21.421**	**16.477**	0.266
Barbara-2	1	10	NLTV	26.048	9.075	**0.427**
			NLABH	**26.198**	**8.768**	0.420

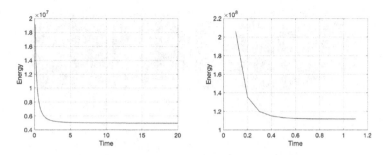

Fig. 5. Energy versus time for restoration experiments. (left) *synthetic* with $\sigma_b = 2$, $\sigma_n = 7$, (right) *Barbara-1* with $\sigma_b = 1$, $\sigma_n = 7$.

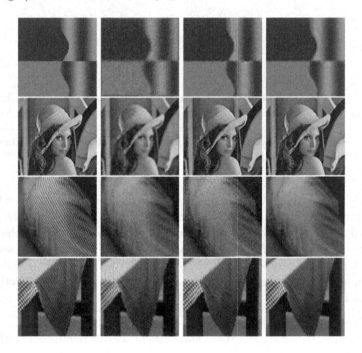

Fig. 6. Restoration results. The first column: original images *synthetic, Lena, Barbara-1*, and *Barbara-2* from top to bottom. The second column: blurry and noisy images, *synthetic*: $\sigma_b = 2$, $\sigma_n = 7$, *Lena*: $\sigma_b = 2$, $\sigma_n = 7$, *Barbara-1*: $\sigma_b = 1$, $\sigma_n = 7$, *Barbara-2*: $\sigma_b = 1$, $\sigma_n = 10$. The third-fourth columns: restored images by NLTV and NLABH.

5   Conclusion

We have proposed in this paper an anisotropic nonlocal fourth order biharmonic model for image denoising and restoration. We have discretized the model using finite difference schemes that are stable in practice. We have presented numerous experimental results on synthetic and real images that show the advantages of the proposed model, by comparison with local fourth order models and nonlocal second order models. We have also shown through experiments that the nonlocal gradient is better suited for edge detection than the nonlocal Laplacian. Future work will provide further analysis of the model and investigate other applications.

References

1. Rudin, L.I., Osher, S., Fatemi, E.: Nonlinear total variation based noise removal algorithms. Physica D: Nonlinear Phenom. **60**(1–4), 259–268 (1992)
2. Perona, P., Malik, J.: Scale-space and edge detection using anisotropic diffusion. IEEE Trans. Pattern Anal. Mach. Intell. **12**(7), 629–639 (1990)
3. Chambolle, A., Lions, P.-L.: Image recovery via total variation minimization and related problems. Numer. Math. **76**(2), 167–188 (1997)
4. Chan, T., Marquina, A., Mulet, P.: High-order total variation-based image restoration. SIAM J. Sci. Comput. **22**(2), 503–516 (2000)
5. You, Y.-L., Kaveh, M.: Fourth-order partial differential equations for noise removal. IEEE Trans. Image Process. **9**(10), 1723–1730 (2000)
6. Lysaker, M., Lundervold, A., Tai, X.-C.: Noise removal using fourth-order partial differential equation with applications to medical magnetic resonance images in space and time. IEEE Trans. Image Process. **12**(12), 1579–1590 (2003)
7. Hajiaboli, M.R.: A self-governing hybrid model for noise removal. In: Wada, T., Huang, F., Lin, S. (eds.) PSIVT 2009. LNCS, vol. 5414, pp. 295–305. Springer, Heidelberg (2009). https://doi.org/10.1007/978-3-540-92957-4_26
8. Buades, A., Coll, B., Morel, J.-M.: A non-local algorithm for image denoising. In: 2005 IEEE Computer Society Conference on Computer Vision and Pattern Recognition (CVPR 2005), vol. 2, ppp. 60–65. IEEE (2005)
9. Gilboa, G., Osher, S.: Nonlocal operators with applications to image processing. Multiscale Model. Simul. **7**(3), 1005–1028 (2009)
10. Lou, Y., Zhang, X., Osher, S., Bertozzi, A.: Image recovery via nonlocal operators. J. Sci. Comput. **42**(2), 185–197 (2010)
11. Jung, M., Bresson, X., Chan, T.F., Vese, L.A.: Nonlocal Mumford-Shah regularizers for color image restoration. IEEE Trans. Image Process. **20**(6), 1583–1598 (2010)
12. Wen, Y., Sun, J., Guo, Z.: A new anisotropic fourth-order diffusion equation model based on image feature for image denoising. CAM report (2020)
13. Bertozzi, A.L., Greer, J.B.: Low-curvature image simplifiers: global regularity of smooth solutions and laplacian limiting schemes. Commun. Pure Appl. Math.: J. Issued Courant Inst. Math. Sci. **57**(6), 764–790 (2004)
14. Wang, Z., Bovik, A.C., Sheikh, H.R., Simoncelli, E.P.: Image quality assessment: from error visibility to structural similarity. IEEE Trans. Image Process. **13**(4), 600–612 (2004)

A Robust Approach to Plagiarism Detection in Handwritten Documents

Om Pandey$^{(\boxtimes)}$, Ishan Gupta, and Bhabani S. P. Mishra

Kalinga Institute of Industrial Technology, Bhubaneswar, Odisha, India
opandey108@gmail.com

Abstract. Plagiarism detection is a widely used technique to uniquely identify quality of work. We address in this paper, the problem of predicting similarities amongst a collection of documents. This technique has widespread uses in academic institutions. In this paper, we propose a simple yet effective method for detection of plagiarism by using a robust word detection and segmentation procedure followed by a convolution neural network (CNN)—Bi-directional Long Short Term Memory (biLSTM) pipeline to extract the text. Our approach also extract and encodes common patterns like scratches in handwriting for improving accuracy on real-world use cases. The extracted information from multiple documents using comparison metrics are used to find the documents which have been plagiarized from a source. Extensive experiments in our research show that this approach may help simplify the examining process and can act as a cheap viable alternative to many modern approaches used to detect plagiarism from handwritten documents.

Keywords: Document matching · Deep learning · Fraud detection · Information retrieval

1 Introduction

The dilemma of plagiarism is increasing rapidly due to an exponential rise in the number of academic institutions around the world to cater to the needs of an ever-increasing population. However, with fewer measures having been kept in place to check the quality of education, we are witnessing hordes of incompetent new graduates who lack the required skills, saturating the already sluggish pool of new job opportunities. This can be avoided at the grass root level by keeping in check, the everyday assignments, and exams, penalizing students for misconduct. The most traditional method to eradicate plagiarism historically is the detection software [1]. Initially many attempts were made for handwritten text matching using HMM [2] and DTW [3]. These model could not be made scalable, which lead to development of newer approaches [4], using advanced techniques like Fischer vectors and semantic indexing to enhance performance. Plagiarism detection using text extraction is a well-known problem in text-processing [5], this, using image matching is also applied to electronic documents [6]. But, these techniques cannot be directly applied to scanned handwritten documents. There have been various

© Springer Nature Switzerland AG 2020
G. Bebis et al. (Eds.): ISVC 2020, LNCS 12510, pp. 682–693, 2020.
https://doi.org/10.1007/978-3-030-64559-5_54

techniques that use geometry or matching key points to detect plagiarism for printed documents [7]. But, due to the high amount of variance in spacing, complex writing style of multiple authors and non-rigidity or conformation to specific style plagiarism detection in handwritten documents have mostly been unsuccessful. Some progress has been made in this field using the effectiveness of CNNs for direct comparison between image patches [8], but the drawback of this approach is that it is a black-box model which can easily be fooled by pixel-pruning. Also, it uses image pairs for comparison which may inappropriately match documents, in case two image patches look similar. Another common feature in handwritten-text recognition that has not been mentioned in literature, is the utilization of contextual information like scratches, cuts and marks. These can act as essential features which can exponentially boost accuracy of prediction.

To our knowledge, this is the first plagiarism detection approach that jointly utilizes not only the semantic and contextual information but also penalizes over patterns in handwritten mistakes for increasing accuracy of the model. By the means of this paper, we tend to propose an efficient, computationally cost-effective and robust plagiarism detection pipeline.

2 Methodology

Various conventional CNNs have been proposed in literature for handwritten text recognition, like [9, 10]. Though, more recently, highly complex, and effective architectures for OCR like [24, 26] have provided a significant boost to the accuracy. But, they are huge in terms of network size and require high amount of computation and training. Some techniques including [23, 27] have also proposed the concept of n-grams to add subjective contextual information to the network. We saw, however, that only a few of these techniques have been revamped for use in other avenues and only theoretically propose plagiarism detection [11]. Almost none of them have discussed handwritten plagiarism detection as a practical use case. Another major drawback is that they do not utilize many salient features like cuts, marks, scratches, etc., which along with positional encoding can add significant information for identifying plagiarism. These features are especially useful in real-world scenarios where such behavior is common in writing. To train and validate our approach on such scenarios we have used created a synthetic ES-700 dataset. Our goal here is to design a technique that is context neutral and feasible for daily use.

2.1 Overview

Our proposed methodology, as illustrated in Fig. 1, can be viewed as a two-part pipelined architecture. Firstly, we extract information from an image using system of detection and segmentation networks (object detectors) that proposes image patches, followed by a CNN-biLSTM for word extraction from the proposed image patches. We use multiple phases of training for each part of the network individually, this helps in efficient text extraction and maximizes the information gain from the document, which would help in fabricating new features. We use SOTA natural language processing techniques even after text extraction to get best possible, most likely word predictions that are fed to multiple comparison metrics for identification of plagiarism.

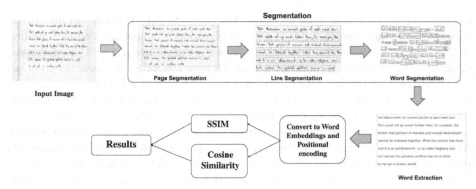

Fig. 1. Overview of proposed system architecture for plagiarism detection

2.2 Extraction and Segmentation Network

For the first phase, as shown in Fig. 2, we perform extraction and segmentation on the page in real-time to extract paragraphs, followed by sentences, and then words. This task was done by training three efficient region proposal network by using the Single-Shot-Detector (SSD) technique [12]. We chose SSD over other region proposal networks based on experiments provided in [13] which show, that it provides a considerable amount of accuracy and is three times faster than other similar architectures. In the process, firstly we segment a paragraphs from the page image. The extracted patch is fed into the sentence extractor network, to extract sentences, patches of which are iteratively fed into the word segmentation network, for word patch proposals (as shown in Fig. 1). These word patches will now be utilized for word retrieval in the next phase. This process of extraction ensured that no part of the information on the page was lost due to recklessness in extraction process. To keep in check, the number of bounding box predictions, non-max suppression was applied, and values above an arbitrary threshold of Intersection over Union (IoU) only were considered positive predictions. The networks optimize over the Mean Square Error, calculated on the IoU [14] overlap of predictions with ground-truth labels. We minimize the objective function using the standard SSD multi-task loss $l(\{p_i\}, \{t_i\})$ defined by:

$$l(\{p_i\}, \{t_i\}) = \frac{1}{N} \times \Sigma_i l_{cls}(p_i, p_i^*) + \lambda \times \frac{1}{N_{reg}} \times \Sigma_i p_i l_{reg}(t_i, t_i^*) \qquad (1)$$

where, ith indexed anchor in a mini-batch is defined by p_i, the predicted probability of it being an object. Here, t_i is a vector representing the 4 parameterized coordinates of the predicted bounding box, and t_i^* vector coordinates are that of the ground-truth box associated with a positive anchor p_i^*. Here, l_{cls} is the classification log loss. We use $l_{reg}(t_i, t_i^*) = R(t_i, t_i^*)$, for defining regression loss where R is the robust loss function as defined in [16]. The terms are being normalized by N and N_{reg} respectively, and are balancing the weight λ. Further clarification on loss function and mathematical aspects, can be found in the original papers [14, 15]. For extracting textual features from an image patch, the effectiveness of Convolutional Neural Networks has been confirmed in various previous studies [17]. Figure 3 illustrates our text extraction module. We use a pre-trained Resnet-50 architecture to act as a feature extractor. The extracted features are then fed into a Bidirectional-LSTM [18] network.

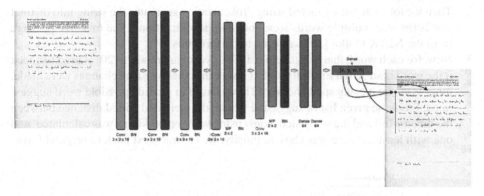

Fig. 2. Extractor network for region proposals

This network captures the relative probability of information occurring in the patch to feed into the probability matrix, for word extraction. The calculations in bidirectional LSTMs are articulated as:

$$\vec{h}_t = lstm\left(\vec{h}_{t-1}, e(w_t)\right); \vec{h}_t = lstm\left(\vec{h}_{t-1}, e(w_t)\right) \qquad (2)$$

e, in (2) is the non-linear function. The concatenation of forward $\left(\vec{h}_t^l\right)$ and back-ward $\left(\vec{h}_t^l\right)$ hidden states is taken as the representation of each word. For word w_t, the representation is denoted as:

$$h_t^l = \left[\vec{h}_t^l; \vec{h}_t^l\right] \qquad (3)$$

In Eq. (3), h_t^l is the hidden state of lth layer Bidirectional LSTM. As shown in Fig. 3, in the output of this CNN-biLSTM, the decoder is used to predict probability distribution over the characters of each word (i.e. over English alphabets used in each word) for each image patch. Also, multiple downsamples of the feature matrix extracted from CNN is done, to parallely feed multiple LSTM networks and combine the extract information. This makes the network robust to images with varying sizes.

2.3 Word Retrieval

In this phase we use multiple techniques to get the extracted text as sensible and close to original text as possible. This phase does not require training as pre-trained libraries are used. From the probability matrix obtained, the greedy search approach iterates over each time-step t to obtain the most probable character at each time step. This output (words) is utilized by a lexicon search model which attempts to match each word with a dictionary. Precisely, this phase was broken into 3 key parts:

1. Firstly, the characters are extracted and we decontract the string. (Contractions are shorted versions of a word or a spoken form of a word. For example, did not → didn't, might have → might've).
2. Then we tokenize the extracted string. Tokenization separates the string into distinct words (in case multiple words were found in decontraction). The tokenize package from the NLTK toolkit [19] was used to perform this.
3. Now, for each word, that was tokenized. The pyenchant module [20] is used to check if the word is an actual English word. If it was an actual word, no changes were made, otherwise, the Norvig spell checker [21] was used to provide possible word suggestions. From the given list of suggested words, the weighted edited distance between the given word and the suggested words using word embeddings was calculated, and one with least distance was chosen. Finally, we contract text back to original form.

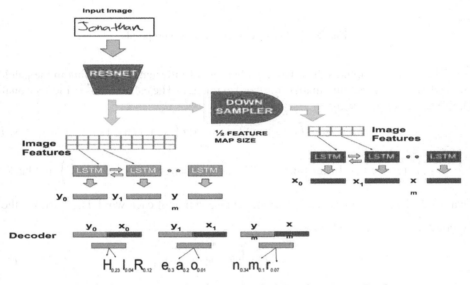

Fig. 3. Network Depiction for Retrieval of Text from Image Patches

In case, a word cannot be guessed for the extracted patch we believed it to be a scratch or a cut marks. We had trained the network to identify such gashes and cuts on paper and encode them.

2.4 Feature Extraction

Finally, the extracted corpus is vectorised and converted to word embeddings using NLTK toolkit. We used positional encoding, not only for words but also for scratched texts, marks, and cuts on the paper which are identified during word detection from extracted patches and stored as special symbols (example of extracted data in Fig. 4) to identify the hidden patterns in the way corrections were being made at similar places in documents. For example, if two people have scratched a word in the same place chances of plagiarism increase slightly. But, if they have scratched a sentence or an entire paragraph in the same place chances of plagiarism increase exponentially. This we found to be an important salient feature and form of contextual information which is generally ignored by most algorithms. This is a common feature that can be leveraged to detect plagiarism especially in handwritten text. Our model was trained to detect such marks of scratches and cuts in order to improve accuracy. These features along with the extracted contextual information, are used for comparison and are necessary to make the model more powerful and robust.

3   Experimental Setup

In this section we describe in detail the datasets used for experimentation. We also provide the experimental setting and the hyper-parameters used for reproducing obtained results and further discuss details regarding the implementation.

3.1   Datasets

We train the model in two stages, firstly on the IAM dataset [22] and then on the ES-700 dataset. Once the network was well-trained to detect words from handwritten images, for the next phase of the training i.e. to detect scratches, misspell etc. we could not find an online dataset, so we made a synthetic *ES-700* dataset.

ES-700 DATASET:
To validate the performance of the architecture on an unrestricted real-world collection, we introduce ES-700 dataset which is collected from the real examination sheets of a class as part of an active Big Data course. It contains nearly 700 handwritten pages from more than 100 students. The content in these documents have been coupled, by taking answer to the same 7 questions in each of the scripts submitted by 100 students. One image in the datasets corresponded to one answer, the contents are mostly in text or diagram format. Most of these image documents follow complex variations in line and word spacing, the layout has misalignment in lines and paragraphs, and a high degree of skewness over the content (example snapshot of dataset, Fig. 4).

3.2   Training Phases

The proposed extraction and segmentation network (triple SSD + CNN-BiLSTM) was first trained on the IAM dataset, this would first make the network robust enough for basic text extraction and recognizing basic handwritten plagiarism by document matching. But, to recognize scratched-out sentences (not words) we freeze the training on the paragraph extraction SSD and train the rest of the network on the ES-700 dataset. This replaced the scratched sentences with a symbol - "/" (example in Fig. 4). This would help us to find patterns, which along with positional encoding would penalize the algorithm in such cases. To recognize scratched-out words (not sentences) we froze training on all the paragraph and sentence extraction layer SSDs training the rest of the network again using the ES-700, this replaced the scratched out words with "*", an example of the output label is shown in Fig. 4 (right). This was the final-stage of training, this network is used to test on both IAM and ES-700 datasets and results were compared to previous approaches using various comparison metrics.

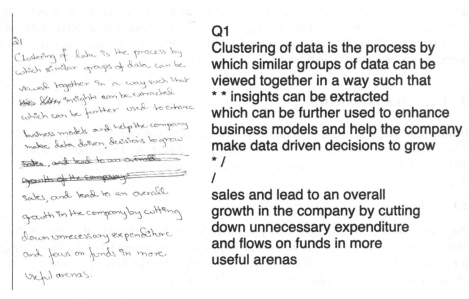

Q1
Clustering of data is the process by which similar groups of data can be viewed together in a way such that * * insights can be extracted which can be further used to enhance business models and help the company make data driven decisions to grow * /

/
sales and lead to an overall growth in the company by cutting down unnecessary expenditure and flows on funds in more useful arenas

Fig. 4. Example snapshot of dataset (left); Corresponding output label (right)

3.3 Implementation Details

The entire code was written in Python 3.5 and aided by MXnet gluon. For sequence to sequence learning, we used a Transformer Encoder-Decoder network as the Bi-LSTM. For calculation of error, a word suggestor gives the word and character error rates using SCTK, the NIST scoring toolkit. We tune the hyper-parameters on the validation set using the micro-F1 score as evaluation metric. The vocabulary size is $\approx$50,000 and the batch size is 32. We set the embedding size to 512. Encoder and Decoder are 2-layer Bidirectional-LSTMs with the hidden size 2048 and 512 respectively. We "pre-train" the model for 30 epochs via the MLE method. Mean Square Error was used as the loss function and the optimizer is Adam [30] with a 0.003 learning rate for pre-training and 0.005 for training. Besides, we use dropout [31] to avoid overfitting and clip the gradients to the maximum norm of 5. Final evaluation was done through SSIM and Cosine similarity for word embedding as it shows better results than other evaluation metrics such as Euclidean distance. Another common metric for plagiarism detection is sum of word matches (SWM) [8], which we do not use as it deals with word distributions, which can be realized by cosine similarity while comparing word-embeddings.

3.4 Evaluation Metrics

In order to find which of the documents were copied, multiple similarity metrics were used in order to compare the documents. We use the SpaCy [30] module—en_core_web_lg because it comes with a word embedding model. Word embeddings were obtained using the Word2Vec [29] for constructing vector representations of words. The vector for each word is a semantic description of how that word is used in context, so two words that are used similarly in text will get similar vector representations. This automates the process of generating word-embeddings for the obtained dictionary words. Cosine Similarity [32] is used to obtain similarity scores for each pair of documents using Natural Language Processing, the formula for cosine similarity is given by:

$$\text{Cos}(\theta) = \frac{\vec{a}.\vec{b}}{||\vec{a}||.||\vec{b}||} = \frac{\Sigma_1^n a_i b_i}{\sqrt{\Sigma_1^n a_i^2}\sqrt{\Sigma_1^n b_i^2}} \tag{4}$$

In order to calculate the similarity between two text snippets, ordinarily the way is to convert the text into its corresponding vector representation, which can be done using various methods like one-hot encoding, after which similarity or difference using different distance metrics such as cosine-similarity and Euclidean distance is calculated. We used SpaCy as the tool for text processing which comes with an inbuilt representation of text as vectors at different levels of Token, Span and Doc objects. The underlying vector representations come from a word embedding model which generally produces a dense multi-dimensional semantic representation of words. Using this vector representation, we calculate similarities and dissimilarities between tokens, named entities, noun phrases, sentences, and documents.

Structural Similarity Index (SSIM) is used to obtain similarity scores for the documents using image processing as it is most effective when used at appropriate scale depending on image resolution and viewing distance, it is a method for predicting the perceived quality of digital pictures. As the name suggests, based on structure it calculates the similarity score, as shown below:

$$\text{SSIM}(x,\ y) = \frac{(2\mu_x\mu_y + c_1)(2\sigma_{xy} + c_2)}{(\mu_x^2 + \mu_y^2 + c_1)(\sigma_x^2 + \sigma_y^2 + c_2)} \tag{5}$$

Here, x and y, denote the two images. μ_x and μ_y, denotes the average of x's and y's pixels. σ_x^2 and σ_y^2, denotes the variance of x's and y's pixels. c_1, c_2 are two variables to stabilize the division with weak denominator.

SSIM can be viewed as a quality measure of one of the images being compared, provided the other image is regarded as of perfect quality. Taking one image from the documents as a reference image for comparing with other images in dataset of documents provides the similarity score between each pair of documents.

4 Results and Discussion

To investigate the usefulness of our approach, in this section we conduct an in-depth analysis of the model and experimental results. The text extracted from the handwritten documents was vectorised into word embeddings. Further, the word embeddings were checked for cosine-similarity, to find the lexical and semantic similarities between all documents pairwise. This was done by making all possible pairs from the given number of documents and applying cosine similarity to calculate the distance between the vectors of word embeddings and obtain a similarity score for each pair. The SSIM was used to find the structural similarities between the documents i.e. finding the patterns in sentence or paragraph construction and similarity in style of handwritten text. Lastly, the Cosine similarity and SSIM scores were aggregated to obtain the final similarity scores for comparing the documents.

We first compare the proposed network architecture on handwritten-text recognition task (or OCR task) on the IAM dataset for which results can be found in Table 1. Our approach fairs well over many other proposed approaches, because of our robust information retrieval technique.

Table 1. Accuracies of different model architectures for hand-written text extraction.

Model architecture	Accuracy score
CNN n-gram [23]	93.6
Boosted Multi-Dimensional LSTM [24]	89.5
Gated CRNN (GRCL) [25]	85.9
Large Multi-Dimensional LSTM [26]	90.7
OCR + BILSTM [27]	85.1
GRCL Fine Tuned [27]	89.2
RESNET-34 with LSTM [28]	35.0
RESNET-18 with LSTM [28]	31.0
Our Methodology	**91.2**

For testing on more robust real world scenarios, we carry out experiments on our ES-700 dataset. To validate the correctness of our approach we performed a human evaluation where we picked a set of 40 images written by various students. We used five humans evaluators and asked them to give a score to the top-1 retrieval on a scale of 0–3. Here, 0 is "almost no similarity", 1 is "vaguely similar", 2 is "partially similar" and 3 is "almost no change or totally similar". To scale the percentages of our results, between 0–3 we use binning with 4 bins of 25% each. The average agreement to the human judgments as evaluated for the top-1 similar document is reported at 2.125 with 3 as the best score. To report, in this paper we select a set of random 5 images, which are answers to the same question by different authors and report the SSIM, Cosine Similarity and Combined scores as mentioned in Tables 2, 3, and 4. The 5 images are compared pairwise. An important *assumption* of our paper is that, we consider the document which is most similar to rest of the documents to be the most likely source of plagiarism.

We see that Table 2 gives comparatively low structural similarity index scores as it compare handwriting of multiple authors which may have varied writing styles but marks

Table 2. SSIM Similarity scores for the five documents pairwise.

Index	Document 1	Document 2	Document 3	Document 4	Document 5
Document 1	100	62.59	56.72	57.34	57.12
Document 2	62.59	100	61.92	61.43	61.81
Document 3	58.72	61.92	100	60.44	60.58
Document 4	57.34	61.43	60.44	100	61.58
Document 5	57.12	61.81	60.58	61.58	100

Table 3. Cosine similarity scores for the five documents pairwise.

Index	Document 1	Document 2	Document 3	Document 4	Document 5
Document 1	100	98.57	98.67	97.34	97.56
Document 2	98.57	100	98.20	96.43	98.36
Document 3	98.67	98.20	100	97.98	98.35
Document 4	97.34	96.43	97.98	100	97.65
Document 5	97.56	98.36	98.35	97.65	100

Table 4. Combined Similarity score comparison for the documents.

Index	SSIM	Cosine	Aggregated
Document 1	59.75	98.43	78.23
Document 2	61.93	97.31	79.91
Document 3	60.41	98.64	79.35
Document 4	60.19	97.35	78.77
Document 5	60.27	97.98	79.12

out the most similar document to all others using image processing. The documents are then processed for extracting texts and finding out semantic similarity using cosine similarity for word embeddings. The maximum similarity score obtained was 98.64 as shown in Table 3 and the index of the author from whom the other documents were plagiarized was 3. But, for a combined average, probable index of authors responsible for plagiarism (source documents) were 2 and 3 as shown in Table 4. The values of SSIM and Cosine similarity in Table 4 are calculated by averaging those scores across all authors (except self). Thus, the plagiarized documents found were 1, 4 and 5. This satisfied our ground-truth labels. For calculation of combined similarity in Table 4 a non-weighted average of SSIM and cosine similarity was used. The suspected documents if needed can also be sorted in most likely order of the amount of plagiarism, based on scratch and scribble count on the paper. Because according to psychological reports

[33, 34], multiple correction on paper is a sign of low moral or self-confidence and can possible indicate plagiarist mentality.

5 Conclusion

In this paper, we focused on various aspects of plagiarism and possible solutions to an effective detection system using various information retrieval methods. The competitive results obtained in the experiments accurately landed as per our predictions enabling us to fulfil the objective of this research. This detection system claims to find possible and most likely source of plagiarism, based on information that is provided. We would like to strengthen this claim in our future works as research into more complex and accurate techniques are developed in this field. Interesting directions for future work may include, improving the accuracy metric using fuzzy clustering to detect multiple sources by feeding data that was obtained after extraction of vectors. Also, the incorporation of complex positional encoding for documents that may span multiple pages. A weighted average can replace the non-weighted average given thresholds and environment details of implementation. As new ways to tackle plagiarism are appearing by the day, we sincerely hope that the obtained results can serve as a possible benchmark for further research into this field.

References

1. Tripathi, R., Tiwari, P., Nithyanandam, K.: Avoiding plagiarism in research through free online plagiarism tools. In: 4th International Symposium on Emerging Trends and Technologies in Libraries and Information Services, pp. 275–280 (2015)
2. Rath, T.M., Manmatha, R.: Word spotting for historical documents. IJDAR (2007)
3. Rodriguez-Serrano, J.A., Perronnin, F.: A model-based sequence similarity with application to handwritten word spotting. PAMI (2012)
4. Rusinol, M., Aldavert, D., Toledo, R., Llados, J.: Efficient segmentation-free keyword spotting in historical document collections. PR (2015)
5. Manning, C.D., Raghavan, P., Schütze, H.: Introduction to Information Retrieval. Cambridge University Press, Cambridge (2008)
6. Potthast, M., et al.: Overview of the 6th International Competition on Plagiarism Detection. In: CLEF (2014)
7. Gandhi, A., Jawahar, C.V.: Detection of cut-and-paste in document images. In: ICDAR (2013)
8. Krishnan, P., Jawahar, C.V.: Matching handwritten document images. In: Leibe, B., Matas, J., Sebe, N., Welling, M. (eds.) Computer Vision—ECCV 2016. ECCV 2016. Lecture Notes in Computer Science, vol. 9905. Springer, Cham, Switzerland (2016)
9. Jiao, L., et al.: A survey of deep learning-based object detection. IEEE Access (2019)
10. Wise, M.J.: YAP3: improved detection of similarities in computer program and other texts. In: Proceedings of SIGCSE'96 Technical Symposium (1996)
11. Batomalaque, M.B., Camacho, C.M.R., Dalida, M.J.P., Delmo, J.A.B.: Image to text conversion technique for anti-plagiarism system. In: International Journal of Advanced Science and Convergence (2019)
12. Gitchell, D., Tran, N.: Sim: A utility for detecting similarity in computer programs. In: Proceedings of the 30th SIGCSE Technical Symposium on Computer Science Education (1999)

13. Zhao, Z.Q., Zheng, P., Zheng, P., Xu, S.T., Wu, X.: Object detection with deep learning: A review. IEEE Trans. Neural. Netw. Learn. Syst. **30**(11), 3212–3232 (2019)
14. Rezatofighi, H., Tsoi, N., Gwak, J., Sadeghian, A., Reid, I., Savarese, S.: Generalized intersection over union: A metric and a loss for bounding box regression. In: Proceedings of the IEEE Conference on Computer Vision and Pattern Recognition (2019)
15. Liu, W., et al.: Ssd: Single shot multibox detector. In: ECCV (2016)
16. Girshick, R.: Fast R-CNN. arXiv:1504.08083 (2015)
17. Xu, L., Ren, J., Liu, C., Jia, J.: Deep Convolutional Neural Network for Image Deconvolution. In: NIPS (2014)
18. Ding, Z., Xia, R., Yu, J., Li, X., Yang, J.: Densely connected bidirectional lstm with applications to sentence classification. In: CCF International Conference on Natural Language Processing and Chinese Computing, Springer, Cham (2018)
19. Loper, E., Bird, S.: NLTK: The Natural Language ToolKit. In: ETMTNLP'02 (2002)
20. Github Homepage. https://pyenchant.github.io/pyenchant/index.html
21. Github Homepage. https://github.com/barrust/pyspellchecker
22. Marti, U., Bunke, H., Bunke, H.: The IAM-database: An english sentence database for off-line handwriting recognition. IJDAR **5** , 39–46 (2002)
23. Poznanski, A., Wolf, L.: Cnn-n-gram for handwriting word recognition in CVPR (2016)
24. Castro, D., Bezerra, B.L.D., Valena, M.: Boosting the deep multidimensional long-short-term memory network for handwritten recognition systems. In: ICFHR (2018)
25. Bluche, T., Messina, R.: Gated convolutional recurrent neural networks for multilingual handwriting recognition. ICDAR (2017)
26. Voigtlaender, P., Doetsch, P., Ney, H.: Handwriting recognition with large multidimensional long short-term memory recurrent neural networks. ICFHR (2016)
27. Ingle, R., Fujii, Y., Deselaers, T., Baccash, J., Popat, A.C.: A Scalable Handwritten Text Recognition System Google Research (2019)
28. Balci, B., Saadati, D., Shiferaw, D.: Handwritten Text Recognition using Deep Learning Stanford Edu. (2017)
29. Mikolov, T., Sutskever, I., Chen, K., Corrado, G., Dean, J.: Distributed Representations of Words and Phrases and their Compositionality. NIPS (2013)
30. Kingma, D.P., Ba, J.L.: Adam: A method for stochastic optimization (2014)
31. Srivastava, N., Hinton, G., Krizhevsky, A., Sutskever, I., Salakhutdinov, R.: Dropout: A simple way to prevent neural networks from overfitting. J. Mach. Learn. Res. **15**, 1929–1958 (2014)
32. Lahitani, A.R., Permanasari, A.E., Setiawan, N.A.: Cosine similarity to determine similarity measure. In: ICIT (2016)
33. Ed.gov Homepage. https://files.eric.ed.gov/fulltext/EJ1112609.pdf
34. p.org Homepage. https://www.plagiarism.org/blog/2017/11/16/what-does-confidence-have-to-do-with-plagiarism

Optical Coherence Tomography Latent Fingerprint Image Denoising

Sboniso Sifiso Mgaga[1,2]([⊠]), Jules-Raymond Tapamo[1],
and Nontokozo Portia Khanyile[2]

[1] University of KwaZulu-Natal, Durban, South Africa
SMgaga@csir.co.za
[2] Council for Scientific and Industrial Research, Pretoria, South Africa
http://www.csir.co.za/

Abstract. Latent fingerprints are fingerprint impressions left on the surfaces a finger comes into contact with. They are found in almost every crime scene. Conventionally, latent fingerprints have been obtained using chemicals or physical methods, thus destructive techniques. Forensic community is moving towards contact-less acquisition methods. The contact-less acquisition presents some advantages over destructive methods; such advantages include multiple acquisitions of the sample and a possibility of further analysis such as touch DNA. This work proposes a speckle-noise denoising method for optical coherence tomography (OCT) latent fingerprint images. The proposed denoising technique was derived from the adaptive threshold and the normal shrinkage. Experimental results have shown that the proposed method suppressed speckle-noise better than the adaptive threshold, NormalShrink, VisuShrink, SUREShrink and BayesShrink.

Keywords: Denoising · Latent fingerprints · Wavelet thresholding · Optical coherence tomography · Biometrics

1 Introduction

Latent fingerprints are finger impressions left on the surfaces a finger comes into contact with. This type of fingerprint is formed by the natural secretion of sweat from eccrine glands that are present in the friction ridges. They can also be made by artificial means such as touching ink, dye or any other substances transferred from ridges on the finger to a surface. They are found in almost every crime scene and are often acquired using different techniques [1, 2, 4, 6, 16, 22, 23].

Traditionally latent fingerprints are collected through destructive methods which include the use of instrumental methods, dyes and chemicals such as iodine, Ninhydrin, silver nitrate [1]. Using chemicals or dyes alters the crime scene, destroying any possibilities of secondary analysis of the sample and using tape to lift the fingerprint may destroy the sample [19].

Supported by organization CSIR.

G. Bebis et al. (Eds.): ISVC 2020, LNCS 12510, pp. 694–705, 2020.
https://doi.org/10.1007/978-3-030-64559-5_55

The forensic science community has been moving towards the use of non-destructive techniques to process crime scenes. These methods involve using an alternative light source to localize the fingerprints from different surfaces. This is then followed by the acquisition of the fingerprint using a contact-less sensor such as a high-resolution digital camera, laser, chromatic white light, reflected ultraviolet imaging systems and OCT [2–4,6,16,23]. These contact-less acquisition methods have advantages over the destructive techniques; such advantages include multiple acquisitions of the sample and the possibility of further analysis such as touch DNA. However, these non-destructive techniques also have their downfall.

The chromatic white light sensor can only acquire visible prints, reflected ultraviolet imaging systems are detrimental to DNA. High-resolution digital cameras, the prints still need to be developed or improve its contrast using traditional techniques, and the OCT produces images that are immense with speckle-noise [20]. It is clear from the work done in [7,18,26] that OCT latent fingerprint images suffer from speckle-noise.

Any unwanted modifications of a signal or image are called noise. Noise signal may appear as additive or multiplicative on an image [15,17]. The linear filters may suppress additive noise signal while multiplicative is a bit complicated. Speckle-noise is a granular interference that inherently exists in and degrades the quality of the optical sensors images such as OCT. This type of noise is multiplicative; thus, linear filters such as median filter are unable to remove it. The methods that use wavelets are recommended for speckle-noise removal [7,13,18,19,25,26].

The process of removing noise from an image is called denoising. In this work, a wavelet-based denoising technique that uses stationary wavelet transform (SWT) as recommended in [19] is proposed. The technique is derived from the adaptive threshold shrinkage [25] and the normal shrinkage (NormalShrink) [14]. The method is implemented in an effort to remove speckle-noise from the latent fingerprint images acquired using the OCT system. This technique is compared some of the well speckle-noise removal methods which include VisuShrink, BayesShrink, SUREShrink, NormalShrink and adaptive threshold [14,21,24,25]. Peak-to-signal-to-noise-ratio (PSNR), Signal-to-noise-ratio (SNR), root mean square error (RMSE) and structural similarity index (SSIM) are used as the quantitative measure of speckle-noise removal.

2   Wavelet Principle

If an image is convolved with low-pass and a high-pass filter in the vertical and horizontal direction respectively, four sub-images of the original image are formed [19,25,26]. The sub-images encompass the full image, but at different resolutions and containing different components of the original image. This includes a sub-image of low frequency in both the horizontal and vertical direction (LL), sub-image with low horizontal frequency but the high vertical frequency (LH), sub-image with high horizontal frequency but the low vertical frequency (HL) and (HH) which has a high frequency in both horizontal and vertical directions. Figure 1 shows the decomposition skeleton of the image up to level 2, where LL is the approximation image, HL, LH and HH represent image details in the horizontal, vertical and diagonal direction respectively. The image may be decomposed using either the convention DWT or the Stationary Wavelet Transform.

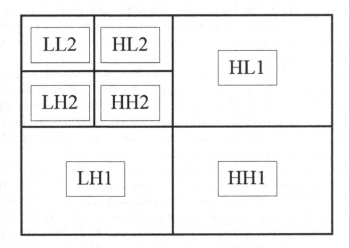

Fig. 1. Image wavelet decomposition

3   OCT Latent Fingerprints

We used a database acquired by spectral-domain OCT (SD-OCT) system. The details about the database and OCT system can be found in our study [x]. The SD-OCT system has a super-luminescent diode with 930 nm central wavelength, an average power of 10 mW and imaging depth of 2.9 mm, scanning speed of 100 kHz. The study was performed on the database that consists of 270 latent fingerprint images. The database was created using 5 participants and six surfaces, from each participant, three fingers were considered (*i.e.* index finger, middle finger thumb). Each finger impression was captured 3 times, hence, $5 \times 6 \times 3 \times 3 = 270$ latent fingerprint images. On Fig. 2, some of the latent fingerprint images in the database are displayed.

4   Proposed Method

The proposed method was derived from NormalShrink [14] and Adaptive threshold [25]. When denoising using wavelets, four components need to be defined [8,19]. These components include wavelet filter, thresholding rule, level of decomposition and shrinkage rule. In this work three wavelet filters which include *haar,*

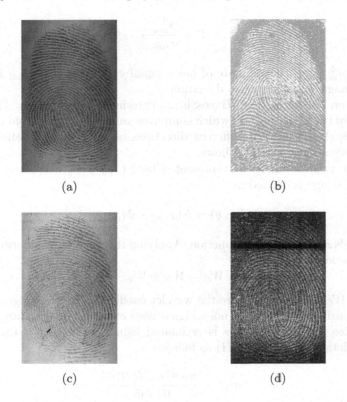

(a)   (b)

(c)   (d)

Fig. 2. Some of the images in OCT latent fingerprint database.

sym4 and *boir2.6* [5,9,11] were experimented. Soft thresholding [19] was used, levels of decomposition were chosen to be 1 & 2 and the proposed technique was the shrinkage rule. The pre-processing step involves normalization, adaptive histogram equalization and median filter.

4.1 Adaptive Threshold Shrinkage

Yinping *et al.* [25] proposed an adaptive threshold method based on the wavelet transform for fingerprint denoising.

Threshold Value Computation: Their proposed method uses the same principles of wavelets decomposition. The difference is how the threshold value T is computed. The threshold value, T, is critical when using wavelets. Conventionally VisuShrink and BayesShrink are used to compute the optimal threshold. The universal threshold is given by:

$$T = \sigma\sqrt{2logN},\tag{1}$$

where σ, is the noise standard deviation and N is the number of high-frequency coefficients found by applying a discrete wavelet transform (DWT) on an image. BayesShrink threshold is defined as follows:

$$T = \frac{\sigma_{noise}^2}{\sigma_{signal}} \tag{2}$$

where σ_{noise}^2, is the estimate of noise signal variance and σ_{signal} is the estimate of image signal standard deviation.

Based on VisuShrink and BayesShrink threshold, Yinping et al. [25] defined an adaptive threshold Shrink, which computes an adaptive threshold of different sub-images (LL) using the different directions of coefficients details (LH, HL, HH). These are achieved as follows:

Let the original image be represented by $F(x, y)$ where $x, y = 1, 2, \ldots, M$. The noisy image is defined as:

$$G(x, y) = F(x, y) + \Phi(x, y) \tag{3}$$

where $\Phi(x, y)$ is the noise function. Applying the wavelet transform, the noisy image function becomes:

$$W_G = W_F + W_\Phi, \tag{4}$$

where W_G, W_F and W_N are the wavelet coefficients of the image containing noise, the original image and noise signal respectively. The standard deviation of the noise signal coefficients is estimated using the median estimator with diagonal detail coefficients (HH) as follows:

$$\sigma_{W_\Phi} = \frac{median(|HH_i|)}{0.6745} \tag{5}$$

where $i = 1, 2, \ldots, k$ k represents wavelet decomposition layers. The signal variance of the image containing noise is computed using the coefficients of each direction detail. These coefficients are as follow:

Let $D = 1, 2, 3$ represent horizontal, vertical and diagonal details respectively, then, $W_G(1, i) \in LH_i$, $W_G(2, i) \in HL_i$ and $W_G(3, i) \in HH_i$. These direction details are used to estimate the noisy $(G(x, y))$ image signal noise variance by 6:

$$\sigma_{W_G}^2(D, i) = \frac{1}{N(i)^2} \sum_{x=1}^{N(i)} \sum_{y=1}^{N(i)} W_G(D, i) \tag{6}$$

analogously the noisy image in terms of variance is defined as,

$$\sigma_{W_G}^2 = \sigma_{W_F}^2 + \sigma_{W_\Phi}^2 \tag{7}$$

where $\sigma_{W_F}^2$ and $\sigma_{W_\Phi}^2$ represent the variance of the original and noise signal respectively. The original image variance is then defined as:

$$\sigma_{W_F}(D, i) = \sqrt{max(\sigma_{W_G}^2(D, i) - \sigma_{W_\Phi}^2(i), 0)}, \tag{8}$$

where $\sigma^2_{W_\Phi}(i)$ is noise in different layers. Finally, the adaptive threshold Shrink is given by:

$$T(D, i) = \begin{cases} \dfrac{\sigma^2_{W_\Phi}(i)}{\sigma_{W_F}(D,i)} & \text{if} \sigma_{W_F}(D, i) \neq 0 \\ max(W_G(D, i)) & \text{if} \sigma_{W_F}(D, i) = 0 \end{cases} \qquad (9)$$

The adaptive threshold shrinkage method [25] is modified using β constant from NormalShrink [10]. The block diagram of the proposed method is shown in Fig. 4.

4.2 Normal Shrinkage

Normal Shrinkage (NormalShrink) technique is a wavelet domain denoising method based on the generalized Gaussian distribution sub-band coefficients modelling [14]. The threshold value of NormalShrink is defined as,

$$T = \beta \frac{\sigma^2}{\sigma_y} \qquad (10)$$

where σ^2 is the noise variance given by (5). The σ_y is the standard deviation of the noisy image signal, which is computed using (6). The β constant is the scale parameter which is computed as,

$$\beta = \sqrt{log\left(\frac{L_k}{J}\right)} \qquad (11)$$

where L_k is the length of sub-band and J is the total number of decomposition levels. The NormalShrink technique outperforms both Bayesian shrinkage and universal threshold noise removal techniques, and it preserves edges efficiently [12].

4.3 Proposed Method

The adaptive threshold shrinkage method [25] is modified using β constant from NormalShrink, and the noise variance estimated from diagonal subband details (HH) is computed using (5). The block diagram of the proposed method is shown in Fig. 4.

The threshold value in (9) is multiplied by the scaling constant β defined in (11), then the new threshold value is computed as:

$$T = \begin{cases} \beta_i \left(\dfrac{\sigma^2_{W_\Phi}(i)}{\sigma_{W_F}(D,i)} \right) & \text{if} \sigma_{W_F}(D, i) \neq 0 \\ \beta_i(max(W_{x,y}(D, i))) & \text{if} \sigma_{W_F}(D, i) = 0 \end{cases} \qquad (12)$$

After calculating the noise variance, the new modified adaptive threshold is applied to noisy OCT latent fingerprint image.

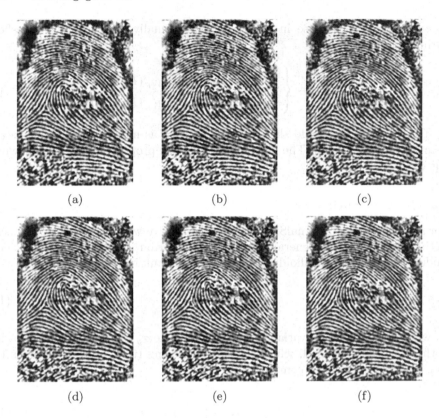

(a)   (b)   (c)

(d)   (e)   (f)

Fig. 3. Haar wavelet filter at level 2 for different wavelet denoising techniques results: (a) VisuShrink, (b) BayesShrink, (c) SUREShrink (d) NormalShrink (e) Adapt. Threshold and (f) Proposed Method.

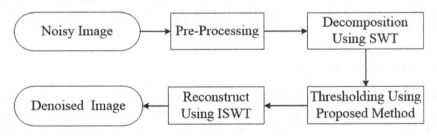

Fig. 4. The basic structure of the proposed wavelet transform based OCT latent fingerprint image denoising technique.

4.4   Quality Assessment Metrics

The PSNR, SNR, mean square error (MSE), RMSE and SSIM are widely used to assess the quality of images. They are defined in Table 1:

Table 1. Quality estimation matrices [7].

Matrix name	Formula	
PSNR	$log_{10}\left(\dfrac{MAX_I^2}{\text{MSE}}\right)$	(13)
SNR	$\dfrac{\sigma(s)}{\sigma(n)}$	(14)
MSE(r, d)	$\dfrac{1}{N}\sum_{i=1}^{N}(r_i - d_i)^2$	(15)
RMSE(r, d)	$\sqrt{\text{MSE(r,d)}}$	(16)
SSIM(w_1, w_2)	$\dfrac{2\mu_{w_1}\mu_{w_2} + C_1)(2\sigma_{w_1 w_2} + C_2}{\mu_{w_1}^2 + \mu_{w_2}^2 + C_1)(\sigma_{w_1}^2 + \sigma_{w_2}^2 + C_2}$	(17)

5   Experimental Results

The results of the proposed method are presented. Some of the denoised images are shown on Fig. 3. The numerical performance of the denoising techniques are presented on Fig. 5 & 6.

6   Discussion

In Fig. 6 VisuShrink outperform the other techniques at level 1 in terms of PSNR, SNR and RMSE. The proposed technique is better than other techniques in terms of SSIM in both level 1 & 2 while BayesShrink is better in terms of PSNR and SNR in level 2. The SUREShrink has better RMSE in level 2. BayesShrink and VisuShrink performed very well with *haar* wavelet filter.

In Fig. 5 the proposed technique dominates the optimal results. This is because *sym*4 and *bior*2.6 wavelet filters are steeper and they have a lot of overlapping windows [5,9,11] that co-operate with the technique adaptiveness.

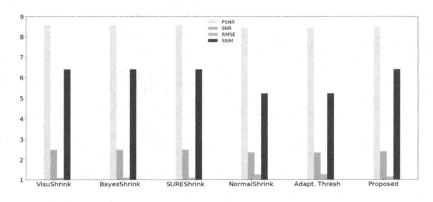

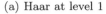

(a) Haar at level 1

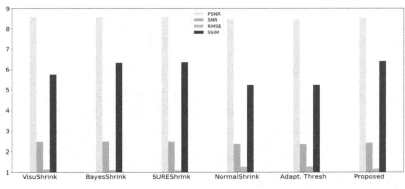

(b) Haar at level 2

Fig. 5. PSNR, SNR and RMSE and SSIM values for each technique with *bior2.6* as a wavelet filter at decomposition level 1 & 2.

The proposed technique performs better with *bior2.6* filter at level 2; this is deduced from the highest value of PSNR (8.6062 dB) and SNR (2.5186 dB). It is observed from Fig. 6 & 5 that the value of SSIM decrease with an increase in decomposition level and the value of RMSE increase with an increase in decomposition levels. The decrease in SSIM and the increase in RMSE value means the image is losing quality. This provides evidence that higher levels of wavelet decomposition distort the image [19].

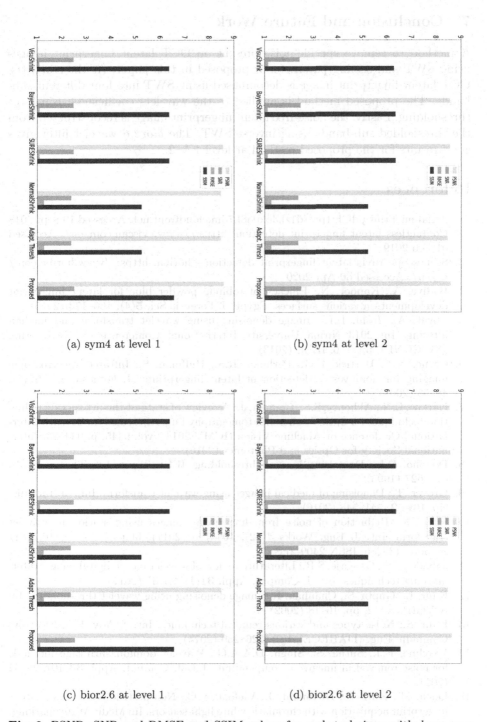

(a) sym4 at level 1

(b) sym4 at level 2

(c) bior2.6 at level 1

(d) bior2.6 at level 2

Fig. 6. PSNR, SNR and RMSE and SSIM values for each technique with *haar* as a wavelet filter at decomposition level 1 & 2.

7   Conclusion and Future Work

A method to remove speckle-noise present on OCT latent fingerprint images using SWT and scaling parameter is proposed in this paper. At the start, the OCT latent fingerprint image is decomposed using SWT into four different sub-bands. The proposed method is applied to the wavelets coefficients using soft thresholding. Lastly, the noise-free latent fingerprint image is reconstructed from the thresholded sub-bands using inverse SWT. The *bior2.6* wavelet filter gives good results for the proposed method at level 1 & 2.

References

1. 02_latent_print.pdf. http://d1zh4ok0q8k7dm.cloudfront.net. Accessed 19 Sept 2018
2. Contactless latent fingerprint detection. https://www.eviscan.com/en/. Accessed 01 Feb 2019
3. Scenescope ruvis latent fingerprint detection - horiba. https://www.horiba.com/us/en/. Accessed 30 Apr 2020
4. Badiye, A., Kapoor, N.: Efficacy of robin® powder blue for latent fingerprint development on various surfaces. Egypt. J. Forensic Sci. **5**(4), 166–173 (2015)
5. Boyat, A., Joshi, B.K.: Image denoising using wavelet transform and median filtering. In: 2013 Nirma University International Conference on Engineering (NUiCONE), pp. 1–6. IEEE (2013)
6. Crane, N.J., Bartick, E.G., Perlman, R.S., Huffman, S.: Infrared spectroscopic imaging for noninvasive detection of latent fingerprints. J. Forensic Sci. **52**(1), 48–53 (2007)
7. Darlow, L.N., Akhoury, S.S., Connan, J.: A review of state-of-the-art speckle reduction techniques for optical coherence tomography fingertip scans. In: Seventh International Conference on Machine Vision (ICMV 2014), vol. 9445, p. 944523. International Society for Optics and Photonics (2015)
8. Donoho, D.L.: De-noising by soft-thresholding. IEEE Trans. Inf. Theory **41**(3), 613–627 (1995)
9. Grover, T.: Denoising of medical images using wavelet transform. Imp. J. Interdiscip. Res. **2**, 541–548 (2016)
10. Iqbal, N.: Reduction of noise from fingerprint images using stationary wavelet trasnform. Int. J. Eng. Works **4**(12), 104–108 (2017). https://doi.org/10.5281/zenodo.1133286. ISSN 2409-277
11. Jabade, V.S., Gengaje, S.R.: Literature review of wavelet based digital image watermarking techniques. Int. J. Comput. Appl. **31**(1), 28–35 (2011)
12. Kaur, L., Gupta, S., Chauhan, R.: Image denoising using wavelet thresholding. In: ICVGIP, vol. 2, pp. 16–18 (2002)
13. Kaur, S.: Noise types and various removal techniques. Int. J. Adv. Res. Electron. Commun. Eng. (IJARECE) **4**(2), 226–230 (2015)
14. Leavline, E.J., Sutha, S., Singh, D.A.A.G.: Wavelet domain shrinkage methods for noise removal in images: a compendium. Int. J. Comput. Appl. **33**(10), 28–32 (2011)
15. Leich, M., Kiltz, S., Dittmann, J., Vielhauer, C.: Non-destructive forensic latent fingerprint acquisition with chromatic white light sensors. In: Media Watermarking, Security, and Forensics III, vol. 7880, p. 78800S. International Society for Optics and Photonics (2011)

16. Lin, A.C.Y., Hsieh, H.M., Tsai, L.C., Linacre, A., Lee, J.C.I.: Forensic applications of infrared imaging for the detection and recording of latent evidence. J. Forensic Sci. **52**(5), 1148–1150 (2007)
17. Maity, A., Pattanaik, A., Sagnika, S., Pani, S.: A comparative study on approaches to speckle noise reduction in images. In: 2015 International Conference on Computational Intelligence and Networks (CINE), pp. 148–155. IEEE (2015)
18. Makinana, S., Khanyile, P.N., Khutlang, R.: Latent fingerprint wavelet transform image enhancement technique for optical coherence tomography. In: 2016 Third International Conference on Artificial Intelligence and Pattern Recognition (AIPR), pp. 1–5, September 2016. https://doi.org/10.1109/ICAIPR.2016.7585203
19. Mgaga, S.S., Khanyile, N.P., Tapamo, J.: A review of wavelet transform based techniques for denoising latent fingerprint images. In: 2019 Open Innovations (OI), pp. 57–62, October 2019. https://doi.org/10.1109/OI.2019.8908252
20. Mgaga, S.S., Khanyile, N.P., Tapamo, J.: Latent fingerprint acquisition using optical coherence tomography. In: 3rd International Conference on Information Communication and Signal Processing (ICICSP) (2020)
21. Nasif, H.: Wavelet denoising, April 2016. https://doi.org/10.13140/RG.2.1.1074.9844
22. Rohatgi, R., Kapoor, A.: Development of latent fingerprints on wet non-porous surfaces with SPR based on basic fuchsin dye. Egypt. J. Forensic Sci. **6**(2), 179–184 (2016)
23. Saitoh, N., Akiba, N.: Ultraviolet fluorescence imaging of fingerprints. Sci. World J. **6**, 691–699 (2006)
24. Xiao, F., Zhang, Y.: A comparative study on thresholding methods in wavelet-based image denoising. Procedia Eng. **15**, 3998–4003 (2011)
25. Yinping, M., Yongxing, H.: Adaptive threshold based on wavelet transform fingerprint image denoising. In: 2012 International Conference on Computer Science and Electronics Engineering, vol. 3, pp. 494–497. IEEE (2012)
26. Zaki, F., Wang, Y., Su, H., Yuan, X., Liu, X.: Noise adaptive wavelet thresholding for speckle noise removal in optical coherence tomography. Biomed. Opt. Express **8**(5), 2720–2731 (2017)

CNN, Segmentation or Semantic Embeddings: Evaluating Scene Context for Trajectory Prediction

Arsal Syed$^{(\boxtimes)}$ (iD) and Brendan Tran Morris (iD)

University of Nevada Las Vegas (UNLV), Las Vegas, NV 89154, USA
syeda3@unlv.nevada.edu, brendan.morris@unlv.edu

Abstract. For autonomous vehicles (AV) and social robot's navigation, it is important for them to completely understand their surroundings for natural and safe interactions. While it is often recognized that scene context is important for understanding pedestrian behavior, it has received less attention than modeling social-context – influence from interactions between pedestrians. In this paper, we evaluate the effectiveness of various scene representations for deep trajectory prediction. Our work focuses on characterizing the impact of scene representations (sematic images vs. semantic embeddings) and scene quality (competing semantic segmentation networks). We leverage a hierarchical RNN autoencoder to encode historical pedestrian motion, their social interaction and scene semantics into a low dimensional subspace and then decode to generate future motion prediction. Experimental evaluation on the ETH and UCY datasets show that using full scene semantics, specifically segmented images, can improve trajectory prediction over using just embeddings.

Keywords: Trajectory prediction · Scene context · RNN autoencoder

1 Introduction

Pedestrian trajectory prediction is an important topic in many applications including autonomous vehicles (AV), social robots, and surveillance systems. In AVs, accurate trajectory prediction of pedestrians enables the vehicle to achieve better control and operate in a safer manner. For surveillance systems, understanding pedestrian behavior can help to detect unusual activity. With the spread of COVID-19, another important application is ensuring a safe distance to meet social distancing guidelines. A recent surveillance implementation was used to predict whether people walking in a scene were maintaining safe distance and generate corresponding alerts if pedestrians are in too close proximity to each other [1]. The task of pedestrian trajectory prediction is challenging in nature due to erratic dynamics and ability to make sudden directional changes. However, when people walk, they tend to follow learned societal norms – for example they avoid collision and give right of way as necessary – but the social context and influences may not be consistent with all of those around them.

© Springer Nature Switzerland AG 2020
G. Bebis et al. (Eds.): ISVC 2020, LNCS 12510, pp. 706–717, 2020.
https://doi.org/10.1007/978-3-030-64559-5_56

Scene context also influences pedestrian motion as they tend to avoid static objects and follow "rules of the road." Before deep learning became popular, pedestrian motion was modeled using hand-crafted features and experimentally validated. One such famous technique was the Social Force (SF) model [2], which used vector functions to incorporate pedestrian interaction. In order to capture scene interaction, the SF model used repulsive and attractive potentials to incorporate interaction with stationary objects. Recently researchers have shifted from manual methods to data driven approaches for pedestrian motion modeling. Usually a video sequence is preprocessed to annotate trajectories and prediction is treated as a sequence-sequence learning task.

Our focus in this paper is to evaluate the importance of scene semantics on pedestrian motion and how to best incorporate those semantics into the learning framework. Recently researchers have explored different ways to incorporate scene context by using convolutional encoding layers of semantic segmentation architectures, like Deeplabv3 [3]. We believe that much of the contextual power of semantic segmentation architectures comes from the decoding layers which is lost when only using the encoding layers. Our experiments show that instead of embeddings, a fully segmented output map shows considerable improvement in trajectory prediction results.

2 Related Work

We review primary work on human trajectory prediction which are classified into two areas: (i) Human-human centric interaction where pedestrian motion is modeled through an occupancy grid map to provide social context. (ii) Pedestrian-scene interaction where influence of static scene objects (sidewalk/roads/exits etc.) is considered for scene context.

2.1 Human-Human Interaction

Social LSTM (S-LSTM) [4] was the primary research work that shifted focus from physics-based modeling approach to a deep learning model. It proposed a LSTM-based framework which models pedestrian interaction through a social pooling mechanism to share hidden state information with neighbors. Gupta et al. proposed Social GAN (S-GAN) [5], a GAN based network in conjunction with LSTM encoder-decoder to model multi-modal behavior of pedestrians. It also used an efficient global pooling technique, in contrast to the local pooling of S-LSTM [4], for social interaction. More recently graph neural networks have become popular where pedestrian motion and their interaction with surroundings is modeled by creating a spatio-temporal graph [6, 7]. However, these models fail to capture scene interactions.

Since pedestrian behavior is stochastic in nature, Variational Autoencoders (VAE) [8] and inverse optimal control [9] techniques have also been used. Similarly, these data driven techniques were extended for vehicle trajectory forecasting where Kim et al. [10] used LSTM models to forecast vehicle trajectory by understanding neighboring vehicle behavior through an occupancy grid map. Deo and Trivedi [11] addressed the social interaction of vehicles through a convolution social pooling layer and then predicted different vehicle maneuvers. Becker et al. [12] proposed the RED predictor to compare the prediction results with linear interpolation as base line. It consists of an RNN-Encoder with a stacked multi-layer perceptron (MLP) and used smooth trajectories to forecast future time steps, which helped in preventing accumulation of error. Compared to other baseline methods like RNN-MLP, RNN-encoder-MLP and Temporal Convolutional Networks (TCN), RED has strong results on the TrajNet [13] challenge despite its simple architecture.

2.2 Human-Scene Interaction

To understand the importance of scene structure, Sadeghian et al. [14] proposed the SoPhie network which was comprised of an attention-based GAN network with VGG-19 as a scene feature extraction module. The attention mechanism focuses on the agents and static objects which are important for trajectory prediction. In [15], Bartoli et al. introduced context-aware trajectory prediction where it used a context based pooling strategy to include static scene features. More recent works like Peek into the Future (PIF) [16] and State Refinement LSTM (SR-LSTM) [17] extended S-LSTM by incorporating scene features and new pooling strategies to improve prediction results. Multi-agent tensor fusion is another recent work which leverages GANs and CNNs to capture dynamic vehicle behavior by fusing the motion of multiple agents and their respective scene context into a tensor. Social Scene-LSTM (SS-LSTM) [18] used an explicit scene context branch paired with social context and self context (dynamics) for prediction. They used a CNN encoder for the scene that was trained from scratch specifically for trajectory prediction. SSeg-LSTM [19] extended the idea of SS-LSTM to explicitly incorporate scene semantics through the use of a semantic segmentation network (SegNet [20]) to encode scene features and showed improvement compared to just CNN-encoding.

Most of recent scene structure techniques have utilized variants of CNN/VGG-16 for embedding scene information. In this work, we focus on evaluating scene encoding techniques and their ability to extract relevant scene features for pedestrian motion. We then further evaluate these methods with semantic segmentation architectures which have not been explored in depth for trajectory prediction problems.

3   Scene Augmented RAE Trajectory Prediction

In order to characterize the importance of scene-context for trajectory prediction, we utilize a network model with three branches to handle dynamics, social interactions, and scene contribution as shown in Fig. 1.

3.1   Encoding Context

For every pedestrian i in a scene, the observed motion is denoted as $X_t^i = \left(x_t^i, y_t^i\right)$ where $t = 1, \ldots, t_{obs}$. The goal is to predict trajectories for future time stamps which is defined as $\hat{Y}_t^i = \left(\hat{x}_t^i, \hat{y}_t^i\right)$ for $t = t_{obs+1}, \ldots, t_{pred}$. The scene branch utilizes a semantic segmentation network to provide scene encoding. Since the scene is static, a single frame is used once for each trajectory. Pedestrian dynamics are encoded as typical using an LSTM on historical positions [4, 5] for each time step. Social interactions between

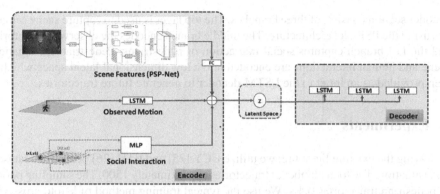

Fig. 1. Our proposed model based on RNN-AE which uses PSP-Net to incorporates Scene Semantics

neighboring pedestrians using a neighborhood pooling strategy similar to [5]. The social interaction tensor is generated based only on the time of prediction t_{obs}. Since the scene is static, only a single fixed frame is used as input for each trajectory.

This work uses PSP-Net [21] for semantic segmentation which has shown improvement in the pixel-level prediction through use of a different global pooling mechanism [22] where it explores the capability of global context information through region-based context aggregation. Previous methods, especially the early Fully Convolution Network (FCN) [23] had numerous problems when it came to parsing a scene. There were several mismatched relationships based on the appearance of objects, for example in the ADE20K [24] dataset it predicted car over water instead of boat. FCN also failed to recognize small scene objects like signboards and streetlights. Given FCN shortcomings, PSP-Net introduced a pyramid pooling module which is effective in capturing the global context prior. It used four modules in a pyramid fashion to fuse the feature context. The coarsest level is the global pooling module, which generates a single output. The subsequent levels divide the feature map into different sub regions and generated a pooled representation of its locations. Google DeepLab variants (notably DeepLab_v3) have become popular for semantic segmentation but only have marginal improvement over PSP-Net in benchmarks [3].

3.2 Decoding Trajectories

Trajectory predictions are generated through a sequence-sequence mapping through an autoencoder (AE). An AE is a self-supervised learning technique which has been extensively used in representation learning tasks. Usually the input to an AE is a set of features which are compressed into a bottleneck dimension and at the output, a decoder is used to reconstruct the original input. The key attribute to AE is the bottleneck representation or latent space without which the network will only memorize the input states. The latent space provides the necessary information to traverse the full network, forcing a learned compression of input data.

RNN-AE (RAE) on the other hand is a formulation of an AE for sequence data which uses an LSTM encoder-decoder architecture. In our pedestrian trajectory problem, the encoder section consists of three branches. The top layer is used to capture scene semantics using the PSP-Net architecture. The middle branch encodes the observed trajectories and the last branch captures social interaction of pedestrians. Pedestrian information, scene and human interactions are encoded into a low dimensional latent space which is then provided as an input to the LSTM-decoder to generate future trajectories.

4 Experiments

Following the existing literature, we utilize UCY [25] and ETH [26] pedestrian datasets for evaluation. The total number of trajectories approximately 1500. The sampling period of pedestrian trajectories 0.4 s. We use the typical training method of k-fold cross validation to train on four and test on the remaining sequence. To evaluate the model, we observe the past trajectories for 3.2 s (8-time stamps) and predict for 4.8 s (12 time stamps).

The evaluation metrics used are Average displacement error (ADE) and final displacement errors (FDE). ADE measures the average prediction performance along the trajectory for all the pedestrians in the scene. FDE on other hand measures the performance for the last or end point of trajectory for the pedestrians in the scene. To keep evaluation consistent for fair comparison, like SGAN [5] we also draw 20 sample trajectories closest to ground truth and then compute ADE and FDE.

$$ADE = \frac{\Sigma_{i=1}^{N} \Sigma_{t=t_{obs+1}}^{T} \left\| \hat{Y}_t^i - Y_t^i \right\|_2}{N * T} \quad FDE = \frac{\Sigma_{i=1}^{N} \left\| \hat{Y}_{t_{pred}}^i - Y_{t_{pred}}^i \right\|_2}{N} \quad (1)$$

Where N refers to number of pedestrians in a scene and $T = t_{pred} - t_{obs} + 1$ is the prediction horizon.

4.1 Implementation Details

Our model uses an LSTM framework to encode observed trajectories and PSP-Net to capture scene features. We utilize the same pooling method training parameters as mentioned in generator module of [5]. The network is trained for 200 epochs with batch size of 32 and learning rate as 0.005. The latent space (z) has dimension of 64. To implement segmentation networks, we annotated different frames across pedestrian datasets and generated image masks. The networks were trained for 20 epochs with batch size of 2 using Adam optimizer.

4.2 Pedestrian Scene Segmentation

We first examined the quality of semantic scene segmentation with different segmentation networks such as fully trained (FT) SegNet and PSP-Net. A visual comparison of segmentation results is provided in Fig. 2 which highlights cleaner results from PSP-Net over SegNet. PSP-Net better identifies light post, trees, and the bench in Hotel. The grass area on the top of Univ is more cleanly segmented against the building. Finally, in ZARA we see that SegNet was not able to parse the lower vehicle correctly.

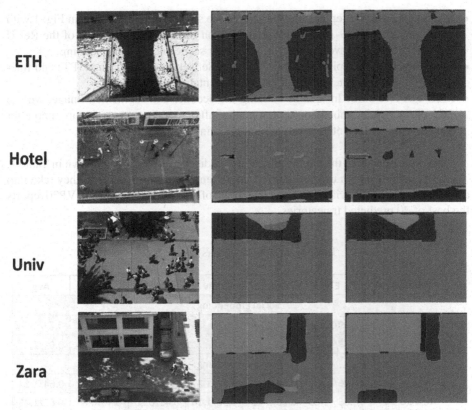

Fig. 2. Segmentation results: scene image (left), fully trained SegNet (middle), and fully trained PSP-Net (right)

In general, PSP-Net had consistent scene segmentation making it more understandable. Hence it is expected that the PSP-Net architecture will produce better trajectory prediction results. We also used SegNet which was pre-trained (PT) using CamVid [26] dataset. Unsurprisingly, it failed to accurately capture scene semantics on UCY-Univ and ETH-Univ dataset which are from a top-down view rather than street level as in CamVid.

4.3 Quantitative Analysis

We compare our prediction results with following baseline models:

- **S-LSTM** [4]: Pedestrian behavior modeled using LSTM and social interaction through hidden layer pooling. It has no scene context.
- **S-GAN** [5]: An adversarial network architecture with generator that uses a global pooling module to capture pedestrian's social interactions. It has no scene context.
- **SoPhie** [14]: An attention-based GAN network which uses VGG-19 tuned for FCN segmentation as backbone to extract scene context.

- **RAE-VGG-16:** We replace the PSP-Net in the scene encoding branch in Fig. 1 with an off-the-shelf VGG-16 encoder pretrained on ImageNet. The output of the ReLU following the last convolution layer is used for scene encoding/embedding.
- **RAE-SegNet:** We replace the PSP-Net with SetNet, both pre-trained (PT) and fine-tuned (FT), to characterize the effect of segmentation quality.
- **RAE-PSPNet-emb:** Instead of utilizing the decoder and segmented image, we use only the semantic embedding representation after encoding into a feature map after concatenating different levels of pyramid pooling module in PSP-Net.

The performance of the various trajectory prediction algorithms is shown in Table 1. The architectures which use scene information tend to perform better as they take into account of where pedestrians walk and their point of interests. Note S-GAN-VP20 reports the best of 20 predicted trajectories.

Table 1. ADE/FDE (meters) comparison

Models	ETH	Hotel	Univ	Zara1	Zara2	Avg
Social Embedding						
S-LSTM [4]	1.09/2.35	0.79/1.76	0.67/1.40	0.47/1.00	0.56/1.17	0.72/1.54
S-GAN-VP20 [5]	0.87/1.62	0.67/1.37	0.76/1.52	0.35/**0.68**	0.42/0.84	0.61/1.21
Scene Embedding						
Sophie (T_o+I_o) [14]	0.86/1.65	0.84/1.80	0.58/1.27	0.34/**0.68**	0.40/0.82	0.64/1.24
RAE-VGG-16	0.86 / 1.65	0.89/1.75	0.56/**1.14**	0.42/0.80	0.40/0.81	0.62/1.23
RAE-PSPNet-emb	0.88/1.70	0.79/1.53	0.56/1.39	0.41/0.97	0.42/0.96	0.61/1.31
Scene Segmentation						
RAE-SegNet-PT	1.11/1.87	0.70/1.38	0.86/1.77	0.57/1.18	0.59/1.21	0.90/1.75
RAE-SegNet-FT	0.84/1.51	0.68/1.36	0.54/1.41	0.33/1.11	**0.36**/0.83	0.55/1.24
RAE-PSPNet (ours)	**0.79/1.48**	**0.64/1.34**	**0.52**/1.40	**0.32**/0.99	**0.36/0.80**	**0.52/1.20**

Social Embedding vs Scene Embedding: From Table 1, we see that Sophie outperforms on ETH, Univ, Zara1, Zara2 and RAE-VGG-16 shows better performance on ETH, Univ and Zara2 when compared with models (S-LSTM and S-GAN-VP20) that do not incorporate scene behavior. This shows that for trajectory prediction, capturing scene features are essential. We want to further investigate how much influence trajectory motion has if we can come up with better methods to encode scene information.

Scene Embedding vs Scene Segmentation: While, semantic embedding only provided marginal improvement of social embedding, there is considerable improvement with scene segmentation. We speculate that much of the representation power from semantic segmentation networks comes from the decoder which needs to produce semantic interpretation and labels from embeddings. The VGG-16 or ResNet (PSPNet-emb) encoders do not provide strong semantic insight, therefore, taking advantage of decoder is necessary to accurately encode scene features.

However, the use of semantic segmentation images alone is not sufficient. As seen in Table 1, RAE-SegNet-PT performs poorly compared to scene embedding models. Since SegNet-PT is trained on driver's view perspective images and not from surveillance point-of-view, it was not able to semantically segment and identify points of interest for the pedestrians. In order to overcome this shortcoming and to keep the evaluation consistent, we trained SegNet from scratch which reduced the trajectory prediction errors. To further test our hypothesis, we experimented with fully training the more advanced segmentation architecture of PSP-Net and found further improved segmentation performance, especially on Hotel and Zara datasets. From Table 1 we see that RAE-PSPNet outperforms all other models with 0.52/1.20 ADE/FDE.

The RAE-PSPNet results are placed in context in Table 2 by comparison with state-of-the-art (SOTA). While there is a clear gap in performance with SOTA, our model uses a RAE which is a simpler model in comparison with more advanced graph convolutional networks or Transformer networks [31]. Further, the SOTA approaches should be able add a scene branch or replace scene embeddings with scene images easily. In order to provide a bound on segmentation-based performance, we replaced the semantic segmentation network with ground truth labeled images. As expected, ground truth segmentation resulted in improved performance across the board versus RAE-PSPNet and approaches performance of some more recent (and more complicated) networks.

Table 2. ADE/FDE (meters) comparison with other state of the art architectures

Models	ETH	Hotel	Univ	Zara1	Zara2	Avg
RAE-PSPNet (ours)	0.79/1.48	0.64/1.34	0.52/1.40	0.32/0.99	0.36/0.80	0.52/1.20
Ground truth	0.75/1.45	0.62/1.33	0.50/1.40	0.29/0.96	0.31/0.75	0.49/1.17
Trajectron++ [28]	**0.35/0.77**	**0.18/0.38**	**0.22/0.48**	**0.14/0.28**	**0.14**/0.75	**0.21/0.45**
Soc-BIGAT [29]	0.69/1.29	0.49/1.01	0.55/1.32	0.30/0.62	0.36/0.75	0.48/1.00
MATF-GAN [30]	1.01/1.75	0.43/0.80	0.44/0.91	0.26/0.45	0.26/0.57	0.48/0.90
TF-based [31]	0.61/1.12	**0.18/0.30**	0.35/0.65	0.22/0.38	0.17/**0.32**	0.31/0.55

4.4 Qualitative Analysis

Here we will discuss different scenarios which shows the importance of semantics and its influence on trajectory prediction. When people walk, they tend to traverse a walkable path, for example pavements, entrances/exits, etc. It is essential for our network to semantically identify the points of interest for pedestrian motion.

In Fig. 3(a) RAE-PSPNet and RAE-SegNet-FT are able to avoid the stopped pedestrians and look to avoid the bench. Since S-GAN does not model scene features, we see a diverging path. Figure 3(b) shows that RAE-PSPNet is able to predict a trajectory that follows the edge of the path next to the snow covering. In Fig. 3(c) we observe

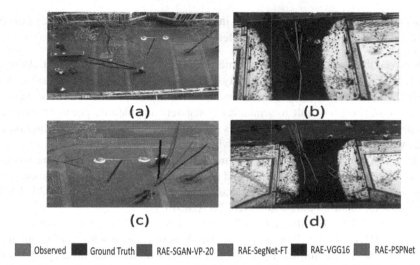

■ Observed ■ Ground Truth ■ RAE-SGAN-VP-20 ■ RAE-SegNet-FT ■ RAE-VGG16 ■ RAE-PSPNet

Fig. 3. Trajectory Prediction Comparison. (a) Similar results for all (but S-GAN). (b–c) RAE-PSPNet with improvement due to strong scene influence. (d) Poor performance from all models.

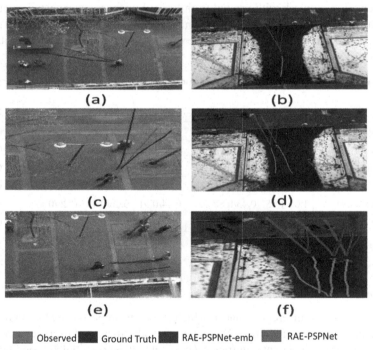

■ Observed ■ Ground Truth ■ RAE-PSPNet-emb ■ RAE-PSPNet

Fig. 4. (a) RAE-PSPNet-emb shows poor results. (b–c) RAE-PSPNet-emb was not able to capture scene information and has bad predictions. (d) Both perform poor but RAE-PSPNet-emb is even worse. (e–f) RAE-PSPNet-emb does better where pedestrians walk in groups.

a rich scene interaction and therefore RAE-PSPNet has successful predictions compared to RAE-SegNet-FT. This is because in Fig. 2 PSP-Net was better able to identify static objects (pole and lamppost) where as SegNet failed to capture those features. Figure 4(d) shows and example where all techniques work poorly and are not able to predict the slowing while the couple turn to the left.

Specific comparison between semantic images and embeddings are shown in Fig. 4. In (a), (c) the semantic obstacle information does not seem to effectively utilized by RAE-PSPNet-emb. In (b), (d) the embedded prediction continues straight up while RAE-PSPNet is able to have predictions that follow the snow bank. When comparing RAE-PSPNet-emb with RAE-PSPNet, it shows that using semantic embedding alone is not enough and that there is value in the decoding steps which generate the fully segmented output image. Figures 4(e–f) shows that RAE-PSPNet has poorer performance than RAE-PSPNet-emb for groups of pedestrians. It may be that the social interaction module is not weighted enough (or scene too much) or needs more complex modeling though something like graph convolution networks.

5 Conclusion

In this work, we evaluated different strategies for encoding scene information for better understanding of pedestrian motion. We leveraged hierarchical RNN based autoencoders to encode semantic context with observed raw motion and social interaction. We then replaced the scene encoding branch with different off-the-shelf feature extraction modules such VGG-16, SegNet, and PSPNet. Our experiments and analysis of pedestrian interaction with various scenarios showed that availability of full and accurate segmented output map can be helpful for forecasting pedestrian trajectories compared to just semantic and scene embeddings. While this work used a RAE, the scene encoding branch can be replaced and scene segmentation applied to other architectures, such as GANs and graph neural networks, without any difficulty and can bring added value for pedestrian motion prediction.

References

1. Punn, N.S., Sonbhadra, S.K., Agarwal, S.: Monitoring COVID-19 social distancing with person detection and tracking via fine-tuned YOLO v3 and Deepsort techniques. arXiv preprint arXiv:2005.01385 (2020)
2. Helbing, D., Molnar, P.: Social force model for pedestrian dynamics. Phys. Rev. E **51**(5), 4282 (1995)
3. Chen, L.-C., Papandreou, G., Schroff, F., Adam, H.: Rethinking atrous convolution for semantic image segmentation. CoRR, abs/1706.05587 (2017)
4. Alahi, A., Goel, K., Ramanathan, V., Robicquet, A., Fei-Fei, L., Savarese, S.: Social LSTM: human trajectory prediction in crowded spaces. In: Proceedings of the IEEE Conference on Computer Vision and Pattern Recognition, pp. 961–971 (2016)
5. Gupta, A., Johnson, J., Fei-Fei, L., Savarese, S., Alahi, A.: Social GAN: socially acceptable trajectories with generative adversarial networks. arXiv preprint arXiv:1803.10892 (2018)

6. Mohamed, A., Qian, K., Elhoseiny, M., Claudel, C.: Social-STGCNN: a social spatio-temporal graph convolutional neural network for human trajectory prediction. In: Proceedings of the IEEE/CVF Conference on Computer Vision and Pattern Recognition, pp. 14 424–14 432 (2020)

7. Kosaraju, V., Sadeghian, A., Martín-Martín, R., Reid, I., Rezatofighi, S.H., Savarese, S.: Social-BIGAT: multimodal trajectory forecasting using bicycle-GAN and graph attention networks. arXiv preprint arXiv:1907.03395 (2019)

8. Bhattacharyya, A., Hanselmann, M., Fritz, M., Schiele, B., Straehle, C.-N.: Conditional flow variational autoencoder for structured sequence prediction. In: BDL@NeurIPS (2019)

9. Kitani, K.M., Ziebart, B.D., Bagnell, J.A., Hebert, M.: Activity forecasting. In: Fitzgibbon, A., Lazebnik, S., Perona, P., Sato, Y., Schmid, C. (eds.) ECCV 2012. LNCS, vol. 7575, pp. 201–214. Springer, Heidelberg (2012). https://doi.org/10.1007/978-3-642-33765-9_15

10. Kim, B., et al.: Probabilistic vehicle trajectory prediction over occupancy grid map via recurrent neural network. arXiv preprint arXiv:1704.07049 (2017)

11. Deo, N., Trivedi, M.M.: Convolutional social pooling for vehicle trajectory prediction. CoRR abs/1805.06771 (2018)

12. Becker, S., Hug, R., Hübner, W., Arens, M.: An evaluation of trajectory prediction approaches and notes on the TrajNet benchmark. arXiv:1805.07663 (2018)

13. Traj Net Challenge. http://trajnet.stanford.edu/

14. Sadeghian, A., Kosaraju, V., Sadeghian, A., Hirose, N., Savarese, S.: SoPhie: an attentive GAN for predicting paths compliant to social and physical constraints. arXiv preprint arXiv: 1806.01482 (2018)

15. Bartoli, F., Lisanti, G., Ballan, L., Del Bimbo, A.: Context aware trajectory prediction. arXiv: 1705.02503 (2017)

16. Liang, J., Jiang, L., Niebles, J.C., Hauptmann, A.G., Fei-Fei, L.: Peeking into the future: predicting future person activities and locations in videos. In: Proceedings of the IEEE Conference on Computer Vision and Pattern Recognition, pp. 5725–5734 (2019)

17. Zhang, P., Ouyang, W., Zhang, P., Xue, J., Zheng, N.: SR-LSTM: state refinement for LSTM towards pedestrian trajectory prediction. In: Proceedings of the IEEE Conference on Computer Vision & Pattern Recognition, pp. 12085–12094 (2019)

18. Xue, H., Huynh, D.Q., Reynolds, M.: SS-LSTM: a hierarchical LSM model for pedestrian trajectory prediction. In: 2018 IEEE Winter Conference on Applications of Computer Vision (WACV), pp. 1186–1194 (2018)

19. Syed, A., Morris, B.T.: SSeg-LSTM: semantic scene segmentation for trajectory prediction. In: 2019 IEEE Intelligent Vehicles Symposium (IV), pp. 2504–2509. IEEE (2019)

20. Badrinarayanan, V., Handa, A., Cipolla, R.: SegNet: a deep convolutional encoder-decoder architecture for robust semantic pixel-wise labelling. arXiv preprint arXiv:1505.07293 (2015)

21. Zhao, H., Shi, J., Qi, X., Wang, X., Jia, J.: Pyramid scene parsing network. In: CVPR (2017)

22. Liu, W., Rabinovich, A., Berg, A.C.: ParseNet: looking wider to see better. arXiv:1506.04579 (2015)

23. Long, J., Shelhamer, E., Darrell, T.: Fully convolutional networks for semantic segmentation. In: Proceedings of the IEEE Conference on Computer Vision and Pattern Recognition, pp. 3431–3440 (2015)

24. Zhou, B., Zhao, H., Puig, X., Fidler, S., Barriuso, A., Torralba, A.: Semantic understanding of scenes through the ADE20K dataset. arXiv:1608.05442 (2016)

25. Lerner, A., Chrysanthou, Y., Lischinski, D.: Crowds by example. In: Computer Graphics Forum, vol. 26, pp. 655–664. Wiley Online Library (2007)

26. Pellegrini, S., Ess, A., Schindler, K., Van Gool, L.: You will never walk alone: modeling social behavior for multi-target tracking. In: 2009 IEEE 12th International Conference on Computer Vision, pp. 261–268 (2009)

27. Brostow, G., Fauqueur, J., Cipolla, R.: Semantic object classes: a high-definition ground truth database. PRL **30**(2), 88–97 (2009)
28. Salzmann, T., Ivanovic, B., Chakravarty, P., Pavone, M.: Trajectron++: multi-agent generative trajectory forecasting with heterogeneous data for control. arXiv preprint arXiv:2001.03093 (2020)
29. Kosaraju, V., Sadeghian, A., Martín-Martín, R., Reid, I., Rezatofighi, H., Savarese, S.: Social-BIGAT: multimodal trajectory forecasting using bicycle-GAN and graph attention networks. In: Advances in Neural Information Processing Systems, pp. 137–146 (2019)
30. Zhao, T., et al.: Multi-agent tensor fusion for contextual trajectory prediction. arXiv preprint arXiv:1904.04776 (2019)
31. Giuliari, F., Hasan, I., Cristani, M., Galasso, F.: Transformer networks for trajectory forecasting. arXiv preprint arXiv:2003.08111 (2020)

Automatic Extraction of Joint Orientations in Rock Mass Using PointNet and DBSCAN

Rushikesh Battulwar[✉], Ebrahim Emami, Masoud Zare Naghadehi, and Javad Sattarvand

University of Nevada, Reno, NV 89512, USA
rbattulwar@nevada.unr.edu

Abstract. Measurement of joint orientation is an essential task for rock mass discontinuity characterization. This work presents a methodology for automatic extraction of joint orientations in a rock mass from 3D point cloud data generated using Unmanned Aerial Vehicles and photogrammetry. Our algorithm first automatically classifies joints on 3D rock surface using state-of-the-art deep network architecture PointNet. It then identifies individual joints by the Density-Based Scan with Noise (DBSCAN) clustering and computes their orientations by fitting least-square planes using Random Sample Consensus. A major case study has been developed to evaluate the performance of the entire methodology. Our results showed the proposed approach outperforms similar approaches in the literature both in terms of accuracy and time complexity. Our experiments show the great potential in the application of 3D deep learning techniques for discontinuity characterization which might be used for the estimation of other parameters as well.

Keywords: Rock mass · Joint detection · Deep learning · 3D point cloud

1 Introduction

Rock mass discontinuities play a significant role in stability of slopes, and most of the highwalls stability analysis methods rely on measurement and characterization of the geological discontinuities since they define the weak planes in a rock mass along which the rock blocks detach and fail [1, 2]. Decisive information on rock joints also helps to predict the flow of groundwater, improve the quality of blasting in open pit mine highwalls, and finally a better stability condition for slopes [3, 4]. Traditionally, acquiring accurate discontinuity information is mostly dependent on the field measurements such as, scanline mapping with a geological compass near steep rock slopes faces. Occasionally, surveyors use a laser scanner mounted on a vehicle to scan the rock face and utilize special software in the office to make the measurements digitally on a computer. Therefore, the current practice approaches present numerous problems. Firstly, apart from being a laborious procedure, the access often does not exist to the rock faces to carry out geological mapping either in person or by a scanner. Additionally, there is a huge variation in the measurements at different locations of the mine, and it is difficult to

© Springer Nature Switzerland AG 2020
G. Bebis et al. (Eds.): ISVC 2020, LNCS 12510, pp. 718–727, 2020.
https://doi.org/10.1007/978-3-030-64559-5_57

accurately estimate the orientation and geometry of geological structures at few sample locations where a scanline crosses the structure. Furthermore, in-person mapping with a compass at the base of a steep slope or driving in such an environment exposes people to multiple types of hazards. Finally, as the mine is being developed, new measurements are required since the slope faces are drastically changed due to new production blasting practices.

Automated characterization of discontinuities from 3D models like point clouds of rock slopes is efficient compared to traditional methods in terms of operational cost and time [5]. There are various parameters suggested by the International Society for Rock Mechanics for quantitative description of discontinuities in rock mass and this study is focused on the measurement of one of the parameters: joint orientations. In this work, a new methodology has been proposed which takes advantage of deep neural networks for detection of joint points in 3D point clouds of rock masses. In our approach, the joint points are first identified using PointNet [6]. The geological information of the joints can then be computed by conducting statistical analysis on the classified points only. The experimental results show, our approach outperforms similar approaches in the literature both in terms of accuracy and time complexity.

The next section briefly discusses the previously presented approaches for joint orientation extraction. The proposed method has been detailed in Sect. 3. We present the results in Sect. 4. An analysis of the results is given in Sect. 4 and finally we conclude in Sect. 5.

2 Background

Several automated or semi-automated approaches have been presented in the literature for measuring joint orientations from 3D point clouds of rock masses. The most popular are the clustering-based methods where 3D points belonging to joints surfaces are identified by statistical analysis of the normal vectors of each point in point cloud using K-means clustering [7], Fuzzy K-means clustering [8], spectral clustering [9], Firefly algorithm with fuzzy K-means algorithm [10], Kernel density estimation [11], Iterative Self-organizing Data Analysis Techniques Algorithm (ISODATA) [12] or fast search and find density peaks (CFSFDP) algorithm. Clustering methods however introduce human bias in the results as prior knowledge of the value of K is required. Further, the results are also influenced by noise points present due to vegetation, sky or debris present in the point clouds. These methods are also characterized by higher computation times for large rock mass point clouds (more than one million points). Once the points forming the joint surfaces are identified, its orientation is determined by fitting a plane to those points using RANSAC or directly computing the normal direction using PCA.

Kong et al. [13] have successfully demonstrated the application of clustering method Density-Based Scan Algorithm with Noise (DBSCAN) for identifying points which are part of the same joint and used RANSAC for computing the dip and dip direction of joint planes.

Region growing-based methods [14–17] have been proposed recently in which joint planes are extracted by randomly selecting seed points from the entire point cloud and then the regions are expanded by adding neighboring points based on preset rules. The region growing criteria is usually based on normal angle or curvature difference between neighboring points These methods are found to be more accurate in terms of joint detection and have significantly lower computation time. However, they require tuning of up to eight or ten parameters to get the most accurate results. The tuning process is basically a trial-and-error approach which is performed by considering a subset from the original point cloud.

Rock discontinuities can also be extracted by iterative plane fitting approaches using RANSAC or PCA [18, 19] or by moving a cube through point clouds and extracting least-square fitting planes [20]. The iterative approaches are relatively inaccurate as well as the optimum size of the sampling cube is difficult to determine. Further, the computation time increases for large rock mass point clouds. Vasuki et al. [21] have presented an approach for joint detection based on the fusion of data from UAV images and digital elevation maps (DEM). While the joint traces are detected on 2D images using image phase congruency and phase symmetry algorithms, the third dimension of the detected features is extracted from DEM. This method shows relatively good accuracy however, it fails to detect in case of faint features due to shadows or poor lighting.

3   Methodology

The proposed method aims to detect exposed joint planes and compute their dip directions and dip angles from 3D point cloud models of rock masses. Figure 1 depicts the major steps of our approach. In the following, each step is discussed in detail.

3.1   Photogrammetric Point Cloud Generation

Generation of 3D models like point cloud representing the surface of rock mass is the first step in this method. The rock mass dataset was collected from various sites along the Donner Pass road, California. DJI Phantom 4 Pro [22] was used to collect overlapping aerial images of the rock face. The mode of flight was manual. This drone has a 20 MP camera sensor and 20–25 min of flying time. The collected images were processed using Agisoft Metashape [23] to generate 3D point cloud models of rock masses. A total of 249 images were collected from three different sites and three rock mass models were generated as shown in Fig. 2. Datasets A and B were used for training and validation of PointNet and Dataset C was used for testing the performance of the overall algorithm. Each of the resulting point clouds has more than one million points with each point having x, y, z information in WGS coordinate system as well as RGB values. It can be seen in Fig. 2 that these rock mass datasets also consist of vegetations, parts of road and rock debris, which makes the joint detection task challenging.

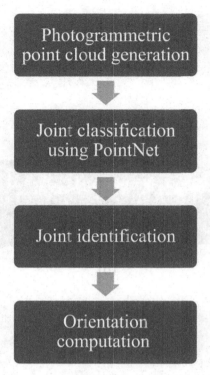

Fig. 1. Flow chart of the proposed methodology

3.2 Joint Classification Using PointNet

Deep Neural Network. PointNet is a highly efficient and effective deep neural net for 3D point cloud classification, part segmentation and semantic segmentation. This deep network directly takes raw point clouds as input and outputs the class labels for the entire point cloud or for each point. In our work, PointNet is deployed to identify joint points from the entire point cloud. This step improves the performance of our algorithm both in terms of accuracy and speed. In particular, PointNet is able to eliminate noise such as vegetation, parts of road and sky, rock debris, etc. Moreover, this elimination speeds up the run time of the subsequent step, by significantly reducing the amount of input points.

Dataset Preparation. Datasets A and B were used for generating training and validation data required by PointNet. The datasets were labelled manually using the "Segment" tool in CloudCompare [24] software such that each point is labelled as joint or non-joint as shown in Fig. 3. In each model, the dark blue colored points are labelled as joint class and the rest of the points are labelled as non-joint class. These datasets were separately divided into 5765 voxels. The voxel size in each case was selected such that each voxel would have more than 2048 points required by PointNet. From this collection, 1000 voxels were selected such that each voxel had a mixture of points from both classes.

(a)

(b)

(c)

Fig. 2. Rock Mass 3D point clouds: (a) Dataset A, (b) Dataset B, and (c) Dataset C

Experimental Work. Each training point was represented by x, y and z information which was normalized to a unit sphere. Training data was also augmented by randomly rotating the data points along all three axes during training. The experiments were performed using Nvidia GTX 2080 Ti graphics cards. During our experiments, the classification accuracy of 77% was obtained on the validation set.

3.3   Joint Identification

The output of PointNet is a set of points which may belong to any joint surfaces. In the next step, points belonging to the individual joint surfaces need to be clustered. In this work, DBSCAN has been used for this purpose. Two parameters are required by DBSCAN: (a) eps, the density parameter used to find neighboring points; (b) min-points, the minimum number of points to form a cluster. DBSCAN is affected by the variation in density of the point cloud. In this work we have adopted the value of eps suggested by Riquelme et al. [11] as will be mentioned in Sect. 4. After this step, all points will be assigned individual clusters representing the joint surfaces.

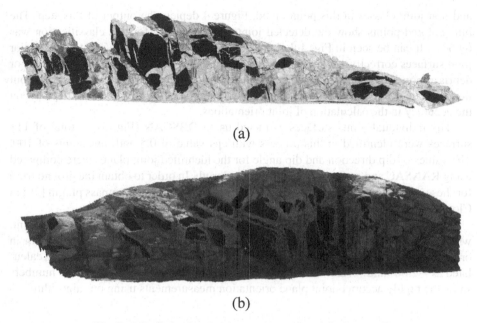

(a)

(b)

Fig. 3. Labelled point clouds:(a) Dataset A and (b) Dataset B

3.4 Orientations Computation

The orientation of individual joints is identified by fitting planes to points of each cluster identified in previous step. The random sample consensus (RANSAC) algorithm [25] was used for fitting planes to joint surfaces. RANSAC computes a plane equation for each joint cluster in the form:

$$ax + by + cz + d = 0 \tag{1}$$

where a, b and c represent unit normal vector of the plane. The dip direction and dip angle for the plane can then be computed by using Eqs. 2 and 3 [13].

$$dip\ direction = q - \tan^{-1}\left(\frac{b}{a}\right) \tag{2}$$

where $q = 90°$, if a > 0; $q = 270$, if a < 0; Dip direction = $0°$, if a = 0 and b ≥ 0; Dip direction = $180°$, if a = 0 and b ≤ 0.

$$dip = q - \tan^{-1}\left(\frac{|c|}{\sqrt{a^2 + b^2}}\right) \tag{3}$$

4 Results and Discussions

Dataset C has been developed for evaluating the performance of the proposed methodology. This point cloud includes 1643220 points. PointNet is first used to classify joint and non-joint classes in this point cloud. Figure 4 depicts the output of this step. The blue colored points show the detected joints. The accuracy for this classification was 69.64%. It can be seen in Fig. 4 that the PointNet is able to classify most of the major joint surfaces correctly while being able to reject the noise points such as vegetation or debris as non-joint points. While the classification accuracy provides some insight about the performance of our algorithm, the real work applicability of this work, depends on the accuracy in the calculation of joint orientations.

The individual joints surfaces extracted using DBSCAN (Fig. 5). A total of 111 surfaces were identified in this process with eps value of 0.5 and min-points of 100. The values of dip direction and dip angle for the identified joint planes were computed using RANSAC and compared with the ground truth. In order to obtain the ground truth for these orientations, manual readings were recorded using the Compass plugin [26] in CloudCompare software.

Our analysis showed that 67 surfaces our of the identified surfaces were actual joint, while the rest were either part of the vegetation or debris. Finally, the average error in orientation values for all identified joints planes compared to the ground truth, was calculated as $-2.06°$ and $-1.24°$ for dip direction and dip angle respectively. These numbers show the highly accurate joint plane orientation measurements using our algorithm.

Fig. 4. Visual results of PointNet semantic classification

In order to further evaluate the performance of our algorithm, the previously published method, Discontinuity Set Extractor (DSE) [27] was used on the same data set. Ten major joint planes were selected for comparison of dip direction and dip angle with ground truth values. Dip direction and dip angle errors summarized in Table 1 clearly show the strength of our algorithm.

Fig. 5. Results of DBSCAN clustering on segmented point cloud

Table 1. Dip direction and dip angle error using DSE and the proposed method

Proposed method		DSE	
Δ Dip direction	Δ Dip angle	Δ Dip direction	Δ Dip angle
−1.15°	0.13°	5.98°	3.54°

As mentioned above, the joint points classification accuracy was lower than the observed accuracy during training and validation. Our investigations suggest the lower accuracy is due to the differences between the test and validation sets due to the limitations of data acquisition in this study. For example, the lower part of the rock cut is part of a road which is horizontal, and some other parts are also planar due to weathering. Nevertheless, the lower accuracy in classification does not seem to reduce accuracy of final orientation values which are of the most significance to a geologist.

Overall, our results demonstrate the significant potential of this method for automatic discontinuity characterization from rock mass point data. The conventional methods [11, 13] based on statistical analysis of geometrical properties (normal directions) require high computation time, which was a motivating factor for the initiation of our research. Our recorded time for processing over one million points using DSE took 3231 s while our method took only 52.31 s to process the same amount of data. It should also be noted that PointNet runs GPU while DSE completely runs on CPU.

Another advantage of the proposed method is elimination of the need for extensive statistical analysis thereby removing the human bias. Moreover, some previous methods based on region growing require numerous parameters tuning which reduces their generality and applicability, while the deployed DBSCAN algorithm in this study requires only 2 parameters to be tuned.

5   Conclusion and Future Work

In this study, we aimed to develop a fast and automatic joint orientation computation algorithm from 3D point clouds of rock mass. Data were collected using UAV and point cloud models were generated using photogrammetry. A labelled dataset was constructed by manually labelling joint surfaces on rock mass point clouds. A popular deep learning architecture was applied for semantic classification of joint surfaces from rock mass point clouds. Then, DBSCAN clustering algorithm was deployed for segmenting points belonging to individual joint surfaces and finally their orientations were computed using RANSAC. The results show that our algorithm is capable of computing the dip directions and angles accurately. The computation time of the proposed method was also significantly lower than a similar approach in the literature. For future work, we plan to investigate the PointNet++ architecture to improve the accuracy of semantic classification. Also, characterization of other discontinuity parameters like spacing, persistence and block size will be investigated.

Acknowledgments. This work has been funded by the US National Institute for Occupational Safety and Health (NIOSH) under Contract No. 75D30119C06044. We are grateful to the funding agency for support.

References

1. Jaboyedoff, M., Couture, R., Locat, P.: Structural analysis of Turtle Mountain (Alberta) using digital elevation model: toward a progressive failure. Geomorphology **103**, 5–16 (2009). https://doi.org/10.1016/j.geomorph.2008.04.012
2. Kainthola, A., Singh, P.K., Singh, T.N.: Stability investigation of road cut slope in basaltic rockmass, Mahabaleshwar, India. Geosci. Front. **6**, 837–845 (2015). https://doi.org/10.1016/j.gsf.2014.03.002
3. Zare, M., Jimenez, R.: On the development of a slope instability index for open-pit mines using an improved systems approach. In: ISRM Regional Symposium - EUROCK 2015, pp. 1041–1046. International Society for Rock Mechanics and Rock Engineering, Salzburg, Austria (2015)
4. Zare Naghadehi, M., Jimenez, R., KhaloKakaie, R., Jalali, S.M.E.: A new open-pit mine slope instability index defined using the improved rock engineering systems approach. Int. J. Rock Mech. Min. Sci. **61**, 1–14 (2013). https://doi.org/10.1016/j.ijrmms.2013.01.012
5. Slob, S., et al.: Method for automated discontinuity analysis of rock slopes with three-dimensional laser scanning. Transp. Res. Rec. J. Transp. Res. Board. **1913**, 187–194 (2005). https://doi.org/10.1177/0361198105191300118
6. Qi, C.R., Su, H., Mo, K., Guibas, L.J.: PointNet: deep learning on point sets for 3D classification and segmentation. In: IEEE Conference on Computer Vision and Pattern Recognition, pp. 79–85. Honolulu, Hawaii (2017)
7. Chen, J., Zhu, H., Li, X.: Automatic extraction of discontinuity orientation from rock mass surface 3D point cloud. Comput. Geosci. **95**, 18–31 (2016). https://doi.org/10.1016/j.cageo.2016.06.015
8. Van Knapen, B., Slob, S.: Identification and characterisation of rock mass discontinuity sets using 3D laser scanning (2006)
9. Jimenez-Rodriguez, R., Sitar, N.: A spectral method for clustering of rock discontinuity sets. Int. J. Rock Mech. Min. Sci. **43**, 1052–1061 (2006). https://doi.org/10.1016/j.ijrmms.2006.02.003
10. Guo, J., Liu, S., Zhang, P., Wu, L., Zhou, W., Yu, Y.: Towards semi-automatic rock mass discontinuity orientation and set analysis from 3D point clouds. Comput. Geosci. **103**, 164–172 (2017). https://doi.org/10.1016/j.cageo.2017.03.017
11. Riquelme, A.J., Abellán, A., Tomás, R., Jaboyedoff, M.: A new approach for semi-automatic rock mass joints recognition from 3D point clouds. Comput. Geosci. **68**, 38–52 (2014). https://doi.org/10.1016/j.cageo.2014.03.014
12. Zhang, P., Li, J., Yang, X., Zhu, H.: Semi-automatic extraction of rock discontinuities from point clouds using the ISODATA clustering algorithm and deviation from mean elevation. Int. J. Rock Mech. Min. Sci. **110**, 76–87 (2018). https://doi.org/10.1016/j.ijrmms.2018.07.009
13. Kong, D., Wu, F., Saroglou, C.: Automatic identification and characterization of discontinuities in rock masses from 3D point clouds. Eng. Geol. **265** (2020). https://doi.org/10.1016/j.enggeo.2019.105442
14. Wang, X., Zou, L., Shen, X., Ren, Y., Qin, Y.: A region-growing approach for automatic outcrop fracture extraction from a three-dimensional point cloud. Comput. Geosci. **99**, 100–106 (2017). https://doi.org/10.1016/j.cageo.2016.11.002

15. Ge, Y., et al.: Automated measurements of discontinuity geometric properties from a 3D-point cloud based on a modified region growing algorithm. Eng. Geol. **242**, 44–54 (2018). https://doi.org/10.1016/j.enggeo.2018.05.007

16. Drews, T., et al.: Validation of fracture data recognition in rock masses by automated plane detection in 3D point clouds. Int. J. Rock Mech. Min. Sci. **109**, 19–31 (2018). https://doi.org/10.1016/j.ijrmms.2018.06.023

17. Hu, L., Xiao, J., Wang, Y.: Efficient and automatic plane detection approach for 3-D rock mass point clouds. Multimed. Tools Appl. (2019). https://doi.org/10.1007/s11042-019-08189-6

18. Ferrero, A.M., Forlani, G., Roncella, R., Voyat, H.I.: Advanced geostructural survey methods applied to rock mass characterization. Rock Mech. Rock Eng. **42**, 631–665 (2009). https://doi.org/10.1007/s00603-008-0010-4

19. Gomes, R.K., De Oliveira, L.P.L., Gonzaga, L., Tognoli, F.M.W., Veronez, M.R., De Souza, M.K.: An algorithm for automatic detection and orientation estimation of planar structures in LiDAR-scanned outcrops. Comput. Geosci. **90**, 170–178 (2016). https://doi.org/10.1016/j.cageo.2016.02.011

20. Gigli, G., Casagli, N.: Semi-automatic extraction of rock mass structural data from high resolution LIDAR point clouds. Int. J. Rock Mech. Min. Sci. **48**, 187–198 (2011). https://doi.org/10.1016/j.ijrmms.2010.11.009

21. Vasuki, Y., Holden, E.J., Kovesi, P., Micklethwaite, S.: Semi-automatic mapping of geological structures using UAV-based photogrammetric data: an image analysis approach. Comput. Geosci. **69**, 22–32 (2014). https://doi.org/10.1016/j.cageo.2014.04.012

22. DJI: DJI Mavic Pro – Specs, Tutorials & Guides. https://www.dji.com/mavic/info

23. Agisoft: Agisoft Metashape. https://www.agisoft.com/

24. CloudCompare (2020). https://www.danielgm.net/cc/

25. Fischler, M.A., Bolles, R.C.: Random sample consensus: a paradigm for model fitting with applications to image analysis and automated cartography. Commun. ACM **24**, 381–395 (1981). https://doi.org/10.1145/358669.358692

26. Thiele, S.T., Grose, L., Samsu, A., Micklethwaite, S., Vollgger, S.A., Cruden, A.R.: Rapid, semi-automatic fracture and contact mapping for point clouds, images and geophysical data. Solid Earth **8**, 1241–1253 (2017). https://doi.org/10.5194/se-8-1241-2017

27. Riquelme, A., Tomás, R., Cano, M., Abellan, A.: Using open-source software for extracting geomechanical parameters of a rock mass from 3D point clouds: discontinuity set extractor and SMRTool (2016)

Feature Map Retargeting to Classify Biomedical Journal Figures

Vinit Veerendraveer Singh$^{(\boxtimes)}$ and Chandra Kambhamettu

Video/Image Modeling and Synthesis (VIMS) Lab, University of Delaware,
Newark, DE 19716, USA
{vinitvs,chandrak}@udel.edu

Abstract. In this work, we propose a layer to retarget feature maps in Convolutional Neural Networks (CNNs). Our "Retarget" layer densely samples values for each feature map channel at locations inferred by our proposed spatial attention regressor. Our layer increments an existing saliency-based distortion layer by replacing its convolutional components with depthwise convolutions. This reformulation with the tuning of its hyper-parameters makes the Retarget layer applicable at any depth of feed-forward CNNs. Keeping in spirit with Content-Aware Image Resizing retargeting methods, we introduce our layers at the bottlenecks of three pre-trained CNNs. We validate our approach on the Image-CLEF2013, ImageCLEF2015, and ImageCLEF2016 document subfigure classification task. Our redesigned DenseNet121 model with the Retarget layer achieved state-of-the-art results under the visual category when no data augmentations were performed. Performing spatial sampling for each channel of the feature maps at deeper layers exponentially increases computational cost and memory requirements. To address this, we experiment with an approximation of the nearest neighbor interpolation and show consistent improvement over the baseline models and other state-of-the-art attention models. The code is available at https://github.com/VimsLab/CNN-Retarget.

Keywords: Feature maps retargeting · Convolutional Neural Networks · Biomedical document image · Classification

1 Introduction

Extracting information from images to solve vision tasks is trivial for humans. However, computer vision methods are not as robust in making such decisions. Modern supervised learning methods alleviate this problem by harnessing the increased availability of annotated image data to improve their decision-making abilities. Among supervised learning methods, CNNs, have achieved state-of-the-art results on numerous image-based vision tasks such as classification, object localization, and segmentation. Standard CNNs [1,2] contain local receptive units with shared weights and spatial sub-sampling units stacked sequentially. The weights in the receptive units are updated to minimize the global loss

© Springer Nature Switzerland AG 2020
G. Bebis et al. (Eds.): ISVC 2020, LNCS 12510, pp. 728–741, 2020.
https://doi.org/10.1007/978-3-030-64559-5_58

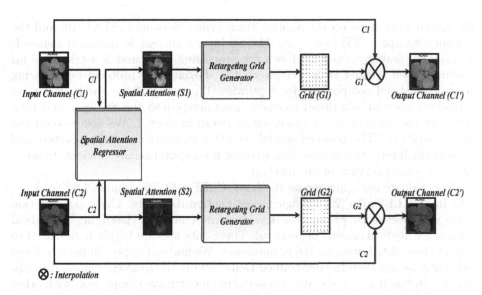

Fig. 1. Overview of our approach. Spatial attention is inferred through a spatial attention regressor. The retargeting grid generator provides a separate grid for each channel. The interpolation algorithm utilizes these grids to densely sample feature map responses with high spatial attention values. Blue color and red color represent lower and higher values of spatial attention, respectively. [Best viewed in color] (Color figure online)

function by gradient-based learning, giving CNNs the ability to extract higher-order task-relevant features for a specific predictive modeling problem. Despite their rich representational power, standard CNNs lack certain modeling capabilities. Most contemporary research improves CNNs' decision-making abilities by designing novel backbone architectures or by incorporating attention modules in them.

Following the success of deep CNNs [1] on the ILSVRC-2012 [3] competition, CNNs with different backbones have been proposed. Most approaches [4–9] make CNNs deeper or wider by stacking and combining convolutional layers under varying configurations. Contrary to creating new backbone architectures, attention modules are introduced into existing CNNs to improve upon their shortcomings. CNNs lack internal mechanisms to handle large geometric transformations, and a few attention-based methods [10–12] model geometrical invariance. Other methods [13–16] refine feature maps through network engineering.

Image retargeting methods in computer graphics preserve and distort the aesthetically valuable content in an image while sub-sampling. CNNs are not subject to such subjective constraints. Depending upon the task's predictive accuracy, CNNs recognize important content in feature maps. In this work, keeping in the spirit of retargeting methods, we amalgamate the idea of distorting feature maps at the CNNs sub-sampling layers. For this, we propose a Retarget layer to explicitly increase the spatial coverage of feature map responses at locations inferred through our proposed spatial attention regressor. Our layer build upon the initial work done on the Spatial Transformer Networks (STN) [10] and the Saliency Sampler (SS) layer [12]. The SS layer's current formulation makes it suitable for training when used as a pre-processing block and is detrimental for training when applied at deeper layers. We alleviate this problem by replacing its convolutional components by depthwise [17] convolutions. Furthermore, we introduce a set of additional learnable parameters into the SS layer and tune a few of its parameters, as discussed in detail in Sect. 3. We also extend the grid sampler in STN to model spatial attention for every channel separately and modify the interpolation algorithm to make it computationally efficient. Figure 1 illustrates the overview of our method.

We evaluate our approach on the ImageCLEF2013 [18], ImageCLEF2015 [19] and ImageCLEF2016 [20] subfigure classification data sets. These classification tasks were released to prompt the development of methods classifying biomedical figures for medical document retrieval. These data sets are highly imbalanced to reflect their distribution on larger databases. We find our approach performs significantly better than the pre-trained DenseNet121 [7], ResNet50 [6], and InceptionV3 [9] baseline models. We also perform an extensive comparison with other state-of-the-art attention models and show significant improvements. State-of-the-art results are achieved on all three datasets when our module is used with the DenseNet121 baseline.

2   Related Work

Modeling spatial transformations on the input data or the feature maps using geometric clues to improve the CNNs decision-making ability is an open research problem. STN [10] can learn either affine, projective, or Thin-Plate Spline (TPS) transformation to spatially manipulate input images to the network. However, identical transformations are applied across all channels to maintain spatial consistency. Finnveden et al. [21] show the problems with using STN to transform intermediate feature maps and proposed sharing the first X layers of the Spatial Transformer module with the classification network. TPS based feature maps can also undergo extreme transformations and fold-overs. Shen et al. [22] applied random scaling, cropping, and translation transformations to the feature maps. However, these transformations are not learned by the network. Deformable convolutional networks (DCN) [11] learn offsets and add them to the regular kernel sampling locations while performing the convolution and pooling operations in CNNs. However, Zhu et al. [23] find that the coverage of the sampling positions learned by DCN can extend beyond the area of interest. They use a teacher network invariant to the information outside of the area of interest and use it to train DCN using a mimicking loss.

Some methods model attention into the CNNs inspired by the human visual system. Traditionally, computational saliency is modeled by identifying regions that stand out in an image while being in accordance with a human observer. Flores et al. [24] proposed an attention mechanism that modulates the feature map responses for the image classification task. They generate these modulation maps by passing saliency maps through a separate convolutional branch, and they experiment fusing these modulation maps at different depths within the networks. Nanni *et al.* [25] follows a similar approach, and they train different saliency maps on separate CNNs and combine the ensemble of these networks using the sum rule. However, saliency maps in both these approaches are pre-computed using other existing methods and not learned by the network itself. Modeling eye movements within CNN has been recently introduced by Sigurdsson *et al.* [26]. However, their approach requires an explicit conversion to a 3D architecture, increasing the computational overhead. Experiments have also been performed to add gaze information captured through external hardware into CNNs [27].

Modeling attention into CNNs by network engineering has also gained popularity. Squeeze-and-excitation (SE) blocks [13] learn per-channel modulation weights by producing an embedding that captures the distribution of channel-wise responses in a feature map. These embeddings get passed through a self-gating mechanism. SE blocks' perform channel-wise multiplication between these learned weights and the feature maps to model the inter-channel dependencies. Wang *et al.* [14] introduced attention modules that consist of a trunk branch that learns task-relevant features and a mask branch that softy weighs those features using a residual learning formulation. Bottleneck Attention Module (BAM) [15] compute the feature map attention across two different dimensions; channel and spatial. Information across both dimensions is combined to refine the original feature maps by a sequence of element-wise additions or element-wise multiplications. Convolutional Block Attention Module (CBAM) [16] refines input feature maps by performing a series of element-wise multiplications with attention learned from the channel and the spatial dimension.

Closely related to our work in this paper; some methods explicitly increase the spatial content at certain areas of input images or feature maps. As mentioned earlier, Recasens *et al.* [12] were the first to realize the role of image retargeting in modern CNN. Their saliency-based sampler can be used within CNN's deeper layers, but this idea was not explored. Their approach to finding saliency is computationally expensive since a different network is required to learn it. Marin *et al.* [28] formulate content-adaptive downsampling as a least-squares problem subject to convex constraints that are solved globally by a set of sparse linear equations. Their method favors locations near semantic boundaries of classes before down-sampling from high-resolution images. This downsampling block is positioned before a few standard image segmentation models leading to better boundary quality for small objects. Poernomo and Kang [29] show they obtain better feature representations in CNNs by downsizing feature maps by their seam carving layer. Their layer finds and discards the pixel path that minimizes the seam cost function [30] gradually until the layer achieves the desired output size. However, they insert their layer only after the first and second layers of a very shallow CNN. Cropping is observed in STN when the determinant of the left 2×2 sub-matrix of the affine transformation matrix has a magnitude less than unity, but they do not explicitly impose such a constraint.

3   Method

In this section of the paper, we elucidate upon the detailed architecture of our spatial attention regressor and elaborate upon the formulation of our Retarget layer.

3.1   Spatial Attention Regressor

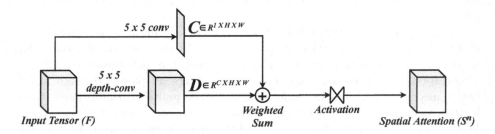

Fig. 2. Detailed architecture: Given an intermediate feature map F, the spatial attention regressor module infers the spatial attention S^n . S^n is computed by applying either softmax activation or min-max scaling on the weighted sum of the outputs of the convolutional branch C and the depthwise convolutional branch D.

Detailed architecture of the spatial attention regressor in illustrated in Fig. 2. This module can infer spatial attention $S^n \in \mathbb{R}^{CXHXW}$ from an input feature map $F \in \mathbb{R}^{CXHXW}$. Here, S^1 would imply the spatial attention for the first channel. This transformation is given by Eq. 1.

$$S^n = Activation\left(W_1 C + W_2 D\right), \tag{1}$$

where $W_1 \in \mathbb{R}^C$ is the weight learned by the network for performing element-wise multiplication with the stacked output of the convolutional branch $C \in \mathbb{R}^{1XHXW}$. W_1 weights are constrained between 0 and 1. W_2 weights, calculated as $1 - W_1$, are used to perform element-wise multiplication with the output of depthwise convolution branch $D \in \mathbb{R}^{CXHXW}$. The size of the convolution filters is set to 5×5 for both C and D. We also experiment with two hyper-parameters for this module; weighted sum of C and D is normalized to have values between 0 and 1 by either the softmax activation function or by performing min-max scaling per channel.

3.2   Retarget Layer

In the original work, saliency in the Saliency Sampler (SS) is learned as a single channel, and it determines the regions to zoom on all the three channels of the input image. No problem arises when SS is used as a pre-processing block to a task network due to spatial consistency in the input images' channels. However, the channels of feature maps at deeper layers of CNNs learn discriminative features required to make a global decision. In its current form, SS cannot be used within the deeper layers of CNNs. This problem arises from the SS layer using a Gaussian distance kernel to regularize pixels merging to the same value while allocating them to the target region. Due to the presence of a Gaussian distance kernel, SS ends up taking a convolutional form. Since convolution operations in CNNs combine information between feature map channels, the SS layer in its convolutional form will combine sampling locations between the channels. In this work, we incorporate a Gaussian distance kernel $D^{\mathcal{G}}$ in a depthwise convolution setting, thus avoiding the mixing of sampling locations between channels. This reformulations is described by Eq. 2 and Eq. 3. u^n and v^n are functions that map feature map responses proportionally to the normalized per-channel weight assigned to them by the learned spatial attention.

$$u^n\left(x,y\right) = \frac{\sum_{x',y'} S^n\left(x',y'\right) D^{\mathcal{G}}\left((x,y),(x',y')\right) x'}{\sum_{x',y'} S^n\left(x',y'\right) D^{\mathcal{G}}\left((x,y),(x',y')\right)} \qquad (2)$$

$$v^n\left(x,y\right) = \frac{\sum_{x',y'} S^n\left(x',y'\right) D^{\mathcal{G}}\left((x,y),(x',y')\right) y'}{\sum_{x',y'} S^n\left(x',y'\right) D^{\mathcal{G}}\left((x,y),(x',y')\right)} \qquad (3)$$

Unlike, SS the Retarget layer learns $\sigma \in \mathbb{R}^C$ without explicitly setting it to a certain value. However, the Retarget layer, like SS, has an undesirable bias to sample towards the image center. This can be avoided by padding spatial attention with border values. However, using larger padding values can cause extreme deformations. We find the size of the padding to be a hyper-parameter for the Retarget layer. In this work, we obtain the padding by dividing the height of input feature maps by a reduction ratio r.

3.3   Faster Interpolation

Interpolation methods use spatial coordinates from a sampling grid to assign values from an input feature map to an output feature map. Both STN and SS use the grid sampler to perform bilinear interpolation on the feature maps, and learned transformations are applied identically across all channels. In this work, we extend the grid sampler introduced in STN to perform spatial sampling separately for each channel of an intermediate feature map F. The use of bilinear interpolation produces blurred outputs since the output value for a single location is obtained by taking a weighted sum of its four nearest corners. However, the blurring of feature maps without any explicit learning can be detrimental to deep CNNs [26] and is also computationally expensive. The nearest-neighbor interpolation only selects the nearest corner value to produce an output, and thus no blurring of feature maps is observed. In our work, we remove the checks to find the nearest-neighbor and estimate sampling locations by using the floor function. Like nearest-neighbor interpolation, gradients are either zero or undefined for the grid.

4   Experiments

4.1   Data Set and Experimental Setup

We evaluate our Retarget layer and our spatial attention regressor for the medical subfigure classification task on three different biomedical document data sets: ImageCLEF2013, ImageCLEF2015, and ImageCLEF2016. Images in these datasets primarily belong to two classes; diagnostic images and generic biomedical illustrations. The distribution of figures into train and test set is given in Table 1. All the data sets exhibit class-imbalance. For example, five classes cover more than 76% of the data in the ImageCLEF2016 dataset. In contrast, some classes contain less than ten figures. Some of the classes show high intra-class similarity; figures in the "Dermatology" class are remarkably similar to the "Other Organs" class. The medical modality figures contain additional noise in the form of writings and drawings. We introduce our Retarget layer along with the spatial attention regressor after the first and second convolutional bottlenecks of the pre-trained DenseNet121, ResNet50, and InceptionV3 architectures. Our training approach is similar to Andrearczyk and Müller [31]; we train all the networks for 25 epochs with an Adam [32] optimizer learning rate set to 0.0001. Average decays β_1 and β_2 are set to 0.9 and 0.999, respectively. However, we do not weigh the loss function since we found accuracy to be very sensitive to changes in it. Besides rescaling each figure to 224×224 for the DenseNet121 and ResNet50 architectures, and 299×299 for InceptionV3 architecture, we do not perform any augmentations or use extra data. We evaluate our method against the baseline (pre-trained architectures without additional attention modules). Then we compare against state-of-the-art attention modules such as SE, BAM, and CBAM introduced into the baseline in their standard settings. Finally, we evaluate the effectiveness of our module under different configurations, namely, the size of the reduction ratio r in the Retarget layer and the choice of the activation function in the spatial attention regressor. We also perform extensive ablation experiments.

Table 1. Distribution of figures and class in the train set and test set

Data set	Number of figures		Number of classes
	Train set	Test set	
ImageCLEF2013	2879	2570	31
ImageCLEF2015	4532	2244	30
ImageCLEF2016	6776	4166	30

4.2   Quantitative Experimental Results

We compare the performance of our module against other competitive attention models in Table 2(a), Table 2(b), and Table 2(c), respectively, when no data augmentation was performed. As shown in Table 2, our module outperforms the

Table 2. Comparision of results of different architectures on the ImageCLEF2013, ImageCLEF2015, and ImageCLEF2016 data sets. The right column in each table reports the classification accuracy (Acc) on the datasets. State-of-the-art number are highlighted in bold.

| (a) | | (b) | | (c) | |
| ImageCLEF2013 Results | | ImageCLEF2015 Results | | ImageCLEF2016 Results | |
Architecture	Acc	Architecture	Acc	Architecture	Acc
DenseNet121	84.16	DenseNet121	75.58	DenseNet121	86.58
DenseNet121$_{SE}$	86.38	DenseNet121$_{SE}$	74.91	DenseNet121$_{SE}$	82.78
DenseNet121$_{BAM}$	85.56	DenseNet121$_{BAM}$	75.17	DenseNet121$_{BAM}$	85.91
DenseNet121$_{CBAM}$	87.31	DenseNet121$_{CBAM}$	71.79	DenseNet121$_{CBAM}$	86.12
DenseNet121$_{Retarget}$	**87.57**	DenseNet121$_{Retarget}$	**75.62**	DenseNet121$_{Retarget}$	**87.13**
ResNet50	81.40	ResNet50	71.34	ResNet50	81.40
ResNet50$_{SE}$	80.54	ResNet50$_{SE}$	67.51	ResNet50$_{SE}$	83.48
ResNet50$_{BAM}$	85.05	ResNet50$_{BAM}$	67.95	ResNet50$_{BAM}$	85.35
ResNet50$_{CBAM}$	85.05	ResNet50$_{CBAM}$	67.51	ResNet50$_{CBAM}$	83.72
ResNet50$_{Retarget}$	85.05	ResNet50$_{Retarget}$	73.93	ResNet50$_{Retarget}$	84.69
InceptionV3	85.94	InceptionV3	73.35	InceptionV3	83.66
InceptionV3$_{SE}$	81.49	InceptionV3$_{SE}$	73.84	InceptionV3$_{SE}$	84.78
InceptionV3$_{BAM}$	83.96	InceptionV3$_{BAM}$	68.27	InceptionV3$_{BAM}$	82.85
InceptionV3$_{CBAM}$	77.39	InceptionV3$_{CBAM}$	68.44	InceptionV3$_{CBAM}$	79.85
InceptionV3$_{Retarget}$	86.77	InceptionV3$_{Retarget}$	74.82	InceptionV3$_{Retarget}$	85.35
DenseNet169 [31]	83.8	SDL [33]	75.00	DenseNet169 [31]	86.20
Ensemble [35]	85.51			SDL [33]	85.93
				CDHVF [34]	85.47

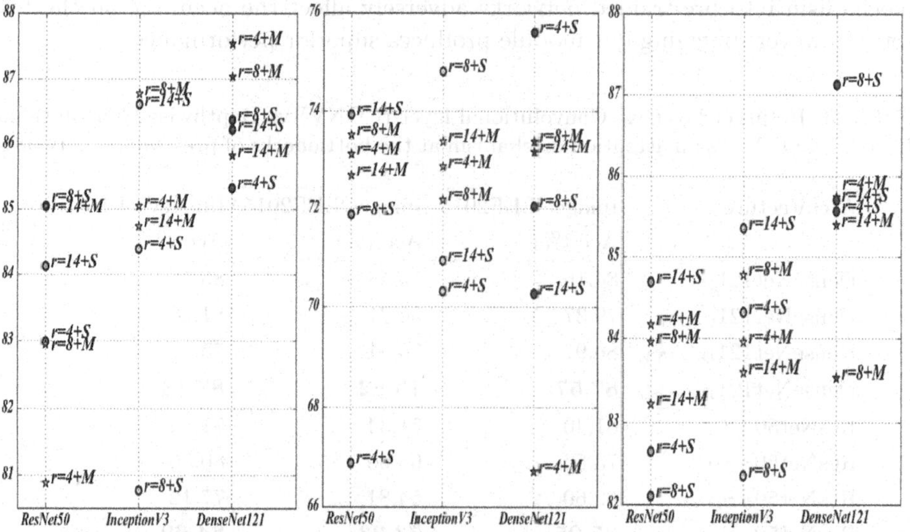

(a)ImageCLEF2013   (b)ImageCLEF2015   (c)ImageCLEF2016

Fig. 3. Accuracy of Retarget layers under different configurations. Reduction ratio r is set to 4, 8, or 14 for all experiments. S represent softmax activation and M represents the min-max scaling.

baseline models and almost outperforms every other attention module on all three pre-trained CNNs. BAM attention module achieved better or comparable results to our module on the ResNet50 trained on ImageCLEF2013 and Image-CLEF2016. Unlike our module, the test accuracy of BAM and CBAM is significantly lower on the InceptionV3 architecture. Our approach also outperforms all the previously reported state-of-the-art methods when no data augmentation is performed. We note that SDL [33] outperforms our approach on the ResNet50 baseline, but their approach uses multiple ResNet50 backbones and a different optimizer. To get insights into the impact of our module's hyper-parameters on test accuracy, we evaluate each model on all the datasets under every possible combination of the reduction ratio and the activation function. As shown in Fig. 3, our module, besides a few configurations, still yields comparable or better accuracy to the other attention modules.

4.3   Ablation Studies

In these experiments, we empirically verify that the improvement to the baseline pre-trained architectures is due to our module's ability to perform significant feature refinement and not due to the increased depth by adding our modules at the bottlenecks. We add auxiliary convolutional layers (CONV) and depthwise convolutional layers (DCONV) at the same bottlenecks locations where our modules were initially placed. The size of the filter is set to 5×5, similar to our spatial attention regressor. Observing the results reported in Table 3, it is obvious that naive plugging of the CONV and DCONV layers as an attention mechanism into pre-trained networks adversely affect the accuracy on the test sets. However, plugging our module produces superior performance.

Table 3. Retarget layer vs. Convolutional layer (CONV) vs Depthwise Convolutional Layer (DCONV) as an attention mechanism at the bottlenecks of pre-trained networks.

Architecture	ImageCLEF2013	ImageCLEF2015	ImageCLEF2016
	Acc (%)	Acc (%)	Acc (%)
DenseNet121	84.16	75.58	86.58
DenseNet121$_{CONV}$	79.37	66.71	81.20
DenseNet121$_{DCONV}$	80.97	70.41	75.20
DenseNet121$_{Retarget}$	**87.57**	**75.62**	**87.13**
ResNet50	81.40	71.34	71.34
ResNet50$_{CONV}$	73.50	65.06	80.50
ResNet50$_{DCONV}$	62.60	54.81	77.12
ResNet50$_{Retarget}$	**85.05**	**73.93**	**84.69**
InceptionV3	85.94	73.53	83.66
InceptionV3$_{CONV}$	74.98	63.01	80.34
InceptionV3$_{DCONV}$	76.22	65.46	76.86
InceptionV3$_{Retarget}$	**86.77**	**74.82**	**85.35**

4.4   Qualitative Results

Qualitative results give insight into the functioning of our module in deeper layers of CNNs. As shown in Fig. 4, retargeting causes the spatial content of the feature map channel to increase at learned locations. The input image in Fig. 4 belongs to the 3D reconstructions category in the ImageCLEF2016 data set. The presence of multiple chemical structures and noise in the form of text makes it challenging to classify. Unlike our approach, which correctly classified this image with a softmax probability of 0.99, the pre-trained baseline DenseNet121 model misclassified this image.

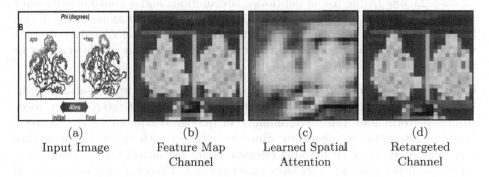

| (a) | (b) | (c) | (d) |
| Input Image | Feature Map Channel | Learned Spatial Attention | Retargeted Channel |

Fig. 4. Visualizing our approach on a channel of a feature map: (a) Input image; (b) Initial response values of the channel; (c) Spatial attention learned by our spatial attention regressor; (d) Channel retargeted by Retarget layer. Blue, green, and red colors represent low, medium, and high channel responses, respectively. [Best viewed in color] (Color figure online)

Our module constructs hierarchical attention when inserted at multiple bottlenecks of the CNNs. As shown in Fig. 5, our module can learn to gradually attend the regions of interest during the CNNs forward pass.

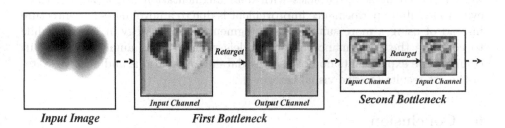

Fig. 5. We observe our module constructs hierarchical attention when placed at multiple bottlenecks. In the illustrated example, the white region and the black regions represent the background and the PET scan, respectively. As expected, our modules gradually reduced background content in the feature map channels.

5   Discussion

Architecture of Spatial Attention Regressor: Naively sending intermediate feature maps to a retargeting function increases the spatial content for high values in feature map channels. Ideally, we want the network to learn where to weigh these responses before retargeting. Although spatial attention can be learned from standard convolutional layers, the number of learnable weights significantly increases at deeper layers of the CNNs. Furthermore, stacking multiple such convolutional layers to infer spatial attention would only further aggravate this problem. On the other hand, our spatial attention regressor is relatively lightweight due to the use of depthwise convolutions and a convolutional layer that only outputs a single channel feature map. Despite our superior results on the three data sets, inferring spatial attention in CNNs is challenging. Adjustment of several hyper-parameters if often required depending on the data set to obtain good performance.

Choice of Interpolation Algorithm: Querying values from spatial coordinates of sampling grids is an expensive operation. Bilinear interpolation algorithms perform four times the number of queries compared to the nearest-neighbor interpolation algorithm. Since we retarget each channel of a feature map separately, the floating-point operations per second (FLOPS) increase significantly. It takes significantly more time to train CNNs with a higher number of channels at their bottlenecks. Hence in our work, we relax the nearest-neighbor interpolation algorithm to avoid additional checks and reduce memory requirements. With GPU efficient programming optimizations, the execution time of performing spatial sampling within the network can be further improved. The Retarget layer can be introduced at different levels CNNs and can be evaluated on much larger data sets with such execution time improvements.

Role of Data Augmentation: Several methods augmented their data by commonly used data augmentations or by increasing the size of their training data set to report results on the ImageCLEF subfigure classification tasks. All previous work reported higher accuracies with data augmentation [31,33,35,36]. However, to attribute performance improvement is due to a novel model architecture instead of using a more suitable data augmentations strategy, it is worthwhile to compare the performance of the models without data augmentation. Our comparative experiments do not use any data augmentations and achieve state-of-the-art results (on the visual category).

6   Conclusion

In this work, we present a Retarget layer and a spatial attention regressor to improve the representational power of pre-trained CNNs. Our approach retargets intermediate feature maps responses for each channel separately, which, to our knowledge, is novel. Also, unlike other methods that perform spatial manipulation in CNNs, our approach does not suffer from extreme deformations. Keeping in spirit with traditional retargeting methods, we introduced our module at the bottlenecks of pre-trained DenseNet121, ResNet50, and InceptionV3 architectures. We conducted extensive experiments on the ImageClef2013, ImageClef2015, and ImageClef2016 subfigure classification data sets under the visual category without data augmentation. We achieved state-of-the-art accuracy on all three data sets by introducing our module in the DenseNet121 model. Compared to other state-of-the-art attention modules, we found that our approach consistently yielded significantly higher accuracy on the ResNet50 and the InceptionV3 architectures.

Acknowledgments. This work was supported by the National Institutes of Health/National Library of Medicine award R01LM012527.

References

1. Krizhevsky, A., Sutskever, I., Hinton, G.E.: ImageNet classification with deep convolutional neural networks. In: Advances in Neural Information Processing Systems, pp. 1097–1105 (2012)
2. LeCun, Y., Bottou, L., Bengio, Y., Haffner, P.: Gradient-based learning applied to document recognition. Proc. IEEE **86**(11), 2278–2324 (1998)
3. Russakovsky, O., et al.: Imagenet large scale visual recognition challenge. Int. J. Comput. Vis. **115**(3), 211–252 (2015)
4. Simonyan, K. and Zisserman, A.: Very deep convolutional networks for large-scale image recognition. arXiv preprint arXiv:1409.1556 (2014)
5. Szegedy, C., et al.: Going deeper with convolutions. In: Proceedings of the IEEE Conference on Computer Vision and Pattern Recognition, pp. 1–9 (2015)
6. He, K., Zhang, X., Ren, S., Sun, J.: Deep residual learning for image recognition. In: Proceedings of the IEEE Conference on Computer Vision and Pattern Recognition, pp. 770–778 (2016)
7. Huang, G., Liu, Z., Van Der Maaten, L., Weinberger, K.Q.: Densely connected convolutional networks. In: Proceedings of the IEEE Conference on Computer Vision and Pattern Recognition, pp. 4700–4708 (2017)
8. Zagoruyko, S., Komodakis, N.: Wide residual networks. arXiv preprint arXiv:1605.07146 (2016)
9. Szegedy, C., Vanhoucke, V., Ioffe, S., Shlens, J., Wojna, Z.: Rethinking the inception architecture for computer vision. In: Proceedings of the IEEE Conference on Computer Vision and Pattern Recognition, pp. 2818–2826 (2016)
10. Jaderberg, M., Simonyan, K., Zisserman, A.: Spatial transformer networks. In: Advances in Neural Information Processing Systems, pp. 2017–2025 (2015)
11. Dai, J., et al.: Deformable convolutional networks. In: Proceedings of the IEEE International Conference on Computer Vision, pp. 764–773 (2017)
12. Recasens, A., Kellnhofer, P., Stent, S., Matusik, W., Torralba, A.: Learning to zoom: a saliency-based sampling layer for neural networks. In: Proceedings of the European Conference on Computer Vision (ECCV), pp. 51–66 (2018)
13. Hu, J., Shen, L. and Sun, G.: Squeeze-and-excitation networks. In: Proceedings of the IEEE Conference on Computer Vision and Pattern Recognition, pp. 7132–7141 (2018)

14. Wang, F., et al.: Residual attention network for image classification. In: Proceedings of the IEEE Conference on Computer Vision and Pattern Recognition, pp. 3156–3164 (2017)
15. Park, J., Woo, S., Lee, J.Y., Kweon, I.S.: BAM: bottleneck attention module. arXiv preprint arXiv:1807.06514 (2018)
16. Woo, S., Park, J., Lee, J.Y. and So Kweon, I.: CBAM: convolutional block attention module. In: Proceedings of the European Conference on Computer Vision (ECCV), pp. 3–19 (2018)
17. Chollet, F.: Xception: deep learning with depthwise separable convolutions. In: Proceedings of the IEEE Conference on Computer Vision and Pattern Recognition, pp. 1251–1258 (2017)
18. Garcia Seco De Herrera, A., Kalpathy-Cramer, J., Demner-Fushman, D., Antani, S., Müller, H.: Overview of the ImageCLEF 2013 medical tasks. In: CEUR Workshop Proceedings, September 2014
19. Garcia Seco De Herrera, A., Müller, H., Bromuri, S.: Overview of the ImageCLEF 2015 medical classification tasks. In: CEUR Workshop Proceedings, August 2015
20. De Herrera, A.G.S., Bromuri, S., Schaer, R., Müller, H.: Overview of the medical tasks in ImageCLEF 2016. CLEF Working Notes, Evora, Portugal (2016)
21. Finnveden, L., Jansson, Y., Lindeberg, T.: The problems with using STNs to align CNN feature maps. arXiv preprint arXiv:2001.05858 (2020)
22. Shen, X., Tian, X., He, A., Sun, S., Tao, D.: Transform-invariant convolutional neural networks for image classification and search. In: Proceedings of the 24th ACM International Conference on Multimedia, pp. 1345–1354, October 2016
23. Zhu, X., Hu, H., Lin, S., Dai, J.: Deformable convnets v2: more deformable, better results. In: Proceedings of the IEEE Conference on Computer Vision and Pattern Recognition, pp. 9308–9316 (2019)
24. Flores, C.F., Gonzalez-Garcia, A., van de Weijer, J., Raducanu, B.: Saliency for fine-grained object recognition in domains with scarce training data. Pattern Recogn. **94**, 62–73 (2019)
25. Nanni, L., Maguolo, G., Pancino, F.: Insect pest image detection and recognition based on bio-inspired methods. Ecolog. Inf. 101089 (2020)
26. Sigurdsson, G.A., Gupta, A., Schmid, C., Alahari, K.: Beyond the camera: neural networks in world coordinates. arXiv preprint arXiv:2003.05614 (2020)
27. Sattar, H., Fritz, M., Bulling, A.: Deep gaze pooling: inferring and visually decoding search intents from human gaze fixations. Neurocomputing **387**, 369–382 (2020)
28. Marin, D., et al.: Efficient segmentation: learning downsampling near semantic boundaries. In: Proceedings of the IEEE International Conference on Computer Vision, pp. 2131–2141 (2019)
29. Poernomo, A., Kang, D.K.: Content-aware convolutional neural network for object recognition task. Int. J. Adv. Smart Converg. 5(3), 1–7 (2016)
30. Avidan, S., Shamir, A.: Seam carving for content-aware image resizing. In: ACM SIGGRAPH 2007 papers, p. 10-es (2007)
31. Andrearczyk, V., Müller, H.: Deep multimodal classification of image types in biomedical journal figures. In: Bellot, P., et al. (eds.) CLEF 2018. LNCS, vol. 11018, pp. 3–14. Springer, Cham (2018). https://doi.org/10.1007/978-3-319-98932-7_1
32. Kingma, D.P., Ba, J.: Adam: a method for stochastic optimization. arXiv preprint arXiv:1412.6980 (2014)
33. Zhang, J., Xie, Y., Wu, Q., Xia, Y.: Medical image classification using synergic deep learning. Med. Image Anal. **54**, 10–19 (2019)

34. Zhang, J., Xia, Y., Xie, Y., Fulham, M., Feng, D.D.: Classification of medical images in the biomedical literature by jointly using deep and handcrafted visual features. IEEE J. Biomed. Health Inf. **22**(5), 1521–1530 (2017)
35. Lee, S.L., Zare, M.R., Muller, H.: Late fusion of deep learning and handcrafted visual features for biomedical image modality classification. IET Image Proc. **13**(2), 382–391 (2018)
36. Stathopoulos, S., Kalamboukis, T.: Medical image classification with weighted latent semantic tensors and deep convolutional neural networks. In: Bellot, P., et al. (eds.) CLEF 2018. LNCS, vol. 11018, pp. 89–100. Springer, Cham (2018). https://doi.org/10.1007/978-3-319-98932-7_8

Automatic 3D Object Detection from RGB-D Data Using PU-GAN

Xueqing Wang[1], Ya-Li Hou[1(✉)], Xiaoli Hao[1], Yan Shen[1], and Shuai Liu[2]

[1] School of Electronics and Information Engineering,
Beijing Jiaotong University, Beijing, China
ylhou@bjtu.edu.cn
[2] School of Engineering, Honghe University, Mengzi, China

Abstract. 3D object detection from RGB-D data in outdoor scenes is crucial in various industrial applications such as autonomous driving, robotics, etc. However, the points obtained from range sensor scans are usually sparse and non-uniform, which seriously limit the detection performance, especially for far-away objects. By learning a rich variety of point distributions from the latent space, we believe that 3D upsampling techniques may fill up the missing knowledge due to the sparsity of the 3D points. Hence, a 3D object detection method using 3D upsampling techniques has been presented in this paper. The main contributions of the paper are two-fold. First, based on the Frustum PointNets pipeline, a 3D object detection method using PU-GAN has been implemented. A state-of-the-art 3D upsampling method, PU-GAN, is used to complement the sparsity of point cloud. Second, some effective strategies have been proposed to improve the detection performance using upsampled dense points. Extensive experimental results on KITTI benchmark show that the impacts of PU-GAN upsampled points on object detection are closely related to the object distances from the camera. They show their superiority when they are applied on objects located at around 30 meters away. By carefully designing the criteria to employ the upsampled points, the developed method can outperform the baseline Frustum PointNets by a large margin for all the categories, including car, pedestrian and cyclist objects.

Keywords: 3D object detection · RGB-D data · PU-GAN

1 Introduction

3D object detection from RGB-D data in outdoor scenes is crucial in various industrial applications such as autonomous driving, robotics, etc. Given RGB-D data as input, 3D object detection is to classify and localize objects, estimate their size and orientations in 3D space. The RGB data are usually 2D images from a camera and the depth data is usually obtained from LiDAR in outdoor scenarios and represented as a point cloud.

Frustum PointNets [1] leverage mature 2D object detectors and directly operate on raw point clouds, which has achieved remarkable performance and become a baseline of 3D detection using RGB-D data. However, the sparsity and non-uniformity of raw point clouds from range sensor scans is still a big headache especially for far-away object

© Springer Nature Switzerland AG 2020
G. Bebis et al. (Eds.): ISVC 2020, LNCS 12510, pp. 742–752, 2020.
https://doi.org/10.1007/978-3-030-64559-5_59

detections. Without sufficient information about the objects of interest, few 3D points often cause inaccurate pose and size estimation.

In recent years, 3D upsampling methods have achieved great progress with the development of deep learning techniques. By learning a rich variety of point distributions from the latent space, we believe that upsampled points may complement the point cloud from the range sensors and finally lead to better object detection performance. Hence, 3D object detection with RGB-D data using 3D upsampling techniques has been studied in this paper. PU-GAN [2] has been used as an example since it is a state-of-the-art work for 3D upsampling and it can achieve a better distribution uniformity and 3D geometry reconstruction quality.

2 Related Work

3D object detection has made great progress thanks to the deep learning, as a fundamental part of 3D scene perception. It is crucial in various industrial applications such as autonomous driving, robotics and augmented reality. Based on the ways to represent RGB-D data, the approaches can be classified into three categories: Front-view image based methods, bird's eye view based methods and 3D based methods.

Front-View Image Based Methods. [3, 4] infer 3D bounding box by combining monocular RGB images and shape priors. [5, 6] use 2D CNN network to extract feature form images for 3D bounding box regression. FVNet [7] first project point clouds onto a cylindrical surface to generate front-view feature maps which retains rich information, and then introduce a proposal generation network to predict 3D region proposals from the generated maps and further extrude objects of interest from the whole point cloud.

Bird's Eye View Based Methods. MV3D [8] achieves relatively high 3D object detection accuracy by fusing LiDAR projections from different perspective. VoxelNet [9] use voxel feature encoding (VFE) layer to extract learning-based features through each voxel, and then the features are stacked as bird's eye view feature maps. Finally, 2D region proposal network (RPN [10]) is trained to complete the 3D detection. SECOND [11] proposes an improved method of sparse convolution [12] for voxel based object detection to increases the speed of training and inference. PointPillars [13] voxelize the whole point cloud into vertical columns (pillars), then encoded features from each pillar are mapped as 2D bird's eye view image for 3D object detection.

3D Based Methods. Frustum PointNets [1] first uses 2D detector to generate 2D box proposals, then frustums are extracted by lifting 2D regions to 3D space, and a PointNet++ [14] framework is used to complete the prediction of 3D box. [15–18] convert image-based depth maps to pseudo LiDAR representations, and then 3D based methods are used to finish the 3D object detection. STD [19] first uses a proposal generation module (PGM) to generate proposals from point-based spherical anchors. Then a PointsPool layer is used to convert proposal features from sparse expression to compact representation.

Although the fusion of RGB images and point data has achieved great success, the sparsity and non-uniformity of point cloud is still a main challenge of 3D object detection. Insufficient 3D points often cause inaccurate pose and size estimation.

3   The Method

The framework of the developed object detection method using PU-GAN is shown in Fig. 1. As a state-of-the-art work of 3D object detection from RGB-D data, the baseline architecture of Frustum PointNets [1] has been followed. A 2D object detector is used to identify the possible object candidates and greatly reduce the search space of point cloud-based 3D object detection. Based on the monocular vision, the camera projection matrix is used to lift 2D proposals to 3D space. In the 3D frustum formed by each proposal, PointNet++ [14] is used to predict the object types, sizes, positions and orientations. At the output, each 3D object is represented by a category label t, a 3D box parameterized by its size h; w; l, its center cx; cy; cz, and the heading angle θ around the up-axis for orientation.

Although the fusion of RGB images and point data for 3D object detection has achieved some remarkable progress, the sparsity of points is still a serious limitation of the detection performance, especially for small objects, like pedestrians in the street. In the KITTI dataset [20], there are less than 50 points for a pedestrian at 30 meters away from the camera and only around 10 points at 60 meters away. Without sufficient 3D points, it is difficult to identify a pedestrian with a high confidence. Motivated by the development of data-driven 3D upsampling techniques in recent years, we believe that 3D upsampling may be able to complement the sparsity of the 3D points by learning various point distributions from a variety of objects. PU-GAN [2] is a recently proposed 3D upsampling method and shows good 3D geometry reconstruction quality even in large scale scenarios. In the developed method, PU-GAN generated dense points are used for 3D object detection. To effectively use the upsampled points, some criteria have been carefully designed to classify the 2D proposals into easy and hard samples. The upsampled points are only used for those difficult to be identified by raw Lidar points.

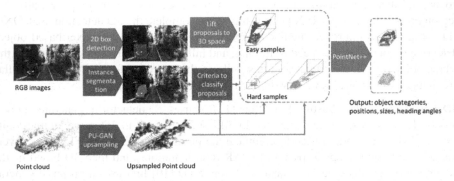

Fig. 1. The proposed framework for 3D object detection using PU-GAN.

PU-GAN Upsampling. To remedy the sparsity of the original lidar points, 3D upsampling techniques are used in the developed method. In recent years, data-driven upsampling approaches have achieved remarkable progress, such as PU-Net [21], EC-Net [22],

MPU [23] etc. In our implementations, PU-GAN [2] is used as an example since it can achieve better uniformity of point distribution and better proximity-to-surface.

Given an original sparse LiDAR point set $P_O = \{X_i, Y_i, Z_i, R_i\}_{i=1}^M$ of M points, PU-GAN aims to produce uniformly-distributed points which can well preserve the underlying geometry of the original object. After the upsampling, a dense point set $P_G = \{X_i, Y_i, Z_i, R_i\}_{i=1}^{rM}$ of rM points can be obtained.

In PU-GAN, the whole process follows the patch-based strategies. S seeds are first picked using the farthest sampling from P_O and a local patch with 256 points around each seed is extracted. Each patch is normalized and fed into a generator, which is guided by a discriminator to generate uniformly distributed dense points. Finally, the upsampled patches are merged into the final output P_G. S is an important parameter for 3D upsampling in a large scale scenario. We have tried different numbers of seeds and use 800 in all our experiments. As shown in Fig. 2, when a small number of seeds is used, the dense points may not be uniform because patches cannot cover the entire scene and only a portion of Lidar points have been upsampled. When the seed number S is 800, the extracted patches can span the entire space and the generated dense points tend to be uniformly distributed in 3D space.

Fig. 2. Upsampled **point cloud data of KITTI dataset from the bird's eye view**. Left: a raw point cloud from KITTI street scene acquired by LiDAR. Middle: upsampled point cloud by PU-GAN with 200 seeds. Right: upsampled point cloud by PU-GAN with 800 seeds.

Criteria to Classify Proposals. A simple way to use PU-GAN for object detection may be to replace all the point clouds from LiDAR with upsampled dense points in the Frustum PointNets architecture. However, the results in our experimental sections show that the effects of upsampled 3D points on object detection are closely related to the object distances. To effectively use 3D upsampling techniques for object detection, some criteria are carefully designed to determine whether Lidar or PU-GAN upsampled points will be used for 3D box estimations.

First, instance segmentation is performed on RGB images to get 2D object masks. In our implementations, Mask R-CNN [24] has been used. Suppose S_O^M and S_G^M are the number of Lidar points and upsampled points from PU-GAN in the mask respectively, we define two criteria to classify the object proposals from a 2D object detector into easy and hard samples, as shown in (1).

$$\begin{cases} crt_1 = S_O^M \\ crt_2 = S_O^M / S_G^M \end{cases} \tag{1}$$

Figure 3 shows the distribution of crt_1 and crt_2 over the distances from the camera. They are plotted based on the ground-truth objects. It can be easily observed that, objects close to the camera tend to have more Lidar points and much higher ratio of Lidar points over upsampled points. We define proposals with crt_1 greater 90 and crt_2 higher than 0.15 as easy samples and it is believed Lidar points are sufficient to make a reliable 3D box estimation for these samples. Other proposals are defined as hard samples and upsampled dense points from PU-GAN will be injected into PointNet++ to predict 3D objects.

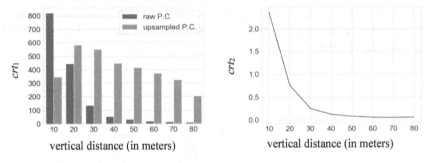

Fig. 3. The distribution of crt_1 and crt_2 over the distances.

Finally, frustums formed by the point clouds are injected into PointNet++ for 3D box estimation. PoinNet++ contains a segmentation network to extract the points of interest in each frustum, a learning-based 3D alignment T-net to refine the centroid of the object based on the masked foreground points, and a PointNet-based 3D box estimation network to finally regress the sizes, positions and heading angles of the 3D objects.

4 Experiments

4.1 Implementation Details

Dataset and Evaluation Metric. All the experimental results are performed on KITTI 3D object detection benchmark [20], which consists of 7481 training images and 7518 test images, as well as the corresponding point clouds. There are a total of 80,256 labeled objects, including three object categories (i.e., car, pedestrian, and cycle). Each category is divided into three different difficulty levels (easy, moderate and hard) according to the object distances and occlusion degrees.

In this experiment, we follow the train/val split as in [8]. The evaluation metric is average precision with the 3D IoU thresholds at 0.7 for car category and 0.5 for pedestrian and cycle categories.

2D Instance Detection. The 2D box proposals come from the same 2D detector model in Frustum PointNets [1]. The open-sourced mask R-CNN [25] is used as the instance segmentation algorithm to obtain the instance masks. The model is pre-trained on the Cityscapes Dataset [26]. For cyclist category, we merge the masks of riders and bicycles to get complete instance mask proposals.

Parameter Settings. The implementation of PU-GAN upsampling method follows the publicly available code in [27]. The farthest sampling strategy is used to choose seeds in the Lidar points and a local patch with 256 points is extracted around each seed. The patches are fed to the generator and upsampled by 12 times. Finally, the upsampled patches are merged and farthest sampling is performed to obtain the final uniformly-distributed points.

The PU-GAN network is trained based on 120 3D models, ranging from simple and smooth models (e.g., Icosahedron) to complex and high-detailed objects (e.g., Statue). A total of 24, 000 patches are collected by cropping 200 patches from each model. These input patches are randomly rotated, scaled to avoid overfitting. The network is trained for 100 epochs with Adam optimizer.

In all the experiments, PointNet++ [14] is used as the backbone of Frustum PointNets for 3D objection. The implementation follows the code in [28]. The models are trained using Adam optimizer with a batch size of 32 frustums, momentum of 0.9. The learning rate is initialized at 0.001 and 0.7 decays every 10 epochs. The models are trained around 80 epochs on one NVIDIA GTX1080Ti GPU. To avoid overfitting, the input frustums are augmented by randomly shifting and expanding the 2D proposals.

4.2 Experimental Results

Results When PU-GAN Points are Applied at Different Distances. To test the impacts of PU-GAN upsampled points on object detection in details, PU-GAN upsampled points are applied on the objects at different distances in this experiment. To decouple the influence of 2D detectors, we use ground truth 2D boxes for region proposals and test the 3D box estimation accuracy. Average precisions of the moderate level in each category are evaluated. In Fig. 3, each point shows the average precision when upsampled points are used for the objects beyond a certain range. For example, when the distance is zero meters, upsampled points are used for all the proposals to estimate the 3D boxes. When the distance is 30 meters, only the proposals beyond 30 meters away from the camera use upsampled points for 3D box estimation and others use original Lidar points. The blue curve is for the car category, the red one is for cyclists and the green one is for pedestrians. The dashed lines indicate the baseline performance of each category in [1].

From Fig. 3, it can be easily observed that the effects of upsampled points on 3D object detection are closely related to the distances of the objects. Using PU-GAN generated dense points for all the objects are not a good option . For objects near the

camera, the accuracy of 3D detection significantly decreases when the generated points
are used instead of Lidar points. The upsampled points show their superiority when they
are applied on the objects beyond 30 meters away from the camera. The superiority
decreases when only the objects beyond 40 meters are considered.

It seems that, PU-GAN upsampling can provide dense and reliable 3D points for
cars, pedestrians and cyclists at around 30 meters away from the camera. For objects
near the camera, Lidar points are dense enough to make a decision on the object types,
locations and orientations. On the other hand, the generated point data from PU-GAN
may not be as accurate as the Lidar points. This may be the reason why the accuracy
decreases when PU-GAN is used for the objects at a short distance. The observations
may also indicate that there is still a large gap for the 3D point upsampling techniques to
be as accurate as real Lidar points for reliable 3D object detection. For far-away objects,
the underlying geometry of the object may not be able to be well indicated by very few
Lidar points, which may mislead the generation of 3D point generation by PU-GAN
(Fig. 4).

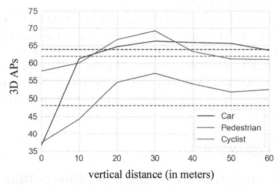

Fig. 4. The 3D APs of the moderate level in each category when PU-GAN generated dense points
are used beyond a certain distance.

Detection When PU-GAN Points are Applied with Our Criteria. In the test stage,
distances of objects are unknown. In this experiment, criteria proposed in Sect. 3 are
tested to verify its efficiency to improve the 3D detection performance using upsampled
dense points. Since objects close to the camera tend to have sufficient and accurate Lidar
point data, dense points generated from PU-GAN are only used for 2D proposals with
S_O^M less than 90 and S_O^M / S_G^M lower than 0.15. Frustum PointNets is used as a baseline for
comparison since it is still a state-of-the-art work of 3D object detection using RGB-D
data. The 3D object detection AP for each category are shown in Table 1. The results of
Frustum PointNets on KITTI *val* set are obtained using the public code in [28] and the
models are trained by ourselves.

Table 1. 3D object detection AP on KITTI *val* set.

Category	Method	3D AP		
		Easy	Mod.	Hard
Car	Frustum PointNet	82.39	**69.86**	**62.73**
	Ours	**82.72**	67.88	60.31
Pedestrian	Frustum PointNet	60.96	53.08	47.41
	Ours	**65.81**	**57.34**	**50.14**
Cyclist	Frustum PointNet	67.33	50.73	47.47
	Ours	**71.57**	**52.05**	**48.25**

From Table 1, it can be observed that significant improvements are achieved for pedestrians and cyclists. The average precision is increased by around 5% and 4% respectively for the easy level in the pedestrian and cyclist category. The moderate level and hard level for pedestrians are improved by 4.26% and 2.73% respectively. The results show the potential of the upsampled dense point data from the data-driven approaches for 3D object detection. To further improve its efficiency in the moderate and hard levels, the 3D upsampling techniques may need more prior knowledge about the geometry of the specific categories. For the car category, the detection performance for the easy level is slightly improved while the moderate and hard level decrease a little bit. The reason may be that the threshold setting for S_O^M and S_O^M/S_G^M is strict for the car category and the current upsampling techniques are not powerful enough to produce reliable points for those difficult cases. In the future, the parameters will be tuned carefully and different thresholds may be considered for the proposals with different category labels.

Figure 5 Gives More Qualitative Results for Comparison. In each group, the upper part is the 3D box detection results shown in RGB images while the lower part is the 3D box detection results shown with Lidar point cloud in bird's eye view. In a), c) and d), it can be observed that the original Frustum PointNets algorithm has large errors in the prediction of 3D bounding box in the illustrated samples. With the developed method, the positions and the orientations of the cars can be better estimated due to the complementary knowledge from the upsampled dense points. In b), a partially-occluded pedestrian is missed in the baseline, but the developed method has successfully detected it.

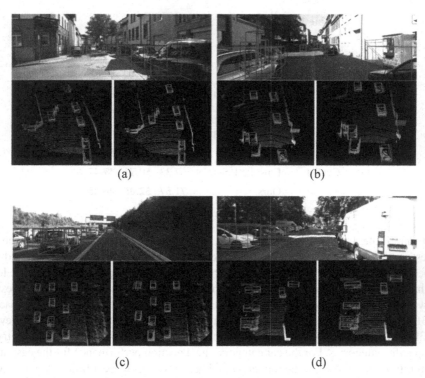

(a)   (b)

(c)   (d)

Fig. 5. Qualitative **comparison of the Frustum PointNets and our method.** In each group, the upper part is the 3D box detection results shown in RGB images: our method (red) and the Frustum PoinNet (blue). The lower part is the 3D box detection results shown with Lidar point cloud in bird's eye view. Groundtruth (green), Frustum PoinNets (blue) and our developed method (red). (Color figure online)

5   Conclusions

In this paper, a 3D object detection method using PU-GAN has been developed. PU-GAN upsampled dense points are tested for object detection at different distances. Extensive experimental results show that the impacts of 3D upsampling on object detection are closely related to object distances from the camera. Two criteria are proposed to better combine the advantages of the lidar points and the generated dense points. The results on KITTI 3D object detection benchmark show the potential of the 3D upsampling method for 3D object detection purpose.

Although our algorithm is based on Frustum PointNet and PU-GAN, the idea to complement the sparsity of LiDAR data by upsampling can be easily applied to other architectures. In the future, more upsampling techniques will be examined for 3D object detectioin. Parameter settings will be discussed in details.

In addition, the results of the paper also indicate that there is still much room for the 3D upsampling techniques to be used for object detection. The accuracy and the ability to produce reliable dense points when there are few original point data need to be improved. The speed of upsampling is also a key to the wide applications of upsampling techniques in object detections.

Acknowledgement. This work is supported by the National Natural Science Foundation of China (No. 61771042, 61702032 and 41761079) and Beijing Natural Science Foundation (No. 4202061).

References

1. Qi, C.R., Liu, W., Wu, C., Su, H., Guibas, L.J.: Frustum pointnets for 3D object detection from RGB-D data. In: CVPR (2018)
2. Li, R., Li, X., Fu, C., Cohen-Or, D., Heng, P.: PU-GAN: a point cloud upsampling adversarial network. In: Proceedings of the IEEE International Conference on Computer Vision (2019)
3. Chen, X., Kundu, K., Zhang, Z., Ma, H., Fidler, S., Sun R.U.: Monocular 3D object detection for autonomous driving. In: Proceedings of the IEEE Conference on Computer Vision and Pattern Recognition, pp. 2147–2156 (2016)
4. Xiang, Y., Choi, W., Lin, Y., Savarese, S.: Data-driven 3D voxel patterns for object category recognition. In: Proceedings of the IEEE Conference on Computer Vision and Pattern Recognition, pp. 1903–1911 (2015)
5. Li, B., Zhang, T., Xia, T.: Vehicle detection from 3D lidar using fully convolutional network. In: RSS (2016)
6. Deng, Z., Latecki, L.J.: Amodal detection of 3D objects: inferring 3D bounding boxes from 2D ones in RGB-depth images. In: Conference on Computer Vision and Pattern Recognition (CVPR) (2017)
7. Zhou, J., Tan, X., Shao, Z., Ma, L.: FVNet: 3D front-view proposal generation for real-time object detection from point clouds. In: 12th International Congress on Image and Signal Processing, BioMedical Engineering and Informatics (CISP-BMEI) (2019)
8. Chen, X., Ma, H., Wan, J., Li, B., Xia, T.: Multi-view 3D object detection network for autonomous driving. In: IEEE CVPR (2017)
9. Zhou, Y., Tuzel, O.: Voxelnet: end-to-end learning for point cloud based 3D object detection. CoRR (2017)
10. Ren, S., He, K., Girshick, R., Sun, J.: Faster R-CNN: towards real-time object detection with region proposal networks. In: Advances in Neural Information Processing Systems, pp. 91–99 (2015)
11. Yan, Y., Mao, Y., Li, B.: Second: sparsely embedded convolutional detection. Sensors (2018)
12. Graham, B., Engelcke, M., van der Maaten, L.: 3D semantic segmentation with submanifold sparse convolutional networks. In: CVPR (2018)
13. Lang, A.H., Vora, S., Caesar, H., Zhou, L., Yang, J., Jbom, O.B.: Pointpillars: fast encoders for object detection from point clouds. In: CVPR (2019)
14. Qi, C.R., Yi, L., Su, H., Guibas, L.J.: Pointnet++: deep hierarchical feature learning on point sets in a metric space. In: NIPS (2017)
15. Wang, Y., Chao, W., Garg, D., Hariharan, B., Campbell, M., Weinberger, K.Q.: Pseudo-lidar from visual depth estimation: bridging the gap in 3D object detection for autonomous driving. In: CVPR (2019)
16. You, Y., et al.: Pseudo-LiDAR++: accurate depth for 3D object detection in autonomous driving (2019)
17. Ma, X., Wang, Z., Li, H., Ouyang, W., Fan, X., Zhang, P.: Accurate monocular object detection via color-embedded 3D reconstruction for autonomous driving. In: ICCV (2019)

18. Weng, X., Kitani, K.: Monocular 3D object detection with pseudo-LiDAR point cloud. In: CVPR (2019)

19. Yang, Z., Sun, Y., Liu, S., Shen, X., Jia, J.: STD: sparse-to-dense 3D object detector for point cloud. In: ICCV (2019)

20. Kitti 3D object detection benchmark. http://www.cvlibs.net/datasets/kitti/eval_object.php?obj_benchmark=3d (2019)

21. Yu, L., Li, X., Fu, C.W., Cohen-Or, D., Heng, P.A.: PU-net: point cloud upsampling network. In: IEEE Conference on Computer Vision and Pattern Recognition (CVPR), pp. 2790–2799 (2018)

22. Yu, L., Li, X., Fu, C.W., Cohen-Or, D., Heng, P.A.: EC-Net: an edge-aware point set consolidation network. In: European Conference on Computer Vision (ECCV), pp. 386–402 (2018)

23. Yifan, W., Wu, S., Huang, H., Cohen-Or, D., Hornung, O.S.: Patch-based progressive 3D point set upsampling. In: CVPR, pp. 5958–5967 (2019)

24. He, K., Gkioxari, G., Doll, P., Girshick, R.: Mask R-CNN. In: ICCV (2017)

25. Wu, Y., Kirillov, A., Massa, F., Lo, W., Girshick, R.: Detectron2 (2019). https://github.com/facebookresearch/detectron2

26. Cordts, M., et al.: The cityscapes dataset for semantic urban scene understanding. In: CVPR (2016)

27. Li, R., Li, X., Fu, C., Cohen-Or, D., Heng, P.: PU-GAN (2019). https://liruihui.github.io/publication/PU-GAN/

28. Qi, C.R., Liu, W., Wu, C., Su, H., Guibas, L.J.: Frustum-pointnets. https://github.com/charlesq34/frustum-pointnets

Nodule Generation of Lung CT Images Using a 3D Convolutional LSTM Network

Kolawole Olulana[1]($\boxtimes$) (iD), Pius Owolawi[1], Chunling Tu[1], and Bolanle Abe[2]

[1] Computer Systems Engineering Department, Tshwane University of Technology,
Pretoria, South Africa
kolawolegolulana@gmail.com, {owolawipa,duc}@tut.ac.za
[2] Electrical Engineering Department, Tshwane University of Technology, Pretoria, South Africa
abebt@tut.ac.za

Abstract. In the US, the American Cancer Society report for 2020 estimates about 228,820 new cases which could result in 135,720 deaths which translates to 371 deaths per day compared to the overall daily cancer death of 1660. The Cancer Society of South Africa (CANSA) reports that lung cancer and other chronic lung diseases are leading causes of death nationally. Research in this area is necessary in order to reduce the number of reported deaths through early detection and diagnosis. A number of studies have been done using datasets for Computed Tomography (CT) images in the diagnosis and prognosis by oncologists, radiologists and medical professionals in the healthcare sector and a number of machine learning methods are being developed using conventional neural networks (CNN) for feature extraction and binary classification with just a few researches making use of combined (hybrid) methods that have shown the capability to increase performance and accuracy in prediction and detection of early stage onset of lung cancer. In this paper, a combined model is proposed using 3D images as input to a combination of a CNN and long short-term memory (LSTM) network which is a type of recurrent neural network (RNN). The hybridization which often lead to increase need for computational resources will be adjusted by improving the nodule generation to focus only on the search space around the lung nodules, this proposed model requires less computation resources, avoiding the need to adding the whole 3D CT image into the network, therefore only the region of interest near candidate regions with nodules will be pre-processed. The results of previous traditional CNN architecture is compared to this combined 3D Convolutional LSTM for nodule generation. In the experiments, the proposed hybrid model overperforms the traditional CNN architecture which shows how much improvement a hybridization of suitable models can contribute to lung cancer research.

Keywords: ConvLSTM · CNN · Deep learning · Hybrid network · Lung cancer diagnosis · LSTM

1 Introduction

According to the World Health Organization (WHO), amongst other types of cancer, lung cancer is responsible for 1.76 million deaths alone in 2018, the highest among any

© Springer Nature Switzerland AG 2020
G. Bebis et al. (Eds.): ISVC 2020, LNCS 12510, pp. 753–760, 2020.
https://doi.org/10.1007/978-3-030-64559-5_60

type of cancer. Early detection of lung cancer can significantly increase survival rate, many cases can be cured by early detection through treatment [1].

The screening of patients plays an important role in improving survival rate where improvement of current machine learning methods can also help in reducing cost, expenses, and help advance current methods used in analyzing CT images compared to present techniques where 2D images with limited information and lower accuracy in detection methods are being used for monitoring the growth of lung nodules [2], using a hybrid model will lead to better results, hence the motivation for the development and deployment of a model using Computed Aided Diagnosis (CAD) services with increased performance and accessibility will go a long way in improving chances of survival of lung cancer. There exists a number of previous studies that have explored the technique of using low-dose CT images to develop 3D images to achieve accurate nodule detection [3, 4] using conventional neural networks alone, however, in this study, a hybrid network will be employed to increase prediction accuracy rate and early detection. Due to the nature of the convolutional long term short term memory (ConvLSTM) network which requires a larger 3D input compared to 2D traditional conventional neural network, the pre-processing step will take into consideration the large search space constraint which can lead to a strain on limited available computation resources, so only the low-level features are selected around the nodules of interest within that search space to generate the image voxels, this would be an important step to reduce processing time and size of input of the network [5]. Use of this low-dose lung image scans make it easier to design the hybrid model with a higher performance than traditional convolutional network as seen in a previous studies where a similar hybrid network was used in weather forecasting, applying this deep learning method would bring more accurate diagnosis and efficiency for medical professionals to overcome the weaknesses seen in other models, it is a better model and more details about the spatial temporal characteristic of the model lead to better performance [6].

In literatures, where hybrid networks have been used in other areas of study [7], there is an observed improved performance, compared to using recurrent neural networks, LSTM models and traditional conventional neutral networks being used alone, hybrid approach can lead to better results in accuracy and early detection [8].

The approach taken in hybrid networks takes advantage of the feature extraction characteristics and spatial temporal characteristics of recurrent neural networks and both combined networks.

In this paper, these layers are collectively referred to as Convolutional LSTM (ConvLSTM) to help distinguish the naming conventions in other architectures, all architectures in this layer have a minimum dimensionality of three, and this would account for samples taken over time in the LSTM aspect of the hybrid network; it can be increased from 3D to 4D and up to 5D if sequence time_steps are needed.

This model will be tested on the LUNA16 dataset where a region of interest within the search space will be selected based on the threshold of Hounsfield radiodensity units [9] of greater than 604($-$400 HU).

2 Method

The proposed 3D ConvLSTM hybrid model for nodule candidate generation is as described in Fig. 1. The inputs and previous hidden states are convolved to produce 3D tensors that flow through each cell. Changes to standard fully connected (LSTM-FC) are highlighted in red. This method covers the nodule generation step and it's accuracy and other performance metrics. The predicted mask is what would be needed in a classification task when pre-processing and nodule generation is completed.

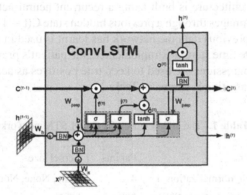

Fig. 1. ConvLSTM Cell.

The entire 3D search space is not of much consequence as interest only lies in the surrounding area of each nodule which is scaled and padded and resized from the original dimension of $(512 \times 512 \times 512)$ volume to $(64 \times 64 \times 64)$; to decrease the GPU memory usage, this adjustment is done to the input batch which is added to the nature in a grid pattern, the output batch is compared with an actual batch for the validation and testing set as discussed further below. The mathematical representation of the model is defined by [10] is as follows

$$\widetilde{\mathbf{f}}^{(\tau)}$$

$$\widetilde{\mathbf{i}}^{(\tau)} = \mathbf{BN}\left(W_h * x^{(\tau)};\ \gamma_x \beta_{hx}\right) + W_{peep} \odot C^{(\tau-1)} + b + \mathbf{BN}\left(W_h * h^{(\tau-1)};\ \gamma_h \beta_h\right)$$

$$\widetilde{\mathbf{o}}^{(\tau)}$$

where

$$\widehat{\mathbf{C}}^{(\tau)} = \tan^{-1}\left(BN\left(W_{hc} * h^{(\tau-1)}; \gamma_h, \beta_h\right) + BN\left(W_{xc} * x^{(\tau)}; \gamma_x, \beta_x\right) + b_c\right)$$

$$\mathbf{C} = \sigma\left(\widetilde{\mathbf{f}}^{(\tau)}\right) \odot C^{(\tau-1)} + \sigma\left(\widetilde{\mathbf{i}}^{(\tau)}\right) \odot \widehat{\mathbf{C}}^{(\tau-1)}$$

$$h^{(\tau)} = \sigma() \odot \tan^{-1}\left(BN\left(C^{(\tau)}; \gamma_c, \beta_c\right)\right) \tag{1}$$

2.1 Network Structure

In the LSTM cell, Wh is the shared weight matrix for the hidden-to-hidden transitions at time step τ, Wx is the shared weights for the input-to-hidden connections, as well as Wpeep is the shared weights matrix for the peephole connections. The b is the bias, as well as C(0), h(0) are the initial states of the memory cell and the hidden state, respectively. Furthermore, one of the batch-normalization (BN) layers with its learned shift; γ and scale; β, are denoted by (x; γ, β) where the bias terms are denoted by b as did in [10].

The network's architecture is built using a recurrent neural network approach that passes the input grid images through a previous hidden state C(t − 1) as a step to the next sequence, such that previous data the network has learnt is used in making decisions.

In the cases where time steps are implemented, the patient's previous CT images are compared. These progressions are used to keep true positives as accurate as possible.

The rest of the transition is shown in Table 1.

Table 1. The architecture of a ConvLSTM network

Layers	Params	Kernel size
Batch_normalization_1	4	None, None, None
Conv3D_1 (Conv3D)	208	1,5,5
Conv3D_2 (Conv3D)	1736	3,3,3
Batch_normalization_2	32	None, None, None
Bidirectional_1	27776	3,3
Bidirectional_2	147712	3,3
Conv3D_3	4616	1,3,3
Conv3D_4	9	1,1,1
Cropping3D_1 (Cropping3D)	0	1,2,2

2.2 Applying the Proposed Method in 3D Image Classification

As shown in Fig. 2 and discussed in [16, 19], the input samples (spatial-temporal data) is fed into the algorithm network to learn how to follow a sequence of data like a physician reading through a number of images meaning that the order is important and takes notes of already noticeable patterns to make better decisions. Similar studies in video prediction and weather forecasting have been successfully modeled with high accuracy [15].

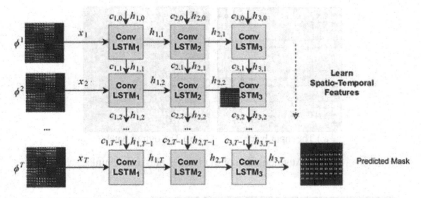

Fig. 2. Flow Diagram of Proposed ConvLSTM.

3 Experimental Results

The proposed model was evaluated against the publicly available LUNA16 dataset and compared with traditional conventional methods, specifically the DeepSeed approach in [3] and DL algorithm in [21].

3.1 Dataset

The LUNA16 dataset contains 226,589 test CT images from 888 studies where than 2.5 mm in a raw format. The annotation was modified accordingly as detailed in [4]. The pre-processing steps are done in preparation of the model for a 3D conventional neural network coupled with a LSTM model. Nodules are defined as non-nodule, nodule if diameter is less than 3 mm, and nodules are otherwise classified as nodules if greater than 3 mm. See this publication for the details of the annotation process.

The pre-processing steps included resizing and selecting lesion being classified as a nodule as defined by a consensus of at least three of the four radiologists involved in classification of the image sets. This dataset was selected because of its 3D images which is the only type of input the hybrid layer will accept

3.2 Implementation Details

The model is compiled using an adam optimizer and binary cross entropy, then runs for 100 steps per epoch to train the parameters; it is trained in 20 epochs [12]. The model was trained on Kaggle using a Nvidia K80 GPU.

The training and validation sets are split with the ratio 80:20. Each input image has a binary segmentation mask to segment lungs. The image size is 64×64 with an input batch of sixteen with a slice count of ten as seen in Fig. 3, for the validation set the slice count was increased to 100 and batch size was reduced to just one (1) as detailed in Fig. 4.

In this study, the 3D network structure emphasized on the memory features of RNN, the memory, M in LSTM to develop a neutral by augmenting the 3D input images in

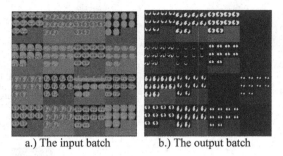

a.) The input batch   b.) The output batch

Fig. 3. Augmentation of 3D images into little chunks.

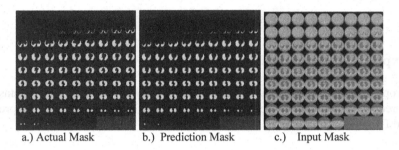

a.) Actual Mask   b.) Prediction Mask   c.)   Input Mask

Fig. 4. The Input mask validation mask and actual mask.

the pre-processing stages to select only the regions of interest by generating cutting 3D voxels around this regions as indicated by the image dataset. Yu Gu et al. [11] have established a dot enhancement filter method to generate 3D matrix of voxel data which was annotated in LUNA16 dataset where the radius of each nodule is used to generate the binary mask.

Once the 3D voxels are generated, each mask is fed into the network input layer, where it goes through the layers starting with the batch normalization (BN) layer where the dimensionality of the input is set to None when BN is the first layer. This layer is followed by the first conventional 3D (conv3D_1) layer; four convolution layers are employed with the same activation and padding but different kernel sizes. It is followed by the second of four conventional layers, conv3D_2 with a RELU activation [17, 18]. The first LSTM bidirectional layer (bidirectional_1) follows the conv3D_2 to account for the recurrent layer for the sequence classification layer as shown in Fig. 1, as labeled as h (t + 1).

At the end of 20 epochs, the binary accuracy converged to 0.9317 and average binary accuracy of 0.9866, average mean square error of 0.0087 and average loss of 0.0709

The output of the prediction step was however output in a single batch due to the small nature of the 3D masks provided by the dataset, it is a resource intensive process to expand the dataset 2D images into 3D images [20]. More work still needs to be done in this area.

3.3 Performance Comparison Top Traditional CNNs

In comparison to 3D DeepSeed [3] and DL algorithm [21], there is a noticeable improved accuracy based on the LUNA16 dataset as shown in Table 2. The ConvLSTM accuracy peaked at 0.972 and its loss converged around 0.0709. It outperformed the DeepSeed and DL Algorithm approach.

Table 2. Comparison of Metrics.

Network	Precision	Recall	Accuracy
ConvLSTM (ours)	0.9820	0.948	0.972
3D CNN Deep Seed	–	0.862	0.862
DL Algorithm	0.82	0.82	0.90

4 Conclusion

In this study, the focus was on improving the accuracy and early detection of the progression of lung cancer progress through the use of hybrid models are able in generation of nodules from low dose lung CT scan images for pre-processing step using the proposed ConvLSTM that combines the capabilities of a recurrent neural network using LSTM network coupled with a conventional CNNs. The expected results of increased accuracies were achieved on the LUNA 16 dataset which consisted of low-dose CT scan images by generating 3D image voxels around the region-of-interest by feeding them into the network.

A 10% improvement on the accuracy was observed compared to the DeepSeed approach.

References

1. Siegel, R.L., Miller, K.D., Jemal, A.: Cancer statistics, pp. 8 (2019)
2. Hawkes, N.: Cancer survival data emphasis importance of early diagnosis, **364**, 1408 (2019)
3. Li, Y., Fan, Y.: DeepSeed: 3D Squeeze-and-Excitation Encoder-Decoder Convolutional Neural Networks for Pulmonary Nodule Detection, pp. 2–4 (2019)
4. Zhu, W., Liu, C., Fan, W., Xie, X.: Deeplung: Deep 3D dual path nets for automated pulmonary nodule detection and classification, pp. 2–7 (2018)
5. Li, W., Cao, P., Zhao, D., Wang, J.: Pulmonary nodule classification with deep convolutional neural networks on computed tomography images, pp. 1–3 (2016)
6. Shi, X., Chen, Z., Wang, H., Yeung, D.-Y., Wong, W.-K., Woo, W.-C.: Convolutional LSTM Network: A Machine Learning Approach for Precipitation Nowcasting, pp. 2–8 (2015)
7. Seijo-Pardo, B., Porto-Díaz, I., Bolón-Canedo, V., Alonso-Betanzos, A.: Ensemble feature selection: Homogeneous and heterogeneous approaches, pp. 6–27 (2017)
8. Gao, R., et al.: Distanced LSTM: Time-Distanced gates in long short-term memory models for lung cancer detection, pp. 2–5 (2019)

9. Kuan, K., et al.: Deep learning for lung cancer detection: Tackling the kaggle data science bowl 2017 Challenge, pp. 2–5 (2017)

10. Sautermeister, B.: Learning approaches to predict future frames in videos, pp. 45–46 (2016)

11. Gu, Y., et al.: Automatic lung nodule detection using multi-scale dot nodule-enhancement filter and weighted support vector machines in chest computed tomography, pp. 2–5 (2019)

12. Ozdemir, O., Russell, R.L., Berlin, D.A.: A 3D probabilistic deep learning system for detection and diagnosis of lung cancer using Low-Dose CT scans, pp. 6–11 (2020)

13. Li, W., Cao, P., Dazhe, Z., Wang, J.: Pulmonary nodule classification with deep convolutional neural networks on computed tomography images, pp. 1–3 (2016)

14. Hu, W.-S.: Feature extraction and classification based on spatial-spectral ConvLSTM neural network for hyperspectral images

15. Oprea, S., et al.: A review on deep learning techniques for video prediction, pp. 9–14 (2020)

16. Zapata-Impata, B.S., Gil, P., Torres, F.: Learning spatio temporal tactile features with a ConvLSTM for the direction of slip detection, pp. 6–7 (2019)

17. Li, Y., Sarvi, M., Khoshelham, K., Haghani, M.: Predicting traffic congestion maps using convolutional long short-term memory, pp. 4–6 (2019)

18. Rahman, S.A., and Adjeroh, D.A.: Deep learning using convolutional LSTM estimates biological age from physical activity, pp. 10 (2019)

19. Li, Y., Xu, H., Bian, M., Xiao, J.: Attention based CNN-ConvLSTM for pedestrian attribute recognition, pp. 4–5 (2020)

20. Feng, S., Zhou, H., Dong, H.: Using deep neural network with small dataset to predict material defects, pp. 302 (2019)

21. Cui, S., et al.: Development and clinical application of deep learning model for lung nodules screening on CT images, pp. 4 (2020)

Conditional GAN for Prediction of Glaucoma Progression with Macular Optical Coherence Tomography

Osama N. Hassan[1]([✉]), Serhat Sahin[2], Vahid Mohammadzadeh[3], Xiaohe Yang[2], Navid Amini[7], Apoorva Mylavarapu[5], Jack Martinyan[5], Tae Hong[7], Golnoush Mahmoudinezhad[4], Daniel Rueckert[1,6], Kouros Nouri-Mahdavi[3], and Fabien Scalzo[2,4,8]

[1] Computing Department, Imperial College London, London, UK
usama@ucla.edu
[2] Department of Electrical and Computer Engineering, UCLA, Los Angeles, USA
[3] Ophthalmology Department, Jules Stein Eye Institute, Los Angeles, USA
[4] Department of Computer Science, UCLA, Los Angeles, USA
[5] David Geffen School of Medicine, UCLA, Los Angeles, USA
[6] Technische Universität München, Munich, Germany
[7] Department of Computer Science, California State University, Los Angeles, USA
[8] Department of Neurology, UCLA, Los Angeles, USA

Abstract. The estimation of glaucoma progression is a challenging task as the rate of disease progression varies among individuals in addition to other factors such as measurement variability and the lack of standardization in defining progression. Structural tests, such as thickness measurements of the retinal nerve fiber layer or the macula with optical coherence tomography (OCT), are able to detect anatomical changes in glaucomatous eyes. Such changes may be observed before any functional damage. In this work, we built a generative deep learning model using the conditional GAN architecture to predict glaucoma progression over time. The patient's OCT scan is predicted from three or two prior measurements. The predicted images demonstrate high similarity with the ground truth images. In addition, our results suggest that OCT scans obtained from only two prior visits may actually be sufficient to predict the next OCT scan of the patient after six months.

Keywords: Generative models · CGAN · Glaucoma progression · OCT.

1 Introduction

Glaucoma is a progressive optic neuropathy and is the second leading cause of blindness worldwide [1]. The number of people with glaucoma worldwide was

---

O. N. Hassan and S. Sahin—Equal contribution.

© Springer Nature Switzerland AG 2020
G. Bebis et al. (Eds.): ISVC 2020, LNCS 12510, pp. 761–772, 2020.
https://doi.org/10.1007/978-3-030-64559-5_61

estimated to be about 60.5 million people in 2010 and it is expected to reach 111.8 million in 2040 [2]. The retinal ganglion cell (RGC) machinery is located in the inner retina and RGC axons form the optic nerve. The role of the optic nerve is to transmit visual information from the photoreceptors to the brain. Glaucoma is characterized by slow degeneration of the RGC and their axons which leads to a functional visual loss in glaucoma patients [3, 4]. The functional visual loss in glaucoma manifests as a progressive loss of vision mainly in the periphery; if glaucoma is not treated, it can eventually lead to complete visual loss and blindness [5].

Due to the progressive and asymptomatic nature of glaucoma, it is crucial for clinicians to diagnose it in its early stages and be able to detect its progression in a timely manner to prevent the progressive functional loss [5–8]. Glaucoma progression can be evaluated with structural and functional measures [9–16]. The estimation of glaucoma progression is challenging as the rate of disease progression varies among individuals [17]. Moreover, measurement variability, the influence of age-related attrition, and the lack of standardization in defining progression make tracking disease deterioration a very challenging task with either structural or functional tests [18–20]. Standard achromatic perimetry and measurement of the visual field (VF) is the most common functional test used to evaluate glaucoma progression [21]. It quantifies visual degradation in the peripheral field of view of the patient. Patients may experience VF loss after a substantial amount of structural change has occurred [22]. Structural tests, such as thickness measurements of the retinal nerve fiber layer or the macula (central retina) with optical coherence tomography (OCT), are able to detect anatomical changes in glaucomatous eyes; such changes may be observed before any functional damage; hence, they may be useful for glaucoma detection especially in early stages [23, 24]. Clinicians also depend on structural tests for the detection of disease progression, especially in early to moderate stages [25, 26]. When the disease becomes more advanced, structural measurements may reach their floor and further changes might be difficult to detect [27]. At this stage, functional tests are considered to be more useful to track disease progression [28].

The gold standard for retinal imaging at present is an optical imaging modality called OCT [29]. OCT is non-invasive and is able to acquire high resolution, in-vivo cross-sectional or 3D images from transparent or semi-transparent biological tissues. With the aid of OCT, it has become possible to image retinal anatomy including individual layers such as the ganglion cell layer and diagnose glaucoma before the visual field defects emerge. OCT systems can be classified into time domain based OCT (TD-OCT) and spectral domain based OCT (SD-OCT). The SD-OCT systems have better resolution, are much faster, have higher reproducibility and are more computationally efficient and therefore, SD-OCT has become the gold standard for imaging of the retinal and the optic nerve head [28]. An example of a retinal OCT cross section is shown in Fig. 1.

The goal of our work is to provide a computational framework for the modeling of glaucoma progression over time based on macular OCT images. A dataset of longitudinal macular OCT images is used. Macular OCT images of around

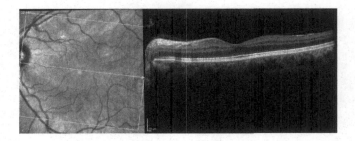

Fig. 1. (Right) A raw macular B-scan of optical coherence tomography passing through the fovea (center of the macula). (Left) An infrared image of the macula and the green square outlines the area in which all the B-scans will be transmitted. (Color figure online)

hundred eyes with more than two years of follow-up were used. We aim to predict structural and functional changes over time. More specifically, assume we have images x_0, x_i to x_{n-1} where each image represents a scan at a specific time point i, the question we address here is how the image x_n looks like and whether the changes are beyond what is expected. A machine learning based algorithm is used to make the prediction and reconstruction of image x_n. Our study primarily uses the generative adversarial networks (GAN) to achieve its prediction goal. The framework of generative model is like a minimax two-player game. The GAN consists of two components: a generator G and a discriminator D. The generator captures the data distribution and predicts the next time-point image based on the input images of previous time points. On the other hand, the discriminator tries to distinguish between the ground-truth image and the image predicted by the generator. The training succeeds when the discriminator is no longer able to tell any difference between the ground-truth images and the predicted images and the generator totally fools the discriminator. Both the generator and discriminator models are constructed using neural networks [30].

2 Dataset and Problem Definition

Our dataset consists of longitudinal macular OCT images of 109 eyes. Each eye is scanned at four to ten visits separated by six months. Each visit has a macular OCT volume that consists of 61 cross-sectional B-scans from the central retina spanning $30 \times 25°$. The hierarchy of the dataset is depicted in Fig. 2.

The objective of this work is to predict glaucoma progression over time by the construction of a future macular cross-sectional image from past measurements. To elaborate, for a cross-sectional image that is available at 3 time points x_0, x_1, x_3, we reconstruct the cross-sectional image at time point x_4. In other words, the model's task is to learn the growth of glaucoma-related features of OCT images over different cross sectional images in individual patients. Moreover, we set no constraints on the baseline which implies that the input images can be at any stage of the disease provided that subsequent images are separated by six months in time.

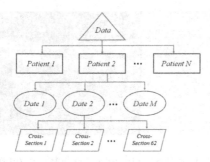

Fig. 2. The hierarchy of the data set. Each patient, at each visit (date) has 61 cross-sectional images (B-scans) of the retina.

3   Methods

We adopted in our work the image-to-image translation framework with conditional generative adversarial network (cGAN) that is presented in [31], with some minor modifications in our implementation of its architecture.

3.1   CGAN Model

The motivation of using GAN in this problem is its flexibility of specifying the objective of the network at high-level by requiring the output of its generator to be indistinguishable from reality; the network then automatically learns the loss function that is necessary to achieve this through its adversarial mechanism. That is, the GAN learns a loss function through its discriminator that attempts to classify the generated image as true or fake while training a generative model that tries to minimize this loss at the same time. This learning-based loss function introduces a general framework to many tasks for which defining a loss function would be otherwise very difficult. In addition, we have chosen to use particularly conditional GAN to enforce the network to constrain each generated output image to the corresponding input; in other words, the output of the GAN network is conditioned on the input images [31]. The cGAN model consists of:

Generator Model. The generator architecture can be divided into two blocks. First, a 3D convolutional neural network (3D-CNN) block to learn the spatio-temporal features in the input image frames (see Fig. 3a) [32]. Second, similar to [31], a U-Net based architecture, as originally proposed in [33], is used as the main block of the generative model. The general architecture is shown in Fig. 3b. The U-Net generator is a decoder-encoder network with long skip connections. The network consists of 4 encoding/down-sampling layers and 4 decoding/up-sampling layers. It uses a skip connection mechanism that copies the learned features from layer i to layer $n - i$, where n is the total number of layers. At each layer of the generator, except for the last layer, rectified linear units (ReLU) are used in the up-sampling part of the network, and their leaky version are

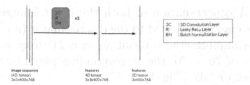

(a) 3D convolutional block to extract the spatio-temporal features.

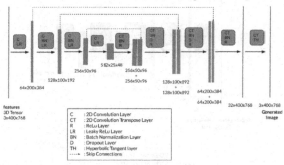

(b) Generator with U-Net-based architecture. Reproduced from [32].

Fig. 3. The components of our proposed model showing the feature extraction block and the generator.

used in the down-sampling part. In addition, batch normalization layers [34] are added to accelerate the training process and dropout layers are used within the up-sampling layers (except for the first and last layers) to add randomness to the generative process.

Discriminator Model The discriminator is a fully CNN classifier. In this study, we adopted the five-layer PatchGAN discriminator that is proposed at [31] and originally discussed at [35].

Although using the L_1 norm in the loss function does not preserve high frequencies and results in blurry images, it preserves the low frequency content and therefore if we use L_1 loss, the GAN discriminator can be designed to be more dedicated to preserving the structural and high frequency content of the generated images while leaving the low frequency preservation task to the L_1 loss. In order for the discriminator to preserve high frequencies, it does not classify the image as a whole. Instead, it treats it as patches and classifies each patch as real or fake. This way the discriminator offers structured loss functionality and penalizes the joint configuration of the output and does not consider the output of each pixel to be conditionally independent in an unstructured fashion. This design modality of the discriminator is called PatchGAN since it penalizes structures at the patch scale. This results in the additional advantages of having a discriminator with fewer parameters and being able to apply the discriminator to arbitrarily large images. The PatchGAN classifies patches of size 70 × 70 as suggested by [31]. A concatenation of both the input images to the generator and the image to be classified are fed to the discriminator (see Fig. 5) and passed through five down-sampling stages resulting in a 2D map in which each pixel has a receptive field of 70 × 70; the corresponding patch in the input image is then classified as real or fake (Fig. 4).

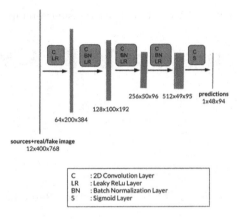

Fig. 4. PatchGAN-based discriminator network. Reproduced from [31].

3.2 Objective and Loss Functions

In a vanilla GAN, the generator loss (L_G) and the discriminator loss $(L_D)$are defined as

$$L_G = F(D(\hat{y}), 1),$$
$$L_D = F(D(\hat{y}), 0) + F(D(y), 1),$$

where F can be a binary cross entropy (BCE) loss or mean squared error (MSE) loss, y is the real ground-truth target image, and $\hat{y}$ is the predicted output of the generator. The discriminator input in this case the output of the generator $\hat{y}$.

However, in conditional GAN, the discriminator input includes both the generator input x and the generator output $\hat{y}$. In addition, we add to the generator loss: L_1 norm loss, to capture the low frequency content, as explained earlier. This can be written as

$$L_G = F(D(x, \hat{y}), 1) + \alpha * L_1(\hat{y}, y),$$
$$L_D = F(D(x, \hat{y}), 0) + F(D(x, y), 1). \tag{1}$$

where the hyper-parameter α is used to emphasize the weight of the L_1 loss and is optimized empirically.

4   Experiments and Results

4.1   Training Details

For training, 26, 592 OCT cross-sections from 101 glaucomatous eyes were prepared. These eyes were imaged in at least four visits. We conducted two different
experiments. In experiment A, the model was trained based on a sequence of four
images using the first 3 visits as the input and the fourth visit as the output of
the model. In experiment B, the model was trained based on a sequence of three
visits using the first two visits as the input and the third visit as the output of
the model. We arranged the training and validation split percentages as 75% and
15% respectively. The less the number of visits that one uses as an input, the
more useful the model becomes when we have limited data for a given patient.

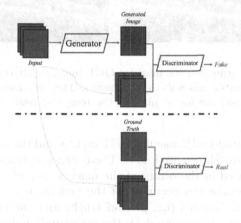

Fig. 5. Training conditional GAN. (Top) the generator optimization step and (Bottom)
the discriminator optimization step.

In GAN training, it is often seen that the discriminator detects the outputs
of the generator as fake images at very early stages of the training process, which
stops the generator from learning. To prevent this issue, we alternated between
four optimization steps on the generator and then one optimization step on
the discriminator as this experimentally resulted in an optimum performance.
In optimization, Adam optimizer was used for the generator with momentum
parameters $\beta_1 = 0.5$ and $\beta_2 = 0.999$. For the discriminator, stochastic gradient
descent (SGD) with momentum (0.5) was used. A batch size of eight was used
in training and dropout was used at rate of 0.5 to provide noise to the GAN
during training.

4.2   Results

The test data split had the scans of 16 patients that was not used during training
the model. For the experiment A, a total of 2, 379 input-output pairs were prepared from 8 patients that have at least four visits, while in the experiment B,

a total of 3, 111 input-output pairs were prepared for the all of the 16 patients' data as they all have at least three visits. Unlike the conventional protocol, we followed [31] in applying dropout and batch normalization, using the test batch statistics, at the test time as well.

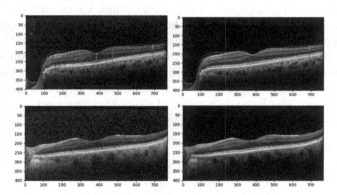

Fig. 6. Examples of ground-truth macular OCT images (left column) vs. the corresponding GAN generated images (right column). The red lines highlight from left-to-right the nasal peak, the foveal pit and the temporal peak. (Color figure online)

Examples of ground-truth macular OCT images and the corresponding GAN-generated images are shown in Fig. 6. These cross-sections pass through the fovea, which is located in the center of the macula and where the visual acuity is the best. To evaluate the accuracy of the generated images, the similarity between the original B-scans (i.e. ground truth) and the constructed B-scans (i.e. predicted B-scan) is measured by the structural similarity index measure (SSIM). SSIM takes into account changes in luminance, contrast, and structure. The SSIM index ranges in [0, 1], where 0 indicates no similarity between two images and 1 implies perfect similarity. The SSIM index has been shown to be in accordance with human visual perception and human grading of image similarity [36]. Since SSIM is measured locally, it is less sensitive to noise compared with other image similarity measurements such as the mean squared error (MSE) and peak signal-to-noise ratio (PSNR) [37]. Another advantage of SSIM over MSE or PNSR is that SSIM measures the perceived change in structural information, taking into account, the inter-dependencies of spatially proximate pixels and not just the error [38]. The SSIM results are summarized in Table 1.

Table 1. Evaluation of the SSIM metric value for the results of experiments "A" and "B".

Experiment	Average SSIM
A (with 3 visits)	0.8325
B (with 2 visits)	0.8336

5   Discussion

The visual inspection of the OCT images (i.e ground-truth) and the GAN generated images (see Fig. 6) initially demonstrates good structural agreement between them. Furthermore, the network has a denoising effect on the images which is evident by comparing the noise in the background of the generated and ground truth images.

The SSIM results are above 0.83 for both experiments, which demonstrates the accuracy for our method. In addition, both experiments have very close SSIM values suggesting that it is actually adequate to use two visits to make the predictions and adding a third visit does not help the model make better predictions. This is practically very useful as it makes it possible to make predictions with limited number of visits.

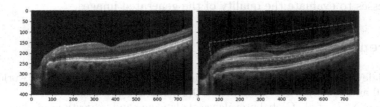

Fig. 7. An example of an artifact that can be generated by the GAN network and result in a corrupted image and wrong predictions. (Left) ground truth and (Right) predicted image. Duplicate image representation can be observed.

A limitation of our method, although uncommon, is the artifacts that can exist in the predicted image. An example of an artifact is shown in Fig. 7 where the network superimposed duplicate cross-sections on top of each other. This is a weakness of the current GAN methods and represents a potential area for further research. Increasing the training dataset size or constraining the cost function with more priors or implementing a hybrid model of both learning-based and rule-based models may help us solve this problem in the future but this remains, for now, an open problem for neural networks based generative models in medical image analysis.

6   Conclusion

Glaucoma is an eye disease that results in irreversible vision loss and is the second leading cause of blindness worldwide. Monitoring glaucoma patients for signs of progression and slowing the decay rate is the ultimate goal of glaucoma treatment. Clinicians depend on retinal structural information obtained with optical coherence tomography for tracking disease progression.

In this work, we built a learning-based generative model using a conditional GAN architecture to predict glaucoma progression over time by reconstructing macular cross-sectional images from three or two prior measurements separated by six-month intervals with no constraints on the stage of the disease at the baseline. We conducted two experiments, one with prior three visits as an input to the model and the other is only with two prior visits as the input. In the first experiment, a total of 2,379 predictions were made for eight patients based on the previous three visits and the predicted images demonstrated a high similarity compared with the ground truth images with an SSIM of 0.8325. In the second experiment, a total of 3,111 predictions were made based on two prior visits resulting in an SSIM of 0.8336. This shows that only two visits may actually be sufficient to use to make the predictions.

A limitation of our method is duplicate image artifacts that were observed in some predicted images and future work may investigate this challenge. In addition, automated segmentation based techniques that are tailored to this problem may be used as an alternative way to accurately measure the layers' thicknesses to evaluate the quality of the generated images.

References

1. Quigley, H.A., Broman, A.T.: The number of people with glaucoma worldwide in 2010 and 2020. Br. J. Ophthalmol. **90**(3), 262–267 (2006)
2. Tham, Y.C., et al.: Global prevalence of glaucoma and projections of glaucoma burden through 2040: a systematic review and meta-analysis. Ophthalmology **121**(11), 2081–2090 (2014)
3. Quigley, H.A., Dunkelberger, G.R., Green, W.R.: Retinal ganglion cell atrophy correlated with automated perimetry in human eyes with glaucoma. Am. J. Ophthalmol. **107**(5), 453–464 (1989)
4. Quigley, H.A., et al.: Retinal ganglion cell death in experimental glaucoma and after axotomy occurs by apoptosis. Invest. Ophthalmol. Vis. Sci. **36**(5), 774–786 (1995)
5. Weinreb, R.N., Aung, T., Medeiros, F.A.: The pathophysiology and treatment of glaucoma: a review. JAMA **311**(18), 1901–1911 (2014)
6. Nouri-Mahdavi, K., Caprioli, J.: Measuring rates of structural and functional change in glaucoma. Br. J. Ophthalmol. **99**(7), 893–898 (2015)
7. Coleman, A.: Glaucoma. Lancet **354**(9192), 1803–1810 (1999)
8. Weinreb, R.N., et al.: Risk assessment in the management of patients with ocular hypertension. Am. J. Ophthalmol. **138**(3), 458–467 (2004)
9. Raza, A.S., Hood, D.C.: Evaluation of the structure-function relationship in glaucoma using a novel method for estimating the number of retinal ganglion cells in the human retina. Invest. Ophthalmol. Vis. Sci. **56**(9), 5548–5556 (2015)
10. Sharma, P., Sample, P.A., Zangwill, L.M., Schuman, J.S.: Diagnostic tools for glaucoma detection and management. Surv. Ophthalmol. **53**(6), S17–S32 (2008)
11. Alexandrescu, C., et al.: Confocal scanning laser ophthalmoscopy in glaucoma diagnosis and management. J. Med. Life **3**(3), 229 (2010)
12. Andreou, P.A., et al.: A comparison of HRT II and GDx imaging for glaucoma detection in a primary care eye clinic setting. Eye **21**(8), 1050–1055 (2007)
13. Belghith, A., et al.: A unified framework for glaucoma progression detection using Heidelberg Retina Tomograph images. Comput. Med. Imaging Graph. **38**(5), 411–420 (2014)

14. Lin, S.C., et al.: Optic nerve head and retinal nerve fiber layer analysis: a report by the American Academy of Ophthalmology. Ophthalmology 114(10), 1937–1949 (2007)
15. Na, J.H., Lee, K.S., Lee, J.R., Lee, Y., Kook, M.S.: The glaucoma detection capability of spectral-domain OCT and GDx-VCC deviation maps in early glaucoma patients with localized visual field defects. Graefe's Arch. Clin. Exp. Ophthalmol. 251(10), 2371–2382 (2013). https://doi.org/10.1007/s00417-013-2362-z
16. Stein, J.D., Talwar, N., LaVerne, A.M., Nan, B., Lichter, P.R.: Trends in use of ancillary glaucoma tests for patients with open-angle glaucoma from 2001 to 2009. Ophthalmology 119(4), 748–758 (2012)
17. Lee, W.J., et al.: Rates of ganglion cell-inner plexiform layer thinning in normal, open-angle glaucoma and pseudoexfoliation glaucoma eyes: a trend-based analysis. Invest. Ophthalmol. Vis. Sci. 60(2), 599–604 (2019)
18. Wadhwani, M., et al.: Test-retest variability of retinal nerve fiber layer thickness and macular ganglion cell-inner plexiform layer thickness measurements using spectral-domain optical coherence tomography. J. Glaucoma 24(5), e109–e115 (2015)
19. Heijl, A., Lindgren, A., Lindgren, G.: Test-retest variability in glaucomatous visual fields. Am. J. Ophthalmol. 108(2), 130–135 (1989)
20. Kim, K.E., Yoo, B.W., Jeoung, J.W., Park, K.H.: Long-term reproducibility of macular ganglion cell analysis in clinically stable glaucoma patients. Invest. Ophthalmol. Vis. Sci. 56(8), 4857–4864 (2015)
21. Caprioli, J., et al.: A method to measure and predict rates of regional visual field decay in glaucoma. Invest. Ophthalmol. Vis. Sci. 52(7), 4765–4773 (2011)
22. Hood, D.C., Kardon, R.H.: A framework for comparing structural and functional measures of glaucomatous damage. Progr. Retinal Eye Res. 26(6), 688–710 (2007)
23. Leung, C.K.S., et al.: Evaluation of retinal nerve fiber layer progression in glaucoma: a study on optical coherence tomography guided progression analysis. Invest. Ophthalmol. Vis. Sci. 51(1), 217–222 (2010)
24. Edlinger, F.S.M., Schrems-Hoesl, L.M., Mardin, C.Y., Laemmer, R., Kruse, F.E., Schrems, W.A.: Structural changes of macular inner retinal layers in early normal-tension and high-tension glaucoma by spectral-domain optical coherence tomography. Graefe's Arch. Clin. Exp. Ophthalmol. 256(7), 1245–1256 (2018). https://doi.org/10.1007/s00417-018-3944-6
25. Anraku, A., Enomoto, N., Takeyama, A., Ito, H., Tomita, G.: Baseline thickness of macular ganglion cell complex predicts progression of visual field loss. Graefe's Arch. Clin. Exp. Ophthalmol. 252(1), 109–115 (2013). https://doi.org/10.1007/s00417-013-2527-9
26. Zhang, X., et al.: Predicting development of glaucomatous visual field conversion using baseline fourier-domain optical coherence tomography. Am. J. Ophthalmol. 163, 29–37 (2016)
27. Miraftabi, A., et al.: Macular SD-OCT outcome measures: comparison of local structure-function relationships and dynamic range. Invest. Ophthalmol. Vis. Sci. 57(11), 4815–4823 (2016)
28. Akman, A., Bayer, A., Nouri-Mahdavi, K.: Optical Coherence Tomography in Glaucoma: A Practical Guide, 1st edn. Springer, Heidelberg (2018). https://doi.org/10.1007/978-3-319-94905-5
29. Parikh, R.S., et al.: Diagnostic capability of optical coherence tomography (Stratus OCT 3) in early glaucoma. Ophthalmology 114(12), 2238–2243 (2007)
30. Goodfellow, I., et al.: Generative adversarial nets. In: Advances in Neural Information Processing Systems, pp. 2672–2680 (2014)

31. Isola, P., Zhu, J.Y., Zhou, T. and Efros, A.A.: Image-to-image translation with conditional adversarial networks. In: Proceedings of the IEEE Conference on Computer Vision and Pattern Recognition, pp. 1125–1134 (2017)
32. Tran, D., et al.: Learning spatiotemporal features with 3d convolutional networks. In: Proceedings of the IEEE International Conference on Computer Vision, pp. 4489–4497 (2015)
33. Ronneberger, O., Fischer, P., Brox, T.: U-net: convolutional networks for biomedical image segmentation. In: Navab, N., Hornegger, J., Wells, W.M., Frangi, A.F. (eds.) MICCAI 2015. LNCS, vol. 9351, pp. 234–241. Springer, Cham (2015). https://doi.org/10.1007/978-3-319-24574-4_28
34. Ioffe, S., Szegedy, C.: Batch normalization: accelerating deep network training by reducing internal covariate shift. arXiv preprint arXiv:1502.03167 (2015)
35. Li, C., Wand, M.: Precomputed real-time texture synthesis with Markovian generative adversarial networks. In: Leibe, B., Matas, J., Sebe, N., Welling, M. (eds.) ECCV 2016. LNCS, vol. 9907, pp. 702–716. Springer, Cham (2016). https://doi.org/10.1007/978-3-319-46487-9_43
36. Wang, Z., Bovik, A.C., Sheikh, H.R., Simoncelli, E.P.: Image quality assessment: from error visibility to structural similarity. IEEE Trans. Image Process. **13**(4), 600–612 (2004)
37. Dosselmann, R., Yang, X.D.: A comprehensive assessment of the structural similarity index. SIViP **5**(1), 81–91 (2011)
38. Marson, A.M., Stern, A.: Horizontal resolution enhancement of autostereoscopy three-dimensional displayed image by chroma subpixel downsampling. J. Displ. Technol. **11**(10), 800–806 (2015)

Author Index

Printed in the United States
By Bookmasters